BENCHMARK SERIES

MICROSOFT® ACCESS® 2013

LEVELS 1 & 2

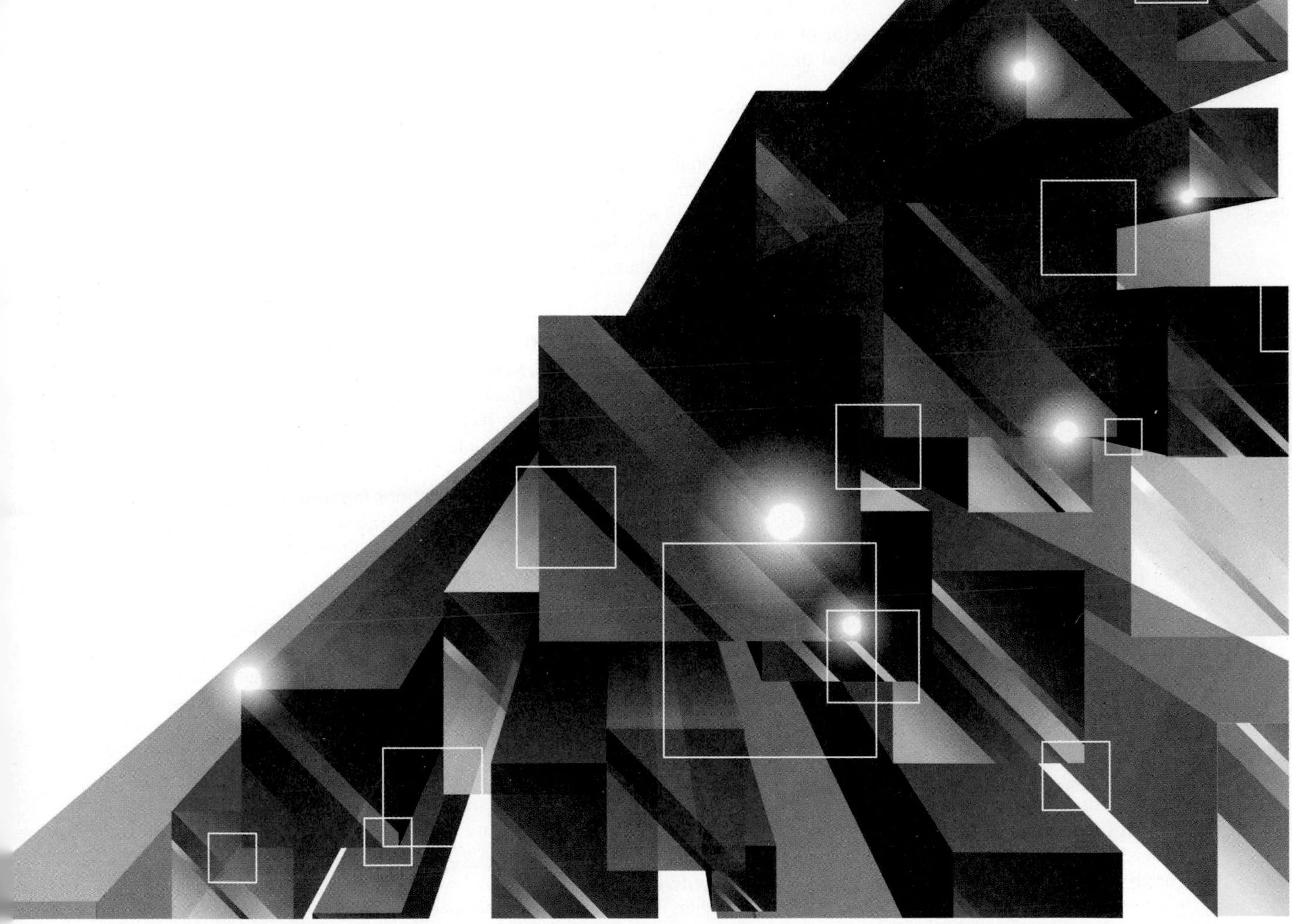

NITA RUTKOSKY
Pierce College at Puyallup
Puyallup, Washington

DENISE SEQUIN
Fanshawe College
London, Ontario

JAN DAVIDSON
Lambton College
Sarnia, Ontario

AUDREY ROGGENKAMP
Pierce College at Puyallup
Puyallup, Washington

IAN RUTKOSKY
Pierce College at Puyallup
Puyallup, Washington

St. Paul

Director of Editorial	Christine Hurney
Director of Production	Timothy W. Larson
Production Editor	Sarah Kearin
Copy Editor	Communicáto, Ltd.; Nan Brooks, Abshier House
Cover Designer	Leslie Anderson
Text Designers	Leslie Anderson and Jaana Bykonich
Desktop Production	Jaana Bykonich, Julie Johnston, Valerie King, Timothy W. Larson, Jack Ross, and Sara Schmidt Boldon
Proofreader	Katherine Lee
Indexer	Terry Casey
VP & Director of Digital Projects	Chuck Bratton
Digital Projects Manager	Tom Modl

Acknowledgements: The authors, editors, and publisher thank the following instructors for their helpful suggestions during the planning and development of the books in the Benchmark Office 2013 Series: Olugbemiga Adekunle, Blue Ridge Community College, Harrisonburg, VA; Letty Barnes, Lake WA Institute of Technology, Kirkland, WA; Erika Nadas, Wilbur Wright College, Chicago, IL; Carolyn Walker, Greenville Technical College, Greenville, SC; Carla Anderson, National College, Lynchburg, VA; Judy A. McLaney, Lurleen B. Wallace Community College, Opp, AL; Sue Canter, Guilford Technical Community College, Jamestown, NC; Reuel Sample, National College, Knoxville, TN; Regina Young, Wiregrass Georgia Technical College, Valdosta, GA; William Roxbury, National College, Stow, OH; Charles Adams, II, Danville Community College, Danville, VA; Karen Spray, Northeast Community College, Norfolk, NE; Deborah Miller, Augusta Technical College, Augusta, GA; Wanda Stuparits, Lanier Technical College, Cumming, GA; Gale Wilson, Brookhaven College, Farmers Branch, TX; Jocelyn S. Pinkard, Arlington Career Institute, Grand Prairie, TX; Ann Blackman, Parkland College, Champaign, IL; Fathia Williams, Fletcher Technical Community College, Houma, LA; Leslie Martin, Gaston College, Dallas, NC; Tom Rose, Kellogg Community College, Battle Creek, MI; Casey Thompson, Wiregrass Georgia Technical College, Douglas, GA; Larry Bush, University of Cincinnati, Clermont College, Amelia, OH; Tim Ellis, Schoolcraft College, Liconia, MI; Miles Cannon, Lanier Technical College, Oakwood, GA; Irvin LaFleur, Lanier Technical College, Cumming, GA; Patricia Partyka, Schoolcraft College, Prudenville, MI.

The authors and publishing team also thanks the following individuals for their contributions to this project: checking the accuracy of the instruction and exercises—Brienna McWade, Traci Post, and Janet Blum, Fanshawe College, London, Ontario; creating annotated model answers and developing lesson plans—Ann Mills, Ivy Tech Community College, Evansville, Indiana; developing rubrics—Marjory Wooten, Laneir Techncial College, Cumming, Georgia.

ISBN 978-0-76385-349-5 (Text)
ISBN 978-0-76385-392-1 (Text + CD)

875 Montreal Way
St. Paul, MN 55102
Email: educate@emcp.com
Website: www.emcp.com

Printed in the United States of America

22 21 20 19 18 17 16 15 14 13 1 2 3 4 5 6 7 8 9 10

Contents

Microsoft Access 2013 Level 2

Preface

Benchmark Series Microsoft Access 2013 is designed for students who want to learn how to use this feature-rich data management tool to track, report, and share information. No prior knowledge of database management systems is required. After successfully completing a course using this textbook, students will be able to

- Create database tables to organize business or personal records
- Modify and manage tables to ensure that data is accurate and up to date
- Perform queries to assist with decision making
- Plan, research, create, revise, and publish database information to meet specific communication needs
- Given a workplace scenario requiring the reporting and analysis of data, assess the information requirements and then prepare the materials that achieve the goal efficiently and effectively

In addition to mastering Access skills, students will learn the essential features and functions of computer hardware, the Windows 8 operating system, and Internet Explorer 10. Upon completing the text, they can expect to be proficient in using Access to organize, analyze, and present information.

Well-designed textbook pedagogy is important, but students learn technology skills from practice and problem solving. Technology provides opportunities for interactive learning as well as excellent ways to quickly and accurately assess student performance. To this end, this textbook is supported with SNAP, Paradigm Publishing's web-based training and assessment learning management system. Details about SNAP as well as additional student courseware and instructor resources can be found on page xiv.

Achieving Proficiency in Access 2013

Since its inception several Office versions ago, the Benchmark Series has served as a standard of excellence in software instruction. Elements of the book function individually and collectively to create an inviting, comprehensive learning environment that produces successful computer users. The following visual tour highlights the text's features.

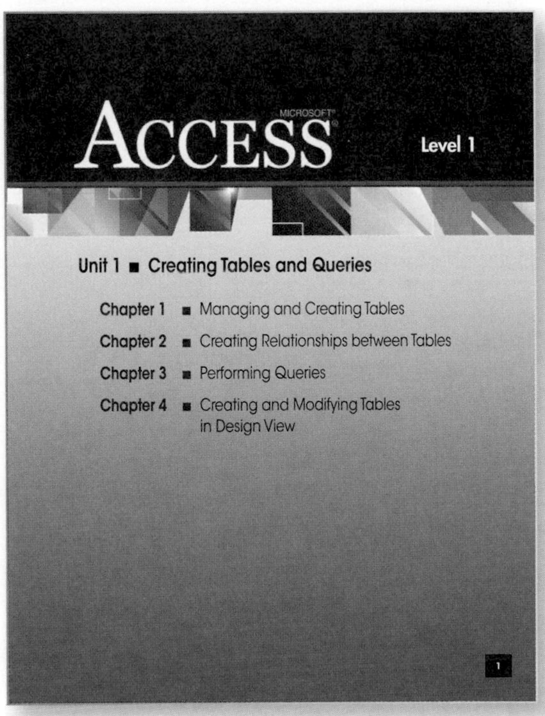

MICROSOFT
ACCESS
Level 1
Unit 1 ■ Creating Tables and Queries
Chapter 1 ■ Managing and Creating Tables
Chapter 2 ■ Creating Relationships between Tables
Chapter 3 ■ Performing Queries
Chapter 4 ■ Creating and Modifying Tables in Design View
1

UNIT OPENERS display the unit's four chapter titles. Each level has two units, which conclude with a comprehensive unit performance assessment.

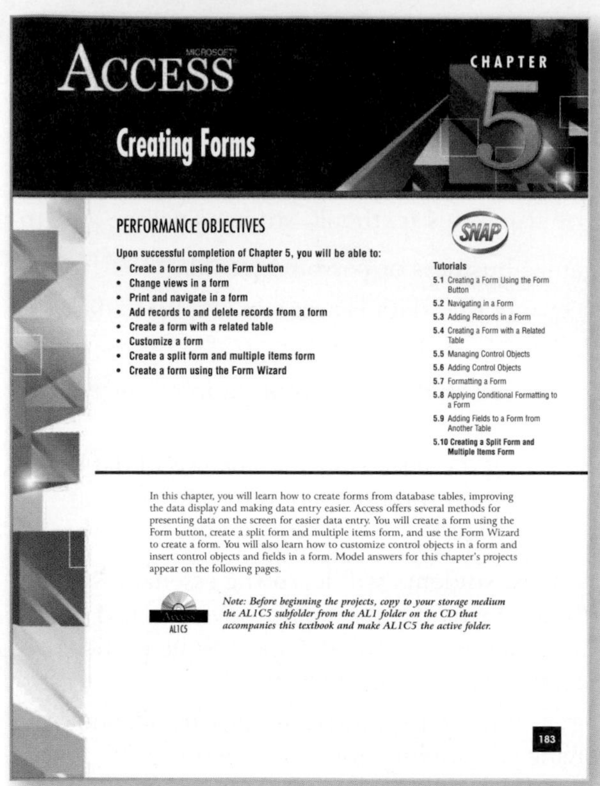

CHAPTER OPENERS present the performance objectives and an overview of the skills taught.

SNAP interactive tutorials are available to support chapter-specific skills at snap2013.emcp.com.

DATA FILES are provided for each chapter. A prominent note reminds students to copy the appropriate chapter data folder and make it active.

PROJECT APPROACH: Builds Skill Mastery within Realistic Context

MODEL ANSWERS provide a preview of the finished chapter projects and allow students to confirm they have created the materials accurately.

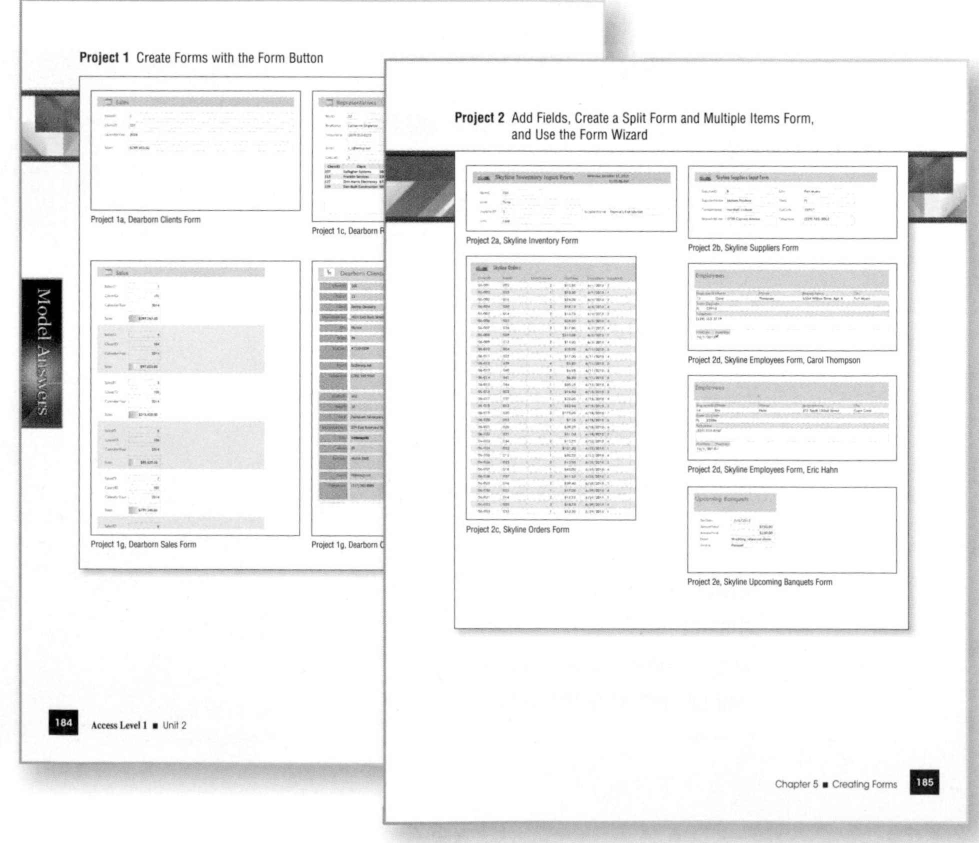

MULTIPART PROJECTS provide a framework for the instruction and practice on software features. A project overview identifies tasks to accomplish and key features to use in completing the work.

Between project parts, the text presents instruction on the features and skills necessary to accomplish the next section of the project.

STEP-BY-STEP INSTRUCTIONS guide students to the desired outcome for each project part. Screen captures illustrate what the student's screen should look like at key points.

Project 1 Create Forms with the Form Button — 7 Parts

You will use the Form button to create forms with fields in the Clients, Representatives, and Sales tables. You will also add, delete, and print records and use buttons in the FORM LAYOUT TOOLS FORMAT tab to apply formatting to control objects in the forms.

Creating Forms

HINT A form allows you to focus on a single record at a time.

Access offers a variety of options for presenting data in a clear and attractive format. For instance, you can view, add, or edit data in a table in Datasheet view. When you enter data in a table in Datasheet view, you will see multiple records at the same time. If a record contains several fields, you may not be able to view all of the fields within the record at the same time. If you create a form, however, all of the fields for a record are generally visible on the screen.

HINT Save a form before making changes or applying formatting to it.

A ***form*** is an object you can use to enter and edit data in a table or query. It is a user-friendly interface for viewing, adding, editing, and deleting records. A form is also useful in helping to prevent incorrect data from being entered and it can be used to control access to specific data.

Several methods are available for creating forms. In this chapter, you will learn how to create forms using the Form, Split Form, and Multiple Items buttons as well as the Form Wizard.

Creating a Form with the Form Button

Quick Steps
Create a Form with the Form Button
1. Click desired table.
2. Click CREATE tab.
3. Click Form button.

The simplest method for creating a form is to click a table in the Navigation pane, click the CREATE tab, and then click the Form button in the Forms groups. Figure 5.1 shows the form you will create in Project 1a with the Sales table in AL1-C5-Dearborn.accdb. Access creates the form using all fields in the table in a vertical layout and displays the form in Layout view with the FORM LAYOUT TOOLS DESIGN tab active.

Changing Views

Form

Form View

Layout View

When you click the Form button to create a form, the form displays in Layout view. This is one of three views for working with forms. Use the Form view to enter and manage records. Use the Layout view to view the data and modify the appearance and contents of the form. Use the Design view to view the structure of the form and modify the form. Change views with the View button in the Views group on the FORM LAYOUT TOOLS DESIGN tab or with buttons in the view area located at the right side of the Status bar.

You can open an existing form in Layout view. To do this, right-click the form name in the Navigation pane and then click *Layout View* at the shortcut menu.

Printing a Form

Print all of the records in a form by clicking the FILE tab, clicking the *Print* option, and then clicking the Quick Print button. If you want to print a specif... a form, click the FILE tab, click the *Print* option, and then click the Pr...

Adding and Deleting Records

Add a new record to the form by clicking the New (blank) record button (contains a right-pointing arrow and a yellow asterisk) that displays on the Record Navigation bar along the bottom of the form. You can also add a new record to a form by clicking the HOME tab and then clicking the New button in the Records group. To delete a record, display the record, click the HOME tab, click the Delete button arrow in the Records group, and then click *Delete Record* at the drop-down list. At the message telling you that the record will be deleted permanently, click Yes. Add records to or delete records from the table from which the form was created and the form will reflect the additions or deletions. Also, if you make additions or deletions to the form, the changes are reflected in the table on which the form was created.

Quick Steps
Add a Record
Click New (blank) record button on Record Navigation bar.
OR
1. Click HOME tab.
2. Click New button.
Delete a Record
1. Click HOME tab.
2. Click Delete button arrow.
3. Click *Delete Record*.
4. Click Yes.

Sorting Records

Sort data in a form by clicking in the field containing data on which you want to sort and then clicking the Ascending button or Descending button in the Sort & Filter group on the HOME tab. Click the Ascending button to sort text in alphabetic order from A to Z or numbers from lowest to highest or click the Descending button to sort text in alphabetic order from Z to A or numbers from highest to lowest.

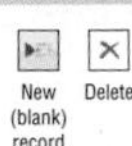

New (blank) record   Delete

Project 1b Adding and Deleting Records in a Form — Part 2 of 7

1. Open the Sales table (not the form) and add a new record by completing the following steps:
   a. Click the New (blank) record button located in the Record Navigation bar.
   b. At the new blank record, type the following information in the specified fields. (Move to the next field by pressing Tab or Enter; move to the previous field by pressing Shift + Tab.)
      SalesID (This is an AutoNumber field, so press Tab.)
      ClientID 127
      CalendarYear 2015
      Sales 176420
2. Close the Sales table.
3. Open the Sales form.
4. Click the Last record button on the Record Navigation bar and notice that the new record you added to the table has been added to the form.

QUICK STEPS provide feature summaries for reference and review.

HINTS provide useful tips on how to use features efficiently and effectively.

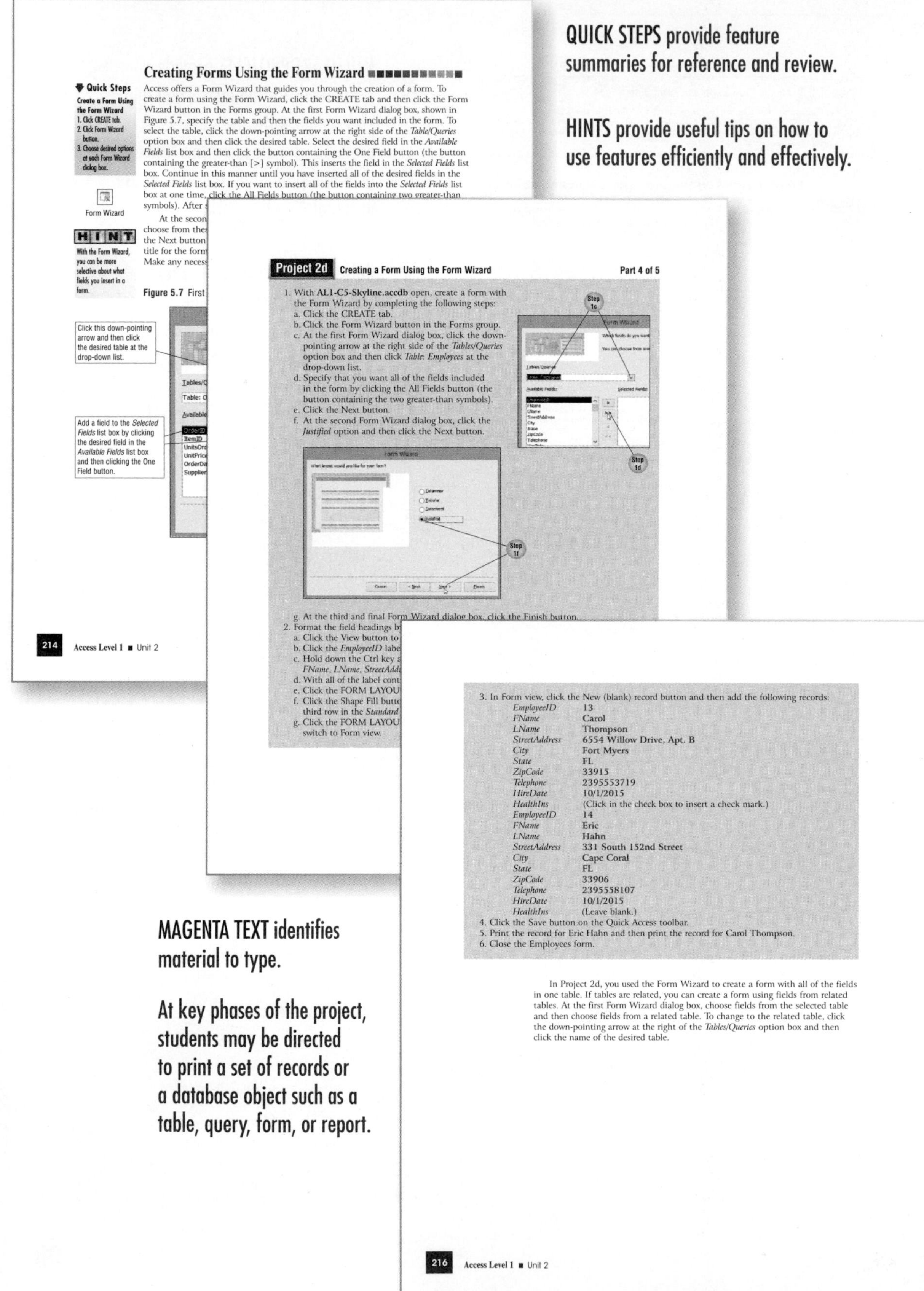

Creating Forms Using the Form Wizard

Quick Steps
Create a Form Using the Form Wizard
1. Click CREATE tab.
2. Click Form Wizard button.
3. Choose desired options at each Form Wizard dialog box.

Form Wizard

HINT
With the Form Wizard, you can be more selective about what fields you insert in a form.

Access offers a Form Wizard that guides you through the creation of a form. To create a form using the Form Wizard, click the CREATE tab and then click the Form Wizard button in the Forms group. At the first Form Wizard dialog box, shown in Figure 5.7, specify the table and then the fields you want included in the form. To select the table, click the down-pointing arrow at the right side of the *Table/Queries* option box and then click the desired table. Select the desired field in the *Available Fields* list box and then click the button containing the One Field button (the button containing the greater-than [>] symbol). This inserts the field in the *Selected Fields* list box. Continue in this manner until you have inserted all of the desired fields in the *Selected Fields* list box. If you want to insert all of the fields into the *Selected Fields* list box at one time, click the All Fields button (the button containing two greater-than symbols). After ...

At the secon... choose from the... the Next button... title for the form... Make any neces...

Figure 5.7 First ...

Click this down-pointing arrow and then click the desired table at the drop-down list.

Add a field to the *Selected Fields* list box by clicking the desired field in the *Available Fields* list box and then clicking the One Field button.

214 Access Level 1 ■ Unit 2

Project 2d Creating a Form Using the Form Wizard — Part 4 of 5

1. With **AL1-C5-Skyline.accdb** open, create a form with the Form Wizard by completing the following steps:
   a. Click the CREATE tab.
   b. Click the Form Wizard button in the Forms group.
   c. At the first Form Wizard dialog box, click the down-pointing arrow at the right side of the *Tables/Queries* option box and then click *Table: Employees* at the drop-down list.
   d. Specify that you want all of the fields included in the form by clicking the All Fields button (the button containing the two greater-than symbols).
   e. Click the Next button.
   f. At the second Form Wizard dialog box, click the *Justified* option and then click the Next button.
   g. At the third and final Form Wizard dialog box, click the Finish button.
2. Format the field headings b...
   a. Click the View button to...
   b. Click the *EmployeeID* labe...
   c. Hold down the Ctrl key a... *FName, LName, StreetAdd...*
   d. With all of the label cont...
   e. Click the FORM LAYOU...
   f. Click the Shape Fill butt... third row in the *Standard*...
   g. Click the FORM LAYOU... switch to Form view.

Step 1c · Step 1d · Step 1f

3. In Form view, click the New (blank) record button and then add the following records:

EmployeeID	13
FName	Carol
LName	Thompson
StreetAddress	6554 Willow Drive, Apt. B
City	Fort Myers
State	FL
ZipCode	33915
Telephone	2395553719
HireDate	10/1/2015
HealthIns	(Click in the check box to insert a check mark.)
EmployeeID	14
FName	Eric
LName	Hahn
StreetAddress	331 South 152nd Street
City	Cape Coral
State	FL
ZipCode	33906
Telephone	2395558107
HireDate	10/1/2015
HealthIns	(Leave blank.)

4. Click the Save button on the Quick Access toolbar.
5. Print the record for Eric Hahn and then print the record for Carol Thompson.
6. Close the Employees form.

In Project 2d, you used the Form Wizard to create a form with all of the fields in one table. If tables are related, you can create a form using fields from related tables. At the first Form Wizard dialog box, choose fields from the selected table and then choose fields from a related table. To change to the related table, click the down-pointing arrow at the right of the *Tables/Queries* option box and then click the name of the desired table.

216 Access Level 1 ■ Unit 2

MAGENTA TEXT identifies material to type.

At key phases of the project, students may be directed to print a set of records or a database object such as a table, query, form, or report.

CHAPTER REVIEW ACTIVITIES: A Hierarchy of Learning Assessments

Chapter Summary

- Microsoft Access is a database management system software program that can organize, store, maintain, retrieve, sort, and print all types of business data.
- In Access, open an existing database by clicking the Open Other Files hyperlink at the Access 2013 opening screen. At the Open backstage area, double-click your SkyDrive or the *Computer* option. At the Open dialog box, navigate to the location of the database and then double-click the desired database.
- Some common objects found in a database include tables, queries, forms, and reports.
- The Navigation pane displays at the left side of the Access screen and displays the objects that are contained in the database.
- Open a database object by double-clicking the object in the Navigation pane. Close an object by clicking the Close button that displays in the upper right corner of the work area.
- When a table is open, the Record Navigation bar displays at the bottom of the screen and contains buttons for displaying records in the table.
- Insert a new record in a table by clicking the New button in the Records group on the HOME tab or by clicking the Ne[w] Navigation bar. Delete a record by clicki[ng] delete, clicking the Delete button arrow [...] *Delete Record* at the drop-down list.
- To add a column to a table, click the first [...] heading and then type the desired data. T[...] and then use the mouse to drag a thick, b[...] column) to the desired location. To delete [...] click the Delete button arrow, and then cl[...]
- Data you enter in a table is automaticall[y ...] a table are not automatically saved.
- Hide, unhide, freeze, and unfreeze colum[ns ...] drop-down list. Display this list by clicki[ng ...] group on the HOME tab.
- Adjust the width of a column (or selecte[d ...] longest entry by double-clicking the colu[mn ...] width of a column by dragging the colum[n ...]
- Rename a table by right-clicking the tabl[e ...] clicking *Rename*, and then typing the new [...] the table name in the Navigation pane a[...]
- Print a table by clicking the FILE tab, cli[cking ...] clicking the Quick Print button. You can [...] clicking the Print Preview button at the P[...]
- With buttons and option on the PRINT [...] page size, orientation, and margins.
- The first principle in database design is t[...] redundant data increases the amount of [...] chances for errors, and takes up addition[al ...]
- A data type defines the type of data Acc[ess ...] type to a field with buttons in the Add &[...]

CHAPTER SUMMARY captures the purpose and execution of key features.

FIELDS tab, by clicking an option from the column heading drop-down list, or with options at the More button drop-down list.

- Rename a column heading by right-clicking the heading, clicking *Rename Field* at the shortcut menu, and then typing the new name.
- Type a name, caption, and description for a column with options at the Enter Field Properties dialog box.
- Use options in the *Quick Start* category in the More Fields button drop-down list to define a data type and assign a field name to a group of related fields.
- Insert a default value in a column with the Default Value button and assign a field size with the *Field Size* text box in the Properties group on the TABLE TOOLS FIELDS tab.
- Use the *Data Type* option box in the Formatting group on the TABLE TOOLS FIELDS tab to change the AutoNumber data type for the first column in a table.

Commands Review

FEATURE	RIBBON TAB, GROUP/OPTION	BUTTON, OPTION	KEYBOARD SHORTCUT
close Access			Alt + F4
close database	FILE, *Close*		
create table	CREATE, Tables		
Currency data type	TABLE TOOLS FIELDS, Add & Delete		
Date & Time data type	TABLE TOOLS FIELDS, Add & Delete		
delete column	HOME, Records	*Delete Column*	
delete record	HOME, Records	*Delete Record*	
Enter Field Properties dialog box	TABLE TOOLS FIELDS, Proper[ties]		
Expression Builder dialog box	TABLE TOOLS FIELDS, Proper[ties]		
freeze column	HOME, Records		
hide column	HOME, Records		
landscape orientation	FILE, *Print*		
new record	HOME, Records		
next field			
Number data type	TABLE TOOLS FIELDS, Add & [Delete]		
Page Setup dialog box	FILE, *Print*		

COMMANDS REVIEW summarizes visually the major features and command options.

Concepts Check Test Your Knowledge SNAP

records in one table that have no matching records in the other related table.

Completion: In the space provided at the right, indicate the correct term, symbol, or command.

1. The Query Design button is located in the Queries group on this tab. ____________
2. Click the Query Design button and the query window displays with this dialog box open. ____________
3. To establish a criterion for a query, click in this row in the column containing the desired field name and then type the criterion. ____________
4. This is the term used for the results of the query. ____________
5. This is the symbol Access automatically inserts before and after a date when writing a criterion for the query. ____________
6. Use this symbol to indicate a wildcard character when writing a query criterion. ____________
7. This is the criterion you would type to return field values greater than $500. ____________
8. This is the criterion you would type to return field values that begin with the letter *L*. ____________
9. This is the criterion you would type to return field values that are not in Oregon. ____________
10. You can sort a field in a query in ascending order or in this order. ____________
11. Multiple criteria entered in the *Criteria* row in the query design grid become this type of statement. ____________
12. This wizard guides you through the steps for preparing a query. ____________
13. This type of query calculates aggregate functions, in which field values are grouped by two fields. ____________
14. Use this type of query to compare two tables and produce a list of the records in one table that have no matching records in the other table. ____________

CONCEPTS CHECK questions assess knowledge recall. Students enrolled in SNAP can complete the concepts check online. SNAP automatically scores student work.

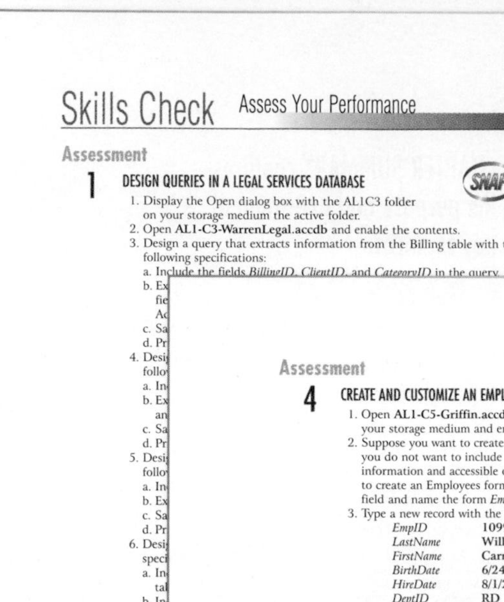

Skills Check Assess Your Performance

Assessment 1

DESIGN QUERIES IN A LEGAL SERVICES DATABASE

1. Display the Open dialog box with the AL1C3 folder on your storage medium the active folder.
2. Open **AL1-C3-WarrenLegal.accdb** and enable the contents.
3. Design a query that extracts information from the Billing table with the following specifications:
   a. Include the fields *BillingID*, *ClientID*, and *CategoryID* in the query
   b. Ex
   fie
   Ac
   c. Sa
   d. Pr
4. Desi
   follo
   a. In
   b. Ex
   an
   c. Sa
   d. Pr
5. Desi
   follo
   a. In
   b. Ex
   c. Sa
   d. Pr
6. Desi
   speci
   a. In
   tal
   b. In
   c. Ex
   d. Sa
   e. Pr
7. Desi
   speci
   a. In
   b. In
   c. In
   d. Ex
   e. Sa
   f. Pr
8. Desi
   speci
   a. In
   b. In
   c. In

122 Access Level 1 ■ Unit 1

SKILLS CHECK exercises ask students to develop both standard and customized kinds of database elements. Versions of the activities marked with a SNAP Grade It icon are available for automatic scoring in SNAP.

Assessment 4

CREATE AND CUSTOMIZE AN EMPLOYEES FORM

1. Open **AL1-C5-Griffin.accdb** from the AL1C5 folder on your storage medium and enable the contents.
2. Suppose you want to create a form for entering employee information but you do not want to include the employees' salaries, since that is confidential information and accessible only to the account manager. Use the Form Wizard to create an Employees form that includes all fields *except* the *AnnualSalary* field and name the form *Employees*.
3. Type a new record with the following information in the specified fields:

EmpID	**1099**
LastName	**Williamson**
FirstName	**Carrie**
BirthDate	**6/24/1986**
HireDate	**8/1/2014**
DeptID	**RD**

4. Switch to layout view, apply the Slice theme, change the theme colors to *Blue Warm*, and change the theme fonts to *Franklin Gothic*.
5. Print the new record you typed.
6. Close the Employees form.

Visual Benchmark Demonstrate Your Proficiency

CREATE AND FORMAT A PROPERTIES FORM

1. Open **AL1-C5-SunProperties.accdb** located in the AL1C5 folder on your storage medium and enable the contents.
2. Create a form with the Properties table and format the form so it appears similar to the form in Figure 5.8 using the following specifications:
   a. Apply the Facet theme and apply the Paper theme colors.
   b. Insert the logo, title,
   the figure. (Insert th
   title control object a
   c. Select all of the obj
   to Maroon 5 (sixth
   d. Select the first colu
   Background 2, Dar
   Theme Colors sectio
   column, sixth row i
   alignment to Align

224 Access Level 1 ■ Unit 2

VISUAL BENCHMARK assessments test students' problem-solving skills and mastery of program features.

Case Study Apply Your Skills

Part 1

You are the office manager at the Lewis Vision Care Center and your center is switching over to Access to manage files. You have already created four basic tables and now need to create relationships and enter data. Open **AL1-C5-LewisCenter.accdb** and then create the following relationships between tables (enforce referential integrity and cascade fields and records):

Field Name	"One" Table	"Many" Table
PatientID	Patients	Billing
ServiceID	Services	Billing
DoctorID	Doctors	Billing

Save and then print the relationships.

Part 2

Before entering data in the tables, create a form for each table and apply a theme of your choosing. Enter data in the forms in the order in which it appears in Figure 5.10 on the next page. Apply any additional formatting to enhance the visual appearance of each form. After entering the information in the forms, print the first record of each form.

Part 3

Apply the following conditions to fields in forms:

- In the Patients form, apply the condition that the city *Tulsa* displays in red and the city *Broken Arrow* displays in blue in the *City* field. Print the first record of the Patients form and then close the form.
- In the Billing form, apply the condition that amounts in the *Fee* field over $99 display in green. Print the second record of the Billing form and then close the form.

Close **AL1-C5-LewisCenter.accdb**.

Part 4

Your center has a procedures manual that describes workplace processes and procedures. Open Word and then create a document for the procedures manual that describes the formatting and conditions you applied to the forms in **AL1-C5-LewisCenter.accdb**. Save the completed document and name it **AL1-C5-CS-Manual**. Print and then close **AL1-C5-CS-Manual.docx**.

226 Access Level 1 ■ Unit 2

CASE STUDY requires analyzing a workplace scenario and then planning and executing multipart projects.

Students strengthen their analytical and writing skills by using Microsoft Word to describe best uses of Access features or to explain the decisions they made in completing the Case Study.

UNIT PERFORMANCE ASSESSMENT: Cross-Disciplinary, Comprehensive Evaluation

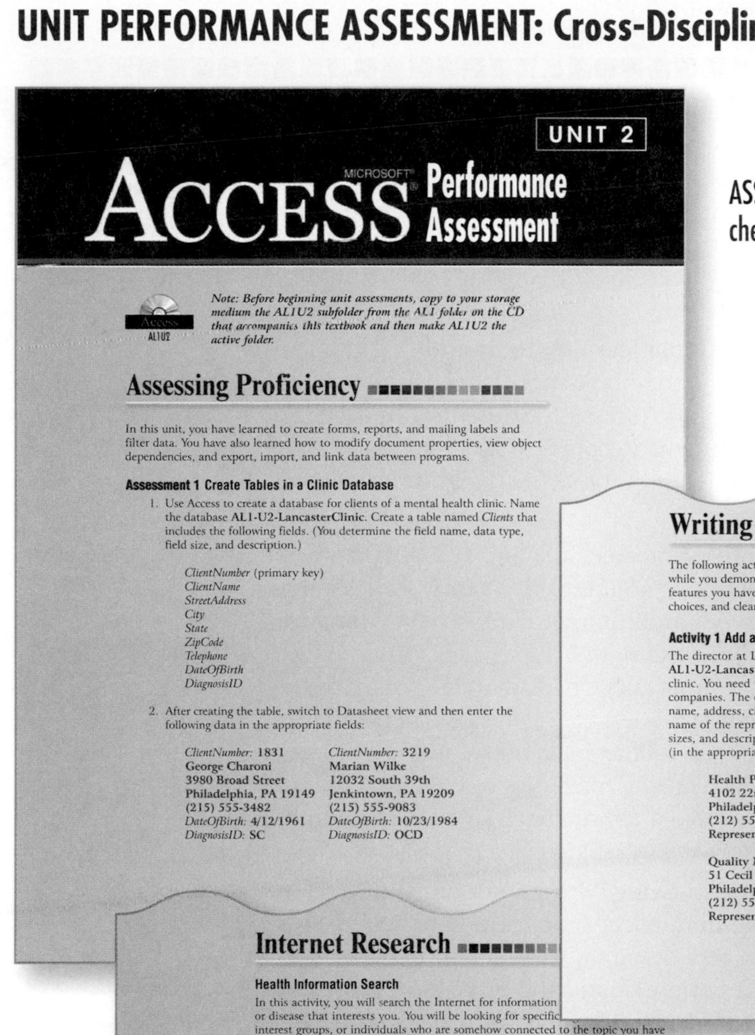

UNIT 2

MICROSOFT® ACCESS Performance Assessment

Note: Before beginning unit assessments, copy to your storage medium the AL1U2 subfolder from the AL1 folder on the CD that accompanies this textbook and then make AL1U2 the active folder.

AL1U2

Assessing Proficiency

In this unit, you have learned to create forms, reports, and mailing labels and filter data. You have also learned how to modify document properties, view object dependencies, and export, import, and link data between programs.

Assessment 1 Create Tables in a Clinic Database

1. Use Access to create a database for clients of a mental health clinic. Name the database **AL1-U2-LancasterClinic**. Create a table named *Clients* that includes the following fields. (You determine the field name, data type, field size, and description.)

   ClientNumber (primary key)
   ClientName
   StreetAddress
   City
   State
   ZipCode
   Telephone
   DateOfBirth
   DiagnosisID

2. After creating the table, switch to Datasheet view and then enter the following data in the appropriate fields:

ClientNumber: 1831	*ClientNumber:* 3219
George Charoni	**Marian Wilke**
3980 Broad Street	**12032 South 39th**
Philadelphia, PA 19149	**Jenkintown, PA 19209**
(215) 555-3482	**(215) 555-9083**
DateOfBirth: **4/12/1961**	*DateOfBirth:* **10/23/1984**
DiagnosisID: **SC**	*DiagnosisID:* **OCD**

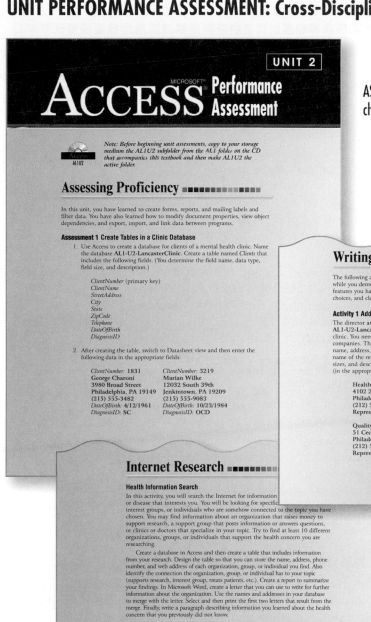

ASSESSING PROFICIENCY checks mastery of features.

WRITING ACTIVITIES involve applying program skills in a communication context.

Writing Activities

The following activities give you the opportunity to practice your writing skills while you demonstrate your understanding of some of the important Access features you have mastered in this unit. Use correct grammar, appropriate word choices, and clear sentence constructions.

Activity 1 Add a Table to the Clinic Database

The director at Lancaster Clinic has asked you to add information to **AL1-U2-LancasterClinic.accdb** on insurance companies contracted by the clinic. You need to create a table that will contain information on insurance companies. The director wants the table to include the insurance company name, address, city, state, and zip code, along with the telephone number and name of the representative. You determine the field names, data types, field sizes, and description for the table and then include the following information (in the appropriate fields):

Health Plus **4102 22nd Street** **Philadelphia, PA 19166** **(212) 555-0990** **Representative: Byron Tolleson**	**Penn-State Health** **5933 Lehigh Avenue** **Philadelphia, PA 19148** **(212) 555-3477** **Representative: Tracey Pavone**
Quality Medical **51 Cecil B. Moore Avenue** **Philadelphia, PA 19168** **(212) 555-4600** **Representative: Lee Stafford**	**Delaware Health** **4418 Front Street** **Philadelphia, PA 19132** **(212) 555-6770** **Representative: Melanie Chon**

Access Level 1 ■ Unit 2 Performance Assessment 325

Internet Research

Health Information Search

In this activity, you will search the Internet for information or disease that interests you. You will be looking for specific interest groups, or individuals who are somehow connected to the topic you have chosen. You may find information about an organization that raises money to support research, a support group that posts information or answers questions, or clinics or doctors that specialize in your topic. Try to find at least 10 different organizations, groups, or individuals that support the health concern you are researching.

Create a database in Access and then create a table that includes information from your research. Design the table so that you can store the name, address, phone number, and web address of each organization, group, or individual you find. Also identify the connection the organization, group, or individual has to your topic (supports research, interest group, treats patients, etc.). Create a report to summarize your findings. In Microsoft Word, create a letter that you can use to write for further information about the organization. Use the names and addresses in your database to merge with the letter. Select and then print the first two letters that result from the merge. Finally, write a paragraph describing information you learned about the health concern that you previously did not know.

326 Access Level 1 ■ Unit 2 Performance Assessment

INTERNET RESEARCH project reinforces research and database development skills.

Job Study

City Improvement Projects

In this activity, you will work with the city council in your area to keep the public informed of the progress being made on improvement projects throughout the city. These projects are paid for through tax dollars voted on by the public, and the city council feels that keeping area residents informed will lead to good voter turnout when it is time to make more improvements.

Your job is to create a database and table in the database that will store the following information for each project: a project ID number, a description of the project, the budgeted dollar amount to be spent, the amount of money spent so far, the amount of time allocated to the project, and the amount of time spent so far. Enter five city improvement projects into the table (using sample data created by you). Create a query based on the table that calculates the percentage of budgeted dollars spent so far and the percentage of budgeted time spent so far. Print the table and the query.

JOB STUDY at the end of Unit 2 presents a capstone assessment requiring critical thinking and problem solving.

Student Courseware

Student Resources CD Each Benchmark Series textbook is packaged with a Student Resources CD containing the data files required for completing the projects and assessments. A CD icon and folder name displayed on the opening page of chapters reminds students to copy a folder of files from the CD to the desired storage medium before beginning the project exercises. Directions for copying folders are printed on the inside back cover.

Internet Resource Center Additional learning tools and reference materials are available at the book-specific website at www.paradigmcollege.net/BenchmarkAccess13. Students can access the same files that are on the Student Resources CD along with study aids, web links, and tips for using computers effectively in academic and workplace settings.

SNAP Training and Assessment Available at snap2013.emcp.com, SNAP is a web-based program offering an interactive venue for learning Microsoft Office 2013, Windows 8, and Internet Explorer 10. Along with a web-based learning management system, SNAP provides multimedia tutorials, performance skill items, Concepts Check matching activities, Grade It Skills Check Assessment activities, comprehensive performance evaluations, a concepts test bank, an online grade book, and a set of course planning tools. A CD of tutorials teaching the basics of Office, Windows, and Internet Explorer is also available if instructors wish to assign additional SNAP tutorial work without using the web-based SNAP program.

eBook For students who prefer studying with an eBook, the texts in the Benchmark Series are available in an electronic form. The web-based, password-protected eBooks feature dynamic navigation tools, including bookmarking, a linked table of contents, and the ability to jump to a specific page. The eBook format also supports helpful study tools, such as highlighting and note taking.

Instructor Resources

Instructor's Guide and Disc Instructor support for the Benchmark Series includes an *Instructor's Guide and Instructor Resources Disc* package. This resource includes planning information, such as Lesson Blueprints, teaching hints, and sample course syllabi; presentation resources, such as PowerPoint slide shows with lecture notes and audio support; and assessment resources, including an overview of available assessment venues, live model answers for chapter activities, and live and PDF model answers for end-of-chapter exercises. Contents of the *Instructor's Guide and Instructor Resources Disc* package are also available on the password-protected section of the Internet Resource Center for this title at www.paradigmcollege.net/BenchmarkAccess13.

Computerized Test Generator Instructors can use the ExamView® Assessment Suite and test banks of multiple-choice items to create customized web-based or print tests.

Blackboard Cartridge This set of files allows instructors to create a personalized Blackboard website for their course and provides course content, tests, and the mechanisms for establishing communication via e-discussions and online group conferences. Available content includes a syllabus, test banks, PowerPoint presentations with audio support, and supplementary course materials. Upon request, the files can be available within 24–48 hours. Hosting the site is the responsibility of the educational institution.

System Requirements

This text is designed for the student to complete projects and assessments on a computer running a standard installation of Microsoft Office Professional Plus 2013 and the Microsoft Windows 8 operating system. To effectively run this suite and operating system, your computer should be outfitted with the following:

- 1 gigahertz (GHz) processor or higher; 1 gigabyte (GB) of RAM (32 bit) or 2 GB of RAM (64 bit)
- 3 GB of available hard-disk space
- .NET version 3.5, 4.0, or 4.5
- DirectX 10 graphics card
- Minimum 1024 × 576 resolution (or 1366 × 768 to use Windows Snap feature)
- Computer mouse, multi-touch device, or other compatible pointing device

Office 2013 will also operate on computers running the Windows 7 operating system.

Screen captures in this book were created using a screen resolution display setting of 1600 × 900. Refer to the *Customizing Settings* section of *Getting Started in Office 2013* following this preface for instructions on changing your monitor's resolution. Figure G.9 on page 10 shows the Microsoft Office Word ribbon at three resolutions for comparison purposes. Choose the resolution that best matches your computer; however, be aware that using a resolution other than 1600 × 900 means that your screens may not match the illustrations in this book.

About the Authors

Nita Rutkosky began teaching business education courses at Pierce College in Puyallup, Washington, in 1978. Since then she has taught a variety of software applications to students in postsecondary Information Technology certificate and degree programs. In addition to *Benchmark Office 2013*, she has co-authored *Marquee Series: Microsoft Office 2013*, *2010*, *2007*, and *2003*; *Signature Series: Microsoft Word 2013*, *2010*, *2007*, and *2003*; *Using Computers in the Medical Office: Microsoft Word, Excel, and PowerPoint 2010*, *2007* and *2003*; and *Computer and Internet Essentials: Preparing for IC3*. She has also authored textbooks on keyboarding, WordPerfect, desktop publishing, and voice recognition for Paradigm Publishing, Inc.

Denise Seguin has served in the Faculty of Business at Fanshawe College of Applied Arts and Technology in London, Ontario, since 1986. She has developed curriculum and taught a variety of office technology, software applications, and accounting courses to students in postsecondary Information Technology diploma programs and in Continuing Education courses. Seguin has served as Program Coordinator for Computer Systems Technician, Computer Systems Technology, Office Administration, and Law Clerk programs and was acting Chair of the School of Information Technology in 2001. In addition to co-authoring the Level 2 *Access 2013* and *Excel 2013* books in the Benchmark Series, she has authored *Computer Concepts and Applications for Microsoft Office 2013* and *Microsoft Outlook 2013*, *2010*, *2007*, *2003*, *2002*, and *2000*. She has also co-authored *Our Digital World* first and second editions; *Marquee Series: Microsoft Office 2013*, *2010*, *2007*, and *2003*; *Office 2003*; *Office XP*; and *Using Computers in the Medical Office: Microsoft Word, Excel, and PowerPoint 2010*, *2007*, and *2003* for Paradigm Publishing, Inc.

Jan Davidson started her teaching career in 1997 as a corporate trainer and postsecondary instructor. Since 2001, she has been a faculty member of the School of Business and Information Technology at Lambton College of Applied Arts and Technology in Sarnia, Ontario. In this role, she has developed curriculum and taught a variety of office technology, software applications, and office administration courses to domestic and international students in postsecondary Office Administration Executive, General, and Medical; Human Resources; and Fashion Business programs. In addition to co-authoring the Level 2 *Access 2013* and *Excel 2013* books in the Benchmark Series, she has written instructor resources and SNAP content for Paradigm Publishing, Inc. since 2006.

Audrey Roggenkamp has been teaching courses in the Business Information Technology department at Pierce College in Puyallup since 2005. Her courses have included keyboarding, skill building, and Microsoft Office programs. In addition to this title, she has co-authored *Marquee Series: Microsoft Office 2013, 2010*, and *2007*; *Signature Series: Microsoft Word 2013, 2010*, and *2007*; *Using Computers in the Medical Office: Microsoft Word, Excel, and PowerPoint 2010, 2007*, and *2003*; and *Computer and Internet Essentials: Preparing for IC3* for Paradigm Publishing, Inc.

Ian Rutkosky teaches Business Technology courses at Pierce College in Puyallup, Washington. In addition to this title, he has coauthored *Computer and Internet Essentials: Preparing for IC3*, *Marquee Series: Microsoft Office 2013*, and *Using Computers in the Medical Office: Microsoft Word, Excel, and PowerPoint 2010*. He is also a co-author and consultant for Paradigm's SNAP training and assessment software.

Getting Started in Office 2013

In this textbook, you will learn to operate several computer programs that combine to make the Microsoft Office 2013 application suite. The programs you will learn are known as ***software***, and they contain instructions that tell the computer what to do. Some of the application programs in the suite include Word, a word processing program; Excel, a spreadsheet program; Access, a database program; and PowerPoint, a presentation program.

Identifying Computer Hardware

The computer equipment you will use to operate the Microsoft Office suite is referred to as ***hardware***. You will need access to a computer system that includes a CPU, monitor, keyboard, printer, drives, and mouse. If you are not sure what equipment you will be operating, check with your instructor. The computer system shown in Figure G.1 consists of six components. Each component is discussed separately in the material that follows.

Figure G.1 Computer System

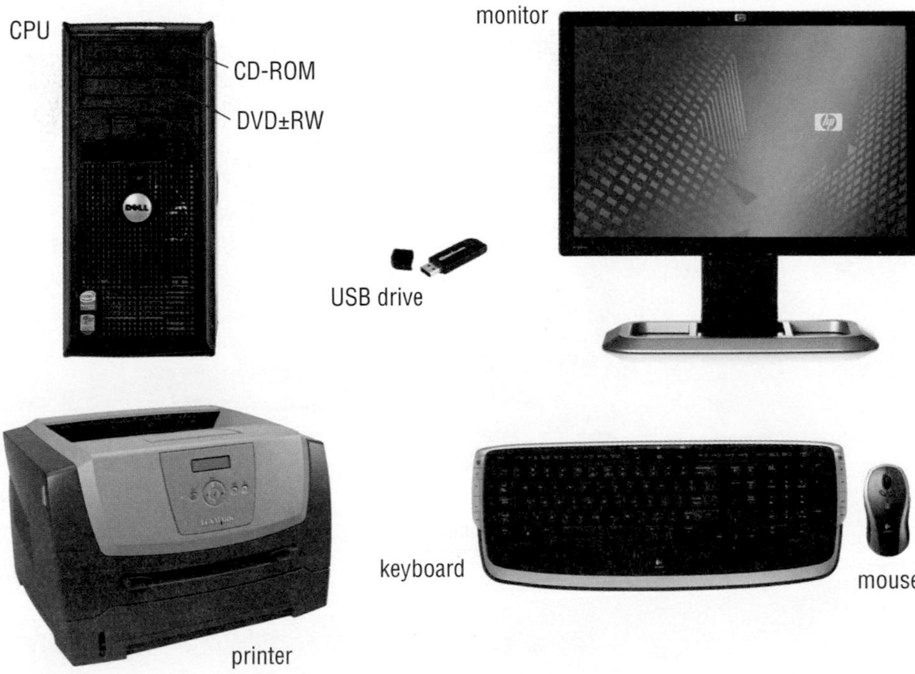

CPU

The ***central processing unit (CPU)*** is the brain of the computer and is where all processing occurs. Silicon chips, which contain miniaturized circuitry, are placed on boards that are plugged into slots within the CPU. Whenever an instruction is given to the computer, it is processed through the circuitry in the CPU.

Monitor

A computer ***monitor*** looks like a television screen. It displays the information in a program and the text you input using the keyboard. The quality of display for monitors varies depending on the type of monitor and the level of resolution. Monitors can also vary in size—generally from 13 inches to 26 inches or larger.

Keyboard

The ***keyboard*** is used to input information into the computer. The number and location of the keys on a keyboard can vary. In addition to letters, numbers, and symbols, most computer keyboards contain function keys, arrow keys, and a numeric keypad. Figure G.2 shows an enhanced keyboard.

The 12 keys at the top of the keyboard, labeled with the letter F followed by a number, are called ***function keys***. Use these keys to perform functions within each of the Office programs. To the right of the regular keys is a group of ***special*** or ***dedicated keys***. These keys are labeled with specific functions that will be performed when you press the key. Below the special keys are arrow keys. Use these keys to move the insertion point in the document screen.

Some keyboards include mode indicator lights. When you select certain modes, a light appears on the keyboard. For example, if you press the Caps Lock key, which disables the lowercase alphabet, a light appears next to Caps Lock. Similarly, pressing the Num Lock key will disable the special functions on the numeric keypad, which is located at the right side of the keyboard.

Figure G.2 Keyboard

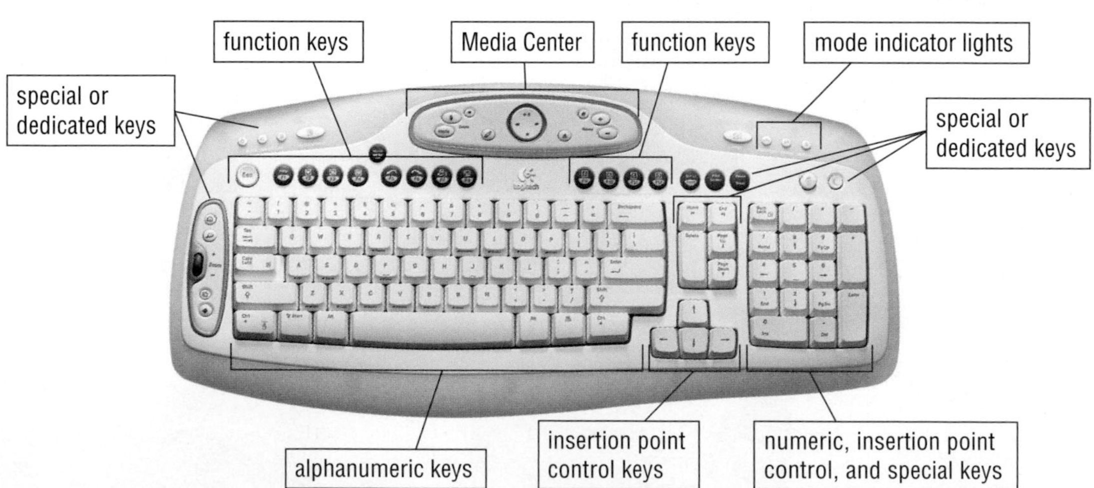

Drives and Ports

Depending on the computer system you are using, Microsoft Office 2013 is installed on a hard drive or as part of a network system. Either way, you will need to have a CD or DVD drive to complete the projects and assessments in this book. If you plan to use a USB drive as your storage medium, you will also need a USB port. You will insert the CD that accompanies this textbook into the CD or DVD drive and then copy folders from the disc to your storage medium. You will also save documents you create to folders on your storage medium.

Printer

An electronic version of a file is known as a ***soft copy***. If you want to create a ***hard copy*** of a file, you need to print it. To print documents you will need to access a printer, which will probably be either a laser printer or an ink-jet printer. A ***laser printer*** uses a laser beam combined with heat and pressure to print documents, while an ***ink-jet printer*** prints a document by spraying a fine mist of ink on the page.

Mouse or Touchpad

Most functions and commands in the Microsoft Office suite are designed to be performed using a mouse or a similar pointing device. A ***mouse*** is an input device that sits on a flat surface next to the computer. You can operate a mouse with your left or right hand. Moving the mouse on the flat surface causes a corresponding pointer to move on the screen, and clicking the left or right mouse buttons allows you to select various objects and commands. Figure G.1 contains an image of a mouse.

If you are working on a laptop computer, you may use a touchpad instead of a mouse. A ***touchpad*** allows you to move the mouse pointer by moving your finger across a surface at the base of the keyboard. You click by using your thumb to press the button located at the bottom of the touchpad.

Using the Mouse

The programs in the Microsoft Office suite can be operated with the keyboard and a mouse. The mouse generally has two buttons on top, which you press to execute specific functions and commands. A mouse may also contain a wheel, which can be used to scroll in a window or as a third button. To use the mouse, rest it on a flat surface or a mouse pad. Put your hand over it with your palm resting on top of the mouse, your wrist resting on the table surface, and your index finger resting on the left mouse button. As you move your hand, and thus the mouse, a corresponding pointer moves on the screen.

When using the mouse, you should understand four terms — point, click, double-click, and drag. When operating the mouse, you may need to point to a specific command, button, or icon. To ***point*** means to position the mouse pointer on the desired item. With the mouse pointer positioned on the desired item, you may need to click a button on the mouse to select the item. To ***click*** means to quickly tap a button on the mouse once. To complete two steps at one time, such as choosing and then executing a function, double-click the mouse button. To ***double-click*** means to tap the left mouse button twice in quick succession. The term ***drag*** means to press and hold the left mouse button, move the mouse pointer to a specific location, and then release the button.

Using the Mouse Pointer

The mouse pointer will look different depending on where you have positioned it and what function you are performing. The following are some of the ways the mouse pointer can appear when you are working in the Office suite:

- The mouse pointer appears as an I-beam (called the ***I-beam pointer***) when you are inserting text in a file. The I-beam pointer can be used to move the insertion point or to select text.
- The mouse pointer appears as an arrow pointing up and to the left (called the ***arrow pointer***) when it is moved to the Title bar, Quick Access toolbar, ribbon, or an option in a dialog box, among other locations.

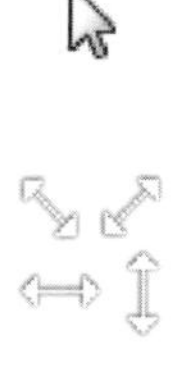

- The mouse pointer becomes a double-headed arrow (either pointing left and right, pointing up and down, or pointing diagonally) when you perform certain functions such as changing the size of an object.

- In certain situations, such as when you move an object or image, the mouse pointer displays with a four-headed arrow attached. The four-headed arrow means that you can move the object left, right, up, or down.

- When a request is being processed or when a program is being loaded, the mouse pointer may appear as a moving circle. The moving circle means "please wait." When the process is completed, the circle is replaced with a normal arrow pointer.

- When the mouse pointer displays as a hand with a pointing index finger, it indicates that more information is available about an item. The mouse pointer also displays as a hand with a pointing index finger when you hover the mouse over a hyperlink.

Choosing Commands

Once a program is open, you can use several methods in the program to choose commands. A ***command*** is an instruction that tells the program to do something. You can choose a command using the mouse or the keyboard. When a program such as Word or PowerPoint is open, the ribbon contains buttons and options for completing tasks, as well as tabs you can click to display additional buttons and options. To choose a button on the Quick Access toolbar or on the ribbon, position the tip of the mouse arrow pointer on the button and then click the left mouse button.

The Office suite provides ***accelerator keys*** you can press to use a command in a program. Press the Alt key on the keyboard to display KeyTips that identify the accelerator key you can press to execute a command. For example, if you press the Alt key in a Word document with the HOME tab active, KeyTips display as shown in Figure G.3. Continue pressing accelerator keys until you execute the desired command. For example, to begin spell checking a document, press the Alt key, press the R key on the keyboard to display the REVIEW tab, and then press the letter S on the keyboard.

Figure G.3 Word HOME Tab KeyTips

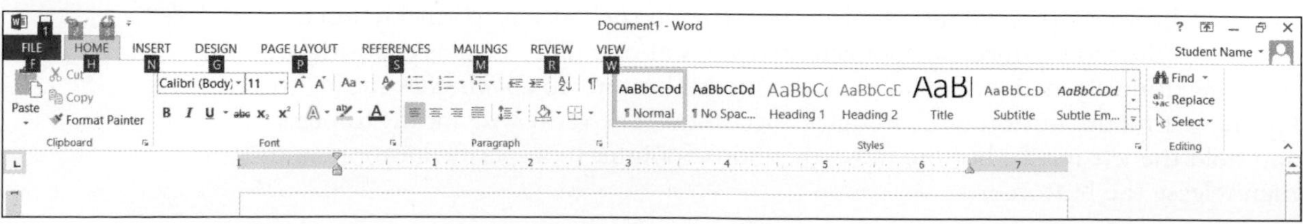

Choosing Commands from Drop-Down Lists

To choose a command from a drop-down list with the mouse, position the mouse pointer on the desired option and then click the left mouse button. To make a selection from a drop-down list with the keyboard, type the underlined letter in the desired option.

Some options at a drop-down list may appear in gray (dimmed), indicating that the option is currently unavailable. If an option at a drop-down list displays preceded by a check mark, it means the option is currently active. If an option at a drop-down list displays followed by an ellipsis (…), clicking that option will display a dialog box.

Choosing Options from a Dialog Box

A ***dialog box*** contains options for applying formatting or otherwise modifying a file or data within a file. Some dialog boxes display with tabs along the top that provide additional options. For example, the Font dialog box shown in Figure G.4 contains two tabs — the Font tab and the Advanced tab. The tab that displays in the front is the active tab. To make a tab active using the mouse, position the arrow pointer on the desired tab and then click the left mouse button. If you are using the keyboard, press Ctrl + Tab or press Alt + the underlined letter on the desired tab.

Figure G.4 Word Font Dialog Box

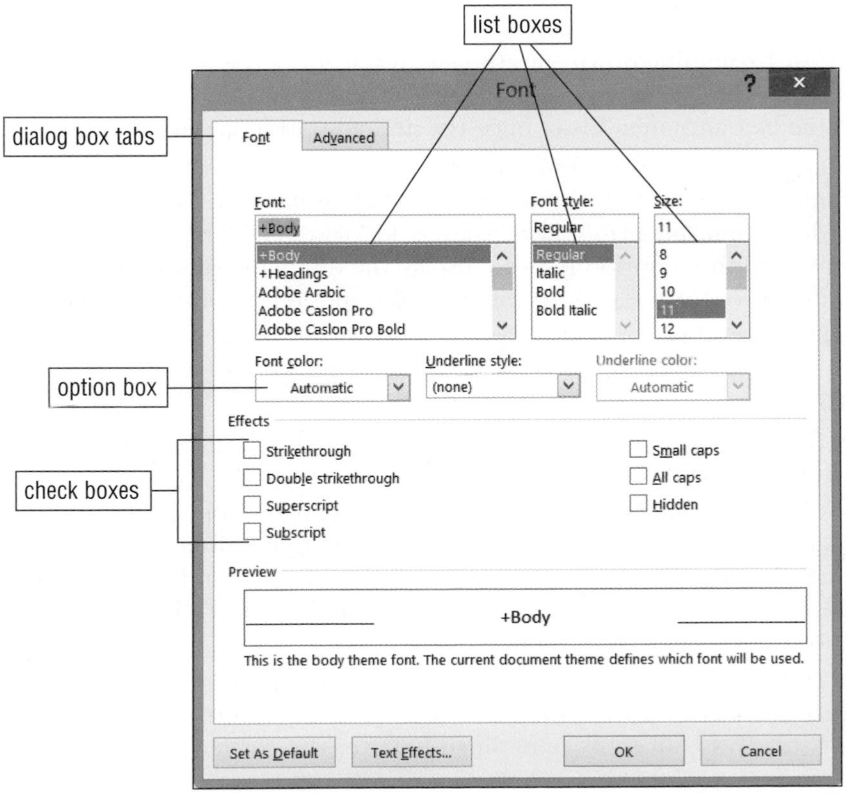

To choose options from a dialog box with the mouse, position the arrow pointer on the desired option and then click the left mouse button. If you are using the keyboard, press the Tab key to move the insertion point forward from option to option. Press Shift + Tab to move the insertion point backward from option to option. You can also hold down the Alt key and then press the underlined letter of the desired option. When an option is selected, it displays with a blue background or surrounded by a dashed box called a ***marquee***. A dialog box contains one or more of the following elements: list boxes, option boxes, check boxes, text boxes, option buttons, measurement boxes, and command buttons.

List Boxes and Option Boxes

The fonts below the *Font* option in the Font dialog box in Figure G.4 are contained in a ***list box***. To make a selection from a list box with the mouse, move the arrow pointer to the desired option and then click the left mouse button.

Some list boxes may contain a scroll bar. This scroll bar will display at the right side of the list box (a vertical scroll bar) or at the bottom of the list box (a horizontal scroll bar). Use a vertical scroll bar or a horizontal scroll bar to move through the list if the list is longer (or wider) than the box. To move down a list using a vertical scroll bar, position the arrow pointer on the down-pointing arrow and hold down the left mouse button. To scroll up through the list, position the arrow pointer on the up-pointing arrow and hold down the left mouse button. You can also move the arrow pointer above the scroll box and click the left mouse button to scroll up the list or move the arrow pointer below the scroll box and click the left mouse button to move down the list. To navigate a list with a horizontal scroll bar, click the left-pointing arrow to scroll to the left of the list or click the right-pointing arrow to scroll to the right of the list.

To use the keyboard to make a selection from a list box, move the insertion point into the box by holding down the Alt key and pressing the underlined letter of the desired option. Press the Up and/or Down Arrow keys on the keyboard to move through the list, and press Enter once the desired option is selected.

In some dialog boxes where there is not enough room for a list box, lists of options are contained in a drop-down list box called an ***option box***. Option boxes display with a down-pointing arrow. For example, in Figure G.4, the font color options are contained in an option box. To display the different color options, click the down-pointing arrow at the right of the *Font color* option box. If you are using the keyboard, press Alt + C.

Check Boxes

Some dialog boxes contain options preceded by a box. A check mark may or may not appear in the box. The Word Font dialog box shown in Figure G.4 displays a variety of check boxes within the *Effects* section. If a check mark appears in the box, the option is active (turned on). If the check box does not contain a check mark, the option is inactive (turned off). Any number of check boxes can be active. For example, in the Word Font dialog box, you can insert a check mark in several of the boxes in the *Effects* section to activate the options.

To make a check box active or inactive with the mouse, position the tip of the arrow pointer in the check box and then click the left mouse button. If you are using the keyboard, press Alt + the underlined letter of the desired option.

Text Boxes

Some options in a dialog box require you to enter text. For example, the boxes below the *Find what* and *Replace with* options at the Excel Find and Replace dialog box shown in Figure G.5 are text boxes. In a text box, you type text or edit existing text. Edit text in a text box in the same manner as normal text. Use the Left and Right Arrow keys on the keyboard to move the insertion point without deleting text and use the Delete key or Backspace key to delete text.

Option Buttons

The Word Insert Table dialog box shown in Figure G.6 contains options in the *AutoFit behavior* section preceded by ***option buttons***. Only one option button can be selected at any time. When an option button is selected, a blue or black circle displays in the button. To select an option button with the mouse, position the tip of the arrow pointer inside the option button or on the option and then click the left mouse button. To make a selection with the keyboard, hold down the Alt key and then press the underlined letter of the desired option.

Measurement Boxes

Some options in a dialog box contain measurements or amounts you can increase or decrease. These options are generally located in a ***measurement box***. For example, the Word Insert Table dialog box shown in Figure G.6 contains the *Number of columns* and *Number of rows* measurement boxes. To increase a number in a measurement box, position the tip of the arrow pointer on the up-pointing arrow at the right of the desired option and then click the left mouse button. To decrease the number, click the down-pointing arrow. If you are using the keyboard, press and hold down Alt + the underlined letter of the desired option and then press the Up Arrow key to increase the number or the Down Arrow key to decrease the number.

Command Buttons

The buttons at the bottom of the Excel Find and Replace dialog box shown in Figure G.5 are called ***command buttons***. Use a command button to execute or cancel a command. Some command buttons display with an ellipsis (...), which means another dialog box will open if you click that button. To choose a command button with the mouse, position the arrow pointer on the desired button and then click the left mouse button. To choose a command button with the keyboard, press the Tab key until the desired command button is surrounded by a marquee and then press the Enter key.

Figure G.5 Excel Find and Replace Dialog Box

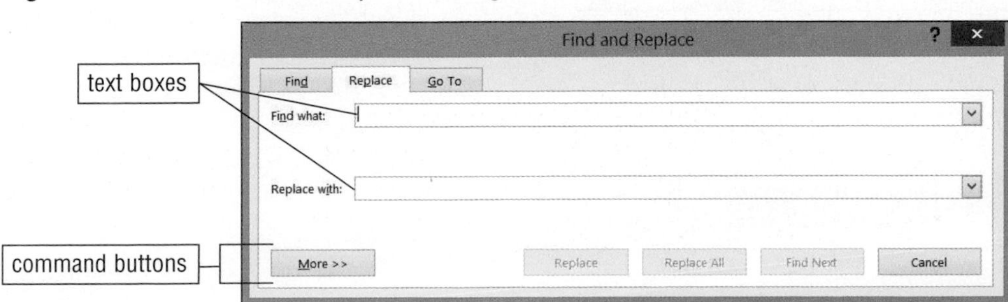

Choosing Commands with Keyboard Shortcuts

Applications in the Office suite offer a variety of keyboard shortcuts you can use to execute specific commands. Keyboard shortcuts generally require two or more keys. For example, the keyboard shortcut to display the Open dialog box in an application is Ctrl + F12. To use this keyboard shortcut, hold down the Ctrl key, press the F12 function on the keyboard, and then release the Ctrl key. For a list of keyboard shortcuts, refer to the Help files.

Choosing Commands with Shortcut Menus

The software programs in the Office suite include shortcut menus that contain commands related to different items. To display a shortcut menu, position the mouse pointer over the item for which you want to view more options, and then click the right mouse button or press Shift + F10. The shortcut menu will appear wherever the insertion point is positioned. For example, if the insertion point is positioned in a paragraph of text in a Word document, clicking the right mouse button or pressing Shift + F10 will cause the shortcut menu shown in Figure G.7 to display in the document screen (along with the Mini toolbar).

To select an option from a shortcut menu with the mouse, click the desired option. If you are using the keyboard, press the Up or Down Arrow key until the desired option is selected and then press the Enter key. To close a shortcut menu without choosing an option, click anywhere outside the shortcut menu or press the Esc key.

Figure G.6 Word Insert Table Dialog Box

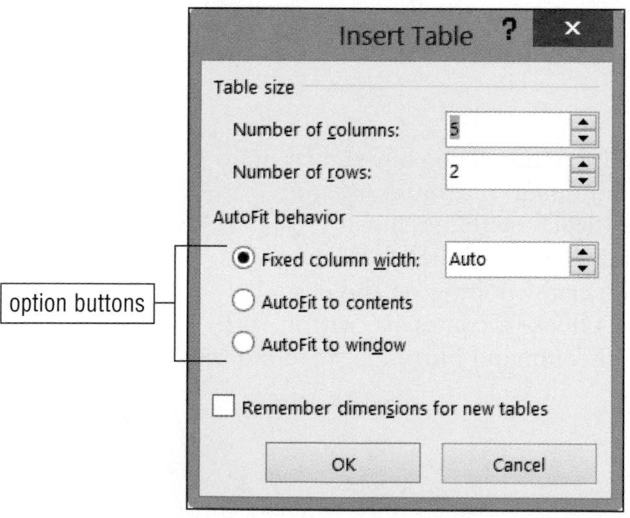

Figure G.7 Word Shortcut Menu

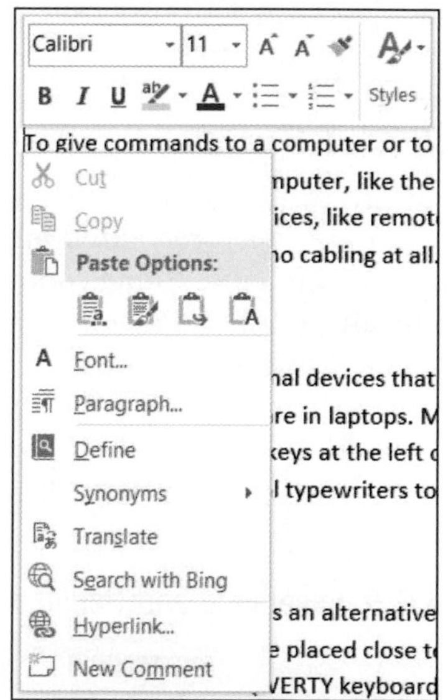

Working with Multiple Programs

As you learn the various programs in the Microsoft Office suite, you will notice many similarities between them. For example, the steps to save, close, and print are virtually the same whether you are working in Word, Excel, or PowerPoint. This consistency between programs greatly enhances a user's ability to transfer knowledge learned in one program to another within the suite. Another benefit to using Microsoft Office is the ability to have more than one program open at the same time and to integrate content from one program with another. For example, you can open Word and create a document, open Excel and create a spreadsheet, and then copy the Excel spreadsheet into Word.

When you open a program, a button containing an icon representing the program displays on the Taskbar. If you open another program, a button containing an icon representing that program displays to the right of the first program button on the Taskbar. Figure G.8 on the next page, shows the Taskbar with Word, Excel, Access, and PowerPoint open. To move from one program to another, click the Taskbar button representing the desired program.

Figure G.8 Taskbar with Word, Excel, Access, and PowerPoint Open

Customizing Settings

Before beginning computer projects in this textbook, you may need to customize your monitor's settings and turn on the display of file extensions. Projects in the chapters in this textbook assume that the monitor display is set at 1600 x 900 pixels and that the display of file extensions is turned on.

Before you begin learning the applications in the Microsoft Office 2013 suite, take a moment to check the display settings on the computer you are using. Your monitor's display settings are important because the ribbon in the Microsoft Office suite adjusts to the screen resolution setting of your computer monitor. A computer monitor set at a high resolution will have the ability to show more buttons in the ribbon than will a monitor set to a low resolution. The illustrations in this textbook were created with a screen resolution display set at 1600 × 900 pixels. In Figure G.9 on the next page, the Word ribbon is shown three ways: at a lower screen resolution (1366 × 768 pixels), at the screen resolution featured throughout this textbook, and at a higher screen resolution (1920 × 1080 pixels). Note the variances in the ribbon in all three examples. If possible, set your display to 1600 × 900 pixels to match the illustrations you will see in this textbook.

Figure G.9 Monitor Resolution

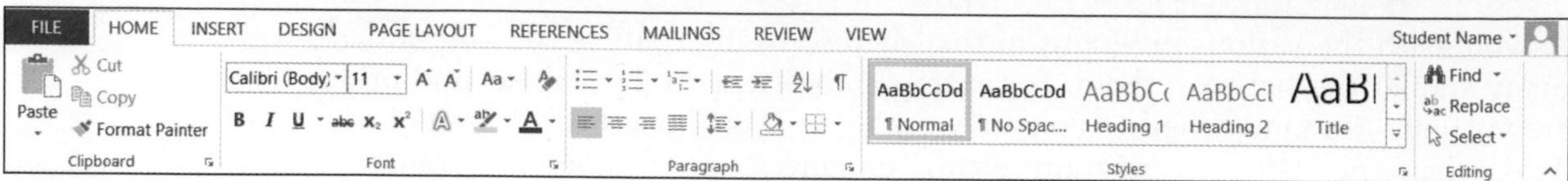

1366 × 768 screen resolution

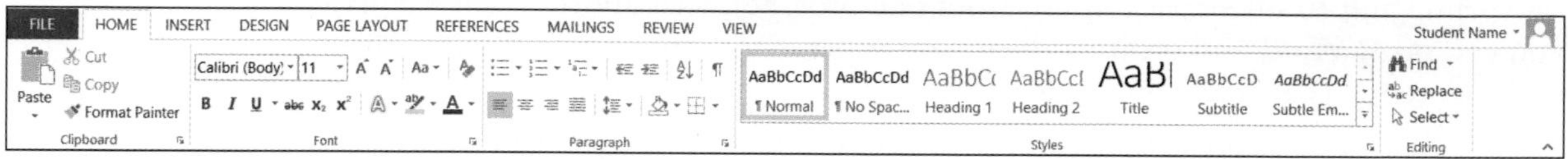

1600 × 900 screen resolution

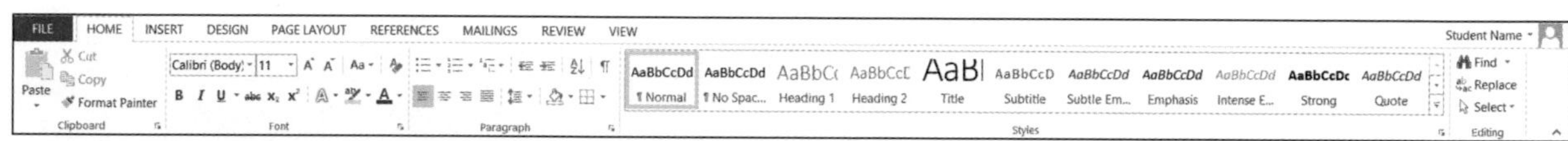

1920 × 1080 screen resolution

Project 1 Setting Monitor Display to 1600 by 900

1. At the Windows 8 desktop, right-click a blank area of the screen.
2. At the shortcut menu, click the *Screen resolution* option.
3. At the Screen Resolution window, click the *Resolution* option box. (This displays a slider bar. Your slider bar may display differently than what you see in the image at the right.)
4. Drag the button on the slider bar until *1600 × 900* displays to the right of the slider bar.
5. Click in the Screen Resolution window to remove the slider bar.
6. Click the Apply button.
7. Click the Keep Changes button.
8. Click the OK button.

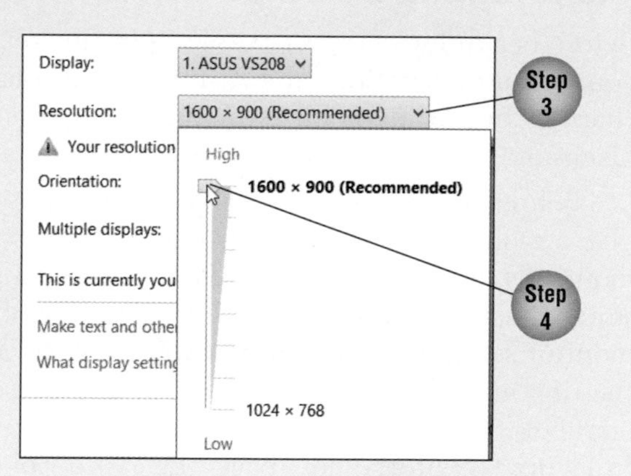

Project 2 Displaying File Extensions

1. At the Windows 8 desktop, position the mouse pointer in the lower left corner of the Taskbar until the Start screen thumbnail displays and then click the right mouse button.
2. At the pop-up list, click the *File Explorer* option.
3. At the Computer window, click the View tab on the ribbon and then click the *File name extensions* check box in the Show/hide group to insert a check mark.
4. Close the Computer window.

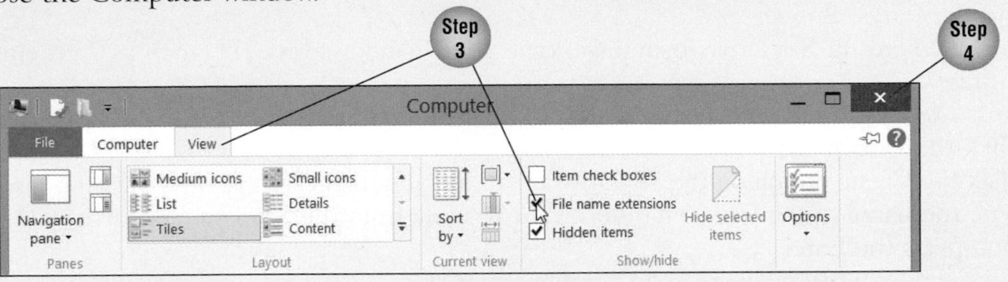

Completing Computer Projects

Some projects in this textbook require that you open an existing file. Project files are saved on the Student Resources CD in individual chapter folders. Before beginning a chapter, copy the necessary folder from the CD to your storage medium (such as a USB flash drive or your SkyDrive) using the Computer window. To maximize storage capacity, delete previous chapter folders before copying a new chapter folder onto your storage medium.

Project 3 Copying a Folder from the Student Resources CD to a USB Flash Drive

1. Insert the CD that accompanies this textbook into your computer's CD/DVD drive.
2. Insert your USB flash drive into an available USB port.
3. At the Windows 8 Start screen, click the Desktop tile.
4. Open File Explorer by clicking the File Explorer button on the Taskbar.
5. Click *Computer* in the Navigation pane at the left side of the File Explorer window.
6. Double-click the CD/DVD drive that displays with the name *BM13StudentResources* preceded by the drive letter.
7. Double-click ***StudentDataFiles*** in the Content pane.
8. Double-click the desired program folder name (and level number, if appropriate) in the Content pane.
9. Click once on the desired chapter (or unit performance assessment) folder name to select it.
10. Click the Home tab and then click the Copy button in the Clipboard group.
11. Click your USB flash drive that displays in the Navigation pane at the left side of the window.
12. Click the Home tab and then click the Paste button in the Clipboard group.
13. Close the File Explorer window by clicking the Close button located in the upper right corner of the window.

Project 4 Copying a Folder from the Student Resources CD to your SkyDrive Account

Note: SkyDrive is updated periodically, so the steps to create folders and upload files may vary from the steps below.

1. Insert the CD that accompanies this textbook into your computer's CD/DVD drive.
2. At the Windows 8 Start screen, click the Desktop tile.
3. Open Internet Explorer by clicking the Internet Explorer button on the Taskbar.
4. At the Internet Explorer home page, click in the Address bar, type **www.skydrive.com**, and then press Enter.
5. At the Microsoft SkyDrive login page, type your Windows Live ID (such as your email address).
6. Press the Tab key, type your password, and then press Enter.
7. Click the Documents tile in your SkyDrive.
8. Click the Create option on the SkyDrive menu bar and then click *Folder* at the drop-down list.
9. Type the name of the folder that you want to copy from the Student Resources CD and then press the Enter key.
10. Click the folder tile you created in the previous step.
11. Click the Upload option on the menu bar.
12. Click the CD/DVD drive that displays in the Navigation pane at the left side of the Choose File to Upload dialog box.
13. Open the chapter folder on the CD that contains the required student data files.
14. Select all of the files in the folder by pressing Ctrl + A and then click the Open button.

Project 5 Deleting a Folder

Note: Check with your instructor before deleting a folder.

1. Insert your storage medium (such as a USB flash drive) into your computer's USB port.
2. At the Windows desktop, open File Explorer by right-clicking the Start screen thumbnail and then clicking *File Explorer* at the shortcut menu.
3. Double-click the drive letter for your storage medium (the drive containing your USB flash drive, such as *Removable Disk (F:)*).
4. Click the chapter folder in the Content pane.
5. Click the Home tab and then click the Delete button in the Organize group.
6. At the message asking if you want to delete the folder, click the Yes button.
7. Close the Computer window by clicking the Close button located in the upper right corner of the window.

Using Windows 8

A computer requires an operating system to provide necessary instructions on a multitude of processes including loading programs, managing data, directing the flow of information to peripheral equipment, and displaying information. Windows 8 is an operating system that provides functions of this type (along with much more) in a graphical environment. Windows is referred to as a ***graphical user interface*** (GUI—pronounced *gooey*) that provides a visual display of information with features such as icons (pictures) and buttons. In this introduction, you will learn these basic features of Windows 8:

- Use the Start screen to launch programs
- Use desktop icons and the Taskbar to launch programs and open files or folders
- Organize and manage data, including copying, moving, creating, and deleting files and folders; and create a shortcut
- Explore the Control Panel and personalize the desktop
- Use the Windows Help and Support features
- Use search tools
- Customize monitor settings

Before using the software programs in the Microsoft Office suite, you will need to start the Windows 8 operating system. To do this, turn on the computer. Depending on your computer equipment configuration, you may also need to turn on the monitor and printer. If you are using a computer that is part of a network system or if your computer is set up for multiple users, a screen will display showing the user accounts defined for your computer system. At this screen, click your user account name; if necessary, type your password; and then press the Enter key. The Windows 8 operating system will start and, after a few moments, the Windows 8 Start screen will display as shown in Figure W.1. (Your Windows 8 Start screen may vary from what you see in Figure W.1.)

Exploring the Start Screen and Desktop

When Windows is loaded, the Windows 8 Start screen displays. This screen contains tiles that open various applications. Open an application by clicking an application's tile or display the Windows 8 desktop by clicking the Desktop tile. Click the Desktop tile and the screen displays as shown in Figure W.2. Think of the desktop in Windows as the top of a desk in an office. A businessperson places necessary tools—such as pencils, pens, paper, files, calculator—on the desktop to perform functions. Like the tools that are located on a desk, the Windows 8 desktop contains tools for operating the computer. These tools are logically grouped and placed in dialog boxes or panels that you can display using icons on the desktop. The desktop contains a variety of features for using your computer and applications installed on the computer.

Figure W.1 Windows 8 Start Screen

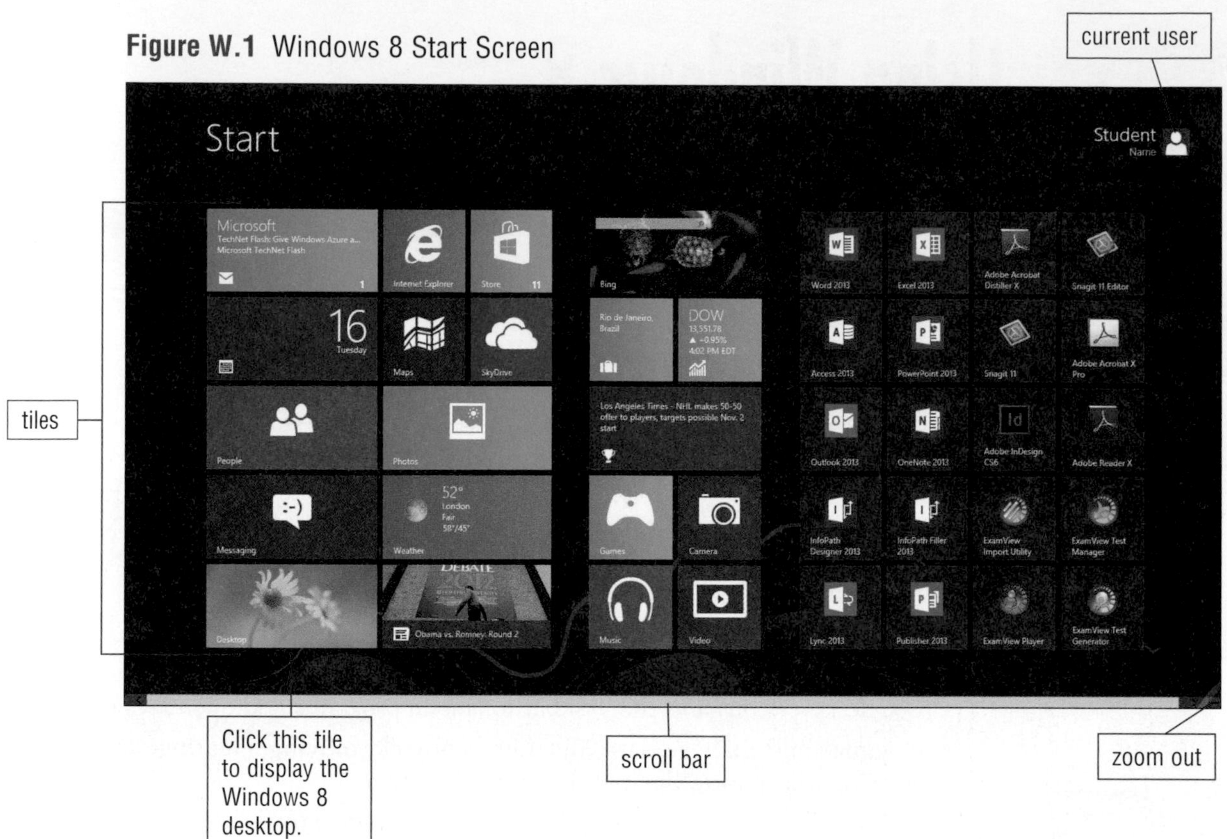

Figure W.2 Windows 8 Desktop

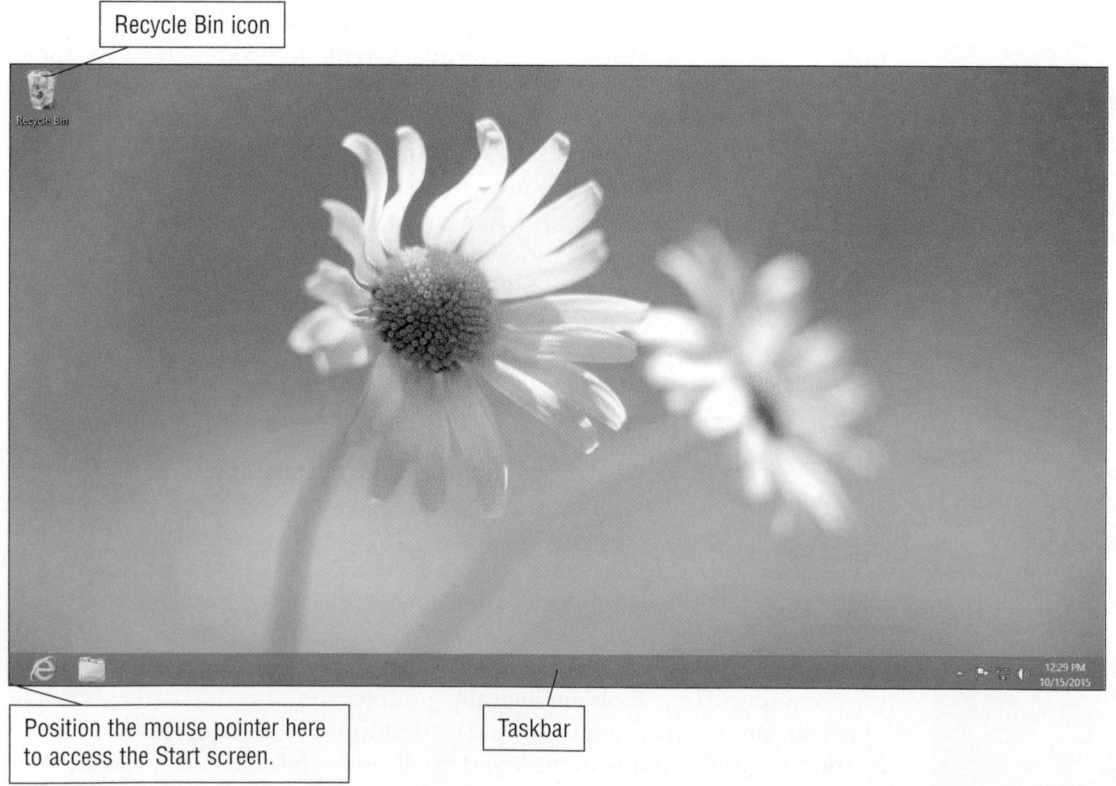

Using Icons

Icons are visual symbols that represent programs, files, or folders. Figure W.2 identifies the Recycle Bin icon on the Windows desktop. The Windows desktop on your computer may contain additional icons. Applications that have been installed on your computer may be represented by an icon on the desktop. Icons that represent files or folders may also display on your desktop. Double-click an icon and the application, file, or folder it represents opens on the desktop.

Using the Taskbar

The bar that displays at the bottom of the desktop (see Figure W.2) is called the ***Taskbar***. The Taskbar, shown in Figure W.3, contains the Start screen area (a spot where you point to access the Start screen), pinned items, a section that displays task buttons representing active tasks, the notification area, and the Show desktop button.

Position the mouse pointer in the lower left corner of the Taskbar to display the Start screen thumbnail. When the Start screen thumbnail displays, click the left mouse button to access the Windows 8 Start screen, shown in Figure W.1. (Your Start screen may look different.) You can also display the Start screen by pressing the Windows key on your keyboard or by pressing Ctrl + Esc. The left side of the Start menu contains tiles you can click to access the most frequently used applications. The name of the active user (the person who is currently logged on) displays in the upper right corner of the Start screen.

To open an application from the Start screen, drag the arrow pointer to the desired tile (referred to as ***pointing***) and then click the left mouse button. When a program is open, a task button representing the program appears on the Taskbar. If multiple programs are open, each program will appear as a task button on the Taskbar (a few specialized tools may not).

Figure W.3 Windows 8 Taskbar

Manipulating Windows

When you open a program, a defined work area known as a ***window*** displays on the screen. A Title bar displays at the top of the window and contains buttons at the right side for minimizing, maximizing, and restoring the size of the window, as well as for closing it. You can open more than one window at a time and the open windows can be cascaded or stacked. Windows 8 contains a Snap feature that causes a window to "stick" to the edge of the screen when the window is moved to the left or right side of the screen. Move a window to the top of the screen and the window is automatically maximized. If you drag down a maximized window, the window is automatically restored down (returned to its previous smaller size).

In addition to moving and sizing a window, you can change the display of all open windows. To do this, position the mouse pointer on the Taskbar and then click the right mouse button. At the pop-up menu that displays, you can choose to cascade all open windows, stack all open windows, or display all open windows side by side.

Project 1 Opening Programs, Switching between Programs, and Manipulating Windows

1. Open Windows 8. (To do this, turn on the computer and, if necessary, turn on the monitor and/or printer. If you are using a computer that is part of a network system or if your computer is set up for multiple users, you may need to click your user account name, type your password, and then press the Enter key. Check with your instructor to determine if you need to complete any additional steps.)
2. When the Windows 8 Start screen displays, open Microsoft Word by positioning the mouse pointer on the *Word 2013* tile and then clicking the left mouse button. (You may need to scroll to the right to display the Word 2013 tile.)
3. When the Microsoft Word program is open, notice that a task button representing Word displays on the Taskbar.
4. Open Microsoft Excel by completing the following steps:
   a. Position the arrow pointer in the lower left corner of the Taskbar until the Start screen thumbnail displays and then click the left mouse button.
   b. At the Start screen, position the mouse pointer on the *Excel 2013* tile and then click the left mouse button.
5. When the Microsoft Excel program is open, notice that a task button representing Excel displays on the Taskbar to the right of the task button representing Word.
6. Switch to the Word program by clicking the Word task button on the Taskbar.
7. Switch to the Excel program by clicking the Excel task button on the Taskbar.
8. Restore down the Excel window by clicking the Restore Down button that displays immediately left of the Close button in the upper right corner of the screen. (This reduces the Excel window so it displays along the bottom half of the screen.)
9. Restore down the Word window by clicking the Restore Down button located immediately left of the Close button in the upper right corner of the screen.

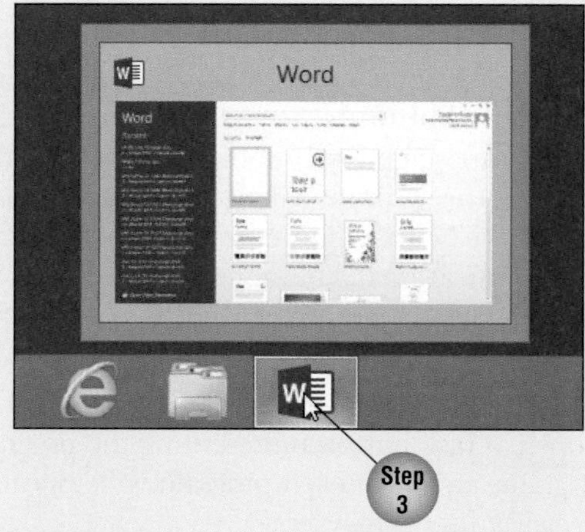

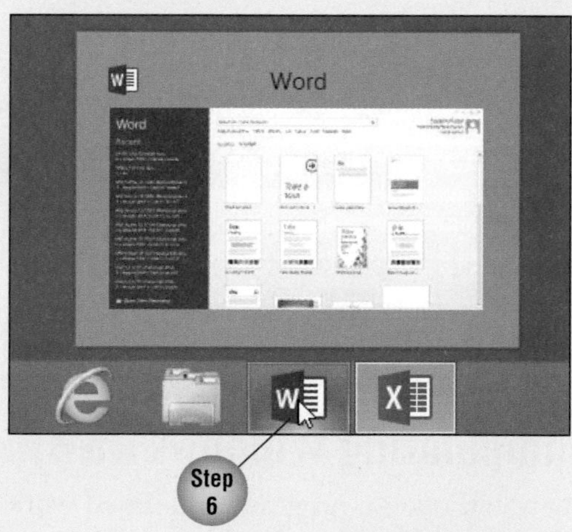

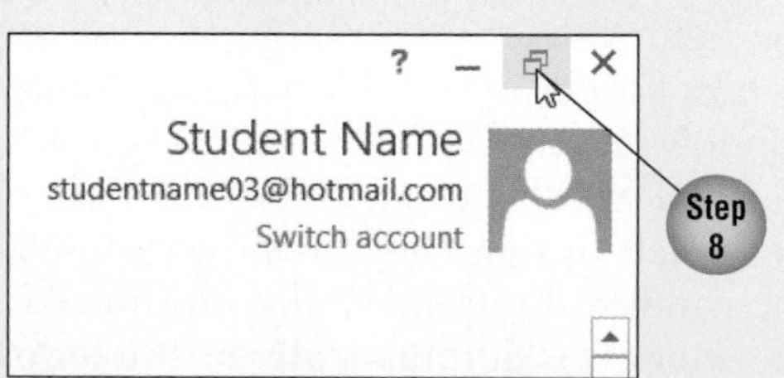

10. Position the mouse pointer at the top of the Word window screen, hold down the left mouse button, drag to the left side of the screen until an outline of the window displays in the left half of the screen, and then release the mouse button. (This "sticks" the window to the left side of the screen.)
11. Position the mouse pointer at the top of the Excel window screen, hold down the left mouse button, drag to the right until an outline of the window displays in the right half of the screen, and then release the mouse button.
12. Minimize the Excel window by clicking the Minimize button that displays in the upper right corner of the Excel window screen.

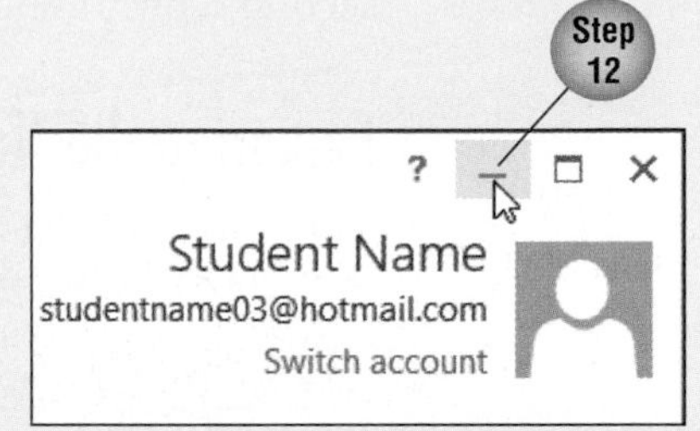

13. Hover your mouse over the Excel button on the Taskbar and then click the Excel window thumbnail that displays. (This displays the Excel window at the right side of the screen.)
14. Cascade the Word and Excel windows by positioning the arrow pointer in an empty area of the Taskbar, clicking the right mouse button, and then clicking *Cascade windows* at the shortcut menu.

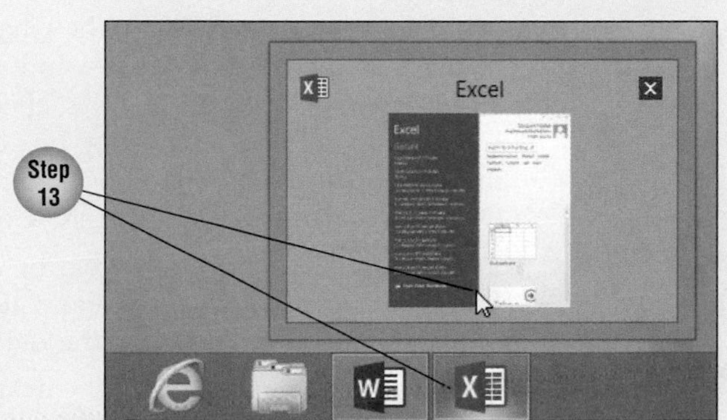

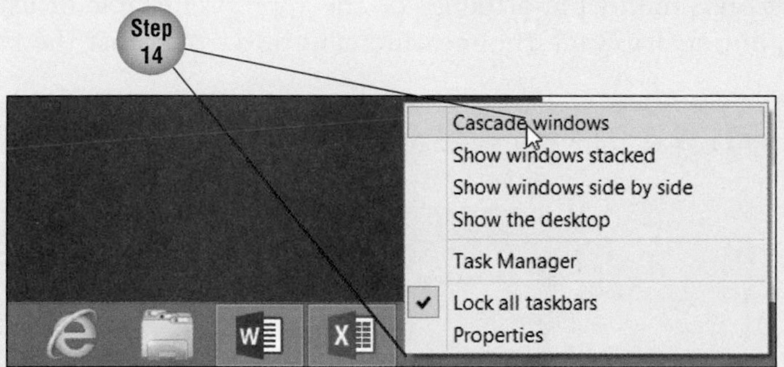

15. After viewing the windows cascaded, display them stacked by right-clicking an empty area of the Taskbar and then clicking *Show windows stacked* at the shortcut menu.
16. Display the desktop by right-clicking an empty area of the Taskbar and then clicking *Show the desktop* at the shortcut menu.
17. Display the windows stacked by right-clicking an empty area of the Taskbar and then clicking *Show open windows* at the shortcut menu.
18. Position the mouse pointer at the top of the Word window screen, hold down the left mouse button, drag the window to the top of the screen, and then release the mouse button. This maximizes the Word window so it fills the screen.
19. Close the Word window by clicking the Close button located in the upper right corner of the window.
20. At the Excel window, click the Maximize button located immediately left of the Close button in the upper right corner of the Excel window.
21. Close the Excel window by clicking the Close button located in the upper right corner of the window.

Using the Pinned Area

The icons that display immediately right of the Start screen area represent ***pinned applications***. Clicking an icon opens the application associated with the icon. Click the first icon to open the Internet Explorer web browser and click the second icon to open a File Explorer window containing Libraries.

Exploring the Notification Area

The notification area is located at the right side of the Taskbar and contains icons that show the status of certain system functions such as a network connection or battery power. The notification area contains icons for managing certain programs and Windows 8 features, as well as the system clock and date. Click the time or date in the notification area and a window displays with a clock and a calendar of the current month. Click the Change date and time settings hyperlink that displays at the bottom of the window and the Date and Time dialog box displays. To change the date and/or time, click the Change date and time button and the Date and Time Settings dialog box displays, similar to the dialog box shown in Figure W.4. (If a dialog box displays telling you that Windows needs your permission to continue, click the Continue button.)

Change the month and year by clicking the left-pointing or right-pointing arrow at the top of the calendar. Click the left-pointing arrow to display the previous month(s) and click the right-pointing arrow to display the next month(s).

To change the day, click the desired day in the monthly calendar that displays in the dialog box. To change the time, double-click either the hour, minute, or seconds number and then type the appropriate time or use the up- and down-pointing arrows in the measurement boxes to adjust the time.

Figure W.4 Date and Time Settings Dialog Box

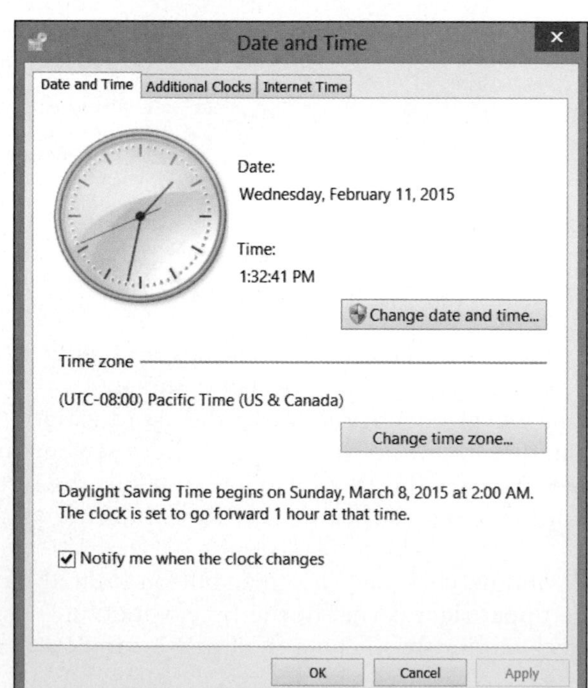

Some applications, when installed, will add an icon to the notification area of the Taskbar. To determine the name of an icon, position the mouse pointer on the icon and, after approximately one second, its label will display. If more icons have been inserted in the notification area than can be viewed at one time, an up-pointing arrow button displays at the left side of the notification area. Click this up-pointing arrow to display the remaining icons.

Setting Taskbar Properties

Customize the Taskbar with options at the Taskbar shortcut menu. Display this menu by right-clicking in an empty portion of the Taskbar. The Taskbar shortcut menu contains options for turning on or off the display of specific toolbars, specifying the display of multiple windows, displaying the Start Task Manager dialog box, locking or unlocking the Taskbar, and displaying the Taskbar Properties dialog box.

With options in the Taskbar Properties dialog box, shown in Figure W.5, you can change settings for the Taskbar. Display this dialog box by right-clicking an empty area on the Taskbar and then clicking *Properties* at the shortcut menu.

Each Taskbar property is controlled by a check box or an option box. If a property's check box contains a check mark, that property is active. Click the check box to remove the check mark and make the option inactive. If an option is inactive, clicking the check box will insert a check mark and turn on the option (make it active). A property option box displays the name of the currently active option. Click the option box to select a different option from the drop-down list.

Figure W.5 Taskbar Properties Dialog Box

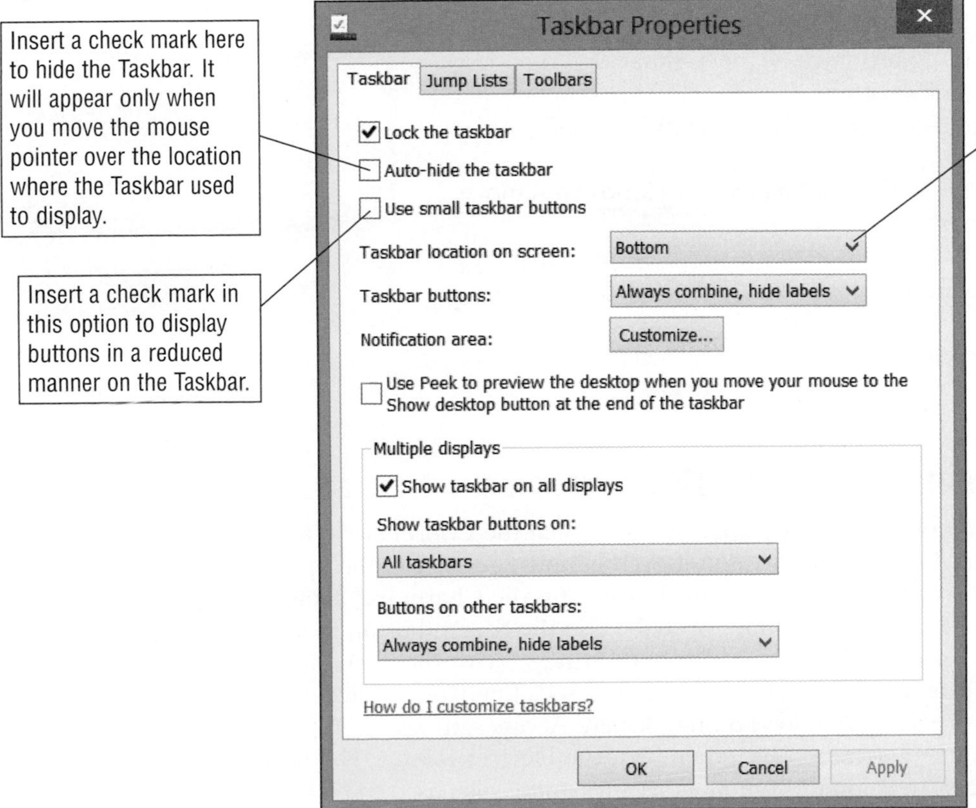

Project 2 Changing Taskbar Properties

1. Make sure the Windows 8 desktop displays.
2. Change the Taskbar properties by completing the following steps:
   a. Position the arrow pointer in an empty area of the Taskbar and then click the right mouse button.
   b. At the shortcut menu that displays, click *Properties*.
   c. At the Taskbar Properties dialog box, click the *Auto-hide the taskbar* check box to insert a check mark.
   d. Click the *Use small taskbar buttons* check box to insert a check mark.
   e. Click the option box (contains the word *Bottom*) that displays at the right side of the *Taskbar location on screen:* option and then click *Right* at the drop-down list.
   f. Click OK to close the dialog box.

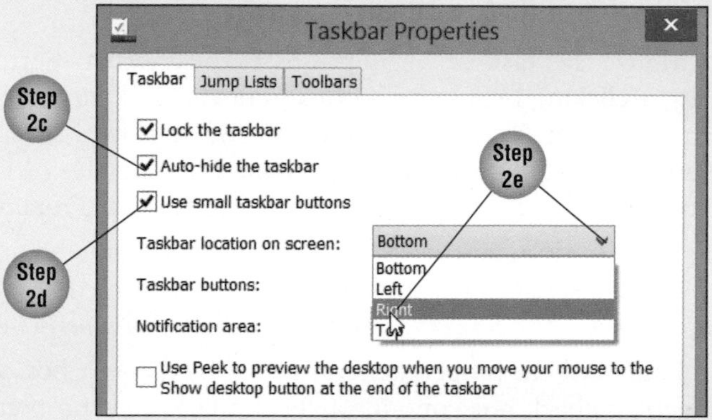

3. Since the *Auto-hide the taskbar* check box contains a check mark, the Taskbar does not display. Display the Taskbar by moving the mouse pointer to the right side of the screen. Notice that the buttons on the Taskbar are smaller than they were before.
4. Return to the default Taskbar properties by completing the following steps:
   a. Move the mouse pointer to the right side of the screen to display the Taskbar.
   b. Right-click an empty area of the Taskbar and then click *Properties* at the shortcut menu.
   c. Click the *Auto-hide the taskbar* check box to remove the check mark.
   d. Click the *Use small taskbar buttons* check box to remove the check mark.
   e. Click the *Taskbar location on screen* option box (displays with the word *Right*) and then click *Bottom* at the drop-down list.
   f. Click OK to close the dialog box.

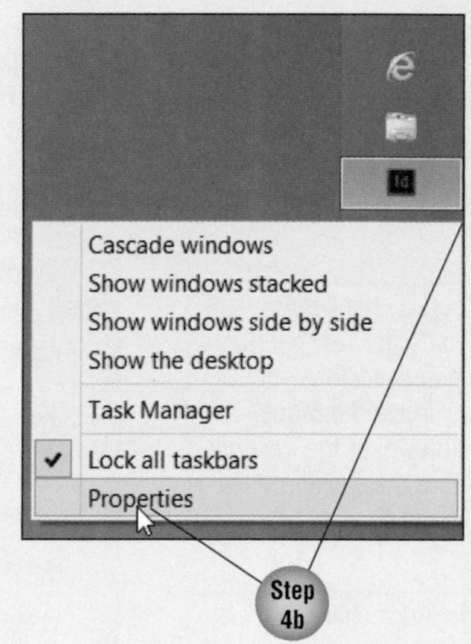

Using the Charm Bar

Windows 8 contains a new feature called the ***Charm bar***. The Charm bar is a bar that displays when you position the mouse pointer in the upper or lower right corner of the screen. Use the buttons on the Charm bar, shown in Figure W.6, to access certain features or tools. Use the Search button to search the computer for applications, files, folders and settings. With the Share button, you can share information with others via email or social networks. Clicking the Start button displays the Windows 8 Start screen. Access settings for various devices such as printers, monitors, and so on with the Devices button. The Settings button gives you access to common computer settings and is also used to power down the computer.

Figure W.6 Charm Bar

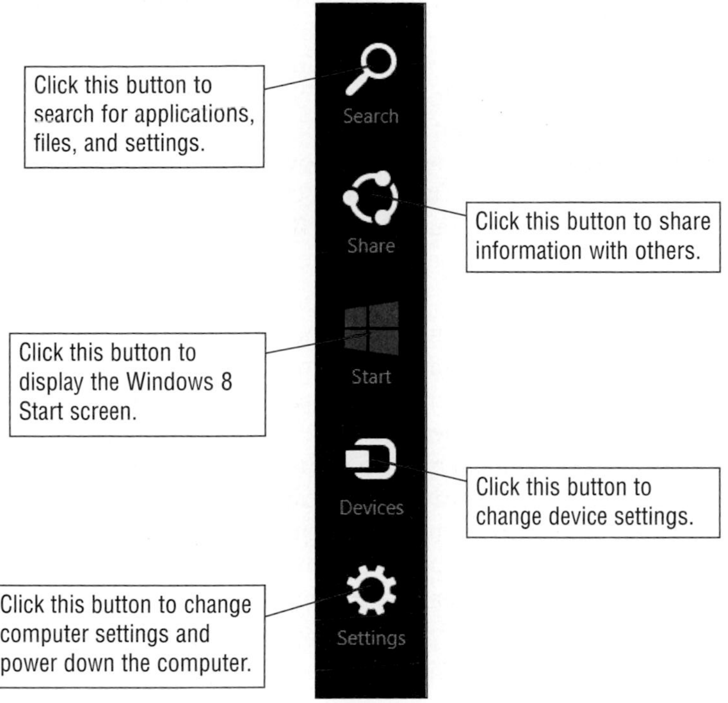

Click this button to search for applications, files, and settings.
Search
Share
Click this button to share information with others.
Click this button to display the Windows 8 Start screen.
Start
Devices
Click this button to change device settings.
Click this button to change computer settings and power down the computer.
Settings

Powering Down the Computer

If you want to shut down Windows, first close any open programs and then display the Charm bar. Click the Settings button on the Charm bar, click the Power tile, and then click the *Shut down* option. The Power tile also contains options for restarting the computer or putting the computer to sleep. Restarting the computer may be useful when installing new applications or if Windows 8 stops working properly. In sleep mode, Windows saves files and information about applications and then powers down the computer to a low-power state. To "wake up" the computer, press the computer's power button.

In a multi-user environment, you can sign out of or lock your account so that no one can tamper with your work. To access these features, display the Windows 8 Start screen and then click your user account tile in the upper right corner. This displays a shortcut menu with three options. The *Lock* option locks the computer, which means that it is still powered on but requires a user password in order to access any applications or files that were previously opened. (To unlock the computer, click the icon on the login screen representing your account, type your password, and then press Enter.) Use the *Sign out* option to sign out of your user account while still keeping the computer turned on so that others may log on to it. Click the *Change account picture* option if you want to change the picture associated with your user account.

Managing Files and Folders

As you begin working with programs in Windows 8, you will create files in which data (information) is saved. A file might be a Word document, an Excel workbook, an Access database, or a PowerPoint presentation. As you begin creating files, consider creating folders in which to store these files. Complete file management tasks such as creating a folder or moving a file at the Computer window. To display the Computer window, shown in Figure W.7, position your mouse pointer in the lower left corner of the screen to display the Start screen thumbnail, click the right mouse button, and then click *File Explorer* at the shortcut menu. The various components of the Computer window are identified in Figure W.7.

In the Content pane of the Computer window, icons display representing each hard disk drive and removable storage medium (such as a CD, DVD, or USB device) connected to your computer. Next to each storage device icon, Windows displays the amount of storage space available as well as a bar with the amount of used space shaded with color. This visual cue allows you to see at a glance the amount of space available relative to the capacity of the device. Double-click a device icon in the Content pane to change the display to show the contents stored on the device. Display contents from another device or folder using the Navigation pane or the Address bar on the Computer window.

Figure W.7 Computer Window

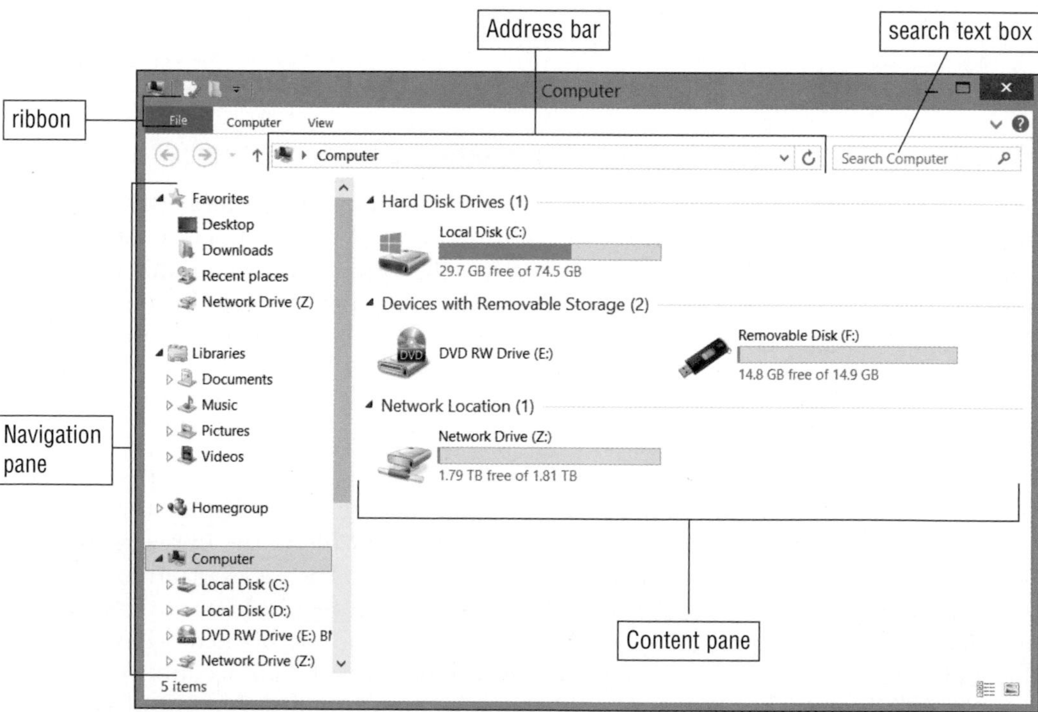

Copying, Moving, and Deleting Files and Folders

File and folder management activities include copying and moving files and folders from one folder or drive to another, as well as deleting files and folders. The Computer window offers a variety of methods for performing these actions. This section will provide you with steps for copying, moving, and deleting files and folders using options from the Home tab (shown in Figure W.8) and the shortcut menu (shown in Figure W.9).

To copy a file to another folder or drive, first display the file in the Content pane. If the file is located in the Documents folder, click the *Documents* folder in the *Libraries* section of the Navigation pane and then, in the Content pane, click the name of the file you want to copy. Click the Home tab on the ribbon and then click the Copy button in the Clipboard group. Use the Navigation pane to navigate to the location where you want to paste the file. Click the Home tab and then click the Paste button at the drop-down list. Complete similar steps to copy and paste a folder to another location.

If the desired file is located on a storage medium such as a CD, DVD, or USB device, double-click the device in the section of the Content pane labeled *Devices with Removable Storage*. (Each removable device is assigned an alphabetic drive letter by Windows, usually starting at E or F and continuing through the alphabet depending on the number of removable devices that are currently in use.) After double-clicking the storage medium in the Content pane, navigate to the desired folder and then click the file to select it. Click the Home tab on the ribbon and then click the Copy button in the Clipboard group. Navigate to the desired folder, click the Home tab, and then click the Paste button in the Clipboard group.

To move a file, click the desired file in the Content pane, click the Home tab on the ribbon, and then click the Cut button in the Clipboard group. Navigate to the desired location, click the Home tab, and then click the Paste button in the Clipboard group.

To delete a file or folder, click the file or folder in the Content pane in the Computer window. Click the Home tab and then click the Delete button in the Organize group. At the message asking if you want to move the file or folder to the Recycle Bin, click the Yes button.

Figure W.8 File Explorer Home tab

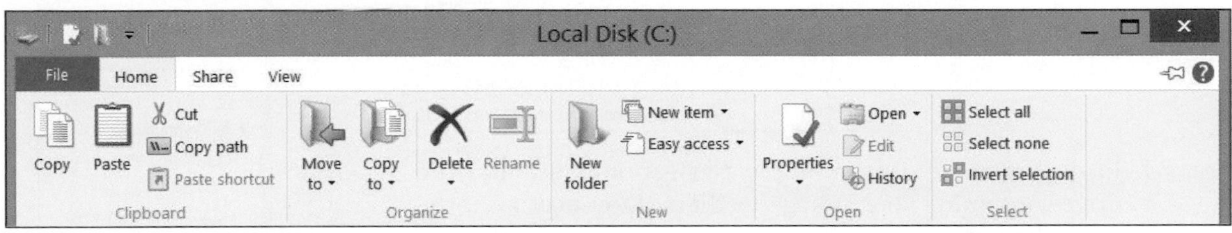

Figure W.9 Shortcut Menu

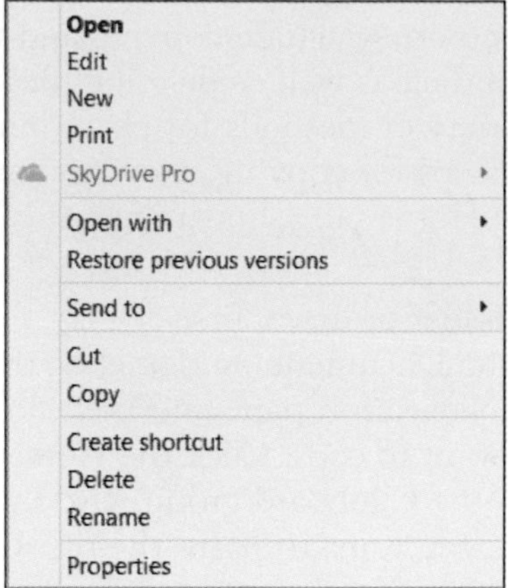

Project 4 Copying a File and Folder and Deleting a File

1. Insert the CD that accompanies this textbook into the appropriate drive.
2. Insert your storage medium (such as a USB flash drive) into the appropriate drive.
3. At the Windows 8 desktop, position the mouse pointer in the lower left corner of the Taskbar to display the Start screen thumbnail, click the right mouse button, and then click *File Explorer* at the shortcut menu.
4. Copy a file from the CD that accompanies this textbook to the drive containing your storage medium by completing the following steps:
   a. In the Content pane, double-click the drive into which you inserted the CD that accompanies this textbook.
   b. Double-click the *StudentDataFiles* folder in the Content pane.
   c. Double-click the *Windows8* folder in the Content pane.
   d. Click ***WordDocument01.docx*** in the Content pane.
   e. Click the Home tab and then click *Copy* in the Clipboard group.

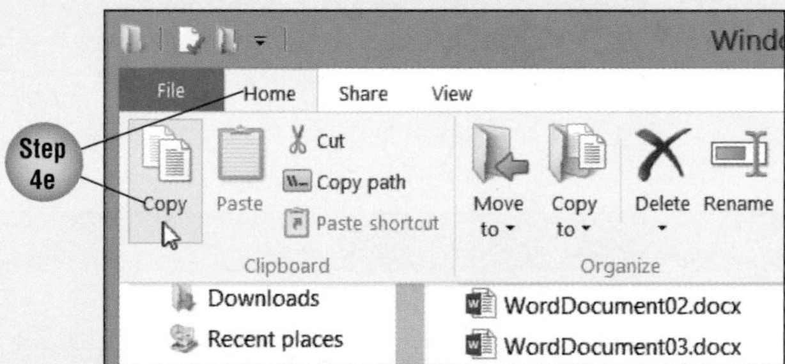

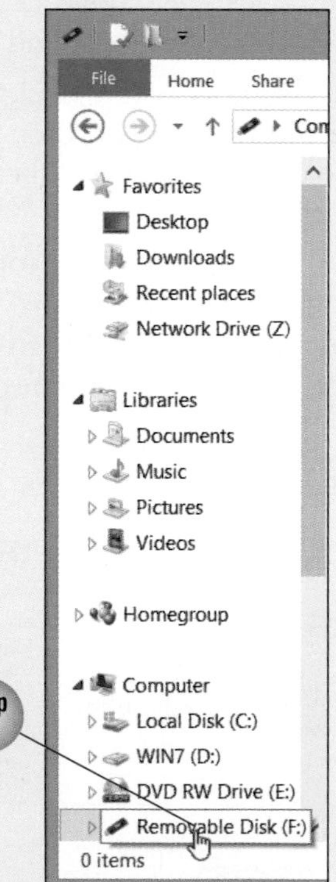

   f. In the Computer section in the Navigation pane, click the drive containing your storage medium. (You may need to scroll down the Navigation pane.)
   g. Click the Home tab and then click the Paste button in the Clipboard group.
5. Delete ***WordDocument01.docx*** from your storage medium by completing the following steps:
   a. Make sure the contents of your storage medium display in the Content pane in the Computer window.

b. Click ***WordDocument01.docx*** in the Content pane to select it.
c. Click the Home tab and then click the Delete button in the Organize group.
d. At the message asking if you want to permanently delete the file, click the Yes button.

6. Copy the Windows8 folder from the CD to your storage medium by completing the following steps:
   a. With the Computer window open, click the drive in the *Computer* section in the Navigation pane that contains the CD that accompanies this book.
   b. Double-click *StudentDataFiles* in the Content pane.
   c. Click the *Windows8* folder in the Content pane.
   d. Click the Home tab and then click the Copy button in the Clipboard group.
   e. In the *Computer* section in the Navigation pane, click the drive containing your storage medium.
   f. Click the Home tab and then click the Paste button in the Clipboard group.
7. Close the Computer window by clicking the Close button located in the upper right corner of the window.

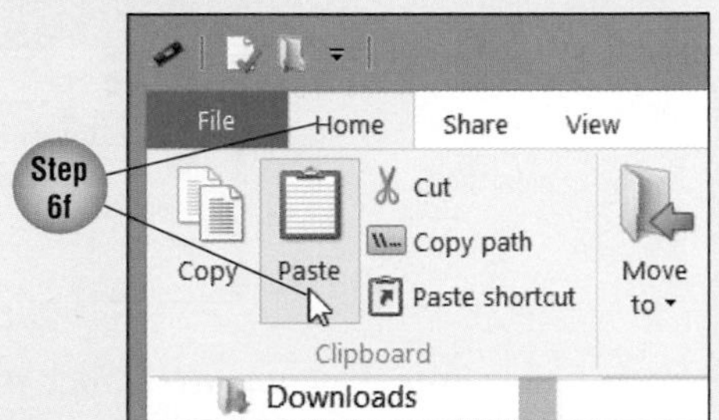

In addition to options on the Home tab, you can use options in a shortcut menu to copy, move, and delete files or folders. To use a shortcut menu, select the desired file(s) or folder(s), position the mouse pointer on the selected item, and then click the right mouse button. At the shortcut menu that displays, click the desired option, such as *Copy*, *Cut*, or *Delete*.

Selecting Files and Folders

You can move, copy, or delete more than one file or folder at the same time. Before moving, copying, or deleting files or folders, select the desired files or folders. To make selecting easier, consider displaying the files in the Content pane in a list or detailed list format. To change the display, click the View tab on the ribbon and then click *List* or *Details* in the Layout group.

To select adjacent files or folders, click the first file or folder, hold down the Shift key, and then click the last file or folder. To select nonadjacent files or folders, click the first file or folder, hold down the Ctrl key, and then click the other files or folders you wish to select.

Project 5 Copying and Deleting Files

1. At the Windows 8 desktop, position the mouse pointer in the lower left corner of the Taskbar to display the Start screen thumbnail, click the right mouse button, and then click *File Explorer* at the shortcut menu.
2. Copy files from the CD that accompanies this textbook to the drive containing your storage medium by completing the following steps:
   a. Make sure the CD that accompanies this textbook and your storage medium are inserted in the appropriate drives.
   b. Double-click the CD drive in the Content pane in the Computer window.

c. Double-click the *StudentDataFiles* folder in the Content pane.
d. Double-click the *Windows8* folder in the Content pane.
e. Change the display to List by clicking the View tab and then clicking *List* in the Layout group list box.

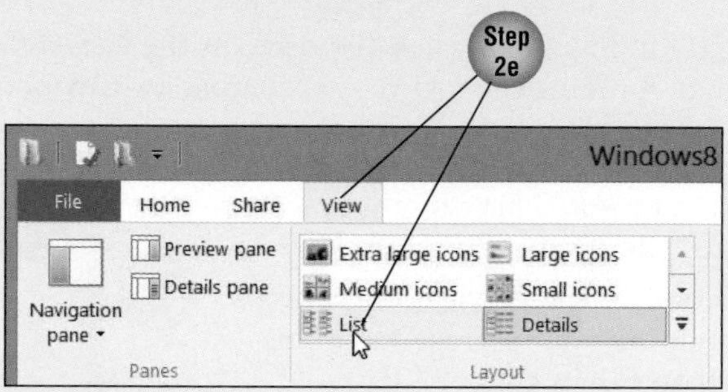

f. Click ***WordDocument01.docx*** in the Content pane.
g. Hold down the Shift key, click ***WordDocument05.docx***, and then release the Shift key. (This selects five documents.)

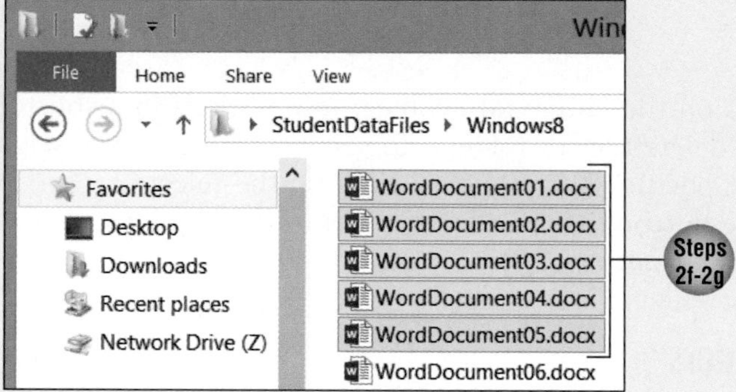

h. Click the Home tab and then click the Copy button in the Clipboard group.
i. In the *Computer* section of the Navigation pane, click the drive containing your storage medium.
j. Click the Home tab and then click the Paste button in the Clipboard group.

3. Delete the files you just copied to your storage medium by completing the following steps:
   a. Change the display by clicking the View tab and then clicking *List* in the Layout group.
   b. Click ***WordDocument01.docx*** in the Content pane.
   c. Hold down the Shift key, click ***WordDocument05.docx***, and then release the Shift key.
   d. Position the mouse pointer on any selected file, click the right mouse button, and then click *Delete* at the shortcut menu.
   e. At the message asking if you are sure you want to permanently delete the files, click Yes.

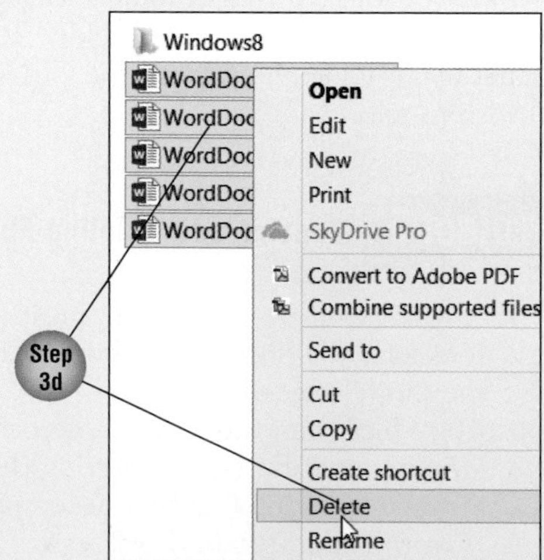

4. Close the Computer window by clicking the Close button located in the upper right corner of the window.

Manipulating and Creating Folders

As you begin working with and creating multiple files, consider creating folders in which you can logically group and store the files. To create a folder, display the Computer window and then display the drive or folder where you want to create the folder in the Content pane. To create the new folder, click the New folder button in the New group on the Home tab; click the New folder button on the Quick Access toolbar; or click in a blank area in the Content pane, click the right mouse button, point to *New* in the shortcut menu, and then click *Folder* at the side menu. Any of the three methods inserts a folder icon in the Content pane and names the folder *New folder*. Type the desired name for the new folder and then press Enter.

Project 6 Creating a New Folder

1. At the Windows 8 desktop, open the Computer window.
2. Create a new folder by completing the following steps:
   a. In the Content pane, double-click the drive that contains your storage medium.
   b. Double-click the *Windows8* folder in the Content pane. (This opens the folder.)
   c. Click the View tab and then click *List* in the Layout group.
   d. Click the Home tab and then click the New folder button in the New group.
   e. Type **SpellCheckFiles** and then press Enter. (This changes the name from *New folder* to *SpellCheckFiles*.)

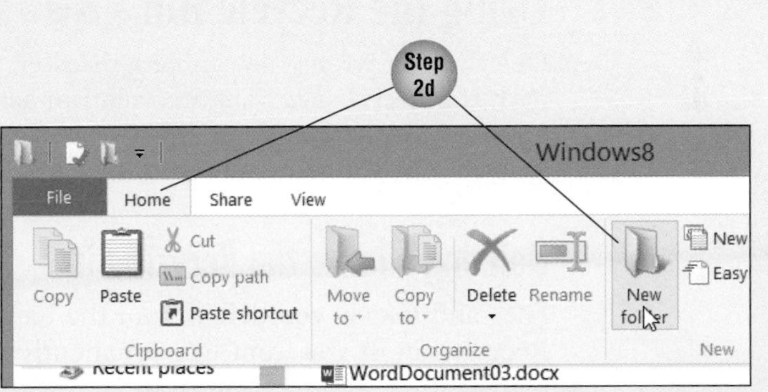

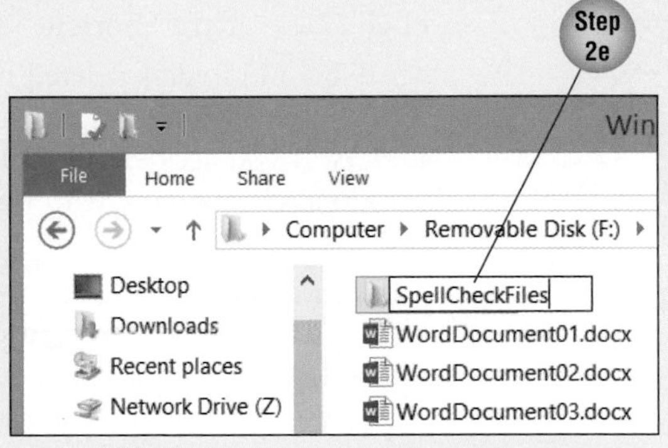

3. Copy **WordSpellCheck01.docx**, **WordSpellCheck02.docx**, and **WordSpellCheck03.docx** into the SpellCheckFiles folder you just created by completing the following steps:
   a. Click the View tab and then click *List* in the Layout group. (Skip this step if *List* is already selected.)
   b. Click ***WordSpellCheck01.docx*** in the Content pane.
   c. Hold down the Shift key, click ***WordSpellCheck03.docx***, and then release the Shift key. (This selects three documents.)
   d. Click the Home tab and then click the Copy button in the Clipboard group.
   e. Double-click the *SpellCheckFiles* folder in the Content pane.
   f. Click the Home tab and then click the Paste button in the Clipboard group.

4. Delete the SpellCheckFiles folder and its contents by completing the following steps:
   a. Click the Back button (contains a left-pointing arrow) located at the left side of the Address bar.
   b. With the SpellCheckFiles folder selected in the Content pane, click the Home tab and then click the Delete button in the Organize group.
   c. At the message asking you to confirm the deletion, click Yes.
5. Close the window by clicking the Close button located in the upper right corner of the window.

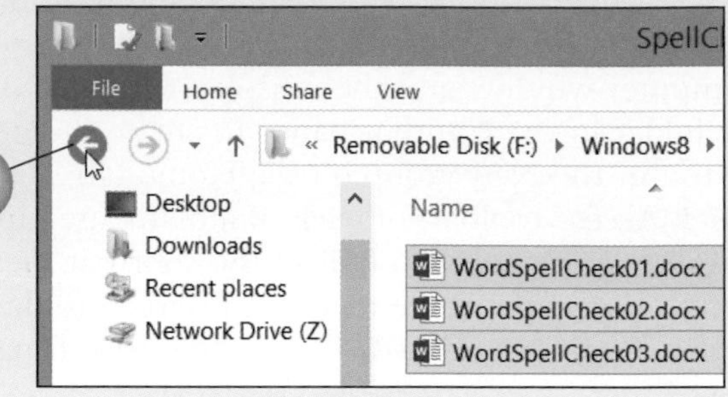

Using the Recycle Bin

Deleting the wrong file can be a disaster, but Windows 8 helps protect your work with the ***Recycle Bin***. The Recycle Bin acts just like an office wastepaper basket; you can "throw away" (delete) unwanted files, but you can also "reach in" to the Recycle Bin and take out (restore) a file if you threw it away by accident.

Deleting Files to the Recycle Bin

Files and folders you delete from the hard drive are sent automatically to the Recycle Bin. If you want to permanently delete files or folders from the hard drive without first sending them to the Recycle Bin, select the desired file(s) or folder(s), right-click one of the selected files or folders, hold down the Shift key, and then click *Delete* at the shortcut menu.

Files and folders deleted from a USB flash drive or disc are deleted permanently. (Recovery programs are available, however, that will help you recover deleted files or folders. If you accidentally delete a file or folder from a USB flash drive or disc, do not do anything more with the USB flash drive or disc until you can run a recovery program.)

You can delete files in the manner described earlier in this section and you can also delete a file by dragging the file icon to the Recycle Bin. To do this, click the desired file in the Content pane in the Computer window, drag the file icon to the Recycle Bin icon on the desktop until the text *Move to Recycle Bin* displays, and then release the mouse button.

Restoring Files from the Recycle Bin

To restore a file from the Recycle Bin, double-click the Recycle Bin icon on the desktop. This opens the Recycle Bin window, shown in Figure W.10. (The contents of the Recycle Bin will vary.) To restore a file, click the file you want restored, click the Recycle Bin Tools Manage tab and then click the Restore the selected items button in the Restore group. This removes the file from the Recycle Bin and returns it to its original location. You can also restore a file by positioning the mouse pointer on the file, clicking the right mouse button, and then clicking *Restore* at the shortcut menu.

Figure W.10 Recycle Bin Window

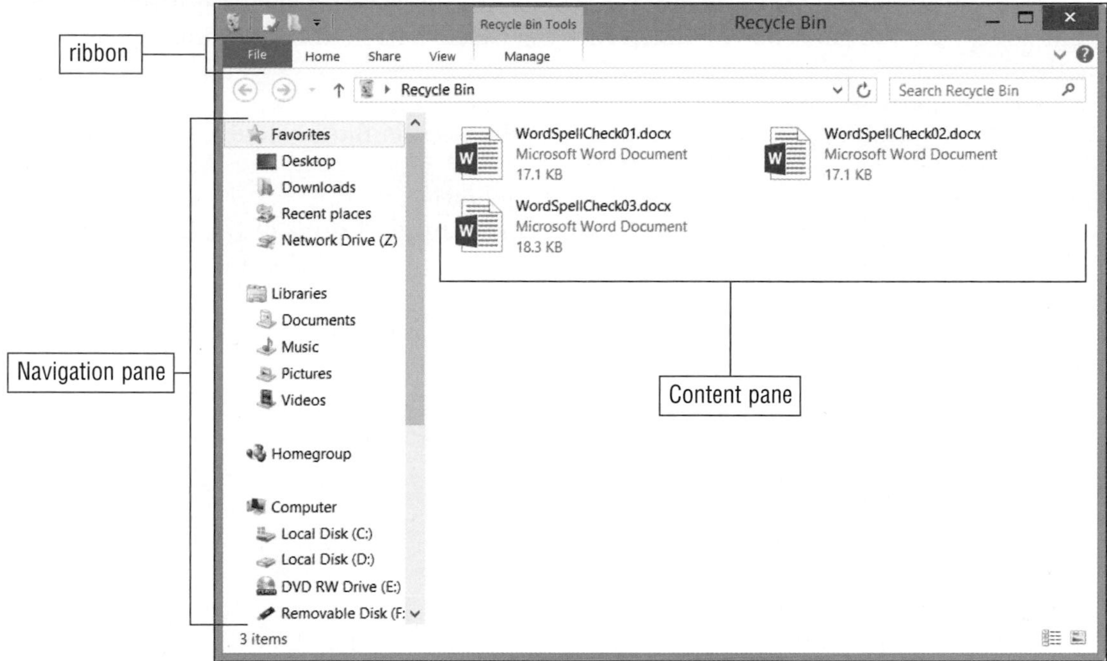

Project 7 Deleting Files to and Restoring Files from the Recycle Bin

Before beginning this project, check with your instructor to determine if you can copy files to the hard drive.

1. At the Windows 8 desktop, open the Computer window.
2. Copy files from your storage medium to the Documents folder on your hard drive by completing the following steps:
   a. In the Content pane, double-click the drive containing your storage medium.
   b. Double-click the *Windows8* folder in the Content pane.
   c. Click the View tab and then click *List* in the Layout group. (Skip this step if *List* is already selected.)
   d. Click ***WordSpellCheck01.docx*** in the Content pane.
   e. Hold down the Shift key, click ***WordSpellCheck03.docx***, and then release the Shift key.
   f. Click the Home tab and then click the Copy button in the Clipboard group.
   g. Click the *Documents* folder in the *Libraries* section of the Navigation pane.
   h. Click the Home tab and then click the Paste button in the Clipboard group.

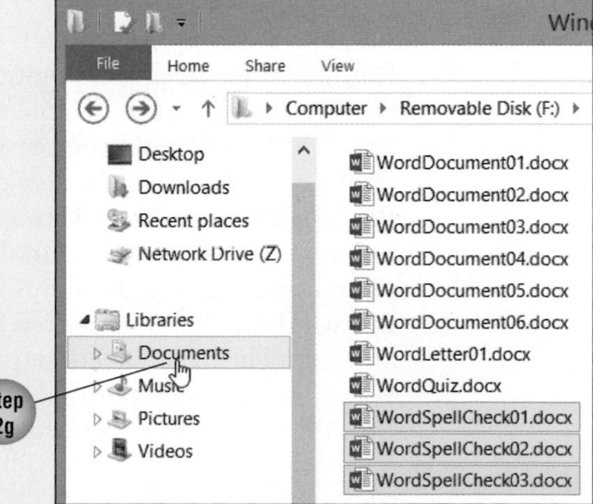

3. With **WordSpellCheck01.docx** through **WordSpellCheck03.docx** selected in the Content pane, click the Home tab and then click the Delete button in the Organize group to delete the files to the Recycle Bin.
4. Close the Computer window.
5. At the Windows 8 desktop, display the contents of the Recycle Bin by double-clicking the Recycle Bin icon.
6. Restore the files you just deleted by completing the following steps:
   a. Select **WordSpellCheck01.docx** through **WordSpellCheck03.docx** in the Recycle Bin Content pane. (If these files are not visible, you will need to scroll down the list of files in the Content pane.)
   b. Click the Recycle Bin Tools Manage tab and then click the Restore the selected items button in the Restore group.

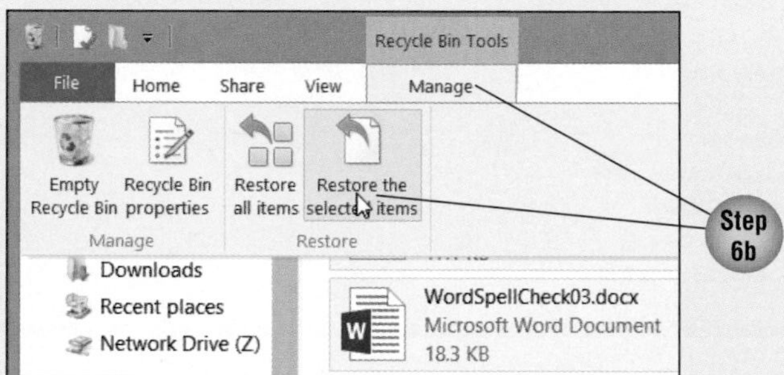

7. Close the Recycle Bin by clicking the Close button located in the upper right corner of the window.
8. Display the Computer window.
9. Click the *Documents* folder in the *Libraries* section of the Navigation pane.
10. Delete the files you restored.
11. Close the Computer window.

Emptying the Recycle Bin

Just like a wastepaper basket, the Recycle Bin can get full. To empty the Recycle Bin, position the arrow pointer on the Recycle Bin icon on the desktop and then click the right mouse button. At the shortcut menu that displays, click the *Empty Recycle Bin* option. At the message asking if you want to permanently delete the items, click Yes. You can also empty the Recycle Bin by displaying the Recycle Bin window and then clicking the Empty Recycle Bin button in the Manage group on the Recycle Bin Tools Manage tab. At the message asking if you want to permanently delete the items, click Yes. To delete a specific file from the Recycle Bin window, click the desired file in the Recycle Bin window, click the Home tab, and then click the Delete button in the Organize group. At the message asking if you want to permanently delete the file, click Yes. When you empty the Recycle Bin, the files cannot be recovered by the Recycle Bin or by Windows 8. If you have to recover a file, you will need to use a file recovery program.

Project 8 Emptying the Recycle Bin

Note: Before beginning this project, check with your instructor to determine if you can delete files/folders from the Recycle Bin.

1. At the Windows 8 desktop, double-click the Recycle Bin icon.
2. At the Recycle Bin window, empty the contents by clicking the Empty Recycle Bin button in the Manage group on the Recycle Bin Tools Manage tab.
3. At the message asking you if you want to permanently delete the items, click Yes.
4. Close the Recycle Bin by clicking the Close button located in the upper right corner of the window.

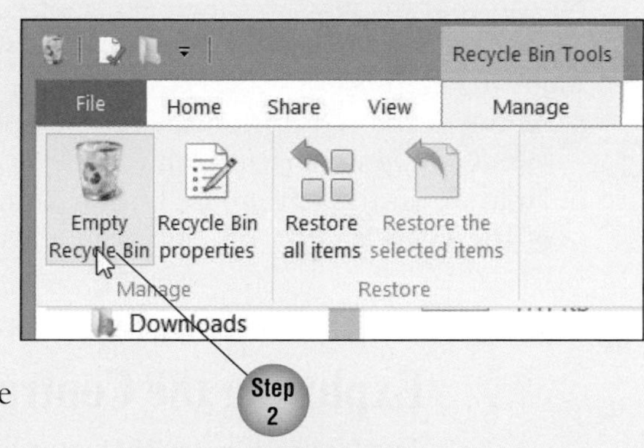

Creating a Shortcut

If you use a file or application on a consistent basis, consider creating a shortcut to the file or application. A ***shortcut*** is a specialized icon that points the operating system to an actual file, folder, or application. If you create a shortcut to a Word document, the shortcut icon is not the actual document but a very small file that contains the path to the document. Double-click the shortcut icon and Windows 8 opens the document in Word.

One method for creating a shortcut is to display the Computer window and then make active the drive or folder where the file is located. Right-click the desired file, point to *Send to*, and then click *Desktop (create shortcut)*. You can easily delete a shortcut icon from the desktop by dragging the shortcut icon to the Recycle Bin icon. This deletes the shortcut icon but does not delete the file to which the shortcut pointed.

Project 9 Creating a Shortcut

1. At the Windows 8 desktop, display the Computer window.
2. Double-click the drive containing your storage medium.
3. Double-click the *Windows8* folder in the Content pane.
4. Change the display of files to a list by clicking the View tab and then clicking *List* in the Layout group. (Skip this step if *List* is already selected.)
5. Create a shortcut to the file named **WordQuiz.docx** by right-clicking ***WordQuiz.docx***, pointing to *Send to*, and then clicking *Desktop (create shortcut)*.
6. Close the Computer window.

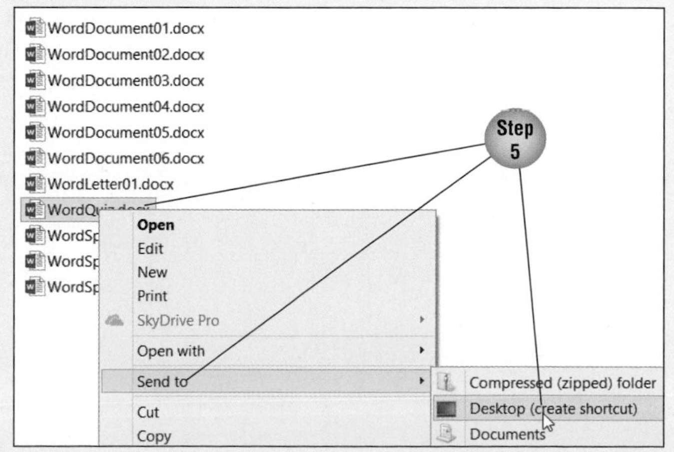

7. Open Word and **WordQuiz.docx** by double-clicking the *WordQuiz.docx* shortcut icon on the desktop.
8. After viewing the file in Word, close Word by clicking the Close button that displays in the upper right corner of the window.
9. Delete the *WordQuiz.docx* shortcut icon by completing the following steps:
   a. At the desktop, position the mouse pointer on the *WordQuiz.docx* shortcut icon.
   b. Hold down the left mouse button, drag the icon on top of the Recycle Bin icon, and then release the mouse button.

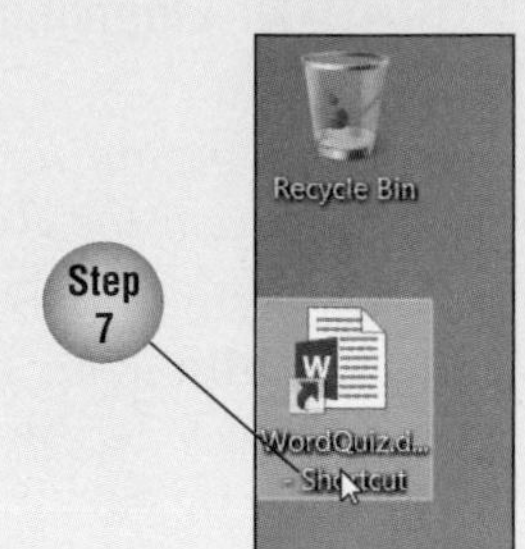

Exploring the Control Panel

The Control Panel, shown in Figure W.11, contains a variety of icons for customizing the appearance and functionality of your computer as well as accessing and changing system settings. Display the Control Panel by right-clicking the Start screen thumbnail and then clicking *Control Panel* at the shortcut menu. The Control Panel organizes settings into categories to make them easier to find. Click a category icon and the Control Panel displays lower-level categories and tasks within each of them.

Hover your mouse over a category icon in the Control Panel and a ScreenTip displays with an explanation of what options are available. For example, if you hover the mouse over the Appearance and Personalization icon, a ScreenTip displays with information about the tasks available in the category, such as changing the appearance of desktop items, applying a theme or screen saver to your computer, or customizing the Taskbar.

If you click a category icon in the Control Panel, the Control Panel displays all of the available subcategories and tasks in the category. Also, the categories display in text form at the left side of the Control Panel. For example, if you click the Appearance and Personalization icon, the Control Panel displays as shown in Figure W.12. Notice how the Control Panel categories display at the left side of the Control Panel and options for changing the appearance and personalizing your computer display in the middle of the Control Panel.

By default, the Control Panel displays categories of tasks in what is called *Category* view. You can change this view to display large or small icons. To change the view, click the down-pointing arrow that displays at the right side of the text *View by* that displays in the upper right corner of the Control Panel, and then click the desired view at the drop-down list (see Figure W.11).

Figure W.11 The Control Panel

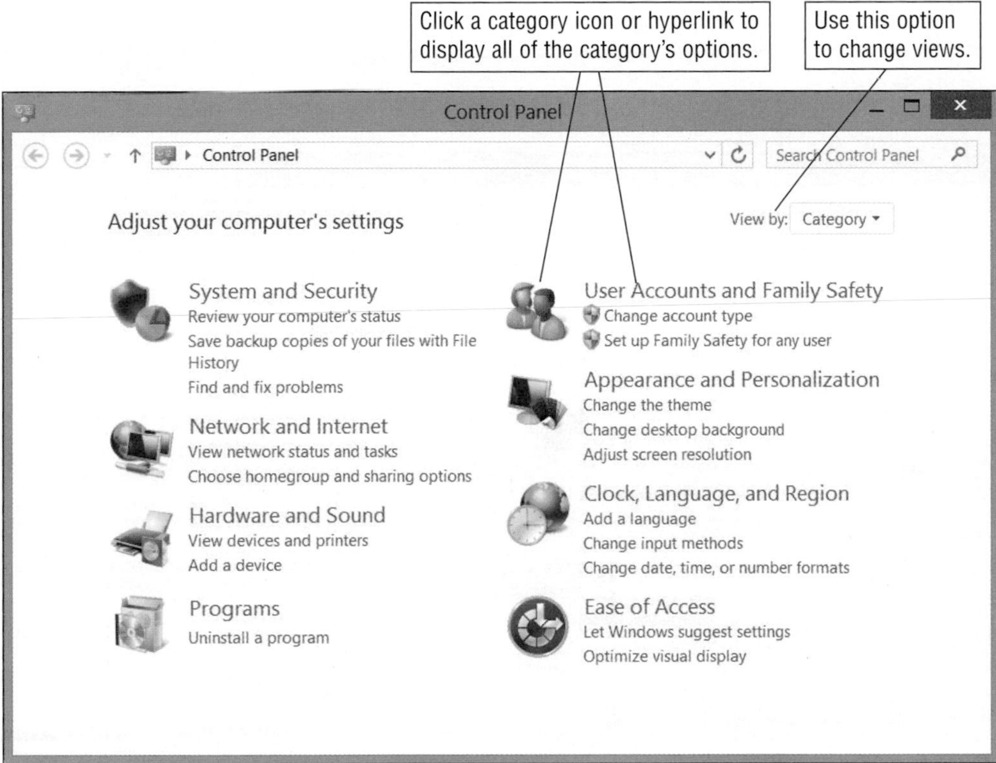

Figure W.12 Appearance and Personalization Window

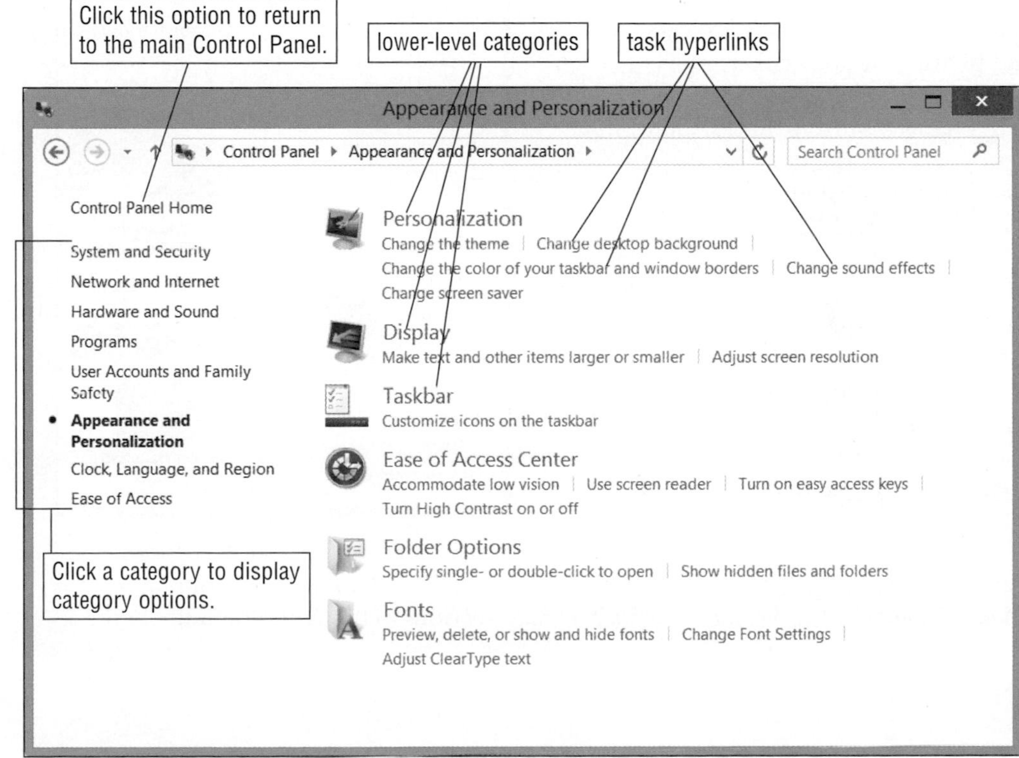

Project 10 Changing the Desktop Theme

1. At the Windows 8 desktop, right-click the Start screen thumbnail and then click *Control Panel* at the shortcut menu.
2. At the Control Panel, click the Appearance and Personalization icon.

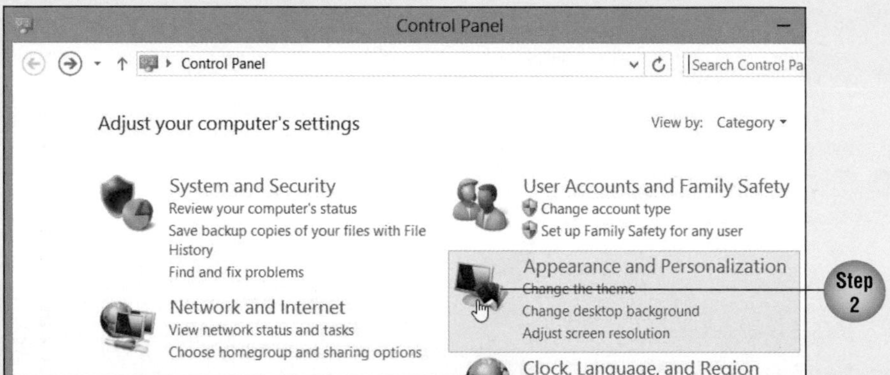

3. Click the Change the theme hyperlink that displays below *Personalization* in the panel at the right in the Control Panel.
4. At the window that displays with options for changing visuals and sounds on your computer, click *Earth* in the *Windows Default Themes* section.

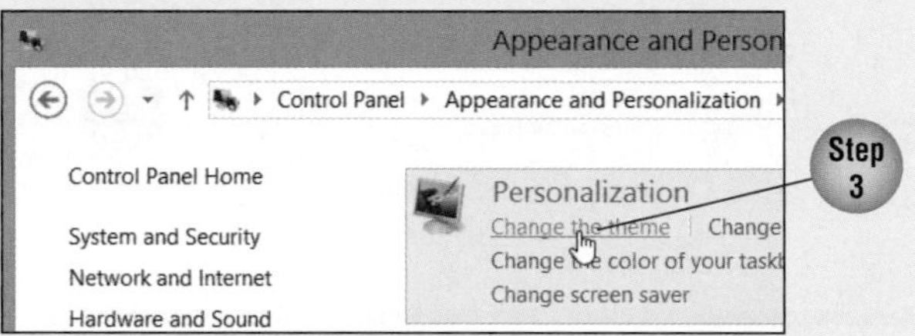

5. Click the Desktop Background hyperlink that displays in the lower left corner of the panel.
6. Click the button that displays below the text *Change picture every* and then click *10 Seconds* at the drop-down list. (This tells Windows to change the picture on your desktop every 10 seconds.)
7. Click the Save changes button that displays in the lower right corner of the Control Panel.
8. Click the Close button located in the upper right corner to close the Control Panel.
9. Look at the picture that displays as the desktop background. Wait for 10 seconds and then look at the second picture that displays.
10. Right-click the Start screen thumbnail and then click *Control Panel* at the shortcut menu.
11. At the Control Panel, click the Appearance and Personalization icon.
12. Click the Change the theme hyperlink that displays below *Personalization* in the panel at the right.

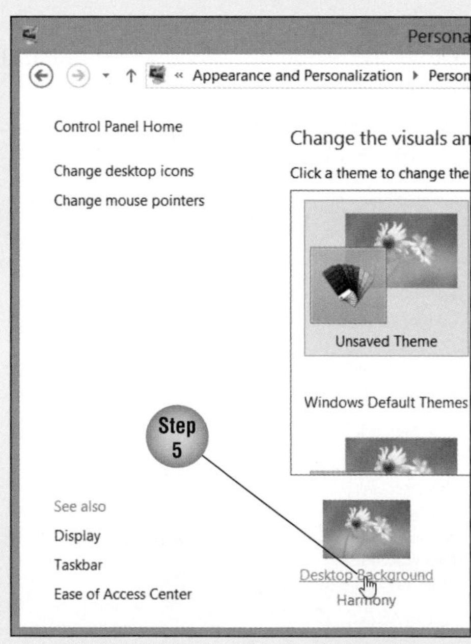

13. At the window that displays with options for changing visuals and sounds on your computer, click *Windows* in the *Windows Default Themes* section. (This is the default theme.)
14. Click the Close button located in the upper right corner of the Control Panel.

Searching in the Control Panel

The Control Panel contains a large number of options for customizing the appearance and functionality of your computer. If you want to customize a feature and are not sure where the options for the feature are located, search for the feature. To do this, display the Control Panel and then type the name of the desired feature. By default, the insertion point is positioned in the *Search Control Panel* text box. When you type the feature name in the text box, options related to the feature display in the Control Panel.

Project 11 Customizing the Mouse

1. Right-click the Start screen thumbnail and then click *Control Panel*.
2. At the Control Panel, type **mouse**. (The insertion point is automatically located in the *Search Control Panel* text box when you open the Control Panel. When you type *mouse*, features for customizing the mouse display in the Control Panel.)
3. Click the Mouse icon that displays in the Control Panel.
4. At the Mouse Properties dialog box, notice the options that display. (The *Switch primary and secondary buttons* option might be useful, for example, if you are left-handed and want to switch the buttons on the mouse.)
5. Click the Cancel button to close the dialog box.
6. At the Control Panel, click the Change the mouse pointer display or speed hyperlink.

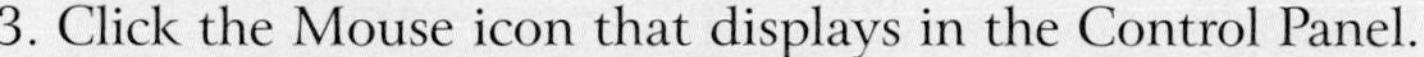

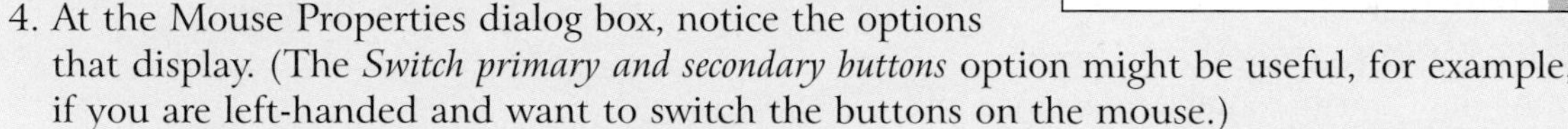

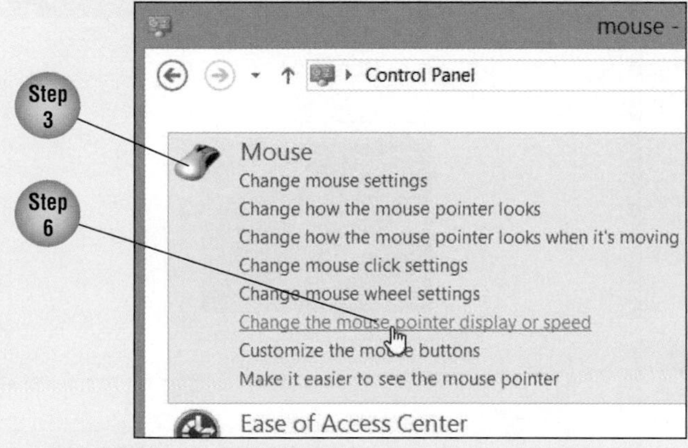

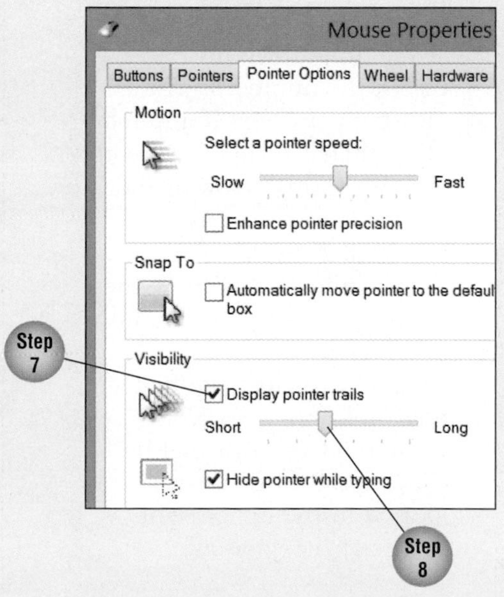

7. At the Mouse Properties dialog box with the Pointer Options tab selected, click the *Display pointer trails* check box in the *Visibility* section to insert a check mark.
8. Drag the button on the slider bar (located below the *Display pointer trails* check box) approximately to the middle of the bar.
9. Click OK to close the dialog box.
10. Close the Control Panel.
11. Move the mouse pointer around the screen to see the pointer trails.

Displaying Personalize Options with a Shortcut Command

In addition to the Control Panel, display customization options with a command from a shortcut menu. Display a shortcut menu by positioning the mouse pointer in the desired position and then clicking the right mouse button. For example, display a shortcut menu with options for customizing the desktop by positioning the mouse pointer in an empty area of the desktop and then clicking the right mouse button. At the shortcut menu that displays, click the desired shortcut command.

Project 12 Customizing with a Shortcut Command

1. At the Windows 8 desktop, position the mouse pointer in an empty area on the desktop, click the right mouse button, and then click *Personalize* at the shortcut menu.
2. At the Control Panel Appearance and Personalization window that displays, click the Change mouse pointers hyperlink that displays at the left side of the window.
3. At the Mouse Properties dialog box, click the Pointer Options tab.
4. Click in the *Display pointer trails* check box to remove the check mark.
5. Click OK to close the dialog box.
6. At the Control Panel Appearance and Personalization window, click the Screen Saver hyperlink that displays in the lower right corner of the window.
7. At the Screen Saver Settings dialog box, click the option button below the *Screen saver* option and then click *Ribbons* at the drop-down list.
8. Check the number in the *Wait* measurement box. If a number other than *1* displays, click the down-pointing arrow at the right side of the measurement box until *1* displays. (This tells Windows to display the screen saver after one minute of inactivity.)
9. Click OK to close the dialog box.
10. Close the Control Panel by clicking the Close button located in the upper right corner of the window.

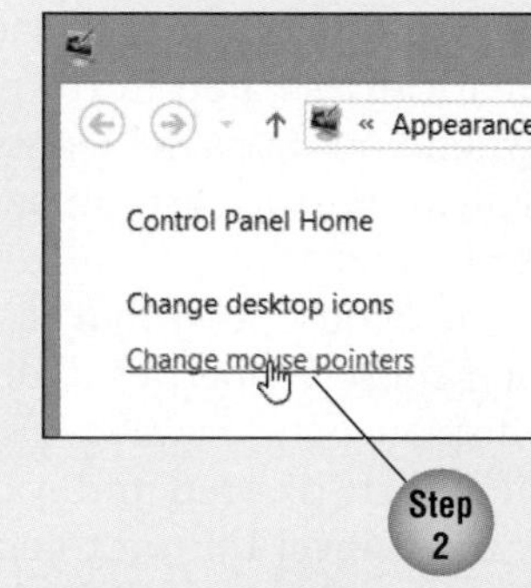

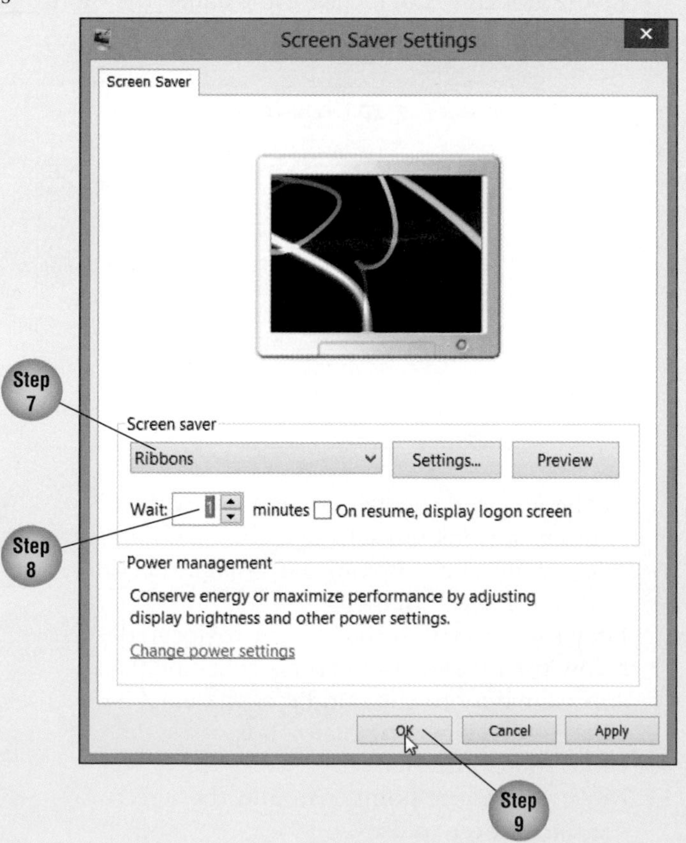

11. Do not touch the mouse or keyboard and wait over one minute for the screen saver to display. After watching the screen saver, move the mouse. (This redisplays the desktop.)
12. Right-click in an empty area of the desktop and then click *Personalize* at the shortcut menu.
13. At the Control Panel Appearance and Personalization window, click the Screen Saver hyperlink.
14. At the Screen Saver Settings dialog box, click the option button below the *Screen saver* option and then click *(None)* at the drop-down list.
15. Click OK to close the dialog box.
16. Close the Control Panel Appearance and Personalization window.

Exploring Windows Help and Support

Windows 8 includes an on-screen reference guide providing information, explanations, and interactive help on learning Windows features. Get help at the Windows Help and Support window, shown in Figure W.13. Display this window by clicking the Start screen thumbnail to display the Windows 8 Start screen. Right-click a blank area of the Start screen, click the All apps button, and then click the *Help and Support* tile in the Windows System group. Use options in the Windows Help and Support window to search for help on a specific feature; display the opening Windows Help and Support window; print the current information; and display information on getting started with Windows 8, setting up a network, and protecting your computer.

Figure W.13 Windows Help and Support Window

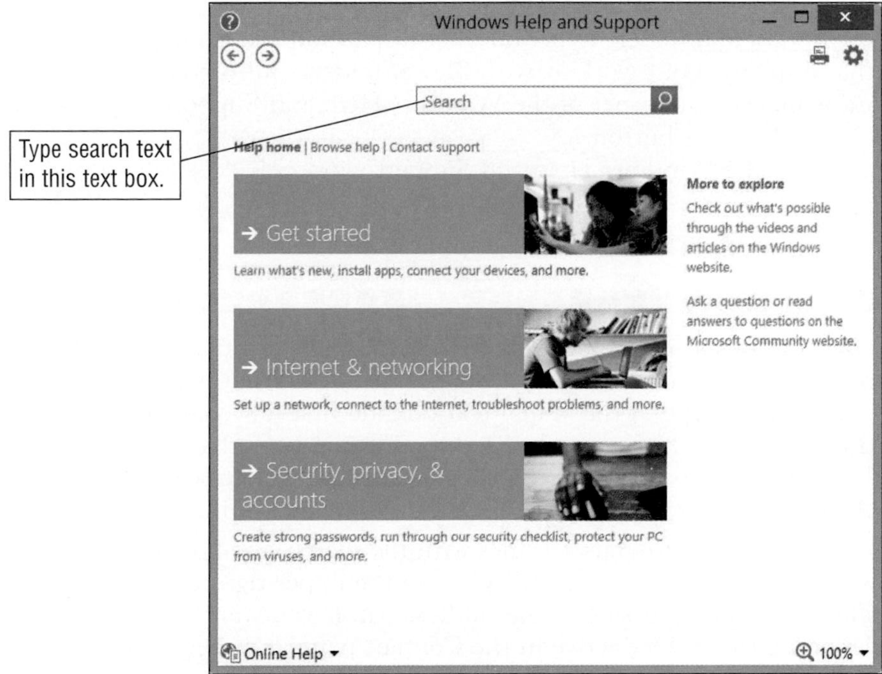

Project 13 Getting Help

1. Display the Windows 8 Help and Support window by following these steps:
   a. At the Windows 8 desktop, position the mouse pointer in the lower left corner of the screen and then click the Start screen thumbnail.
   b. Position the mouse in a blank area of the Windows 8 Start screen and then click the right mouse button.
   c. Click the All apps button that appears in the lower right corner of the Start screen and then scroll to the right of the Start screen.
   d. Click the *Help and Support* tile located in the *Windows System* category.
2. At the Windows Help and Support window, click the Get started hyperlink.
3. Click a hyperlink that interests you, read the information, and then click the Back button. (The Back button is located in the upper left corner of the window.)
4. Click another hyperlink that interests you and then read the information.
5. Click the Help home hyperlink that displays below the search text box. (This returns you to the opening Windows Help and Support window.)
6. Click in the search text box, type **delete files**, and then press Enter.
7. Click the How to work with files and folders hyperlink that displays in the window.
8. Read the information that displays about working with files or folders and then click the Print button located in the upper right corner of the Windows Help and Support window.
9. At the Print dialog box, click the Print button.
10. Click the Close button to close the Windows Help and Support window.

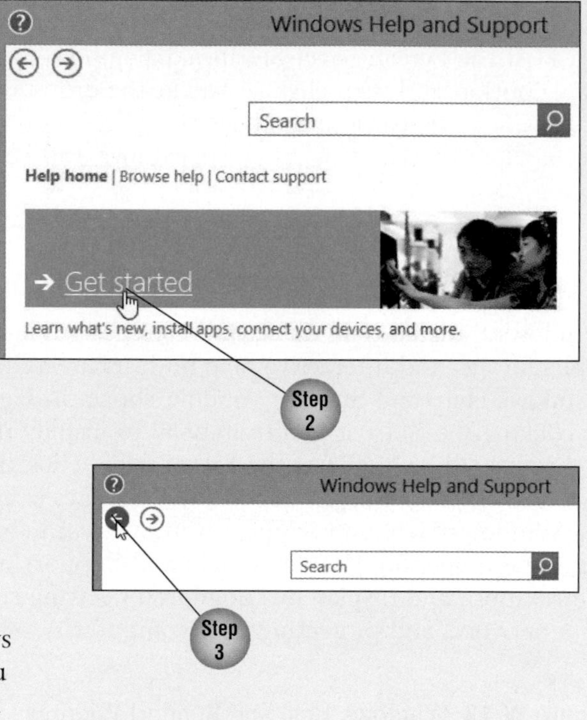

Using Search Tools

The Charm bar contains a search tool you can use to quickly find an application or file on your computer. To use the search tool, display the Charm bar, click the Search button and then type in the search text box the first few characters of the application or file for which you are searching. As you type characters in the text box, a list displays with application names or file names that begin with the characters. As you continue typing characters, the search tool refines the list.

You can also search for programs or files with the search text box in the Computer window. The search text box displays in the upper right corner of the Computer window at the right side of the Address bar. If you want to search a specific folder, make that folder active in the Content pane and then type the search text in the text box.

When conducting a search, you can use the asterisk (*) as a wildcard character in place of any letters, numbers, or symbols within a file name. For example, in the following project you will search for file names containing *check* by typing ***check** in the search text box. The asterisk indicates that the file name can start with any letter but it must contain the letters *check* somewhere in the file name.

Project 14 Searching for Programs and Files

1. At the Windows 8 desktop, display the Charm bar and then click the Search button.
2. With the insertion point positioned in the search text box, type **paint**. (Notice as you type the letters that Windows displays applications that begin with the same letters you are typing or that are associated with the same letters in a keyword. Notice that the Paint program displays below the heading *Apps* at the top of the list. Depending on the contents stored in the computer you are using, additional items may display below Paint.)

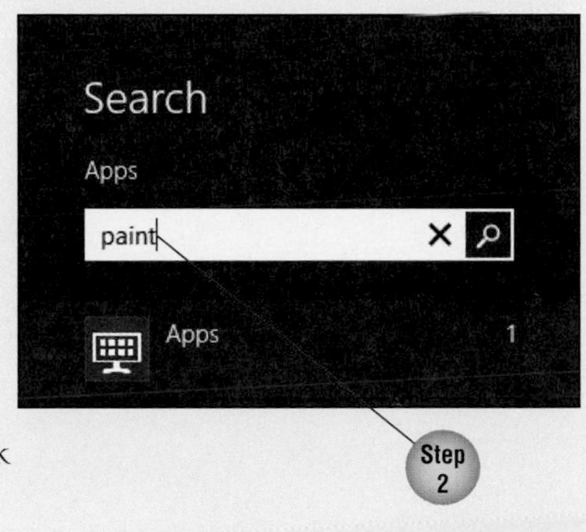

3. Click *Paint* that displays below the *Apps* heading.
4. Close the Paint window.
5. Right-click the Start screen thumbnail and then click *File Explorer*.
6. At the Computer window, double-click the icon representing your storage medium.
7. Double-click the *Windows8* folder.
8. Click in the search text box located at the right of the Address bar and then type **document**. (As you begin typing the letters, Windows filters the list of files in the Content pane to those that contain the letters you type. Notice that the Address bar displays *Search Results in Windows8* to indicate that the files that display matching your criteria are limited to the current folder.)

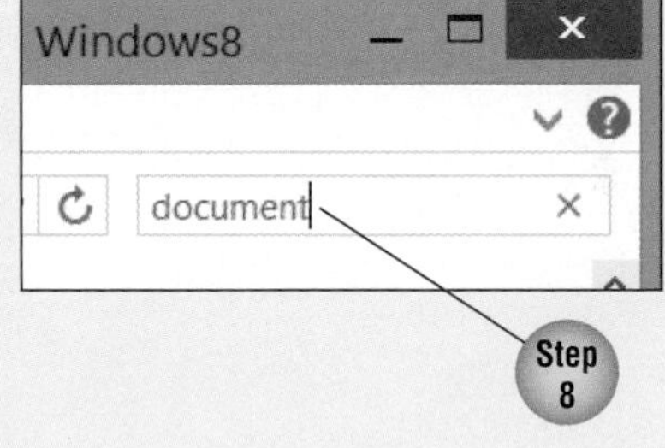

9. Select the text *document* that displays in the search text box and then type ***check**. (Notice that the Content pane displays file names containing the letters *check* no matter how the file name begins.)
10. Double-click ***WordSpellCheck02.docx*** to open the document in Word.
11. Close the document and then close Word by clicking the Close button located in the upper right corner of the window.
12. Close the Computer window.

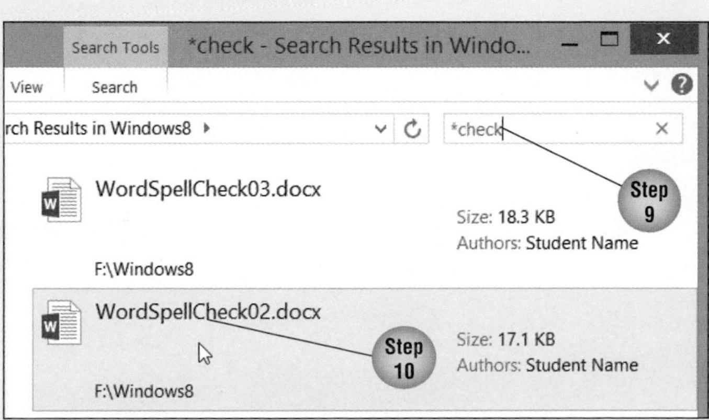

Browsing the Internet Using Internet Explorer 10

Microsoft Internet Explorer 10 is a web browser with options and features for displaying sites as well as navigating and searching for information on the Internet. The ***Internet*** is a network of computers connected around the world. Users access the Internet for several purposes: to communicate using instant messaging and/or email, to subscribe to newsgroups, to transfer files, to socialize with other users around the globe on social websites, and to access virtually any kind of information imaginable.

Using the Internet, people can find a phenomenal amount of information for private or public use. To use the Internet, three things are generally required: an ***Internet Service Provider (ISP)***, software to browse the Web (called a ***web browser***), and a ***search engine***. In this section, you will learn how to:

- Navigate the Internet using URLs and hyperlinks
- Use search engines to locate information
- Download web pages and images

You will use the Microsoft Internet Explorer web browser to locate information on the Internet. A ***Uniform Resource Locator***, referred to as a ***URL***, identifies a location on the Internet. The steps for browsing the Internet vary but generally include opening Internet Explorer, typing the URL for the desired site, navigating the various pages of the site, navigating to other sites using links, and then closing Internet Explorer.

To launch Internet Explorer 10, click the Internet Explorer icon on the Taskbar at the Windows desktop. Figure IE.1 identifies the elements of the Internet Explorer 10 window. The web page that displays in your Internet Explorer window may vary from what you see in Figure IE.1.

If you know the URL for a desired website, click in the Address bar, type the URL, and then press Enter. The website's home page displays in a tab within the Internet Explorer window. The format of a URL is *http://server-name.path*. The first part of the URL, *http*, stands for HyperText Transfer Protocol, which is the protocol or language used to transfer data within the World Wide Web. The colon and slashes separate the protocol from the server name. The server name is the second component of the URL. For example, in the URL http://www.microsoft.com, the server name is *microsoft*. The last part of the URL specifies the domain to which the server belongs. For example, *.com* refers to "commercial" and establishes that the URL is a commercial company. Examples of other domains include *.edu* for "educational," *.gov* for "government," and *.mil* for "military."

Internet Explorer 10 has been streamlined to provide users with more browsing space and reduced clutter. By default, Microsoft has turned off many features in Internet Explorer 10 such as the Menu bar, Command bar, and Status bar. You can turn these features on by right-clicking the empty space above the Address bar and to the right of the new tab button (see Figure IE.1) and then clicking the desired option at the drop-down list that displays. For example, if you want to turn on the Menu bar (the bar that contains File, Edit, and so on), right-click the empty space above the Address bar and then click *Menu bar* at the drop-down list. (This inserts a check mark next to *Menu bar*.)

Figure IE.1 Internet Explorer Window

Project 1 Browsing the Internet Using URLs

1. Make sure you are connected to the Internet through an Internet Service Provider and that the Windows 8 desktop displays. (Check with your instructor to determine if you need to complete steps for accessing the Internet such as typing a user name and password to log on.)
2. Launch Microsoft Internet Explorer by clicking the Internet Explorer icon located at the left side of the Windows Taskbar, which is located at the bottom of the Windows desktop.
3. Turn on the Command bar by right-clicking the empty space above the Address bar or to the right of the new tab button (see Figure IE.1) and then clicking *Command bar* at the drop-down list.

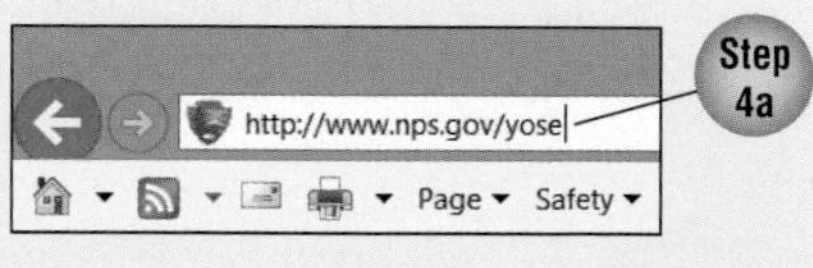

4. At the Internet Explorer window, explore the website for Yosemite National Park by completing the following steps:
   a. Click in the Address bar, type **www.nps.gov/yose**, and then press Enter.
   b. Scroll down the home page for Yosemite National Park by clicking the down-pointing arrow on the vertical scroll bar located at the right side of the Internet Explorer window.

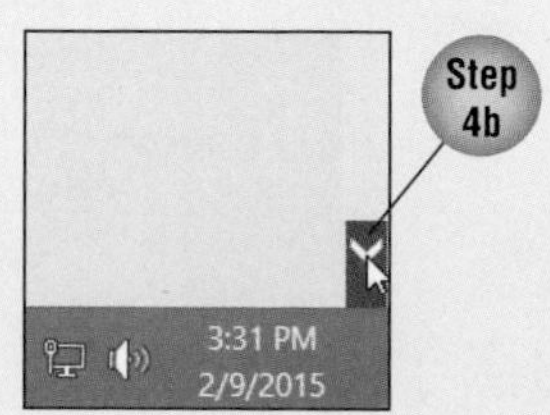

c. Print the home page by clicking the Print button located on the Command bar. (Note that some websites have a printer-friendly button you can click to print the page.)
5. Explore the website for Glacier National Park by completing the following steps:
   a. Click in the Address bar, type **www.nps.gov/glac**, and then press Enter.
   b. Print the home page by clicking the Print button located on the Command bar.
6. Close Internet Explorer by clicking the Close button (contains an X) located in the upper right corner of the Internet Explorer window.

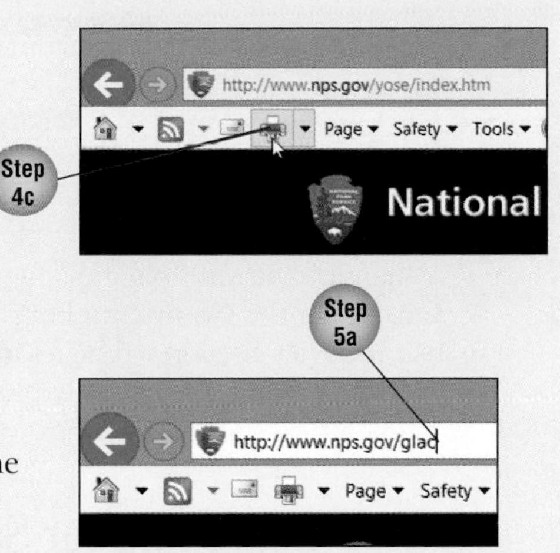

Navigating Using Hyperlinks

Most web pages contain ***hyperlinks*** that you click to connect to another page within the website or to another site on the Internet. Hyperlinks may display in a web page as underlined text in a specific color or as images or icons. To use a hyperlink, position the mouse pointer on the desired hyperlink until the mouse pointer turns into a hand and then click the left mouse button. Use hyperlinks to navigate within and between sites on the Internet. The Internet Explorer window contains a Back button (see Figure IE.1) that, when clicked, takes you to the previous web page viewed. If you click the Back button and then want to return to the previous page, click the Forward button. You can continue clicking the Back button to back your way out of several linked pages in reverse order since Internet Explorer maintains a history of the websites you visit.

Project 2 Navigating Using Hyperlinks

1. Make sure you are connected to the Internet and then click the Internet Explorer icon on the Windows Taskbar.
2. At the Internet Explorer window, display the White House web page and navigate in the page by completing the following steps:
   a. Click in the Address bar, type **whitehouse.gov**, and then press Enter.
   b. At the White House home page, position the mouse pointer on a hyperlink that interests you until the pointer turns into a hand and then click the left mouse button.
   c. At the linked web page, click the Back button. (This returns you to the White House home page.)
   d. At the White House home page, click the Forward button to return to the previous web page viewed.
   e. Print the web page by clicking the Print button on the Command bar.

3. Display the website for Amazon.com and navigate in the site by completing the following steps:
   a. Click in the Address bar, type **www.amazon.com**, and then press Enter.
   b. At the Amazon.com home page, click a hyperlink related to books.
   c. When a book web page displays, click the Print button on the Command bar.

4. Close Internet Explorer by clicking the Close button (contains an X) located in the upper right corner of the Internet Explorer window.

Searching for Specific Sites

If you do not know the URL for a specific site or you want to find information on the Internet but do not know what site to visit, complete a search with a search engine. A ***search engine*** is software created to search quickly and easily for desired information. A variety of search engines are available on the Internet, each offering the opportunity to search for specific information. One method for searching for information is to click in the Address bar, type a keyword or phrase related to your search, and then press Enter. Another method for completing a search is to visit the website for a search engine and use options at the site.

Bing is Microsoft's online search portal and is the default search engine used by Internet Explorer. Bing organizes search results by topic category and provides related search suggestions.

Project 3 Searching for Information by Topic

1. Start Internet Explorer.
2. At the Internet Explorer window, search for sites on bluegrass music by completing the following steps:
   a. Click in the Address bar.
   b. Type **bluegrass music** and then press Enter.
   c. When a list of sites displays in the Bing results window, click a site that interests you.
   d. When the page displays, click the Print button.

Step 2b

bluegrass music

Page

3. Use the Yahoo! search engine to find sites on bluegrass music by completing the following steps:
   a. Click in the Address bar, type **www.yahoo.com**, and then press Enter.
   b. At the Yahoo! website, with the insertion point positioned in the search text box, type **bluegrass music** and then press Enter. (Notice that the sites displayed vary from sites displayed in the earlier search.)

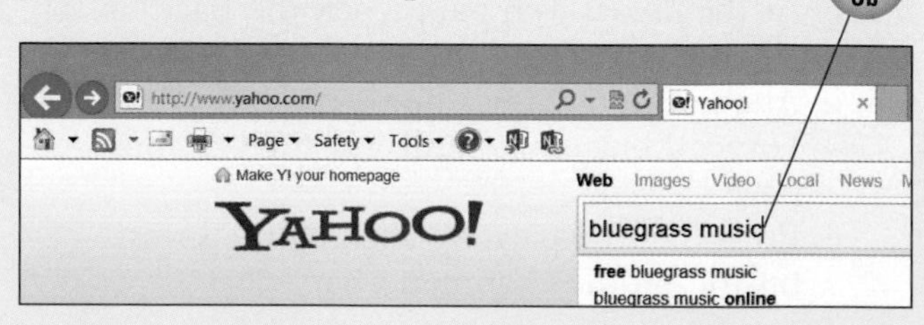

c. Click hyperlinks until a website displays that interests you.
d. Print the page.

4. Use the Google search engine to find sites on jazz music by completing the following steps:
   a. Click in the Address bar, type **www.google.com**, and then press Enter.
   b. At the Google website, with the insertion point positioned in the search text box, type **jazz music** and then press Enter.
   c. Click a site that interests you.
   d. Print the page.
5. Close Internet Explorer.

Using a Metasearch Engine

Bing, Yahoo!, and Google are search engines that search the Web for content and display search results. In addition to individual search engines, you can use a metasearch engine, such as Dogpile, that sends your search text to other search engines and then compiles the results in one list. With a metasearch engine, you type the search text once and then access results from a wider group of search engines. The Dogpile metasearch engine provides search results from Google, Yahoo!, and Yandex.

Project 4 Searching with a Metasearch Search Engine

1. Start Internet Explorer.
2. Click in the Address bar.
3. Type **www.dogpile.com** and then press Enter.
4. At the Dogpile website, type **jazz music** in the search text box and then press Enter.
5. Click a hyperlink that interests you.
6. Close the Internet Explorer window. If a message displays asking if you want to close all tabs, click the Close all tabs button.

Completing Advanced Searches for Specific Sites

The Internet contains an enormous amount of information. Depending on what you are searching for on the Internet and the search engine you use, some searches can result in several thousand "hits" (sites). Wading through a large number of sites can be very time-consuming and counterproductive. Narrowing a search to very specific criteria can greatly reduce the number of hits for a search. To narrow a search, use the advanced search options offered by the search engine.

Project 5 Narrowing a Search

1. Start Internet Explorer.
2. Search for sites on skydiving in Oregon by completing the following steps:
   a. Click in the Address bar, type **www.yahoo.com**, and then press Enter.
   b. At the Yahoo! home page, click the Search button next to the search text box.
   c. Click the More hyperlink located above the search text box and then click *Advanced Search* at the drop-down list.

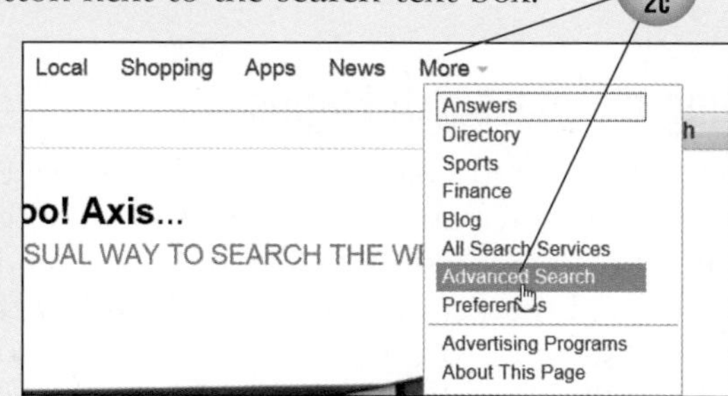

   d. At the Advanced Web Search page, click in the search text box next to *all of these words*.
   e. Type **skydiving Oregon tandem static line**. (This limits the search to web pages containing all of the words typed in the search text box.)
   f. Click the Yahoo! Search button.

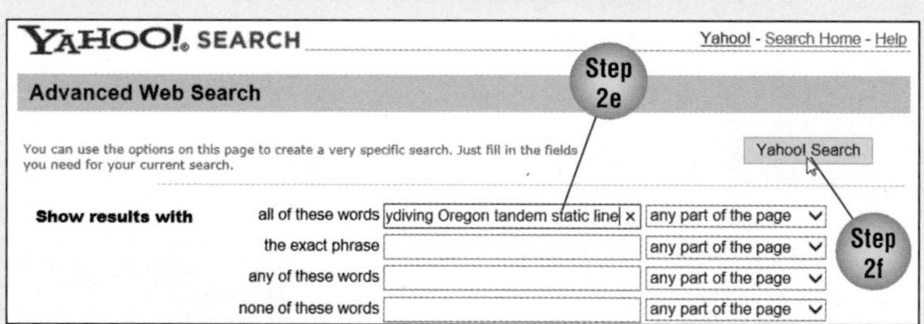

   g. When the list of websites displays, click a hyperlink that interests you.
   h. Click the Back button until the Yahoo! Advanced Web Search page displays.
   i. Click in the *the exact phrase* text box and then type **skydiving in Oregon**.
   j. Click the *Only .com domains* option in the *Site/Domain* section.
   k. Click the Yahoo! Search button.
   l. When the list of websites displays, click a hyperlink that interests you.
   m. Print the page.

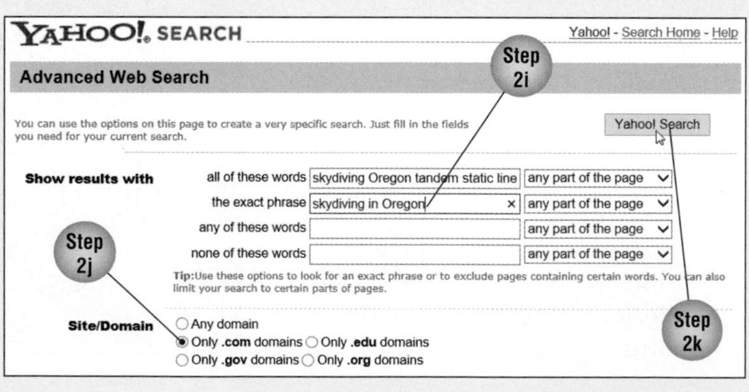

3. Close Internet Explorer.

Downloading Images, Text, and Web Pages from the Internet

The image(s) and/or text that display when you open a web page, as well as the web page itself, can be saved as a separate file. This separate file can be viewed, printed, or inserted in another file. The information you want to save in a separate file is downloaded from the Internet by Internet Explorer and saved in a folder of your choosing with the name you specify. Copyright laws protect much of the information on the Internet. Before using information downloaded from the Internet, check the site for restrictions. If you do use information, make sure you properly cite the source.

Project 6 Downloading Images and Web Pages

1. Start Internet Explorer.
2. Download a web page and image from Banff National Park by completing the following steps:
   a. Search for websites related to Banff National Park.
   b. From the list of sites that displays, choose a site that contains information about Banff National Park and at least one image of the park.
   c. Make sure the Command bar is turned on. (If the Command bar is turned off, turn it on by right-clicking the empty space above the Address bar or to the right of the new tab button and then clicking *Command bar* at the drop-down list.)

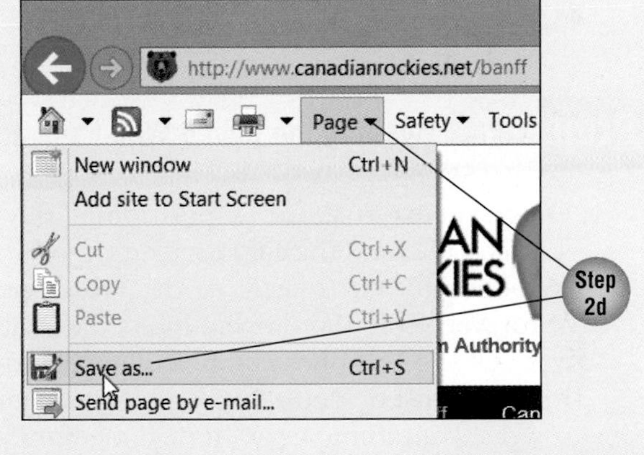

   d. Save the web page as a separate file by clicking the Page button on the Command bar and then clicking *Save as* at the drop-down list.
   e. At the Save Webpage dialog box, type **BanffWebPage**.
   f. Click the down-pointing arrow for the *Save as type* option and then click *Web Archive, single file (*.mht)*.
   g. Navigate to the drive containing your storage medium and then click the Save button.

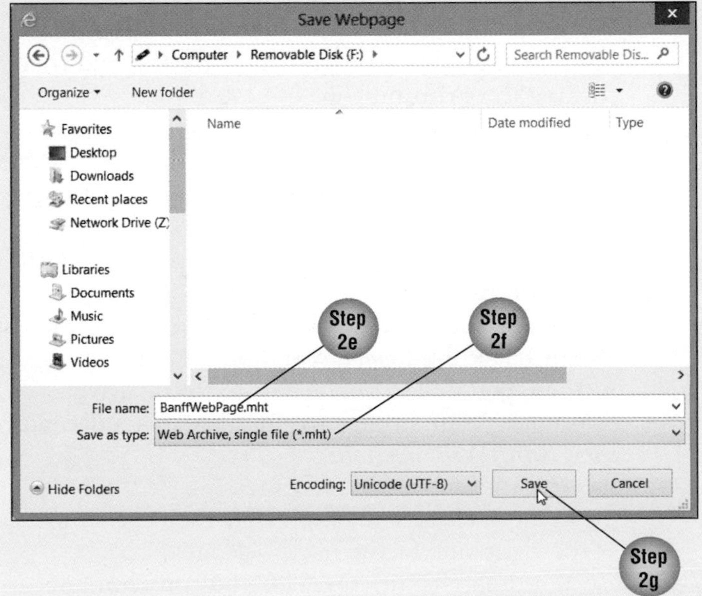

3. Save an image file by completing the following steps:
   a. Right-click an image that displays at the website.
   b. At the shortcut menu that displays, click *Save picture as*.

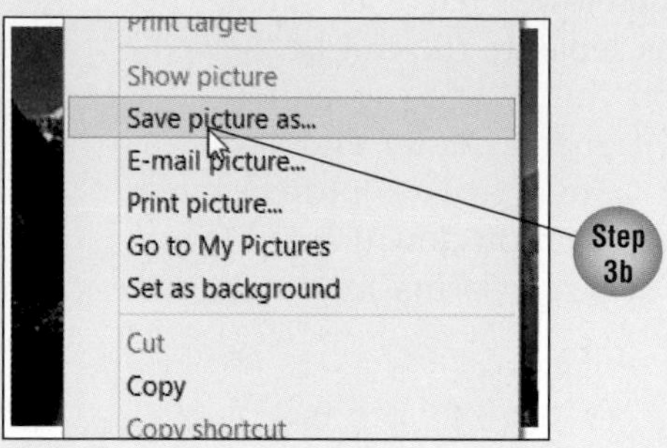

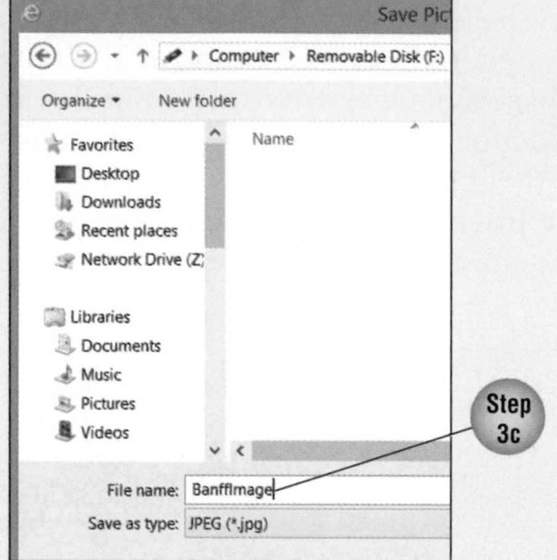

   c. At the Save Picture dialog box, type **BanffImage** in the *File name* text box.
   d. Navigate to the drive containing your storage medium and then click the Save button.
4. Close Internet Explorer.

Project 7 Opening the Saved Web Page and Image in a Word Document

1. Open Microsoft Word by positioning the mouse pointer in the lower left corner of the Taskbar, clicking the Start screen thumbnail, and then clicking the *Word 2013* tile in the Windows 8 Start screen. At the Word opening screen, click the *Blank document* template.
2. With Microsoft Word open, insert the image in a document by completing the following steps:
   a. Click the INSERT tab and then click the Pictures button in the Illustrations group.
   b. At the Insert Picture dialog box, navigate to the drive containing your storage medium and then double-click ***BanffImage.jpg***.
   c. When the image displays in the Word document, print the document by pressing Ctrl + P and then clicking the Print button.
   d. Close the document by clicking the FILE tab and then clicking the *Close* option. At the message asking if you want to save the changes, click the Don't Save button.

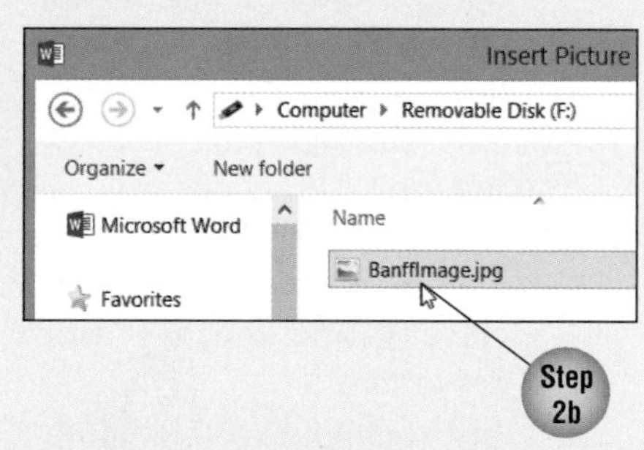

3. Open the **BanffWebPage.mht** file by completing the following steps:
   a. Click the FILE tab and then click the *Open* option.
   b. Double-click the *Computer* option.
   c. At the Open dialog box, navigate to the drive containing your storage medium and then double-click ***BanffWebPage.mht***.
   d. Preview the web page(s) by pressing Ctrl + P. At the Print backstage area, preview the page shown at the right side of the backstage area.

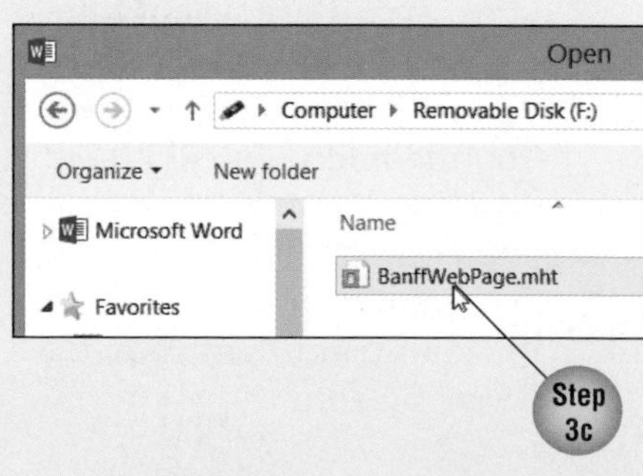

4. Close Word by clicking the Close button (contains an X) that displays in the upper right corner of the screen.

MICROSOFT®

ACCESS®

Level 1

Unit 1 ■ Creating Tables and Queries

MICROSOFT®

ACCESS®

CHAPTER 1

Managing and Creating Tables

PERFORMANCE OBJECTIVES

Upon successful completion of Chapter 1, you will be able to:

- **Open and close objects in a database**
- **Insert, delete, and move rows and columns in a table**
- **Hide, unhide, freeze, and unfreeze columns**
- **Adjust table column width**
- **Preview and print a table**
- **Design and create a table**
- **Rename column headings**
- **Insert a column name, caption, and description**
- **Insert Quick Start fields**
- **Assign a default value and field size**

Tutorials

1.1 Opening and Closing an Access Database and Table
1.2 Using the Recent List
1.3 Navigating in Objects
1.4 Adding Records in a Table
1.5 Deleting Records in a Table
1.6 Adjusting Column Width
1.7 Previewing and Printing a Table
1.8 Creating a New Database; Creating a Table in Datasheet View
1.9 Creating a Table Using Quick Start Fields
1.10 Modifying Field Size, Caption, and Default Value Properties

Managing information is an integral part of operating a business. Information can come in a variety of forms, such as data about customers, including names, addresses, and telephone numbers; product data; and purchasing and buying data. Most companies today manage data using a system software program. Microsoft Office Professional Plus includes a database management system software program named *Access*. With Access, you can organize, store, maintain, retrieve, sort, and print all types of business data.

This chapter contains just a few ideas on how to manage data with Access. With a properly designed and maintained database management system, a company can operate smoothly with logical, organized, and useful information. Model answers for this chapter's projects appear on the following pages.

AL1C1

Note: Before beginning the projects, copy to your storage medium the AL1C1 subfolder from the AL1 folder on the CD that accompanies this textbook. Make sure you have copied the files from the CD to your storage medium. Open all database files from your removable storage device and not directly from the CD since Access database files on the CD are read-only. Steps on how to copy a folder are presented on the inside of the back cover of this textbook. Do this every time you start a chapter's projects.

Project 1 Establish Relationships between Tables

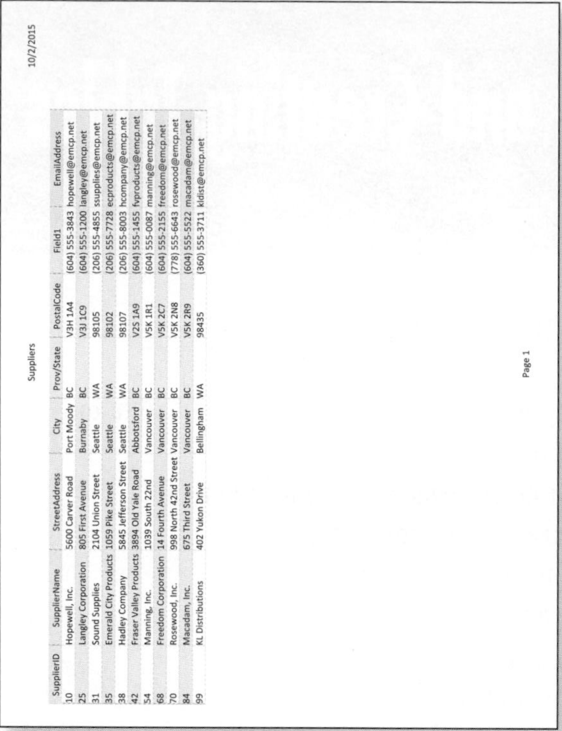

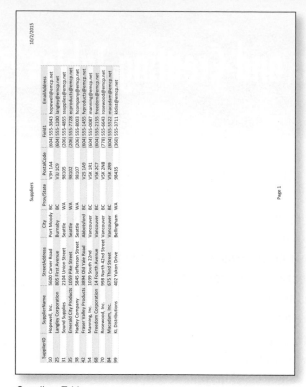

Suppliers 10/2/2015

SupplierID	SupplierName	StreetAddress	City	Prov/State	PostalCode	Field1	EmailAddress
10	Hopewell, Inc.	5600 Carver Road	Port Moody	BC	V3H 1A4	(604) 555-3843	hopewell@emcp.net
25	Langley Corporation	805 First Avenue	Burnaby	BC	V3J 1C9	(604) 555-1200	langley@emcp.net
31	Sound Supplies	2104 Union Street	Seattle	WA	98105	(206) 555-4855	ssupplies@emcp.net
35	Emerald City Products	1059 Pike Street	Seattle	WA	98102	(206) 555-7728	ecproducts@emcp.net
38	Hadley Company	5845 Jefferson Street	Seattle	WA	98107	(206) 555-8003	hcompany@emcp.net
42	Fraser Valley Products	3894 Old Yale Road	Abbotsford	BC	V2S 1A9	(604) 555-1455	fvproducts@emcp.net
54	Manning, Inc.	1039 South 22nd	Vancouver	BC	V5K 1R1	(604) 555-0087	manning@emcp.net
68	Freedom Corporation	14 Fourth Avenue	Vancouver	BC	V5K 2C7	(604) 555-2155	freedom@emcp.net
70	Rosewood, Inc.	998 North 42nd Street	Vancouver	BC	V5K 2N8	(778) 555-6643	rosewood@emcp.net
84	Macadam, Inc.	675 Third Street	Vancouver	BC	V5K 2R9	(604) 555-5522	macadam@emcp.net
99	KL Distributions	402 Yukon Drive	Bellingham	WA	98435	(360) 555-3711	kldist@emcp.net

Page 1

Suppliers Table

Products 10/2/2015

ProductID	Product	SupplierID	UnitsInStock	UnitsOnOrder	ReorderLevel
101-S1B	SL 0-degrees down sleeping bag, black	54	16	0	15
101-S1R	SL 0-degrees down sleeping bag, red	54	17	0	15
101-S2B	SL 15-degrees synthetic sleeping bag, blac	54	21	0	15
101-S2R	SL 15-degrees synthetic sleeping bag, red	54	12	15	15
101-S3B	SL 20-degrees synthetic sleeping bag, blac	54	8	15	15
101-S3R	SL 20-degrees synthetic sleeping bag, red	54	4	10	10
209-L	Gordon wool ski hat, L	68	21	25	25
209-XL	Gordon wool ski hat, XL	68	14	25	25
209-XXL	Gordon wool ski hat, XXL	68	10	20	20
210-L	Tech-lite ski hat, L	68	17	25	25
210-M	Tech-lite ski hat, M	68	6	15	15
210-XL	Tech-lite ski hat, XL	68	22	0	20
299-M1	HT waterproof hiking boots, MS13	31	8	0	10
299-M2	HT waterproof hiking boots, MS12	31	2	10	10
299-M3	HT waterproof hiking boots, MS11	31	6	10	10
299-M4	HT waterproof hiking boots, MS10	31	7	0	10
299-M5	HT waterproof hiking boots, MS9	31	9	10	10
299-W1	HT waterproof hiking boots, WS11	31	5	8	8
299-W2	HT waterproof hiking boots, WS10	31	9	0	8
299-W3	HT waterproof hiking boots, WS9	31	3	10	10
299-W4	HT waterproof hiking boots, WS8	31	2	10	10
299-W5	HT waterproof hiking boots, WS7	31	3	10	10
299-W6	HT waterproof hiking boots, WS6	31	11	0	10
371-L	Lite-tech ski gloves, ML	68	3	10	10
371-M	Lite-tech ski gloves, MM	68	5	0	15
371-XL	Lite-tech ski gloves, MXL	68	3	10	10
371-XXL	Lite-tech ski gloves, MXXL	68	12	0	10
375-L	Lite-tech ski gloves, WL	68	22	0	20
375-M	Lite-tech ski gloves, WM	68	3	20	20
375-S	Lite-tech ski gloves, WS	68	6	20	20
442-1A	Polar backpack, 150BR	42	12	0	10
442-1B	Polar backpack, 150RW	42	9	10	10
443-1A	Polar backpack, 250BR	42	14	0	15
443-1B	Polar backpack, 250RW	42	6	15	15
558-C	ICE snow goggles, clear	68	18	0	15
559-B	ICE snow goggles, bronze	68	22	0	20

Page 1

Products Table, Page 1

Products 10/2/2015

ProductID	Product	SupplierID	UnitsInStock	UnitsOnOrder	ReorderLevel
602-XR	Binoculars, 8 x 42	35	3	5	5
602-XT	Binoculars, 10.5 x 45	35	5	0	4
602-XX	Binoculars, 10 x 50	35	7	0	5
647-1	Two-person dome tent	99	10	15	15
648-2	Three-person dome tent	99	5	0	10
651-1	K-2 one-person tent	99	8	0	10
652-2	K-2 two-person tent	99	12	0	10
804-50	AG freestyle snowboard, X50	70	7	0	10
804-60	AG freestyle snowboard, X60	70	8	0	5
897-L	Lang blunt snowboard	70	8	0	7
897-W	Lang blunt snowboard, wide	70	4	0	3
901-S	Solar battery pack	38	16	0	15
917-S	Silo portable power pack	38	8	0	10

Page 2

Products Table, Page 2

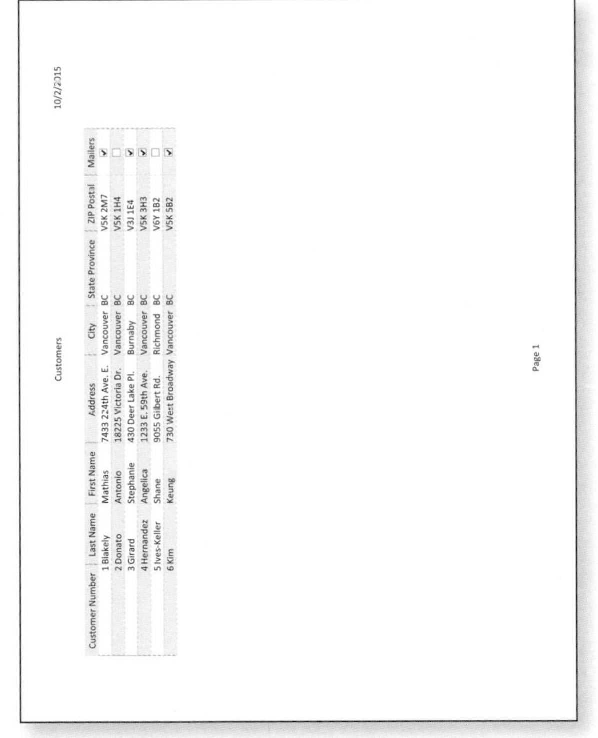

Customers 10/2/2015

Customer Number	Last Name	First Name	Address	City	State Province	ZIP Postal	Mailers
1	Blakely	Mathias	7433 224th Ave. E.	Vancouver	BC	V5K 2M7	☑
2	Donato	Antonio	18225 Victoria Dr.	Vancouver	BC	V5K 1H4	☐
3	Girard	Stephanie	430 Deer Lake Pl.	Burnaby	BC	V3J 1E4	☑
4	Hernandez	Angelica	1233 E. 59th Ave.	Vancouver	BC	V5K 3H3	☑
5	Ives-Keller	Shane	9055 Gilbert Rd.	Richmond	BC	V6Y 1B2	☐
6	Kim	Keung	730 West Broadway	Vancouver	BC	V5K 5B2	☑

Page 1

Customers Table

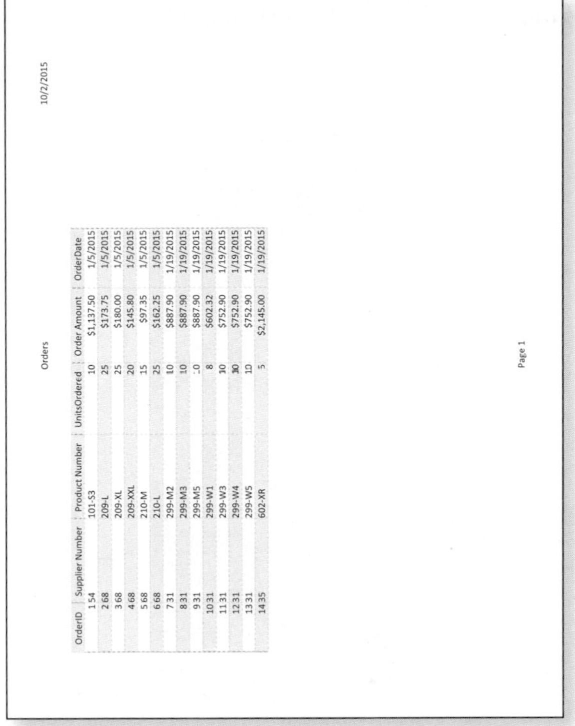

Orders 10/2/2015

OrderID	Supplier Number	Product Number	UnitsOrdered	Order Amount	OrderDate
1	54	101-S3	10	$1,137.50	1/5/2015
2	68	209-L	25	$173.75	1/5/2015
3	68	209-XL	25	$180.00	1/5/2015
4	68	209-XXL	20	$145.80	1/5/2015
5	68	210-M	15	$97.35	1/5/2015
6	68	210-L	25	$162.25	1/5/2015
7	31	299-M2	10	$887.90	1/19/2015
8	31	299-M3	10	$887.90	1/19/2015
9	31	299-M5	10	$887.90	1/19/2015
10	31	299-W1	8	$602.32	1/19/2015
11	31	299-W3	10	$752.90	1/19/2015
12	31	299-W4	10	$752.90	1/19/2015
13	31	299-W5	10	$752.90	1/19/2015
14	35	602-XR	5	$2,145.00	1/19/2015

Page 1

Orders Table

Project 1 Explore an Access Database — 1 Part

You will open a database and open and close objects in the database, including tables, queries, forms, and reports.

Exploring a Database

A ***database*** is comprised of a series of objects (such as tables, queries, forms, and reports) that you use to enter, manage, view, and print data. Data in a database is organized into tables, which contain information for related items (such as customers, employees, orders, and products). To view the various objects in a database, you will open a previously created database and then navigate in the database and open objects.

To create a new database or open a previously created database, click the Access 2013 tile at the Windows 8 Start screen. (This step may vary depending on your system configuration.) This displays the Access 2013 opening screen, as shown in Figure 1.1. At this opening screen, you can open a recently opened database, a blank database, a database from the Open backstage area, or a database based on a template.

Quick Steps

Create a New Database
1. Open Access.
2. Click Blank desktop database template.
3. Type database name.
4. Click Create button.

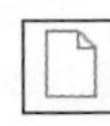

Create

To create a new blank database, click the Blank desktop database template. At the Blank desktop database window that displays, type a name for the database in the *File Name* text box, and then click the Create button. If you want to save the database in a particular location, click the Browse button at the right side of the *File Name* text box. At the File New Database dialog box that displays, navigate to the desired location or folder, type the database name in the *File name* text box, and then click OK.

Figure 1.1 Access 2013 Opening Screen

Click this template to create a blank database.

Click the Open Other Files hyperlink to display the Open backstage area, where you can navigate to the desired folder and then double-click the name of the database file.

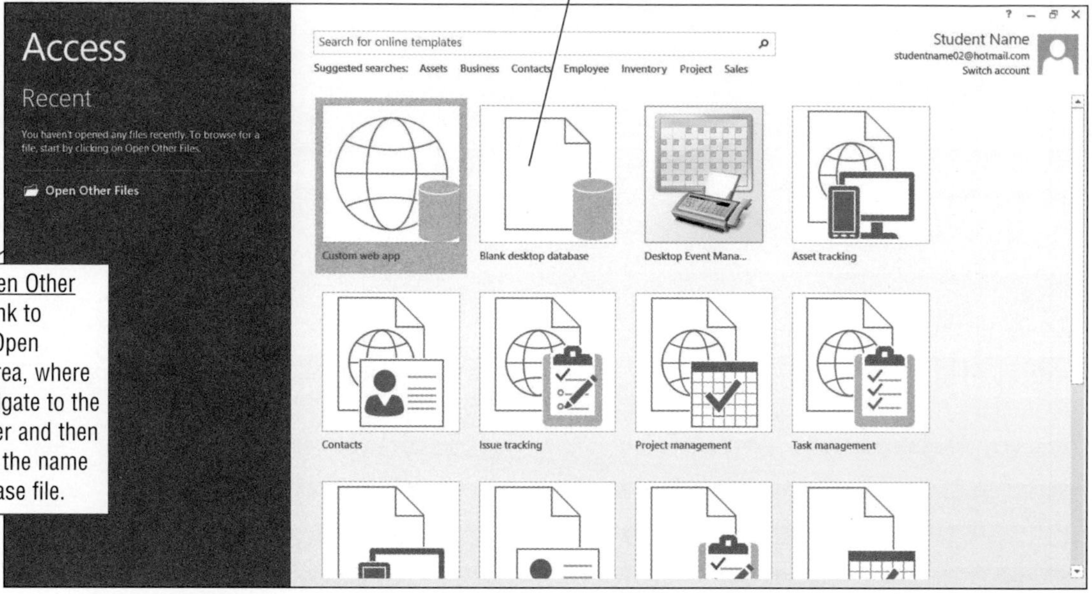

Opening a Database

Quick Steps

Open a Database

1. Open Access.
2. Click Open Other Files hyperlink.
3. Double-click SkyDrive or *Computer* option.
4. Navigate to desired location.
5. Double-click database.

To open an existing Access database, click the Open Other Files hyperlink that displays in the left panel at the Access 2013 opening screen. This displays the Open backstage area. You can also display the Open backstage area with the keyboard shortcut Ctrl + O or by inserting an Open button on the Quick Access toolbar and clicking that button. At the Open backstage area, click the desired location, such as your SkyDrive or the *Computer* option, and then click the Browse button. (If you are opening a database from your computer or USB flash drive, double-click the *Computer* option.) At the Open dialog box that displays, navigate to the desired folder and then double-click the desired database name in the Content pane.

If you are opening a database from your SkyDrive, Access requires you to save a copy of the database to a location such as your computer's hard drive or a USB flash drive. Any changes you make to the database will be saved to the local copy of the database but not the database on your SkyDrive. If you want to save the database back to your SkyDrive, you will need to upload the database by opening a web browser, going to skydrive.com, logging in to your SkyDrive account, and then clicking the Upload link. Microsoft constantly updates the skydrive.com website, so these steps may vary.

When you click your SkyDrive or the *Computer* option at the Open backstage area, a list of the most recently accessed folders displays in the Recent Folders list in the *Computer* section. Open a folder from this list by clicking the folder name.

At the Open backstage area with *Recent* selected in the middle panel, a list of the most recently opened databases displays in the Recent list. Open a database from this list by clicking the database name. When you open a database, the Access screen displays, as shown in Figure 1.2. Refer to Table 1.1 for descriptions of the Access screen elements.

Figure 1.2 Access Screen

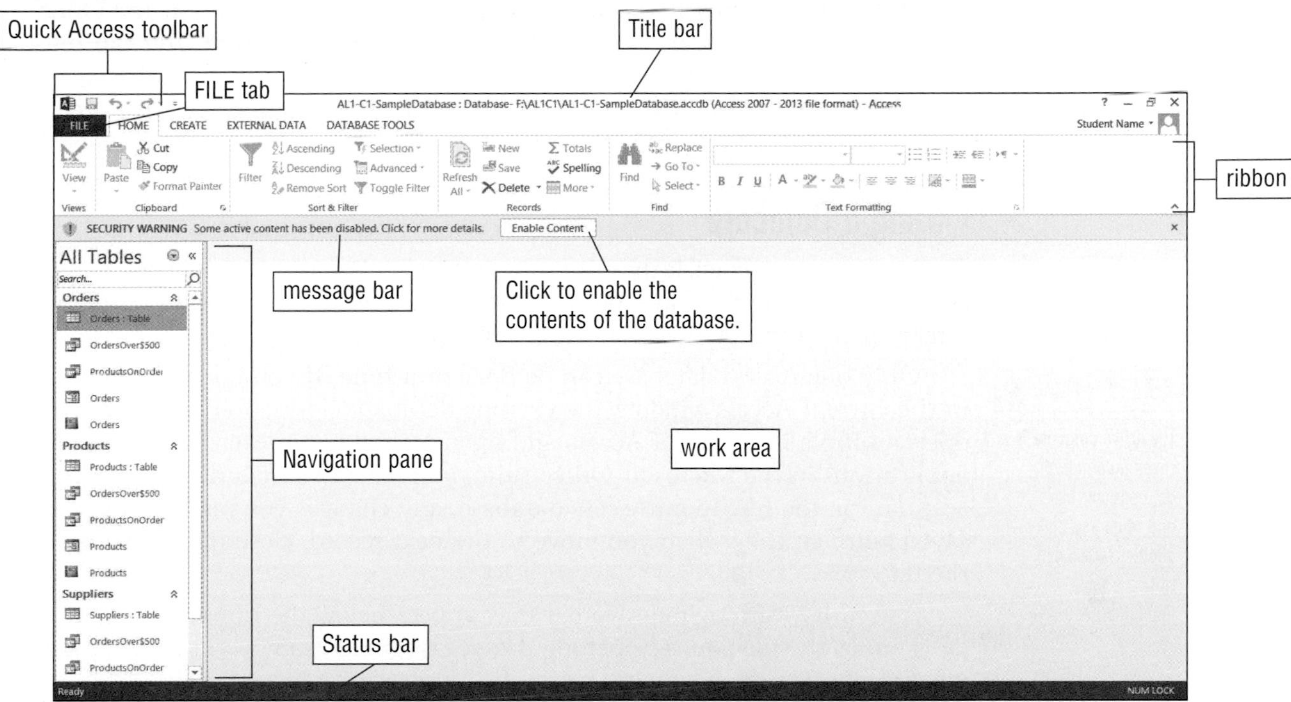

Table 1.1 Access Screen Elements

Feature	*Description*
FILE tab	When clicked, displays the backstage area that contains options for working with and managing databases.
message bar	Displays security alerts if the database being opened contains potentially unsafe content.
Navigation pane	Displays the names of objects within the database grouped by categories.
Quick Access toolbar	Contains buttons for commonly used commands.
ribbon	Contains the tabs with commands and buttons divided into groups.
Status bar	Displays messages, the current view, and view buttons.
tabs	Contain commands and features organized into groups.
Title bar	Displays the database name followed by the program name.
work area	Displays opened objects.

Pinning a Database File or Folder to the Recent List

If you want a database to remain in the Recent list at the Open backstage area, "pin" the database to the list. To do this, position the mouse pointer over the desired database file name and then click the small, left-pointing stick pin that displays at the right side of the list. When you click the stick pin, it changes to a down-pointing stick pin. The next time you display the Open backstage area, the database file name you pinned displays at the top of the Recent list.

You can also pin a folder name to the Recent Folders list in the same manner as you pin a database file name. The Recent Folders list displays at the Open backstage area when you click the SkyDrive or *Computer* option. You can pin more than one database file name to the Recent list or more than one folder name to the Recent Folders list. To "unpin" a database or folder name, click the stick pin to change it from a down-pointing pin to a left-pointing pin.

Closing a Database

Close

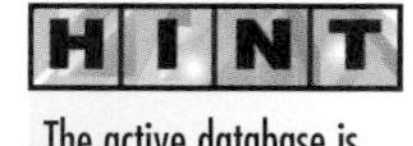

The active database is saved automatically on a periodic basis and when you make another record active, close the table, or close the database.

To close a database, click the FILE tab and then click the *Close* option. Close Access by clicking the Close button that displays in the upper right corner of the screen or with the keyboard shortcut Alt + F4.

Only one Access database can be open at a time. If you open a new database in the current Access window, the existing database closes. You can, however, open multiple instances of Access and open a database in each instance. In other applications in the Microsoft Office suite, you have to save a revised file after you edit data in the file. In an Access database, any changes you make to data are saved automatically when you move to the next record, close the table, or close the database.

A security warning message bar may appear below the ribbon if Access determines the file you are opening did not originate from a trusted location on your computer and may have viruses or other security hazards. This often occurs when you copy a file from another medium (such as a CD or the Web). Active content in the file is disabled until you click the Enable Content button. The message bar closes when you identify the database as a trusted source. Before making any changes to the database, you must click the Enable Content button.

The Navigation pane at the left side of the Access screen displays the objects contained in the database. Some common objects found in a database include tables, queries, forms, and reports. Refer to Table 1.2 for descriptions of these four types of objects.

Opening and Closing Objects

Database objects display in the Navigation pane. Control what displays in the pane by clicking the menu bar at the top of the Navigation pane and then clicking the desired option at the drop-down list or by clicking the button on the menu bar containing the down-pointing triangle. (The name of this button changes

Table 1.2 Database Objects

Object Type	*Description*
table	Organizes data in fields (columns) and records (rows). A database must contain at least one table. The table is the base upon which other objects are created.
query	Displays data from a table or related tables that meets a conditional statement and/or performs calculations. For example, all records from a specific month can be displayed or only those records containing a specific city.
form	Allows fields and records to be presented in a layout different from the datasheet. Used to facilitate data entry and maintenance.
report	Prints data from tables or queries.

depending on what is selected.) For example, to display a list of all saved objects in the database, click the *Object Type* option at the drop-down list. This view displays the objects grouped by type: *Tables*, *Queries*, *Forms*, and *Reports*. To open an object, double-click the object in the Navigation pane. The object opens in the work area and a tab displays with the object name at the left side of the object.

To view more of an object, consider closing the Navigation pane by clicking the Shutter Bar Open/Close Button located in the upper right corner of the Navigation pane or by using the keyboard shortcut F11. Click the button or press F11 again to reopen the Navigation pane. You can open more than one object in the work area. Each object opens with a visible tab. Navigate to objects by clicking the object tab. To close an object, click the Close button that displays in the upper right corner of the work area or use the keyboard shortcut Ctrl + F4.

Hide the Navigation pane by clicking the Shutter Bar Open/Close Button or by pressing F11.

Shutter Bar Open/Close Button

Project 1 Opening and Closing a Database and Objects in a Database — Part 1 of 1

1. Open Access by clicking the Access 2013 tile at the Windows 8 Start screen.
2. At the Access 2013 opening screen, click the Open Other Files hyperlink that displays in the left panel.
3. At the Open backstage area, click the desired location in the middle panel of the backstage area. (For example, click your SkyDrive if you are using your SkyDrive account or click the *Computer* option if you are opening a database from your computer's hard drive or a USB flash drive.)
4. Click the Browse button (or click *AL1C1* if it displays in the Recent Folders list).
5. At the Open dialog box, navigate to the AL1C1 folder on your storage medium and then double-click ***AL1-C1-SampleDatabase.accdb***. (This database contains data on orders, products, and suppliers for a specialty hiking and backpacking outfitters store named Pacific Trek.)
6. Click the Enable Content button in the message bar if a security warning message appears. (The message bar will display immediately below the ribbon.)
7. With the database open, click the Navigation pane menu bar and then click *Object Type* at the drop-down list. (This option displays the objects grouped by type: *Tables*, *Queries*, *Forms*, and *Reports*.)
8. Double-click *Suppliers* in the Tables group in the Navigation pane. This opens the Suppliers table in the work area, as shown in Figure 1.3.
9. Close the Suppliers table by clicking the Close button in the upper right corner of the work area.
10. Double-click *OrdersOver$500* in the Queries group in the Navigation pane. A query displays data that meets a conditional statement. This query displays orders that meet the criterion of being more than $500.
11. Close the query by clicking the Close button in the upper right corner of the work area.
12. Double-click *SuppliersNotVancouver* in the Queries group in the Navigation pane and notice that the query displays information about suppliers but excludes those located in Vancouver.

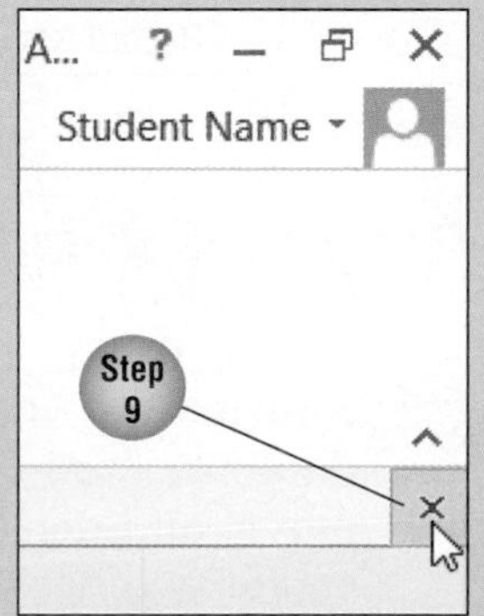

13. Click the Close button in the work area.
14. Double-click *Orders* in the Forms group in the Navigation pane. This displays an order form. A form is used to view and edit data in a table one record at a time.
15. Click the Close button in the work area.
16. Double-click *Orders* in the Reports group in the Navigation pane. This displays a report with information about orders and order amounts.
17. Close the Navigation pane by clicking the Shutter Bar Open/ Close Button located in the upper right corner of the pane.
18. After viewing the report, click the Shutter Bar Open/Close Button again to open the Navigation pane.
19. Click the Close button in the work area to close the report.
20. Close the database by clicking the FILE tab and then clicking the *Close* option.
21. Close Access by clicking the Close button (contains an X) that displays in the upper right corner of the screen.

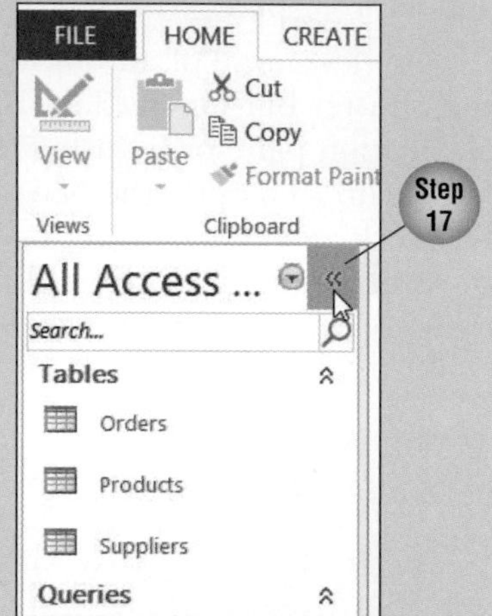

Figure 1.3 Open Suppliers Table

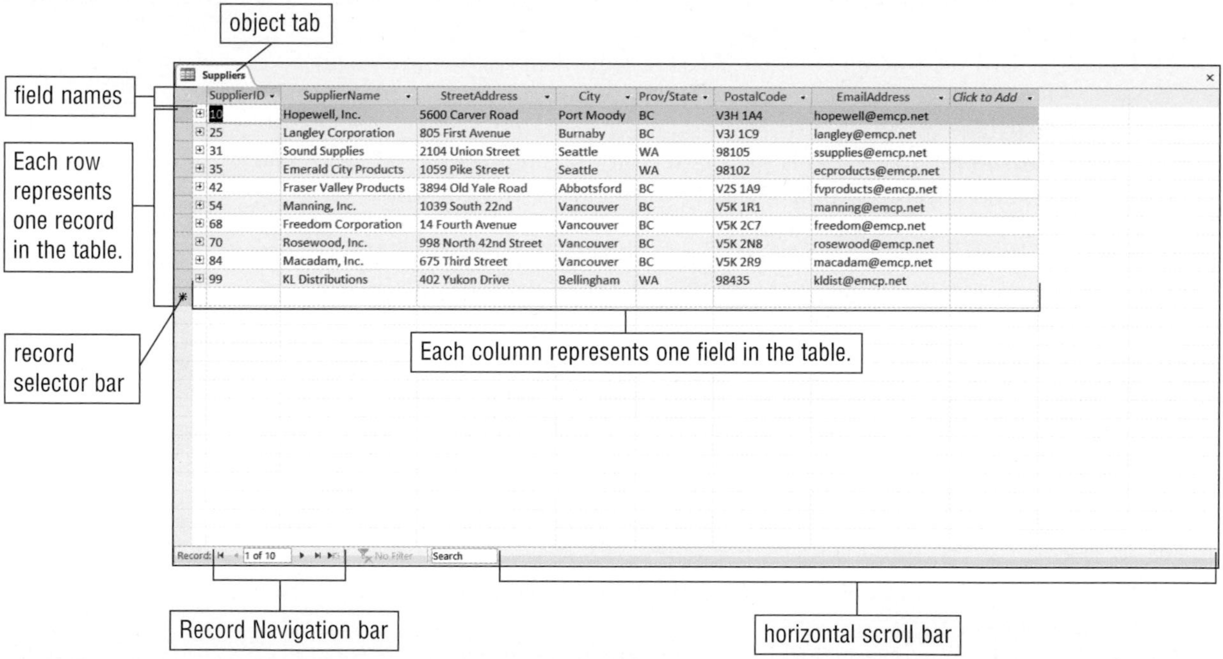

SupplierID	SupplierName	StreetAddress	City	Prov/State	PostalCode	EmailAddress	Click to Add
10	Hopewell, Inc.	5600 Carver Road	Port Moody	BC	V3H 1A4	hopewell@emcp.net	
25	Langley Corporation	805 First Avenue	Burnaby	BC	V3J 1C9	langley@emcp.net	
31	Sound Supplies	2104 Union Street	Seattle	WA	98105	ssupplies@emcp.net	
35	Emerald City Products	1059 Pike Street	Seattle	WA	98102	ecproducts@emcp.net	
42	Fraser Valley Products	3894 Old Yale Road	Abbotsford	BC	V2S 1A9	fvproducts@emcp.net	
54	Manning, Inc.	1039 South 22nd	Vancouver	BC	V5K 1R1	manning@emcp.net	
68	Freedom Corporation	14 Fourth Avenue	Vancouver	BC	V5K 2C7	freedom@emcp.net	
70	Rosewood, Inc.	998 North 42nd Street	Vancouver	BC	V5K 2N8	rosewood@emcp.net	
84	Macadam, Inc.	675 Third Street	Vancouver	BC	V5K 2R9	macadam@emcp.net	
99	KL Distributions	402 Yukon Drive	Bellingham	WA	98435	kldist@emcp.net	

Project 2 Manage Tables in a Database — 7 Parts

Pacific Trek is an outfitting store specializing in hiking and backpacking gear. Information about the store, including suppliers and products, is contained in a database. You will open the database and then insert and delete records; insert, move, and delete fields; preview and print tables; rename and delete a table; and create two new tables for the database.

Managing Tables

In a new database, tables are the first objects created, since all other database objects rely on a table as the source for their data. Managing the tables in the database is important for keeping the database up to date and may include inserting or deleting records, inserting or deleting fields, renaming fields, creating a hard copy of the table by printing the table, and renaming and deleting tables.

Inserting and Deleting Records

When you open a table, it displays in Datasheet view in the work area. The Datasheet view displays the contents of a table in a column and row format similar to an Excel worksheet. Columns contain the field data, with the field names in the header row at the top of the table, and rows contain the records. A Record Navigation bar displays at the bottom of the screen just above the Status bar and contains buttons to navigate in the table. Figure 1.4 identifies the buttons and other elements on the Record Navigation bar.

To add a new record to the open table, make sure the HOME tab is active and then click the New button in the Records group. This moves the insertion point to the first field in the blank row at the bottom of the table and the *Current Record* box on the Record Navigation bar indicates what record you are creating (or editing). You can also create a new record by clicking the New (blank) record button on the Record Navigation bar.

When working in a table, press the Tab key to make the next field active or press Shift + Tab to make the previous field active. You can also click in the desired field using the mouse. When you begin typing data for the first field in the record, another row of cells is automatically inserted below the current row and a pencil icon displays in the record selector bar at the beginning of the current record. The pencil icon indicates that the record is being edited and that the changes to the data have not been saved. When you enter the data in the last field in the record and then move the insertion point out of the field, the pencil icon is removed, indicating that the data is saved.

When managing a table, you may need to delete a record when you no longer want the data in the record. One method for deleting a record is to click in one of the fields in the record, make sure the HOME tab is active, click the Delete button arrow, and then click *Delete Record* at the drop-down list. At the message that displays asking if you want to delete the record, click the Yes button. When you click in a field in a record, the Delete button displays in a dimmed manner unless specific data is selected.

When you are finished entering data in a record in a table, the data is automatically saved. Changes to the layout of a table, however, are not automatically saved. For example, if you delete a column in a table, when you close the table you will be asked if you are sure you want to delete the selected field.

Quick Steps

Add a New Record
1. Open table.
2. Click New button on HOME tab.
3. Type data.

OR
1. Open table.
2. Click New (blank) record button on Record Navigation bar.
3. Type data.

Delete a Record
1. Open table.
2. Click Delete button arrow on HOME tab.
3. Click *Delete Record.*
4. Click Yes button.

New

Delete

Figure 1.4 Record Navigation Bar

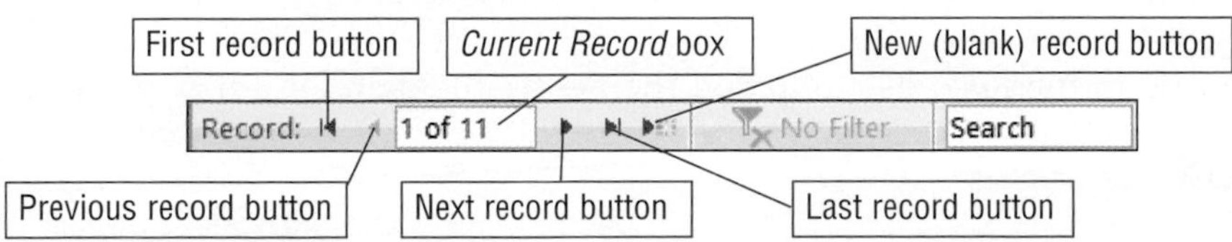

Project 2a Inserting and Deleting Records in a Table

Part 1 of 7

1. Open Access.
2. At the Access 2013 opening screen, click the Open Other Files hyperlink.
3. At the Open backstage area, double-click the *Computer* option or your SkyDrive (depending on where your AL1C1 folder is located).
4. At the Open dialog box, navigate to the AL1C1 folder on your storage medium or SkyDrive and then double-click ***AL1-C1-PacTrek.accdb***.
5. Click the Enable Content button in the message bar if a security warning message appears. (The message bar will display immediately below the ribbon.)
6. With the database open, make sure the Navigation pane displays object types. (If it does not, click the Navigation pane menu bar and then click *Object Type* at the drop-down list.)
7. Double-click *Suppliers* in the Tables group in the Navigation pane. (This opens the table in Datasheet view.)
8. With the Suppliers table open and the HOME tab active, create a new record by completing the following steps:
   a. Click the New button in the Records group on the HOME tab. (This moves the insertion point to the first field in the blank record at the bottom of the table and the *Current Record* box in the Record Navigation bar indicates what record you are creating or editing.)
   b. Type 38. (This inserts *38* in the field immediately below *99*.)
   c. Press the Tab key (to make the next field active) and then type **Hadley Company**.
   d. Press the Tab key and then type **5845 Jefferson Street**.
   e. Press the Tab key and then type **Seattle**.
   f. Press the Tab key and then type **WA**.
   g. Press the Tab key and then type **98107**.
   h. Press the Tab key and then type **hcompany@emcp.net**.
   i. Press the Tab key and then type **Jurene Miller**.

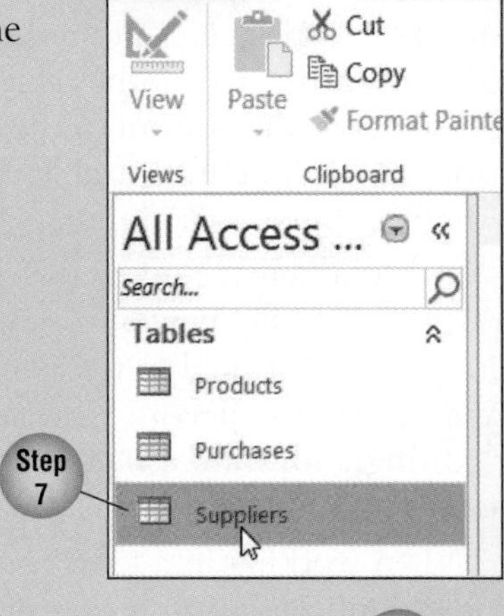

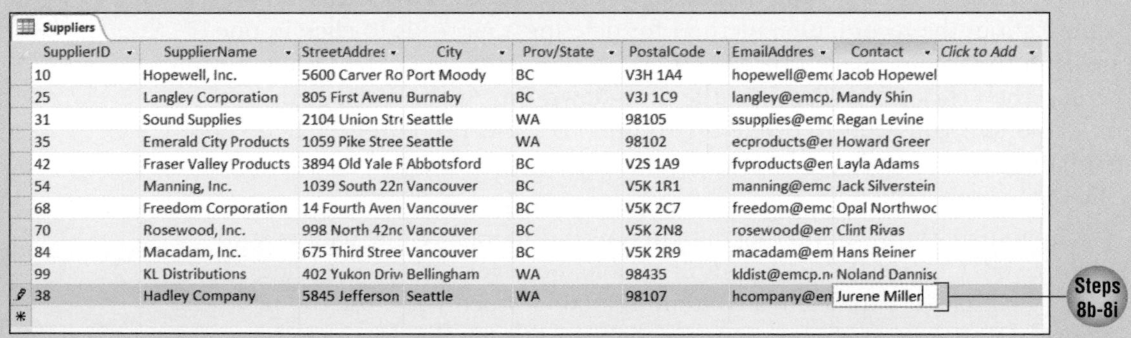

Suppliers

SupplierID	SupplierName	StreetAddres	City	Prov/State	PostalCode	EmailAddres	Contact	Click to Add
10	Hopewell, Inc.	5600 Carver Ro	Port Moody	BC	V3H 1A4	hopewell@emc	Jacob Hopewel	
25	Langley Corporation	805 First Avenu	Burnaby	BC	V3J 1C9	langley@emcp.	Mandy Shin	
31	Sound Supplies	2104 Union Str	Seattle	WA	98105	ssupplies@emc	Regan Levine	
35	Emerald City Products	1059 Pike Stree	Seattle	WA	98102	ecproducts@er	Howard Greer	
42	Fraser Valley Products	3894 Old Yale F	Abbotsford	BC	V2S 1A9	fvproducts@en	Layla Adams	
54	Manning, Inc.	1039 South 22n	Vancouver	BC	V5K 1R1	manning@emc	Jack Silverstein	
68	Freedom Corporation	14 Fourth Aven	Vancouver	BC	V5K 2C7	freedom@emc	Opal Northwoc	
70	Rosewood, Inc.	998 North 42nc	Vancouver	BC	V5K 2N8	rosewood@em	Clint Rivas	
84	Macadam, Inc.	675 Third Stree	Vancouver	BC	V5K 2R9	macadam@em	Hans Reiner	
99	KL Distributions	402 Yukon Driv	Bellingham	WA	98435	kldist@emcp.n	Noland Dannisc	
38	Hadley Company	5845 Jefferson	Seattle	WA	98107	hcompany@en	Jurene Miller	

9. Close the Suppliers table by clicking the Close button in the work area.
10. Open the Products table by double-clicking *Products* in the Tables group in the Navigation pane. (This opens the table in Datasheet view.)
11. Insert two new records by completing the following steps:
   a. Click the New button in the Records group and then enter the data for a new record as shown in Figure 1.5. (See the record that begins with *901-S*.)

b. After you type the last field entry in the record for product number 901-S, press the Tab key. This moves the insertion point to the blank field below *901-S*.
c. Type the new record as shown in Figure 1.5. (See the record that begins with *917-S*.)

12. With the Products table open, delete a record by completing the following steps:
    a. Click in the field containing the data *780-2*.
    b. Click the Delete button arrow in the Records group (notice that the button displays in a dimmed manner) and then click *Delete Record* at the drop-down list.
    c. At the message asking if you want to delete the record, click the Yes button.
13. Close the Products table by clicking the Close button in the work area.

Figure 1.5 Project 2a, Step 11

Products

ProductID	Product	SupplierID	UnitsInStock	UnitsOnOrder	ReorderLevel	Click to Add
559-B	ICE snow goggles, bronze	68	22	0	20	
602-XR	Binoculars, 8 x 42	35	3	5	5	
602-XT	Binoculars, 10.5 x 45	35	5	0	4	
602-XX	Binoculars, 10 x 50	35	7	0	5	
647-1	Two-person dome tent	99	10	15	15	
648-2	Three-person dome tent	99	5	0	10	
651-1	K-2 one-person tent	99	8	0	10	
652-2	K-2 two-person tent	99	12	0	10	
780-2	Two-person tent	99	17	10	20	
804-50	AG freestyle snowboard, X50	70	7	0	10	
804-60	AG freestyle snowboard, X60	70	8	0	5	
897-L	Lang blunt snowboard	70	8	0	7	
897-W	Lang blunt snowboard, wide	70	4	0	3	
901-S	Solar battery pack	38	16	0	15	
917-S	Silo portable power pack	38	8	0	10	
*						

Step 11

Inserting, Moving, and Deleting Fields

When managing a database, you may determine that you need to add additional information to a table. For example, you might decide that you want to insert a field for contact information, a field for cell phone numbers, or a field for the number of items in stock. To insert a new field in a table, open the table in Datasheet view and then click in the first field below the *Click to Add* heading. Type the desired data in the field for the first record, press the Down Arrow key to make the field below active, and then type the desired data for the second record. Continue in this manner until you have entered data in the new field for all records in the table. Instead of pressing the Down Arrow key to move the

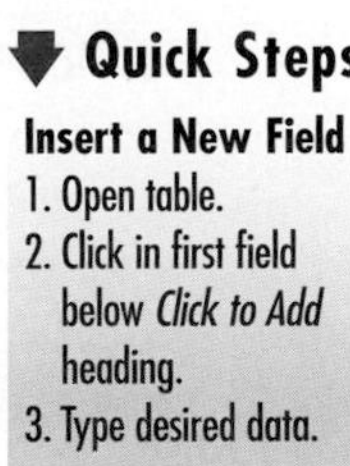
Quick Steps
Insert a New Field
1. Open table.
2. Click in first field below Click to Add heading.
3. Type desired data.

insertion point down to the next field, you can click in the desired field using the mouse or you can press the Tab key until the desired field is active.

A new field is added to the right of existing fields. Move a field by positioning the mouse pointer on the field heading until the pointer displays as a down-pointing black arrow and then clicking the left mouse button. This selects the entire column. With the field column selected, position the mouse pointer on the heading; hold down the left mouse button; drag to the left or right until a thick, black vertical line displays in the desired location; and then release the mouse button. The thick, black vertical line indicates where the field column will be positioned when you release the mouse button. In addition, the pointer displays with the outline of a gray box attached to it, indicating that you are performing a move operation.

Delete a field column in a manner similar to deleting a row. Click in one of the fields in the column, make sure the HOME tab is active, click the Delete button arrow, and then click *Delete Column* at the drop-down list. At the message that displays asking if you want to delete the column, click the Yes button.

Quick Steps

Move a Field Column
1. Select column.
2. Position mouse pointer on heading.
3. Hold down left mouse button.
4. Drag to desired location.
5. Release mouse button.

Delete a Field Column
1. Click in field.
2. Click Delete button arrow on HOME tab.
3. Click *Delete Column*.
4. Click Yes button.

Project 2b Inserting, Moving, and Deleting Fields — Part 2 of 7

1. With **AL1-C1-PacTrek.accdb** open, you decide to add a new field to the Suppliers table. Do this by completing the following steps:
   a. Double-click *Suppliers* in the Tables group in the Navigation pane.
   b. Click in the field immediately below the heading *Click to Add*.
   c. Type **(604) 555-3843** and then press the Down Arrow key on your keyboard.
   d. Type the remaining telephone numbers as shown at the right.

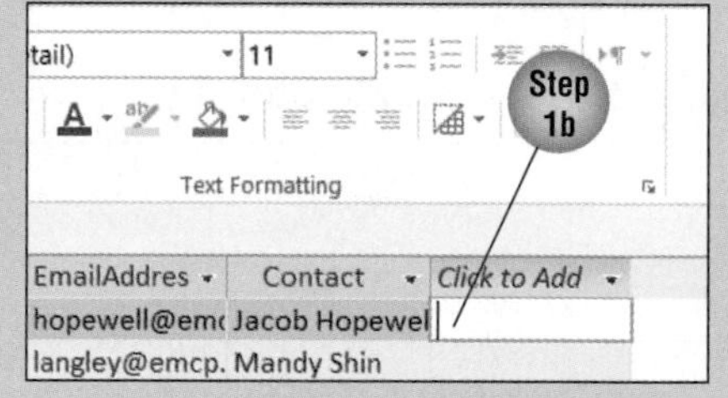

Contact	Field1	Click
Jacob Hopewel	(604) 555-3843	
Mandy Shin	(604) 555-1200	
Regan Levine	(206) 555-4855	
Howard Greer	(206) 555-7728	
Jurene Miller	(206) 555-8003	
Layla Adams	(604) 555-1455	
Jack Silverstein	(604) 555-0087	
Opal Northwoc	(604) 555-2155	
Clint Rivas	(778) 555-6643	
Hans Reiner	(604) 555-5522	
Noland Dannis(	(360) 555-3711	

Step 1d

2. Move the field column so it is positioned immediately left of the *EmailAddress* field by completing the following steps:
   a. Position the mouse pointer on the heading *Field1* until the pointer displays as a down-pointing black arrow and then click the left mouse button. (This selects the column.)
   b. Position the mouse pointer on the heading. (The pointer displays as the normal, white arrow pointer.) Hold down the left mouse button; drag to the left until the thick, black vertical line displays immediately left of the *EmailAddress* field; and then release the mouse button.

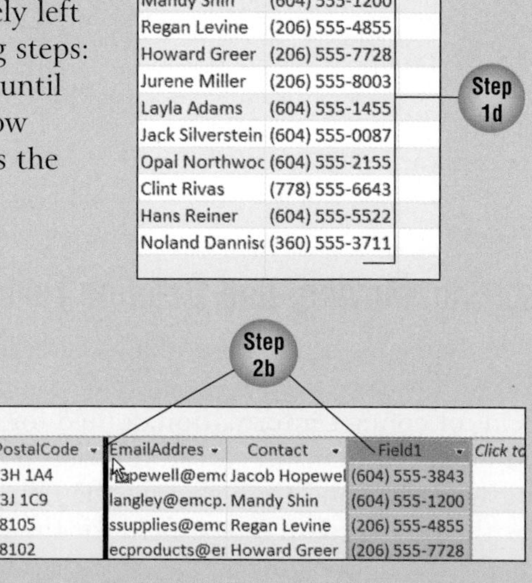

PostalCode	EmailAddres	Contact	Field1	Click to
V3H 1A4	hopewell@emc	Jacob Hopewel	(604) 555-3843	
V3J 1C9	langley@emcp.	Mandy Shin	(604) 555-1200	
98105	ssupplies@emc	Regan Levine	(206) 555-4855	
98102	ecproducts@er	Howard Greer	(206) 555-7728	

3. You realize that you no longer need the supplier contact information so you decide to delete the field. Do this by completing the following steps:
   a. Position the mouse pointer on the heading *Contact* until the pointer displays as a down-pointing black arrow and then click the left mouse button. (This selects the column.)

b. Click the Delete button arrow in the Records group and then click *Delete Column* at the drop-down list.
c. At the message asking if you want to permanently delete the selected fields, click the Yes button.
4. Close the Suppliers table. At the message that displays asking if you want to save the changes to the layout of the table, click the Yes button.

Hiding, Unhiding, Freezing, and Unfreezing Column Fields

You can hide columns of data in a table if you do not want the data visible or you want to make it easier to view two nonadjacent columns containing data you want to compare. To hide a column, click in any field in the column you want to hide, click the More button in the Records group on the HOME tab, and then click *Hide Fields* at the drop-down list. Hide adjacent columns by selecting the columns, clicking the More button in the Records group, and then clicking *Hide Fields* at the drop-down list. To unhide columns, click the More button and then click *Unhide Fields*. At the Unhide Columns dialog box that displays, insert a check mark in the check boxes for those columns you want to be visible.

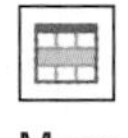
More

Another method for comparing column fields side by side is to freeze a column. Freezing a column is also helpful when not all of the columns of data are visible at one time. To freeze a column, click in any field in the column you want to freeze, click the More button, and then click *Freeze Fields* at the drop-down list. To freeze adjacent columns, select the columns first, click the More button, and then click *Freeze Fields* at the drop-down list. To unfreeze all columns in a table, click the More button and then click *Unfreeze All Fields* at the drop-down list.

Changing Column Width

When entering data in the Suppliers and Products table, did you notice that not all of the data was visible? To remedy this, you can adjust the widths of columns so that all data is visible. You can adjust the width of one column in a table to accommodate the longest entry in the column by positioning the arrow pointer on the column boundary at the right side of the column until the pointer turns into a left-and-right-pointing arrow with a vertical line in the middle and then double-clicking the left mouse button.

Adjust the widths of adjacent columns by selecting the columns first and then double-clicking on one of the selected column boundaries. To select adjacent columns, position the arrow pointer on the first column heading until the pointer turns into a down-pointing black arrow, hold down the left mouse button, drag to the last column you want to adjust, and then release the mouse button. With the columns selected, double-click one of the column boundaries.

You can also adjust the width of a column by dragging the boundary to the desired position. To do this, position the arrow pointer on the column boundary until it turns into a left-and-right-pointing arrow with a vertical line in the middle, hold down the left mouse button, drag until the column is the desired width, and then release the mouse button.

Quick Steps

Change a Table Column Width
Double-click column boundary.
OR
Select columns and then double-click column boundary.
OR
Drag column boundary to desired position.

Automatically adjust column widths in an Access table in the same manner as adjusting column widths in an Excel worksheet.

Project 2c Hiding, Unhiding, Freezing, and Unfreezing Columns and Changing Column Widths Part 3 of 7

1. With **AL1-C1-PacTrek.accdb** open, open the Suppliers table.
2. Hide the *PostalCode* column by clicking in any field in the *PostalCode* column, clicking the More button in the Records group on the HOME tab, and then clicking *Hide Fields* at the drop-down list.
3. Unhide the column by clicking the More button and then clicking *Unhide Fields* at the drop-down list. At the Unhide Columns dialog box, click in the *PostalCode* check box to insert a check mark, and then click the Close button.

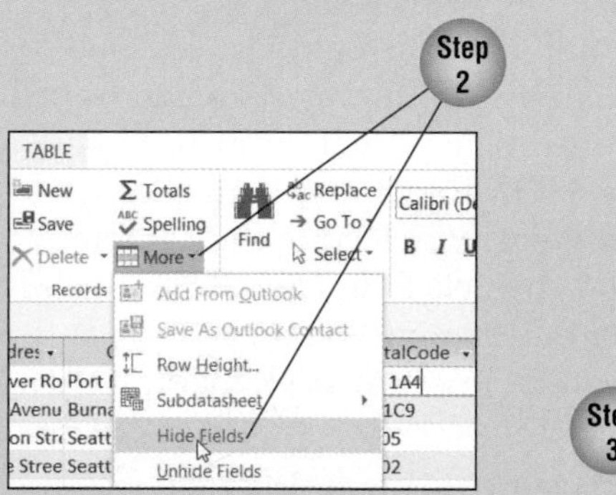

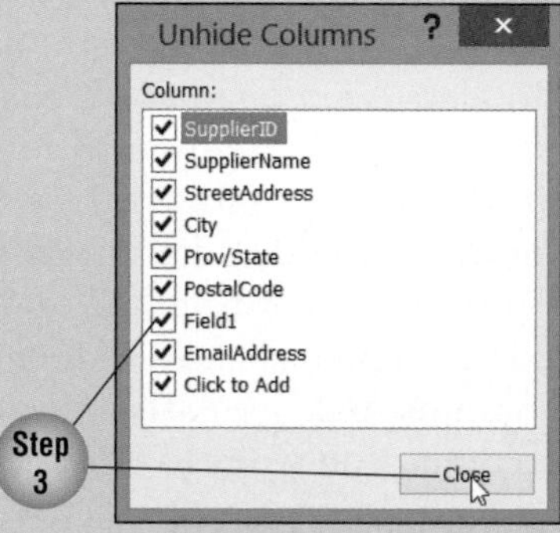

4. Adjust the width of the *SupplierID* column by positioning the arrow pointer on the column boundary at the right side of the *SupplierID* column until it turns into a left-and-right-pointing arrow with a vertical line in the middle and then double-clicking the left mouse button.

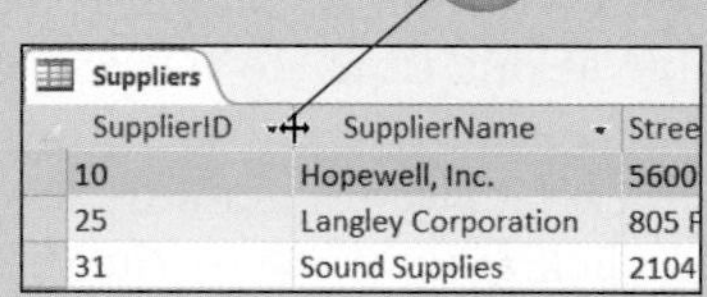

5. Adjust the width of the remaining columns by completing the following steps:
   a. Position the arrow pointer on the *SupplierName* heading until the pointer turns into a down-pointing black arrow, hold down the left mouse button, drag to the *EmailAddress* heading, and then release the mouse button.
   b. With the columns selected, double-click one of the column boundaries.
   c. Click in any field in the table to deselect the columns.
6. Increase the width of the *EmailAddress* column by positioning the arrow pointer on the column boundary at the right side of the *EmailAddress* column until it turns into a left-and-right-pointing arrow with a vertical line in the middle, holding down the left mouse button while dragging all of the way to the right side of the screen, and then releasing the mouse button. (Check the horizontal scroll bar located toward the bottom of the table and notice that the scroll bar contains a scroll box.)
7. Position the mouse pointer on the scroll box on the horizontal scroll bar and then drag to the left until the *SupplierID* field is visible.
8. Freeze the *SupplierID* column by clicking in any field in the *SupplierID* column, clicking the More button in the Records group, and then clicking *Freeze Fields* at the drop-down list.

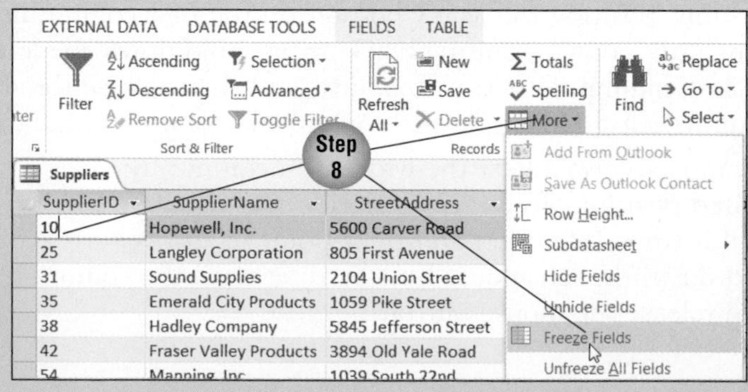

9. Using the mouse, drag the scroll box along the horizontal scroll to the right and then to the left and notice that the *SupplierID* column remains visible on the screen.
10. Unfreeze the column by clicking the More button in the Records group and then clicking *Unfreeze All Fields* at the drop-down list.
11. Double-click on the column boundary at the right side of the *EmailAddress* column.
12. Close the Suppliers table and click the Yes button at the message that asks if you want to save the changes to the layout.
13. Open the Products table and then complete steps similar to those in Step 5 to select and then adjust the column widths.
14. Close the Products table and click the Yes button at the message that asks if you want to save the changes to the layout.

Renaming and Deleting a Table

Managing tables might include actions such as renaming and deleting a table. Rename a table by right-clicking the table name in the Navigation pane, clicking *Rename* at the shortcut menu, typing the new name, and then pressing Enter. Delete a table from a database by right-clicking the table name in the Navigation pane, clicking the Delete button in the Records group on the HOME tab, and then clicking the Yes button at the message asking if you want to permanently delete the table. Another method is to right-click the table in the Navigation pane, click *Delete* at the shortcut menu, and then click the Yes at the message. If you are deleting a table from your computer's hard drive, the message asking if you want to permanently delete the table will not display. This is because Access automatically sends the deleted table to the Recycle Bin, where it can be retrieved if necessary.

Quick Steps

Rename a Table
1. Right-click table name in Navigation pane.
2. Click *Rename*.
3. Type new name.
4. Press Enter

Delete a Table
1. Right-click table name in Navigation pane.
2. Click *Delete*.
3. Click Yes, if necessary.

Printing Tables

In some situations, you may want to print a table. To do this, open the table, click the FILE tab, and then click the *Print* option. This displays the Print backstage area, as shown in Figure 1.6. Click the Quick Print button to send the table directly to the printer without making any changes to the printer setup or the table formatting. Click the Print button to display the Print dialog box, where you can specify the printer, page range, and specific records to print. Click OK to close the dialog box and send the table to the printer. By default, Access prints a table on letter-size paper in portrait orientation.

Quick Steps

Print a Table
1. Click FILE tab.
2. Click *Print* option.
3. Click Quick Print button.

OR

1. Click FILE tab.
2. Click *Print* option.
3. Click Print button.
4. Click OK.

Figure 1.6 Print Backstage Area

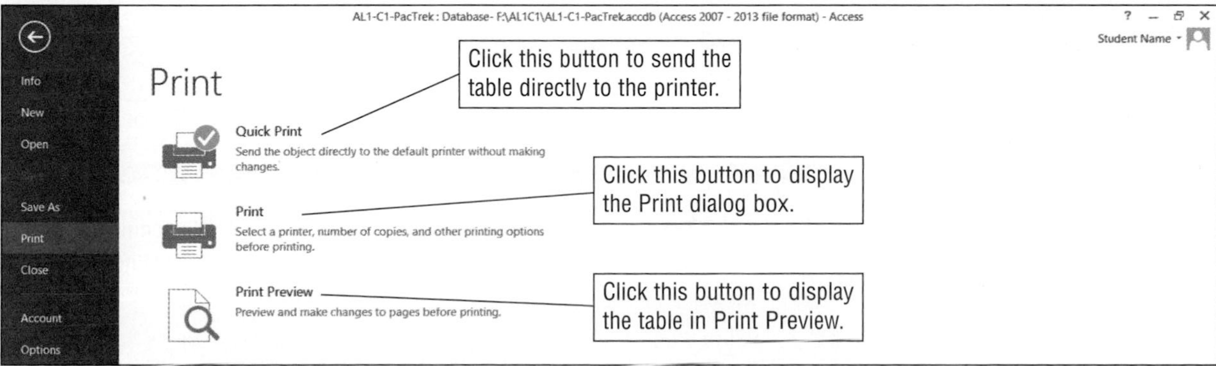

Previewing a Table

Quick Steps

Preview a Table
1. Click FILE tab.
2. Click *Print* option.
3. Click Print Preview button.

Print Preview

Print

Close Print Preview

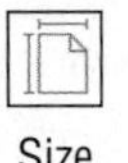

Size

Margins

Before printing a table, you may want to display the table in Print Preview to see how the table will print on the page. To display a table in Print Preview, as shown in Figure 1.7, click the Print Preview button at the Print backstage area.

Use options in the Zoom group on the PRINT PREVIEW tab to increase or decrease the size of the page display. You can also change the size of the page display using the Zoom slider bar located at the right side of the Status bar. If your table spans more than one page, use buttons on the Navigation bar to display the next or previous page.

Print a table from Print Preview by clicking the Print button located at the left side of the PRINT PREVIEW tab. Click the Close Print Preview button if you want to close Print Preview and continue working in the table without printing it.

Changing Page Size and Margins

By default, Access prints a table in standard letter size (8.5 inches wide and 11 inches tall). Click the Size button in the Page Size group on the PRINT PREVIEW tab and a drop-down list displays with options for changing the page size to legal, executive, envelope, and so on. Access uses default top, bottom, left, and right margins of 1 inch. Change these default margins by clicking the Margins button in the Page Size group and then clicking one of the predesigned margin options.

Figure 1.7 Print Preview

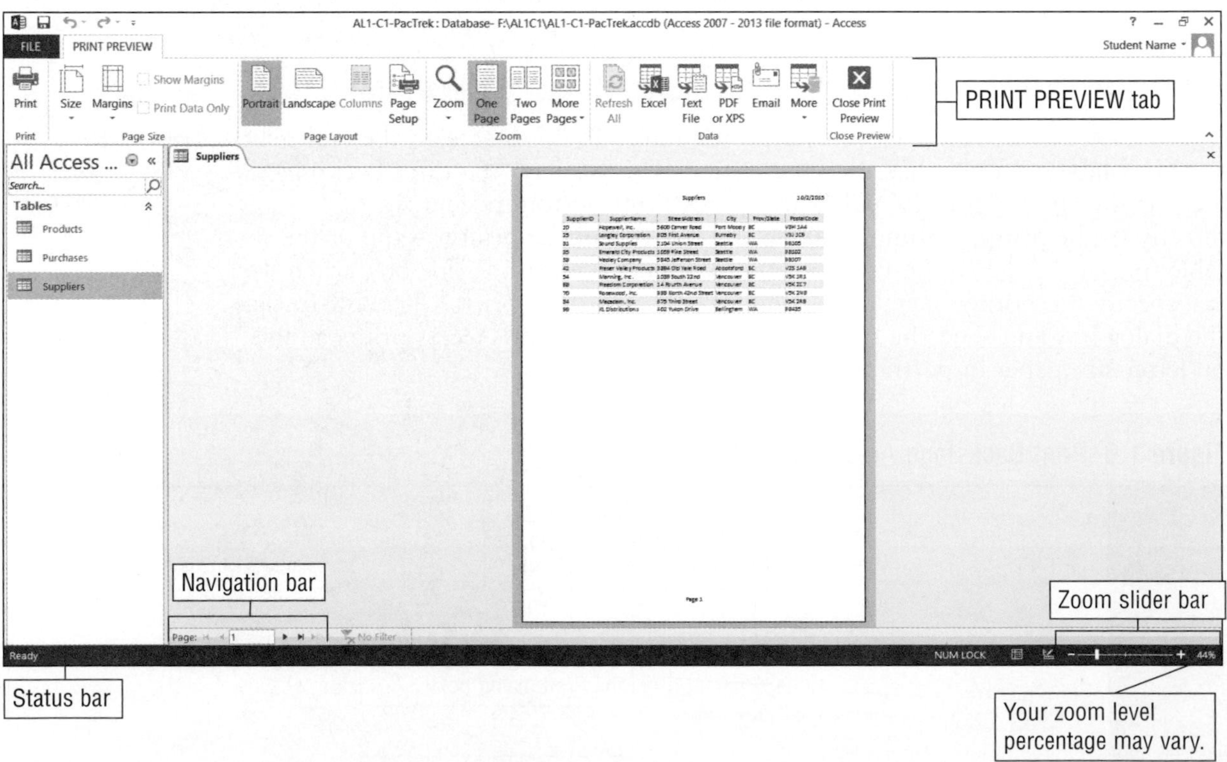

Changing Page Layout

The PRINT PREVIEW tab contains the Page Layout group with buttons for controlling how data is printed on the page. By default, Access prints a table in portrait orientation, which prints the text on the page so that it is taller than it is wide (like a page in this textbook). If a table contains a number of columns, changing to landscape orientation allows more columns to fit on a page. Landscape orientation rotates the printout to be wider than it is tall. To change from the default portrait orientation to landscape orientation, click the Landscape button in the Page Layout group on the PRINT PREVIEW tab.

Landscape

Click the Page Setup button in the Page Layout group and the Page Setup dialog box displays as shown in Figure 1.8. At the Page Setup dialog box with the Print Options tab selected, notice that the default margins are 1 inch. Change these defaults by typing a different number in the desired margin text box. By default, the table name prints at the top center of the page and the current date prints in the upper right corner of the page. In addition, the word *Page* followed by the page number prints at the bottom of the page. If you do not want the name of the table, date, and page number to print, remove the check mark from the *Print Headings* option at the Page Setup dialog box with the Print Options tab selected.

Quick Steps

Display Page Setup Dialog Box
1. Click FILE tab.
2. Click *Print* option.
3. Click Print Preview button.
4. Click Page Setup button.

Click the Page tab at the Page Setup dialog box and the dialog box displays as shown in Figure 1.9. Change the orientation with options in the *Orientation* section and change the paper size with options in the *Paper* section. Click the *Size* option box arrow and a drop-down list displays with paper sizes similar to the options available at the *Size* button drop-down list in the Page Size group on the PRINT PREVIEW tab. Specify the printer with options in the *Printer for (table name)* section of the dialog box.

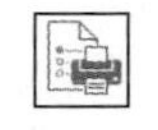
Page Setup

Figure 1.8 Page Setup Dialog Box with Print Options Tab Selected

Enter measurements in these boxes to change the page margins.

Page Setup

Print Options | Page

Margins (inches)

Top: 1

Bottom: 1

Left: 1

Right: 1

Sample

Print Headings

Split Form

Print Form Only

Print Datasheet Only

OK | Cancel

Remove the check mark from this check box if you do not want the table name, date, and page number printed.

Figure 1.9 Page Setup Dialog Box with Page Tab Selected

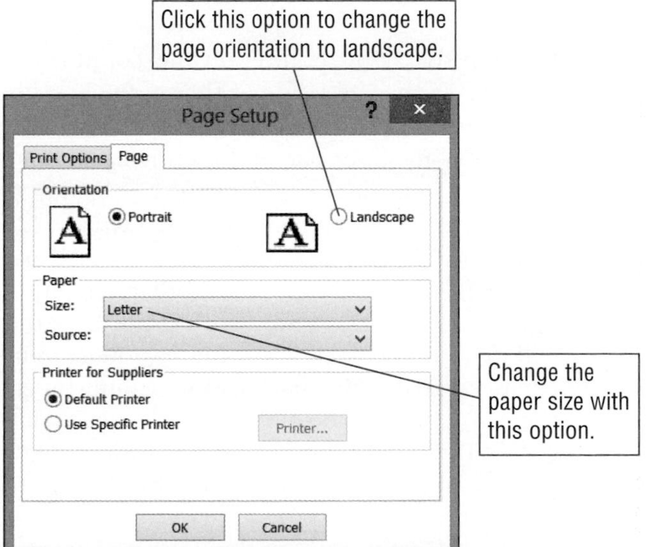

Project 2d Previewing, Changing Page Layout, Renaming, Deleting, and Printing Tables Part 4 of 7

1. With **AL1-C1-PacTrek.accdb** open, open the Suppliers table.
2. Preview and then print the Suppliers table in landscape orientation by completing the following steps:
   a. Click the FILE tab and then click the *Print* option.
   b. At the Print backstage area, click the Print Preview button.
   c. Click the Two Pages button in the Zoom group on the PRINT PREVIEW tab. (This displays two pages of the table.)
   d. Click the Zoom button arrow in the Zoom group on the PRINT PREVIEW tab and then click *75%* at the drop-down list.

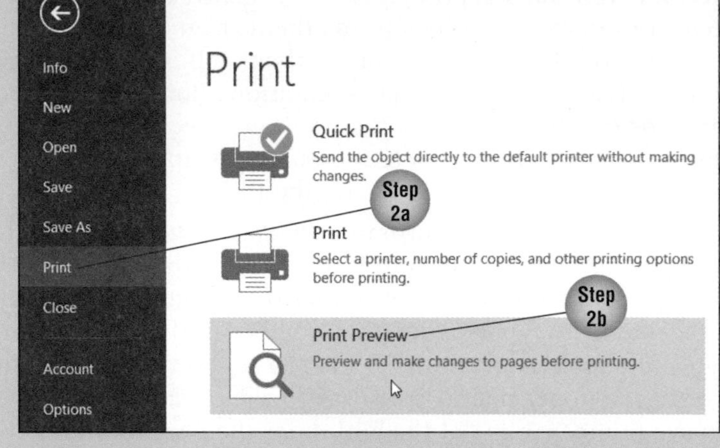

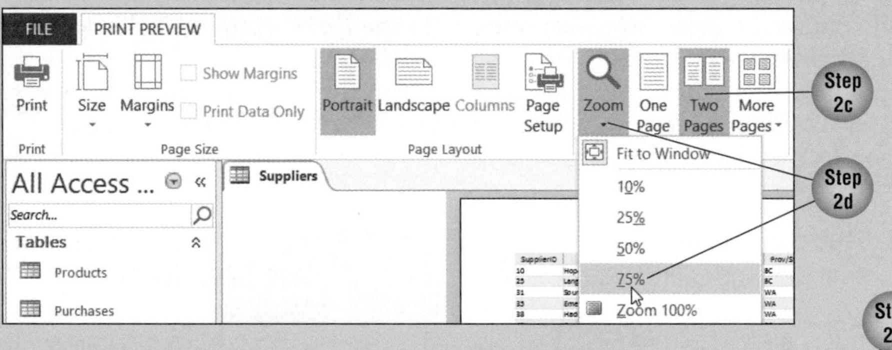

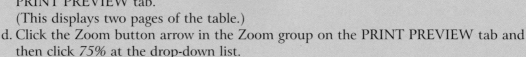

   e. Position the arrow pointer on the Zoom slider bar button that displays at the right side of the Status bar, hold down the left mouse button, drag to the right until *100%* displays at the right of the Zoom slider bar, and then release the mouse button.
   f. Return the display to a full page by clicking the One Page button in the Zoom group on the PRINT PREVIEW tab.
   g. Click the Margins button in the Page Size group on the PRINT PREVIEW tab and then click the *Narrow* option at the drop-down list. (Notice how the data will print on the page with the narrow margins.)
   h. Change the margins back to the default by clicking the Margins button in the Page Size group and then clicking the *Normal* option at the drop-down list.
   i. Change to landscape orientation by clicking the Landscape button in the Page Layout group. (Check the Next Page button on the Record Navigation bar and notice that it is dimmed. This indicates that the table will print on only one page.)

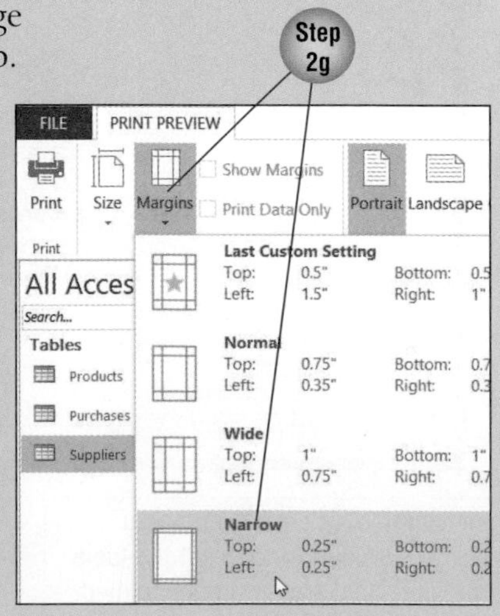

j. Print the table by clicking the Print button located at the left side of the PRINT PREVIEW tab and then clicking the OK button at the Print dialog box.
3. Close the Suppliers table.
4. Open the Products table and then print the table by completing the following steps:
   a. Click the FILE tab and then click the *Print* option.
   b. At the Print backstage area, click the Print Preview button.
   c. Click the Page Setup button in the Page Layout group on the PRINT PREVIEW tab. (This displays the Page Setup dialog box with the Print Options tab selected.)
   d. At the Page Setup dialog box, click the Page tab.
   e. Click the *Landscape* option.

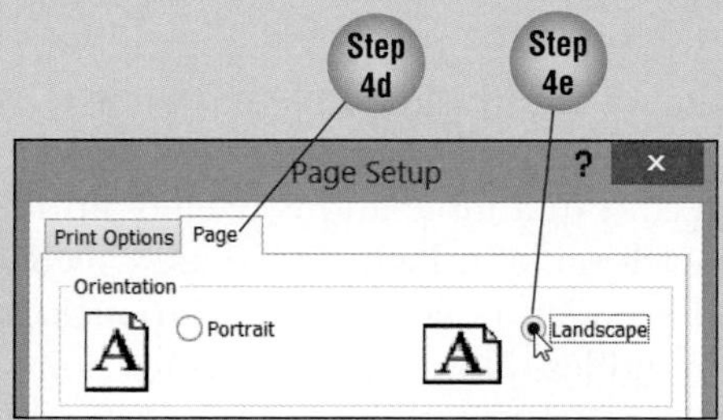

   f. Click the Print Options tab.
   g. Select the current measurement in the *Top* text box and then type **0.5**.
   h. Select the current measurement in the *Bottom* text box and then type **0.5**.
   i. Select the current measurement in the *Left* text box and then type **1.5**.
   j. Click OK to close the dialog box.
   k. Click the Print button on the PRINT PREVIEW tab and then click the OK button at the Print dialog box. (This table will print on two pages.)

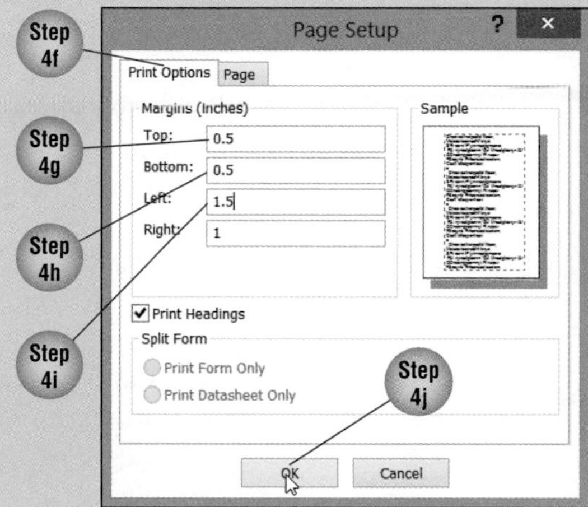

5. Close the Products table.
6. Rename the Purchases table by right-clicking *Purchases* in the Navigation pane, clicking *Rename* at the shortcut menu, typing **Orders**, and then pressing Enter.
7. Delete the Orders table by right-clicking *Orders* in the Navigation pane and then clicking *Delete* at the shortcut menu. If a message displays asking if you want to permanently delete the table, click Yes.

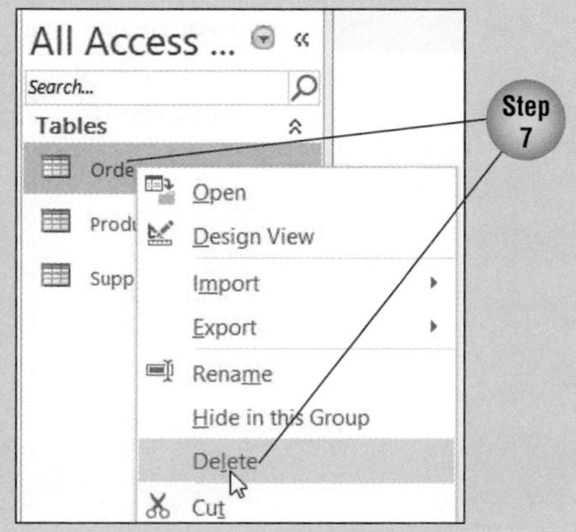

Designing a Table

Tables are the first objects created in a new database and all other objects in a database rely on tables for data. Designing a database involves planning the number of tables needed and the fields that will be included in each table. Each table in a database should contain information about only one subject. For example, the Suppliers table in the AL1-C1-PacTrek.accdb database contains data only about suppliers and the Products table contains data only about products.

Database designers often create a visual representation of the database's structure in a diagram similar to the one shown in Figure 1.10. Each table is represented by a box with the table name at the top. Within each box, the fields that will be stored in the table are listed with the field names that will be used when the table is created.

Notice that one field in each table has an asterisk next to its name. The field with the asterisk is called the ***primary key***. A primary key holds data that uniquely identifies each record in a table and is usually an identification number. The lines drawn between each table in Figure 1.10 are called ***join lines,*** and they represent links established between tables (called ***relationships***) so that data can be extracted from one or more tables. Notice the join lines point to a common field name included in each table that is to be linked. (You will learn how to join, or relate, tables in Chapter 2.) A database with related tables is called a ***relational database***.

Notice the join line in the database diagram that connects the *SupplierID* field in the Suppliers table with the *SupplierID* field in the Products table and another join line that connects the *SupplierID* field in the Suppliers table with the *SupplierID* field in the Orders table. In the database diagram, a join line connects the *ProductID* field in the Products table with the *ProductID* field in the Orders table.

Organize data in tables to minimize or eliminate duplication.

When designing a database, you need to consider certain design principles. The first principle is to reduce redundant (duplicate) data, for several reasons. Redundant data increases the amount of data entry required, increases the chances for errors and inconsistencies, and takes up additional storage space. The Products table contains a *SupplierID* field and that field reduces the redundant

Figure 1.10 Database Diagram

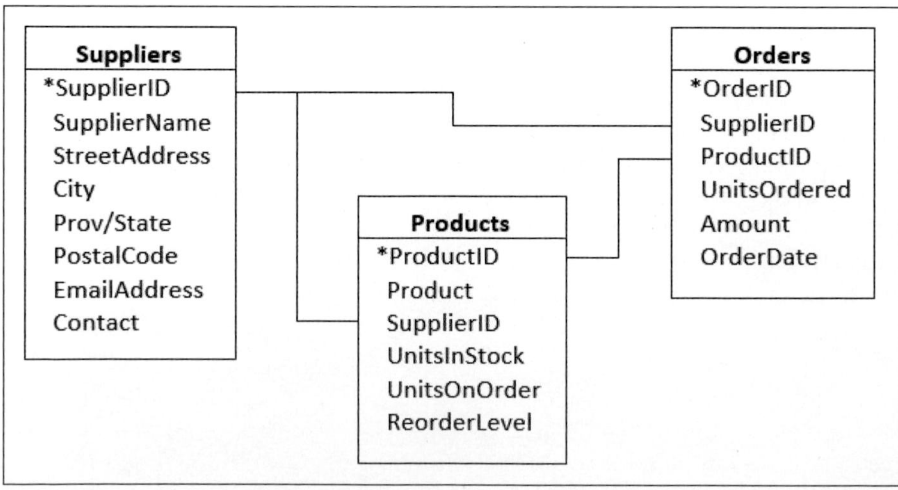

data needed in the table. For example, rather than typing the supplier information in the Suppliers table *and* the Products table, you type the information once in the Suppliers table and then "join" the tables with the connecting field *SupplierID*. If you need information on suppliers as well as specific information about products, you can draw the information into one object, such as a query or report using data from both tables. When you create the Orders table, you will use the *SupplierID* field and the *ProductID* field rather than typing all of the information for the suppliers and the product description. Typing a two-letter unique identifier number for a supplier greatly reduces the amount of typing required to create the Orders table. Inserting the *ProductID* field in the Orders table eliminates the need to type the product description for each order; instead, you type a unique five-, six-, or seven-digit identifier number.

Creating a Table

Creating a new table generally involves determining fields, assigning a data type to each field, modifying properties, designating the primary key, and naming the table. This process is referred to as ***defining the table structure***.

A database table contains fields that describe a person, customer, client, object, place, idea, or event.

The first step in creating a table is to determine the fields. A ***field***, commonly called a column, is one piece of information about a person, place, or item. Each field contains data about one aspect of the table subject, such as a company name or product number. All fields for one unit, such as a customer or product, are considered a ***record***. For example, in the Suppliers table in the AL1-C1-PacTrek.accdb database, a record is all of the information pertaining to one supplier. A collection of records becomes a ***table***.

When designing a table, determine fields for information to be included on the basis of how you plan to use the data. When organizing fields, be sure to consider not only current needs for the data but also any future needs. For example, a company may need to keep track of customer names, addresses, and telephone numbers for current mailing lists. In the future, the company may want to promote a new product to customers who purchase a specific type of product. For this information to be available at a later date, a field that identifies product type must be included in the database. When organizing fields, consider all potential needs for the data but also try to keep the fields logical and manageable.

Table

You can create a table in Access in Datasheet view or in Design view. To create a table in Datasheet view, open the desired database (or create a new database), click the CREATE tab, and then click the Table button in the Tables group. This inserts a blank table in the work area with the tab labeled *Table1*, as shown in Figure 1.11. Notice the column with the field name *ID* has been created automatically. Access creates *ID* as an AutoNumber field in which the field value is assigned automatically by Access as you enter each record. In many tables, you can use this AutoNumber field to create the unique identifier for the table. For example, in Project 2e, you will create an Orders table and use the ID AutoNumber field to assign automatically a number to each order, since each order must contain a unique number.

Assign a data type to each field that determines the type of information that can be entered into the field.

When creating a new field (column), determine the type of data you will insert in the field. For example, one field might contain text such as a name or product description, another field might contain an amount of money, and another might contain a date. The data type defines the type of information Access will allow to be entered into the field. For example, Access will not allow alphabetic

Figure 1.11 Blank Table

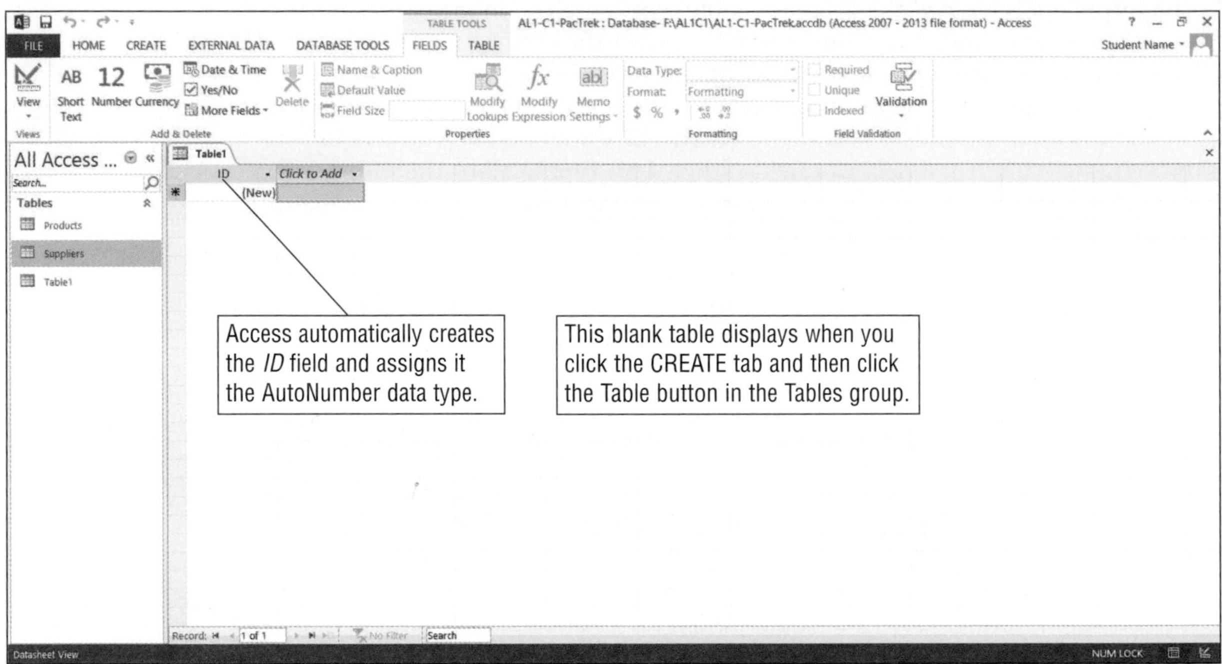

characters to be entered into a field with a data type set to Date & Time.

Access automatically creates the *ID* field and assigns it the AutoNumber data type.
This blank table displays when you click the CREATE tab and then click the Table button in the Tables group.

More Fields

The Add & Delete group on the TABLE TOOLS FIELDS tab contains five buttons for assigning data types plus a More Fields button. Descriptions of the five data types assigned by the buttons are provided in Table 1.3.

Table 1.3 Data Types

Data Type Button	*Description*
Short Text	Alphanumeric data up to 255 characters in length—for example, a name, an address, or a value such as a telephone number or social security number that is used as an identifier and not for calculating.
Number	Positive or negative values that can be used in calculations; not to be used for values that will calculate monetary amounts (see Currency).
Currency	Values that involve money; Access will not round off during calculations.
Date & Time	Used to ensure dates and times are entered and sorted properly.
Yes/No	Data in the field will be either *Yes* or *No*; *True* or *False*, *On* or *Off*.

In Project 2e, you will create the Orders table, as shown in Figure 1.12. Looking at the diagram in Figure 1.10, you will assign the following data types to the columns:

OrderID:	AutoNumber (Access automatically assigns this data type to the first column)
SupplierID:	Short Text (the supplier numbers are identifiers, not numbers for calculating)
ProductID:	Short Text (the product numbers are identifiers, not numbers for calculating)
UnitsOrdered:	Number (the unit numbers are values for calculating)
Amount:	Currency
OrderDate:	Date & Time

When you click a data type button, Access inserts a field to the right of the *ID* field and selects the field heading *Field1*. Type a name for the field; press the Enter key; and Access selects the next field column, named *Click to Add*, and displays a drop-down list of data types. This drop-down list contains the same five data types as the buttons in the Add & Delete group as well as additional data types. Click the desired data type at the drop-down list, type the desired field name, and then press Enter. Continue in this manner until you have entered all field names for the table. When naming a field, consider the following guidelines:

- Each field must have a unique name.
- The name should describe the contents of the field.
- A field name can contain up to 64 characters.
- A field name can contain letters and numbers. Some symbols are permitted but others are excluded, so avoid using symbols other than the underscore (to separate words) and the number symbol (to indicate an identifier number).
- Do not use spaces in field names. Although a space is an accepted character, most database designers avoid using spaces in field names and object names. Use field compound words for field names or the underscore character as a word separator. For example, a field name for a person's last name could be named *LastName*, *Last_Name*, or *LName*.
- Abbreviate field names so that they are as short as possible but still easily understood. For example, a field such as *CompanyName* could be shortened to *CoName* and a field such as *EmailAddress* could be shortened to *Email*.

Avoid using spaces in field names.

Project 2e **Creating a Table and Entering Data** **Part 5 of 7**

1. With **AL1-C1-PacTrek.accdb** open, create a new table and specify data types and column headings by completing the following steps:
   a. Click the CREATE tab.
   b. Click the Table button in the Tables group.
   c. Click the Short Text button in the Add & Delete group.

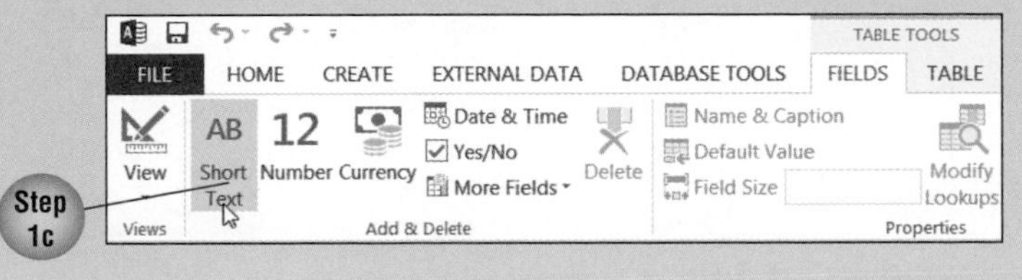

d. With the *Field1* column heading selected, type **SupplierID** and then press the Enter key. (This displays a drop-down list of data types below the *Click to Add* heading.)

e. Click the *Short Text* option at the drop-down list.

f. Type **ProductID** and then press Enter.

g. Click *Number* at the drop-down list, type **UnitsOrdered**, and then press Enter.

h. Click *Currency* at the drop-down list, type **Amount**, and then press Enter.

i. Click *Date & Time* at the drop-down list and then type **OrderDate**. (Do not press the Enter key since this is the last column in the table.)

2. Enter the first record in the table, as shown in Figure 1.12, by completing the following steps:
   a. Click twice in the first field below the *SupplierID* column heading. (The first time you click the mouse button, the row is selected. Clicking the second time makes active only the field below *SupplierID*.)
   b. Type the data in the fields as shown in Figure 1.12. Press the Tab key to move to the next field or press Shift + Tab to move to the previous field. Access will automatically insert the next number in the sequence in the first column (the *ID* column). When typing the money amounts in the *Amount* column, you do not need to type the dollar sign or the comma. Access will automatically insert them when you make the next field active.
3. When the 14 records have been entered, click the Save button on the Quick Access toolbar.
4. At the Save As dialog box, type **Orders** and then press the Enter key. (This saves the table with the name *Orders*.)
5. Close the Orders table by clicking the Close button located in the upper right corner of the work area.

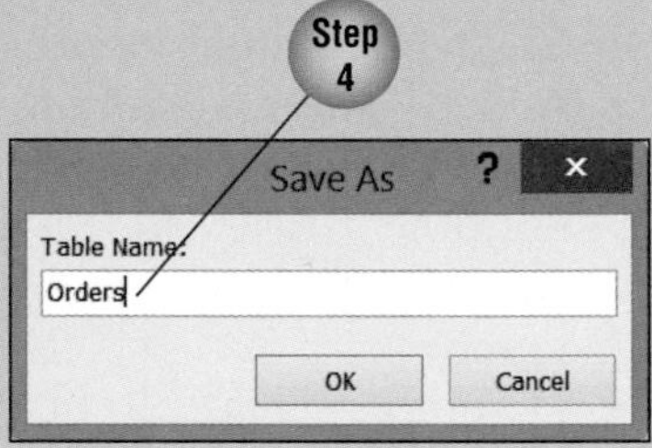

Figure 1.12 Project 2e

Orders

ID	SupplierID	ProductID	UnitsOrderec	Amount	OrderDate	Click to Add
1	54	101-S3	10	$1,137.50	1/5/2015	
2	68	209-L	25	$173.75	1/5/2015	
3	68	209-XL	25	$180.00	1/5/2015	
4	68	209-XXL	20	$145.80	1/5/2015	
5	68	210-M	15	$97.35	1/5/2015	
6	68	210-L	25	$162.25	1/5/2015	
7	31	299-M2	10	$887.90	1/19/2015	
8	31	299-M3	10	$887.90	1/19/2015	
9	31	299-M5	10	$887.90	1/19/2015	
10	31	299-W1	8	$602.32	1/19/2015	
11	31	299-W3	10	$752.90	1/19/2015	
12	31	299-W4	10	$752.90	1/19/2015	
13	31	299-W5	10	$752.90	1/19/2015	
14	35	602-XR	5	$2,145.00	1/19/2015	
(New)			0	$0.00		

Renaming a Field Heading

When you click a data type button or click a data type at the data type drop-down list, the default heading (such as *Field1*) is automatically selected. You can type a name for the field heading that takes the place of the selected text. If you create a field heading and then decide to change the name, right-click the heading, click *Rename Field* at the shortcut menu (which selects the current column heading), and then type the new name.

Inserting a Name, Caption, and Description

When you create a table that others will use, consider providing additional information so users understand the fields in the table and what should be entered in each one. Along with the field heading name, you can provide a caption and description for each field with options at the Enter Field Properties dialog box, shown in Figure 1.13. Display this dialog by clicking the Name & Caption button in the Properties group on the TABLE TOOLS FIELDS tab.

Name & Caption

At the Enter Field Properties dialog box, type the desired name for the field heading in the *Name* text box. If you want a more descriptive name for the field heading, type the heading in the *Caption* text box. The text you type will display as the field heading but the actual field name will still be part of the table structure. Creating a caption is useful if you abbreviate a field name or want to show spaces between words in a field name. A caption also provides more information for others using the database. The name is what Access uses for the table and the caption is what displays to users.

The *Description* text box is another source for providing information about the field to others using the database. Type information in the text box that specifies what should be entered in the field. The text you type in the *Description* text box displays at the left side of the Status bar when a field in the column is active. For example, if you type *Enter the total amount of the order* in the *Description* text box for the *Amount* field column, that text will display at the left side of the Status bar when a field in the column is active.

Figure 1.13 Enter Field Properties Dialog Box

Enter Field Properties
?
×
Name
SupplierID
Caption
Description
OK
Cancel
Type in the *Caption* text box a more descriptive name for the field heading.
Type information in the *Description* text box that specifies what should be entered in the field.

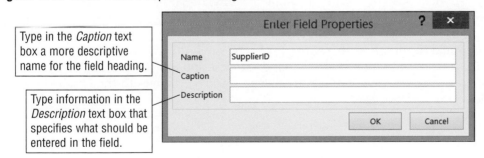

Project 2f Inserting a Name, Caption, and Description Part 6 of 7

1. With **AL1-C1-PacTrek.accdb** open, open the Orders table.
2. Access automatically named the first field *ID*. You want to make the heading more descriptive so you decide to rename the heading. To do this, right-click the *ID* heading and then click *Rename Field* at the drop-down list.
3. Type **OrderID** and then press the Enter key.
4. To provide more information for others using the table, you decide to add information for the *SupplierID* field by creating a caption and description. To do this, complete the following steps:
   a. Click the *SupplierID* field heading. (This selects the entire column.)
   b. Click the TABLE TOOLS FIELDS tab.
   c. Click the Name & Caption button in the Properties group. (At the Enter Field Properties dialog box, notice that *SupplierID* is already inserted in the *Name* text box.)
   d. At the Enter Field Properties dialog box, click in the *Caption* text box and then type **Supplier Number**.
   e. Click in the *Description* text box and then type **Supplier identification number**.
   f. Click OK to close the dialog box. (Notice that the field name now displays as *Supplier Number*. The field name is still *SupplierID* but what displays is *Supplier Number*.)
5. Click the *ProductID* field heading and then complete steps similar to those in Steps 4c through 4f to create the caption *Product Number* and the description *Product identification number*.
6. Click the *Amount* field heading and then complete steps similar to those in Steps 4c through 4f to create the caption *Order Amount* and the description *Total amount of order*.
7. Click the Save button on the Quick Access toolbar to save the changes to the Orders table.
8. Close the Orders table.

Step 2

Orders

Sort Smallest to Largest
Sort Largest to Smallest
Copy
Paste
Field Width
Hide Fields
Unhide Fields
Freeze Fields
Unfreeze All Fields
Find...
Insert Field
Modify Lookups
Modify Expression
Rename Field
Delete Field

Step 4a

Step 4b

Step 4c

FILE HOME CREATE EXTERNAL DATA DATABASE TOOLS FIELDS TABLE
TABLE TOOLS
View, Short Text, Number, Currency, Date & Time, Yes/No, More Fields, Delete, Name & Caption, Default Value, Field Size 255, Modify Lookups
Views, Add & Delete, Properties
All Access ...
Orders
OrderID SupplierID ProductID UnitsOrd
1 54 101-S3 10

Step 4d

Enter Field Properties
Name: SupplierID
Caption: Supplier Number
Description: Supplier identification number
OK Cancel

Step 4e

Step 4f

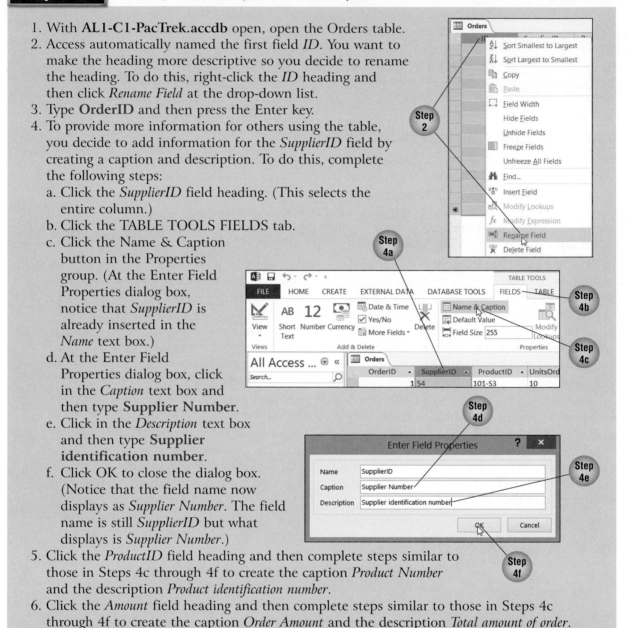

Inserting Quick Start Fields

Short Text

The Add & Delete group on the TABLE TOOLS FIELDS tab contains buttons for specifying data types. You used the Short Text button to specify the data type for the *SupplierID* field when you created the Orders table. You also used the field heading drop-down list to choose a data type. In addition to these two methods, you can specify a data type by clicking the More Fields button in the Add & Delete group on the TABLE TOOLS FIELDS tab. When you click this button, a drop-down list displays with data types grouped into categories such as *Basic Types*, *Number*, *Date and Time*, *Yes/No*, and *Quick Start*.

The options in the *Quick Start* category not only define a data type but also assign a field name. Additionally, with options in the *Quick Start* category, you can add a group of related fields in one step. For example, if you click the *Name* option in the *Quick Start* category, Access inserts the *LastName* field in one column and the *FirstName* field in the next column. Both fields are automatically assigned a short text data type. If you click the *Address* option in the *Quick Start* category, Access inserts five fields, including *Address*, *City*, *StateProvince*, *ZIPPostal*, and *CountryRegion*—all with the short text data type assigned.

Assigning a Default Value

The Properties group on the TABLE TOOLS FIELDS tab contains additional buttons for defining field properties in a table. If most records in a table are likely to contain the same field value in a column, consider inserting that value by default. Do this by clicking the Default Value button in the Properties group. At the Expression Builder dialog box, type the desired default value and then click OK.

Default Value

For example, in Project 2g, you will create a new table in the AL1-C1-PacTrek database containing information on customers, most of whom live in Vancouver, British Columbia. You will create a default value of *Vancouver* for the *City* field and a default value of *BC* for the *Prov/State* field. You can replace the default value with different text, so if a customer lives in Abbotsford instead of Vancouver, simply type *Abbotsford* in the *City* field instead.

Assigning a Field Size

The default field size property varies depending on the data type. For example, if you assign a short text data type to a field, the maximum length of the data you can enter in the field is 255 characters. You can decrease this number depending on what data will be entered in the field. You can also change the field size number to control how much data is entered and help reduce errors. For example, if you have a field for states and you want a two-letter state abbreviation inserted in each field in the column, you can assign a field size of 2 characters. If someone entering data into the table tries to type more than two letters, Access will not accept the additional text. To change field size, click in the *Field Size* text box in the Properties group on the TABLE TOOLS FIELDS tab and then type the desired number.

Changing the AutoNumber Field

Access automatically applies the AutoNumber data type to the first field in a table and assigns a unique number to each record in the table. In many cases, letting Access automatically assign a number to a record is a good idea. Some situations may arise, however, when you want the unique value in the first field to be something other than a number.

If you try to change the AutoNumber data type in the first column by clicking one of the data type buttons in the Add & Delete group on the TABLE TOOLS FIELDS tab, Access creates another field. To change the AutoNumber data type for the first field, click the down-pointing arrow at the right side of the *Data Type* option box in the Formatting group on the TABLE TOOLS FIELDS tab and then click the desired data type at the drop-down list.

Project 2g **Creating a Customers Table** Part 7 of 7

1. The owners of Pacific Trek have decided to publish a semiannual product catalog and have asked customers who want to receive the catalog to fill out a form and include on the form whether or not they want to receive notices of upcoming sales in addition to the catalog. Create a table to store the data for customers by completing the following steps:
   a. With **AL1-C1-PacTrek.accdb** open, click the CREATE tab.
   b. Click the Table button in the Tables group.
   c. With the *Click to Add* field heading active, click the More Fields button in the Add & Delete group on the TABLE TOOLS FIELDS tab.
   d. Scroll down the drop-down list and then click *Name* located in the *Quick Start* category. (This inserts the *Last Name* and *First Name* field headings in the table.)

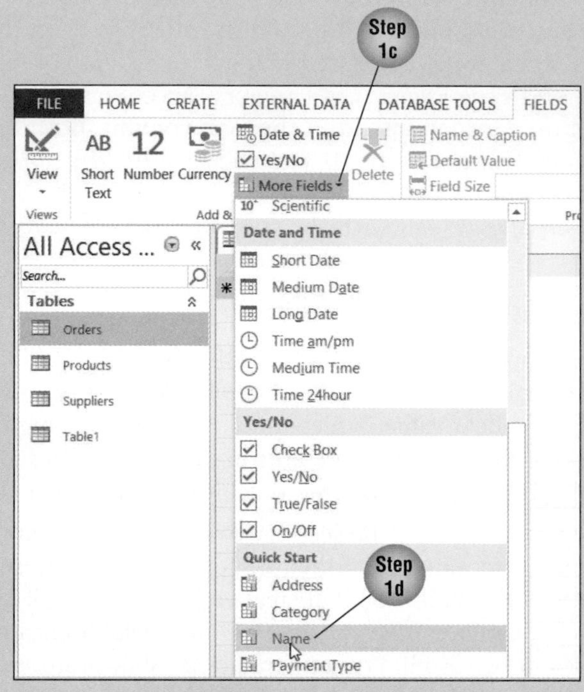

   e. Click the *Click to Add* field heading that displays immediately right of the *First Name* field heading. (The data type drop-down list displays. You are going to use the More Fields button rather than the drop-down list to create the next fields.)
   f. Click the More Fields button, scroll down the drop-down list, and then click *Address* in the *Quick Start* category. (This inserts five more fields in the table.)
   g. Scroll to the right in the table to display the *Click to Add* field heading that follows the *Country Region* column heading. (You can scroll in the table using the horizontal scroll bar that displays to the right of the Record Navigation bar.)
   h. Click the *Click to Add* field heading and then click *Yes/No* at the drop-down list.
   i. With the name *Field1* selected, type **Mailers**. (When entering records in the table, you will insert a check mark in the field check box if a customer wants to receive sales promotion mailers. If a customer does not want to receive the mailers, you will leave the check box blank.)

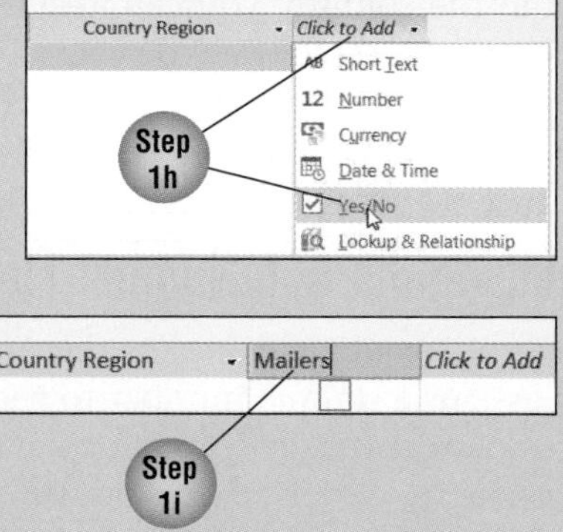

2. Rename and create a caption and description for the *ID* column heading by completing the following steps:
   a. Scroll to the beginning of the table and then click the *ID* column heading. (You can scroll in the table using the horizontal scroll bar that displays to the right of the Record Navigation bar.)
   b. Click the Name & Caption button in the Properties group on the TABLE TOOLS FIELDS tab.

c. At the Enter Field Properties dialog box, select the text *ID* that displays in the *Name* text box and then type **CustomerID**.
d. Press the Tab key and then type **Customer Number** in the *Caption* text box.
e. Press the Tab key and then type **Access will automatically assign the record the next number in the sequence.**
f. Click OK to close the Enter Field Properties dialog box. (Notice the description that displays at the left side of the Status bar.)

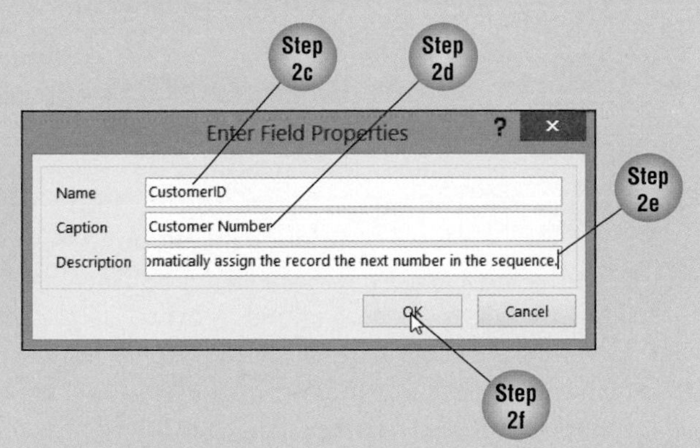

3. Add a description to the *Last Name* column by completing the following steps:
   a. Click the *Last Name* column heading.
   b. Click the Name & Caption button in the Properties group.
   c. At the Enter Field Properties dialog box notice that Access named the field *LastName* but provided the caption *Last Name*. You do not want to change the name and caption so press the Tab key twice to make the *Description* text box active and then type **Customer last name**.
   d. Click OK to close the dialog box.
4. You know that a customer's last name will not likely exceed 30 characters, so you decide to limit the field size. To do this, click in the *Field Size* text box in the Properties group (this selects *255*), type **30**, and then press the Enter key.

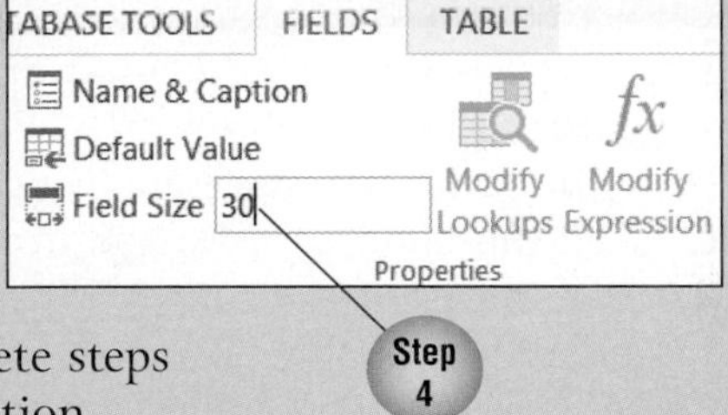

5. Click the *First Name* column heading and then complete steps similar to those in Steps 3 and 4 to create the description *Customer first name* and change the field size to 30 characters.
6. Since most of Pacific Trek's customers live in the city of Vancouver, you decide to make it the default field value. To do this, complete the following steps:

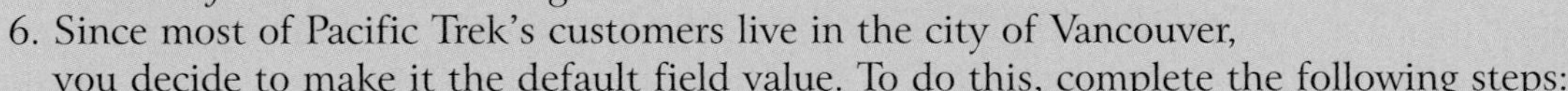

   a. Click the *City* column heading.
   b. Click the Default Value button in the Properties group.
   c. At the Expression Builder dialog box, type **Vancouver**.
   d. Click the OK button to close the dialog box.

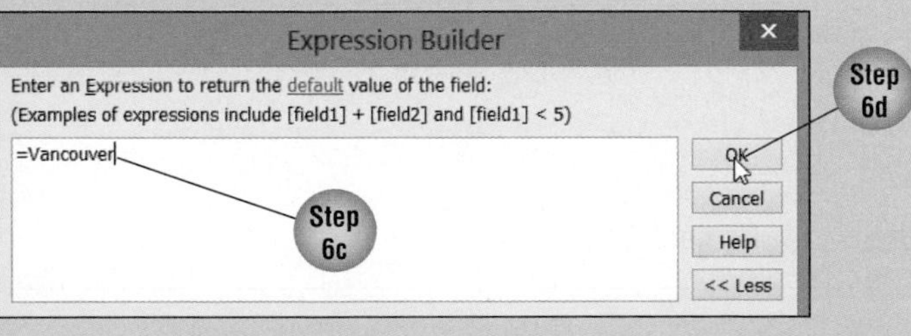

7. Change the name of the *State Province* field name and insert a default value by completing the following steps:
   a. Right-click the *State Province* column heading and then click *Rename Field* at the shortcut menu.
   b. Type **Province**.
   c. Click the Default Value button in the Properties group.
   d. Type **BC** in the Expression Builder dialog box and then click the OK button.
8. Click the *ZIP Postal* column heading and then limit the field size to 7 characters by clicking

in the *Field Size* text box (which selects *255*), typing 7, and then pressing the Enter key.

9. Since most customers want to be sent the sales promotional mailers, you decide to insert a check mark as the default value in the check boxes in the *Yes/No* column. To do this, complete the following steps:
   a. Click the *Mailers* field heading.
   b. Click the Default Value button in the Properties group.
   c. At the Expression Builder dialog box, press the Backspace key two times to delete *No* and then type **Yes**.
   d. Click OK to close the dialog box.
10. Delete the *Country Region* field by clicking the *Country Region* field heading and then clicking the Delete button in the Add & Delete group.
11. Save the table by completing the following steps:
   a. Click the Save button on the Quick Access toolbar.
   b. At the Save As dialog box, type **Customers** and then press Enter.
12. Enter the six records in the table shown in Figure 1.14. To remove a check mark in the *Mailers* column, press the spacebar.
13. Adjust the column widths to accommodate the longest entry in each column by completing the following steps:
   a. Position the arrow pointer on the *Customer Number* field heading until the pointer turns into a down-pointing black arrow, hold down the left mouse button, drag to the *Mailers* field heading, and then release the mouse button.
   b. With the columns selected, double-click one of the column boundaries.
14. Click the Save button to save the Customers table.
15. Print the Customers table by completing the following steps:
   a. Click the FILE tab and then click the *Print* option.
   b. At the Print backstage area, click the Print Preview button.
   c. Click the Landscape button in the Page Layout group on the PRINT PREVIEW tab.
   d. Click the Print button that displays at the left side of the PRINT PREVIEW tab.
   e. At the Print dialog box, click OK.
16. Close the Customers table.
17. Open the Orders table.
18. Automatically adjust the column widths to accommodate the longest entry in each column.
19. Click the Save button to save the Orders table.
20. Print the table in landscape orientation (refer to Step 15) and then close the table.
21. Close **AL1-C1-PacTrek.accdb**.

Figure 1.14 Project 2g

Customers

	Customer Number	Last Name	First Name	Address	City	State Province	ZIP Postal	Mailers
	1	Blakely	Mathias	7433 224th Ave. E.	Vancouver	BC	V5K 2M7	✔
	2	Donato	Antonio	18225 Victoria Dr.	Vancouver	BC	V5K 1H4	☐
	3	Girard	Stephanie	430 Deer Lake Pl.	Burnaby	BC	V3J 1E4	✔
	4	Hernandez	Angelica	1233 E. 59th Ave.	Vancouver	BC	V5K 3H3	✔
	5	Ives-Keller	Shane	9055 Gilbert Rd.	Richmond	BC	V6Y 1B2	☐
	6	Kim	Keung	730 West Broadway	Vancouver	BC	V5K 5B2	✔
*	(New)				Vancouver	BC		✔

Chapter Summary

- Microsoft Access is a database management system software program that can organize, store, maintain, retrieve, sort, and print all types of business data.
- In Access, open an existing database by clicking the Open Other Files hyperlink at the Access 2013 opening screen. At the Open backstage area, double-click your SkyDrive or the *Computer* option. At the Open dialog box, navigate to the location of the database and then double-click the desired database.
- Some common objects found in a database include tables, queries, forms, and reports.
- The Navigation pane displays at the left side of the Access screen and displays the objects that are contained in the database.
- Open a database object by double-clicking the object in the Navigation pane. Close an object by clicking the Close button that displays in the upper right corner of the work area.
- When a table is open, the Record Navigation bar displays at the bottom of the screen and contains buttons for displaying records in the table.
- Insert a new record in a table by clicking the New button in the Records group on the HOME tab or by clicking the New (blank) record button in the Record Navigation bar. Delete a record by clicking in a field in the record you want to delete, clicking the Delete button arrow on the HOME tab, and then clicking *Delete Record* at the drop-down list.
- To add a column to a table, click the first field below the *Click to Add* column heading and then type the desired data. To move a column, select the column and then use the mouse to drag a thick, black, vertical line (representing the column) to the desired location. To delete a column, click the column heading, click the Delete button arrow, and then click *Delete Column* at the drop-down list.
- Data you enter in a table is automatically saved while changes to the layout of a table are not automatically saved.
- Hide, unhide, freeze, and unfreeze columns with options at the More button drop-down list. Display this list by clicking the More button in the Records group on the HOME tab.
- Adjust the width of a column (or selected columns) to accommodate the longest entry by double-clicking the column boundary. You can also adjust the width of a column by dragging the column boundary.
- Rename a table by right-clicking the table name in the Navigation pane, clicking *Rename*, and then typing the new name. Delete a table by right-clicking the table name in the Navigation pane and then clicking *Delete*.
- Print a table by clicking the FILE tab, clicking the *Print* option, and then clicking the Quick Print button. You can also preview a table before printing by clicking the Print Preview button at the Print backstage area.
- With buttons and option on the PRINT PREVIEW tab, you can change the page size, orientation, and margins.
- The first principle in database design is to reduce redundant data, because redundant data increases the amount of data entry required, increases the chances for errors, and takes up additional storage space.
- A data type defines the type of data Access will allow in the field. Assign a data type to a field with buttons in the Add & Delete group on the TABLE TOOLS

FIELDS tab, by clicking an option from the column heading drop-down list, or with options at the More button drop-down list.

- Rename a column heading by right-clicking the heading, clicking *Rename Field* at the shortcut menu, and then typing the new name.
- Type a name, caption, and description for a column with options at the Enter Field Properties dialog box.
- Use options in the *Quick Start* category in the More Fields button drop-down list to define a data type and assign a field name to a group of related fields.
- Insert a default value in a column with the Default Value button and assign a field size with the *Field Size* text box in the Properties group on the TABLE TOOLS FIELDS tab.
- Use the *Data Type* option box in the Formatting group on the TABLE TOOLS FIELDS tab to change the AutoNumber data type for the first column in a table.

Commands Review

FEATURE	RIBBON TAB, GROUP/OPTION	BUTTON, OPTION	KEYBOARD SHORTCUT
close Access			Alt + F4
close database	FILE, *Close*		
create table	CREATE, Tables		
Currency data type	TABLE TOOLS FIELDS, Add & Delete		
Date & Time data type	TABLE TOOLS FIELDS, Add & Delete		
delete column	HOME, Records	, *Delete Column*	
delete record	HOME, Records	, *Delete Record*	
Enter Field Properties dialog box	TABLE TOOLS FIELDS, Properties		
Expression Builder dialog box	TABLE TOOLS FIELDS, Properties		
freeze column	HOME, Records	, *Freeze Fields*	
hide column	HOME, Records	, *Hide Fields*	
landscape orientation	FILE, *Print*	Print Preview,	
new record	HOME, Records		Ctrl + +
next field			Tab
Number data type	TABLE TOOLS FIELDS, Add & Delete	12	
Page Setup dialog box	FILE, *Print*	Print Preview,	

FEATURE	RIBBON TAB, GROUP/OPTION	BUTTON, OPTION	KEYBOARD SHORTCUT
page size	FILE, *Print*	Print Preview,	
page margins	FILE, *Print*	Print Preview,	
portrait orientation	FILE, *Print*	Print Preview,	
previous field			Shift + Tab
Print backstage area	FILE, *Print*		
Print dialog box	FILE, *Print*	Print	Ctrl + P
Print Preview	FILE, *Print*	Print Preview	
Short Text data type	TABLE TOOLS FIELDS, Add & Delete	AB	
unfreeze column	HOME, Records	, *Unfreeze Fields*	
unhide column	HOME, Records	, *Unhide Fields*	
Yes/No data type	TABLE TOOLS FIELDS, Add & Delete		

Concepts Check Test Your Knowledge

Completion: In the space provided at the right, indicate the correct term, symbol, or command.

1. Click this template at the Access 2013 opening screen to create a new database. ____________________
2. This toolbar contains buttons for commonly used commands. ____________________
3. This displays the names of objects within a database grouped by categories. ____________________
4. When you open a table, it displays in this view. ____________________
5. Use buttons on this bar to navigate in a table. ____________________
6. To add a new record, click the New button in this group on the HOME tab. ____________________
7. At the Print backstage area, click this button to send the table directly to the printer. ____________________
8. The Landscape button is located in this group on the PRINT PREVIEW tab. ____________________

9. All fields for one unit, such as an employee or customer, are considered to be this. ____________

10. Assign this data type to values that involve money. ____________

11. Click this button in the Properties group on the TABLE TOOLS FIELDS tab to display the Enter Field Properties dialog box. ____________

12. With options in this category in the More Fields button drop-down list, you can define a data type and also assign a field name. ____________

13. If you want to assign the same field value to a column, click this button to display the Expression Builder dialog box and then type the desired value. ____________

Skills Check Assess Your Performance

The database designer for Griffin Technologies has created the database diagram shown in Figure 1.15 to manage data about company employees. You will open the Griffin database and maintain and create tables that follow the diagram.

Figure 1.15 Griffin Technologies Database Diagram

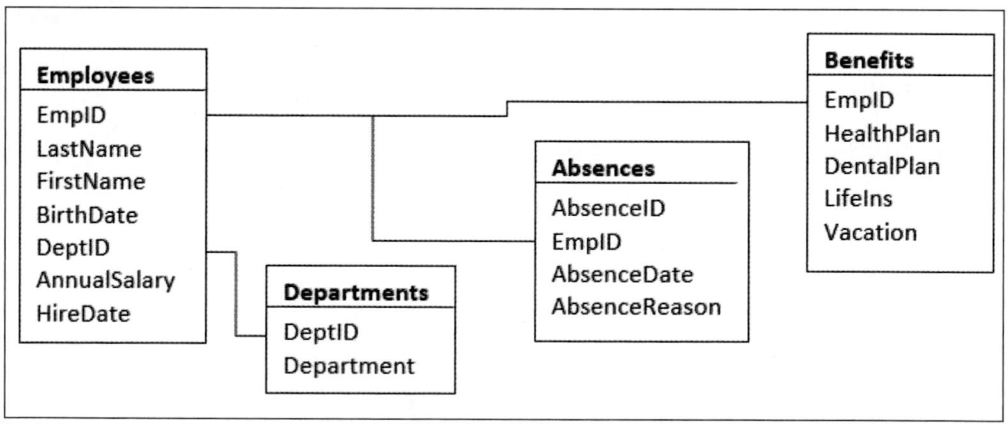

Assessment 1

INSERTING AND DELETING ROWS AND COLUMNS

1. In Access, open **AL1-C1-Griffin.accdb** from the AL1C1 folder on your storage medium and enable the contents.
2. Double-click *Employees* in the Tables group in the Navigation pane.
3. Delete the record for Scott Jorgensen (employee number 1025).
4. Delete the record for Leanne Taylor (employee number 1060).

5. Insert the following records:

EmpID: **1010**	EmpID: **1052**
LastName: **Harrington**	LastName: **Reeves**
FirstName: **Tyler**	FirstName: **Carrie**
Birthdate: **9/7/1976**	Birthdate: **12/4/1978**
AnnualSalary: **$53,350**	AnnualSalary: **$38,550**
HireDate: **10/1/2010**	HireDate: **10/1/2012**

6. Close the Employees table.
7. Looking at the database diagram in Figure 1.15, you realize that the Employees table includes a *DeptID* field. Open the Employees table, insert the new field in the Employees table, and name it *DeptID*. Change the field size to 2 characters (since department abbreviations are only one or two letters in length). At the message telling you that some data may be lost, click the Yes button. Type the department identification for each record as shown below (the records are listed from left to right):

1001: HR	1002: RD	1003: IT	1005: DP	1010: DP
1013: RD	1015: HR	1020: A	1023: IT	1030: PR
1033: A	1040: DP	1043: HR	1045: RD	1050: IT
1052: PR	1053: HR	1063: DP	1065: DP	1080: IT
1083: HR	1085: PR	1090: RD	1093: A	1095: RD

8. Move the *DeptID* column so it is positioned between the *BirthDate* column and the *AnnualSalary* column.
9. Automatically adjust the widths of the columns.
10. Save the table.
11. Display the table in Print Preview, change the top margin to 1.5 inches, change the left margin to 1.25 inches, and then print the table.
12. Close the Employees table.

Assessment 2

CREATE A DEPARTMENTS TABLE

SNAP Grade It

1. You entered a one- or two-letter abbreviation representing each department within the company. Creating the abbreviations saved you from having to type the entire department name for each record. You need to create the Departments table that will provide the department name for each abbreviation. Create a new table in the **AL1-C1-Griffin.accdb** database with the column headings and data shown in Figure 1.16 by completing the following steps:
   a. Click the CREATE tab and then click the Table button.
   b. Click the *ID* column heading, click the down-pointing arrow at the right side of the *Data Type* option box in the Formatting group, and then click *Short Text* at the drop-down list.
   c. Limit the field size to 2 characters and rename the heading as *DeptID*.
   d. Click the *Click to Add* column heading, click *Short Text* at the drop-down list, and then type **Department**.
   e. Type the data in the fields as shown in Figure 1.16 on the next page.
   f. Automatically adjust the widths of the columns.
2. Save the table and name it *Departments*.
3. Print and then close the table.

Figure 1.16 Departments Table

DeptID	Department	Click to Add
A	Accounting	
DP	Design and Production	
HR	Human Resources	
IT	Information Technology Services	
PR	Public Relations	
RD	Research and Development	
*		

Assessment

3 CREATE A BENEFITS TABLE

1. Create a new table in **AL1-C1-Griffin.accdb** with the data shown in Figure 1.17 and with the following specifications:
   a. Name the fields as shown in the Benefits table in the diagram in Figure 1.15 and create the caption names for the fields as shown in Figure 1.17. (For example, name the life insurance field *LifeIns* and create the caption *Life Insurance*.)
   b. For the first column (EmpID), click the *ID* column heading, click the down-pointing arrow at the right side of the *Data Type* option box in the Formatting group, and then click *Short Text* at the drop-down list. Limit the field size to 4 characters and rename the field as *EmpID*.
   c. Apply the Yes/No data type to the second column, make the default value a check mark (by typing **Yes** at the Expression Builder dialog box), and provide the description *A check mark indicates the employee has signed up for the health plan*.

Figure 1.17 Benefits Table

EmployeeID	Health Plan	Dental Plan	Life Insurance	Vacation	Click to Add
103	✓	✓	$100,000.00	4 weeks	
105	✓	✓	$200,000.00	3 weeks	
106		✓	$150,000.00	3 weeks	
109	✓	✓	$200,000.00	3 weeks	
110	✓	✓	$185,000.00	4 weeks	
112		✓	$200,000.00	3 weeks	
117			$100,000.00	3 weeks	
120	✓	✓	$200,000.00	4 weeks	
122			$75,000.00	2 weeks	
125	✓	✓	$125,000.00	3 weeks	
128	✓	✓	$200,000.00	3 weeks	
130	✓	✓	$200,000.00	3 weeks	
132			$50,000.00	2 weeks	
138	✓		$125,000.00	2 weeks	
141	✓	✓	$85,000.00	3 weeks	
143	✓	✓	$175,000.00	3 weeks	
149	✓		$100,000.00	2 weeks	
152	✓	✓	$150,000.00	2 weeks	
153	✓	✓	$200,000.00	2 weeks	
155		✓	$150,000.00	1 week	
159	✓		$75,000.00	1 week	
163	✓	✓	$125,000.00	1 week	
165	✓		$150,000.00	1 week	
170		✓	$185,000.00	1 week	
173	✓	✓	$125,000.00	1 week	
*	✓	✓			

d. Apply the Yes/No data type to the third column, make the default value a check mark (by typing **Yes** at the Expression Builder dialog box), and provide the description *A check mark indicates the employee has signed up for the dental plan.*
e. Apply the Currency data type to the fourth column.
f. Apply the Short Text data type to the fifth column and limit the field size to 8 characters.
g. Type the data in each record as shown in Figure 1.17.
h. Automatically adjust the column widths.
i. Save the table and name it *Benefits*.

2. Display the table in Print Preview, change the top and left margins to 1.5 inches, and then print the table.
3. Close the Benefits table.

Assessment 4

SORT DATA

1. With **AL1-C1-Griffin.accdb** open, open the Employees table.
2. Experiment with the buttons in the Sort & Filter group on the HOME tab and determine how to sort columns of data in ascending and descending order.
3. Sort the records in the Employees table in ascending order by last name.
4. Save, print, and then close the Employees table.
5. Open the Benefits table and then sort the records in descending order by life insurance amounts.
6. Save, print, and then close the Benefits table.

Visual Benchmark Demonstrate Your Proficiency

CREATE AN ABSENCES TABLE

1. With **AL1-C1-Griffin.accdb** open, create the Absences table shown in Figure 1.18 (using the field names as shown in Figure 1.15 on page 36) with the following specifications:
   a. Use the default AutoNumber data type for column 1. Apply the appropriate data type to the other columns.
   b. Create an appropriate caption and description for the *EmpID*, *AbsenceDate*, and *AbsenceReason* columns.
   c. Apply the default value of Sick Day to the *AbsenceReason* column. (You will need to type **"Sick Day"** in the Expression Builder dialog box.)
2. Save the table and name it *Absences*.
3. Print the table in landscape orientation with top and left margins of 1.5 inches.
4. Close the Absences table and then close **AL1-C1-Griffin.accdb**.

Figure 1.18 Visual Benchmark

Absences

AbsenceID	EmpID	Absent Date	Absent Reason	Click to Add
1	141	1/2/2015	Sick Day	
2	141	1/5/2015	Sick Day	
3	105	1/6/2015	Sick Day	
4	163	1/9/2015	Sick Day	
5	125	1/9/2015	Bereavement	
6	125	1/12/2015	Bereavement	
7	125	1/12/2015	Bereavement	
8	117	1/13/2015	Sick Day	
9	170	1/14/2015	Personal Day	
10	153	1/16/2015	Sick Day	
11	153	1/19/2015	Sick Day	
12	103	1/19/2015	Personal Day	
13	109	1/20/2015	Sick Day	
14	109	1/22/2015	Sick Day	
15	167	1/23/2015	Personal Day	
16	138	1/29/2015	Sick Day	
17	159	1/30/2015	Sick Day	
* (New)			Sick Day	

Case Study Apply Your Skills

You are the office manager for Elite Limousines, and your company is switching over to Access for managing company data. The database designer has provided you with the database diagram in Figure 1.19. She wants you to follow the diagram when creating the database.

Figure 1.19 Elite Limousines Database Diagram

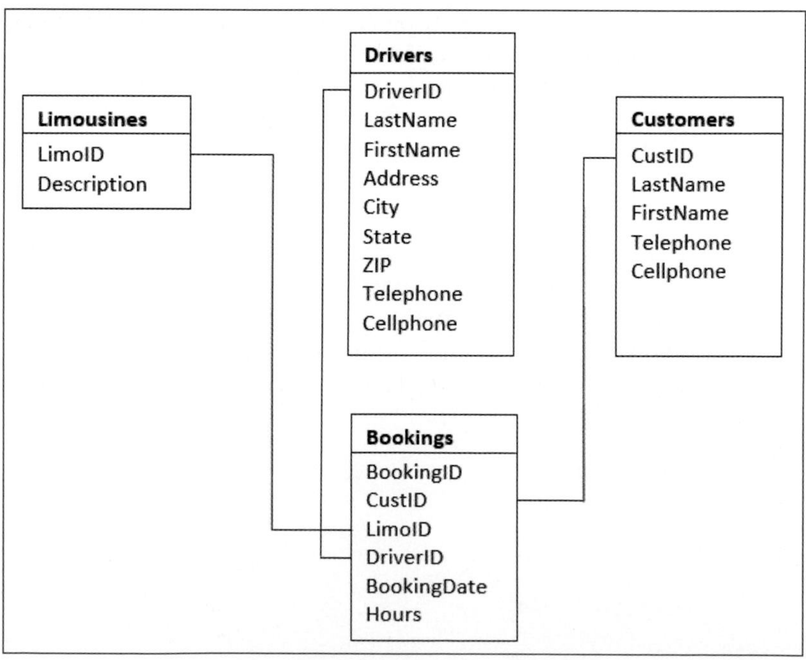

Part 1

Create a new database named **AL1-C1-Elite.accdb** and then create the Limousines table shown in the database diagram in Figure 1.19. The database designer has asked you to include an appropriate caption and description for each field and to change the field size for the *LimoID* field. Type the following records in the table:

LimoID: **01**
Description: **2011 White stretch**

LimoID: **02**
Description: **2011 Black stretch**

LimoID: **04**
Description: **2012 Black minibus**

LimoID: **06**
Description: **2012 Black standard**

LimoID: **08**
Description: **2014 Black SUV stretch**

LimoID: **10**
Description: **2015 Black stretch**

Part 2

With **AL1-C1-Elite.accdb** open, create the Drivers table shown in the database diagram shown in Figure 1.19. Include appropriate captions and descriptions for each field and change the field sizes where appropriate. Type the following records in the table:

DriverID#: **101**
LastName: **Brennan**
FirstName: **Andrea**
Address: **4438 Gowan Rd.**
City: **Las Vegas**
State: **NV**
ZIP: **89115**
Telephone: **(702) 555-3481**
Cellphone: **(702) 555-1322**

DriverID: **114**
LastName: **Gould**
FirstName: **Randall**
Address: **330 Aura Ave.**
City: **Las Vegas**
State: **NV**
ZIP: **89052**
Telephone: **(702) 555-1239**
Cellphone: **(702) 555-7474**

DriverID: **120**
LastName: **Martinelli**
FirstName: **Albert**
Address: **107 Cameo Dr.**
City: **Las Vegas**
State: **NV**
ZIP: **89138**
Telephone: **(702) 555-0349**
Cellphone: **(702) 555-6649**

DriverID: **125**
LastName: **Nunez**
FirstName: **Frank**
Address: **4832 Helena St.**
City: **Las Vegas**
State: **NV**
ZIP: **89129**
Telephone: **(702) 555-3748**
Cellphone: **(702) 555-2210**

Part 3

With **AL1-C1-Elite.accdb** open, create the Customers table shown in the database diagram in Figure 1.19. Include appropriate captions and descriptions for the fields and change the field sizes where appropriate. Type the following records in the table:

CustID: **1001**
LastName: **Spencer**
FirstName: **Maureen**
Telephone: **(513) 555-3943**
Cellphone: **(513) 555-4884**

CustID: **1002**
LastName: **Tsang**
FirstName: **Lee**
Telephone: **(702) 555-4775**
Cellphone: **(702) 555-4211**

CustID: **1028**
LastName: **Gabriel**
FirstName: **Nicholas**
Telephone: **(612) 555-7885**
Cellphone: **(612) 555-7230**

CustID: **1031**
LastName: **Marshall**
FirstName: **Patricia**
Telephone: **(702) 555-6410**
Cellphone: **(702) 555-0137**

CustID: **1010**
LastName: **Chavez**
FirstName: **Blake**
Telephone: **(206) 555-3774**
Cellphone: **(206) 555-3006**

CustID: **1044**
LastName: **Vanderhage**
FirstName: **Vernon**
Telephone: **(213) 555-8846**
Cellphone: **(213) 555-4635**

Part 4

With **AL1-C1-Elite.accdb** open, create the Bookings table shown in the database diagram in Figure 1.19. Include appropriate captions and descriptions for the fields and change the field sizes where appropriate. Type the following records in the table:

BookingID: (AutoNumber)
CustID: **1044**
LimoID: **02**
DriverID: **114**
BookingDate: **7/1/2015**
Hours: **6**

BookingID: (AutoNumber)
CustID: **1001**
LimoID: **10**
DriverID: **120**
BookingDate: **7/1/2015**
Hours: **8**

BookingID: (AutoNumber)
CustID: **1002**
LimoID: **04**
DriverID: **101**
BookingDate: **7/6/2015**
Hours: **8**

BookingID: (AutoNumber)
CustID: **1028**
LimoID: **02**
DriverID: **125**
BookingDate: **7/6/2015**
Hours: **4**

BookingID: (AutoNumber)
CustID: **1010**
LimoID: **06**
DriverID: **125**
BookingDate: **7/3/2015**
Hours: **3**

BookingID: (AutoNumber)
CustID: **1031**
LimoID: **08**
DriverID: **120**
BookingDate: **7/7/2015**
Hours: **5**

Automatically adjust the column widths of each table to accommodate the longest entry in each column. Print each table so all records fit on one page.

MICROSOFT®

ACCESS®

Creating Relationships between Tables

PERFORMANCE OBJECTIVES

Upon successful completion of Chapter 2, you will be able to:

- **Define a primary key in a table**
- **Create a one-to-many relationship**
- **Specify referential integrity**
- **Print, edit, and delete relationships**
- **Create a one-to-one relationship**
- **View and edit a subdatasheet**

Tutorials

2.1 Defining a Primary Key

2.2 Printing, Editing, and Deleting Relationships

2.3 Creating a Relationship between Two Tables in a Database

2.4 Creating a One-to-One Relationship between Tables

2.5 Editing a Relationship; Enforcing Referential Integrity; Viewing a Subdatasheet

Access is a relational database program you can use to create tables that are related or connected within the same database. When a relationship is established between tables, you can view and edit records in related tables with a subdatasheet. In this chapter, you will learn how to identify a primary key in a table that is unique to that table, how to join tables by creating a relationship between them, and how to view and edit subdatasheets. Model answers for this chapter's projects appear on the following pages.

AL1C2

Note: Before beginning the projects, copy the AL1C2 subfolder from the AL1 folder on the CD that accompanies this textbook to your storage medium and make AL1C2 the active folder.

Project 1 Establish Relationships between Tables

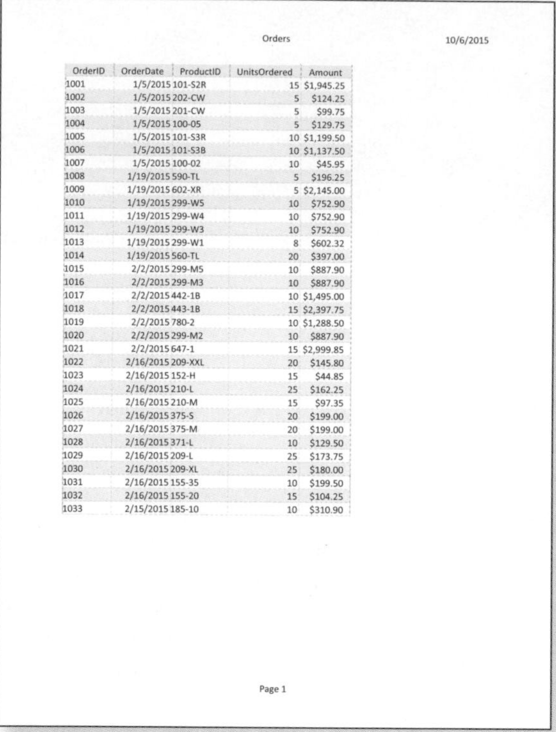

Orders 10/6/2015

OrderID	OrderDate	ProductID	UnitsOrdered	Amount
1001	1/5/2015	101-S2R	15	$1,945.25
1002	1/5/2015	202-CW	5	$124.25
1003	1/5/2015	201-CW	5	$99.75
1004	1/5/2015	100-05	5	$129.75
1005	1/5/2015	101-S3R	10	$1,199.50
1006	1/5/2015	101-S3B	10	$1,137.50
1007	1/5/2015	100-02	10	$45.95
1008	1/19/2015	590-TL	5	$196.25
1009	1/19/2015	602-XR	5	$2,145.00
1010	1/19/2015	299-W5	10	$752.90
1011	1/19/2015	299-W4	10	$752.90
1012	1/19/2015	299-W3	10	$752.90
1013	1/19/2015	299-W1	8	$602.32
1014	1/19/2015	560-TL	20	$397.00
1015	2/2/2015	299-M5	10	$887.90
1016	2/2/2015	299-M3	10	$887.90
1017	2/2/2015	442-1B	10	$1,495.00
1018	2/2/2015	443-1B	15	$2,397.75
1019	2/2/2015	780-2	10	$1,288.50
1020	2/2/2015	299-M2	10	$887.90
1021	2/2/2015	647-1	15	$2,999.85
1022	2/16/2015	209-XXL	20	$145.80
1023	2/16/2015	152-H	15	$44.85
1024	2/16/2015	210-L	25	$162.25
1025	2/16/2015	210-M	15	$97.35
1026	2/16/2015	375-S	20	$199.00
1027	2/16/2015	375-M	20	$199.00
1028	2/16/2015	371-L	10	$129.50
1029	2/16/2015	209-L	25	$173.75
1030	2/16/2015	209-XL	25	$180.00
1031	2/16/2015	155-35	10	$199.50
1032	2/16/2015	155-20	15	$104.25
1033	2/15/2015	185-10	10	$310.90

Page 1

Orders Table

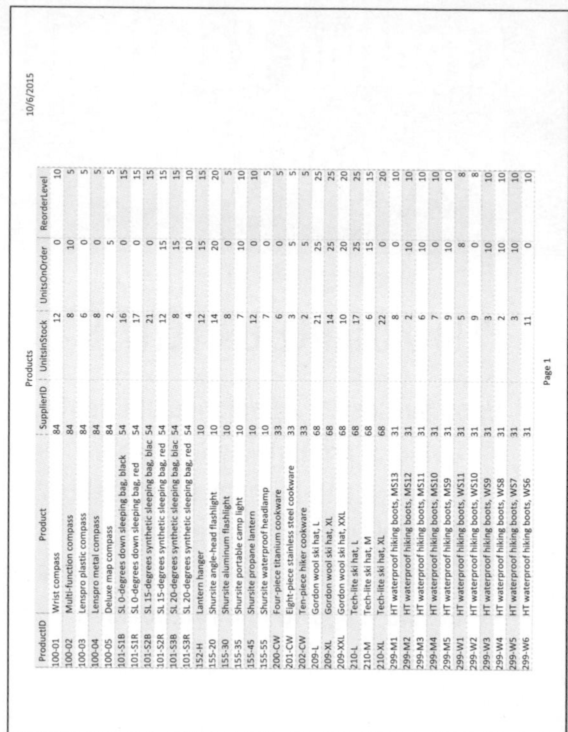

10/6/2015 Products

ProductID	Product	SupplierID	UnitsInStock	UnitsOnOrder	ReorderLevel
100-01	Wrist compass	84	12	0	10
100-02	Multi-function compass	84	8	10	5
100-03	Lenspro plastic compass	84	6	0	5
100-04	Lenspro metal compass	84	8	0	5
100-05	Deluxe map compass	84	2	5	5
101-S1B	SL 0-degrees down sleeping bag, black	54	16	0	15
101-S1R	SL 0-degrees down sleeping bag, red	54	17	0	15
101-S2B	SL 15-degrees synthetic sleeping bag, blac	54	21	0	15
101-S2R	SL 15-degrees synthetic sleeping bag, red	54	12	15	15
101-S3B	SL 20-degrees synthetic sleeping bag, blac	54	8	15	15
101-S3R	SL 20-degrees synthetic sleeping bag, red	54	4	10	10
152-H	Lantern hanger	10	12	15	15
155-20	Shursite angle-head flashlight	10	14	20	20
155-30	Shursite aluminum flashlight	10	8	0	5
155-35	Shursite portable camp light	10	7	10	10
155-45	Shursite propane lantern	10	12	0	10
155-55	Shursite waterproof headlamp	10	7	0	5
200-CW	Four-piece titanium cookware	33	6	0	5
201-CW	Eight-piece stainless steel cookware	33	3	5	5
202-CW	Ten-piece hiker cookware	33	2	5	5
209-L	Gordon wool ski hat, L	68	21	25	25
209-XL	Gordon wool ski hat, XL	68	14	25	25
209-XXL	Gordon wool ski hat, XXL	68	10	20	20
210-L	Tech-lite ski hat, L	68	17	25	25
210-M	Tech-lite ski hat, M	68	6	15	15
210-XL	Tech-lite ski hat, XL	68	22	0	20
299-M1	HT waterproof hiking boots, MS13	31	8	0	10
299-M2	HT waterproof hiking boots, MS12	31	2	10	10
299-M3	HT waterproof hiking boots, MS11	31	6	10	10
299-M4	HT waterproof hiking boots, MS10	31	7	0	10
299-M5	HT waterproof hiking boots, MS9	31	9	10	10
299-W1	HT waterproof hiking boots, WS11	31	5	8	8
299-W2	HT waterproof hiking boots, WS10	31	9	0	8
299-W3	HT waterproof hiking boots, WS9	31	3	10	10
299-W4	HT waterproof hiking boots, WS8	31	2	10	10
299-W5	HT waterproof hiking boots, WS7	31	3	10	10
299-W6	HT waterproof hiking boots, WS6	31	11	0	10

Page 1

Products Table, Page 1

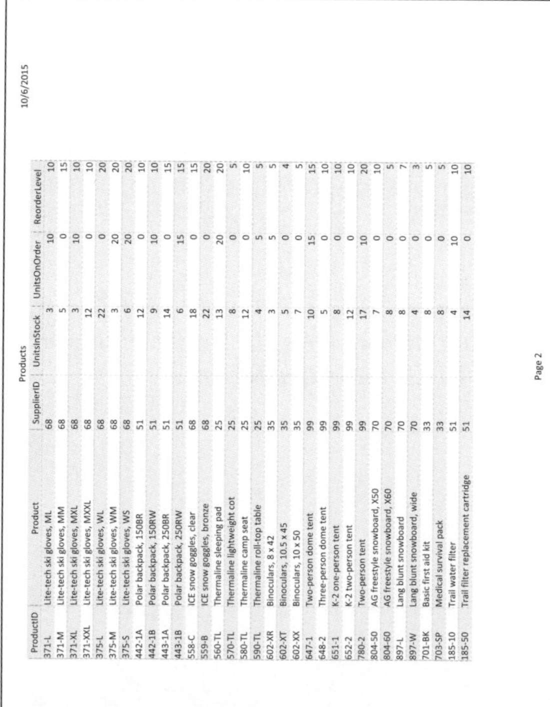

10/6/2015 Products

ProductID	Product	SupplierID	UnitsInStock	UnitsOnOrder	ReorderLevel
371-L	Lite-tech ski gloves, ML	68	3	10	10
371-M	Lite-tech ski gloves, MM	68	5	0	15
371-XL	Lite-tech ski gloves, MXL	68	3	10	10
371-XXL	Lite-tech ski gloves, MXXL	68	12	0	10
375-L	Lite-tech ski gloves, WL	68	22	0	20
375-M	Lite-tech ski gloves, WM	68	3	20	20
375-S	Lite-tech ski gloves, WS	68	6	20	20
442-1A	Polar backpack, 150BR	51	12	0	10
442-1B	Polar backpack, 150RW	51	9	10	10
443-1A	Polar backpack, 250BR	51	14	0	15
443-1B	Polar backpack, 250RW	51	6	15	15
558-C	ICE snow goggles, clear	68	18	0	15
559-B	ICE snow goggles, bronze	68	22	0	20
560-TL	Thermaline sleeping pad	25	13	20	20
570-TL	Thermaline lightweight cot	25	8	0	5
580-TL	Thermaline camp seat	25	12	0	10
590-TL	Thermaline roll-top table	25	4	5	5
602-XR	Binoculars, 8 x 42	35	3	5	5
602-XT	Binoculars, 10.5 x 45	35	5	0	4
602-XX	Binoculars, 10 x 50	35	7	0	5
647-1	Two-person dome tent	99	10	15	15
648-2	Three-person dome tent	99	5	0	10
651-1	K-2 one-person tent	99	8	0	10
652-2	K-2 two-person tent	99	12	0	10
780-2	Two-person tent	99	17	10	20
804-50	AG freestyle snowboard, X50	70	7	0	10
804-60	AG freestyle snowboard, X60	70	8	0	5
897-L	Lang blunt snowboard	70	8	0	7
897-W	Lang blunt snowboard, wide	70	4	0	3
701-BK	Basic first aid kit	33	8	0	5
703-SP	Medical survival pack	33	8	0	5
185-10	Trail water filter	51	4	10	10
185-50	Trail filter replacement cartridge	51	14	0	10

Page 2

Products Table, Page 2

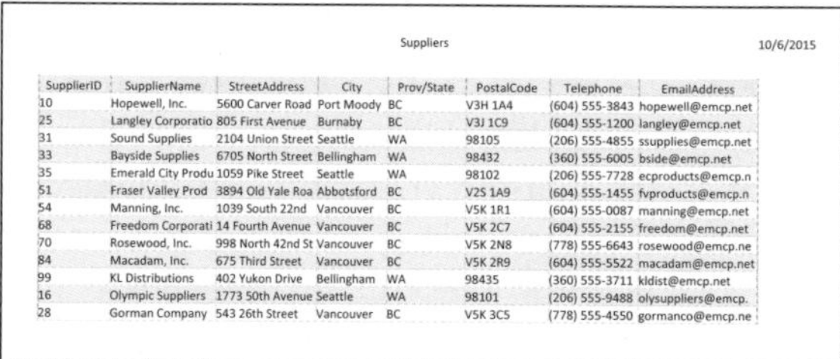

Suppliers 10/6/2015

SupplierID	SupplierName	StreetAddress	City	Prov/State	PostalCode	Telephone	EmailAddress
10	Hopewell, Inc.	5600 Carver Road	Port Moody	BC	V3H 1A4	(604) 555-3843	hopewell@emcp.net
25	Langley Corporatio	805 First Avenue	Burnaby	BC	V3J 1C9	(604) 555-1200	langley@emcp.net
31	Sound Supplies	2104 Union Street	Seattle	WA	98105	(206) 555-4855	ssupplies@emcp.net
33	Bayside Supplies	6705 North Street	Bellingham	WA	98432	(360) 555-6005	bside@emcp.net
35	Emerald City Produ	1059 Pike Street	Seattle	WA	98102	(206) 555-7728	ecproducts@emcp.n
51	Fraser Valley Prod	3894 Old Yale Roa	Abbotsford	BC	V2S 1A9	(604) 555-1455	fvproducts@emcp.n
54	Manning, Inc.	1039 South 22nd	Vancouver	BC	V5K 1R1	(604) 555-0087	manning@emcp.net
68	Freedom Corporati	14 Fourth Avenue	Vancouver	BC	V5K 2C7	(604) 555-2155	freedom@emcp.net
70	Rosewood, Inc.	998 North 42nd St	Vancouver	BC	V5K 2N8	(778) 555-6643	rosewood@emcp.ne
84	Macadam, Inc.	675 Third Street	Vancouver	BC	V5K 2R9	(604) 555-5522	macadam@emcp.net
99	KL Distributions	402 Yukon Drive	Bellingham	WA	98435	(360) 555-3711	kldist@emcp.net
16	Olympic Suppliers	1773 50th Avenue	Seattle	WA	98101	(206) 555-9488	olysuppliers@emcp.
28	Gorman Company	543 26th Street	Vancouver	BC	V5K 3C5	(778) 555-4550	gormanco@emcp.ne

Suppliers Table

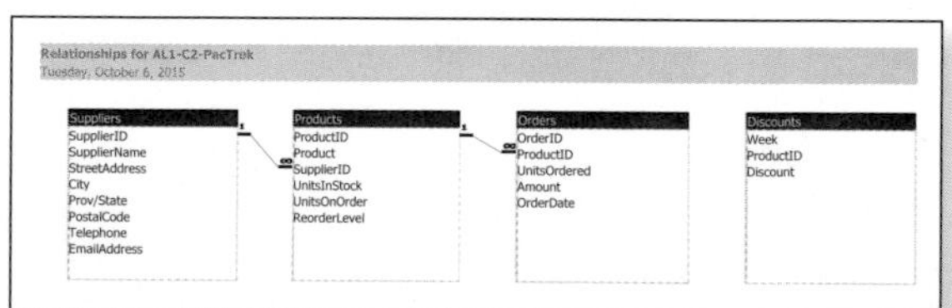

Relationships Report

Project 2 Create Relationships and Display Subdatasheets in a Database

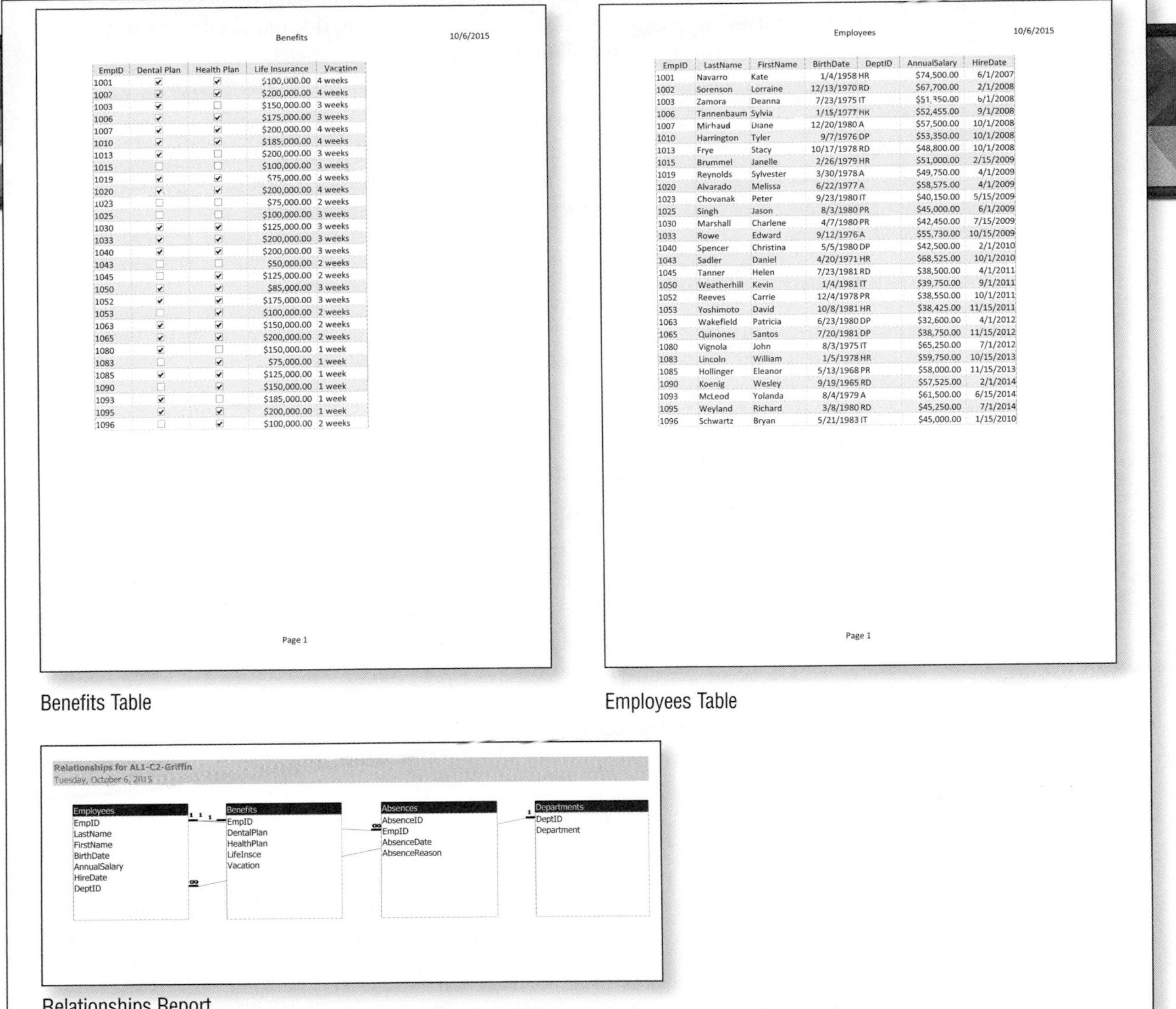

Benefits 10/6/2015

EmpID	Dental Plan	Health Plan	Life Insurance	Vacation
1001	☑	☑	$100,000.00	4 weeks
1002	☑	☑	$200,000.00	4 weeks
1003	☑	☐	$150,000.00	3 weeks
1006	☑	☑	$175,000.00	3 weeks
1007	☑	☑	$200,000.00	4 weeks
1010	☑	☑	$185,000.00	4 weeks
1013	☑	☐	$200,000.00	3 weeks
1015	☐	☐	$100,000.00	3 weeks
1019	☑	☑	$75,000.00	3 weeks
1020	☑	☑	$200,000.00	4 weeks
1023	☐	☐	$75,000.00	2 weeks
1025	☐	☐	$100,000.00	3 weeks
1030	☑	☑	$125,000.00	3 weeks
1033	☑	☑	$200,000.00	3 weeks
1040	☑	☑	$200,000.00	3 weeks
1043	☐	☐	$50,000.00	2 weeks
1045	☐	☑	$125,000.00	2 weeks
1050	☑	☑	$85,000.00	3 weeks
1052	☑	☑	$175,000.00	3 weeks
1053	☐	☑	$100,000.00	2 weeks
1063	☑	☑	$150,000.00	2 weeks
1065	☑	☑	$200,000.00	2 weeks
1080	☑	☐	$150,000.00	1 week
1083	☐	☑	$75,000.00	1 week
1085	☑	☑	$125,000.00	1 week
1090	☐	☑	$150,000.00	1 week
1093	☑	☐	$185,000.00	1 week
1095	☑	☑	$200,000.00	1 week
1096	☐	☑	$100,000.00	2 weeks

Page 1

Benefits Table

Employees 10/6/2015

EmpID	LastName	FirstName	BirthDate	DeptID	AnnualSalary	HireDate
1001	Navarro	Kate	1/4/1958	HR	$74,500.00	6/1/2007
1002	Sorenson	Lorraine	12/13/1970	RD	$67,700.00	2/1/2008
1003	Zamora	Deanna	7/23/1975	IT	$51,350.00	6/1/2008
1006	Tannenbaum	Sylvia	1/15/1977	HR	$52,455.00	9/1/2008
1007	Michaud	Diane	12/20/1980	A	$57,500.00	10/1/2008
1010	Harrington	Tyler	9/7/1976	DP	$53,350.00	10/1/2008
1013	Frye	Stacy	10/17/1978	RD	$48,800.00	10/1/2008
1015	Brummel	Janelle	2/26/1979	HR	$51,000.00	2/15/2009
1019	Reynolds	Sylvester	3/30/1978	A	$49,750.00	4/1/2009
1020	Alvarado	Melissa	6/22/1977	A	$58,575.00	4/1/2009
1023	Chovanak	Peter	9/23/1980	IT	$40,150.00	5/15/2009
1025	Singh	Jason	8/3/1980	PR	$45,000.00	6/1/2009
1030	Marshall	Charlene	4/7/1980	PR	$42,450.00	7/15/2009
1033	Rowe	Edward	9/12/1976	A	$55,730.00	10/15/2009
1040	Spencer	Christina	5/5/1980	DP	$42,500.00	2/1/2010
1043	Sadler	Daniel	4/20/1971	HR	$68,525.00	10/1/2010
1045	Tanner	Helen	7/23/1981	RD	$38,500.00	4/1/2011
1050	Weatherhill	Kevin	1/4/1981	IT	$39,750.00	9/1/2011
1052	Reeves	Carrie	12/4/1978	PR	$38,550.00	10/1/2011
1053	Yoshimoto	David	10/8/1981	HR	$38,425.00	11/15/2011
1063	Wakefield	Patricia	6/23/1980	DP	$32,600.00	4/1/2012
1065	Quinones	Santos	7/20/1981	DP	$38,750.00	11/15/2012
1080	Vignola	John	8/3/1975	IT	$65,250.00	7/1/2012
1083	Lincoln	William	1/5/1978	HR	$59,750.00	10/15/2013
1085	Hollinger	Eleanor	5/13/1968	PR	$58,000.00	11/15/2013
1090	Koenig	Wesley	9/19/1965	RD	$57,525.00	2/1/2014
1093	McLeod	Yolanda	8/4/1979	A	$61,500.00	6/15/2014
1095	Weyland	Richard	3/8/1980	RD	$45,250.00	7/1/2014
1096	Schwartz	Bryan	5/21/1983	IT	$45,000.00	1/15/2010

Page 1

Employees Table

Relationships Report

Project 1 Establish Relationships between Tables — 4 Parts

You will specify primary keys in tables, establish one-to-many relationships between tables, specify referential integrity, and print the relationships. You will also edit and delete a relationship.

Creating Related Tables

Generally, a database management system fits into one of two categories: a file management system (also sometimes referred to as a ***flat file database***) or a relational database management system. A flat file management system stores all data in a single directory and cannot contain multiple tables. This type of management system is a simple way to store data but becomes more inefficient as more data is added. In a

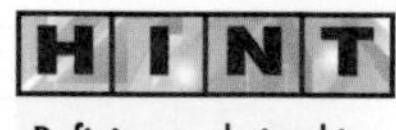

Defining a relationship between tables is one of the most powerful features of a relational database management system.

relational database management system, like Access, relationships are defined between sets of data, allowing greater flexibility in manipulating data and eliminating data redundancy (entering the same data in more than one place).

In Project 1, you will define relationships between tables in the AL1-C2-PacTrek.accdb database. Because the tables in the database will be related, information on the same product does not need to be repeated in a table on orders. If you used a flat file management system to maintain product information, you would need to repeat the product description for each order.

Determining Relationships

Taking time to plan a database is extremely important. Creating a database with related tables takes even more consideration. You need to determine how to break down the required data and what tables to create to eliminate redundancies. One idea to help you determine what tables are necessary in a database is to think of the word *about*. For example, the Pacific Trek store needs a table *about* products, another *about* suppliers, and another *about* orders. A table should be about only one subject, such as products, suppliers, or orders.

Along with determining the necessary tables for a database, you need to determine the relationship between tables. The ability to relate, or "join," tables is what makes Access a relational database system. As you learned in Chapter 1, database designers often create a visual representation of the database's structure in a diagram. Figure 2.1 displays the database diagram for the AL1-C2-PacTrek.accdb database. (Some of the fields in the tables have been slightly modified from the database you used in Chapter 1.)

Defining the Primary Key

A database table can contain two different types of keys: a primary key and a foreign key. In the database diagram in Figure 2.1, notice that one field in each table contains an asterisk. The asterisk indicates a ***primary key field***, which is a field that holds data that uniquely identifies each record in a table. For example,

Figure 2.1 AL1-C2-PacTrek.accdb Database Diagram

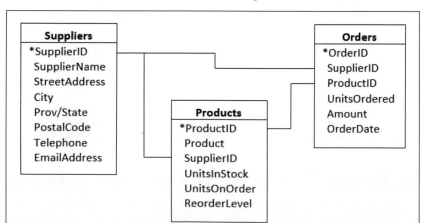

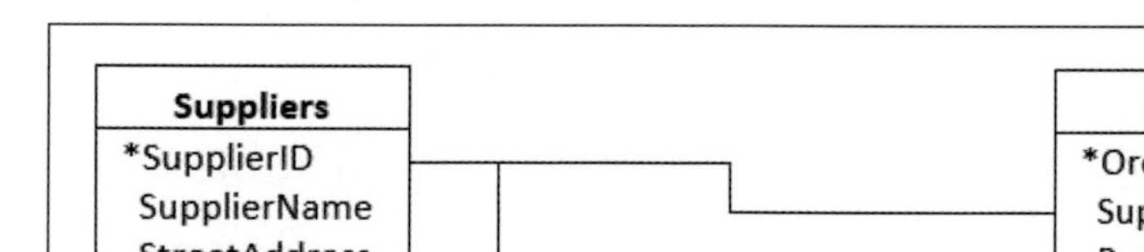

the *SupplierID* field in the Suppliers table contains a unique supplier number for each record in the table and the *ProductID* field in the Products table contains a unique product number for each product. A table can have only one primary key field and it is the field by which the table is sorted whenever the table is opened.

When a new record is added to a table, Access checks to ensure that there is no existing record with the same data in the primary key. If there is, Access displays an error message indicating there are duplicate values and does not allow the record to be saved. When adding a new record to a table, the primary key field cannot be left blank. Access expects a value in each record in the table and this is referred to as ***entity integrity***. If a value is not entered in a field, Access actually enters a null value. A null value cannot be given to a primary key field. Access will not let you close a database containing a primary key field with a null value.

By default, Access includes the *ID* field as the first field in a table, assigns the AutoNumber data type, and identifies the field as the primary key. The AutoNumber data type assigns the first record a field value of *1* and each new record is assigned the next sequential number. You can use this default field as the primary key or define your own. To determine what field is the primary key or to define a primary key field, you must display the table in Design view. To do this, open the table and then click the View button located at the left side of the HOME tab. You can also display the table in Design view by clicking the View button arrow and then clicking *Design View* at the drop-down list. To add or remove a primary key from a field, click the desired field in the *Field Name* column and then click the Primary Key button in the Tools group on the TABLE TOOLS DESIGN tab. A key icon is inserted in the field selector bar (the blank column to the left of the field names) for the desired field. Figure 2.2 displays the Products table in Design view with the *ProductID* field identified as the primary key.

Quick Steps

Define a Primary Key
1. Open table.
2. Click View button.
3. Click desired field.
4. Click Primary Key button.
5. Click Save button.

Primary Key

Figure 2.2 Products Table in Design View

A key icon in the field selector bar specifies the primary key field.

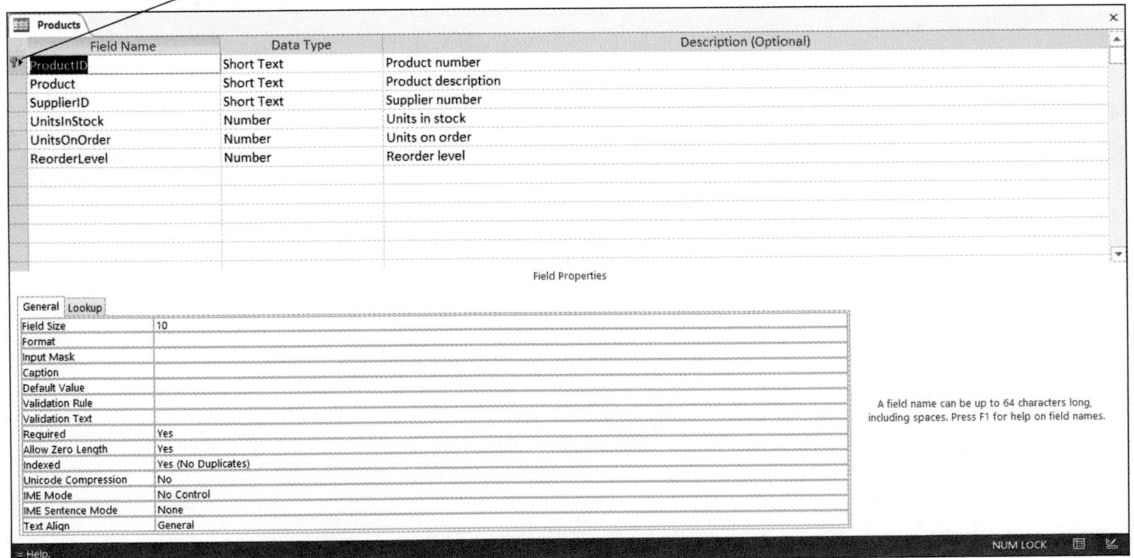

Access uses a primary key to associate data from multiple tables.

You must enter a value in the primary key in every record.

Typically, a primary key field in one table becomes the ***foreign key field*** in a related table. For example, the primary key field *SupplierID* in the Suppliers table is considered the foreign key field in the Orders table. In the Suppliers table, each entry in the *SupplierID* field must be unique since it is the primary key field but the same supplier number may appear more than once in the *SupplierID* field in the Orders table (for instance, in a situation when more than one product is ordered from the same supplier).

Data in the foreign key field must match data in the primary key field of the related table. For example, any supplier number you enter in the *SupplierID* field in the Orders table must be contained in the Suppliers table. In other words, you would not make an order to a supplier that does not exist in the Suppliers table. Figure 2.3 identifies the primary and foreign keys in the tables in the AL1-C2-PacTrek.accdb database. Primary keys are identified with *(PK)* and foreign keys are identified with *(FK)* in the figure.

Figure 2.3 AL1-C2-PacTrek.accdb Database Diagram with Primary and Foreign Keys Identified

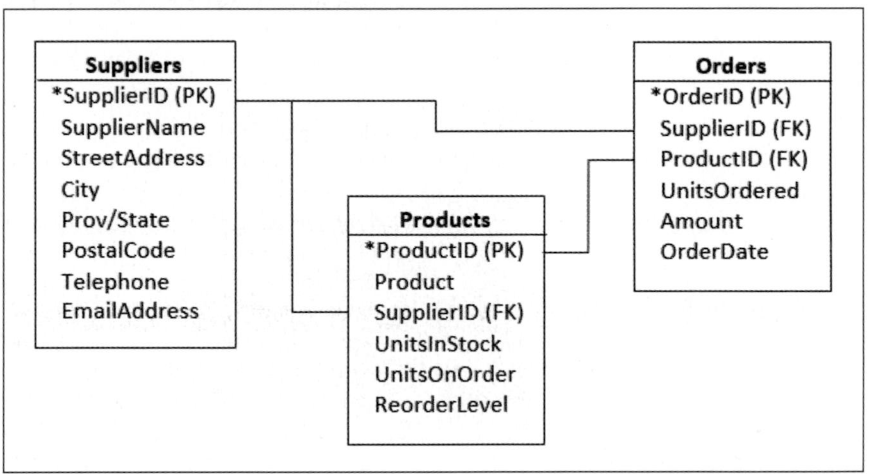

Project 1a Defining a Primary Key Field — Part 1 of 4

1. Open Access.
2. At the Access 2013 opening screen, click the Open Other Files hyperlink that displays at the left side of the screen.
3. At the Open backstage area, double-click the *Computer* option or your SkyDrive (depending on where your student data files are located).
4. At the Open dialog box, navigate to the AL1C2 folder on your storage medium and then double-click the database ***AL1-C2-PacTrek.accdb***.
5. Click the Enable Content button in the message bar if the security warning message appears. (The message bar will display immediately below the ribbon.)
6. Open the Products table.
7. View the primary key field by completing the following steps:
   a. Click the View button located at the left side of the HOME tab. (This displays the table in Design view.)

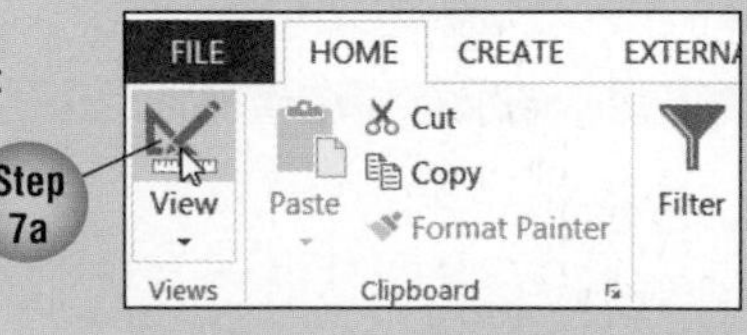

b. In Design view, notice the *Field Name*, *Data Type*, and *Description* columns and notice the information that displays for each field. The first field, *ProductID* is the primary key field and is identified by the key icon that displays in the field selector bar.
c. Click the View button to return to the Datasheet view.
d. Close the Products table.

8. Open the Suppliers table, click the View button to display the table in Design view, and then notice the *SupplierID* field is defined as the primary key field.
9. Click the View button to return to Datasheet view and then close the table.
10. Open the Orders table. (The first field in the Orders table has been changed from the AutoNumber field automatically assigned by Access in the AL1-C2-PacTrek.accdb database to a Short Text data type field.)
11. Define the *OrderID* field as the primary key field by completing the following steps:
    a. Click the View button located at the left side of the HOME tab.
    b. With the table in Design view and the *OrderID* field selected in the *Field Name* column, click the Primary Key button located in the Tools group on the TABLE TOOLS DESIGN tab.

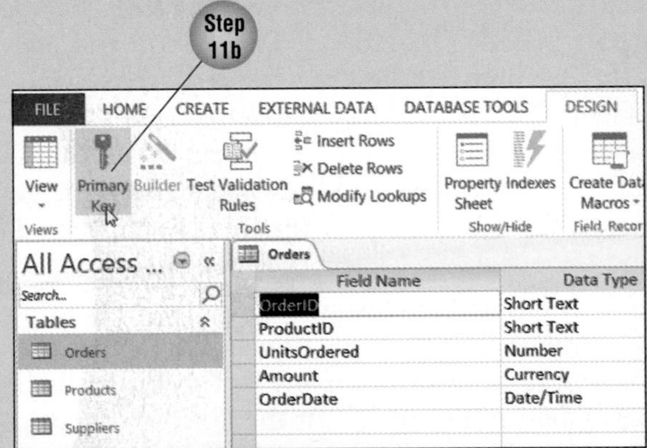

    c. Click the Save button on the Quick Access toolbar.
    d. Click the View button to return the table to Datasheet view.
12. Move the *OrderDate* field by completing the following steps:
    a. Click the *OrderDate* field heading. (This selects the column.)
    b. Position the mouse pointer on the heading; hold down the left mouse button; drag to the left until the thick, black vertical line displays immediately left of the *ProductID* field; and then release the mouse button.

Step 12b

Orders

OrderID	ProductID	UnitsOrderec	Amount	OrderDate	Click to Add
1001	101-S2R	15	$1,945.25	1/5/2015	
1002	202-CW	5	$124.25	1/5/2015	
1003	201-CW	5	$99.75	1/5/2015	
1004	100-05	5	$129.75	1/5/2015	

13. Automatically adjust the column widths.
14. Save and then close the Orders table.

Relating Tables in a One-to-Many Relationship

In Access, one table can be related to another, which is generally referred to as performing a ***join***. When tables with a common field are joined, data can be extracted from both tables as if they were one large table. Relate tables to ensure the integrity of the data. For example, in Project 1b, you will create a relationship between the Suppliers table and the Products table. The relationship you establish will ensure that a supplier number cannot be entered in the Products table without first being entered in the Suppliers table. This type of relationship is called a ***one-to-many relationship***, which means that one record in the Suppliers table will match zero, one, or many records in the Products table.

In a one-to-many relationship, the table containing the "one" is referred to as the ***primary table*** and the table containing the "many" is referred to as the ***related table***. Access follows a set of rules that provide ***referential integrity***, which enforces consistency between related tables. These rules are enforced when data is updated in related tables. The referential integrity rules ensure that a record added to a related table has a matching record in the primary table.

Quick Steps

Create a One-to-Many Relationship
1. Click DATABASE TOOLS tab.
2. Click Relationships button.
3. At Show Table dialog box, add tables.
4. In Relationships window, drag "one" field from primary table to "many" field in related table.
5. At Edit Relationships dialog box, enforce referential integrity.
6. Click Create button.
7. Click Save button.

Relationships

To create a one-to-many relationship, open the database containing the tables to be related. Click the DATABASE TOOLS tab and then click the Relationships button in the Relationships group. This displays the Show Table dialog box, as shown in Figure 2.4. At the Show Table dialog box, each table that will be related must be added to the Relationships window. To do this, click the first table name to be included and then click Add (or double-click the desired table). Continue in this manner until all necessary table names have been added to the Relationships window and then click the Close button.

At the Relationships window, such as the one shown in Figure 2.5, use the mouse to drag the common field from the primary table's field list box (the "one") to the related table's field list box (the "many"). This causes the Edit Relationships dialog box to display, as shown in Figure 2.6. At the Edit Relationships dialog box, check to make sure the correct field name displays in the *Table/Query* and *Related Table/Query* list boxes and the relationship type at the bottom of the dialog box displays as *One-To-Many*.

Specify the relationship options by choosing *Enforce Referential Integrity*, as well as *Cascade Update Related Fields* and/or *Cascade Delete Related Records*, and then click the Create button. This causes the Edit Relationships dialog box to close and the Relationships window to display showing the relationship between the tables.

Figure 2.4 Show Table Dialog Box

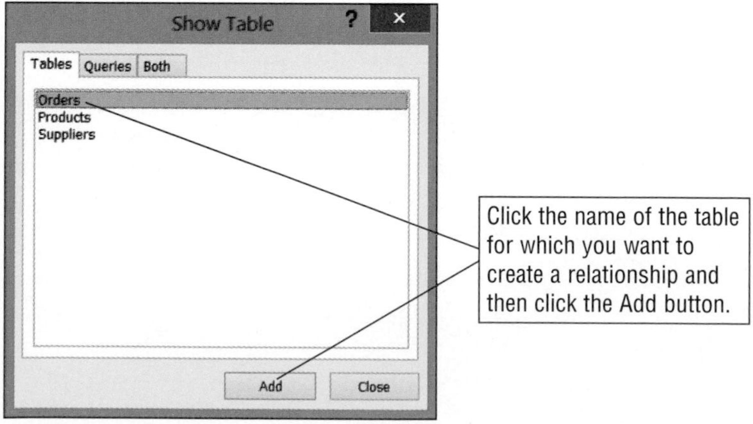
Show Table
Tables
Queries
Both
Orders
Products
Suppliers
Add
Close
Click the name of the table for which you want to create a relationship and then click the Add button.

Figure 2.5 Relationships Window

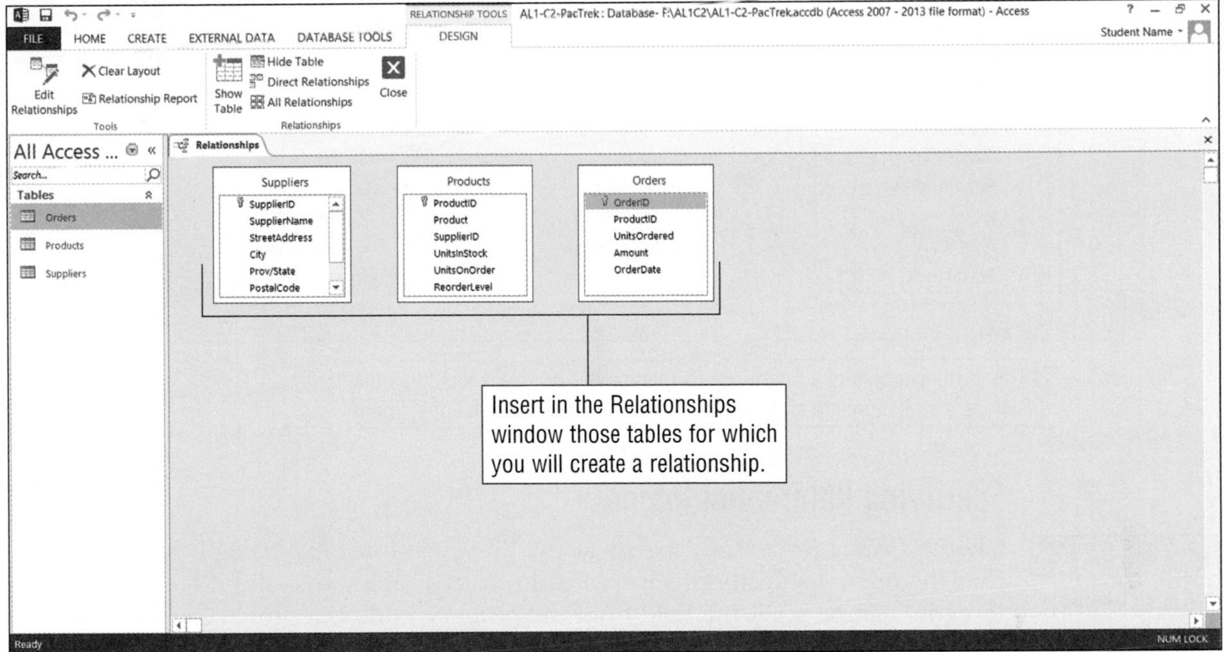
Insert in the Relationships window those tables for which you will create a relationship.

Figure 2.6 Edit Relationships Dialog Box

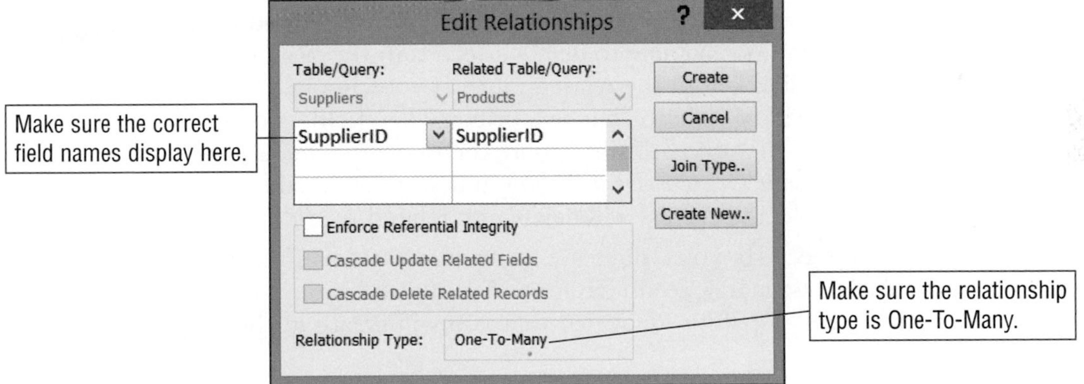
Make sure the correct field names display here.
Make sure the relationship type is One-To-Many.

In Figure 2.7, the *Suppliers* field list box displays with a black line attached along with the number *1* (signifying the "one" side of the relationship). The black line is connected to the *Products* field list box along with the infinity symbol, ∞ (signifying the "many" side of the relationship). The black line, called the ***join line***, is thick at both ends if the *Enforce Referential Integrity* option is chosen. If this option is not chosen, the line is thin at both ends. Click the Save button on the Quick Access toolbar to save the relationship. Close the Relationships window by clicking the Close button located in the upper right corner of the window.

Figure 2.7 One-to-Many Relationship

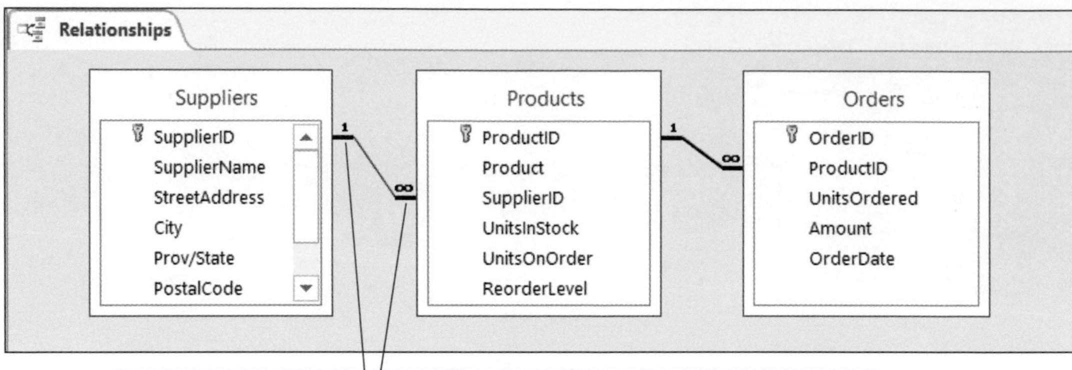

This is an example of a one-to-many relationship, where 1 identifies the "one" side of the relationship and the infinity symbol (∞) identifies the "many" side.

Specifying Referential Integrity

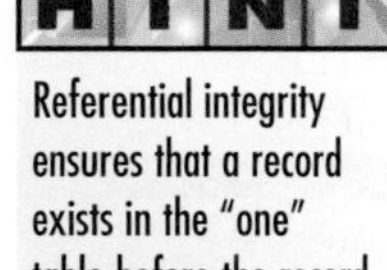

Referential integrity ensures that a record exists in the "one" table before the record can be entered in the "many" table.

Choose *Enforce Referential Integrity* at the Edit Relationships dialog box to ensure that the relationships between records in related tables are valid. Referential integrity can be set if the field from the primary table is a primary key and the related fields have the same data type. When referential integrity is established, a value for the primary key must first be entered in the primary table before it can be entered in the related table.

If you select only *Enforce Referential Integrity* and the related table contains a record, you will not be able to change a primary key field value in the primary table. You will not be able to delete a record in the primary table if its key value equals a foreign key in the related table. If you choose *Cascade Update Related Fields*, you will be able to change a primary key field value in the primary table and Access will automatically update the matching value in the related table. Choose *Cascade Delete Related Records* and you will be able to delete a record in the primary table and Access will delete any related records in the related table.

In Project 1b, you will create a one-to-many relationship between tables in the AL1-C2-PacTrek.accdb database. Figure 2.8 displays the Relationships window with the relationships identified that you will create in the project.

Figure 2.8 Relationships in the AL1-C2-PacTrek Database

A one-to-many relationship with referential integrity and cascade updated and deleted records all selected.

A one-to-many relationship with referential integrity selected. (Notice the join line is thick in the middle, indicating that cascade updated and cascade deleted records are not selected.)

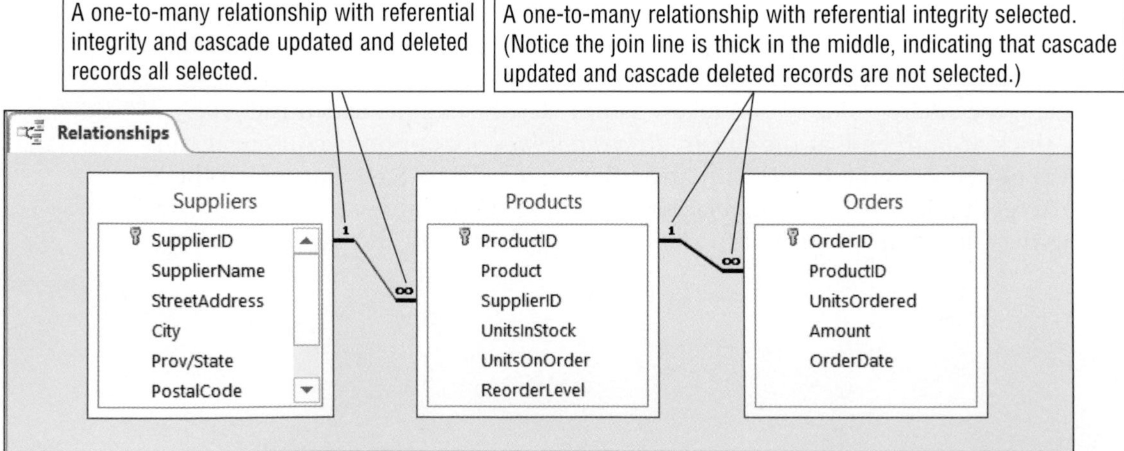

Printing Relationships

You can print a report displaying the relationships between tables. To do this, display the Relationships window and then click the Relationship Report button in the Tools group. This displays the relationships report in Print Preview. Click the Print button in the Print group on the PRINT PREVIEW tab and then click OK at the Print dialog box. After printing the relationships report, click the Close button to close the relationships report.

Quick Steps

Print a Relationship

1. Click DATABASE TOOLS tab.
2. Click Relationships button.
3. Click Relationships Report button.
4. Click Print button.
5. Click OK.
6. Click Close button.

Relationship Report

Project 1b **Creating Relationships between Tables** **Part 2 of 4**

1. With **AL1-C2-PacTrek.accdb** open, click the DATABASE TOOLS tab and then click the Relationships button in the Relationships group. (The Show Table dialog box should display in the Relationships window. If it does not display, click the Show Table button in the Relationships group on the RELATIONSHIP TOOLS DESIGN tab.)

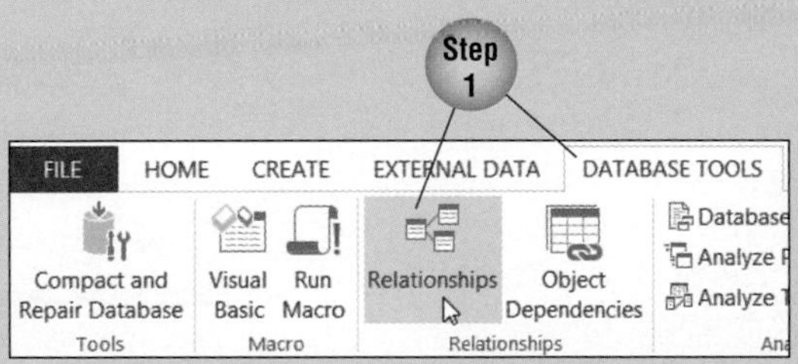

2. At the Show Table dialog box with the Tables tab selected, add the Suppliers, Products, and Orders tables to the Relationships window by completing the following steps:
   a. Click *Suppliers* in the list box and then click the Add button.
   b. Click *Products* in the list box and then click the Add button.
   c. Click *Orders* in the list box and then click the Add button.
3. Click the Close button to close the Show Table dialog box.

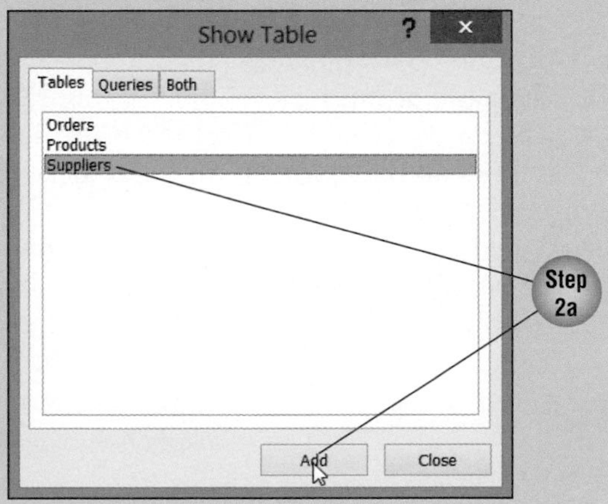

4. At the Relationships window, drag the *SupplierID* field from the *Suppliers* field list box to the *Products* field list box by completing the following steps:
   a. Position the arrow pointer on the *SupplierID* field that displays in the *Suppliers* field list box.
   b. Hold down the left mouse button, drag the arrow pointer (with a field icon attached) to the *SupplierID* field in the *Products* field list box, and then release the mouse button. (This causes the Edit Relationships dialog box to display.)

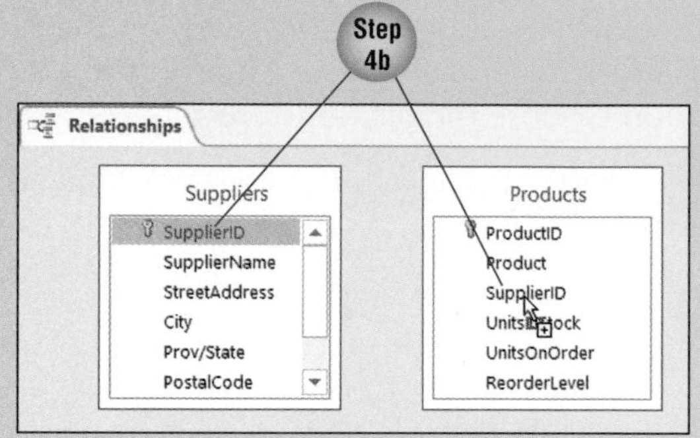

5. At the Edit Relationships dialog box, make sure *SupplierID* displays in the *Table/Query* and *Related Table/Query* list boxes and the relationship type at the bottom of the dialog box displays as *One-To-Many*.
6. Enforce the referential integrity of the relationship by completing the following steps:
   a. Click the *Enforce Referential Integrity* check box to insert a check mark. (This makes the other two options available.)
   b. Click the *Cascade Update Related Fields* check box to insert a check mark.
   c. Click the *Cascade Delete Related Records* check box to insert a check mark.

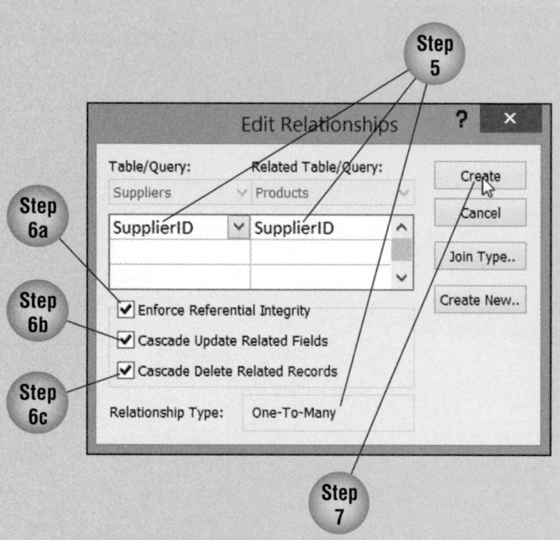

7. Click the Create button. (This causes the Edit Relationships dialog box to close and the Relationships window to display, showing a black line (thick on the ends and thin in the middle) connecting the *SupplierID* field in the *Suppliers* field list box to the *SupplierID* field in the *Products* field list box. A *1* appears at the Suppliers table side and an infinity symbol (∞) appears at the Products table side of the black line.)
8. Click the Save button on the Quick Access toolbar to save the relationship.
9. Create a one-to-many relationship between the Products table and the Orders table with the *ProductID* field by completing the following steps:
   a. Position the arrow pointer on the *ProductID* field that displays in the *Products* field list box.
   b. Hold down the left mouse button, drag the arrow pointer (with a field icon attached) to the *ProductID* field in the *Orders* field list box, and then release the mouse button.

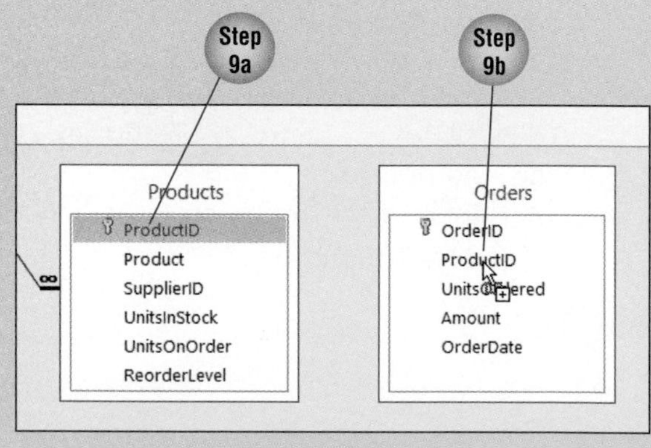

c. At the Edit Relationships dialog box, make sure *ProductID* displays in the *Table/Query* and *Related Table/Query* list boxes and the relationship type displays as *One-To-Many*.
d. Click the *Enforce Referential Integrity* check box. (Do not insert check marks in the other two check boxes.)
e. Click the Create button.

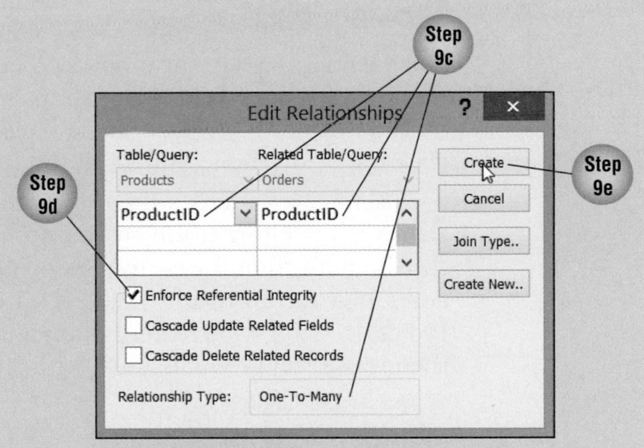

10. Click the Save button on the Quick Access toolbar to save the relationships.
11. Print the relationships by completing the following steps:
    a. At the Relationships window, click the Relationship Report button in the Tools group. This displays the relationships report in Print Preview. (If a security notice displays, click the Open button.)

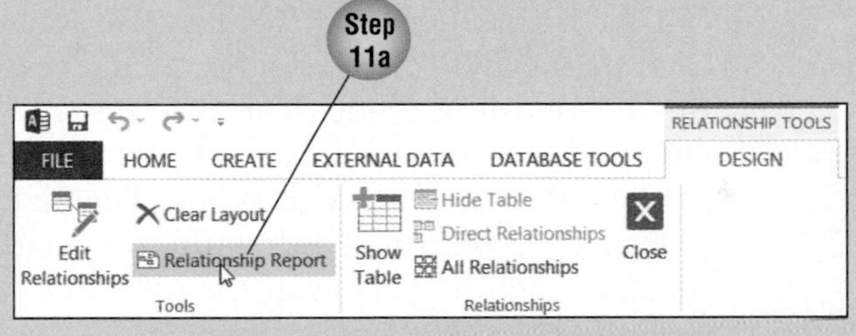

    b. Click the Print button in the Print group at the left side of the PRINT PREVIEW tab.

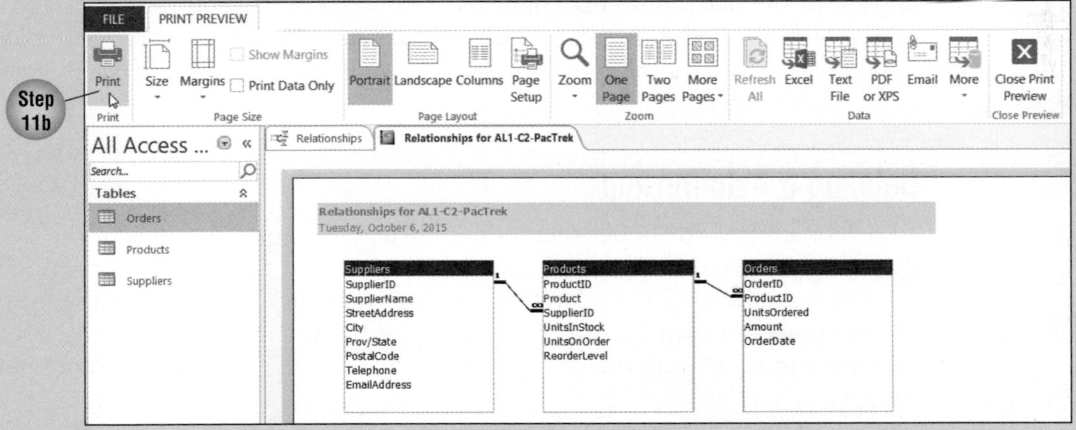

    c. Click OK at the Print dialog box.
    d. Close the report by clicking the Close button that displays in the upper right corner of the work area.
    e. At the message asking if you want to save changes to the design of the report, click No.
12. Close the Relationships window by clicking the Close button that displays in the upper right corner of the work area.

Showing Tables

Show Table

Once a relationship is established between tables and the Relationships window is closed, clicking the Relationships button causes the Relationships window to display without the Show Table dialog box. To display the Show Table dialog box, click the Show Table button in the Relationships group.

Pacific Trek offers a discount on one product each week. You want to keep track of this information so you decide to create a Discounts table that includes the discount item for each week of the first three months of the year. (You will add a new record to this field each week when the discount item is chosen.) In Project 1c, you will create the Discounts table shown in Figure 2.9 on page 59 and then relate the Products table with the Discounts table using the *ProductID* field.

Editing a Relationship

Quick Steps

Edit a Relationship

1. Click DATABASE TOOLS tab.
2. Click Relationships button.
3. Click Edit Relationships button.
4. Make desired changes at Edit Relationships dialog box.
5. Click OK.

Edit Relationships

You can edit a relationship between tables or delete the relationship altogether. To edit a relationship, open the database containing the tables with the relationship, click the DATABASE TOOLS tab, and then click the Relationships button in the Relationships group. This displays the Relationships window with the related tables. Click the Edit Relationships button located in the Tools group to display the Edit Relationships dialog box. The dialog box will be similar to the one shown in Figure 2.6 on page 51. Identify the relationship you want to edit by clicking the down-pointing arrow at the right side of the *Table/Query* option box and then clicking the table name containing the "one" field. Click the down-pointing arrow at the right side of the *Related Table/Query* option box and then click the table name containing the "many" field.

To edit a specific relationship, position the arrow pointer on the middle portion of the black line that connects the related tables and then click the right mouse button. At the shortcut menu that displays, click the *Edit Relationship* option. This displays the Edit Relationships dialog box with the specific related field in both list boxes.

Deleting a Relationship

Quick Steps

Delete a Relationship

1. Click DATABASE TOOLS tab.
2. Click Relationships button.
3. Right-click black line connecting related tables.
4. Click *Delete*.
5. Click Yes.

To delete a relationship between tables, display the related tables in the Relationships window. Position the arrow pointer on the middle portion of the black line connecting the related tables and then click the right mouse button. At the shortcut menu that displays, click *Delete*. At the message asking if you are sure you want to permanently delete the selected relationship from your database, click Yes.

Project 1c Creating a Table and Creating and Editing Relationships Part 3 of 4

1. With **AL1-C2-PacTrek.accdb** open, create the Discounts table shown in Figure 2.9 on page 59 by completing the following steps:
   a. Click the CREATE tab.
   b. Click the Table button in the Tables group.
   c. Click the Short Text button in the Add & Delete group. (This creates and then selects the *Field1* heading that displays to the right of the *ID* column.)

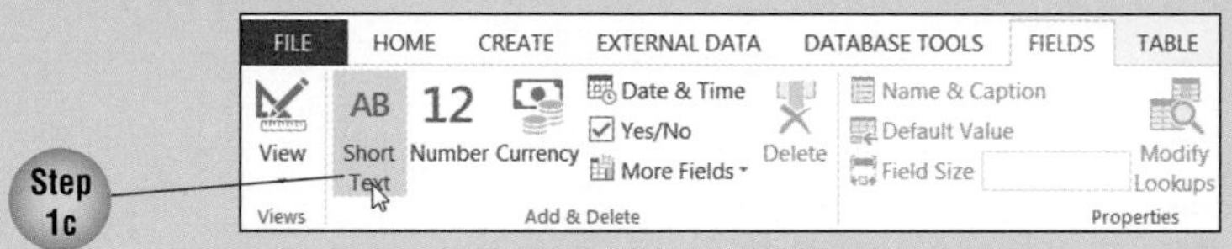

   d. Type **ProductID** and then press Enter.
   e. Click the *Short Text* option at the drop-down list and then type **Discount**.
   f. Click the *ID* heading (the first column), click the down-pointing arrow at the right side of the *Data Type* option box in the Formatting group, and then click *Date/Time* at the drop-down list.

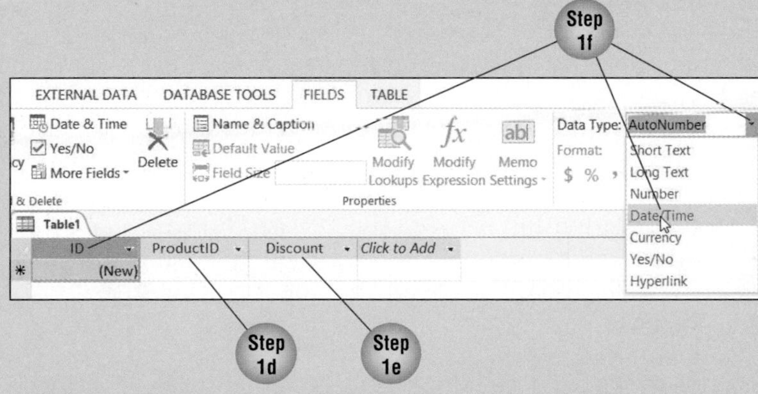

   g. Right-click the *ID* heading, click *Rename Field* at the shortcut menu, type **Week**, and then press Enter.
   h. Type the 13 records in the Discounts table shown in Figure 2.9 on page 59.
2. After typing the records, save the table by completing the following steps:
   a. Click the Save button on the Quick Access toolbar.
   b. At the Save As dialog box, type **Discounts** and then press Enter.
3. Close the Discounts table.
4. Create a relationship from the Products table to the Discounts table by completing the following steps:
   a. Click the DATABASE TOOLS tab and then click the Relationships button in the Relationships group.
   b. Display the Show Table dialog box by clicking the Show Table button in the Relationships group.
   c. At the Show Table dialog box, double-click the Discounts table.
   d. Click the Close button to close the Show Table dialog box.

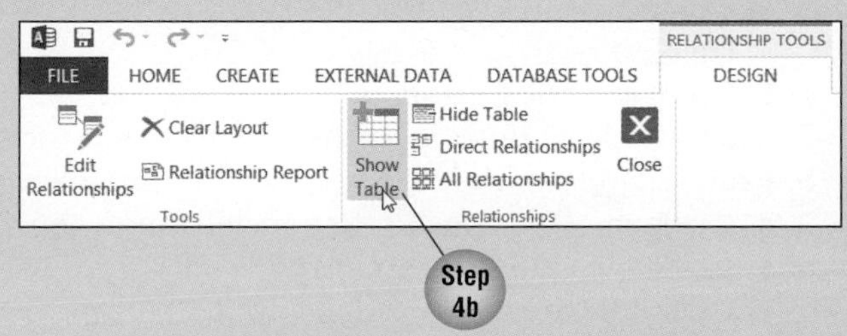

5. At the Relationships window, create a one-to-many relationship between the Products table and the Discounts table with the *ProductID* field by completing the following steps:
   a. Drag the *ProductID* field from the *Products* field list box to the *ProductID* field in the *Discounts* field list box.

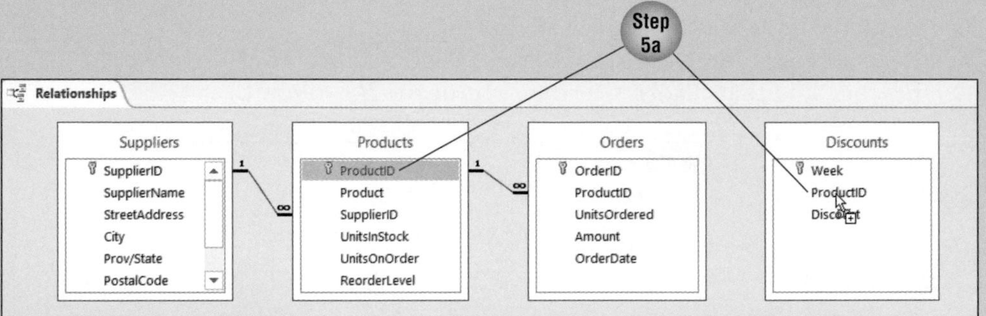

   b. At the Edit Relationships dialog box, make sure *ProductID* displays in the *Table/Query* and *Related Table/Query* list boxes and the relationship type at the bottom of the dialog box displays as *One-To-Many*.
   c. Click the *Enforce Referential Integrity* check box.
   d. Click the *Cascade Update Related Fields* check box.
   e. Click the *Cascade Delete Related Records* check box.
   f. Click the Create button. (At the Relationships window, notice the join line that displays between the Products table and the Discounts table. If a message occurs telling you that the relationship cannot be created, click the Cancel button. Open the Discounts table, check to make sure the product numbers are entered correctly in the *ProductID* field, and then close the Discounts table. Try again to create the relationship.)
6. Edit the one-to-many relationship between the *ProductID* field in the Products table and the Orders table and specify that you want to cascade updated and related fields and cascade and delete related records by completing the following steps:
   a. Click the Edit Relationships button located in the Tools group on the RELATIONSHIP TOOLS DESIGN tab.
   b. At the Edit Relationships dialog box, click the down-pointing arrow at the right side of the *Table/Query* option box and then click *Products* at the drop-down list.
   c. Click the down-pointing arrow at the right side of the *Related Table/Query* option box and then click *Orders* at the drop-down list.
   d. Click the *Cascade Update Related Fields* check box.
   e. Click the *Cascade Delete Related Records* check box.
   f. Click the OK button.

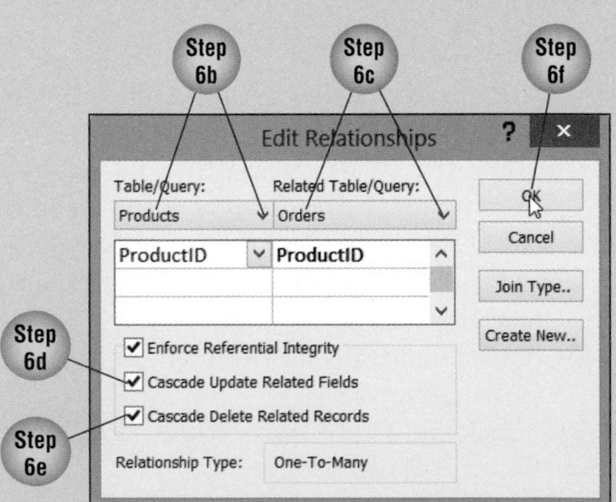

7. Click the Save button on the Quick Access toolbar to save the relationship.
8. Print the relationships by completing the following steps:
   a. Click the Relationship Report button in the Tools group.
   b. Click the Print button in the Print group.
   c. Click OK at the Print dialog box.

d. Close the report by clicking the Close button that displays in the upper right corner of the work area.
e. At the message asking if you want to save changes to the design of the report, click No.
9. Delete the relationship between the Products table and the Discounts table by completing the following steps:
a. Position the arrow pointer on the thin portion of the black line connecting the *ProductID* field in the *Products* field list box with the *ProductID* field in the *Discounts* field list box and then click the right mouse button.
b. Click the *Delete* option at the shortcut menu.

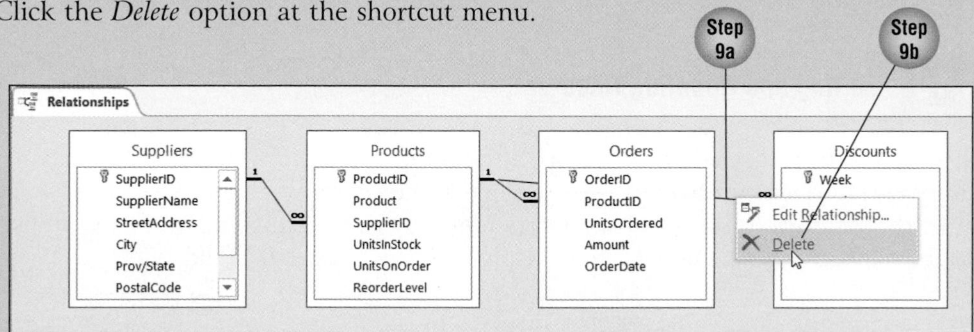

c. At the message asking if you are sure you want to permanently delete the selected relationship from your database, click Yes.
10. Click the Save button on the Quick Access toolbar to save the relationship.
11. Print the relationships by completing the following steps:
a. Click the RELATIONSHIP TOOLS DESIGN tab and then click the Relationship Report button in the Tools group.
b. Click the Print button in the Print group.
c. Click OK at the Print dialog box.
d. Close the report by clicking the Close button that displays in the upper right corner of the work area.
e. At the message asking if you want to save changes to the design of the report, click No.
12. Close the Relationships window by clicking the Close button that displays in the upper right corner of the work area.

Figure 2.9 Discounts Table

Discounts

Week	ProductID	Discount	Click to Add
1/5/2015	155-45	20%	
1/12/2015	652-2	15%	
1/19/2015	443-1A	20%	
1/26/2015	202-CW	15%	
2/2/2015	804-60	10%	
2/9/2015	652-2	15%	
2/16/2015	101-S1B	5%	
2/23/2015	560-TL	20%	
3/2/2015	652-2	20%	
3/9/2015	602-XX	15%	
3/16/2015	100-05	10%	
3/23/2015	652-2	15%	
3/30/2015	202-CW	15%	

Inserting and Deleting Records in Related Tables

In the relationship established in Project 1b, a record must first be added to the Suppliers table before a related record can be added to the Products table. This is because you chose the *Enforce Referential Integrity* option at the Edit Relationships dialog box. Because you chose the two options *Cascade Update Related Fields* and *Cascade Delete Related Records*, records in the Suppliers table (the primary table) can be updated or deleted and related records in the Products table (the related table) are automatically updated or deleted.

Project 1d — Editing and Updating Records — Part 4 of 4

1. With **AL1-C2-PacTrek.accdb** open, open the Suppliers table.
2. Change two supplier numbers in the Suppliers table (Access will automatically change them in the Products table and the Orders table) by completing the following steps:
   a. Double-click the field value *15* that displays in the *SupplierID* field.
   b. Type 33.
   c. Double-click the field value *42* that displays in the *SupplierID* field.
   d. Type 51.
   e. Click the Save button on the Quick Access toolbar.
   f. Close the Suppliers table.
   g. Open the Products table and notice that supplier number *15* changed to *33* and supplier number *42* changed to *51*.
   h. Close the Products table.

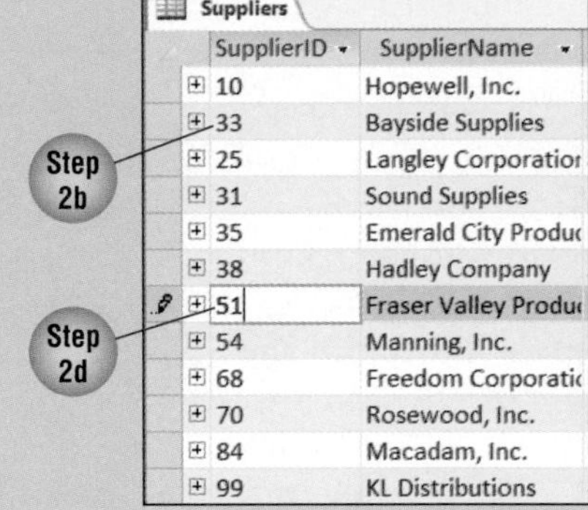

SupplierID	SupplierName
10	Hopewell, Inc.
33	Bayside Supplies
25	Langley Corporatio
31	Sound Supplies
35	Emerald City Produ
38	Hadley Company
51	Fraser Valley Produ
54	Manning, Inc.
68	Freedom Corporati
70	Rosewood, Inc.
84	Macadam, Inc.
99	KL Distributions

3. Open the Suppliers table and then add the following records:

   SupplierID: 16
   SupplierName: **Olympic Suppliers**
   StreetAddress: **1773 50th Avenue**
   City: **Seattle**
   Prov/State: **WA**
   PostalCode: **98101**
   Telephone: **(206) 555-9488**
   EmailAddress: **olysuppliers@emcp.net**

   SupplierID: 28
   SupplierName: **Gorman Company**
   StreetAddress: **543 26th Street**
   City: **Vancouver**
   Prov/State: **BC**
   PostalCode: **V5K 3C5**
   Telephone: **(778) 555-4550**
   EmailAddress: **gormanco@emcp.net**

Suppliers

SupplierID	SupplierName	StreetAddress	City	Prov/State	PostalCode	Telephone	EmailAddress	Click to Add
10	Hopewell, Inc.	5600 Carver Road	Port Moody	BC	V3H 1A4	(604) 555-3843	hopewell@emcp.net	
25	Langley Corporatio	805 First Avenue	Burnaby	BC	V3J 1C9	(604) 555-1200	langley@emcp.net	
31	Sound Supplies	2104 Union Street	Seattle	WA	98105	(206) 555-4855	ssupplies@emcp.net	
33	Bayside Supplies	6705 North Street	Bellingham	WA	98432	(360) 555-6005	bside@emcp.net	
35	Emerald City Produ	1059 Pike Street	Seattle	WA	98102	(206) 555-7728	ecproducts@emcp.ne	
38	Hadley Company	5845 Jefferson Stre	Seattle	WA	98107	(206) 555-8003	hcompany@emcp.net	
51	Fraser Valley Produ	3894 Old Yale Roa	Abbotsford	BC	V2S 1A9	(604) 555-1455	fvproducts@emcp.ne	
54	Manning, Inc.	1039 South 22nd	Vancouver	BC	V5K 1R1	(604) 555-0087	manning@emcp.net	
68	Freedom Corporati	14 Fourth Avenue	Vancouver	BC	V5K 2C7	(604) 555-2155	freedom@emcp.net	
70	Rosewood, Inc.	998 North 42nd Str	Vancouver	BC	V5K 2N8	(778) 555-6643	rosewood@emcp.net	
84	Macadam, Inc.	675 Third Street	Vancouver	BC	V5K 2R9	(604) 555-5522	macadam@emcp.net	
99	KL Distributions	402 Yukon Drive	Bellingham	WA	98435	(360) 555-3711	kldist@emcp.net	
16	Olympic Suppliers	1773 50th Avenue	Seattle	WA	98101	(206) 555-9488	olysuppliers@emcp.n	
28	Gorman Company	543 26th Street	Vancouver	BC	V5K 3C5	(778) 555-4550	gormanco@emcp.net	

Step 3

4. Delete the record for supplier number 38 (Hadley Company). At the message telling you that relationships that specify cascading deletes are about to cause records in this table and related tables to be deleted, click Yes.
5. Display the table in Print Preview, change to landscape orientation, and then print the table.
6. Close the Suppliers table.
7. Open the Products table and then add the following records to the table:

ProductID: 701-BK	*ProductID:* 703-SP
Product: Basic first aid kit	*Product:* Medical survival pack
SupplierID: 33	*SupplierID:* 33
UnitsInStock: 8	*UnitsInStock:* 8
UnitsOnOrder: 0	*UnitsOnOrder:* 0
ReorderLevel: 5	*ReorderLevel:* 5
ProductID: 185-10	*ProductID:* 185-50
Product: Trail water filter	*Product:* Trail filter replacement cartridge
SupplierID: 51	*SupplierID:* 51
UnitsInStock: 4	*UnitsInStock:* 14
UnitsOnOrder: 10	*UnitsOnOrder:* 0
ReorderLevel: 10	*ReorderLevel:* 10

8. Display the Products table in Print Preview, change to landscape orientation, change the top and bottom margins to 0.4 inch and then print the table. (The table will print on two pages.)
9. Close the Products table.
10. Open the Orders table and then add the following record:
    OrderID: 1033
    OrderDate: 2/15/2015
    ProductID: 185-10
    UnitsOrdered: 10
    Amount: $310.90
11. Print and then close the Orders table.
12. Close **AL1-C2-PacTrek.accdb**.

Project 2 Create Relationships and Display Subdatasheets in a Database — 2 Parts

You will open a company database and then create one-to-many relationships between tables, as well as a one-to-one relationship. You will also display and edit subdatasheets.

Creating One-to-One Relationships

You can create a ***one-to-one relationship*** between tables in which each record in the first table matches only one record in the second table and one record in the second table matches only one record in the first table. A one-to-one relationship is not as common as a one-to-many relationship, since the type of information used to create the relationship can be stored in one table. A one-to-one relationship is generally used when you want to break a large table with many fields into two smaller tables.

The Relationships window displays any relationship you have defined between tables.

In Project 2a, you will create a one-to-one relationship between the Employees table and the Benefits table. Each record in the Employees table and each record in the Benefits table pertains to one employee. These two tables could be merged into one but the data in each table is easier to manage when separated. Figure 2.10 shows the relationships you will define between the tables in AL1-C2-Griffin.accdb. The Benefits table and the Departments table have been moved down so you can more easily see the relationships.

Figure 2.10 AL1-C2-Griffin.accdb Table Relationships

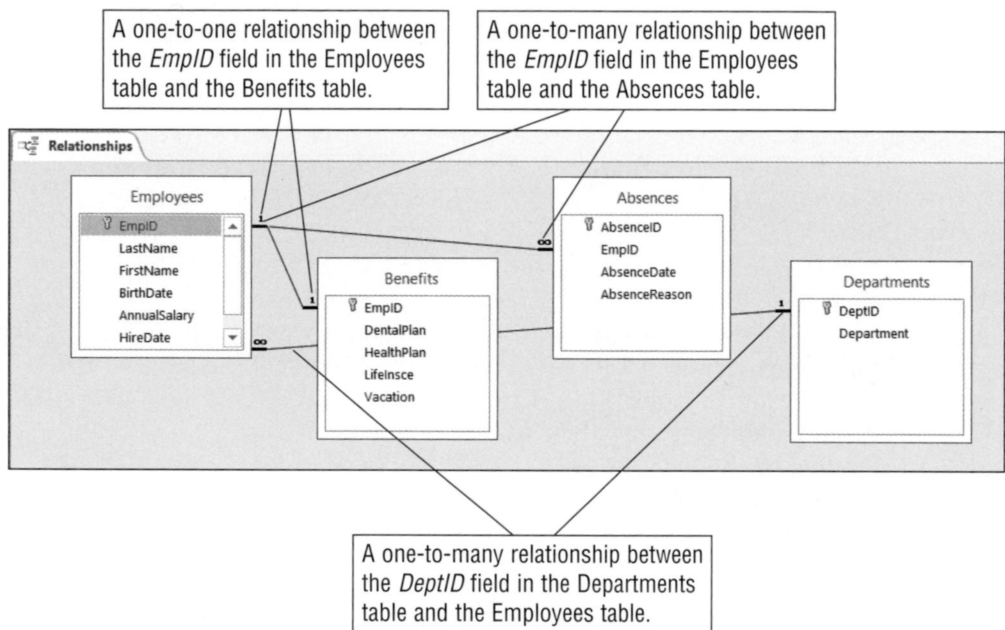

Project 2a Creating One-to-Many and One-to-One Relationships — Part 1 of 2

1. Open **AL1-C2-Griffin.accdb** and enable the contents.
2. Click the DATABASE TOOLS tab.
3. Click the Relationships button in the Relationships group.
4. At the Show Table dialog box with the Tables tab selected, add all of the tables to the Relationships window by completing the following steps:
   a. Double-click *Employees* in the list box. (This inserts the table in the Relationships window.)
   b. Double-click *Benefits* in the list box.
   c. Double-click *Absences* in the list box.
   d. Double-click *Departments* in the list box.
   e. Click the Close button to close the Show Table dialog box.
5. At the Relationships window, create a one-to-many relationship with the *EmpID* field in the Employees table as the "one" and the *EmpID* field in the Absences table the "many" by completing the following steps:
   a. Position the arrow pointer on the *EmpID* field that displays in the *Employees* field list box.

b. Hold down the left mouse button, drag the arrow pointer (with a field icon attached) to the *EmpID* field in the *Absences* field list box, and then release the mouse button. (This causes the Edit Relationships dialog box to display.)

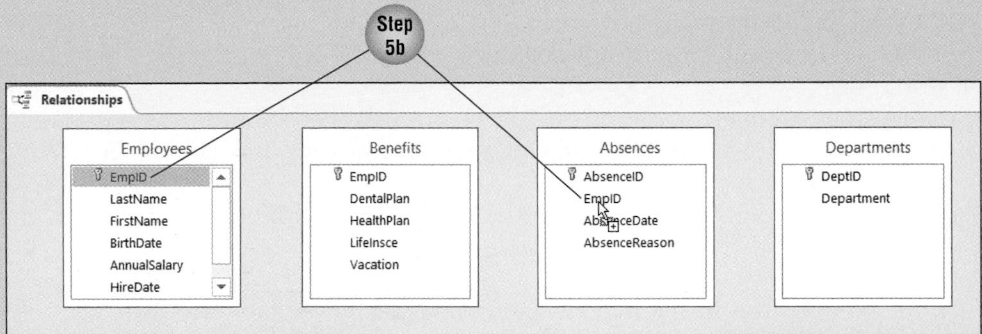

c. At the Edit Relationships dialog box, make sure *EmpID* displays in the *Table/Query* and *Related Table/Query* list boxes and the relationship type at the bottom of the dialog box displays as *One-To-Many*.
d. Click the *Enforce Referential Integrity* check box to insert a check mark.
e. Click the *Cascade Update Related Fields* check box to insert a check mark.
f. Click the *Cascade Delete Related Records* check box to insert a check mark.
g. Click the Create button. (A *1* appears at the *Employees* field list box side and an infinity symbol (∞) appears at the *Absences* field list box side of the black line.)

6. Complete steps similar to those in Step 5 to create a one-to-many relationship with the *DeptID* field in the Departments table the "one" and the *DeptID* field in the Employees table the "many." (You may need to scroll down the Employees field list box to display the *DeptID* field.)
7. Create a one-to-one relationship with the *EmpID* field in the Employees table and the *EmpID* field in the Benefits table by completing the following steps:
   a. Position the arrow pointer on the *EmpID* field in the *Employees* field list box.
   b. Hold down the left mouse button, drag the arrow pointer to the *EmpID* field in the *Benefits* field list box, and then release the mouse button. (This displays the Edit Relationships dialog box; notice at the bottom of the dialog box that the relationship type displays as *One-To-One*.)
   c. Click the *Enforce Referential Integrity* check box to insert a check mark.
   d. Click the *Cascade Update Related Fields* check box.
   e. Click the *Cascade Delete Related Records* check box.
   f. Click the Create button. (Notice that a *1* appears at the side of the *Employees* field list box and at the side of the *Benefits* field list box, indicating a one-to-one relationship.)

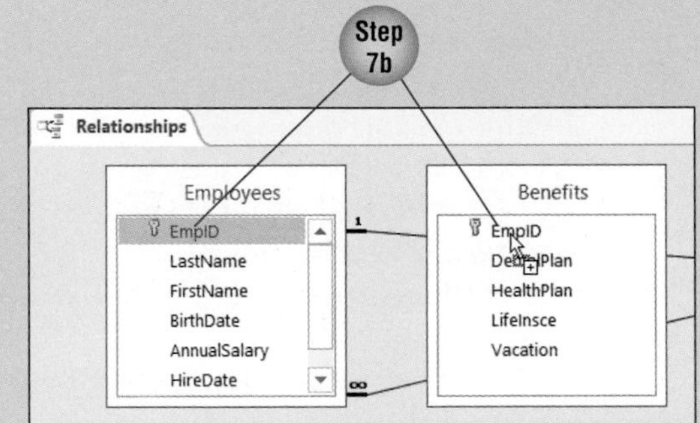

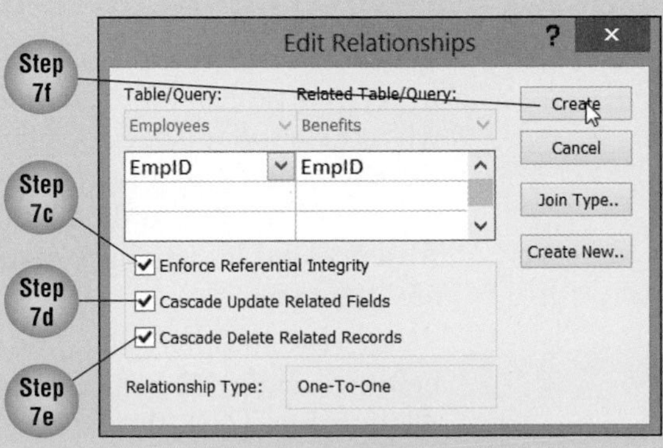

8. Click the Save button on the Quick Access toolbar to save the relationships.
9. Print the relationships by completing the following steps:
   a. Click the Relationship Report button in the Tools group.
   b. Click the Print button in the Print group.
   c. Click OK at the Print dialog box.
   d. Close the report by clicking the Close button that displays in the upper right corner of the work area.
   e. At the message asking if you want to save changes to the design of the report, click No.
10. Close the Relationships window by clicking the Close button that displays in the upper right corner of the work area.
11. Add a record to and delete a record from the Employees and Benefits tables by completing the following steps:
   a. Open the Employees table.
   b. Click the New button in the Records group on the HOME tab and then type the following data in the specified field:
      EmpID: **1096**
      LastName: **Schwartz**
      FirstName: **Bryan**
      BirthDate: **5/21/1983**
      DeptID: **IT**
      AnnualSalary: **$45,000.00**
      HireDate: **1/15/2010**
   c. Delete the record for Trevor Sargent (employee number 1005). At the message telling you that relationships that specify cascading deletes are about to cause records in this table and related tables to be deleted, click Yes.
   d. Print and then close the Employees table.
12. Open the Benefits table and notice that the record for Trevor Sargent is deleted but the new employee record you entered in the Employees table is not reflected in the Benefits table. Add a new record for Bryan Schwartz with the following information:
      EmpID: **1096**
      Dental Plan: (Press spacebar to remove check mark.)
      Health Plan: (Leave check mark.)
      Life Insurance: **$100,000.00**
      Vacation: **2 weeks**
13. Print and then close the Benefits table.

Displaying Related Records in Subdatasheets

When a relationship is established between tables, you can view and edit records in related tables with a ***subdatasheet***. Figure 2.11 displays the Employees table with the subdatasheet displayed for employee Kate Navarro. The subdatasheet displays the fields in the Benefits table related to Kate Navarro. Use this sub-datasheet to view and edit information in both the Employees table and Absences table. Changes made to fields in a subdatasheet affect the table and any related table.

Access automatically inserts a plus symbol (referred to as an ***expand indicator***) before each record in a table that is joined to another table by a one-to-many relationship. Click the expand indicator and if the table is related to only one other table, a subdatasheet containing fields from the related table displays below the record, as shown in Figure 2.11. To remove the subdatasheet, click the minus sign (referred to as a ***collapse indicator***) preceding the record. (The plus symbol turns into the minus symbol when a subdatasheet displays.)

If a table has more than one relationship defined, clicking the expand indicator will display the Insert Subdatasheet dialog box, as shown in Figure 2.12. At this dialog box, click the desired table in the Tables list box and then click OK. You can also display the Insert Subdatasheet dialog box by clicking the More button in the Records group on the HOME tab, pointing to *Subdatasheet*, and then clicking *Subdatasheet*. Display subdatasheets for all records by clicking the More button, pointing to *Subdatasheet*, and then clicking *Expand All*. Remove all subdatasheets by clicking the More button, pointing to *Subdatasheet*, and then clicking *Collapse All*.

If a table is related to two or more tables, specify the desired subdatasheet at the Insert Subdatasheet dialog box. If you decide to display a different subdatasheet, remove the subdatasheet first, before selecting the next subdatasheet. Do this by clicking the More button, pointing to *Subdatasheet*, and then clicking *Remove*.

Quick Steps

Display a Subdatasheet

1. Open table.
2. Click expand indicator at left side of desired record.
3. Click desired table at Insert Subdatasheet dialog box.
4. Click OK.

Figure 2.11 Table with Subdatasheet Displayed

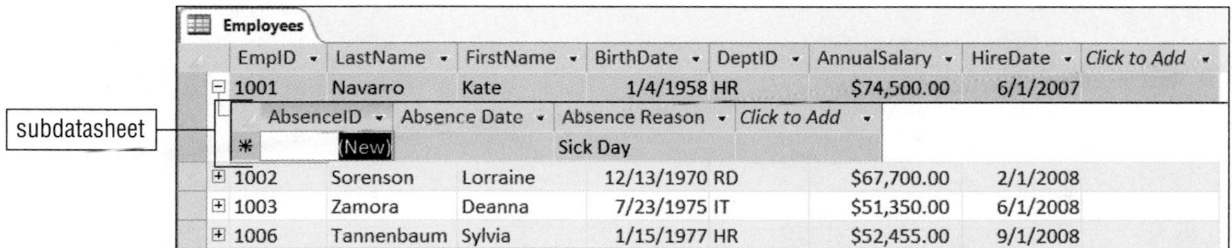

Figure 2.12 Insert Subdatasheet Dialog Box

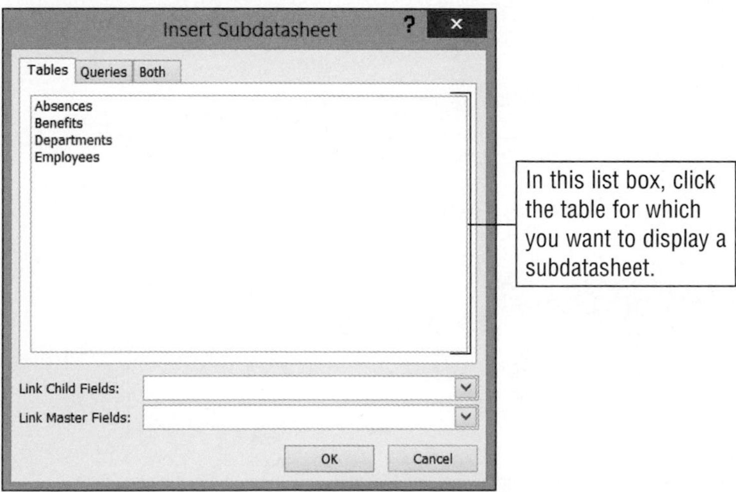

Project 2b Viewing and Editing a Subdatasheet Part 2 of 2

1. With the **AL1-C2-Griffin.accdb** database open, open the Employees table.
2. Display a subdatasheet by clicking the expand indicator (plus symbol) that displays at the left side of the first row (the row for Kate Navarro).

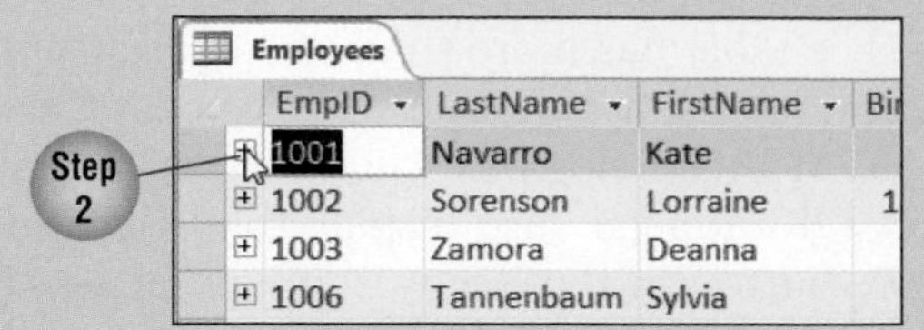

3. Remove the subdatasheet by clicking the collapse indicator (minus sign) that displays at the left side of the record for Kate Navarro.
4. Display subdatasheets for all of the records by clicking the More button in the Records group, pointing to *Subdatasheet*, and then clicking *Expand All*.

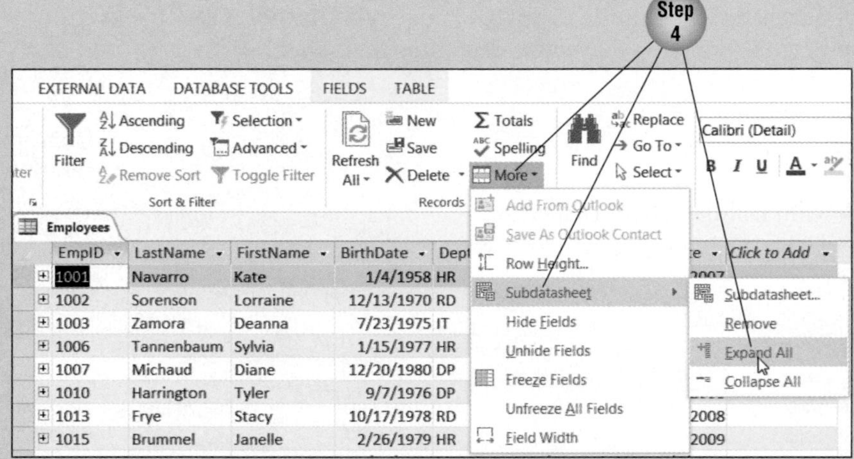

5. Remove the display of all subdatasheets by clicking the More button, pointing to *Subdatasheet*, and then clicking *Collapse All*.
6. Remove the connection between the Employees table and Absences table by clicking the More button, pointing to *Subdatasheet*, and then clicking *Remove*. (Notice that the expand indicators [plus symbols] no longer display before each record.)

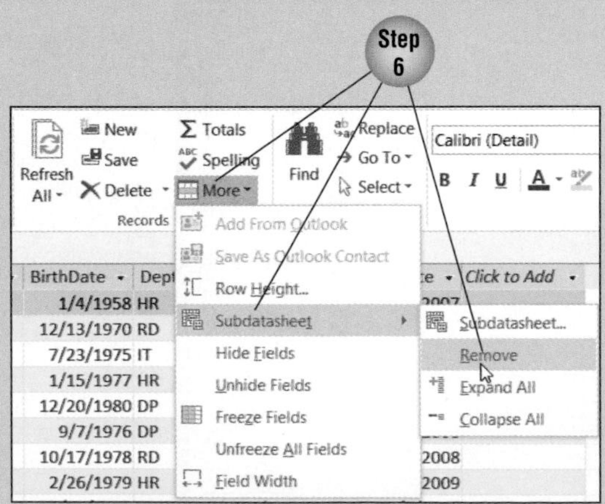

7. Suppose that the employee, Diane Michaud, has moved to a different department and has had an increase in salary. Display the Benefits subdatasheet and make changes to fields in the Employees table and Benefits table by completing the following steps:
   a. Click the More button in the Records group, point to *Subdatasheet*, and then click *Subdatasheet* at the side menu.
   b. At the Insert Subdatasheet dialog box, click *Benefits* in the list box and then click OK.
   c. Change the department ID for the record for *Diane Michaud* from *DP* to *A*.
   d. Change the salary from *$56,250.00* to *$57,500.00*.
   e. Click the expand indicator (plus symbol) that displays at the left side of the record for Diane Michaud.
   f. Insert a check mark in the *Dental Plan* check box and change the vacation from 3 weeks to 4 weeks.
   g. Click the collapse indicator (minus symbol) that displays at the left side of the record for Diane Michaud.

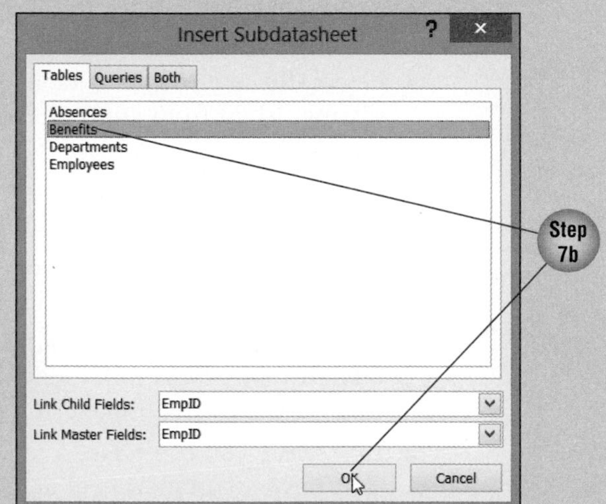

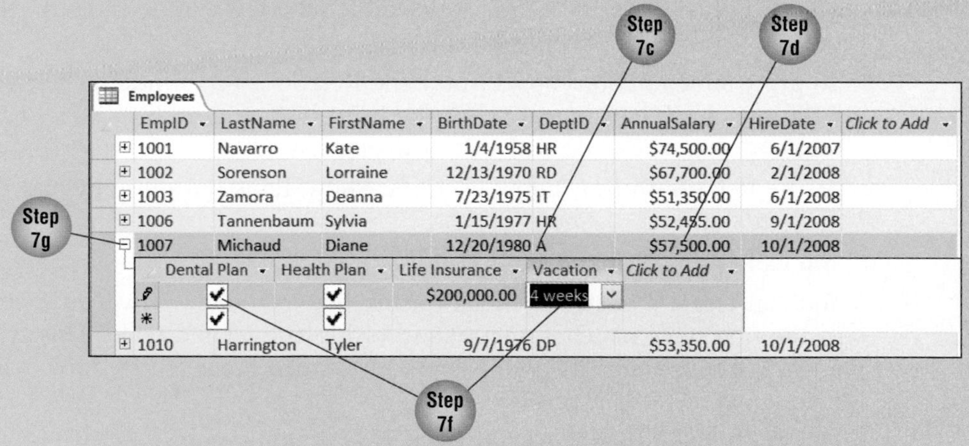

8. Click the Save button on the Quick Access toolbar.
9. Print and then close the Employees table.
10. Open, print, and then close the Benefits table.
11. Close the **AL1-C2-Griffin.accdb** database.

Chapter Summary

- Access is a relational database software program in which you can create tables that are related or connected.
- When planning a table, take time to determine how to break down the required data and what relationships need to be defined to eliminate data redundancies.
- Generally, one field in a table must be unique so that one record can be distinguished from another. A field with a unique value is considered a primary key field.
- A table can have only one primary key field and it is the field by which the table is sorted whenever it is opened.
- In a field defined as a primary key field, duplicate values are not allowed. Access also expects a value in each record in the primary key field.
- Typically, a primary key field in one table becomes the foreign key field in a related table. Data in a foreign key field must match data in the primary key field of the related tables.
- In Access, you can relate a table to another by performing a join. When tables that have a common field are joined, you can extract data from both tables as if they were one large table.
- You can create a one-to-many relationship between tables. In this relationship, a record must be added to the "one" table before it can be added to the "many" table.
- To print table relationships, display the Relationships window, click the Relationship Report button, click the Print button on the PRINT PREVIEW tab, and then click OK at the Print dialog box.
- At the Relationships window, click the Show Table button to display the Show Table dialog box.
- You can edit or delete a relationship between tables.
- You can create a one-to-one relationship between tables in which each record in the first table matches only one record in the related table. This type of relationship is generally used when you want to break a large table with many fields into two smaller tables.
- When a relationship is established between tables, you can view and edit fields in related tables with a subdatasheet.
- To display a subdatasheet for a record, click the expand indicator (plus symbol) that displays to the left of the record. To display subdatasheets for all records, click the More button in the Records group on the HOME tab, point to *Subdatasheet*, and then click *Expand All*.
- Display the Insert Subdatasheet dialog box by clicking the More button in the Reports group on the HOME tab, pointing to *Subdatasheet*, and then clicking *Subdatasheet*.
- Turn off the display of a subdatasheet by clicking the collapse indicator (minus symbol) at the beginning of the record. To turn off the display of subdatasheets for all records, click the More button, point to *Subdatasheet*, and then click *Collapse All*.

Commands Review

FEATURE	RIBBON, GROUP	BUTTON	OPTION
Edit Relationships dialog box	RELATIONSHIP TOOLS DESIGN, Tools		
Insert Subdatasheet dialog box	HOME, Records		*Subdatasheet, Subdatasheet*
primary key	TABLE TOOLS DESIGN, Tools		
print relationships report	RELATIONSHIP TOOLS DESIGN, Tools		
Relationships window	DATABASE TOOLS, Relationships		
Show Table dialog box	RELATIONSHIP TOOLS DESIGN, Relationships		

Concepts Check

Test Your Knowledge

Completion: In the space provided at the right, indicate the correct term, symbol, or command.

1. In Access, one table can be related to another, which is generally referred to as performing this. ____________________
2. A database table can contain a foreign key field and this type of key field. ____________________
3. Open a table, click the View button on the HOME tab, and the table displays in this view. ____________________
4. In a one-to-many relationship, the table containing the "one" is referred to as this. ____________________
5. In a one-to-many relationship, the table containing the "many" is referred to as this. ____________________
6. In a one-to-many relationship, Access follows a set of rules that enforces consistency between related tables and is referred to as this. ____________________
7. In related tables, this symbol displays near the black line next to the field list box of the related table. ____________________
8. The black line that connects the field list boxes of related tables is referred to as this. ____________________

9. Establish this type of relationship between tables in which each record in the first table matches only one record in the second table and only one record in the second table matches each record in the first table. ________________

10. The plus symbol that displays at the beginning of a record in a related table is referred to as this. ________________

11. The minus symbol that displays at the beginning of a record in a related table with a subdatasheet displayed is referred to as this. ________________

12. Display subdatasheets for all records by clicking the More button, pointing to *Subdatasheet*, and then clicking this option. ________________

Skills Check Assess Your Performance

The database designer for Copper State Insurance has created the database diagram shown in Figure 2.13 to manage company data. You will open the Copper State Insurance database and maintain and create tables that follow the diagram.

Figure 2.13 Copper State Insurance Database Design

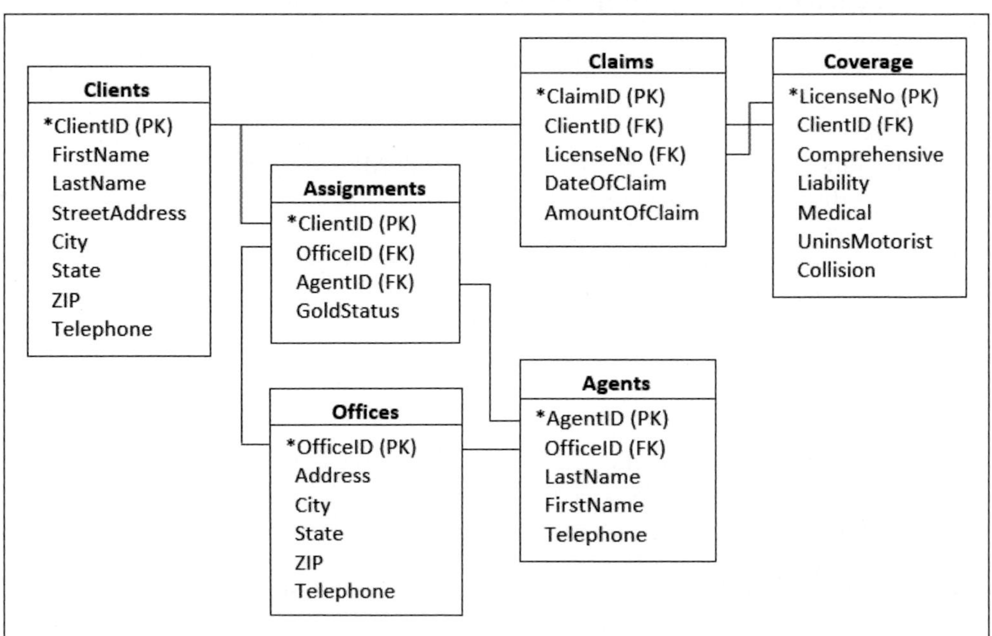

Assessment 1

CREATE RELATIONSHIPS IN AN INSURANCE COMPANY DATABASE

1. Open **AL1-C2-CopperState.accdb** and enable the contents.
2. Open the Claims table.
3. Display the table in Design view, define the *ClaimID* field as the primary key field, click the Save button on the Quick Access toolbar, and then close the Claims table.
4. Display the Relationships window and then insert the Clients, Claims, and Coverage tables.
5. Create a one-to-many relationship with the *ClientID* field in the Clients table the "one" and the *ClientID* field in the Claims table the "many." Enforce referential integrity and cascade fields and records.
6. Create a one-to-many relationship with the *ClientID* field in the Clients table the "one" and the *ClientID* field in the Coverage table the "many." Enforce referential integrity and cascade fields and records.
7. Create a one-to-many relationship with the *LicenseNo* field in the Coverage table the "one" and the *LicenseNo* field in the Claims table the "many." Enforce referential integrity and cascade fields and records.
8. Save and then print the relationships.
9. Close the relationships report without saving it and close the Relationships window.

Assessment 2

CREATE A NEW TABLE AND RELATE THE TABLE

1. With **AL1-C2-CopperState.accdb** open, create the Offices table shown in Figure 2.14. Change the data type of the first column to *Short Text*. (Do this with the *Data Type* option box in the Formatting group on the TABLE TOOLS FIELDS tab.) Change the field size to 2 characters. Change the default value for the *State* field to *AZ*.
2. After typing the records, adjust the column widths to accommodate the longest entry in each column and then save the Offices table.
3. Print and then close the Offices table.
4. Display the Relationships window and then add the Offices table and the Assignments table to the window.
5. Create a one-to-many relationship with the *OfficeID* field in the Offices table the "one" and the *OfficeID* field in the Assignments table the "many." Enforce referential integrity and cascade fields and records.
6. Create a one-to-one relationship with the *ClientID* field in the Clients table and the *ClientID* field in the Assignments table. Enforce referential integrity and cascade fields and records.
7. Save and then print the relationships in landscape orientation. To do this, click the Landscape button in the Page Layout group in Print Preview.
8. Close the relationships report without saving it and then close the Relationships window.

Figure 2.14 Assessment 2 Offices Table

Offices

	OfficeID	Address	City	State	ZIP	Telephone	Click to Add
	GN	North 51st Avenue	Glendale	AZ	85305	(653) 555-8800	
	GW	West Bell Road	Glendale	AZ	85312	(623) 555-4300	
	PG	Grant Street West	Phoenix	AZ	85003	(602) 555-6200	
	PM	McDowell Road	Phoenix	AZ	85012	(602) 555-3800	
	SE	East Thomas Road	Scottsdale	AZ	85251	(480) 555-5500	
	SN	North 68th Street	Scottsdale	AZ	85257	(480) 555-9000	
*				AZ			

Assessment

3 DELETE AND EDIT RECORDS IN TABLES

SNAP Grade It

1. With **AL1-C2-CopperState.accdb** open, open the Clients table.
2. Delete the record for Harold McDougal (client number 9879). (At the message telling you that relationships that specify cascading deletes are about to cause records in this table and related tables to be deleted, click Yes.)
3. Delete the record for Vernon Cook (client number 7335). (At the message telling you that relationships that specify cascading deletes are about to cause records in this table and related tables to be deleted, click Yes.)
4. Change the client number for Paul Vuong from *4300* to *2560*.
5. Print the Clients table in landscape orientation and then close the table.
6. Open the Claims table, print the table, and then close the table. (The Claims table initially contained two entries for client number 9879 and one entry for 7335. These entries were deleted automatically when you deleted the records in the Clients table.)

Assessment

4 DISPLAY AND EDIT RECORDS IN A SUBDATASHEET

1. With **AL1-C2-CopperState.accdb** open, open the Clients table.
2. Click the expand indicator (plus symbol) that displays at the left side of the record for Erin Hagedorn. At the Insert Subdatasheet dialog box, click *Claims* in the list box and then click OK.
3. Change the amount of the claim from *$1,450.00* to *$1,797.00*, change Erin's street address from *4818 Oakes Boulevard* to *763 51st Avenue*, and change her zip code from *85018* to *85014*.
4. Click the collapse indicator (minus symbol) that displays at the left side of the record for Erin Hagedorn.
5. Remove the connection between the Clients and Claims tables by clicking the More button in the Records group on the HOME tab, pointing to *Subdatasheet*, and then clicking *Remove*.
6. Click the More button in the Records group, point to *Subdatasheet*, and then click *Subdatasheet*.
7. At the Insert Subdatasheet dialog box, click *Coverage* in the list box and then click OK.
8. Expand all records by clicking the More button, pointing to *Subdatasheet*, and then clicking *Expand All*.
9. Change the telephone number for Claire Azevedo (client number 1379) from *480-555-2154* to *480-555-2143* and insert check marks in the *Medical* field and the *UninsMotorist* field.
10. Change the last name of Joanne Donnelly (client number 1574) to *Marquez* and remove the check mark from the *Collision* field.
11. At the record for Brenda Lazzuri (client number 3156), insert check marks in the *UninsMotorist* field and *Collision* field for both vehicles.
12. Click in any field heading and then collapse all records.
13. Remove the connection between the Clients and Coverage tables.
14. Save, print, and then close the Clients table. (Make sure the table displays in landscape orientation.)
15. Open the Coverage table, print the table, and then close the table.
16. Close **AL1-C2-CopperState.accdb**.

Visual Benchmark Demonstrate Your Proficiency

CREATE A BOOKINGS TABLE

1. Open **AL1-C2-CarefreeTravel.accdb** and then create the Bookings table shown in Figure 2.15. You determine the data types and field sizes. Create a more descriptive caption for each field name and create a description for each field.
2. Save, print, and then close the Bookings table.
3. Create a relationship between the Agents table and Bookings table. You determine what table contains the "one" and what table contains the "many." Enforce referential integrity and cascade fields and records.
4. Create a relationship between the Tours table and Bookings table. You determine what table contains the "one" and what table contains the "many." Enforce referential integrity and cascade fields and records.
5. Save and then print the relationships and then close the Relationships window.
6. Open the Agents table.
7. Change the AgentID for Wayne Postovic from *137* to *115*.
8. Change Jenna Williamson's last name from *Williamson* to *Parr*.
9. Print and then close the Agents table.
10. Open the Bookings table, print the table, and then close the table. (Notice that the *137* AgentID in the Bookings table is changed to *115*. This is because the tables are related and the changes you make in the primary table are made automatically in the related table.)
11. Close **AL1-C2-CarefreeTravel.accdb**.

Figure 2.15 Visual Benchmark Bookings Table

Bookings

	BookingID	BookingDate	TourID	AgentID	NumberPersons	*Click to Add*
	1	6/1/2015	AF02	114	8	
	2	6/1/2015	HC01	109	2	
	3	6/3/2015	CR02	103	2	
	4	6/4/2015	AK01	137	4	
	5	6/5/2015	HC01	109	2	
	6	6/6/2015	AT02	109	4	
	7	6/8/2015	HS02	104	2	
	8	6/10/2015	HC01	125	2	
	9	6/11/2015	AK01	142	4	
	10	6/13/2015	AT01	112	2	
	11	6/15/2015	HC03	129	2	
*	(New)				0	

Case Study Apply Your Skills

You are the manager for Gold Star Cleaning Services and your company is switching over to Access for managing company data. The database designer has provided you with the database diagram in Figure 2.17. He wants you to follow the diagram when creating the database.

Figure 2.17 Gold Star Cleaning Services Database Diagram

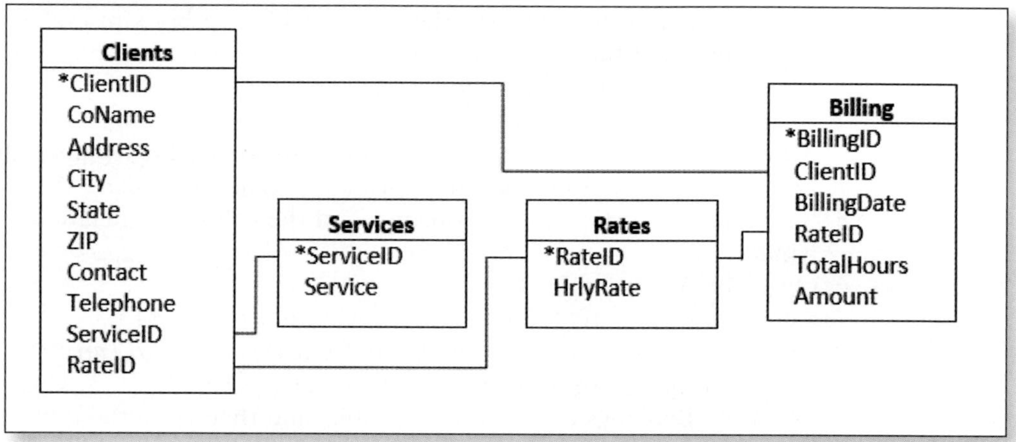

Part 1

Create a new database named **AL1-C2-GoldStar.accdb** and then create the Clients table shown in the database diagram. The database designer has asked you to include an appropriate caption and description for each field. Specify a field size of 3 characters for the *ClientID* field, 4 characters for the *ServiceID* field, and 1 character for the *RateID* field. You determine the field sizes for the *State*, *ZIP*, and *Telephone* fields. The designer also wants you to set the default value for the *City* field to *St. Louis* and the *State* field to *MO*. Type the following records in the table:

ClientID: **101**
CoName: **Smithson Realty**
Address: **492 Papin Street**
City: (default value)
State: (default value)
ZIP: **63108**
Contact: **Danielle Snowden**
Telephone: **(314) 555-3588**
ServiceID: **GS-1**
RateID: **B**

*ClientID:***102**
CoName: **Air-Flow Systems**
Address: **1058 Pine Street**
City: (default value)
State: (default value)
ZIP: **63186**
Contact: **Nick Cline**
Telephone: **(314) 555-9452**
ServiceID: **GS-3**
RateID: **A**

ClientID: **107**
CoName: **Mainstreet Mortgage**
Address: **North 22nd Street**
City: (default value)
State: (default value)
ZIP: **63134**
Contact: **Ted Farrell**
Telephone: **(314) 555-7744**
ServiceID: **GS-1**
RateID: **D**

ClientID: **110**
CoName: **Firstline Finances**
Address: **104 Scott Avenue**
City: (default value)
State: (default value
ZIP: **63126**
Contact: **Robert Styer**
Telephone: **(314) 555-8343**
ServiceID: **GS-2**
RateID: **A**

ClientID: **112**
CoName: **GB Construction**
Address: **988 Lucas Avenue**
City: (default value)
State: (default value)
ZIP: **63175**
Contact: **Joy Ewing**
Telephone: **(314) 555-0036**
ServiceID: **GS-1**
RateID: **C**

ClientID: **115**
CoName: **Simko Equipment**
Address: **1200 Market Street**
City: (default value)
State: (default value)
ZIP: **63140**
Contact: **Dale Aldrich**
Telephone: **(314) 555-3315**
ServiceID: **GS-3**
RateID: **C**

Create the Services table shown in the database diagram. Change the *ServiceID* field size to 4 characters. Type the following records in the table:

ServiceID: **GS-1**
Service: **Deep cleaning all rooms and surfaces, garbage removal, recycling, carpet cleaning, disinfecting**

ServiceID: **GS-2**
Service: **Deep cleaning all rooms and surfaces, garbage removal, disinfecting**

ServiceID: **GS-3**
Service: **Deep cleaning all rooms and surfaces, disinfecting**

Create the Rates table shown in the database diagram. Change the *RateID* field size to 1 character. Type the following records in the table:

RateID: **A**
HrlyRate: **$75.50**

RateID: **B**
HrlyRate: **$65.00**

RateID: **C**
HrlyRate: **$59.75**

RateID: **D**
HrlyRate: **$50.50**

Create the Billing table shown in the database diagram. Change the *BillingID* field size to 2 characters, the *ClientID* field size to 3 characters, and the *RateID* field size to 1 character. Apply the appropriate data types to the fields. Type the following records in the table:

BillingID: **40**
ClientID: **101**
BillingDate: **4/1/2015**
RateID: **B**
TotalHours: **26**
Amount: **$1,690.00**

BillingID: **41**
ClientID: **102**
BillingDate: **4/1/2015**
RateID: **A**
TotalHours: **32**
Amount: **$2,416.00**

BillingID: **42**
ClientID: **107**
BillingDate: **4/1/2015**
RateID: **D**
TotalHours: **15**
Amount: **$747.50**

BillingID: **43**
ClientID: **110**
BillingDate: **4/1/2015**
RateID: **A**
TotalHours: **30**
Amount: **$2,265.00**

BillingID: **44**
ClientID: **112**
BillingDate: **4/1/2015**
RateID: **C**
TotalHours: **20**
Amount: **$1,195.00**

BillingID: **45**
ClientID: **115**
BillingDate: **4/1/2015**
RateID: **C**
TotalHours: **22**
Amount: **$1,314.50**

Automatically adjust the column widths of each table to accommodate the longest entry in each column and then print each table on one page. ***Hint: Check the table in Print Preview and, if necessary, change to landscape orientation and change the margins.***

Part 2

With **AL1-C2-GoldStar.accdb** open, create the one-to-many relationships required to connect the tables. (Refer to Figure 2.17 as a guide.) You will need to increase the size of the Clients field list box to view all of the fields. To do this, position the mouse pointer on the bottom border of the Clients field list box in the Relationships window until the pointer turns into a white arrow pointing up and down. Hold down the left mouse button, drag down to the desired position, and then release the mouse button. Print the relationships report.

Part 3

Open the Services table and then make the following changes to the field values in the *ServiceID* field:

Change *GS-1* to *GS-A*
Change *GS-2* to *GS-B*
Change *GS-3* to *GS-C*

Print and then close the Services table. Open the Clients table, delete the record for client number 112, and then insert the following record:

ClientID: **108**
Name: **Cedar Ridge Products**
Address: **6400 Olive Street**
City: (default value)
State: (default value)
ZIP: **63114**
Contact: **Penny Childers**
Telephone: **(314) 555-7660**
ServiceID: **GS-B**
RateID: **B**

Print and then close the Clients table. Open the Billing table, print the table, and then close the table. Close **AL1-C2-GoldStar.accdb**.

MICROSOFT® ACCESS®

Performing Queries

PERFORMANCE OBJECTIVES

Upon successful completion of Chapter 3, you will be able to:

- **Design queries to extract specific data from tables**
- **Modify queries**
- **Design queries with *Or* and *And* criteria**
- **Use the Simple Query Wizard to create queries**
- **Create a calculated field**
- **Use aggregate functions in queries**
- **Create crosstab, duplicate, and unmatched queries**

Tutorials

3.1 Creating a Query in Design View
3.2 Extracting Records Using Criteria Statements
3.3 Creating a Query in Design View Using Multiple Tables
3.4 Extracting Records Using AND Criteria; Sorting Query Results
3.5 Renaming and Deleting Objects
3.6 Extracting Records Using OR Criteria
3.7 Creating Queries Using the Simple Query Wizard
3.8 Performing Calculations in a Query
3.9 Using Aggregate Functions
3.10 Creating a Crosstab Query
3.11 Creating a Find Duplicates Query
3.12 Creating a Find Unmatched Query

One of the primary uses of a database is to extract the specific information needed to answer questions and make decisions. A company might need to know information such as how much inventory is currently on hand, which products have been ordered, which accounts are past due, or which customers live in a particular city. You can extract specific information from a table or multiple tables by completing a query. You will learn how to perform a variety of queries on information in tables in this chapter. Model answers for this chapter's projects appear on the following pages.

AL1C3

Note: Before beginning the projects, copy the AL1C3 subfolder from the AL1 folder on the CD that accompanies this textbook to your storage medium and make AL1C3 the active folder.

Project 1 Design Queries

Project 1a

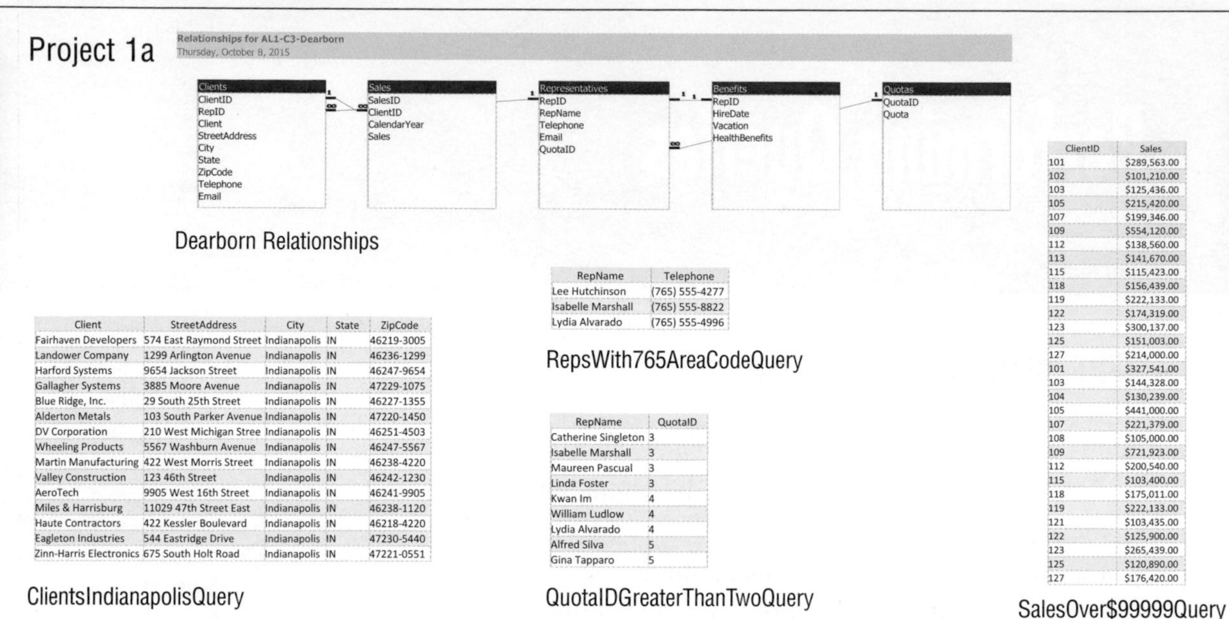

Dearborn Relationships

Client	StreetAddress	City	State	ZipCode
Fairhaven Developers	574 East Raymond Street	Indianapolis	IN	46219-3005
Landower Company	1299 Arlington Avenue	Indianapolis	IN	46236-1299
Harford Systems	9654 Jackson Street	Indianapolis	IN	46247-9654
Gallagher Systems	3885 Moore Avenue	Indianapolis	IN	47229-1075
Blue Ridge, Inc.	29 South 25th Street	Indianapolis	IN	46227-1355
Alderton Metals	103 South Parker Avenue	Indianapolis	IN	47220-1450
DV Corporation	210 West Michigan Stree	Indianapolis	IN	46251-4503
Wheeling Products	5567 Washburn Avenue	Indianapolis	IN	46247-5567
Martin Manufacturing	422 West Morris Street	Indianapolis	IN	46238-4220
Valley Construction	123 46th Street	Indianapolis	IN	46242-1230
AeroTech	9905 West 16th Street	Indianapolis	IN	46241-9905
Miles & Harrisburg	11029 47th Street East	Indianapolis	IN	46238-1120
Haute Contractors	422 Kessler Boulevard	Indianapolis	IN	46218-4220
Eagleton Industries	544 Eastridge Drive	Indianapolis	IN	47230-5440
Zinn-Harris Electronics	675 South Holt Road	Indianapolis	IN	47221-0551

ClientsIndianapolisQuery

RepName	Telephone
Lee Hutchinson	(765) 555-4277
Isabelle Marshall	(765) 555-8822
Lydia Alvarado	(765) 555-4996

RepsWith765AreaCodeQuery

RepName	QuotaID
Catherine Singleton	3
Isabelle Marshall	3
Maureen Pascual	3
Linda Foster	3
Kwan Im	4
William Ludlow	4
Lydia Alvarado	4
Alfred Silva	5
Gina Tapparo	5

QuotaIDGreaterThanTwoQuery

ClientID	Sales
101	$289,563.00
102	$101,210.00
103	$125,436.00
105	$215,420.00
107	$199,346.00
109	$554,120.00
112	$138,560.00
113	$141,670.00
115	$115,423.00
118	$156,439.00
119	$222,133.00
122	$174,319.00
123	$300,137.00
125	$151,003.00
127	$214,000.00
101	$327,541.00
103	$144,328.00
104	$130,239.00
105	$441,000.00
107	$221,379.00
108	$105,000.00
109	$721,923.00
112	$200,540.00
115	$103,400.00
118	$175,011.00
119	$222,133.00
121	$103,435.00
122	$125,900.00
123	$265,439.00
125	$120,890.00
127	$176,420.00

SalesOver$99999Query

Project 1b

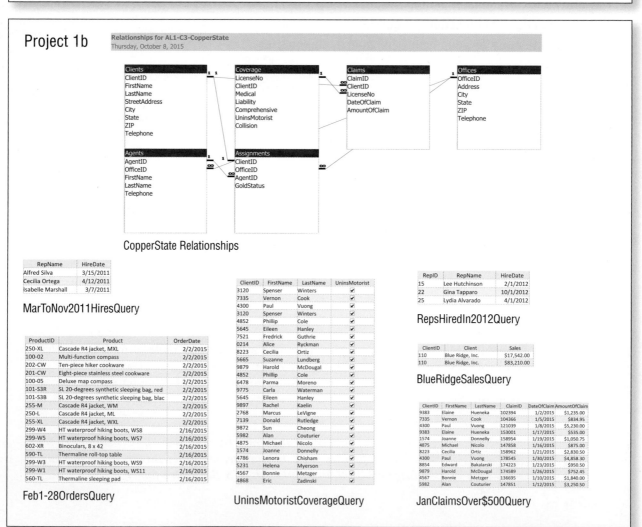

Relationships for AL1-C3-CopperState
Thursday, October 8, 2015

Clients: ClientID, FirstName, LastName, StreetAddress, City, State, ZIP, Telephone

Coverage: LicenseNo, ClientID, Medical, Liability, Comprehensive, UninsMotorist, Collision

Claims: ClaimID, ClientID, LicenseNo, DateOfClaim, AmountOfClaim

Offices: OfficeID, Address, City, State, ZIP, Telephone

Agents: AgentID, OfficeID, FirstName, LastName, Telephone

Assignments: ClientID, OfficeID, AgentID, GoldStatus

CopperState Relationships

RepName	HireDate
Alfred Silva	3/15/2011
Cecilia Ortega	4/12/2011
Isabelle Marshall	3/7/2011

MarToNov2011HiresQuery

RepID	RepName	HireDate
15	Lee Hutchinson	2/1/2012
22	Gina Tapparo	10/1/2012
25	Lydia Alvarado	4/1/2012

RepsHiredIn2012Query

ProductID	Product	OrderDate
250-XL	Cascade R4 jacket, MXL	2/2/2015
100-02	Multi-function compass	2/2/2015
202-CW	Ten-piece hiker cookware	2/2/2015
201-CW	Eight-piece stainless steel cookware	2/2/2015
100-05	Deluxe map compass	2/2/2015
101-S3R	SL 20-degrees synthetic sleeping bag, red	2/2/2015
101-S3B	SL 20-degrees synthetic sleeping bag, blac	2/2/2015
255-M	Cascade R4 jacket, WM	2/2/2015
250-L	Cascade R4 jacket, ML	2/2/2015
255-XL	Cascade R4 jacket, WXL	2/2/2015
299-W4	HT waterproof hiking boots, WS8	2/16/2015
299-W5	HT waterproof hiking boots, WS7	2/16/2015
602-XR	Binoculars, 8 x 42	2/16/2015
590-TL	Thermaline roll-top table	2/16/2015
299-W3	HT waterproof hiking boots, WS9	2/16/2015
299-W1	HT waterproof hiking boots, WS11	2/16/2015
560-TL	Thermaline sleeping pad	2/16/2015

Feb1-28OrdersQuery

ClientID	FirstName	LastName	UninsMotorist
3120	Spenser	Winters	☑
7335	Vernon	Cook	☑
4300	Paul	Vuong	☑
3120	Spenser	Winters	☑
4852	Phillip	Cole	☑
5645	Eileen	Hanley	☑
7521	Fredrick	Guthrie	☑
0214	Alice	Ryckman	☑
8223	Cecilia	Ortiz	☑
5665	Suzanne	Lundberg	☑
9879	Harold	McDougal	☑
4852	Phillip	Cole	☑
6478	Parma	Moreno	☑
9775	Carla	Waterman	☑
5645	Eileen	Hanley	☑
9897	Rachel	Kaelin	☑
2768	Marcus	LeVigne	☑
7139	Donald	Rutledge	☑
9872	Sun	Cheong	☑
5982	Alan	Couturier	☑
4875	Michael	Nicolo	☑
1574	Joanne	Donnelly	☑
4786	Lenora	Chisham	☑
5231	Helena	Myerson	☑
4567	Bonnie	Metzger	☑
4868	Eric	Zadinski	☑

UninsMotoristCoverageQuery

ClientID	Client	Sales
110	Blue Ridge, Inc.	$17,542.00
110	Blue Ridge, Inc.	$83,210.00

BlueRidgeSalesQuery

ClientID	FirstName	LastName	ClaimID	DateOfClaim	AmountOfClaim
9383	Elaine	Hueneka	102394	1/2/2015	$1,235.00
7335	Vernon	Cook	104366	1/5/2015	$834.95
4300	Paul	Vuong	121039	1/8/2015	$5,230.00
9383	Elaine	Hueneka	153001	1/17/2015	$535.00
1574	Joanne	Donnelly	158954	1/19/2015	$1,050.75
4875	Michael	Nicolo	147858	1/16/2015	$875.00
8223	Cecilia	Ortiz	158962	1/21/2015	$2,830.50
4300	Paul	Vuong	178545	1/30/2015	$4,858.30
8854	Edward	Bakalarski	174223	1/23/2015	$950.50
9879	Harold	McDougal	174589	1/26/2015	$752.45
4567	Bonnie	Metzger	136695	1/10/2015	$1,840.00
5982	Alan	Couturier	147851	1/12/2015	$3,250.50

JanClaimsOver$500Query

Project 1c

ProductID	SupplierID	UnitsOrdered	Amount
442-1B	42	10	$1,495.00
780-2	99	10	$1,288.50
250-XL	60	10	$1,285.00
250-L	60	10	$1,285.00
101-S3R	54	10	$1,199.50
101-S3B	54	10	$1,137.50
299-M3	31	10	$887.90
299-M2	31	10	$887.90
299-M5	31	10	$887.90
299-W4	31	10	$752.90
299-W5	31	10	$752.90
299-W3	31	10	$752.90
299-W1	31	8	$602.32
255-XL	60	5	$599.50
255-M	60	5	$599.50
560-TL	25	20	$397.00
155-35	10	10	$199.50
375-S	68	20	$199.00
375-M	68	20	$199.00
590-TL	25	5	$196.25
209-XL	68	25	$180.00
209-L	68	25	$173.75
210-L	68	25	$162.25
209-XXL	68	20	$145.80
100-05	84	5	$129.75
371-L	68	10	$129.50
202-CW	15	5	$124.25
155-20	10	15	$104.25
201-CW	15	5	$99.75
210-M	68	15	$97.35
100-02	84	10	$45.95
152-H	10	15	$44.85

OrdersLessThan$1500Query

OfficeID	FirstName	LastName
GW	Carlos	Alvarez
GW	Joanne	Donnelly
GW	Cecilia	Ortiz
GW	Donald	Rutledge
GW	Paul	Vuong

GWClientsQuery

RepName	Client	Sales
Andre Kulisek	HE Systems	$721,923.00
Andre Kulisek	HE Systems	$554,120.00
Lee Hutchinson	Harford Systems	$441,000.00
Linda Foster	Bering Company	$327,541.00
Kwan Im	Eagleton Industries	$300,137.00
Linda Foster	Bering Company	$289,563.00
Kwan Im	Eagleton Industries	$265,439.00
Craig Johnson	Miles & Harrisburg	$222,133.00
Craig Johnson	Miles & Harrisburg	$222,133.00
Catherine Singleton	Gallagher Systems	$221,379.00
Lee Hutchinson	Harford Systems	$215,420.00
Catherine Singleton	Zinn-Harris Electronics	$214,000.00
Gina Tapparo	DV Corporation	$200,540.00
Catherine Singleton	Gallagher Systems	$199,346.00
Catherine Singleton	Zinn-Harris Electronics	$176,420.00
David DeBruler	AeroTech	$175,011.00
Jaren Newman	Haute Contractors	$174,319.00
David DeBruler	AeroTech	$156,439.00
Cecilia Ortega	Dover Industries	$151,003.00
Alfred Silva	Clearwater Service	$144,328.00
Catherine Singleton	Franklin Services	$141,670.00
Gina Tapparo	DV Corporation	$138,560.00
Robin Rehberg	Landower Company	$130,239.00
Jaren Newman	Haute Contractors	$125,900.00
Alfred Silva	Clearwater Service	$125,436.00
Cecilia Ortega	Dover Industries	$120,890.00
Craig Johnson	Wheeling Products	$115,423.00
Edward Harris	Karris Supplies	$105,000.00
William Ludlow	Madison Electrics	$103,435.00
Craig Johnson	Wheeling Products	$103,400.00
Kwan Im	Fairhaven Developers	$101,210.00

SalesMoreThan$100000Query

Project 1d

RepName	Client	Sales
William Ludlow	Madison Electrics	$99,450.00
Robin Rehberg	Landower Company	$97,653.00
Kwan Im	Fairhaven Developers	$95,630.00
Isabelle Marshall	Providence, Inc.	$85,628.00
Maureen Pascual	Blue Ridge, Inc.	$83,210.00
Isabelle Marshall	Providence, Inc.	$75,462.00
Catherine Singleton	Franklin Services	$65,411.00
Lydia Alvarado	Martin Manufacturing	$61,539.00
Edward Harris	Karris Supplies	$61,349.00
Jaren Newman	Paragon Corporation	$51,237.00
Alfred Silva	Alderton Metals	$45,230.00
Lydia Alvarado	Martin Manufacturing	$35,679.00
Craig Johnson	Hoosier Corporation	$31,935.00
Kwan Im	Milltown Contractors	$31,230.00
Craig Johnson	Hoosier Corporation	$24,880.00
Lee Hutchinson	Valley Construction	$22,478.00
Jaren Newman	Paragon Corporation	$20,137.00
Maureen Pascual	Blue Ridge, Inc.	$17,542.00
Lee Hutchinson	Valley Construction	$15,248.00
Alfred Silva	Northstar Services	$15,094.00
Alfred Silva	Alderton Metals	$9,547.00
Alfred Silva	Northstar Services	$9,457.00
Kwan Im	Milltown Contractors	$2,356.00

SalesLessThan$100000Query

RepName	Vacation
Alfred Silva	3 weeks
Cecilia Ortega	3 weeks
Isabelle Marshall	3 weeks
Craig Johnson	3 weeks
Gina Tapparo	3 weeks
Edward Harris	3 weeks

RepsWith3WeekVacationsQuery

Project 1e

RepName	Vacation
William Ludlow	4 weeks
Alfred Silva	3 weeks
Cecilia Ortega	3 weeks
Robin Rehberg	4 weeks
Isabelle Marshall	3 weeks
Craig Johnson	3 weeks
Gina Tapparo	3 weeks
Edward Harris	3 weeks

RepsWith3Or4WeekVacationsQuery

Client	City	Sales
Fairhaven Developers	Indianapolis	$101,210.00
Landower Company	Indianapolis	$130,239.00
Harford Systems	Indianapolis	$215,420.00
Harford Systems	Indianapolis	$441,000.00
Gallagher Systems	Indianapolis	$199,346.00
Gallagher Systems	Indianapolis	$221,379.00
DV Corporation	Indianapolis	$138,560.00
DV Corporation	Indianapolis	$200,540.00
Wheeling Products	Indianapolis	$115,423.00
Wheeling Products	Indianapolis	$103,400.00
AeroTech	Indianapolis	$156,439.00
AeroTech	Indianapolis	$175,011.00
Miles & Harrisburg	Indianapolis	$222,133.00
Miles & Harrisburg	Indianapolis	$222,133.00
Haute Contractors	Indianapolis	$174,319.00
Haute Contractors	Indianapolis	$125,900.00
Eagleton Industries	Indianapolis	$300,137.00
Eagleton Industries	Indianapolis	$265,439.00
Zinn-Harris Electronics	Indianapolis	$214,000.00
Zinn-Harris Electronics	Indianapolis	$176,420.00

SalesOver$100000IndianapolisQuery

SupplierID	SupplierName	Product
25	Langley Corporation	Thermaline sleeping pad
25	Langley Corporation	Thermaline light-weight cot
25	Langley Corporation	Thermaline camp seat
25	Langley Corporation	Thermaline roll-top table
31	Sound Supplies	HT waterproof hiking boots, MS13
31	Sound Supplies	HT waterproof hiking boots, MS12
31	Sound Supplies	HT waterproof hiking boots, MS11
31	Sound Supplies	HT waterproof hiking boots, MS10
31	Sound Supplies	HT waterproof hiking boots, MS9
31	Sound Supplies	HT waterproof hiking boots, WS11
31	Sound Supplies	HT waterproof hiking boots, WS10
31	Sound Supplies	HT waterproof hiking boots, WS9
31	Sound Supplies	HT waterproof hiking boots, WS8
31	Sound Supplies	HT waterproof hiking boots, WS7
31	Sound Supplies	HT waterproof hiking boots, WS6
42	Fraser Valley Products	Polar backpack, 150BR
42	Fraser Valley Products	Polar backpack, 150RW
42	Fraser Valley Products	Polar backpack, 250BR
42	Fraser Valley Products	Polar backpack, 250RW

Suppliers25-31-42Query

OrderID	SupplierName	Product	UnitsOrdered
1017	Freedom Corporation	Gordon wool ski hat, L	25
1009	Freedom Corporation	Gordon wool ski hat, XL	25
1008	Freedom Corporation	Gordon wool ski hat, XXL	20
1012	Freedom Corporation	Tech-lite ski hat, L	25
1013	Freedom Corporation	Tech-lite ski hat, M	15
1016	Freedom Corporation	Lite-tech ski gloves, ML	10
1015	Freedom Corporation	Lite-tech ski gloves, WM	20
1014	Freedom Corporation	Lite-tech ski gloves, WS	20

SkiHatsGlovesOnOrderQuery

ProductID	Product	SupplierName
443-1B	Polar backpack, 250RW	Fraser Valley Products
101-S1B	SL 0-degrees down sleeping bag, black	Manning, Inc.
101-S1R	SL 0-degrees down sleeping bag, red	Manning, Inc.
101-S2B	SL 15-degrees synthetic sleeping bag, blac	Manning, Inc.
101-S2R	SL 15-degrees synthetic sleeping bag, red	Manning, Inc.
101-S3B	SL 20-degrees synthetic sleeping bag, blac	Manning, Inc.
101-S3R	SL 20-degrees synthetic sleeping bag, red	Manning, Inc.
299-M1	HT waterproof hiking boots, MS13	Sound Supplies
299-M2	HT waterproof hiking boots, MS12	Sound Supplies
299-M3	HT waterproof hiking boots, MS11	Sound Supplies
299-M4	HT waterproof hiking boots, MS10	Sound Supplies
299-M5	HT waterproof hiking boots, MS9	Sound Supplies
299-W1	HT waterproof hiking boots, WS11	Sound Supplies
299-W2	HT waterproof hiking boots, WS10	Sound Supplies
299-W3	HT waterproof hiking boots, WS9	Sound Supplies
299-W4	HT waterproof hiking boots, WS8	Sound Supplies
299-W5	HT waterproof hiking boots, WS7	Sound Supplies

BootsSleepingBagsBackpacksQuery

FirstName	LastName	Medical	Liability	Comprehensive	UninsMotorist	Collision
Brenda	Lazzuri	☐	☑	☐	☐	☐
Edward	Bakalarski	☐	☑	☐	☐	☐
Brenda	Lazzuri	☐	☑	☐	☐	☐
Bret	Mardock	☐	☑	☐	☐	☐
Carlos	Alvarez	☐	☑	☐	☐	☐

ClientsWithOnlyLiabilityQuery

Project 1f

ClientID	Client	Sales
101	Bering Company	$289,563.00
101	Bering Company	$327,541.00
102	Fairhaven Developers	$101,210.00
102	Fairhaven Developers	$95,630.00
103	Clearwater Service	$125,436.00
103	Clearwater Service	$144,328.00
104	Landower Company	$97,653.00
104	Landower Company	$130,239.00
105	Harford Systems	$215,420.00
105	Harford Systems	$441,000.00
106	Providence, Inc.	$85,628.00
106	Providence, Inc.	$75,462.00
107	Gallagher Systems	$199,346.00
107	Gallagher Systems	$221,379.00
108	Karris Supplies	$61,349.00
108	Karris Supplies	$105,000.00
109	HE Systems	$554,120.00
109	HE Systems	$721,923.00
110	Blue Ridge, Inc.	$17,542.00
110	Blue Ridge, Inc.	$83,210.00
111	Alderton Metals	$9,547.00
111	Alderton Metals	$45,230.00
112	DV Corporation	$138,560.00
112	DV Corporation	$200,540.00
113	Franklin Services	$141,670.00
113	Franklin Services	$65,411.00
114	Milltown Contractors	$2,356.00
114	Milltown Contractors	$31,230.00
115	Wheeling Products	$115,423.00
115	Wheeling Products	$103,400.00
116	Martin Manufacturing	$35,679.00
116	Martin Manufacturing	$61,539.00
117	Valley Construction	$15,248.00
117	Valley Construction	$22,478.00
118	AeroTech	$156,439.00
118	AeroTech	$175,011.00
119	Miles & Harrisburg	$222,133.00
119	Miles & Harrisburg	$222,133.00
120	Paragon Corporation	$51,237.00
120	Paragon Corporation	$20,137.00
121	Madison Electrics	$99,450.00
121	Madison Electrics	$103,435.00
122	Haute Contractors	$174,319.00

ClientSalesQuery, Page 1

ClientID	Client	Sales
122	Haute Contractors	$125,900.00
123	Eagleton Industries	$300,137.00
123	Eagleton Industries	$265,439.00
124	Hoosier Corporation	$24,880.00
124	Hoosier Corporation	$31,935.00
125	Dover Industries	$151,003.00
125	Dover Industries	$120,890.00
126	Northstar Services	$9,457.00
126	Northstar Services	$15,094.00
127	Zinn-Harris Electronics	$214,000.00
127	Zinn-Harris Electronics	$176,420.00

ClientSalesQuery, Page 2

SupplierID	SupplierName	ProductID	Amount
42	Fraser Valley Products	443-1B	$2,397.75
25	Langley Corporation	560-TL	$397.00
25	Langley Corporation	590-TL	$196.25
35	Emerald City Products	602-XR	$2,145.00
99	KL Distributions	647-1	$2,999.85
99	KL Distributions	780-2	$1,288.50
84	Macadam, Inc.	100-02	$45.95
84	Macadam, Inc.	100-05	$129.75
54	Manning, Inc.	101-S2R	$1,945.25
54	Manning, Inc.	101-S3B	$1,137.50
54	Manning, Inc.	101-S3R	$1,199.50
10	Hopewell, Inc.	152-H	$44.85
10	Hopewell, Inc.	155-20	$104.25
10	Hopewell, Inc.	155-35	$199.50
15	Bayside Supplies	201-CW	$99.75
15	Bayside Supplies	202-CW	$124.25
68	Freedom Corporation	209-L	$173.75
68	Freedom Corporation	209-XL	$180.00
68	Freedom Corporation	209-XXL	$145.80
68	Freedom Corporation	210-L	$162.25
68	Freedom Corporation	210-M	$97.35
60	Cascade Gear	250-L	$1,285.00
60	Cascade Gear	250-XL	$1,285.00
60	Cascade Gear	255-M	$599.50
60	Cascade Gear	255-XL	$599.50
31	Sound Supplies	299-M2	$887.90
31	Sound Supplies	299-M3	$887.90
31	Sound Supplies	299-M5	$887.90
31	Sound Supplies	299-W1	$602.32
31	Sound Supplies	299-W3	$752.90
31	Sound Supplies	299-W4	$752.90
31	Sound Supplies	299-W5	$752.90
68	Freedom Corporation	371-L	$129.50
68	Freedom Corporation	375-M	$199.00
68	Freedom Corporation	375-S	$199.00
42	Fraser Valley Products	442-1B	$1,495.00

ProductOrderAmountsQuery

Project 1g

SupplierName	StreetAddress	City	Prov/State	PostalCode
Bayside Supplies	6705 North Street	Bellingham	WA	98432
Hadley Company	5845 Jefferson Street	Seattle	WA	98107
Cascade Gear	540 Broadway	Seattle	WA	98106
Sound Supplies	2104 Union Street	Seattle	WA	98105
Emerald City Products	1059 Pike Street	Seattle	WA	98102
KL Distributions	402 Yukon Drive	Bellingham	WA	96435

SuppliersNotBCQuery

Client	StreetAddress	City	State	ZipCode
Bering Company	4521 East Sixth Street	Muncie	IN	47310-5500
Clearwater Service	10385 North Gavin Street	Muncie	IN	47308-1236
Providence, Inc.	12490 141st Street	Muncie	IN	47306-3410
Paragon Corporation	4500 Meridian Street	Muncie	IN	47302-4338
Dover Industries	4839 Huchins Road	Muncie	IN	47306-4839
Northstar Services	5135 West Second Street	Muncie	IN	47301-7774

ClientsMuncieQuery

ClientID	FirstName	LastName	StreetAddress	City	State	ZIP	ClaimID	AmountOfClaim
7335	Vernon	Cook	1230 South Mesa	Phoenix	AZ	85018	104366	$834.95
1331	Erin	Hagedorn	4818 Oakes Boulevard	Phoenix	AZ	85018	198745	$1,797.00
9879	Harold	McDougal	7115 Elizabeth Lane	Phoenix	AZ	85009	174589	$752.45
9775	Carla	Waterman	3979 19th Avenue	Phoenix	AZ	85031	241485	$4,500.00
6478	Parma	Moreno	610 Sheridan Avenue	Phoenix	AZ	85031	200147	$925.75
4868	Eric	Zadinski	1301 North Meridian	Phoenix	AZ	85031	210369	$2,675.00
9879	Harold	McDougal	7115 Elizabeth Lane	Phoenix	AZ	85009	247823	$775.75

PhoenixClientClaimsOver$500Query

Project 1h

EmpID	FirstName	LastName	AnnualSalary	PensionContrib
101	Joseph	Ammons	$52,350.00	1570.5
102	Walter	Irving	$50,750.00	1522.5
103	Francine	Prescott	$52,500.00	1575
104	Mary	Vanderhoff	$59,750.00	1792.5
105	Corey	Gadeau	$60,150.00	1804.5
106	Stephanie	Wendt	$42,000.00	1260
108	Nathan	Holmes	$53,350.00	1600.5
110	Thomas	Byrnes	$42,500.00	1275
111	Ray	Bannerman	$32,600.00	978
112	Noreen	Blanca	$38,750.00	1162.5
114	Blaine	Kaiser	$64,500.00	1935
115	Sean	O'Callaghan	$52,455.00	1573.65
116	Silas	Workman	$51,000.00	1530
118	Glenn	Ishimoto	$68,525.00	2055.75
119	Lucinda	Larsen	$38,425.00	1152.75
121	Patricia	Ochoa	$59,750.00	1792.5
124	Antonio	Silvestri	$51,350.00	1540.5
125	Debra	Tapparo	$40,150.00	1204.5
126	Michelle	Vincent	$39,750.00	1192.5
127	Kurt	Ziegler	$65,250.00	1957.5
129	Shilo	Alvarado	$45,000.00	1350
130	Norman	Curis	$42,450.00	1273.5
133	Brett	Dupree	$58,550.00	1756.5
134	Sally	Farrell	$58,000.00	1740
135	Dorothy	Griswold	$67,700.00	2031
137	Leslie	Jacobsen	$48,800.00	1464
138	Susan	Masui	$38,500.00	1155
139	Jerry	Prentiss	$57,525.00	1725.75
140	Kathleen	Schreiber	$45,250.00	1357.5

PensionContributionsQuery

EmpID	FirstName	LastName	AnnualSalary	Salary&Pension
101	Joseph	Ammons	$52,350.00	53920.5
102	Walter	Irving	$50,750.00	52272.5
103	Francine	Prescott	$52,500.00	54075
104	Mary	Vanderhoff	$59,750.00	61542.5
105	Corey	Gadeau	$60,150.00	61954.5
106	Stephanie	Wendt	$42,000.00	43260
108	Nathan	Holmes	$53,350.00	54950.5
110	Thomas	Byrnes	$42,500.00	43775
111	Ray	Bannerman	$32,600.00	33578
112	Noreen	Blanca	$38,750.00	39912.5
114	Blaine	Kaiser	$64,500.00	66435
115	Sean	O'Callaghan	$52,455.00	54028.65
116	Silas	Workman	$51,000.00	52530
118	Glenn	Ishimoto	$68,525.00	70580.75
119	Lucinda	Larsen	$38,425.00	39577.75
121	Patricia	Ochoa	$59,750.00	61542.5
124	Antonio	Silvestri	$51,350.00	52890.5
125	Debra	Tapparo	$40,150.00	41354.5
126	Michelle	Vincent	$39,750.00	40942.5
127	Kurt	Ziegler	$65,250.00	67207.5
129	Shilo	Alvarado	$45,000.00	46350
130	Norman	Curis	$42,450.00	43723.5
133	Brett	Dupree	$58,550.00	60306.5
134	Sally	Farrell	$58,000.00	59740
135	Dorothy	Griswold	$67,700.00	69731
137	Leslie	Jacobsen	$48,800.00	50264
138	Susan	Masui	$38,500.00	39655
139	Jerry	Prentiss	$57,525.00	59250.75
140	Kathleen	Schreiber	$45,250.00	46607.5

Salary&PensionQuery

Product	OrderID	UnitsOrdered	Amount	Total
Two-person tent	1001	10	$1,288.50	$12,885.00
HT waterproof hiking boots, MS9	1002	10	$887.90	$8,879.00
HT waterproof hiking boots, MS11	1003	10	$887.90	$8,879.00
Polar backpack, 250RW	1004	15	$2,397.75	$35,966.25
HT waterproof hiking boots, MS12	1005	10	$887.90	$8,879.00
Two-person dome tent	1006	15	$2,999.85	$44,997.75
Polar backpack, 150RW	1007	10	$1,495.00	$14,950.00
Gordon wool ski hat, XXL	1008	20	$145.80	$2,916.00
Gordon wool ski hat, XL	1009	25	$180.00	$4,500.00
Shursite portable camp light	1010	10	$199.50	$1,995.00
Lantern hanger	1011	15	$44.85	$672.75
Tech-lite ski hat, L	1012	25	$162.25	$4,056.25
Tech-lite ski hat, M	1013	15	$97.35	$1,460.25
Lite-tech ski gloves, WS	1014	20	$199.00	$3,980.00
Lite-tech ski gloves, WM	1015	20	$199.00	$3,980.00
Lite-tech ski gloves, ML	1016	10	$129.50	$1,295.00
Gordon wool ski hat, L	1017	25	$173.75	$4,343.75
Shursite angle-head flashlight	1018	15	$104.25	$1,563.75
Cascade R4 jacket, MXL	1019	10	$1,285.00	$12,850.00
Multi-function compass	1020	10	$45.95	$459.50
Ten-piece hiker cookware	1021	5	$124.25	$621.25
Eight-piece stainless steel cookware	1022	5	$99.75	$498.75
Deluxe map compass	1023	5	$129.75	$648.75
SL 20-degrees synthetic sleeping bag, re	1024	10	$1,199.50	$11,995.00
SL 20-degrees synthetic sleeping bag, bla	1025	10	$1,137.50	$11,375.00
Cascade R4 jacket, WM	1026	5	$599.50	$2,997.50
SL 15-degrees synthetic sleeping bag, re	1027	15	$1,945.25	$29,178.75
Cascade R4 jacket, ML	1028	10	$1,285.00	$12,850.00
Cascade R4 jacket, WXL	1029	5	$599.50	$2,997.50
HT waterproof hiking boots, WS8	1030	10	$752.90	$7,529.00
HT waterproof hiking boots, WS7	1031	10	$752.90	$7,529.00
Binoculars, 8 x 42	1032	5	$2,145.00	$10,725.00
Thermaline roll-top table	1033	5	$196.25	$981.25
HT waterproof hiking boots, WS9	1034	10	$752.90	$7,529.00
HT waterproof hiking boots, WS11	1035	8	$602.32	$4,818.56
Thermaline sleeping pad	1036	20	$397.00	$7,940.00

UnitsOrderedTotalQuery

Project 2 Create Aggregate Functions, Crosstab, Find Duplicates, and Find Unmatched Queries

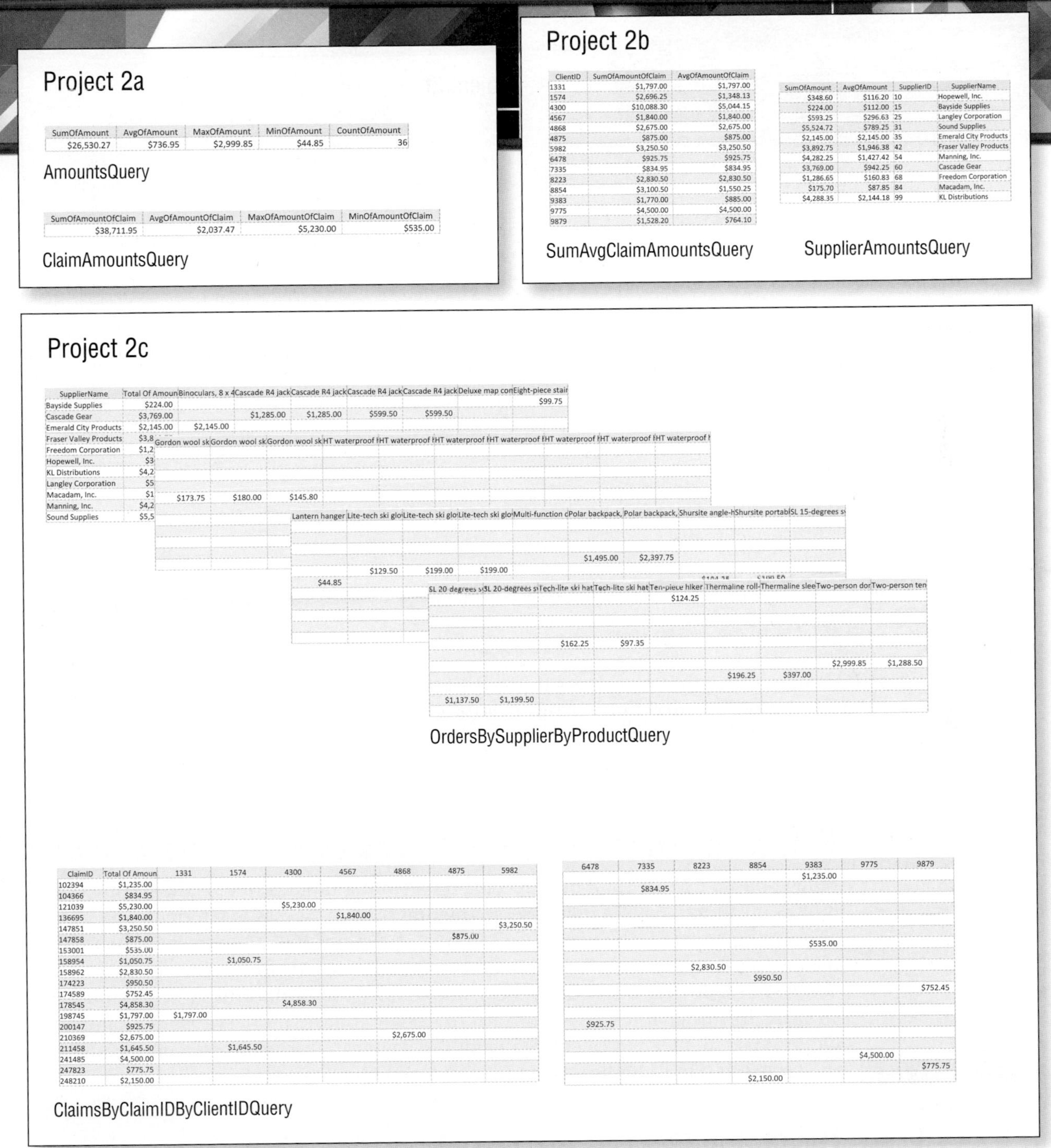

Project 2a

SumOfAmount	AvgOfAmount	MaxOfAmount	MinOfAmount	CountOfAmount
$26,530.27	$736.95	$2,999.85	$44.85	36

AmountsQuery

SumOfAmountOfClaim	AvgOfAmountOfClaim	MaxOfAmountOfClaim	MinOfAmountOfClaim
$38,711.95	$2,037.47	$5,230.00	$535.00

ClaimAmountsQuery

Project 2b

ClientID	SumOfAmountOfClaim	AvgOfAmountOfClaim
1331	$1,797.00	$1,797.00
1574	$2,696.25	$1,348.13
4300	$10,088.30	$5,044.15
4567	$1,840.00	$1,840.00
4868	$2,675.00	$2,675.00
4875	$875.00	$875.00
5982	$3,250.50	$3,250.50
6478	$925.75	$925.75
7335	$834.95	$834.95
8223	$2,830.50	$2,830.50
8854	$3,100.50	$1,550.25
9383	$1,770.00	$885.00
9775	$4,500.00	$4,500.00
9879	$1,528.20	$764.10

SumAvgClaimAmountsQuery

SumOfAmount	AvgOfAmount	SupplierID	SupplierName
$348.60	$116.20	10	Hopewell, Inc.
$224.00	$112.00	15	Bayside Supplies
$593.25	$296.63	25	Langley Corporation
$5,524.72	$789.25	31	Sound Supplies
$2,145.00	$2,145.00	35	Emerald City Products
$3,892.75	$1,946.38	42	Fraser Valley Products
$4,282.25	$1,427.42	54	Manning, Inc.
$3,769.00	$942.25	60	Cascade Gear
$1,286.65	$160.83	68	Freedom Corporation
$175.70	$87.85	84	Macadam, Inc.
$4,288.35	$2,144.18	99	KL Distributions

SupplierAmountsQuery

Project 2c

SupplierName	Total Of Amoun	Binoculars, 8 x 4	Cascade R4 jack	Cascade R4 jack	Cascade R4 jack	Cascade R4 jack	Deluxe map con	Eight-piece stair
Bayside Supplies	$224.00							$99.75
Cascade Gear	$3,769.00		$1,285.00	$1,285.00	$599.50	$599.50		
Emerald City Products	$2,145.00	$2,145.00						
Fraser Valley Products	$3,8							
Freedom Corporation	$1,2							
Hopewell, Inc.	$3							
KL Distributions	$4,2							
Langley Corporation	$5							
Macadam, Inc.	$1							
Manning, Inc.	$4,2							
Sound Supplies	$5,5							

Gordon wool sk	Gordon wool sk	Gordon wool sk	HT waterproof I	HT waterproof I	HT waterproof I	HT waterproof I	HT waterproof I	HT waterproof I	HT waterproof I
$173.75	$180.00	$145.80							

Lantern hanger	Lite-tech ski glo	Lite-tech ski glo	Lite-tech ski glo	Multi-function c	Polar backpack,	Polar backpack,	Shursite angle-h	Shursite portabl	SL 15-degrees s
					$1,495.00	$2,397.75			
	$129.50	$199.00	$199.00						
$44.85							[illegible]	[illegible]	

SL 20 degrees s	SL 20-degrees s	Tech-lite ski hat	Tech-lite ski hat	Ten-piece hiker	Thermaline roll-	Thermaline slee	Two-person dor	Two-person ten
				$124.25				
		$162.25	$97.35					
							$2,999.85	$1,288.50
					$196.25	$397.00		
$1,137.50	$1,199.50							

OrdersBySupplierByProductQuery

ClaimID	Total Of Amoun	1331	1574	4300	4567	4868	4875	5982
102394	$1,235.00							
104366	$834.95							
121039	$5,230.00			$5,230.00				
136695	$1,840.00				$1,840.00			
147851	$3,250.50							$3,250.50
147858	$875.00						$875.00	
153001	$535.00							
158954	$1,050.75		$1,050.75					
158962	$2,830.50							
174223	$950.50							
174589	$752.45							
178545	$4,858.30			$4,858.30				
198745	$1,797.00	$1,797.00						
200147	$925.75							
210369	$2,675.00					$2,675.00		
211458	$1,645.50		$1,645.50					
241485	$4,500.00							
247823	$775.75							
248210	$2,150.00							

6478	7335	8223	8854	9383	9775	9879
				$1,235.00		
	$834.95					
				$535.00		
		$2,830.50				
			$950.50			
						$752.45
$925.75						
					$4,500.00	
						$775.75
			$2,150.00			

ClaimsByClaimIDByClientIDQuery

Project 2d

SupplierName	SupplierID	StreetAddress	City	Prov/State	PostalCode	EmailAddress	Telephone
Langley Corporation	25	805 First Avenue	Burnaby	BC	V3J 1C9	langley@emcp.net	(604) 555-1200
Langley Corporation	29	1248 Larson Avenue	Burnaby	BC	V5V 9K2	lc@emcp.net	(604) 555-1200

DuplicateSuppliersQuery

Project 2e

SupplierName Field	NumberOfDups
Bayside Supplies	2
Cascade Gear	4
Fraser Valley Products	2
Freedom Corporation	8
Hopewell, Inc.	3
KL Distributions	2
Langley Corporation	2
Macadam, Inc.	2
Manning, Inc.	3
Sound Supplies	7

SupplierOrdersCountQuery

Project 2f

ProductID	Product	SupplierID	UnitsInStock	UnitsOnOrder	ReorderLevel
558-C	ICE snow goggles, clear	68	18	0	15
559-B	ICE snow goggles, bronze	68	22	0	20
570-TL	Thermaline light-weight cot	25	8	0	5
580-TL	Thermaline camp seat	25	12	0	10
602-XT	Binoculars, 10.5 x 45	35	5	0	4
602-XX	Binoculars, 10 x 50	35	7	0	5
648-2	Three-person dome tent	99	5	0	10
651-1	K-2 one-person tent	99	8	0	10
652-2	K-2 two-person tent	99	12	0	10
804-50	AG freestyle snowboard, X50	70	7	0	10
804-60	AG freestyle snowboard, X60	70	8	0	5
897-L	Lang blunt snowboard	70	8	0	7
897-W	Lang blunt snowboard, wide	70	4	0	3
901-S	Solar battery pack	38	16	0	15
917-S	Silo portable power pack	38	8	0	10
100-01	Wrist compass	84	12	0	10
100-03	Lenspro plastic compass	84	6	0	5
100-04	Lenspro metal compass	84	8	0	5
101-S1B	SL 0-degrees down sleeping bag, black	54	16	0	15
101-S1R	SL 0-degrees down sleeping bag, red	54	17	0	15
101-S2B	SL 15-degrees synthetic sleeping bag, blac	54	21	0	15
155-30	Shursite aluminum flashlight	10	8	0	5
155-45	Shursite propane lantern	10	12	0	10
155-55	Shursite waterproof headlamp	10	7	0	5
200-CW	Four-piece titanium cookware	15	6	0	5
210-XL	Tech-lite ski hat, XL	68	22	0	20
250-M	Cascade R4 jacket, MM	60	6	0	5
250-XXL	Cascade R4 jacket, MXXL	60	5	0	0
255-L	Cascade R4 jacket, WL	60	6	0	5
299-M1	HT waterproof hiking boots, MS13	31	8	0	10
299-M4	HT waterproof hiking boots, MS10	31	7	0	10

Products Without Matching Orders

Project 1 Design Queries — 8 Parts

You will design and run a number of queries including queries with fields from one table and queries with fields from more than one table. You will also use the Simple Query Wizard to design queries.

Extracting Data with Queries

Being able to extract (pull out) specific data from a table is one of the most important functions of a database. Extracting data in Access is referred to as performing a query. The word ***query*** means "question" and to perform a query means to ask a question. Access provides several methods for performing a query. You can design your own query, use a simple query wizard, or use complex query wizards. In this chapter, you will learn to design your own query; use the Simple Query Wizard; create a calculated field; use aggregate functions in a query; and use the Crosstab, Find Duplicates, and Unmatched Query wizards.

The first step in designing a query is to choose the fields that you want to display in the query results datasheet.

Designing Queries

Designing a query consists of identifying the table from which you are gathering data, the field or fields from which the data will be drawn, and the criteria for selecting the data. To design a query and perform the query, open a database, click the CREATE tab, and then click the Query Design button in the Queries group. This displays a query window in the work area and also displays the Show Table dialog box, as shown in Figure 3.1.

Query Design

Figure 3.1 Query Window with Show Table Dialog Box

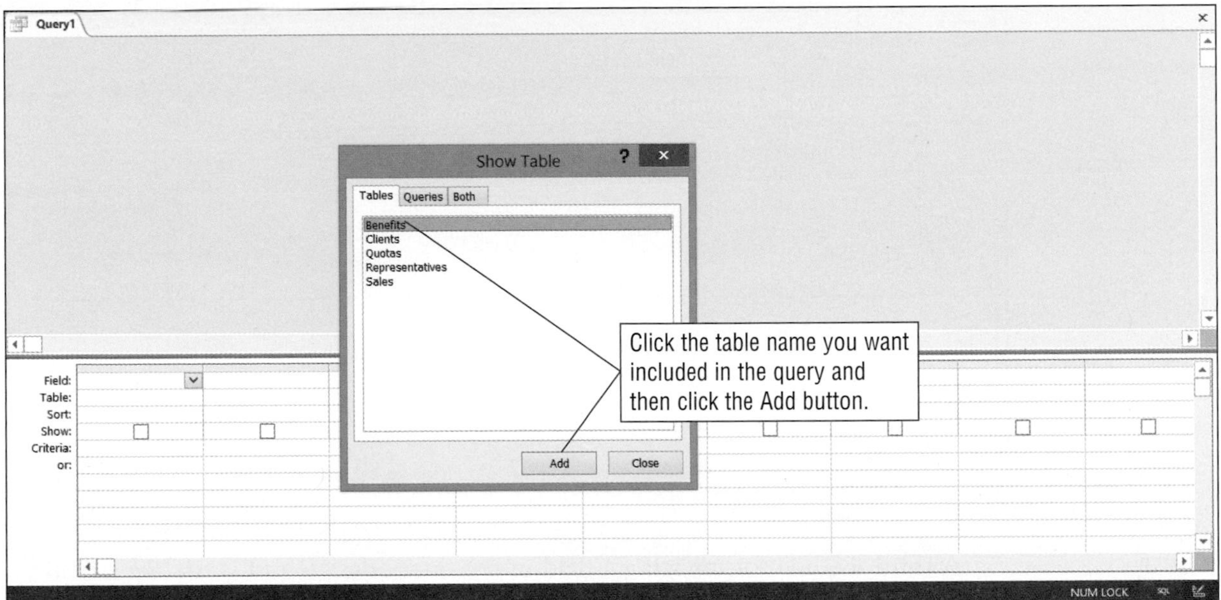

Click the table name in the Show Table dialog box that you want included in the query and then click the Add button or double-click the desired table. This inserts a field list box for the table. Add any other tables required for the query. When all tables have been added, click the Close button. In the query window, click the down-pointing arrow at the right of the first *Field* row field in the query design grid and then click the desired field from the drop-down list. Figure 3.2 displays a sample query window.

To establish a criterion, click inside the *Criteria* row field in the column containing the desired field name in the query design grid and then type the criterion. With the fields and criteria established, click the Run button in the Results group on the QUERY TOOLS DESIGN tab. Access searches the specified tables for records that match the criteria and then displays those records in the query results datasheet. If you plan to use the query in the future, save the query and name it. If you will not need the query again, close the query results datasheet without saving it.

To insert a field in the query design grid, click the down-pointing arrow at the right side of a *Field* row field and then click the desired field at the drop-down list. You can also double-click a field in a table field list box to insert the field in the first available *Field* row field in the query design grid. For example, suppose you want to find out how many purchase orders were issued on a specific date. To do this, double-click *PurchaseOrderID* in the table field list box (which inserts *PurchaseOrderID* in the first *Field* row field in the query design grid) and then double-click *OrderDate* in the table field list box (which inserts *OrderDate* in the second *Field* row field in the query design grid). In this example, both fields are needed, so the purchase order ID is displayed along with the specific order date. After inserting the fields, you insert the criterion. The criterion for this example is something like *#1/15/2015#*. After you insert the criterion, click the Run button in the Results group and the results of the query display in the query results datasheet.

Quick Steps

Design a Query
1. Click CREATE tab.
2. Click Query Design button.
3. At Show Table dialog box, click desired table, and then click Add button.
4. Add any additional tables.
5. In query design grid, click down-pointing arrow in *Field* row field and click desired field from drop-down list.
6. Insert criterion.
7. Click Run button.
8. Save query.

Run

Figure 3.2 Query Window

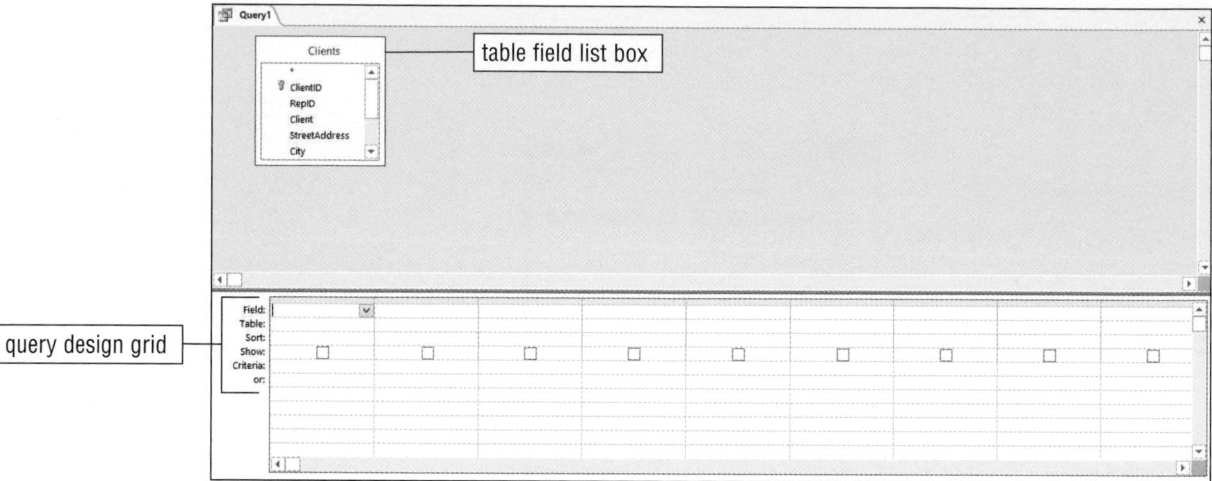

A third method for inserting a field in the query design grid is to drag a field from the table field list box to the desired field in the query design grid. To do this, position the mouse pointer on the desired field in the table field list box, hold down the left mouse button, drag to the desired *Field* row field in the query design grid, and then release the mouse button.

Establishing Query Criteria

Quick Steps

Establish a Query Criterion

1. At query window, click in desired *Criteria* row field in query design grid.
2. Type criterion and then press Enter.
3. Click Run button.

Insert fields in the *Field* row fields in the query design grid in the order in which you want the fields to display in the query results datasheet.

Access inserts quotation marks around text criteria and pound symbols around date criteria.

Performing a query does not require specific criteria to be established. In the example described on the previous page, if the criterion for the date was not included, the query would return all purchase order numbers with the dates. (*Return* is the term used for the results of the query.) While this information may be helpful, you could easily find this information in the table. The value of performing a query is to extract specific information from a table. To do this, you must insert a criterion like the one described in the example.

Access makes writing a criterion fairly simple by inserting the necessary symbols in the criterion. If you type a city name, such as *Indianapolis*, in the *Criteria* row field and then press Enter, Access changes the criterion to "*Indianapolis*". The quotation marks are inserted by Access and are necessary for the query to run properly. You can either let Access put the proper symbols in the *Criteria* row field, or you can type the criterion with the symbols. Table 3.1 shows some examples of criteria, including what is typed and what is returned.

In the criteria examples, the asterisk is used as a so-called ***wildcard character***, or a symbol that can be used to indicate any character. This is consistent with many other software applications. Two of the criteria examples in Table 3.1 use less-than and greater-than symbols. You can use these symbols for fields containing numbers, values, dates, amounts, and so forth. In the next several projects, you will design queries to extract specific information from different tables in databases.

Table 3.1 Criteria Examples

Typing This Criterion	*Returns This Result*
"Smith"	Field value that matches *Smith*
"Smith" Or "Larson"	Field value that matches either *Smith* or *Larson*
Not "Smith"	Field value that is not *Smith* (the opposite of "Smith")
"s*"	Field value that begins with *S* or *s* and ends in anything
"*s"	Field value that begins with anything and ends in *S* or *s*
"[A-D]*"	Field value that begins with *A*, *B*, *C*, or *D* and ends in anything
#01/01/2015#	Field value that matches the date 01/01/2015
<#04/01/2015#	Field value that is less than (before) 04/01/2015
>#04/01/2015#	Field value that is greater than (after) 04/01/2015
Between #01/01/2015# And #03/31/2015#	Field value that is between 01/01/2015 and 03/31/2015

Project 1a Performing Queries on Tables

Part 1 of 8

1. Open **AL1-C3-Dearborn.accdb** from the AL1C3 folder on your storage medium and enable the contents.
2. Create the following relationships and enforce referential integrity (and cascade fields and records) for each relationship:
   a. Create a one-to-many relationship with the *ClientID* field in the *Clients* field list box the "one" and the *ClientID* field in the *Sales* field list box the "many."
   b. Create a one-to-one relationship with the *RepID* field in the *Representatives* field list box the "one" and the *RepID* field in the *Benefits* field list box the "one."
   c. Create a one-to-many relationship with the *RepID* field in the *Representatives* field list box the "one" and the *RepID* field in the *Clients* field list box the "many."
   d. Create a one-to-many relationship with the *QuotaID* field in the *Quotas* field list box the "one" and the *QuotaID* field in the *Representatives* field list box the "many."
3. Click the Save button on the Quick Access toolbar.
4. Print the relationships by completing the following steps:
   a. Click the Relationship Report button in the Tools group on the RELATIONSHIP TOOLS DESIGN tab.
   b. At the relationship report window, click the Landscape button in the Page Layout group on the PRINT PREVIEW tab.
   c. Click the Print button that displays at the left side of the PRINT PREVIEW tab.
   d. At the Print dialog box, click OK.
5. Close the relationship report window without saving the report.
6. Close the Relationships window.

7. Extract records of those clients located in Indianapolis by completing the following steps:
   a. Click the CREATE tab.
   b. Click the Query Design button in the Queries group.
   c. At the Show Table dialog box with the Tables tab selected (see Figure 3.1), click *Clients*

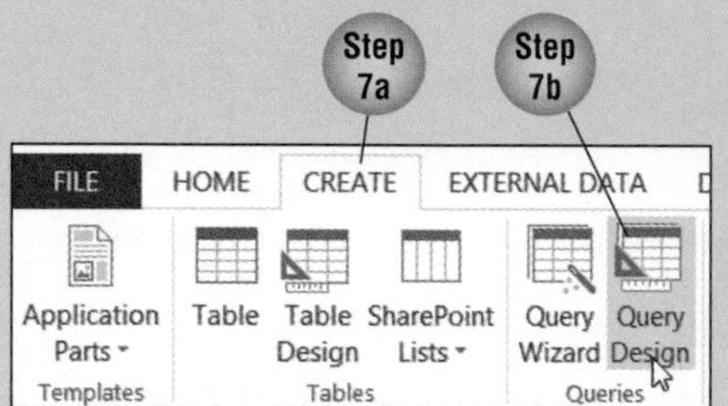

   in the list box, click the Add button, and then click the Close button.
   d. Insert fields from the *Clients* field list box to the *Field* row fields in the query design grid by completing the following steps:
      1) Click the down-pointing arrow located at the right of the first *Field* row field in the query design grid and then click *Client* in the drop-down list.
      2) Click inside the next *Field* row field (to the right of *Client*) in the query design grid, click the down-pointing arrow, and then click *StreetAddress* in the drop-down list.
      3) Click inside the next *Field* row field (to the right of *StreetAddress*), click the down-pointing arrow, and then click *City* in the drop-down list.
      4) Click inside the next *Field* row field (to the right of *City*), click the down-pointing arrow, and then click *State* in the drop-down list.
      5) Click inside the next *Field* row field (to the right of *State*), click the down-pointing arrow, and then select *ZipCode* in the drop-down list.

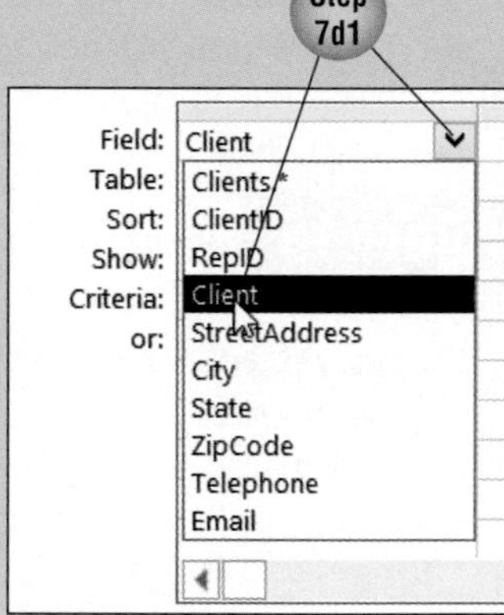

Step 7d2 · Step 7d3 · Step 7d4 · Step 7d5

Field:	Client	StreetAddress	City	State	ZipCode
Table:	Clients	Clients	Clients	Clients	Clients
Sort:					
Show:	✔	✔	✔	✔	✔
Criteria:					
or:					

e. Insert the criterion text telling Access to display only those suppliers located in Indianapolis by completing the following steps:
   1) Click in the *Criteria* row field in the *City* column in the query design grid. (This positions the insertion point in the field.)
   2) Type **Indianapolis** and then press Enter. (This changes the criterion to "Indianapolis".)

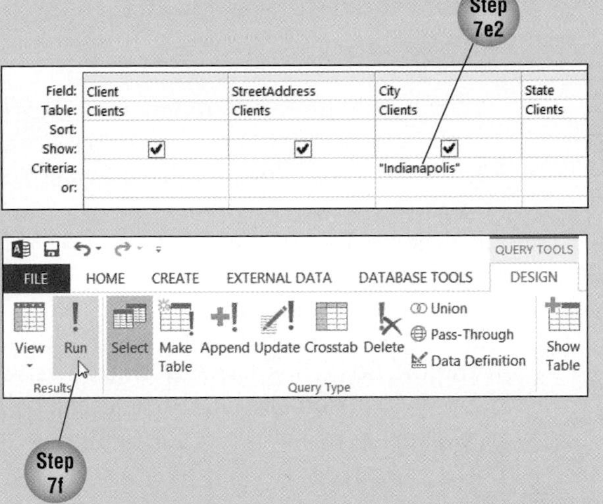

f. Return the results of the query by clicking the Run button in the Results group on the QUERY TOOLS DESIGN tab. (This displays the results in the query results datasheet.)
g. Save the results of the query by completing the following steps:
   1) Click the Save button on the Quick Access toolbar.
   2) At the Save As dialog box, type **ClientsIndianapolisQuery** and then press Enter or click OK. (See Project 1a query results on page 78.)
h. Print the query results datasheet by clicking the FILE tab, clicking the *Print* option, and then clicking the Quick Print button.
i. Close ClientsIndianapolisQuery.

8. Extract those records with quota identification numbers greater than 2 by completing the following steps:
   a. Click the CREATE tab and then click the Query Design button in the Queries group.
   b. Double-click *Representatives* in the Show Table dialog box and then click the Close button.
   c. In the query window, double-click *RepName*. (This inserts the field in the first *Field* row field in the query design grid.)
   d. Double-click *QuotaID*. (This inserts the field in the second *Field* row field in the query design grid.)
   e. Insert the query criterion by completing the following steps:
      1) Click in the *Criteria* row field in the *QuotaID* column in the query design grid.
      2) Type >2 and then press Enter. (Access will automatically insert quotation marks around *2* since the data type for the field is identified as *Short Text* [rather than *Number*].)

Field:	RepName	QuotaID
Table:	Representatives	Representatives
Sort:		
Show:	✔	✔
Criteria:		>"2"
or:		

Step 8e2

   f. Return the results of the query by clicking the Run button in the Results group.
   g. Save the query and name it *QuotaIDGreaterThanTwoQuery*. (See Project 1a query results on page 78.)
   h. Print and then close the query.

9. Extract those sales greater than $99,999 by completing the following steps:
   a. Click the CREATE tab and then click the Query Design button.
   b. Double-click *Sales* in the Show Table dialog box and then click the Close button.
   c. At the query window, double-click *ClientID*. (This inserts the field in the first *Field* row field in the query design grid.)
   d. Insert the *Sales* field in the second *Field* row field.

e. Insert the query criterion by completing the following steps:
   1) Click in the *Criteria* row field in the *Sales* column in the query design grid.
   2) Type **>99999** and then press Enter. (Access will not insert quotation marks around *99999* since the field is identified as *Currency*.)

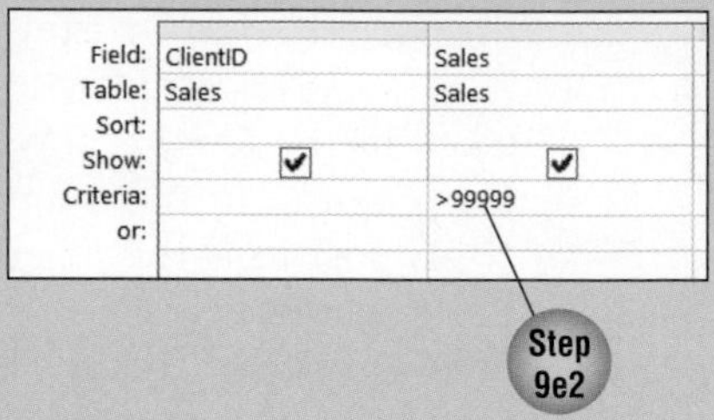

Field:	ClientID	Sales
Table:	Sales	Sales
Sort:		
Show:	✔	✔
Criteria:		>99999
or:		

Step 9e2

f. Return the results of the query by clicking the Run button in the Results group.

g. Save the query and name it *SalesOver$99999Query*. (See Project 1a query results on page 78.)

h. Print and then close the query.

10. Extract records of those representatives with a telephone number that begins with the 765 area code by completing the following steps:
    a. Click the CREATE tab and then click the Query Design button.
    b. Double-click *Representatives* in the Show Table dialog box and then click the Close button.
    c. Insert the *RepName* field in the first *Field* row field.
    d. Insert the *Telephone* field in the second *Field* row field.
    e. Insert the query criterion by completing the following steps:
       1) Click in the *Criteria* row field in the *Telephone* column.
       2) Type **"(765*"** and then press Enter. (You need to type the quotation marks in this criterion because the criterion contains a left parenthesis.)

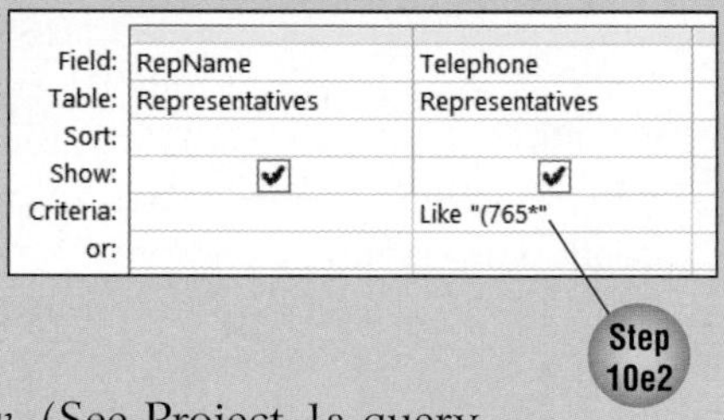

Field:	RepName	Telephone
Table:	Representatives	Representatives
Sort:		
Show:	✔	✔
Criteria:		Like "(765*"
or:		

Step 10e2

    f. Return the results of the query by clicking the Run button in the Results group.
    g. Save the query and name it *RepsWith765AreaCodeQuery*. (See Project 1a query results on page 78.)
    h. Print and then close the query.

In Project 1a, you performed several queries on specific tables. You can also perform queries on fields from more than one table. In Project 1b, you will perform queries on related tables.

When completing steps in Project 1b, you will be instructed to open AL1-C3-CopperState.accdb. Two of the tables in the database contain yes/no check boxes. When designing a query, you can extract records that contain a check mark or records that do not contain a check mark. If you want to extract records that contain a check mark, click in the *Criteria* row field in the desired column in the query design grid, type a *1*, and then press Enter. When you press the Enter key, Access changes the *1* to *True*. If you want to extract records that do not contain a check mark, type *0* in the *Criteria* row field and then press Enter. Access changes the 0 to *False*.

You can use the Zoom box when entering a criterion in a query to provide a larger area for typing. To display the Zoom box, press Shift + F2 or right-click in the desired *Criteria* row field and then click *Zoom* at the shortcut menu. Type the desired criterion in the Zoom box and then click OK.

Project 1b Performing Queries on Related Tables — Part 2 of 8

1. With **AL1-C3-Dearborn.accdb** open, extract information on representatives hired between March 2011 and November 2011 and include the representatives' names by completing the following steps:
   a. Click the CREATE tab and then click the Query Design button.
   b. Double-click *Representatives* in the Show Table dialog box.
   c. Double-click *Benefits* in the Show Table dialog box and then click the Close button.
   d. At the query window, double-click *RepName* in the *Representatives* field list box.
   e. Double-click *HireDate* in the *Benefits* field list box.

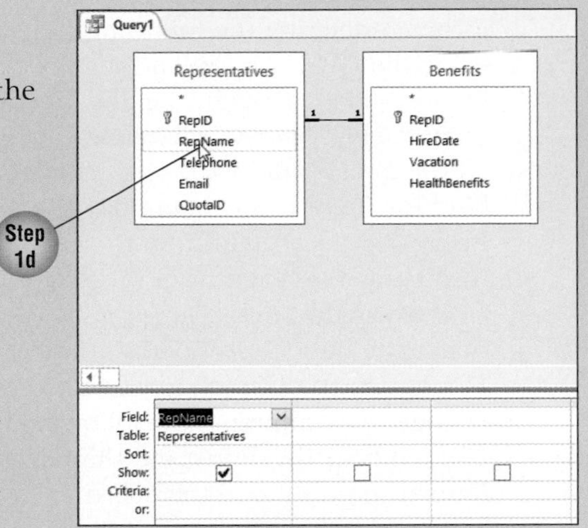

   f. Insert the query criterion in the Zoom box by completing the following steps:
      1) Click in the *Criteria* row field in the *HireDate* column.
      2) Press Shift + F2 to display the Zoom box.
      3) Type **Between 3/1/2011 And 11/30/2011**. (Make sure you type zeros and not capital *O*s.)
      4) Click OK.

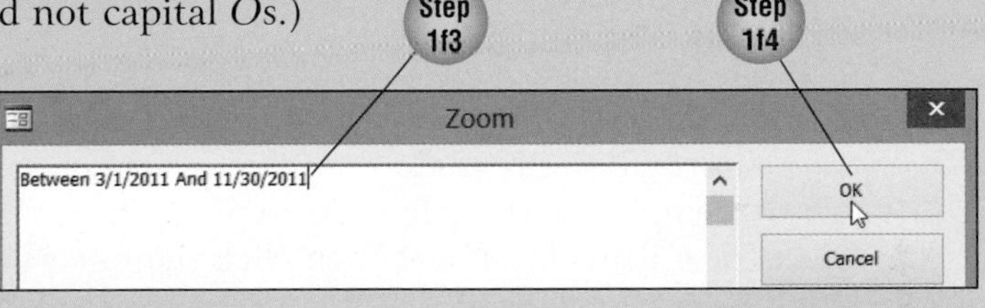

   g. Return the results of the query by clicking the Run button in the Results group.
   h. Save the query and name it *MarToNov2011HiresQuery*. (See Project 1b query results on page 78.)
   i. Print and then close the query.
2. Extract records of those representatives who were hired in 2012 by completing the following steps:
   a. Click the CREATE tab and then click the Query Design button.
   b. Double-click *Representatives* in the Show Table dialog box.
   c. Double-click *Benefits* in the Show Table dialog box and then click the Close button.
   d. At the query window, double-click the *RepID* field in the *Representatives* field list box.
   e. Double-click *RepName* in the *Representatives* field list box.
   f. Double-click *HireDate* in the *Benefits* field list box.
   g. Insert the query criterion by completing the following steps:
      1) Click in the *Criteria* row field in the *HireDate* column.
      2) Type ***2012** and then press Enter.

Field:	RepID	RepName	HireDate
Table:	Representatives	Representatives	Benefits
Sort:			
Show:	☑	☑	☑
Criteria:			Like "*2012"
or:			

Step 2g2

   h. Return the results of the query by clicking the Run button in the Results group.
   i. Save the query and name it *RepsHiredIn2012Query*. (See Project 1b query results on page 78.)
   j. Print and then close the query.

3. Suppose you need to determine sales for a company but you can only remember that the company name begins with *Blue*. Create a query that finds the company and identifies the sales by completing the following steps:
   a. Click the CREATE tab and then click the Query Design button.
   b. Double-click *Clients* in the Show Table dialog box.
   c. Double-click *Sales* in the Show Table dialog box and then click the Close button.
   d. At the query window, insert the *ClientID* field from the *Clients* field list box in the first *Field* row field in the query design grid.
   e. Insert the *Client* field from the *Clients* field list box in the second *Field* row field.
   f. Insert the *Sales* field from the *Sales* field list box in the third *Field* row field.
   g. Insert the query criterion by completing the following steps:
      1) Click in the *Criteria* row field in the *Client* column.
      2) Type **Blue*** and then press Enter.
   h. Return the results of the query by clicking the Run button in the Results group.
   i. Save the query and name it *BlueRidgeSalesQuery*. (See Project 1b query results on page 78.)
   j. Print and then close the query.

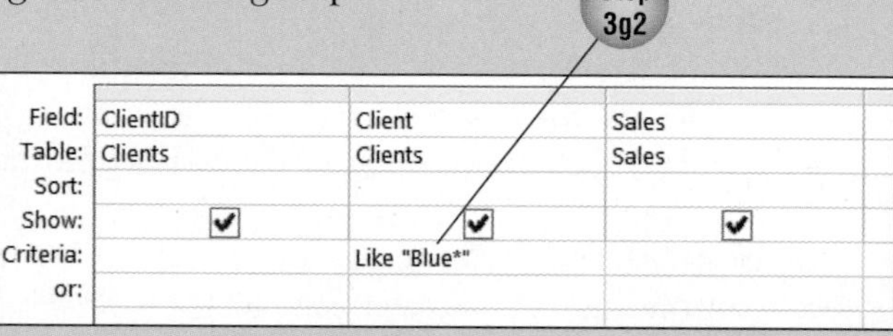

Field:	ClientID	Client	Sales
Table:	Clients	Clients	Sales
Sort:			
Show:	✔	✔	✔
Criteria:		Like "Blue*"	
or:			

4. Close **AL1-C3-Dearborn.accdb**.
5. Display the Open dialog box with the AL1C3 folder on your storage medium active.
6. Open **AL1-C3-PacTrek.accdb** and enable the contents.
7. Extract information on products ordered between February 1, 2015, and February 28, 2015, by completing the following steps:
   a. Click the CREATE tab and then click the Query Design button.
   b. Double-click *Products* in the Show Table dialog box.
   c. Double-click *Orders* in the Show Table dialog box and then click the Close button.
   d. At the query window, insert the *ProductID* field from the *Products* field list box in the first *Field* row field.
   e. Insert the *Product* field from the *Products* field list box in the second *Field* row field.
   f. Insert the *OrderDate* field from the *Orders* field list box in the third *Field* row field.
   g. Insert the query criterion by completing the following steps:
      1) Click in the *Criteria* row field in the *OrderDate* column.
      2) Type **Between 2/1/2015 And 2/28/2015** and then press Enter. (Make sure you type zeros and not capital *O*s.)
   h. Return the results of the query by clicking the Run button in the Results group.
   i. Save the query and name it *Feb1-28OrdersQuery*. (See Project 1b query results on page 78.)
   j. Print and then close the query.

Field:	ProductID	Product	OrderDate
Table:	Products	Products	Orders
Sort:			
Show:	✔	✔	✔
Criteria:			Between #2/1/2015# An
or:			

Step
7g2

8. Close **AL1-C3-PacTrek.accdb**.
9. Open **AL1-C3-CopperState.accdb** and enable the contents.
10. Display the Relationships window and create the following additional relationships (enforce referential integrity and cascade fields and records):
    a. Create a one-to-many relationship with the *AgentID* field in the Agents field list box the "one" and the *AgentID* field in the Assignments field list box the "many."

b. Create a one-to-many relationship with the *OfficeID* field in the Offices field list box the "one" and the *OfficeID* field in the Assignments field list box the "many."
   c. Create a one-to-many relationship with the *OfficeID* field in the Offices field list box the "one" and the *OfficeID* field in the Agents field list box the "many."
11. Save and then print the relationships.
12. Close the relationship report without saving it and then close the Relationships window.
13. Extract records of clients that have uninsured motorist coverage by completing the following steps:
   a. Click the CREATE tab and then click the Query Design button.
   b. Double-click *Clients* in the Show Table dialog box.
   c. Double-click *Coverage* in the Show Table dialog box and then click the Close button.
   d. At the query window, insert the *ClientID* field from the *Clients* field list box in the first *Field* row field.
   e. Insert the *FirstName* field from the *Clients* field list box in the second *Field* row field.
   f. Insert the *LastName* field from the *Clients* field list box in the third *Field* row field.
   g. Insert the *UninsMotorist* field from the *Coverage* field list box in the fourth *Field* row field. (You may need to scroll down the Coverage field list box to display the *UninsMotorist* field.)
   h. Insert the query criterion by clicking in the *Criteria* row field in the *UninsMotorist* column, typing 1, and then pressing the Enter key. (Access changes the *1* to *True*.)

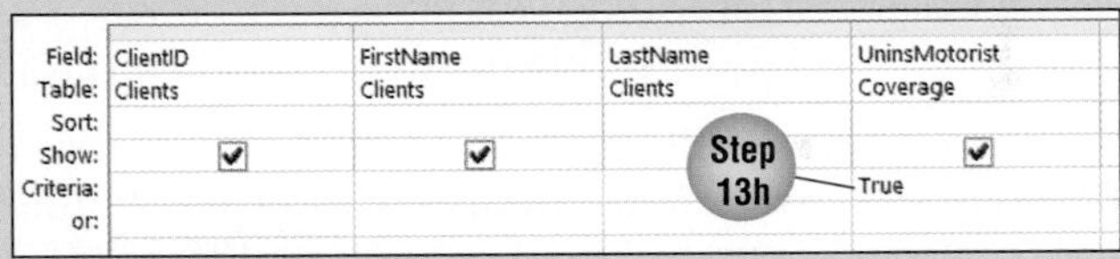

Field:	ClientID	FirstName	LastName	UninsMotorist
Table:	Clients	Clients	Clients	Coverage
Sort:				
Show:	✔	✔		✔
Criteria:				True
or:				

   i. Click the Run button in the Results group.
   j. Save the query and name it *UninsMotoristCoverageQuery*. (See Project 1b query results on page 78.)
   k. Print and then close the query.
14. Extract records of claims in January over $500 by completing the following steps:
   a. Click the CREATE tab and then click the Query Design button.
   b. Double-click *Clients* in the Show Table dialog box.
   c. Double-click *Claims* in the Show Table dialog box and then click the Close button.
   d. At the query window, insert the *ClientID* field from the *Clients* field list box in the first *Field* row field.
   e. Insert the *FirstName* field from the *Clients* field list box in the second *Field* row field.
   f. Insert the *LastName* field from the *Clients* field list box in the third *Field* row field.
   g. Insert the *ClaimID* field from the *Claims* field list box in the fourth *Field* row field.
   h. Insert the *DateOfClaim* field from the *Claims* field list box in the fifth *Field* row field.
   i. Insert the *AmountOfClaim* field from the *Claims* field list box in the sixth *Field* row field.
   j. Click in the *Criteria* row field in the *DateOfClaim* column, type **Between 1/1/2015 And 1/31/2015**, and then press Enter.
   k. With the insertion point positioned in the *Criteria* row field in the *AmountOfClaim* column, type **>500** and then press Enter.

Field:	ClientID	FirstName	LastName	ClaimID	DateOfClaim	AmountOfClaim
Table:	Clients	Clients	Clients	Claims	Claims	Claims
Sort:						
Show:	✔	✔	✔	✔	✔	✔
Criteria:					Between #1/1/2015# An	>500
or:						

Step 14j Step 14k

   l. Click the Run button in the Results group.
   m. Save the query and name it *JanClaimsOver$500Query*. (See Project 1b query results on page 78.)
   n. Print and then close the query.

Quick Steps

Sort Fields in a Query

1. At query window, click in *Sort* row field in query design grid.
2. Click down arrow in *Sort* row field.
3. Click *Ascending* or *Descending*.

Sorting and Showing or Hiding Fields in a Query

When designing a query, you can specify the sort order of a field or fields. Click inside one of the columns in the *Sort* row field and a down-pointing arrow displays at the right of the field. Click this down-pointing arrow and a drop-down list displays with the choices *Ascending*, *Descending*, and *(not sorted)*. Click *Ascending* to sort from lowest to highest or click *Descending* to sort from highest to lowest. You can hide specific fields in the query result by removing the check mark from the check box in the *Show* row in the design grid for the field you do not want to show.

Arranging Fields in a Query

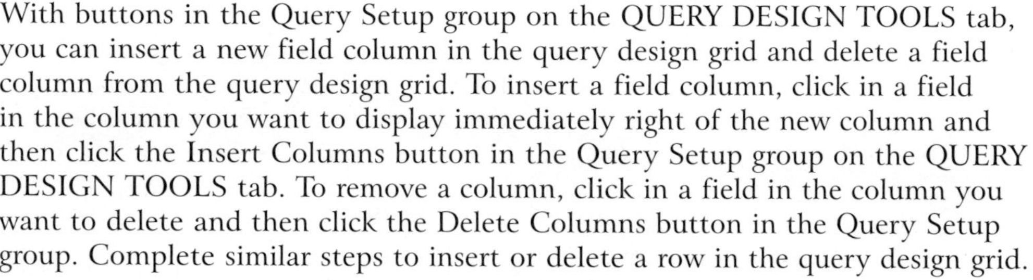

With buttons in the Query Setup group on the QUERY DESIGN TOOLS tab, you can insert a new field column in the query design grid and delete a field column from the query design grid. To insert a field column, click in a field in the column you want to display immediately right of the new column and then click the Insert Columns button in the Query Setup group on the QUERY DESIGN TOOLS tab. To remove a column, click in a field in the column you want to delete and then click the Delete Columns button in the Query Setup group. Complete similar steps to insert or delete a row in the query design grid.

Insert Columns

Delete Columns

You can also rearrange columns in the query design grid by selecting the desired field column and then dragging the column to the desired position. To select a column in the query design grid, position the mouse pointer at the top of the column until the pointer turns into a small, black, down-pointing arrow and then click the left mouse button. Position the mouse pointer toward the top of the selected column until the mouse displays as a pointer, hold down the left mouse button, drag to the desired position in the design grid, and then release the mouse button. As you drag the column, a thick, black, vertical line displays identifying the location where the column will be inserted.

Project 1c **Performing Queries on Related Tables and Sorting in Field Values** **Part 3 of 8**

1. With **AL1-C3-CopperState.accdb** open, extract information on clients with agents from the West Bell Road Glendale office and sort the information alphabetically by client last name by completing the following steps:
   a. Click the CREATE tab and then click the Query Design button.
   b. Double-click *Assignments* in the Show Table dialog box.
   c. Double-click *Clients* in the Show Table dialog box and then click the Close button.
   d. At the query window, insert the *OfficeID* field from the *Assignments* field list box in the first *Field* row field.
   e. Insert the *AgentID* field from the *Assignments* field list box in the second *Field* row field.
   f. Insert the *FirstName* field from the *Clients* field list box in the third *Field* row field.
   g. Insert the *LastName* field from the *Clients* field list box in the fourth *Field* row field.

h. Click in the *Criteria* row field in the *OfficeID* column, type **GW**, and then press Enter.

i. Sort the *LastName* field in ascending alphabetical order (A–Z) by completing the following steps:

  1) Click in the *Sort* row field in the *LastName* column. (This causes a down-pointing arrow to display at the right side of the field.)

  2) Click the down-pointing arrow at the right side of the *Sort* row field and then click *Ascending*.

j. Specify that you do not want the *AgentID* field to show in the query results by clicking in the check box in the *Show* row field in the *AgentID* column to remove the check mark.

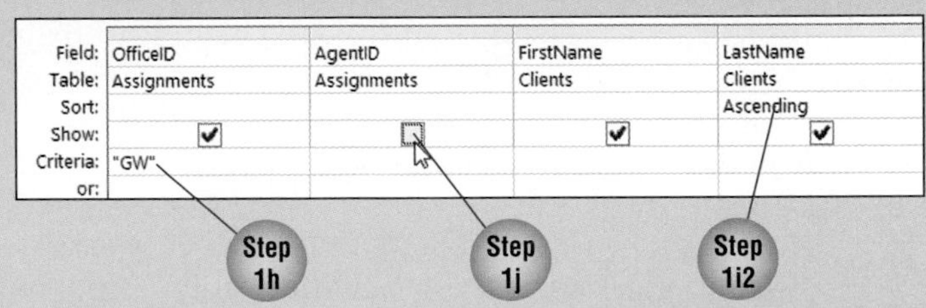

k. Click the Run button in the Results group.

l. Save the query and name it *GWClientsQuery*. (See Project 1c query results on page 79.)

m. Print and then close the query.

2. Close **AL1-C3-CopperState.accdb**.

3. Open **AL1-C3-PacTrek.accdb**.

4. Extract information on orders less than $1,500 by completing the following steps:

  a. Click the CREATE tab and then click the Query Design button.

  b. Double-click *Products* in the Show Table dialog box.

  c. Double-click *Orders* in the Show Table dialog box and then click the Close button.

  d. At the query window, insert the *ProductID* field from the *Products* field list box in the first *Field* row field.

  e. Insert the *SupplierID* field from the *Products* field list box in the second *Field* row field.

  f. Insert the *UnitsOrdered* field from the Orders field list box in the third *Field* row field.

  g. Insert the *Amount* field from the Orders field list box in the fourth *Field* row field.

  h. Insert the query criterion by completing the following steps:

    1) Click in the *Criteria* row field in the *Amount* column.

    2) Type **<1500** and then press Enter. (Make sure you type zeros and not capital *O*s.)

Field:	ProductID	SupplierID	UnitsOrdered	Amount
Table:	Products	Products	Orders	Orders
Sort:				
Show:	✔	✔	✔	✔
Criteria:				<1500
or:				

Step 4h2

  i. Sort the *Amount* field values from highest to lowest by completing the following steps:

    1) Click in the *Sort* row field in the *Amount* column. (This causes a down-pointing arrow to display at the right side of the field.)

    2) Click the down-pointing arrow at the right side of the *Sort* field and then click *Descending*.

Ordered	Amount
s	Orders
	Descending
✔	Ascending
	Descending
	(not sorted)

Step 4i2

  j. Return the results of the query by clicking the Run button in the Results group.

  k. Save the query and name it *OrdersLessThan$1500Query*. (See Project 1c query results on page 79.)

  l. Print and then close the query.

5. Close **AL1-C3-PacTrek.accdb**.

6. Open **AL1-C3-Dearborn.accdb**.

7. Design a query by completing the following steps:

  a. Click the CREATE tab and then click the Query Design button.

  b. Double-click *Representatives* in the Show Table dialog box.

c. Double-click *Clients* in the Show Table dialog box.
d. Double-click *Sales* in the Show Table dialog box and then click the Close button.
e. At the query window, insert the *RepID* field from the *Representatives* field list box in the first *Field* row field.
f. Insert the *RepName* field from the *Representatives* field list box in the second *Field* row field.
g. Insert the *ClientID* field from the *Clients* field list box in the third *Field* row field.
h. Insert the *Sales* field from the *Sales* field list box in the fourth *Field* row field.

8. Move the *RepName* field by completing the following steps:
   a. Position the mouse pointer at the top of the *RepName* column until the pointer turns into a small, black, down-pointing arrow and then click the left mouse button. (This selects the entire column.)

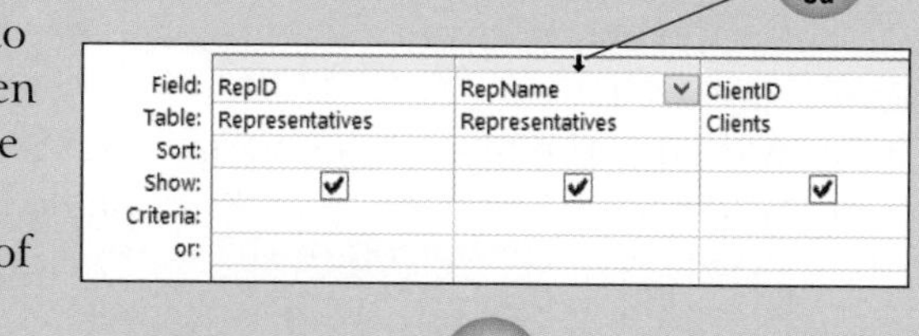

   b. Position the mouse pointer toward the top of the selected column until the pointer turns into a white arrow.
   c. Hold down the left mouse button; drag to the right until a thick, black horizontal line displays between the *ClientID* column and the *Sales* column; and then release the mouse button.

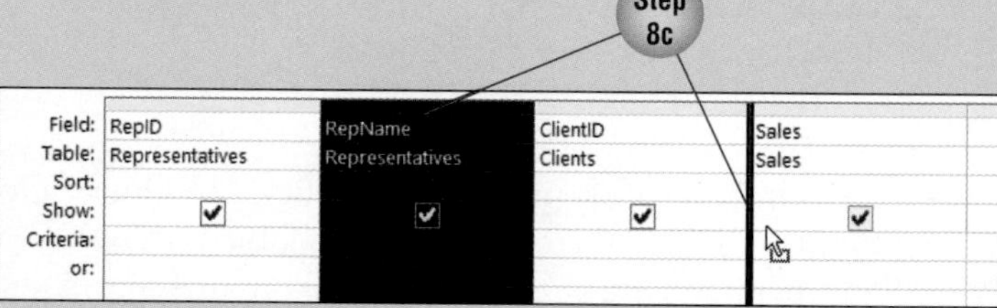

9. Delete the *RepID* field by clicking in a field in the column and then clicking the Delete Columns button in the Query Setup group.
10. Insert a new field column and insert a new field in the column by completing the following steps:
    a. Click in the *Sales* field and then click the Insert Columns button in the Query Setup group.
    b. Click the down-pointing arrow at the right side of the new field and then click *Clients.Client* at the drop-down list.

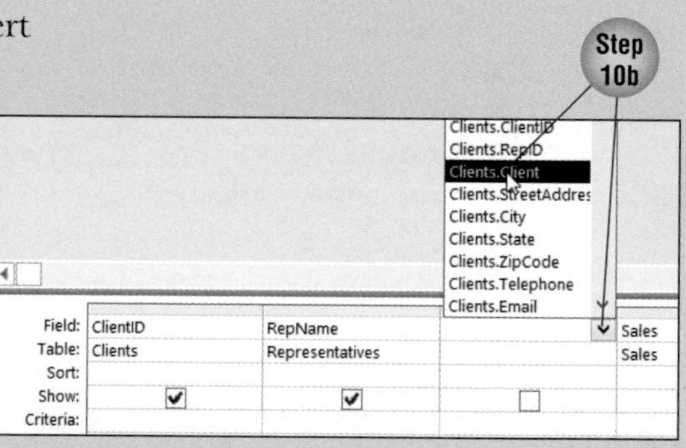

11. Hide the *ClientID* field so it does not display in the query results by clicking the *Show* check box in the *ClientID* column to remove the check mark.
12. Insert the query criterion that extracts information on sales over $100,000 by completing the following steps:
    a. Click in the *Criteria* row field in the *Sales* column.
    b. Type **>100000** and then press Enter. (Make sure you type zeros and not capital *O*s.)
13. Sort the *Sales* field values from highest to lowest by completing the following steps:
    a. Click in the *Sort* row field in the *Sales* column.
    b. Click the down-pointing arrow at the right side of the *Sort* row field and then click *Descending*.
14. Return the results of the query by clicking the Run button in the Results group.
15. Save the query and name it *SalesMoreThan$100000Query*. (See Project 1c query results on page 79.)
16. Print and then close the query.

Modifying a Query

You can modify a saved query and use it for a new purpose. For example, suppose that after designing the query that displays sales of more than $100,000, you decide that you want to find sales that are less than $100,000. Rather than design a new query, open the existing query, make any needed changes, and then run the query.

To modify an existing query, double-click the query in the Navigation pane. (This displays the query in Datasheet view.) Click the View button to display the query in Design view. You can also open a query in Design view by right-clicking the query in the Navigation pane and then clicking *Design View* at the shortcut menu. Make the desired changes and then click the Run button in the Results group. Click the Save button on the Quick Access toolbar to save the query with the same name. If you want to save the query with a new name, click the FILE tab, click the *Save As* option, click the *Save Object As* option, and then click the Save As button. At the Save As dialog box, type a name for the query and then press Enter.

If your database contains a number of queries, you can group and display them in the Navigation pane. To do this, click the down-pointing arrow in the Navigation pane menu bar and then click *Object Type* at the drop-down list. This displays objects grouped in categories, such as *Tables* and *Queries*.

Quick Steps

Modify a Query

1. Double-click query in Navigation pane.
2. Click View button.
3. Make desired changes to query.
4. Click Run button.
5. Click Save button.

Save time designing a new query by modifying an existing query.

Renaming and Deleting a Query

If you modify a query, you may want to rename it. To do this, right-click the query name in the Navigation pane, click *Rename* at the shortcut menu, type the new name, and then press Enter. If you no longer need the query in the database, delete it by clicking the query name in the Navigation pane, clicking the Delete button in the Records group on the HOME tab, and then clicking the Yes button at the message asking if you want to permanently delete the query. Another method is to right-click the query in the Navigation pane, click *Delete* at the shortcut menu, and then click the Yes at the message. If you are deleting a query from your computer's hard drive, the message asking if you want to permanently delete the query will not display. This is because Access automatically sends the deleted query to the Recycle Bin, where it can be retrieved if necessary.

Project 1d **Modifying Queries** **Part 4 of 8**

1. With **AL1-C3-Dearborn.accdb** open, find sales less than $100,000 by completing the following steps:
   a. Double-click *SalesMoreThan$100000Query* in the Queries group in the Navigation pane.
   b. Click the View button in the Views group to switch to Design view.
   c. Click in the *Criteria* row field containing the text *>100000* and then edit the text so it displays as *<100000*.

Field:	RepName	Client	Sales
Table:	Representatives	Clients	Sales
Sort:			Descending
Show:	✔	✔	✔
Criteria:			<100000
or:			

Step 1c

   d. Click the Run button in the Results group.

2. Save the query with a new name by completing the following steps:
   a. Click the FILE tab, click the *Save As* option, click the *Save Object As* option, and then click the Save As button.
   b. At the Save As dialog box, type **SalesLessThan$100000Query** and then press Enter. (See Project 1d query results on page 79.)
   c. Print and then close the query.

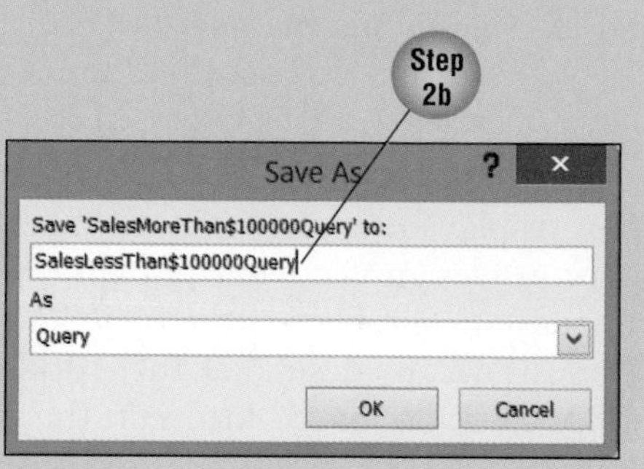

3. Modify an existing query and find employees with three weeks of vacation by completing the following steps:
   a. Right-click *MarToNov2011HiresQuery* in the Queries group in the Navigation pane and then click *Design View* at the shortcut menu.
   b. Click in the *Field* row field containing the text *HireDate*.
   c. Click the down-pointing arrow that displays at the right side of the field and then click *Vacation* at the drop-down list.
   d. Select the current text in the *Criteria* row field in the *Vacation* column, type **3 weeks**, and then press Enter.
   e. Click the Run button in the Results group.
   f. Save and then close the query.

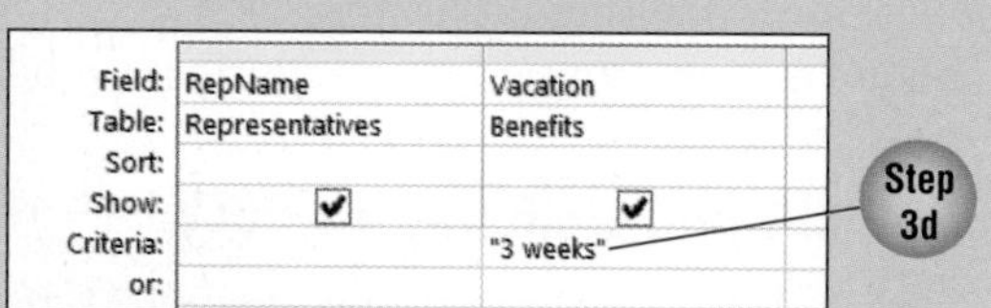

4. Rename the query by completing the following steps:
   a. Right-click *MarToNov2011HiresQuery* in the Navigation pane and then click *Rename* at the shortcut menu.
   b. Type **RepsWith3WeekVacationsQuery** and then press Enter. (See Project 1d query results on page 79.)
   c. Open, print and then close the query.
5. Delete the *SalesOver$99999Query* by right-clicking the query name in the Navigation pane and then clicking *Delete* at the shortcut menu. If a message displays asking if you want to permanently delete the query, click Yes.

Designing Queries with *Or* and *And* Criteria

The query design grid contains an *or* row that you can use to design a query that instructs Access to display records matching any of the criteria. Multiple criterion statements on different rows in a query become an Or statement, which means that any of the criterion can be met for a record to be displayed in the query results datasheet. For example, to display a list of employees with three weeks of vacation *or* four weeks of vacation, type *3 weeks* in the *Criteria* row field for the *Vacation* column and then type *4 weeks* in the field immediately below *3 weeks* in the *or* row. Other examples include finding clients that live in *Muncie* or *Lafayette* and finding representatives with quotas of *1* or *2*.

HINT
You can design a query that combines *And* and *Or* statements.

You can also select records by entering criteria statements into more than one *Criteria* field. Multiple criteria all entered in the same row become an *And* statement, for which each criterion must be met for Access to select the record. For example, you can search for clients in the Indianapolis area with sales greater than $100,000.

Project 1e Designing Queries with *Or* and *And* Criteria Part 5 of 8

1. With **AL1-C3-Dearborn.accdb** open, modify an existing query and find employees with three weeks or four weeks of vacation by completing the following steps:
   a. Double-click the *RepsWith3WeekVacationsQuery*.
   b. Click the View button in the Views group to switch to Design view.
   c. Click in the empty field below "*3 weeks*" in the *or* row, type **4 weeks**, and then press Enter.
   d. Click the Run button in the Results group.

Field:	RepName	Vacation
Table:	Representatives	Benefits
Sort:		
Show:	✔	✔
Criteria:		"3 weeks"
or:		"4 weeks"

Step 1c

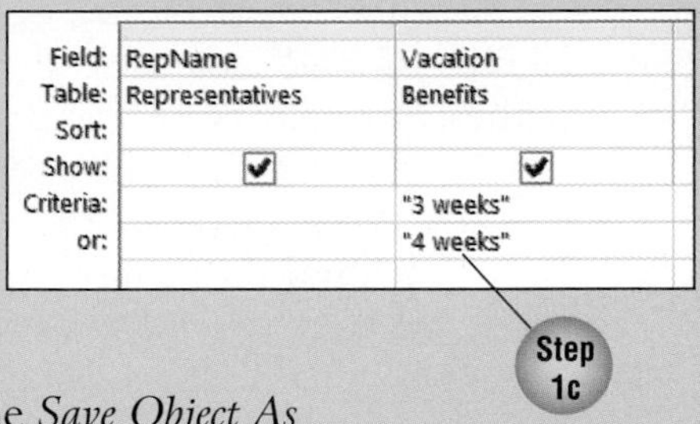

2. Save the query with a new name by completing the following steps:
   a. Click the FILE tab, click the *Save As* option, click the *Save Object As* option, and then click the Save As button.
   b. At the Save As dialog box, type **RepsWith3Or4WeekVacationsQuery** and then press Enter. (See Project 1e query results on page 79.)
   c. Print and then close the query.
3. Design a query that finds records of clients in the Indianapolis area with sales over $100,000 by completing the following steps:
   a. Click the CREATE tab and then click the Query Design button.
   b. Double-click *Clients* in the Show Table dialog box.
   c. Double-click *Sales* in the Show Table dialog box and then click the Close button.
   d. At the query window, insert the *Client* field from the *Clients* field list box in the first *Field* row field.
   e. Insert the *City* field from the *Clients* field list box in the second *Field* row field.
   f. Insert the *Sales* field from the *Sales* field list box in the third *Field* row field.
   g. Insert the query criteria by completing the following steps:
      1) Click in the *Criteria* row field in the *City* column.
      2) Type **Indianapolis** and then press Enter.
      3) With the insertion point positioned in the *Criteria* row field in the *Sales* column, type **>100000** and then press Enter.
   h. Click the Run button in the Results group. 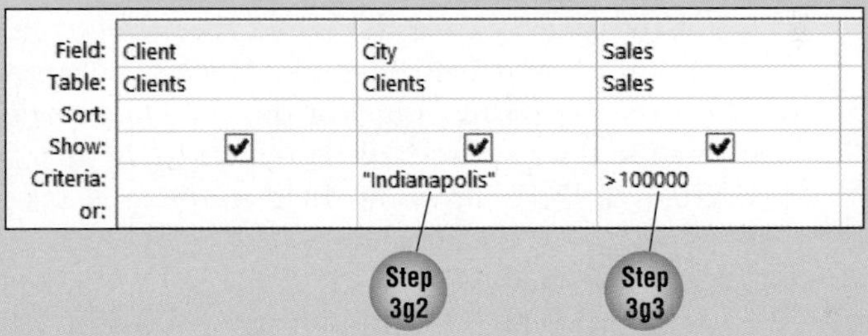

Field:	Client	City	Sales
Table:	Clients	Clients	Sales
Sort:			
Show:	✔	✔	✔
Criteria:		"Indianapolis"	>100000
or:			

Step 3g2 Step 3g3

   i. Save the query and name it *SalesOver$100000IndianapolisQuery*. (See Project 1e query results on page 79.)
   j. Print and then close the query.
4. Close **AL1-C3-Dearborn.accdb**.
5. Open **AL1-C3-PacTrek.accdb**.
6. Design a query that finds products available from supplier numbers 25, 31, and 42 by completing the following steps:
   a. Click the CREATE tab and then click the Query Design button.
   b. Double-click *Suppliers* in the Show Table dialog box.
   c. Double-click *Products* in the Show Table dialog box and then click the Close button.
   d. At the query window, insert the *SupplierID* field from the *Suppliers* field list box in the first *Field* row field.

e. Insert the *SupplierName* field from the *Suppliers* field list box in the second *Field* row field.
f. Insert the *Product* field from the *Products* field list box in the third *Field* row field.
g. Insert the query criteria by completing the following steps:
   1) Click in the *Criteria* row field in the *SupplierID* column.
   2) Type **25** and then press the Down Arrow key on your keyboard. (This makes active the field below *25*.)
   3) Type **31** and then press the Down Arrow key on your keyboard. (This makes active the field below *31*.)
   4) Type **42** and then press Enter.

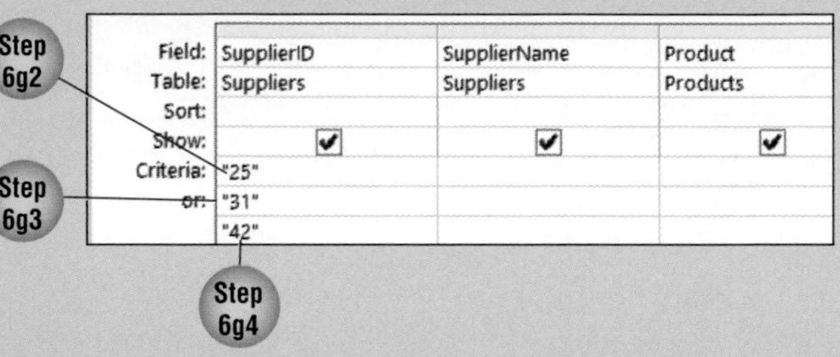

h. Click the Run button in the Results group.
i. Save the query and name it *Suppliers25-31-42Query*. (See Project 1e query results on page 79.)
j. Print and then close the query.

7. Design a query that finds ski hats or gloves on order and the numbers ordered by completing the following steps:
   a. Click the CREATE tab and then click the Query Design button.
   b. Double-click *Orders* in the Show Table dialog box.
   c. Double-click *Suppliers* in the Show Table dialog box.
   d. Double-click *Products* in the Show Table dialog box and then click the Close button.
   e. At the query window, insert the *OrderID* field from the *Orders* field list box in the first *Field* row field.
   f. Insert the *SupplierName* field from the *Suppliers* field list box in the second *Field* row field.
   g. Insert the *Product* field from the *Products* field list box in the third *Field* row field.
   h. Insert the *UnitsOrdered* field from the *Orders* field list box in the fourth *Field* row field.
   i. Insert the query criteria by completing the following steps:
      1) Click in the *Criteria* row field in the *Product* column.
      2) Type ***ski hat*** and then press the Down Arrow key on your keyboard. (You need to type the asterisk before and after *ski hat* so the query will find any product that includes the words *ski hat* in the description, no matter what text comes before or after the words.)
      3) Type ***gloves*** and then press Enter.

Step 7i2

Field:	OrderID	SupplierName	Product	UnitsOrdered
Table:	Orders	Suppliers	Products	Orders
Sort:				
Show:	✔	✔	✔	✔
Criteria:			Like "*ski hat*"	
or:			Like "*gloves*"	

Step 7i3

   j. Click the Run button in the Results group.
   k. Save the query and name it *SkiHatsGlovesOnOrderQuery*. (See Project 1e query results on page 79.)
   l. Print and then close the query.

8. Design a query that finds boots, sleeping bags, or backpacks and the suppliers that produce them by completing the following steps:
   a. Click the CREATE tab and then click the Query Design button.
   b. Double-click *Products* in the Show Table dialog box.
   c. Double-click *Suppliers* in the Show Table dialog box and then click the Close button.
   d. At the query window, insert the *ProductID* field from the *Products* field list box in the first *Field* row field.
   e. Insert the *Product* field from the *Products* field list box in the second *Field* row field.
   f. Insert the *SupplierName* field from the *Suppliers* field list box in the third *Field* row field.
   g. Insert the query criteria by completing the following steps:
      1) Click in the *Criteria* row field in the *Product* column.
      2) Type ***boots*** and then press the Down Arrow key on your keyboard.
      3) Type ***sleeping bag*** and then press the Down Arrow key on your keyboard.
      4) Type ***backpack*** and then press Enter.

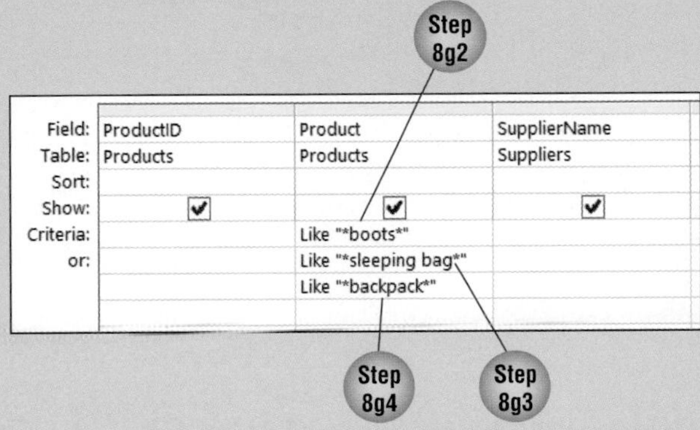

   h. Click the Run button in the Results group.
   i. Save the query and name it *BootsSleepingBagsBackpacksQuery*. (See Project 1e query results on page 79.)
   j. Print and then close the query.
9. Close **AL1-C3-PacTrek.accdb**.
10. Open **AL1-C3-CopperState.accdb**.
11. Design a query that finds clients that have only liability auto coverage by completing the following steps:
    a. Click the CREATE tab and then click the Query Design button.
    b. Double-click *Clients* in the Show Table dialog box.
    c. Double-click *Coverage* in the Show Table dialog box and then click the Close button.
    d. At the query window, insert the *ClientID* field from the *Clients* field list box in the first *Field* row field.
    e. Insert the *FirstName* field from the *Clients* field list box in the second *Field* row field.
    f. Insert the *LastName* field from the *Clients* field list box in the third *Field* row field.
    g. Insert the *Medical* field from the *Coverage* field list box in the fourth *Field* row field.
    h. Insert the *Liability* field from the *Coverage* field list box in the fifth *Field* row field.
    i. Insert the *Comprehensive* field from the *Coverage* field list box in the sixth *Field* row field.
    j. Insert the *UninsMotorist* field from the *Coverage* field list box in the seventh *Field* row field. (You may need to scroll down the *Coverage* field list box to display the *UninsMotorist* field.)
    k. Insert the *Collision* field from the *Coverage* field list box in the eighth *Field* row field. (You may need to scroll down the *Coverage* field list box to display the *Collision* field.)

l. Insert the query criteria by completing the following steps:
   1) Click in the *Criteria* row field in the *Medical* column, type 0, and then press Enter. (Access changes the *0* to *False*.)
   2) With the insertion point in the *Liability* column, type 1 and then press Enter. (Access changes the *1* to *True*.)
   3) With the insertion point in the *Comprehensive* column, type 0 and then press Enter.
   4) With the insertion point in the *UninsMotorist* column, type 0 and then press Enter.
   5) With the insertion point in the *Collision* column, type 0 and then press Enter.

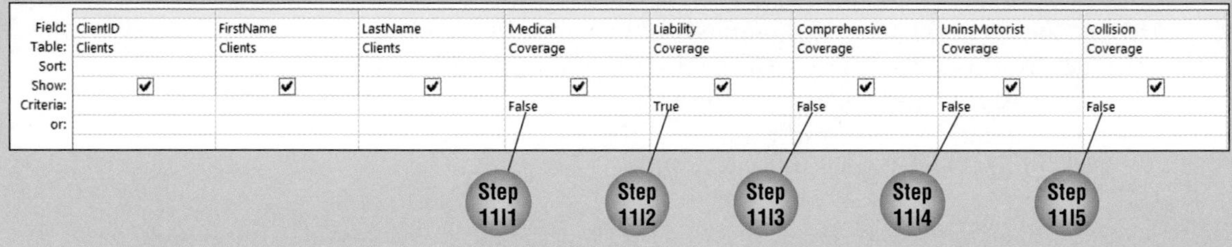
Field: ClientID FirstName LastName Medical Liability Comprehensive UninsMotorist Collision
Table: Clients Clients Clients Coverage Coverage Coverage Coverage Coverage
Sort:
Show:
Criteria: False True False False False
or:
Step 11l1
Step 11l2
Step 11l3
Step 11l4
Step 11l5

m. Click the Run button in the Results group.
n. Save the query and name it *ClientsWithOnlyLiabilityQuery*. (See Project 1e query results on page 79.)
o. Print the query in landscape orientation.
p. Close the query.

12. Close **AL1-C3-CopperState.accdb**.

Performing Queries with the Simple Query Wizard

Query Wizard

The Simple Query Wizard provided by Access guides you through the steps for preparing a query. To use this wizard, open the database, click the CREATE tab, and then click the Query Wizard button in the Queries group. At the New Query dialog box, make sure *Simple Query Wizard* is selected in the list box and then click the OK button. At the first Simple Query Wizard dialog box, shown in Figure 3.3, specify the table(s) in the *Tables/Queries* option box. After specifying the table(s), insert the fields you want included in the query in the *Selected Fields* list box and then click the Next button.

Figure 3.3 First Simple Query Wizard Dialog Box

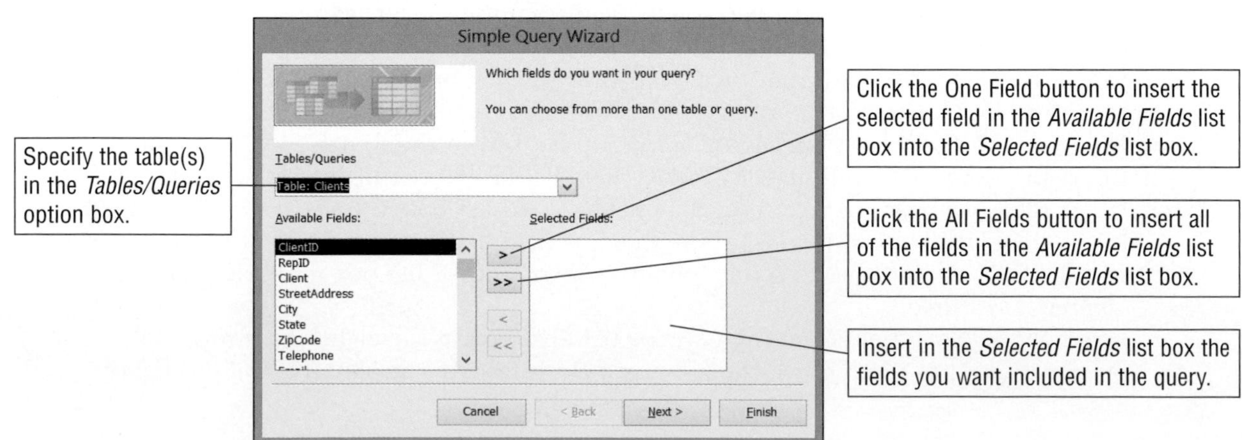
Simple Query Wizard
Which fields do you want in your query?
You can choose from more than one table or query.
Tables/Queries
Table: Clients
Available Fields:
Selected Fields:
ClientID
RepID
Client
StreetAddress
City
State
ZipCode
Telephone
>
>>
<
<<
Cancel
< Back
Next >
Finish
Specify the table(s) in the Tables/Queries option box.
Click the One Field button to insert the selected field in the Available Fields list box into the Selected Fields list box.
Click the All Fields button to insert all of the fields in the Available Fields list box into the Selected Fields list box.
Insert in the Selected Fields list box the fields you want included in the query.

At the second Simple Query Wizard dialog box, specify whether you want a detail or summary query and then click the Next button. At the third (and last) Simple Query Wizard dialog box, shown in Figure 3.4, type a name for the completed query or accept the name provided by the wizard. At this dialog box, you can also specify that you want to open the query to view the information or modify the query design. If you want to extract specific information, be sure to choose the *Modify the query design* option. After making any necessary changes, click the Finish button.

If you do not modify the query design in the last Simple Query Wizard dialog box, the query displays all records for the fields identified in the first Simple Query Wizard dialog box. In Project 1f, you will perform a query without modifying the design, and in Project 1g, you will modify the query design.

Quick Steps

Create a Query with the Simple Query Wizard

1. Click CREATE tab.
2. Click Query Wizard button.
3. Make sure *Simple Query Wizard* is selected in list box and then click OK.
4. Follow query steps.

Figure 3.4 Last Simple Query Wizard Dialog Box

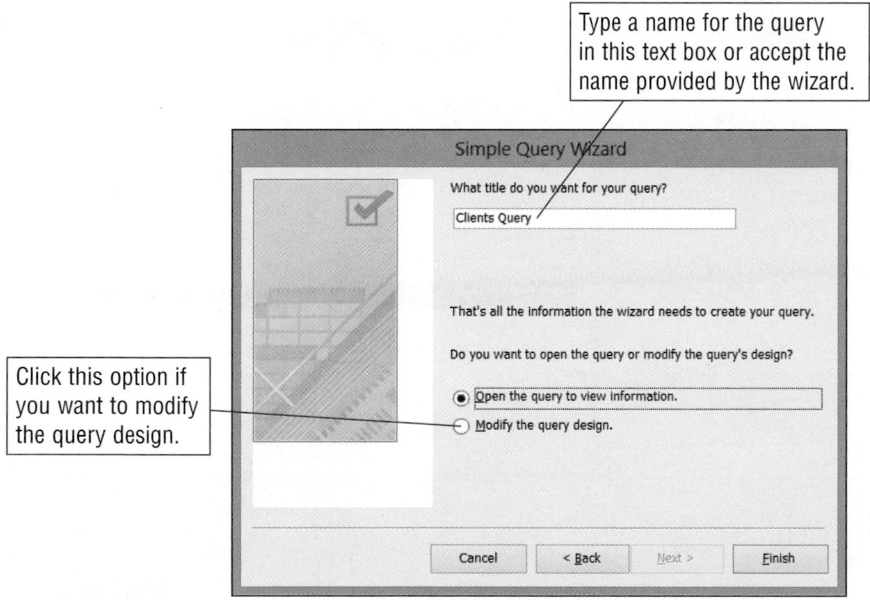

Project 1f Performing Queries with the Simple Query Wizard — Part 6 of 8

1. Open **AL1-C3-Dearborn.accdb** and then use the Simple Query Wizard to create a query that displays client names along with sales by completing the following steps:
   a. Click the CREATE tab and then click the Query Wizard button in the Queries group.
   b. At the New Query dialog box, make sure *Simple Query Wizard* is selected in the list box and then click OK.
   c. At the first Simple Query Wizard dialog box, click the down-pointing arrow at the right of the *Tables/Queries* option box and then click *Table: Clients*.

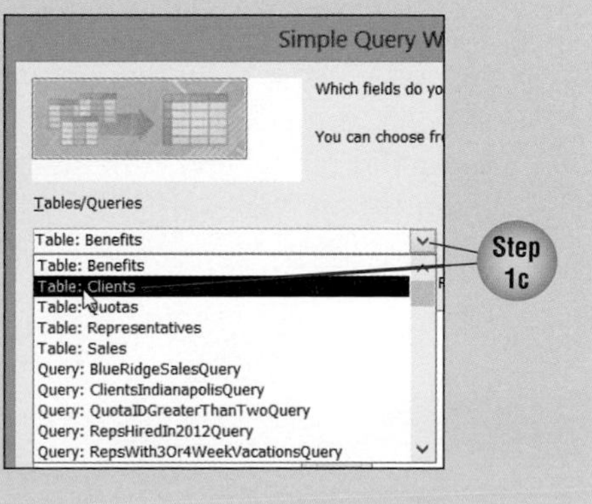

d. With *ClientID* selected in the *Available Fields* list box, click the One Field button (the button containing the greater-than symbol, >). This inserts the *ClientID* field in the *Selected Fields* list box.
e. Click *Client* in the *Available Fields* list box and then click the One Field button.
f. Click the down-pointing arrow at the right of the *Tables/Queries* option box and then click *Table: Sales*.
g. Click *Sales* in the *Available Fields* list box and then click the One Field button.
h. Click the Next button.
i. At the second Simple Query Wizard dialog box, click the Next button.
j. At the last Simple Query Wizard dialog box, select the name in the *What title do you want for your query?* text box, type **ClientSalesQuery**, and then press Enter.

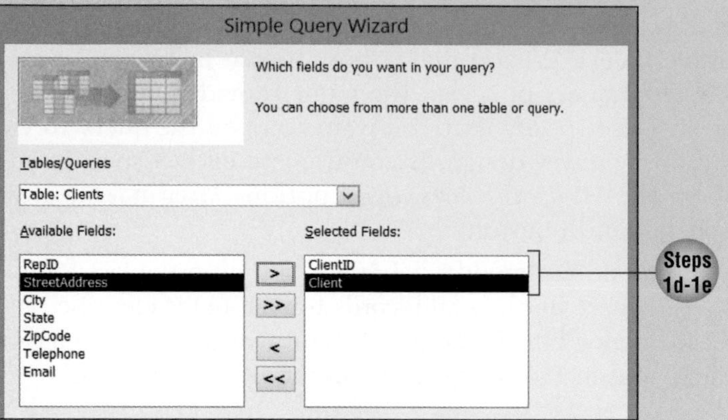

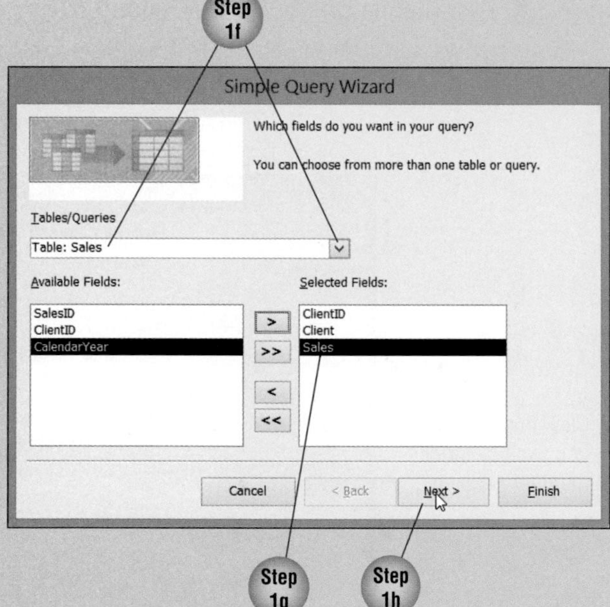

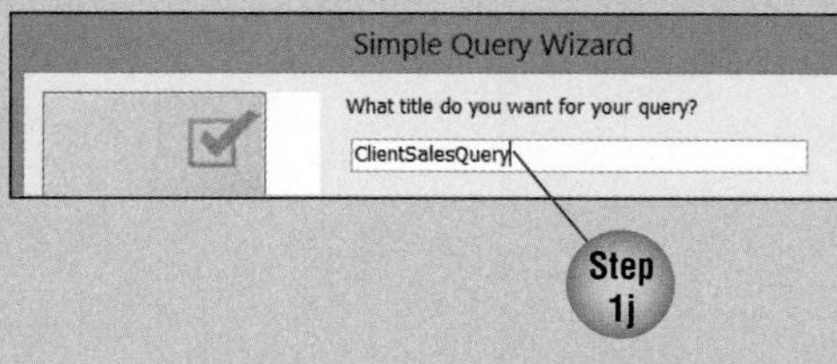

k. When the results of the query display, print the results. (See Project 1f query results on page 80.)

2. Close the query.
3. Close **AL1-C3-Dearborn.accdb**.
4. Open **AL1-C3-PacTrek.accdb**.
5. Create a query that displays the products on order, order amounts, and supplier names by completing the following steps:
   a. Click the CREATE tab and then click the Query Wizard button.
   b. At the New Query dialog box, make sure *Simple Query Wizard* is selected in the list box and then click OK.

c. At the first Simple Query Wizard dialog box, click the down-pointing arrow at the right side of the *Tables/Queries* option box and then click *Table: Suppliers*.
d. With *SupplierID* selected in the *Available Fields* list box, click the One Field button. (This inserts the *SupplierID* field in the *Selected Fields* list box.)
e. With *SupplierName* selected in the *Available Fields* list box, click the One Field button.
f. Click the down-pointing arrow at the right of the *Tables/Queries* option box and then click *Table: Orders*.
g. Click *ProductID* in the *Available Fields* list box and then click the One Field button.
h. Click *Amount* in the *Available Fields* list box and then click the One Field button.
i. Click the Next button.
j. At the second Simple Query Wizard dialog box, click the Next button.

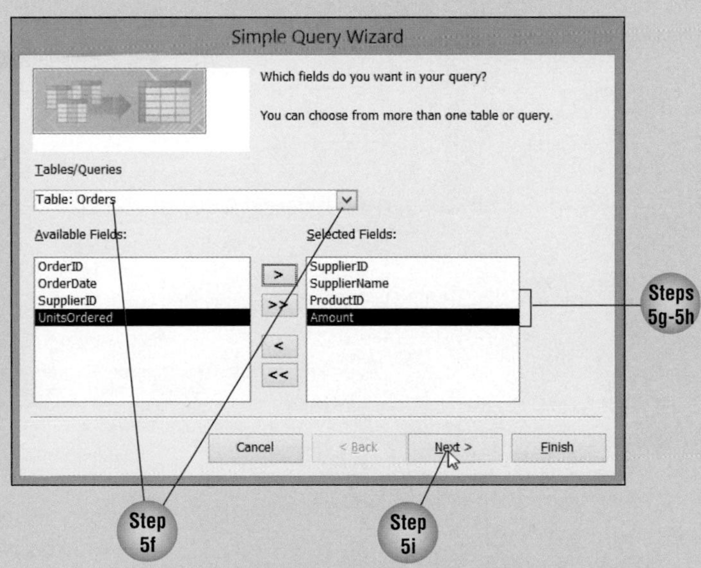

k. At the last Simple Query Wizard dialog box, select the text in the *What title do you want for your query?* text box, type **ProductOrderAmountsQuery**, and then press Enter.
l. When the results of the query display, print the results. (See Project 1f query results on page 80.)
m. Close the query.

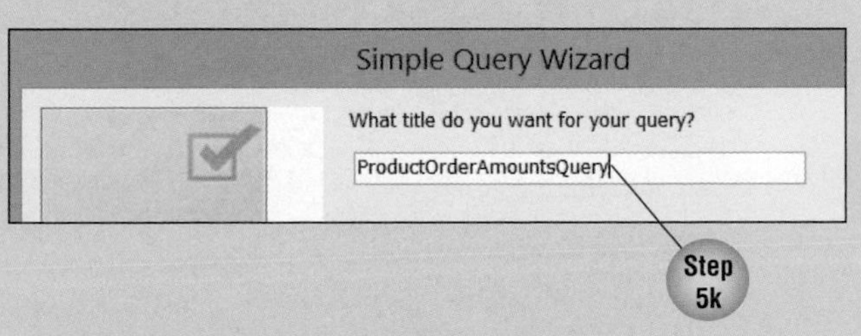

To extract specific information when using the Simple Query Wizard, tell the wizard that you want to modify the query design. This displays the query window with the query design grid, where you can insert query criteria.

Project 1g **Performing and Modifying Queries with the Simple Query Wizard** **Part 7 of 8**

1. With **AL1-C3-PacTrek.accdb** open, use the Simple Query Wizard to create a query that displays suppliers outside British Columbia by completing the following steps:
   a. Click the CREATE tab and then click the Query Wizard button.
   b. At the New Query dialog box, make sure *Simple Query Wizard* is selected and then click OK.
   c. At the first Simple Query Wizard dialog box, click the down-pointing arrow at the right side of the *Tables/Queries* option box and then click *Table: Suppliers*.
   d. Insert the following fields in the *Selected Fields* list box:
      SupplierName
      StreetAddress
      City
      Prov/State
      PostalCode
   e. Click the Next button.
   f. At the last Simple Query Wizard dialog box, select the current text in the *What title do you want for your query?* text box and then type **SuppliersNotBCQuery**.
   g. Click the *Modify the query design* option and then click the Finish button.
   h. At the query window, complete the following steps:
      1) Click in the *Criteria* row field in the *Prov/State* column in the query design grid.
      2) Type **Not BC** and then press Enter.

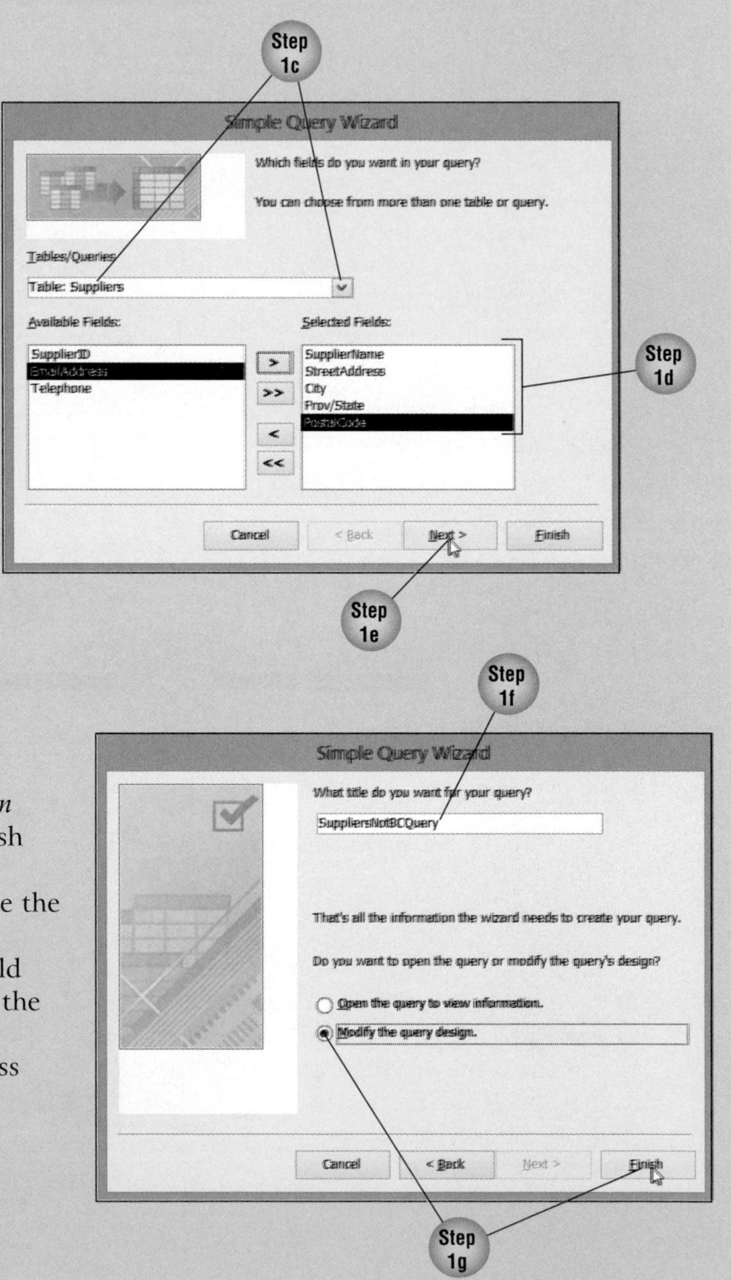

i. Specify that the fields are to be sorted in descending order by postal code by completing the following steps:
   1) Click in the *Sort* row field in the *PostalCode* column.
   2) Click the down-pointing arrow that displays at the right side of the field and then click *Descending*.

Field:	[SupplierName]	[StreetAddress]	[City]	[Prov/State]	[PostalCode]
Table:	Suppliers	Suppliers	Suppliers	Suppliers	Suppliers
Sort:					Descending
Show:	✔	✔	✔	✔	Ascending
Criteria:				Not "BC"	Descending
or:					(not sorted)

Step 1i2

j. Click the Run button in the Results group. (This displays suppliers that are not located in British Columbia and displays the records sorted by postal code in descending order. See Project 1g query results on page 80.)
k. Save, print, and then close the query.

2. Close **AL1-C3-PacTrek.accdb**.
3. Open **AL1-C3-Dearborn.accdb**.
4. Use the Simple Query Wizard to create a query that displays clients in Muncie by completing the following steps:
   a. Click the CREATE tab and then click the Query Wizard button.
   b. At the New Query dialog box, make sure *Simple Query Wizard* is selected and then click OK.
   c. At the first Simple Query Wizard dialog box, click the down-pointing arrow at the right of the *Tables/Queries* option box and then click *Table: Clients*. (You may need to scroll up the list to display this table.)
   d. Insert the following fields in the *Selected Fields* list box:
      Client
      StreetAddress
      City
      State
      ZipCode
   e. Click the Next button.
   f. At the last Simple Query Wizard dialog box, select the current text in the *What title do you want for your query?* text box and then type **ClientsMuncieQuery**.
   g. Click the *Modify the query design* option and then click the Finish button.
   h. At the query window, complete the following steps:
      1) Click in the *Criteria* row field in the *City* column in the query design grid.
      2) Type **Muncie** and then press Enter.

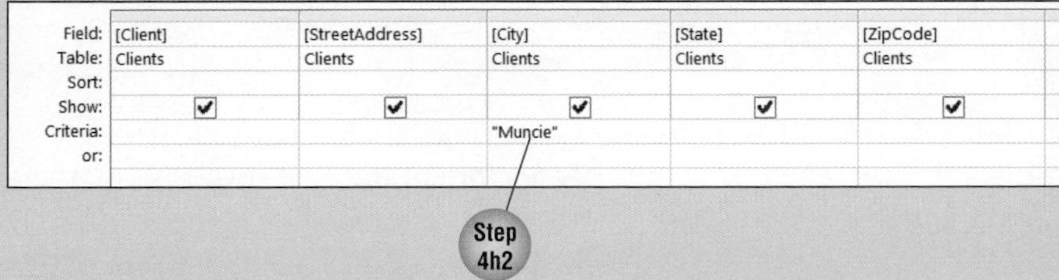

   i. Click the Run button in the Results group. (This displays clients located in Muncie. See Project 1g query results on page 80.)
   j. Save, print, and then close the query.

5. Close **AL1-C3-Dearborn.accdb**.
6. Open **AL1-C3-CopperState.accdb**.
7. Use the Simple Query Wizard to display clients that live in Phoenix with claims over $500 by completing the following steps:
   a. Click the CREATE tab and then click the Query Wizard button in the Queries group.
   b. At the New Query dialog box, make sure *Simple Query Wizard* is selected in the list box and then click OK.
   c. At the first Simple Query Wizard dialog box, click the down-pointing arrow at the right of the *Tables/Queries* option box and then click *Table: Clients*.
   d. Insert the following fields in the *Selected Fields* list box:
      ClientID
      FirstName
      LastName
      StreetAddress
      City
      State
      ZIP
   e. Click the down-pointing arrow at the right of the *Tables/Queries* option box and then click *Table: Claims*.
   f. With *ClaimID* selected in the *Available Fields* list box, click the One Field button.
   g. Click *AmountOfClaim* in the *Available Fields* list box and then click the One Field button.
   h. Click the Next button.
   i. At the second Simple Query Wizard dialog box, click the Next button.
   j. At the last Simple Query Wizard dialog box, select the current text in the *What title do you want for your query?* text box and then type **PhoenixClientClaimsOver$500Query**.
   k. Click the *Modify the query design* option and then click the Finish button.
   l. At the query window, complete the following steps:
      1) Click in the *Criteria* row field in the *City* column in the query design grid.
      2) Type "**Phoenix**" and then press Enter. (Type the quotation marks to tell Access that this is a criterion, otherwise Access will insert the query name *PhoenixClientClaimsOver$500Query* in the *Criteria* field.)
      3) Click in the *Criteria* row field in the *AmountOfClaim* column. (You may need to scroll to the right to display this field.)
      4) Type **>500** and then press Enter.

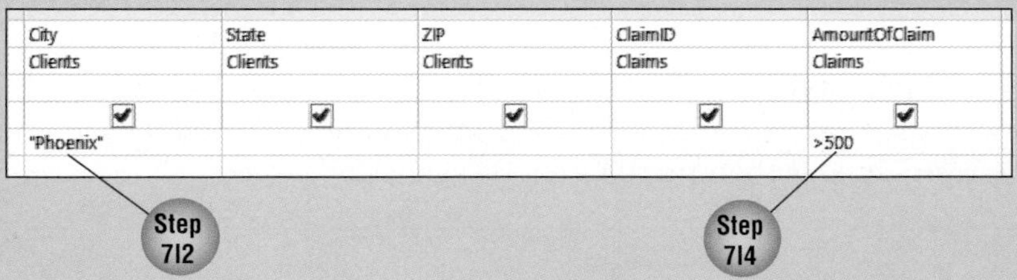

City	State	ZIP	ClaimID	AmountOfClaim
Clients	Clients	Clients	Claims	Claims
✔	✔	✔	✔	✔
"Phoenix"				>500

Step 7l2

Step 7l4

   m. Click the Run button in the Results group. (This displays clients located in Phoenix with claims greater than $500. See Project 1g query results on page 80.)
   n. Save the query, print the query in landscape orientation, and then close the query.
8. Close **AL1-C3-CopperState.accdb**.

Creating Calculated Fields

In a query, you can calculate values from a field by inserting a ***calculated field*** in a *Field* row field in the query design grid. To insert a calculated field, click in the *Field* row field, type the desired field name followed by a colon, and then type the equation. For example, to determine pension contributions as 3% of an employee's annual salary, type *PensionContribution:[AnnualSalary]*0.03* in the *Field* row field. Use brackets to specify field names and use mathematical operators to perform the equation. Some basic operators include the plus (+) for addition, the hyphen (-) for subtraction, the asterisk (*) for multiplication, and the forward slash (/) for division.

Type a calculated field in the field or in the Expression Builder dialog box. To display the Expression Builder dialog box, display the query in Design view, click in the field where you want the calculated field expression inserted, and then click the Builder button in the Query Setup group on the QUERY TOOLS DESIGN tab. You can type field names in the Expression Builder and when you click OK, the equation is inserted in the field with the correct symbols. For example, you can type *AnnualSalary*0.03* in the Expression Builder and when you click OK, *Expr1: [AnnualSalary]*0.03* is inserted in the *Criteria* row field. If you do not type a name for the field, Access creates the alias *Expr1* for the field name. If you want a specific name for the field, such as *PensionContribution*, first type that in the Expression Builder, followed by a colon, and then type the expression.

Builder

Project 1h **Creating a Calculated Field in a Query** **Part 8 of 8**

1. Open **AL1-C3-MRInvestments.accdb** and enable the contents.
2. Create a query that displays employer pension contributions at 3% of employees' annual salary by completing the following steps:
   a. Click the CREATE tab and then click the Query Design button.
   b. Double-click *Employees* in the Show Table dialog box and then click the Close button.
   c. At the query window, insert the *EmpID* field from the *Employees* field list box in the first *Field* row field.
   d. Insert the *FirstName* field in the second *Field* row field.
   e. Insert the *LastName* field in the third *Field* row field.
   f. Insert the *AnnualSalary* field in the fourth *Field* row field.
   g. Click in the fifth *Field* row field.
   h. Type **PensionContribution:[AnnualSalary]*0.03** and then press Enter.
   i. Click the Run button in the Results group.
   j. Save the query and name it *PensionContributionsQuery*. (See Project 1h query results on page 80.)
   k. Print and then close the query.

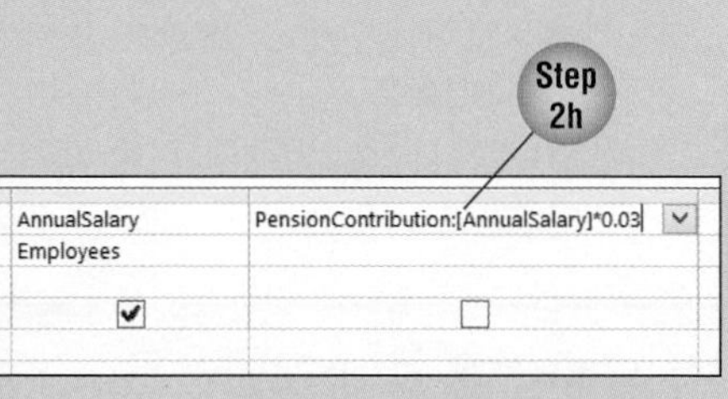

3. Modify *PensionContributionsQuery* and use the Expression Builder to write an equation finding the total amount of annual salary plus a 3% employer pension contribution by completing the following steps:
   a. Right-click *PensionContributionsQuery* in the Queries group in the Navigation pane and then click *Design View* at the shortcut menu.
   b. Click in the field containing *PensionContribution:[AnnualSalary]*0.03*.
   c. Click the Builder button in the Query Setup group on the QUERY TOOLS DESIGN tab.

d. In the Expression Builder, select the existing expression *PensionContribution: [AnnualSalary]*0.03*.
e. Type **Salary&Pension: [AnnualSalary]*1.03** and then click OK.
4. Click the Run button in the Results group.
5. Save the query by completing the following steps:
a. Click the FILE tab, click the *Save As* option, click the *Save Object As* option, and then click the Save As button.
b. At the Save As dialog box, type **Salary&PensionQuery** and then click OK. (See Project 1h query results on page 80.)

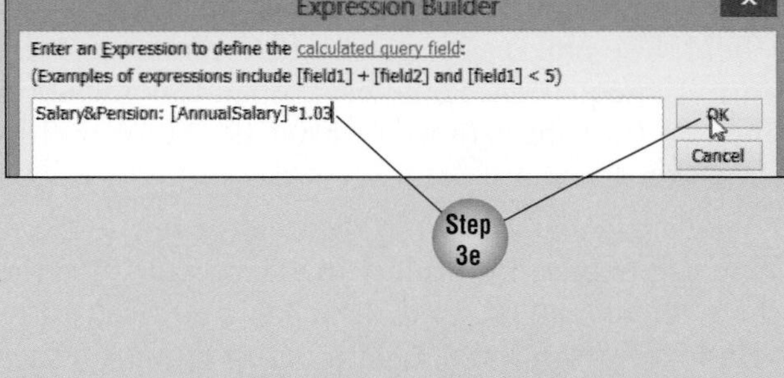

6. Print and then close the query.
7. Close **AL1-C3-MRInvestments.accdb**.
8. Open **AL1-C3-PacTrek.accdb**.
9. Create a query that displays orders and total order amounts by completing the following steps:
a. Click the CREATE tab and then click the Query Design button.
b. Double-click *Products* in the Show Table dialog box.
c. Double-click *Orders* in the Show Table dialog box and then click the Close button.
d. At the query window, insert the *Product* field from the *Products* field list box in the first *Field* row field.
e. Insert the *OrderID* field from the *Orders* field list box in the second *Field* row field.
f. Insert the *UnitsOrdered* field from the *Orders* field list box in the third *Field* row field.
g. Insert the *Amount* field from the *Orders* field list box in the fourth *Field* row field.
h. Click in the fifth *Field* row field.
i. Click the Builder button in the Query Setup group on the QUERY TOOLS DESIGN tab.
j. Type **Total:Amount*UnitsOrdered** in the Expression Builder and then click OK.
k. Click the Run button in the Results group.
l. Adjust the width of the columns to fit the longest entries.

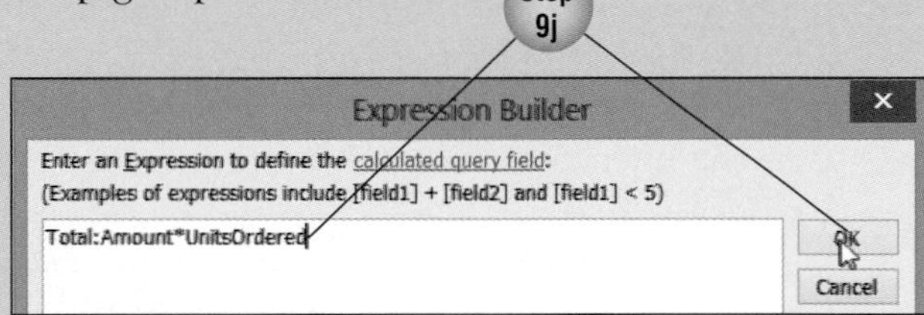

m. Save the query and name it *UnitsOrderedTotalQuery*. (See Project 1h query results on page 80.)
n. Print and then close the query.

Project 2 Create Aggregate Functions, Crosstab, Find Duplicates, and Find Unmatched Queries — 6 Parts

You will create an aggregate functions query that determines the total, average, minimum, and maximum order amounts and then calculate total and average order amounts grouped by supplier. You will also use the Crosstab, Find Duplicates, and Find Unmatched query wizards to design queries.

Designing Queries with Aggregate Functions

You can include an ***aggregate function***—such as Sum, Avg, Min, Max, or Count—in a query to calculate statistics from numeric field values of all the records in the table. When an aggregate function is used, Access displays one row in the query results datasheet with the formula result for the function used. For example, in a table with a numeric field containing annual salary amounts, you can use the Sum function to calculate the total of all salary amount values.

To display the aggregate function list, click the Totals button in the Show/Hide group on the QUERY TOOLS DESIGN tab. Access adds a *Total* row to the design grid with a drop-down list from which you select the desired function. Access also inserts the words *Group By* in the *Total* row field. Click the down-pointing arrow and then click the desired aggregate function from the drop-down list. In Project 2a, Step 1, you will create a query in Design view and use aggregate functions to find the total of all sales, average sales amount, maximum and minimum sales, and total number of sales. The completed query will display as shown in Figure 3.5. Access automatically determines the column heading names.

Quick Steps

Design a Query with an Aggregate Function

1. At query window, click Totals button.
2. Click down-pointing arrow in *Total* row field.
3. Click desired aggregate function.

Totals

Figure 3.5 Query Results for Project 2a, Step 1

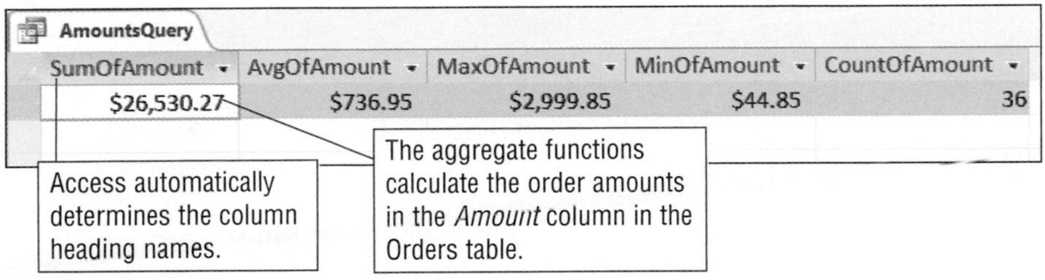

Project 2a **Using Aggregate Functions in Queries** **Part 1 of 6**

1. With **AL1-C3-PacTrek.accdb** open, create a query with aggregate functions that determines total, average, maximum, and minimum order amounts, as well as the total number of orders, by completing the following steps:
   a. Click the CREATE tab and then click the Query Design button.
   b. At the Show Table dialog box, make sure *Orders* is selected in the list box, click the Add button, and then click the Close button.
   c. Insert the *Amount* field in the first, second, third, fourth, and fifth *Field* row fields. (You may need to scroll down the *Orders* field list box to display the *Amount* field.)
   d. Click the Totals button in the Show/Hide group on the QUERY TOOLS DESIGN tab. (This adds a *Total* row to the design grid between *Table* and *Sort* with the default option of *Group By*.)

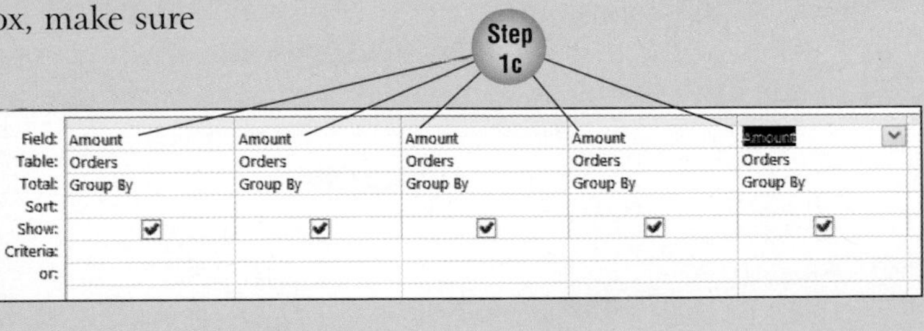

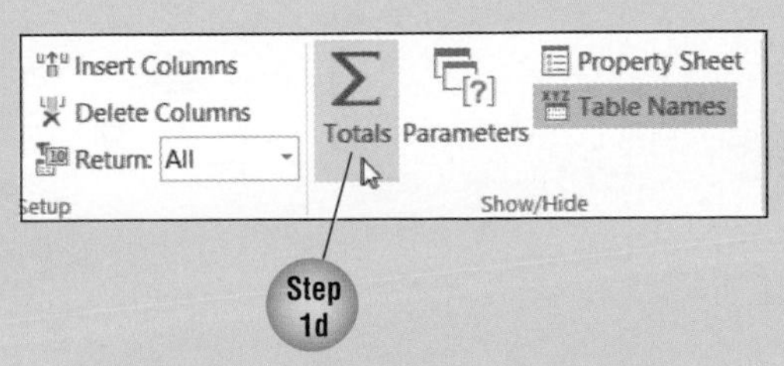

e. Specify a Sum function for the first *Total* row field by completing the following steps:
   1) Click in the first *Total* row field.
   2) Click the down-pointing arrow that displays at the right side of the field.
   3) Click *Sum* at the drop-down list.

f. Complete steps similar to those in Step 1e to insert *Avg* in the second *Total* row field.

g. Complete steps similar to those in Step 1e to insert *Max* in the third *Total* row field.

h. Complete steps similar to those in Step 1e to insert *Min* in the fourth *Total* row field.

i. Complete steps similar to those in Step 1e to insert *Count* in the fifth *Total* row field.

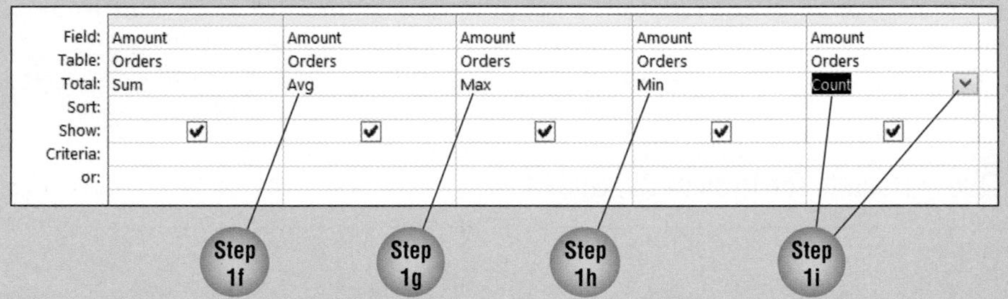

j. Click the Run button in the Results group. (Notice the headings that Access assigns to the columns.)

k. Automatically adjust the widths of the columns.

l. Save the query and name it *AmountsQuery*. (See Project 2a query results on page 81.)

m. Print and then close the query.

2. Close **AL1-C3-PacTrek.accdb**.
3. Open **AL1-C3-CopperState.accdb**.
4. Create a query with aggregate functions that determines total, average, maximum, and minimum claim amounts by completing the following steps:
   a. Click the CREATE tab and then click the Query Design button.
   b. At the Show Table dialog box, double-click *Claims*.
   c. Click the Close button to close the Show Table dialog box.
   d. Insert the *AmountOfClaim* field in the first, second, third, and fourth *Field* row fields.
   e. Click the Totals button in the Show/Hide group.
   f. Click in the first *Total* row field, click the down-pointing arrow that displays at the right side of the field, and then click *Sum* at the drop-down list.

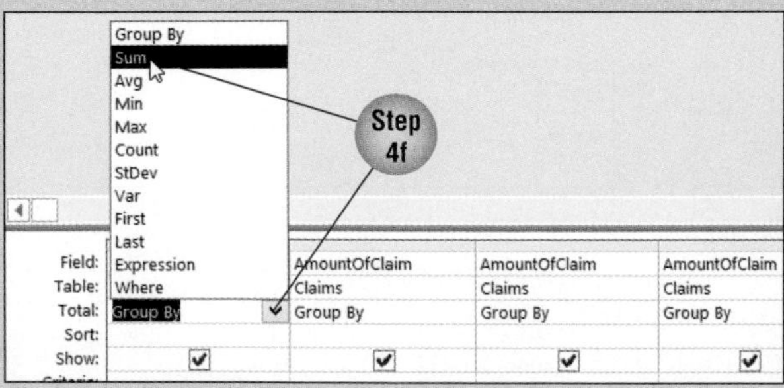

g. Click in the second *Total* row field, click the down-pointing arrow, and then click *Avg* at the drop-down list.
h. Click in the third *Total* row field, click the down-pointing arrow, and then click *Max* at the drop-down list.
i. Click in the fourth *Total* row field, click the down-pointing arrow, and then click *Min* at the drop-down list.
j. Click the Run button in the Results group. (Notice the headings that Access chooses for the columns.)
k. Automatically adjust the widths of the columns.
l. Save the query and name it *ClaimAmountsQuery*. (See Project 2a query results on page 81.)
m. Print the query in landscape orientation and then close the query.

Using the *Group By* option in the *Total* field, you can add a field to the query on which you want Access to group records for statistical calculations. For example, to calculate the total of all orders for a specific supplier, add the *SupplierID* field to the design grid with the *Total* field set to *Group By*. In Project 2b, Step 1, you will create a query in Design view and use aggregate functions to find the total of all order amounts and the average order amounts grouped by supplier number.

Project 2b Using Aggregate Functions and Grouping Records — Part 2 of 6

1. With **AL1-C3-CopperState.accdb** open, determine the sum and average of client claims by completing the following steps:
   a. Click the CREATE tab and then click the Query Design button.
   b. At the Show Table dialog box, double-click *Clients* in the list box.
   c. Double-click *Claims* in the list box and then click the Close button.
   d. Insert the *ClientID* field from the *Clients* field list box to the first *Field* row field.
   e. Insert the *AmountOfClaim* field from the *Claims* field list box to the second *Field* row field.
   f. Insert the *AmountOfClaim* field from the *Claims* field list box to the third *Field* row field.
   g. Click the Totals button in the Show/Hide group.
   h. Click in the second *Total* row field, click the down-pointing arrow, and then click *Sum* at the drop-down list.
   i. Click in the third *Total* row field, click the down-pointing arrow, and then click *Avg* at the drop-down list.
   j. Make sure *Group By* displays in the first *Total* row field.

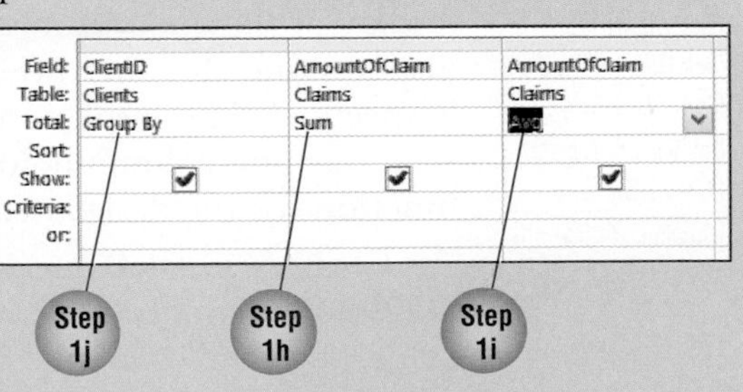

   k. Click the Run button in the Results group.
   l. Automatically adjust column widths.
   m. Save the query and name it *SumAvgClaimAmountsQuery*. (See Project 2b query results on page 81.)
   n. Print and then close the query.
2. Close **AL1-C3-CopperState.accdb**.

3. Open **AL1-C3-PacTrek.accdb**.
4. Determine the total and average order amounts for each supplier by completing the following steps:
   a. Click the CREATE tab and then click the Query Design button.
   b. At the Show Table dialog box, make sure *Orders* is selected in the list box and then click the Add button.
   c. Click *Suppliers* in the list box, click the Add button, and then click the Close button.
   d. Insert the *Amount* field from the *Orders* field list box to the first *Field* row field. (You may need to scroll down the *Orders* field list box to display the *Amount* field.)
   e. Insert the *Amount* field from the *Orders* field list box to the second *Field* row field.
   f. Insert the *SupplierID* field from the *Suppliers* field list box to the third *Field* row field.
   g. Insert the *SupplierName* field from the *Suppliers* field list box to the fourth *Field* row field.
   h. Click the Totals button in the Show/Hide group.
   i. Click in the first *Total* row field, click the down-pointing arrow, and then click *Sum* at the drop-down list.
   j. Click in the second *Total* row field, click the down-pointing arrow, and then click *Avg* at the drop-down list.
   k. Make sure *Group By* displays in the third and fourth *Total* row fields.
   l. Click the Run button in the Results group.
   m. Automatically adjust column widths.
   n. Save the query and name it *SupplierAmountsQuery*. (See Project 2b query results on page 81.)
   o. Print and then close the query.

Field:	Amount	Amount	SupplierID	SupplierName
Table:	Orders	Orders	Suppliers	Suppliers
Total:	Sum	Avg	Group By	Group By
Sort:				
Show:	☑	☑	☑	☑
Criteria:				
or:				

Step 4i   Step 4j   Step 4k

Creating Crosstab Queries

Quick Steps

Create a Crosstab Query
1. Click CREATE tab.
2. Click Query Wizard button.
3. Double-click *Crosstab Query Wizard*.
4. Complete wizard steps.

A ***crosstab query*** calculates aggregate functions, such as Sum and Avg, in which field values are grouped by two fields. A wizard is included that guides you through the steps to create the query. The first field selected causes one row to display in the query results datasheet for each group. The second field selected displays one column in the query results datasheet for each group. A third field is specified that is the numeric field to be summarized. The intersection of each row and column holds a value that is the result of the specified aggregate function for the designated row and column group.

Create a crosstab query from fields in one table. If you want to include fields from more than one table, you must first create a query containing the desired fields, and then create the crosstab query. For example, in Project 2c, Step 2, you will create a new query that contains fields from each of the three tables in AL1-C3-PacTrek.accdb. Using this query, you will use the Crosstab Query Wizard to create a query that summarizes the order amounts by supplier name and product ordered. Figure 3.6 displays the results of that crosstab query. The first column displays the supplier names, the second column displays the total amount for each supplier, and the remaining columns display the amounts by suppliers for specific items.

Figure 3.6 Crosstab Query Results for Project 2c, Step 2

Order amounts are grouped by supplier name and individual product.

OrdersBySupplierByProductQuery

SupplierName	Total Of Amc	Binoculars, 8	Cascade R4 ja	Cascade R4 ja	Cascade R4 ja	Cascade R4 ja	Deluxe map c	Eight-piece st
Bayside Supplies	$224.00							$99.75
Cascade Gear	$3,769.00		$1,285.00	$1,285.00	$599.50	$599.50		
Emerald City Products	$2,145.00	$2,145.00						
Fraser Valley Products	$3,892.75							
Freedom Corporation	$1,286.65							
Hopewell, Inc.	$348.60							
KL Distributions	$4,288.35							
Langley Corporation	$593.25							
Macadam, Inc.	$175.70						$129.75	
Manning, Inc.	$4,282.25							
Sound Supplies	$5,524.72							

Project 2c Creating Crosstab Queries

Part 3 of 6

1. With **AL1-C3-PacTrek.accdb** open, create a query containing fields from the three tables by completing the following steps:
   a. Click the CREATE tab and then click the Query Design button.
   b. At the Show Table dialog box with *Orders* selected in the list box, click the Add button.
   c. Double-click *Products* in the list box.
   d. Double-click *Suppliers* in the list box and then click the Close button.
   e. Insert the following fields to the specified *Field* row fields:
      1) From the *Orders* field list box, insert the *ProductID* field in the first *Field* row field.
      2) From the *Products* field list box, insert the *Product* field in the second *Field* row field.
      3) From the *Orders* field list box, insert the *UnitsOrdered* field in the third *Field* row field.
      4) From the *Orders* field list box, insert the *Amount* field in the fourth *Field* row field.
      5) From the *Suppliers* field list box, insert the *SupplierName* field in the fifth *Field* row field.
      6) From the *Orders* field list box, insert the *OrderDate* field in the sixth *Field* row field.

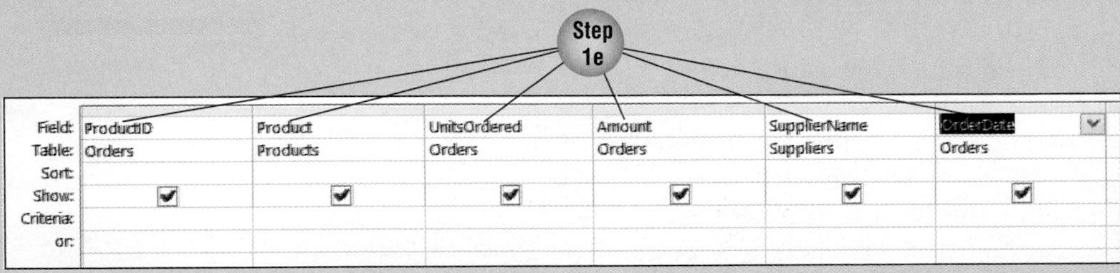

   f. Click the Run button to run the query.
   g. Save the query and name it *ItemsOrderedQuery*.
   h. Close the query.

2. Create a crosstab query that summarizes the orders by supplier name and by product ordered by completing the following steps:
   a. Click the CREATE tab and then click the Query Wizard button.
   b. At the New Query dialog box, double-click *Crosstab Query Wizard* in the list box.
   c. At the first Crosstab Query Wizard dialog box, click the *Queries* option in the *View* section and then click *Query: ItemsOrderedQuery* in the list box.
   d. Click the Next button.
   e. At the second Crosstab Query Wizard dialog box, click *SupplierName* in the *Available Fields* list box and then click the One Field button. (This inserts *SupplierName* in the *Selected Fields* list box and specifies that you want *SupplierName* for the row headings.)
   f. Click the Next button.
   g. At the third Crosstab Query Wizard dialog box, click *Product* in the list box. (This specifies that you want *Product* for the column headings.)
   h. Click the Next button.
   i. At the fourth Crosstab Query Wizard dialog box, click *Amount* in the *Fields* list box and then click *Sum* in the *Functions* list box.
   j. Click the Next button.
   k. At the fifth Crosstab Query Wizard dialog box, select the current text in the *What do you want to name your query?* text box and then type **OrdersBySupplierByProductQuery**.
   l. Click the Finish button. (See Project 2c query results on page 81.)

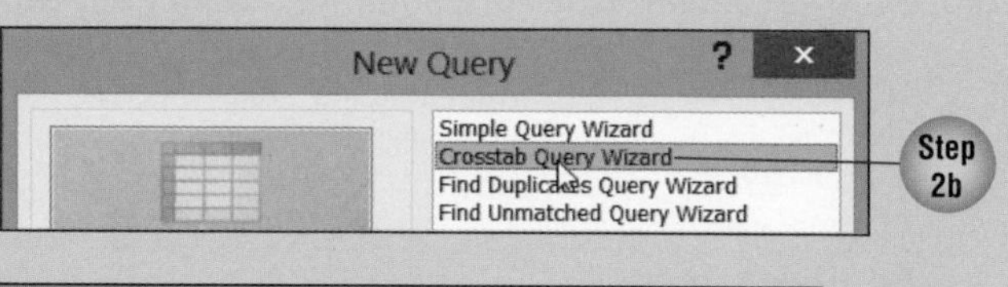

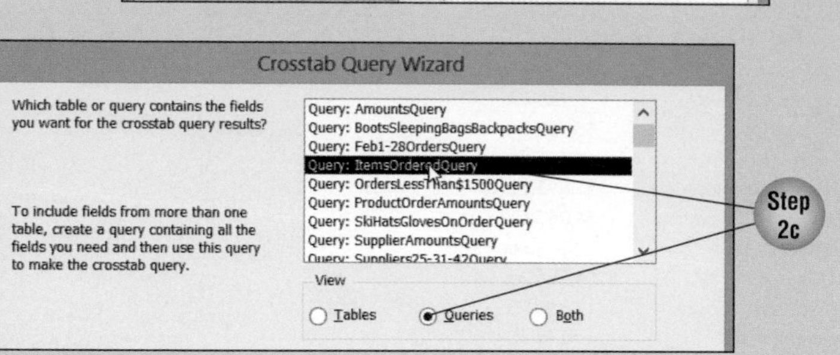

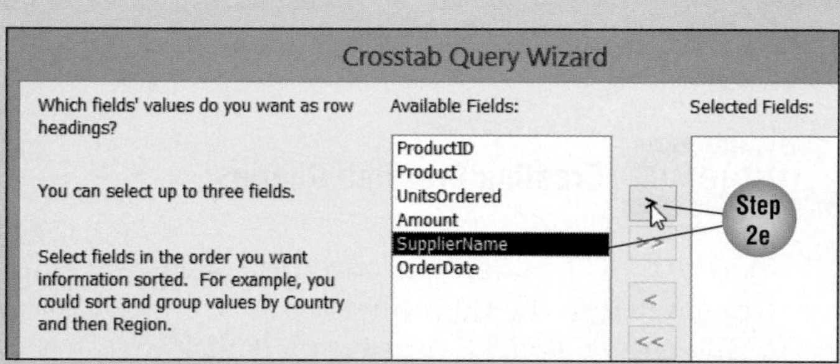

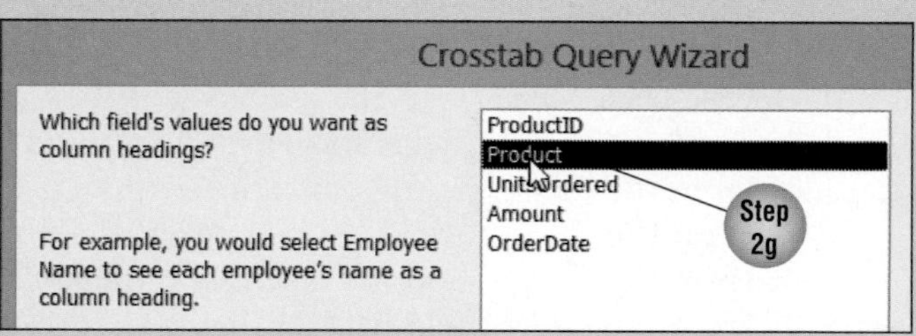

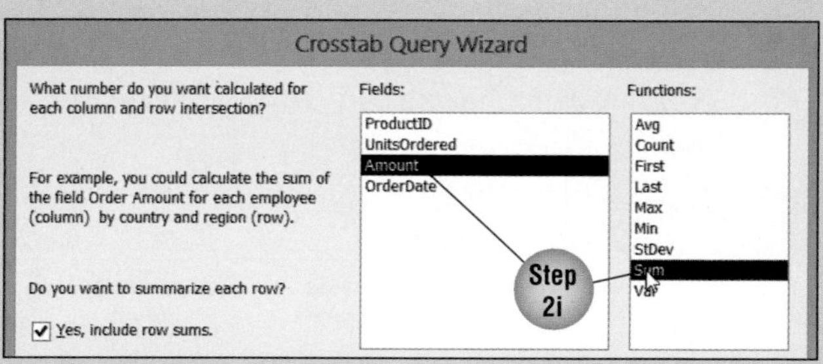

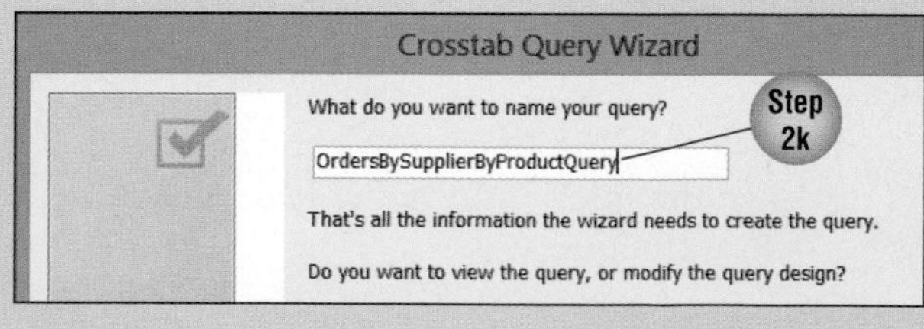

3. Display the query in Print Preview, change the orientation to landscape, change the left and right margins to 0.5 inch, and then print the query. (The query will print on four pages.)

4. Close the query.
5. Close **AL1-C3-PacTrek.accdb**.
6. Open **AL1-C3-CopperState.accdb**.
7. Create a crosstab query from fields in one table that summarizes clients' claims by completing the following steps:
   a. Click the CREATE tab and then click the Query Wizard button.
   b. At the New Query dialog box, double-click *Crosstab Query Wizard* in the list box.
   c. At the first Crosstab Query Wizard dialog box, click *Table: Claims* in the list box.
   d. Click the Next button.
   e. At the second Crosstab Query Wizard dialog box, click the One Field button. (This inserts the *ClaimID* field in the *Selected Fields* list box.)
   f. Click the Next button.
   g. At the third Crosstab Query Wizard dialog, make sure *ClientID* is selected in the list box and then click the Next button.
   h. At the fourth Crosstab Query Wizard dialog box, click *AmountOfClaim* in the *Fields* list box and click *Sum* in the *Functions* list box.
   i. Click the Next button.
   j. At the fifth Crosstab Query Wizard dialog box, select the current text in the *What do you want to name your query?* text box and then type **ClaimsByClaimIDByClientIDQuery**.
   k. Click the Finish button. (See Project 2c query results on page 81.)
8. Change the orientation to landscape and then print the query. The query will print on two pages.
9. Close the query.
10. Close **AL1-C3-CopperState.accdb**.

Creating Find Duplicates Queries

Use a ***find duplicates query*** to search a specified table or query for duplicate field values within a designated field or fields. Create this type of query, for example, if you suspect a record (such as a product record) has inadvertently been entered twice (perhaps under two different product numbers). A find duplicates query has many applications. Here are a few other examples of how you can use a find duplicates query:

- In an orders table, find records with the same customer number so you can identify loyal customers.
- In a customers table, find records with the same last name and mailing address so you can send only one mailing to a household and save on printing and postage costs.
- In an employee expenses table, find records with the same employee number so you can see which employee is submitting the most claims.

Access provides the Find Duplicates Query Wizard to build the query based on the selections made in a series of dialog boxes. To use this wizard, open the desired database, click the CREATE tab, and then click the Query Wizard button. At the New Query dialog box, double-click *Find Duplicates Query Wizard* in the list box and then complete the steps provided by the wizard.

In Project 2d, you will assume that you have been asked to update the address for a supplier in AL1-C3-PacTrek.accdb. Instead of updating the address, you create a new record. You will then use the Find Duplicates Query Wizard to find duplicate field values in the Suppliers table.

Quick Steps

Create a Find Duplicates Query
1. Click CREATE tab.
2. Click Query Wizard button.
3. Double-click *Find Duplicates Query Wizard*.
4. Complete wizard steps.

Project 2d Creating a Find Duplicates Query

Part 4 of 6

1. Open **AL1-C3-PacTrek.accdb** and then open the Suppliers table.
2. Add the following record to the table:

   SupplierID# **29**
   SupplierName **Langley Corporation**
   StreetAddress **1248 Larson Avenue**
   City **Burnaby**
   Prov/State **BC**
   PostalCode **V5V 9K2**
   EmailAddress **lc@emcp.net**
   Telephone **(604) 555-1200**
3. Close the Suppliers table.
4. Use the Find Duplicates Query Wizard to find any duplicate supplier names by completing the following steps:
   a. Click the CREATE tab and then click the Query Wizard button.
   b. At the New Query dialog box, double-click *Find Duplicates Query Wizard*.
   c. At the first wizard dialog box, click *Table: Suppliers* in the list box.

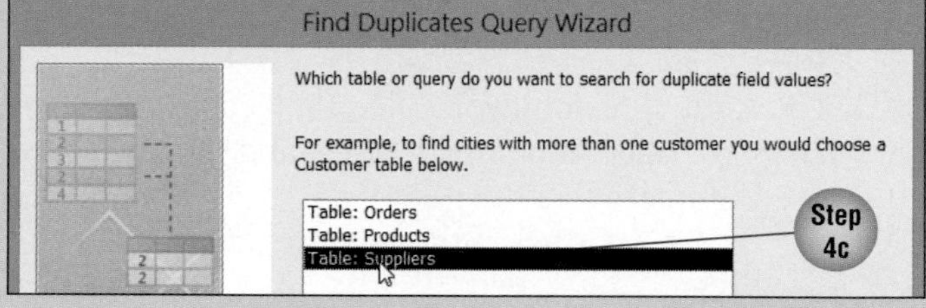

   d. Click the Next button.
   e. At the second wizard dialog box, click *SupplierName* in the *Available fields* list box and then click the One Field button. (This moves the *SupplierName* field to the *Duplicate-value fields* list box.)

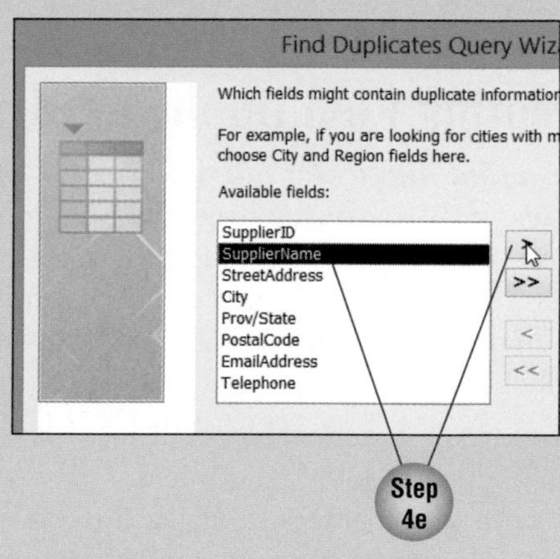

   f. Click the Next button.
   g. At the third wizard dialog box, click the All Fields button (the button containing the two greater-than symbols, >>). This moves all the fields to the *Additional query fields* list box. You are doing this because if you find a duplicate supplier name, you want to view all the fields to determine which record is accurate.
   h. Click the Next button.
   i. At the fourth (and last) wizard dialog box, type **DuplicateSuppliersQuery** in the *What do you want to name your query?* text box.
   j. Click the Finish button. (See Project 2d query results on page 81.)
   k. Change the orientation to landscape and then print the query.
5. As you look at the query results, you realize that an inaccurate record was entered for the Langley Corporation, so you decide to delete one of the records. To do this, complete the following steps:

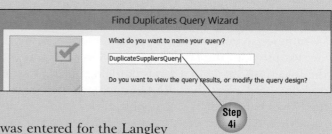

a. With the query open, click in the record selector bar next to the record with a supplier ID of *29*. (This selects the entire row.)

b. Click the HOME tab and then click the Delete button in the Records group.

c. At the message asking you to confirm, click the Yes button.

d. Close the query.

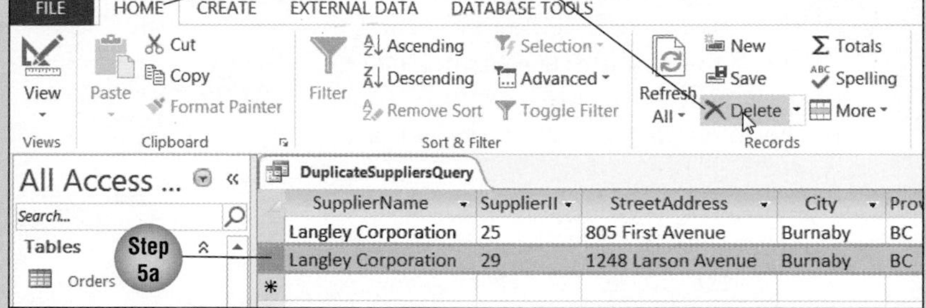

6. Change the street address for Langley Corporation by completing the following steps:
   a. Open the Suppliers table in Datasheet view.
   b. Change the address for Langley Corporation from *805 First Avenue* to *1248 Larson Avenue*. Leave the other fields as displayed.
   c. Close the Suppliers table.

In Project 2d, you used the Find Duplicates Query Wizard to find records containing the same field.In Project 2e, you will use the Find Duplicates Query Wizard to find information on the suppliers you order from the most. You could use this information to negotiate for better prices or to ask for discounts.

Project 2e Finding Duplicate Orders

Part 5 of 6

1. With **AL1-C3-PacTrek.accdb** open, create a query with the following fields (in the order shown) from the specified tables:

SupplierID	Suppliers table
SupplierName	Suppliers table
ProductID	Orders table
Product	Products table

2. Run the query.
3. Save the query with the name *SupplierOrdersQuery* and then close the query.
4. Use the Find Duplicates Query Wizard to find the suppliers you order from the most by completing the following steps:
   a. Click the CREATE tab and then click the Query Wizard button.
   b. At the New Query dialog box, double-click *Find Duplicates Query Wizard*.
   c. At the first wizard dialog box, click the *Queries* option in the *View* section and then click *Query: SupplierOrdersQuery*. (You may need to scroll down the list to display this query.)

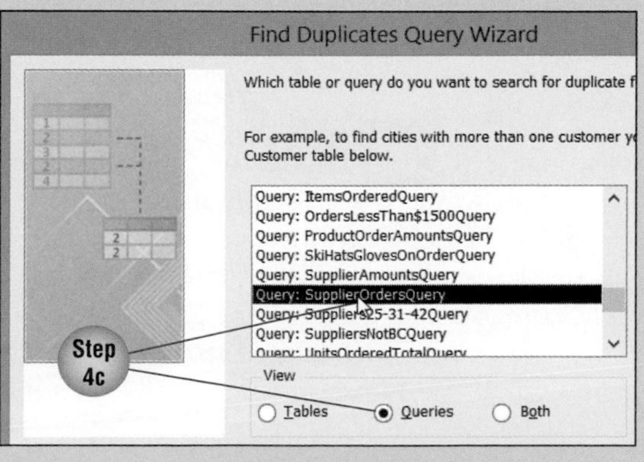

d. Click the Next button.
e. At the second wizard dialog box, click *SupplierName* in the *Available fields* list box and then click the One Field button.
f. Click the Next button.
g. At the third wizard dialog box, click the Next button.
h. At the fourth (and last) wizard dialog box, type **SupplierOrdersCountQuery** in the *What do you want to name your query?* text box.

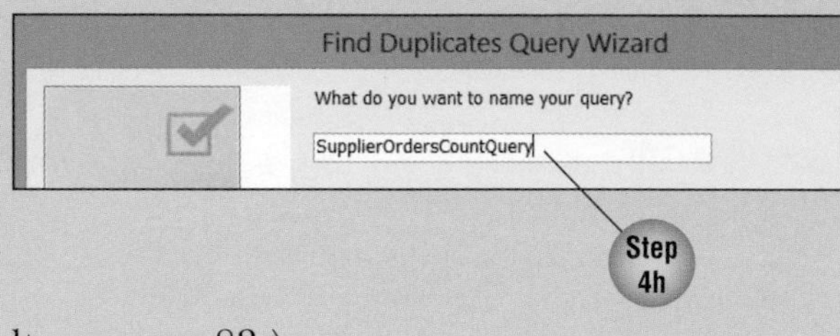

i. Click the Finish button.
j. Adjust the widths of the columns to fit the longest entries.
k. Print the query. (See Project 2e query results on page 82.)

5. Close the query.

Creating Find Unmatched Queries

Quick Steps

Create a Find Unmatched Query
1. Click CREATE tab.
2. Click Query Wizard button.
3. Double-click *Find Unmatched Query Wizard.*
4. Complete wizard steps.

Create a ***find unmatched query*** to compare two tables and produce a list of the records in one table that have no matching record in the other table. This type of query is useful to produce lists such as customers who have never placed orders and invoices that have no records of payment. Access provides the Find Unmatched Query Wizard to build the select query by guiding you through a series of dialog boxes.

In Project 2f, you will use the Find Unmatched Query Wizard to find all of the products that have no units on order. This information is helpful in identifying which products are not selling and might need to be discontinued or returned. To use the Find Unmatched Query Wizard, click the CREATE tab and then click the Query Wizard button in the Queries group. At the New Query dialog box, double-click *Find Unmatched Query Wizard* in the list box and then follow the wizard steps.

Project 2f **Creating a Find Unmatched Query** **Part 6 of 6**

1. With **AL1-C3-PacTrek.accdb** open, use the Find Unmatched Query Wizard to find all products that do not have units on order by completing the following steps:
   a. Click the CREATE tab and then click the Query Wizard button.
   b. At the New Query dialog box, double-click *Find Unmatched Query Wizard.*
   c. At the first wizard dialog box, click *Table: Products* in the list box. (This is the table containing the fields you want to see in the query results.)

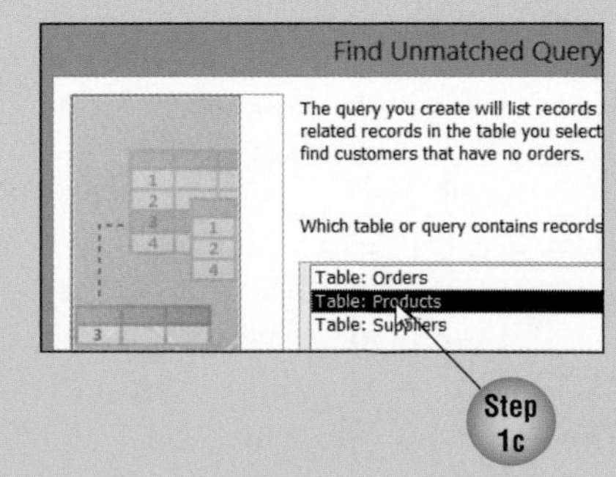

   d. Click the Next button.
   e. At the second wizard dialog box, make sure *Table: Orders* is selected in the list box. (This is the table containing the related records.)
   f. Click the Next button.

g. At the third wizard dialog box, make sure *ProductID* is selected in both the *Fields in 'Products'* list box and in the *Fields in 'Orders'* list box.
h. Click the Next button.
i. At the fourth wizard dialog box, click the All Fields button to move all of the fields from the *Available fields* list box to the *Selected fields* list box.
j. Click the Next button.
k. At the fifth wizard dialog box, click the Finish button. (Let the wizard determine the query name: *Products Without Matching Orders*. See Project 2f query results on page 82.)

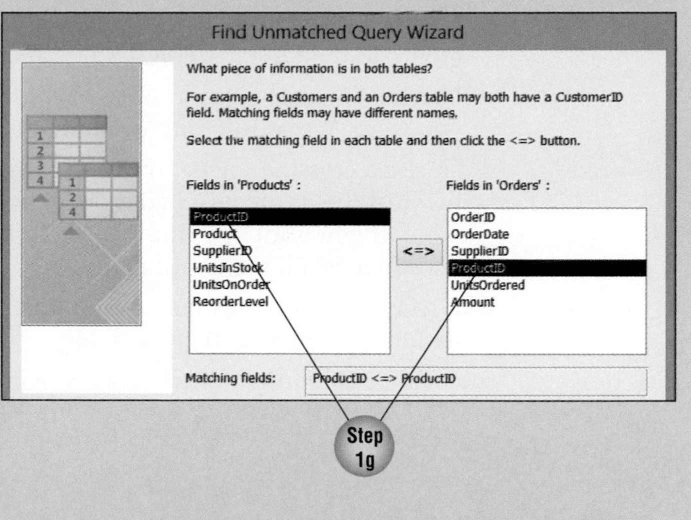

2. Print the query in landscape orientation and then close the query.
3. Close **AL1-C3-PacTrek.accdb**.

Chapter Summary

- One of the most important uses of a database is to select the information needed to answer questions and make decisions. Data can be extracted from an Access database by performing a query, which can be accomplished by designing a query or using a query wizard.
- Designing a query consists of identifying the table, the field or fields from which the data will be drawn, and the criteria for selecting the data.
- In designing a query, type the criterion (or criteria) for extracting the specific data. Access inserts any necessary symbols in the criterion when the Enter key is pressed.
- In a criterion, quotation marks surround field values and pound symbols (#) surround dates. Use the asterisk (*) as a wildcard character.
- You can perform a query on fields within one table or on fields from related tables.
- When designing a query, you can specify the sort order of a field or fields.
- You can modify an existing query and use it for a new purpose.
- Enter a criterion in the *or* row in the query design grid to instruct Access to display records that match any of the criteria.
- Multiple criteria entered in the *Criteria* row in the query design grid become an *And* statement, where each criterion must be met for Access to select the record.
- The Simple Query Wizard guides you through the steps for preparing a query. You can modify a query you create with the wizard.
- You can insert a calculated field in a *Field* row field when designing a query.

- Include an aggregate function (such as Sum, Avg, Min, Max, or Count) to calculate statistics from numeric field values. Click the Totals button in the Show/Hide group on the QUERY TOOLS DESIGN tab to display the aggregate function list.
- Use the *Group By* option in the *Total* row field to add a field to a query on which you want Access to group records for statistical calculations.
- Create a crosstab query to calculate aggregate functions (such as Sum and Avg), in which fields are grouped by two. Create a crosstab query from fields in one table. If you want to include fields from more than one table, create a query first and then create the crosstab query.
- Use a find duplicates query to search a specified table for duplicate field values within a designated field or fields.
- Create a find unmatched query to compare two tables and produce a list of the

Commands Review

FEATURE	RIBBON TAB, GROUP	BUTTON, OPTION
add *Total* row to query design	QUERY TOOLS DESIGN, Show/Hide	Σ
Crosstab Query Wizard	CREATE, Queries	, *Crosstab Query Wizard*
Find Duplicates Query Wizard	CREATE, Queries	, *Find Duplicates Query Wizard*
Find Unmatched Query Wizard	CREATE, Queries	, *Find Unmatched Query Wizard*
New Query dialog box	CREATE, Queries	
query results	QUERY TOOLS DESIGN, Results	!
query window	CREATE, Queries	
Simple Query Wizard	CREATE, Queries	, *Simple Query Wizard*

Concepts Check Test Your Knowledge

records in one table that have no matching records in the other related table.

Completion: In the space provided at the right, indicate the correct term, symbol, or command.

1. The Query Design button is located in the Queries group on this tab. ____________________
2. Click the Query Design button and the query window displays with this dialog box open. ____________________
3. To establish a criterion for a query, click in this row in the column containing the desired field name and then type the criterion. ____________________
4. This is the term used for the results of the query. ____________________
5. This is the symbol Access automatically inserts before and after a date when writing a criterion for the query. ____________________
6. Use this symbol to indicate a wildcard character when writing a query criterion. ____________________
7. This is the criterion you would type to return field values greater than $500. ____________________
8. This is the criterion you would type to return field values that begin with the letter *L*. ____________________
9. This is the criterion you would type to return field values that are not in Oregon. ____________________
10. You can sort a field in a query in ascending order or in this order. ____________________
11. Multiple criteria entered in the *Criteria* row in the query design grid become this type of statement. ____________________
12. This wizard guides you through the steps for preparing a query. ____________________
13. This type of query calculates aggregate functions, in which field values are grouped by two fields. ____________________
14. Use this type of query to compare two tables and produce a list of the records in one table that have no matching records in the other table. ____________________

Skills Check Assess Your Performance

Assessment 1

DESIGN QUERIES IN A LEGAL SERVICES DATABASE

1. Display the Open dialog box with the AL1C3 folder on your storage medium the active folder.
2. Open **AL1-C3-WarrenLegal.accdb** and enable the contents.
3. Design a query that extracts information from the Billing table with the following specifications:
   a. Include the fields *BillingID*, *ClientID*, and *CategoryID* in the query.
   b. Extract those records with the *SE* category. (Type "**SE**" in the *Criteria* row field in the *CategoryID* column. You need to type the quotation marks to tell Access that SE is a criterion and not a built-in Access function.)
   c. Save the query and name it *SECategoryBillingQuery*.
   d. Print and then close the query.
4. Design a query that extracts information from the Billing table with the following specifications:
   a. Include the fields *BillingID*, *ClientID*, and *Date*.
   b. Extract those records in the *Date* field with dates between 6/8/2015 and 6/15/2015.
   c. Save the query and name it *June8-15BillingQuery*.
   d. Print and then close the query.
5. Design a query that extracts information from the Clients table with the following specifications:
   a. Include the fields *FirstName*, *LastName*, and *City*.
   b. Extract those records with cities other than Kent in the *City* field.
   c. Save the query and name it *ClientsNotInKentQuery*.
   d. Print and then close the query.
6. Design a query that extracts information from two tables with the following specifications:
   a. Include the fields *BillingID*, *ClientID*, *Date*, and *RateID* from the Billing table.
   b. Include the field *Rate* from the Rates table.
   c. Extract those records with rate IDs greater than *2*.
   d. Save the query and name it *RateIDGreaterThan2Query*.
   e. Print and then close the query.
7. Design a query that extracts information from three tables with the following specifications:
   a. Include the fields *AttorneyID*, *FName*, and *LName* from the Attorneys table.
   b. Include the fields *FirstName* and *LastName* from the Clients table.
   c. Include the fields *Date* and *Hours* from the Billing table.
   d. Extract those records with an attorney ID of *12*.
   e. Save the query and name it *Attorney12Query*.
   f. Print and then close the query.
8. Design a query that extracts information from four tables with the following specifications:
   a. Include the fields *AttorneyID*, *FName*, and *LName* from the Attorneys table.
   b. Include the field *Category* from the Categories table.
   c. Include the fields *RateID* and *Rate* from the Rates table.

d. Include the fields *Date* and *Hours* from the Billing table.
e. Extract those records with an attorney ID of *17* and a rate ID of *4*.
f. Save the query and name it *Attorney17RateID4Query*.
g. Print the query in landscape orientation and then close the query.

9. Open the Attorney17RateID4Query query, click the View button on the HOME tab to display the query in Design view, and then modify the query so it displays records with a rate ID of *4* and attorney IDs of *17* and *19* by making the following changes:
   a. Click below the field value "*17*" in the *AttorneyID* column and then type **19**.
   b. Click below the field value "*4*" in the *RateID* column, type **4**, and then press Enter.
   c. Run the query.
   d. Save the query with the new name *Attorney17&19RateID4Query*. ***Hint: Do this at the Save As dialog box. Display this dialog box by clicking the FILE tab,* clicking *the* Save As *option, clicking the* Save Object As *option, and then clicking the Save As button.***
   e. Print the query in landscape orientation and then close the query.

Assessment 2

USE THE SIMPLE QUERY WIZARD AND DESIGN QUERIES

1. With **AL1-C3-WarrenLegal.accdb** open, use the Simple Query Wizard to extract specific information from three tables with the following specifications:
   a. At the first Simple Query Wizard dialog box, include the following fields:
      From Attorneys table: *AttorneyID*, *FName*, and *LName*
      From Categories table: *Category*
      From Billing table: *Hours*
   b. At the second Simple Query Wizard dialog box, click Next.
   c. At the third Simple Query Wizard dialog box, click the *Modify the query design* option and then click the Finish button.
   d. At the query window, insert *14* in the *Criteria* row field in the *AttorneyID* column.
   e. Run the query.
   f. Save the query with the default name.
   g. Print and then close the query.
2. Create a query in Design view with the Billing table with the following specifications:
   a. Insert the *Hours* field from the *Billing* field list box to the first, second, third, and fourth *Field* row fields.
   b. Click the Totals button in the Show/Hide group.
   c. Insert *Sum* in the first *Total* row field.
   d. Insert *Min* in the second *Total* row field.
   e. Insert *Max* in the third *Total* row field.
   f. Insert *Count* in the fourth *Total* row field.
   g. Run the query.
   h. Automatically adjust the widths of the columns.
   i. Save the query and name it *HoursAmountQuery*.
   j. Print and then close the query.
3. Create a query in Design view with the following specifications:
   a. Add the Attorneys table and Billing table to the query window.
   b. Insert the *FName* field from the *Attorneys* field list box to the first *Field* row field.
   c. Insert the *LName* field from the *Attorneys* field list box to the second *Field* row field.

d. Insert the *AttorneyID* field from the *Billing* field list box to the third *Field* row field. (You will need to scroll down the *Billing* field list box to display the *AttorneyID* field.)
e. Insert the *Hours* field from the *Billing* field list box to the fourth *Field* row field.
f. Click the Totals button in the Show/Hide group.
g. Insert *Sum* in the fourth *Total* row field in the *Hours* column.
h. Run the query.
i. Save the query and name it *AttorneyHoursQuery*.
j. Print and then close the query.

4. Create a query in Design view with the following specifications:
   a. Add the Attorneys, Clients, Categories, and Billing tables to the query window.
   b. Insert the *AttorneyID* field from the *Attorneys* field list box to the first *Field* row field.
   c. Insert the *ClientID* field from the *Clients* field list box to the second *Field* row field.
   d. Insert the *Category* field from the *Categories* field list box to the third *Field* row field.
   e. Insert the *Hours* field from the *Billing* field list box to the fourth *Field* row field.
   f. Run the query.
   g. Save the query and name it *AttorneyClientHours*.
   h. Print and then close the query.

Assessment 3

CREATE A CROSSTAB QUERY AND USE THE FIND DUPLICATES AND FIND UNMATCHED QUERY WIZARDS

1. With **AL1-C3-WarrenLegal.accdb** open, create a crosstab query that summarizes the hours by attorney by category with the following specifications:
   a. At the first Crosstab Query Wizard dialog box, click the *Queries* option in the *View* section and then click *Query: AttorneyClientHours* in the list box.
   b. At the second Crosstab Query Wizard dialog box with *AttorneyID* selected in the *Available Fields* list box, click the One Field button.
   c. At the third Crosstab Query Wizard dialog box, click *Category* in the list box.
   d. At the fourth Crosstab Query Wizard dialog box, click *Hours* in the *Fields* list box and click *Sum* in the *Functions* list box.
   e. At the fifth Crosstab Query Wizard dialog box, select the current name in the *What do you want to name your query?* text box and then type **HoursByAttorneyByCategory**.
   f. Display the query in Print Preview, change to landscape orientation, change the left and right margins to 0.5 inch, and then print the query.
   g. Close the query.
2. Use the Find Duplicates Query Wizard to find those clients with the same last name with the following specifications:
   a. At the first wizard dialog box, click *Table: Clients* in the list box.
   b. At the second wizard dialog box, click *LastName* in the *Available fields* list box and then click the One Field button.
   c. At the third wizard dialog box, click the All Fields button.

d. At the fourth wizard dialog box, name the query *DuplicateLastNamesQuery*.
e. Print the query in landscape orientation and then close the query.

3. Use the Find Unmatched Query Wizard to find all clients who do not have any billing hours with the following specifications:
   a. At the first wizard dialog box, click *Table: Clients* in the list box.
   b. At the second wizard dialog box, click *Table: Billing* in the list box.
   c. At the third wizard dialog box, make sure *ClientID* is selected in both the *Fields in 'Clients'* list box and in the *Fields in 'Billing'* list box.
   d. At the fourth wizard dialog box, click the All Fields button to move all fields from the *Available fields* list box to the *Selected fields* list box.
   e. At the fifth wizard dialog box, click the Finish button. (Let the wizard determine the query name: *Clients Without Matching Billing*.)
4. Print the query in landscape orientation and then close the query.

Assessment 4

DESIGN AND HIDE FIELDS IN A QUERY

1. You can use the check boxes in the query design grid *Show* row to show or hide fields in the query. Experiment with these check boxes and then with **AL1-C3-WarrenLegal.accdb** open design the following query:
   a. At the Show Table dialog box, add the Clients table, the Billing table, and the Rates table.
   b. At the query window, insert the following fields in *Field* row fields:
      Clients table: *FirstName*
      LastName
      Billing table: *Hours*
      Rates table: *Rate*
   c. Insert in the fifth *Field* row field the calculated field *Total:[Hours]*[Rate]*.
   d. Hide the *Hours* and *Rate* fields.
   e. Run the query.
   f. Save the query and name it *ClientBillingQuery*.
   g. Print and then close the query. (The query will print on two pages.)
2. Close **AL1-C3-WarrenLegal.accdb**.

Visual Benchmark Demonstrate Your Proficiency

CREATING RELATIONSHIPS AND DESIGNING A QUERY

1. Open **AL1-C3-MRInvestments.accdb** from the AL1C3 folder on your storage medium and, if necessary, enable the contents.
2. Display the Relationships window and then create the relationships shown in Figure 3.7. Enforce referential integrity and cascade fields and records. (The tables in Figure 3.7 have been rearranged in the Relationships window so you have a better view of the relationships.)
3. Save and then print the relationships.
4. Close the relationship report without saving it and then close the Relationships window.
5. Design the query shown in Figure 3.8.

6. Run the query.
7. Save the query with an appropriate name and then print the query.
8. Close **AL1-C3-MRInvestments.accdb**.

Figure 3.7 Visual Benchmark Relationships Window

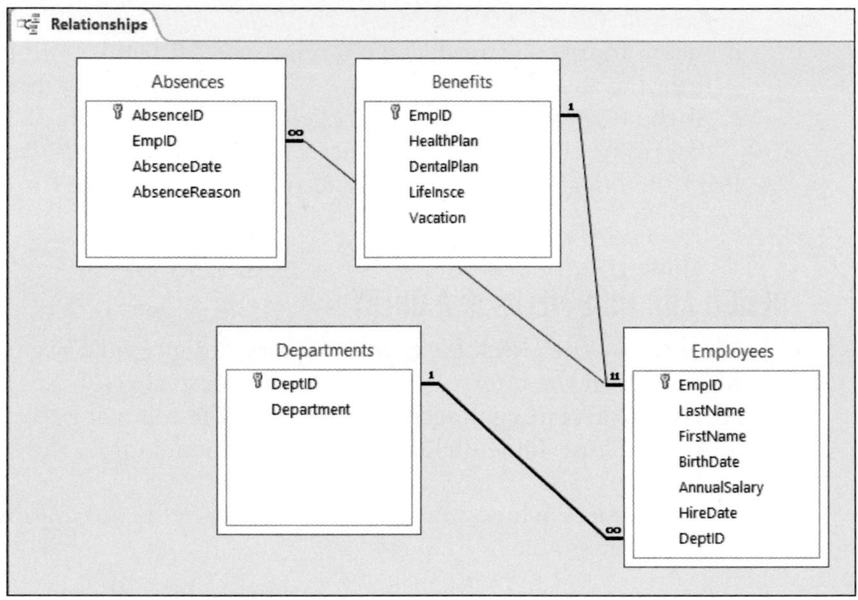

Figure 3.8 Visual Benchmark Query

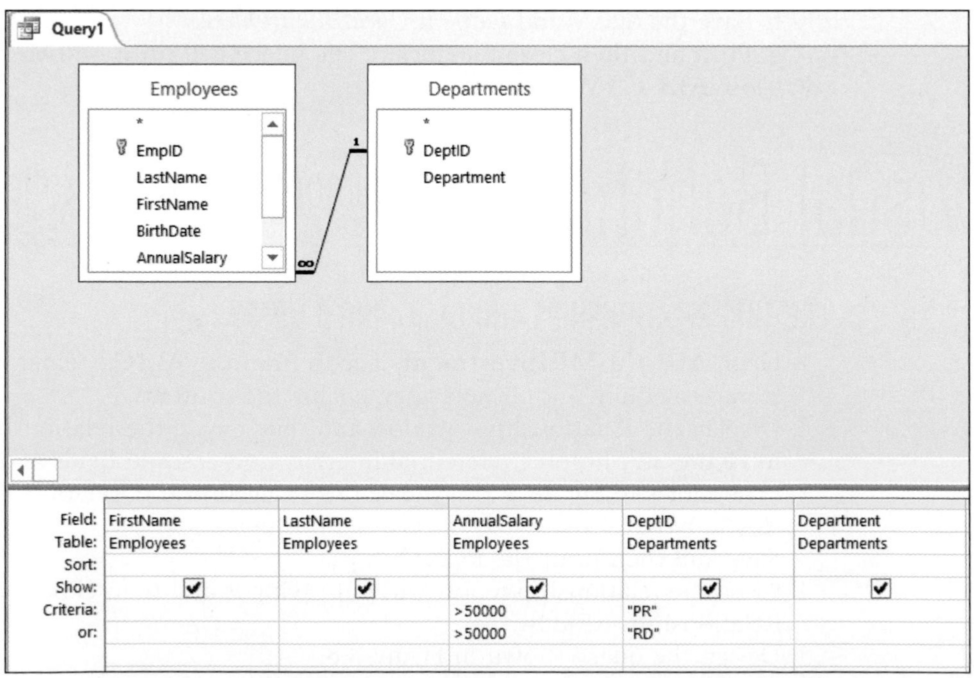

Field:	FirstName	LastName	AnnualSalary	DeptID	Department
Table:	Employees	Employees	Employees	Departments	Departments
Sort:					
Show:	✔	✔	✔	✔	✔
Criteria:			>50000	"PR"	
or:			>50000	"RD"	

Case Study Apply Your Skills

Part 1

You work for the Skyline Restaurant in Fort Myers, Florida. Your supervisor is reviewing the restaurant's operations and has asked for a number of query reports. Before running the queries, you realize that the tables in the restaurant database, **AL1-C3-Skyline.accdb**, are not related. Open **AL1-C3-Skyline.accdb**, enable the contents, and then create the following relationships (enforce referential integrity and cascade fields and records):

Field Name	"One" Table	"Many" Table
EmployeeID	Employees	Banquets
ItemID	Inventory	Orders
SupplierID	Suppliers	Orders
SupplierID	Suppliers	Inventory
EventID	Events	Banquets

Save and then print the relationships. Close the relationship report without saving it and then close the Relationships window.

Part 2

As part of the review of the restaurant's records, your supervisor has asked you for the following information. Create a separate query for each bulleted item listed below and save, name, and print the queries. (You determine the query names.)

- Suppliers in Fort Myers: From the Suppliers table, include the supplier identification number, supplier name, city, and telephone number.
- Suppliers not located in Fort Myers: From the Suppliers table, include the supplier identification number and supplier name, city, and telephone number.
- Employees hired in 2012: From the Employees table, include the employee identification number, first and last names, and hire date.
- Employees signed up for health insurance: From the Employees table, include employee first and last names and the health insurance field.
- Wedding receptions (event identification "WR") booked in the banquet room: From the Banquets table, include the reservation identification number; reservation date; event identification; and first name, last name, and telephone number of the person making the reservation.
- Banquet reservations between 6/14/2015 and 6/30/2015 and the employees making the reservations: From the Banquets table, include the reservation identification number; reservation date; and first name, last name, and telephone number of the person making the reservation; from the Employees table include the employee first and last names.
- Banquet reservations that have not been confirmed and the employees making the reservations: From the Banquets table, include the reservation identification number; reservation date; confirmed field; and first and last names of person making the reservation; from the Employees table, include employee first and last names.
- Banquet room reserved by someone whose last name begins with the letters *Wie:* From the Employees table, include the first and last names of the employee who booked the reservation; from the Banquets table, include the first and last names and telephone number of the person making the reservation.

- A query that inserts a calculated field that multiplies the number of units ordered by the unit price for all orders for supplier number *2:* From the Orders table, include the order identification number, the supplier identification number, the units ordered, and the unit price; from the Inventory table, include the item field.

Part 3

Use the Find Duplicates Query Wizard to find duplicate items in the Orders table with the following specifications:

- At the first wizard dialog box, specify the Orders table.
- At the second wizard dialog box, specify *ItemID* as the duplicate value field.
- At the third wizard dialog, specify that you want all of the fields in the query.
- At the fourth wizard dialog box, determine the query name.
- Print and then close the query.

Use the Find Unmatched Query Wizard to find all of the employees who have not made banquet reservations with the following specifications:

- At the first wizard dialog box, specify the Employees table.
- At the second wizard dialog box, specify the Banquets table.
- At the third wizard dialog box, specify the *EmployeeID* field in both list boxes.
- At the fourth wizard dialog box, specify that you want all of the fields in the query.
- At the fifth wizard dialog box, determine the query name.
- Print the query in landscape orientation with 0.5-inch left and right margins and then close the query.

Use the Crosstab Query Wizard to create a query that summarizes order amounts by supplier with the following specifications:

- At the first wizard dialog box, specify the Orders table.
- At the second wizard dialog box, specify the *SupplierID* field for row headings.
- At the third wizard dialog box, specify the *ItemID* field for column headings.
- At the fourth wizard dialog box, click *UnitPrice* in the *Fields* list box and click *Sum* in the *Functions* list box.
- At the fifth wizard dialog box, determine the query name.
- Automatically adjust the columns in the query. (You will need to scroll to the right to view and adjust all of the columns containing data.)
- Print the query in landscape orientation and then close the query.

Part 4

Design three additional queries that require fields from at least two tables. Run the queries and then save and print the queries. In Microsoft Word, write the query information (including specific information about each query) and format the document to enhance the visual appearance. Save the document and name it **AL1-C3-CS-Queries**. Print and then close **AL1-C3-CS-Queries.docx**. Close **AL1-C3-Skyline.accdb**.

MICROSOFT® ACCESS®

Creating and Modifying Tables in Design View

PERFORMANCE OBJECTIVES

Upon successful completion of Chapter 4, you will be able to:

- **Create a table in Design view**
- **Assign a default value**
- **Use the Input Mask Wizard and the Lookup Wizard**
- **Validate field entries**
- **Insert, move, and delete fields in Design view**
- **Insert a *Total* row**
- **Sort records in a table**
- **Print selected records in a table**
- **Complete a spelling check**
- **Find and replace data in records in a table**
- **Apply text formatting**
- **Use the Help feature**

Tutorials

- **4.1** Creating a Table in Design View
- **4.2** Creating an Input Mask and Formatting a Field
- **4.3** Validating Field Entries
- **4.4** Creating a Lookup Field
- **4.5** Modifying Table Structure in Design View; Inserting a *Total* Row
- **4.6** Sorting Records in a Table
- **4.7** Formatting Table Data and Printing Specific Records
- **4.8** Completing a Spelling Check
- **4.9** Finding and Replacing Data in Records
- **4.10** Using Help

In Chapter 1, you learned how to create a table in Datasheet view. You can also create a table in Design view, where you can establish the table's structure and properties before entering data. In this chapter, you will learn how to create a table in Design view and use the Input Mask Wizard and Lookup Wizards; insert, move, and delete fields in Design view; sort records; check spelling in a table; find and replace data; apply text formatting to a table; and use the Access Help feature. Model answers for this chapter's projects appear on the following pages.

Note: Before beginning the projects, copy the AL1C4 subfolder from the AL1 folder on the CD that accompanies this textbook to your storage medium and make AL1C4 the active folder.

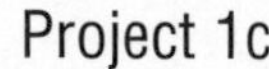

Project 1 Create and Modify Tables in a Property Management Database

Project 1c

EmpID	EmpCategory	FName	LName	Address	City	State	ZIP	Telephone	HealthIns	DentalIns	LifeIns
02-59	Hourly	Christina	Solomon	12241 East 51st	Citrus Heights	CA	95611	(916) 555-8844	☑	☑	$100,000.00
03-23	Salaried	Douglas	Ricci	903 Mission Road	Roseville	CA	95678	(916) 555-4125	☑	☐	$25,000.00
03-55	Hourly	Tatiana	Kasadev	6558 Orchard Drive	Citrus Heights	CA	95610	(916) 555-8534	☑	☐	$0.00
04-14	Salaried	Brian	West	12232 142nd Avenue East	Citrus Heights	CA	95611	(916) 555-0967	☑	☑	$50,000.00
04-32	Temporary	Kathleen	Addison	21229 19th Street	Citrus Heights	CA	95621	(916) 555-3408	☑	☑	$50,000.00
05-20	Hourly	Teresa	Villanueva	19453 North 42nd Street	Citrus Heights	CA	95611	(916) 555-2302	☑	☑	$0.00
05-31	Salaried	Marcia	Griswold	211 Haven Road	North Highlands	CA	95660	(916) 555-1449	☐	☐	$100,000.00
06-24	Temporary	Tiffany	Gentry	12312 North 20th	Roseville	CA	95661	(916) 555-0043	☑	☑	$50,000.00
06-33	Hourly	Joanna	Gallegos	6850 York Street	Roseville	CA	95747	(956) 555-7446	☐	☐	$25,000.00
07-20	Salaried	Jesse	Scholtz	3412 South 21st Street	Fair Oaks	CA	95628	(916) 555-4204	☑	☐	$0.00
07-23	Salaried	Eugene	Bond	530 Laurel Road	Orangevale	CA	95662	(916) 555-9412	☑	☐	$100,000.00

Step 11, Employees Table

EmpID	FName	LName	Address	City	State	ZIP	Telephone	EmpCategory	HealthIns	LifeIns
02-59	Christina	Solomon	12241 East 51st	Citrus Heights	CA	95611	(916) 555-8844	Hourly	☑	$100,000.00
03-23	Douglas	Ricci	903 Mission Road	Roseville	CA	95678	(916) 555-4125	Salaried	☑	$25,000.00
03-55	Tatiana	Kasadev	6558 Orchard Drive	Citrus Heights	CA	95610	(916) 555-8534	Hourly	☑	$0.00
04-14	Brian	West	12232 142nd Avenue East	Citrus Heights	CA	95611	(916) 555-0967	Salaried	☑	$50,000.00
04-32	Kathleen	Addison	21229 19th Street	Citrus Heights	CA	95621	(916) 555-3408	Temporary	☑	$50,000.00
05-20	Teresa	Villanueva	19453 North 42nd Street	Citrus Heights	CA	95611	(916) 555-2302	Hourly	☑	$0.00
05-31	Marcia	Griswold	211 Haven Road	North Highlands	CA	95660	(916) 555-1449	Salaried	☐	$100,000.00
06-24	Tiffany	Gentry	12312 North 20th	Roseville	CA	95661	(916) 555-0043	Temporary	☑	$50,000.00
06-33	Joanna	Gallegos	6850 York Street	Roseville	CA	95747	(956) 555-7446	Hourly	☐	$25,000.00
07-20	Jesse	Scholtz	3412 South 21st Street	Fair Oaks	CA	95628	(916) 555-4204	Salaried	☑	$0.00
07-23	Eugene	Bond	530 Laurel Road	Orangevale	CA	95662	(916) 555-9412	Salaried	☑	$100,000.00

Step 16, Employees Table

PymntID	RenterID	PymntDate	PymntAmount	LateFee
1	130	3/1/2015	$1,800.00	
2	111	3/1/2015	$1,900.00	
3	136	3/1/2015	$1,250.00	
4	110	3/1/2015	$1,300.00	
5	135	3/2/2015	$1,900.00	
6	123	3/2/2015	$1,000.00	
7	117	3/2/2015	$1,100.00	
8	134	3/3/2015	$1,400.00	
9	131	3/3/2015	$1,200.00	
10	118	3/3/2015	$900.00	
11	125	3/5/2015	$1,650.00	
12	119	3/5/2015	$1,500.00	
13	133	3/8/2015	$1,650.00	
14	129	3/9/2015	$1,650.00	
15	115	3/12/2015	$1,375.00	$25.00
16	121	3/12/2015	$950.00	$25.00
17	127	3/19/2015	$1,300.00	$50.00
Total			**$23,825.00**	**$100.00**

Payments Table

Project 1d

RenterID	FirstName	LastName	PropID	EmpID	CreditScore	LeaseBegDate	LeaseEndDate
118	Mason	Ahn	1004	07-23	538	3/1/2015	2/28/2016
119	Michelle	Bertram	1001	03-23	621	3/1/2015	2/28/2016
110	Greg	Hamilton	1029	04-14	624	1/1/2015	12/31/2015
121	Travis	Jorgenson	1010	04-14	590	3/1/2015	2/28/2016
135	Marty	Lobdell	1006	04-14	510	6/1/2015	5/31/2016
129	Susan	Lowrey	1002	04-14	634	4/1/2015	3/31/2016
130	Ross	Molaski	1027	03-23	688	5/1/2015	4/30/2016
136	Nadine	Paschal	1022	05-31	702	6/1/2015	5/31/2016
111	Julia	Perez	1013	07-20	711	1/1/2015	12/31/2015
115	Dana	Rozinski	1026	02-59	538	2/1/2015	1/31/2016
131	Danielle	Rubio	1020	07-20	722	5/1/2015	4/30/2016
133	Katie	Smith	1018	07-23	596	5/1/2015	4/30/2016
123	Richard	Terrell	1014	07-20	687	3/1/2015	2/28/2016
117	Miguel	Villegas	1007	07-20	695	2/1/2015	1/31/2016
125	Rose	Wagoner	1015	07-23	734	4/1/2015	3/31/2016
134	Carl	Weston	1009	03-23	655	6/1/2015	5/31/2016
127	William	Young	1023	05-31	478	4/1/2015	3/31/2016

Step 2c, Renters Table

RenterID	FirstName	LastName	PropID	EmpID	CreditScore	LeaseBegDate	LeaseEndDate
125	Rose	Wagoner	1015	07-23	734	4/1/2015	3/31/2016
131	Danielle	Rubio	1020	07-20	722	5/1/2015	4/30/2016
111	Julia	Perez	1013	07-20	711	1/1/2015	12/31/2015
136	Nadine	Paschal	1022	05-31	702	6/1/2015	5/31/2016
117	Miguel	Villegas	1007	07-20	695	2/1/2015	1/31/2016
130	Ross	Molaski	1027	03-23	688	5/1/2015	4/30/2016
123	Richard	Terrell	1014	07-20	687	3/1/2015	2/28/2016
134	Carl	Weston	1009	03-23	655	6/1/2015	5/31/2016
129	Susan	Lowrey	1002	04-14	634	4/1/2015	3/31/2016
110	Greg	Hamilton	1029	04-14	624	1/1/2015	12/31/2015
119	Michelle	Bertram	1001	03-23	621	3/1/2015	2/28/2016
133	Katie	Smith	1018	07-23	596	5/1/2015	4/30/2016
121	Travis	Jorgenson	1010	04-14	590	3/1/2015	2/28/2016
118	Mason	Ahn	1004	07-23	538	3/1/2015	2/28/2016
115	Dana	Rozinski	1026	02-59	538	2/1/2015	1/31/2016
135	Marty	Lobdell	1006	04-14	510	6/1/2015	5/31/2016
127	William	Young	1023	05-31	478	4/1/2015	3/31/2016

Step 3c, Renters Table

PropID	CatID	MoRent	Address	City	State	ZIP
1007	A	$1,100.00	904 Everson Road	Fair Oaks	CA	95628
1004	A	$900.00	1932 Oakville Drive	North Highlands	CA	95660
1010	A	$950.00	19334 140th East	Citrus Heights	CA	95621
1014	A	$1,000.00	9045 Valley Avenue	Citrus Heights	CA	95611

Step 6f, Properties Table

PropID	CatID	MoRent	Address	City	State	ZIP
1007	A	$1,100.00	904 Everson Road	Fair Oaks	CA	95628
1004	A	$900.00	1932 Oakville Drive	North Highlands	CA	95660
1010	A	$950.00	19334 140th East	Citrus Heights	CA	95621
1014	A	$1,000.00	9045 Valley Avenue	Citrus Heights	CA	95611
1029	C	$1,300.00	155 Aldrich Road	Roseville	CA	95678
1002	C	$1,650.00	2650 Crestline Drive	Citrus Heights	CA	95611
1001	C	$1,500.00	4102 Tenth Street	Citrus Heights	CA	95611
1026	C	$1,375.00	10057 128th Avenue	Citrus Heights	CA	95611
1023	C	$1,300.00	750 Birch Drive	Orangevale	CA	95662
1009	C	$1,400.00	159 Meridian Street	Orangevale	CA	95662
1019	C	$1,700.00	765 Chellis Street	Fair Oaks	CA	95628
1018	C	$1,650.00	9945 North 20th Road	North Highlands	CA	95660
1017	D	$1,300.00	4500 Maple Lane	Orangevale	CA	95662
1011	D	$1,350.00	348 Hampton Avenue	Citrus Heights	CA	95611
1008	D	$1,575.00	5009 North Garden	Roseville	CA	95661
1020	D	$1,200.00	23390 South 22nd Street	Citrus Heights	CA	95610
1006	S	$1,900.00	3412 Mango Street	Orangevale	CA	95662
1003	S	$1,800.00	10234 122nd Avenue	North Highlands	CA	95660
1012	S	$1,775.00	1212 Fairhaven Road	North Highlands	CA	95660
1013	S	$1,900.00	2606 30th Street	Citrus Heights	CA	95610
1016	S	$1,825.00	21388 South 42nd Street	Citrus Heights	CA	95621
1030	S	$1,950.00	5430 112th Southeast	Citrus Heights	CA	95611
1021	S	$1,875.00	652 Seventh Street	Fair Oaks	CA	95628
1024	S	$1,650.00	1195 24th Street	North Highlands	CA	95660
1027	S	$1,800.00	2203 Center Road	Orangevale	CA	95662
1028	S	$1,750.00	488 Franklin Drive	Fair Oaks	CA	95628
1022	T	$1,250.00	4572 152nd Avenue	Citrus Heights	CA	95621
1005	T	$1,350.00	12110 55th Southeast	Citrus Heights	CA	95611
1025	T	$1,200.00	3354 North 62nd Street	Citrus Heights	CA	95610
1015	T	$1,650.00	560 Tenth Street East	North Highlands	CA	95660

Step 7f, Properties Table

Project 1d–*continued*

PymntID	RenterID	PymntDate	PymntAmount	LateFee
1	130	3/1/2015	$1,800.00	
2	111	3/1/2015	$1,900.00	
3	136	3/1/2015	$1,250.00	
4	110	3/1/2015	$1,300.00	
5	135	3/2/2015	$1,900.00	
6	123	3/2/2015	$1,000.00	
7	117	3/2/2015	$1,100.00	
8	134	3/3/2015	$1,400.00	
9	131	3/3/2015	$1,200.00	
10	118	3/3/2015	$900.00	
11	125	3/5/2015	$1,650.00	
12	119	3/5/2015	$1,500.00	
13	133	3/8/2015	$1,650.00	
14	129	3/9/2015	$1,650.00	
15	115	3/12/2015	$1,375.00	$25.00
16	121	3/12/2015	$950.00	$25.00
17	127	3/19/2015	$1,300.00	$50.00
Total			$23,825.00	$100.00

Step 8g, Payments Table

RenterID	FirstName	LastName	PropID	EmpID	CreditScore	LeaseBegDate	LeaseEndDate
110	Greg	Hamilton	1029	04-14	624	1/1/2015	12/31/2015
111	Julia	Perez	1013	07-20	711	1/1/2015	12/31/2015
115	Dana	Rozinski	1026	02-59	538	2/1/2015	1/31/2016
117	Miguel	Villegas	1007	07-20	695	2/1/2015	1/31/2016
118	Mason	Ahn	1004	07-23	538	3/1/2015	2/28/2016
119	Michelle	Bertram	1001	03-23	621	3/1/2015	2/28/2016
121	Travis	Jorgenson	1010	04-14	590	3/1/2015	2/28/2016
123	Richard	Terrell	1014	07-20	687	3/1/2015	2/28/2016
125	Rose	Wagoner	1015	07-23	734	4/1/2015	3/31/2016
127	William	Young	1023	05-31	478	4/1/2015	3/31/2016
129	Susan	Lowrey	1002	04-14	634	4/1/2015	3/31/2016
130	Ross	Molaski	1027	03-23	688	5/1/2015	4/30/2016
131	Danielle	Rubio	1020	07-20	722	5/1/2015	4/30/2016
133	Katie	Smith	1018	07-23	596	5/1/2015	4/30/2016
134	Carl	Weston	1009	03-23	655	6/1/2015	5/31/2016
135	Marty	Lobdell	1006	04-14	510	6/1/2015	5/31/2016
136	Nadine	Paschal	1022	05-31	702	6/1/2015	5/31/2016

Step 10j, Renters Table

Project 1e

EmpID	FName	LName	Address	City	State	ZIP	Telephone	EmpCategory	HealthIns
02-59	Christina	Solomon	12241 East 51st	Citrus Heights	CA	95611	(916) 555-8844	Hourly	☑
03-23	Douglas	Ricci	903 Mission Road	Roseville	CA	95678	(916) 555-4125	Salaried	☑
03-55	Tatiana	Kasadev	6558 Orchard Drive	Citrus Heights	CA	95610	(916) 555-8534	Hourly	☑
04-14	Brian	West	12232 142nd Avenue East	Citrus Heights	CA	95611	(916) 555-0967	Salaried	☑
04-32	Kathleen	Addison	21229 19th Street	Citrus Heights	CA	95621	(916) 555-3408	Temporary	☑
05-20	Teresa	Villanueva	19453 North 42nd Street	Citrus Heights	CA	95611	(916) 555-2302	Hourly	☑
05-31	Marcia	Griswold	211 Haven Road	North Highlands	CA	95660	(916) 555-1449	Salaried	☐
06-24	Tiffany	Gentry	12312 North 20th	Roseville	CA	95661	(916) 555-0043	Temporary	☑
06-33	Joanna	Gallegos	6850 York Street	Roseville	CA	95747	(956) 555-7446	Hourly	☐
07-20	Jesse	Scholtz	3412 South 21st Street	Fair Oaks	CA	95628	(916) 555-4204	Salaried	☑
07-23	Eugene	Bond	530 Laurel Road	Orangevale	CA	95662	(916) 555-9412	Salaried	☑
02-72	Robin	Wilder	9945 Valley Avenue	Citrus Heights	CA	95610	(916) 555-6522	Salaried	☐

Employees Table

Project 1f

PropID	CatID	MoRent	Address	City	State	ZIP
1007	A	$1,100.00	904 Everson Road	Fair Oaks	CA	95628
1004	A	$900.00	1932 Oakville Drive	North Highlands	CA	95668
1010	A	$950.00	19334 140th East	Citrus Heights	CA	95621
1014	A	$1,000.00	9045 Valley Avenue	Citrus Heights	CA	95611
1029	C	$1,300.00	155 Aldrich Road	Roseville	CA	95678
1002	C	$1,650.00	2650 Crestline Drive	Citrus Heights	CA	95611
1001	C	$1,500.00	4102 Tenth Street	Citrus Heights	CA	95611
1026	C	$1,375.00	10057 128th Avenue	Citrus Heights	CA	95611
1023	C	$1,300.00	750 Birch Drive	Orangevale	CA	95662
1009	C	$1,400.00	159 Meridian Street	Orangevale	CA	95662
1019	C	$1,700.00	765 Chellis Street	Fair Oaks	CA	95628
1018	C	$1,650.00	9945 North 20th Road	North Highlands	CA	95660
1017	D	$1,300.00	4500 Maple Lane	Orangevale	CA	95662
1011	D	$1,350.00	348 Hampton Avenue	Citrus Heights	CA	95611
1008	D	$1,575.00	5009 North Garden	Roseville	CA	95661
1020	D	$1,200.00	23390 South 22nd Street	Citrus Heights	CA	95610
1006	S	$1,900.00	3412 Mango Street	Orangevale	CA	95662
1003	S	$1,800.00	10234 122nd Avenue	North Highlands	CA	95668
1012	S	$1,775.00	1212 Fairhaven Road	North Highlands	CA	95660
1013	S	$1,900.00	2606 30th Street	Citrus Heights	CA	95610
1016	S	$1,825.00	21388 South 42nd Street	Citrus Heights	CA	95621
1030	S	$1,950.00	5430 112th Southeast	Citrus Heights	CA	95611
1021	S	$1,875.00	652 Seventh Street	Fair Oaks	CA	95628
1024	S	$1,650.00	1195 24th Street	North Highlands	CA	95660
1027	S	$1,800.00	2203 Center Road	Orangevale	CA	95662
1028	S	$1,750.00	488 Franklin Drive	Fair Oaks	CA	95628
1022	T	$1,250.00	4572 152nd Avenue	Citrus Heights	CA	95621
1005	T	$1,350.00	12110 55th Southeast	Citrus Heights	CA	95611
1025	T	$1,200.00	3354 North 62nd Street	Citrus Heights	CA	95610
1015	T	$1,650.00	560 Tenth Street East	North Highlands	CA	95668

PropertiesTable

Relationships Report

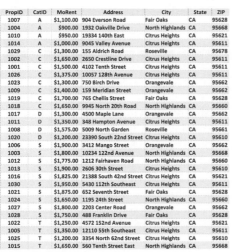

FName	LName	HealthIns
Christina	Solomon	☑
Douglas	Ricci	☑
Tatiana	Kasadev	☑
Brian	West	☑
Kathleen	Addison	☑
Teresa	Villanueva	☑
Tiffany	Gentry	☑
Jesse	Scholtz	☑
Eugene	Bond	☑

EmpsWithHealthInsQuery

PropID	Category	Address	City	State	ZIP
1010	Apartment	19334 140th East	Citrus Heights	CA	95621
1014	Apartment	9045 Valley Avenue	Citrus Heights	CA	95611
1001	Condominium	4102 Tenth Street	Citrus Heights	CA	95611
1002	Condominium	2650 Crestline Drive	Citrus Heights	CA	95611
1026	Condominium	10057 128th Avenue	Citrus Heights	CA	95611
1013	Single-family house	2606 30th Street	Citrus Heights	CA	95610
1016	Single-family house	21388 South 42nd Street	Citrus Heights	CA	95621
1030	Single-family house	5430 112th Southeast	Citrus Heights	CA	95611
1011	Duplex	348 Hampton Avenue	Citrus Heights	CA	95611
1020	Duplex	23390 South 22nd Street	Citrus Heights	CA	95610
1005	Townhouse	12110 55th Southeast	Citrus Heights	CA	95611
1022	Townhouse	4572 152nd Avenue	Citrus Heights	CA	95621
1025	Townhouse	3354 North 62nd Street	Citrus Heights	CA	95610

CitrusHeightsPropsQuery

Project 1f–*continued*

PymntID	PymntDate	PymntAmount	FirstName	LastName
4	3/1/2015	$1,300.00	Greg	Hamilton
2	3/1/2015	$1,900.00	Julia	Perez
7	3/2/2015	$1,100.00	Miguel	Villegas
10	3/3/2015	$900.00	Mason	Ahn
12	3/5/2015	$1,500.00	Michelle	Bertram
6	3/2/2015	$1,000.00	Richard	Terrell
11	3/5/2015	$1,650.00	Rose	Wagoner
1	3/1/2015	$1,800.00	Ross	Molaski
9	3/3/2015	$1,200.00	Danielle	Rubio
8	3/3/2015	$1,400.00	Carl	Weston
5	3/2/2015	$1,900.00	Marty	Lobdell
3	3/1/2015	$1,250.00	Nadine	Paschal

Pymnts3/1To3/5Query

Category	PropID	MoRent	Address	City	State	ZIP
Apartment	1010	$950.00	19334 140th East	Citrus Heights	CA	95621
Apartment	1014	$1,000.00	9045 Valley Avenue	Citrus Heights	CA	95611
Condominium	1001	$1,500.00	4102 Tenth Street	Citrus Heights	CA	95611
Condominium	1009	$1,400.00	159 Meridian Street	Orangevale	CA	95662
Condominium	1023	$1,300.00	750 Birch Drive	Orangevale	CA	95662
Condominium	1026	$1,375.00	10057 128th Avenue	Citrus Heights	CA	95611
Duplex	1011	$1,350.00	348 Hampton Avenue	Citrus Heights	CA	95611
Duplex	1017	$1,300.00	4500 Maple Lane	Orangevale	CA	95662
Duplex	1020	$1,200.00	23390 South 22nd Street	Citrus Heights	CA	95610
Townhouse	1005	$1,350.00	12110 55th Southeast	Citrus Heights	CA	95611
Townhouse	1022	$1,250.00	4572 152nd Avenue	Citrus Heights	CA	95621
Townhouse	1025	$1,200.00	3354 North 62nd Street	Citrus Heights	CA	95610

RentLessThan$1501InCHAndOVQuery

EmpID	FName	LName	Address	City	State	ZIP
07-20	Jesse	Scholtz	4102 Tenth Street	Citrus Heights	CA	95611
07-20	Jesse	Scholtz	2650 Crestline Drive	Citrus Heights	CA	95611
07-20	Jesse	Scholtz	12110 55th Southeast	Citrus Heights	CA	95611
07-20	Jesse	Scholtz	19334 140th East	Citrus Heights	CA	95621
07-20	Jesse	Scholtz	348 Hampton Avenue	Citrus Heights	CA	95611
07-20	Jesse	Scholtz	2606 30th Street	Citrus Heights	CA	95610
07-20	Jesse	Scholtz	9045 Valley Avenue	Citrus Heights	CA	95611
07-20	Jesse	Scholtz	21388 South 42nd Street	Citrus Heights	CA	95621
07-20	Jesse	Scholtz	23390 South 22nd Street	Citrus Heights	CA	95610
07-20	Jesse	Scholtz	4572 152nd Avenue	Citrus Heights	CA	95621
07-20	Jesse	Scholtz	3354 North 62nd Street	Citrus Heights	CA	95610
07-20	Jesse	Scholtz	10057 128th Avenue	Citrus Heights	CA	95611
07-20	Jesse	Scholtz	5430 112th Southeast	Citrus Heights	CA	95611

Emp07-20CHPropsQuery

Project 1 Create and Modify Tables in a Property Management Database — 8 Parts

You will open the Sun Properties database, create two new tables in Design view, modify existing tables, and sort data in tables. You will also complete a spelling check on data in tables, find data in a table and replace it with other data, create relationships and perform queries, and get help using the Access Help feature.

Creating Tables in Design View

Quick Steps

Create a Table in Design View

1. Open database.
2. Click CREATE tab.
3. Click Table button.
4. Click View button.
5. Type name for table.
6. Press Enter or click OK.
7. Type field names, specify data types, and include descriptions.
8. Click Save button.

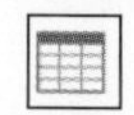
Table

View

In Datasheet view, you can create a table by assigning each column a data type and typing the field name. Once the columns are defined, you enter the data into records. You can also create a table in Design view, where you can set field properties before you begin entering data. To display a table in Design view, open the desired database, click the CREATE tab, and then click the Table button. This opens a new blank table in Datasheet view. Display the table in Design view by clicking the View button that displays at the left side of the TABLE TOOLS FIELDS tab in the Views group. When you click the View button in a new table, Access displays the Save As dialog box, where you type the table name and then press Enter or click OK. Figure 4.1 displays the Properties table in Design view in AL1-C4-SunProperties.accdb.

In Design view, each row in the top section of the work area represents one field in the table and is used to define the field name, the field data type, and a description. The *Field Properties* section in the lower half of the work area displays the properties for the active field. The properties vary depending on the active field. In the lower right corner of Design view, Help information displays about an option as you make an option active in the Design window. In Figure 4.1, the *PropID* field name is active in Design view, so Access displays information on field names in the Help area.

Figure 4.1 Properties Table in Design View

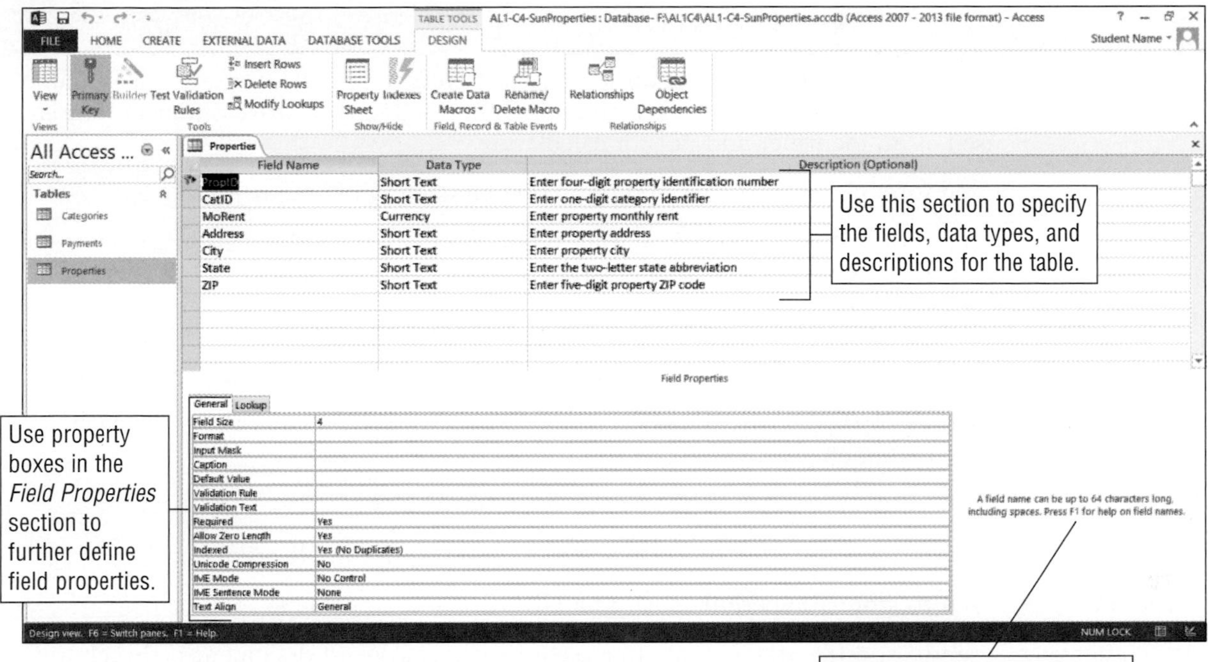

Define each field in the table in the rows in the top section of Design view. When you create a new table in Design view, Access automatically assigns the first field the name *ID* and assigns the AutoNumber data type. You can leave this field name or type a new name and you can also change the data type. To create a new field in the table, click in the field in the *Field Name* column, type the field name, and then press the Tab key or Enter key. This makes active the *Data Type* field. Click the down-pointing arrow in the *Data Type* field and then click the desired data type at the drop-down list. In Chapter 1, you created tables in Datasheet view and assigned data types of Short Text, Date/Time, Currency, and Yes/No. The *Data Type* field drop-down list includes these data types plus additional types, as described in Table 4.1.

When you click the desired data type at the drop-down list and then press the Tab key, the *Description* field becomes active. Type a description in the field that provides useful information to someone entering data in the table. When typing a description, consider identifying the field's purpose or contents or providing instructional information for data entry. The description you type displays in the Status bar when the field is active in the table in Datasheet view.

When creating the table, continue typing field names, assigning data types to fields, and typing field descriptions. When you have completed the table design, save the table by clicking the Save button on the Quick Access toolbar. Return to Datasheet view by clicking the View button in the Views group on the TABLE TOOLS DESIGN tab. In Datasheet view, type the records for the table.

Save

Table 4.1 Data Types

Data Type	*Description*
Short Text	Used for alphanumeric data up to 255 characters in length—for example, a name, address, or value (such as a telephone number or social security number) that is used as an identifier and not for calculating.
Long Text	Used for alphanumeric data up to 64,000 characters in length.
Number	Used for positive and negative values that can be used in calculations. Do not use for values that will calculate monetary amounts (see Currency).
Date/Time	Used to ensure dates and times are entered and sorted properly.
Currency	Used for values that involve money. Access will not round off during calculations.
AutoNumber	Used to automatically number records sequentially (incrementing by 1); each new record is numbered as it is typed.
Yes/No	Used for values of *Yes* or *No*, *True* or *False*, or *On* or *Off*.
OLE Object	Used to embed or link objects created in other Office applications.
Hyperlink	Used to store a hyperlink, such as a URL.
Attachment	Used to add file attachments to a record such as a Word document or Excel workbook.
Calculated	Used to display the Expression Builder dialog box, where an expression is entered to calculate the value of the calculated column.
Lookup Wizard	Used to enter data in the field from another existing table or to display a list of values in a drop-down list from which the user chooses.

Project 1a Creating a Table in Design View

Part 1 of 8

1. Open Access and then open **AL1-C4-SunProperties.accdb** located in the AL1C4 folder on your storage medium.
2. Click the Enable Content button in the message bar. (The message bar will display immediately below the ribbon.)
3. View the Properties table in Design view by completing the following steps:
   a. Open the Properties table.
   b. Click the View button in the Views group on the HOME tab.
   c. Click each field name and then look at the information that displays in the *Field Properties* section.
   d. Click in various options in the work area and then read the information that displays in the Help area located in the lower right corner of Design view.
   e. Click the View button to return the table to Datasheet view.
   f. Close the Properties table.

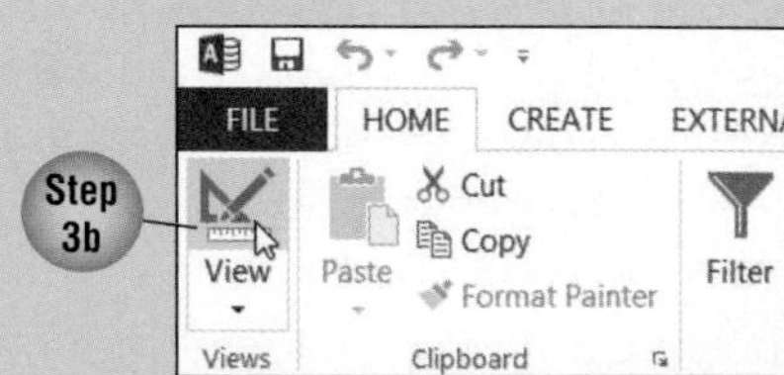

4. Create a new table in Design view, as shown in Figure 4.2, by completing the following steps:
   a. Click the CREATE tab and then click the Table button in the Tables group.
   b. Click the View button in the Views group on the TABLE TOOLS FIELDS tab.
   c. At the Save As dialog box, type **Renters** and then press Enter.
   d. Type **RenterID** in the *Field Name* column in the first row and then press the Tab key.
   e. Change the data type to Short Text by clicking the down-pointing arrow located in the *Data Type* column and then clicking *Short Text* at the drop-down list.
   f. Change the field size from the default of 255 characters to 3 characters by selecting *255* in the *Field Size* property box in the *Field Properties* section and then typing **3**.
   g. Click in the *Description* column for the *RenterID* row, type **Enter three-digit renter identification number**, and then press the Tab key.

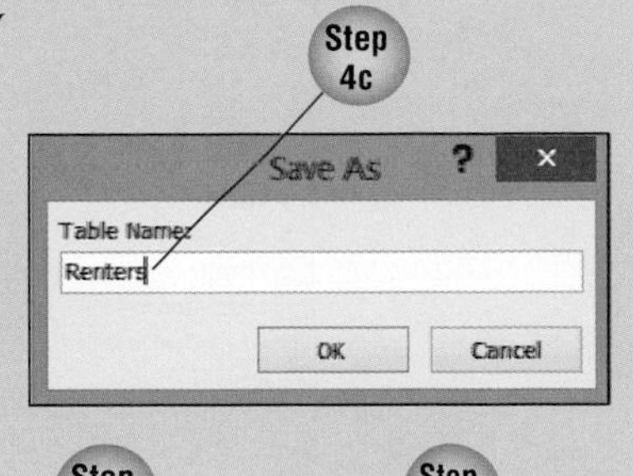

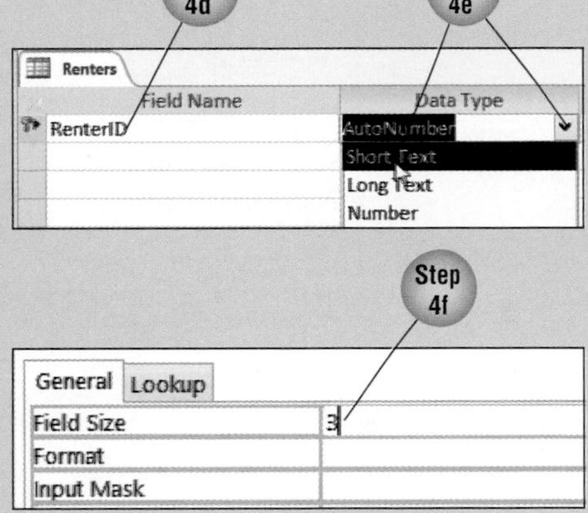

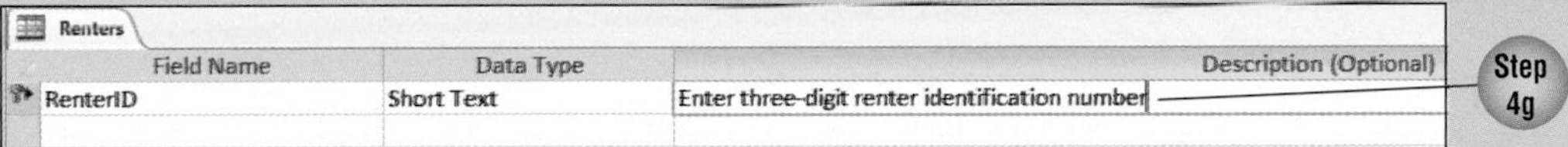

   h. Type **FirstName** in the *Field Name* column and then press the Tab key.
   i. Select *255* in the *Field Size* property box in the *Field Properties* section and then type **20**.
   j. Click in the *Description* column for the *FirstName* row, type **Enter renter's first name**, and then press the Tab key.
   k. Type **LastName** in the *Field Name* column and then press the Tab key.
   l. Change the field size to 30 characters (at the *Field Size* property box).
   m. Click in the *Description* column for the *LastName* row, type **Enter renter's last name**, and then press the Tab key.
   n. Enter the remaining field names, data types, and descriptions as shown in Figure 4.2. (Change the field sizes to 4 characters for the *PropID* field, 5 characters for the *EmpID* field, and 3 characters for the *CreditScore* field.)
   o. After all of the fields are entered, click the Save button on the Quick Access toolbar.
   p. Make sure the *RenterID* field is identified as the primary key. (A key icon displays in the *RenterID* field selector bar.)
   q. Click the View button to return the table to Datasheet view.
5. Enter the records in the Renters table as shown in Figure 4.3.
6. After all of the records are entered, automatically adjust the column widths.
7. Save and then close the Renters table.

Figure 4.2 Project 1a Renters Table in Design View

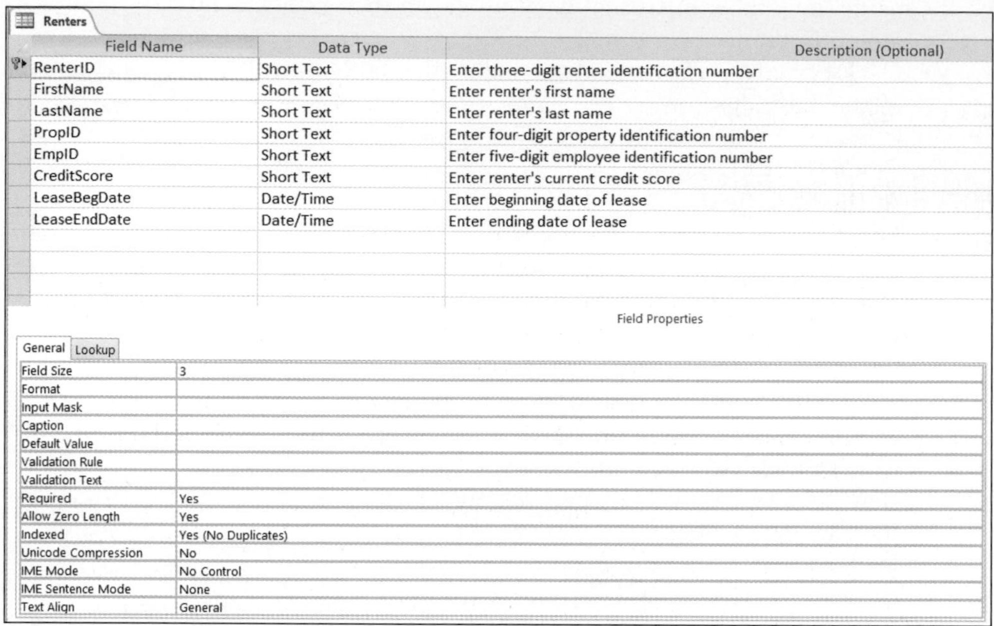

Renters

Field Name	Data Type	Description (Optional)
RenterID	Short Text	Enter three-digit renter identification number
FirstName	Short Text	Enter renter's first name
LastName	Short Text	Enter renter's last name
PropID	Short Text	Enter four-digit property identification number
EmpID	Short Text	Enter five-digit employee identification number
CreditScore	Short Text	Enter renter's current credit score
LeaseBegDate	Date/Time	Enter beginning date of lease
LeaseEndDate	Date/Time	Enter ending date of lease

Field Properties

General | Lookup

Field Size	3
Format	
Input Mask	
Caption	
Default Value	
Validation Rule	
Validation Text	
Required	Yes
Allow Zero Length	Yes
Indexed	Yes (No Duplicates)
Unicode Compression	No
IME Mode	No Control
IME Sentence Mode	None
Text Align	General

Figure 4.3 Project 1a Renters Table in Datasheet View

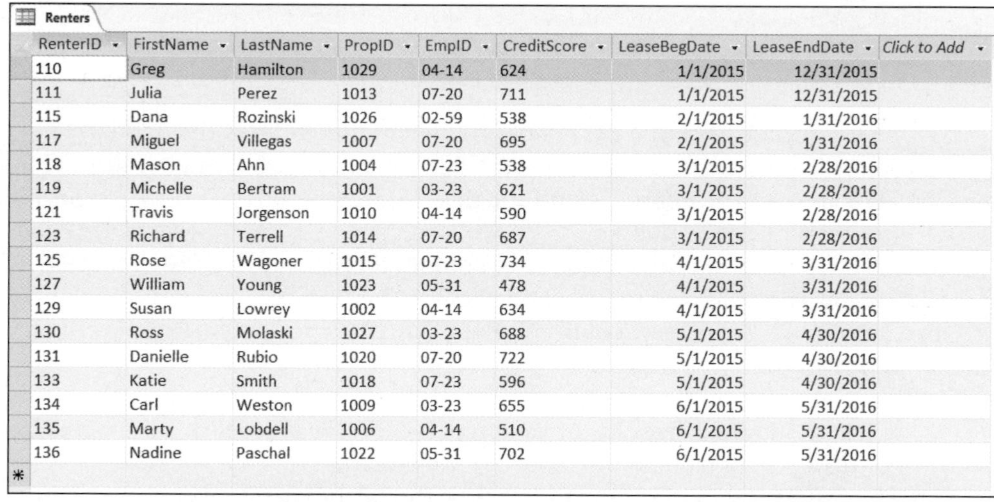

Renters

RenterID	FirstName	LastName	PropID	EmpID	CreditScore	LeaseBegDate	LeaseEndDate	Click to Add
110	Greg	Hamilton	1029	04-14	624	1/1/2015	12/31/2015	
111	Julia	Perez	1013	07-20	711	1/1/2015	12/31/2015	
115	Dana	Rozinski	1026	02-59	538	2/1/2015	1/31/2016	
117	Miguel	Villegas	1007	07-20	695	2/1/2015	1/31/2016	
118	Mason	Ahn	1004	07-23	538	3/1/2015	2/28/2016	
119	Michelle	Bertram	1001	03-23	621	3/1/2015	2/28/2016	
121	Travis	Jorgenson	1010	04-14	590	3/1/2015	2/28/2016	
123	Richard	Terrell	1014	07-20	687	3/1/2015	2/28/2016	
125	Rose	Wagoner	1015	07-23	734	4/1/2015	3/31/2016	
127	William	Young	1023	05-31	478	4/1/2015	3/31/2016	
129	Susan	Lowrey	1002	04-14	634	4/1/2015	3/31/2016	
130	Ross	Molaski	1027	03-23	688	5/1/2015	4/30/2016	
131	Danielle	Rubio	1020	07-20	722	5/1/2015	4/30/2016	
133	Katie	Smith	1018	07-23	596	5/1/2015	4/30/2016	
134	Carl	Weston	1009	03-23	655	6/1/2015	5/31/2016	
135	Marty	Lobdell	1006	04-14	510	6/1/2015	5/31/2016	
136	Nadine	Paschal	1022	05-31	702	6/1/2015	5/31/2016	
*								

Assigning a Default Value

In Chapter 1, you learned how to specify a default value for a field in a table in Datasheet view using the Default Value button in the Properties group on the TABLE TOOLS FIELDS tab. In addition to this method, you can create a default value for a field in Design view with the *Default Value* property box in the *Field Properties* section. Click in the *Default Value* property box and then type the desired field value.

In Project 1b, you will create a health insurance field with a Yes/No data type. Since most of the agents of Sun Properties have signed up for health insurance benefits, you set the default value for the field to *Yes*. If you add a new field that contains a default value to an existing table, the existing records do not reflect the default value. Only new records entered in the table reflect the default value.

Using the Input Mask

For some fields, you may want to control the data entered in the field. For example, in a zip code field, you may want the nine-digit zip code entered (rather than the five-digit zip code) or you may want the three-digit area code included in a telephone number. Use the *Input Mask* field property to set a pattern for how data is entered in a field. An input mask ensures that data in records conforms to a standard format. Access includes an Input Mask Wizard that guides you through creating an input mask. The Input Mask is available for fields with a data type of Short Text or Date/Time.

Use the Input Mask Wizard when assigning a data type to a field. In Design view, click in the Input Mask property box in the *Field Properties* section and then run the Input Mask Wizard by clicking the Build button (contains three black dots) that appears at the right side of the Input Mask property box. This displays the first Input Mask Wizard dialog box, as shown in Figure 4.4. In the *Input Mask* list box, choose which input mask you want your data to look like and then click the Next button. At the second Input Mask Wizard dialog box, as shown in Figure 4.5, specify the appearance of the input mask and the desired placeholder character and then click the Next button. At the third Input Mask Wizard dialog box, specify whether you want the data stored with or without the symbol in the mask and then click the Next button. At the fourth dialog box, click the Finish button.

Quick Steps

Use the Input Mask Wizard

1. Open table in Design view.
2. Type text in *Field Name* column.
3. Press Tab key.
4. Change data type to *Short Text* or *Date/Time*.
5. Click Save button.
6. Click in *Input Mask* property box.
7. Click Build button.
8. Complete wizard steps.

Build

HINT

An input mask is a set of characters that control what you can and cannot enter in a field.

Figure 4.4 First Input Mask Wizard Dialog Box

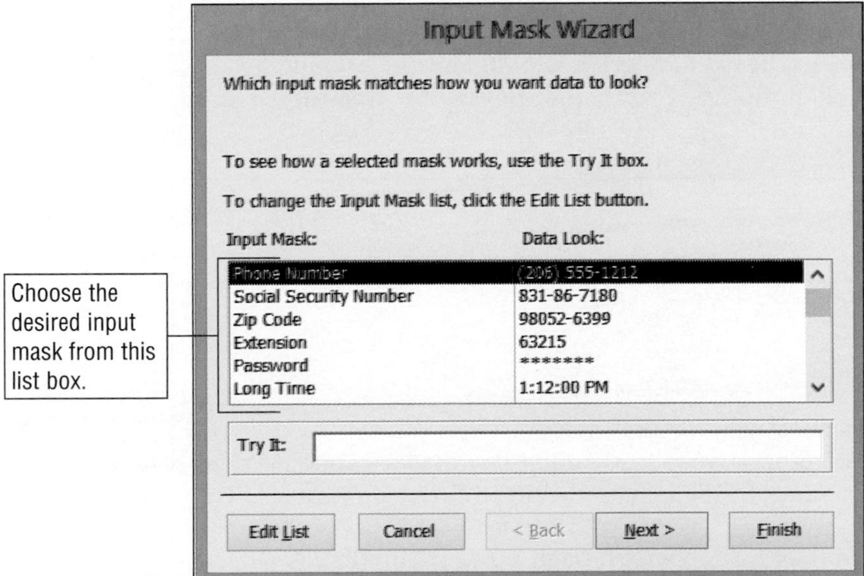

Figure 4.5 Second Input Mask Wizard Dialog Box

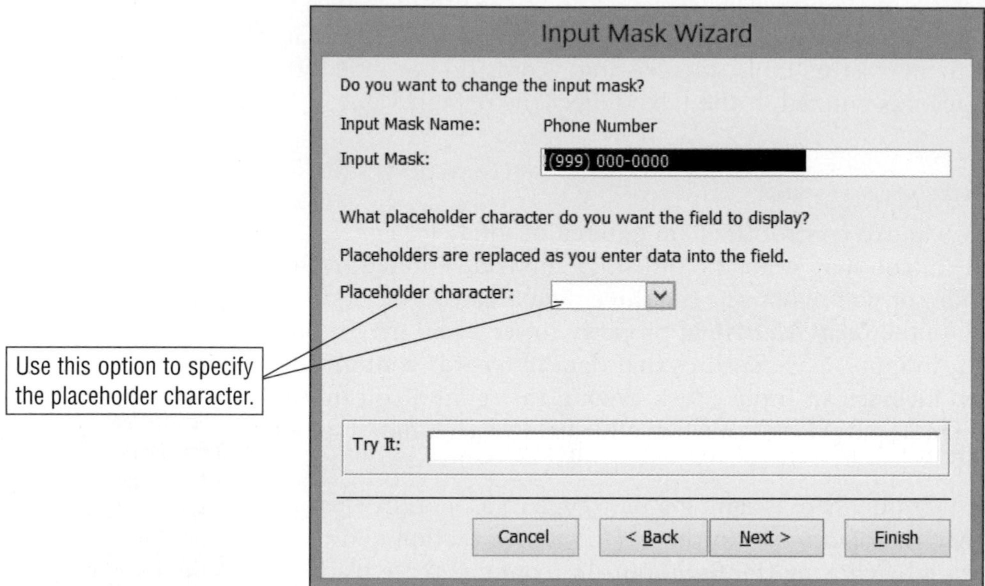

Project 1b Creating an Employees Table

Part 2 of 8

1. With **AL1-C4-SunProperties.accdb** open, create the Employees table in Design view as shown in Figure 4.6 on page 140. Begin by clicking the CREATE tab and then clicking the Table button.
2. Click the View button to switch to Design view.
3. At the Save As dialog box, type **Employees** and then press Enter.
4. Type **EmpID** in the *Field Name* column in the first row and then press the Tab key.
5. Change the data type to Short Text by clicking the down-pointing arrow located in the *Data Type* column and then clicking *Short Text* at the drop-down list.
6. Change the field size from the default of 255 characters to 5 characters by selecting *255* in the *Field Size* property box in the *Field Properties* section and then typing **5**.
7. Click in the *Description* column for the *EmpID* row, type **Enter five-digit employee identification number**, and then press the Tab key.

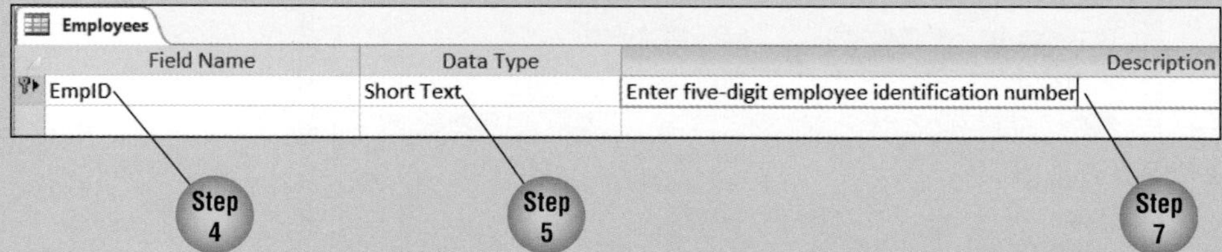

8. Type **FName** in the *Field Name* column and then press the Tab key.
9. Select *255* in the *Field Size* property box in the *Field Properties* section and then type **20**.
10. Click in the *Description* column for the *FName* row, type **Enter employee's first name**, and then press the Tab key.
11. Complete steps similar to those in Steps 8 through 10 to create the *LName*, *Address*, and *City* fields as shown in Figure 4.6. Change the field size for the *LName* field and *Address* field to 30 characters and change the *City* field to 20 characters.

12. Create the *State* field with a default value of *CA,* since all employees live in California, by completing the following steps:
    a. Type **State** in the *Field Name* column in the row below the *City* row and then press the Tab key.
    b. Click in the *Default Value* property box in the *Field Properties* section and then type **CA**.
    c. Click in the *Description* column for the *State* row, type **CA automatically entered as state**, and then press the Tab key.
13. Type **ZIP** and then press the Tab key.
14. Select *255* that displays in the *Field Size* property box in the *Field Properties* section and then type **5**.
15. Click in the *Description* column for the *ZIP* row, type **Enter five-digit ZIP code**, and then press the Tab key.
16. Type **Telephone** and then press the Tab key.
17. Create an input mask for the telephone number by completing the following steps:
    a. Click the Save button on the Quick Access toolbar to save the table. (You must save the table before using the Input Mask Wizard.)
    b. Click in the *Input Mask* property box in the *Field Properties* section.
    c. Click the Build button (contains three black dots) that displays at the right side of the *Input Mask* property box.

    d. At the first Input Mask Wizard dialog box, make sure *Phone Number* is selected in the *Input Mask* list box and then click the Next button.
    e. At the second Input Mask Wizard dialog box, click the down-pointing arrow at the right side of the *Placeholder character* option box and then click # at the drop-down list.

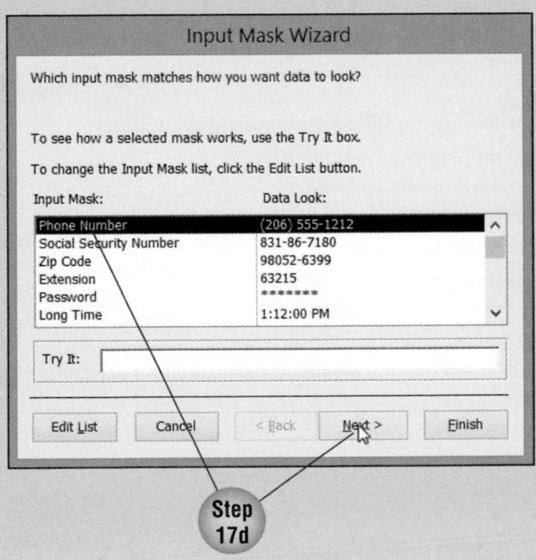

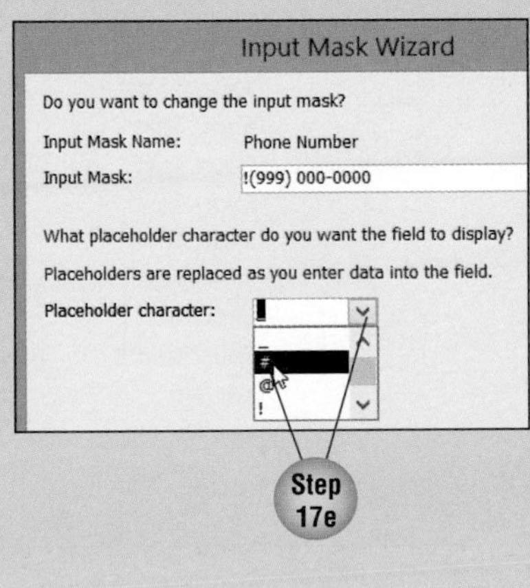

f. Click the Next button.
g. At the third Input Mask Wizard dialog box, click the *With the symbols in the mask, like this* option.
h. Click the Next button.
i. At the fourth Input Mask Wizard dialog box, click the Finish button.

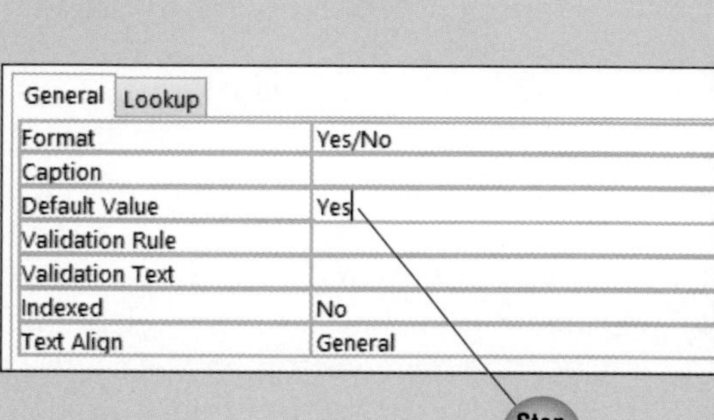

18. Click in the *Description* column in the *Telephone* row, type **Enter employee's telephone number**, and then press the Tab key.
19. Type **HealthIns** and then press the Tab key.
20. Click the down-pointing arrow in the *Data Type* column and then click *Yes/No* at the drop-down list.
21. Click in the *Default Value* property box in the *Field Properties* section, delete the text *No*, and then type **Yes**.

General | Lookup

Format	Yes/No
Caption	
Default Value	Yes
Validation Rule	
Validation Text	
Indexed	No
Text Align	General

Step 21

22. Click in the *Description* column for the *HealthIns* row, type **Leave check mark if employee is signed up for health insurance**, and then press the Tab key.
23. Type **DentalIns** and then press the Tab key.
24. Click the down-pointing arrow in the *Data Type* column and then click *Yes/No* at the drop-down list. (The text in the *Default Value* property box will remain as *No*.)
25. Click in the *Description* column for the *DentalIns* row, type **Insert check mark if employee is signed up for dental insurance**, and then press the Tab key.
26. After all of the fields are entered, click the Save button on the Quick Access toolbar.
27. Click the View button to return the table to Datasheet view.
28. Enter the records in the Employees table as shown in Figure 4.7.
29. After all of the records are entered, automatically adjust the widths of the columns in the table.
30. Save and then close the Employees table.

Figure 4.6 Project 1b Employees Table in Design View

Employees

Field Name	Data Type	Description (Optional)
EmpID	Short Text	Enter five-digit employee identification number
FName	Short Text	Enter employee's first name
LName	Short Text	Enter employee's last name
Address	Short Text	Enter employee's address
City	Short Text	Enter employee's city
State	Short Text	CA automatically entered as state
ZIP	Short Text	Enter five-digit ZIP code
Telephone	Short Text	Enter employee's telephone number
HealthIns	Yes/No	Leave check mark if employee is signed up for health insurance
DentalIns	Yes/No	Insert check mark if employee is signed up for dental insurance

Field Properties

Figure 4.7 Project 1b Employees Table in Datasheet View

	EmpID	FName	LName	Address	City	State	ZIP	Telephone	HealthIns	DentalIns
	02-59	Christina	Solomon	12241 East 51st	Citrus Heights	CA	95611	(916) 555-8844	✔	✔
	03-23	Douglas	Ricci	903 Mission Road	Roseville	CA	95678	(916) 555-4125	✔	☐
	03-55	Tatiana	Kasadev	6558 Orchard Drive	Citrus Heights	CA	95610	(916) 555-8534	✔	☐
	04-14	Brian	West	12232 142nd Avenue East	Citrus Heights	CA	95611	(916) 555-0967	✔	✔
	04-32	Kathleen	Addison	21229 19th Street	Citrus Heights	CA	95621	(916) 555-3408	✔	✔
	05-20	Teresa	Villanueva	19453 North 42nd Street	Citrus Heights	CA	95611	(916) 555-2302	✔	✔
	05-31	Marcia	Griswold	211 Haven Road	North Highlands	CA	95660	(916) 555-1449	☐	☐
	06-24	Tiffany	Gentry	12312 North 20th	Roseville	CA	95661	(916) 555-0043	✔	✔
	06-33	Joanna	Gallegos	6850 York Street	Roseville	CA	95747	(956) 555-7446	☐	☐
	07-20	Jesse	Scholtz	3412 South 21st Street	Fair Oaks	CA	95628	(916) 555-4204	✔	☐
	07-23	Eugene	Bond	530 Laurel Road	Orangevale	CA	95662	(916) 555-9412	✔	☐
*						CA			✔	☐

Validating Field Entries

Use the *Validation Rule* property box in the *Field Properties* section in Design view to enter a statement containing a conditional test that is checked each time data is entered into a field. If data is entered that fails to satisfy the conditional test, Access does not accept the entry and displays an error message. By entering a conditional statement in the *Validation Rule* property box that checks each entry against the acceptable range, you can reduce errors. Enter in the *Validation Text* property box the content of the error message that you want to display.

HINT

Enter a validation rule in a field to control what is entered in the field and to reduce errors. Create validation text that displays when someone enters invalid data in the field.

Using the Lookup Wizard

Like the Input Mask Wizard, the Lookup Wizard can be used to control the data entered in a field. Use the Lookup Wizard to confine the data entered into a field to a specific list of items. For example, in Project 1c, you will use the Lookup Wizard to restrict the new *EmpCategory* field to one of three choices: *Salaried*, *Hourly*, and *Temporary*. When the user clicks in the field in the datasheet, a down-pointing arrow displays. The user clicks this down-pointing arrow to display a drop-down list of available entries and then clicks the desired item.

Use the Lookup Wizard when assigning a data type to a field. Click in the desired field in the *Data Type* column and then click the down-pointing arrow that displays at the right side of the field. At the drop-down list that displays, click *Lookup Wizard*. This displays the first Lookup Wizard dialog box, as shown in Figure 4.8. At this dialog box, indicate that you want to enter the field choices by clicking the *I will type in the values that I want* option and then click the Next button. At the second Lookup Wizard dialog box, shown in Figure 4.9, click in the blank text box below *Col1* and then type the first choice. Press the Tab key and then type the second choice. Continue in this manner until you have entered all the desired choices and then click the Next button. At the third Lookup Wizard dialog box, make sure the proper name displays in the *What label would you like for your lookup column?* text box and then click the Finish button.

Quick Steps

Use the Lookup Wizard

1. Open table in Design view.
2. Type text in *Field Name* column.
3. Press Tab key.
4. Click down-pointing arrow.
5. Click *Lookup Wizard.*
6. Complete wizard steps.

Figure 4.8 First Lookup Wizard Dialog Box

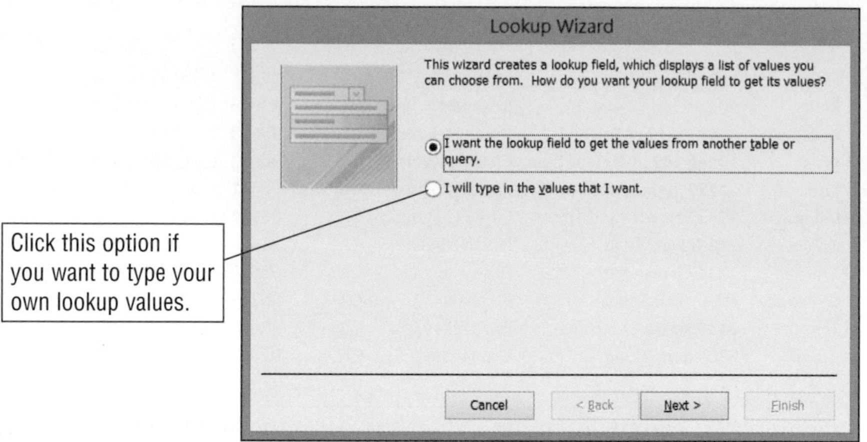

Figure 4.9 Second Lookup Wizard Dialog Box

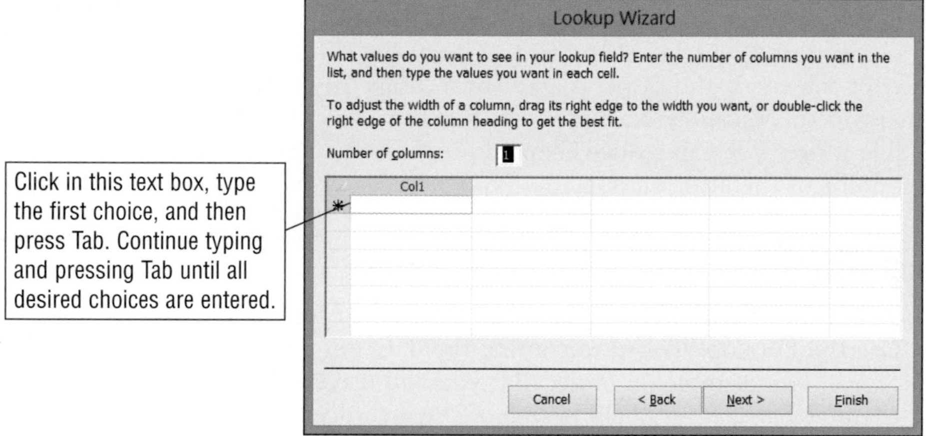

Inserting, Moving, and Deleting Fields in Design View

Quick Steps

Insert a Field in Design View

1. Open table in Design view.
2. Click in row that will follow new field.
3. Click Insert Rows button.

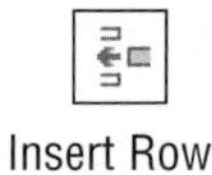

Insert Rows

In Chapter 1, you learned how to insert, move, and delete fields in a table in Datasheet view. You can also perform these tasks in Design view. To insert a new field in a table in Design view, position the insertion point in a field in the row that will be located immediately *below* the new field and then click the Insert Rows button in the Tools group on the TABLE TOOLS DESIGN tab. Another option is to position the insertion point on any text in the row that will display immediately *below* the new field, click the right mouse button, and then click *Insert Rows* at the shortcut menu. If you insert a row for a new field and then change your mind, immediately click the Undo button on the Quick Access toolbar. Remember that a *row* in the Design view creates a *field* in the table.

You can move a field in a table to a different location in Datasheet view or Design view. To move a field in Design view, click in the field selector bar at the left side of the row you want to move. With the row selected, position the arrow pointer in the field selector bar at the left side of the selected row, hold down the left mouse button, drag the arrow pointer with a gray square attached until a thick black line displays in the desired position, and then release the mouse button.

Delete a field in a table and all data entered in that field is also deleted. When you delete a field, it cannot be undone with the Undo button. Delete a field only if you are sure you really want it and the data associated with it completely removed from the table. To delete a field in Design view, click in the field selector bar at the left side of the row you want to delete and then click the Delete Rows button in the Tools group. At the message asking if you want to permanently delete the field and all of the data in the field, click Yes. You can also delete a row by positioning the mouse pointer in the row you want to delete, clicking the right mouse button, and then clicking *Delete Rows* at the shortcut menu.

Quick Steps

Delete a Field in Design View
1. Open table in Design view.
2. Click in row to be deleted.
3. Click Delete Rows button.
4. Click Yes.

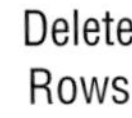
Delete Rows

Inserting a Total Row

You can add a *Total* row in a table in Datasheet view and then choose from a list of functions to find the sum, average, maximum, minimum, count, standard deviation, or variance result in a numeric column. To insert a *Total* row, click the Totals button in the Records group on the HOME tab. Access adds a row to the bottom of the table with the label *Total* at the left. Click in the *Total* row, click the down-pointing arrow that appears, and then click the desired function at the drop-down list.

Quick Steps

Insert a Total Row
1. Open table in Datasheet view.
2. Click Totals button.
3. Click in *Total* row.
4. Click down-pointing arrow.
5. Click desired function.

Totals

Project 1c **Validating Field Entries; Using the Lookup Wizard; and Inserting, Moving, and Deleting a Field** **Part 3 of 8**

1. With **AL1-C4-SunProperties.accdb** open, open the Employees table.
2. Insert in the Employees table a new field and apply a validation rule by completing the following steps:
   a. Click the View button to switch to Design view.
   b. Click in the empty field immediately below the *DentalIns* field in the *Field Name* column and then type **LifeIns**.
   c. Press the Tab key.
   d. Click the down-pointing arrow at the right side of the *Data Type* field and then click *Currency* at the drop-down list.
   e. Click in the *Validation Rule* property box, type **<=100000**, and then press Enter.
   f. With the insertion point positioned in the *Validation Text* property box, type **Enter a value that is equal to or less than $100,000**.
   g. Click in the field in the *Description* column for the *LifeIns* row and then type **Enter optional life insurance amount.**
   h. Click the Save button on the Quick Access toolbar. Since the validation rule was created *after* data was entered into the table, Access displays a warning message indicating that some data may not be valid. At this message, click No.
   i. Click the View button to switch to Datasheet view.
3. Click in the first empty field in the *LifeIns* column, type **200000**, and then press the Down Arrow key.

Step 2e

General | Lookup

Format	Currency
Decimal Places	Auto
Input Mask	
Caption	
Default Value	0
Validation Rule	<=100000
Validation Text	Enter a value that is equal to or less than $100,000
Required	No

4. Access displays the error message telling you to enter an amount that is equal to or less than $100,000. At this error message, click OK.
5. Edit the amount in the field so it displays as *100000* and then press the Down Arrow key.
6. Type the following entries in the remaining fields in the *LifeIns* column:
   Record 2: **25000**
   Record 3: **0**
   Record 4: **50000**
   Record 5: **50000**
   Record 6: **0**
   Record 7: **100000**
   Record 8: **50000**
   Record 9: **25000**
   Record 10: **0**
   Record 11: **100000**
7. Insert the field *EmpCategory* in the Employees table and use the Lookup Wizard to specify field choices by completing the following steps:
   a. Click the View button to change to Design view.
   b. Click on any character in the *FName* field entry in the *Field Name* column.
   c. Click the Insert Rows button in the Tools group.
   d. With the insertion point positioned in the new blank field in the *Field Name* column, type **EmpCategory**.
   e. Press the Tab key. (This moves the insertion point to the *Data Type* column.)
   f. Click the down-pointing arrow at the right side of the *Data Type* field and then click *Lookup Wizard* at the drop-down list.
   g. At the first Lookup Wizard dialog box, click the *I will type in the values that I want* option and then click the Next button.

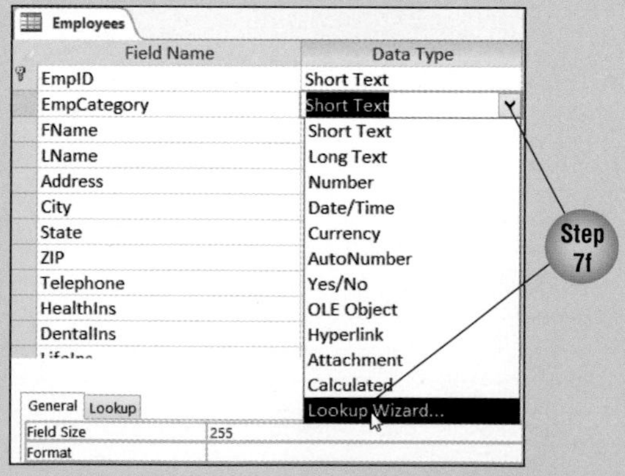

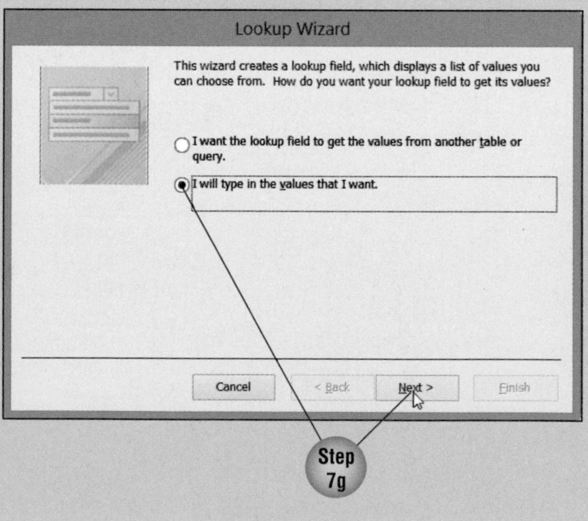

h. At the second Lookup Wizard dialog box, click in the blank text box below *Col1*, type **Salaried**, and then press the Tab key.
i. Type **Hourly** and then press the Tab key.
j. Type **Temporary**.
k. Click the Next button.
l. At the third Lookup Wizard dialog box, click the Finish button.
m. Press the Tab key and then type **Click down-pointing arrow and then click employee category** in the *Description* column.

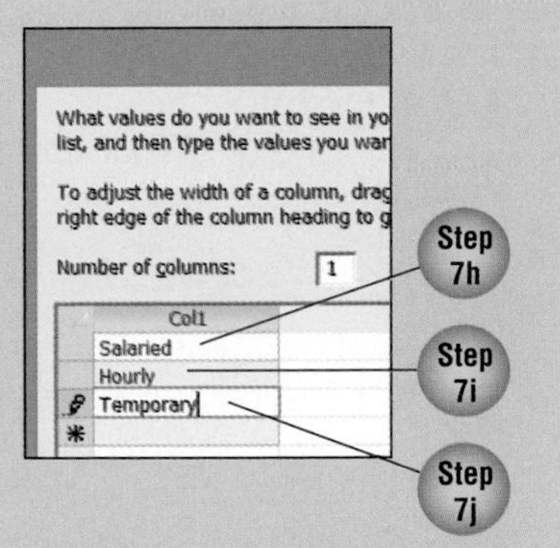

8. Click the Save button on the Quick Access toolbar.
9. Click the View button to switch to Datasheet view.
10. Insert information in the *EmpCategory* column by completing the following steps:
    a. Click in the first blank field in the new *EmpCategory* field.
    b. Click the down-pointing arrow at the right side of the field and then click *Hourly* at the drop-down list.
    c. Click in the next blank field in the *EmpCategory* column, click the down-pointing arrow, and then click *Salaried* at the drop-down list.
    d. Continue entering information in the *EmpCategory* column by completing similar steps. Choose the following in the specified record:
        Third record: *Hourly*
        Fourth record: *Salaried*
        Fifth record: *Temporary*
        Sixth record: *Hourly*
        Seventh record: *Salaried*
        Eighth record: *Temporary*
        Ninth record: *Hourly*
        Tenth record: *Salaried*
        Eleventh record: *Salaried*

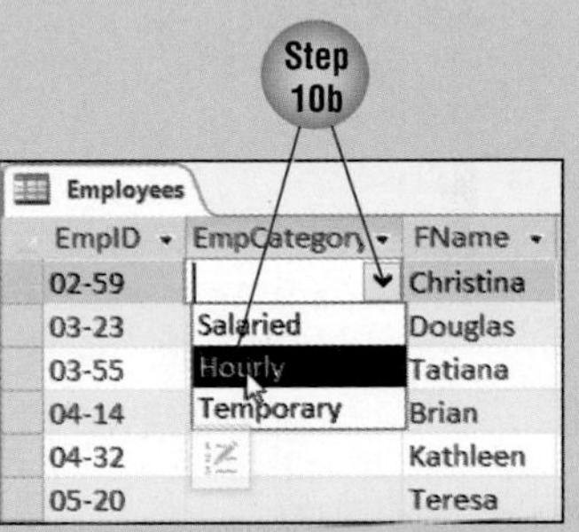

11. Print the Employees table. (The table will print on two pages.)
12. After looking at the printed table, you decide to move the *EmpCategory* field. You also need to delete the *DentalIns* field, since Sun Properties no longer offers dental insurance benefits to employees. Move the *EmpCatgory* field and delete the *DentalIns* field in Design view by completing the following steps:
    a. With the Employees table open, click the View button to switch to Design view.
    b. Click in the field selector bar at the left side of the *EmpCategory* field to select the row.
    c. Position the arrow pointer in the *EmpCategory* field selector bar, hold down the left mouse button, drag down until a thick black line displays below the *Telephone* field, and then release the mouse button.

Employees

Field Name	Data Type
EmpID	Short Text
EmpCategory	Short Text
FName	Short Text
LName	Short Text
Address	Short Text
City	Short Text
State	Short Text
ZIP	Short Text
Telephone	Short Text
HealthIns	Yes/No
DentalIns	Yes/No

Step 12c

13. Delete the *DentalIns* field by completing the following steps:
    a. Click in the field selector bar at the left side of the *DentalIns* row. (This selects the row.)
    b. Click the Delete Rows button in the Tools group.
    c. At the message asking if you want to permanently delete the field and all of the data in the field, click Yes.

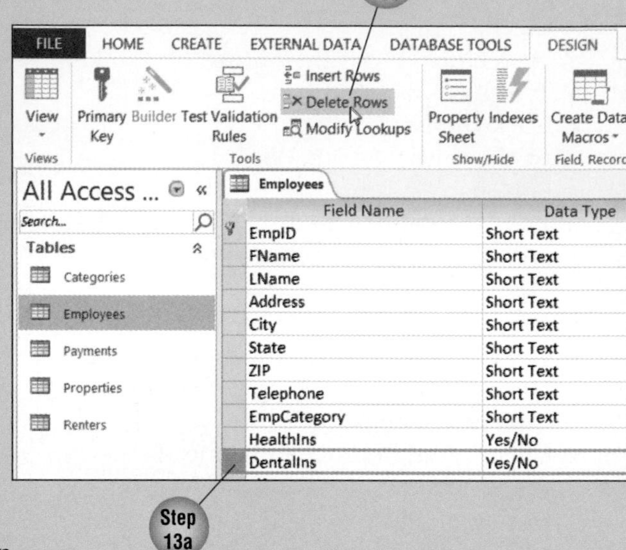

14. Click the Save button on the Quick Access toolbar.
15. Click the View button to switch to Datasheet view.
16. Print the Employees table. (The table will print on two pages.)
17. Close the Employees table.
18. Open the Payments table and then insert a new field and apply a validation rule by completing the following steps:
    a. Click the View button to switch to Design view.
    b. Click in the empty field immediately below the *PymntAmount* field in the *Field Name* column and then type **LateFee**.
    c. Press the Tab key.
    d. Click the down-pointing arrow at the right side of the *Data Type* field and then click *Currency* at the drop-down list.
    e. Click in the *Validation Rule* property box, type **<=50**, and then press Enter.
    f. With the insertion point positioned in the *Validation Text* property box, type **Late fee must be $50 or less**.
    g. Click in the box in the *Description* column for the *LateFee* field and then type **Enter a late fee amount if applicable**.

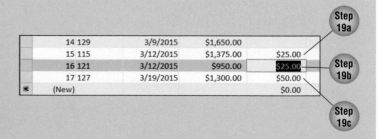

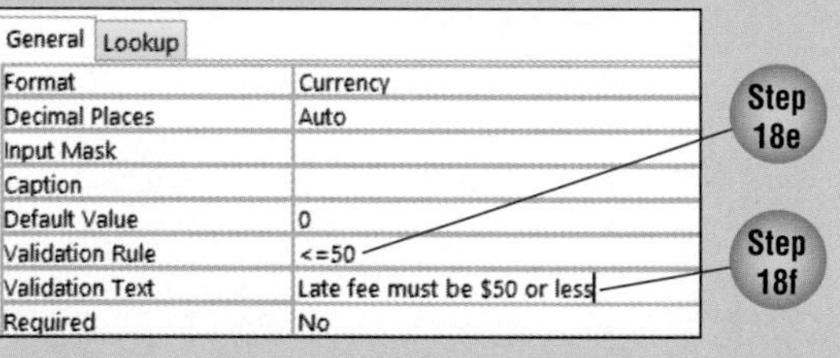

    h. Click the Save button on the Quick Access toolbar. Since the validation rule was created *after* data was entered into the table, Access displays a warning message indicating that some data may not be valid. At this message, click No.
    i. Click the View button to switch to Datasheet view.
19. Insert late fees for the last three records by completing the following steps:
    a. Click in the *LateFee* field for record 15, type **25**, and then press the Down Arrow key.
    b. With the *LateFee* field for record 16 active, type **25** and then press the Down Arrow key.
    c. With the *LateFee* field for record 17 active, type **50** and then press the Up Arrow key.

	14 129	3/9/2015	$1,650.00	
	15 115	3/12/2015	$1,375.00	$25.00
	16 121	3/12/2015	$950.00	$25.00
	17 127	3/19/2015	$1,300.00	$50.00
*	(New)			$0.00

Step 19a
Step 19b
Step 19c

20. Insert a *Total* row by completing the following steps:
    a. In Datasheet view, click the Totals button in the Records group on the HOME tab.
    b. Click in the blank field in the *PymntAmount* column in the *Total* row.
    c. Click the down-pointing arrow at the left side of the field and then click *Sum* at the drop-down list.
    d. Click in the blank field in the *LateFee* column in the *Total* row.
    e. Click the down-pointing arrow at the left side of the field and then click *Sum* at the drop-down list.
    f. Click in any other field.
21. Save, print, and then close the Payments table.

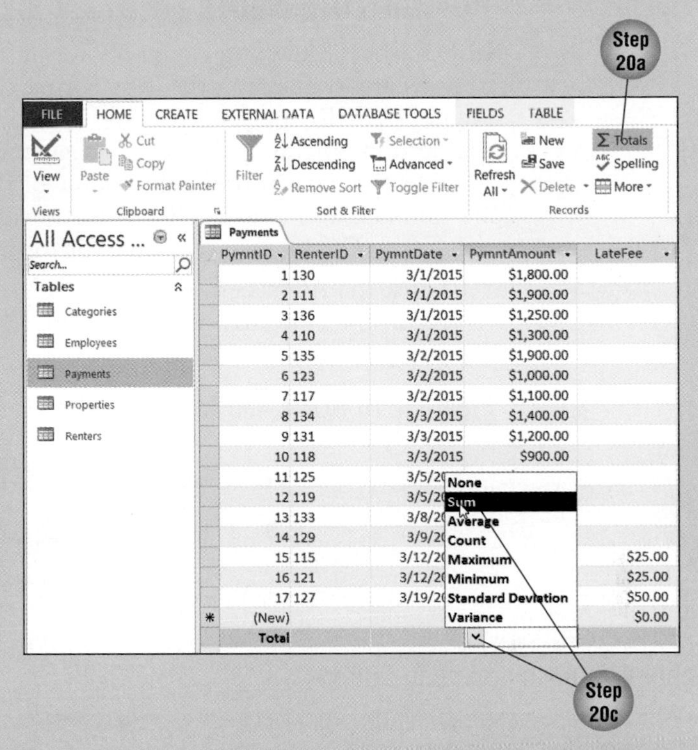

Sorting Records

The Sort & Filter group on the HOME tab contains two buttons for sorting data in records. When you click the Ascending button to sort data in the active field, text is sorted in alphabetical order from A to Z and numbers are sorted from lowest to highest. When you click the Descending button to sort data in the active field, text is sorted in alphabetical order from Z to A and numbers are sorted from highest to lowest.

Quick Steps

Sort Records

1. Open table in Datasheet view.
2. Click in field in desired column.
3. Click Ascending button or Descending button.

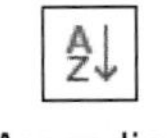

Ascending

Descending

Printing Specific Records

If you want to print specific records in a table, select the records and then display the Print dialog box by clicking the FILE tab, clicking the *Print* option, and then clicking the Print button. At the Print dialog box, click the *Selected Record(s)* option in the *Print Range* section and then click OK. To select specific records, display the table in Datasheet view, click the record selector of the first record, and then drag to select the desired records. The record selector is the light gray square that displays at the left side of the record. When you position the mouse pointer on the record selector, the pointer turns into a right-pointing black arrow.

Quick Steps

Print Selected Records

1. Open table and select records.
2. Click FILE tab.
3. Click *Print* option.
4. Click Print button.
5. Click *Selected Record(s)*.
6. Click OK.

Formatting Table Data

In Datasheet view, you can apply formatting to data in a table. Formatting options are available in the Text Formatting group on the HOME tab, as shown in Figure 4.10. To apply formatting, open a table in Datasheet view and then click the desired button in the Text Formatting group. The button formatting is applied to all of the data in the table. (Some of the buttons in the Text Formatting group are dimmed and unavailable. These buttons are available for fields formatted as rich text.) The buttons available for formatting a table are shown in Table 4.2.

Click the Align Left, Center, or Align Right button and formatting is applied to text in the currently active column. Click one of the other buttons shown in

Figure 4.10 HOME Tab Text Formatting Group

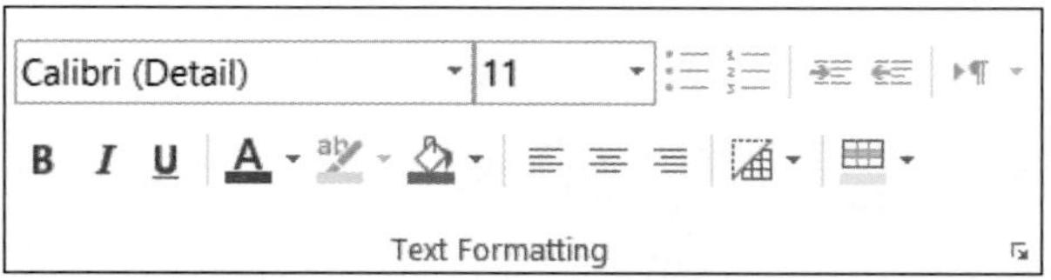

Table 4.2 Text Formatting Buttons

Button	Name	Description
Calibri (Detail)	Font	Change the text font.
11	Font Size	Change the text size.
B	Bold	Bold the text.
I	Italic	Italicize the text.
U	Underline	Underline the text.
A	Font Color	Change the text color.
	Background Color	Apply a background color to all fields.
	Align Left	Align all text in the currently active column at the left side of the fields.
	Center	Center all text in the currently active column in the center of the fields.
	Align Right	Align all text in the currently active column at the right side of the fields.
	Gridlines	Specify whether to display vertical and/or horizontal gridlines.
	Alternate Row Color	Apply a specified color to alternating rows in the table.

Table 4.2 and formatting is applied to all columns and rows of data in the table. The exception is the Background Color button, which applies formatting to all fields in the table.

When creating a table, you specify a data type for a field, such as the Short Text, Date/Time, or Currency data type. If you want to format text in a field rather than all of the fields in a column or the entire table, choose the Long Text data type and then specify rich text formatting. For example, in Project 1d, you will format specific credit scores in the *CreditScore* field column. To be able to format specific scores, you change the data type to Long Text and then specify rich text formatting. Use the Long Text data type only for fields containing text—not for fields containing currency amounts, numbers, and dates.

By default, the Long Text data type uses plain text formatting. To change to rich text, click in the *Text Format* property box in the *Field Properties* section (displays with the text *Plain Text*), click the down-pointing arrow that displays at the right side of the property box, and then click *Rich Text* at the drop-down list.

Project 1d Sorting, Printing, and Formatting Records and Fields in Tables Part 4 of 8

1. With **AL1-C4-SunProperties.accdb** open, open the Renters table.
2. With the table in Datasheet view, sort records in ascending alphabetical order by last name by completing the following steps:
   a. Click any last name in the *LastName* field in the table.
   b. Click the Ascending button in the Sort & Filter group on the HOME tab.
   c. Print the Renters table in landscape orientation.

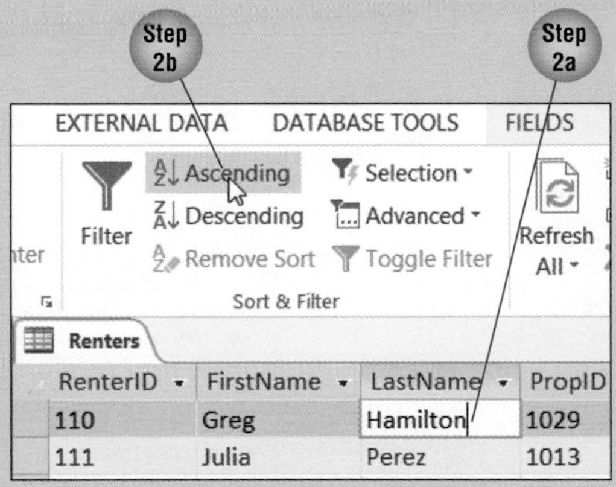

3. Sort records in descending order (highest to lowest) by credit score number by completing the following steps:
   a. Click any number in the *CreditScore* field.
   b. Click the Descending button in the Sort & Filter group.
   c. Print the Renters table in landscape orientation.
4. Close the Renters table without saving the changes.
5. Open the Properties table.
6. Sort and then print selected records with the apartment property type by completing the following steps:
   a. Click any entry in the *CatID* field.
   b. Click the Ascending button in the Sort & Filter group.
   c. Position the mouse pointer on the record selector of the first record with *A* for a category ID, hold down the mouse button, and then drag to select the four records with a category ID of *A*.

d. Click the FILE tab and then click the *Print* option.
e. Click the Print button.
f. At the Print dialog box, click the *Selected Record(s)* option in the *Print Range* section.
g. Click OK.

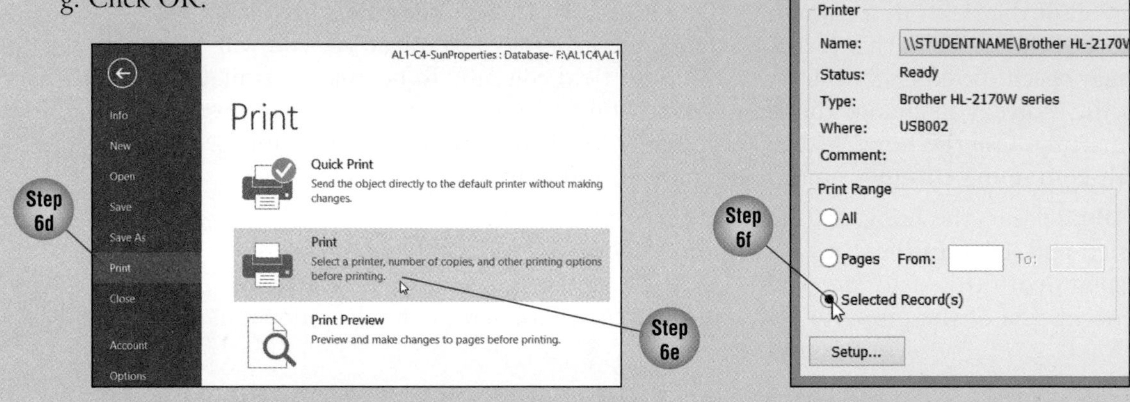

7. With the Properties table open, apply the following text formatting:
   a. Click in any field in the *CatID* column and then click the Center button in the Text Formatting group on the HOME tab.

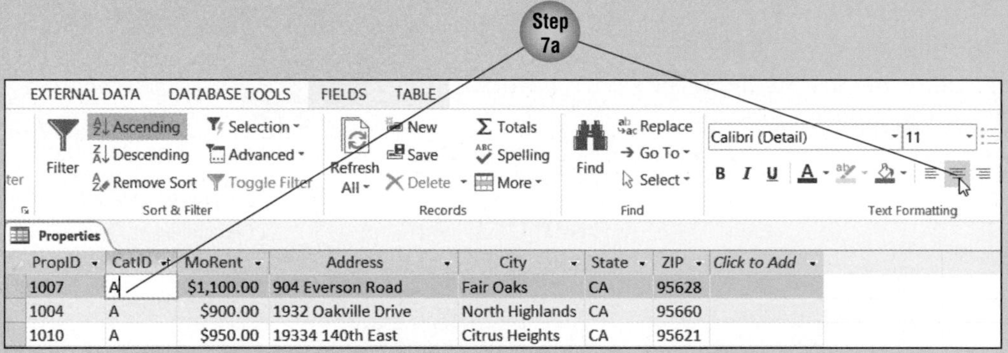

   b. Click in any field in the *PropID* column and then click the Center button in the Text Formatting group.
   c. Click the Bold button in the Text Formatting group. (This applies bold to all text in the table.)
   d. Click the Font Color button arrow and then click *Dark Blue* (fourth column, first row in the *Standard Colors* section).
   e. Adjust the column widths.
   f. Save, print, and then close the Properties table.

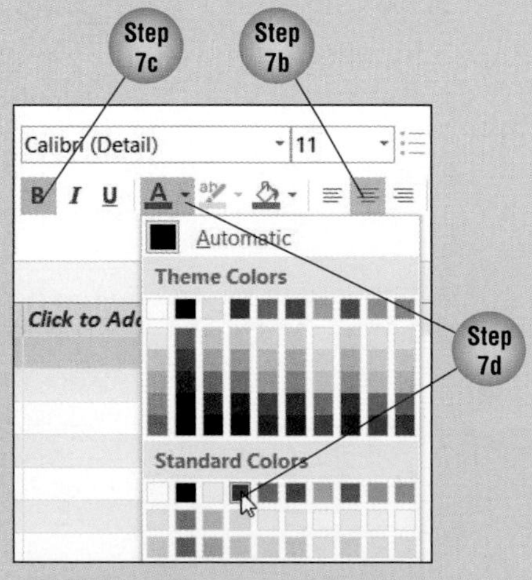

8. Open the Payments table and apply the following text formatting:
   a. With the first field active in the *PymntID* column, click the Center button in the Text Formatting group on the HOME tab.

b. Click in any field in the *RenterID* column and then click the Center button in the Text Formatting group.
c. Click the Font button arrow, scroll down the drop-down list that displays, and then click *Candara*. (Fonts are listed in alphabetical order in the drop-down list.)
d. Click the Font Size button arrow and then click *12* at the drop-down list.
e. Click the Alternate Row Color button arrow and then click *Green 2* (seventh column, third row in the *Standard Colors* section).

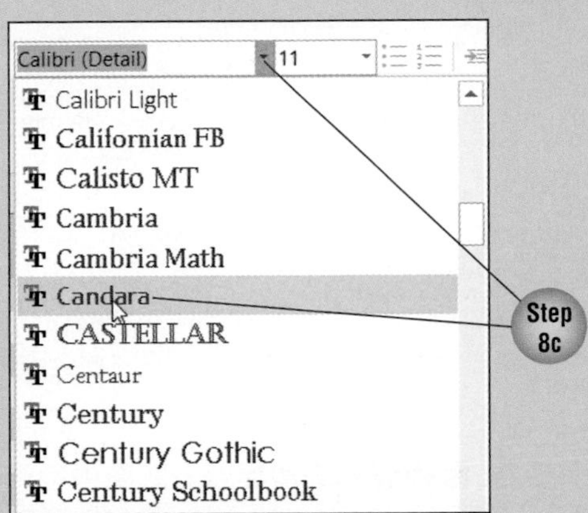

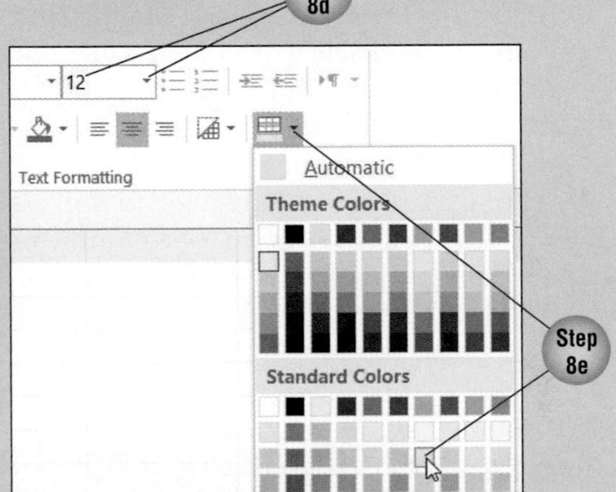

f. Adjust the column widths.
g. Save, print, and then close the Payments table.

9. Open the Renters table and then apply the following formatting to columns in the table:
   a. With the first field active in the *RenterID* column, click the Center button in the Text Formatting group on the HOME tab.
   b. Click in any field in the *PropID* column and then click the Center button.
   c. Click in any field in the *EmpID* column and then click the Center button
   d. Click in any field in the *CreditScore* column and then click the Center button.
10. Change the data type for the *CreditScore* field to Long Text with rich text formatting and apply formatting by completing the following steps:
   a. Click the View button to switch to Design view.
   b. Click in the *Data Type* column in the *CreditScore* row, click the down-pointing arrow that displays in the field, and then click *Long Text* at the drop-down list.
   c. Click in the *Text Format* property box in the *Field Properties* section (displays with the words *Plain Text*), click the down-pointing arrow that displays at the right side of the property box, and then click *Rich Text* at the drop-down list.

d. At the message that displays telling you that the field will be converted to rich text, click the Yes button.
e. Click the Save button on the Quick Access toolbar.
f. Click the View button to switch to Datasheet view.
g. Double-click the field value *538* that displays in the *CreditScore* column in the row for Dana Rozinski. (Double-clicking in the field selects the field value *538*.)
h. With *538* selected, click the Font Color button in the Text Formatting group. (This changes the number to red. If the font color does not change to red, click the Font Color button arrow and then click *Red* in the second column, bottom row of the *Standard Colors* section.)
i. Change the font to red for any credit scores below 600.
j. Print the Renters table in landscape orientation and then close the table.

Quick Steps

Complete a Spelling Check
1. Open table in Datasheet view.
2. Click Spelling button.
3. Change or ignore spelling as needed.
4. Click OK.

Spelling

You can also begin a spelling check with the keyboard shortcut F7.

Completing a Spelling Check

The spelling check feature in Access finds misspelled words and suggests replacement words. It also finds duplicate words and irregular capitalizations. When you spell check an object in a database, such as a table, the spelling check compares the words in your table with the words in its dictionary. If a match is found, the word is passed over. If no match is found, the spelling check selects the word and suggests possible replacements.

To complete a spelling check, open the desired table in Datasheet view and then click the Spelling button in the Records group on the HOME tab. If the spelling check does not find a match for a word in your table, the Spelling dialog box displays with replacement options. Figure 4.11 displays the Spelling dialog box with the word *Citruis* selected and possible replacements displayed in the *Suggestions* list box. At the Spelling dialog box, you can choose to ignore the word (for example, if the spelling check has selected a proper name), change to one of the replacement options, or add the word to the dictionary or AutoCorrect feature. You can also complete a spelling check on other objects in a database, such as a query, form, and report. (You will learn about forms and reports in future chapters.)

Figure 4.11 Spelling Dialog Box

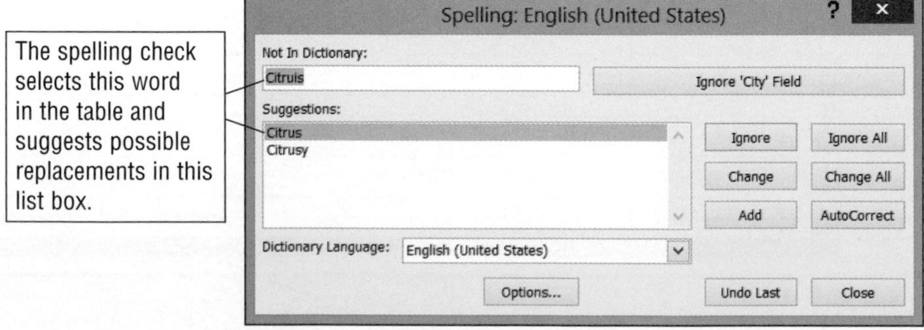

Project 1e Checking Spelling in a Table Part 5 of 8

1. With **AL1-C4-SunProperties.accdb** open, open the Employees table.
2. Delete the *LifeIns* field by completing the following steps:
   a. Click the View button to switch to the Design view.
   b. Click in the field selector bar at the left side of the *LifeIns* row. (This selects the row.)
   c. Click the Delete Rows button in the Tools group.
   d. At the message asking if you want to permanently delete the field and all of the data in the field, click Yes.
   e. Click the Save button on the Quick Access toolbar.
   f. Click the View button to switch to Datasheet view.
3. Add the following record to the Employees table. (Type the misspelled words as shown below. You will correct the spelling in a later step.)

EmpID	**02-72**
FName	**Roben**
LName	**Wildre**
Address	**9945 Valley Avenue**
City	**Citruis Heights**
State	(CA automatically inserted)
ZIP	**95610**
Telephone	**9165556522**
EmpCategory	(choose *Salaried*)
HealthIns	No (Remove check mark)

4. Save the Employees table.
5. Click in the first entry in the *EmpID* column.
6. Click the Spelling button in the Records group on the HOME tab.
7. The spelling check selects the name *Kasadev*. This is a proper name, so click the Ignore button to tell the spelling check to leave the name as written.
8. The spelling check selects the name *Scholtz*. This is a proper name, so click the Ignore button to tell the spelling check to leave the name as written.
9. The spelling check selects *Roben*. The proper spelling *(Robin)* is selected in the *Suggestions* list box, so click the Change button.
10. The spelling check selects *Wildre*. The proper spelling *(Wilder)* is selected in the *Suggestions* list box, so click the Change button.

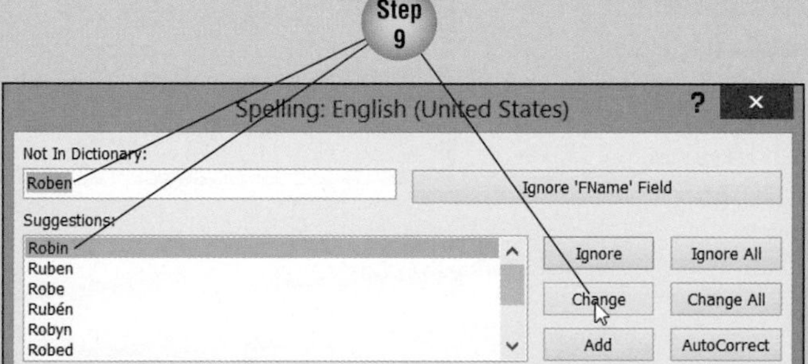

11. The spelling check selects *Citruis*. The proper spelling *(Citrus)* is selected in the *Suggestions* list box, so click the Change button.
12. At the message telling you that the spelling check is complete, click the OK button.
13. Print the Employees table in landscape orientation and then close the table.

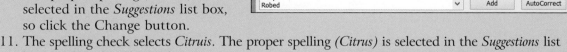

Finding and Replacing Data

Quick Steps

Find Data
1. Open table in Datasheet view.
2. Click Find button.
3. Type data in *Find What* text box.
4. Click Find Next button.

Find and Replace Data
1. Open table in Datasheet view.
2. Click Replace button.
3. Type find data in *Find What* text box.
4. Type replace data in *Replace With* text box.
5. Click Find Next button.
6. Click Replace button or Find Next button.

Find

Replace

Press Ctrl + F to display the Find and Replace dialog box with the Find tab selected.

Press Ctrl + H to display the Find and Replace dialog box with the Replace tab selected.

If you need to find a specific entry in a field in a table, consider using options at the Find and Replace dialog box with the Find tab selected, as shown in Figure 4.12. Display this dialog box by clicking the Find button in the Find group on the HOME tab. At the Find and Replace dialog box, enter the data you want to locate in the *Find What* text box. By default, Access looks only in the specific column where the insertion point is positioned. Click the Find Next button to find the next occurrence of the data or click the Cancel button to close the Find and Replace dialog box.

The *Look In* option defaults to the column where the insertion point is positioned. You can choose to look in the entire table by clicking the down-pointing arrow at the right side of the *Look In* option and then clicking the table name at the drop-down list. The *Match* option has a default setting of *Whole Field*. You can change this to *Any Part of Field* or *Start of Field*. The *Search* option has a default setting of *All*, which means that Access will search all of the data in a specific column. This can be changed to *Up* or *Down*. If you want to find data that contains specific uppercase and lowercase letters, insert a check mark in the *Match Case* check box and Access will return results that match the case formatting of the search text you entered.

Use the Find and Replace dialog box with the Replace tab selected to search for specific data and replace it with other data. Display this dialog box by clicking the Replace button in the Find group on the HOME tab.

Figure 4.12 Find and Replace Dialog Box with Find Tab Selected

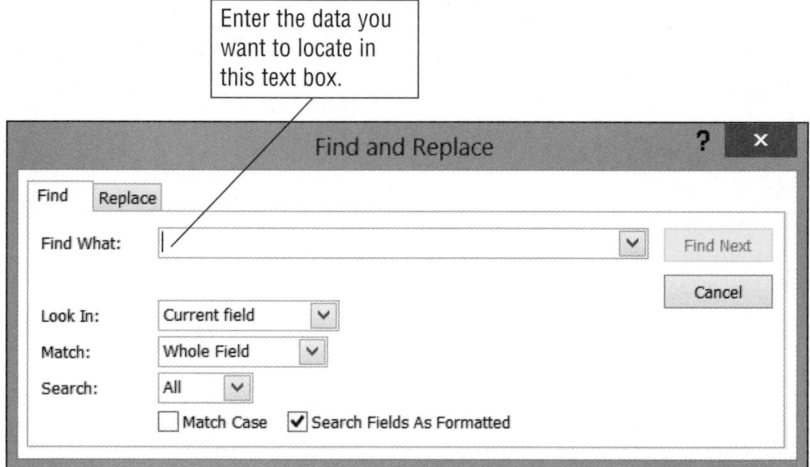

Project 1f — Finding and Replacing Data, Creating Relationships, and Performing Queries — Part 6 of 8

1. With **AL1-C4-SunProperties.accdb** open, open the Properties table.
2. Find records containing the zip code *95610* by completing the following steps:
   a. Click in the first field in the *ZIP* column.
   b. Click the Find button in the Find group on the HOME tab.
   c. At the Find and Replace dialog box with the Find tab selected, type **95610** in the *Find What* text box.
   d. Click the Find Next button. (Access finds and selects the first occurrence of *95610*. If the Find and Replace dialog box covers the data, drag the dialog box to a different location on the screen.)

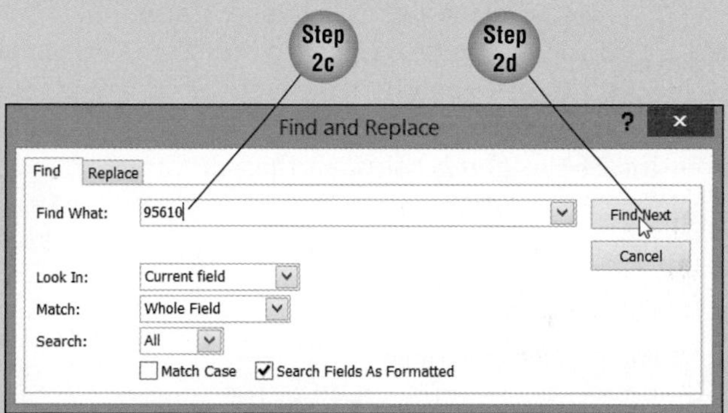

   e. Continue clicking the Find Next button until a message displays telling you that Access has finished searching the records. At this message, click OK.
   f. Click the Cancel button to close the Find and Replace dialog box.
3. Suppose a new zip code has been added to the city of North Highlands and you need to change to this new zip for some of the North Highlands properties. Complete the following steps to find *95660* and replace it with *95668*:
   a. Click in the first field in the *ZIP* column.
   b. Click the Replace button in the Find group.
   c. At the Find and Replace dialog box with the Replace tab selected, type **95660** in the *Find What* text box.
   d. Press the Tab key. (This moves the insertion point to the *Replace With* text box.)
   e. Type **95668** in the *Replace With* text box.
   f. Click the Find Next button.
   g. When Access selects the first occurrence of *95660*, click the Replace button.
   h. When Access selects the second occurrence of *95660*, click the Find Next button.

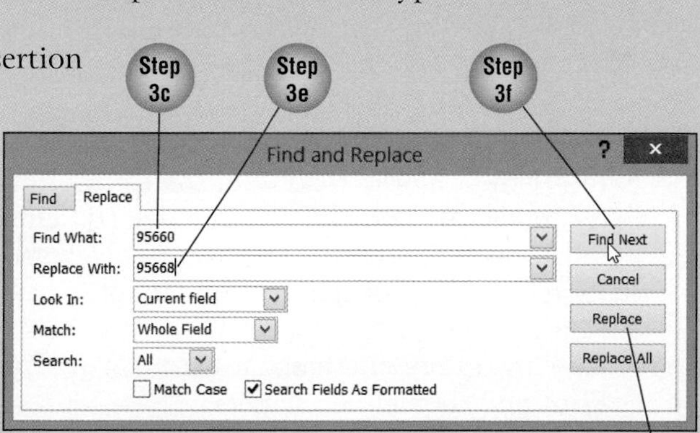

   i. When Access selects the third occurrence of *95660*, click the Replace button.
   j. When Access selects the fourth occurrence of *95660*, click the Find Next button.
   k. When Access selects the fifth occurrence of *95660*, click the Find Next button.
   l. When Access selects the sixth occurrence of *95660*, click the Replace button.
   m. Access selects the first occurrence of *95660* (record 1018) in the table. Click the Cancel button to close the Find and Replace dialog box.
4. Print and then close the Properties table.

5. Display the Relationships window and then create the following relationships (enforce referential integrity and cascade fields and records):
   a. Create a one-to-many relationship with the *CatID* field in the Categories table the "one" and the *CatID* field in the Properties table the "many."
   b. Create a one-to-many relationship with the *EmpID* field in the Employees table the "one" and the *EmpID* field in the Renters table the "many."
   c. Create a one-to-many relationship with the *PropID* field in the Properties table the "one" and the *PropID* field in the Renters table the "many."
   d. Create a one-to-many relationship with the *RenterID* field in the Renters table the "one" and the *RenterID* field in the Payments table the "many."
   e. Save the relationships and then print the relationships in landscape orientation.
   f. Close the relationships report without saving it and then close the Relationships window.
6. Design a query that displays employees with health insurance benefits with the following specifications:
   a. Insert the Employees table in the query window.
   b. Insert the *EmpID* field in the first *Field* row field.
   c. Insert the *FName* field in the second *Field* row field.
   d. Insert the *LName* field in the third *Field* row field.
   e. Insert the *HealthIns* field in the fourth *Field* row field.
   f. Click in the check box in the *Show* row field in the *EmpID* column to remove the check mark. (This hides the EmpID numbers in the query results.)

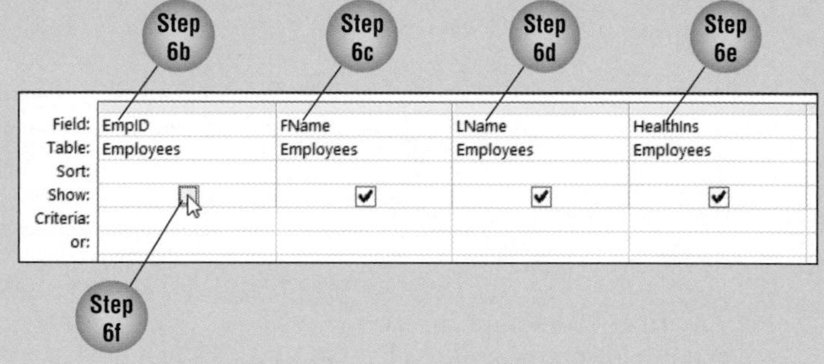

   g. Extract those employees with health benefits. (Type a *1* for the criteria.)
   h. Run the query.
   i. Save the query and name it *EmpsWithHealthInsQuery*.
   j. Print and then close the query.
7. Design a query that displays all properties in the city of Citrus Heights with the following specifications:
   a. Insert the Properties table and the Categories table in the query window.
   b. Insert the *PropID* field from the Properties table in the first *Field* row field.
   c. Insert the *Category* field from the Categories table in the second *Field* row field.
   d. Insert the *Address*, *City*, *State*, and *ZIP* fields from the Properties table to the third, fourth, fifth, and sixth *Field* row fields, respectively.
   e. Extract those properties in the city of Citrus Heights.
   f. Run the query.
   g. Save the query and name it *CitrusHeightsPropsQuery*.
   h. Print and then close the query.
8. Design a query that displays rent payments made between 3/1/2015 and 3/5/2015 with the following specifications:
   a. Insert the Payments table and the Renters table in the query window.
   b. Insert the *PymntID*, *PymntDate*, and *PymntAmount* fields from the Payments table in the first, second, and third *Field* row fields, respectively.
   c. Insert the *FirstName* and *LastName* fields from the Renters table in the fourth and fifth *Field* row fields, respectively.

d. Extract those payments made between 3/1/2015 and 3/5/2015.
e. Run the query.
f. Save the query and name it *Pymnts3/1To3/5Query*.
g. Print and then close the query.

9. Design a query that displays properties in Citrus Heights or Orangevale that rent for less than $1,501 a month as well as the type of property with the following specifications:
a. Insert the Categories table and the Properties table in the query window.
b. Insert the *Category* field from the Categories table.
c. Insert the *PropID*, *MoRent*, *Address*, *City*, *State*, and *ZIP* fields from the Properties table.
d. Extract those properties in Citrus Heights and Orangevale that rent for less than $1,501.
e. Run the query.
f. Save the query and name it *RentLessThan$1501InCHAndOVQuery*.
g. Print the query in landscape orientation and then close the query.

10. Design a query that displays properties in Citrus Heights assigned to employee identification number *07-20* with the following specifications:
a. Insert the Employees table and Properties table in the query window.
b. Insert the *EmpID*, *FName*, and *LName* fields from the Employees table.
c. Insert the *Address*, *City*, *State*, and *ZIP* fields from the Properties table.
d. Extract those properties in Citrus Heights assigned to EmpID 07-20.
e. Run the query.
f. Save the query and name it *Emp07-20CHPropsQuery*.
g. Print and then close the query.

Using Help

Microsoft Access includes a Help feature that contains information about Access features and commands. This on-screen reference manual is similar to Windows Help and the Help features in Word, PowerPoint, and Excel. Click the Microsoft Access Help button (the question mark) located in the upper right corner of the screen or press the keyboard shortcut F1 to display the Access Help window, as shown in Figure 4.13. In this window, type a topic, feature, or question in the search text box and then press the Enter key. Topics related to the search text display in the Access Help window. Click a topic that interests you. If the topic window contains a Show All hyperlink in the upper right corner, click this hyperlink to expand the topic options to show additional help information related to the topic. When you click the Show All hyperlink, it becomes the Hide All hyperlink.

Quick Steps
Use the Help Feature
1. Click Microsoft Access Help button.
2. Type topic or feature.
3. Press Enter.
4. Click desired topic.

Help

Press F1 to display the Access Help window.

Getting Help on a Button

When you position the mouse pointer on a button, a ScreenTip displays with information about the button. Some button ScreenTips display with a Help icon and the text *Tell me more*. Click this hyperlinked text or press F1 and the Access Help window opens with information about the button feature.

Figure 4.13 Access Help Window

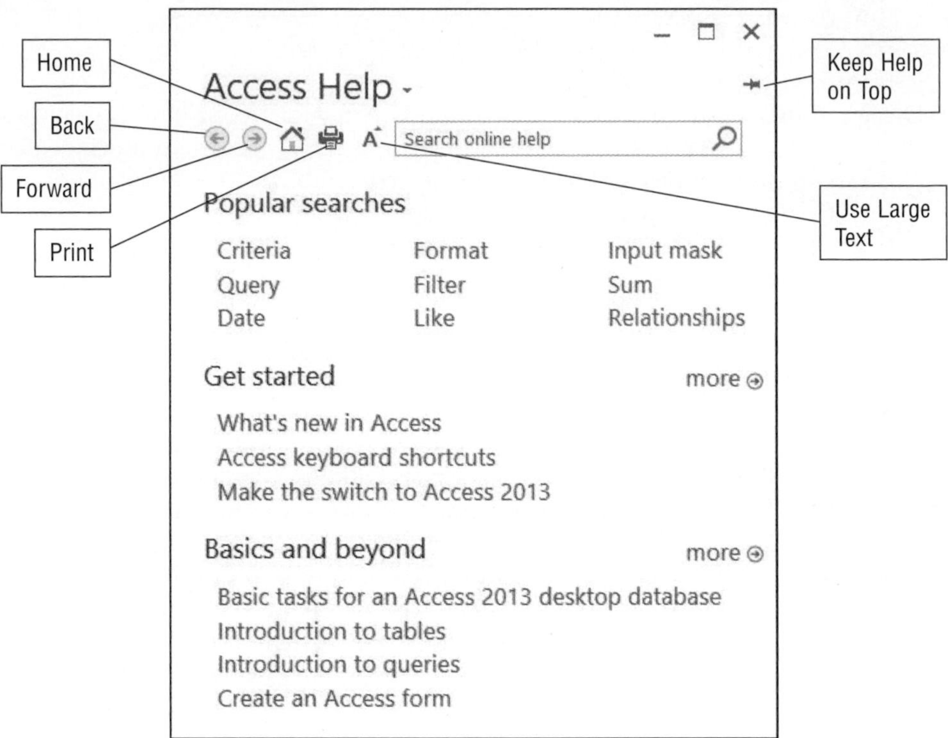

Project 1g Using the Help Feature

Part 7 of 8

1. With **AL1-C4-SunProperties.accdb** open, click the Microsoft Access Help button located in the upper right corner of the screen.
2. At the Access Help window, type **input mask** in the search text box and then press Enter.
3. When the list of topics displays, click the Guide data entry by using input masks hyperlink. (If this article is not available, choose a similar article.)
4. Read the information on creating an input mask. (If you want a printout of the information, click the Print button located toward the top of the Access Help window and then click the Print button at the Print dialog box.)
5. Close the Access Help window by clicking the Close button located in the upper right corner of the window.

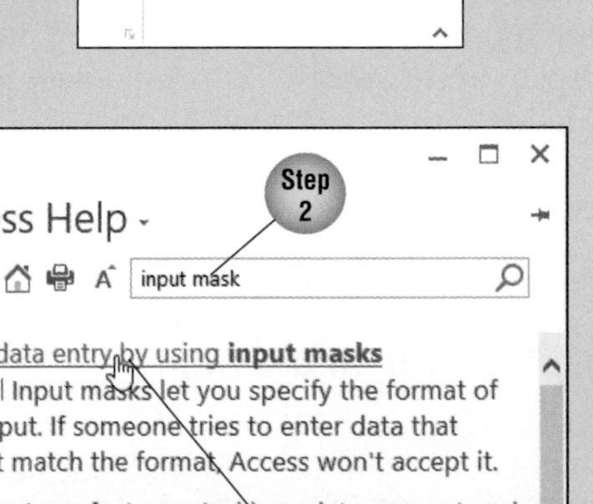

6. Click the CREATE tab.
7. Hover the mouse over the Table button and then click the Tell me more hyperlink that displays toward the bottom of the ScreenTip.
8. At the Access Help window, read the information on tables and then click the Close button located in the upper right corner of the Access Help window.

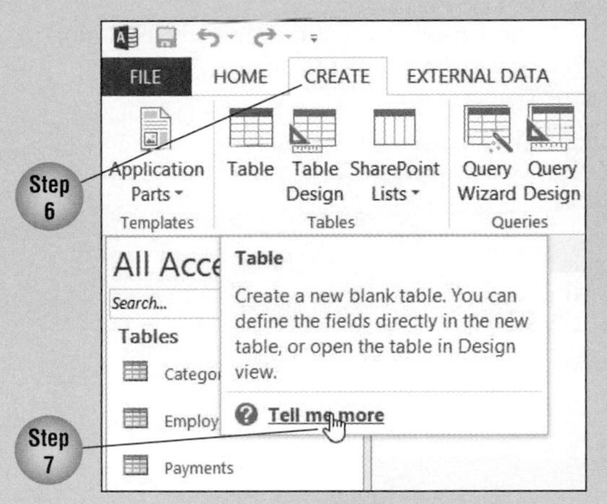

Getting Help in a Dialog Box or Backstage Area

Some dialog boxes and backstage areas provide a Help button you can click to display the Access Help window with specific information about the dialog box or backstage area. After reading and/or printing the information, close the dialog box by clicking the Close button located in the upper right corner of the dialog box or close the backstage area by clicking the Back button or pressing the Esc key.

Project 1h **Getting Help in a Dialog Box and Backstage View** **Part 8 of 8**

1. With **AL1-C4-SunProperties.accdb** open, click the DATABASE TOOLS tab.
2. Click the Relationships button. (Make sure the Show Table dialog box displays. If it does not, click the Show Table button in the Relationships group.)
3. Click the Help button that displays in the upper right corner of the Show Table dialog box.

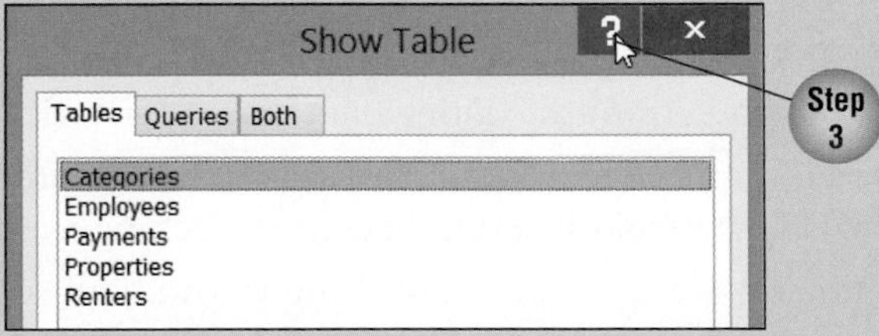

4. Click the Guide to table relationships hyperlink. (If this article is not available, choose a similar article.)
5. Read the information that displays about table relationships and then close the Access Help window.
6. Close the Show Table dialog box and then close the Relationships window.
7. Click the FILE tab and then click the *Open* option.

8. At the Open backstage area, click the Microsoft Access Help button that displays in the upper right corner.
9. Read the information that displays in the Access Help window.
10. Close the Access Help window and then press the Esc key to return to the database.
11. Close **AL1-C4-SunProperties.accdb**.

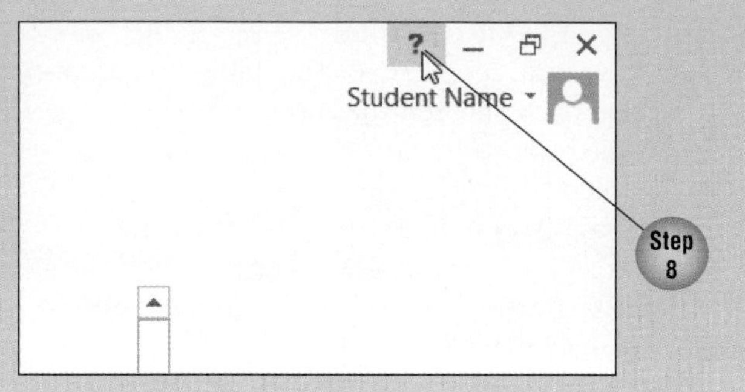

Chapter Summary

- You can create a table in Datasheet view or Design view. Click the View button on the TABLE TOOLS FIELDS tab or the HOME tab to switch between Datasheet view and Design view.
- Define each field in a table in the rows in the top section of Design view. Access automatically assigns the first field the name *ID* and assigns the AutoNumber data type.
- In Design view, specify a field name, data type, and description for each field.
- Assign a data type in Design view by clicking in the *Data Type* field in the desired row, clicking the down-pointing arrow at the right side of the field, and then clicking the desired data type at the drop-down list.
- Create a default value for a field in Design view with the *Default Value* property box in the *Field Properties* section.
- Use the Input Mask Wizard to set a pattern for how data is entered in a field.
- Use the *Validation Rule* property box in the *Field Properties* section in Design view to enter a statement containing a conditional test. Enter in the *Validation Text* property box the error message you want to display if the data entered violates the validation rule.
- Use the Lookup Wizard to confine data entered in a field to a specific list of items.
- Insert a field in Design view by clicking in the row immediately below where you want the new field inserted and then clicking the Insert Rows button.
- Move a field in Design view by clicking in the field selector bar of the field you want to move and then dragging with the mouse to the desired position.
- Delete a field in Design view by clicking in the field selector bar at the left side of the row you want deleted and then clicking the Delete Rows button.
- Insert a *Total* row in a table in Datasheet view by clicking the Totals button in the Records group on the HOME tab, clicking the down-pointing arrow in the *Total* row field, and then clicking the desired function at the drop-down list.
- Click the Ascending button in the Sort & Filter group on the HOME tab to sort records in ascending order and click the Descending button to sort records

in descending order.

- To print specific records in a table, select the records, display the Print dialog box, make sure *Selected Record(s)* is selected, and then click OK.
- Apply formatting to a table in Datasheet view with buttons in the Text Formatting group on the HOME tab. Depending on the button you click in the Text Formatting group, formatting is applied to all of the data in a table or data in a specific column in the table.
- If you want to format text in a specific field, change the data type to Long Text and then specify rich text formatting. Do this in Design view with the *Text Format* property box in the *Field Properties* section.
- Use the spelling check to find misspelled words in a table and consider possible replacement words.
- Use options at the Find and Replace dialog box with the Find tab selected to search for specific field entries in a table. Use options at the Find and Replace dialog box with the Replace tab selected to search for specific data and replace it with other data.
- Click the Microsoft Access Help button or press F1 to display the Access Help window. At this window, type a topic in the search text box and then press Enter.
- The ScreenTip for some buttons displays with a Help icon and the text *Tell me more*. Click this hyperlinked text or press F1 and the Access Help window opens with information about the button.
- Some dialog boxes and backstage areas contain a Help button you can click to display information specific to the dialog box or backstage area.

Commands Review

FEATURE	RIBBON TAB, GROUP	BUTTON, OPTION	KEYBOARD SHORTCUT
Access Help window		?	F1
align text left	HOME, Text Formatting		
align text right	HOME, Text Formatting		
alternate row color	HOME, Text Formatting		
background color	HOME, Text Formatting		
bold formatting	HOME, Text Formatting	B	
center text	HOME, Text Formatting		
delete field	TABLE TOOLS DESIGN, Tools		
Design view	HOME, Views OR TABLE TOOLS FIELDS, Views		

FEATURE	RIBBON TAB, GROUP	BUTTON, OPTION	KEYBOARD SHORTCUT
Find and Replace dialog box with Find tab selected	HOME, Find		Ctrl + F
Find and Replace dialog box with Replace tab selected	HOME, Find		Ctrl + H
font	HOME, Text Formatting	Calibri (Detail)	
font color	HOME, Text Formatting		
font size	HOME, Text Formatting	11	
gridlines	HOME, Text Formatting		
insert field	TABLE TOOLS DESIGN, Tools		
italic formatting	HOME, Text Formatting		
sort records ascending	HOME, Sort & Filter		
sort records descending	HOME, Sort & Filter		
spelling check	HOME, Records		F7
Total row	HOME, Records		
underline formatting	HOME, Text Formatting		

Concepts Check Test Your Knowledge

Completion: In the space provided at the right, indicate the correct term, symbol, or command.

1. The lower half of the work area in Design view that displays the properties for the active field is referred to as this. ____________________
2. When you create a new table in Design view, Access automatically assigns the first field the name *ID* and assigns this data type. ____________________
3. The description you type in the *Description* field displays in this location when the field is active in the table in Datasheet view. ____________________
4. Use this field property to set a pattern for how data is entered in a field. ____________________
5. Use this property box in Design view to enter a statement containing a conditional test that is checked each time data is entered into a field. ____________________

6. Use this wizard to confine the data entered in a field to a specific list of items. ________________
7. To insert a new field in a table in Design view, click this button. ________________
8. To insert a *Total* row in a table, click the Totals button in this group on the HOME tab. ________________
9. The Ascending and Descending sort buttons are located in this group on the HOME tab. ________________
10. Click this button to change the text size of data in a table. ________________
11. Click this button to align all text in the active column in the center of the fields. ________________
12. Click this button to specify a color for alternating rows in a table. ________________
13. Use options at the Find and Replace dialog box with this tab selected to search for specific data and replace it with other data. ________________
14. This is the keyboard shortcut to display the Access Help window. ________________

Skills Check Assess Your Performance

Assessment 1

CREATE AN EMPLOYEES TABLE WITH THE INPUT MASK AND LOOKUP WIZARDS

1. Open Access and then create a new database by completing the following steps:
   a. At the Access 2013 opening screen, click the Blank desktop database template.
   b. Type **AL1-C4-Hudson** in the *File Name* text box.
   c. Click the Browse button.
   d. At the File New Database dialog box, navigate to the AL1C4 folder on your storage medium and then click OK.
   e. Click the Create button.
2. Create the Employees table in Design view as shown in Figure 4.14 with the following specifications:
   a. Limit the *EmpID* field size to 4 characters, the *FirstName* and *LastName* fields to 20 characters, and the *Address* field to 30 characters.
   b. Create a default value of *Pueblo* for the *City* field since most of the employees live in Pueblo.

Figure 4.14 Employees Table in Design View

Field Name	Data Type	Description
EmpID	Short Text	Enter four-digit employee identification number
FirstName	Short Text	Enter employee first name
LastName	Short Text	Enter employee last name
Address	Short Text	Enter employee street address
City	Short Text	Pueblo automatically inserted
State	Short Text	CO automatically inserted
ZIP	Short Text	Enter employee ZIP code
Telephone	Short Text	Enter employee telephone number
Status	Short Text	Click down-pointing arrow and then click employee status
HireDate	Date/Time	Enter employee hire date

   c. Create a default value of *CO* for the *State* field, since all of the employees live in Colorado.
   d. Create an input mask for the telephone number.
   e. Use the Lookup Wizard to specify field choices for the *Status* field and include the following choices: *Full-time*, *Part-time*, *Temporary*, and *Contract*.
3. Save the table, switch to Datasheet view, and then enter the records as shown in Figure 4.15.
4. Adjust the column widths.
5. Save the table and then print it in landscape orientation.
6. Switch to Design view and then add a row immediately above the *FirstName* row. Type **Title** in the *Field Name* field, limit the field size to 20 characters, and type the description **Enter employee job title**.
7. Delete the *HireDate* field.
8. Move the *Status* field so it is positioned between the *EmpID* row and the *Title* row.
9. Save the table and then switch to Datasheet view.
10. Enter the following information in the *Title* field:

EmpID	Title	EmpID	Title
1466	**Design Director**	2301	**Assistant**
1790	**Assistant**	2440	**Assistant**
1947	**Resources Director**	3035	**Clerk**
1955	**Accountant**	3129	**Clerk**
1994	**Assistant**	3239	**Assistant**
2019	**Production Director**	4002	**Contractor**
2120	**Assistant**	4884	**Contractor**

11. Apply the following text formatting to the table:
   a. Change the font to Arial and the font size to 10 points.
   b. Center the data in the *EmpID* field column and the *State* field column.
   c. Apply the Aqua Blue 2 alternating row color (ninth column, third row in the *Standard Colors* section) to the table.
12. Adjust the column widths.
13. Save the table and then print it in landscape orientation with left and right margins of 0.5 inch.

Figure 4.15 Employees Table in Datasheet View

Employees

	EmpID	FirstName	LastName	Address	City	State	ZIP	Telephone	Status	HireDate	Click
	1466	Samantha	O'Connell	9105 Pike Avenue	Pueblo	CO	81011	(719) 555-7658	Full-time	8/15/2013	
	1790	Edward	Sorrell	9958 Franklin Avenue	Pueblo	CO	81006	(719) 555-3724	Full-time	11/15/2009	
	1947	Brandon	Byrne	102 Hudson Avenue	Pueblo	CO	81012	(719) 555-1202	Full-time	8/1/2011	
	1955	Leland	Hughes	4883 Caledonia Road	Pueblo	CO	81005	(719) 555-1211	Full-time	3/1/2013	
	1994	Rosa	Martinez	310 Graham Avenue	Pueblo	CO	81004	(719) 555-8394	Part-time	8/15/2010	
	2019	Jean	Perrault	123 Chinook Lake	Pueblo	CO	81012	(719) 555-4027	Full-time	11/15/2009	
	2120	Michael	Turek	5503 East 27th Street	Boone	CO	81025	(719) 555-5423	Full-time	3/15/2011	
	2301	Gregory	Nitsche	12055 East 18th Street	Pueblo	CO	81007	(719) 555-6657	Part-time	3/15/2010	
	2440	Bethany	Rosario	858 West 27th Street	Pueblo	CO	81012	(719) 555-9481	Part-time	2/15/2014	
	3035	Alia	Shandra	7740 West Second Street	Avondale	CO	81022	(719) 555-0059	Temporary	2/1/2013	
	3129	Gloria	Cushman	6590 East 14th Street	Pueblo	CO	81006	(719) 555-0332	Temporary	5/1/2015	
	3239	Rudolph	Powell	8874 Hood Avenue	Pueblo	CO	81008	(719) 555-2223	Temporary	4/1/2015	
	4002	Alice	Murray	4300 East 14th Street	Pueblo	CO	81003	(719) 555-4230	Contract	9/12/2009	
	4884	Simon	Banister	1022 Division Avenue	Boone	CO	81025	(719) 555-2378	Contract	5/15/2015	
*					Pueblo	CO					

14. Find all occurrences of *Director* and replace them with *Manager*. ***Hint: Position the insertion point in the first entry in the* Title *column and then display the Find and Replace dialog box. At the dialog box, change the* Match *option to* Any Part of Field.**
15. Find all occurrences of *Assistant* and replace them with *Associate*.
16. Save the table, print it in landscape orientation with left and right margins of 0.5 inch, and then close it.

Assessment 2

CREATE A PROJECTS TABLE

1. With **AL1-C4-Hudson.accdb** open, create a Projects table in Design view. Include the following fields (making sure the *ProjID* field is identified as the primary key) and create an appropriate description for each field:

Field Name	**Data Type**
ProjID	Short Text (field size = 4 characters)
EmpID	Short Text (field size = 4 characters)
BegDate	Date/Time
EndDate	Date/Time
EstCosts	Currency

2. Save the table, switch to Datasheet view, and then type the following data in the specified field:

ProjID	08-A	*ProjID*	08-B
EmpID	2019	*EmpID*	1466
BegDate	8/1/2015	*BegDate*	8/15/2015
EndDate	10/31/2015	*EndDate*	12/15/2015
EstCosts	$5,250.00	EstCosts	$2,000.00
ProjID	10-A	*ProjID*	10-B
EmpID	1947	*EmpID*	2019
BegDate	10/1/2015	*BegDate*	10/1/2015
EndDate	1/15/2016	*EndDate*	12/15/2015
EstCosts	$10,000.00	*EstCosts*	$3,500.00
ProjID	11-A	*ProjID*	11-B
EmpID	1466	*EmpID*	1947

BegDate	**11/1/2015**	*BegDate*	**11/1/2015**
EndDate	**2/1/2016**	*EndDate*	**3/31/2016**
EstCosts	**$8,000.00**	*EstCosts*	**$12,000.00**

3. Adjust the column widths.
4. Save, print, and then close the Projects table.

Assessment 3

CREATE AN EXPENSES TABLE WITH A VALIDATION RULE AND INPUT MASK

1. With **AL1-C4-Hudson.accdb** open, create an Expenses table in Design view. Include the following fields (making sure the *ItemID* field is identified as the primary key) and include an appropriate description for each field:

Field Name	**Data Type**
ItemID	AutoNumber
EmpID	Short Text (field size = 4 characters)
ProjID	Short Text (field size = 4 characters)
Amount	Currency (Type a condition in the *Validation Rule* property box that states the entry must be $500 or less. Type an appropriate error message in the *Validation Text* property box.)
DateSubmitted	Date/Time (Use the Input Mask to control the date so it is entered as a short date.)

2. Save the table, switch to Datasheet view, and then type the following data in the fields (recall that Access automatically fills in the *ItemID* field):

EmpID	**1466**	*EmpID*	**2019**
ProjID	**08-B**	*ProjID*	**08-A**
Amount	**$245.79**	*Amount*	**$500.00**
DateSubmitted	**09/04/2015**	*DateSubmitted*	**09/10/2015**
EmpID	**4002**	*EmpID*	**1947**
ProjID	**08-B**	*ProjID*	**10-A**
Amount	**$150.00**	*Amount*	**$500.00**
DateSubmitted	**09/18/2015**	*DateSubmitted*	**10/03/2015**
EmpID	**2019**	*EmpID*	**1947**
ProjID	**10-B**	*ProjID*	**10-A**
Amount	**$487.25**	*Amount*	**$85.75**
DateSubmitted	**10/22/2015**	*DateSubmitted*	**10/24/2015**
EmpID	**1466**	*EmpID*	**1790**
ProjID	**08-B**	*ProjID*	**08-A**
Amount	**$175.00**	*Amount*	**$110.50**
DateSubmitted	**10/29/2015**	*DateSubmitted*	**10/30/2015**
EmpID	**2120**	*EmpID*	**1466**
ProjID	**10-A**	*ProjID*	**08-B**
Amount	**$75.00**	*Amount*	**$300.00**
DateSubmitted	**11/05/2015**	*DateSubmitted*	**11/07/2015**
EmpID	**1466**	*EmpID*	**2019**
ProjID	**11-A**	*ProjID*	**10-B**
Amount	**$75.00**	*Amount*	**$300.00**
DateSubmitted	**11/14/2015**	*DateSubmitted*	**11/19/2015**

3. Adjust the column widths.
4. Insert a *Total* row with the following specifications:
   a. Click the Totals button in the Records group on the HOME tab.
   b. Click in the blank field in the *Amount* column in the *Total* row.
   c. Click the down-pointing arrow at the left side of the field and then click *Sum* at the drop-down list.
   d. Click in any other field.
5. Save, print, and then close the Expenses table.
6. Create a one-to-many relationship where *EmpID* in the Employees table is the "one" and *EmpID* in the Expenses table is the "many." (Enforce referential integrity and cascade fields and records.)
7. Create a one-to-many relationship where *EmpID* in the Employees table is the "one" and *EmpID* in the Projects table is the "many." (Enforce referential integrity and cascade fields and records.)
8. Create a one-to-many relationship where *ProjID* in the Projects table is the "one" and *ProjID* in the Expenses table is the "many." (Enforce referential integrity and cascade fields and records.)
9. Save the relationships, print the relationships, and then close the relationship report and the Relationships window.
10. Design and run a query that displays all full-time employees with the following specifications:
    a. Insert the Employees table in the query window.
    b. Insert the *EmpID, FirstName, LastName,* and *Status* fields.
    c. Click in the check box in the *Show* row field in the *EmpID* column to remove the check mark. (This hides the EmpID numbers in the query results.)
    d. Extract full-time employees.
    e. Save the query and name it *FTEmpsQuery*.
    f. Print and then close the query.
11. Design and run a query that displays projects managed by employee number 1947 with the following specifications:
    a. Insert the Employees table and Projects table in the query window.
    b. Insert the *EmpID, FirstName,* and *LastName* fields from the Employees table.
    c. Insert the *ProjID* field from the Projects table.
    d. Extract those projects managed by employee number 1947.
    e. Save the query and name it *ProjsManagedByEmp1947Query*.
    f. Print and then close the query.
12. Design and run a query that displays expense amounts over $250 and the employees submitting the expenses with the following specifications:
    a. Insert the Expenses table and Employees table in the query window.
    b. Insert the *ItemID, Amount,* and *DateSubmitted* fields from the Expenses table.
    c. Insert the *FirstName* and *LastName* fields from the Employees table.
    d. Hide the *ItemID* field in the query results by clicking in the check box in the *Show* row field in the *ItemID* column to remove the check mark.
    e. Extract those expense amounts over $250.
    f. Save the query and name it *ExpensesOver$250Query*.
    g. Print and then close the query.
13. Design and run a query that displays expenses submitted by employee number 1947 with the following specifications:
    a. Insert the Employees table and Expenses table in the query window.
    b. Insert the *EmpID, FirstName,* and *LastName* fields from the Employees table.
    c. Insert the *ProjID, Amount,* and *DateSubmitted* from the Expenses table.

d. Click in the check box in the *Show* row field in the *EmpID* column to remove the check mark. (This hides the EmpID numbers in the query results.)
e. Extract those expenses submitted by employee number 1947.
f. Save the query and name it *ExpSubmittedBy1947Query*.
g. Print and then close the query.

Assessment 4

EDIT THE EMPLOYEES TABLE

1. With **AL1-C4-Hudson.accdb** open, open the Employees table.
2. Display the table in Design view, click in the *ZIP* field row in the *Data Type* column, and then click in the *Input Mask* property box in the *Field Properties* section.
3. Use the Input Mask Wizard to create a nine-digit zip code input mask.
4. Save the table and then switch to Datasheet view.
5. Delete the records for employee number 3035 (Alia Shandra), employee number 3129 (Gloria Cushman), and employee number 4884 (Simon Banister).
6. Insert the following new records:

EmpID	**2286**	EmpID	**2970**
Status	**Full-time**	Status	**Full-time**
Title	**Associate**	Title	**Associate**
FirstName	**Erica**	FirstName	**Daniel**
LastName	**Bonari**	LastName	**Ortiz**
Address	**4850 55th Street**	Address	**12021 Cedar Lane**
City	(Pueblo automatically inserted)	City	(Pueblo automatically inserted)
State	(CO automatically inserted)	State	(CO automatically inserted)
ZIP	**81005-5002**	ZIP	**81011-1255**
Telephone	**(719) 555-1293**	Telephone	**(719) 555-0790**

7. Adjust the width of the *ZIP* column. (Only the two new records will contain the nine-digit zip code.)
8. Save the Employees table.
9. Display the table in Print Preview, change to landscape orientation, and then change the left and right margins to 0.5 inch. Print and then close the table.
10. Close **AL1-C4-Hudson.accdb**.

Visual Benchmark Demonstrate Your Proficiency

DESIGN AND FORMAT A QUERY

1. Open **AL1-C4-AlpineServices.accdb** from the AL1C4 folder on your storage medium and enable the contents.
2. Design and run the query that displays in Figure 4.16. (Make sure you include the calculated field to determine the order totals and the *Total* row.)
3. Change the font for the data in the query to 12-point Candara, add an alternating row color, and adjust column widths so your query displays in a manner similar to the query in Figure 4.16.
4. Save, print the query in landscape orientation, and then close the query.
5. Close **AL1-C4-AlpineServices.accdb**.

Figure 4.16 Visual Benchmark

OrderTotal

OrderDate	SupplierName	ProductID	UnitsOrdered	UnitPrice	Total
5/4/2015	Manning, Inc.	101-S2R	15	$129.95	1949.25
5/4/2015	Manning, Inc.	101-S3B	15	$119.95	1799.25
5/4/2015	Freedom Corporation	209-L	25	$6.95	173.75
5/4/2015	Freedom Corporation	209-XL	25	$7.20	180
5/4/2015	Freedom Corporation	209-XXL	20	$7.29	145.8
5/4/2015	Freedom Corporation	210-M	15	$6.49	97.35
5/4/2015	Freedom Corporation	210-L	25	$6.49	162.25
5/18/2015	Sound Supplies	299-M2	10	$88.79	887.9
5/18/2015	Sound Supplies	299-M3	10	$88.79	887.9
5/18/2015	Sound Supplies	299-M5	10	$88.79	887.9
5/18/2015	Sound Supplies	299-W1	8	$75.29	602.32
5/18/2015	Sound Supplies	299-W3	10	$75.29	752.9
5/18/2015	Sound Supplies	299-W4	10	$75.29	752.9
5/18/2015	Sound Supplies	299-W5	10	$75.29	752.9
5/18/2015	Emerald City Products	602-XR	5	$429.00	2145
Total				**$1,280.85**	**12177.37**

Case Study Apply Your Skills

Part 1

You work for Blue Ridge Enterprises and your supervisor has asked you to create a database with information about representatives and clients. Create a new database named **AL1-C4-BlueRidge.accdb** and then create a Representatives table with the following fields:

- Create a field for the representative identification number, change the data type to Short Text, and limit the field size to 3 characters. (This is the primary key field.)
- Create a field for the representative's first name and limit the field size to 20 characters.
- Create a field for the representative's last name and limit the field size to 20 characters.
- Create a field for the representative's telephone number and use the Input Mask Wizard.
- Create a field for the insurance plan and use the Lookup Wizard and include four options: *Platinum*, *Premium*, *Standard*, and *None*.
- Create a field for the yearly bonus amount, type a validation rule that states the bonus must be less than $10,001, and include an error message. (You determine the message.)

In Datasheet view, enter six records in the table. (You determine the data to enter.) When entering the data, make sure that at least two representatives will receive a yearly bonus over $5,000 and that at least two representatives are signed up for the *Platinum* insurance plan. Insert a *Total* row that sums the yearly bonus amounts. Change the font for the data in the table to Cambria, change the font size to 10 points, and apply a light green alternating row color. Center the data in the representative identification column. Adjust the column widths and then save the Representatives table. Print the table in landscape orientation and then close the table.

Part 2

With **AL1-C4-BlueRidge.accdb** open, create a second table named Clients (containing information on companies doing business with Blue Ridge Enterprises) with the following fields:

- Create a field for the client identification number and limit the field size to 2 characters. (This is the primary key field.)
- Create a field for the representative identification number (using the same field name you used in Part 1 in the Representatives table) and limit the field size to 3 characters.
- Create fields for the company name, address, city, state (or province), and zip (or postal code). Insert the city you live in as the default value for the city field and insert the two-letter state or province abbreviation where you live as the default value for the state or province field.
- Create a field for the client's telephone number and use the Input Mask.
- Create a field for the client's type of business and insert the word *Wholesaler* as the default value.

In Datasheet view, enter at least eight companies. (You determine the data to enter.) Make sure you use the representative identification numbers in the Clients table that match numbers in the Representatives table. Identify at least one company as a *Retailer*, rather than a *Wholesaler*, and make at least one representative represent two or more companies. Change the font for the data in the table to Cambria, change the font size to 10 points, and apply a light green alternating row color (the same color you chose in Part 1). Center the data in the client identification column, the representative identification column, and the state (or province) column. Adjust the column widths and then save the Clients table. Print the table in landscape orientation and then close the table.

Part 3

Create a one-to-many relationship with the representative identification number in the Representatives table as the "one" and the representative identification number in the Clients table as the "many." Save the relationship, print the relationships report, and then close the report without saving it.

Part 4

Your supervisor has asked you for specific information about representatives and clients. To provide answers to your supervisor, create and print the following queries:

- Create a query that extracts records of representatives earning a yearly bonus over $5,000. (You determine the fields to insert in the query window.) Save, print, and then close the query.
- Create a query that extracts records of representatives signed up for the Platinum insurance plan. (You determine the fields to insert in the query window.) Save, print, and then close the query.
- Create a query that extracts records of wholesale clients. (You determine the fields to insert in the query window.) Save, print, and then close the query.
- Create a query that extracts records of companies represented by a specific representative. (Use a representative identification number you entered in Part 2 that represents two or more companies.) Save, print, and then close the query.

MICROSOFT® ACCESS® Performance Assessment

Note: The Student Resources CD does not include an Access Level 1, Unit 1 subfolder of files because no data files are required for the Unit 1 assessments. You will create all of the files yourself. Before beginning the assessments, create a folder for the new files and name it AL1U1.

Assessing Proficiency

In this unit, you have learned to design, create, and modify tables and to create one-to-many relationships and one-to-one relationships between tables. You have also learned how to perform queries on data in tables.

Assessment 1 Create Tables in a Cornerstone Catering Database

1. Use Access to create tables for Cornerstone Catering. Name the database **AL1-U1-Cornerstone**. Create a table named *Employees* that includes the following fields. If no data type is specified for a field, use the Short Text data type. You determine the field size and specify the same field size for a field that is contained in different tables. For example, if you specify a field size of 2 characters for the *EmployeeID* field in the Employees table, specify a field size of 2 characters for the *EmployeeID* field in the Events table. Provide a description for each field.

   EmployeeID (primary key)
   FirstName
   LastName
   CellPhone (Use the Input Mask Wizard for this field.)

2. After creating the table, switch to Datasheet view and then enter the following data in the appropriate fields:

   EmployeeID 10
   FirstName Erin
   LastName Jergens
   CellPhone (505) 555-3193

   EmployeeID 14
   FirstName Mikio
   LastName Ogami
   CellPhone (505) 555-1087

   EmployeeID 19
   FirstName Martin
   LastName Vaughn
   CellPhone (505) 555-4461

   EmployeeID 21
   FirstName Isabelle
   LastName Baptista
   CellPhone (505) 555-4425

EmployeeID	24	*EmployeeID*	26
FirstName	Shawn	*FirstName*	Madison
LastName	Kettering	*LastName*	Harris
CellPhone	(505) 555-3885	*CellPhone*	(505) 555-2256
EmployeeID	28	*EmployeeID*	30
FirstName	Victoria	*FirstName*	Isaac
LastName	Lamesa	*LastName*	Hobart
CellPhone	(505) 555-6650	*CellPhone*	(505) 555-7430
EmployeeID	32	*EmployeeID*	35
FirstName	Lester	*FirstName*	Manuela
LastName	Franklin	*LastName*	Harte
CellPhone	(505) 555-0440	*CellPhone*	(505) 555-1221

3. Change the font for data in the table to Cambria, change the font size to 10 points, and apply a light blue alternating row color. Center-align the data in the *EmployeeID* column.
4. Adjust the column widths.
5. Save, print, and then close the Employees table.
6. Create a table named *Plans* that includes the following fields:

   PlanCode (primary key)
   Plan

7. After creating the table, switch to Datasheet view and then enter the following data in the appropriate fields:

PlanCode	A	*PlanCode*	B
Plan	Sandwich Buffet	*Plan*	Cold Luncheon Buffet
PlanCode	C	*PlanCode*	D
Plan:	Hot Luncheon Buffet	*Plan*	Combination Dinner
PlanCode	E	*PlanCode*	F
Plan:	Vegetarian Luncheon Buffet	*Plan:*	Vegetarian Dinner Buffet
PlanCode	G	*PlanCode*	H
Plan:	Seafood Luncheon Buffet	*Plan*	Seafood Dinner Buffet

8. Change the font for data in the table to Cambria, change the font size to 10 points, and apply a light blue alternating row color. Center-align the data in the *PlanCode* column.
9. Adjust the column widths.
10. Save, print, and then close the Plans table.
11. Create a table named *Prices* that includes the following fields:

    PriceCode (primary key)
    PricePerPerson (Identify as the Currency data type.)

12. After creating the table, switch to Datasheet view and then enter the following data in the appropriate fields:

PriceCode	1	*PriceCode*	2
PricePerPerson	$11.50	*PricePerPerson*	$12.75
PriceCode	3	*PriceCode*	4
PricePerPerson	$14.50	*PricePerPerson*	$16.00
PriceCode	5	*PriceCode*	6
PricePerPerson	$18.50	*PricePerPerson*	$21.95

13. Change the font for data in the table to Cambria, change the font size to 10 points, and apply a light blue alternating row color. Center-align the data in both columns.
14. Adjust the column widths.
15. Save, print, and then close the Prices table.
16. Create a table named *Clients* that includes the following fields:

    ClientID (primary key)
    ClientName
    StreetAddress
    City
    State (Insert *NM* as the default value.)
    ZIP
    Telephone (Use the Input Mask Wizard for this field.)

17. After creating the table, switch to Datasheet view and then enter the following data in the appropriate fields:

ClientID	104	*ClientID*	155
ClientName	Sarco Corporation	*ClientName*	Creative Concepts
StreetAddress	340 Cordova Road	*StreetAddress*	1026 Market Street
City	Santa Fe	*City*	Los Alamos
State	NM	*State*	NM
ZIP	87510	*ZIP*	87547
Telephone	(505) 555-3880	*Telephone*	(505) 555-1200
ClientID	218	*ClientID*	286
ClientName	Allenmore Systems	*ClientName*	Sol Enterprises
StreetAddress	7866 Second Street	*StreetAddress*	120 Cerrillos Road
City	Espanola	*City*	Santa Fe
State	NM	*State*	NM
ZIP	87535	*ZIP*	87560
Telephone	(505) 555-3455	*Telephone*	(505) 555-7700
ClientID	295	*ClientID*	300
ClientName	Benson Productions	*ClientName*	Old Town Corporation
StreetAddress	555 Junction Road	*StreetAddress*	1035 East Adams Way
City	Santa Fe	*City*	Santa Fe
State	NM	*State*	NM
ZIP	87558	*ZIP*	87561
Telephone	(505) 555-8866	*Telephone*	(505) 555-2125

ClientID	305	*ClientID*	350
ClientName	Cromwell Company	*ClientName*	GH Manufacturing
StreetAddress	752 Rialto Way	*StreetAddress*	9550 Stone Road
City	Santa Fe	*City*	Los Alamos
State	NM	*State*	NM
ZIP	87512	*ZIP*	87547
Telephone	(505) 555-7500	*Telephone*	(505) 555-3388

18. Change the font for data in the table to Cambria, change the font size to 10 points, and apply a light blue alternating row color. Center-align the data in the *ClientID* column.
19. Adjust the column widths.
20. Save the table and then print it in landscape orientation.
21. Close the Clients table.
22. Create a table named *Events* that includes the following fields:

    EventID (primary key) (Identify as the AutoNumber data type.)
    ClientID
    EmployeeID
    DateOfEvent (Identify as the Date/Time data type.)
    PlanCode
    PriceCode
    NumberOfPeople (Identify as the Number data type.)

23. After creating the table, switch to Datasheet view and then enter the following data in the appropriate fields:

EventID	(AutoNumber)	*EventID*	(AutoNumber)
ClientID	218	*ClientID*	104
EmployeeID	14	*EmployeeID*	19
DateOfEvent	7/11/2015	*DateOfEvent*	7/12/2015
PlanCode	B	*PlanCode*	D
PriceCode	3	*PriceCode*	5
NumberOfPeople	250	*NumberOfPeople*	120

EventID	(AutoNumber)	*EventID*	(AutoNumber)
ClientID	155	*ClientID*	286
EmployeeID	24	*EmployeeID*	10
DateOfEvent	7/17/2015	*DateOfEvent*	7/18/2015
PlanCode	A	*PlanCode*	C
PriceCode	1	*PriceCode*	4
NumberOfPeople	300	*NumberOfPeople*	75

EventID	(AutoNumber)	*EventID*	(AutoNumber)
ClientID	218	*ClientID*	104
EmployeeID	14	*EmployeeID*	10
DateOfEvent	7/19/2015	*DateOfEvent*	7/22/2015
PlanCode	C	*PlanCode*	B
PriceCode	4	*PriceCode*	3
NumberOfPeople	50	*NumberOfPeople*	30

EventID	(AutoNumber)	*EventID*	(AutoNumber)
ClientID	305	*ClientID*	295
EmployeeID	30	*EmployeeID*	35
DateOfEvent	7/24/2015	*DateOfEvent*	7/25/2015
PlanCode	H	*PlanCode*	E
PriceCode	6	*PriceCode*	4
NumberOfPeople	150	*NumberOfPeople*	75

EventID	(AutoNumber)	*EventID*	(AutoNumber)
ClientID	300	*ClientID*	350
EmployeeID	32	*EmployeeID*	28
DateOfEvent	7/26/2015	*DateOfEvent*	7/30/2015
PlanCode	B	*PlanCode*	D
PriceCode	3	*PriceCode*	6
NumberOfPeople	200	*NumberOfPeople*	100

24. Change the font for data in the table to Cambria, change the font size to 10 points, and apply a light blue alternating row color. Center-align the data in all of the columns except the *DateOfEvent* column.
25. Adjust the column widths.
26. Save the table and then print it in landscape orientation.
27. Close the Events table.

Assessment 2 Create Relationships between Tables

1. With **AL1-U1-Cornerstone.accdb** open, create the following one-to-many relationships and enforce referential integrity:
   a. *ClientID* in the Clients table is the "one" and *ClientID* in the Events table is the "many."
   b. *EmployeeID* in the Employees table is the "one" and *EmployeeID* in the Events table is the "many."
   c. *PlanCode* in the Plans table is the "one" and *PlanCode* in the Events table is the "many."
   d. *PriceCode* in the Prices table is the "one" and *PriceCode* in the Events table is the "many."
2. Save and then print the relationships in landscape orientation.
3. Close the relationship report without saving it and then close the Relationships window.

Assessment 3 Modify Tables

1. With **AL1-U1-Cornerstone.accdb** open, open the Plans table in Datasheet view and then add the following record at the end of the table:

   PlanCode **I**
   Plan **Hawaiian Luau Dinner Buffet**

2. Adjust the column widths.
3. Save, print, and then close the Plans table.
4. Open the Events table in Datasheet view and then add the following record at the end of the table:

EventID	(AutoNumber)	*PlanCode*	**I**
ClientID	**104**	*PriceCode*	**5**
EmployeeID	**21**	*NumberOfPeople*	**125**
Date	**7/31/2015**		

5. Save, print (in landscape orientation), and then close the Events table.

Assessment 4 Design Queries

1. With **AL1-U1-Cornerstone.accdb** open, create a query to extract records from the Events table with the following specifications:
   a. Include the fields *ClientID*, *DateOfEvent*, and *PlanCode*.
   b. Extract those records with a PlanCode of C. (You will need to type "C" in the *Criteria* row.)
   c. Run the query.
   d. Save the query and name it *PlanCodeCQuery*.
   e. Print and then close the query.
2. Extract records from the Clients table with the following specifications:
   a. Include the fields *ClientName*, *City*, and *Telephone*.
   b. Extract those records with a city of Santa Fe.
   c. Run the query.
   d. Save the query and name it *SantaFeClientsQuery*.
   e. Print and then close the query.
3. Extract information from two tables with the following specifications:
   a. From the Clients table, include the fields *ClientName* and *Telephone*.
   b. From the Events table, include the fields *DateOfEvent*, *PlanCode*, and *NumberOfPeople*.
   c. Extract those records with dates between July 1, 2015, and July 15, 2015.
   d. Run the query.
   e. Save the query and name it *July1-15EventsQuery*.
   f. Print and then close the query.

Assessment 5 Design a Query with a Calculated Field Entry

1. With **AL1-U1-Cornerstone.accdb** open, create a query in Design view with the Events table and Prices table and insert the following fields in the specified locations:
   a. Insert *EventID* from the Events table to the first *Field* row field.
   b. Insert *DateOfEvent* from the Events table to the second *Field* row field.
   c. Insert *NumberOfPeople* from the Events table to the third *Field* row field.
   d. Insert *PricePerPerson* from the Prices table to the fourth *Field* row field.
2. Insert the following calculated field entry in the fifth *Field* row field: *Amount: [NumberOfPeople]*[PricePerPerson]*.

3. Run the query.
4. Save the query and name it *EventAmountsQuery*.
5. Print and then close the query.

Assessment 6 Design a Query with Aggregate Functions

1. With **AL1-U1-Cornerstone.accdb** open, create a query in Design view using EventAmountsQuery with the following specifications:
   a. Click the CREATE tab and then click the Query Design button.
   b. At the Show Tables dialog box, click the Queries tab.
   c. Double-click *EventAmountsQuery* in the list box and then click the Close button.
   d. Insert the *Amount* field in the first, second, third, and fourth *Field* row field.
   e. Click the Totals button in the Show/Hide group.
   f. Insert *Sum* in the first *Total* row field.
   g. Insert *Avg* in the second *Total* row field.
   h. Insert *Min* in the third *Total* row field.
   i. Insert *Max* in the fourth *Total* row field.
2. Run the query.
3. Automatically adjust the column widths.
4. Save the query and name it *AmountTotalsQuery*.
5. Print and then close the query.

Assessment 7 Design a Query Using Fields from Tables and a Query

1. With **AL1-U1-Cornerstone.accdb** open, create a query in Design view using the Employees table, Clients table, Events table, and EventAmountsQuery with the following specifications:
   a. Click the CREATE tab and then click the Query Design button.
   b. At the Show Tables dialog box, double-click *Employees*.
   c. Double-click *Clients*.
   d. Double-click *Events*.
   e. Click the Queries tab, double-click *EventAmountsQuery* in the list box, and then click the Close button.
   f. Insert the *LastName* field from the *Employees* field list box to the first *Field* row field.
   g. Insert the *ClientName* field from the *Clients* field list box to the second *Field* row field.
   h. Insert the *Amount* field from *EventAmountsQuery* field list box to the third *Field* row field.
   i. Insert the *DateOfEvent* field from the *Events* field list box to the fourth *Field* row field.
2. Run the query.
3. Save the query and name it *EmployeeEventsQuery*.
4. Close the query.
5. Using the Crosstab Query Wizard, create a query that summarizes the total event amounts by employee by client using the following specifications:
   a. At the first Crosstab Query Wizard dialog box, click the *Queries* option in the *View* section and then click *Query: EmployeeEventsQuery* in the list box.
   b. At the second Crosstab Query Wizard dialog box, click *LastName* in the *Available Fields* list box and then click the One Field button.

c. At the third Crosstab Query Wizard dialog box, make sure *ClientName* is selected in the list box.
d. At the fourth Crosstab Query Wizard dialog box, make sure *Amount* is selected in the *Fields* list box and then click *Sum* in the *Functions* list box.
e. At the fifth Crosstab Query Wizard dialog box, type **AmountsByEmployeeByClientQuery** in the *What do you want to name your query?* text box.
6. Automatically adjust the column widths.
7. Print the query in landscape orientation and then close the query.

Assessment 8 Use the Find Duplicates Query Wizard

1. With **AL1-U1-Cornerstone.accdb** open, use the Find Duplicates Query Wizard to find employees who are responsible for at least two events with the following specifications:
   a. At the first wizard dialog box, double-click *Table: Events* in the list box.
   b. At the second wizard dialog box, click *EmployeeID* in the *Available fields* list box and then click the One Field button.
   c. At the third wizard dialog box, move the *DateOfEvent* field and the *NumberOfPeople* field from the *Available fields* list box to the *Additional query fields* list box.
   d. At the fourth wizard dialog box, name the query *DuplicateEventsQuery*.
2. Print and then close the query.

Assessment 9 Use the Find Unmatched Query Wizard

1. With **AL1-U1-Cornerstone.accdb** open, use the Find Unmatched Query Wizard to find employees who do not have upcoming events scheduled with the following specifications:
   a. At the first wizard dialog box, click *Table: Employees* in the list box.
   b. At the second wizard dialog box, click *Table: Events* in the list box.
   c. At the third wizard dialog box, make sure *EmployeeID* is selected in the *Fields in 'Employees'* list box and in the *Fields in 'Events'* list box.
   d. At the fourth wizard dialog box, click the All Fields button to move all fields from the *Available fields* list box to the *Selected fields* list box.
   e. At the fifth wizard dialog box, click the Finish button. (Let the wizard determine the query name: *Employees Without Matching Events*.)
2. Print and then close the *Employees Without Matching Events* query.

Writing Activities

The following activity gives you the opportunity to practice your writing skills along with demonstrating an understanding of some of the important Access features you have mastered in this unit. Use correct grammar, appropriate word choices, and clear sentence constructions.

Create a Payroll Table and Word Report

The manager of Cornerstone Catering has asked you to add information to the **AL1-U1-Cornerstone.accdb** database on employee payroll. You need to create another table that will contain information on payroll. The manager wants the table to include the following information (you determine the appropriate field name, data type, field size, and description):

Employee Number	10	*Employee Number*	14
Status	Full-time	*Status*	Part-time
Monthly Salary	$2,850	*Monthly Salary*	$1,500
Employee Number	19	*Employee Number*	21
Status	Part-time	*Status*	Full-time
Monthly Salary	$1,400	*Monthly Salary*	$2,500
Employee Number	24	*Employee Number*	26
Status	Part-time	*Status*	Part-time
Monthly Salary	$1,250	*Monthly Salary*	$1,000
Employee number	28	*Employee number*	30
Status	Full-time	*Status*	Part-time
Monthly salary	$2,500	*Monthly salary*	$3,000
Employee number	32	*Employee number*	35
Status	Full-time	*Status*	Full-time
Monthly salary	$2,300	*Monthly salary*	$2,750

Print and then close the payroll table. Open Word and then write a report to the manager detailing how you created the table. Include a title for the report, steps on how the table was created, and any other pertinent information. Save the completed report and name it **AL1-U1-Act01-TableRpt**. Print and then close **AL1-U1-Act01-TableRpt.docx** and then close Word.

Internet Research

Vehicle Search

In this activity, you will search the Internet for information on different vehicles before doing actual test drives. Learning about a major product, such as a vehicle, can increase your chances of finding a good buy, potentially guide you away from making a poor purchase, and help speed up the process of narrowing the search to the type of vehicle that will meet your needs. Before you begin, list the top five criteria you would look for in a vehicle. For example, it must be a four-door vehicle, needs to be four-wheel drive, and so on.

Using key search words, find at least two websites that provide vehicle reviews. Use the search engines provided within the different review sites to find vehicles that fulfill the criteria you listed. Create a database in Access and create a table in that database that will contain the results from your vehicle search. Design the table to accommodate the types of data you need to record for each vehicle that meets your requirements. Include at least the make, model, year, price, description, and special problems in the table. Also include the ability to rate the vehicle as poor, fair, good, or excellent. You will decide on the rating of each vehicle depending on your findings. Print the table you created and then close the database.

MICROSOFT®

ACCESS®

Level 1

Unit 2 ■ Creating Forms and Reports

MICROSOFT®

ACCESS®

Creating Forms

PERFORMANCE OBJECTIVES

Upon successful completion of Chapter 5, you will be able to:

- **Create a form using the Form button**
- **Change views in a form**
- **Print and navigate in a form**
- **Add records to and delete records from a form**
- **Create a form with a related table**
- **Customize a form**
- **Create a split form and multiple items form**
- **Create a form using the Form Wizard**

Tutorials

- **5.1** Creating a Form Using the Form Button
- **5.2** Navigating in a Form
- **5.3** Adding Records in a Form
- **5.4** Creating a Form with a Related Table
- **5.5** Managing Control Objects
- **5.6** Adding Control Objects
- **5.7** Formatting a Form
- **5.8** Applying Conditional Formatting to a Form
- **5.9** Adding Fields to a Form from Another Table
- **5.10** Creating a Split Form and Multiple Items Form

In this chapter, you will learn how to create forms from database tables, improving the data display and making data entry easier. Access offers several methods for presenting data on the screen for easier data entry. You will create a form using the Form button, create a split form and multiple items form, and use the Form Wizard to create a form. You will also learn how to customize control objects in a form and insert control objects and fields in a form. Model answers for this chapter's projects appear on the following pages.

AL1C5

Note: Before beginning the projects, copy to your storage medium the AL1C5 subfolder from the AL1 folder on the CD that accompanies this textbook and make AL1C5 the active folder.

Project 1 Create Forms with the Form Button

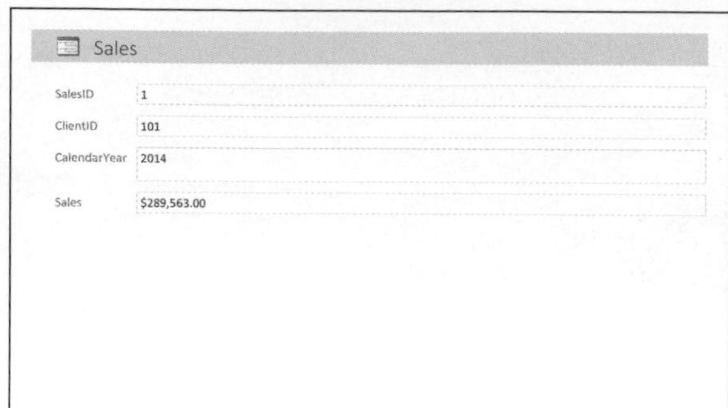

Project 1a, Dearborn Clients Form

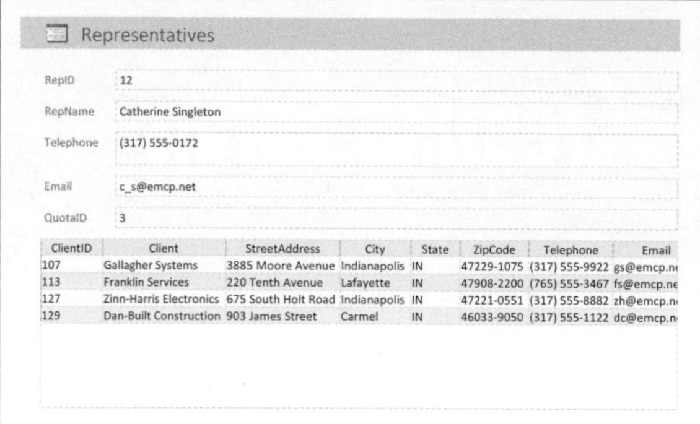

ClientID	Client	StreetAddress	City	State	ZipCode	Telephone	Email
107	Gallagher Systems	3885 Moore Avenue	Indianapolis	IN	47229-1075	(317) 555-9922	gs@emcp.n
113	Franklin Services	220 Tenth Avenue	Lafayette	IN	47908-2200	(765) 555-3467	fs@emcp.ne
127	Zinn-Harris Electronics	675 South Holt Road	Indianapolis	IN	47221-0551	(317) 555-8882	zh@emcp.n
129	Dan-Built Construction	903 James Street	Carmel	IN	46033-9050	(317) 555-1122	dc@emcp.n

Project 1c, Dearborn Representatives Form

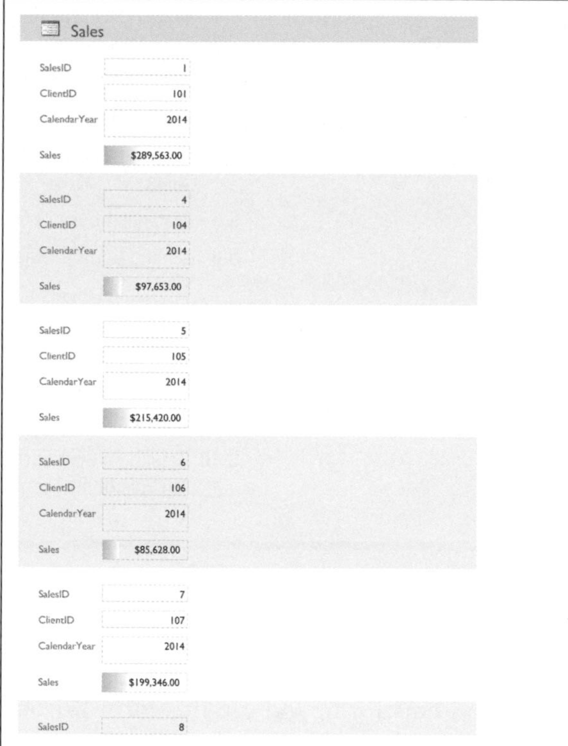

Project 1g, Dearborn Sales Form

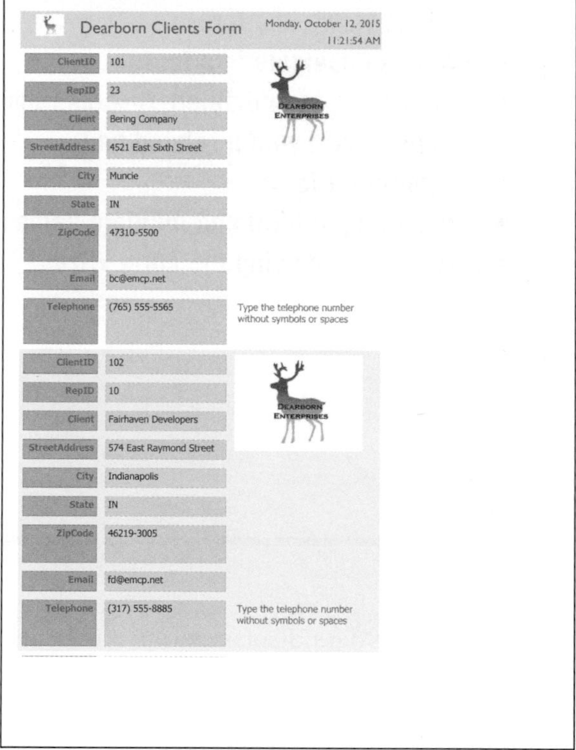

Project 1g, Dearborn Clients Form

Model Answers

Project 2 Add Fields, Create a Split Form and Multiple Items Form, and Use the Form Wizard

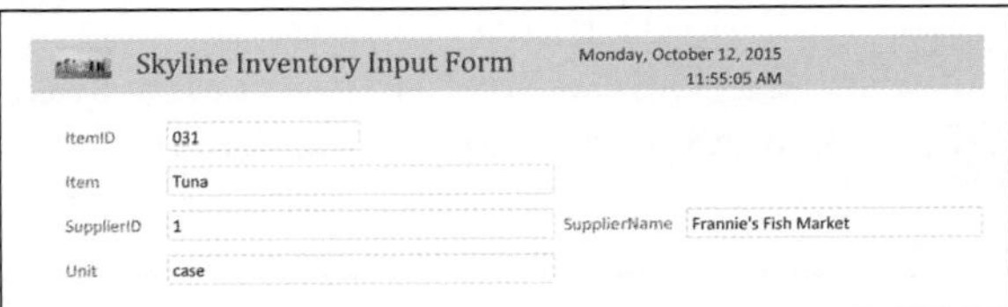

Project 2a, Skyline Inventory Form

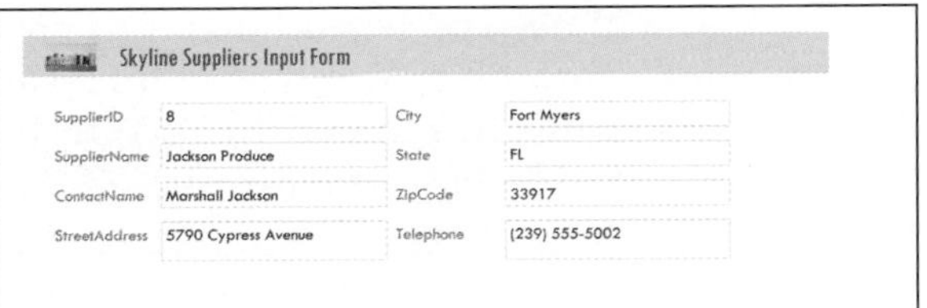

Project 2b, Skyline Suppliers Form

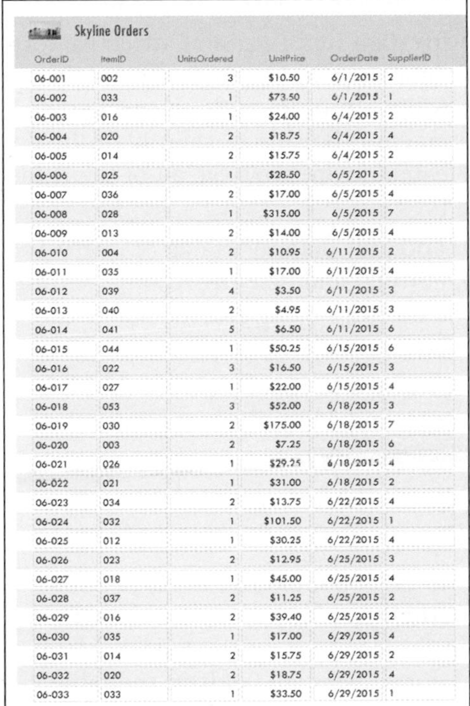

Skyline Orders

OrderID	ItemID	UnitsOrdered	UnitPrice	OrderDate	SupplierID
06-001	002	3	$10.50	6/1/2015	2
06-002	033	1	$73.50	6/1/2015	1
06-003	016	1	$24.00	6/4/2015	2
06-004	020	2	$18.75	6/4/2015	4
06-005	014	2	$15.75	6/4/2015	2
06-006	025	1	$28.50	6/5/2015	4
06-007	036	2	$17.00	6/5/2015	4
06-008	028	1	$315.00	6/5/2015	7
06-009	013	2	$14.00	6/5/2015	4
06-010	004	2	$10.95	6/11/2015	2
06-011	035	1	$17.00	6/11/2015	4
06-012	039	4	$3.50	6/11/2015	3
06-013	040	2	$4.95	6/11/2015	3
06-014	041	5	$6.50	6/11/2015	6
06-015	044	1	$50.25	6/15/2015	6
06-016	022	3	$16.50	6/15/2015	3
06-017	027	1	$22.00	6/15/2015	4
06-018	053	3	$52.00	6/18/2015	3
06-019	030	2	$175.00	6/18/2015	7
06-020	003	2	$7.25	6/18/2015	6
06-021	026	1	$29.25	6/18/2015	4
06-022	021	1	$31.00	6/18/2015	2
06-023	034	2	$13.75	6/22/2015	4
06-024	032	1	$101.50	6/22/2015	1
06-025	012	1	$30.25	6/22/2015	4
06-026	023	2	$12.95	6/25/2015	3
06-027	018	1	$45.00	6/25/2015	4
06-028	037	2	$11.25	6/25/2015	2
06-029	016	2	$39.40	6/25/2015	2
06-030	035	1	$17.00	6/29/2015	4
06-031	014	2	$15.75	6/29/2015	2
06-032	020	2	$18.75	6/29/2015	4
06-033	033	1	$33.50	6/29/2015	1

Project 2c, Skyline Orders Form

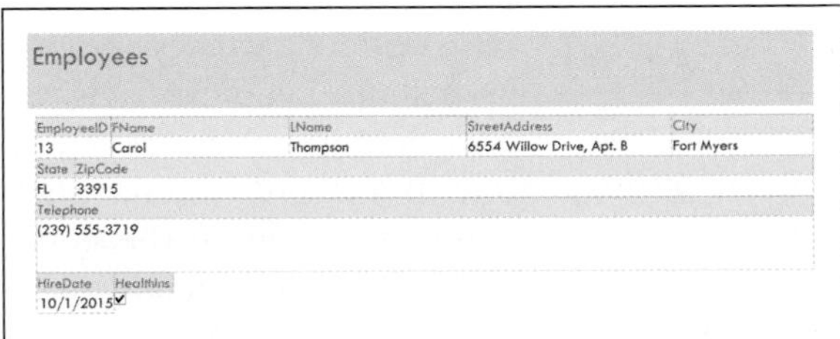

Project 2d, Skyline Employees Form, Carol Thompson

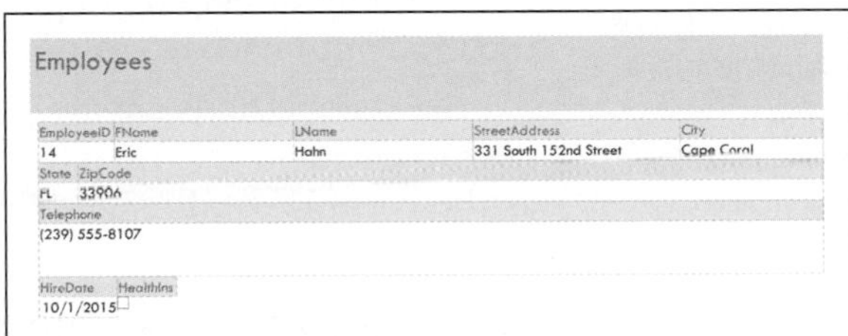

Project 2d, Skyline Employees Form, Eric Hahn

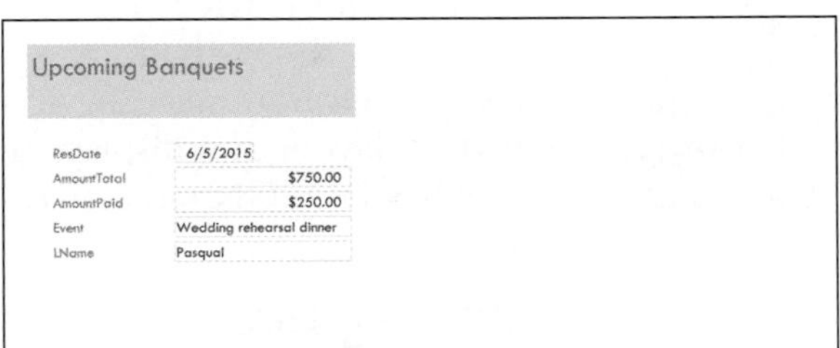

Project 2e, Skyline Upcoming Banquets Form

Project 1 Create Forms with the Form Button 7 Parts

You will use the Form button to create forms with fields in the Clients, Representatives, and Sales tables. You will also add, delete, and print records and use buttons in the FORM LAYOUT TOOLS FORMAT tab to apply formatting to control objects in the forms.

Creating Forms

A form allows you to focus on a single record at a time.

Save a form before making changes or applying formatting to it.

Access offers a variety of options for presenting data in a clear and attractive format. For instance, you can view, add, or edit data in a table in Datasheet view. When you enter data in a table in Datasheet view, you will see multiple records at the same time. If a record contains several fields, you may not be able to view all of the fields within the record at the same time. If you create a form, however, all of the fields for a record are generally visible on the screen.

A ***form*** is an object you can use to enter and edit data in a table or query. It is a user-friendly interface for viewing, adding, editing, and deleting records. A form is also useful in helping to prevent incorrect data from being entered and it can be used to control access to specific data.

Several methods are available for creating forms. In this chapter, you will learn how to create forms using the Form, Split Form, and Multiple Items buttons as well as the Form Wizard.

Creating a Form with the Form Button

Quick Steps

Create a Form with the Form Button
1. Click desired table.
2. Click CREATE tab.
3. Click Form button.

The simplest method for creating a form is to click a table in the Navigation pane, click the CREATE tab, and then click the Form button in the Forms groups. Figure 5.1 shows the form you will create in Project 1a with the Sales table in AL1-C5-Dearborn.accdb. Access creates the form using all fields in the table in a vertical layout and displays the form in Layout view with the FORM LAYOUT TOOLS DESIGN tab active.

Changing Views

Form

Form View

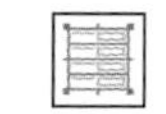

Layout View

When you click the Form button to create a form, the form displays in Layout view. This is one of three views for working with forms. Use the Form view to enter and manage records. Use the Layout view to view the data and modify the appearance and contents of the form. Use the Design view to view the structure of the form and modify the form. Change views with the View button in the Views group on the FORM LAYOUT TOOLS DESIGN tab or with buttons in the view area located at the right side of the Status bar.

You can open an existing form in Layout view. To do this, right-click the form name in the Navigation pane and then click *Layout View* at the shortcut menu.

Printing a Form

Print all of the records in a form by clicking the FILE tab, clicking the *Print* option, and then clicking the Quick Print button. If you want to print a specific record in a form, click the FILE tab, click the *Print* option, and then click the Print button.

Figure 5.1 Form Created from Data in the Sales Table

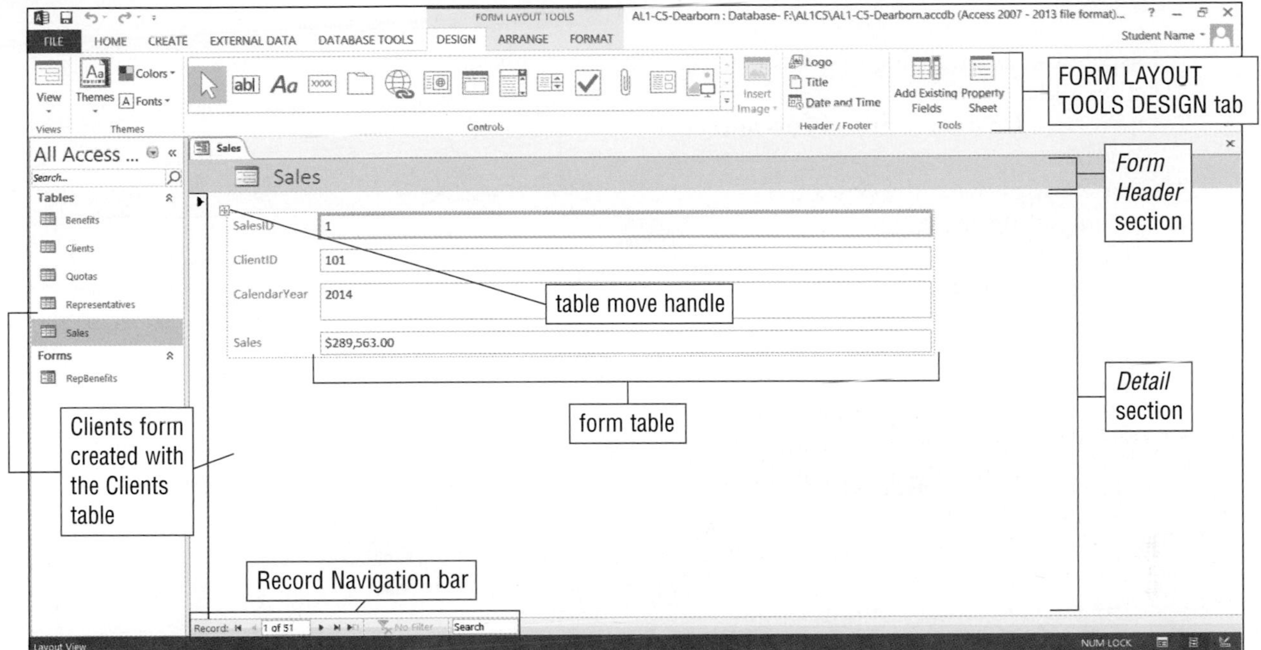

At the Print dialog box that displays, click the *Selected Record(s)* option and then click OK. You can also print a range of records by clicking the *Pages* option in the *Print Range* section of the Print dialog box and then entering the beginning record number in the *From* text box and the ending record number in the *To* text box.

Quick Steps

Print a Specific Record

1. Display form.
2. Click FILE tab.
3. Click *Print* option.
4. Click Print button.
5. Click *Selected Record(s)*.
6. Click OK.

Deleting a Form

If you no longer need a form in a database, delete the form. Delete a form by clicking the form name in the Navigation pane, clicking the Delete button in the Records group on the HOME tab, and then clicking the Yes button at the message asking if you want to permanently delete the form. Another method is to right-click the form name in the Navigation pane, click *Delete* at the shortcut menu, and then click Yes at the message. If you are deleting a form from your computer's hard drive, the message asking if you want to permanently delete the form will not display. This is because Access automatically sends the deleted form to the Recycle Bin, where it can be retrieved if necessary.

Navigating in a Form

When a form displays in Form view or Layout view, navigation buttons display along the bottom of the form in the Record Navigation bar, as identified in Figure 5.1. Use these navigation buttons to display the first, previous, next, or last record in the form or add a new record. Navigate to a specific record by clicking in the *Current Record* box, selecting the current number, typing the number of the record you want to view, and then pressing Enter. You can also navigate using the keyboard. Press the Page Down key to move forward or press the Page Up key to move back a single record. Press Ctrl + Home to display the first record or Press Ctrl + End to display the last record.

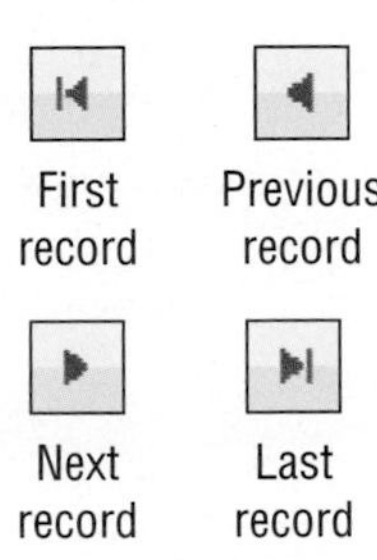

Project 1a Creating a Form with the Sales Table and Deleting a Form Part 1 of 7

1. Display the Open dialog box with the AL1C5 folder on your storage medium the active folder.
2. Open **AL1-C5-Dearborn.accdb** and enable the contents.
3. Create a form with the Sales table by completing the following steps:
   a. Click the Sales table in the Tables group in the Navigation pane.
   b. Click the CREATE tab.
   c. Click the Form button in the Forms group.
4. Switch to Form view by clicking the View button in the Views group on the FORM LAYOUT TOOLS DESIGN tab.
5. Navigate in the form by completing the following steps:
   a. Click the Next record button in the Record Navigation bar to display the next record.
   b. Click in the *Current Record* box, select any numbers that display, type 15, and then press Enter.
   c. Click the First record button in the Record Navigation bar to display the first record.
6. Save the form by completing the following steps:
   a. Click the Save button on the Quick Access toolbar.
   b. At the Save As dialog box, with *Sales* inserted in the *Form Name* text box, click OK.
7. Print the current record in the form by completing the following steps:
   a. Click the FILE tab and then click the *Print* option.
   b. Click the Print button.
   c. At the Print dialog box, click the *Selected Record(s)* option in the *Print Range* section and then click OK.
8. Close the Sales form.
9. Delete the RepBenefits form by right-clicking *RepBenefits* in the Navigation pane, clicking *Delete* at the shortcut menu, and then clicking Yes at the message asking if you want to permanently delete the form.

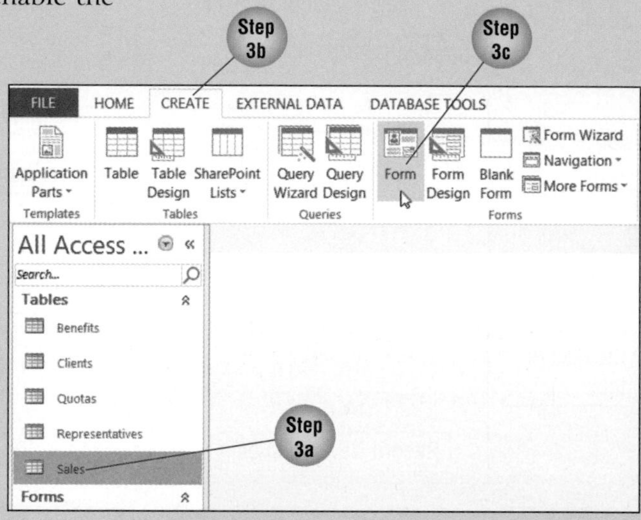

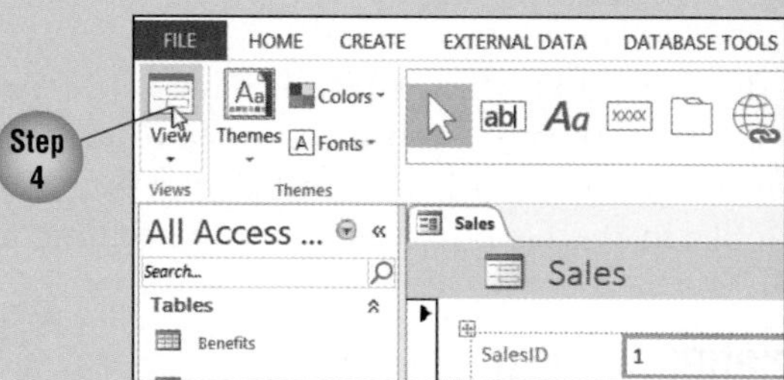

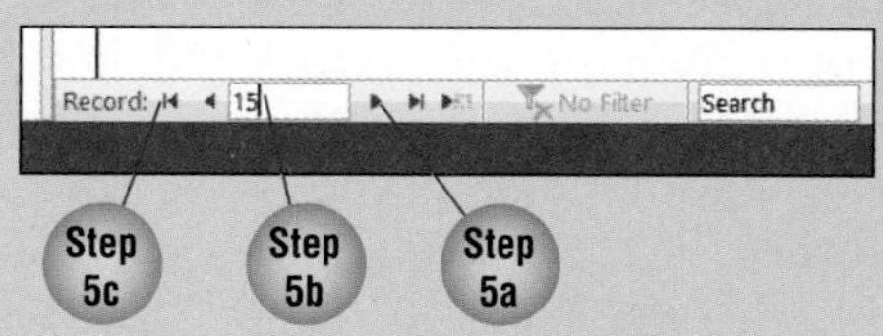

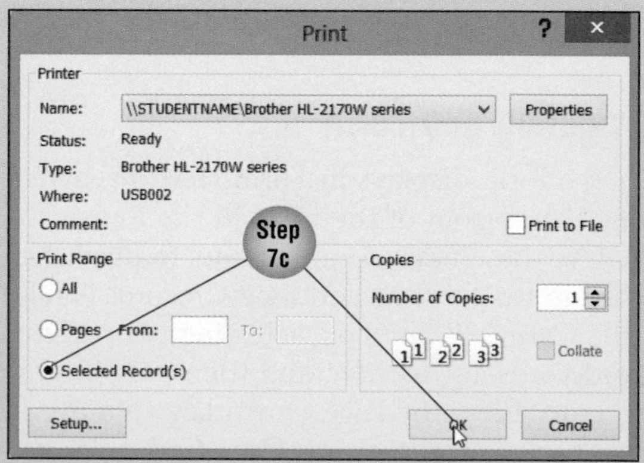

Adding and Deleting Records

Add a new record to the form by clicking the New (blank) record button (contains a right-pointing arrow and a yellow asterisk) that displays on the Record Navigation bar along the bottom of the form. You can also add a new record to a form by clicking the HOME tab and then clicking the New button in the Records group. To delete a record, display the record, click the HOME tab, click the Delete button arrow in the Records group, and then click *Delete Record* at the drop-down list. At the message telling you that the record will be deleted permanently, click Yes. Add records to or delete records from the table from which the form was created and the form will reflect the additions or deletions. Also, if you make additions or deletions to the form, the changes are reflected in the table on which the form was created.

Quick Steps

Add a Record
Click New (blank) record button on Record Navigation bar.
OR
1. Click HOME tab.
2. Click New button.

Delete a Record
1. Click HOME tab.
2. Click Delete button arrow.
3. Click *Delete Record.*
4. Click Yes.

New (blank) record

Delete

Sorting Records

Sort data in a form by clicking in the field containing data on which you want to sort and then clicking the Ascending button or Descending button in the Sort & Filter group on the HOME tab. Click the Ascending button to sort text in alphabetic order from A to Z or numbers from lowest to highest or click the Descending button to sort text in alphabetic order from Z to A or numbers from highest to lowest.

Project 1b Adding and Deleting Records in a Form

Part 2 of 7

1. Open the Sales table (not the form) and add a new record by completing the following steps:
   a. Click the New (blank) record button located in the Record Navigation bar.

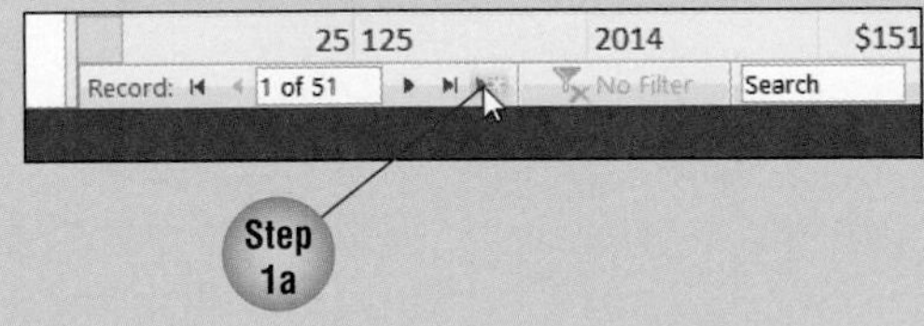

   b. At the new blank record, type the following information in the specified fields. (Move to the next field by pressing Tab or Enter; move to the previous field by pressing Shift + Tab.)

SalesID	(This is an AutoNumber field, so press Tab.)
ClientID	127
CalendarYear	2015
Sales	176420

2. Close the Sales table.
3. Open the Sales form.
4. Click the Last record button on the Record Navigation bar and notice that the new record you added to the table has been added to the form.

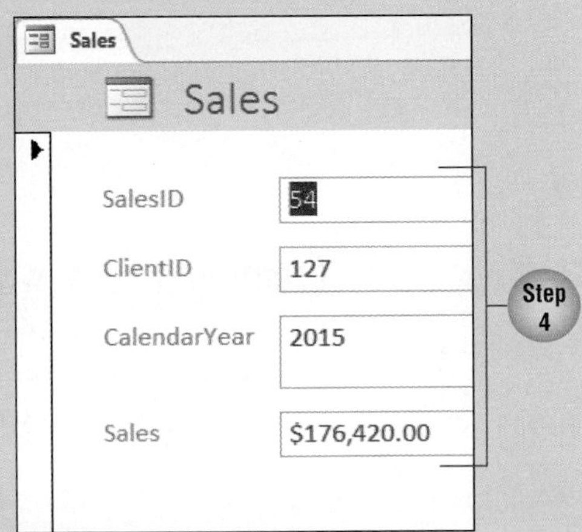

5. Delete the second record (sales ID 3) in the form by completing the following steps:
   a. Click the First record button in the Record Navigation bar.
   b. Click the Next record button in the Record Navigation bar.
   c. With Record 2 active, click the Delete button arrow in the Records group on the HOME tab and then click *Delete Record* at the drop-down list.

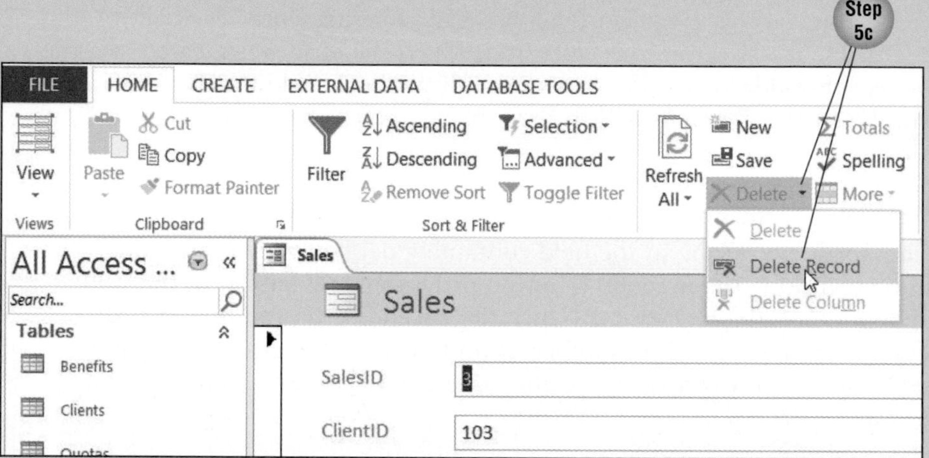

   d. At the message that displays telling you that you will not be able to undo the deletion, click the Yes button.
6. Click the New (blank) record button in the Record Navigation bar and then type the following information in the specified fields:

SalesID	(Press Tab.)
ClientID	**103**
CalendarYear	**2014**
Sales	**110775**

7. Sort the records in the form by completing the following steps:
   a. Click in the field containing the data *103* and then click the Ascending button in the Sort & Filter group on the HOME tab.
   b. Click in the field containing the data *$289,563.00* and then click the Descending button in the Sort & Filter group.
   c. Click in the field containing the data *36* and then click the Ascending button in the Sort & Filter group.
8. Close the Sales form.

Creating a Form with a Related Table

When you created the form with the Sales table, only the Sales table fields displayed in the form. If you create a form with a table that has a one-to-many relationship established, Access adds a datasheet to the form that is based on the related table.

For example, in Project 1c, you will create a form with the Representatives table, and since it is related to the Clients table by a one-to-many relationship, Access inserts a datasheet at the bottom of the form containing all of the records in the Clients table. Figure 5.2 displays the form you will create in Project 1c. Notice the datasheet that displays at the bottom of the form.

If you have created only a single one-to-many relationship, the datasheet for the related table displays in the form. If you have created multiple one-to-many relationships in a table, Access will not display any datasheets when you create a form with the table.

Figure 5.2 Representatives Form with Clients Datasheet

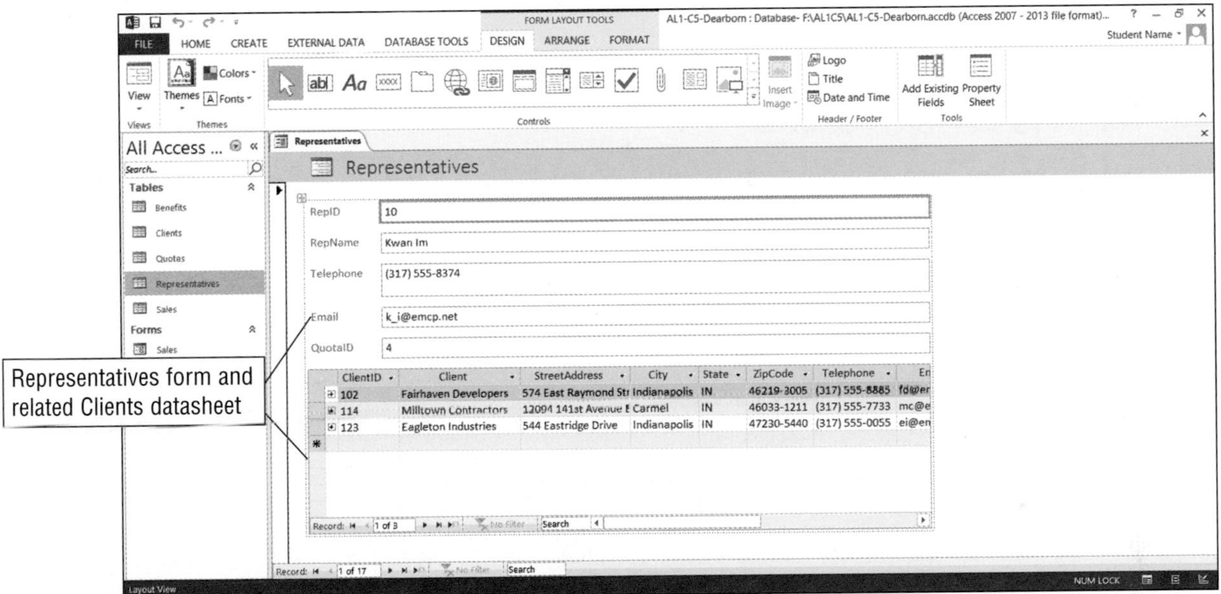

Project 1c Creating a Form with a Related Table Part 3 of 7

1. With **AL1-C5-Dearborn.accdb** open, create a form with the Representatives table by completing the following steps:
   a. Click the Representatives table in the Navigation pane.
   b. Click the CREATE tab.
   c. Click the Form button in the Forms group.
2. Insert a new record in the Clients table for representative 12 (Catherine Singleton) by completing the following steps:
   a. Click twice on the Next record button in the Record Navigation bar at the bottom of the form window (not the Record Navigation bar in the Clients datasheet) to display the record for Catherine Singleton.
   b. Click in the cell immediately below *127* in the *ClientID* field in the Clients datasheet.

c. Type the following information in the specified fields:

ClientID	**129**
Client	**Dan-Built Construction**
StreetAddress	**903 James Street**
City	**Carmel**
State	**IN**
ZipCode	**460339050**
Telephone	**3175551122**
Email	**dc@emcp.net**

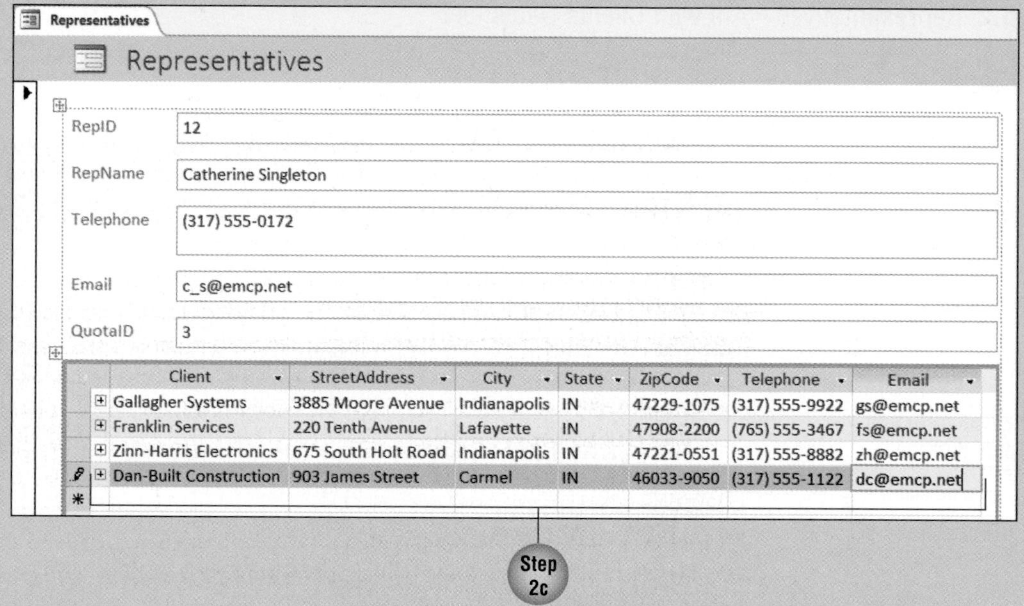

3. Click the Save button on the Quick Access toolbar and at the Save As dialog box with *Representatives* in the *Form Name* text box, click OK.
4. Print the current record in the form by completing the following steps:
   a. Click the FILE tab and then click the *Print* option.
   b. Click the Print button.
   c. At the Print dialog box, click the *Select Record(s)* option in the *Print Range* section and then click OK.
5. Close the Representatives form.

Customizing Forms

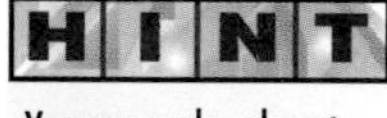

You can make almost all changes to a form in Layout view.

A form is comprised of a series of ***control objects***, which are objects that display titles or descriptions, accept data, or perform actions. Control objects are contained in the *Form Header* section and *Detail* section of the form. (Refer to Figure 5.1 on page 187.) The control objects in the *Detail* section are contained within a form table.

You can customize control objects in the *Detail* section and data in the *Form Header* section with buttons on the FORM LAYOUT TOOLS ribbon with the DESIGN tab, ARRANGE tab, or FORMAT tab selected. When you open a form in Layout view, the FORM LAYOUT TOOLS DESIGN tab is active. This tab contains options for applying a theme, inserting controls, inserting header or footer data, and adding existing fields.

Applying Themes

Themes

Access provides a number of themes for formatting objects in a database. A ***theme*** is a set of formatting choices that include a color theme (a set of colors) and a font theme (a set of heading and body text fonts). To apply a theme, click the Themes button in the Themes group on the FORM LAYOUT TOOLS DESIGN tab. At the drop-down gallery that displays, click the desired theme. Position the mouse pointer over a theme and the ***live preview feature*** will display the form with the theme formatting applied. With the live preview feature, you can see how the theme formatting affects your form before you make your final choice. When you apply a theme, any new objects you create in the database will be formatted with the theme.

Themes available in Access are the same as the themes available in Word, Excel, and PowerPoint.

You can further customize the formatting of a form with the Colors button and the Fonts button in the Themes group on the FORM LAYOUT TOOLS DESIGN tab. If you want to customize the theme colors, click the Colors button in the Themes group and then click the desired option at the drop-down list. Change the theme fonts by clicking the Themes button and then clicking the desired option at the drop-down list.

Colors

Font

Inserting Data in the Form Header

Use buttons in the Header/Footer group on the FORM LAYOUT TOOLS DESIGN tab to insert a logo, form title, or date and time. Click the Logo button and the Insert Picture dialog box displays. Browse to the folder containing the desired image and then double-click the image file. Click the Title button and the current title is selected. Type the new title and then press the Enter key. Click the Date and Time button in the Header/Footer group and the Date and Time dialog box displays. At this dialog box, choose the desired date and time format and then click OK. The date and time are inserted at the right side of the *Form Header* section.

Logo

Title

Date and Time

You can resize and move control objects in the *Form Header* section. To resize an object, click the object to select it and then drag a left or right border to increase or decrease the width. To increase or decrease the height of the object, as well as the *Form Header* section, drag a top or bottom border. To move a selected object in the *Form Header* section, position the mouse pointer over the selected object until the pointer displays with a four-headed arrow attached. Hold down the left mouse button, drag the object to the desired position, and then release the mouse button.

Modifying a Control Object

When Access creates a form from a table, the first column in the form contains the label control objects and displays the field names from the table. The second column contains the text box control objects that display the field values you entered in the table. The width of either column can be resized. To do this, click in any control object in the desired column, position the mouse pointer on the right or left border of the selected control object until the pointer displays as a black left-and-right-pointing arrow. Hold down the left mouse button, drag left or right to change the width of the column, and then release the mouse button. Complete similar steps to change the height of the row containing the selected control object. As you drag a border, a line and character count displays at the left side of the Status bar. Use the line and character count numbers to move the border to a precise location.

To delete a control object from the form, click the desired object and then press the Delete key. You can also right-click the object and then click *Delete* at the shortcut menu. If you want to delete a form row, right-click an object in the row you want to delete and then click *Delete Row* at the shortcut menu. To delete a column, right-click in one of the objects in the column you want to delete and then click *Delete Column* at the shortcut menu. In addition to the label and text box control objects, the sizes and positions of objects in the *Form Header* section, such as the logo and title, can be modified.

Inserting a Control

Select

Text Box

Each cell can contain only one control object.

The Controls group on the FORM LAYOUT TOOLS DESIGN tab contains a number of control objects you can insert in a form. By default, the Select button is active. With this button active, use the mouse pointer to select control objects. You can insert a new label control and text box control object in your form by clicking the Text Box button in the Controls group and then clicking in the desired position in the form. Click in the label control object, select the default text, and then type the label text. You can enter text in a label control object in Layout view but you cannot enter data in a text box control object. In Form view, you can enter data in a text box control object but you cannot edit text in a label control object. The Controls group contains a number of additional buttons for inserting control objects in a form, such as a hyperlink, combo box, or image.

Project 1d **Creating a Form and Customizing the Design of a Form** **Part 4 of 7**

1. With **AL1-C5-Dearborn.accdb** open, create a form with the Clients table and delete the datasheet by completing the following steps:
   a. Click the Clients table in the Navigation pane.
   b. Click the CREATE tab.
   c. Click the Form button in the Forms group.
   d. Click in the SalesID field in the datasheet that displays below the form.
   e. Click the table move handle that displays in the upper left corner of the datasheet (see image at right).
   f. Press the Delete key.
2. Apply a theme to the form by clicking the Themes button in the Themes group on the FORM LAYOUT TOOLS DESIGN tab and then clicking *Facet* at the drop-down gallery (first row, second column).

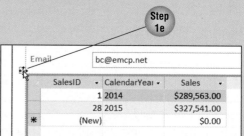

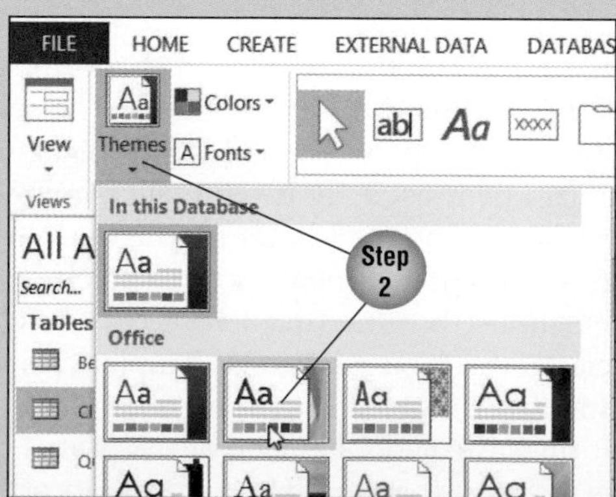

3. Change the theme fonts by clicking the Fonts button in the Themes group and then clicking *Gill Sans MT* at the drop-down gallery. (You will need to scroll down the list to display *Gill Sans MT*.)
4. Change the theme colors by clicking the Colors button in the Themes group and then clicking *Orange* at the drop-down gallery.
5. Insert a logo image in the *Form Header* section by completing the following steps:
   a. Right-click the logo object that displays in the *Form Header* section (located to the left of the title *Clients*) and then click *Delete* at the shortcut menu.
   b. Click the Logo button in the Header/Footer group.
   c. At the Insert Picture dialog box, navigate to the AL1C5 folder on your storage medium and then double-click the file named ***DearbornLogo.jpg***.
6. Change the title by completing the following steps:
   a. Click the Title button in the Header/Footer group. (This selects *Clients* in the *Form Header* section.)
   b. Type **Dearborn Clients Form** and then press Enter.
7. Insert the date and time in the *Form Header* section by completing the following steps:
   a. Click the Date and Time button in the Header/Footer group.
   b. At the Date and Time dialog box, click OK.
8. Size the control object containing the title by completing the following steps:
   a. Click in any field outside the title and then click the title to select the header control object.
   b. Position the mouse pointer on the right border of the selected object until the pointer displays as a black left-and-right-pointing arrow.
   c. Hold down the left mouse button, drag to the left until the right border is immediately right of the title, and then release the mouse button.

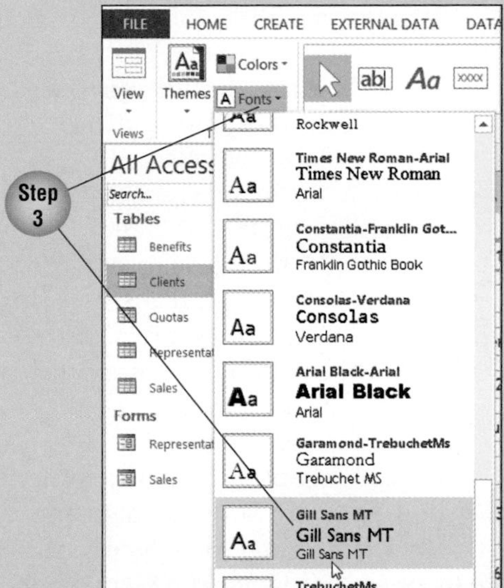

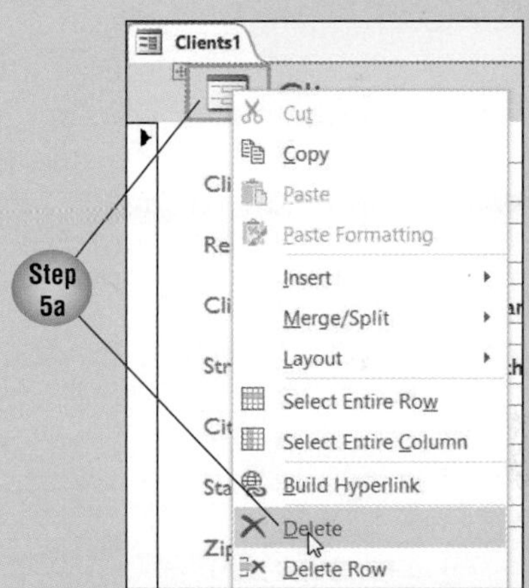

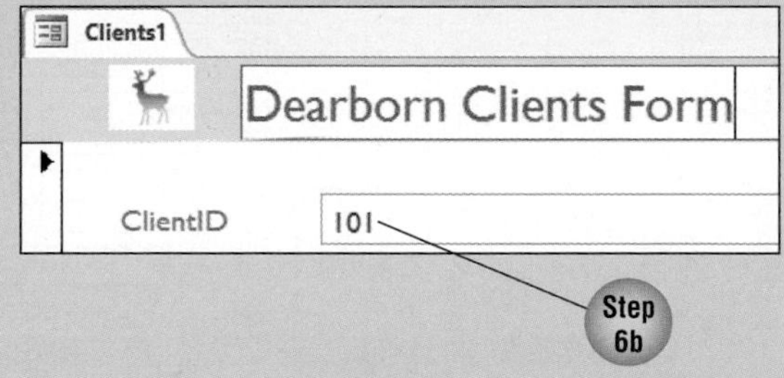

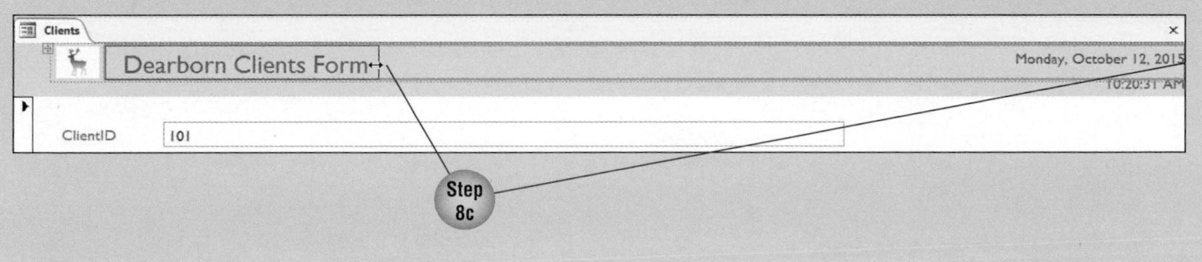

9. Size and move the control objects containing the date and time by completing the following steps:
   a. Click the date to select the control object.
   b. Hold down the Shift key, click the time, and then release the Shift key. (Both control objects should be selected.)
   c. Position the mouse pointer on the left border of the selected objects until the pointer displays as a black left-and-right-pointing arrow.
   d. Hold down the left mouse button, drag to the right until the border displays immediately left of the date, and then release the mouse button.
   e. Position the mouse pointer in the selected objects until the pointer displays with a four-headed arrow attached.
   f. Hold down the left mouse button and then drag the outline of the date and time objects to the left until the outline displays near the title.

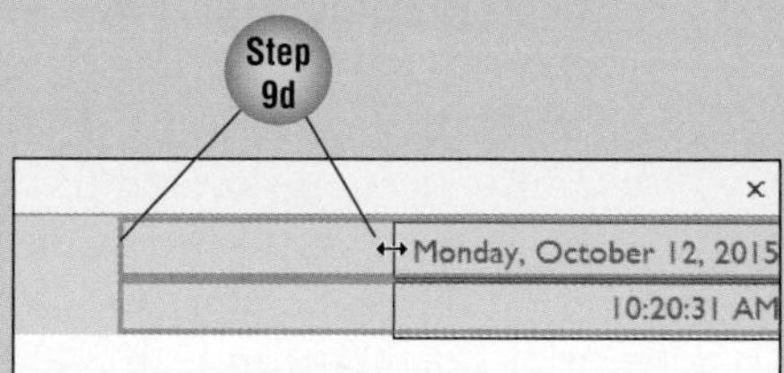

10. Decrease the size of the second column of control objects in the *Detail* section by completing the following steps:
    a. Click in the text box control object containing the client number *101*. (This selects and inserts an orange border around the object.)
    b. Position the mouse pointer on the right border of the selected object until the pointer displays as a black left-and-right-pointing arrow.
    c. Hold down the left mouse button, drag to the left until *Lines: 1 Characters: 30* displays at the left side of the Status bar, and then release the mouse button.

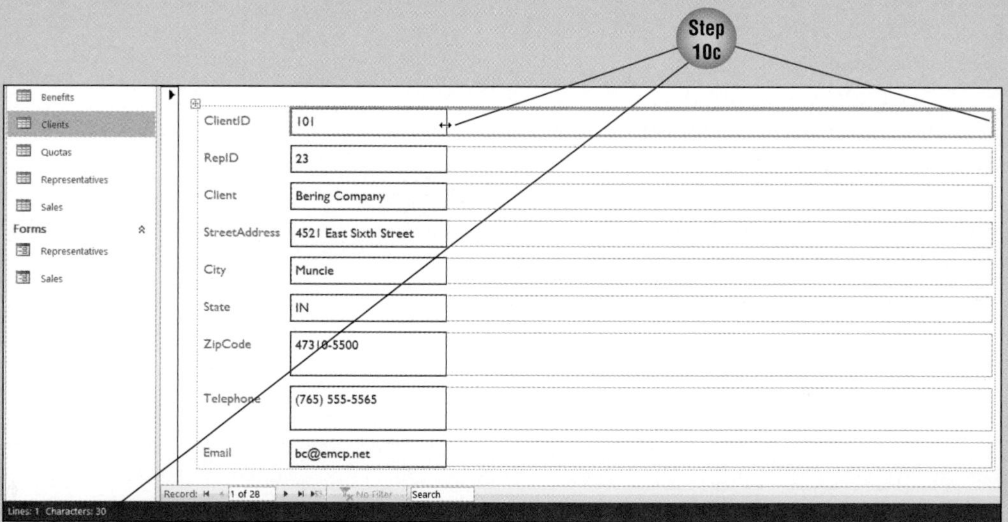

11. Insert a label control object by completing the following steps:
    a. Click the Label button in the Controls group.

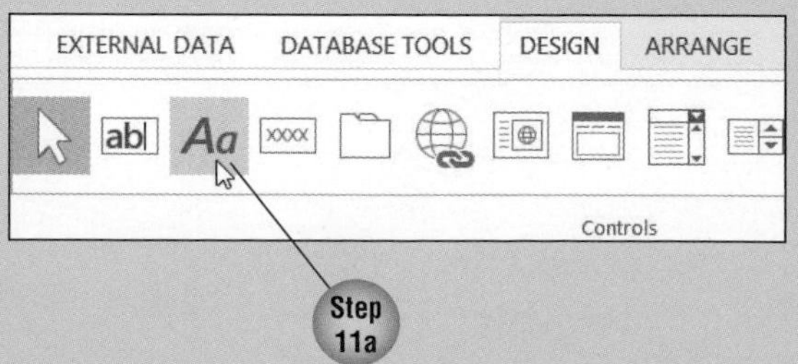

b. Click immediately right of the text box containing the telephone number *(765) 555-5565*. (This inserts the label to the right of the *Telephone* text box.)
c. With the insertion point positioned inside the label, type **Type the telephone number without symbols or spaces** and then press the Enter key.

12. Change the size of the new label control object by completing the following steps:
    a. Position the arrow pointer on the right border of the new label control object until the pointer displays as a black left-and-right-pointing arrow.
    b. Hold down the left mouse button, drag the border to the right until *Lines: 6 Characters: 32* displays at the left side of the Status bar, and then release the mouse button. The text line in the label should break after the word *number*.
    c. Decrease the height of the new label control object by dragging the bottom border up so it is positioned just below the second line of text.

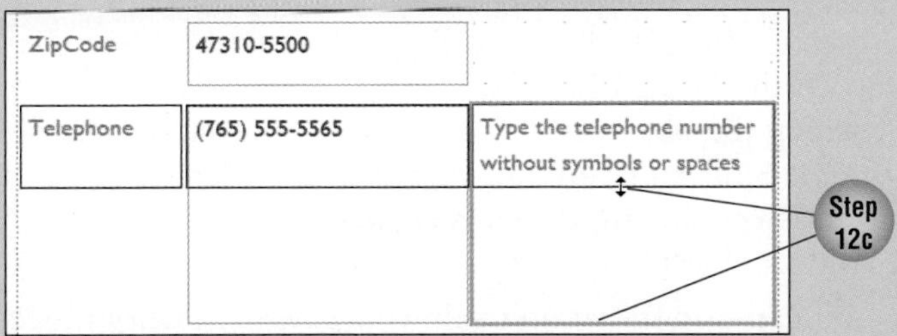

13. Click the Save button on the Quick Access toolbar. At the Save As dialog box with *Clients* in the *Form Name* text box, click OK.

Moving a Form Table

The control objects in the *Detail* section in a form in Layout view are contained within the form table. Click in a control object and the table is selected and the table move handle is visible. The table move handle is a small square with a four-headed arrow inside that displays in the upper left corner of the table. (Refer to Figure 5.1 on page 187.) Move the table and all of the control objects within the table by dragging the table move handle using the mouse. When you position the mouse pointer on the table move handle and then hold down the left mouse button, all of the control objects are selected. You can also click the table move handle to select the control objects.

You can move a control object by dragging it to the desired location.

Arranging Objects

With options on the FORM LAYOUT TOOLS ARRANGE tab, you can select, insert, delete, arrange, merge, and split cells. When you inserted a label control object to the right of the *Telephone* text box control in Project 1d, empty cells were inserted in the form above and below the new label control object. Select a control object or cell by clicking in the desired object or cell. Select adjacent objects or cells by holding down the Shift key while clicking in the desired objects or cells. To select nonadjacent objects or cells, hold down the Ctrl key while clicking in the desired objects or cells.

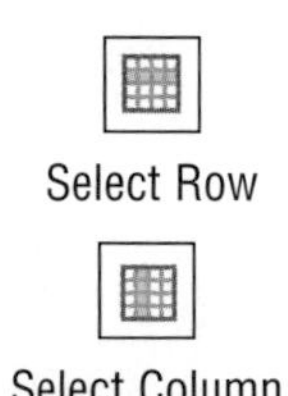

Select Row

Select Column

Select a row of control objects and cells by clicking the Select Row button in the Rows & Columns group or by right-clicking in an object or cell and then clicking *Select Entire Row* at the shortcut menu. To select a column of control objects and cells, click the Select Column button in the Rows & Columns group or right-click an object or cell and then click *Select Entire Column* at the shortcut menu. You can also select a column by positioning the mouse pointer at the top of the column until the pointer displays as a small, black, down-pointing arrow and then clicking the left mouse button.

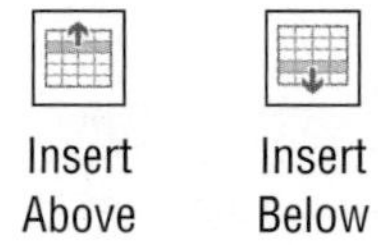

Insert Above Insert Below

The Rows & Columns group contains buttons for inserting a row or column of blank cells. To insert a new row, select a cell or object in a row and then click the Insert Above button to insert a row of blank cells above the current row or click the Insert Below button to insert a row of blank cells below the current row. Complete similar steps to insert a new column of blank cells to the left or right of the current column.

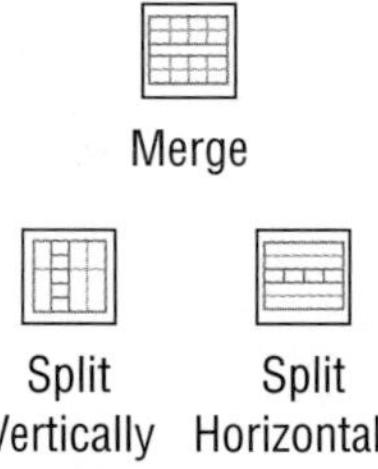

Merge

Split Vertically Split Horizontally

Merge adjacent selected cells by clicking the Merge button in the Merge/Split group on the FORM LAYOUT TOOLS ARRANGE tab. Split a control object or cell by clicking the object or cell to make it active and then clicking the Split Vertically button or Split Horizontally button in the Merge/Split group. When you split a control object, an empty cell is created to the right of the control object or below the control object.

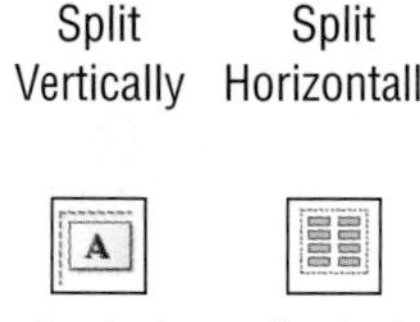

Control Margins Control Padding

You can also move up or down a row of control objects. To do this, select the desired row and then click the Move Up button in the Move group to move the row above the current row or click the Move Down button to move the row below the current row. Use the Control Margins button in the Position group to increase or decrease margins within control objects. The Position group also contains a Control Padding button you can use to increase or decrease spacing between control objects.

The Table group is located at the left side of the FORM LAYOUT TOOLS ARRANGE tab. It contains buttons for applying gridlines to control objects and changing the layout of the objects to a stacked layout or columnar layout.

Project 1e Arranging Objects in a Form

1. With the Clients form in **AL1-C5-Dearborn.accdb** open in Design view, select and merge cells by completing the following steps:
   a. Click to the right of the text box control object containing the text *101*. (This selects the empty cell.)
   b. Hold down the Shift key and then click to the right of the text box control containing the text *Muncie*. (This selects five adjacent cells.)
   c. Click the FORM LAYOUT TOOLS ARRANGE tab.
   d. Click the Merge button in the Merge/Split group.

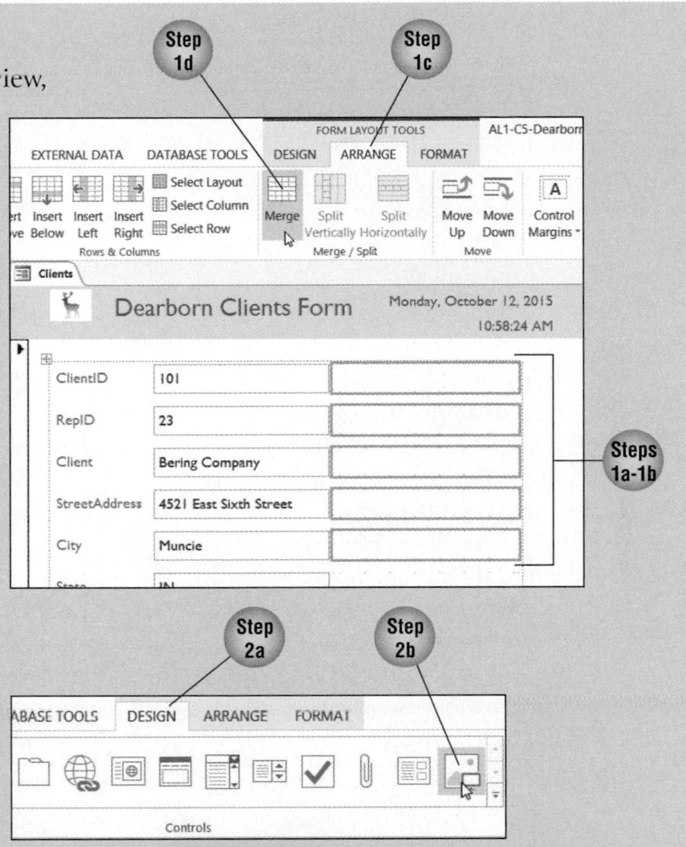

2. With the cells merged, insert an image control object and then insert an image by completing the following steps:
   a. Click the FORM LAYOUT TOOLS DESIGN tab.
   b. Click the Image button in the Controls group.
   c. Move the mouse pointer (which displays as a plus symbol next to an image icon) to the location of the merged cell until the cell displays with pink fill color and then click the left mouse button.

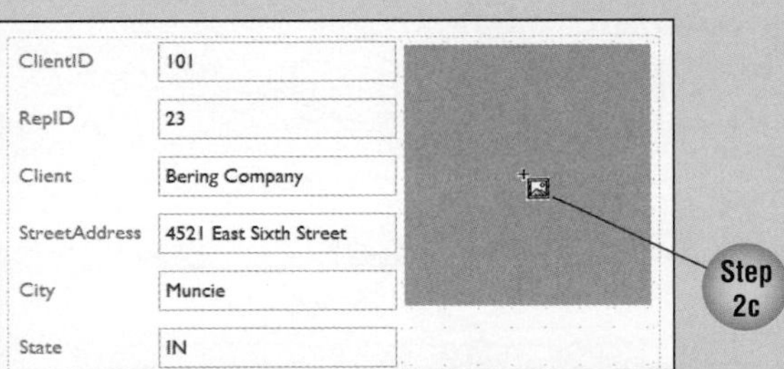

   d. At the Insert Picture dialog box, navigate to the AL1C5 folder on your storage medium and then double-click ***Dearborn.jpg***.

3. Move down the telephone row by completing the following steps:
   a. Click the FORM LAYOUT TOOLS ARRANGE tab.
   b. Click in the control object containing the text *Telephone*.
   c. Click the Select Row button in the Rows & Columns group.
   d. Click the Move Down button in the Move group.

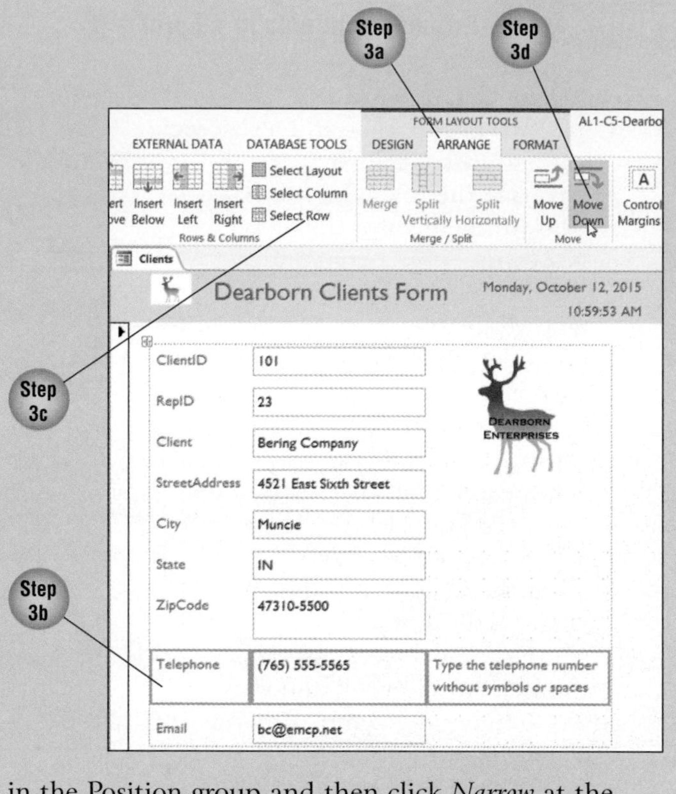

4. Decrease the margins within objects and cells, increase the spacing (padding) between objects and cells in the form, and apply gridlines by completing the following steps:
   a. If necessary, click the FORM LAYOUT TOOLS ARRANGE tab.
   b. Click the Select Layout button in the Rows & Columns group. (This selects all objects and cells in the form.)
   c. Click the Control Margins button in the Position group and then click *Narrow* at the drop-down list.

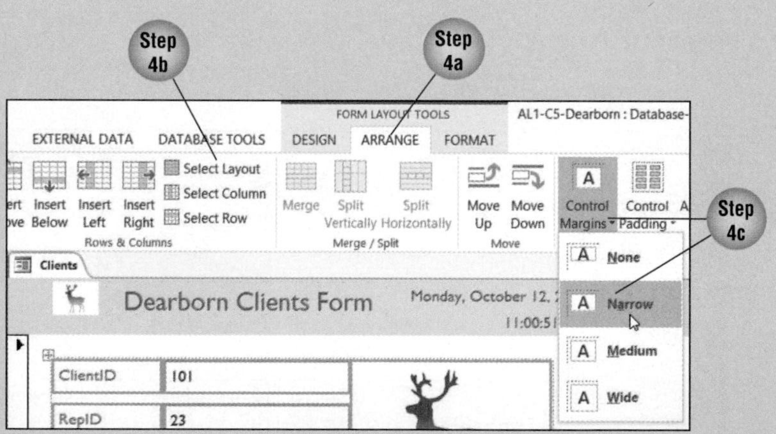

   d. Click the Control Padding button in the Position group and then click *Medium* at the drop-down list.

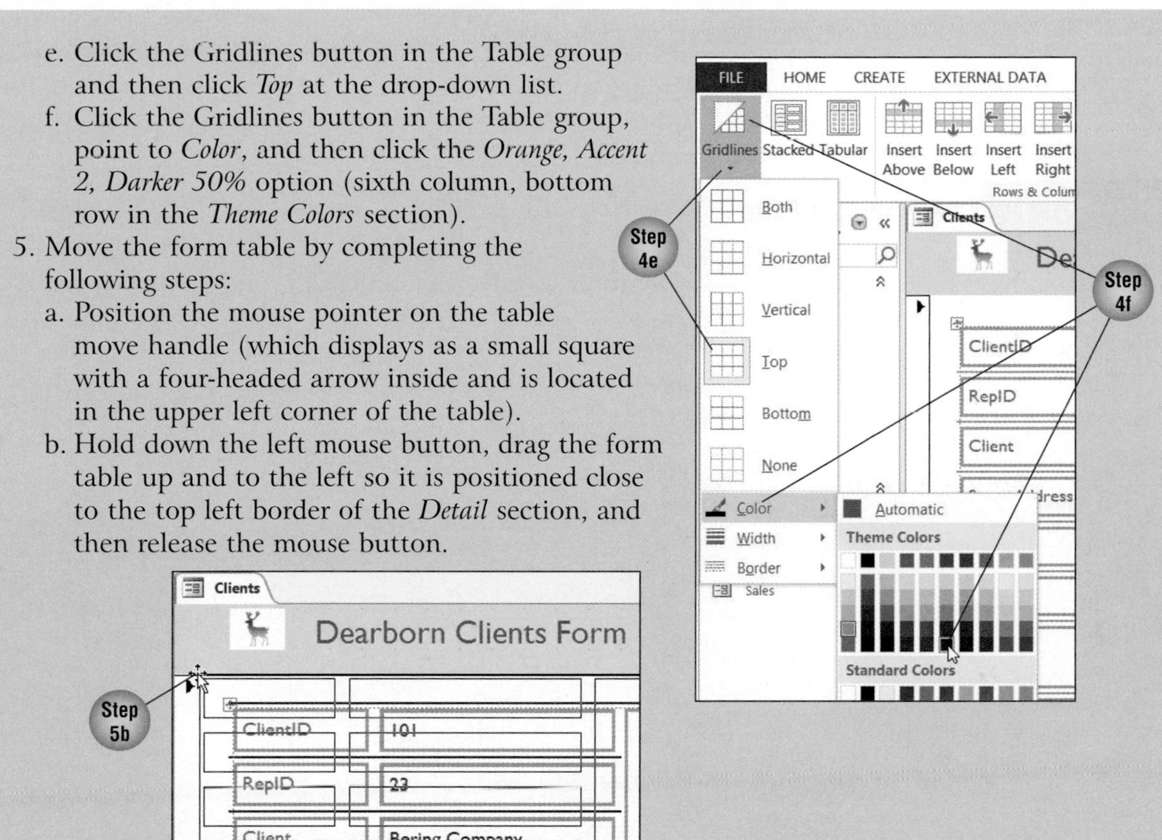

   e. Click the Gridlines button in the Table group and then click *Top* at the drop-down list.
   f. Click the Gridlines button in the Table group, point to *Color*, and then click the *Orange, Accent 2, Darker 50%* option (sixth column, bottom row in the *Theme Colors* section).
5. Move the form table by completing the following steps:
   a. Position the mouse pointer on the table move handle (which displays as a small square with a four-headed arrow inside and is located in the upper left corner of the table).
   b. Hold down the left mouse button, drag the form table up and to the left so it is positioned close to the top left border of the *Detail* section, and then release the mouse button.
6. Click in the control object containing the field name *ClientID*.
7. Save the Clients form.

Formatting a Form

Click the FORM LAYOUT TOOLS FORMAT tab and buttons and options display for applying formatting to a form or specific objects in a form. If you want to apply formatting to a specific object, click the object in the form or click the Object button arrow in the Selection group and then click the desired object at the drop-down list. To format all objects in the form, click the Select All button in the Selection group. This selects all objects in the form, including objects in the *Form Header* section. If you want to select all of the objects in the *Detail* section (and not the *Form Header* section), click an object in the *Detail* section and then click the table move handle.

Object

Select All

With buttons in the Font, Number, Background, and Control Formatting groups, you can apply formatting to a control object or cell and to selected objects and cells in a form. Use buttons in the Font group to change the font, apply a different font size, apply text effects (such as bold and underline), and change the alignment of data in objects. If the form contains data with a Number or Currency data type, use buttons in the Number group to apply specific formatting

to numbers. Insert a background image in the form using the Background Image button and apply formatting to objects or cells with buttons in the Control Formatting group. Depending on what is selected in the form, some of the buttons may not be active.

Project 1f Formatting a Form

Part 6 of 7

1. With the Clients form in **AL1-C5-Dearborn.accdb** open and in Layout view, change the font and font size of text in the form by completing the following steps:
   a. Click in any control object in the form.
   b. Select all control objects and cells in the form by clicking the table move handle that displays in the upper left corner of the *Detail* section.

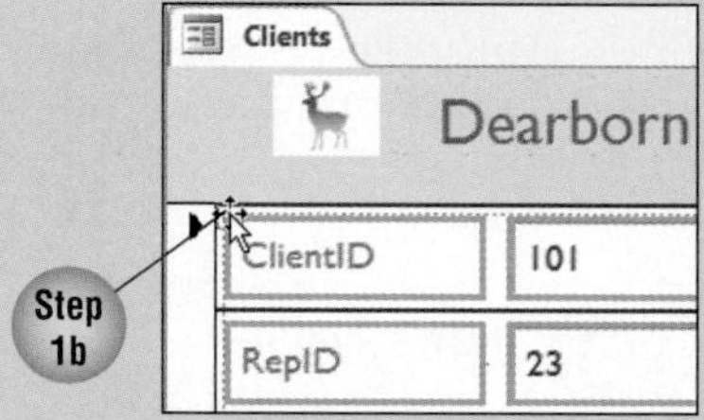

   c. Click the FORM LAYOUT TOOLS FORMAT tab.
   d. Click the Font button arrow, scroll down the drop-down list, and then click *Tahoma*. (Fonts are alphabetized in the drop-down list.)
   e. Click the Font Size button arrow and then click *10* at the drop-down list.

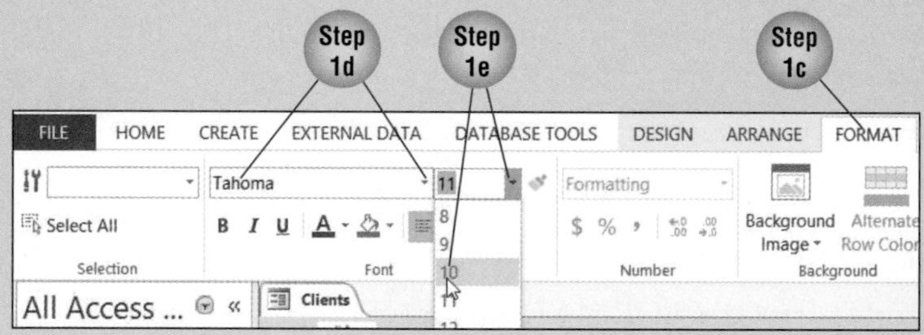

2. Apply formatting and change the alignment of the first column by completing the following steps:
   a. Click the control object containing the field name *ClientID*, hold down the Shift key, click the bottom control object containing the field name *Telephone*, and then release the Shift key.
   b. Click the Bold button in the Font group.
   c. Click the Shape Fill button in the Control Formatting group and then click the *Brown, Accent 3, Lighter 60%* color option (seventh column, third row in the *Theme Colors* section).
   d. Click the Shape Outline button in the Control Formatting group and then click the *Brown, Accent 3, Darker 50%* option (seventh column, bottom row in the *Theme Colors* section).
   e. Click the Align Right button in the Font group.

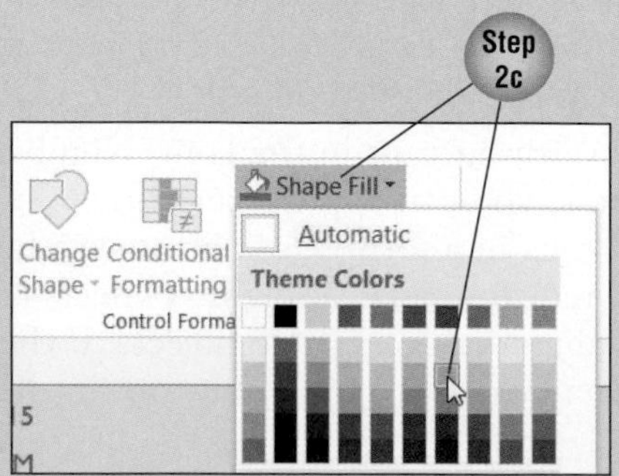

3. Apply shape fill to the second column by completing the following steps:
   a. Click the text box control object containing the text *101*.
   b. Position the mouse pointer at the top border of the selected object until the pointer displays as a small, black, down-pointing arrow and then click the left mouse button. (Make sure all of the objects in the second column are selected.)

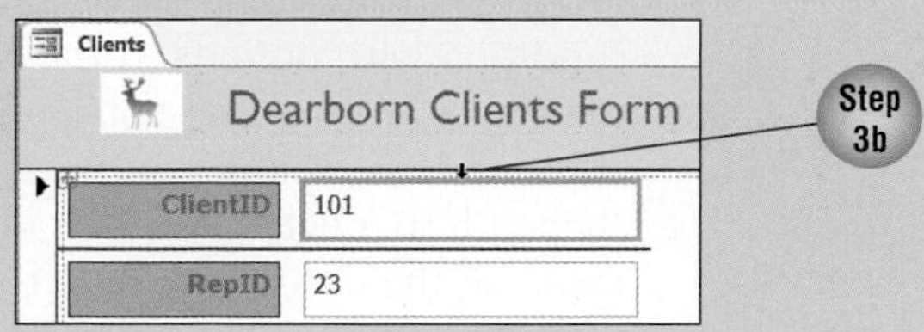

   c. Click the Shape Fill button in the Control Formatting group and then click the *Brown, Accent 3, Lighter 80%* color option (seventh column, second row in the *Theme Colors* section).
4. Remove the gridlines by completing the following steps:
   a. Click the FORM LAYOUT TOOLS ARRANGE tab.
   b. Click the Select Layout button in the Rows & Columns group.
   c. Click the Gridlines button in the Table group and then click *None* at the drop-down list.
5. Click the Save button on the Quick Access toolbar to save the Clients form.
6. Insert a background image by completing the following steps:
   a. Click the FORM LAYOUT TOOLS FORMAT tab.
   b. Click the Background Image button in the Background group and then click *Browse* at the drop-down list.
   c. Navigate to the AL1C5 folder on your storage medium and then double-click ***Mountain.jpg***.
   d. View the form and background image in Print Preview. (To display Print Preview, click the FILE tab, click the *Print* option, and then click the Print Preview button.)
   e. After viewing the form in Print Preview, return to the form by clicking the Close Print Preview button.
7. Click the Undo button on the Quick Access toolbar to remove the background image. (If this does not remove the image, close the form without saving it and then reopen the form.)
8. Save the Clients form.

Applying Conditional Formatting

Conditional Formatting

With the Conditional Formatting button in the Control Formatting group on the FORM LAYOUT TOOLS FORMAT tab, you can apply formatting to data that meets a specific criterion or apply conditional formatting to data in all records in a form. For example, you can apply conditional formatting to sales amounts in a form that displays amounts higher than a specified number in a different color or you can apply conditional formatting to states' names and specify a color for companies in a particular state. You can also include conditional formatting that inserts data bars that visually compare data among records. The data bars provide a visual representation of the comparison of data in records. For example, in Project 1g, you will insert data bars in the *Sales* field that provide a visual representation of how the sales amount in one record compares to the sales amounts in other records.

To apply conditional formatting, click the Conditional Formatting button in the Control Formatting group and the Conditional Formatting Rules Manager dialog box displays. At this dialog box, click the New Rule button and the New Formatting Rule dialog box displays, as shown in Figure 5.3. In the *Select a rule type* list box, choose the *Check values in the current record or use an expression* option if the conditional formatting is applied to a field in the record that matches a specific condition. Click the *Compare to other records* option if you want to insert data bars in a field in all records that compare the data among the records.

If you want to apply conditional formatting to a field, specify the field and field condition with options in the *Edit the rule description* section of the dialog box. Specify the type of formatting you want applied to data in a field that meets the specific criterion. For example, in Project 1g, you will specify that you want to change the shape fill to a light green for all *City* fields containing *Indianapolis*. When you have made all the desired changes to the dialog box, click OK to close the dialog box and then click OK to close the Conditional Formatting Rules Manager dialog box.

To insert data bars in a field, click the Conditional Formatting button, click the New Rule button at the Conditional Formatting Rules Manager dialog box, and then click the *Compare to other records* option in the *Select a rule type* list box. This changes the options in the dialog box, as shown in Figure 5.4. Make the desired changes in the *Edit the rule description* section.

Figure 5.3 New Formatting Rule Dialog Box with the *Check values in the current record or use an expression* Option Selected

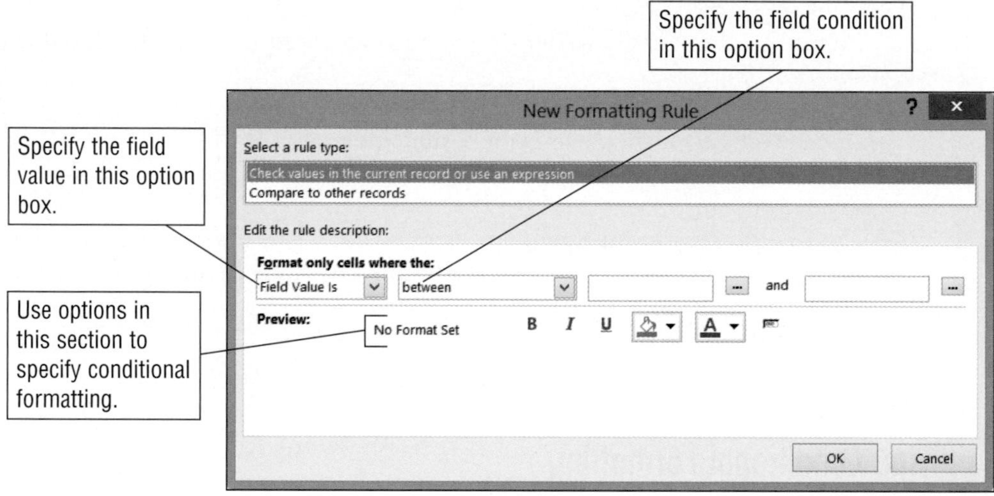

Figure 5.4 New Formatting Rule Dialog Box with the *Compare to other records* Option Selected

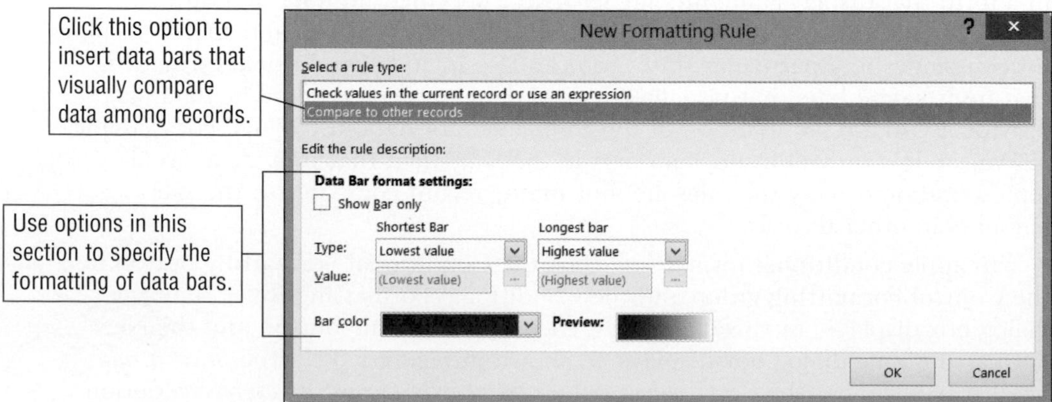

Project 1g Applying Conditional Formatting to Fields in Forms Part 7 of 7

1. With the Clients form in **AL1-C5-Dearborn.accdb** open and in Layout view, apply conditional formatting so that the *City* field displays all Indianapolis entries with a light green shape fill by completing the following steps:
   a. Click in the text box control object containing the text *Muncie*.
   b. Click the FORM LAYOUT TOOLS FORMAT tab.
   c. Click the Conditional Formatting button in the Control Formatting group.
   d. At the Conditional Formatting Rules Manager dialog box, click the New Rule button.

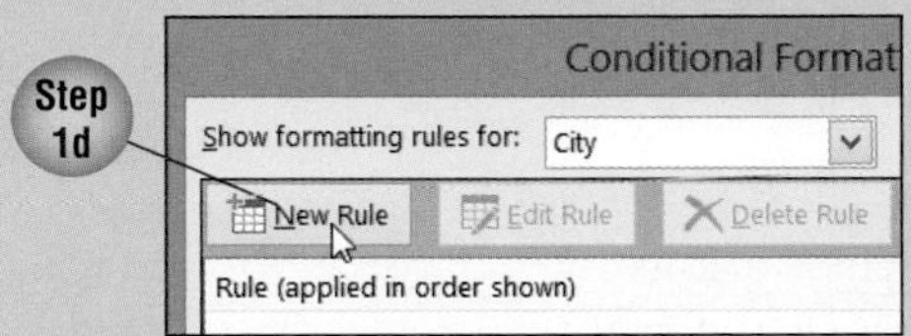

   e. At the New Formatting Rule dialog box, click the down-pointing arrow at the right side of the option box containing the word *between* and then click *equal to* at the drop-down list.
   f. Click in the text box to the right of the *equal to* option box and then type **Indianapolis**.
   g. Click the Background color button arrow and then click the *Green 3* color option (seventh column, fourth row).
   h. Click OK to close the New Formatting Rule dialog box.
   i. Click OK to close the Conditional Formatting Rules Manager dialog box.

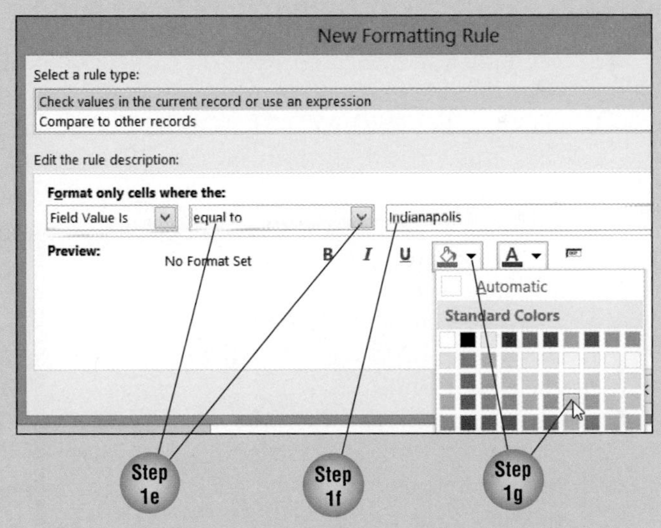

2. Click the HOME tab and then click the View button to switch to Form view.
3. Click the Next record button to display the next record in the form. Continue clicking the Next record button to view records and notice that *Indianapolis* entries display with a light green shape fill.
4. Click the First record button in the Record Navigation bar.
5. Click the Save button on the Quick Access toolbar.
6. Print page 1 of the form by completing the following steps:
   a. Click the FILE tab and then click the *Print* option.
   b. Click the Print button.
   c. At the Print dialog box, click the *Pages* option in the *Print Range* section, type 1 in the *From* text box, press the Tab key, and then type 1 in the *To* text box.
   d. Click OK.
7. Close the Clients form.
8. Open the Sales form and switch to Layout View by clicking the View button in the Views group on the HOME tab.

9. With the text box control object containing the sales ID number *1* selected, drag the right border to the left until *Lines: 1 Characters: 21* displays at the left side of the Status bar.

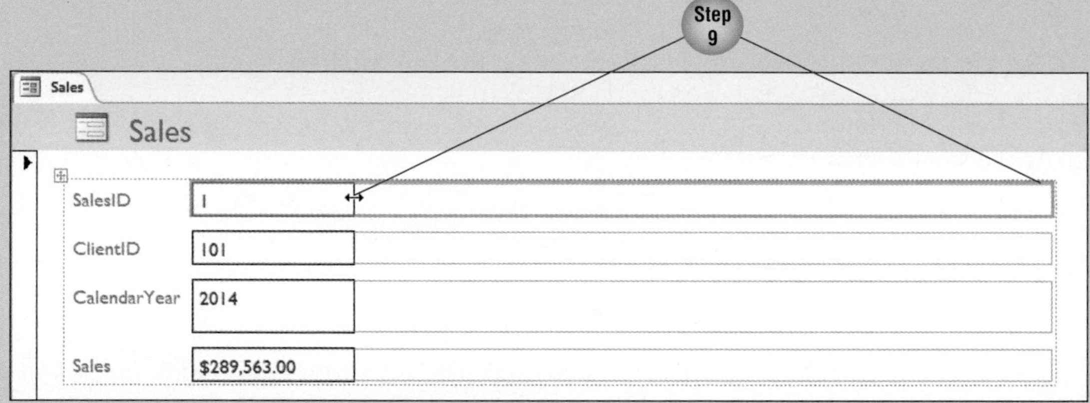

10. Change the alignment of text by completing the following steps:
    a. Right-click the selected text box control object (the object containing *1*) and then click *Select Entire Column* at the shortcut menu.
    b. Click the FORM LAYOUT TOOLS FORMAT tab.
    c. Click the Align Right button in the Font group.
11. Apply data bars to the *Sales* field by completing the following steps:
    a. Click in the text box control object containing the text *$289,563.00*.
    b. Make sure the FORM LAYOUT TOOLS FORMAT tab is active.
    c. Click the Conditional Formatting button.
    d. At the Conditional Formatting Rules Manager dialog box, click the New Rule button.
    e. At the New Formatting Rule dialog box, click the *Compare to other records* option in the *Select a rule type* list box.
    f. Click the down-pointing arrow at the right side of the *Bar color* option box and then click the *Green 4* color option (seventh column, fifth row).

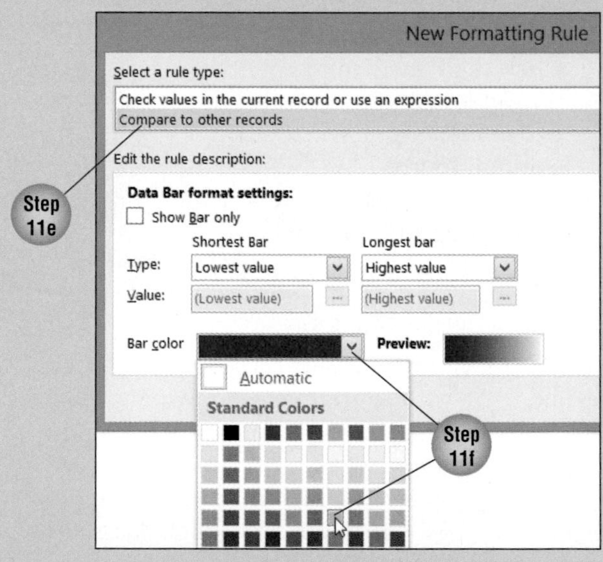

    g. Click OK to close the New Formatting Rule dialog box and then click OK to close the Conditional Formatting Rules Manager dialog box.
12. Click the Next record button in the Record Navigation bar to display the next record. Continue clicking the Next record button and notice the data bars that display in the *Sales* field.
13. Click the First record button in the Record Navigation bar.
14. Click the Save button on the Quick Access toolbar.

15. Print page 1 of the form by completing the following steps:
    a. Click the FILE tab and then click the *Print* option.
    b. Click the Print button.
    c. At the Print dialog box, click the *Pages* option in the *Print Range* section, type 1 in the *From* text box, press the Tab key, type 1 in the *To* text box, and then click OK.
16. Close the Sales form.
17. Close **AL1-C5-Dearborn.accdb**.

Project 2 Add Fields, Create a Split Form and Multiple Items Form, and Use the Form Wizard — 5 Parts

You will open the Skyline database, create a form and add related fields to the form, create a split and multiple items form, and create a form using the Form Wizard.

Adding Existing Fields

If you create a form and then realize that you forgot a field or want to insert an existing field in the form, display the form in Layout view and then click the Add Existing Fields button located in the Tools group on the FORM LAYOUT TOOLS DESIGN tab. When you click the Add Existing Fields button, the Field List task pane opens and displays at the right side of the screen. This task pane displays the fields available in the current view, fields available in related tables, and fields available in other tables. Figure 5.5 displays the Field List task pane that you will open in Project 2a.

Add Existing Fields

In the *Fields available for this view* section, Access displays all fields in any tables used to create the form. So far, you have been creating a form with all fields in one table. In the *Fields available in related tables* section, Access displays tables that are related to the table(s) used to create the form. To display the fields in the related table, click the plus symbol that displays before the table name in the Field List task pane and the list expands to display all of the field names.

Alt + F8 is the keyboard shortcut to display the Field List task pane.

To add a field to the form, double-click the desired field in the Field List task pane. This inserts the field below the existing fields in the form. You can also drag a field from the Field List task pane into the form. To do this, position the mouse pointer on the desired field in the Field List task pane, hold down the left mouse button, drag into the form window, and then release the mouse button. A pink insert indicator bar displays as you drag the field in the existing fields in the form. When you drag over a cell, the cell displays with pink fill. When the insert indicator bar is in the desired position or the desired cell is selected, release the mouse button.

Use the Field List task pane to add fields from a table or query to your form.

You can insert multiple fields in a form from the Field List task pane. To do this, hold down the Ctrl key while clicking the desired fields and then drag the fields into the form. If you try to drag a field from a table in the *Fields available in other tables* section, the Specify Relationship dialog box will display. To move a field from the Field List task pane to the form, the field must be located in a table that is related to the table(s) used to create the form.

Figure 5.5 Field List Task Pane

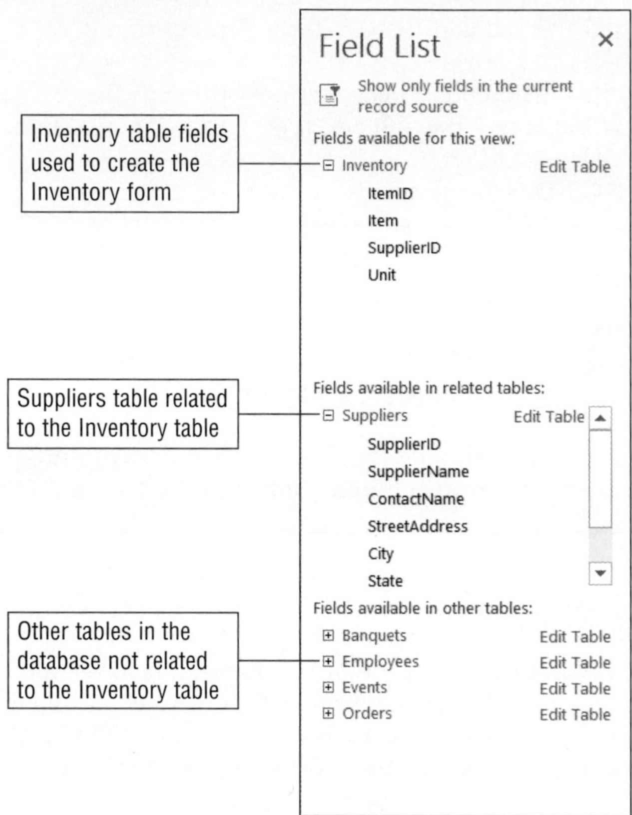

Project 2a Adding Existing Fields to a Form

Part 1 of 5

1. Display the Open dialog box with the AL1C5 folder on your storage medium the active folder, open **AL1-C5-Skyline.accdb**, and enable the contents.
2. Create a form with the Inventory table by clicking the Inventory table in the Navigation pane, clicking the CREATE tab, and then clicking the Form button in the Forms group.
3. With the text box control object containing the text *001* selected, drag the right border to the left until the selected object is approximately one-half the original width.

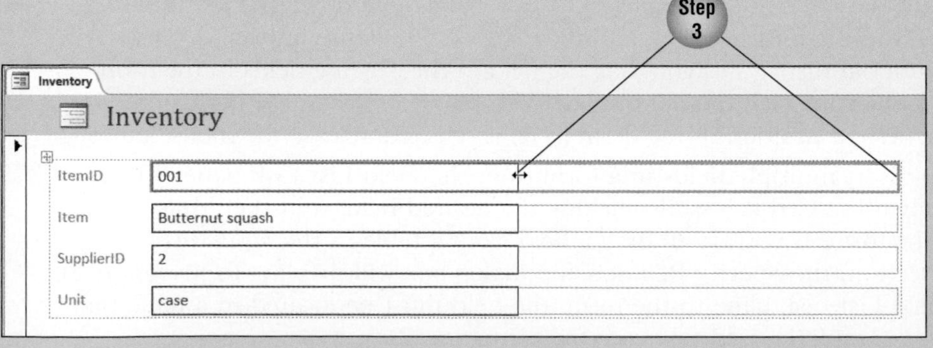

4. With the text box control object still selected, click the FORM LAYOUT TOOLS ARRANGE tab and then click the Split Horizontally button in the Merge/Split group. (This splits the text box control object into one object and one empty cell.)
5. You decide that you want to add the supplier name to the form so the name displays when the form is entered. Add the supplier name field by completing the following steps:
   a. Click the FORM LAYOUT TOOLS DESIGN tab.
   b. Click the Add Existing Fields button in the Tools group.
   c. Click the Show all tables hyperlink that displays toward the top of the Field List task pane.
   d. Click the plus symbol that displays immediately left of the Suppliers table name located in the *Fields available in related tables* section of the Field List task pane.

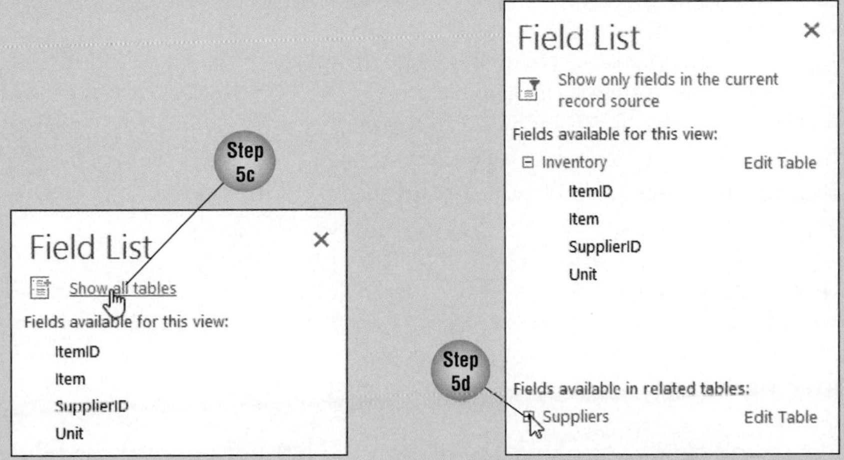

   e. Position the mouse pointer on the *SupplierName* field, hold down the left mouse button, drag into the form until the pink insert indicator bar displays immediately right of the text box control containing *2* (the text box control that displays at the right side of the *SupplierID* label control), and then release the mouse button. Access inserts the field as a Lookup field (a down-pointing arrow displays at the right side of the field).

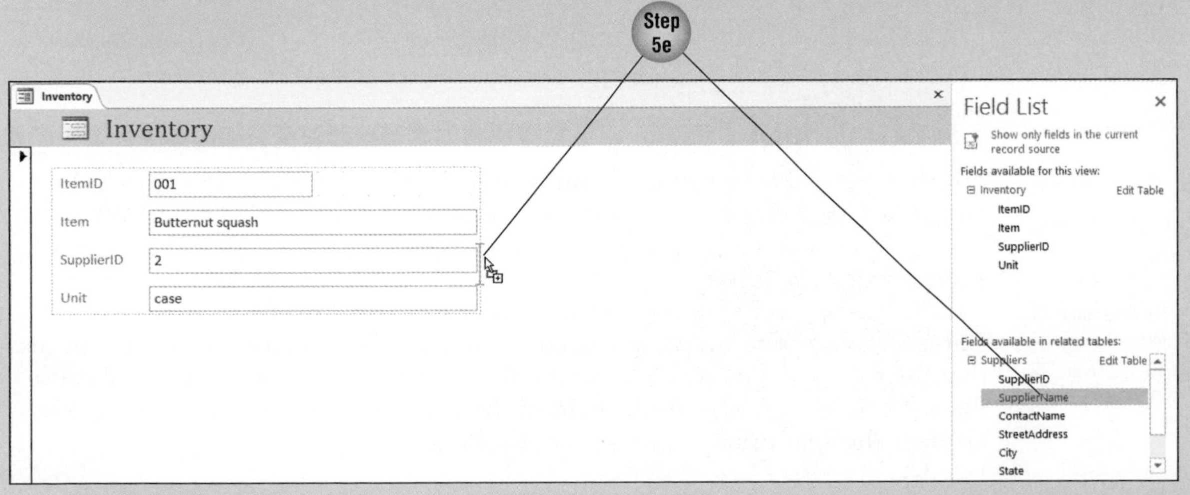

f. Change the *SupplierName* field from a Lookup field to a text box by clicking the Options button that displays below the field and then clicking *Change to Text Box* at the drop-down list. (This removes the down-pointing arrow at the right side of the field.)

g. Close the Field List task pane by clicking the Close button located in the upper right corner of the task pane.

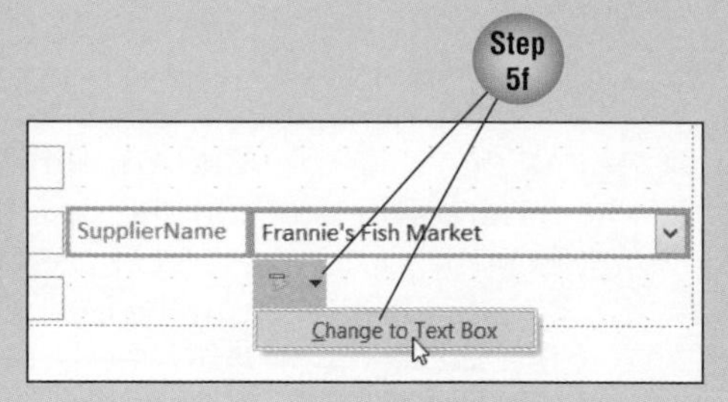

6. Insert a logo image in the *Form Header* section by completing the following steps:
   a. Right-click the logo object that displays in the *Form Header* section (located to the left of the title *Inventory*) and then click *Delete* at the shortcut menu.
   b. Click the Logo button in the Header/Footer group.
   c. At the Insert Picture dialog box, navigate to the AL1C5 folder on your storage medium and then double-click the file named ***Cityscape.jpg***.
7. Change the title by completing the following steps:
   a. Click the Title button in the Header/Footer group. (This selects *Inventory* in the *Form Header* section.)
   b. Type **Skyline Inventory Input Form** and then press Enter.
8. Insert the date and time in the *Form Header* section by clicking the Date and Time button in the Header/Footer group and then clicking OK at the Date and Time dialog box.
9. Click in any field outside the title, click the title to select the header control object, and then drag the right border of the title control object to the left until the border displays near the title.
10. Select the date and time control objects, drag in the left border until the border displays near the date and time, and then drag the objects so they are positioned near the title.
11. Scroll through the records in the form.
12. Click the First record button in the Record Navigation bar.
13. Click the Save button on the Quick Access toolbar and save the form with the name *Inventory*.
14. Print the current record.
15. Close the Inventory form.

Creating Split Forms

Quick Steps

Create a Split Form
1. Click desired table.
2. Click CREATE tab.
3. Click More Forms button.
4. Click *Split Form*.

More Forms

Another method for creating a form is to use the *Split Form* option at the More Forms button drop-down list in the Forms group on the CREATE tab. When you use this option to create a form, Access splits the screen in the work area and provides two views of the form. The top half of the work area displays the form in Layout view and the bottom half of the work area displays the form in Datasheet view. The two views are connected and are ***synchronous***, which means that displaying or modifying a specific field in the Form view portion will cause the same action to occur in the field in the Datasheet view portion. Figure 5.6 displays the split form you will create for Project 2b.

Figure 5.6 Split Form

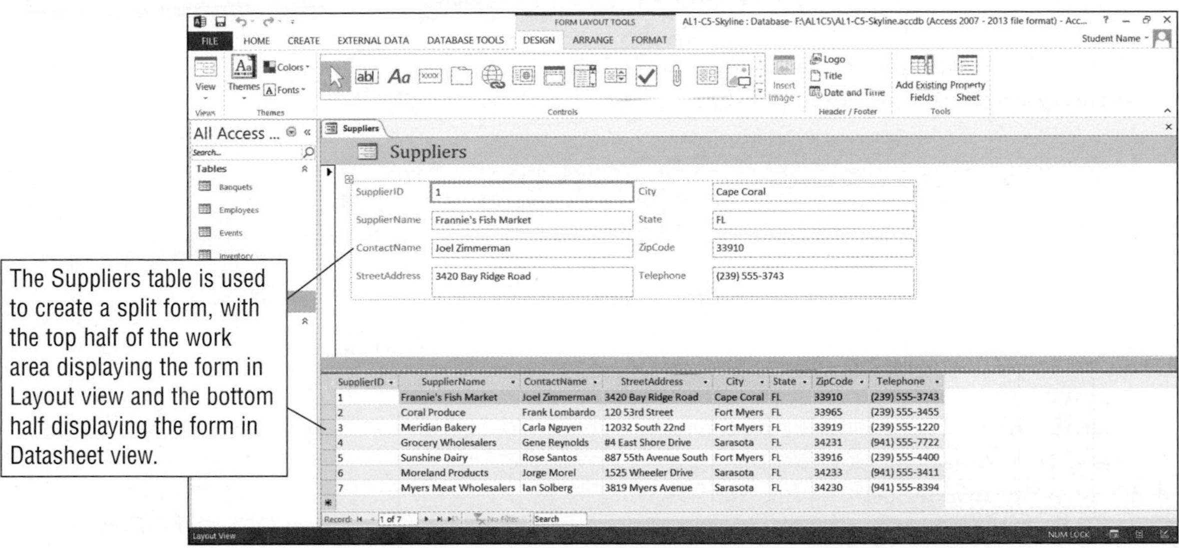

Project 2b Creating a Split Form

Part 2 of 5

1. With **AL1-C5-Skyline.accdb** open, create a split form with the Suppliers table by completing the following steps:
   a. Click the Suppliers table in the Navigation pane.
   b. Click the CREATE tab.
   c. Click the More Forms button in the Forms group and then click *Split Form* at the drop-down list.

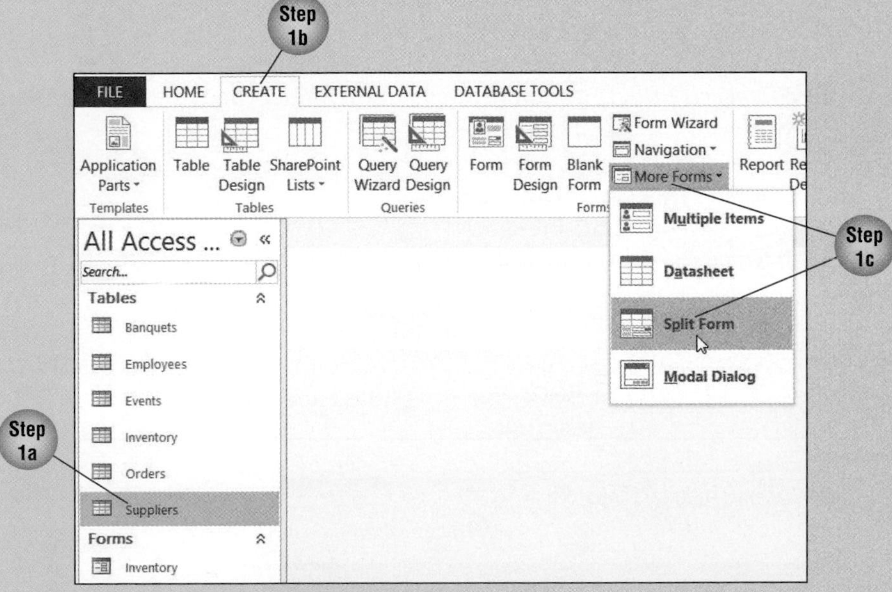

   d. Click several times on the Next record button in the Record Navigation bar. (As you display records, notice that the current record in the Form view in the top portion of the window is the same record selected in Datasheet view in the lower portion of the window.)
   e. Click the First record button.

2. Apply a theme by clicking the Themes button in the Themes group on the FORM LAYOUT TOOLS DESIGN tab and then clicking *Integral* at the drop-down gallery (third column, first row).
3. Insert a logo image in the *Form Header* section by completing the following steps:
   a. Right-click the logo object that displays in the *Form Header* section (located to the left of the title *Suppliers*) and then click *Delete* at the shortcut menu.
   b. Click the Logo button in the Header/Footer group.
   c. At the Insert Picture dialog box, navigate to the AL1C5 folder on your storage medium and then double-click ***Cityscape.jpg***.
4. Change the title by completing the following steps:
   a. Click the Title button in the Header/Footer group. (This selects *Suppliers* in the *Form Header* section.)
   b. Type **Skyline Suppliers Input Form** and then press Enter.
   c. Click in any field outside the title, click the title again to select the header control object, and then drag the right border to the left until the border displays near the title.
5. Click the text box control object containing the supplier identification number *1*, and then drag the right border of the text box control object to the left until *Lines: 1 Characters: 35* displays at the left side of the Status bar.
6. Click the text box control object containing the city *Cape Coral* and drag the right border of the text box control object to the left until *Lines: 1 Characters: 35* displays at the left side of the Status bar.
7. Insert a new record in the Suppliers form by completing the following steps:
   a. Click the View button to switch to Form view.
   b. Click the New (blank) record button in the Record Navigation bar.
   c. Click in the *SupplierID* field in the Form view portion of the window and then type the following information in the specified fields:

SupplierID	**8**
SupplierName	**Jackson Produce**
ContactName	**Marshall Jackson**
StreetAddress	**5790 Cypress Avenue**
City	**Fort Myers**
State	**FL**
ZipCode	**33917**
Telephone	**2395555002**

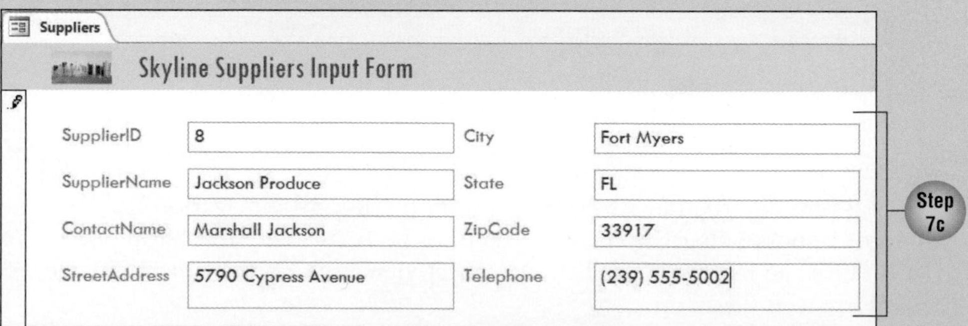

8. Click the Save button on the Quick Access toolbar and save the form with the name *Suppliers*.
9. Print the current form by completing the following steps:
   a. Click the FILE tab and then click the *Print* option.
   b. Click the Print button.
   c. At the Print dialog box, click the Setup button.
   d. At the Page Setup dialog box, click the *Print Form Only* option in the *Split Form* section of the dialog box and then click OK.
   e. At the Print dialog box, click the *Selected Record(s)* option and then click OK.
10. Close the Suppliers form.

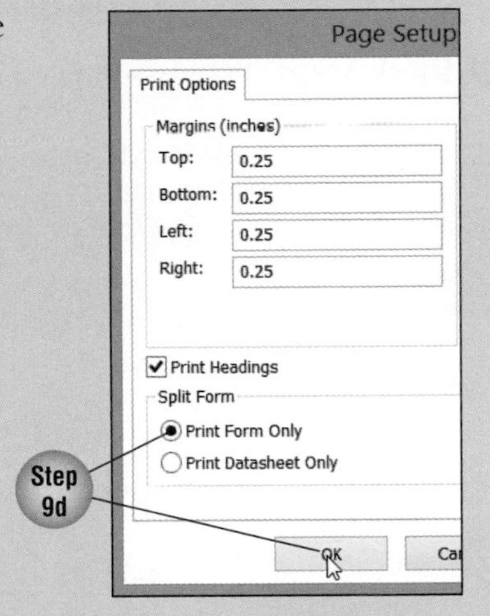

Creating Multiple Items Forms

When you create a form with the Form button, a single record displays. You can use the *Multiple Items* option at the More Forms button drop-down list to create a form that displays multiple records. The advantage to creating a multiple items form over displaying the table in Datasheet view is that you can customize the form using buttons in the FORM LAYOUT TOOLS ribbon with the DESIGN, ARRANGE, or FORMAT tab selected.

Quick Steps

Create a Multiple Items Form

1. Click desired table.
2. Click CREATE tab.
3. Click More Forms button.
4. Click *Multiple Items*.

Project 2c **Creating a Multiple Items Form** **Part 3 of 5**

1. With **AL1-C5-Skyline.accdb** open, create a multiple items form by completing the following steps:
   a. Click the Orders table in the Navigation pane.
   b. Click the CREATE tab.
   c. Click the More Forms button in the Forms group and then click *Multiple Items* at the drop-down list.
2. Insert the **Cityscape.jpg** image as the logo.
3. Insert the title *Skyline Orders*.
4. Click in any field outside the title, click the title again to select the header control object, and then drag the right border to the left until the border displays near the title.
5. Save the form with the name *Orders*.
6. Print the first page of the form by completing the following steps:
   a. Click the FILE tab and then click the *Print* option.
   b. Click the Print button.
   c. At the Print dialog box, click the *Pages* option in the *Print Range* section.
   d. Type 1 in the *From* text box, press the Tab key, and then type 1 in the *To* text box.
   e. Click OK.
7. Close the Orders form.

Creating Forms Using the Form Wizard

Quick Steps

Create a Form Using the Form Wizard
1. Click CREATE tab.
2. Click Form Wizard button.
3. Choose desired options at each Form Wizard dialog box.

Form Wizard

With the Form Wizard, you can be more selective about what fields you insert in a form.

Access offers a Form Wizard that guides you through the creation of a form. To create a form using the Form Wizard, click the CREATE tab and then click the Form Wizard button in the Forms group. At the first Form Wizard dialog box, shown in Figure 5.7, specify the table and then the fields you want included in the form. To select the table, click the down-pointing arrow at the right side of the *Table/Queries* option box and then click the desired table. Select the desired field in the *Available Fields* list box and then click the button containing the One Field button (the button containing the greater-than [>] symbol). This inserts the field in the *Selected Fields* list box. Continue in this manner until you have inserted all of the desired fields in the *Selected Fields* list box. If you want to insert all of the fields into the *Selected Fields* list box at one time, click the All Fields button (the button containing two greater-than symbols). After specifying the fields, click the Next button.

At the second Form Wizard dialog box, specify the layout for the records. You can choose from these layout type options: *Columnar*, *Tabular*, *Datasheet*, and *Justified*. Click the Next button and the third and final Form Wizard dialog box displays. It offers a title for the form and also provides the option *Open the form to view or enter information*. Make any necessary changes in this dialog box and then click the Finish button.

Figure 5.7 First Form Wizard Dialog Box

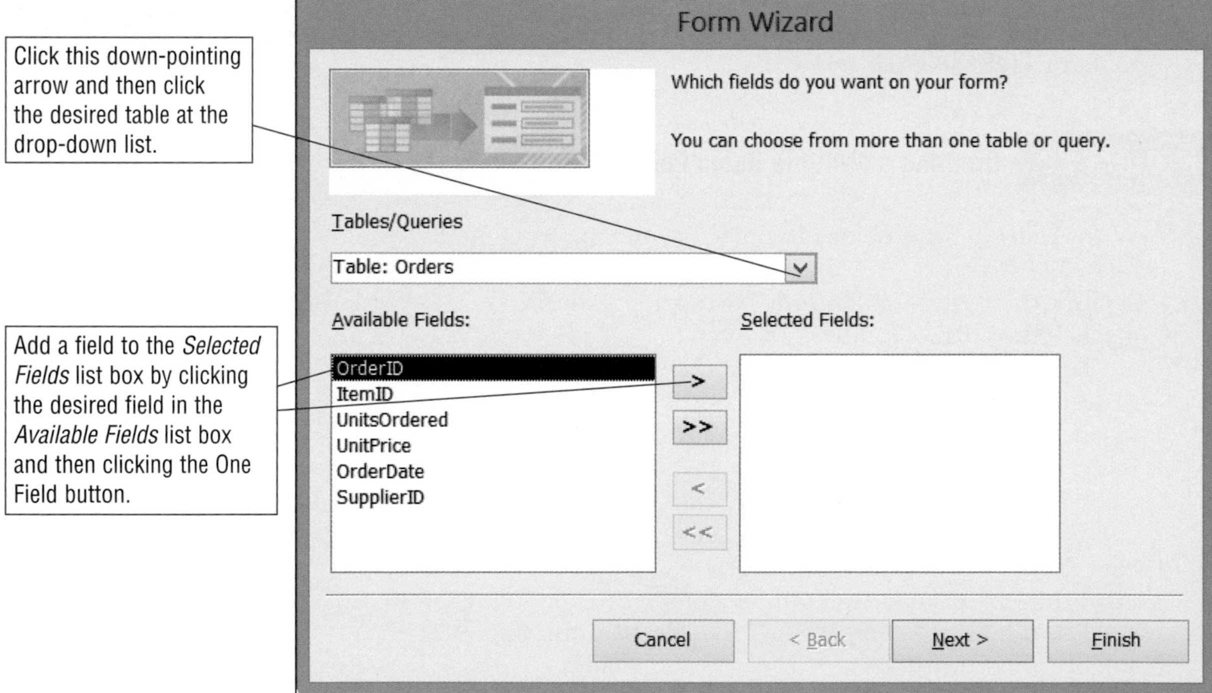

Project 2d Creating a Form Using the Form Wizard

Part 4 of 5

1. With **AL1-C5-Skyline.accdb** open, create a form with the Form Wizard by completing the following steps:
   a. Click the CREATE tab.
   b. Click the Form Wizard button in the Forms group.
   c. At the first Form Wizard dialog box, click the down-pointing arrow at the right side of the *Tables/Queries* option box and then click *Table: Employees* at the drop-down list.
   d. Specify that you want all of the fields included in the form by clicking the All Fields button (the button containing the two greater-than symbols).
   e. Click the Next button.
   f. At the second Form Wizard dialog box, click the *Justified* option and then click the Next button.

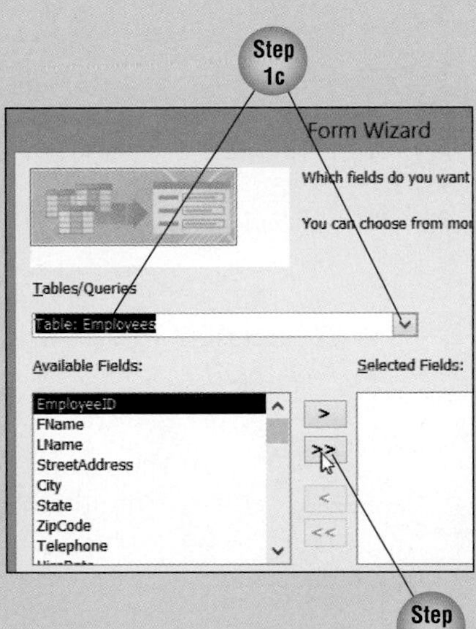

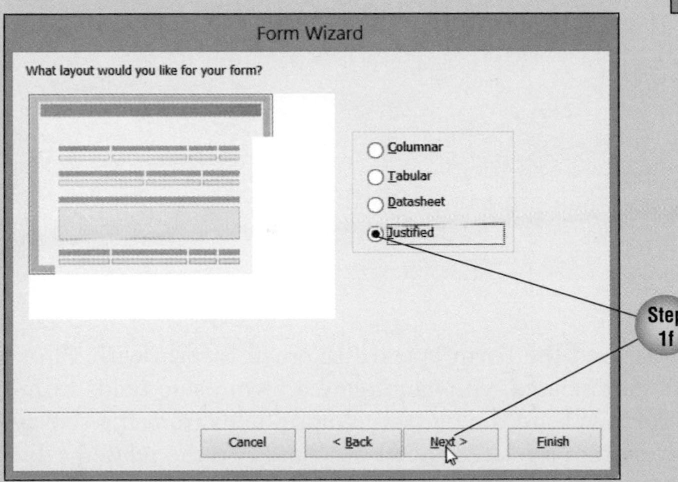

   g. At the third and final Form Wizard dialog box, click the Finish button.
2. Format the field headings by completing the following steps:
   a. Click the View button to switch to Layout view.
   b. Click the *EmployeeID* label control object. (This selects the object.)
   c. Hold down the Ctrl key and then click on each of the following label control objects: *FName*, *LName*, *StreetAddress*, *City*, *State*, *ZipCode*, *Telephone*, *HireDate*, and *HealthIns*.
   d. With all of the label control objects selected, release the Ctrl key.
   e. Click the FORM LAYOUT TOOLS FORMAT tab.
   f. Click the Shape Fill button and then click the *Aqua Blue 2* color option (ninth column, third row in the *Standard Colors* section).
   g. Click the FORM LAYOUT TOOLS DESIGN tab and then click the View button to switch to Form view.

3. In Form view, click the New (blank) record button and then add the following records:

EmployeeID	**13**
FName	**Carol**
LName	**Thompson**
StreetAddress	**6554 Willow Drive, Apt. B**
City	**Fort Myers**
State	**FL**
ZipCode	**33915**
Telephone	**2395553719**
HireDate	**10/1/2015**
HealthIns	(Click in the check box to insert a check mark.)
EmployeeID	**14**
FName	**Eric**
LName	**Hahn**
StreetAddress	**331 South 152nd Street**
City	**Cape Coral**
State	**FL**
ZipCode	**33906**
Telephone	**2395558107**
HireDate	**10/1/2015**
HealthIns	(Leave blank.)

4. Click the Save button on the Quick Access toolbar.
5. Print the record for Eric Hahn and then print the record for Carol Thompson.
6. Close the Employees form.

In Project 2d, you used the Form Wizard to create a form with all of the fields in one table. If tables are related, you can create a form using fields from related tables. At the first Form Wizard dialog box, choose fields from the selected table and then choose fields from a related table. To change to the related table, click the down-pointing arrow at the right of the *Tables/Queries* option box and then click the name of the desired table.

Project 2e Creating a Form with Related Tables

Part 5 of 5

1. With **AL1-C5-Skyline.accdb** open, create a form with related tables by completing the following steps:
   a. Click the CREATE tab.
   b. Click the Form Wizard button in the Forms group.
   c. At the first Form Wizard dialog box, click the down-pointing arrow at the right of the *Tables/Queries* option box and then click *Table: Banquets*.
   d. Click *ResDate* in the *Available Fields* list box and then click the One Field button. (This inserts *ResDate* in the *Selected Fields* list box.)
   e. Click *AmountTotal* in the *Available Fields* list box, click the One Field button.
   f. With *AmountPaid* selected in the *Available Fields* list box, click the One Field button.
   g. Click the down-pointing arrow at the right side of the *Tables/Queries* option box and then click *Table: Events* at the drop-down list.
   h. Click *Event* in the *Available Fields* list box and then click the One Field button.
   i. Click the down-pointing arrow at the right side of the *Tables/Queries* option box and then click *Table: Employees* at the drop-down list.
   j. Click *LName* in the *Available Fields* list box and then click the One Field button.
   k. Click the Next button.
   l. At the second Form Wizard dialog box, click the Next button.
   m. At the third Form Wizard dialog box, click the Next button.
   n. At the fourth Form Wizard dialog box, select the text in the *What title do you want for your form?* text box, type **Upcoming Banquets**, and then click the Finish button.
2. When the first record displays, print the record.
3. Save and then close the form.
4. Close **AL1-C5-Skyline.accdb**.

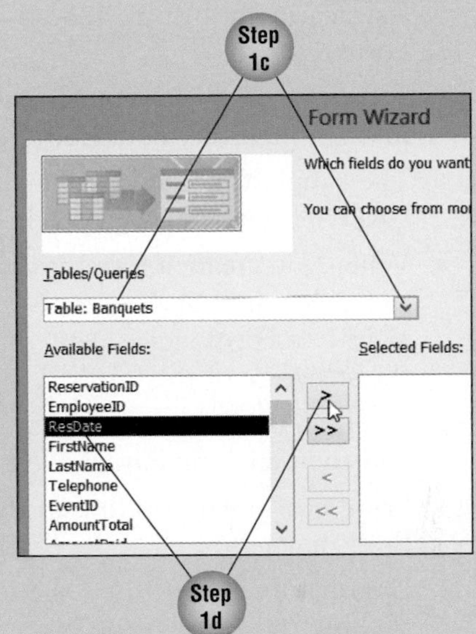

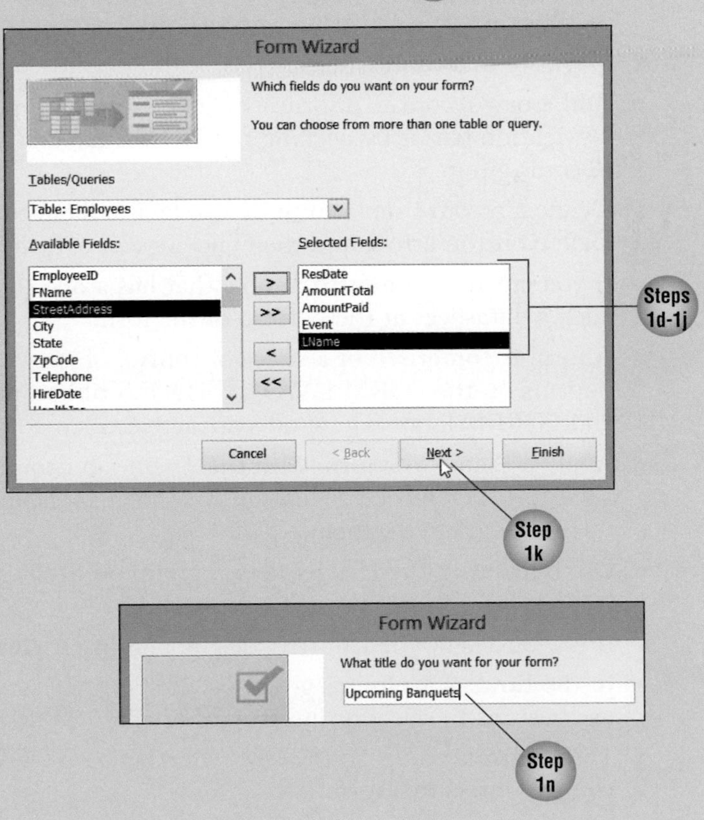

Chapter Summary

- Creating a form generally improves the ease of entering data into a table. Some methods for creating a form include using the Form, Split Form, and Multiple Items buttons or the Form Wizard.
- A form is an object you can use to enter and edit data in a table or query and to help prevent incorrect data from being entered in a database.
- The simplest method for creating a form is to click a table in the Navigation pane, click the CREATE button, and then click the Form button in the Forms group.
- When you create a form, it displays in Layout view. Use this view to display data and modify the appearance and contents of the form. Other form views include Form view and Design view. Use Form view to enter and manage records and use Design view to view and modify the structure of the form.
- Open an existing form in Layout view by right-clicking the form in the Navigation pane and then clicking *Layout View* at the shortcut menu.
- Print a form with options at the Print dialog box. To print an individual record, display the Print dialog box, click the *Selected Record(s)* option, and then click OK.
- Delete a form with the Delete button in the Records group on the HOME tab or by right-clicking the form in the Navigation pane and then clicking *Delete* at the shortcut menu. A message may display asking you to confirm the deletion.
- Navigate in a form with buttons in the Record Navigation bar.
- Add a new record to a form by clicking the New (blank) record button in the Record Navigation bar or by clicking the HOME tab and then clicking the New button in the Records group.
- Delete a record from a form by displaying the record, clicking the HOME tab, clicking the Delete button arrow, and then clicking *Delete Record* at the drop-down list.
- If you create a form with a table that has a one-to-many relationship established, Access adds a datasheet at the bottom of the form.
- A form is comprised of a series of control objects. Customize these control objects with buttons on the FORM LAYOUT TOOLS ribbon under the DESIGN tab, ARRANGE tab, and FORMAT tab. These tabs are active when a form displays in Layout view.
- Apply a theme to a form with the Themes button in the Themes group on the FORM LAYOUT TOOLS DESIGN tab. Use the Colors and Fonts buttons in the Themes group to further customize a theme.
- Use buttons in the Header/Footer group on the FORM LAYOUT TOOLS DESIGN tab to insert a logo, form title, and date and time.
- In Layout view, you can size, delete, and insert control objects.
- In the Rows & Columns group on the FORM LAYOUT TOOLS ARRANGE tab, you can use buttons to select or insert rows or columns.
- The Controls group on the FORM LAYOUT TOOLS DESIGN tab contains control objects you can insert in a form.
- Merge cells in a form by selecting cells and then clicking the Merge button in the Merge/Split group on the FORM LAYOUT TOOLS ARRANGE tab. Split selected cells by clicking the Split Vertically or Split Horizontally button.

- Format control objects and cells in a form with buttons on the FORM LAYOUT TOOLS FORMAT tab.
- Use the Conditional Formatting button in the Control Formatting group on the FORM LAYOUT TOOLS FORMAT tab to apply specific formatting to data that matches a specific criterion.
- Click the Add Existing Fields button in the Tools group on the FORM LAYOUT TOOLS DESIGN tab to display the Field List task pane. Add fields to the form by double-clicking a field or dragging the field from the task pane.
- Create a split form by clicking the More Forms button on the CREATE tab and then clicking *Split Form* in the drop-down list. Access displays the form in Form view in the top portion of the work area and in Datasheet view in the bottom portion of the work area. The two views are connected and synchronous.
- Create a Multiple Items form by clicking the More Forms button on the CREATE tab and then clicking *Multiple Items* in the drop-down list.
- The Form Wizard walks you through the steps for creating a form and lets you specify the fields you want included in the form, a layout for the records, and a name for the form.
- You can create a form with the Form Wizard that contains fields from tables connected by a one-to-many relationship.

Commands Review

FEATURE	RIBBON TAB, GROUP	BUTTON, OPTION
Conditional Formatting Rules Manager dialog box	FORM LAYOUT TOOLS FORMAT, Control Formatting	
Field List task pane	FORM LAYOUT TOOLS DESIGN, Tools	
form	CREATE, Forms	
Form Wizard	CREATE, Forms	
multiple items form	CREATE, Forms	, *Multiple Items*
split form	CREATE, Forms	, *Split Form*

Concepts Check Test Your Knowledge

Completion: In the space provided at the right, indicate the correct term, symbol, or command.

1. The simplest method for creating a form is to click this tab and then click the Form button. ____________
2. When you click the Form button to create a form, the form displays in this view. ____________
3. To print the current record in a form, click this option at the Print dialog box and then click OK. ____________
4. Navigate in a form using buttons in this bar. ____________
5. Click this button to add a new record to a form. ____________
6. The FORM LAYOUT TOOLS DESIGN tab is active when a form displays in this view. ____________
7. The Themes group on the FORM LAYOUT TOOLS DESIGN tab contains three buttons: the Themes button, the Colors button, and this button. ____________
8. Click the Logo button on the FORM LAYOUT TOOLS DESIGN tab and this dialog box displays. ____________
9. To select nonadjacent objects or cells, hold down this key on the keyboard while clicking the desired objects or cells. ____________
10. This group on the FORM LAYOUT TOOLS ARRANGE tab contains buttons for selecting and inserting rows and columns in a form. ____________
11. With this button in the Control Formatting group on the FORM LAYOUT TOOLS FORMAT tab, you can apply formatting to data that meets a specific criterion. ____________
12. Click the Add Existing Fields button in the Tools group on the FORM LAYOUT TOOLS DESIGN tab and this task pane displays. ____________
13. Create a split form or multiple items form with options at this button's drop-down list. ____________
14. When you create a form with the *Split Form* option, the form displays in this view in the top half of the work area. ____________

Skills Check Assess Your Performance

Assessment 1

CREATE AND CUSTOMIZE A SALES FORM

1. Display the Open dialog box with the AL1C5 folder on your storage medium the active folder.
2. Open **AL1-C5-PacTrek.accdb** and enable the contents.
3. Use the Form button in the Forms group on the CREATE tab to create a form with the Suppliers table.
4. Switch to Form view and then add the following records to the Suppliers form:

SupplierID	**12**
SupplierName	**Seaside Suppliers**
StreetAddress	**4120 Shoreline Drive**
City	**Vancouver**
Prov/State	**BC**
PostalCode	**V2V 8K4**
EmailAddress	**seaside@emcp.net**
Telephone	**6045557945**

SupplierID	**34**
SupplierName	**Carson Company**
StreetAddress	**120 Plaza Center**
City	**Vancouver**
Prov/State	**BC**
PostalCode	**V2V 1K6**
EmailAddress	**carson@emcp.net**
Telephone	**6045551955**

5. Delete the record containing information on Manning, Inc.
6. Switch to Layout view and then apply the Organic theme to the form.
7. Select and delete the logo object in the *Form Header* section and then click the Logo button in the Header/Footer group. At the Insert Picture dialog box, navigate to the AL1C5 folder on your storage medium and then double-click ***River.jpg***.
8. Create the title *Pacific Trek Suppliers* for the form. Click in any field outside the title and then click in the title (which selects the header control object). Drag the right border of the title control object to the left until the border displays near the title.
9. Insert the date and time in the *Form Header* section.
10. Select the date and time control objects, drag in the left border until the border displays near the date and time, and then drag the objects so they are positioned near the title.
11. Click the text box control object containing the supplier number and then drag the right border to the left until *Lines: 1 Characters: 30* displays at the left side of the Status bar.

12. Select the fields in the first column (*SupplierID* through *Telephone*) and then apply the following formatting:
    a. Apply bold formatting.
    b. Apply the Dark Blue font color (ninth column, bottom row in the *Standard Colors* section).
    c. Apply the Align Right alignment.
    d. Apply the Light Blue 2 shape fill (fifth column, third row in the *Standard Colors* section).
    e. Apply the Dark Blue shape outline color (ninth column, bottom row in the *Standard Colors* section).
13. Select the second column and then apply the following formatting:
    a. Apply the Light Blue 1 shape fill (fifth column, second row in the *Standard Colors* section).
    b. Apply the Dark Blue shape outline color (ninth column, bottom row in the *Standard Colors* section).
14. Switch to Form view.
15. Save the form with the name *Suppliers*.
16. Make active the record for supplier number 12 (one of the new records you entered) and then print the record. (Make sure you print only the record for supplier number 12.)
17. Make active the record for supplier number 34 and then print the record.
18. Close the Suppliers table.

Assessment 2

CREATE AND CUSTOMIZE AN ORDERS FORM

1. With **AL1-C5-PacTrek.accdb** open, create a form with the Orders table using the Form button on the CREATE tab.
2. Insert a field from a related table by completing the following steps:
    a. Display the Field List task pane and then, if necessary, click the Show all tables hyperlink.
    b. Expand the Suppliers table in the *Fields available in related tables* section.
    c. Drag the field named *SupplierName* into the form and position it between *SupplierID* and *ProductID*.
    d. Change the *SupplierName* field from a Lookup field to a text box by clicking the Options button that displays below the field and then clicking *Change to Text Box* at the drop-down list.
    e. Close the Field List task pane.
3. Click the text box control object containing the text *1010* and then drag the right border to the left until *Lines: 1 Characters: 30* displays at the left side of the Status bar.
4. Select all of the objects in the *Detail* section by clicking an object in the *Detail* section and then clicking the table move handle (the small, square button with a four-headed arrow inside). With the objects selected, apply the following formatting:
    a. Change the font to Cambria and the font size to 12 points.
    b. Apply the Align Right alignment.

5. Select the first column and then apply the following formatting:
   a. Apply the Green 2 shape fill (seventh column, third row in the *Standard Colors* section).
   b. Apply bold formatting.
6. Apply conditional formatting that changes the font color to blue for any *Amount* field entry that contains an amount greater than $999. ***Hint: Click the text box control object containing the amount $199.50, click the Conditional Formatting button, click the New Rule button, change the second option in the* Edit the rule description *section to* greater than, *and then enter 999 in the third option box (without the dollar sign).***
7. Save the form with the name *Orders*.
8. Print the fifteenth record in the form and then close the form.

Assessment

3 CREATE A SPLIT FORM WITH THE PRODUCTS TABLE

1. With **AL1-C5-PacTrek.accdb** open, create a form with the Products table using the *Split Form* option from the More Forms button drop-down list.
2. Decrease the width of the second column until *Lines: 1 Characters: 35* displays at the left side of the Status bar
3. Select the first column and then apply the following formatting:
   a. Apply bold formatting.
   b. Apply the Aqua Blue 1 shape fill (ninth column, second row in the *Standard Colors* section).
   c. Apply the Blue shape outline color (eighth column, bottom row in the *Standard Colors* section).
4. Click in the text box control object containing the number *0* (the *UnitsOnOrder* number) and then apply conditional formatting that displays the number in red in any field value equal to zero.
5. Change to Form view, create a new record, and then enter the following information in the specified fields:

ProductID	**205-CS**
Product	**Timberline solo cook set**
SupplierID	**15**
UnitsInStock	**8**
UnitsOnOrder	**0**
ReorderLevel	**5**

6. Save the form with the name *Products*.
7. Print the current record (the record you just typed). ***Hint: At the Print dialog box, click the Setup button. At the Page Setup dialog box, click the* Print Form Only *option.***
8. Close the Products form.
9. Close **AL1-C5-PacTrek.accdb**.

Assessment

4 CREATE AND CUSTOMIZE AN EMPLOYEES FORM

Grade It

1. Open **AL1-C5-Griffin.accdb** from the AL1C5 folder on your storage medium and enable the contents.
2. Suppose you want to create a form for entering employee information but you do not want to include the employees' salaries, since that is confidential information and accessible only to the account manager. Use the Form Wizard to create an Employees form that includes all fields *except* the *AnnualSalary* field and name the form *Employees*.
3. Type a new record with the following information in the specified fields:

EmpID	**1099**
LastName	**Williamson**
FirstName	**Carrie**
BirthDate	**6/24/1986**
HireDate	**8/1/2014**
DeptID	**RD**

4. Switch to layout view, apply the Slice theme, change the theme colors to *Blue Warm*, and change the theme fonts to *Franklin Gothic*.
5. Print the new record you typed.
6. Close the Employees form.

Visual Benchmark Demonstrate Your Proficiency

CREATE AND FORMAT A PROPERTIES FORM

1. Open **AL1-C5-SunProperties.accdb** located in the AL1C5 folder on your storage medium and enable the contents.
2. Create a form with the Properties table and format the form so it appears similar to the form in Figure 5.8 using the following specifications:
   a. Apply the Facet theme and apply the Paper theme colors.
   b. Insert the logo, title, date, and time in the *Form Header* section, as shown in the figure. (Insert the file **SunPropLogo.jpg** for the logo. Adjust the size of the title control object and then move the date and time, as shown in the figure.)
   c. Select all of the objects in the *Detail* section and then change the font color to Maroon 5 (sixth column, sixth row in the *Standard Colors* section).
   d. Select the first column; apply bold formatting; apply Light Yellow, Background 2, Darker 10% shape fill (third column, second row in the *Theme Colors* section); apply the Maroon 5 shape outline color (sixth column, sixth row in the *Standard Colors* section); and then change the alignment to Align Right.

e. Decrease the size of the second column as shown in the figure.
f. Insert a new column to the right of the second column, merge cells in the new column to accommodate the sun image, and then insert the image **SunProp.jpg** (as a control object). Adjust the width of the third column so the image displays as shown in Figure 5.8.
g. Apply conditional formatting to the *MoRent* field that displays in green any rent amount greater than $999.
h. Adjust the position of the control objects so that the form displays similar to what is shown in Figure 5.8.

3. Save the form with the name *Properties* and then print the current record.
4. Close the form and then close **AL1-C5-SunProperties.accdb**.

Figure 5.8 Visual Benchmark

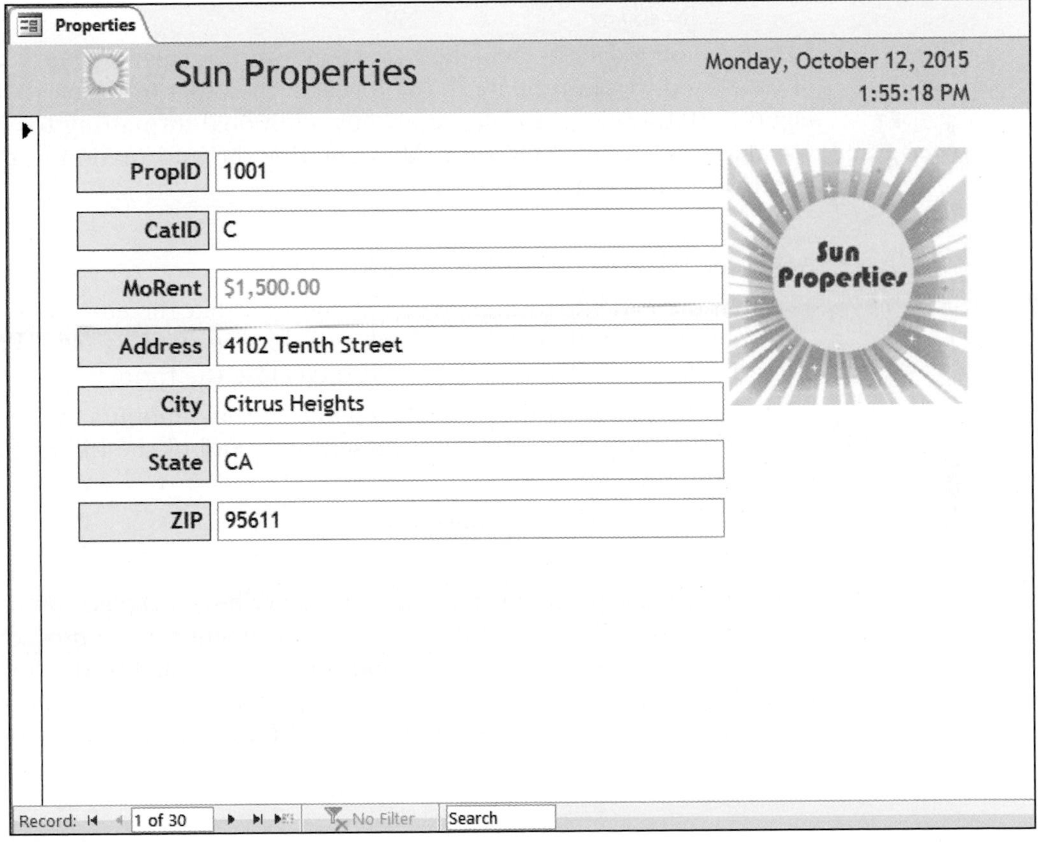

Case Study Apply Your Skills

Part 1

You are the office manager at the Lewis Vision Care Center and your center is switching over to Access to manage files. You have already created four basic tables and now need to create relationships and enter data. Open **AL1-C5-LewisCenter.accdb** and then create the following relationships between tables (enforce referential integrity and cascade fields and records):

Field Name	**"One" Table**	**"Many" Table**
PatientID	Patients	Billing
ServiceID	Services	Billing
DoctorID	Doctors	Billing

Save and then print the relationships.

Part 2

Before entering data in the tables, create a form for each table and apply a theme of your choosing. Enter data in the forms in the order in which it appears in Figure 5.10 on the next page. Apply any additional formatting to enhance the visual appearance of each form. After entering the information in the forms, print the first record of each form.

Part 3

Apply the following conditions to fields in forms:

- In the Patients form, apply the condition that the city *Tulsa* displays in red and the city *Broken Arrow* displays in blue in the *City* field. Print the first record of the Patients form and then close the form.
- In the Billing form, apply the condition that amounts in the *Fee* field over $99 display in green. Print the second record of the Billing form and then close the form.

Close **AL1-C5-LewisCenter.accdb**.

Part 4

Your center has a procedures manual that describes workplace processes and procedures. Open Word and then create a document for the procedures manual that describes the formatting and conditions you applied to the forms in **AL1-C5-LewisCenter.accdb**. Save the completed document and name it **AL1-C5-CS-Manual**. Print and then close **AL1-C5-CS-Manual.docx**.

Figure 5.10 Case Study Part 2

Patients form

Patient number 030
Rhonda J. Mahler
130 East 41st Street
Tulsa, OK 74155
(918) 555-3107

Patient number 076
Patrick S. Robbins
3281 Aspen Avenue
Tulsa, OK 74108
(918) 555-9672

Patient number 092
Oren L. Vargas
21320 Tenth Street
Broken Arrow, OK 74012
(918) 555-1188

Patient number 085
Michael A. Dempsey
506 Houston Street
Tulsa, OK 74142
(918) 555-5541

Patient number 074
Wendy L. Holloway
23849 22nd Street
Broken Arrow, OK 74009
(918) 555-8842

Patient number 023
Maggie M. Winters
4422 South 121st
Tulsa, OK 74142
(918) 555-8833

Doctors form

Doctor number 1
Carolyn Joswick
(918) 555-4772

Doctor number 2
Gerald Ingram
(918) 555-9890

Doctor number 3
Kay Feather
(918) 555-7762

Doctor number 4
Sean Granger
(918) 555-1039

Doctor number 5
Jerome Deltoro
(918) 555-8021

Services form

Co = Consultation
C = Cataract Testing
V = Vision Screening
S = Surgery
G = Glaucoma Testing
E = Emergency

Billing form

Patient number 076
Doctor number 2
Date of visit = 4/1/2015
Service ID = C
Fee = $85

Patient number 076
Doctor number 3
Date of visit = 4/1/2015
Service ID = V
Fee = $150

Patient number 085
Doctor number 1
Date of visit = 4/1/2015
Service ID = Co
Fee = $0

Patient number 074
Doctor number 3
Date of visit = 4/1/2015
Service ID = V
Fee = $150

Patient number 023
Doctor number 5
Date of visit = 4/1/2015
Service ID = S
Fee = $750

Patient number 092
Doctor number 1
Date of visit = 4/1/2015
Service ID = G
Fee = $85

MICROSOFT®

ACCESS®

Creating Reports and Mailing Labels

PERFORMANCE OBJECTIVES

Upon successful completion of Chapter 6, you will be able to:

- **Create a report using the Report button**
- **Display a report in Print Preview**
- **Create a report with a query**
- **Format and customize a report**
- **Group and sort records in a report**
- **Create a report using the Report Wizard**
- **Create mailing labels using the Label Wizard**

Tutorials

6.1 Creating and Editing a Report
6.2 Modifying a Report
6.3 Adding a Calculation to a Report
6.4 Applying Conditional Formatting to a Report
6.5 Grouping, Sorting, and Adding Totals to a Report
6.6 Creating a Report Using the Report Wizard
6.7 Creating Mailing Labels

In this chapter, you will learn how to prepare reports from data in a table using the Report button in the Reports group on the CREATE tab and using the Report Wizard. You will also learn how to format and customize a report and create mailing labels using the Label Wizard. Model answers for this chapter's projects appear on the following pages.

Note: Before beginning the projects, copy to your storage medium the AL1C6 subfolder from the AL1 folder on the CD that accompanies this textbook and make AL1C6 the active folder.

Project 1 Create and Customize Reports Using Tables and Queries

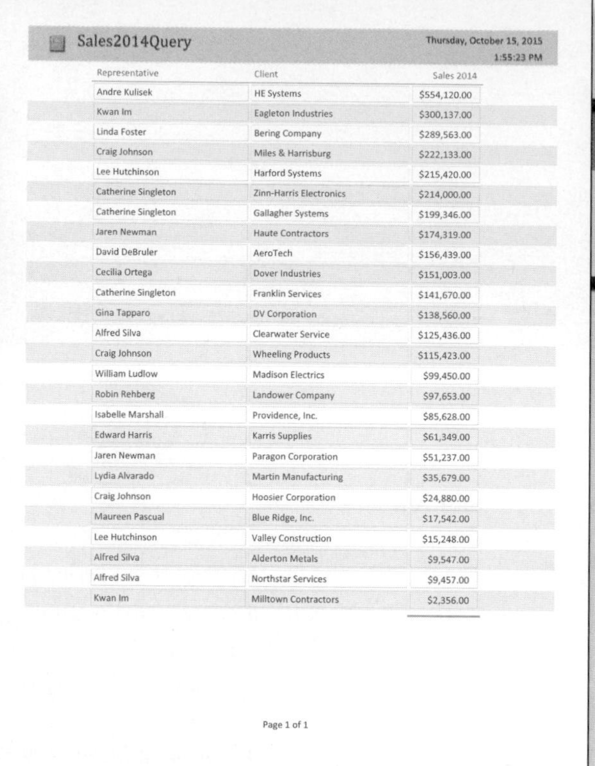

Sales2014Query — Thursday, October 15, 2015 1:55:23 PM

Representative	Client	Sales 2014
Andre Kulisek	HE Systems	$554,120.00
Kwan Im	Eagleton Industries	$300,137.00
Linda Foster	Bering Company	$289,563.00
Craig Johnson	Miles & Harrisburg	$222,133.00
Lee Hutchinson	Harford Systems	$215,420.00
Catherine Singleton	Zinn-Harris Electronics	$214,000.00
Catherine Singleton	Gallagher Systems	$199,346.00
Jaren Newman	Haute Contractors	$174,319.00
David DeBruler	AeroTech	$156,439.00
Cecilia Ortega	Dover Industries	$151,003.00
Catherine Singleton	Franklin Services	$141,670.00
Gina Tapparo	DV Corporation	$138,560.00
Alfred Silva	Clearwater Service	$125,436.00
Craig Johnson	Wheeling Products	$115,423.00
William Ludlow	Madison Electrics	$99,450.00
Robin Rehberg	Landower Company	$97,653.00
Isabelle Marshall	Providence, Inc.	$85,628.00
Edward Harris	Karris Supplies	$61,349.00
Jaren Newman	Paragon Corporation	$51,237.00
Lydia Alvarado	Martin Manufacturing	$35,679.00
Craig Johnson	Hoosier Corporation	$24,880.00
Maureen Pascual	Blue Ridge, Inc.	$17,542.00
Lee Hutchinson	Valley Construction	$15,248.00
Alfred Silva	Alderton Metals	$9,547.00
Alfred Silva	Northstar Services	$9,457.00
Kwan Im	Milltown Contractors	$2,356.00

Page 1 of 1

Project 1b, Dearborn 2014Sales Report

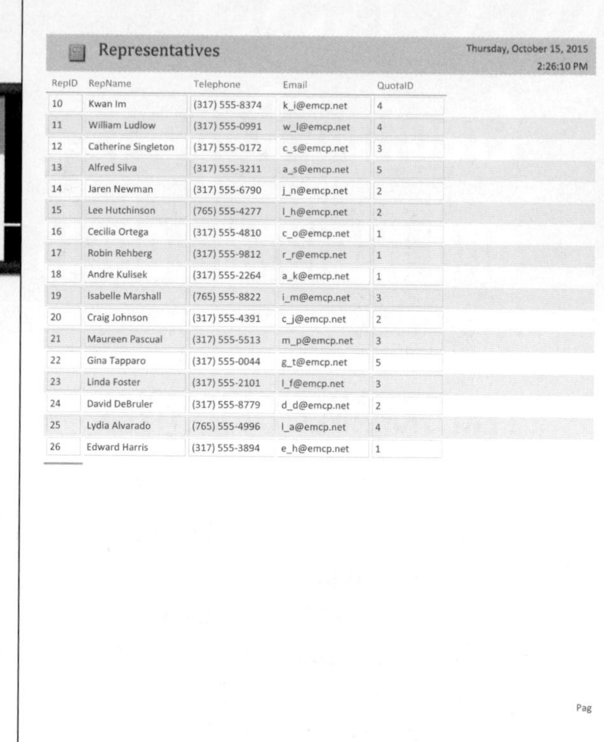

Representatives — Thursday, October 15, 2015 2:26:10 PM

RepID	RepName	Telephone	Email	QuotaID
10	Kwan Im	(317) 555-8374	k_i@emcp.net	4
11	William Ludlow	(317) 555-0991	w_l@emcp.net	4
12	Catherine Singleton	(317) 555-0172	c_s@emcp.net	3
13	Alfred Silva	(317) 555-3211	a_s@emcp.net	5
14	Jaren Newman	(317) 555-6790	j_n@emcp.net	2
15	Lee Hutchinson	(765) 555-4277	l_h@emcp.net	2
16	Cecilia Ortega	(317) 555-4810	c_o@emcp.net	1
17	Robin Rehberg	(317) 555-9812	r_r@emcp.net	1
18	Andre Kulisek	(317) 555-2264	a_k@emcp.net	1
19	Isabelle Marshall	(765) 555-8822	i_m@emcp.net	3
20	Craig Johnson	(317) 555-4391	c_j@emcp.net	2
21	Maureen Pascual	(317) 555-5513	m_p@emcp.net	3
22	Gina Tapparo	(317) 555-0044	g_t@emcp.net	5
23	Linda Foster	(317) 555-2101	l_f@emcp.net	3
24	David DeBruler	(317) 555-8779	d_d@emcp.net	2
25	Lydia Alvarado	(765) 555-4996	l_a@emcp.net	4
26	Edward Harris	(317) 555-3894	e_h@emcp.net	1

Pag

Project 1b, Dearborn Representatives Report

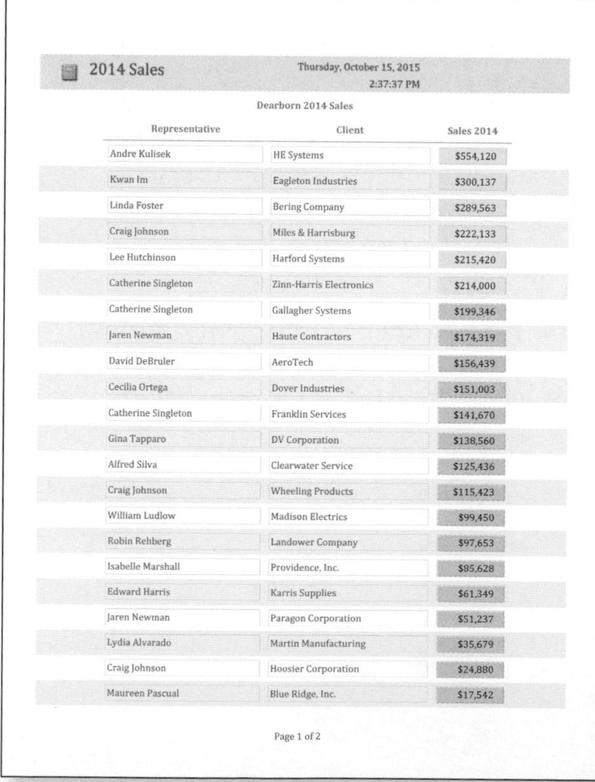

2014 Sales — Thursday, October 15, 2015 2:37:37 PM

Dearborn 2014 Sales

Representative	Client	Sales 2014
Andre Kulisek	HE Systems	$554,120
Kwan Im	Eagleton Industries	$300,137
Linda Foster	Bering Company	$289,563
Craig Johnson	Miles & Harrisburg	$222,133
Lee Hutchinson	Harford Systems	$215,420
Catherine Singleton	Zinn-Harris Electronics	$214,000
Catherine Singleton	Gallagher Systems	$199,346
Jaren Newman	Haute Contractors	$174,319
David DeBruler	AeroTech	$156,439
Cecilia Ortega	Dover Industries	$151,003
Catherine Singleton	Franklin Services	$141,670
Gina Tapparo	DV Corporation	$138,560
Alfred Silva	Clearwater Service	$125,436
Craig Johnson	Wheeling Products	$115,423
William Ludlow	Madison Electrics	$99,450
Robin Rehberg	Landower Company	$97,653
Isabelle Marshall	Providence, Inc.	$85,628
Edward Harris	Karris Supplies	$61,349
Jaren Newman	Paragon Corporation	$51,237
Lydia Alvarado	Martin Manufacturing	$35,679
Craig Johnson	Hoosier Corporation	$24,880
Maureen Pascual	Blue Ridge, Inc.	$17,542

Page 1 of 2

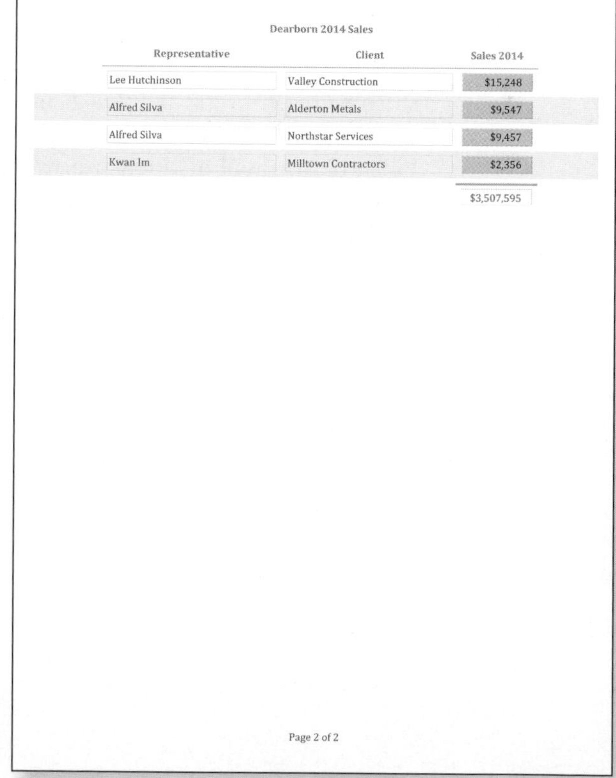

Dearborn 2014 Sales

Representative	Client	Sales 2014
Lee Hutchinson	Valley Construction	$15,248
Alfred Silva	Alderton Metals	$9,547
Alfred Silva	Northstar Services	$9,457
Kwan Im	Milltown Contractors	$2,356
		$3,507,595

Page 2 of 2

Project 1c, Dearborn 2014Sales Report

Model Answers

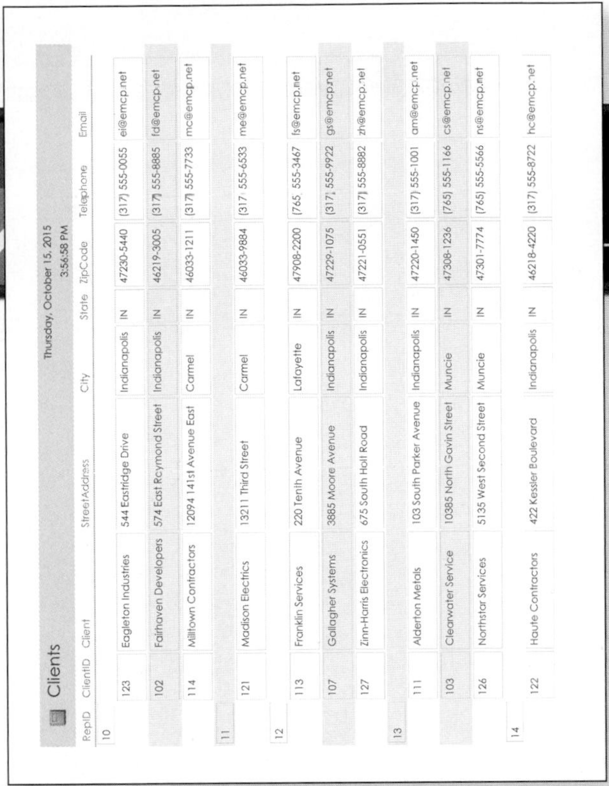

Clients — Thursday, October 15, 2015, 3:56:58 PM

RepID	ClientID	Client	StreetAddress	City	State	ZipCode	Telephone	Email
10								
	123	Eagleton Industries	544 Eastridge Drive	Indianapolis	IN	47230-5440	(317) 555-0055	ei@emcp.net
	102	Fairhaven Developers	574 East Raymond Street	Indianapolis	IN	46219-3005	(317) 555-8885	fd@emcp.net
	114	Milltown Contractors	12094 141st Avenue East	Carmel	IN	46033-1211	(317) 555-7733	mc@emcp.net
11								
	121	Madison Electrics	13211 Third Street	Carmel	IN	46033-9884	(317) 555-6533	me@emcp.net
12								
	113	Franklin Services	220 Tenth Avenue	Lafayette	IN	47908-2200	(765) 555-3467	fs@emcp.net
	107	Gallagher Systems	3885 Moore Avenue	Indianapolis	IN	47229-1075	(317) 555-9922	gs@emcp.net
	127	Zinn-Harris Electronics	675 South Holt Road	Indianapolis	IN	47221-0551	(317) 555-8882	zh@emcp.net
13								
	111	Alderton Metals	103 South Parker Avenue	Indianapolis	IN	47220-1450	(317) 555-1001	am@emcp.net
	103	Clearwater Service	10385 North Gavin Street	Muncie	IN	47308-1236	(765) 555-1166	cs@emcp.net
	126	Northstar Services	5135 West Second Street	Muncie	IN	47301-7774	(765) 555-5566	ns@emcp.net
14								
	122	Haute Contractors	422 Kessler Boulevard	Indianapolis	IN	46218-4220	(317) 555-8722	hc@emcp.net

Project 1d, Dearborn ClientsGroupedRpt Report

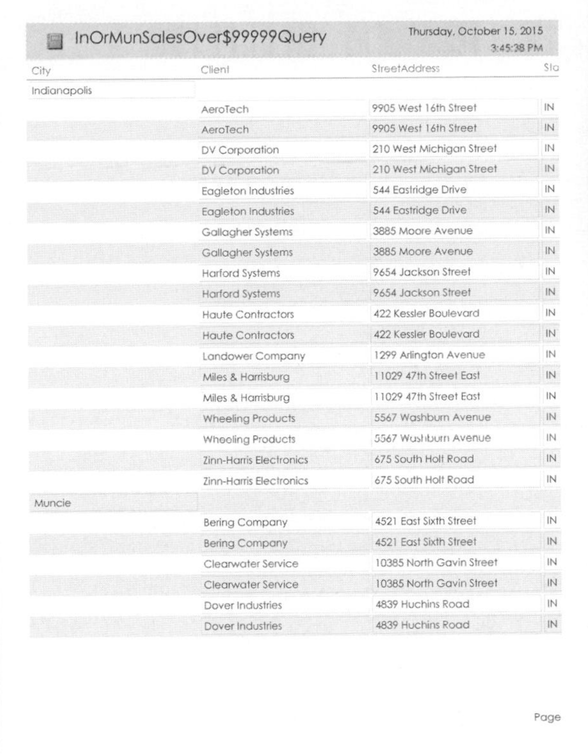

InOrMunSalesOver$99999Query — Thursday, October 15, 2015, 3:45:38 PM

City	Client	StreetAddress	Sta
Indianapolis			
	AeroTech	9905 West 16th Street	IN
	AeroTech	9905 West 16th Street	IN
	DV Corporation	210 West Michigan Street	IN
	DV Corporation	210 West Michigan Street	IN
	Eagleton Industries	544 Eastridge Drive	IN
	Eagleton Industries	544 Eastridge Drive	IN
	Gallagher Systems	3885 Moore Avenue	IN
	Gallagher Systems	3885 Moore Avenue	IN
	Harford Systems	9654 Jackson Street	IN
	Harford Systems	9654 Jackson Street	IN
	Haute Contractors	422 Kessler Boulevard	IN
	Haute Contractors	422 Kessler Boulevard	IN
	Landower Company	1299 Arlington Avenue	IN
	Miles & Harrisburg	11029 47th Street East	IN
	Miles & Harrisburg	11029 47th Street East	IN
	Wheeling Products	5567 Washburn Avenue	IN
	Wheeling Products	5567 Washburn Avenue	IN
	Zinn-Harris Electronics	675 South Holt Road	IN
	Zinn-Harris Electronics	675 South Holt Road	IN
Muncie			
	Bering Company	4521 East Sixth Street	IN
	Bering Company	4521 East Sixth Street	IN
	Clearwater Service	10385 North Gavin Street	IN
	Clearwater Service	10385 North Gavin Street	IN
	Dover Industries	4839 Huchins Road	IN
	Dover Industries	4839 Huchins Road	IN

Page

Project 1d, Dearborn InOrMunOver$99999 Report

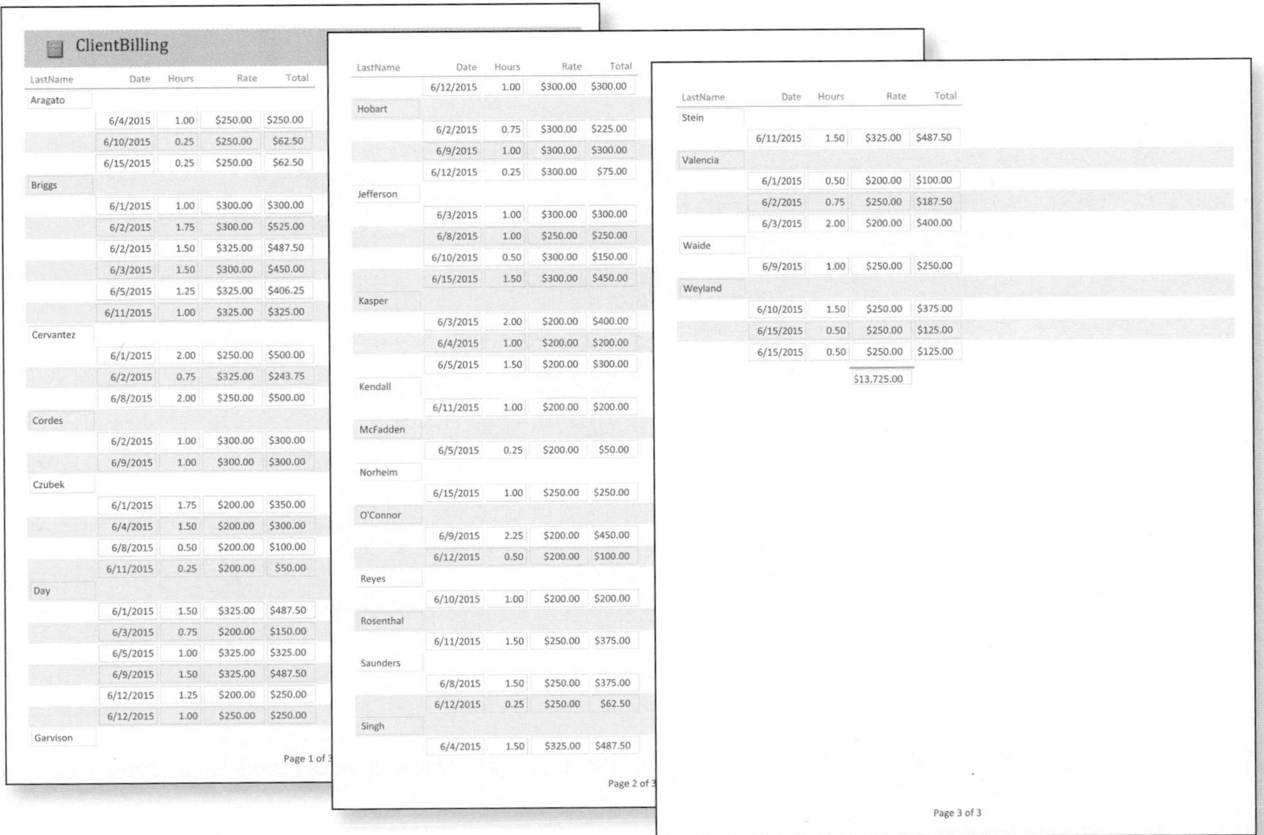

ClientBilling

LastName	Date	Hours	Rate	Total
Aragato				
	6/4/2015	1.00	$250.00	$250.00
	6/10/2015	0.25	$250.00	$62.50
	6/15/2015	0.25	$250.00	$62.50
Briggs				
	6/1/2015	1.00	$300.00	$300.00
	6/2/2015	1.75	$300.00	$525.00
	6/2/2015	1.50	$325.00	$487.50
	6/3/2015	1.50	$300.00	$450.00
	6/5/2015	1.25	$325.00	$406.25
	6/11/2015	1.00	$325.00	$325.00
Cervantez				
	6/1/2015	2.00	$250.00	$500.00
	6/2/2015	0.75	$325.00	$243.75
	6/8/2015	2.00	$250.00	$500.00
Cordes				
	6/2/2015	1.00	$300.00	$300.00
	6/9/2015	1.00	$300.00	$300.00
Czubek				
	6/1/2015	1.75	$200.00	$350.00
	6/4/2015	1.50	$200.00	$300.00
	6/8/2015	0.50	$200.00	$100.00
	6/11/2015	0.25	$200.00	$50.00
Day				
	6/1/2015	1.50	$325.00	$487.50
	6/3/2015	0.75	$200.00	$150.00
	6/5/2015	1.00	$325.00	$325.00
	6/9/2015	1.50	$325.00	$487.50
	6/12/2015	1.25	$200.00	$250.00
	6/12/2015	1.00	$250.00	$250.00
Garvison				

Page 1 of 3

LastName	Date	Hours	Rate	Total
	6/12/2015	1.00	$300.00	$300.00
Hobart				
	6/2/2015	0.75	$300.00	$225.00
	6/9/2015	1.00	$300.00	$300.00
	6/12/2015	0.25	$300.00	$75.00
Jefferson				
	6/3/2015	1.00	$300.00	$300.00
	6/8/2015	1.00	$250.00	$250.00
	6/10/2015	0.50	$300.00	$150.00
	6/15/2015	1.50	$300.00	$450.00
Kasper				
	6/3/2015	2.00	$200.00	$400.00
	6/4/2015	1.00	$200.00	$200.00
	6/5/2015	1.50	$200.00	$300.00
Kendall				
	6/11/2015	1.00	$200.00	$200.00
McFadden				
	6/5/2015	0.25	$200.00	$50.00
Norheim				
	6/15/2015	1.00	$250.00	$250.00
O'Connor				
	6/9/2015	2.25	$200.00	$450.00
	6/12/2015	0.50	$200.00	$100.00
Reyes				
	6/10/2015	1.00	$200.00	$200.00
Rosenthal				
	6/11/2015	1.50	$250.00	$375.00
Saunders				
	6/8/2015	1.50	$250.00	$375.00
	6/12/2015	0.25	$250.00	$62.50
Singh				
	6/4/2015	1.50	$325.00	$487.50

Page 2 of 3

LastName	Date	Hours	Rate	Total
Stein				
	6/11/2015	1.50	$325.00	$487.50
Valencia				
	6/1/2015	0.50	$200.00	$100.00
	6/2/2015	0.75	$250.00	$187.50
	6/3/2015	2.00	$200.00	$400.00
Waide				
	6/9/2015	1.00	$250.00	$250.00
Weyland				
	6/10/2015	1.50	$250.00	$375.00
	6/15/2015	0.50	$250.00	$125.00
	6/15/2015	0.50	$250.00	$125.00
			$13,725.00	

Page 3 of 3

Project 1d, Warren Legal ClientBillingRpt Report

Project 2 Use Wizards to Create Reports and Labels

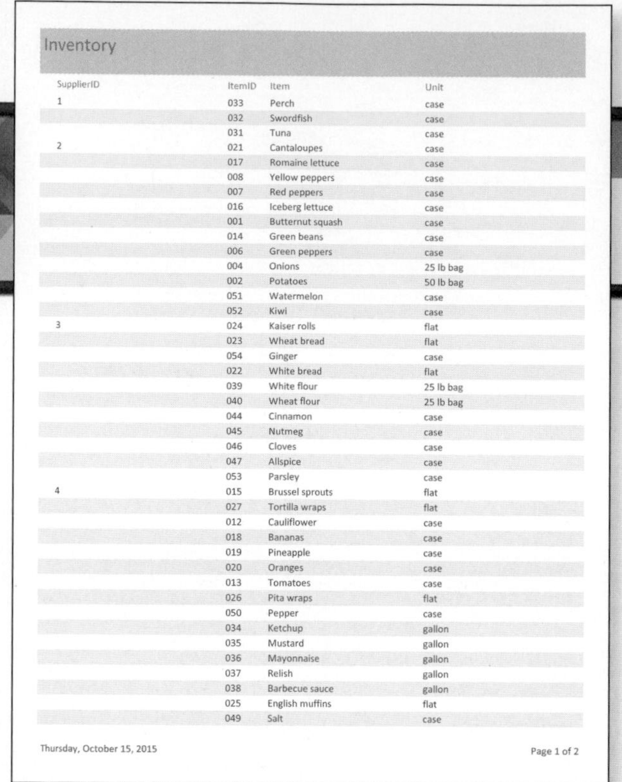

Inventory

SupplierID	ItemID	Item	Unit
1	033	Perch	case
	032	Swordfish	case
	031	Tuna	case
2	021	Cantaloupes	case
	017	Romaine lettuce	case
	008	Yellow peppers	case
	007	Red peppers	case
	016	Iceberg lettuce	case
	001	Butternut squash	case
	014	Green beans	case
	006	Green peppers	case
	004	Onions	25 lb bag
	002	Potatoes	50 lb bag
	051	Watermelon	case
	052	Kiwi	case
3	024	Kaiser rolls	flat
	023	Wheat bread	flat
	054	Ginger	case
	022	White bread	flat
	039	White flour	25 lb bag
	040	Wheat flour	25 lb bag
	044	Cinnamon	case
	045	Nutmeg	case
	046	Cloves	case
	047	Allspice	case
	053	Parsley	case
4	015	Brussel sprouts	flat
	027	Tortilla wraps	flat
	012	Cauliflower	case
	018	Bananas	case
	019	Pineapple	case
	020	Oranges	case
	013	Tomatoes	case
	026	Pita wraps	flat
	050	Pepper	case
	034	Ketchup	gallon
	035	Mustard	gallon
	036	Mayonnaise	gallon
	037	Relish	gallon
	038	Barbecue sauce	gallon
	025	English muffins	flat
	049	Salt	case

Thursday, October 15, 2015 Page 1 of 2

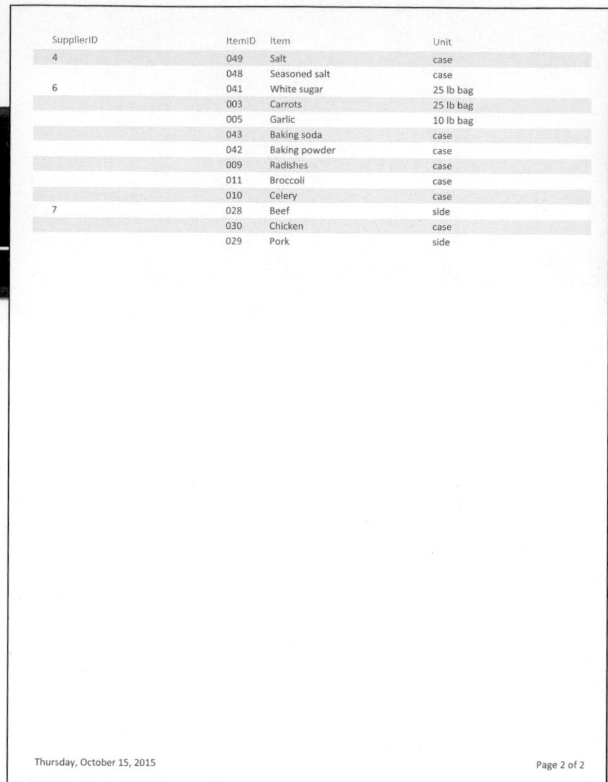

SupplierID	ItemID	Item	Unit
4	049	Salt	case
	048	Seasoned salt	case
6	041	White sugar	25 lb bag
	003	Carrots	25 lb bag
	005	Garlic	10 lb bag
	043	Baking soda	case
	042	Baking powder	case
	009	Radishes	case
	011	Broccoli	case
	010	Celery	case
7	028	Beef	side
	030	Chicken	case
	029	Pork	side

Thursday, October 15, 2015 Page 2 of 2

Project 2a, Skyline Inventory Report

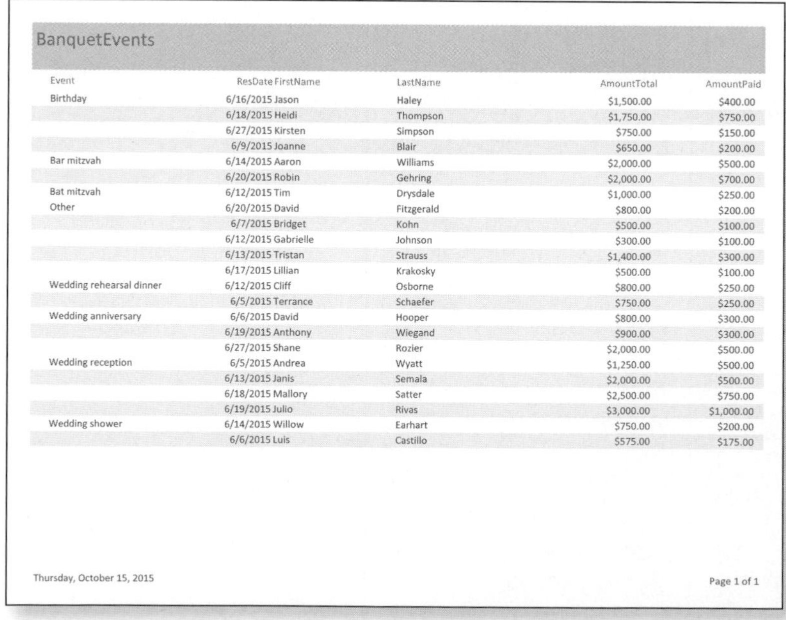

BanquetEvents

Event	ResDate	FirstName	LastName	AmountTotal	AmountPaid
Birthday	6/16/2015	Jason	Haley	$1,500.00	$400.00
	6/18/2015	Heidi	Thompson	$1,750.00	$750.00
	6/27/2015	Kirsten	Simpson	$750.00	$150.00
	6/9/2015	Joanne	Blair	$650.00	$200.00
Bar mitzvah	6/14/2015	Aaron	Williams	$2,000.00	$500.00
	6/20/2015	Robin	Gehring	$2,000.00	$700.00
Bat mitzvah	6/12/2015	Tim	Drysdale	$1,000.00	$250.00
Other	6/20/2015	David	Fitzgerald	$800.00	$200.00
	6/7/2015	Bridget	Kohn	$500.00	$100.00
	6/12/2015	Gabrielle	Johnson	$300.00	$100.00
	6/13/2015	Tristan	Strauss	$1,400.00	$300.00
	6/17/2015	Lillian	Krakosky	$500.00	$100.00
Wedding rehearsal dinner	6/12/2015	Cliff	Osborne	$800.00	$250.00
	6/5/2015	Terrance	Schaefer	$750.00	$250.00
Wedding anniversary	6/6/2015	David	Hooper	$800.00	$300.00
	6/19/2015	Anthony	Wiegand	$900.00	$300.00
	6/27/2015	Shane	Rozier	$2,000.00	$500.00
Wedding reception	6/5/2015	Andrea	Wyatt	$1,250.00	$500.00
	6/13/2015	Janis	Semala	$2,000.00	$500.00
	6/18/2015	Mallory	Satter	$2,500.00	$750.00
	6/19/2015	Julio	Rivas	$3,000.00	$1,000.00
Wedding shower	6/14/2015	Willow	Earhart	$750.00	$200.00
	6/6/2015	Luis	Castillo	$575.00	$175.00

Thursday, October 15, 2015 Page 1 of 1

Project 2b, Skyline BanquetEvents Report

Haley Brown 3219 North 33rd Street Auburn, WA 98001	Margaret Kasper 40210 42nd Avenue Auburn, WA 98001	Abigail Jefferson 1204 Meridian Road Auburn, WA 98001
Doris Sturtevant 3713 Nelton Road Auburn, WA 98001	Carlina McFadden 7809 52nd Street East Auburn, WA 98001	Ewan Aragato 904 Marine View Drive Auburn, WA 98002
Tricia O'Connor 3824 Sanders Court Auburn, WA 98002	Carol Kendall 24 Ferris Parkway Kent, WA 98003	James Weyland 2533 145th Street East Kent, WA 98031
Janice Saunders 2757 179th Avenue East Kent, WA 98032	Jeffrey Day 317 Meridian Street Kent, WA 98033	Mindy Garvison 68 Queens Avenue Kent, WA 98033
Kevin Stein 12034 South 22nd Avenue Kent, WA 98035	Jean Briggs 2110 West Valley Avenue Kent, WA 98036	Arthur Norheim 10533 Ashton Boulevard Kent, WA 98036
Consuelo Day 13321 North Lake Drive Kent, WA 98036	Christina Miles 13043 South 25th Avenue Kent, WA 98036	Matthew Waide 18391 North 45th Street Renton, WA 98055

Karl Cordes 240 Mill Avenue Renton, WA 98055	Mira Valencia 114 Springfield Avenue Renton, WA 98056	Charles Hobart 11000 132nd Street Renton, WA 98056
Taylor Reyes 201 Northwest Boulevard Renton, WA 98056	Eric Rosenthal 1230 Maplewood Road Auburn, WA 98071	Jennifer Czubek 8790 34th Avenue Renton, WA 98228
Maddie Singh 450 Mill Avenue Renton, WA 98228	Chris Cervantez 8722 Riverside Road Renton, WA 98228	Arthur Jefferson 23110 North 33rd Street Renton, WA 98230

Project 2c, WarrenLegal Mailing Labels

Project 1 Create and Customize Reports Using Tables and Queries — 4 Parts

You will create reports with the Report button using tables and queries. You will change the report views; select, move, and resize control objects; sort records; customize reports; apply conditional formatting; and group and sort fields in a report.

Creating Reports

The primary purposes for inserting data in a form are to improve the display of the data and to make data entry easier. You can also insert data in a report. The purpose for doing this is to control what data appears on the page when printed. Reports generally answer specific questions (queries). For example, a report could answer the question *What customers have submitted claims?* or *What products do we currently have on order?* The record source for a report can be a table or query. Create a report with the Report button in the Reports group or use the Report Wizard, which walks you through the process of creating a report.

Quick Steps

Create a Report
1. Click desired table or query in Navigation pane.
2. Click CREATE tab.
3. Click Report button.

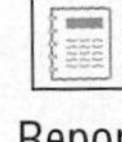

Report

Create a report to control what data appears on the page when printed.

Creating a Report with the Report Button

To create a report with the Report button, click the desired table or query in the Navigation pane, click the CREATE tab, and then click the Report button in the Reports group. This displays the report in columnar style in Layout view with the REPORT LAYOUT TOOLS DESIGN tab active, as shown in Figure 6.1. Access creates the report using all of the fields in the table or query.

Figure 6.1 Report Created with Sales Table

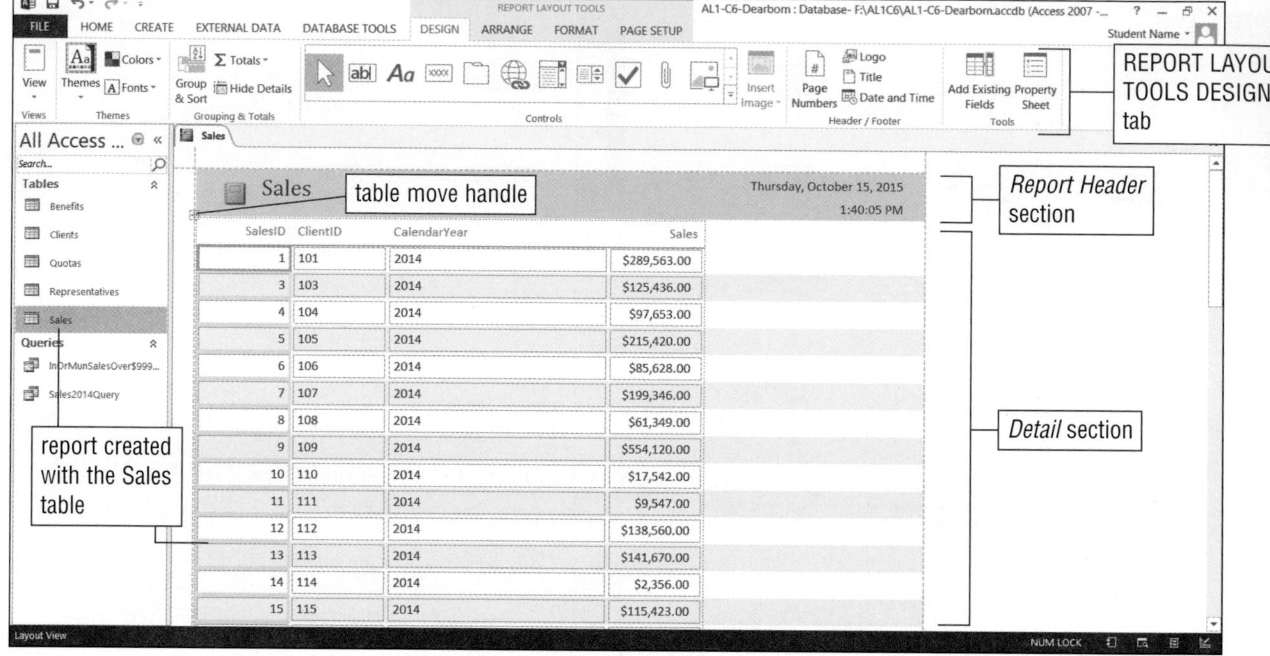

Modifying the Record Source

The record source for a report is the table or query used to create the report. If changes are made to the record source, such as adding or deleting records, those changes are reflected in the report. For example, in Project 1a, you will create a report based on the Sales table. You will then add a record to the Sales table (the record source for the report) and the added record will display in the Sales report.

Project 1a Creating a Report with the Report Button Part 1 of 4

1. Display the Open dialog box with the AL1C6 folder on your storage medium the active folder.
2. Open **AL1-C6-Dearborn.accdb** and enable the contents.
3. Create a report based on the Sales table by completing the following steps:
   a. Click the Sales table in the Navigation pane.
   b. Click the CREATE tab.
   c. Click the Report button in the Reports group.

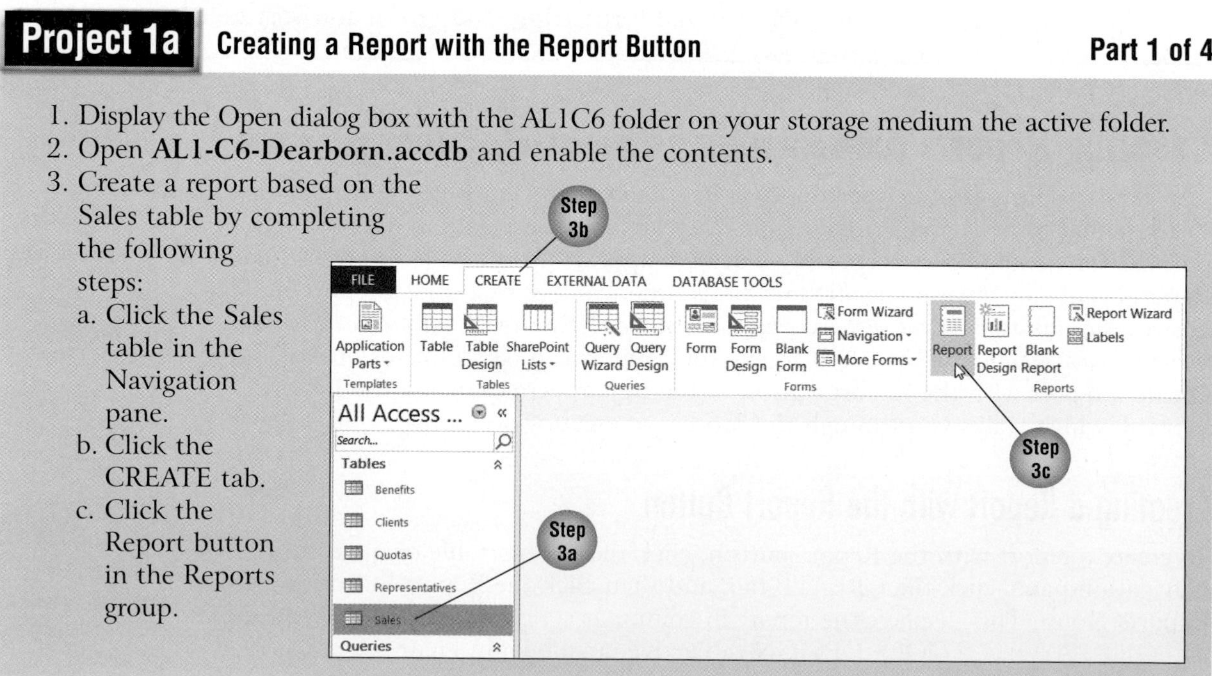

d. Save the report by clicking the Save button on the Quick Access toolbar and then clicking OK at the Save As dialog box. (This saves the report with the default name, *Sales*.)
e. Close the Sales report.

4. Add a record to the Sales table by completing the following steps:
   a. Double-click the Sales table in the Navigation pane. (Make sure you open the Sales table and not the Sales report.)
   b. Click the New button in the Records group on the HOME tab.
   c. Press the Tab key to accept the default number in the *SalesID* field.
   d. Type **127** in the *ClientID* field and then press the Tab key.
   e. Type **2015** in the *CalendarYear* field and then press the Tab key.
   f. Type **176420** in the *Sales* field.
   g. Close the Sales table.
5. Open the Sales report and then scroll down to the bottom. Notice that the new record you added to the Sales table displays in the report.
6. Close the Sales report.
7. Use the query named *Sales2014Query* to create a report by completing the following steps:
   a. Click *Sales2014Query* in the Queries group in the Navigation pane.
   b. Click the CREATE tab.
   c. Click the Report button in the Reports group.
8. Access automatically inserted a total amount for the *Sales* column of the report. Delete this amount by scrolling down to the bottom of the report, clicking the total amount at the bottom of the *Sales* column, and then pressing the Delete key. (This deletes the total amount but not the underline above the amount.)
9. Save the report by clicking the Save button on the Quick Access toolbar, typing **2014Sales** in the *Report Name* text box in the Save As dialog box, and then clicking OK.

Modifying Control Objects

A report, like a form, is comprised of control objects, such as logos, titles, labels, and text boxes. You can select an object in a report by clicking the object. A selected object displays with an orange border. If you click a data field in the report, Access selects all of the objects in the column except the column heading.

Like a form, a report contains a *Header* section and a *Detail* section. Select all of the control objects in the report in both the *Header* and *Detail* sections by pressing Ctrl + A. Control objects in the *Detail* section are contained in a report table. To select the control objects in the report table, click in any cell in the report and then click the table move handle. The table move handle is a small square with a four-headed arrow inside that displays in the upper left corner of the table (see Figure 6.1). Move the table and all of the control objects within the table by dragging the table move handle using the mouse.

Adjust column widths in a report by dragging the column border left or right. In addition to adjusting column width, you can change the position of a selected column. To do this, select the desired column, position the mouse pointer in the column heading until the pointer displays with a four-headed arrow attached, and then drag the column left or right to the desired position. As you drag the column, a vertical pink bar displays indicating where the column will be placed when you release the mouse button.

Some control objects in a report, such as a column heading or title, are label control objects. Edit a label control by double-clicking in the object and then making the desired change. For example, if you want to rename a label control, double-click in the label control and then edit or type the desired text.

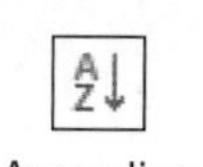
Ascending

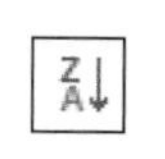
Descending

Quick Steps

Sort Records
1. Click in field containing data.
2. Click Ascending button or click Descending button.

Sorting Records

Sort data in a report by clicking in the field containing the data you want to sort and then clicking the Ascending button or Descending button in the Sort & Filter group on the HOME tab. Click the Ascending button to sort text in alphabetical order from A to Z or sort numbers from lowest to highest or click the Descending button to sort text in alphabetical order from Z to A or sort numbers from highest to lowest.

Displaying and Customizing a Report in Print Preview

Print Preview

View

When you create a report, the report displays in the work area in Layout view. In addition to Layout view, three other views are available: Report, Print Preview, and Design. Use Print Preview to display the report as it will appear when printed. To change to Print Preview, click the Print Preview button in the view area located at the right side of the Status bar. You can also click the View button arrow in the Views group on the HOME tab or REPORT LAYOUT TOOLS DESIGN tab and then click *Print Preview* at the drop-down list.

In Print Preview, send the report to the printer by clicking the Print button on the PRINT PREVIEW tab. Use options in the Page Size group to change the page size and margins. If you want to print only the report data and not the column headings, report title, shading, and gridlines, insert a check mark in the *Print Data Only* check box. Use options in the Page Layout group to specify the page orientation, specify columns, and display the Page Setup dialog box. Click the Page Setup button and the Page Setup dialog box displays with options for customizing margins, orientation, size, and columns.

Deleting a Report

If you no longer need a report in a database, delete the report. Delete a report by clicking the report name in the Navigation pane, clicking the Delete button in the Records group on the HOME tab, and then clicking the Yes button at the message asking if you want to permanently delete the report. Another method is to right-click the report in the Navigation pane, click *Delete* at the shortcut menu, and then click the Yes at the message. If you are deleting a report from your computer's hard drive, the message asking if you want to permanently delete the report will not display. This is because Access automatically sends the deleted report to the Recycle Bin, where it can be retrieved if necessary.

Finding Data in a Report

You can find specific data in a report with options at the Find dialog box. Display this dialog box by clicking the Find button in the Find group on the HOME tab. At the Find dialog box, enter the data you want to search for in the *Find What* text box. The *Match* option at the Find dialog box is set at *Whole Field* by default. At this setting, the data you enter must match the entire entry in a field. If you want to search for partial data in a field, change the *Match* option to *Any Part of Field* or *Start of Field*. If you want the text you enter in the *Find What* text box to match the case in a field entry, click the *Match Case* option check box to insert a check mark. Access will search the entire report by default. You can change this to *Up* if you want to search from the currently active field to the beginning of the report or *Down* if you want to search from the currently active field to the end of the report. Click the Find Next button to find data that matches the data in the *Find What* text box.

Project 1b **Adjusting Control Objects, Renaming Labels, Finding and Sorting Data, Displaying a Report in Print Preview, and Deleting a Report** **Part 2 of 4**

1. With the 2014Sales report open, reverse the order of the *RepName* and *Client* columns by completing the following steps:
   a. Make sure the report displays in Layout view.
   b. Click the *RepName* column heading.
   c. Hold down the Shift key and then click in the last control object in the *RepName* column (the control object containing *Catherine Singleton*).
   d. Position the mouse pointer inside the *RepName* column heading until the pointer displays with a four-headed arrow attached.
   e. Hold down the left mouse button, drag to the left until the vertical pink bar displays to the left of the *Client* column, and then release the mouse button.

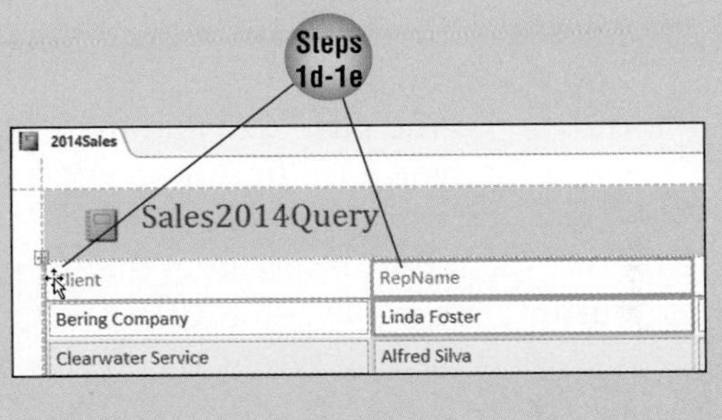

2. Sort the data in the *Sales* column in descending order by completing the following steps:
   a. Click the HOME tab.
   b. Click in any field in the *Sales* column.
   c. Click the Descending button in the Sort & Filter group.
3. Rename the *RepName* label control as *Representative* by double-clicking in the label control object containing the text *RepName*, selecting *RepName*, and then typing **Representative**.
4. Double-click in the *Sales* label control and then rename it *Sales 2014*.

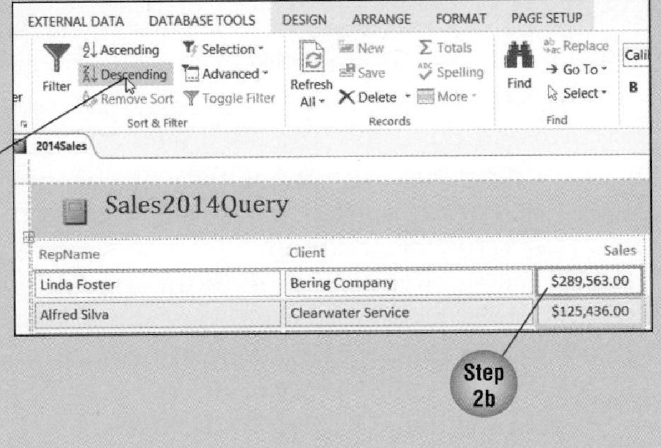

5. Move the report table by completing the following steps:
   a. Click in a cell in the report.
   b. Position the mouse pointer on the table move handle (which displays as a small square with a four-headed arrow inside and is located in the upper left corner of the table).
   c. Hold down the left mouse button, drag the report table to the right until it is centered between the left and right sides of the *Detail* section, and then release the mouse button. (When you drag with the mouse, you will see only outlines of some of the control objects.)

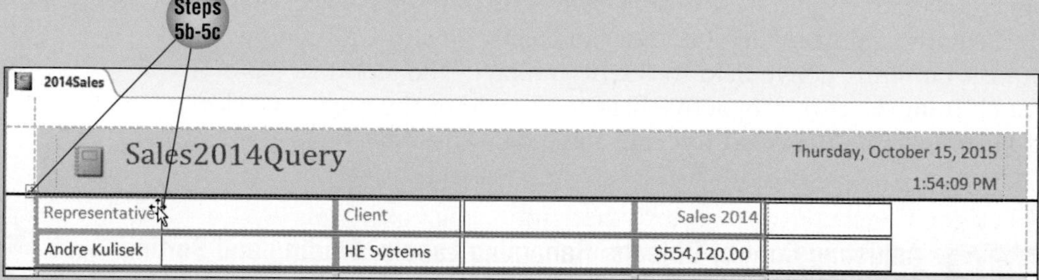

6. Display the report in Print Preview by clicking the Print Preview button in the view area at the right side of the Status bar.

7. Click the One Page button (already active) in the Zoom group to display the entire page.
8. Click the Zoom button arrow in the Zoom group and then click *50%* at the drop-down list.
9. Click the One Page button in the Zoom group.
10. Print the report by clicking the Print button on the PRINT PREVIEW tab and then clicking OK at the Print dialog box.
11. Close Print Preview by clicking the Close Print Preview button located at the right side of the PRINT PREVIEW tab.
12. Save and then close the 2014Sales report.
13. Create a report with the Representatives table by completing the following steps:
    a. Click *Representatives* in the Tables group in the Navigation pane.
    b. Click the CREATE tab.
    c. Click the Report button in the Reports group.
14. Adjust the width of the second column by completing the following steps:
    a. Click in the *RepName* column heading.
    b. Drag the right border of the selected column heading to the left until the border displays near the longest entry in the column.
15. Complete steps similar to those in Step 14 to decrease the width of the third column (*Telephone*) and the fourth column (*Email*).
16. Search for fields containing a quote of *2* by completing the following steps:
    a. Click in the *RepID* column heading.
    b. Click the HOME tab and then click the Find button in the Find group.

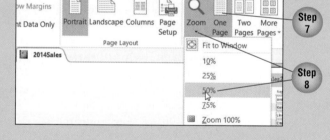

c. At the Find dialog box, type **2** in the *Find What* text box.
d. Make sure the *Match* option is set to *Whole Field*. (If not, click the down-pointing arrow at the right side of the *Match* option and then click *Whole Field* at the drop-down list.)
e. Click the Find Next button.
f. Continue clicking the Find Next button until a message displays telling you that Access has finished searching the records. At this message, click OK.
g. Click the Cancel button to close the Find dialog box.

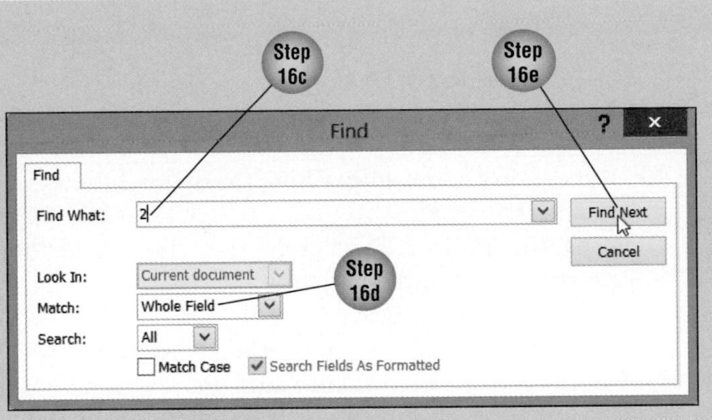

17. Suppose you want to find information on a representative and you remember the first name but not the last name. Search for a field containing the first name *Lydia* by completing the following steps:
    a. Click in the *RepID* column heading.
    b. Click the Find button in the Find group.
    c. At the Find dialog box, type **Lydia** in the *Find What* text box.
    d. Click the down-pointing arrow at the right side of the *Match* option and then click *Any Part of Field* at the drop-down list.
    e. Click the Find Next button. (Access will find and select the representative name *Lydia Alvarado*.)
    f. Click the Cancel button to close the Find dialog box.

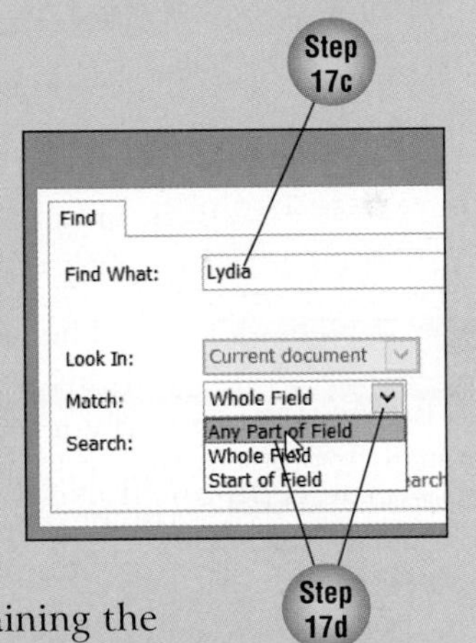

18. Click the control object at the bottom of the *RepID* column containing the number *17* and then press the Delete key. (This does not delete the underline above the amount.)
19. Switch to Print Preview by clicking the View button arrow in the Views group on the REPORT LAYOUT TOOLS DESIGN tab and then clicking *Print Preview* at the drop-down list.
20. Click the Margins button in the Page Size group and then click *Normal* at the drop-down list.

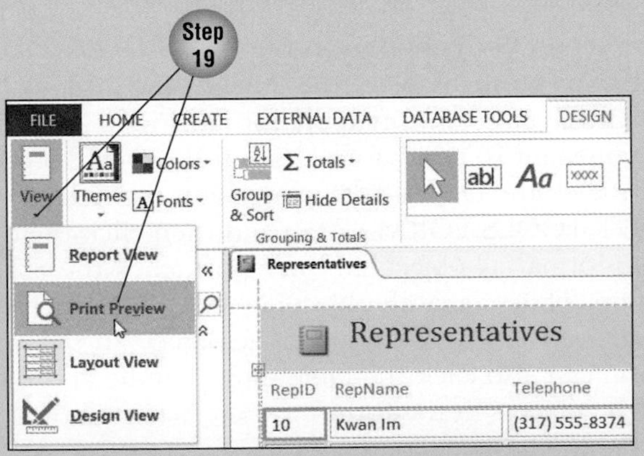

21. Print the first page of the report (the second page contains only shading) by completing the following steps:
    a. Click the Print button that displays at the left side of the PRINT PREVIEW tab.
    b. At the Print dialog box, click the *Pages* option in the *Print Range* section.
    c. Type 1 in the *From* text box, press the Tab key, and then type 1 in the *To* text box.
    d. Click OK.
22. Close Print Preview by clicking the Close Print Preview button.
23. Save the report with the name *Representatives*.
24. Close the Representatives report.
25. Delete the Sales report by right-clicking the Sales report in the Navigation pane, clicking *Delete* at the shortcut menu, and then clicking Yes at the message that displays.

Customizing Reports

Customize a report in much the same manner as you customize a form. When you first create a report, the report displays in Layout view and the REPORT LAYOUT TOOLS DESIGN tab is active. Customize control objects in the *Detail* section and the *Header* section with buttons on the REPORT LAYOUT TOOLS ribbon using the DESIGN tab, ARRANGE tab, FORMAT tab, or PAGE SETUP tab selected.

The themes available in Access are the same as the themes available in Word, Excel, and PowerPoint.

Totals

The REPORT LAYOUT TOOLS DESIGN tab contains many of the same options at the FORM LAYOUT TOOLS DESIGN tab. Use options on this tab to apply a theme, insert controls, insert header or footer data, and add existing fields. The tab also contains the Grouping & Totals group, which you will learn about in the next section. Use the Totals button in the Grouping & Totals group to perform functions such as finding the sum, average, maximum, or minimum of the numbers in a column. To use the Totals button, click the column heading of the column containing the data you want to total, click the Totals button, and then click the desired function at the drop-down list. Use the Page Number button on the REPORT LAYOUT TOOLS DESIGN tab to insert and format page numbers.

Click the REPORT LAYOUT TOOLS ARRANGE tab and options display for inserting and selecting rows, splitting cells horizontally and vertically, moving data up or down, controlling margins, and changing the padding between objects and cells. The options on the REPORT LAYOUT TOOLS ARRANGE tab are the same as the options on the FORM LAYOUT TOOLS ARRANGE tab.

Customize the formatting of control objects with options at the REPORT LAYOUT TOOLS FORMAT tab.

Select and format data in a report with options on the REPORT LAYOUT TOOLS FORMAT tab. The options on this tab are the same as the options on the FORM LAYOUT TOOLS FORMAT tab. You can apply formatting to a report or specific objects in a report. If you want to apply formatting to a specific object, click the object in the report or click the Object button arrow in the Selection group on the REPORT LAYOUT TOOLS FORMAT tab and then click the desired object at the drop-down list. To format all objects in the report, click the Select All button in the Selection group. This selects all objects in the report, including objects in the *Header* section. If you want to select all of the objects in the report, click the table move handle. You can also click the table move handle and then drag with the mouse to move the objects in the form.

With buttons in the Font, Number, Background, and Control Formatting groups, you can apply formatting to a control object or cell and to selected objects or cells in a report. Use buttons in the Font group to change the font, apply a different font size, apply text effects (such as bold and underline), and change the alignment of data in objects. Insert a background image in the report using the Background button and apply formatting to objects or cells with buttons in the Control Formatting group. Depending on what is selected in the report, some of the buttons may not be active.

Background

Click the REPORT LAYOUT TOOLS PAGE SETUP tab and the buttons that display are buttons that are also available in Print Preview. For example, you can change the page size and page layout of the report and display the Page Setup dialog box.

Project 1c Applying Formatting to a Report

Part 3 of 4

1. With **AL1-C6-Dearborn.accdb** open, open the 2014Sales report.
2. Display the report in Layout view.
3. Click the Themes button in the Themes group on the REPORT LAYOUT TOOLS DESIGN tab and then click *Ion* at the drop-down gallery (fourth column, first row).

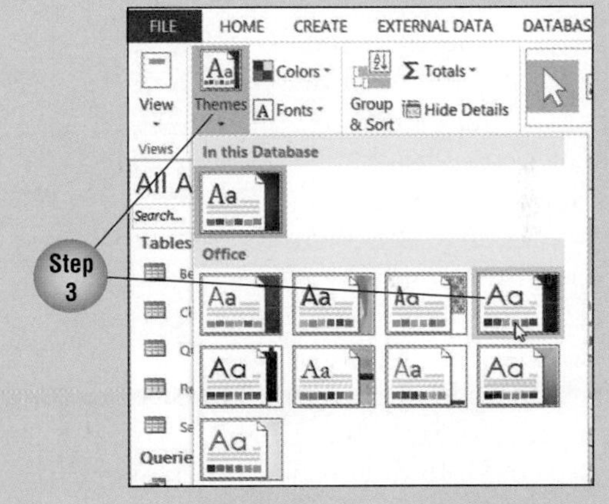

4. Click the Title button in the Header/Footer group (which selects the current title), type **2014 Sales**, and then press Enter.
5. Insert new control objects by completing the following steps:
   a. Click in the *Representative* cell.
   b. Click the REPORT LAYOUT TOOLS ARRANGE tab.
   c. Click the Insert Above button in the Rows & Columns group.
6. Merge the cells in the new row by completing the following steps:
   a. Click in the blank cell immediately above the *Representative* cell.
   b. Hold down the Shift key and then click immediately above the *Sales 2014* cell. (This selects three cells.)
   c. Click the Merge button in the Merge/Split group.
   d. Type **Dearborn 2014 Sales** in the new cell.

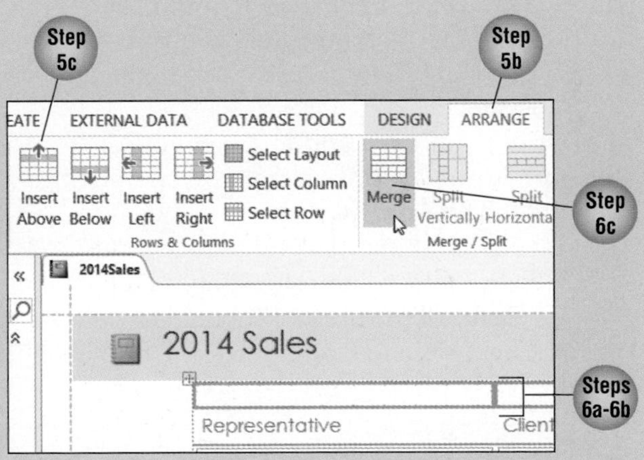

7. Split a cell by completing the following steps:
   a. Click in the *2014 Sales* title in the *Header* section.
   b. Split the cell containing the title by clicking the Split Horizontally button in the Merge/Split group.
   c. Click in the empty cell immediately right of the cell containing the title *Sales 2014* and then press the Delete key. (Deleting the empty cell causes the date and time to move to the left in the *Header* section.)
8. Change the report table margins and padding by completing the following steps:
   a. Click in any cell in the *Detail* section and then click the table move handle that displays in the upper left corner of the *Dearborn 2014 Sales* cell. (This selects the control objects in the report table in the *Detail* section.)

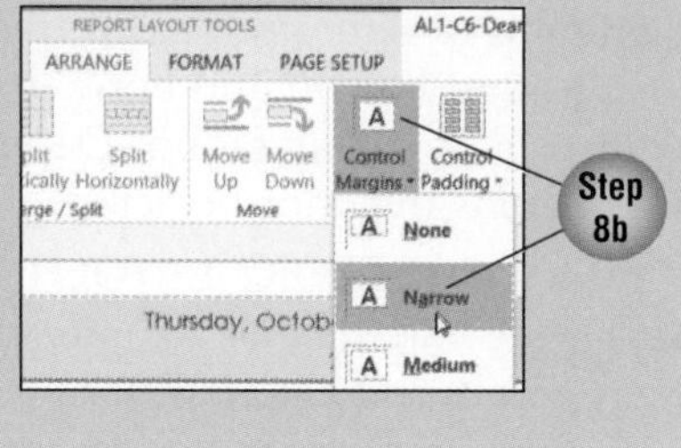

b. Click the Control Margins button in the Position group and then click *Narrow* at the drop-down list.
c. Click the Control Padding button in the Position group and then click *Medium* at the drop-down list.

9. Click in the *Dearborn 2014 Sales* cell and then drag down the bottom border so all of the text in the cell is visible.
10. Change the font for all control objects in the report by completing the following steps:
    a. Press Ctrl + A to select all control objects in the report. (An orange border displays around selected objects.)
    b. Click the REPORT LAYOUT TOOLS FORMAT tab.
    c. Click the Font button arrow in the Font group and then click *Cambria* at the drop-down list. (You may need to scroll down the list to display *Cambria*.)

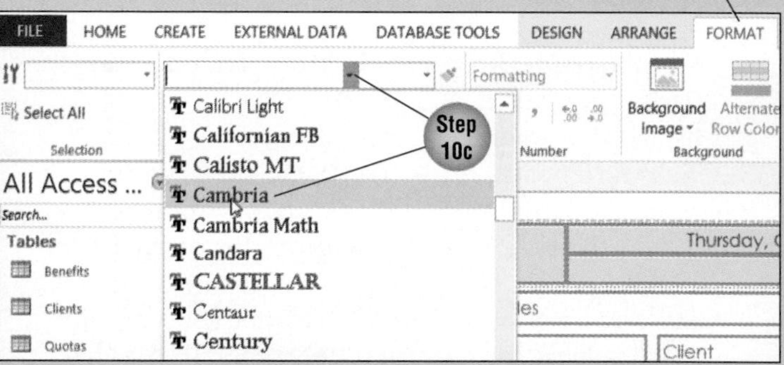

11. Apply bold formatting and change the alignment of the column headings by completing the following steps:
    a. Click *Dearborn 2014 Sales* to select the control object.
    b. Hold down the Shift key and then click *Sales 2014*. (This selects four cells.)
    c. Click the Bold button in the Font group.
    d. Click the Center button in the Font group.

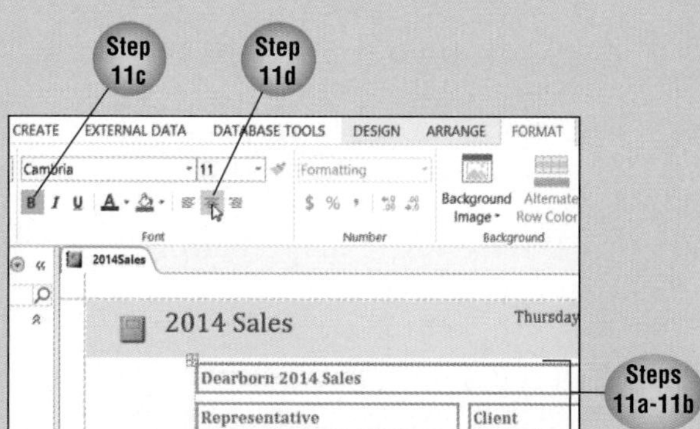

12. Format amounts and apply conditional formatting to the amounts by completing the following steps:
    a. Click the first field value below the *Sales 2014* column heading. (This selects all of the amounts in the column.)
    b. Click twice on the Decrease Decimals button in the Number group.

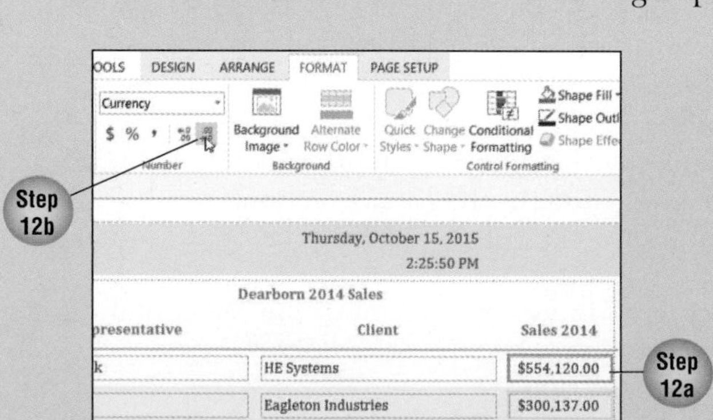

    c. Click the Conditional Formatting button in the Control Formatting group.

d. At the Conditional Formatting Rules Manager dialog box, click the New Rule button.
e. At the New Formatting Rule dialog box, click the down-pointing arrow at the right side of the second option box in the *Edit the rule description* section and then click *greater than* at the drop-down list.
f. Click in the text box immediately right of the option box containing *greater than* and then type **199999**.
g. Click the Background color button arrow and then click the *Green 2* color option (seventh column, third row).
h. Click the OK button.
i. At the Conditional Formatting Rules Manager dialog box, click the New Rule button.
j. At the New Formatting Rule dialog box, click the down-pointing arrow at the right side of the second option box in the *Edit the rule description* section and then click *less than* at the drop-down list.
k. Click in the text box immediately right of the option containing *less than* and then type **200000**.
l. Click the Background color button arrow and then click the *Maroon 2* color option (sixth column, third row).
m. Click OK to close the New Formatting Rule dialog box.
n. Click OK to close the Conditional Formatting Rules Manager dialog box.

13. Sum the totals in the *Sales 2014* column by completing the following steps:
    a. Click in the *Sales 2014* column heading.
    b. Click the REPORT LAYOUT TOOLS DESIGN tab.
    c. Click the Totals button in the Grouping & Totals group and then click *Sum* at the drop-down list.
14. Click in the *Sales 2014* sum amount (located at the bottom of the *Sales 2014* column) and then drag down the bottom border so the entire amount is visible in the cell.

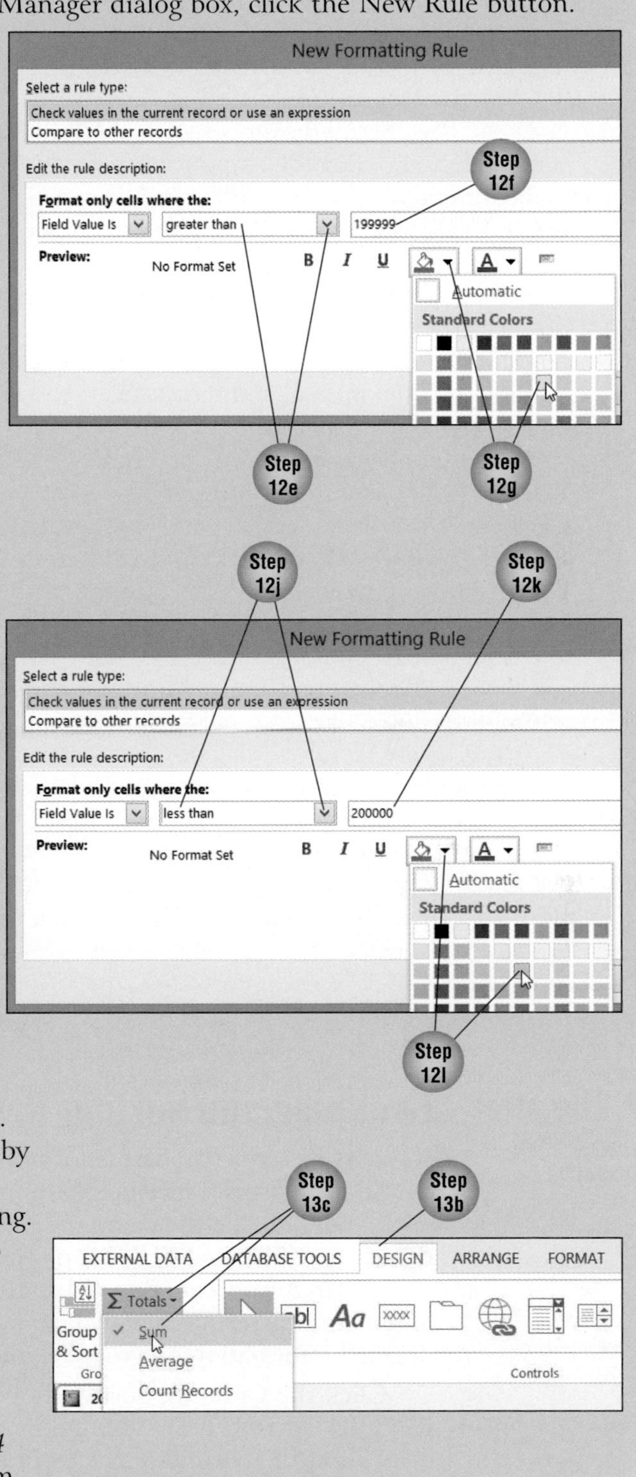

15. Change the top margin by completing the following steps:
    a. Click in the *Representative* column heading and then click the REPORT LAYOUT TOOLS PAGE SETUP tab.
    b. Click the Page Setup button in the Page Layout group.
    c. At the Page Setup dialog box with the Print Options tab selected, select the current measurement in the *Top* measurement box and then type **0.5**.
    d. Click OK to close the Page Setup dialog box.
16. Change the page size by clicking the Size button in the Page Size group and and then clicking *Legal* at the drop-down list.

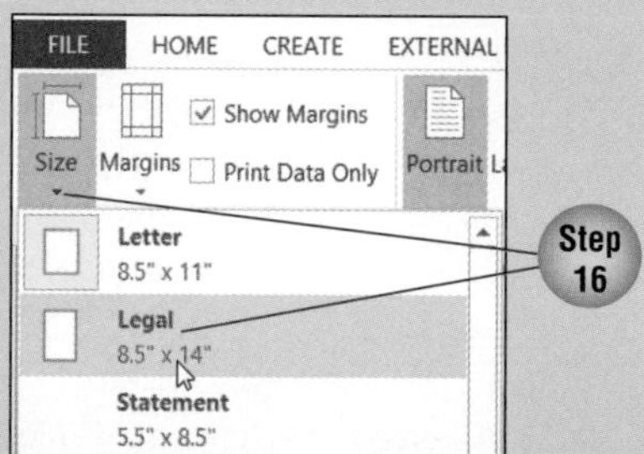

17. Display the report in Print Preview by clicking the FILE tab, clicking the *Print* option, and then clicking the Print Preview button.
18. Click the One Page button in the Zoom group and notice that the entire report will print on one legal-sized page.
19. Click the Close Print Preview button to return to the report.
20. Change the page size by clicking the PAGE LAYOUT TOOLS PAGE SETUP tab, clicking the Size button in the Page Size group, and then clicking *Letter* at the drop-down list.
21. Insert and then remove a background image by completing the following steps:
    a. Click the REPORT LAYOUT TOOLS FORMAT tab.
    b. Click the Background Image button in the Background group and then click *Browse* at the drop-down list.
    c. At the Insert Picture dialog box, navigate to the AL1C6 folder on your storage medium and then double-click ***Mountain.jpg***.
    d. Scroll through the report and notice how the image displays in the report.
    e. Click the Undo button on the Quick Access toolbar to remove the background image. (You may need to click the Undo button more than once.)
22. Print the report by clicking the FILE tab, clicking the *Print* option, and then clicking the Quick Print button.
23. Save and then close the report.

Quick Steps

Group and Sort Records
1. Open desired report in Layout view.
2. Click Group & Sort button.
3. Click Add a group button.
4. Click desired group field.

Group & Sort

Add a group

Grouping and Sorting Records

A report presents database information in a printed form and generally displays data that answers a specific question. To make the data in a report easy to understand, divide the data into groups. For example, you can divide data in a report by regions, sales, dates, or any other division that helps clarify the data for the reader. Access contains a powerful group and sort feature that you can use in a report. In this section, you will complete basic group and sort functions. For more detailed information on grouping and sorting, refer to the Access help files.

Click the Group & Sort button in the Grouping & Totals group on the REPORT LAYOUT TOOLS DESIGN tab and the Group, Sort, and Total pane displays at the bottom of the work area, as shown in Figure 6.2. Click the Add a group button in the Group, Sort, and Total pane and Access adds a new grouping level row to the pane, along with a list of available fields. Click the field on which you want to group data in the report and Access adds the grouping level in the report. With options in the grouping level row, change the group, specify the sort order, and expand the row to display additional options.

Figure 6.2 Group, Sort, and Total Pane

Clients

Thursday, October 15, 2015
3:35:14 PM

ClientID	RepID	Client	StreetAddress	City	State	ZipCode	Telephone	Email
101	23	Bering Company	4521 East Sixth Street	Muncie	IN	47310-5500	(765) 555-5565	bc@emcp.net
102	10	Fairhaven Developers	574 East Raymond Street	Indianapolis	IN	46219-3005	(317) 555-8885	fd@emcp.net
103	13	Clearwater Service	10385 North Gavin Street	Muncie	IN	47308-1236	(765) 555-1166	cs@emcp.net
104	17	Landower Company	1299 Arlington Avenue	Indianapolis	IN	46236-1299	(317) 555-1255	lc@emcp.net
105	15	Harford Systems	9654 Jackson Street	Indianapolis	IN	46247-9654	(317) 555-7665	hs@emcp.net
106	19	Providence, Inc.	12490 141st Street	Muncie	IN	47306-3410	(765) 555-3210	pi@emcp.net
107	12	Gallagher Systems	3885 Moore Avenue	Indianapolis	IN	47229-1075	(317) 555-9922	gs@emcp.net
108	26	Karris Supplies	12003 East 16th Street	Fishers	IN	46038-1200	(317) 555-2005	ks@emcp.net
109	18	HE Systems	321 Midland Avenue	Greenwood	IN	46143-3120	(317) 555-3311	he@emcp.net
110	21	Blue Ridge, Inc.	29 South 25th Street	Indianapolis	IN	46227-1355	(317) 555-7742	br@emcp.net

Group, Sort, and Total

Add a group　Add a sort

Group records by a specific field by clicking this button and then clicking the desired field.

Sort records by a specific field by clicking this button and then clicking the desired field.

When you specify a grouping level, Access automatically sorts that level in ascending order (from A to Z or lowest to highest). You can then sort additional data within the report by clicking the Add a sort button in the Group, Sort, and Total pane. This inserts a sorting row in the pane below the grouping level row, along with a list of available fields. At this list, click the field on which you want to sort. For example, in Project 1d, you will specify that a report is grouped by city (which will display in ascending order) and then specify that the client names display in alphabetical order within the city.

HINT
Grouping allows you to separate groups of records visually.
Add a sort

To delete a grouping or sorting level in the Group, Sort, and Total pane, click the Delete button that displays at the right side of the level row. After specifying the grouping and sorting levels, close the Group, Sort, and Total pane by clicking the Close button located in the upper right corner of the pane.

Project 1d Grouping and Sorting Data — Part 4 of 4

1. With **AL1-C6-Dearborn.accdb** open, create a report with the Clients table using the Report button on the CREATE tab.
2. Click each column heading individually and then decrease the size of each column so the right border is just right of the longest entry.
3. Change the orientation to landscape by completing the following steps:
   a. Click the REPORT LAYOUT TOOLS PAGE SETUP tab.
   b. Click the Landscape button in the Page Layout group.
4. Group the report by representative ID and then sort by clients by completing the following steps:
   a. Click the REPORT LAYOUT TOOLS DESIGN tab.
   b. Click the Group & Sort button in the Grouping & Totals group.

c. Click the Add a group button in the Group, Sort, and Total pane.

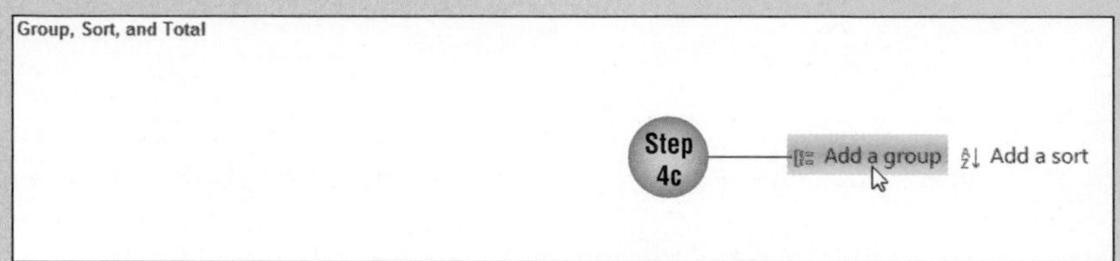

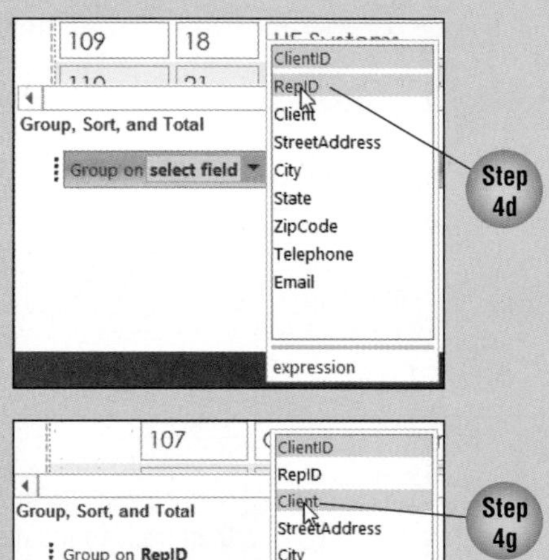

d. Click the *RepID* field in the list box.

e. Scroll through the report and notice that the records are grouped by the *RepID* field. Also, notice that the client names within each RepID field group are not in alphabetic order.

f. Click the Add a sort button in the Group, Sort, and Total pane.

g. Click the *Client* field in the list box.

h. Scroll through the report and notice that client names are now alphabetized within *RepID* field groups.

i. Close the Group, Sort, and Total pane by clicking the Close button located in the upper right corner of the pane.

5. Save the report and name it *ClientsGroupedRpt*.
6. Print the first page of the report by completing the following steps:
   a. Click the FILE tab, click the *Print* option, and then click the Print button.
   b. At the Print dialog box, click the *Pages* option in the *Print Range* section.
   c. Type 1 in the *From* text box, press the Tab key, and then type 1 in the *To* text box.
   d. Click OK.
7. Close the ClientsGroupedRpt report.
8. Create a report with the InOrMunSalesOver$99999Query query using the Report button on the CREATE tab.
9. Make sure the report displays in Layout view.
10. Group the report by city and then sort by clients by completing the following steps:
    a. Click the Group & Sort button in the Grouping & Totals group on the REPORT LAYOUT TOOLS DESIGN tab.
    b. Click the Add a group button in the Group, Sort, and Total pane.
    c. Click the *City* field in the list box.
    d. Click the Add a sort button in the Group, Sort, and Total pane and then click the *Client* field in the list box.
    e. Close the Group, Sort, and Total pane by clicking the Close button located in the upper right corner of the pane.
11. Print the first page of the report. (Refer to Step 6.)
12. Save the report and name it *InMunSalesOver$99999*.
13. Close the report.
14. Close **AL1-C6-Dearborn.accdb**.
15. Display the Open dialog box with the AL1C6 folder on your storage medium the active folder, open **AL1-C6-WarrenLegal.accdb**, and enable the contents.

16. Design a query that extracts records from three tables with the following specifications:
    a. Add the Billing, Clients, and Rates tables to the query window.
    b. Insert the *LastName* field from the *Clients* field list box to the first *Field* row field.
    c. Insert the *Date* field from the *Billing* field list box to the second *Field* row field.
    d. Insert the *Hours* field from the *Billing* field list box to the third *Field* row field.
    e. Insert the *Rate* field from the *Rates* field list box to the fourth *Field* row field.
    f. Click in the fifth *Field* row field, type **Total: [Hours]*[Rate]**, and then press Enter.

	Step 16b	Step 16c	Step 16d	Step 16e	Step 16f
Field:	LastName	Date	Hours	Rate	Total: [Hours]*[Rate]
Table:	Clients	Billing	Billing	Rates	
Sort:					
Show:	✔	✔	✔	✔	✔
Criteria:					
or:					

    g. Run the query.
    h. Save the query and name it *ClientBilling*.
    i. Close the query.
17. Create a report with the ClientBilling query using the Report button on the CREATE tab.
18. Click each column heading individually and then decrease the size of each column so the right border is near the longest entry.
19. Apply Currency formatting to the numbers in the *Total* column by completing the following steps:
    a. Click the REPORT LAYOUT TOOLS FORMAT tab.
    b. Click in the first field below the *Total* column (the field containing the number *350*).
    c. Click the Apply Currency Format button in the Number group.
    d. If necessary, increase the size of the *Total* column so the entire amounts (including the dollar signs) are visible.

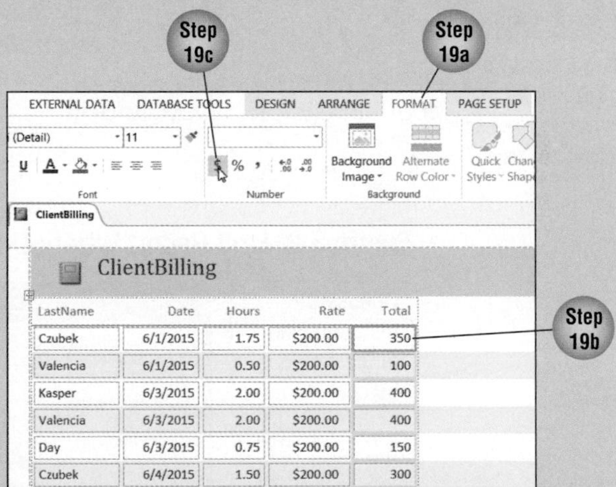

20. Group the report by last name by completing the following steps:
    a. Click the REPORT LAYOUT TOOLS DESIGN tab.
    b. Click the Group & Sort button in the Grouping & Totals group.
    c. Click the Add a group button in the Group, Sort, and Total pane.
    d. Click the *LastName* field in the list box.
    e. Click the Add a sort button in the Group, Sort, and Total pane.
    f. Click the *Date* field in the list box.
    g. Close the Group, Sort, and Total pane by clicking the Close button located in the upper right corner of the pane.
21. Scroll to the bottom of the report and, if necessary, increase the size of the column and row so the total amount in the *Rate* column is visible.
22. Save the report and name it *ClientBillingRpt*.
23. Print and then close the report. (The report will print on three pages.)
24. Close **AL1-C6-WarrenLegal.accdb**.

Project 2 Use Wizards to Create Reports and Labels 3 Parts

You will create reports using the Report Wizard and prepare mailing labels using the Label Wizard.

Creating Reports Using the Report Wizard

Quick Steps

Create a Report Using the Report Wizard
1. Click CREATE tab.
2. Click Report Wizard button.
3. Choose desired options at each Report Wizard dialog box.

Report Wizard

Use the Report Wizard to select specific fields and specify how data is grouped and sorted.

Access offers a Report Wizard that will guide you through the steps for creating a report. To create a report using the wizard, click the CREATE tab and then click the Report Wizard button in the Reports group. At the first wizard dialog box, shown in Figure 6.3, choose the desired table or query with options from the *Tables/Queries* option box. Specify the fields you want included in the report by inserting them in the *Selected Fields* list box and then clicking the Next button.

At the second Report Wizard dialog box, shown in Figure 6.4, specify the grouping level of data in the report. To group data by a specific field, click the field in the list box at the left side of the dialog box and then click the One Field button. Use the button containing the left-pointing arrow to remove an option as a grouping level. Use the up-pointing and down-pointing arrows to change the priority of the field.

Specify a sort order with options at the third Report Wizard dialog box, shown in Figure 6.5. To specify a sort order, click the down-pointing arrow at the right of the option box preceded by the number *1* and then click the field name. The default sort order is ascending. You can change this to descending by clicking the button that displays at the right side of the text box. After identifying the sort order, click the Next button.

Figure 6.3 First Report Wizard Dialog Box

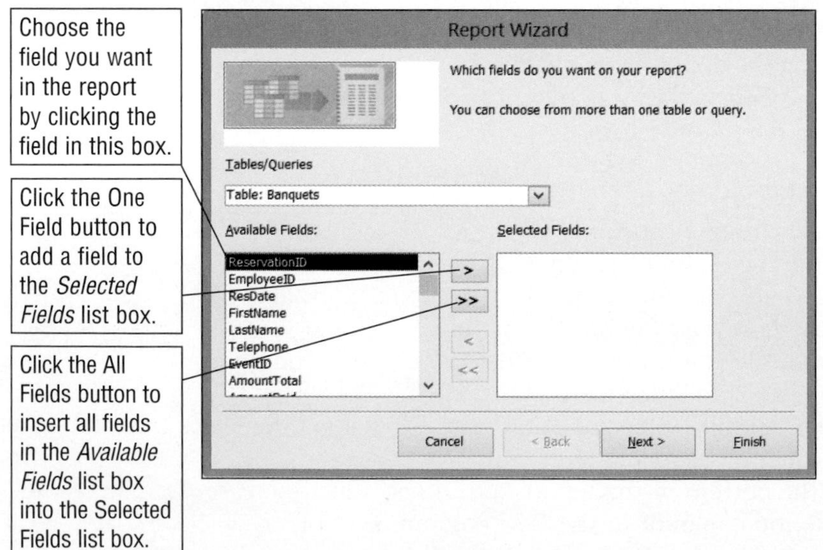
Choose the field you want in the report by clicking the field in this box.
Click the One Field button to add a field to the *Selected Fields* list box.
Click the All Fields button to insert all fields in the *Available Fields* list box into the Selected Fields list box.
Report Wizard
Which fields do you want on your report?
You can choose from more than one table or query.
Tables/Queries
Table: Banquets
Available Fields:
Selected Fields:
ReservationID
EmployeeID
ResDate
FirstName
LastName
Telephone
EventID
AmountTotal
>
>>
<
<<
Cancel
< Back
Next >
Finish

Figure 6.4 Second Report Wizard Dialog Box

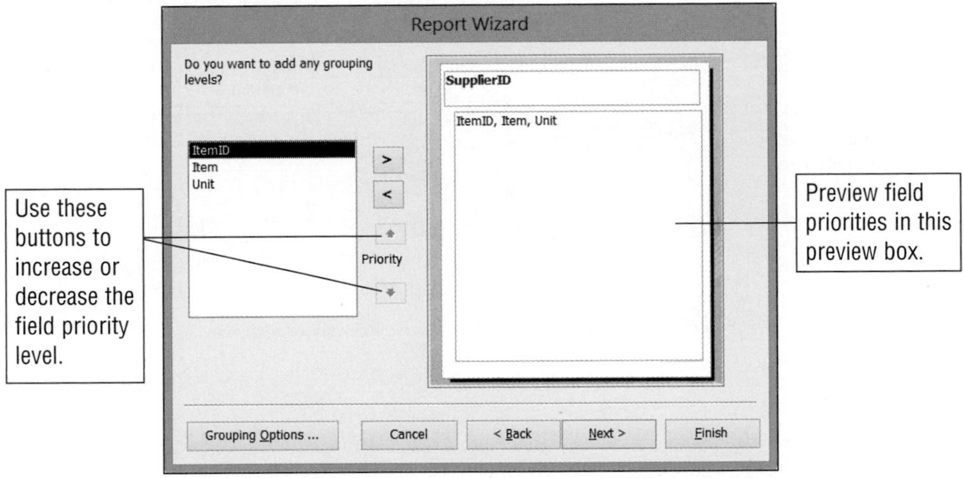

Figure 6.5 Third Report Wizard Dialog Box

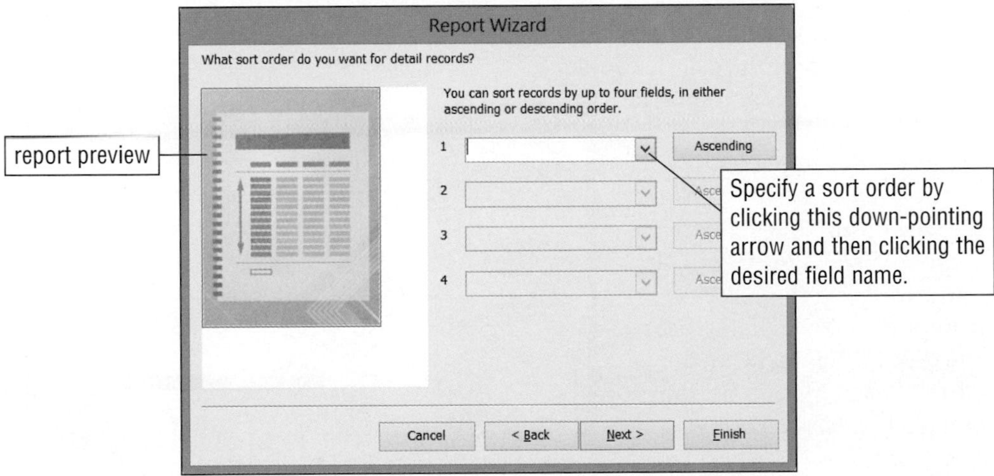

Use options at the fourth Report Wizard dialog box, shown in Figure 6.6, to specify the layout and orientation of the report. The *Layout* section has the default setting of *Stepped*. You can change this to *Block* or *Outline*. By default, the report will print in portrait orientation. You can change to landscape orientation in the *Orientation* section of the dialog box. Access will adjust field widths in the report so all of the fields fit on one page. If you do not want Access to make this adjustment, remove the check mark from the *Adjust the field width so all fields fit on a page* option.

At the fifth and final Report Wizard dialog box, type a name for the report and then click the Finish button.

Figure 6.6 Fourth Report Wizard Dialog Box

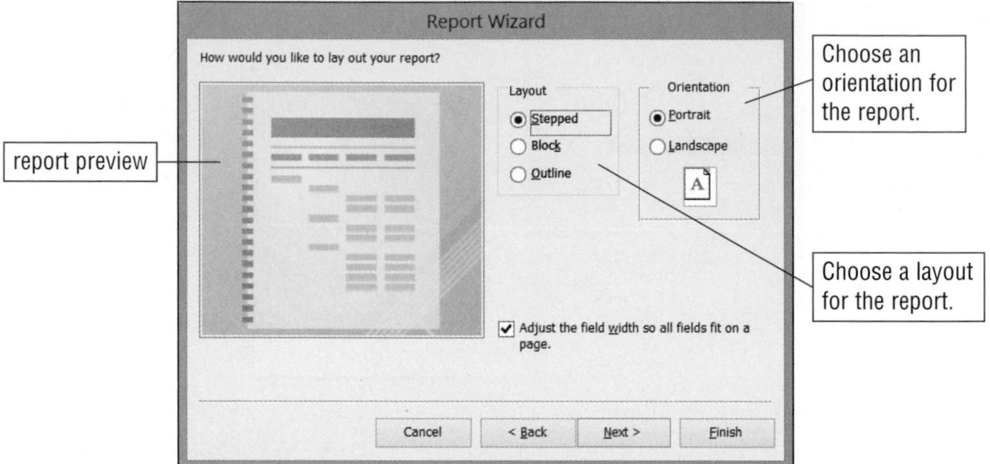

Project 2a Using the Report Wizard to Prepare a Report

Part 1 of 3

1. Display the Open dialog box with the AL1C6 folder on your storage medium the active folder.
2. Open **AL1-C6-Skyline.accdb** and enable the contents.
3. Create a report using the Report Wizard by completing the following steps:
   a. Click the CREATE tab.
   b. Click the Report Wizard button in the Reports group.
   c. At the first Report Wizard dialog box, click the down-pointing arrow at the right side of the *Tables/Queries* option box and then click *Table: Inventory* at the drop-down list.
   d. Click the All Fields button to insert all of the Inventory fields in the *Selected Fields* list box.
   e. Click the Next button.
   f. At the second Report Wizard dialog box, make sure *SupplierID* displays in blue at the top of the preview page at the right side of the dialog box and then click the Next button.
   g. At the third Report Wizard dialog box, click the Next button. (You want to use the sorting defaults.)
   h. At the fourth Report Wizard dialog box, click the *Block* option in the *Layout* section and then click the Next button.

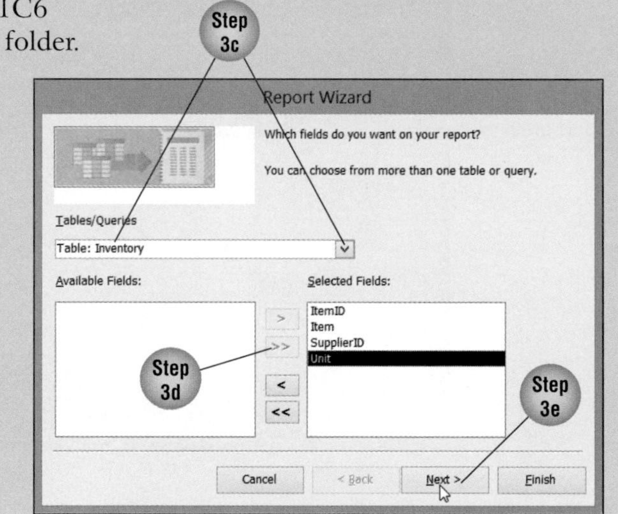

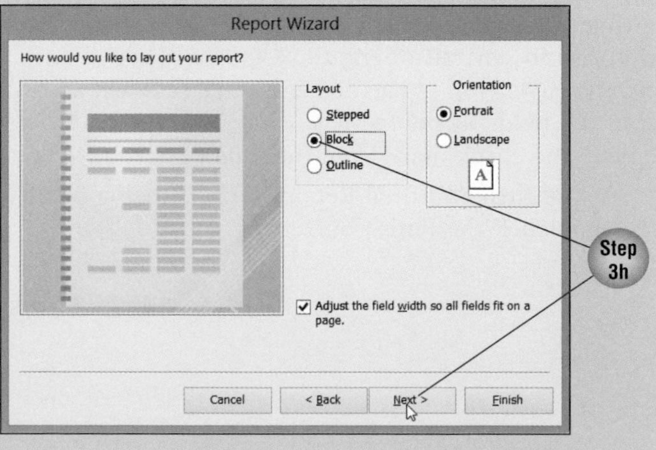

i. At the fifth Report Wizard dialog box, make sure *Inventory* displays in the *What title do you want for your report?* text box and then click the Finish button. (The report displays in Print Preview.)

4. With the report in Print Preview, click the Print button at the left side of the PRINT PREVIEW tab and then click OK at the Print dialog box. (The report will print on two pages.)
5. Close Print Preview.
6. Switch to Report view by clicking the View button on the REPORT DESIGN TOOLS DESIGN tab.
7. Close the Inventory report.

If you create a report with fields from only one table, you will choose options from five Report Wizard dialog boxes. If you create a report with fields from more than one table, you will choose options from six Report Wizard dialog boxes. After choosing the tables and fields at the first dialog box, the second dialog box that displays asks how you want to view the data. For example, if you specify fields from a Suppliers table and fields from an Orders table, the second Report Wizard dialog box will ask you if you want to view data "by Suppliers" or "by Orders."

Project 2b Creating a Report with Fields from Multiple Tables — Part 2 of 3

1. With **AL1-C6-Skyline.accdb** open, create a report with the Report Wizard by completing the following steps:
   a. Click the CREATE tab.
   b. Click the Report Wizard button in the Reports group.
   c. At the first Report Wizard dialog box, click the down-pointing arrow at the right side of the *Tables/Queries* option box and then click *Table: Events* at the drop-down list.
   d. Click the *Event* field in the *Available Fields* list box and then click the One Field button.
   e. Click the down-pointing arrow at the right side of the *Tables/Queries* option box and then click *Table: Banquets* at the drop-down list.
   f. Insert the following fields in the *Selected Fields* list box:
      ResDate
      FirstName
      LastName
      AmountTotal
      AmountPaid
   g. After inserting the fields, click the Next button.
   h. At the second Report Wizard dialog box, make sure *by Events* is selected and then click the Next button.

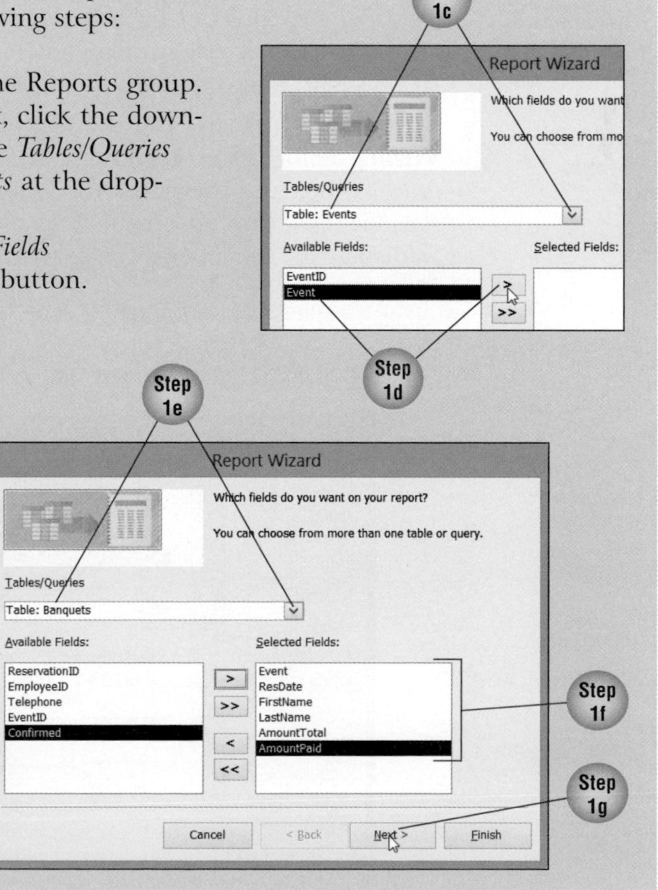

i. At the third Report Wizard dialog box, click the Next button. (The report preview shows that the report will be grouped by event.)
j. At the fourth Report Wizard dialog box, click the Next button. (You want to use the sorting defaults.)
k. At the fifth Report Wizard dialog box, click the *Block* option in the *Layout* section, click *Landscape* in the *Orientation* section, and then click the Next button.
l. At the sixth Report Wizard dialog box, select the current name in the *What title do you want for your report?* text box, type **BanquetEvents**, and then click the Finish button.

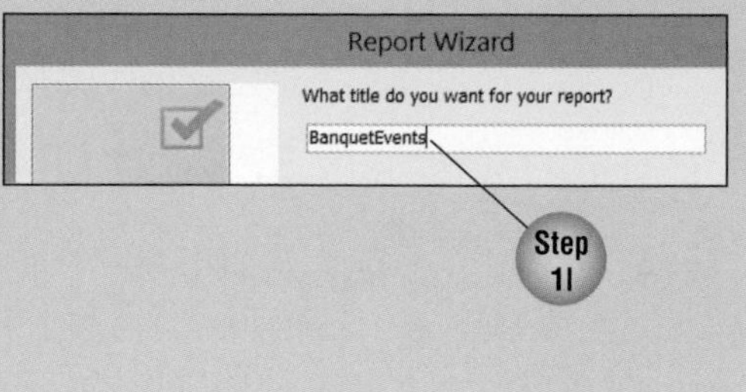

2. Close Print Preview and then change to Layout view.
3. Print and then close the BanquetEvents report.
4. Close **AL1-C6-Skyline.accdb**.

Preparing Mailing Labels

Quick Steps
Create Mailing Labels Using the Label Wizard
1. Click desired table.
2. Click CREATE tab.
3. Click Labels button.
4. Choose desired options at each Label Wizard dialog box.

Labels

Access includes a mailing label wizard that walks you through the steps for creating mailing labels with fields in a table. To create mailing labels, click the desired table, click the CREATE tab, and then click the Labels button in the Reports group. At the first Label Wizard dialog box, shown in Figure 6.7, specify the label size, units of measure, and label type and then click the Next button. At the second Label Wizard dialog box, shown in Figure 6.8, specify the font name, size, weight, and color and then click the Next button.

Specify the fields you want included in the mailing labels at the third Label Wizard dialog box, shown in Figure 6.9. To do this, click the field in the *Available fields* list box and then click the One Field button. This moves the field to the *Prototype label* box. Insert the fields in the *Prototype label* box as you want the text to display on the label. After inserting the fields in the *Prototype label* box, click the Next button.

Figure 6.7 First Label Wizard Dialog Box

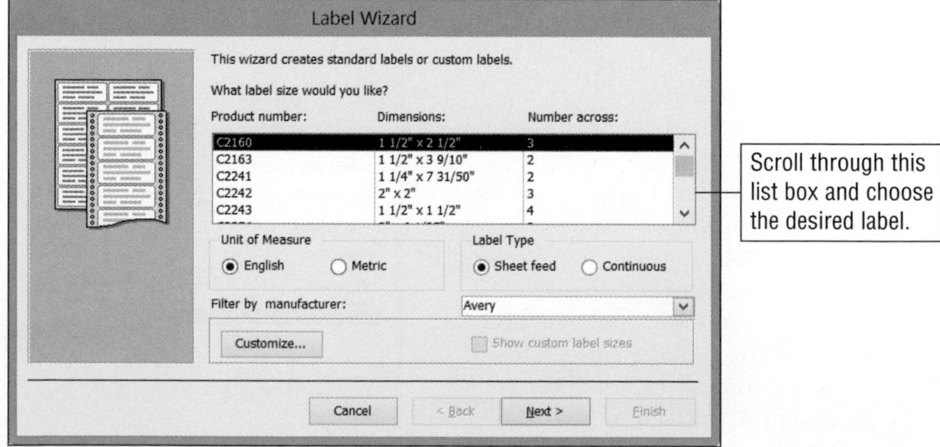

Figure 6.8 Second Label Wizard Dialog Box

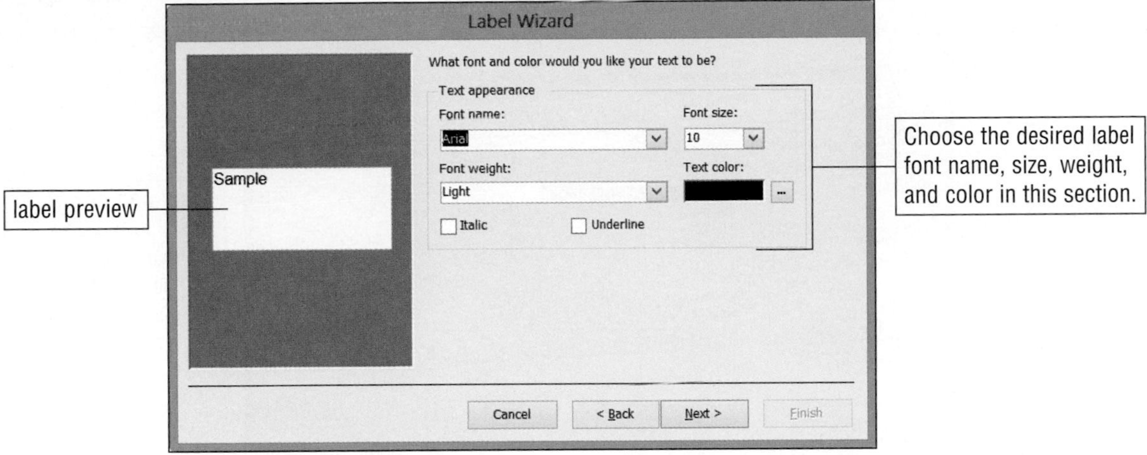

Figure 6.9 Third Label Wizard Dialog Box

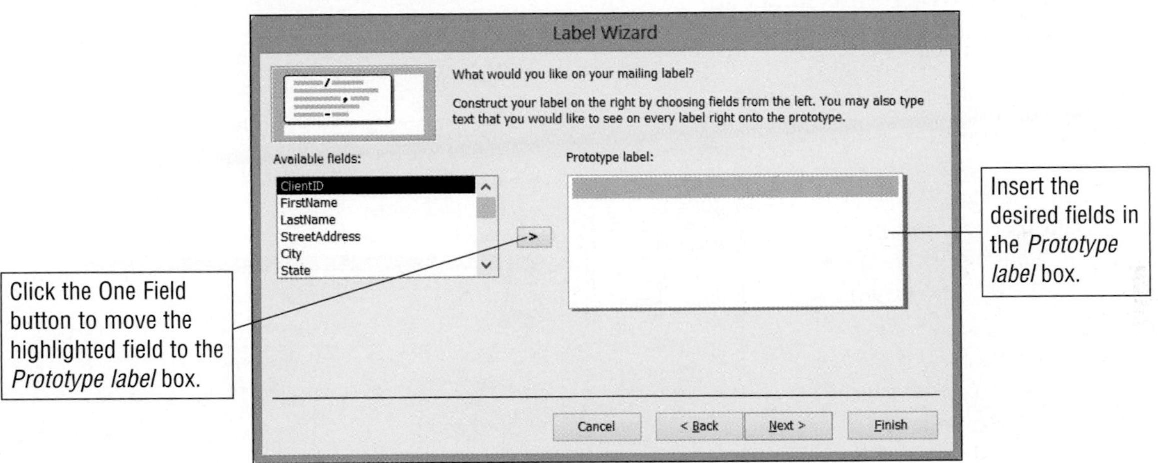

At the fourth Label Wizard dialog box, shown in Figure 6.10, specify a field from the database by which the labels will be sorted. If you want the labels sorted (for example, by last name, postal code, etc.), insert the field in the *Sort by* list box and then click the Next button.

At the last Label Wizard dialog box, type a name for the label file and then click the Finish button. After a few moments, the labels display on the screen in Print Preview. Print the labels and/or close Print Preview.

Figure 6.10 Fourth Label Wizard Dialog Box

Project 2c Preparing Mailing Labels **Part 3 of 3**

1. Open **AL1-C6-WarrenLegal.accdb**.
2. Click *Clients* in the Tables group in the Navigation pane.
3. Click the CREATE tab and then click the Labels button in the Reports group.
4. At the first Label Wizard dialog box, make sure *English* is selected in the *Unit of Measure* section, *Avery* is selected in the *Filter by manufacturer* list box, *Sheet feed* is selected in the *Label Type* section, and *C2160* is selected in the *Product number* list box and then click the Next button.
5. At the second Label Wizard dialog box, if necessary, change the font size to 10 points and then click the Next button.
6. At the third Label Wizard dialog box, complete the following steps to insert the fields in the *Prototype label* box:
   a. Click *FirstName* in the *Available fields* list box and then click the One Field button.
   b. Press the spacebar, make sure *LastName* is selected in the *Available fields* list box, and then click the One Field button.
   c. Press the Enter key. (This moves the insertion point down to the next line in the *Prototype label* box.)
   d. With *StreetAddress* selected in the *Available fields* list box, click the One Field button.
   e. Press the Enter key.
   f. With *City* selected in the *Available fields* list box, click the One Field button.
   g. Type a comma (,) and then press the spacebar.

h. With *State* selected in the *Available fields* list box, click the One Field button.
i. Press the spacebar.
j. With *ZipCode* selected in the *Available fields* list box, click the One Field button.
k. Click the Next button.

7. At the fourth Label Wizard dialog box, sort by zip code. To do this, click *ZipCode* in the *Available fields* list box and then click the One Field button.
8. Click the Next button.
9. At the last Label Wizard dialog box, click the Finish button. (The Label Wizard automatically names the label report *Labels Clients*.)
10. Print the labels by clicking the Print button that displays at the left side of the PRINT PREVIEW tab and then click OK at the Print dialog box.
11. Close Print Preview.
12. Switch to Report view by clicking the View button on the REPORT DESIGN TOOLS DESIGN tab.
13. Close the labels report and then close **AL1-C6-WarrenLegal.accdb**.

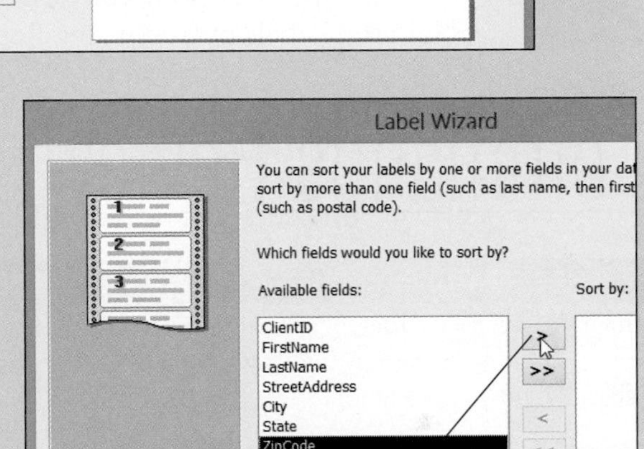

Chapter Summary

- Create a report with data in a table or query to control how data appears on the page when printed.
- Create a report with the Report button in the Reports group on the CREATE tab.
- Four views are available for viewing a report: Report view, Print Preview, Layout view, and Design view.
- Use options on the PRINT PREVIEW tab to specify how a report prints.
- In Layout view, you can select a report control object and then size or move the object. You can also change the column width by clicking a column heading and then dragging the border to the desired width.
- Sort data in a record using the Ascending button or Descending button in the Sort & Filter group on the HOME tab.
- Customize a report with options on the REPORT LAYOUT TOOLS ribbon with the DESIGN tab, ARRANGE tab, FORMAT tab, or PAGE SETUP tab selected.

- To make data in a report easier to understand, divide the data into groups using the Group, Sort, and Total pane. Display this pane by clicking the Group & Sort button in the Grouping & Totals group on the REPORT LAYOUT TOOLS DESIGN tab.
- Use the Report Wizard to guide you through the steps for creating a report. Begin the wizard by clicking the CREATE tab and then clicking the Report Wizard button in the Reports group.
- Create mailing labels with data in a table using the Label Wizard. Begin the wizard by clicking the desired table, clicking the CREATE tab, and then clicking the Labels button in the Reports group.

Commands Review

FEATURE	RIBBON TAB, GROUP	BUTTON
Group, Sort, and Total pane	REPORT LAYOUT TOOLS DESIGN, Grouping & Totals	
Labels Wizard	CREATE, Reports	
report	CREATE, Reports	
Report Wizard	CREATE, Reports	

Concepts Check Test Your Knowledge

Completion: In the space provided at the right, indicate the correct term, symbol, or command.

1. The Report button is located in the Reports group on this tab. ____________________
2. Press these keys on the keyboard to select all control objects in a report in Layout view. ____________________
3. The Ascending button is located in this group on the HOME tab. ____________________
4. Four views are available in a report, including Layout view, Report view, Design view, and this view. ____________________
5. With options on this tab, you can insert controls, insert header or footer data, and add existing fields. ____________________

6. Click this button in the Grouping & Totals group on the REPORT LAYOUT TOOLS DESIGN tab to perform functions such as finding the sum, average, maximum, and minimum of the numbers in a column. ____________________

7. The Group & Sort button is located in this group on the REPORT LAYOUT TOOLS DESIGN tab. ____________________

8. Click the Group & Sort button and this pane displays. ____________________

9. Use this to guide you through the steps for creating a report. ____________________

10. To create mailing labels, click the desired table, click the CREATE tab, and then click the Labels button in this group. ____________________

Skills Check Assess Your Performance

Assessment 1

CREATE AND FORMAT REPORTS IN THE HILLTOP DATABASE

1. Open **AL1-C6-Hilltop.accdb** and enable the contents.
2. Create a report with the Inventory table using the Report button.
3. With the report in Layout view, apply the following formatting:
   a. Center the data below each of the following column headings: *EquipmentID*, *AvailableHours*, *ServiceHours*, and *RepairHours*.
   b. Select all of the control objects and then change the font to Constantia.
   c. Select the money amounts below the *PurchasePrice* column heading and then click the Decrease Decimals button (in the Number group) until the amounts display without any places past the decimal point.
   d. Click in the *$473,260.00* amount and then click the Decrease Decimals button until the amount displays with no places past the decimal point.
   e. If necessary, increase the height of the total amount row so the entire amount is visible.
   f. Change the title of the report to *Inventory Report*.
4. Save the report and name it *InventoryReport*.
5. Print and then close InventoryReport.
6. Create a query in Design view with the following specifications:
   a. Add the Customers, Equipment, Invoices, and Rates tables to the query window.
   b. Insert the *Customer* field from the *Customers* field list box in the first *Field* row field.
   c. Insert the *Equipment* field from the *Equipment* field list box in the second *Field* row field.
   d. Insert the *Hours* field from the *Invoices* field list box in the third *Field* row field.
   e. Insert the *Rate* field from the *Rates* field list box in the fourth *Field* row field.
   f. Click in the fifth *Field* row field, type **Total: [Hours]*[Rate]**, and then press Enter.

g. Run the query.
h. Save the query and name it *CustomerRentals* and then close the query.
7. Create a report with the CustomerRentals query using the Report button.
8. With the report in Layout view, apply the following formatting:
a. Decrease the widths of the columns so the right border of each column displays near the right side of the longest entry.
b. Select the money amounts and then click the Decrease Decimals button until the amounts display with no places past the decimal point.
c. Click in the *Total* column and then total the amounts by clicking the REPORT LAYOUT TOOLS DESIGN tab, clicking the Totals button in the Grouping & Totals group, and then clicking *Sum* at the drop-down list.
d. Click the total amount (located at the bottom of the *Total* column), click the REPORT LAYOUT TOOLS FORMAT tab, and then click the Apply Currency Format button in the Number group.
e. Increase the height of the total amount row so the entire amount is visible.
f. Select and then delete the amount that displays at the bottom of the *Rate* column.
g. Display the Group, Sort, and Total pane; group the records by *Customer*; sort by *Equipment*; and then close the pane.
h. Apply the Integral theme. (Do this with the Themes button in the Themes group on the REPORT LAYOUT TOOLS DESIGN tab.)
i. Select the five column headings and change the font color to black.
j. Change the title of the report to *Rentals*.
9. Save the report and name it *RentalReport*.
10. Print and then close RentalReport.

Assessment 2

CREATE REPORTS USING THE REPORT WIZARD

1. With **AL1-C6-Hilltop.accdb** open, create a report using the Report Wizard with the following specifications:
a. At the first Report Wizard dialog box, insert the following fields in the *Selected Fields* list box:

From the Equipment table:	*Equipment*
From the Inventory table:	*PurchaseDate*
	PurchasePrice
	AvailableHours

b. Do not make any changes at the second Report Wizard dialog box.
c. Do not make any changes at the third Report Wizard dialog box.
d. At the fourth Report Wizard dialog box, choose the *Columnar* option.
e. At the fifth and last Report Wizard dialog box, click the Finish button. (This accepts the default report name *Equipment*.)
2. Print and then close the report.

3. Create a report using the Report Wizard with the following specifications:
   a. At the first Report Wizard dialog box, insert the following fields in the *Selected Fields* list box:

From the Customers table:	*Customer*
From the Invoices table:	*BillingDate* *Hours*
From the Equipment table:	*Equipment*
From the Rates table:	*Rate*

   b. Do not make any changes at the second Report Wizard dialog box.
   c. Do not make any changes at the third Report Wizard dialog box.
   d. Do not make any changes at the fourth Report Wizard dialog box.
   e. At the fifth Report Wizard dialog box, choose the *Block* option.
   f. At the sixth and last Report Wizard dialog box, name the report *Rentals*.
4. Print and then close the report.

Assessment 3

CREATE MAILING LABELS

1. With **AL1-C6-Hilltop.accdb** open, click *Customers* in the Tables group in the Navigation pane.
2. Use the Label Wizard to create mailing labels (you determine the label type) with customer names and addresses and sort the labels by customer names. Name the mailing label report *CustomerMailingLabels*.
3. Print the mailing labels.
4. Close the mailing labels report.

Assessment 4

ADD A FIELD TO A REPORT

1. In Chapter 5, you added a field list to an existing form using the Field List task pane. Experiment with adding a field to an existing report and then complete the following:
   a. Open the RentalReport report (created in Assessment 1) in Layout view.
   b. Display the Field List task pane and display all of the tables.
   c. Drag the *BillingDate* field from the Invoices table so the field is positioned between the *Equipment* column and *Hours* column.
   d. At the message indicating that Access will modify the RecordSource property and asking if you want to continue, click Yes.
   e. Close the Field List task pane.
2. Save, print, and then close the report.
3. Close **AL1-C6-Hilltop.accdb**.

Visual Benchmark Demonstrate Your Proficiency

DESIGN A QUERY AND CREATE A REPORT WITH THE QUERY

1. Open **AL1-C6-Skyline.accdb** and then create and run the query shown in Figure 6.11.
2. Save the query and name it *Suppliers2&4Orders* and then close the query.
3. Use the Report button to create the report shown in Figure 6.12 using the *Suppliers2&4Orders* query with the following specifications:
   a. Apply the Facet theme.
   b. Adjust the column widths and change the alignment of data as shown in Figure 6.12.
   c. Change the title as shown in Figure 6.12.
   d. Select the column headings and then apply the Black font color.
   e. Insert the total of the amounts in the *Total* column. Format the total amount as shown in Figure 6.12.
   f. Delete the sum amount at the bottom of the *UnitPrice* column.
4. Save the report and name it *Suppliers2&4OrdersRpt*.
5. Print the report, close the report, and then close **AL1-C6-Skyline.accdb**.

Figure 6.11 Visual Benchmark Query

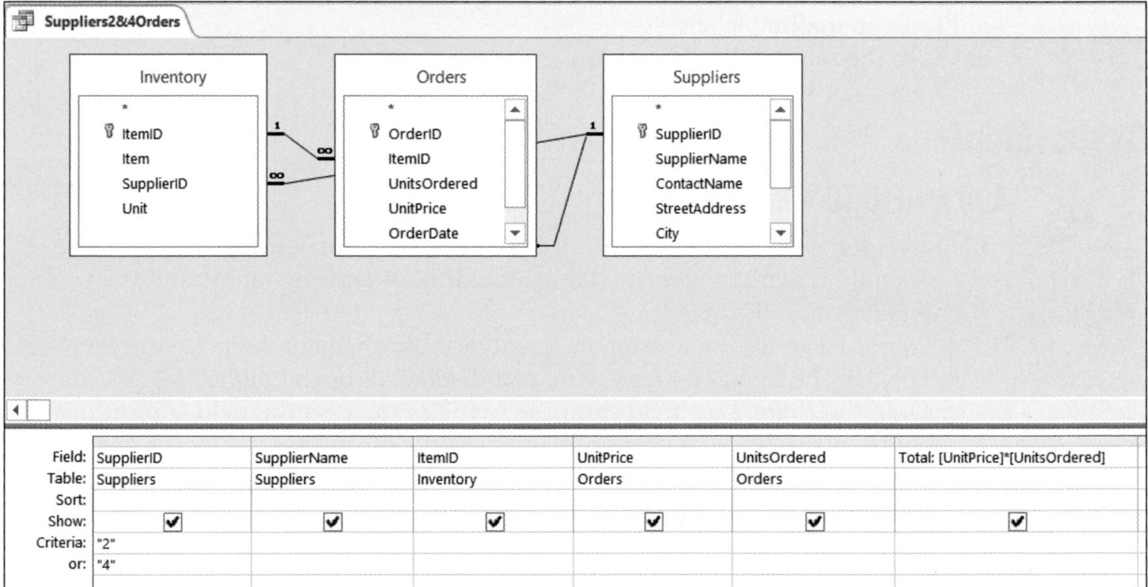

Figure 6.12 Visual Benchmark Report

Suppliers 2 and 4 Orders

Thursday, October 15, 2015
4:45:53 PM

SupplierID	SupplierName	ItemID	UnitPrice	UnitsOrdered	Total
2	Coral Produce	002	$10.50	3	$31.50
2	Coral Produce	016	$24.00	1	$24.00
4	Grocery Wholesalers	020	$18.75	2	$37.50
2	Coral Produce	014	$15.75	2	$31.50
4	Grocery Wholesalers	025	$28.50	1	$28.50
4	Grocery Wholesalers	036	$17.00	2	$34.00
4	Grocery Wholesalers	013	$14.00	2	$28.00
2	Coral Produce	004	$10.95	2	$21.90
4	Grocery Wholesalers	035	$17.00	1	$17.00
4	Grocery Wholesalers	027	$22.00	1	$22.00
4	Grocery Wholesalers	026	$29.25	1	$29.25
2	Coral Produce	021	$31.00	1	$31.00
4	Grocery Wholesalers	034	$13.75	2	$27.50
4	Grocery Wholesalers	012	$30.25	1	$30.25
4	Grocery Wholesalers	018	$45.00	1	$45.00
2	Coral Produce	016	$39.40	2	$78.80
4	Grocery Wholesalers	035	$17.00	1	$17.00
2	Coral Produce	014	$15.75	2	$31.50
4	Grocery Wholesalers	020	$18.75	2	$37.50
					$603.70

Case Study Apply Your Skills

Part 1

As the office manager at Millstone Legal Services, you need to enter records for three new clients in **AL1-C6-Millstone.accdb**. Using the following information, enter the data in the appropriate tables:

Client number 42
Martin Costanzo
1002 Thomas Drive
Casper, WY 82602
(307) 555-5001
Mr. Costanzo saw Douglas Sheehan regarding divorce proceedings with a billing date of 3/15/2015 and a fee of $150.

Client number 43
Susan Nordyke
23193 Ridge Circle East
Mills, WY 82644
(307) 555-2719
Ms. Nordyke saw Loretta Ryder regarding support enforcement with a billing date of 3/15/2015 and a fee of $175.

Client number 44
Monica Sommers
1105 Riddell Avenue
Casper, WY 82609
(307) 555-1188
Ms. Sommers saw Anita Leland regarding a guardianship with a billing date of 3/15/2015 and a fee of $250.

Part 2

Create and print the following queries, reports, and labels:

- Create a report with the Clients table. Apply formatting to enhance the appearance of the report.
- Create a query that displays the client ID, first name, and last name; attorney last name; billing date; and fee. Name the query *ClientBilling*.
- Create a report with the ClientBilling query. Group the records in the report by attorney last name (the *LName* field in the drop-down list) and sort alphabetically in ascending order by client last name (the *LastName* field in the drop-down list). Apply formatting to enhance the appearance of the report.
- Produce a telephone directory by creating a report that includes client last names, first names, and telephone numbers. Sort the records in the report alphabetically by last name in ascending order.
- Edit the ClientBilling query so it includes a criterion that displays only billing dates between 3/10/2015 and 3/13/2015. Save the query with Save Object As and name it *ClientBilling10-13*.
- Create a report with the ClientBilling10-13 query. Apply formatting to enhance the appearance of the report.
- Create mailing labels for the clients.

Part 3

Apply the following conditions to fields in reports and then print the reports:

- In the Clients report, apply the condition that the city *Casper* displays in the Red font color and the city *Mills* displays the Blue font color in the *City* field.
- In the ClientBilling report, apply the condition that fees over $199 display in the Green font color and fees less than $200 display in the Blue font color.

Part 4

Your center has a manual that describes processes and procedures in the workplace. Open Word and create a document for the manual that describes how to create a report using the Report button and Report Wizard and how to create mailing labels using the Label Wizard. Save the completed document and name it **AL1-C6-CS-Manual**. Print and then close **AL1-C6-CS-Manual.docx**.

MICROSOFT® ACCESS®

CHAPTER 7

Modifying, Filtering, and Viewing Data

PERFORMANCE OBJECTIVES

Upon successful completion of Chapter 7, you will be able to:

- **Filter data by selection and form**
- **Remove a filter**
- **View object dependencies**
- **Compact and repair a database**
- **Encrypt a database with a password**
- **View and customize document properties**
- **Save a database in an earlier version of Access**
- **Save a database object in PDF file format**

Tutorials

7.1 Filtering Records

7.2 Viewing Object Dependencies

7.3 Compacting, Repairing, and Backing Up a Database

7.4 Encrypting a Database with a Password and Modifying Document Properties

7.5 Saving Databases and Database Objects in Different Formats

You can filter data in a database object to view specific records without having to change the design of the object. In this chapter, you will learn how to filter data by selection and form. You will also learn how to view object dependencies, manage a database with options at the Info backstage area, save a database in an earlier version of Access, and save a database object in PDF file format. Model answers for this chapter's projects appear on the following pages.

Note: Before beginning the projects, copy to your storage medium the AL1C7 subfolder from the AL1 folder on the CD that accompanies this textbook and make AL1C7 the active folder.

Project 1 Filter Records

Project 1a

EmployeeID	FName	LName	StreetAddress	City	State	ZipCode
02	Wayne	Weber	17362 North Tenth	Fort Myers	FL	33994
03	Owen	Pasqual	4010 Shannon Drive	Fort Myers	FL	33910
04	Vadim	Sayenko	1328 St. Paul Avenue	Fort Myers	FL	33907
07	Donald	Sellars	23103 Summer Highway	Fort Myers	FL	33919
09	Elizabeth	Mohr	1818 Brookdale Road	Fort Myers	FL	33902
11	Nicole	Bateman	5001 150th Street	Fort Myers	FL	33908

Skyline Employees Filtered Records, Page 1

Telephone	HireDate	HealthIns
(239) 555-6041	4/1/2010	☐
(239) 555-3492	4/15/2009	☐
(239) 555-9487	6/15/2009	☑
(239) 555-4348	6/6/2012	☑
(239) 555-0430	5/1/2011	☑
(239) 555-2631	2/1/2013	☐

Skyline Employees Filtered Records, Page 2

Project 1b

ResDate	FirstName	LastName	Telephone	Event	EmployeeID
6/5/2015	Terrance	Schaefer	(239) 555-6239	Wedding rehearsal dinner	03
6/5/2015	Andrea	Wyatt	(239) 555-4282	Wedding reception	01
6/6/2015	Luis	Castillo	(239) 555-4001	Wedding shower	11
6/6/2015	David	Hooper	(941) 555-2338	Wedding anniversary	04
6/7/2015	Bridget	Kohn	(239) 555-1299	Other	02
6/9/2015	Joanne	Blair	(239) 555-7783	Birthday	03
6/12/2015	Tim	Drysdale	(941) 555-0098	Bat mitzvah	02
6/12/2015	Gabrielle	Johnson	(239) 555-1882	Other	05
6/12/2015	Cliff	Osborne	(239) 555-7823	Wedding rehearsal dinner	12
6/13/2015	Janis	Semala	(239) 555-0476	Wedding reception	06
6/13/2015	Tristan	Strauss	(941) 555-7746	Other	03
6/14/2015	Aaron	Williams	(239) 555-3821	Bar mitzvah	04
6/14/2015	Willow	Earhart	(239) 555-0034	Wedding shower	04

Skyline Banquet Reservations Query

BanquetReservations

Friday, October 16, 2015
1:41:29 PM

ResDate	FirstName	LastName	Telephone	Event	EmployeeID
6/9/2015	Joanne	Blair	(239) 555-7783	Birthday	03
6/5/2015	Terrance	Schaefer	(239) 555-6239	Wedding rehearsal dinner	03

Skyline Banquet Report

Project 1c

ItemID	Item	SupplierID	Unit
003	Carrots	6	25 lb bag
005	Garlic	6	10 lb bag
009	Radishes	6	case
010	Celery	6	case
011	Broccoli	6	case
041	White sugar	6	25 lb bag
042	Baking powder	6	case
043	Baking soda	6	case

Skyline Filtered Inventory Records, Step 2c

ItemID	Item	SupplierID	Unit
006	Green peppers	2	case
007	Red peppers	2	case
008	Yellow peppers	2	case

Skyline Filtered Inventory Records, Step 3d

ResDate	FirstName	LastName	Telephone	Event	EmployeeID
6/6/2015	Luis	Castillo	(239) 555-4001	Wedding shower	11
6/14/2015	Willow	Earhart	(239) 555-0034	Wedding shower	04
6/9/2015	Joanne	Blair	(239) 555-7783	Birthday	03
6/16/2015	Jason	Haley	(239) 555-6641	Birthday	06
6/18/2015	Heidi	Thompson	(941) 555-3215	Birthday	01
6/27/2015	Kirsten	Simpson	(941) 555-4425	Birthday	02
6/14/2015	Aaron	Williams	(239) 555-3821	Bar mitzvah	04
6/20/2015	Robin	Gehring	(239) 555-0126	Bar mitzvah	06
6/12/2015	Tim	Drysdale	(941) 555-0098	Bat mitzvah	02
6/7/2015	Bridget	Kohn	(239) 555-1299	Other	02
6/12/2015	Gabrielle	Johnson	(239) 555-1882	Other	05
6/13/2015	Tristan	Strauss	(941) 555-7746	Other	03
6/17/2015	Lillian	Krakosky	(239) 555-8890	Other	03
6/20/2015	David	Fitzgerald	(941) 555-3792	Other	01
6/5/2015	Terrance	Schaefer	(239) 555-6239	Wedding rehearsal dinner	03
6/12/2015	Cliff	Osborne	(239) 555-7823	Wedding rehearsal dinner	12
6/6/2015	David	Hooper	(941) 555-2338	Wedding anniversary	04
6/19/2015	Anthony	Wiegand	(239) 555-7853	Wedding anniversary	11
6/27/2015	Shane	Rozier	(239) 555-1033	Wedding anniversary	12

Skyline Filtered Banquet Reservations Records, Step 6c

ResDate	FirstName	LastName	Telephone	Event	EmployeeID
6/14/2015	Aaron	Williams	(239) 555-3821	Bar mitzvah	04
6/20/2015	Robin	Gehring	(239) 555-0126	Bar mitzvah	06
6/12/2015	Tim	Drysdale	(941) 555-0098	Bat mitzvah	02

Skyline Filtered Banquet Reservations Records, Step 7d

Project 1d

ReservationID	EmployeeID	ResDate	FirstName	LastName	Telephone	EventID	AmountTotal	AmountPaid	Confirmed
1	03	6/5/2015	Terrance	Schaefer	(239) 555-6239	RD	$750.00	$250.00	☑
6	03	6/9/2015	Joanne	Blair	(239) 555-7783	BD	$650.00	$200.00	☑
11	03	6/13/2015	Tristan	Strauss	(941) 555-7746	OT	$1,400.00	$300.00	☐
15	03	6/17/2015	Lillian	Krakosky	(239) 555-8890	OT	$500.00	$100.00	☐

Skyline Filtered Banquets Records, Step 3c

ItemID	Item	SupplierID	Unit
001	Butternut squash	2	case
002	Potatoes	2	50 lb bag
004	Onions	2	25 lb bag
006	Green peppers	2	case
007	Red peppers	2	case
008	Yellow peppers	2	case
014	Green beans	2	case
016	Iceberg lettuce	2	case
017	Romaine lettuce	2	case
021	Cantaloupes	2	case
028	Beef	7	side
029	Pork	7	side
030	Chicken	7	case
051	Watermelon	2	case
052	Kiwi	2	case

Skyline Filtered Inventory Records, Step 6h

Model Answers

Project 2 View Object Dependencies, Manage a Database, and Save a Database in a Different File Format

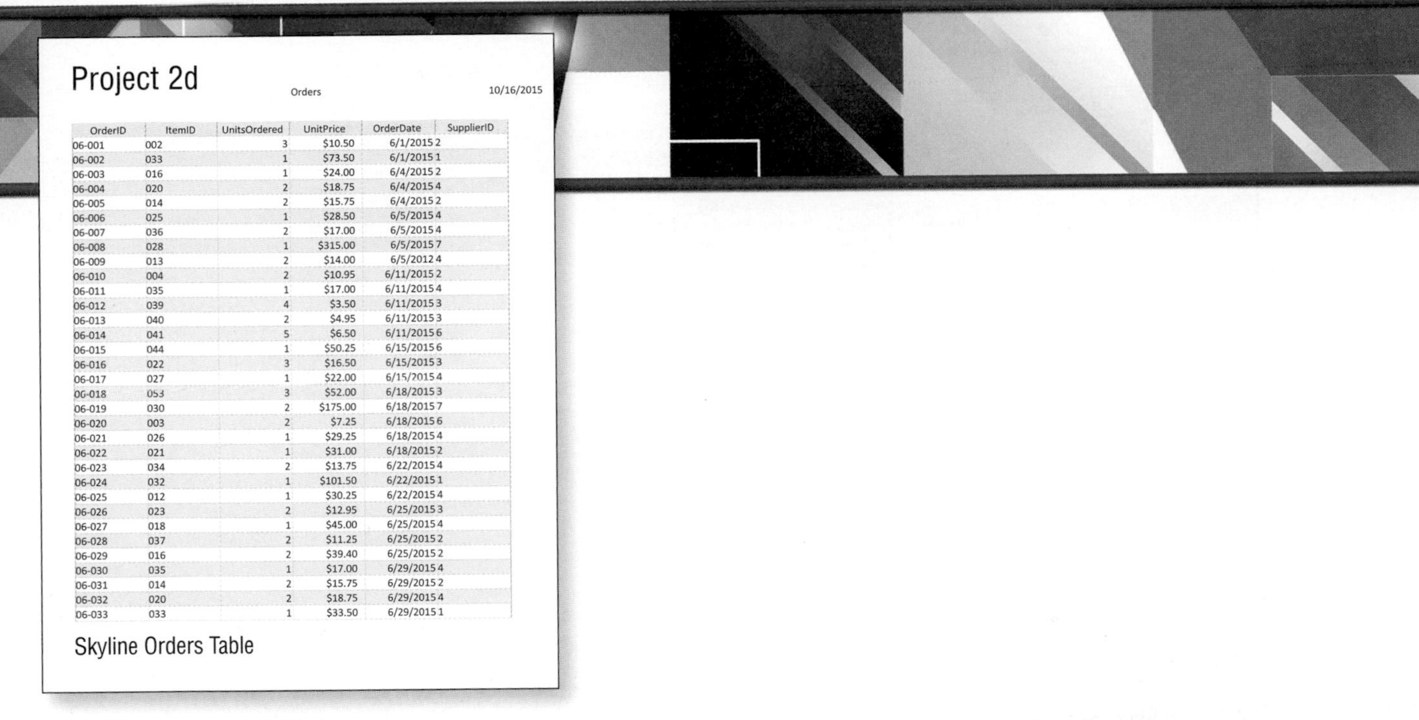

Project 2d

Orders 10/16/2015

OrderID	ItemID	UnitsOrdered	UnitPrice	OrderDate	SupplierID
06-001	002	3	$10.50	6/1/2015	2
06-002	033	1	$73.50	6/1/2015	1
06-003	016	1	$24.00	6/4/2015	2
06-004	020	2	$18.75	6/4/2015	4
06-005	014	2	$15.75	6/4/2015	2
06-006	025	1	$28.50	6/5/2015	4
06-007	036	2	$17.00	6/5/2015	4
06-008	028	1	$315.00	6/5/2015	7
06-009	013	2	$14.00	6/5/2012	4
06-010	004	2	$10.95	6/11/2015	2
06-011	035	1	$17.00	6/11/2015	4
06-012	039	4	$3.50	6/11/2015	3
06-013	040	2	$4.95	6/11/2015	3
06-014	041	5	$6.50	6/11/2015	6
06-015	044	1	$50.25	6/15/2015	6
06-016	022	3	$16.50	6/15/2015	3
06-017	027	1	$22.00	6/15/2015	4
06-018	053	3	$52.00	6/18/2015	3
06-019	030	2	$175.00	6/18/2015	7
06-020	003	2	$7.25	6/18/2015	6
06-021	026	1	$29.25	6/18/2015	4
06-022	021	1	$31.00	6/18/2015	2
06-023	034	2	$13.75	6/22/2015	4
06-024	032	1	$101.50	6/22/2015	1
06-025	012	1	$30.25	6/22/2015	4
06-026	023	2	$12.95	6/25/2015	3
06-027	018	1	$45.00	6/25/2015	4
06-028	037	2	$11.25	6/25/2015	2
06-029	016	2	$39.40	6/25/2015	2
06-030	035	1	$17.00	6/29/2015	4
06-031	014	2	$15.75	6/29/2015	2
06-032	020	2	$18.75	6/29/2015	4
06-033	033	1	$33.50	6/29/2015	1

Skyline Orders Table

Project 1 Filter Records — 4 Parts

You will filter records in a table, query, and report in the Skyline database using the Filter button, Selection button, Toggle Filter button, and shortcut menu. You will also remove filters and filter by form.

Filtering Data

You can place a set of restrictions, called a ***filter***, on records in a table, query, form, or report to isolate temporarily specific records. A filter, like a query, lets you view specific records without having to change the design of the table, query, form, or report. Access provides a number of buttons and options for filtering data. You can filter data using the Filter button in the Sort & Filter group on the HOME tab, right-click specific data in a record and then specify a filter, and use the Selection and Advanced buttons in the Sort & Filter group.

Quick Steps

Filter Records
1. Open desired object.
2. Click in entry of desired field column to filter.
3. Click Filter button.
4. Select desired sorting option at drop-down list.

Filter

Filtering Using the Filter Button

Use the Filter button in the Sort & Filter group on the HOME tab to filter records in an object (a table, query, form, or report). To use this button, open the desired object, click in any entry in the field column on which you want to filter, and then click the Filter button. This displays a drop-down list with sorting options and a list of all of the field entries. In a table, display this drop-down list by clicking the

Figure 7.1 *City* Field Drop-down List

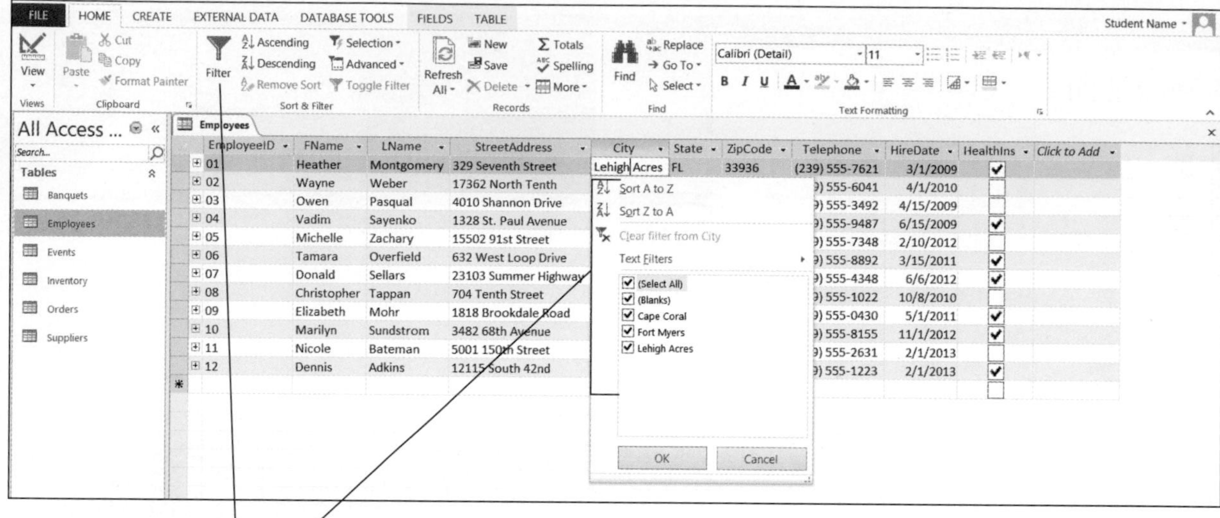

To filter on the *City* field, click in any entry in the field column and then click the Filter button. This displays a drop-down list with sorting options and a list of all field entries.

Filters available depend on the type of data selected in a column.

filter arrow that displays at the right side of a column heading. Figure 7.1 displays the drop-down list that displays when you click in the *City* field and then click the Filter button. To sort on a specific criterion, click the *(Select All)* check box to remove all check marks from the list of field entries. Click the item in the list box on which you want to sort and then click OK.

When you open a table, query, or form, the Record Navigation bar contains the dimmed words *No Filter* preceded by a filter icon with a delete symbol (X). If you filter records in one of these objects, *Filtered* displays in place of *No Filter*, the delete symbol is removed, and the text and filter icon display with an orange background. In a report, if you apply a filter to records, the word *Filtered* displays at the right side of the Status bar.

Removing a Filter

Quick Steps

Remove a Filter

1. Click in field column containing filter.
2. Click Filter button.
3. Click *Clear filter from xxx*.

OR

1. Click Advanced button.
2. Click *Clear All Filters* at drop-down list.

Toggle Filter

When you filter data, the underlying data in the object is not deleted. You can switch back and forth between the data and filtered data by clicking the Toggle Filter button in the Sort & Filter group on the HOME tab. If you click the Toggle Filter button and turn off the filter, all of the data in the table, query, or form displays and the message *Filtered* in the Record Navigation bar changes to *Unfiltered*.

Clicking the Toggle Filter button may redisplay all of the data in an object, but it does not remove the filter. To remove the filter, click in the field column containing the filter and then click the Filter button in the Sort & Filter group on the HOME tab. At the drop-down list that displays, click *Clear filter from xxx* (where *xxx* is the name of the field). You can remove all of the filters from an object by clicking the Advanced button in the Sort & Filter group and then clicking the *Clear All Filters* option.

Project 1a Filtering Records in a Table, Form, and Report

1. Display the Open dialog box with the AL1C7 folder on your storage medium the active folder.
2. Open **AL1-C7-Skyline.accdb** and enable the contents.
3. Filter records in the Employees table by completing the following steps:
   a. Open the Employees table.
   b. Click in any entry in the *City* field.
   c. Click the Filter button in the Sort & Filter group on the HOME tab. (This displays a drop-down list of options for the *City* field.)

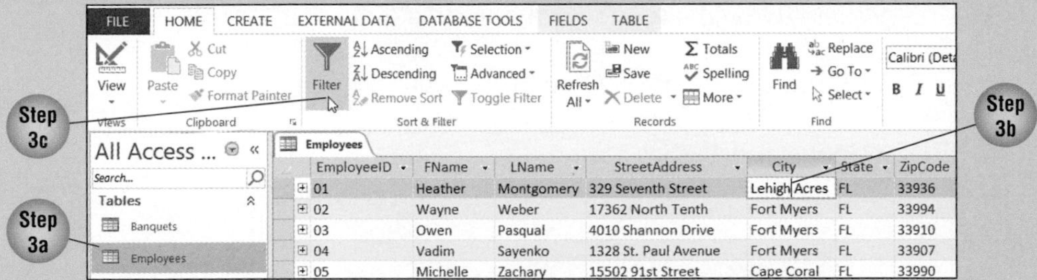

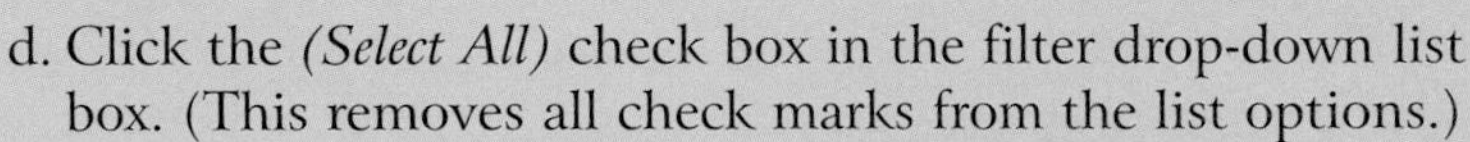

   d. Click the *(Select All)* check box in the filter drop-down list box. (This removes all check marks from the list options.)
   e. Click the *Fort Myers* check box in the list box. (This inserts a check mark in the check box.)
   f. Click OK. (Access displays only those records with a city field of *Fort Myers* and also displays *Filtered* and the filter icon with an orange background in the Record Navigation bar.)
   g. Print the filtered records by pressing Ctrl + P (the keyboard shortcut to display the print dialog box) and then clicking OK at the Print dialog box.
4. Toggle the display of filtered data by clicking the Toggle Filter button in the Sort & Filter group on the HOME tab. (This redisplays all of the data in the table.)
5. Remove the filter by completing the following steps:
   a. Click in any entry in the *City* field.
   b. Click the Filter button in the Sort & Filter group.
   c. Click the *Clear filter from City* option at the drop-down list. (Notice that the message on the Record Navigation bar changes to *No Filter* and dims the words.)

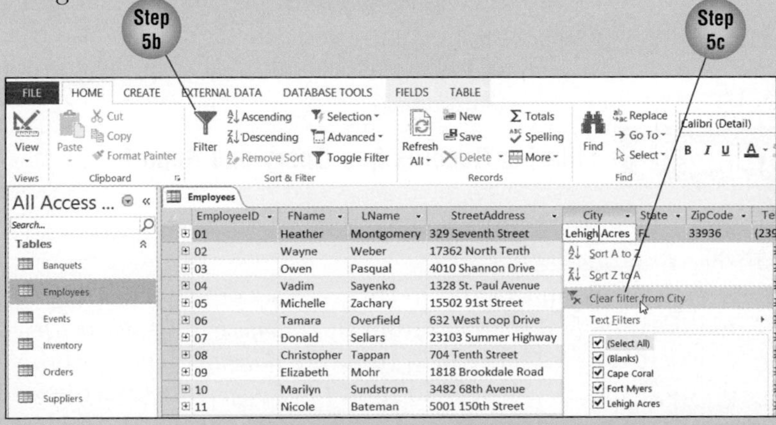

6. Save and then close the Employees table.
7. Create a form by completing the following steps:
   a. Click *Orders* in the Tables group in the Navigation pane.
   b. Click the CREATE tab and then click the Form button in the Forms group.
   c. Click the Form View button in the view area at the right side of the Status bar.
   d. Save the form with the name *Orders*.
8. Filter the records and display only those records with a supplier identification number of 2 by completing the following steps:
   a. Click in the *SupplierID* field containing the text *2*.
   b. Click the Filter button in the Sort & Filter group.
   c. At the filter drop-down list, click *(Select All)* to remove all of the check marks from the list options.
   d. Click the *2* option to insert a check mark.
   e. Click OK.
   f. Navigate through the records and notice that only the records with a supplier identification number of 2 display.
9. Close the Orders form.

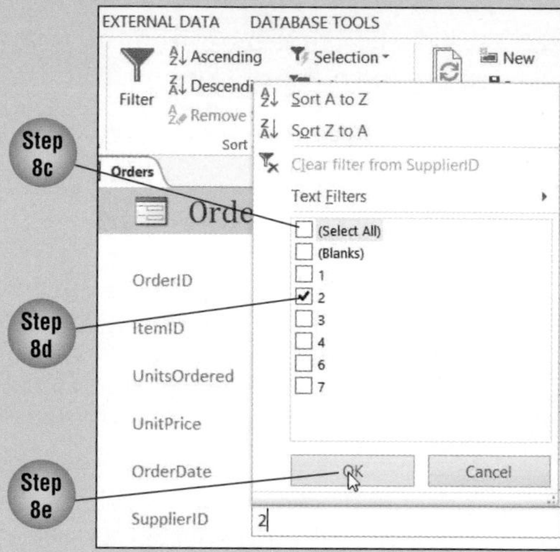

Filtering on Specific Values

When you filter on a specific field, you can display a list of unique values for that field. If you click the Filter button for a field containing text, the drop-down list for the specific field will contain a *Text Filters* option. Click this option and a values list displays next to the drop-down list. The options in the values list vary depending on the type of data in the field. If you click the Filter button for a field containing number values, the option in the drop-down list displays as *Number Filters* and if you are filtering dates, the option in the drop-down list displays as *Date Filters*. Use the options in the values list to refine a filter for a specific field. For example, you can use the values list to display money amounts within a specific range or order dates from a certain time period. You can also use the values list to find fields that are "equal to" or "not equal to" text in the current field.

Project 1b **Filtering Records in a Query and Report** **Part 2 of 4**

1. With **AL1-C7-Skyline.accdb** open, create a query in Design view with the following specifications:
   a. Add the Banquets and Events tables to the query window.
   b. Insert the *ResDate* field from the *Banquets* field list box to the first *Field* row field.
   c. Insert the *FirstName* field from the *Banquets* field list box to the second *Field* row field.
   d. Insert the *LastName* field from the *Banquets* field list box to the third *Field* row field.
   e. Insert the *Telephone* field from the *Banquets* field list box to the fourth *Field* row field.
   f. Insert the *Event* field from the *Events* field list box to the fifth *Field* row field.
   g. Insert the *EmployeeID* field from the *Banquets* field list box to the sixth *Field* row field.
   h. Run the query.
   i. Save the query and name it *BanquetReservations*.

2. Filter records of reservations on or before June 15, 2015, in the query by completing the following steps:
   a. With the BanquetReservations query open, make sure the first entry is selected in the *ResDate* field.
   b. Click the Filter button in the Sort & Filter group on the HOME tab.
   c. Point to the *Date Filters* option in the drop-down list box.
   d. Click *Before* in the values list.
   e. At the Custom Filter dialog box, type **6/15/2015** and then click OK.

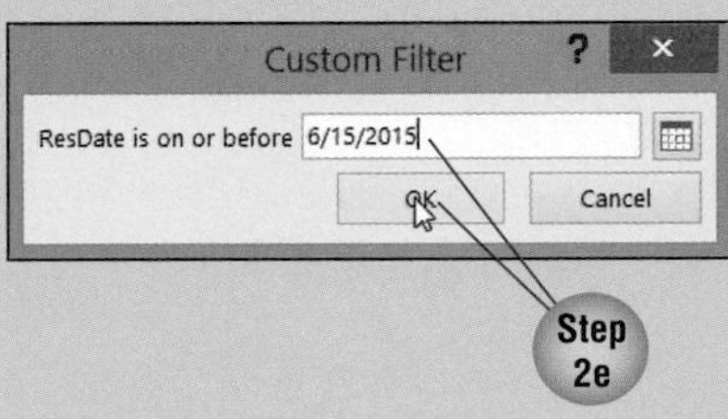

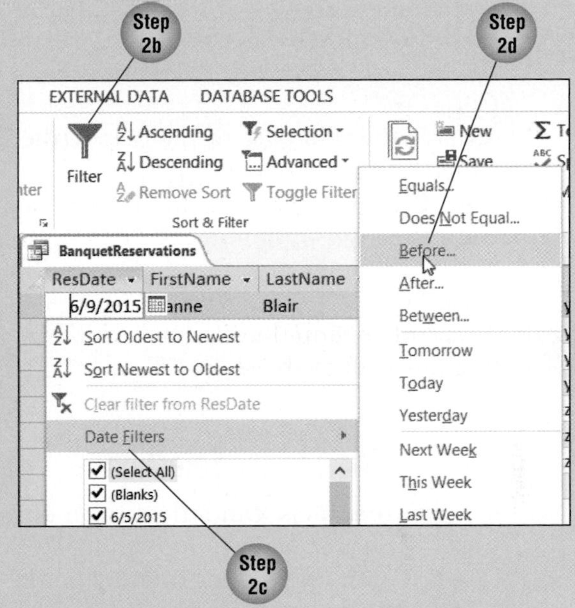

   f. Print the filtered query by pressing Ctrl + P and then clicking OK at the Print dialog box.
3. Remove the filter by clicking the filter icon that displays at the right side of the *ResDate* column heading and then clicking *Clear filter from ResDate* at the drop-down list.
4. Save and then close the BanquetReservations query.
5. Create a report by completing the following steps:
   a. Click *BanquetReservations* in the Queries group in the Navigation pane.
   b. Click the CREATE tab and then click the Report button in the Reports group.
   c. Delete the total amount at the bottom of the *ResDate* column.
   d. With the report in Layout view, decrease the column widths so the right column border displays near the longest entry in each column.
   e. Click the Report View button in the view area at the right side of the Status bar.
   f. Save the report and name it *BanquetReport*.

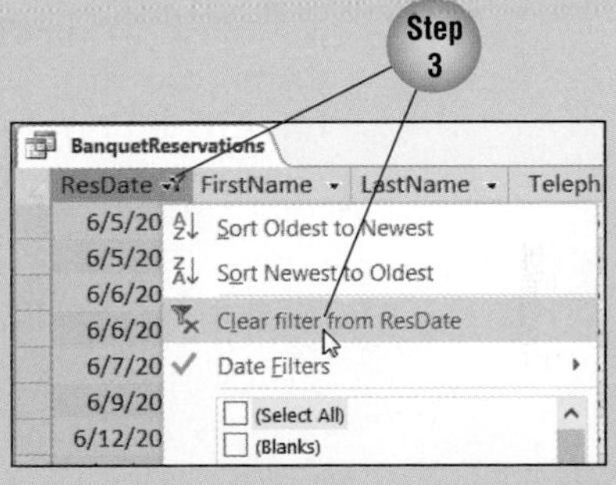

6. Filter the records and display all records of events except *Other* events by completing the following steps:
   a. Click in the first entry in the *Event* field.
   b. Click the Filter button in the Sort & Filter group.
   c. Point to the *Text Filters* option in the drop-down list box and then click *Does Not Equal* at the values list.
   d. At the Custom Filter dialog box, type **Other** and then click OK.

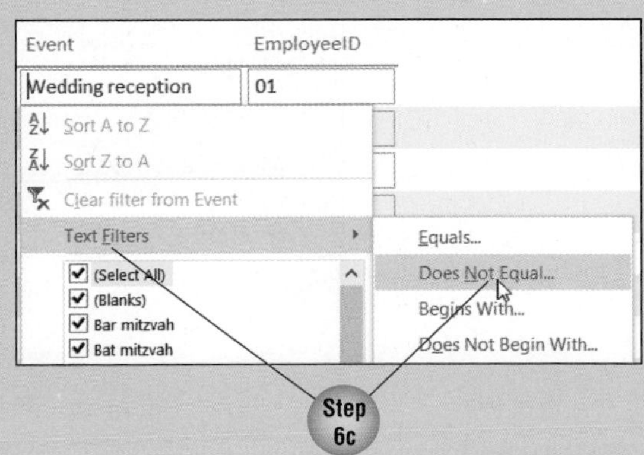

7. Further refine the filter by completing the following steps:
   a. Click in the first entry in the *EmployeeID* field.
   b. Click the Filter button.
   c. At the filter drop-down list, click the *(Select All)* check box to remove all of the check marks from the list options.
   d. Click the *03* check box to insert a check mark.
   e. Click OK.
8. Print only the first page of the report (the second page contains only shading) by completing the following steps:
   a. Press Ctrl + P to display the Print dialog box.
   b. Click the *Pages* option in the *Print Range* section.
   c. Type 1 in the *From* text box, press the Tab key, and then type 1 in the *To* text box.
   d. Click OK.
9. Save and then close the BanquetReport report.

Filtering by Selection

Selection

If you click in a field in an object and then click the Selection button in the Sort & Filter group on the HOME tab, a drop-down list displays below the button with options for filtering on the data in the field. For example, if you click in a field containing the city name *Fort Myers*, clicking the Selection button will cause a drop-down list to display as shown in Figure 7.2. Click one of the options at the drop-down list to filter records. You can select specific text in a field entry and then filter based on the specific text. For example, in Project 1c you will select the word *peppers* in the entry *Green peppers* and then filter records containing the word *peppers*.

Figure 7.2 Selection Button Drop-down List

To filter by selection, click in a field containing the text on which to filter and then click the Selection button. This displays a drop-down list of filtering options.

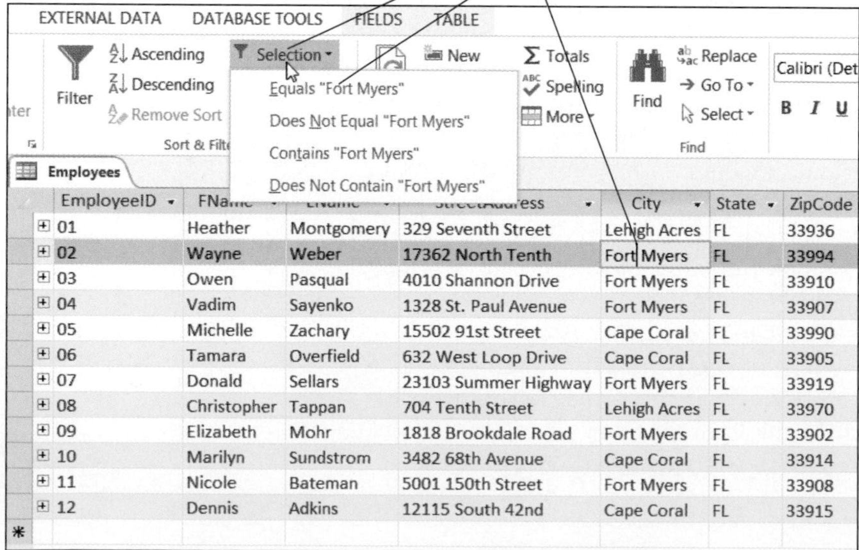

Filtering by Shortcut Menu

If you right-click a field entry, a shortcut menu displays with options to sort the text, display a values list, or filter on a specific value. For example, if you right-click the field entry *Birthday* in the *Event* field, a shortcut menu displays, as shown in Figure 7.3. Click a sort option to sort text in the field in ascending or descending order, point to the *Text Filters* option to display a values list, or click one of the values filters located toward the bottom of the menu. You can also select specific text within a field entry and then right-click the selection to display the shortcut menu.

Figure 7.3 Filtering Shortcut Menu

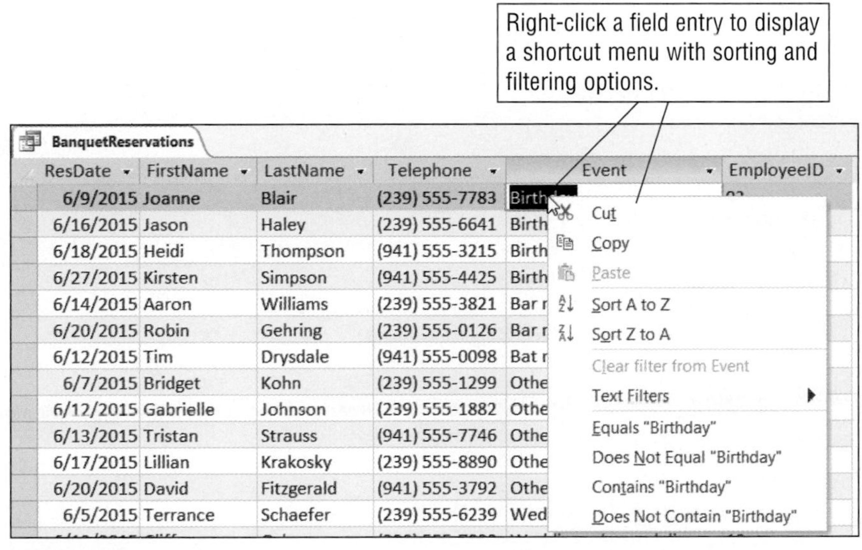

Project 1c **Filtering Records by Selection** **Part 3 of 4**

1. With **AL1-C7-Skyline.accdb** open, open the Inventory table.
2. Filter only those records with a supplier number of 6 by completing the following steps:
   a. Click in the first entry containing *6* in the *SupplierID* field.
   b. Click the Selection button in the Sort & Filter group on the HOME tab and then click *Equals "6"* at the drop-down list.
   c. Print the filtered table by pressing Ctrl + P and then clicking OK at the Print dialog box.
   d. Click the Toggle Filter button in the Sort & Filter group.

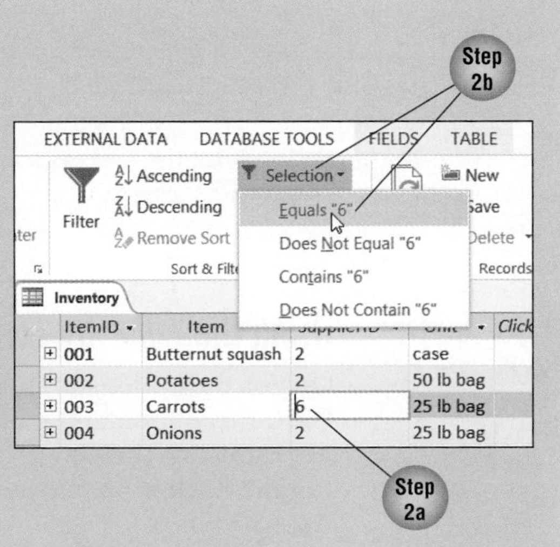

3. Filter any records in the *Item* field containing the word *peppers* by completing the following steps:
   a. Click in an entry in the *Item* field containing the text *Green peppers*.
   b. Using the mouse, select the word *peppers*.
   c. Click the Selection button and then click *Contains "peppers"* at the drop-down list.
   d. Print the filtered table by pressing Ctrl + P and then clicking OK at the Print dialog box.
4. Close the Inventory table without saving the changes.
5. Open the BanquetReservations query.
6. Filter records in the *Event* field except *Wedding reception* by completing the following steps:
   a. Right-click in the first *Wedding reception* entry in the *Event* field.
   b. Click *Does Not Equal "Wedding reception"* at the shortcut menu.
   c. Print the filtered query.
   d. Click the Toggle Filter button in the Sort & Filter group.
7. Filter any records in the *Event* field containing the word *mitzvah* by completing the following steps:
   a. Click in an entry in the *Event* field containing the entry *Bar mitzvah*.
   b. Using the mouse, select the word *mitzvah*.
   c. Right-click on the selected word and then click *Contains "mitzvah"* at the shortcut menu.
   d. Print the filtered query.
8. Close the BanquetReservations query without saving the changes.

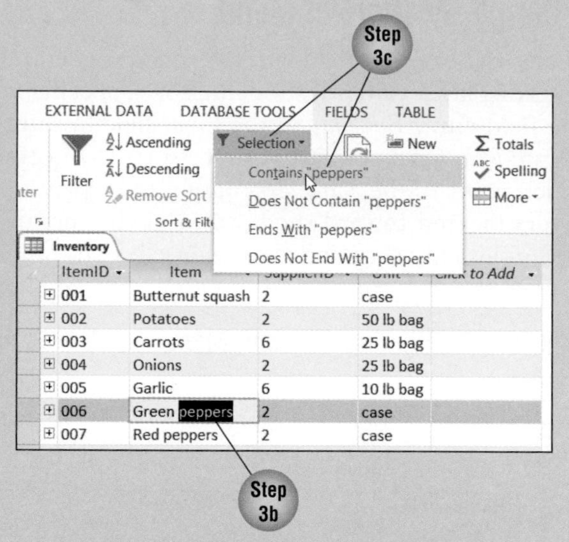

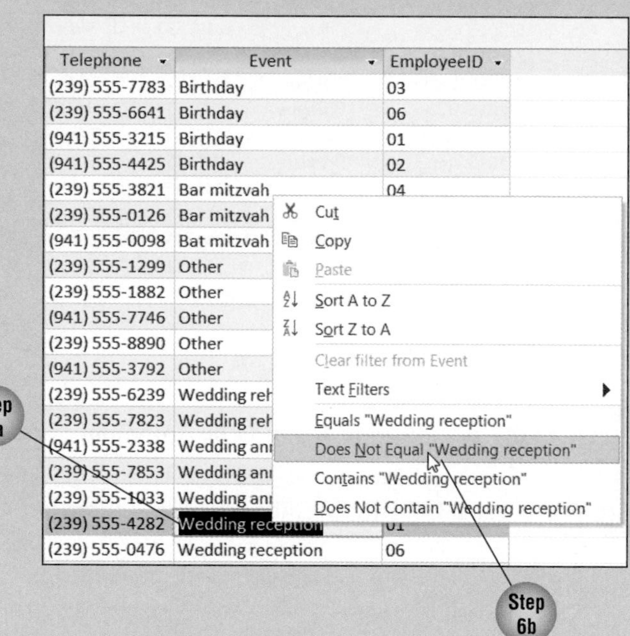

Quick Steps

Use the *Filter By Form* Option

1. Click Advanced button.
2. Click *Filter By Form*.
3. Click in empty field below desired column to filter.
4. Click down-pointing arrow.
5. Click item to filter.

Advanced

Using the *Filter By Form* Option

One of the options from the Advanced button drop-down list is *Filter By Form*. Click this option and a blank record displays in a Filter by Form window in the work area. In the Filter by Form window, the Look for tab and the Or tab display toward the bottom of the form. The Look for tab is active by default and tells Access to look for whatever data you insert in a field. Click in the empty field below the desired column and a down-pointing arrow displays at the right side of the field. Click the down-pointing arrow and then click the item on which you want to filter. Click the Toggle Filter button to display the desired records. Add an additional value to a filter by clicking the Or tab at the bottom of the form.

Project 1d Using the *Filter By Form* Option to Display Specific Records Part 4 of 4

1. With **AL1-C7-Skyline.accdb** open, open the Banquets table.
2. Filter records for a specific employee identification number by completing the following steps:
   a. Click the Advanced button in the Sort & Filter group on the HOME tab and then click *Filter By Form* at the drop-down list.

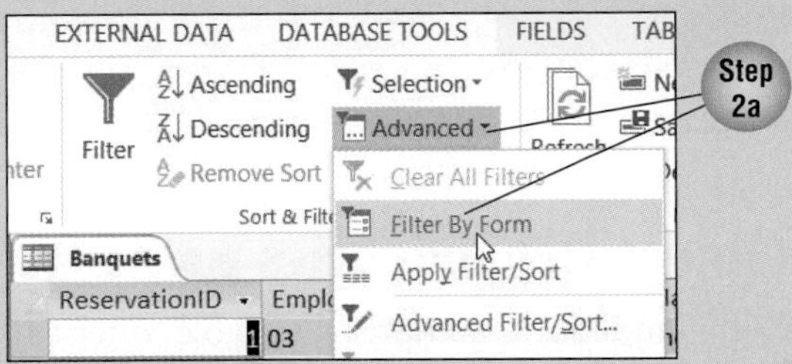

   b. At the Filter by Form window, click in the blank record below the *EmployeeID* field.
   c. Click the down-pointing arrow at the right side of the field and then click *03* at the drop-down list.
   d. Click the Toggle Filter button in the Sort & Filter group.

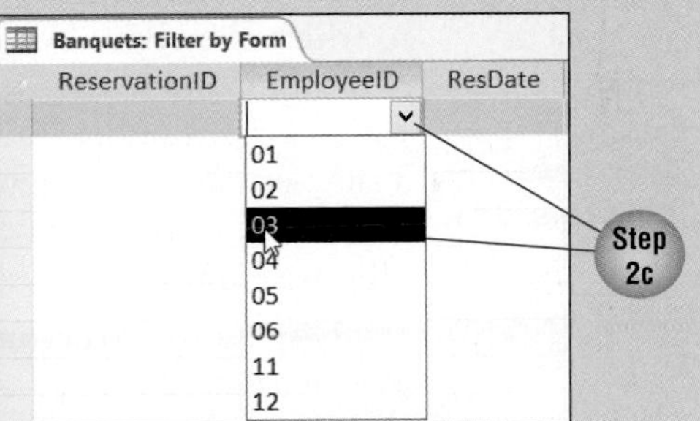

3. Print the filtered table by completing the following steps:
   a. Click the FILE tab, click the *Print* option, and then click the Print Preview button.
   b. Change the orientation to landscape and the left and right margins to 0.5 inch.
   c. Click the Print button and then click OK at the Print dialog box.
   d. Click the Close Print Preview button.
4. Close the Banquets table without saving the changes.
5. Open the Inventory table.
6. Filter records for the supplier number 2 or 7 by completing the following steps:
   a. Click the Advanced button in the Sort & Filter group on the HOME tab and then click *Filter By Form* at the drop-down list.
   b. At the Filter by Form window, click in the blank record below the *SupplierID* field.
   c. Click the down-pointing arrow at the right side of the field and then click *2* at the drop-down list.
   d. Click the Or tab located toward the bottom of the form.
   e. If necessary, click in the blank record below the *SupplierID* field.
   f. Click the down-pointing arrow at the right side of the field and then click *7* at the drop-down list.
   g. Click the Toggle Filter button in the Sort & Filter group.
   h. Print the filtered table.
   i. Click the Toggle Filter button to redisplay all records in the table.
   j. Click the Advanced button and then click *Clear All Filters* from the drop-down list.
7. Close the Inventory table without saving the changes.

Project 2 View Object Dependencies, Manage a Database, and Save a Database in a Different File Format

4 Parts

You will display object dependencies in the Skyline database, compact and repair the database, encrypt it with a password, view and customize document properties, save an object in the database in PDF file format, and save the database in a previous version of Access.

Quick Steps

View Object Dependencies
1. Open desired database.
2. Click object in Navigation pane.
3. Click DATABASE TOOLS tab.
4. Click Object Dependencies button.

Object Dependencies

Viewing Object Dependencies

The structure of a database is comprised of table, query, form, and report objects. Tables are related to other tables by the relationships that have been created. Queries, forms, and reports draw the source data from the records in the tables to which they have been associated, and forms and reports can include subforms and subreports, which further expand the associations between objects. A database with a large number of interdependent objects is more complex to work with than a simpler database. Viewing a list of the objects within a database and viewing the dependencies between objects can be beneficial to ensure an object is not deleted or otherwise modified, causing an unforeseen effect on another object.

Display the structure of a database—including tables, queries, forms, and reports, as well as relationships—at the Object Dependencies task pane. Display this task pane by opening the database, clicking the desired object in the Navigation pane, clicking the DATABASE TOOLS tab, and then clicking the Object Dependencies button in the Relationships group. The Object Dependencies task pane, shown in Figure 7.4, displays the objects in AL1-C7-Skyline.accdb that depend on the Banquets table.

Figure 7.4 Object Dependencies Task Pane

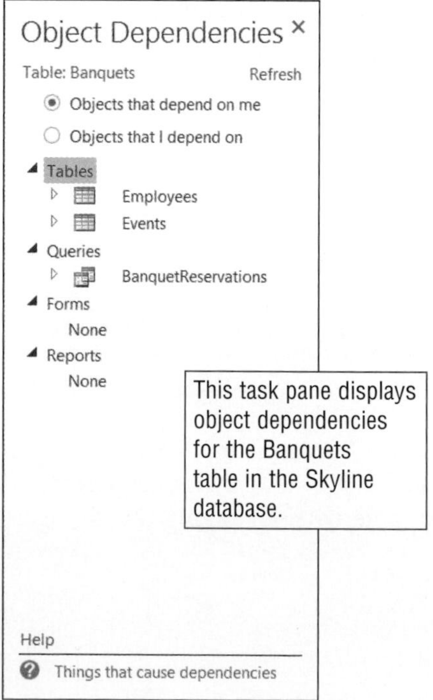

This task pane displays object dependencies for the Banquets table in the Skyline database.

By default, *Objects that depend on me* is selected in the Object Dependencies task pane and the list box displays the names of the objects for which the selected object is the source. Next to each object in the task pane list is an expand button (a right-pointing, white triangle). Clicking the expand button next to an object shows the other objects that depend on it. For example, if a query is based on the Banquets and Events tables and the query is used to generate a report, clicking the expand button next to the query name will show the report name. Clicking an object name in the Object Dependencies task pane opens the object in Design view.

Project 2a Viewing Object Dependencies — Part 1 of 4

1. With **AL1-C7-Skyline.accdb** open, display the structure of the database by completing the following steps:
   a. Click *Banquets* in the Tables group in the Navigation pane.
   b. Click the DATABASE TOOLS tab and then click the Object Dependencies button in the Relationships group. (This displays the Object Dependencies task pane. By default, *Objects that depend on me* is selected and the task pane lists the names of the objects for which the Banquets table is the source.)

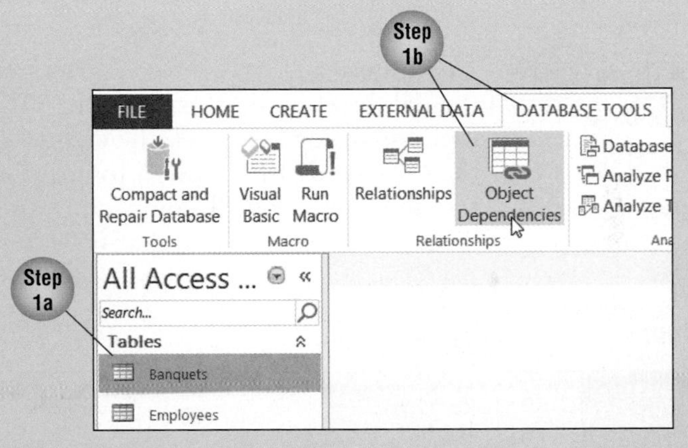

   c. Click the expand button (the right-pointing, white triangle that turns pink when you hover your mouse pointer over it) to the left of *Employees* in the *Tables* section. (This displays all of the objects that depend on the Employees table.)
   d. Click the *Objects that I depend on* option located toward the top of the Object Dependencies task pane.

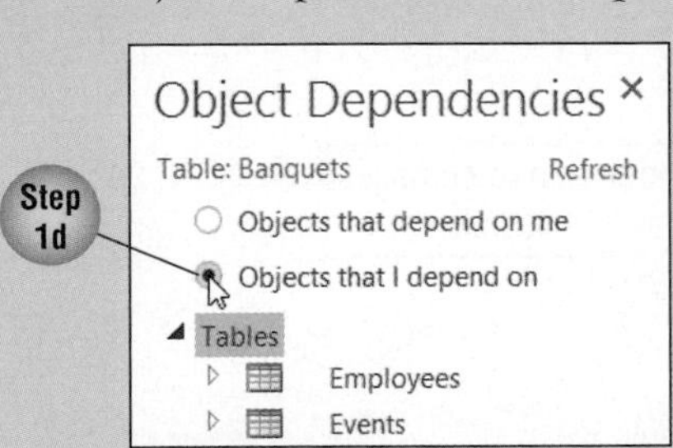

   e. Click *Events* in the Tables group in the Navigation pane. (Make sure to click *Events* in the Navigation pane and not the Object Dependencies task pane.)
   f. Click the Refresh hyperlink in the upper right corner of the Object Dependencies task pane.
   g. Click the *Objects that depend on me* option located toward the top of the Object Dependencies task pane.

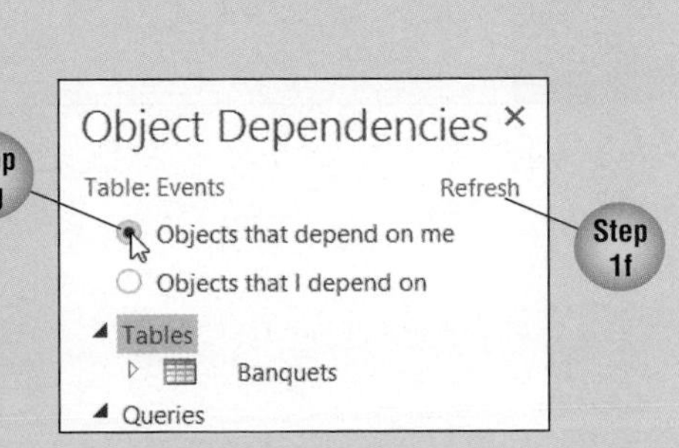

2. Close the Object Dependencies task pane.

Using Options at the Info Backstage Area

The Info backstage area contains options for compacting and repairing a database, encrypting a database with a password, and displaying and customizing database properties. Display the Info backstage area, shown in Figure 7.5, by opening a database and then clicking the FILE tab.

Compacting and Repairing a Database

Quick Steps

Compact and Repair a Database

1. Open database.
2. Click FILE tab.
3. Click Compact & Repair Database button.

Compact & Repair Database

To optimize the performance of your database, compact and repair it on a regular basis. As you work with a database, data in it can become fragmented, causing the amount of space the database takes on the storage medium or in the folder to be larger than necessary. To compact and repair a database, open the database, click the FILE tab and then click the Compact & Repair Database button.

You can tell Access to compact and repair a database each time you close the database. To do this, click the FILE tab and then click *Options*. At the Access Options dialog box, click the *Current Database* option in the left panel. Click the *Compact on Close* option to insert a check mark and then click OK to close the dialog box. Before compacting and repairing a database in a multi-user environment, make sure that no other user has the database open.

Figure 7.5 Info Backstage Area

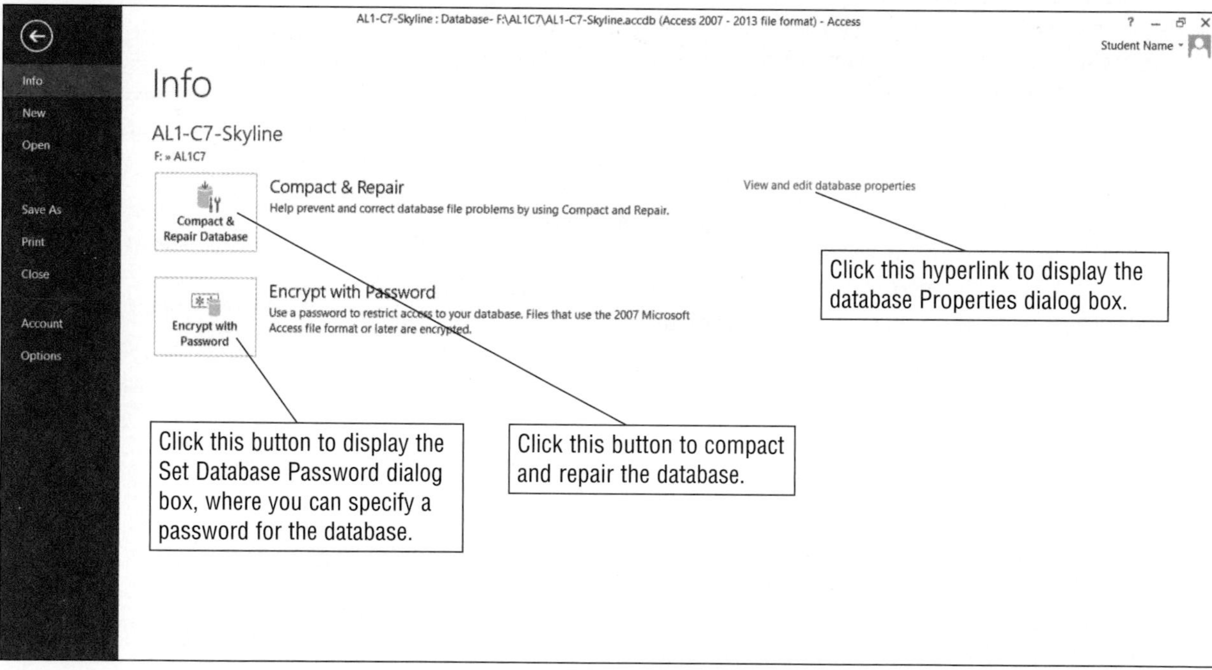
AL1-C7-Skyline : Database- F:\AL1C7\AL1-C7-Skyline.accdb (Access 2007 - 2013 file format) - Access
Student Name
Info
New
Open
Save As
Print
Close
Account
Options
Info
AL1-C7-Skyline
F: » AL1C7
Compact & Repair Database
Compact & Repair
Help prevent and correct database file problems by using Compact and Repair.
Encrypt with Password
Encrypt with Password
Use a password to restrict access to your database. Files that use the 2007 Microsoft Access file format or later are encrypted.
View and edit database properties
Click this hyperlink to display the database Properties dialog box.
Click this button to display the Set Database Password dialog box, where you can specify a password for the database.
Click this button to compact and repair the database.

Encrypting a Database with a Password

If you want to prevent unauthorized access to a database, encrypt the database with a password to ensure that it can be opened only by someone who knows the password. Be careful when encrypting a database with a password because if you lose the password, you will be unable to use the database. You will not be able to remove the password from a database if you do not remember the password.

To encrypt a database with a password, you must open the database in Exclusive mode. To do this, display the Open dialog box, navigate to the desired folder, and then click the database to select it. Click the down-pointing arrow at the right side of the Open button located in the lower right corner of the dialog box and then click *Open Exclusive* at the drop-down list. When the database opens, click the FILE tab and then click the Encrypt with Password button in the Info backstage area. This displays the Set Database Password dialog box, as shown in Figure 7.6. At this dialog box, type a password in the *Password* text box, press the Tab key, and then type the password again. The text you type will display as asterisks. Click OK to close the Set Database Password dialog box. To remove a password from a database, open the database in Exclusive mode, click the FILE tab, and then click the Decrypt Database button. At the Unset Database Password dialog box, type the password and then click OK.

Quick Steps

Open a Database in Exclusive Mode
1. Display Open dialog box.
2. Click desired database.
3. Click down-pointing arrow at right of Open button.
4. Click *Open Exclusive*.

Encrypt a Database with a Password
1. Open database in Exclusive mode.
2. Click FILE tab.
3. Click Encrypt with Password button.
4. Type password, press Tab, and type password again.
5. Click OK.

Encrypt with Password

Decrypt Database

When encrypting a database with a password, use a password that combines uppercase and lowercase letters, numbers, and symbols.

Figure 7.6 Set Database Password Dialog Box

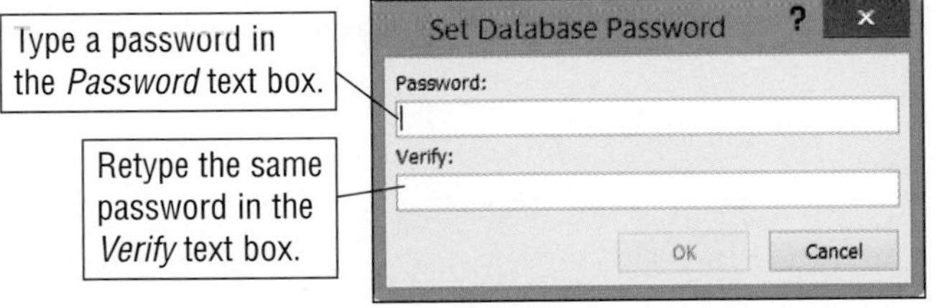

Project 2b **Compact and Repair and Encrypt a Database** **Part 2 of 4**

1. With **AL1-C7-Skyline.accdb** open, compact and repair the database by completing the following steps:
   a. Click the FILE tab. (This displays the Info backstage area.)
   b. Click the Compact & Repair Database button.
2. Close **AL1-C7-Skyline.accdb**.
3. Open the database in Exclusive mode by completing the following steps:
   a. Display the Open dialog box and make AL1C7 the active folder.
   b. Click **AL1-C7-Skyline.accdb** in the Content pane to select it.

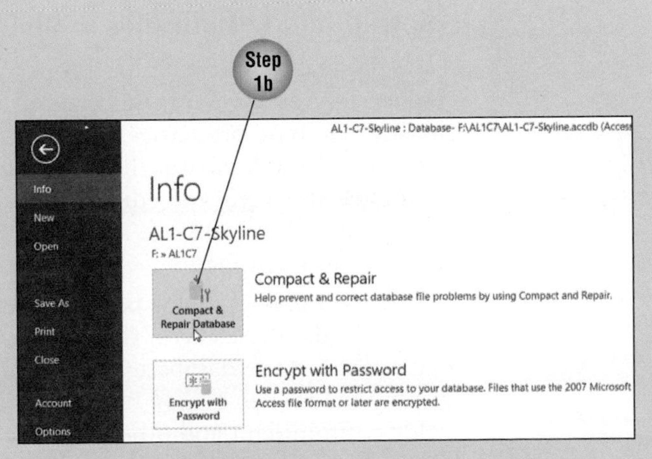

c. Click the down-pointing arrow at the right side of the Open button that displays in the lower right corner of the dialog box and then click *Open Exclusive* at the drop-down list.

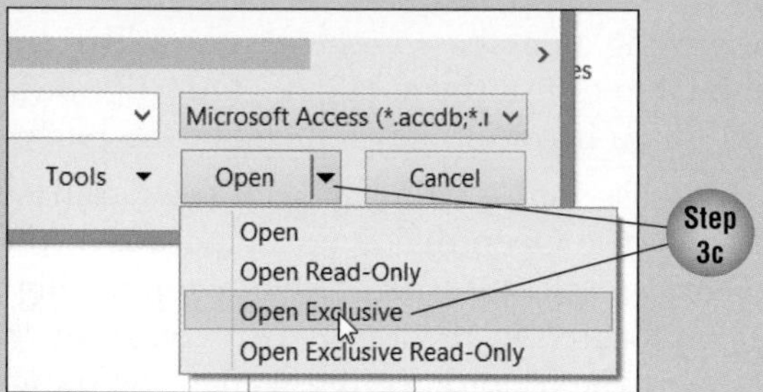

4. Encrypt the database with a password by completing the following steps:
   a. Click the FILE tab.
   b. At the Info backstage area, click the Encrypt with Password button.
   c. At the Set Database Password dialog box, type your first and last names in all lowercase letters with no space, press the Tab key, and then type your first and last names again in lowercase letters.
   d. Click OK to close the dialog box.
   e. If a message displays with information about encrypting with a block cipher, click OK.

5. Close **AL1-C7-Skyline.accdb**.
6. Display the Open dialog box with AL1C7 the active folder and then open **AL1-C7-Skyline.accdb** in Exclusive mode.
7. At the Password Required dialog box, type your password and then click OK.
8. Remove the password by completing the following steps:
   a. Click the FILE tab.
   b. Click the Decrypt Database button.
   c. At the Unset Database Password dialog box, type your first and last names in lowercase letters and then press the Enter key.

Viewing and Customizing Database Properties

Each database you create has properties associated with it, such as the type of file, its location, and when it was created, accessed, and modified. You can view and modify database properties at the Properties dialog box. To view properties for the currently open database, click the FILE tab to display the Info backstage area and then click the View and edit database properties hyperlink that displays at the right side of the backstage area. This displays the Properties dialog box, similar to what is shown in Figure 7.7.

The Properties dialog box for an open database contains tabs with information about the database. With the General tab selected, the dialog box displays information about the database type, size, and location. Click the Summary tab to display fields such as *Title*, *Subject*, *Author*, *Category*, *Keywords*, and *Comments*. Some fields contain data and others are blank. You can insert, edit, or delete text in the fields. Move the insertion point to a field by clicking in the field or by pressing the Tab key until the insertion point is positioned in the desired field.

Figure 7.7 Properties Dialog Box

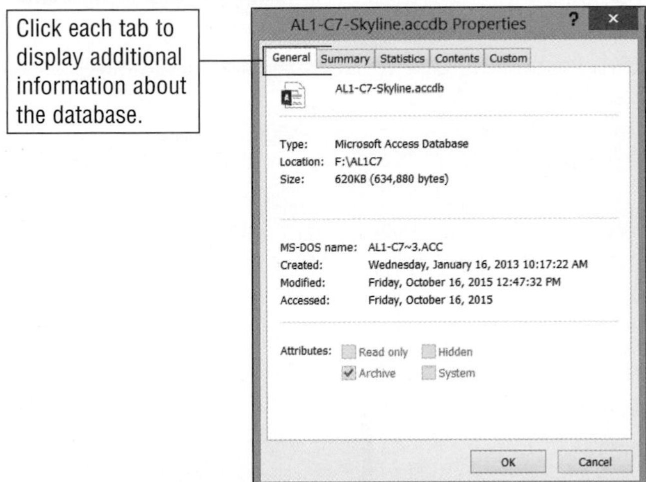

Click the Statistics tab to display information such as the dates the database was created, modified, accessed, and printed. Click the Contents tab and look in the *Document contents* section to see the objects in the database, including tables, queries, forms, reports, macros, and modules.

Use options at the Properties dialog box with the Custom tab selected to add custom properties to the database. For example, you can add a property that displays the date the database was completed, information on the department in which the database was created, and much more. The list box below the *Name* option box displays the predesigned properties provided by Access. You can choose a predesigned property or create your own.

To choose a predesigned property, select the desired property in the list box, specify what type of property it is (such as value, date, number, yes/no), and then type a value. For example, to specify the department in which the database was created, you would click *Department* in the list box, make sure the *Type* displays as *Text*, click in the *Value* text box, and then type the name of the department.

Project 2c **Viewing and Customizing Database Properties** **Part 3 of 4**

1. With **AL1-C7-Skyline.accdb** open, click the FILE tab and then click the View and edit database properties hyperlink that displays at the right side of the backstage area.

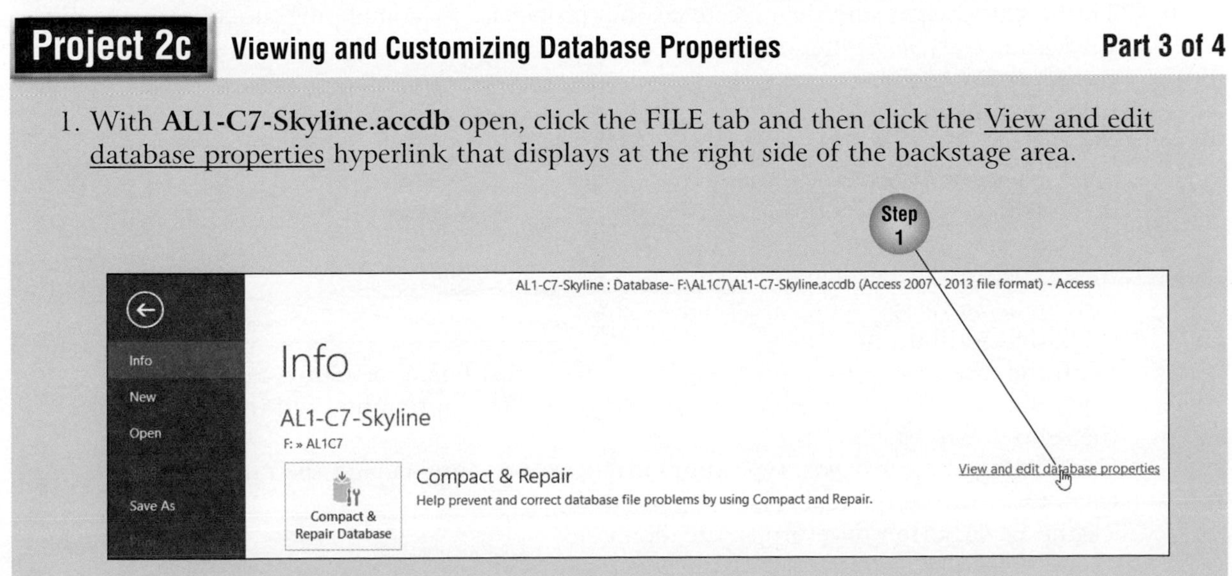

2. At the AL1-C7-Skyline.accdb Properties dialog box, click the General tab and then read the information that displays in the dialog box.
3. Click the Summary tab and then type the following text in the specified text boxes:

Title	**AL1-C7-Skyline database**
Subject	**Restaurant and banquet facilities**
Author	*(type your first and last names)*
Category	**restaurant**
Keywords	**restaurant, banquet, event, Fort Myers**
Comments	**This database contains information on Skyline Restaurant employees, banquets, inventory, and orders.**

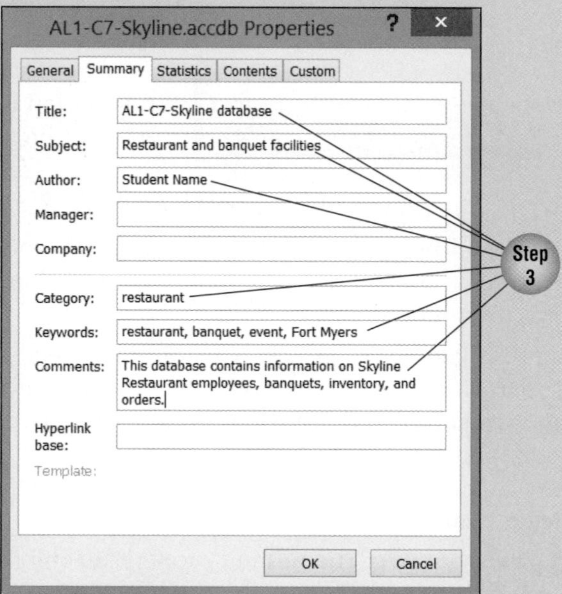

4. Click the Statistics tab and read the information that displays in the dialog box.
5. Click the Contents tab and notice that the *Document contents* section of the dialog box displays the objects in the database.
6. Click the Custom tab and then create custom properties by completing the following steps:
   a. Click the *Date completed* option in the *Name* list box.
   b. Click the down-pointing arrow at the right of the *Type* option box and then click *Date* at the drop-down list.
   c. Click in the *Value* text box and then type the current date in this format: *dd/mm/yyyy*.

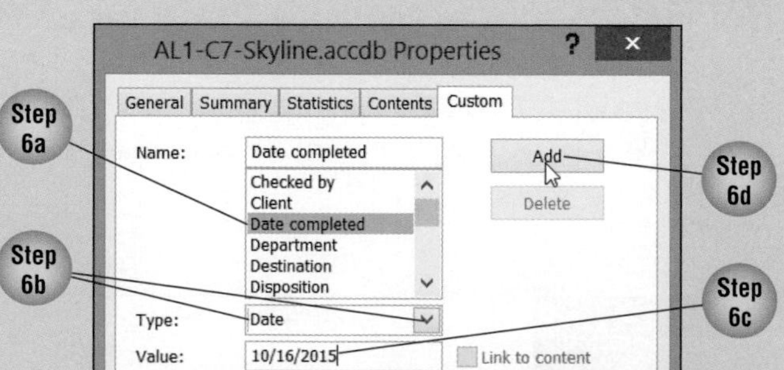

   d. Click the Add button.
   e. With the insertion point positioned in the *Name* text box, type **Course**.
   f. Click the down-pointing arrow at the right of the *Type* option box and then click *Text* at the drop-down list.
   g. Click in the *Value* text box, type your current course number, and then press Enter.
   h. Click OK to close the dialog box.
7. Click the Back button to return to the database.

Saving Databases and Database Objects

An Access 2013, Access 2010, or Access 2007 database is saved with the file extension *.accdb*. Earlier versions of Access (such as 2003, 2002, and 2000) use the file extension *.mdb*. To open an Access 2013, 2010, or 2007 database in an earlier version, you need to save the database in the .mdb file format.

To save an Access database in the 2002 to 2003 file format, open the database, click the FILE tab, and then click the *Save As* option. This displays the Save As backstage area, as shown in Figure 7.9. Click the *Access 2002-2003 Database (*.mdb)* option in the *Save Database As* section and then click the Save As button that displays at the bottom of the *Save Database As* section. This displays the Save As dialog box with the *Save as type* option set to *Microsoft Access Database (2002-2003) (*.mdb)* and the current database file name with the file extension *.mdb* inserted in the *File name* text box. At this dialog box, click the Save button.

With an object open in a database, clicking the *Save Object As* option in the *File Types* section of the Save As backstage area displays options for saving the object. Click the *Save Object As* option to save the selected object in the database or click the *PDF or XPS* option if you want to save the object in PDF or XPS file format. The letters *PDF* stand for *portable document format*, a file format developed by Adobe Systems that captures all of the elements of a file as an electronic image. An XPS file is a Microsoft file format for publishing content in an easily viewable format. The letters *XPS* stand for *XML paper specification* and the letters *XML* stand for *extensible markup language*, which is a set of rules for encoding files electronically.

Quick Steps

Save a Database in an Earlier Version

1. Open database.
2. Click FILE tab.
3. Click *Save As* option.
4. Click desired version in Save Database As category.
5. Click Save As button.

An Access 2007, 2010, or 2013 database cannot be opened with an earlier version of Access.

Saving an Object in PDF or XPS File Format

To save an object in PDF or XPS file format, open the desired object, click the FILE tab, and then click the *Save As* option. At the Save As backstage area, click the *Save Object As* option in the *File Types* section, click the *PDF or XPS* option in the *Save the current database object* section, and then click the Save As button. This displays the Publish as PDF or XPS dialog box with the name of the object inserted in the *File name* text box followed by the file extension *.pdf*, and the *Save as type* option set at *PDF (*.pdf)*. Click the Publish button and the object is saved

Quick Steps

Save an Object in PDF File Format

1. Click desired object in Navigation pane.
2. Click FILE tab.
3. Click *Save As* option.
4. Click *Save Object As* option.
5. Click *PDF or XPS* option.
6. Click Save As button.

Figure 7.9 Save As Backstage Area with *Save Database As* Option Selected

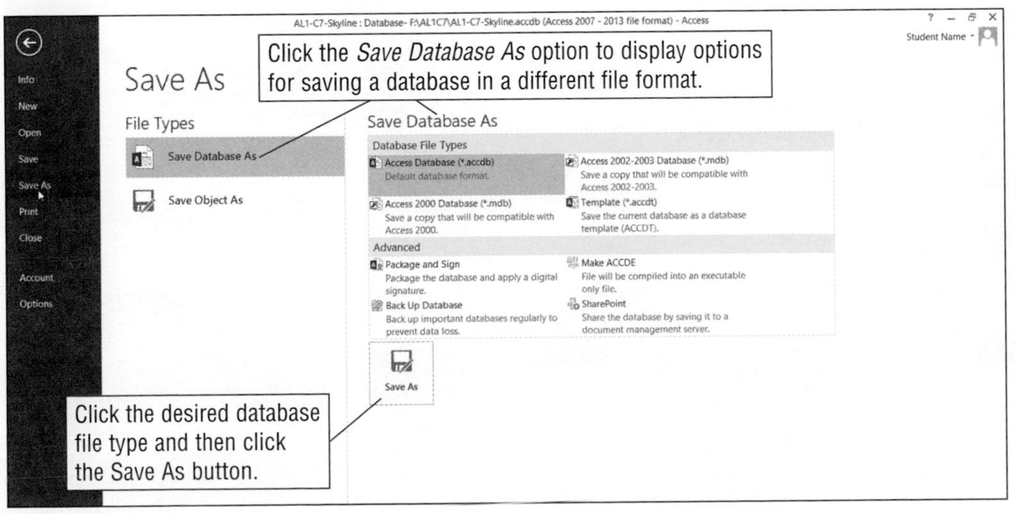

in PDF file format. If you want the object to open in Adobe Reader, click the *Open file after publishing* check box to insert a check box. With this check box active, the object will open in Adobe Reader when you click the Publish button.

You can open a PDF file in Adobe Reader, Internet Explorer, Microsoft Word, or Windows Reader. You can open an XPS file in Internet Explorer, Windows Reader, or XPS Viewer. One method for opening a PDF or XPS file is to open File Explorer, navigate to the folder containing the file, right-click on the file, and then point to *Open with*. This displays a side menu with the programs you can choose to open the file.

Backing Up a Database

Databases often contain important company information, and loss of this information can cause major problems. Backing up a database is important to minimize the chances of losing critical company data and is especially important when several people update and manage a database.

To back up a database, open the database, click the FILE tab, and then click the *Save As* option. At the Save As backstage area, click the *Back Up Database* option in the *Advanced* section and then click the Save As button. This displays the Save As dialog box with a default database file name, which is the original database name followed by the current date, in the *File name* text box. Click the Save button to save the backup database while keeping the original database open.

Project 2d **Saving a Database in a Previous Version, Saving an Object in PDF Format, and Backing Up a Database** **Part 4 of 4**

1. With **AL1-C7-Skyline.accdb** open, save the Orders table in PDF file format by completing the following steps:
   a. Open the Orders table.
   b. Click the FILE tab and then click the *Save As* option.
   c. At the Save As backstage area, click the *Save Object As* option in the *File Types* section.
   d. Click the *PDF or XPS* option in the *Save the current database object* section.
   e. Click the Save As button.

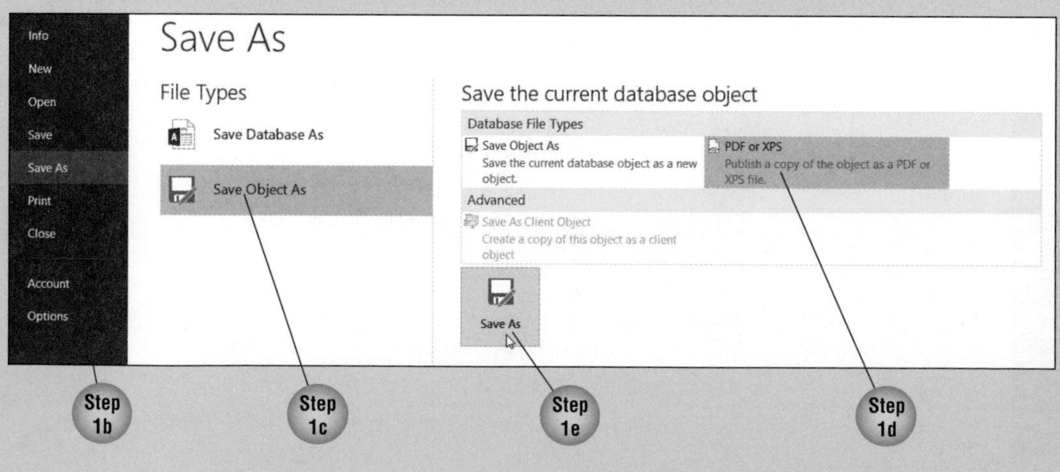

f. At the Publish as PDF or XPS dialog box, make sure the AL1C7 folder on your storage medium is the active folder and then click the *Open file after publishing* check box to insert a check mark. (Skip this step if the check box already contains a check mark.)
g. Click the Publish button.
h. When the Orders table opens in Adobe Reader, scroll through the file and then close the file by clicking the Close button located in the upper right corner of the screen.

2. Close the Orders table.
3. Save the database in a previous version of Access by completing the following steps:
   a. Click the FILE tab and then click the *Save As* option.
   b. At the Save As backstage area, click the *Access 2002-2003 Database (*.mdb)* option in the *Save Database As* section.
   c. Click the Save As button.

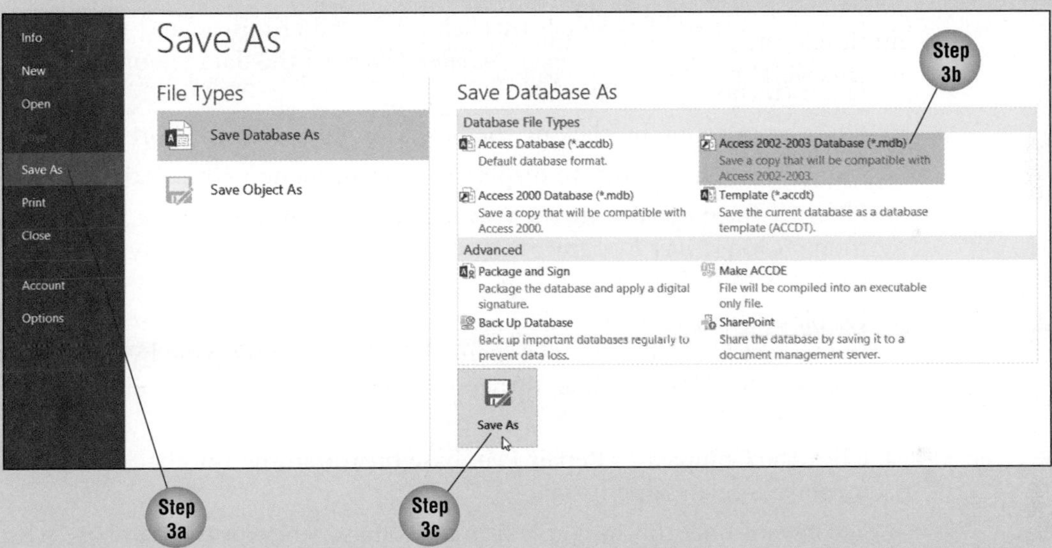

   d. At the Save As dialog box, make sure the AL1C7 folder on your storage medium is the active folder and then click the Save button. This saves the database with the same name (**AL1-C7-Skyline**) but with the file extension *.mdb*.
   e. Notice that the Title bar displays the database file name *AL1-C7-Skyline : Database (Access 2002 - 2003 file format)*.
4. Close the database.
5. Open AL1-C7-Skyline.accdb. (Make sure you open the AL1-C7-Skyline database with the .accdb file extension.)
6. Create a backup of the database by completing the following steps:
   a. Click the FILE tab and then click the *Save As* option.
   b. At the Save As backstage area, click the *Back Up Database* option in the *Advanced* section and then click the Save As button.
   c. At the Save As dialog box, notice that the database name in the *File name* text box displays the original file name followed by the current date (year, month, day).
   d. Make sure the AL1C7 folder on your storage medium is the active folder and then click the Save button. (This saves the backup copy of the database to your folder and the original database remains open.)
7. Close **AL1-C7-Skyline.accdb**.

Chapter Summary

- A set of restrictions called a filter can be set on records in a table or form. A filter lets you select specific field values.
- Filter records with the Filter button in the Sort & Filter group on the HOME tab.
- Click the Toggle Filter button in the Sort & Filter group to switch back and forth between data and filtered data.
- Remove a filter by clicking the Filter button in the Sort & Filter group and then clicking the *Clear filter from xxx* (where *xxx* is the name of the field).
- Another method for removing a filter is to click the Advanced button in the Sort & Filter group and then click *Clear All Filters*.
- Display a list of filter values by clicking the Filter button and then pointing to *Text Filters* (if the data is text), *Number Filters* (if the data is numbers), or *Date Filters* (if the data is dates).
- Filter by selection by clicking the Selection button in the Sort & Filter group.
- Right-click a field entry to display a shortcut menu with filtering options.
- Filter by form by clicking the Advanced button in the Sort & Filter group and then clicking *Filter By Form* at the drop-down list. This displays a blank record with two tabs: Look for and Or.
- Display the structure of a database and relationships between objects at the Object Dependencies task pane. Display this task pane by clicking the DATABASE TOOLS tab and then clicking the Object Dependencies button in the Relationships group.
- Click the Compact & Repair Database button in the Info backstage area to optimize database performance.
- To prevent unauthorized access to a database, encrypt the database with a password. To encrypt a database, you must first open it in Exclusive mode using the Open button drop-down list in the Open dialog box. While in Exclusive mode, encrypt a database with a password using the Encrypt with Password button in the Info backstage area.
- To view properties for the current database, click the View and edit database properties hyperlink in the Info backstage area. The Properties dialog box contains a number of tabs containing information about the database.
- Save a database in a previous version of Access using options in the *Save Database As* section of the Save As backstage area.
- To save a database object in PDF or XPS file format, display the Save As backstage area, click the *Save Object As* option, click the *PDF or XPS* option, and then click the Save As button.
- Backup a database to maintain critical data. Backup a database with the *Back Up Database* option at the Save As backstage area.

Commands Review

FEATURE	RIBBON TAB, GROUP/OPTION	BUTTON, OPTION
filter	HOME, Sort & Filter	
filter by form	HOME, Sort & Filter	, *Filter By Form*
filter by selection	HOME, Sort & Filter	
Info backstage area	FILE, *Info*	
Object Dependencies task pane	DATABASE TOOLS, Relationships	
remove filter	HOME, Sort & Filter	, *Clear filter from xxx* OR , *Clear All Filters*
toggle filter	HOME, Sort & Filter	

Concepts Check

Test Your Knowledge

Completion: In the space provided at the right, indicate the correct term, symbol, or command.

1. The Filter button is located in this group on the HOME tab. ____________________
2. When you filter data, you can switch between the filtered and unfiltered data by clicking this button. ____________________
3. Remove all filtering from an object by pressing the Filter button or clicking this button and then clicking *Clear All Filters*. ____________________
4. In the Filter by Form window, these two tabs display toward the bottom of the form. ____________________
5. Display the structure of a database at this task pane. ____________________
6. Optimize database performance by doing this to the database. ____________________
7. Before encrypting a database with a password, you must open the database in this mode. ____________________
8. Display the Set Database Password dialog box by clicking this button in the Info backstage area. ____________________
9. Data in this dialog box provides details about a database, such as its title, author name, and subject. ____________________
10. Save a database object in PDF file format with the *PDF or XPS* option in this backstage area. ____________________

Skills Check Assess Your Performance

Assessment 1

FILTER RECORDS IN TABLES

1. Display the Open dialog box with the AL1C7 folder on your storage medium the active folder.
2. Open **AL1-C7-WarrenLegal.accdb** and enable the contents.
3. Open the Clients table and then filter the records to display the following records:
   a. Display only those records of clients who live in Renton. When the records of clients in Renton display, print the results in landscape orientation and then remove the filter. ***Hint: Change to landscape orientation in Print Preview.***
   b. Display only those records of clients with the zip code of 98033. When the records of clients with the zip code 98033 display, print the results in landscape orientation and then remove the filter.
4. Close the Clients table without saving the changes.
5. Open the Billing table and then filter the records by selection to display the following records:
   a. Display only those records with a category of CC. Print the records and then remove the filter.
   b. Display only those records with an attorney ID of 12. Print the records and then remove the filter.
   c. Display only those records with dates between 6/1/2015 and 6/10/2015. Print the records and then remove the filter.
6. Close the Billing table without saving the changes.
7. Open the Clients table and then use the *Filter By Form* option to display clients in Auburn or Renton. (Be sure to use the Or tab at the bottom of the table.) Print the table in landscape orientation and then remove the filter.
8. Close the Clients table without saving the changes.
9. Open the Billing table and then use the *Filter By Form* option to display category G or P. Print the table and then remove the filter.
10. Close the Billing table without saving the changes.
11. Close **AL1-C7-WarrenLegal.accdb**.

Assessment 2

SAVE A TABLE AND DATABASE IN DIFFERENT FILE FORMATS

1. Open **AL1-C7-Hilltop.accdb** in Exclusive mode and enable the contents.
2. Create a password for the database (you determine the password), and with the Set Database Password dialog box open, create a screen capture of the screen with the dialog box by completing the following steps:
   a. Press the Print Screen button on your keyboard.
   b. Open a blank document in Microsoft Word.
   c. Click the Paste button located in the Clipboard group on the HOME tab. (This pastes the screen capture image in the Word document.)
   d. Click the FILE tab, click the *Print* option, and then click the Print button at the Print backstage area.
   e. Close Word by clicking the Close button located in the upper right corner of the screen. At the message asking if you want to save the document, click the Don't Save button.

3. Click OK to close the Set Database Password dialog box.
4. At the message telling you that block cipher is incompatible with row level locking, click OK.
5. Close the database.
6. Open **AL1-C7-Hilltop.accdb** in Exclusive mode and enter the password when prompted.
7. Remove the password. ***Hint: Do this with the Decrypt Database button in the Info backstage area.***
8. Open the Invoices table and then save the table in PDF file format with the default file name. Specify that you want the object to open when published.
9. When the table opens in Adobe Reader, print the table by clicking the Print button located toward the upper left side of the screen and then clicking OK at the Print dialog box. (If the Print button is not visible, click the FILE option, click *Print* at the drop-down list, and then click OK at the Print dialog box.)
10. Close Adobe Reader and then close the Invoices table.
11. Save **AL1-C7-Hilltop.accdb** in the *Access 2002-2003 Database (*.mdb)* file format.
12. With the database open, make a screen capture using the Print Screen key on the keyboard. Open Word, paste the screen capture image in the Word document, print the document, and then close Word without saving the changes.
13. Close the database.

Assessment 3

DELETE AND RENAME OBJECTS

1. Open **AL1-C7-Hilltop.accdb**. (Make sure you open the AL1-C7-Hilltop database with the .accdb file extension.)
2. Right-click an object in the Navigation pane, experiment with options in the shortcut menu, and then complete these steps using the shortcut menu:
   a. Delete the Inventory form.
   b. Rename the form Equipment as *EquipForm*.
   c. Rename the report InvReport as *InventoryReport*.
   d. Export (using the shortcut menu) the *EquipmentQuery* to a Word RTF file. ***Hint: Click the Browse button at the Export - RTF File dialog box and make the folder AL1C7 the active folder.***
   e. Open the *EquipmentQuery.rtf* file in Word, print the file, and then close Word.
3. Close **AL1-C7-Hilltop.accdb**.

Visual Benchmark Demonstrate Your Proficiency

DESIGN A QUERY AND FILTER THE QUERY

1. Open **AL1-C7-PacTrek.accdb** and enable the contents.
2. Create and run the query shown in Figure 7.10.
3. Save the query and name it *ProductsOnOrderQuery*.
4. Print the query.
5. Filter the query so the records display as shown in Figure 7.11. ***Hint: Filter the supplier names as shown in Figure 7.11 and then filter the*** **UnitsOnOrder** ***field to show records that do not equal 0.***
6. Print the filtered query.
7. Remove the filters and then close the query without saving the changes.
8. Close **AL1-C7-PacTrek.accdb**.

Figure 7.10 Visual Benchmark Query

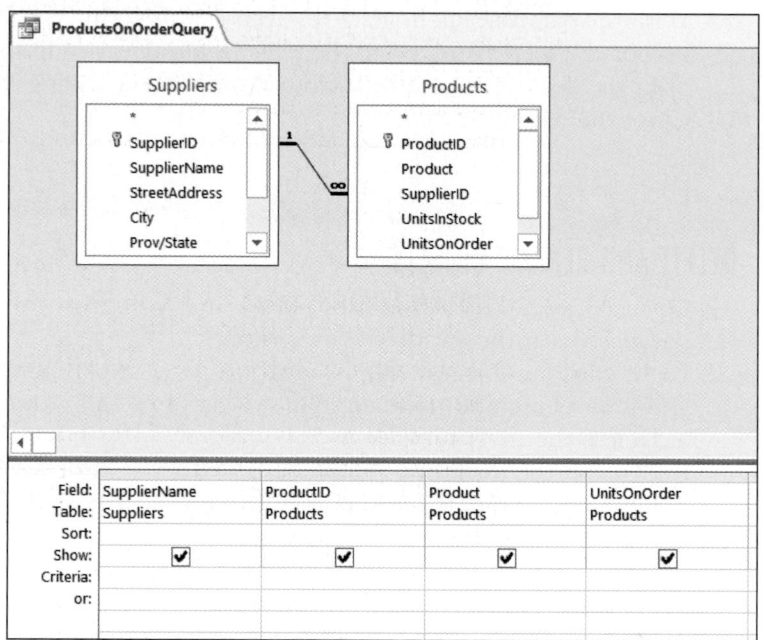

Figure 7.11 Visual Benchmark Filtered Query

ProductsOnOrderQuery

SupplierName	ProductID	Product	UnitsOnOrder
Hopewell, Inc.	152-H	Lantern hanger	15
Hopewell, Inc.	155-20	Shursite angle-head flashlight	20
Hopewell, Inc.	155-35	Shursite portable camp light	10
Cascade Gear	250-L	Cascade R4 jacket, ML	10
Cascade Gear	250-XL	Cascade R4 jacket, MXL	10
Cascade Gear	255-M	Cascade R4 jacket, WM	5
Cascade Gear	255-XL	Cascade R4 jacket, WXL	5
*			

Case Study Apply Your Skills

Part 1

As the office manager at Summit View Medical Services, you are responsible for maintaining clinic records. Open **AL1-C7-SummitView.accdb**, enable the contents, and then insert the following additional services into the appropriate table:

- Edit the *Doctor visit* entry in the Services table so it displays as *Clinic visit*.
- Add the entry *X-ray* with a service identification of *X*.
- Add the entry *Cholesterol screening* with a service identification of *CS*.

Add the following new patient information in the database in the appropriate tables:

Patient number 121
Brian M. Gould
2887 Nelson Street
Helena, MT 59604
(406) 555-3121
Mr. Gould saw Dr. Wallace for a clinic visit on 4/6/2015, which has a fee of $75.

Patient number 122
Ellen L. Augustine
12990 148th Street
East Helena, MT 59635
(406) 555-0722
Ms. Augustine saw Dr. Kennedy for cholesterol screening on 4/6/2015, which has a fee of $90.

Patient number 123
Jeff J. Masura
3218 Eldridge Avenue
Helena, MT 59624
(406) 555-6212
Mr. Masura saw Dr. Rowe for an x-ray on 4/6/2015, which has a fee of $75.

Add the following information to the Billing table:

- Patient 109 came for cholesterol screening with Dr. Kennedy on 4/6/2015 with a $90 fee.
- Patient 106 came for immunizations with Dr. Pena on 4/6/2015 with a $100 fee.
- Patient 114 came for an x-ray with Dr. Kennedy on 4/6/2015 with a $75 fee.

Part 2

Create the following filters and queries:

- Open the Billing table and then filter and print the records for the date 4/2/2015. Clear the filter and then filter and print the records with a doctor number of 18. Save and then close the table.
- Create a report that displays the patient's first name, last name, street address, city, state, and zip code. Apply formatting to enhance the appearance of the report. Filter and print the records of those patients living in Helena, remove the filter, and then filter and print the records of those patients living in East Helena. Close the report.
- Design a query that includes the doctor number, doctor last name, patient number, date of visit, and fee. Save the query with the name *DoctorBillingFees* and then print the query. Filter and print the records for Dr. Kennedy and Dr. Pena, remove the filter, and then filter and print the records for the dates 4/5/2015 and 4/6/2015. Save and then close the query.

Part 3

You want to make the Billing table available for viewing on computers without Access, so you decide to save the table in PDF file format. Save the Billing table in PDF file format, print the table in Adobe Reader, and then close Adobe Reader. Close **AL1-C7-SummitView.accdb**.

Part 4

Your clinic has a manual that describes processes and procedures in the workplace. Open Word and then create a document for the manual that describes the steps you followed to create the *DoctorBillingFees* query and to create and print the two filters. Save the completed document and name it **AL1-C7-CS-Manual**. Print and then close **AL1-C7-CS-Manual.docx**.

MICROSOFT® ACCESS®

Exporting and Importing Data

CHAPTER 8

PERFORMANCE OBJECTIVES

Upon successful completion of Chapter 8, you will be able to:

- **Export Access data to Excel**
- **Export Access data to Word**
- **Merge Access data with a Word document**
- **Exporting an Access object to a PDF or XPS file**
- **Import data to a new table**
- **Link data to a new table**
- **Use the Office Clipboard**

Tutorials

8.1 Exporting Access Data to Excel

8.2 Exporting Access Data to Word

8.3 Merging Access Data with a Word Document

8.4 Importing and Linking Data to a New Table

8.5 Using the Office Clipboard

Microsoft Office 2013 is a suite of programs that allows easy data exchange between programs. In this chapter, you will learn how to export data from Access to Excel and Word, merge Access data with a Word document, export an Access object to a PDF or XPS file, import and link data to a new table, and copy and paste data between programs. You will also learn how to copy and paste data between applications. Model answers for this chapter's projects appear on the following pages.

Note: Before beginning the projects, copy to your storage medium the AL1C8 subfolder from the AL1 folder on the CD that accompanies this textbook and make AL1C8 the active folder.

Project 1 Export Data to Excel and Export and Merge Data to Word

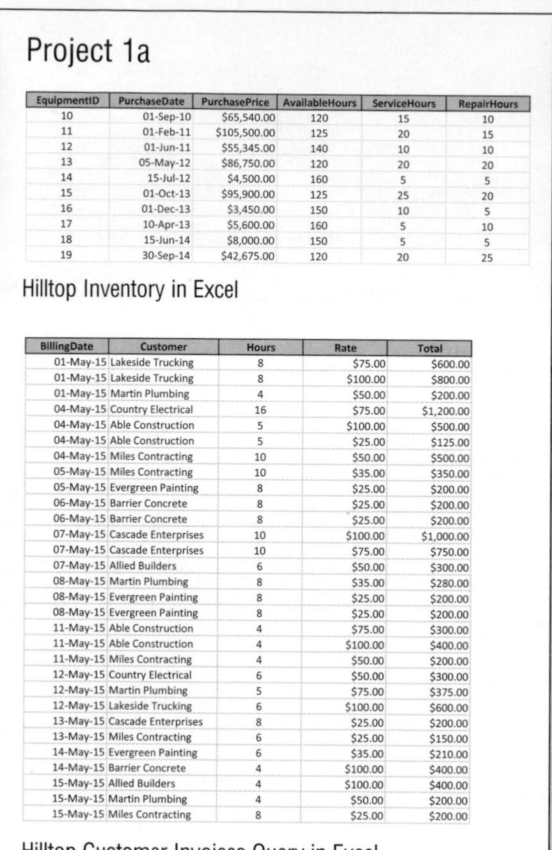

Project 1a

EquipmentID	PurchaseDate	PurchasePrice	AvailableHours	ServiceHours	RepairHours
10	01-Sep-10	$65,540.00	120	15	10
11	01-Feb-11	$105,500.00	125	20	15
12	01-Jun-11	$55,345.00	140	10	10
13	05-May-12	$86,750.00	120	20	20
14	15-Jul-12	$4,500.00	160	5	5
15	01-Oct-13	$95,900.00	125	25	20
16	01-Dec-13	$3,450.00	150	10	5
17	10-Apr-13	$5,600.00	160	5	10
18	15-Jun-14	$8,000.00	150	5	5
19	30-Sep-14	$42,675.00	120	20	25

Hilltop Inventory in Excel

BillingDate	Customer	Hours	Rate	Total
01-May-15	Lakeside Trucking	8	$75.00	$600.00
01-May-15	Lakeside Trucking	8	$100.00	$800.00
01-May-15	Martin Plumbing	4	$50.00	$200.00
04-May-15	Country Electrical	16	$75.00	$1,200.00
04-May-15	Able Construction	5	$100.00	$500.00
04-May-15	Able Construction	5	$25.00	$125.00
04-May-15	Miles Contracting	10	$50.00	$500.00
05-May-15	Miles Contracting	10	$35.00	$350.00
05-May-15	Evergreen Painting	8	$25.00	$200.00
06-May-15	Barrier Concrete	8	$25.00	$200.00
06-May-15	Barrier Concrete	8	$25.00	$200.00
07-May-15	Cascade Enterprises	10	$100.00	$1,000.00
07-May-15	Cascade Enterprises	10	$75.00	$750.00
07-May-15	Allied Builders	6	$50.00	$300.00
08-May-15	Martin Plumbing	8	$35.00	$280.00
08-May-15	Evergreen Painting	8	$25.00	$200.00
08-May-15	Evergreen Painting	8	$25.00	$200.00
11-May-15	Able Construction	4	$75.00	$300.00
11-May-15	Able Construction	4	$100.00	$400.00
11-May-15	Miles Contracting	4	$50.00	$200.00
12-May-15	Country Electrical	6	$50.00	$300.00
12-May-15	Martin Plumbing	5	$75.00	$375.00
12-May-15	Lakeside Trucking	6	$100.00	$600.00
13-May-15	Cascade Enterprises	8	$25.00	$200.00
13-May-15	Miles Contracting	6	$25.00	$150.00
14-May-15	Evergreen Painting	6	$35.00	$210.00
14-May-15	Barrier Concrete	4	$100.00	$400.00
15-May-15	Allied Builders	4	$100.00	$400.00
15-May-15	Martin Plumbing	4	$50.00	$200.00
15-May-15	Miles Contracting	8	$25.00	$200.00

Hilltop Customer Invoices Query in Excel

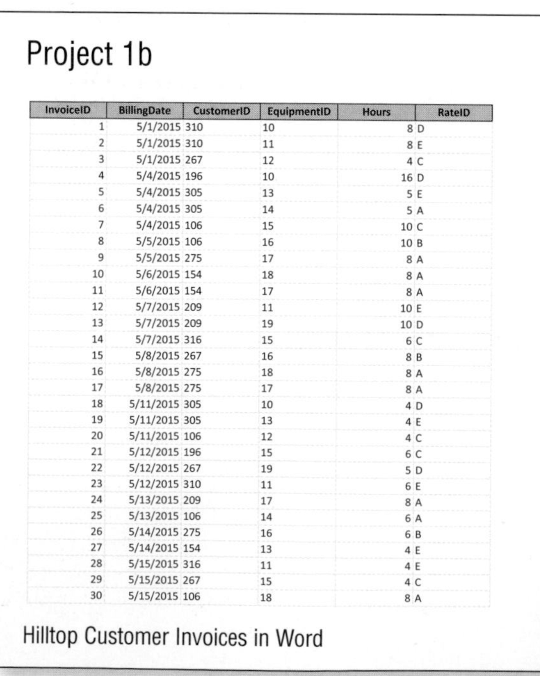

Project 1b

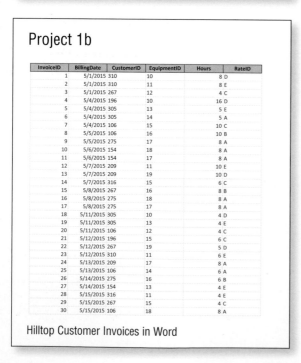

InvoiceID	BillingDate	CustomerID	EquipmentID	Hours	RateID
1	5/1/2015	310	10	8	D
2	5/1/2015	310	11	8	E
3	5/1/2015	267	12	4	C
4	5/4/2015	196	10	16	D
5	5/4/2015	305	13	5	E
6	5/4/2015	305	14	5	A
7	5/4/2015	106	15	10	C
8	5/5/2015	106	16	10	B
9	5/5/2015	275	17	8	A
10	5/6/2015	154	18	8	A
11	5/6/2015	154	17	8	A
12	5/7/2015	209	11	10	E
13	5/7/2015	209	19	10	D
14	5/7/2015	316	15	6	C
15	5/8/2015	267	16	8	B
16	5/8/2015	275	18	8	A
17	5/8/2015	275	17	8	A
18	5/11/2015	305	10	4	D
19	5/11/2015	305	13	4	E
20	5/11/2015	106	12	4	C
21	5/12/2015	196	15	6	C
22	5/12/2015	267	19	5	D
23	5/12/2015	310	11	6	E
24	5/13/2015	209	17	8	A
25	5/13/2015	106	14	6	A
26	5/14/2015	275	16	6	B
27	5/14/2015	154	13	4	E
28	5/15/2015	316	11	4	E
29	5/15/2015	267	15	4	C
30	5/15/2015	106	18	8	A

Hilltop Customer Invoices in Word

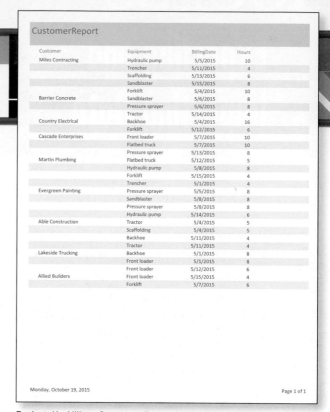

CustomerReport

Customer	Equipment	BillingDate	Hours
Miles Contracting	Hydraulic pump	5/5/2015	10
	Trencher	5/11/2015	4
	Scaffolding	5/13/2015	6
	Sandblaster	5/15/2015	8
	Forklift	5/4/2015	10
Barrier Concrete	Sandblaster	5/6/2015	8
	Pressure sprayer	5/6/2015	8
	Tractor	5/14/2015	4
Country Electrical	Backhoe	5/4/2015	16
	Forklift	5/12/2015	6
Cascade Enterprises	Front loader	5/7/2015	10
	Flatbed truck	5/7/2015	10
	Pressure sprayer	5/13/2015	8
Martin Plumbing	Flatbed truck	5/12/2015	5
	Hydraulic pump	5/8/2015	8
	Forklift	5/15/2015	4
	Trencher	5/1/2015	4
Evergreen Painting	Pressure sprayer	5/5/2015	8
	Sandblaster	5/8/2015	8
	Pressure sprayer	5/8/2015	8
	Hydraulic pump	5/14/2015	6
Able Construction	Tractor	5/4/2015	5
	Scaffolding	5/4/2015	5
	Backhoe	5/11/2015	4
	Tractor	5/11/2015	4
Lakeside Trucking	Backhoe	5/1/2015	8
	Front loader	5/1/2015	8
	Front loader	5/12/2015	6
Allied Builders	Front loader	5/15/2015	4
	Forklift	5/7/2015	6

Monday, October 19, 2015

Page 1 of 1

Project 1b, Hilltop Customer Report in Access

CustomerReport

Customer	Equipment	BillingDate	Hours
Miles Contracting	Hydraulic pump	5/5/2015	10
	Trencher	5/11/2015	4
	Scaffolding	5/13/2015	6
	Sandblaster	5/15/2015	8
	Forklift	5/4/2015	10
Barrier Concrete	Sandblaster	5/6/2015	8
	Pressure sprayer	5/6/2015	8
	Tractor	5/14/2015	4
Country Electrical	Backhoe	5/4/2015	16
	Forklift	5/12/2015	6
Cascade Enterprises	Front loader	5/7/2015	10
	Flatbed truck	5/7/2015	10
	Pressure sprayer	5/13/2015	8
Martin Plumbing	Flatbed truck	5/12/2015	5
	Hydraulic pump	5/8/2015	8
	Forklift	5/15/2015	4
	Trencher	5/1/2015	4
Evergreen Painting	Pressure sprayer	5/5/2015	8
	Sandblaster	5/8/2015	8
	Pressure sprayer	5/8/2015	8
	Hydraulic pump	5/14/2015	6
Able Construction	Tractor	5/4/2015	5
	Scaffolding	5/4/2015	5
	Backhoe	5/11/2015	4
	Tractor	5/11/2015	4
Lakeside Trucking	Backhoe	5/1/2015	8
	Front loader	5/1/2015	8
	Front loader	5/12/2015	6
Allied Builders	Front loader	5/15/2015	4
	Forklift	5/7/2015	6

Friday, October 19, 2012

Page 1 of 1

Project 1b, Hilltop Customer Report in Word

Model Answers

October 19, 2015

Miles Contracting
640 Smith Road
Aurora, CO 80041-6400

Ladies and Gentlemen:

Please join us June 1 for our annual equipment sales auction. Some of the choice items up for auction include three forklifts, two flatbed trucks, a front loader, and a bulldozer. We will also be auctioning painting equipment including pressure sprayers, ladders, and scaffolding.

The auction begins at 7:30 a.m. in the parking lot of our warehouse at 2605 Evans Avenue in Denver. For a listing of all equipment available for auction, stop by our store or call us at (303) 555-9066 and we will mail you the list.

Sincerely,

Lou Galloway
Manager

XX
HilltopLetter.docx

October 19, 2015

Barrier Concrete
220 Colorado Boulevard
Denver, CO 80125-2204

Ladies and Gentlemen:

Please join us June 1 for our annual equipment sales auction. Some of the choice items up for auction include three forklifts, two flatbed trucks, a front loader, and a bulldozer. We will also be auctioning painting equipment including pressure sprayers, ladders, and scaffolding.

The auction begins at 7:30 a.m. in the parking lot of our warehouse at 2605 Evans Avenue in Denver. For a listing of all equipment available for auction, stop by our store or call us at (303) 555-9066 and we will mail you the list.

Sincerely,

Lou Galloway
Manager

XX
HilltopLetter.docx

Project 1c, Hilltop Letters

October 19, 2015

Vernon Cook
1230 South Mesa
Phoenix, AZ 85018

Ladies and Gentlemen:

At the Grant Street West office of Copper State Insurance, we have hired two additional insurance representatives as well as one support staff member to ensure that we meet all your insurance needs. To accommodate the new staff, we have moved to a larger office just a few blocks away. Our new address is 3450 Grant Street West, Suite 110, Phoenix AZ 85003. Our telephone number, (602) 555-6300, has remained the same.

If you have any questions or concerns about your insurance policies or want to discuss adding or changing current coverage, please stop by or give us a call. We are committed to providing our clients with the most comprehensive automobile insurance coverage in the county.

Sincerely,

Lou Galloway
Manager

XX
AL1-C8-CSLtrs.docx

October 19, 2015

Helena Myerson
9032 45th Street East
Phoenix, AZ 85009

Ladies and Gentlemen:

At the Grant Street West office of Copper State Insurance, we have hired two additional insurance representatives as well as one support staff member to ensure that we meet all your insurance needs. To accommodate the new staff, we have moved to a larger office just a few blocks away. Our new address is 3450 Grant Street West, Suite 110, Phoenix AZ 85003. Our telephone number, (602) 555-6300, has remained the same.

If you have any questions or concerns about your insurance policies or want to discuss adding or changing current coverage, please stop by or give us a call. We are committed to providing our clients with the most comprehensive automobile insurance coverage in the county.

Sincerely,

Lou Galloway
Manager

XX
AL1-C8-CSLtrs.docx

Project 1d, Copper State Main Document

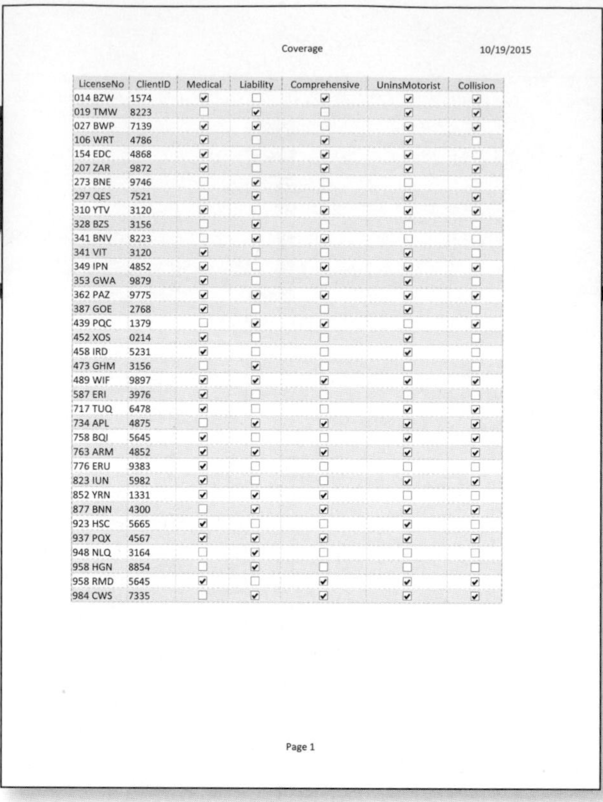

Coverage 10/19/2015

LicenseNo	ClientID	Medical	Liability	Comprehensive	UninsMotorist	Collision
014 BZW	1574	☑	☐	☑	☑	☑
019 TMW	8223	☐	☑	☐	☑	☑
027 BWP	7139	☑	☑	☐	☑	☑
106 WRT	4786	☑	☐	☑	☑	☐
154 EDC	4868	☑	☐	☑	☑	☐
207 ZAR	9872	☑	☐	☑	☑	☑
273 BNE	9746	☐	☑	☐	☐	☐
297 QES	7521	☐	☑	☐	☑	☑
310 YTV	3120	☑	☐	☑	☑	☑
328 BZS	3156	☐	☑	☐	☐	☐
341 BNV	8223	☐	☑	☑	☐	☐
341 VIT	3120	☑	☐	☐	☑	☐
349 IPN	4852	☑	☐	☑	☑	☑
353 GWA	9879	☑	☐	☐	☑	☐
362 PAZ	9775	☑	☑	☑	☑	☑
387 GOE	2768	☑	☐	☐	☑	☐
439 PQC	1379	☐	☑	☑	☐	☑
452 XOS	0214	☑	☐	☐	☑	☐
458 IRD	5231	☑	☐	☐	☑	☐
473 GHM	3156	☐	☑	☐	☐	☐
489 WIF	9897	☑	☑	☑	☑	☑
587 ERI	3976	☑	☐	☐	☐	☐
717 TUQ	6478	☑	☐	☐	☑	☑
734 APL	4875	☐	☑	☑	☑	☑
758 BQI	5645	☑	☐	☐	☑	☑
763 ARM	4852	☑	☑	☑	☑	☑
776 ERU	9383	☑	☐	☐	☐	☐
823 IUN	5982	☑	☐	☐	☑	☑
852 YRN	1331	☑	☑	☑	☐	☐
877 BNN	4300	☐	☑	☑	☑	☑
923 HSC	5665	☑	☐	☐	☑	☐
937 PQX	4567	☑	☑	☑	☑	☑
948 NLQ	3164	☐	☑	☐	☐	☐
958 HGN	8854	☐	☑	☐	☐	☐
958 RMD	5645	☑	☐	☑	☑	☑
984 CWS	7335	☐	☑	☑	☑	☑

Page 1

Project 1e, Copper State Coverage Table

Project 2 Import and Link Excel Worksheets with an Access Table

Project 2a

PolicyID	ClientID	Premium
110-C-39	0214	$1,450
115-C-41	3120	$935
120-B-33	3156	$424
122-E-30	1331	$745
127-E-67	3164	$893
129-D-55	3976	$770
131-C-90	4300	$1,255
135-E-31	4567	$1,510
136-E-77	4786	$635
139-B-59	4852	$338
141-E-84	4875	$951
143-D-20	1379	$920
145-D-12	5231	$1,175
147-C-10	5645	$1,005
150-C-36	5665	$805
152-B-01	5982	$411
155-E-88	6478	$988
168-B-65	7139	$1,050
170-C-20	7335	$875
173-D-77	7521	$556
180-E-05	8223	$721
185-E-19	2768	$734
188-D-63	8854	$1,384
192-C-29	1574	$1,390

Copper State Policies Table in Access

Project 2b

PolicyID	ClientID	Premium
110-C-39	0214	$ 1,450
122-E-30	1331	$ 850
143-D-20	1379	$ 920
192-C-29	1574	$ 1,390
185-E-19	2768	$ 734
115-C-41	3120	$ 935
120-B-33	3156	$ 424
127-E-67	3164	$ 893
129-D-55	3976	$ 770
131-C-90	4300	$ 1,255
135-E-31	4567	$ 1,510
136-E-77	4786	$ 635
139-B-59	4852	$ 338
141-E-84	4875	$ 951
145-D-12	5231	$ 1,175
147-C-10	5645	$ 1,005
150-C-36	5665	$ 805
152-B-01	5982	$ 411
155-E-88	6478	$ 988
168-B-65	7139	$ 1,050
170-C-20	7335	$ 875
173-D-77	7521	$ 556
180-E-05	8223	$ 721
188-D-63	8854	$ 1,384
190-C-28	3120	$ 685

Policies Table in Excel

Project 3 Collect Data in Word and Paste It into an Access Table

Project 3

CustomerID	Customer	StreetAddress	City	State	ZipCode
106	Miles Contracting	640 Smith Road	Aurora	CO	80041-6400
154	Barrier Concrete	220 Colorado Boulevard	Denver	CO	80125-2204
196	Country Electrical	12032 Sixth Avenue	Aurora	CO	80023-5473
209	Cascade Enterprises	24300 Quincy Avenue	Englewood	CO	80118-3800
267	Martin Plumbing	1010 Santa Fe Drive	Littleton	CO	80135-4886
275	Evergreen Painting	1045 Calfax Avenue	Denver	CO	80130-4337
305	Able Construction	8800 Evans Avenue	Denver	CO	80128-3488
310	Lakeside Trucking	566 Jewell Avenue	Denver	CO	80125-1298
316	Allied Builders	550 Alameda Avenue	Denver	CO	80135-7643
178	Stone Construction	9905 Broadway	Englewood	CO	80118-9008
225	Laughlin Products	997 Speer Boulevard	Denver	CO	80129-7446

Hilltop Customers Table

Project 1 Export Data to Excel and Export and Merge Data to Word

5 Parts

You will export a table and query to Excel and export a table and report to Word. You will also merge data in an Access table and query with a Word document.

Exporting Data

One of the advantages of using the Microsoft Office suite is the ability to exchange data between programs. Access, like other programs in the suite, offers a feature to export data from Access into Excel and/or Word. The Export group on the EXTERNAL DATA tab contains buttons for exporting a table, query, form, or report to other programs, such as Excel and Word.

Quick Steps

Export Data to Excel

1. Click desired table, query, or form.
2. Click EXTERNAL DATA tab.
3. Click Excel button in Export group.
4. Make desired changes at Export - Excel Spreadsheet dialog box.
5. Click OK.

Excel

Exporting Data to Excel

Use the Excel button in the Export group on the EXTERNAL DATA tab to export data in a table, query, or form to an Excel worksheet. Click the object containing the data you want to export to Excel, click the EXTERNAL DATA tab, and then click the Excel button in the Export group. The first Export - Excel Spreadsheet wizard dialog box displays, as shown in Figure 8.1.

Figure 8.1 Export - Excel Spreadsheet Wizard Dialog Box

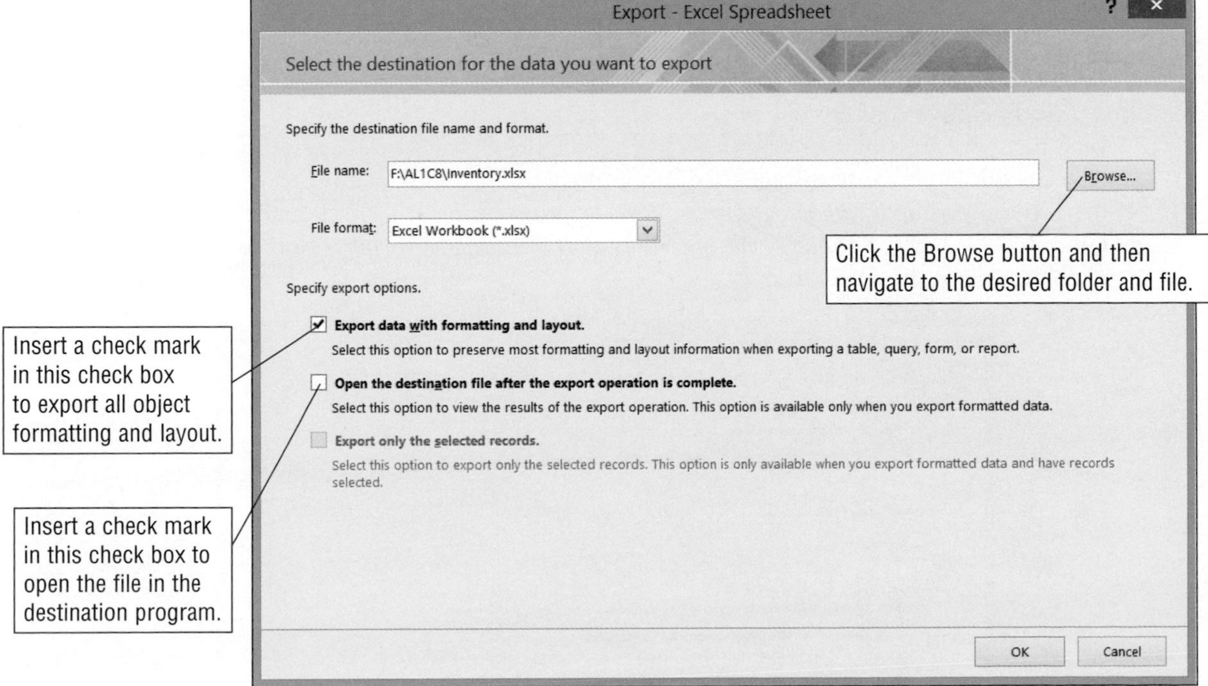

Data exported from Access to Excel is saved as an Excel workbook with the .xlsx file extension.

You can export only one database object at a time.

At the first wizard dialog box, Access uses the name of the object as the Excel workbook name. You can change this by selecting the current name and then typing a new name. You can also specify the file format with the *File format* option. Click the *Export data with formatting and layout* check box to insert a check mark. This exports all data formatting to the Excel workbook. If you want Excel to open with the exported data, click the *Open the destination file after the export operation is complete* option to insert a check mark. When you have made all desired changes, click the OK button. This opens Excel with the data in a workbook. Make any desired changes to the workbook and then save, print, and close the workbook. When you close Excel, Access displays with a second wizard dialog box, asking if you want to save the export steps. At this dialog box, insert a check mark in the *Save export steps* check box if you want to save the export steps or leave the check box blank and then click the Close button.

Project 1a Exporting a Table and Query to Excel — Part 1 of 5

1. Display the Open dialog box with the AL1C8 folder on your storage medium the active folder.
2. Open **AL1-C8-Hilltop.accdb** and enable the contents.
3. Save the Inventory table in the Tables group as an Excel workbook by completing the following steps:
   a. Click *Inventory* in the Tables group in the Navigation pane.
   b. Click the EXTERNAL DATA tab and then click the Excel button in the Export group.
   c. At the Export - Excel Spreadsheet wizard dialog box, click the Browse button.
   d. At the File Save dialog box, navigate to the AL1C8 folder on your storage medium and then click the Save button.
   e. Click the *Export data with formatting and layout* option to insert a check mark in the check box.
   f. Click the *Open the destination file after the export operation is complete* option to insert a check mark in the check box.

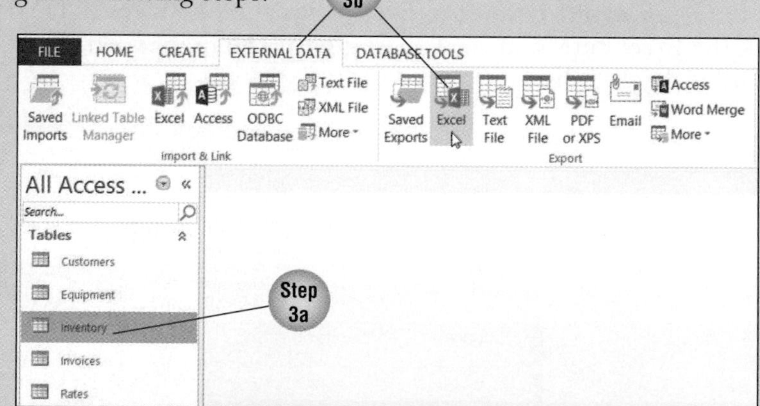

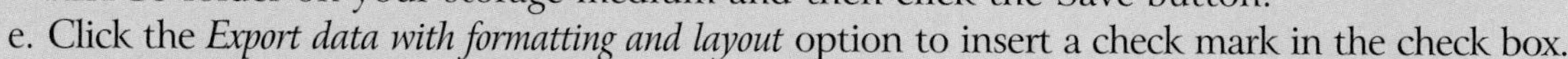

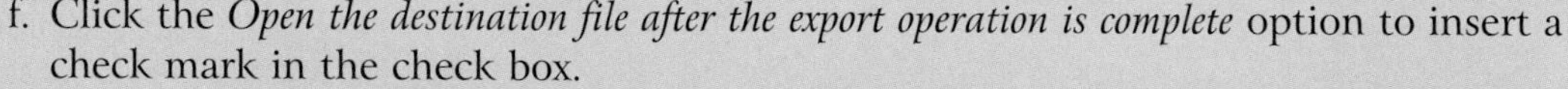

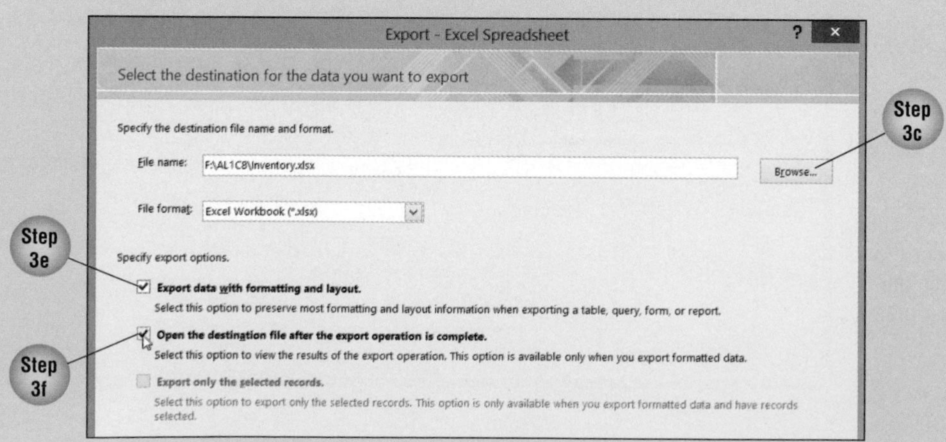

g. Click OK.

h. When the data displays on the screen in Excel as a worksheet, select cells A2 through A11 and then click the Center button in the Alignment group on the HOME tab.

i. Select cells D2 through F11 and then click the Center button.

j. Click the Save button on the Quick Access toolbar.

k. Print the worksheet by pressing Ctrl + P and then clicking the Print button at the Print backstage area.

l. Close the worksheet and then close Excel.

Step 3h

	A	B	C	D	E	F
1	EquipmentID	PurchaseDate	PurchasePrice	AvailableHours	ServiceHours	RepairHours
2	10	01-Sep-10	$65,540.00	120	15	10
3	11	01-Feb-11	$105,500.00	125	20	15
4	12	01-Jun-11	$55,345.00	140	10	10
5	13	05-May-12	$86,750.00	120	20	20
6	14	15-Jul-12	$4,500.00	160	5	5
7	15	01-Oct-13	$95,900.00	125	25	20
8	16	01-Dec-13	$3,450.00	150	10	5
9	17	10-Apr-13	$5,600.00	160	5	10
10	18	15-Jun-14	$8,000.00	150	5	5
11	19	30-Sep-14	$42,675.00	120	20	25
12						
13						

4. In Access, click the Close button to close the second wizard dialog box.
5. Design a query that extracts records from three tables with the following specifications:
   a. Add the Invoices, Customers, and Rates tables to the query window.
   b. Insert the *BillingDate* field from the *Invoices* field list box to the first *Field* row field.
   c. Insert the *Customer* field from the *Customers* field list box to the second *Field* row field.
   d. Insert the *Hours* field from the *Invoices* field list box to the third *Field* row field.
   e. Insert the *Rate* field from the *Rates* field list box to the fourth *Field* row field.
   f. Click in the fifth *Field* row field, type **Total: [Hours]*[Rate]**, and then press Enter.

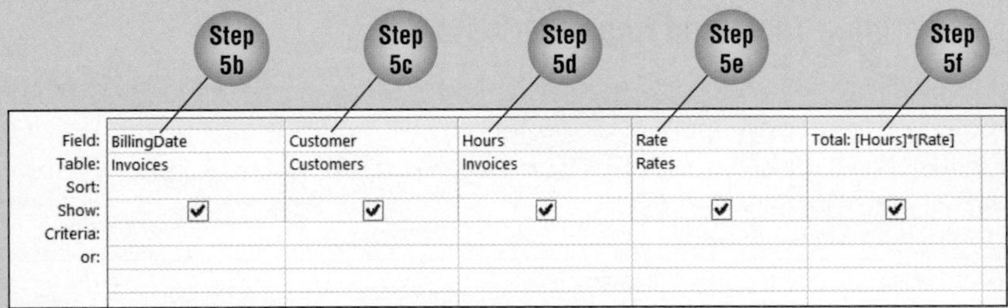

   g. Run the query.
   h. If necessary, automatically adjust the column width of the *Customer* field.
   i. Save the query and name it *CustomerInvoices*.
   j. Close the query.
6. Export the *CustomerInvoices* in the Queries group to Excel by completing the following steps:
   a. Click *CustomerInvoices* in the Queries group in the Navigation pane.
   b. Click the EXTERNAL DATA tab and then click the Excel button in the Export group.
   c. At the Export - Excel Spreadsheet wizard dialog box, click the *Export data with formatting and layout* option to insert a check mark in the check box.
   d. Click the *Open the destination file after the export operation is complete* option to insert a check mark in the check box.

e. Click OK.
f. When the data displays on the screen in Excel as a worksheet, select cells C2 through C31 and then click the Center button in the Alignment group on the HOME tab.
g. Click the Save button on the Quick Access toolbar.
h. Print the worksheet by pressing Ctrl + P and then clicking the Print button at the Print backstage area.
i. Close the worksheet and then close Excel.

7. In Access, click the Close button to close the second wizard dialog box.

Exporting Data to Word

Quick Steps

Export Data to Word
1. Click desired table, query, form, or report.
2. Click EXTERNAL DATA tab.
3. Click More button in Export group.
4. Click *Word*.
5. Make desired changes at Export - RTF File wizard dialog box.
6. Click OK.

More

Export data from Access to Word in a similar manner as exporting to Excel. To export data to Word, select the desired object in the Navigation pane, click the EXTERNAL DATA tab, click the More button in the Export group, and then click *Word* at the drop-down list. At the Export - RTF File wizard dialog box, make desired changes and then click OK. Word automatically opens and the data displays in a Word document that is saved automatically with the same name as the database object. The difference is that the file extension .rtf is added to the name. An RTF file is saved in rich-text format, which preserves formatting such as fonts and styles. You can export a document saved with the .rtf extension in Word and other Windows word processing or desktop publishing programs.

Project 1b **Exporting a Table and Report to Word** **Part 2 of 5**

1. With **AL1-C8-Hilltop.accdb** open, click *Invoices* in the Tables group in the Navigation pane.
2. Click the EXTERNAL DATA tab, click the More button in the Export group, and then click *Word* at the drop-down list.

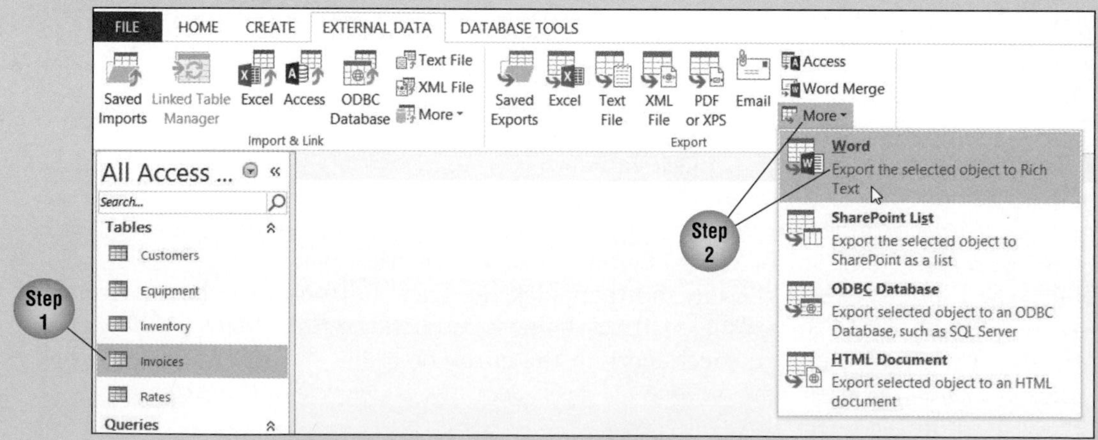

3. At the Export - RTF File wizard dialog box, click the Browse button.
4. At the File Save dialog box, make sure the AL1C8 folder on your storage medium is active and then click the Save button.
5. At the Export - RTF File wizard dialog box, click the *Open the destination file after the export operation is complete* check box to insert a check mark.

6. Click OK.
7. With the **Invoices.rtf** file open in Word, print the document by pressing Ctrl + P and then clicking the Print button at the Print backstage area.
8. Close the **Invoices.rtf** file and then close Word.
9. In Access, click the Close button to close the wizard dialog box.
10. Create a report with the Report Wizard by completing the following steps:
    a. Click the CREATE tab and then click the Report Wizard button in the Reports group.
    b. At the first Report Wizard dialog box, insert the following fields in the *Selected Fields* list box:
        From the Customers table:
            Customer
        From the Equipment table:
            Equipment
        From the Invoices table:
            BillingDate
            Hours
    c. After inserting the fields, click the Next button.
    d. At the second Report Wizard dialog box, make sure *by Customers* is selected in the list box in the upper left corner and then click the Next button.
    e. At the third Report Wizard dialog box, click the Next button.
    f. At the fourth Report Wizard dialog box, click the Next button.
    g. At the fifth Report Wizard dialog box, click *Block* in the *Layout* section and then click the Next button.
    h. At the sixth and final Report Wizard dialog box, select the current name in the *What title do you want for your report?* text box, type **CustomerReport**, and then click the Finish button.

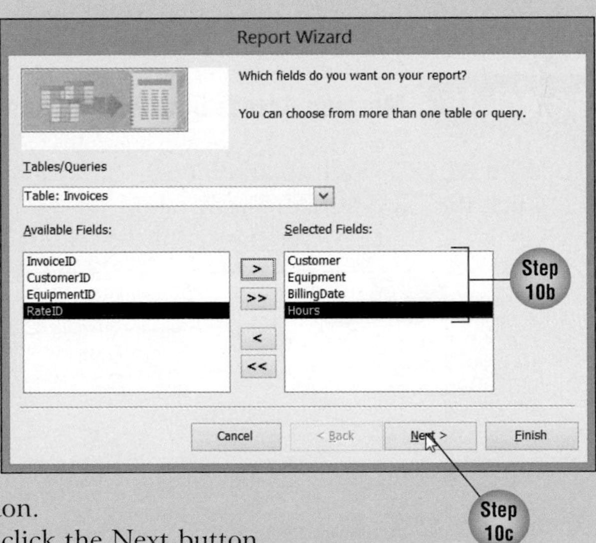

i. When the report displays in Print Preview, click the Print button at the left side of the PRINT PREVIEW tab and then click OK at the Print dialog box.
j. Save and then close the CustomerReport report.
11. Export the CustomerReport report to Word by completing the following steps:
a. Click *CustomerReport* in the Reports group in the Navigation pane.
b. Click the EXTERNAL DATA tab, click the More button in the Export group, and then click *Word* at the drop-down list.
c. At the Export - RTF File wizard dialog box, click the *Open the destination file after export operation is complete* option to insert a check mark in the check box and then click OK.
d. When the data displays on the screen in Word, print the document by pressing Ctrl + P and then clicking the Print button at the Print backstage area.
e. Save and then close the CustomerReport document.
f. Close Word.
12. In Access, click the Close button to close the second wizard dialog box.

Quick Steps

Merge Data with Word
1. Click desired table or query.
2. Click EXTERNAL DATA tab.
3. Click Word Merge button.
4. Make desired choices at each dialog box.

Word Merge

Merging Access Data with a Word Document

You can merge data from an Access table with a Word document. When merging data, the data in the Access table is considered the data source and the Word document is considered the main document. When the merge is completed, the merged documents display in Word.

To merge data, click the desired table in the Navigation pane, click the EXTERNAL DATA tab, and then click the Word Merge button. When merging Access data, you can either type the text in the main document or merge Access data with an existing Word document.

Project 1c **Merging Access Data with a Word Document** **Part 3 of 5**

1. With **AL1-C8-Hilltop.accdb** open, click *Customers* in the Tables group in the Navigation pane.
2. Click the EXTERNAL DATA tab.
3. Click the Word Merge button in the Export group.

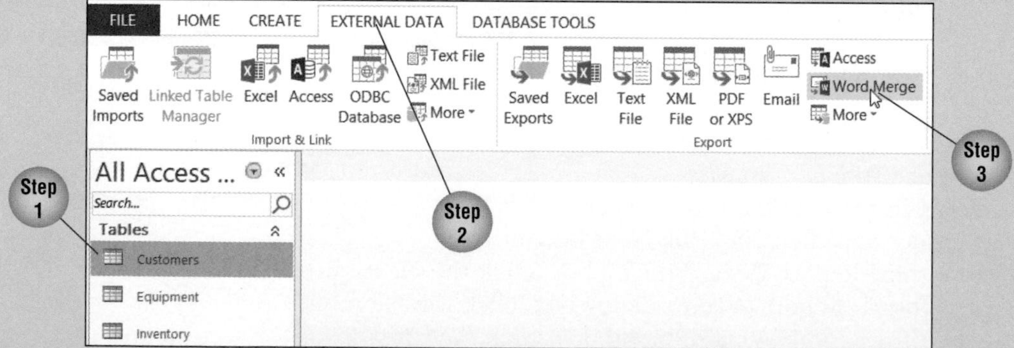

4. At the Microsoft Word Mail Merge Wizard dialog box, make sure *Link your data to an existing Microsoft Word document* is selected and then click OK.
5. At the Select Microsoft Word Document dialog box, make sure the AL1C8 folder on your storage medium is the active folder and then double-click the document named ***HilltopLetter.docx***.

6. Click the Word button on the Taskbar.
7. Click the Maximize button located at the right side of the HilltopLetter.docx Title bar and then close the Mail Merge task pane.
8. Press the down arrow key six times (not the Enter key) and then type the current date.
9. Press the down arrow key four times and then insert fields for merging from the Customers table by completing the following steps:
   a. Click the Insert Merge Field button arrow located in the Write & Insert Fields group and then click *Customer* in the drop-down list. (This inserts the «*Customer*» field in the document.)
   b. Press Enter, click the Insert Merge Field button arrow, and then click *StreetAddress* in the drop-down list.
   c. Press Enter, click the Insert Merge Field button arrow, and then click *City* in the drop-down list.
   d. Type a comma (,) and then press the spacebar.
   e. Click the Insert Merge Field button arrow and then click *State* in the drop-down list.
   f. Press the spacebar, click the Insert Merge Field button arrow, and then click *ZipCode* in the drop-down list.
   g. Replace the letters *XX* that display toward the bottom of the letter with your initials.
   h. Click the Finish & Merge button in the Finish group and then click *Edit Individual Documents* in the drop-down list.
   i. At the Merge to New Document dialog box, make sure *All* is selected and then click OK.
   j. When the merge is completed, save the new document and name it **AL1-C8-HilltopLtrs** in the AL1C8 folder on your storage medium.
10. Print just the first two pages (two letters) of **AL1-C8-HilltopLtrs.docx**.
11. Close **AL1-C8-HilltopLtrs.docx** and then close **HilltopLetter.docx** without saving the changes.
12. Close Word.
13. Close **AL1-C8-Hilltop.accdb**.

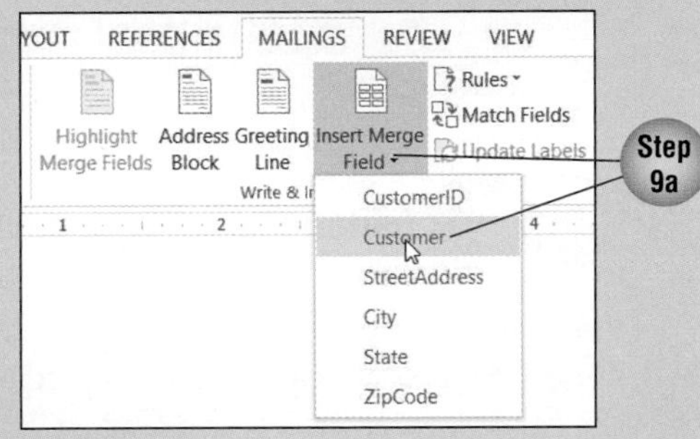

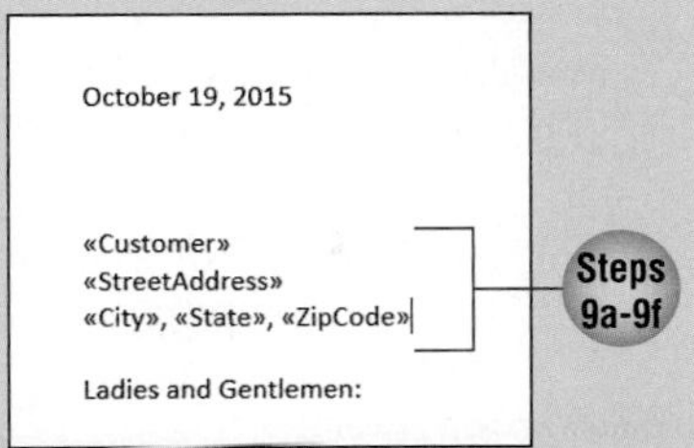

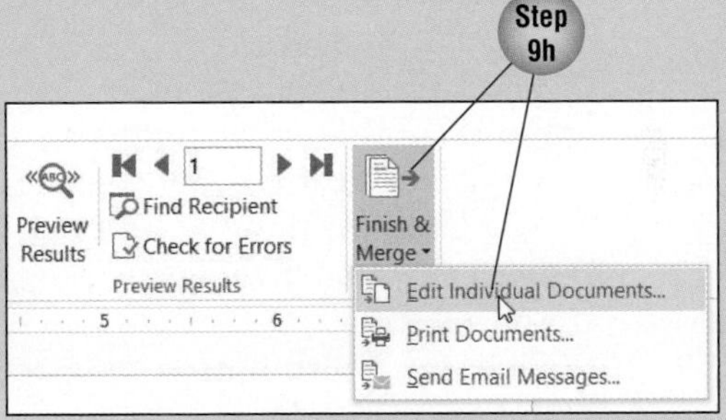

Merging Query Data with a Word Document

You can perform a query in a database and then use the query to merge with a Word document. In Project 1c, you merged a table with an existing Word document. You can also merge a table or query and then type the Word document. You will create a query in Project 1d and then merge data in the query with a new document in Word.

In Project 1c, you inserted a number of merge fields for the inside address of a letter. You can also insert a field that will insert all of the fields required for the inside address of a letter with the Address Block button in the Write & Insert Fields group on the MAILINGS tab. When you click the Address Block button, the Insert Address Block dialog box displays with a preview of how the

Address Block

fields will be inserted in the document to create the inside address. The dialog box also contains buttons and options for customizing the fields. Click OK and the *«AddressBlock»* field is inserted in the document. The *«AddressBlock»* field is an example of a composite field, which groups a number of fields.

In Project 1c, you could not use the *«AddressBlock»* composite field because the *Customer* field was not recognized by Word as a field for the inside address. In Project 1d, you will create a query that contains the *FirstName* and *LastName* fields, which Word recognizes and uses for the *«AddressBlock»* composite field.

Project 1d Performing a Query and Then Merging with a Word Document Part 4 of 5

1. Display the Open dialog box with the AL1C8 folder on your storage medium the active folder.
2. Open **AL1-C8-CopperState.accdb** and enable the contents.
3. Perform a query with the Query Wizard and modify the query by completing the following steps:
   a. Click the CREATE tab and then click the Query Wizard button in the Queries group.
   b. At the New Query dialog box, make sure Simple Query Wizard is selected and then click OK.
   c. At the first Simple Query Wizard dialog box, click the down-pointing arrow at the right of the *Tables/Queries* option box and then click *Table: Clients*.
   d. Click the All Fields button to insert all of the fields in the *Selected Fields* list box.
   e. Click the Next button.
   f. At the second Simple Query Wizard dialog box, make the following changes:
      1) Select the current name in the *What title do you want for your query?* text box and then type **ClientsPhoenixQuery**.
      2) Click the *Modify the query design* option.
      3) Click the Finish button.
   g. At the query window, click in the *Criteria* field in the *City* column, type **Phoenix**, and then press Enter.
   h. Click the Run button in the Results group. (Only clients living in Phoenix will display.)
   i. Save and then close the query.

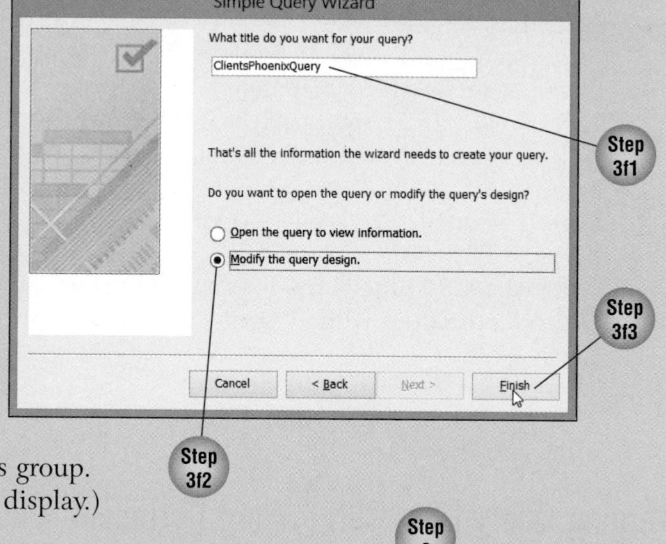

4. Click *ClientsPhoenixQuery* in the Queries group in the Navigation pane.
5. Click the EXTERNAL DATA tab and then click the Word Merge button in the Export group.
6. At the Microsoft Word Mail Merge Wizard dialog box, click the *Create a new document and then link the data to it* option and then click OK.

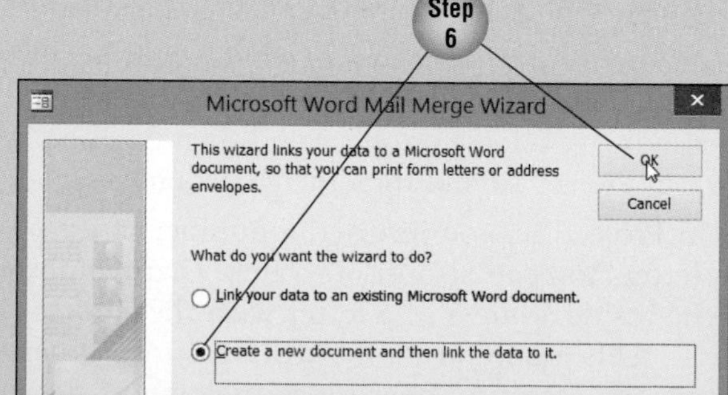

7. Click the Word button on the Taskbar.
8. Click the Maximize button located at the right side of the Document1 Title bar and then close the Mail Merge task pane.
9. Complete the following steps to type text and insert the *«AddressBlock»* composite field in the blank Word document:
   a. Click the HOME tab and then click the *No Spacing* style option in the Styles group.
   b. Press Enter six times.
   c. Type the current date.
   d. Press Enter four times.
   e. Click the MAILINGS tab.
   f. Insert the *«AddressBlock»* composite field by clicking the Address Block button in the Write & Insert Fields group on the MAILINGS tab and then clicking OK at the Insert Address Block dialog box. (This inserts the *«AddressBlock»* composite field in the document.)
   g. Press Enter twice and then type the salutation **Ladies and Gentlemen:**.
   h. Press Enter twice and then type the following paragraphs of text (press the Enter key twice after typing the first paragraph):

      At the Grant Street West office of Copper State Insurance, we have hired two additional insurance representatives as well as one support staff member to ensure that we meet all your insurance needs. To accommodate the new staff, we have moved to a larger office just a few blocks away. Our new address is 3450 Grant Street West, Suite 110, Phoenix AZ 85003. Our telephone number, (602) 555-6300, has remained the same.

      If you have any questions or concerns about your insurance policies or want to discuss adding or changing current coverage, please stop by or give us a call. We are committed to providing our clients with the most comprehensive automobile insurance coverage in the county.

   i. Press Enter twice and then type the following complimentary close at the left margin (press Enter four times after typing *Sincerely,*):

      Sincerely,

      Lou Galloway
      Manager

      XX (Type your initials instead of XX.)
      AL1-C8-CSLtrs.docx

   j. Click the Finish & Merge button in the Finish group on the MAILINGS tab and then click *Edit Individual Documents* in the drop-down menu.
   k. At the Merge to New Document dialog box, make sure *All* is selected, and then click OK.
   l. When the merge is complete, save the new document in the AL1C8 folder on your storage medium and name it **AL1-C8-CSLtrs**.
10. Print the first two pages (two letters) of **AL1-C8-CSLtrs.docx**.
11. Close **AL1-C8-CSLtrs.docx**.
12. Save the main document as **AL1-C8-CSMainDoc** in the AL1C8 folder on your storage medium and then close the document.
13. Close Word.

Exporting an Access Object to a PDF or XPS File

Quick Steps

Export an Access Object to a PDF File

1. Click object in the Navigation pane.
2. Click EXTERNAL DATA tab.
3. Click PDF or XPS button.
4. Navigate to desired folder.
5. Click Publish button.

PDF or XPS

With the PDF or XPS button in the Export group on the EXTERNAL DATA tab, you can export an Access object to a PDF or XPS file. As you learned in Chapter 7, the letters *PDF* stand for *portable document format*, which is a file format that captures all of the elements of a file as an electronic image. The letters *XPS* stand for *XML paper specification* and the letters *XML* stand for *extensible markup language*, which is a set of rules for encoding files electronically.

To export an Access object to PDF or XPS file format, click the desired object, click the EXTERNAL DATA tab, and then click the PDF or XPS button in the Export group. This displays the Publish as PDF or XPS dialog box with the *PDF (*.pdf)* option selected in the *Save as type* option box. If you want to save the Access object in XPS file format, click the *Save as type* option box and then click *XPS Document (*.xps)* at the drop-down list. At the Save As dialog box, type a name in the *File name* text box and then click the Publish button.

To open a PDF or XPS file in your web browser, open the browser, click *File* on the browser Menu bar, and then click *Open* at the drop-down list. At the Open dialog box, click the Browse button. At the browser window Open dialog box, change the *Files of type* to *All Files (*.*)*, navigate to the desired folder, and then double-click the file.

Project 1e **Exporting an Access Object to a PDF File** **Part 5 of 5**

1. With **AL1-C8-CopperState.accdb** open, export the Coverage table to PDF file format by completing the following steps:
   a. Click *Coverage* in the Tables group in the Navigation pane.
   b. Click the EXTERNAL DATA tab.
   c. Click the PDF or XPS button in the Export group.
   d. At the Publish as PDF or XPS dialog box, navigate to the AL1C8 folder on your storage medium, click the *Open file after publishing* check box to insert a check mark, and then click the Publish button.
   e. When the Coverage table data displays in Adobe Reader, scroll through the file and notice how it displays.

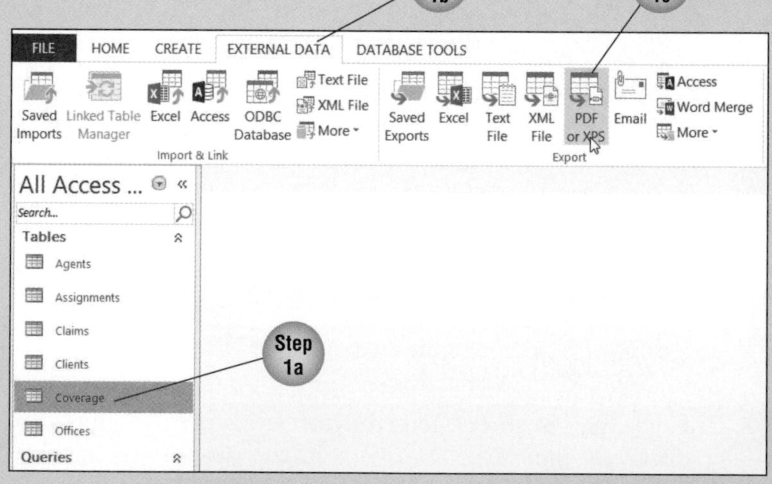

   f. Print the PDF file by clicking the Print button that displays at the left side of the toolbar and then clicking OK at the Print dialog box.
   g. Close Adobe Reader by positioning the mouse pointer at the top of the window (mouse turns into a hand), holding down the left mouse button, dragging down to the bottom of the screen, and then releasing the mouse button.
   h. At the Windows 8 Start screen, click the Desktop icon.
2. In Access, click the Close button to close the wizard dialog box.

Project 2 Import and Link Excel Worksheets with an Access Table — 2 Parts

You will import an Excel worksheet into an Access table. You will also link an Excel worksheet to an Access table and then add a new record to the Access table.

Importing and Linking Data to New Tables

In this chapter, you have learned how to export Access data to Excel and Word. You can also import data from other programs into an Access table. For example, you can import data from an Excel worksheet and create a new table in a database using data from the worksheet. Data in the original program is not connected to the data imported into an Access table. If you make changes to the data in the original program, those changes are not reflected in the Access table. If you want the imported data connected to the original program, link the data.

Quick Steps

Import Data into a New Table

1. Click EXTERNAL DATA tab.
2. Click desired application in Import & Link group.
3. Click Browse button.
4. Double-click desired file name.
5. Make desired choices at each wizard dialog box.

Store data in Access and analyze it using Excel.

You can import and link data between Access databases.

Importing Data into a New Table

To import data, click the EXTERNAL DATA tab and then determine where you would like to retrieve data with options in the Import & Link group. At the Import dialog box that displays, click Browse and then double-click the desired file name. This activates the Import Wizard and displays the first wizard dialog box. The appearance of the dialog box varies depending on the file selected. Complete the steps of the Import Wizard, specifying information such as the range of data, whether the first row contains column headings, whether to store the data in a new table or existing table, the primary key, and the name of the table.

Project 2a Importing an Excel Worksheet into an Access Table — Part 1 of 2

1. With **AL1-C8-CopperState.accdb** open, import an Excel worksheet into a new table in the database by completing the following steps:
   a. Click the EXTERNAL DATA tab and then click the Excel button in the Import & Link group.
   b. At the Get External Data - Excel Spreadsheet dialog box, click the Browse button and then make the AL1C8 folder on your storage medium the active folder.
   c. Double-click ***AL1-C8-Policies.xlsx*** in the list box.
   d. Click OK at the Get External Data - Excel Spreadsheet dialog box.
   e. At the first Import Spreadsheet Wizard dialog box, make sure the *First Row Contains Column Headings* check box contains a check mark and then click the Next button.

f. At the second Import Spreadsheet Wizard dialog box, click the Next button.

g. At the third Import Spreadsheet Wizard dialog box, click the *Choose my own primary key* option (which inserts *PolicyID* in the option box located to the right of the option) and then click the Next button.

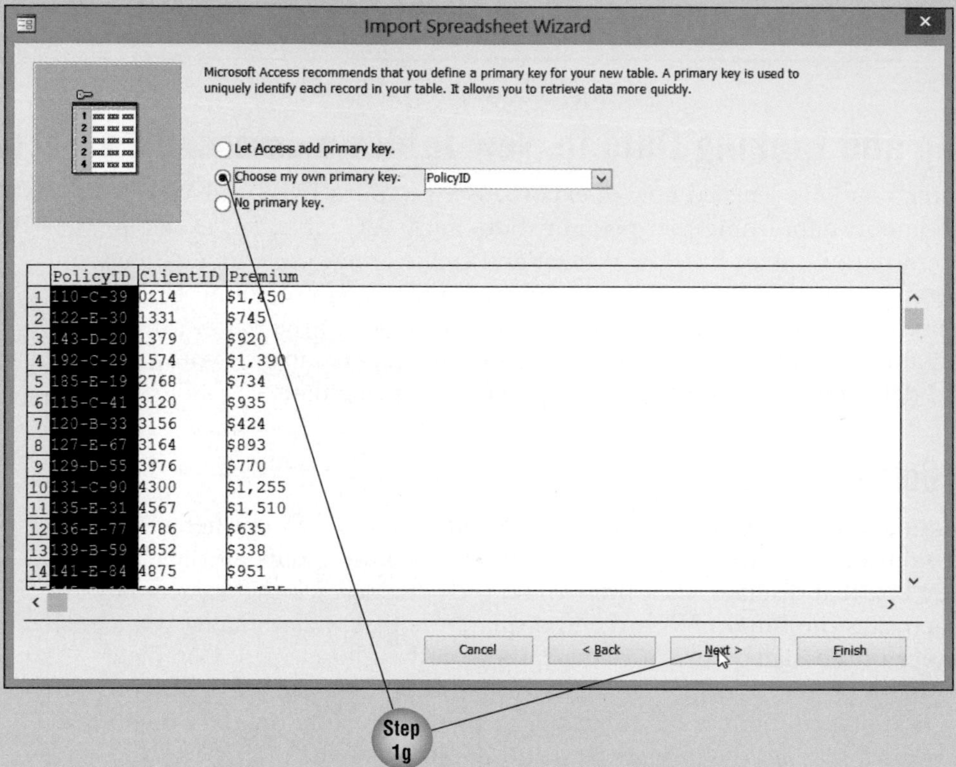

h. At the fourth Import Spreadsheet Wizard dialog box, type **Policies** in the *Import to Table* text box and then click the Finish button.

i. At the Get External Data - Excel Spreadsheet dialog box, click the Close button.

2. Open the new Policies table in Datasheet view.
3. Print and then close the Policies table.

Linking Data to an Excel Worksheet

Imported data is not connected to the source program. If you know that you will use your data only in Access, import it. However, if you want to update the data in a program other than Access, link the data. Changes made to linked data in the source program file are reflected in the destination program file. For example, you can link an Excel worksheet with an Access table and when you make changes in the Excel worksheet, the changes are reflected in the Access table.

To link data to a new table, click the EXTERNAL DATA tab and then click the Excel button in the Import & Link group. At the Get External Data - Excel Spreadsheet dialog box, click the Browse button, double-click the desired file name, click the *Link to a data source by creating a linked table* option, and then click OK. This activates the Link Wizard and displays the first wizard dialog box. Complete the steps of the Link Wizard, specifying the same basic information as the Import Wizard.

Quick Steps

Link Data to an Excel Worksheet

1. Click EXTERNAL DATA tab.
2. Click Excel button in Import & Link group.
3. Click Browse button.
4. Double-click desired file name.
5. Click *Link to a data source by creating a linked table.*
6. Make desired choices at each wizard dialog box.

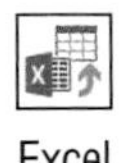

Excel

Project 2b Linking an Excel Worksheet to an Access Table **Part 2 of 2**

1. With **AL1-C8-CopperState.accdb** open, click the EXTERNAL DATA tab and then click the Excel button in the Import & Link group.
2. At the Get External Data - Excel Spreadsheet dialog box, click the Browse button, make sure the AL1C8 folder on your storage medium is active, and then double-click ***AL1-C8-Policies.xlsx***.
3. At the Get External Data - Excel Spreadsheet dialog box, click the *Link to the data source by creating a linked table* option and then click OK.

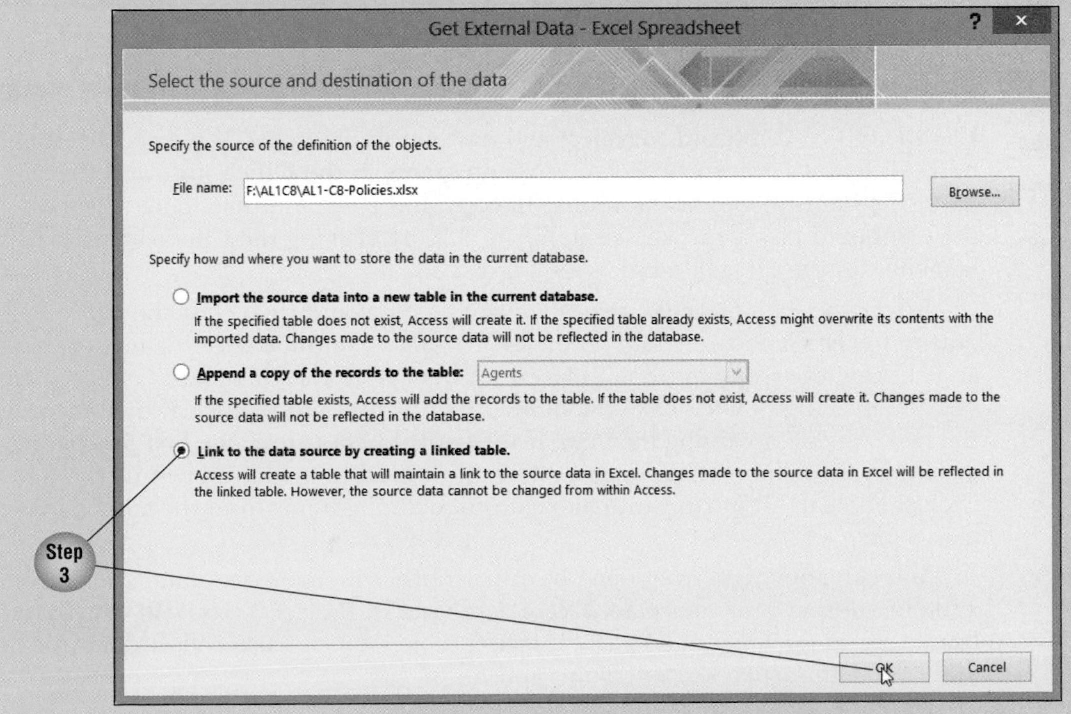

4. At the first Link Spreadsheet Wizard dialog box, make sure the *First Row Contains Column Headings* option contains a check mark and then click the Next button.
5. At the second Link Spreadsheet Wizard dialog box, type **LinkedPolicies** in the *Linked Table Name* text box and then click the Finish button.
6. At the message stating the linking is finished, click OK.
7. Open the new LinkedPolicies table in Datasheet view.
8. Close the LinkedPolicies table.
9. Open Excel, open the **AL1-C8-Policies.xlsx** workbook, and then make the following changes:
   a. Change the amount *$745* in cell C3 to *$850*.
   b. Add the following information in the specified cells:
      A26: **190-C-28**
      B26: **3120**
      C26: **685**

22	170-C-20	7335	$ 875
23	173-D-77	7521	$ 556
24	180-E-05	8223	$ 721
25	188-D-63	8854	$ 1,384
26	190-C-28	3120	$ 685
27			

Step 9b

10. Save, print, and then close **AL1-C8-Policies.xlsx**.
11. Close Excel.
12. With Access the active program and **AL1-C8-CopperState.accdb** open, open the LinkedPolicies table. Notice the changes you made in Excel are reflected in the table.
13. Close the LinkedPolicies table.
14. Close **AL1-C8-CopperState.accdb**.

Project 3 Collect Data in Word and Paste It into an Access Table — 1 Part

You will open a Word document containing Hilltop customer names and addresses and then copy the data and paste it into an Access table.

Using the Office Clipboard

Quick Steps
Display the Clipboard Task Pane
Click Clipboard task pane launcher.

Use the Office Clipboard to collect and paste multiple items. You can collect up to 24 different items in Access or other programs in the Office suite and then paste the items in various locations. To copy and paste multiple items, display the Clipboard task pane, shown in Figure 8.2, by clicking the Clipboard task pane launcher on the HOME tab.

Select the data or object that you want to copy and then click the Copy button in the Clipboard group on the HOME tab. Continue selecting text or items and clicking the Copy button. To insert an item from the Clipboard task pane to a field in an Access table, make the desired field active and then click the button in the task pane representing the item. If the copied item is text, the first 50 characters display in the Clipboard task pane. After all desired items have been inserted, click the Clear All button to remove any remaining items from the Clipboard task pane.

You can copy data from one object to another in an Access database or from a file in another program to an Access database. In Project 3, you will copy data from a Word document and paste it into a table. You can also collect data from other programs, such as PowerPoint and Excel.

Figure 8.2 Office Clipboard Task Pane

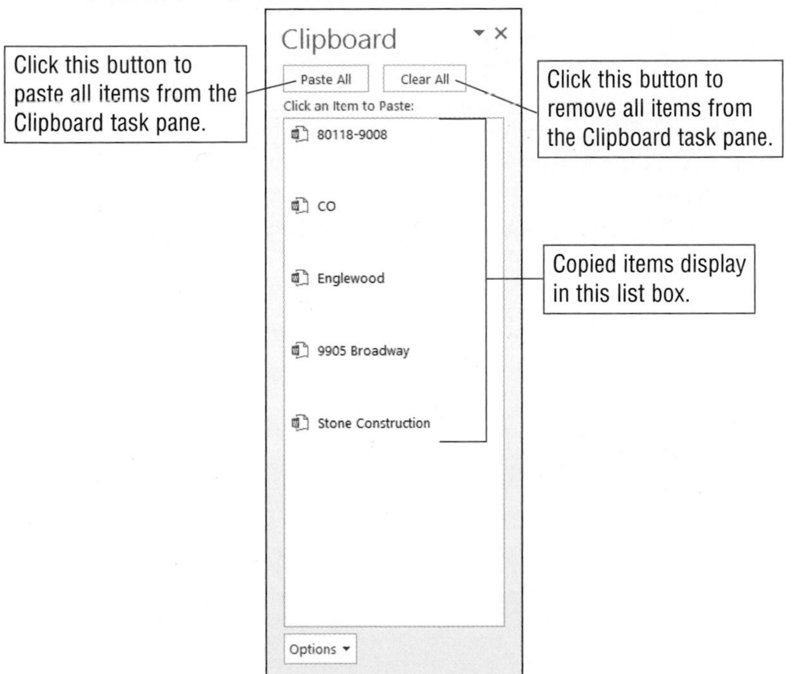

Project 3 Collecting Data in Word and Pasting It into an Access Table

Part 1 of 1

1. Open **AL1-C8-Hilltop.accdb**.
2. Open the Customers table.
3. Copy data from Word and paste it into the Customers table by completing the following steps:
   a. Open Word, make AL1C8 the active folder, and then open **HilltopCustomers.docx**.
   b. Make sure the HOME tab is active.
   c. Click the Clipboard task pane launcher to display the Clipboard task pane.
   d. Select the first company name, *Stone Construction*, and then click the Copy button in the Clipboard group.

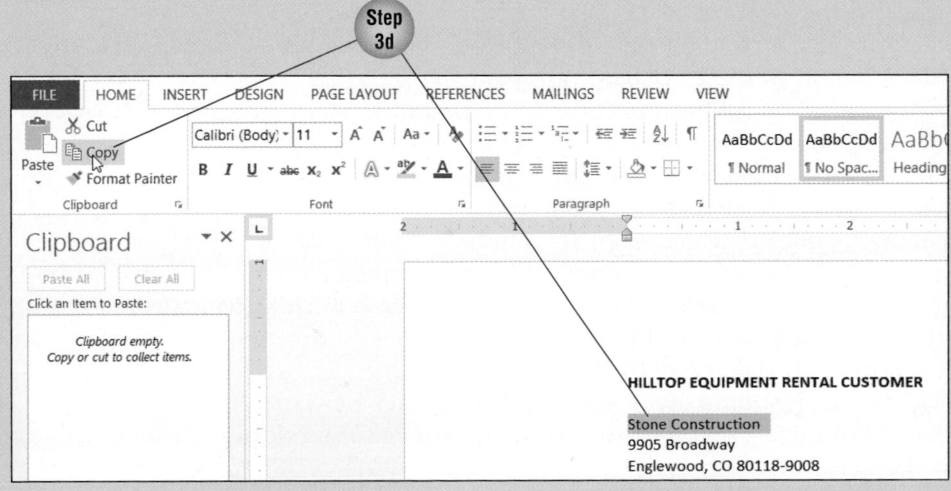

e. Select the street address, *9905 Broadway*, and then click the Copy button.
f. Select the city, *Englewood*, and then click the Copy button.
g. Select the state, *CO* (selecting only the two letters and not the space after the letters), and then click the Copy button.
h. Select the zip code, *80118-9008*, and then click the Copy button.
i. Click the button on the Taskbar representing Access. (Make sure the Customer table is open and displays in Datasheet view.)
j. Click in the first empty cell in the *CustomerID* field and then type 178.
k. Display the Clipboard task pane by clicking the HOME tab and then clicking the Clipboard task pane launcher.
l. Close the Navigation pane by clicking the Shutter Bar Open/Close Button.
m. Click in the first empty cell in the *Customer* field and then click *Stone Construction* in the Clipboard task pane.

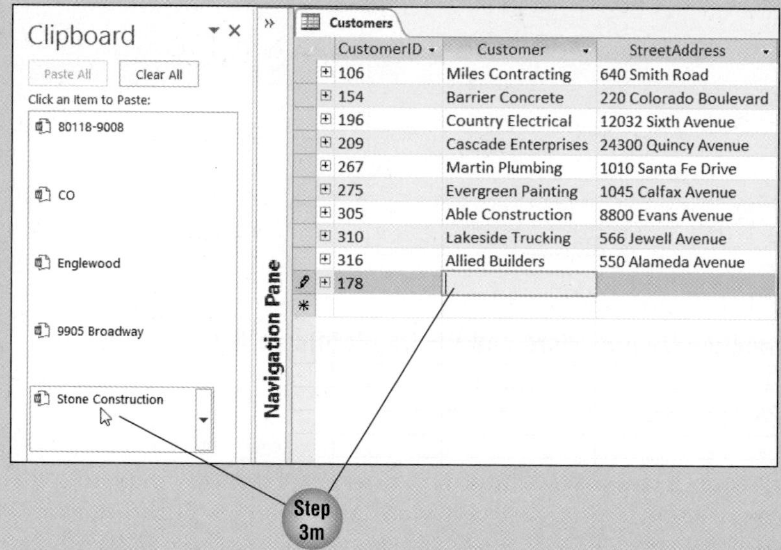

n. Click in the *StreetAddress* field and then click *9905 Broadway* in the Clipboard task pane.
o. Click in the *City* field and then click *Englewood* in the Clipboard task pane.
p. Click in the *State* field and then click *CO* in the Clipboard task pane.
q. Click in the *ZipCode* field, make sure the insertion point is positioned at the left side of the field, and then click *80118-9008* in the Clipboard task pane.
r. Click the Clear All button in the Clipboard task pane. (This removes all entries from the Clipboard.)

Step 3r

Clipboard
Paste All Clear All
Click an Item to Paste:
80118-9008

4. Complete steps similar to those in 3d through 3q to copy the information for Laughlin Products and paste it into the Customers table. (The customer ID number is 225.)
5. Click the Clear All button in the Clipboard task pane.
6. Close the Clipboard task pane by clicking the Close button (which contains an *X*) located in the upper right corner of the task pane.
7. Save, print, and then close the Customers table.
8. Open the Navigation pane by clicking the Shutter Bar Open/Close Button.
9. Make Word the active program, close **HilltopCustomers.docx** without saving changes, and then close Word.
10. Close **AL1-C8-Hilltop.accdb**.

Chapter Summary

- Use the Excel button in the Export group on the EXTERNAL DATA tab to export data in a table, query, or form to an Excel worksheet.
- Export data in a table, query, form, or report to a Word document by clicking the More button and then clicking *Word* at the drop-down list. Access exports the data to an RTF (rich-text format) file.
- Export an Access object to a PDF or XPS file with the PDF or XPS button in the Export group on the EXTERNAL DATA tab.
- You can merge Access data with a Word document. The Access data is the data source and the Word document is the main document. To merge data, click the desired table or query, click the EXTERNAL DATA tab, and then click the Word Merge button in the Export group.
- Use the Excel button in the Import group on the EXTERNAL DATA tab to import Excel data to an Access table.
- You can link imported data. Changes made to the data in the source program file are reflected in the destination source file.
- If you want to link imported data, click the *Link to the data source by creating a linked table* option at the Get External Data dialog box.
- Use the Clipboard task pane to collect up to 24 different items in Access or other programs and paste them in various locations.
- Display the Clipboard task pane by clicking the Clipboard task pane launcher on the HOME tab.

Commands Review

FEATURE	RIBBON TAB, GROUP	BUTTON
Clipboard task pane	HOME, Clipboard	
export object to Excel	EXTERNAL DATA, Export	
export object to PDF or XPS	EXTERNAL DATA, Export	
export object to Word	EXTERNAL DATA, Export	, *Word*
import Excel data	EXTERNAL DATA, Import & Link	
merge Access data with Word	EXTERNAL DATA, Export	

Concepts Check Test Your Knowledge

Completion: In the space provided at the right, indicate the correct term, symbol, or command.

1. Click this tab to display the Export group. ____________
2. Click this button in the Export group to display the Export - Excel Spreadsheet wizard dialog box. ____________
3. At the first Export - Excel Spreadsheet wizard dialog box, click this option if you want Excel to open with the exported data. ____________
4. To export Access data to Word, click this button in the Export group on the EXTERNAL DATA tab and then click *Word* at the drop-down list. ____________
5. When you export Access data to Word, the document is saved in this file format. ____________
6. When merging data, the data in the Access table is considered this. ____________
7. To merge data, click this button in the Export group on the EXTERNAL DATA tab. ____________
8. Import an Excel worksheet into an Access database with the Excel button in this group on the EXTERNAL DATA tab. ____________
9. If you want imported data connected to the original program, do this to the data. ____________
10. Use this task pane to collect and paste multiple items. ____________

Skills Check Assess Your Performance

Assessment 1

EXPORT A FORM TO EXCEL AND A REPORT TO WORD

1. Open **AL1-C8-WarrenLegal.accdb** from the AL1C8 folder on your storage medium and enable the contents.
2. Create a form named *Billing* using the Form Wizard with the following fields:

   From the Billing table: *BillingID*
   ClientID
   BillingDate
   Hours

   From the Rates table: *Rate*

3. When the form displays, close it.
4. Export the Billing form to an Excel worksheet.
5. Make the following changes to the Excel Billing worksheet:
   a. Select columns A through E and then adjust the column widths.
   b. Select cells A2 through B42 and then click the Center button in the Alignment group on the HOME tab.
   c. Save the Billing worksheet.
   d. Print and then close the Billing worksheet.
   e. Close Excel.
6. In Access, close the Export Wizard.
7. Create a report named *ClientBilling* using the Report Wizard (at the fifth wizard dialog box, change the layout to *Block*) with the following fields:

   From the Clients table: *FirstName*
   LastName

   From the Billing table: *BillingDate*
   Hours

   From the Rates table: *Rate*

8. Close the report.
9. Create a Word document with the ClientBilling report and save it to the AL1C8 folder on your storage medium with the default name. In the Word document, make the following changes:
   a. Press Ctrl + A to select the entire document, change the font color to Black, and then deselect the text.
   b. Insert a space between *Client* and *Billing* in the title.
   c. Position the insertion point immediately right of the word *Billing*, press the spacebar, and then type **of Legal Services**.
10. Save and then print **ClientBilling.rtf**.
11. Close the document and then close Word.
12. In Access, close the wizard dialog box.

Assessment

2 MERGE TABLE AND QUERY DATA WITH A WORD DOCUMENT

1. With **AL1-C8-WarrenLegal.accdb** open, merge data in the Clients table to a new Word document using the Word Merge button.
2. Maximize the Word document, close the Mail Merge task pane, and then compose a letter with the following elements:
   a. Click the HOME tab and then click the *No Spacing* style option in the Styles group.
   b. Press Enter six times, type the current date, and then press Enter four times.
   c. Click the MAILINGS tab and then insert the *«AddressBlock»* composite field.
   d. Press Enter twice and then type the salutation **Ladies and Gentlemen:**.
   e. Press Enter twice and then type the following text (press Enter twice after typing the first paragraph of text):

      The last time you visited our offices, you may have noticed how crowded we were. To alleviate the overcrowding, we are leasing new offices in the Meridian Building and will be moving in at the beginning of next month.

      Stop by and see our new offices at our open house planned for the second Friday of next month. Drop by any time between 2:00 and 5:30 p.m. We look forward to seeing you.

   f. After typing the second paragraph, press Enter twice, type **Sincerely,**, and then press Enter four times. Type **Marjorie Shaw**, press the Enter key, and then type **Senior Partner**. Press Enter twice, type your initials, press Enter, and then type **AL1-C8-WLLtrs.docx**.
3. Merge to a new document and then save the document with the name **AL1-C8-WLLtrs**.
4. Print only the first two letters in the document and then close **AL1-C8-WLLtrs.docx**.
5. Save the main document and name it **AL1-C8-WLLtrMD1**. Close the document and then close Word.
6. With **AL1-C8-WarrenLegal.accdb** open, extract the records from the Clients table of those clients located in Kent and then name the query *ClientsKentQuery*. (Include all of the fields from the table in the query.)
7. Merge the ClientsKentQuery to a new Word document using the Word Merge button.
8. Maximize the Word document, close the Mail Merge task pane, and then compose a letter with the following elements:
   a. Click the HOME tab and then click the *No Spacing* style option in the Styles group.
   b. Press Enter six times, type the current date, and then press Enter four times.
   c. Click the MAILINGS tab and then insert the *«AddressBlock»* composite field.
   d. Insert a proper salutation (refer to step 2d).

e. Compose a letter to clients that includes the following information:

The City of Kent Municipal Court has moved from 1024 Meeker Street to a new building located at 3201 James Avenue. All court hearings after the end of this month will be held at the new address. If you need directions to the new building, please call our office.

f. Include an appropriate complimentary close for the letter (refer to Step 2f). Use the name *Thomas Zeiger* and the title *Attorney* in the complimentary close and add your reference initials and the document name (**AL1-C8-WLKentLtrs.docx**).

9. Merge the letter to a new document and then save the document with the name **AL1-C8-WLKentLtrs**.
10. Print only the first two letters in the document and then close **AL1-C8-WLKentLtrs.docx**.
11. Save the main document and name it **AL1-C8-WLLtrMD2**, close the document, and then close Word.

Assessment 3

LINK AN EXCEL WORKBOOK

1. With **AL1-C8-WarrenLegal.accdb** open, link **AL1-C8-Cases.xlsx** into a new table named *Cases*.
2. Open the Cases table in Datasheet view.
3. Print and then close the Cases table.
4. Open Excel, open the **AL1-C8-Cases.xlsx** workbook and then add the following data in the specified cells:

   A8: **57-D**
   B8: **130**
   C8: **1,100**

   A9: **42-A**
   B9: **144**
   C9: **3,250**

   A10: **29-C**
   B10: **125**
   C10: **900**

5. Apply the Accounting formatting with a dollar sign and no decimal places to cells C8, C9, and C10.
6. Save, print, and then close **AL1-C8-Cases.xlsx**.
7. Close Excel.
8. In Access, open the Cases table in Datasheet view. (Notice the changes you made in Excel are reflected in the table.)
9. Print and then close the Cases table.
10. Close **AL1-C8-WarrenLegal.accdb**.

Visual Benchmark Demonstrate Your Proficiency

CREATE A REPORT AND EXPORT THE REPORT TO WORD

1. Open **AL1-C8-Dearborn.accdb** and enable the contents.
2. Use the Report Wizard to create the report shown in Figure 8.3. (Use the Quotas table and Representatives table when creating the report and choose the *Block* layout at the fifth wizard dialog box.) Save the report and name it *RepQuotas* and then print the report.
3. Use the RepQuotas report and export it to Word (to your AL1C8 folder). Format the report in Word as shown in Figure 8.4. Print the Word document and then close Word.
4. In Access, close **AL1-C8-Dearborn.accdb**.

Figure 8.3 Visual Benchmark Report

RepQuotas

RepQuotas

Quota	RepName	Telephone
$100,000.00	Robin Rehberg	(317) 555-9812
	Andre Kulisek	(317) 555-2264
	Edward Harris	(317) 555-3894
	Cecilia Ortega	(317) 555-4810
$150,000.00	David DeBruler	(317) 555-8779
	Jaren Newman	(317) 555-6790
	Lee Hutchinson	(765) 555-4277
	Craig Johnson	(317) 555-4391
$200,000.00	Isabelle Marshall	(765) 555-8822
	Maureen Pascual	(317) 555-5513
	Linda Foster	(317) 555-2101
	Catherine Singleton	(317) 555-0172
$250,000.00	Kwan Im	(317) 555-8374
	William Ludlow	(317) 555-0991
	Lydia Alvarado	(765) 555-4996
$300,000.00	Gina Tapparo	(317) 555-0044

Figure 8.4 Visual Benchmark Word Document

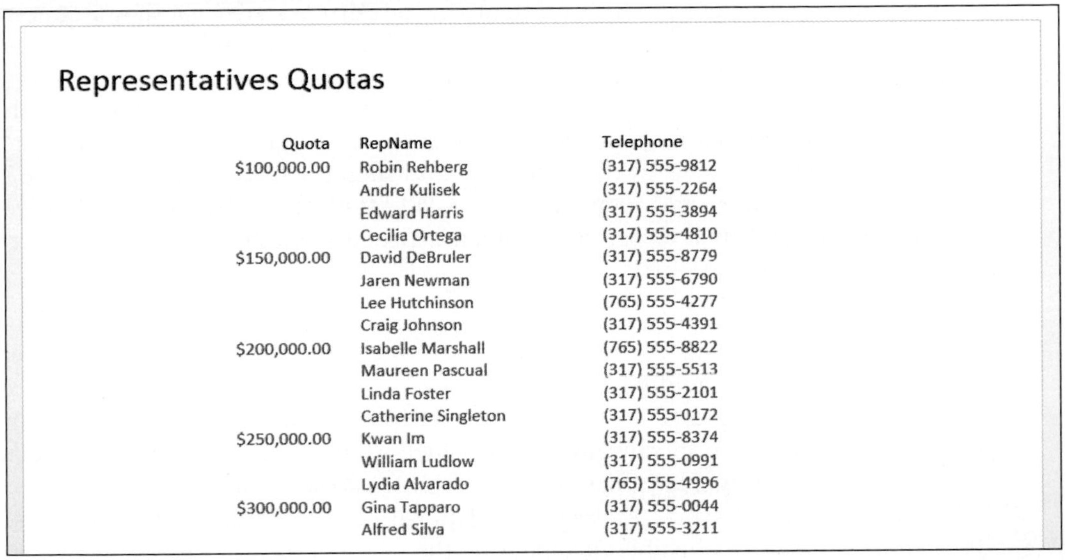

Representatives Quotas

Quota	RepName	Telephone
$100,000.00	Robin Rehberg	(317) 555-9812
	Andre Kulisek	(317) 555-2264
	Edward Harris	(317) 555-3894
	Cecilia Ortega	(317) 555-4810
$150,000.00	David DeBruler	(317) 555-8779
	Jaren Newman	(317) 555-6790
	Lee Hutchinson	(765) 555-4277
	Craig Johnson	(317) 555-4391
$200,000.00	Isabelle Marshall	(765) 555-8822
	Maureen Pascual	(317) 555-5513
	Linda Foster	(317) 555-2101
	Catherine Singleton	(317) 555-0172
$250,000.00	Kwan Im	(317) 555-8374
	William Ludlow	(317) 555-0991
	Lydia Alvarado	(765) 555-4996
$300,000.00	Gina Tapparo	(317) 555-0044
	Alfred Silva	(317) 555-3211

Case Study Apply Your Skills

Part 1

As the office manager at Woodland Dermatology Center, you are responsible for managing the center database. In preparation for an upcoming meeting, open **AL1-C8-Woodland.accdb** and prepare the following with data in the database:

- Create a query that displays the patient identification number, first name, and last name; doctor last name; date of visit; and fee. Name the query *PatientBilling*.
- Export the PatientBilling query to an Excel worksheet. Apply formatting to enhance the appearance of the worksheet and then print the worksheet.
- Create mailing labels for the patients. ***Hint: Use the Labels button on the CREATE tab.***
- Export the patient labels to a Word (.rtf) document and then print the document.
- Import and link the **AL1-C8-Payroll.xlsx** Excel worksheet to a new table named *WeeklyPayroll*. Print the WeeklyPayroll table.

You have been given some updated information about the weekly payroll and need to make the following changes to the **AL1-C8-Payroll.xlsx** worksheet:

- Change the hours for Irene Vaughn to *30*
- Change the wage for Monica Saunders to *$10.50*
- Change the hours for Dale Jorgensen to *20*.

After making and saving the changes, open, print, and then close the WeeklyPayroll table.

Part 2

The center is expanding and will be offering cosmetic dermatology services at the beginning of next month to residents in the Altoona area. Design a query that extracts records of patients living in the city of Altoona and then merge the query with Word. At the Word document, write a letter describing the new services, which include microdermabrasion, chemical peels, laser resurfacing, sclerotherapy, and photorejuvenation, as well as an offer for a free facial and consultation. Insert the appropriate fields in the document and then complete the merge. Save the merged document and name it **AL1-C8-WLDLtr**. Print the first two letters of the document and then close the document. Close the main document without saving it and then close Word.

Part 3

Help

The Woodland database contains critical information and you need to determine how often you should back up the database. (You learned how to back up a database in Chapter 7.) Use the Access Help files to learn more about the backup process and, more specifically, about guidelines for when to back up a database. Search the Access Help files using the phrase *backing up a database* and then read the hyperlinked article Protect your data with backup and restore processes. Since you are responsible for updating the clinic procedures manual, create a Word document that describes how often you think the Woodland database should be backed up and the rationale behind your backup plan. Include steps for creating a backup of the database. Save the completed document and name it **AL1-C8-CS-Manual**. Print and then close **AL1-C8-CS-Manual.docx**.

UNIT 2

MICROSOFT® ACCESS® Performance Assessment

Note: Before beginning unit assessments, copy to your storage medium the AL1U2 subfolder from the AL1 folder on the CD that accompanies this textbook and then make AL1U2 the active folder.

Assessing Proficiency

In this unit, you have learned to create forms, reports, and mailing labels and filter data. You have also learned how to modify document properties, view object dependencies, and export, import, and link data between programs.

Assessment 1 Create Tables in a Clinic Database

1. Use Access to create a database for clients of a mental health clinic. Name the database **AL1-U2-LancasterClinic**. Create a table named *Clients* that includes the following fields. (You determine the field name, data type, field size, and description.)

   ClientNumber (primary key)
   ClientName
   StreetAddress
   City
   State
   ZipCode
   Telephone
   DateOfBirth
   DiagnosisID

2. After creating the table, switch to Datasheet view and then enter the following data in the appropriate fields:

   ClientNumber: **1831**
   George Charoni
   3980 Broad Street
   Philadelphia, PA 19149
   (215) 555-3482
   DateOfBirth: **4/12/1961**
   DiagnosisID: **SC**

   ClientNumber: **3219**
   Marian Wilke
   12032 South 39th
   Jenkintown, PA 19209
   (215) 555-9083
   DateOfBirth: **10/23/1984**
   DiagnosisID: **OCD**

ClientNumber: 2874
Arthur Shroeder
3618 Fourth Avenue
Philadelphia, PA 19176
(215) 555-8311
DateOfBirth: **3/23/1961**
DiagnosisID: **OCD**

ClientNumber: 5831
Roshawn Collins
12110 52nd Court East
Cheltenham, PA 19210
(215) 555-4779
DateOfBirth: **11/3/1968**
DiagnosisID: **SC**

ClientNumber: 4419
Lorena Hearron
3112 96th Street East
Philadelphia, PA 19132
(215) 555-3281
DateOfBirth: **7/2/1987**
DiagnosisID: **AD**

ClientNumber: 1103
Raymond Mandato
631 Garden Boulevard
Jenkintown, PA 19209
(215) 555-0957
DateOfBirth: **9/20/1982**
DiagnosisID: **MDD**

3. Automatically adjust the column widths.
4. Save, print, and then close the Clients table.
5. Create a table named *Diagnoses* that includes the following fields:

   DiagnosisID (primary key)
   Diagnosis

6. After creating the table, switch to Datasheet view and then enter the following data in the appropriate fields:

   DiagnosisID: **AD**
   Diagnosis: **Adjustment Disorder**

   DiagnosisID: **MDD**
   Diagnosis: **Manic-Depressive Disorder**

   DiagnosisID: **OCD**
   Diagnosis: **Obsessive-Compulsive Disorder**

   DiagnosisID: **SC**
   Diagnosis: **Schizophrenia**

7. Automatically adjust the column widths.
8. Save, print, and then close the Diagnoses table.
9. Create a table named *Fees* that includes the following fields. (You determine the field name, data type, field size, and description.)

   FeeCode (primary key)
   HourlyFee

10. After creating the table, switch to Datasheet view and then enter the following data in the appropriate fields:

FeeCode: A
HourlyFee: $75.00

FeeCode: B
HourlyFee: $80.00

FeeCode: C
HourlyFee: $85.00

FeeCode: D
HourlyFee: $90.00

FeeCode: E
HourlyFee: $95.00

FeeCode: F
HourlyFee: $100.00

FeeCode: G
HourlyFee: $105.00

FeeCode: H
HourlyFee: $110.00

11. Automatically adjust the column widths.
12. Save, print, and then close the Fees table.
13. Create a table named *Employees* that includes the following fields. (You determine the field name, data type, field size, and description.)

ProviderNumber (primary key)
ProviderName
Title
Extension

14. After creating the table, switch to Datasheet view and then enter the following data in the appropriate fields:

ProviderNumber: 29
ProviderName: James Schouten
Title: Psychologist
Extension: 399

ProviderNumber: 33
ProviderName: Janice Grisham
Title: Psychiatrist
Extension: 11

ProviderNumber: 15
ProviderName: Lynn Yee
Title: Child Psychologist
Extension: 102

ProviderNumber: 18
ProviderName: Craig Chilton
Title: Psychologist
Extension: 20

15. Automatically adjust the column widths.
16. Save, print, and then close the Employees table.
17. Create a table named *Billing* that includes the following fields. (You determine the field name, data type, field size, and description.)

BillingNumber (primary key; apply the AutoNumber data type)
ClientNumber
DateOfService (apply the Date/Time data type)
Insurer
ProviderNumber
Hours (Apply the Number data type, the *Field Size* option in the *Field Properties* section to *Double*, and the *Decimal Places* option in the *Field Properties* section in Design view to *1*. Two of the records will contain a number requiring this format.)
FeeCode

18. After creating the table, switch to Datasheet view and then enter the following data in the appropriate fields:

ClientNumber: 4419 *DateOfService:* 3/2/2015 *Insurer:* Health Plus *ProviderNumber:* 15 *Hours:* 2 *FeeCode:* B	*ClientNumber:* 1831 *DateOfService:* 3/2/2015 *Insurer:* Self *ProviderNumber:* 33 *Hours:* 1 FeeCode: H
ClientNumber: 3219 *DateOfService:* 3/3/2015 *Insurer:* Health Plus *ProviderNumber:* 15 *Hours:* 1 *FeeCode:* D	*ClientNumber:* 5831 *DateOfService:* 3/3/2015 *Insurer:* Penn-State Health *ProviderNumber:* 18 *Hours:* 2 FeeCode: C
ClientNumber: 4419 *DateOfService:* 3/4/2015 *Insurer:* Health Plus *ProviderNumber:* 15 *Hours:* 1 *FeeCode:* A	*ClientNumber:* 1103 *DateOfService:* 3/4/2015 *Insurer:* Penn-State Health *ProviderNumber:* 18 *Hours:* 0.5 FeeCode: A
ClientNumber: 1831 *DateOfService:* 3/5/2015 *Insurer:* Self *ProviderNumber:* 33 *Hours:* 1 *FeeCode:* H	*ClientNumber:* 5831 *DateOfService:* 3/5/2015 *Insurer:* Penn-State Health *ProviderNumber:* 18 *Hours:* 0.5 *FeeCode:* C

19. Automatically adjust the column widths.
20. Save, print in landscape orientation, and then close the Billing table.

Assessment 2 Relate Tables and Create Forms in a Clinic Database

1. With **AL1-U2-LancasterClinic.accdb** open, create the following one-to-many relationships and enforce referential integrity and cascade fields and records:
   a. *ClientNumber* in the Clients table is the "one" and *ClientNumber* in the Billing table is the "many."
   b. *DiagnosisID* in the Diagnoses table is the "one" and *DiagnosisID* in the Clients table is the "many."
   c. *ProviderNumber* in the Employees table is the "one" and *ProviderNumber* in the Billing table is the "many."
   d. *FeeCode* in the Fees table is the "one" and *FeeCode* in the Billing table is the "many."
2. Create a form with the data in the Clients table.

3. After creating the form, add the following record to the Clients form:

   ClientNumber: **1179**
   Timothy Fierro
   1133 Tenth Southwest
   Philadelphia, PA 19178
   (215) 555-5594
   DateOfBirth: **12/7/1990**
   DiagnosisID: **AD**

4. Save the form with the default name, print the form in landscape orientation, and then close the form.
5. Add the following records to the Billing table:

ClientNumber: **1179**	*ClientNumber:* **1831**
DateOfService: **3/6/2015**	*DateOfService:* **3/6/2015**
Insurer: **Health Plus**	*Insurer:* **Self**
ProviderNumber: **15**	*ProviderNumber:* **33**
Hours: **0.5**	*Hours:* **1**
FeeCode: **C**	FeeCode: **H**

6. Save and then print the Billing table in landscape orientation.
7. Close the Billing table.

Assessment 3 Create Forms Using the Form Wizard

1. With **AL1-U2-LancasterClinic.accdb** open, create a form with fields from related tables using the Form Wizard with the following specifications:
   a. At the first Form Wizard dialog box, insert the following fields in the *Selected Fields* list box:

      From the Clients table: *ClientNumber*
      DateOfBirth
      DiagnosisID

      From the Billing table: *Insurer*
      ProviderNumber

   b. Do not make any changes at the second Form Wizard dialog box.
   c. Do not make any changes at the third Form Wizard dialog box.
   d. At the fourth Form Wizard dialog box, type the name **ProviderInformation** in the *Form* text box.
2. When the first record displays, print the first record.
3. Close the form.

Assessment 4 Create Labels with the Label Wizard

1. With **AL1-U2-LancasterClinic.accdb** open, use the Label Wizard to create mailing labels with the client names and addresses and sort by zip code. Name the mailing label report **ClientMailingLabels**.
2. Print the mailing labels.
3. Close the mailing labels report.

Assessment 5 Filter Records in Tables

1. With **AL1-U2-LancasterClinic.accdb** open, open the Billing table and then filter the records to display the following records:
   a. Display only those records with the Health Plus insurer. Print the results in landscape orientation and then remove the filter.
   b. Display only those records with a client ID number of 4419. Print the results and then remove the filter.
2. Filter records by selection to display the following records:
   a. Display only those records with a fee code of C. Print the results and then remove the filter.
   b. Display only those records between the dates of 3/2/2015 and 3/4/2015. Print the results and then remove the filter.
3. Close the Billing table without saving the changes.
4. Open the Clients table and then use the *Filter By Form* option to display clients in Jenkintown or Cheltenham. Print the results and then remove the filter.
5. Close the Clients table without saving the changes.

Assessment 6 Export a Table to Excel

1. With **AL1-U2-LancasterClinic.accdb** open, export the Billing table to an Excel workbook to your AL1U2 folder.
2. Apply formatting to the cells in the Excel workbook to enhance the appearance of the data.
3. Change the page orientation to landscape.
4. Save, print, and then close the workbook.
5. Close Excel.

Assessment 7 Merge Records to Create Letters in Word

1. With **AL1-U2-LancasterClinic.accdb** open, merge data in the Clients table to a blank Word document. ***Hint: Use the Word Merge button in the Export group on the EXTERNAL DATA tab.*** You determine the fields to use in the inside address (you cannot use the *AddressBlock* field) and an appropriate salutation. Type **March 12, 2015**, as the date of the letter and type the following text in the body of the document:

   The building of a new wing for the Lancaster Clinic will begin April 1, 2015. We are excited about this new addition to our clinic. With the new facilities, we will be able to offer additional community and group services along with enhanced child-play therapy treatment.

   During the construction, the main entrance will be moved to the north end of the building. Please use this entrance until the construction of the wing is completed. We apologize in advance for any inconvenience this causes you.

   Include an appropriate complimentary close for the letter. Use the name and title *Marianne Lambert, Clinic Director* for the signature and add your reference initials and the document name (**AL1-U2-A7-LCLtrs.docx**).
2. Merge to a new document and then save the document with the name **AL1-U2-A7-LCLtrs**.

3. Print the first two letters of the document and then close **AL1-U2-A7-LCLtrs.docx**.
4. Save the main document as **AL1-U2-A7-ConstLtrMD** and then close the document.
5. Close Word.

Assessment 8 Import and Link Excel Data to an Access Table

1. With **AL1-U2-LancasterClinic.accdb** open, import and link **AL1-U2-StaffHours.xlsx** to a new table named *StaffHours*.
2. Open the StaffHours table in Datasheet view.
3. Print and then close the StaffHours table.
4. Open **AL1-U2-StaffHours.xlsx** in Excel.
5. Insert a formula in cell D2 that multiplies B2 with C2 and then copy the formula down to cells D3 through D7.
6. Save and then close **AL1-U2-StaffHours.xlsx**.
7. Close Excel.
8. In Access with **AL1-U2-LancasterClinic.accdb** open, open the StaffHours table.
9. Print and then close the StaffHours table.

Writing Activities

The following activities give you the opportunity to practice your writing skills while you demonstrate your understanding of some of the important Access features you have mastered in this unit. Use correct grammar, appropriate word choices, and clear sentence constructions.

Activity 1 Add a Table to the Clinic Database

The director at Lancaster Clinic has asked you to add information to **AL1-U2-LancasterClinic.accdb** on insurance companies contracted by the clinic. You need to create a table that will contain information on insurance companies. The director wants the table to include the insurance company name, address, city, state, and zip code, along with the telephone number and name of the representative. You determine the field names, data types, field sizes, and description for the table and then include the following information (in the appropriate fields):

Health Plus
4102 22nd Street
Philadelphia, PA 19166
(212) 555-0990
Representative: Byron Tolleson

Penn-State Health
5933 Lehigh Avenue
Philadelphia, PA 19148
(212) 555-3477
Representative: Tracey Pavone

Quality Medical
51 Cecil B. Moore Avenue
Philadelphia, PA 19168
(212) 555-4600
Representative: Lee Stafford

Delaware Health
4418 Front Street
Philadelphia, PA 19132
(212) 555-6770
Representative: Melanie Chon

Save the insurance company table, print it in landscape orientation, and then close the table. Open Word and then write a report to the clinic director detailing how you created the table. Include a title for the report, steps on how you created the table, and any other pertinent information. Save the completed report and name it **AL1-U2-Act1-LCRpt**. Print and then close **AL1-U2-Act1-LCRpt.docx**.

Activity 2 Merge Records to Create Letters to Insurance Companies

Merge data in the insurance company database to a blank Word document. You determine the fields to use in the inside address (you cannot use the Address Block button) and an appropriate salutation. Compose a letter to the insurance companies informing them that Lancaster Clinic is providing mental health counseling services to people who have health insurance through their employers. You are sending an informational brochure about Lancaster Clinic and are requesting information from the insurance companies on services and service limitations. Include an appropriate complimentary close for the letter. Use the name and title *Marianne Lambert, Clinic Director* for the signature and add your reference initials. When the merge is completed, name the document containing the merged letters **AL1-U2-Act2-LCIns**. Print the first two letters in the merged document and then close **AL1-U2-Act2-LCIns.docx**. Close the main document without saving it and then close Word. Close **AL1-U2-LancasterClinic.accdb**.

Internet Research

Health Information Search

In this activity, you will search the Internet for information on a health concern or disease that interests you. You will be looking for specific organizations, interest groups, or individuals who are somehow connected to the topic you have chosen. You may find information about an organization that raises money to support research, a support group that posts information or answers questions, or clinics or doctors that specialize in your topic. Try to find at least 10 different organizations, groups, or individuals that support the health concern you are researching.

Create a database in Access and then create a table that includes information from your research. Design the table so that you can store the name, address, phone number, and web address of each organization, group, or individual you find. Also identify the connection the organization, group, or individual has to your topic (supports research, interest group, treats patients, etc.). Create a report to summarize your findings. In Microsoft Word, create a letter that you can use to write for further information about the organization. Use the names and addresses in your database to merge with the letter. Select and then print the first two letters that result from the merge. Finally, write a paragraph describing information you learned about the health concern that you previously did not know.

Job Study

City Improvement Projects

In this activity, you will work with the city council in your area to keep the public informed of the progress being made on improvement projects throughout the city. These projects are paid for through tax dollars voted on by the public, and the city council feels that keeping area residents informed will lead to good voter turnout when it is time to make more improvements.

Your job is to create a database and table in the database that will store the following information for each project: a project ID number, a description of the project, the budgeted dollar amount to be spent, the amount of money spent so far, the amount of time allocated to the project, and the amount of time spent so far. Enter five city improvement projects into the table (using sample data created by you). Create a query based on the table that calculates the percentage of budgeted dollars spent so far and the percentage of budgeted time spent so far. Print the table and the query.

Index

E

F

G

H

I

Q

R

S

T

U

V

W

X

Y

Z

MICROSOFT®

ACCESS®

Level 2

Unit 1 ■ Advanced Tables, Relationships, Queries, and Forms

MICROSOFT®

ACCESS®

Designing the Structure of Tables

PERFORMANCE OBJECTIVES

Upon successful completion of Chapter 1, you will be able to:

- **Design the structure of a table to optimize efficiency and accuracy of data**
- **Select the appropriate field data type based on analysis of the source data**
- **Disallow blank field values**
- **Allow or disallow zero-length strings in a field**
- **Create a custom format for Short Text, numeric, and Date/Time data type fields**
- **Create a custom input mask**
- **Define rich text formatting for a Long Text data type field**
- **Store the history of changes to a Long Text data type field**
- **Define and use an Attachment data type field with multiple attachments**

Tutorials

1.1 Diagramming a Database
1.2 Creating Tables in Design View
1.3 Restricting Data Entry and Data
1.4 Creating a Custom Format for Text, Numeric, and Date/Time Fields
1.5 Restricting Data Entry Using Input Masks
1.6 Working with Long Text Fields
1.7 Creating an Attachment Data Type Field
1.8 Attaching Files to Records

Designing tables in Access is the most important task when creating a database, because tables are the objects upon which all other objects are based. All queries, forms, and reports rely on tables as the source of their data. Designing a new database involves planning the number of tables needed, the fields to be included in each table, and the methods to be used to check and/or validate new data as it is entered. In this chapter, you will learn the basic steps involved in planning a new database by analyzing existing data. In addition to organizing the data structure, you will also learn to select appropriate data types and use field properties to control, restrict, or otherwise validate data.

Note that readers are assumed to have prior knowledge of the steps in creating a new table, including changing the data type and field size and assigning the primary key, as well as the meanings of the terms *field*, *record*, *table*, and *database*. Model answers for this chapter's projects appear on the following page.

Note: Before beginning the projects, copy to your storage medium the AL2C1 subfolder from the AL2 folder on the CD that accompanies this textbook. Steps on how to copy a folder are presented on the inside of the back cover of this textbook. Do this every time you start a chapter's projects.

Model Answers

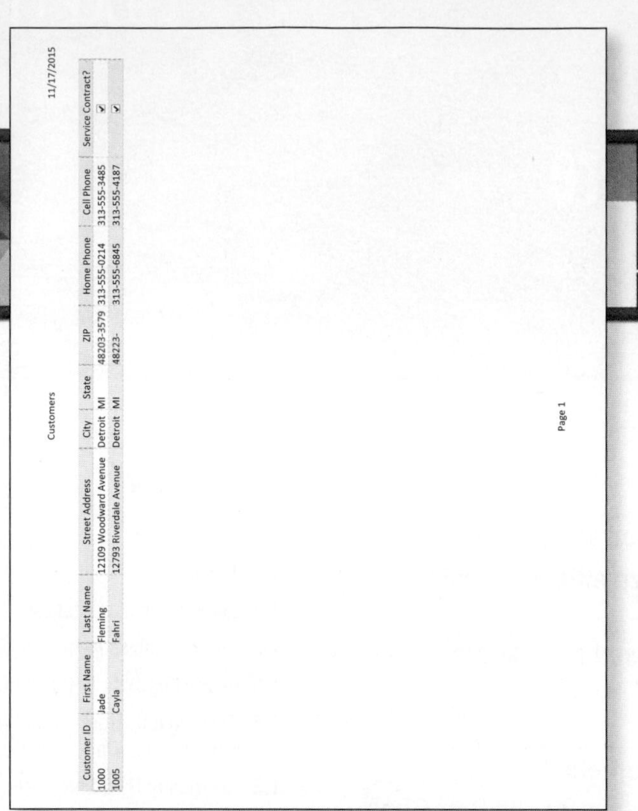

11/17/2015 Customers

Customer ID	First Name	Last Name	Street Address	City	State	ZIP	Home Phone	Cell Phone	Service Contract?
1000	Jade	Fleming	12109 Woodward Avenue	Detroit	MI	48203-3579	313-555-0214	313-555-3485	☑
1005	Cayla	Fahri	12793 Riverdale Avenue	Detroit	MI	48223-	313-555-6845	313-555-4187	☑

Page 1

Project 1 Create Tables by Analyzing Sample Data and Applying Database Design Techniques Project 1c, Customers Table

11/17/2015 WorkOrders

WO	CustID	TechID	WODate	Descr	ServDate	Hours	Rate	Parts	Comments
65012	1000	11	Mon Sep 07 2015	Bi-annual deskt	Mon Sep 07 2015	1.25	30.00	$10.15	"H" key is sticki
65013	1000	10	Mon Sep 07 2015	Replace keyboa	Thu Sep 10 2015	0.50	28.50	$22.75	Serial Number

Page 1

Project 1f, WorkOrders Table

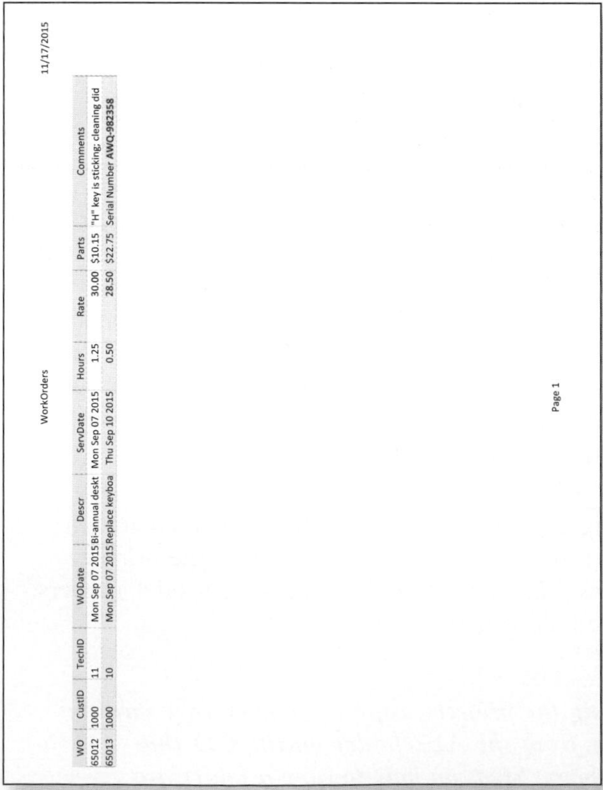

11/17/2015 WorkOrders

WO	CustID	TechID	WODate	Descr	ServDate	Hours	Rate	Parts	Comments
65012	1000	11	Mon Sep 07 2015	Bi-annual deskt	Mon Sep 07 2015	1.25	30.00	$10.15	"H" key is sticking; cleaning did
65013	1000	10	Mon Sep 07 2015	Replace keyboa	Thu Sep 10 2015	0.50	28.50	$22.75	Serial Number **AWQ-982358**

Page 1

Project 2 Work with Long Text and Attachment Data Type Fields
Project 2a, WorkOrders Table

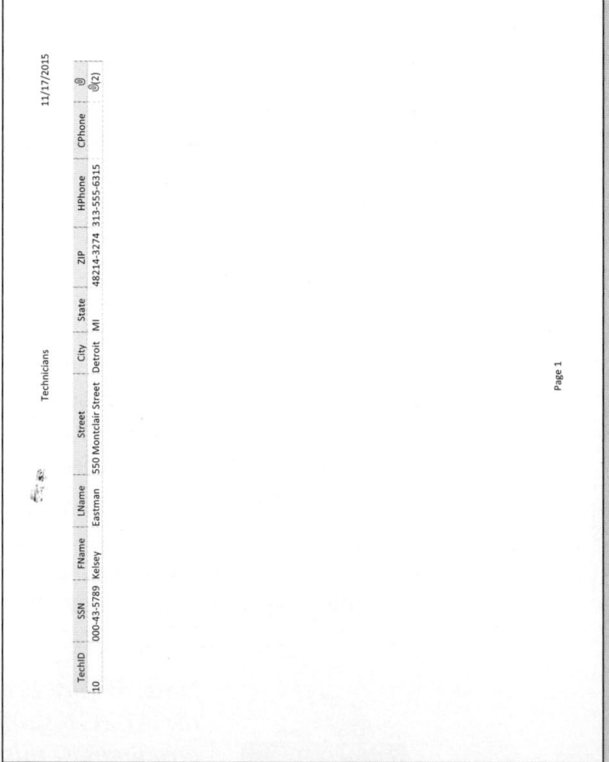

11/17/2015 Technicians

TechID	SSN	FName	LName	Street	City	State	ZIP	HPhone	CPhone	@
10	000-43-5789	Kelsey	Eastman	550 Montclair Street	Detroit	MI	48214-3274	313-555-6315		(2)

Page 1

Project 2b, Technicians Table

Project 1 Create Tables by Analyzing Sample Data and Applying Database Design Techniques — 6 Parts

You will use sample data to decide how to structure a new database to track computer service work orders using best practices for table design, and then you will create the tables.

Designing Tables and Fields for a New Database

Most of the databases you will encounter in the workplace will have been created by database designers. Even so, an introduction to the process involved in creating a new database will help you to better understand the reasons behind how objects are organized and related. Creating a new database from scratch involves careful advance planning.

Database designers spend considerable time analyzing existing data and asking questions of users and managers. Designers want to know how data will be used so that they can identify the forms, queries, and reports that will need to be generated. Often, designers begin by modeling a required report from the database to see the data used to populate the report. The designer then compiles a ***data dictionary*** (a list of fields and attributes of each field) from which he or she can map out the number of required tables.

In Project 1, you will analyze a sample work order for RSR Computer Services. RSR started out as a small computer service company, and the owners used Excel worksheets to enter information from service records and to produce revenue reports. The company's success has created a need for a relational database to track customer information. The owners want to be able to generate queries and reports to use in decision making. Examine the data in the sample work order shown in Figure 1.1. The work order form that the technicians have been filling out at the customer site will be used as the input source document for the database.

Figure 1.1 Sample Work Order for RSR Computer Services

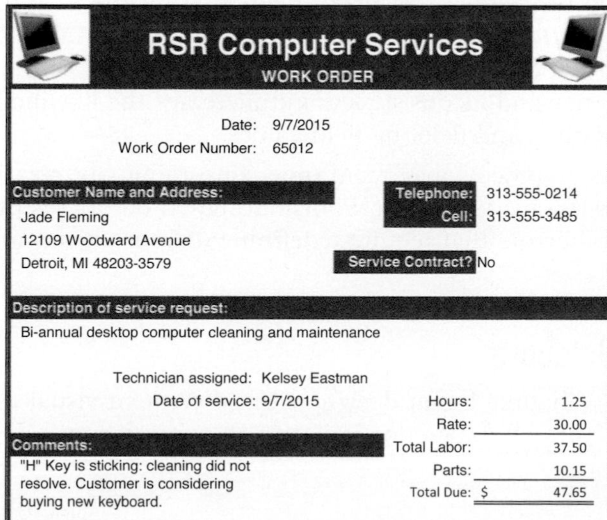

RSR Computer Services
WORK ORDER

Date: 9/7/2015
Work Order Number: 65012

Customer Name and Address:
Jade Fleming
12109 Woodward Avenue
Detroit, MI 48203-3579

Telephone: 313-555-0214
Cell: 313-555-3485
Service Contract? No

Description of service request:
Bi-annual desktop computer cleaning and maintenance

Technician assigned: Kelsey Eastman
Date of service: 9/7/2015

Hours: 1.25
Rate: 30.00
Total Labor: 37.50
Parts: 10.15
Total Due: $ 47.65

Comments:
"H" Key is sticking: cleaning did not resolve. Customer is considering buying new keyboard.

Designers analyze all input documents and output requirements to capture the entire set of data elements that needs to be created. Once all data has been identified, the designer maps out the number of tables required to hold the data. During the process of mapping the tables and fields to be associated with each table, the designer follows these guidelines and techniques:

- Consider each table an ***entity*** that describes a single person, place, object, event, or other subject. Each table should store facts that are related only to that subject.
- Segment data until it is in the smallest units you want to manipulate. For example, in the work order shown in Figure 1.1, the customer's name and address should be split into separate fields for first name, last name, street address, city, state, and zip code. Using this approach provides maximum flexibility for generating other objects and allows you to sort or filter by any individual data element.
- Do not include fields that can be calculated by using data from other fields. For example, the total labor and total due amounts in the work order can be calculated using other numeric data elements.
- Identify fields that can be used to answer questions from the data. Queries and reports can be designed to extract information based on the results of a conditional expression (sometimes referred to as ***Boolean logic***). For example, in the work order in Figure 1.1, the technician enters whether or not the customer has a service contract. A field that stores a Yes or No (true or false) condition for the service contract data element allows the business to generate reports of customers that have subscribed to a service contract (true condition) and those that have not subscribed (false condition).
- Identify a field in each table that will hold data that uniquely identifies each record. This field becomes the primary key. If the source documents used to design the database do not reveal a unique identifier, Access automatically provides an ID field with the AutoNumber data type in a new table that can be used as a primary key.
- Identify each table that will relate to another table and the field you will use to join the two when you create relationships. Identifying relationships at this stage helps you determine if you need to add a field to a related table to allow you to join the tables.
- Keep in mind that relational databases are built on the concept that data redundancy should be avoided, except for fields that will be used to join tables in a relationship. (***Data redundancy*** means that data in one table is repeated in another table.) Repeating fields in multiple tables wastes storage space, promotes inefficiency and inconsistency, and increases the likelihood of errors when adding, updating, and deleting field values.

The database design process may seem time consuming, but creating a well-designed database will save time later. Poorly designed databases often contain logical and structural errors that require redefining data or objects after live data has been entered.

Diagramming a Database

Recall from Level 1, Chapter 1 that designers often create a visual representation of a database's structure in a diagram similar to the one shown in Figure 1.2.

Figure 1.2 Diagram of Table Structure for RSR Computer Services Database

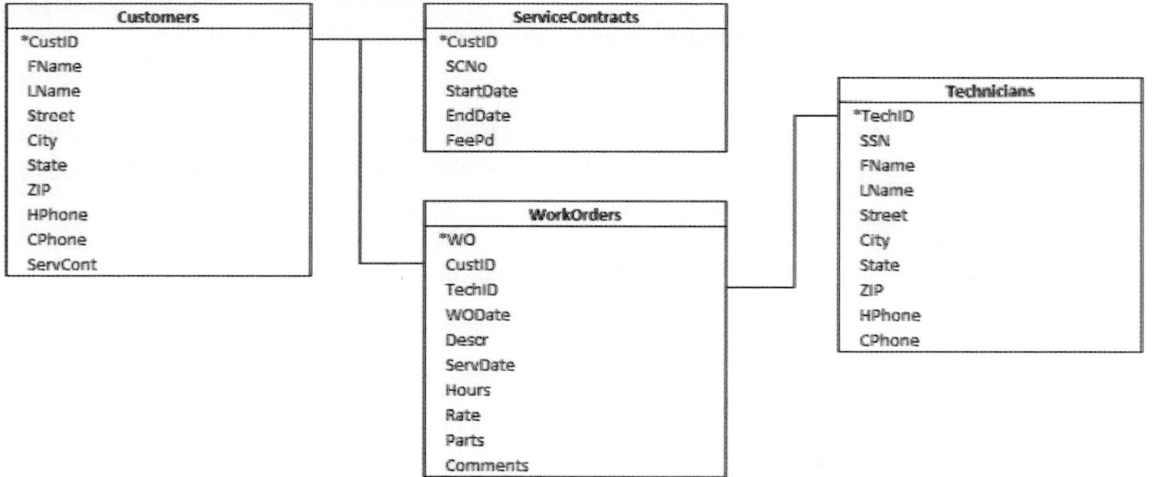

In the database diagram, each table is represented in a box with the table name at the top. Within each box, the fields that will be stored in the table are listed with the field names that will be used when the table is created. The primary key field is denoted with an asterisk. Tables that will be joined are connected with lines at their common fields. You will begin to build this database in the remainder of this chapter, and you will create the relationships in Chapter 2.

Notice that many of the field names in the diagram are abbreviated. Although a field name can contain up to 64 characters, field names that are short enough to be understood are easier to manage and to type into expressions. For abbreviated field names, the Caption property is used to display descriptive headings that contain spaces and/or longer words when viewing the data in a datasheet, form, or report.

Words such as *Name* and *Date* are reserved words in Access and cannot be used as field names. Access prompts you when you try to save a table containing field names that use reserved words.

Also notice that none of the field names contain spaces. Spaces are allowed in field names, but most database designers avoid using them. Instead, designers indicate spaces between words by changing the case, using an underscore character (_), or using a hyphen (-).

Assigning Data Types

The designer assigns each field a data type based on the types of entries he or she wants to allow into the field and the operations that will be used to manipulate the data. Selecting the appropriate data type is important because restrictions will be placed on a field based on its data type. For example, in a field designated with the Number data type, only numbers, a period to represent a decimal point, and a plus or minus sign can be entered into the field in a datasheet or form. Table 1.1 on the next page identifies the available data types.

Table 1.1 Data Types

Data Type	*Description*
Short Text	Alphanumeric data up to 255 characters, such as names and addresses. Short text fields can also store values that are used as identifiers and not for calculating, such as customer numbers, telephone numbers, and social security numbers.
Long Text	Alphanumeric data longer than 255 characters with up to 65,535 characters displayed in the field. Long Text data type fields are used to store longer passages of text in a record. Rich text formatting can be added in a Long Text data type field, such as bold, italics, or font color.
Number	Positive or negative values that can be used in calculations. Number data should not be used for monetary values (see Currency).
Date/Time	Accepts only valid dates and times into the field. Used to ensure dates and times are entered and sorted properly.
Currency	Holds monetary values. Access does not round off during calculations.
AutoNumber	Automatically assigned by Access by sequentially incrementing the field value by 1 when a new record is added.
Yes/No	Each entry in the field is restricted to conditional logic of Yes or No, True or False, On or Off.
OLE Object	Stores an embedded or linked object created in another Microsoft Office application.
Hyperlink	Links to a URL.
Attachment	Attaches a file to the record, such as a picture, Word document, or Excel worksheet.
Calculated	The field value is calculated using a mathematical expression that uses data from other fields within the same table.

Using the Field Size Property to Restrict Field Length

By default, Short Text data type fields are set to a width of 255 characters in the Field Size property. Access uses only the amount of space needed for the data entered, even when the field size allows for more characters, but it can still be helpful to change this property to a smaller value.

One reason to change the Field Size property to a smaller value is that it is a way to restrict the length of the data allowed into the field. For example, if RSR Computer Services has developed a four-character numbering system for customer numbers, setting the field size for the *CustID* field to 4 characters will ensure that no one enters a customer number longer than four characters by accident. Access will disallow all characters typed after the fourth character.

Figure 1.3 shows the table structure diagram for the RSR Computer Services database expanded to include each field's data type and Field Size property. You will use this diagram to create the tables in Project 1a.

Figure 1.3 Expanded Table Structure Diagram with Data Types and Field Sizes for Project 1a

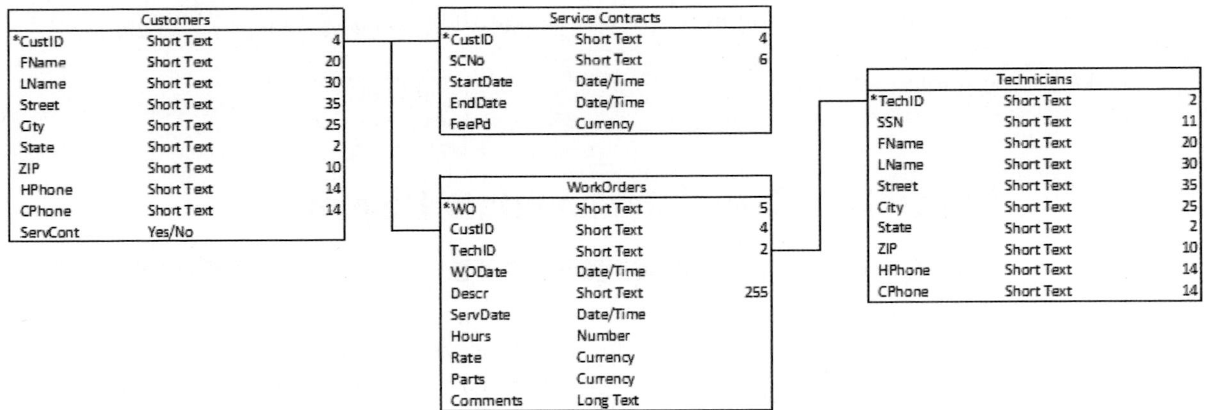

Project 1a Creating Tables in Design View

Part 1 of 6

1. Start Access.
2. At the Access 2013 opening screen, complete the following steps to create a new database to store the work orders for RSR Computer Services:
   a. Click the Blank desktop database template.
   b. At the Blank desktop database window that displays, click the Browse button and navigate to the AL2C1 folder on your storage medium, select the current text in the *File Name* text box, type **AL2-C1-RSRCompServ**, and then click OK.
   c. Click the Create button located below the *File Name* text box.

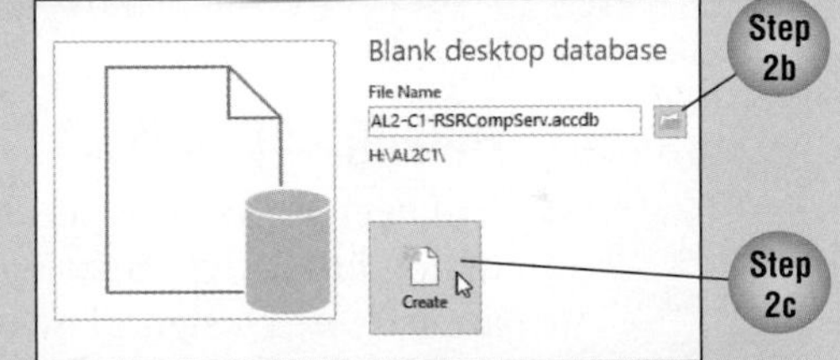

3. Close the Table1 blank table datasheet that displays. You will work with tables in Design view to access all of the field properties available for fields.
4. Click the CREATE tab and then click the Table Design button in the Tables group. Create the fields shown in the Customers table in Figure 1.3, including the data type and field size settings.
5. Assign the primary key to the *CustID* field.
6. Save the table and name it *Customers*.

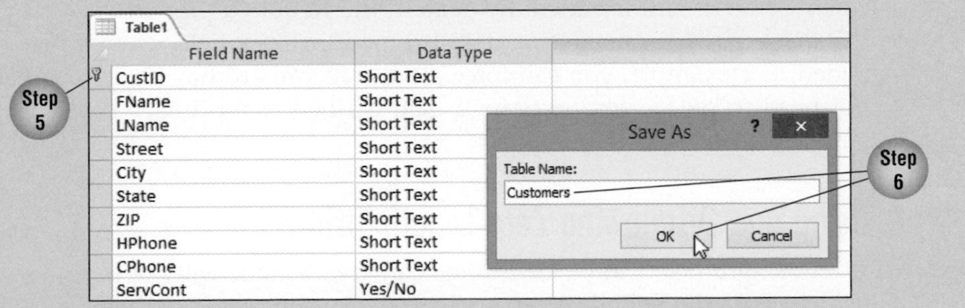

7. Close the table.
8. Create the ServiceContracts, WorkOrders, and Technicians tables shown in Figure 1.3 by completing steps similar to those in Steps 4–7. Assign the primary key in each table using the fields denoted with an asterisk in Figure 1.3.
9. Make sure all tables are closed.

Restricting Data Entry and Data Display Using Field Properties

The properties that are available for a field depend on the field's data type. For example, a Yes/No data type field has 7 properties, whereas a Short Text data type field has 14 and a Number data type field has 11. Use the options available in the *Field Properties* section in Design view to place restrictions on data accepted into a field and ensure that data is entered and displayed consistently. Field properties should be defined before other objects, such as forms and reports, are created, because the properties carry over to the other objects. Taking the time to define the properties when the table is created reduces the number of changes you have to make if you decide to modify properties later on.

You have already used the Field Size property in Project 1a to restrict the lengths of entries allowed in fields. In this section, you will learn to apply other field properties to further control data entry and display.

Quick Steps

Add a Caption to an Existing Field
1. Open table in Design view.
2. Activate desired field.
3. Click in *Caption* property box.
4. Type descriptive text.
5. Save table.

Require Data in a Field
1. Open table in Design view.
2. Activate desired field.
3. Click in *Required* property box.
4. Click down-pointing arrow.
5. Click *Yes*.
6. Save table.

Set the *Required* field to *Yes* and *Allow Zero Length* to *No* to make sure a field value (and not a space) will be entered at the time the record is added.

Adding Captions

In Level 1, you learned about using the Caption property in the Name & Caption dialog box when creating a new table using a Table datasheet. The same property appears in Design view in the *Field Properties* section. Recall that the Caption property allows you to enter a more descriptive title for a field if the field name has been truncated or abbreviated. You can also use spaces between words in field name captions, rather than the underscore or hyphen characters used in the field names themselves. In the absence of a caption, Access displays the field name in datasheets, queries, forms, and reports.

Requiring Data in a Field

Use the Required property to make sure that a certain field is never left empty when a new record is added. By default, the Required property is set to *No*. Change this value to *Yes* to make sure data is typed into the field when a new record is added. For example, you can force all new records to have a zip code entry. You do not need to set this property for a field defined as a primary key, since a primary key field cannot be left empty.

Using and Disallowing Zero-Length Strings

A zero-length field can be used to indicate that a value will not be entered into the field because the field does not apply to the current record. When you are entering a new record and leave a field blank, Access records a null value in the field. For example, if you are adding a new record for a customer and you do not know his or her cell phone number, you can leave the field empty with the intention of updating it at a later time. This is an example of leaving the field blank with a null value. Alternatively, if you know the customer does not own a cell phone, you can enter a zero-length string in the field to indicate no field value applies to this record.

To enter a zero-length string, type two double quotation marks with no space between them (""). When viewing the field in a datasheet, query, form, or report, you cannot distinguish between a field with a null value and a field with a zero-length string, because both display as blanks. However, you can create a control in a form or report that returns a user-defined message in the blank fields, to help you distinguish one from another. For example, you could display the word *Unknown* in a field with a null value and the phrase *Not applicable* in a field with a zero-length string.

By default, Short Text, Long Text, and Hyperlink data type fields allow zero-length strings. Change the Allow Zero Length property to *No* to disallow zero-length strings.

You can also press the spacebar to insert a zero-length string.

Quick Steps

Disallow a Zero-Length String in a Field

1. Open table in Design view.
2. Activate desired field.
3. Click in *Allow Zero Length* property box.
4. Click down-pointing arrow.
5. Click *No*.
6. Save table.

Project 1b Modifying Field Properties to Add Captions and Disallow Blank Values in a Field

Part 2 of 6

1. With **AL2-C1-RSRCompServ.accdb** open, add captions to the fields in the Customers table by completing the following steps:
   a. Right-click *Customers* in the Tables group in the Navigation pane and then click *Design View* at the shortcut menu.
   b. With *CustID* the active field, click in the *Caption* property box in the *Field Properties* section and then type **Customer ID**.
   c. Click in the *FName* field row to activate the field, click in the *Caption* property box in the *Field Properties* section, and then type **First Name**.
   d. Add captions to the following fields by completing a step similar to Step 1c:

      LName **Last Name**
      Street **Street Address**
      HPhone **Home Phone**
      CPhone **Cell Phone**
      ServCont **Service Contract?**

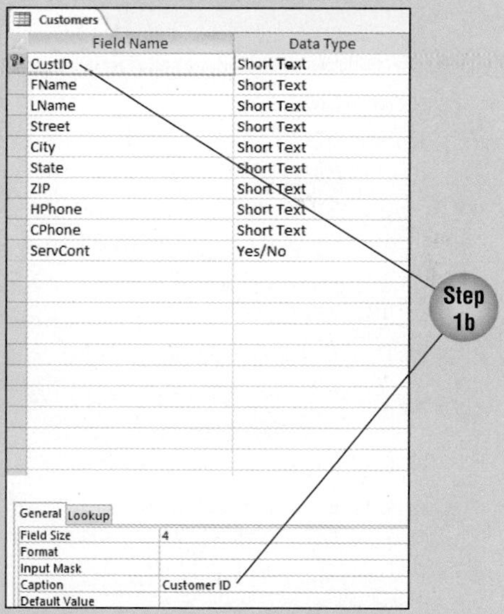

   e. Click the Save button on the Quick Access toolbar.
   f. Click the View button (not the button arrow) to switch to Datasheet view and then select all columns in the datasheet. If necessary, click the Shutter Bar Open/Close button (the two left-pointing chevrons located at the top of the Navigation pane) to minimize the Navigation pane.
   g. Click the More button in the Records group on the HOME tab, click *Field Width* at the drop-down list, and then click the Best Fit button at the Column Width dialog box to adjust the widths to the lengths of the longest entries.
   h. To deselect the columns, click in the *Customer ID* field in the first row of the datasheet.

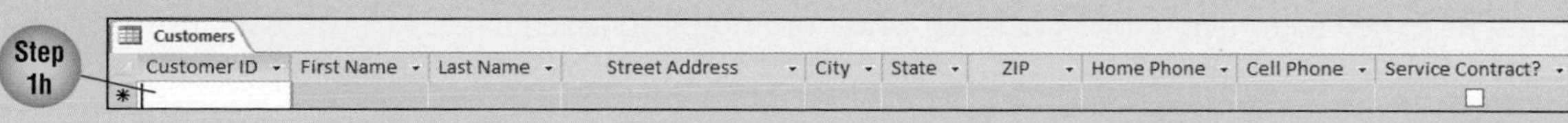

2. Switch to Design View and then click the Shutter Bar Open/Close button (the two right-pointing chevrons) to redisplay the Navigation pane if you minimized the pane in Step 1f.
3. Ensure that no record is entered without an entry in the *ZIP* field and disallow blank values in the field, including zero-length strings, by completing the following steps:
   a. Click in the *ZIP* field row to activate the field.
   b. Click in the *Required* property box in the *Field Properties* section (which currently displays *No*), click the down-pointing arrow that appears, and then click *Yes* at the drop-down list.

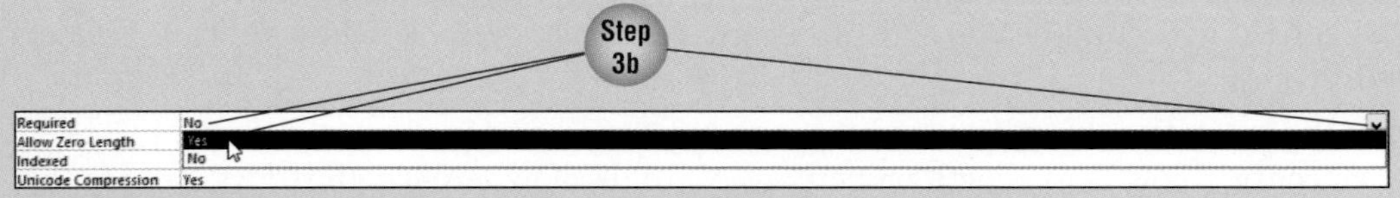

   c. Double-click in the *Allow Zero Length* property box (which currently displays *Yes*) to change the *Yes* to *No*.

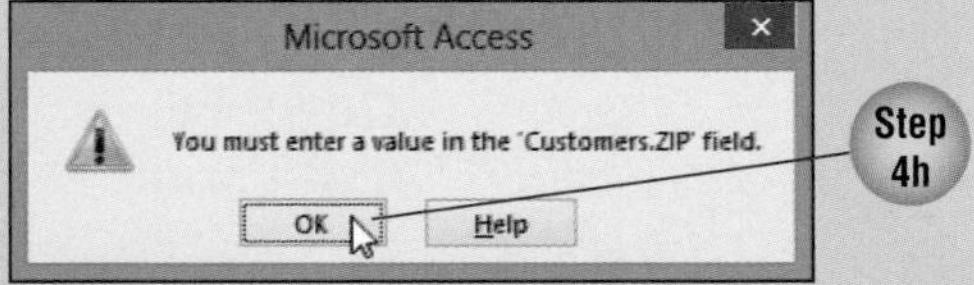

   d. Save the changes to the table design.
4. Use a new record to test the restrictions on the *ZIP* field by completing the following steps:
   a. Switch to Datasheet view.
   b. Add the following data in the fields indicated:

Customer ID	**1000**
First Name	**Jade**
Last Name	**Fleming**
Street Address	**12109 Woodward Avenue**
City	**Detroit**
State	**MI**

   c. At the *ZIP* field, press Enter or Tab to move past the field, leaving it blank.
   d. Type **313-555-0214** in the *Home Phone* field.
   e. Type **313-555-3485** in the *Cell Phone* field.
   f. Press the spacebar in the *Service Contract?* field to insert a check mark in the check box.
   g. Press Enter. Access displays an error message, since the record cannot be saved without an entry in the *ZIP* field.
   h. Click OK at the Microsoft Access message box.
   i. Click in the *ZIP* field, type **48203-3579**, and then press Enter four times to move to the *Customer ID* field in the second row of the datasheet.

Microsoft Access

You must enter a value in the 'Customers.ZIP' field.

OK | Help

Step 4h

5. Double-click the right boundaries of the *Street Address* and *ZIP* columns to adjust the widths so that you can read the entire field values in the columns.

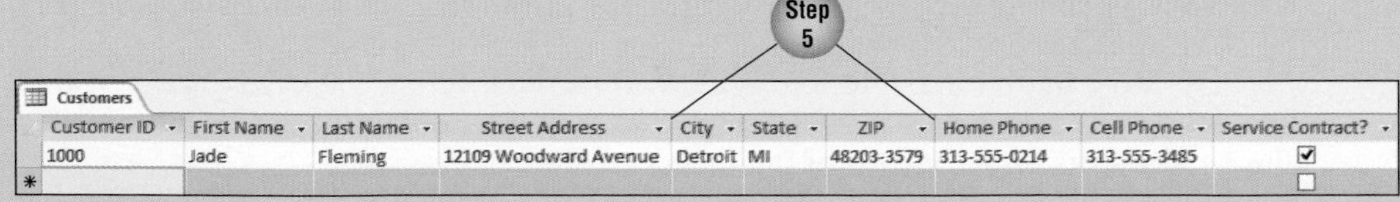

6. Close the Customers table. Click Yes when prompted to save changes to the layout of the table.

Creating a Custom Format for a Text Data Type Field

The Format property controls how data is displayed in the field in the datasheet, query, form, or report. The formats available for use depend on the field's data type. Some data types have predefined formats available, which can be selected from a drop-down list in the *Format* property box. No predefined formats exist for Short Text or Long Text data type fields. If no predefined format exists or if the predefined format options do not meet your needs, you can create your own custom format. Table 1.2 displays commonly used format codes for Short Text and Long Text data type fields.

The Format property does not control how data is entered into the field. Rather, formatting a field controls the display of accepted field values. Refer to the section on input masks (starting on page 18) to learn how to control new data as the data is being entered.

Quick Steps

Format a Text Field

1. Open table in Design view.
2. Activate desired field.
3. Click in *Format* property box.
4. Type desired format codes.
5. Save table.

Table 1.2 Format Codes for Short Text and Long Text Data Type Fields

Code	*Description*	*Format Property Example*
@	Used as a placeholder, one symbol for each character position. Unused positions in a field value are replaced with blank spaces to the left of the text entered into the field.	@@@@ Field value entered is 123. Access displays one blank space followed by 123, left-aligned in the field.
!	Placeholder positions are filled with characters from left to right instead of the default right to left sequence.	!@@@@ Field value entered is 123. Access displays 123 left-aligned in the field with one blank space after the 3.
>	All text is converted to uppercase.	> Field value entered is mi. Access displays MI in the field.
<	All text is converted to lowercase.	< Field value entered is Jones@EMCP.NET. Access displays jones@emcp.net in the field.
[color]	Text is displayed in the font color specified. Available colors are black, blue, cyan, green, magenta, red, yellow, and white.	[red]@@@@@-@@@@ Field value entered is 482033579. Access displays 48203-3579.

Project 1c Formatting Short Text Data Type Fields Using a Custom Format — Part 3 of 6

1. With **AL2-C1-RSRCompServ.accdb** open, format the *State* field to ensure all text is displayed in uppercase letters by completing the following steps:
   a. Right-click *Customers* in the Tables group in the Navigation pane and then click *Design View* at the shortcut menu.
   b. Click in the *State* field row to activate the field.
   c. Click in the *Format* property box and then type **>**.
   d. Save the table.

General	Lookup
Field Size	2
Format	>
Input Mask	

Step 1c

2. Format the *ZIP* field to fill the field with characters from left to right, display the text in red, and provide for the five-plus-four-character US zip code, separated by a hyphen, by completing the following steps:
   a. Click in the *ZIP* field row to activate the field.
   b. Click in the *Format* property box and then type **![red]@@@@@-@@@@**.
   c. Save the table.

General	Lookup
Field Size	10
Format	![red]@@@@@-@@@@
Input Mask	

Step 2b

3. Test the custom formats in the *State* and *ZIP* fields using a new record by completing the following steps:
   a. Switch to Datasheet view.
   b. Add the following data in a new record. Type the text for the *State* field as indicated, in lowercase text. Notice that when you move to the next field, Access automatically converts the lowercase text to uppercase. As you type the ZIP text, notice that the text is displayed in red. Since no field values are entered for the last four characters of the *ZIP* field, Access displays blank spaces in these positions.

Customer ID	**1005**
First Name	**Cayla**
Last Name	**Fahri**
Street Address	**12793 Riverdale Avenue**
City	**Detroit**
State	**mi**
ZIP	**48223**
Home Phone	**313-555-6845**
Cell Phone	**313-555-4187**
Service Contract?	Press spacebar for *Yes*

4. Look at the data in the *ZIP* field for the first record. This data was entered before you formatted the *ZIP* field. Since a hyphen was typed when the data was entered in Project 1b and the field is now formatted to automatically add the hyphen, two hyphen characters appear in the existing record. Update the record by editing the *ZIP* field value for record 1 to remove the extra hyphen.

Step 4

Customers

Customer ID	First Name	Last Name	Street Address	City	State	ZIP	Home Phone	Cell Phone	Service Contract?
1000	Jade	Fleming	12109 Woodward Avenue	Detroit	MI	48203-3579	313-555-0214	313-555-3485	☑
1005	Cayla	Fahri	12793 Riverdale Avenue	Detroit	MI	48223-	313-555-6845	313-555-4187	☑

5. Display the datasheet in Print Preview. Change the orientation to landscape. Set the top margin to 1 inch and the bottom, left, and right margins to 0.25 inch. Print the datasheet and then close Print Preview.
6. Close the Customers table.

Creating a Custom Format for a Numeric Data Type Field

Access provides predefined formats for Number, AutoNumber, and Currency data type fields that include options for displaying a fixed number of places past the decimal point, commas for numbers in the thousands, the currency symbol, percentages, and exponential notation. Table 1.3 displays format codes that you can use to create a custom format. Use the placeholders shown in Table 1.3 in combination with other characters (such as a dollar symbol, comma, and period) to create the desired custom numeric format.

You can specify up to four formats for a numeric data type field to include different options for displaying positive values, negative values, zero values, and null values. Examine the following custom format code:

#,###.00;-#,###.00[red];0.00;"Unknown"

Notice that the four sections are separated with semicolons (;). The first section, *#,###.00*, defines the format for positive values, which includes the comma in thousands and two places past the decimal point with zeros used if no decimal value is entered. The second section, *-#,###.00[red]*, defines negative values with the same placeholders as positive but starts the field with a minus symbol and displays the numbers in red. The third section, *0.00*, instructs Access to show *0.00* in the field if a zero is entered. Finally, a field value that is left blank will display the text *Unknown* (italics for emphasis only) in the field. Notice that the example shown indicates the text that you want shown in the field includes quotation marks at the beginning and end.

Quick Steps

Format a Numeric Data Type Field

1. Open table in Design view.
2. Activate desired field.
3. Click in *Format* property box.
4. Type desired format codes or select from predefined list.
5. Save table.

Table 1.3 Format Codes for Numeric Data Type Fields

Code	*Description*	*Format Property Example*
#	Used as a placeholder to display a number.	#.## Field value entered is 123.45. Access displays 123.45 in the field. Notice that the number of placeholder positions does not restrict the data entered into the field.
0	Used as a placeholder to display a number. Access displays a 0 in place of a position for which no value is entered.	000.00 Field value entered is 55.4. Access displays 055.40 in the field.
%	Value is multiplied times 100 and a percent symbol is added.	#.0% Field value entered is .1242. Access displays 12.4% in the field. Notice that having only one place past the decimal point causes rounding up or down to occur.

Project 1d Formatting Numeric Data Type Fields Using a Custom Format and a Predefined Format

Part 4 of 6

1. With **AL2-C1-RSRCompServ.accdb** open, format the *Rate* field in the WorkOrders table with a custom format by completing the following steps:
   a. Open the WorkOrders table in Design view.
   b. Make the *Rate* field active.
   c. Click in the *Format* property box, delete the current entry, and then type **#.00[blue];;;"Not Available"**. Notice that three semicolons are typed after the first custom format option, *#.00[blue]*. When you do not need a custom format for negative or zero values in a property, include the semicolon to indicate that there is no format setting. Since an hourly rate is never a negative value or zero value, you do not need to include custom formats for these situations.
   d. Save the table.
2. Format the *Hours* field using a predefined format and change the field size by completing the following steps:
   a. Make the *Hours* field active.
   b. Click in the *Field Size* property box, click the down-pointing arrow that appears, and then click *Double* at the drop-down list. The default setting for a Number data type field is *Long Integer*, which stores only whole numbers (meaning that a decimal value entered into the field is rounded). Changing the field size property to *Double* allows you to store decimal values.
   c. Click in the *Format* property box, click the down-pointing arrow that appears, and then click *Standard* at the drop-down list.
   d. Click in the *Decimal Places* property box, click the down-pointing arrow that appears, and then click *2* at the pop-up list.
   e. Save the table.

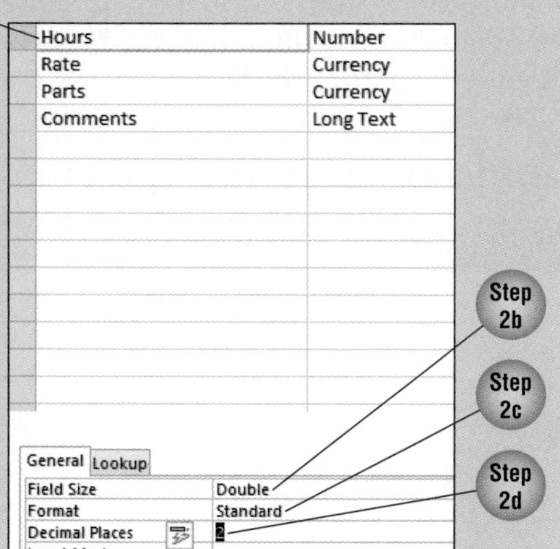

3. Switch to Datasheet view.
4. Add the following data in a new record to test the custom format and the predefined format. Notice when you move past the *Rate* field, the value is displayed in blue.

WO	**65012**
CustID	**1000**
TechID	**11**
WODate	**09-07-2015**
Descr	**Bi-annual desktop computer cleaning and maintenance**
ServDate	**09-07-2015**
Hours	**1.25**
Rate	**30**
Parts	**10.15**
Comments	**"H" key is sticking; cleaning did not resolve. Customer is considering buying a new keyboard.**

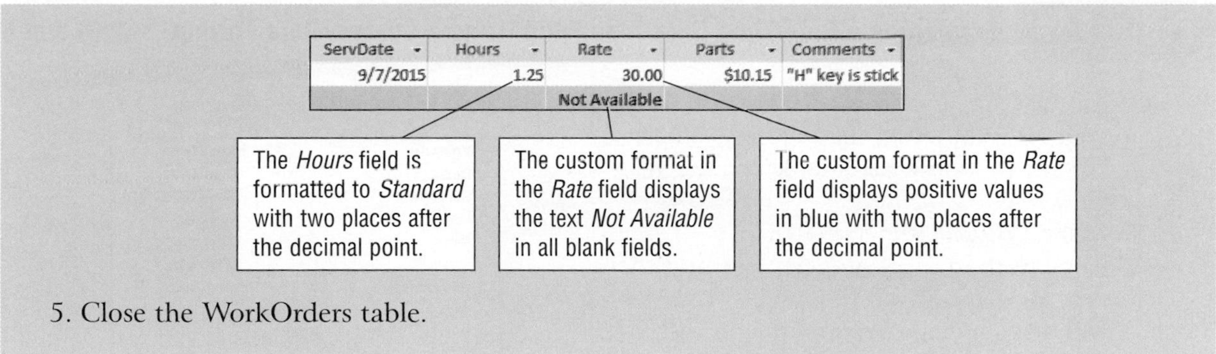

ServDate
Hours
Rate
Parts
Comments
9/7/2015
1.25
30.00
$10.15
"H" key is stick
Not Available
The *Hours* field is formatted to *Standard* with two places after the decimal point.
The custom format in the *Rate* field displays the text *Not Available* in all blank fields.
The custom format in the *Rate* field displays positive values in blue with two places after the decimal point.

5. Close the WorkOrders table.

Creating a Custom Format for a Date/Time Data Type Field

Access provides predefined formats for fields with a Date/Time data type. These formats provide a variety of combinations of month, day, and year options for dates and hour and minute display options for time. If the predefined display formats do not meet your needs, you can create your own custom formats using a combination of the codes described in Table 1.4, along with the desired symbols (such as hyphens and slashes) between parts of the date. If you do not specify a format option for a Date/Time data type field, Access displays the date in the format m/d/yyyy. For example, in Project 1d, the date entered into the *WODate* field displays as 9/7/2015.

A custom format for a Date/Time data type field can contain two sections separated by a semicolon. The first section specifies the format for displaying dates. To add a format for displaying times, type a semicolon and then add the format codes for the time.

Quick Steps

Format a Date/Time Data Type Field

1. Open table in Design view.
2. Activate desired field.
3. Click in *Format* property box.
4. Type desired format codes or select from predefined list.
5. Save table.

Table 1.4 Format Codes for Date/Time Data Type Fields

Code	*Description*
d or dd	Displays the day of the month as one digit (d) or two digits (dd).
ddd or dddd	Displays the day of the week abbreviated (ddd) or in full (dddd).
m or mm	Displays the month as one digit (m) or two digits (mm).
mmm or mmmm	Displays the month abbreviated (mmm) or in full (mmmm).
yy or yyyy	Displays the year as the last two digits (yy) or all four digits (yyyy).
h or hh	Displays the hour as one digit (h) or two digits (hh).
n or nn	Displays the minutes as one digit (n) or two digits (nn).
s or ss	Displays the seconds as one digit (s) or two digits (ss).
AM/PM	Displays 12-hour clock values followed by AM or PM.

Project 1e Formatting a Date/Time Data Type Field Using a Custom Date Format — Part 5 of 6

1. With **AL2-C1-RSRCompServ.accdb** open, format the *WODate* field with a custom format by completing the following steps:
   a. Open the WorkOrders table in Design view.
   b. Make *WODate* the active field.
   c. Click in the *Format* property box and then type **ddd mmm dd yyyy**. This format will display dates beginning with the day of the week in abbreviated form, followed by the month in abbreviated form, the day of the month as two digits, and the year as four digits. Spaces separate the four sections of the date.
   d. Save the table.

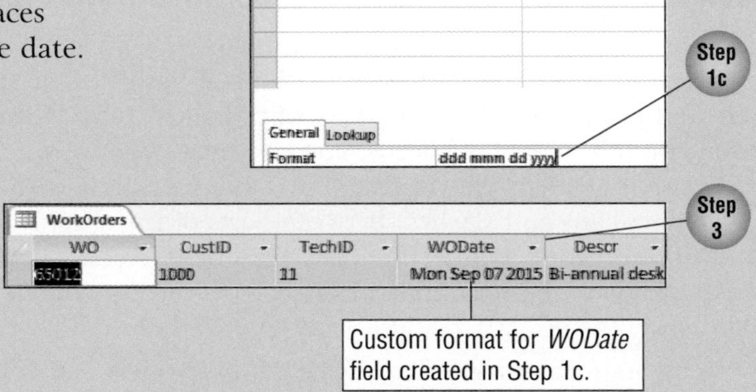

2. Switch to Datasheet view.
3. If necessary, adjust the column width of the *WODate* field to allow reading the entire entry.
4. Switch to Design view.
5. Format the *ServDate* field using the same custom format as used for *WODate* by completing steps similar to those in Steps 1b–1c.
6. Save the table and then switch to Datasheet view.
7. Double-click the right column boundary to adjust the column width of the *ServDate* field and view the custom date format.

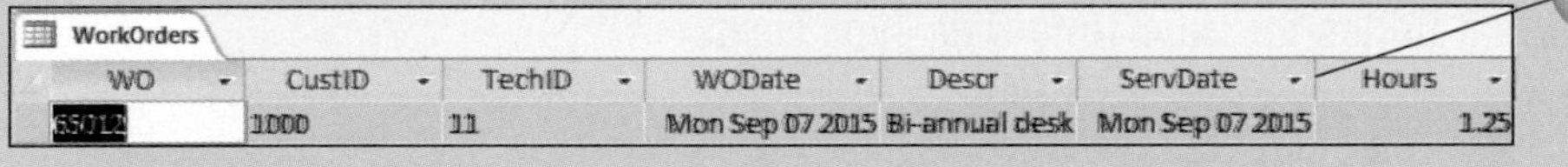

8. Close the WorkOrders table. Click *Yes* when prompted to save changes to the table layout.

Restricting Data Entry Using Input Masks

Quick Steps

Create a Custom Input Mask

1. Open table in Design view.
2. Activate desired field.
3. Click in *Input Mask* property box.
4. Type input mask codes.
5. Save table.

Whereas a format controls how the data is displayed, an ***input mask*** controls the type of data and pattern in which the data is entered into a field. In Project 1e, you created a date format to display the date as *Mon Sep 7 2015*. When confirming dates with clients, it is good practice to give out the day of the week, as well as the day of the month. To type the date consistently and efficiently into the *ServDate* or *WODate* field, you will create an input mask in Project 1f to enter the date by typing *sep072015*. Access knows that this date is a Monday and displays *Mon Sep 7 2015*.

As you learned in Level 1, Chapter 4, Access provides the Input Mask Wizard, which can be used to create an input mask for a text or date field. Commonly used input masks are predefined within the wizard for telephone numbers, social security numbers, zip codes, dates, and times. To create your own input mask without the wizard, use the codes described in Table 1.5.

Table 1.5 Commonly Used Input Mask Codes

Code	*Description*
0	Required digit.
9	Optional digit.
#	Digit, space, plus or minus symbol. If no data is typed at this position, Access leaves a blank space.
L	Required letter.
?	Optional letter.
A	Required letter or digit.
a	Optional letter or digit.
&	Required character or space.
C	Optional character or space.
!	Field is filled from left to right instead of right to left.
\	Character is displayed that immediately follows in the field.

An input mask can contain up to three sections, which are separated by semicolons. The first section contains the input mask codes for the data entry in the field. The second section instructs Access to store or not store the display characters used in the field (such as hyphens and brackets). A zero indicates that Access should store the characters. Leaving the second section blank means the display characters will not be stored. The third section specifies the placeholder character to display in the field when the field becomes active for data entry.

The following is an example of an input mask to store a four-digit customer identification number with a pound symbol (#) as the placeholder: 0000;;#. The first section, *0000*, contains the four required digits for the customer identification. Since the mask contains no display characters (hyphens, slashes, etc.), the second section is blank. The pound symbol after the second semicolon is the placeholder character.

In addition to the symbols in Table 1.5, you can include the format code > to force characters to be uppercase or the format code < to force characters to be lowercase. You can also use decimal points, hyphens, slashes, and other punctuation symbols between parts of the mask.

If you create a custom input mask for a date field that also contains a custom format, make sure the two properties do not conflict. For example, a format code that displays dates with the year first followed by the month and then the day will be confusing if the input mask requires the date to be entered as month first followed by day and then year.

Project 1f Creating Custom Input Masks Part 6 of 6

1. With **AL2-C1-RSRCompServ.accdb** open, create a custom input mask for the work order numbers by completing the following steps:
   a. Open the WorkOrders table in Design view.
   b. With *WO* the active field, click in the *Input Mask* property box and then type **00000;;_**. This mask requires a five-digit work order number to be entered. The underscore is used as the placeholder character that displays when the field becomes active.

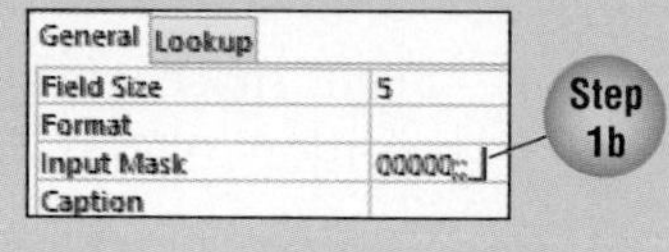

   c. Save the table.
2. Create an input mask to require the two date fields to be entered as three characters for the month, with the first letter uppercase, followed by two digits for the day and four digits for the year by completing the following steps:
   a. Make *WODate* the active field.
   b. Click in the *Input Mask* property box and then type **>L<LL\-00\-0000;0;_**. This mask requires three letters for the month, with the first letter converted to uppercase and the remaining two letters converted to lowercase. The \- symbols instruct Access to display the hyphen character after the month as data is entered. Two digits are required for the day, followed by another hyphen character and then four digits for the year. The *0* after the first semicolon instructs Access to store the display characters. Ending the mask, the underscore character is again used as the placeholder character.

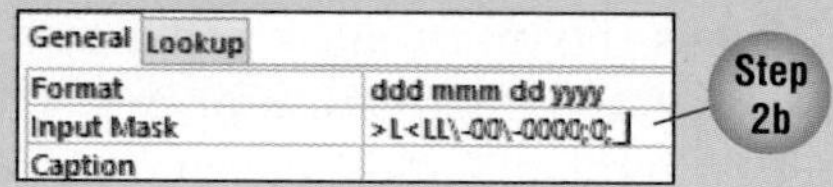

   c. Make *ServDate* the active field, click in the *Input Mask* property box, and then type **>L<LL\-00\-0000;0;_**.
   d. Save the table.
3. Switch to Datasheet view.
4. Test the input masks using a new record by completing the following steps:
   a. Click the New button in the Records group on the HOME tab.
   b. Type **6501**. Notice that as soon as you type the first character, the placeholders appear in the field.
   c. Press Tab or Enter to move to the next field in the datasheet. Since the mask contains five zeros indicating five required digits, Access displays a message box informing you that the value entered is not appropriate for the input mask.
   d. Click OK at the Microsoft Access message box.

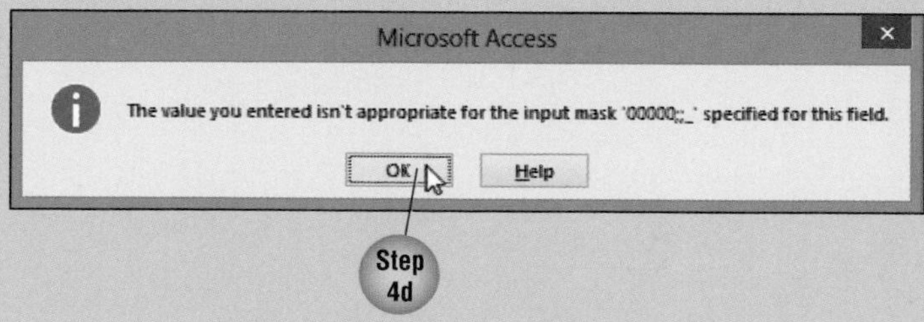

e. Type **3** in the last position in the *WO* field and then press Tab or Enter to move to the next field.
f. Type **1000** in the *CustID* field and then press Tab or Enter.
g. Type **10** in the *TechID* field and then press Tab or Enter.
h. Type **sep072015** in the *WODate* field and then press Tab or Enter. Notice that the placeholder characters and hyphens appear as soon as you type the first letter. Notice also that the first character is converted to uppercase and that you do not need to type the hyphen characters, since Access moves automatically to the next position after the month and day are typed.
i. Type **Replace keyboard** in the *Descr* field and then press Tab or Enter.
j. Type **sep102015** in the *ServDate* field and then press Tab or Enter.
k. Complete the remainder of the record as follows:

Hours	**.5**
Rate	**28.50**
Parts	**22.75**
Comments	**Serial Number AWQ-982358**

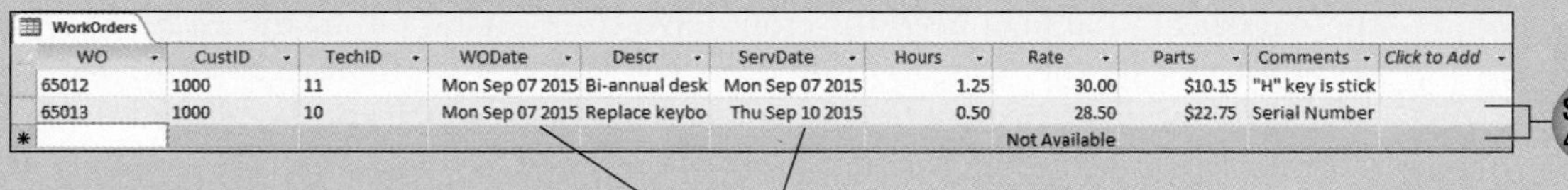

WorkOrders

WO	CustID	TechID	WODate	Descr	ServDate	Hours	Rate	Parts	Comments	Click to Add
65012	1000	11	Mon Sep 07 2015	Bi-annual desk	Mon Sep 07 2015	1.25	30.00	$10.15	"H" key is stick	
65013	1000	10	Mon Sep 07 2015	Replace keybo	Thu Sep 10 2015	0.50	28.50	$22.75	Serial Number	
*							Not Available			

Notice that once the date is accepted into the field, the custom Format property controls how the date is presented in the datasheet, with the abbreviated day of the week at the beginning of the field and spaces between month, day, and year instead of hyphens.

5. Display the datasheet in Print Preview. Change the orientation to landscape. Set the top and bottom margins to 1 inch and the left, and right margins to 0.25 inch. Print the datasheet and then close Print Preview.
6. Close the WorkOrders table.

Other field properties that you should consider for data accuracy when designing database tables include the Default Value, Validation Rule, and Validation Text properties. Use the Default Value property to populate the field in a new record with the field value that is used most often. For example, when most employees live in the same city and state, you can use default values for those fields to ensure consistent spelling and capitalization within a table. The text appears automatically in the fields when new records are added to the table. The user can accept the default value by pressing Tab or Enter to move past the field or type new data in the field. In Level 1, you learned how to create a default value using the Default Value button in the Properties group on the TABLE TOOLS FIELDS tab. In Design view, the Default Value property is located below the Caption property.

Use the Validation Rule and Validation Text properties to enter conditional statements that are checked against new data entered into the field. Invalid entries that do not meet the conditional statement test are rejected. For example, a validation rule on a field used to store labor rates can check that a minimum labor rate value is entered in each record. In Level 1, you learned to add a validation rule using the Validation button in the Field Validation group on the TABLE TOOLS FIELDS tab. In Design view, the Validation Rule and Validation Text properties are located just above the Required property.

Project 2 Work with Long Text and Attachment Data Type Fields 2 Parts

You will edit properties for a Long Text data type field, apply rich text formatting to text, and attach files to records using an Attachment data type field.

Quick Steps

Enable Rich Text Formatting in a Long Text Data Type Field
1. Open table in Design view.
2. Select desired field defined as Long Text.
3. Double-click in *Text Format* property box.
4. Click Yes
5. Save table.

Track Changes in a Long Text Data Type Field
1. Open table in Design view.
2. Select desired field defined as Long Text.
3. Double-click in *Append Only* property box.
4. Click Yes.
5. Save table.

Working with Long Text Data Type Fields

By default, Access formats a Long Text data type field as plain text, but you can apply formatting attributes to text by enabling rich text formatting. Enabling rich text formatting in a Long Text data type field allows you to change the font, apply bold or italic formatting, or add font color to text, among other formatting options. To add rich text formatting capability, change the Text Format property to *Rich Text*.

The Append Only property for a Long Text data type field is set to *No* by default. Change the property to *Yes* to track changes made to the field value in the datasheet. You may need to scroll down the General tab in the *Field Properties* section to locate the Append Only property. When this property is set to *Yes*, Access maintains a history of additions to the field, which can be viewed in the datasheet. Changing the Append Only property to *No* causes Access to delete any existing history.

In Project 2a, you change the text format of the *Comments* field from *Plain Text* to *Rich Text* and then apply bold red formatting to the serial number of the new keyboard. These formatting changes make it easier to find important information—in this case, the serial number—in the Comments field. Changing the Append Only property from *No* to *Yes* allows you to keep track of the dates for any comments entered into the field.

Project 2a Enabling Rich Text Formatting and Maintaining a History of Changes in a Long Text Data Type Field Part 1 of 2

1. With **AL2-C1-RSRCompServ.accdb** open, enable rich text formatting and turn on tracking of history in a field defined as a Long Text data type field by completing the following steps:
   a. Open the WorkOrders table in Design view.
   b. Make *Comments* the active field.
   c. Double-click in the *Text Format* property box (which currently reads *Plain Text*). It should now read *Rich Text*.
   d. At the Microsoft Access message box indicating that the field will be converted to rich text, click Yes.

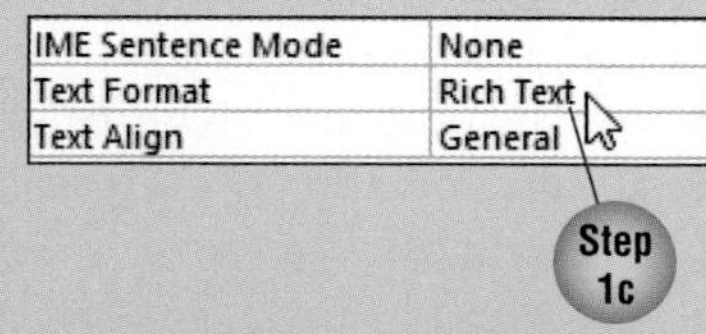

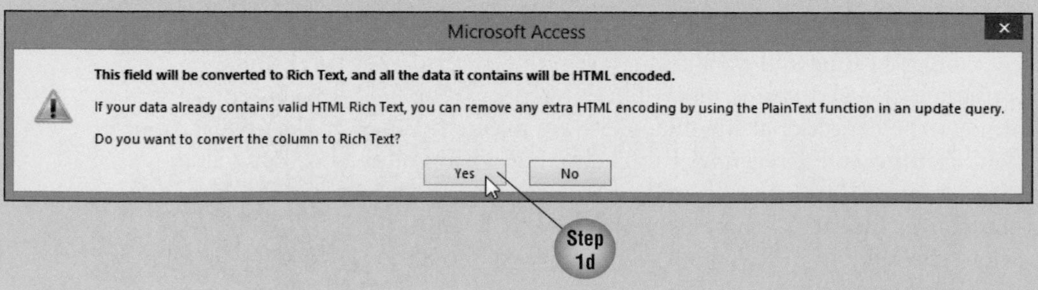

e. If necessary, scroll down the General tab in the *Field Properties* section until you can see the *Append Only* property box.

f. Double-click in the *Append Only* property box to change *No* to *Yes*.

Text Format	Rich Text
Text Align	General
Append Only	Yes

Step 1f

g. Save the table.

2. Switch to Datasheet view.
3. Minimize the Navigation pane and then adjust all of the column widths except the *Descr* and *Comments* fields to best fit.
4. Change the column width of the *Comments* field to 25 characters.
5. Select the serial number text *AWQ-982358* in the second record in the *Comments* field and then apply bold formatting and the Red font color using the buttons in the Text Formatting group on the HOME tab. Click at the end of the serial number to deselect the text.

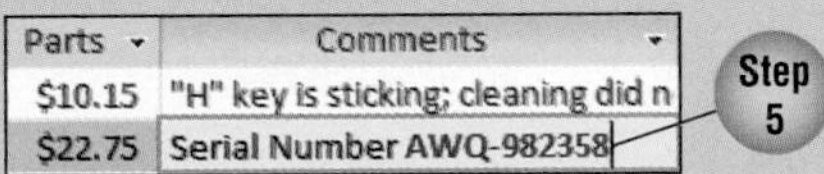

6. Click in the *Comments* field in the first record. Press the End key to move the insertion point to the end of the existing text. Press the spacebar once, update the record by typing **Microsoft wireless keyboard was recommended.**, and then press Enter to save the changes and move to the next row.
7. Right-click in the first record's *Comments* field and then click *Show column history* at the shortcut menu.
8. Click OK after reading the text in the History for Comments dialog box.

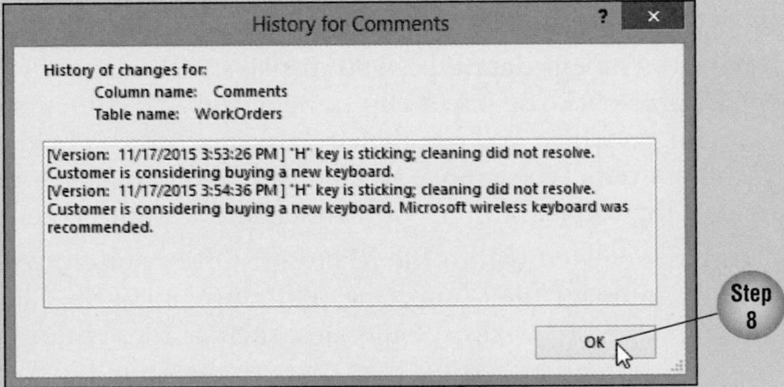

9. Click in the first record's *Comments* field. Press the End key to move the insertion point to the end of the current text. Press the spacebar once, type **See work order 65013 for replacement keyboard request.**, and then press Enter.
10. Right-click in the first record's *Comments* field and then click *Show column history* at the shortcut menu.

11. Click OK after reading the text in the History for Comments dialog box.
12. Display the datasheet in Print Preview. Change the orientation to landscape. Set the top and bottom margins to 1 inch and the left, and right margins to 0.25 inch. Print the datasheet and then close Print Preview.

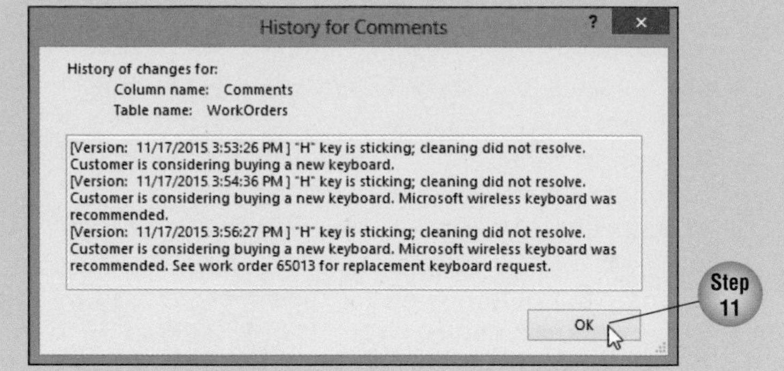

13. Close the WorkOrders table. Click Yes when prompted to save changes to the layout of the table and then redisplay the Navigation pane.

Creating an Attachment Data Type Field and Attaching Files to Records

Use an Attachment data type field to store several files in a single field attached to a record. The attachments can be opened within Access and viewed in the program from which the document originated. For example, you can attach a Word document to a field in a record. Opening the attached file in the Access table causes Microsoft Word to start and the document to display. A file that is attached to a record cannot be larger than 256 megabytes (MB).

An Attachment data type field displays with a paper clip in Datasheet view. Double-click the paper clip to open the Attachments dialog box, shown in Figure 1.4, in which you can manage attached files. A field that is created with an Attachment data type cannot be changed. You can attach multiple files to a record, provided the total size of all files attached does not exceed 2 gigabytes (GB).

Any file created within the Microsoft Office suite can be attached to a record or an image file (.bmp, .jpg, .gif, .png), a log file (.log), a text file (.txt), or a compressed file (.zip). Some files, such as files ending with *.com* or *.exe*, are considered potential security risks and are therefore blocked by Access.

Figure 1.4 Attachments Dialog Box

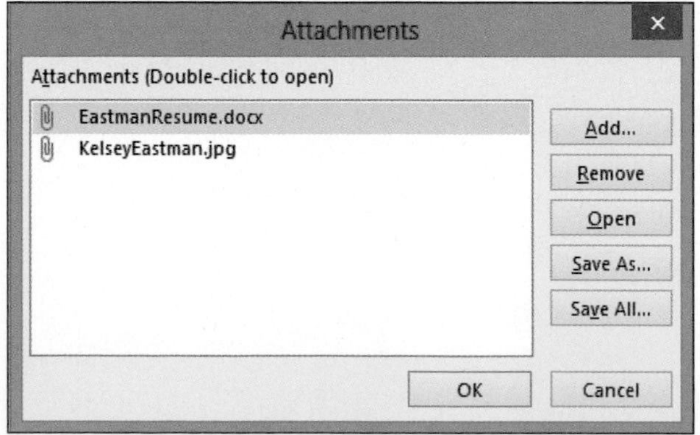

Quick Steps

Create an Attachment Data Type Field
1. Open table in Design view.
2. Click in first blank field row.
3. Type desired field name.
4. Click in *Data Type* column.
5. Click down-pointing arrow.
6. Click *Attachment*.
7. Save table.

Attach Files to a Record
1. Open table in Datasheet view.
2. Double-click paper clip in desired record.
3. Click Add button.
4. Navigate to drive and/or folder location.
5. Double-click file name.
6. Click OK.

View an Attached File
1. Open table in Datasheet view.
2. Double-click paper clip in desired record.
3. Double-click file name.
4. View file contents.
5. Exit source program.
6. Click OK.

Project 2b Creating an Attachment Data Type Field, Attaching Files to a Record, and Viewing the Contents of Attached Files

1. With **AL2-C1-RSRCompServ.accdb** open, create a new field in which you will store file attachments by completing the following steps:
   a. Open the Technicians table in Design view.
   b. Click in the blank row below *CPhone*, type **Attachments**, and then press Tab or Enter.
   c. Click the down-pointing arrow in the *Data Type* column and then click *Attachment* at the drop-down list.
   d. Save the table.

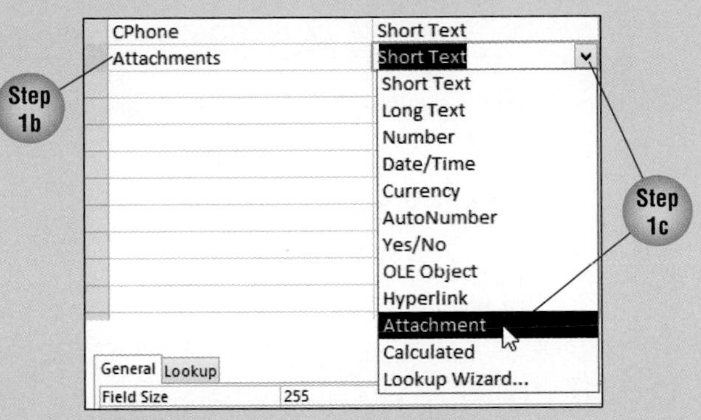

2. Switch to Datasheet view.
3. Add the following data in the first row of the datasheet:

TechID	**10**
SSN	**000-43-5789**
FName	**Kelsey**
LName	**Eastman**
Street	**550 Montclair Street**
City	**Detroit**
State	**MI**
ZIP	**48214-3274**
HPhone	**313-555-6315**
CPhone	"" (Recall that double quotation marks indicate a zero-length field.)

4. Attach two files to the record for Kelsey Eastman by completing the following steps:
   a. Double-click the paper clip in the first row of the datasheet. Attachment data type fields display a paper clip in each record in a column, with a paper clip in the field name row. The number in brackets next to the paper clip indicates the number of files attached to the record.
   b. At the Attachments dialog box, click the Add button.
   c. At the Choose File dialog box, navigate to the AL2C1 folder on your storage medium.
   d. Click the file named ***EastmanResume.docx***.
   e. Hold down the Ctrl key and click the file named ***KelseyEastman.jpg***.
   f. Click the Open button.
   g. Click OK. Access closes the Attachments dialog box and displays *(2)* next to the paper clip in the first record.

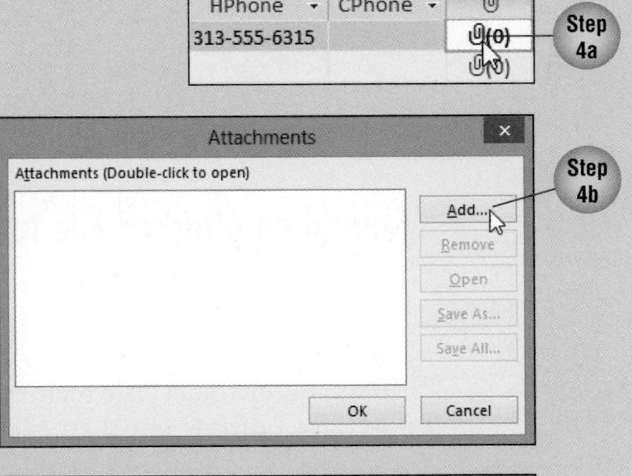

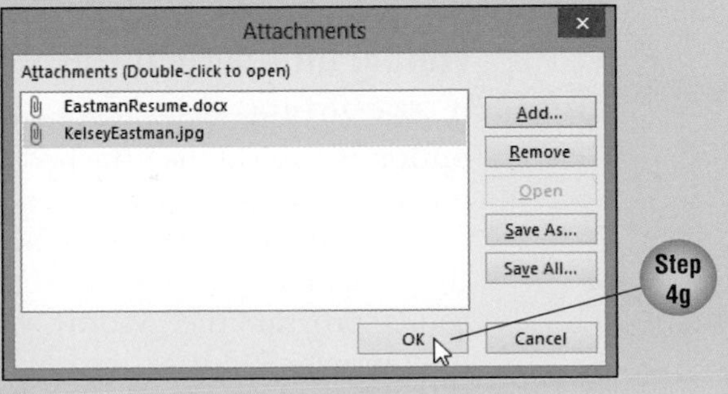

5. Open the attached files by completing the following steps:
   a. Double-click the paper clip in the first row of the datasheet to open the Attachments dialog box.
   b. Double-click ***EastmanResume.docx*** in the *Attachments* list box to open the Word document.
   c. Read the resume in Microsoft Word and then exit Word.

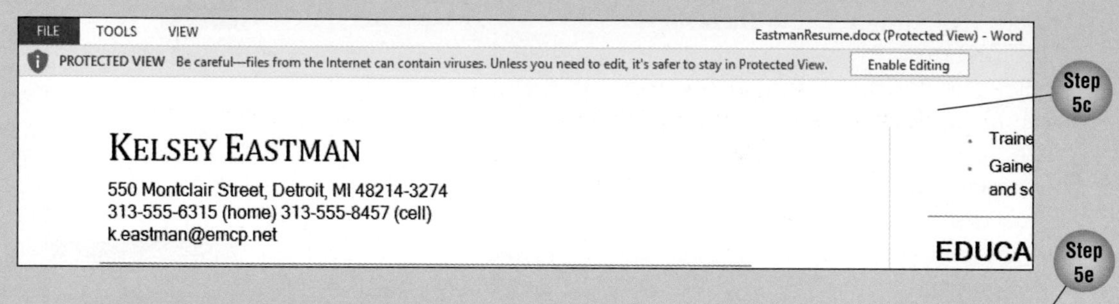

   d. Double-click ***KelseyEastman.jpg*** in the *Attachments* list box to open the picture file.
   e. View the picture and then exit the photo viewer program.
   f. Click OK to close the Attachments dialog box.
6. Adjust all column widths to best fit.
7. Display the datasheet in Print Preview. Change the orientation to landscape, print the datasheet, and then close Print Preview.
8. Close the Technicians table. Click Yes when prompted to save changes to the table layout.
9. Close **AL2-C1-RSRCompServ.accdb**.

Saving an Attached File to Another Location

You can export a file that is attached to a record to save a copy of the document in another location by selecting the file and then clicking the Save As button in the Attachments dialog box. At the Save Attachment dialog box, navigate to the drive and/or folder to which you want to save the duplicate copy of the file, click the Save button, and then click OK to close the Attachments dialog box.

Editing an Attached File

Access 2013 provides two new options for editing an attachment. The first option is to save the attached file to another location, as noted above. After you make the necessary changes and save the file, remove the original attachment from the database and then attach the edited file. The second option is to open the attachment directly in Access. When you save the changes you made in the source program (i.e., Word), you will be asked to save the file to your SkyDrive or computer. Go back into Access, remove the attachment from the database, and then reattach the file to the field.

Removing an Attached File

To remove a file attached to a record in a database, open the Attachments dialog box in the record containing the file attachment, click the file name for the file you want to remove, click the Remove button, and then click OK to close the Attachments dialog box.

Chapter Summary

- Database designers plan the tables for a new database by analyzing sample data, input documents, and output requirements to generate the entire set of data elements needed.
- Once all data has been identified, the designer maps out the number of tables required.
- Each table holds data only for a single topic and data is split into the smallest unit that will be manipulated.
- Designers also consider the relationships that will be needed in case a field needs to be added to a table to join tables.
- Data redundancy should be avoided, which means fields should not be repeated in another table except for those fields needed to join tables in a relationship.
- A diagram of a database portrays the database tables, providing field names, data types, field sizes, and notation of the primary keys.
- A field is assigned a data type by selecting a type appropriate for the kind of data that will be accepted into the field.
- Changing the Field Size property can be used as a way to restrict entries in the field to a maximum length, thus preventing having longer entries added to the field by accident.
- Change the Required property to *Yes* to force an entry into the field when a new record is added to the table.
- Leaving a field blank when a new record is entered results in having a null value stored in the field.
- A zero-length field is entered into a record by typing two double quotation marks, with no space between them. This method is used to indicate a field value does not apply to the current record.
- You can disallow zero-length strings by changing the Allow Zero Length property to *No*.
- The Format property controls the display of data accepted into a field. Custom formats can be created by typing the appropriate format codes in the *Format* property box.
- A custom numeric format can contain four sections: one section for positive values, one section for negative values, one section for zero values, and the last section for null values.
- Use an input mask to control the type and pattern of data entered into the field.

- Create a custom input mask for a Short Text or Date/Time data type field by typing the appropriate input mask codes in the *Input Mask* property box.
- A Long Text data type field can be formatted using rich text formatting options in the Text Formatting group on the HOME tab by changing the Text Format property to *Rich Text*.
- Change the Append Only property of a Long Text data type field to *Yes* to track changes made to field values.
- An attachment data type field can be used to store files associated with a record.
- Double-click the paper clip in the Attachment data type field for a record to add, view, save, or remove a file attachment.

Commands Review

FEATURE	RIBBON TAB, GROUP	BUTTON	KEYBOARD SHORTCUT
create table in Design view	CREATE, Tables		
minimize Navigation pane		«	F11
redisplay Navigation pane		»	F11
switch to Datasheet view from Design view	TABLE TOOLS DESIGN, Views		
switch to Design view from Datasheet view	HOME, Views		

Concepts Check Test Your Knowledge 

Completion: In the space provided at the right, indicate the correct term, command, or number.

1. Use this data type to store alphanumeric text longer than 255 characters. ________________
2. Use this data type for a field that will hold numeric data that is not a monetary value. ________________
3. This data type is restricted to field values used to test conditional logic that can be one of only two conditions. ________________
4. The properties that display for a field in the *Field Properties* section in Design view are dependent on this option. ________________
5. This property is used to display a more descriptive title for the field in the datasheet. ________________
6. To ensure a field is never left empty, set this property to *Yes*. ________________
7. Typing two double quotation marks with no space between them assigns this field value. ________________
8. Use this format code to convert all text in the field to uppercase. ________________
9. This placeholder in a custom numeric format instructs Access to display a 0 if the position is not used. ________________
10. Type this entry in the *Format* property box of a Date/Time data type field to display dates beginning with the day of the week abbreviated, followed by the month as two digits, the day of the month as two digits, and the year as two digits, with all sections separated with hyphen characters. ________________
11. Type this entry in the *Input Mask* property box to require a three-digit identification number to be entered with the pound symbol (#) used as the placeholder. ________________
12. Rich text formatting is enabled for a Long Text data type field by changing this property option to *Rich Text*. ________________
13. For a Long Text data type field with the Append Only property active, right-click in a record and then click this option at the shortcut menu to display a dialog box with the history of the text changes made to the field. ________________
14. Create a field with this data type to store a file with the record. ________________
15. Add a file to the record by double-clicking this object in the record in Datasheet view. ________________

Skills Check Assess Your Performance

Assessment 1

CREATE A NEW DATABASE

1. Create a new blank database named **AL2-C1-BenchmarkGolf.accdb**.
2. Create the tables shown in Figure 1.6 to store membership records for the Benchmark Golf and Country Club. Be sure to set the primary key and assign data types and field sizes.
3. Close any tables that have been left open.

Figure 1.6 Assessment 1

Members		
*MemberID	Short Text	3
FName	Short Text	20
LName	Short Text	30
Street	Short Text	35
City	Short Text	25
State	Short Text	2
ZIP	Short Text	10
HPhone	Short Text	14
CPhone	Short Text	14
BirthDate	Date/Time	
Category	Short Text	10
FamilyMem	Yes/No	

FamilyMembers		
*FamilyMemID	Short Text	3
MemberID	Short Text	3
FName	Short Text	20
LName	Short Text	30
BirthDate	Date/Time	
SocialMem	Yes/No	

MemberTypes		
*Category	Short Text	10
AnnualFee	Currency	
MonthlyFee	Currency	
Restrictions	Long Text	

Assessment 2

ADD CAPTIONS AND DISALLOW BLANK VALUES

1. With **AL2-C1-BenchmarkGolf.accdb** open, create captions for the fields as follows:

Members Table

Field Name	Caption
MemberID	**ID Number**
FName	**First Name**
LName	**Last Name**
Street	**Street Address**
ZIP	**ZIP Code**
HPhone	**Home Phone**
CPhone	**Cell Phone**
BirthDate	**Birth Date**
FamilyMem	**Family Member?**

FamilyMembers Table

Field Name	Caption
FamilyMemID	Family ID Number
MemberID	Member ID Number
FName	First Name
LName	Last Name
BirthDate	Birth Date
SocialMem	Social Member?

MemberTypes Table

Field Name	Caption
AnnualFee	Annual Fee
MonthlyFee	Monthly Fee

2. Make the *ZIP* field a required field and disallow zero-length strings.
3. Save and then close all tables.

Assessment 3

CREATE CUSTOM FORMATS AND INPUT MASKS

1. With **AL2-C1-BenchmarkGolf.accdb** open, create the following custom formats:
   a. Display the state text in uppercase characters.
   b. Display all birth dates with the month in abbreviated form, followed by the day of the month as two digits and the year as four digits. Use single spaces to separate the sections.
   c. Display the monthly fee in blue with two places past the decimal point values. The decimal values will show zeros if a zero is entered.
2. Create the following custom input masks:
   a. In the *MemberID* field in the Members table and the *FamilyMemID* field in the FamilyMembers table, require all three digits, display the underscore character as the placeholder, and do not store the display characters.
   b. Require the *ZIP* field in the Members table to be entered in the pattern of five required digits followed by a hyphen and then four required digits. Display the pound symbol (#) as the placeholder and do not store the display characters.
   c. Use the Input Mask Wizard to create the standard input mask for the two telephone fields in the Members table. Do not store the display characters. When the mask is finished, edit the codes in the property to make the three characters in the area code required digits, as opposed to the optional digits that the wizard created.
   d. Create an input mask for both *BirthDate* fields that will match the custom format pattern created in Step 1b, except include hyphens between the sections. Store the display characters in the field and display the underscore character as the placeholder. For example, the custom format should display the date as *May 03 1964* in the datasheet. ***Hints: You do not need to worry about the first letter of the month being uppercase, since the Format property will automatically use proper capitalization. Also, once you have the input mask created correctly, you can copy and paste the entry to the other* BirthDate *field.***
3. Save and then close all tables.

Assessment

4 ADD RECORDS

SNAP Grade It

1. With **AL2-C1-BenchmarkGolf.accdb** open, add the following records. Type the text in the *State* field as shown to test your format code. As you type the zip codes, telephone numbers, and dates, be careful to watch the placeholders and enter data in the required pattern.

Members Table

Field	Record 1	Record 2
ID Number	100	110
First Name	Hilary	Jesse
Last Name	Sampson	Reynolds
Street Address	300 South Saguaro Drive	7229 E University Drive
City	Apache Junction	Mesa
State	Az	Az
ZIP Code	85220 4956	85207 6501
Home Phone	602 555 1587	480 555 1385
Cell Phone	602 555 3496	480 555 1699
Birth Date	May 03 1964	Oct 15 1977
Category	Gold	Silver
Family Member?	Yes	No

FamilyMembers Table

Field	Record 1	Record 2
Family ID Number	610	611
Member ID Number	100	100
First Name	Kayla	Roy
Last Name	Sampson	Sampson
Birth Date	Jul 18 1996	Mar 16 1994
Social Member?	No	No

MemberTypes Table

Field	Record 1	Record 2	Record 3
Category	Gold	Silver	Bronze
Annual Fee	2500	1775	1550
Monthly Fee	60	52	35
Restrictions	Unlimited weekdays and weekends; weekend ballot first	Unlimited weekdays; weekend ballot second	Unlimited weekdays; weekends after 3 P.M.

2. Adjust all column widths to best fit and print each table in landscape orientation. ***Note: The Members table will print on 2 pages.***
3. Close any tables that have been left open, saving layout changes.
4. Close **AL2-C1-BenchmarkGolf.accdb**.

Visual Benchmark Demonstrate Your Proficiency

CREATE A NEW DATABASE

1. Create a new blank database named **AL2-C1-PawsParadise.accdb**.
2. Create the tables shown in the database diagram in Figure 1.7, including setting the primary key and assigning data types and field sizes. The tables are to be used by Paws Paradise Boarding Inc. to store the records of dog owners, dogs, and kennel categories.
3. Analyze the datasheets shown in Figure 1.8 and make the necessary changes to field properties. The datasheets show captions, default values, custom formats, and rich text formatting in the records. Use the following information to set other field properties not visible in the datasheet:
   a. Make *ZIP* a required field and then use the Input Mask Wizard to create the default input mask for a zip code. Store the display characters.
   b. Use the Input Mask Wizard to create the default input mask for both telephone fields and then edit the masks to change the area code to three required digits. Store the display characters.
4. Add the records shown in the datasheets to the tables.
5. Adjust all column widths to best fit and print each table in landscape orientation.
6. Save and then close all tables.
7. Close the **AL2-C1-PawsParadise.accdb** database.

Figure 1.7 Visual Benchmark Database Diagram

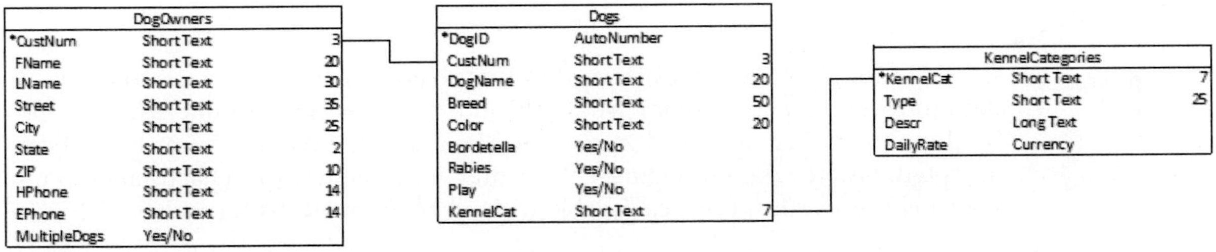

DogOwners
*CustNum ShortText 3
FName ShortText 20
LName ShortText 30
Street ShortText 35
City ShortText 25
State ShortText 2
ZIP ShortText 10
HPhone ShortText 14
EPhone ShortText 14
MultipleDogs Yes/No
Dogs
*DogID AutoNumber
CustNum ShortText 3
DogName ShortText 20
Breed ShortText 50
Color ShortText 20
Bordetella Yes/No
Rabies Yes/No
Play Yes/No
KennelCat ShortText 7
KennelCategories
*KennelCat Short Text 7
Type Short Text 25
Descr Long Text
DailyRate Currency

Figure 1.8 Visual Benchmark Datasheets

DogOwners

Customer Number	First Name	Last Name	Street Address	City	State	ZIP Code	Home Telephone	Emergency Telephone	Multiple Dogs?
100	Shawn	Jenkins	101 Davis Street	Bradford	PA	16701-	(814) 555-8446	(814) 555-7469	☑
110	Valerie	McTague	12 Bishop Street	Bradford	PA	16701-	(814) 555-3456	(814) 555-1495	☐
115	Glen	Waters	35 Vista Avenue	Bradford	PA	16701-2760	(814) 555-7496	(814) 555-6124	☐

Dogs

Dog ID	Customer Number	Dog's Name	Breed	Color	Bordetella Vaccine Checked?	Rabies Vaccine Checked?	Play with other dogs?	Kennel Category
1	100	Abby	Labrador Retriever	Black	☑	☑	☑	VIP
2	100	Winnie	Cocker Spaniel	Buff	☑	☑	☑	VIP
3	110	Chloe	Poodle	White	☑	☑	☐	Deluxe
4	115	Barney	Pug	Black	☐	☐	☐	InOut
(New)					☑	☑	☑	

KennelCategories

Kennel Category	Kennel Type	Description	Daily Rate
DayCare	Day Care Boarding	Grassy play area where dogs can play with staff and other dogs throughout the day.	$16.50
Deluxe	Deluxe Suite	Designed for ***geriatric or special needs dogs***. Raised beds and quiet location.	$29.50
InOut	Indoor/Outdoor Suite	Indoor kennel attached to covered outdoor patio.	$25.50
VIP	V.I.P. Suite	***Indoor upgraded kennel*** attached to covered outdoor patio and grass play area.	$38.50

Case Study Apply Your Skills

Part 1

You work as an intern at Bestar Plumbing Service. Examine the customer invoice shown in Figure 1.9. This is a typical invoice for which the owner would like to start using an Access database. Design tables for the data using the invoice and the following additional information from the owner:

- Customer numbers are assigned using the first three letters of the customer's last name (all uppercase) followed by a hyphen character and three digits.
- Some invoices include plumbing parts with a labor charge. Individual parts are not itemized on the customer invoice. The service technician enters all parts used on a single line on the invoice.
- Bestar has two labor rates: $41.75 for a senior service technician and $28.00 for an apprentice technician.

Using Microsoft Word, create a document that diagrams the tables, including table names, field names, data types, and field sizes. Use an asterisk to denote the primary key field in each table. Ask your instructor for the required format of the diagram in text boxes or tables in Word or if a handwritten diagram is acceptable. Save the Word document and name it **AL2-C1-CS-P1-BestarPlumbing**. Save, print, and close **AL2-C1-CS-P1-BestarPlumbing.docx**.

Part 2

Using the table diagram created in Part 1, create a new database named **AL2-C1-BestarPlumbing.accdb** and then create the tables and set the primary key for each table.

Part 3

Consider the field properties learned in this chapter that can be used to ensure data integrity and consistency. Modify field properties in your tables that can be used to restrict data accepted into the field and display the data after it has been accepted. Use the data in Figure 1.9 to enter a sample record in each table to test your field properties. Print each table with all column widths set to best fit.

Figure 1.9 Case Study, Part 1

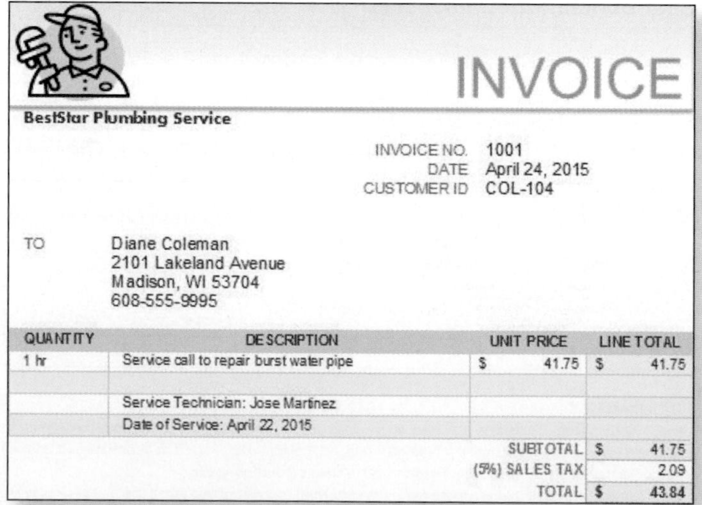

INVOICE

BestStar Plumbing Service

INVOICE NO. 1001
DATE April 24, 2015
CUSTOMER ID COL-104

TO Diane Coleman
2101 Lakeland Avenue
Madison, WI 53704
608-555-9995

QUANTITY	DESCRIPTION	UNIT PRICE	LINE TOTAL
1 hr	Service call to repair burst water pipe	$ 41.75	$ 41.75
	Service Technician: Jose Martinez		
	Date of Service: April 22, 2015		
		SUBTOTAL	$ 41.75
		(5%) SALES TAX	2.09
		TOTAL	$ 43.84

MICROSOFT®

ACCESS®

Building Relationships and Lookup Fields

PERFORMANCE OBJECTIVES

Upon successful completion of Chapter 2, you will be able to:

- **Create and edit relationships between tables, including one-to-many, one-to-one, and many-to-many relationships**
- **Define a table with a multiple-field primary key**
- **Create and modify a lookup field to populate records with data from another table**
- **Create a lookup field that allows having multiple values in records**
- **Create single-field and multiple-field indexes**
- **Define the term *normalization***
- **Determine if a table is in first, second, or third normal form**

Tutorials

2.1 Creating a One-to-Many Relationship

2.2 Creating a Second One-to-Many Relationship

2.3 Editing Relationship Options

2.4 Establishing a Many-to-Many Relationship

2.5 Defining a Multiple-Field Primary Key

2.6 Creating a Field to Look Up Values in Another Table

2.7 Creating a Field that Allows Multiple Values

2.8 Creating Indexes

2.9 Normalizing a Database

Once table design has been completed, establishing relationships and relationship options between tables involves analyzing the type of relationship that exists between two tables. Some database designers draw a relationship diagram to depict the primary table and the related table's matching record frequency. In this chapter, you will create and edit relationships and lookup fields, multiple-field primary keys, multiple-value fields, and indexes. The concept of database normalization and three forms of normalization are introduced to complete the examination of database design fundamentals. Model answers for this chapter's projects appear on the following page.

AL2C2

Note: Before beginning the projects, copy to your storage medium the AL2C2 subfolder from the AL2 folder on the CD that accompanies this textbook and then make AL2C2 the active folder.

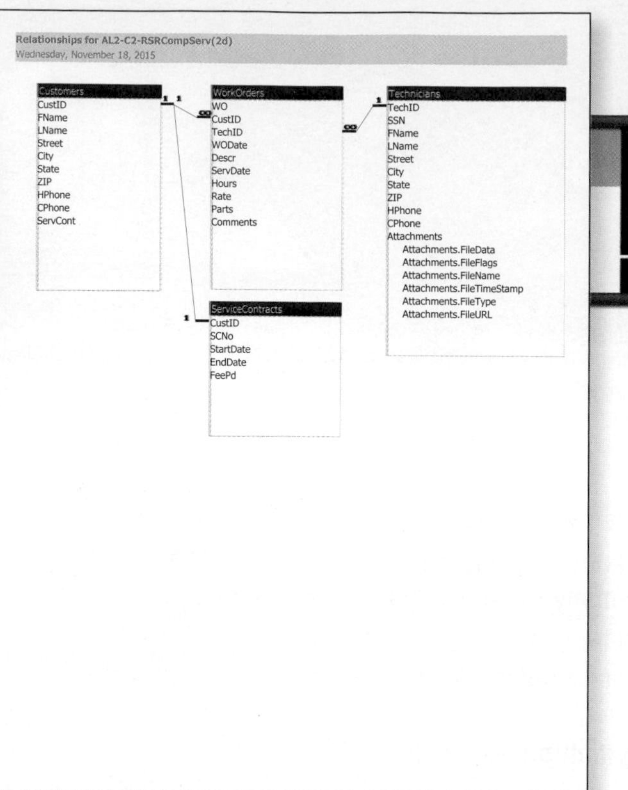

Project 1 Create and Edit Relationships

Project 1d, Relationships Report

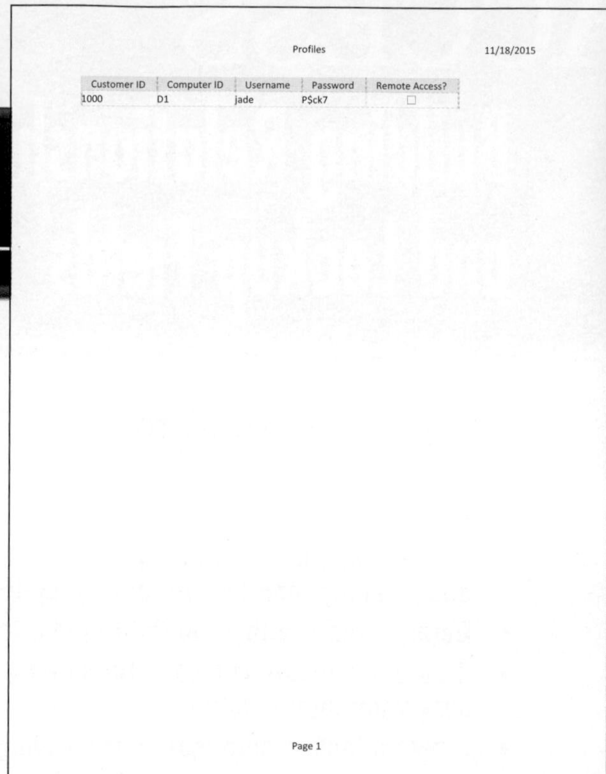

Profiles 11/18/2015

Customer ID	Computer ID	Username	Password	Remote Access?
1000	D1	jade	P$ck7	☐

Page 1

Project 2 Create a Table with a Multiple-Field Primary Key and Lookup Fields

Project 2c, Profiles Datasheet

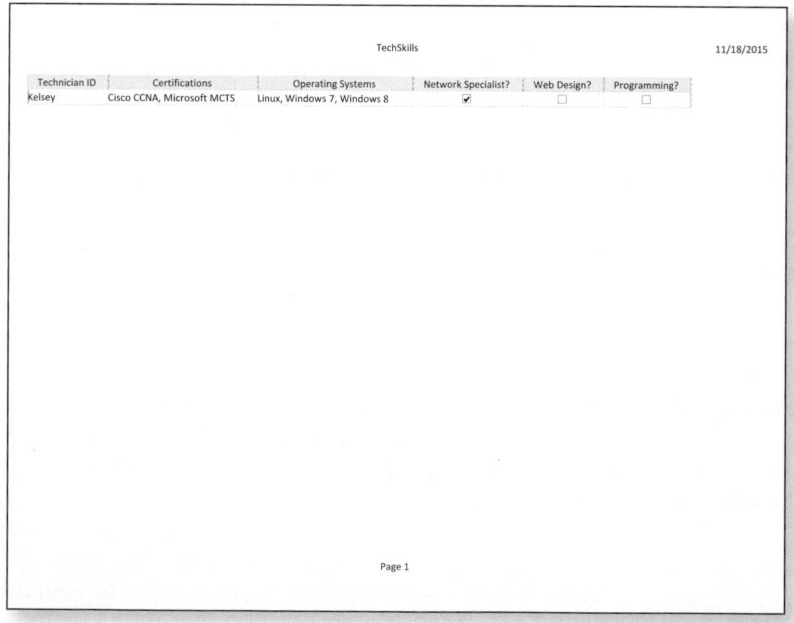

TechSkills 11/18/2015

Technician ID	Certifications	Operating Systems	Network Specialist?	Web Design?	Programming?
Kelsey	Cisco CCNA, Microsoft MCTS	Linux, Windows 7, Windows 8	☑	☐	☐

Page 1

Project 2e, TechSkills Table

Project 1 Create and Edit Relationships 4 Parts

You will create relationships and edit relationship options for the tables designed to track work orders for RSR Computer Services.

Building Relationships

After you determine which tables to relate to one another, the next step in designing your database is to examine the types of relationships that exist between the tables. A relationship is based on an association between two tables. For example, in the database created in Chapter 1 for RSR Computer Services, there is an association between the Customers table and the WorkOrders table. A customer is associated with all of his or her work orders involving computer maintenance requests, and each work order is associated with the individual customer for which the service was requested.

Not sure if two tables should be related? Consider if you will need to extract data from both tables in the same query, form, or report. If yes, then the tables should be joined in a relationship.

When building relationships, consider the associations between tables and how these associations affect the data that will be entered into the tables. In the database diagram presented in Chapter 1, relationships were shown with lines connecting the common field name between tables. In this chapter, you consider the type of relationship that should exist between the tables and the relationship options you want to use to place restrictions on data entry. Access provides for three types of relationships: one-to-many, one-to-one, and many-to-many. In Access Level 1, Chapter 2, you learned about one-to-many and one-to-one relationships. You will begin by reviewing these two relationship types before you learn how to establish a many-to-many relationship.

Relationships

Establishing a One-to-Many Relationship

In the computer service database in Chapter 1, the relationship between the Customers table and the WorkOrders table exists because a work order involves computer maintenance for a specific customer. The customer is identified by the customer number stored in the Customers table. In the Customers table, only one record exists per customer. In the WorkOrders table, the same customer number can be associated with several work orders. This means the relationship between the Customers table and WorkOrders table is a ***one-to-many relationship***. One-to-many relationships are the most common type of relationship created in Access.

A common field is needed to join the Customers table and WorkOrders table, so the *CustID* field is included in both tables. In the Customers table, *CustID* is the primary key field because it contains a unique identification number for each customer. In the WorkOrders table, *CustID* cannot be the primary key, because the same customer can be associated with several computer service work orders. In the WorkOrders table, *CustID* is the ***foreign key***. A foreign key is a field included in a table for the purpose of creating a relationship to a field that is a primary key in another table. The Customers-to-WorkOrders one-to-many relationship can be illustrated using a diagram similar to the one shown in Figure 2.1 on the next page.

Quick Steps

Create a One-to-Many Relationship

1. Click DATABASE TOOLS tab.
2. Click Relationships button.
3. Add tables from Show Table dialog box.
4. Close Show Table dialog box.
5. Drag primary key field name from primary table to foreign key field name in related table.
6. Click Create button.

Figure 2.1 One-to-Many Relationship between Customers Table and WorkOrders Table

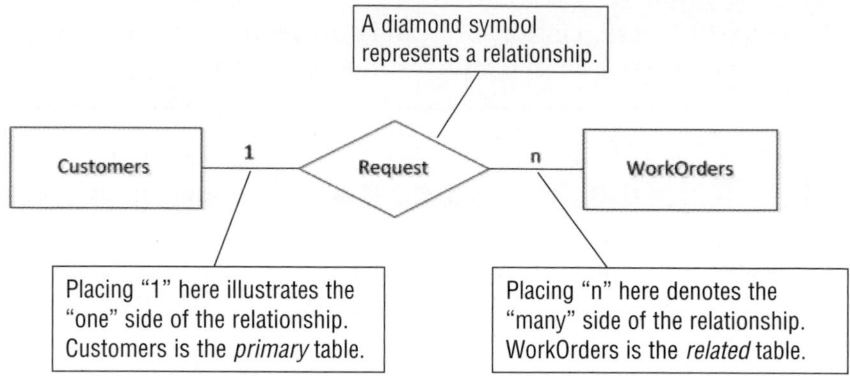

When diagramming a database, designers may choose to show relationships in a separate illustration. In the diagram shown in Figure 2.1, table names are displayed in rectangles with lines drawn to a diamond symbol, which represents a relationship. Inside the diamond, a word (usually a verb) describes the action that relates the two tables. For example, in the relationship shown in Figure 2.1, the word *Request* is used to show that "Customers *Request* WorkOrders." On the join line, a *1* is placed next to the table that represents the primary table, or the "one" side of the relationship, and an *n* is placed next to the related table, or the "many" side of the relationship.

Project 1a Creating a One-to-Many Relationship

Part 1 of 4

1. Open **AL2-C2-RSRCompServ.accdb**. This database has the same structure as the database created in Chapter 1. However, additional field properties have been defined and several records have been added to each table to provide data with which to test relationships and lookup fields.
2. If the security warning appears in the message bar to indicate that some active content has been disabled, click the Enable Content button.
3. Create a one-to-many relationship between the Customers table and WorkOrders table by completing the following steps:
   a. Click the DATABASE TOOLS tab.
   b. Click the Relationships button in the Relationships group.
   c. At the Show Table dialog box with the Tables tab active and *Customers* selected in the list box, hold down the Ctrl key, click *WorkOrders*, and then click the Add button.
   d. Click the Close button to close the Show Table dialog box.
   e. Resize each table's field list box by dragging the bottom border of each box until all of the field names are shown.

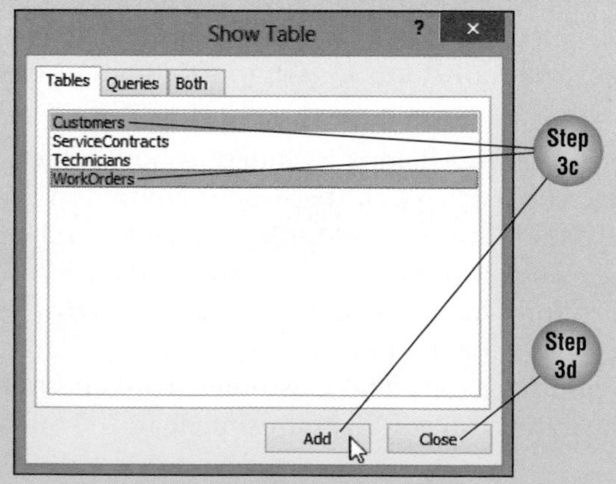

f. Drag the *CustID* field from the Customers table field list box to the *CustID* field in the WorkOrders table field list box. Be careful to drag the common field name from the primary table (Customers) to the related table (WorkOrders) and not vice versa.

g. At the Edit Relationships dialog box, notice that *One-To-Many* appears in the *Relationship Type* section. Access detected this type of relationship because the field used to join the tables is a primary key in only one of the tables. Establishing this relationship makes *CustID* a foreign key in the WorkOrders table. Always check that the correct table and field names are shown in the *Table/Query* and *Related Table/Query* option boxes. If the table name and/or the common field name is not shown correctly, click the Cancel button. Errors can occur if you drag the mouse starting or ending at the wrong table or field. If this happens, return to Step 3f and try again.

h. Click the Create button.

Bottom border of each table field list box is resized to show all field names at Step 3e.

4. Click the Close button in the Relationships group on the RELATIONSHIP TOOLS DESIGN tab.
5. Click Yes at the message box asking if you want to save changes to the layout of the Relationships window.

Another one-to-many relationship exists between the Technicians table and the WorkOrders table. A technician is associated with all of the work orders that he or she has been assigned and a work order is associated with the technician that carried out the service request. The Technicians-to-WorkOrders relationship diagram is shown in Figure 2.2.

Figure 2.2 One-to-Many Relationship between Technicians Table and WorkOrders Table

Project 1b Creating a Second One-to-Many Relationship Part 2 of 4

1. With **AL2-C2-RSRCompServ.accdb** open, display the Relationships window by clicking the DATABASE TOOLS tab and then clicking the Relationships button in the Relationships group.
2. Click the Show Table button in the Relationships group on the RELATIONSHIP TOOLS DESIGN tab.
3. Double-click *Technicians* in the list box at the Show Table dialog box with the Tables tab selected. Move the Show Table dialog box if necessary to verify the Technicians table has been added and then click the Close button.
4. Drag the bottom border and right border of the Technicians table field list box until all of the field names are fully visible.
5. Drag the *TechID* field from the Technicians table field list box to the *TechID* field in the WorkOrders table field list box.
6. Check that the correct table and field names appear in the *Table/Query* and *Related Table/Query* option boxes. If necessary, click Cancel and repeat Step 5.
7. Click the Create button at the Edit Relationships dialog box.
8. Click the Close button in the Relationships group on the RELATIONSHIP TOOLS DESIGN tab.
9. Click Yes at the message box asking if you want to save changes to the layout of the Relationships window.

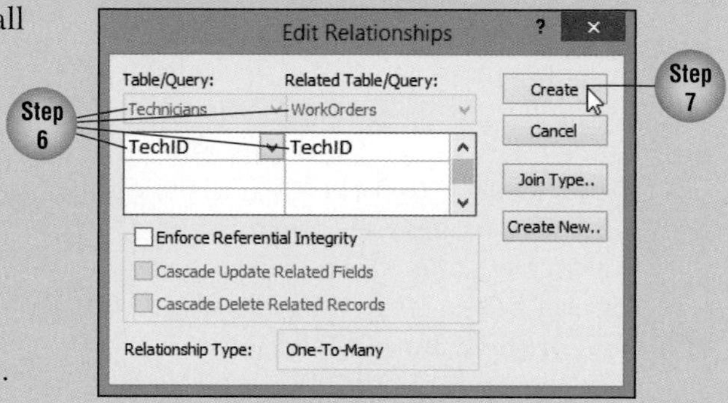

This join line represents the one-to-many relationship created between Technicians and WorkOrders in Steps 1–7.

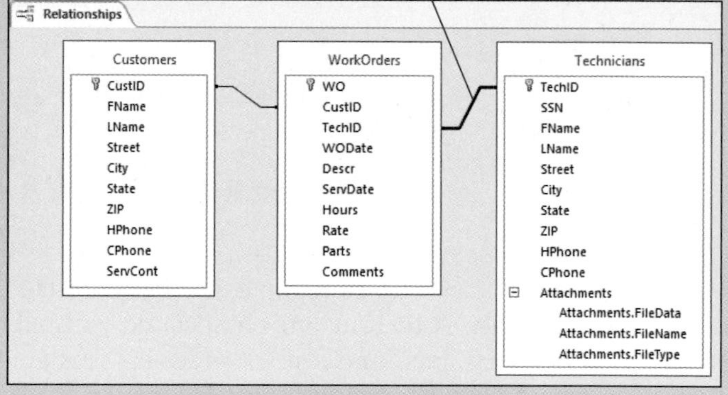

Quick Steps

Edit a Relationship
1. Click DATABASE TOOLS tab.
2. Click Relationships button.
3. Click black join line between tables.
4. Click Edit Relationships button.
5. Select desired options.
6. Click OK.

Edit Relationships

Editing Relationship Options

At the Edit Relationships dialog box, shown in Figure 2.3, you can elect to turn on relationship options and/or specify the type of join to create. To open the Edit Relationships dialog box, click the DATABASE TOOLS tab, click the Relationships button, click the black join line for the relationship you wish to edit, and then click the Edit Relationships button.

Once the Edit Relationships dialog box is open, you can select the desired options. The *Cascade Update Related Fields* and *Cascade Delete Related Records* options do not become active unless referential integrity is turned on, which you can do by clicking the *Enforce Referential Integrity* check box to insert a check mark.

Figure 2.3 Edit Relationships Dialog Box

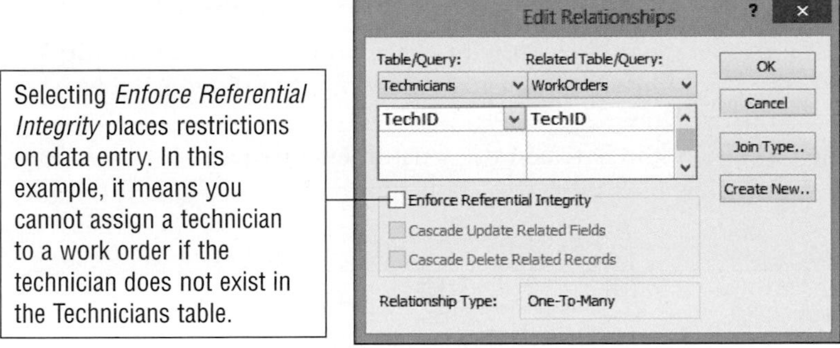

Activating referential integrity in a one-to-many relationship is a good way of ensuring that orphan records do not occur. An ***orphan record*** is a record in a related table for which no "parent" record exists in the primary table. Assigning a technician to a work order in the WorkOrders table with no matching technician record in the Technicians table results in an orphan record in the WorkOrders table. Once referential integrity has been turned on, Access checks for the existence of a matching record in the primary table as each new record is added to the related table. If no match is found, Access does not allow the record to be saved.

To enable referential integrity, the primary key and foreign key fields must be the same data type. If you receive an error message when attempting to enforce referential integrity, open each table in Design view and compare the data types for the fields used to join the tables.

For example, suppose that referential integrity has not been activated and you make a typing mistake that causes you to accidentally enter an unassigned *TechID* to a work order. If the customer later has a question for the technician about the service, you will not know which technician to contact. However, if referential integrity is activated before the record is saved, Access checks the Technicians table and verifies that the *TechID* exists. If it does not exist, the error message shown in Figure 2.4 will display. Click OK at the message and then enter a *TechID* that exists in the Technicians table.

When you click in the *Enforce Referential Integrity* check box to insert a check mark, the *Cascade Update Related Fields* and *Cascade Delete Related Records* check boxes become available. When you insert a check mark in the *Cascade Update Related Fields* check box, Access automatically updates all occurrences of the same data in the foreign key field in the related table when a change is made to the primary key field in the primary table. When you insert a check mark in the *Cascade Delete Related Records* check box, it means that if a record is deleted from the primary table for which related records exist in the related table, Access automatically deletes the related records.

You will learn about join types and situations in which changing the join type is warranted in Chapter 3.

Figure 2.4 Referential Integrity Error Message

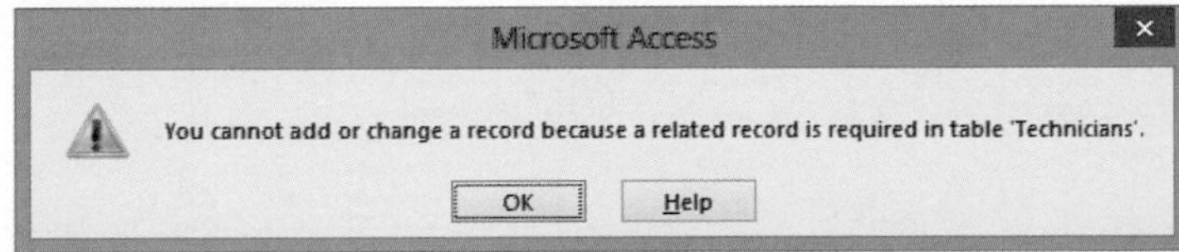

Project 1c Editing Relationships

Part 3 of 4

1. With **AL2-C2-RSRCompServ.accdb** open, edit the one-to-many relationship between the Customers table and the WorkOrders table by completing the following steps:
   a. Open the Relationships window.
   b. Click to select the black join line between the Customers table and WorkOrders table.
   c. Click the Edit Relationships button in the Tools group on the RELATIONSHIP TOOLS DESIGN tab.

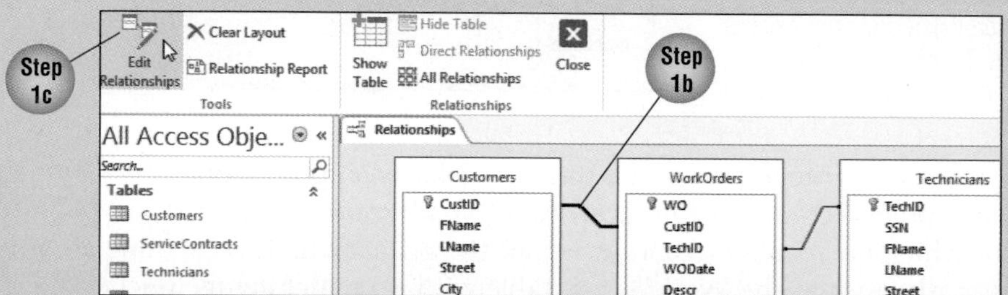

   d. At the Edit Relationships dialog box, click the *Enforce Referential Integrity* check box, the *Cascade Update Related Fields* check box, and the *Cascade Delete Related Records* check box to insert check marks.
   e. Click OK at the Edit Relationships dialog box. The *1* at the primary table (the "one") side of the join line and the infinity symbol (∞) at the related table (the "many" side) of the join line indicate referential integrity has been activated.

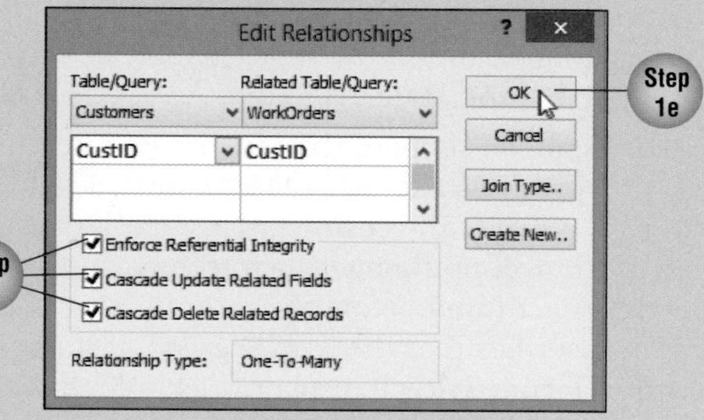

2. Edit the one-to-many relationship between the Technicians table and the WorkOrders table by completing the following steps:
   a. Double-click the black join line between the Technicians table and the WorkOrders table in the Relationships window. (You can also right-click the join line and then click *Edit Relationship* at the shortcut menu.)
   b. At the Edit Relationships dialog box, click to insert check marks in the *Enforce Referential Integrity* check box, the *Cascade Update Related Fields* check box, and the *Cascade Delete Related Records* check box.
   c. Click OK.

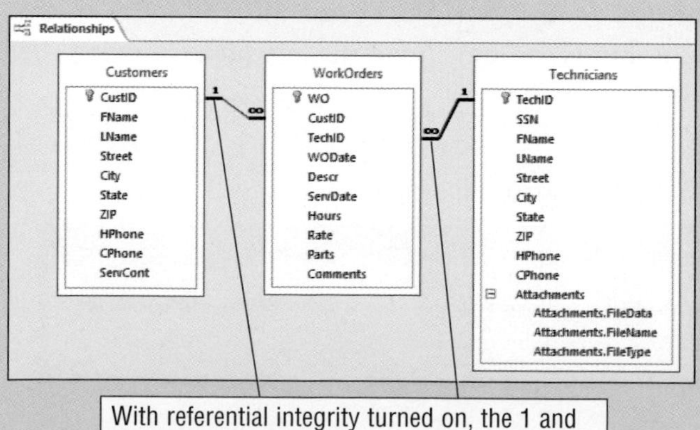

With referential integrity turned on, the 1 and the infinity symbol (∞) display on the join lines.

3. Close the Relationships window.

Establishing a One-to-One Relationship

In the database for RSR Computer Services, a table is used to store service contract information for each customer. This table, named *ServiceContracts*, is associated with the Customers table. Only one record exists for a customer in the Customers table and each customer subscribes to only one service contract in the ServiceContracts table. This means that the two tables have a one-to-one relationship, as shown in Figure 2.5.

When a new customer is added to the database, his or her name and contact information are entered into the Customers table and then the service contract information (including start date, end date, and fee paid) is entered into the ServiceContracts table. When referential integrity is enforced, the Customers table is placed in the *Table/Query* option box and the ServiceContracts table is placed in the *Related Table/Query* option box; otherwise, when you go to enter data an error message will appear, as shown in Figure 2.4 on page 41. To print the relationship, first create the Relationship Report by clicking the relationship report button in the Tools group. When Access displays the report in Print Preview, click the Print button on the PRINT PREVIEW tab.

Quick Steps

Create a One-to-One Relationship

1. Click DATABASE TOOLS tab.
2. Click Relationships button.
3. Add tables from Show Table dialog box.
4. Close Show Table dialog box.
5. Drag primary key field name from primary table to primary key field name in related table.
6. Select desired relationship options.
7. Click Create button.

Relationship Report

Figure 2.5 One-to-One Relationship between Customers Table and ServiceContracts Table

Project 1d **Creating a One-to-One Relationship** **Part 4 of 4**

1. With **AL2-C2-RSRCompServ.accdb** open, first create a one-to-one relationship between the Customers table and the ServiceContracts table by completing the following steps:
   a. Open the Relationships window.
   b. Click the Show Table button in the Relationships group.
   c. Double-click *ServiceContracts* in the Tables list box and then click the Close button.
   d. Drag the *CustID* field from the Customers table field list box to the *CustID* field in the ServiceContracts table field list box.
   e. At the Edit Relationships dialog box, check that the correct table and field names appear in the *Table/Query* and *Related Table/Query* option boxes. If necessary, click Cancel and repeat Step 1d.
   f. Notice that *One-To-One* appears in the *Relationship Type* section. Access detected this type of relationship because the field used to join the tables is a primary key in both tables.
   g. Click the *Enforce Referential Integrity* check box, *Cascade Update Related Fields* check box, and *Cascade Delete Related Records* check box to insert check marks.
   h. Click the Create button.

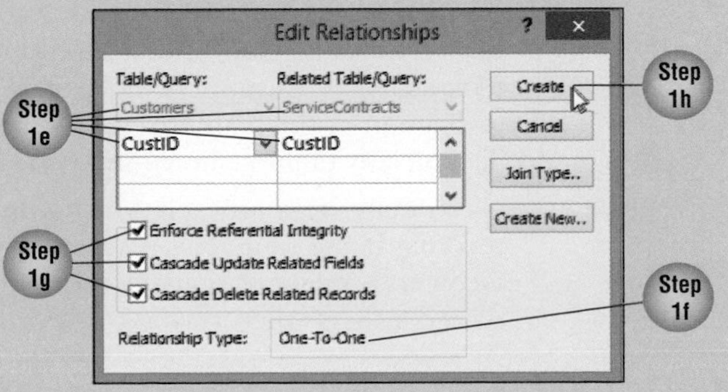

2. Drag the Title bar of the ServiceContracts table field list box to the approximate location shown in the Relationships window below. By moving the table field list box, you are better able to view the join line and the *1* at each end of the join line between Customers and ServiceContracts.

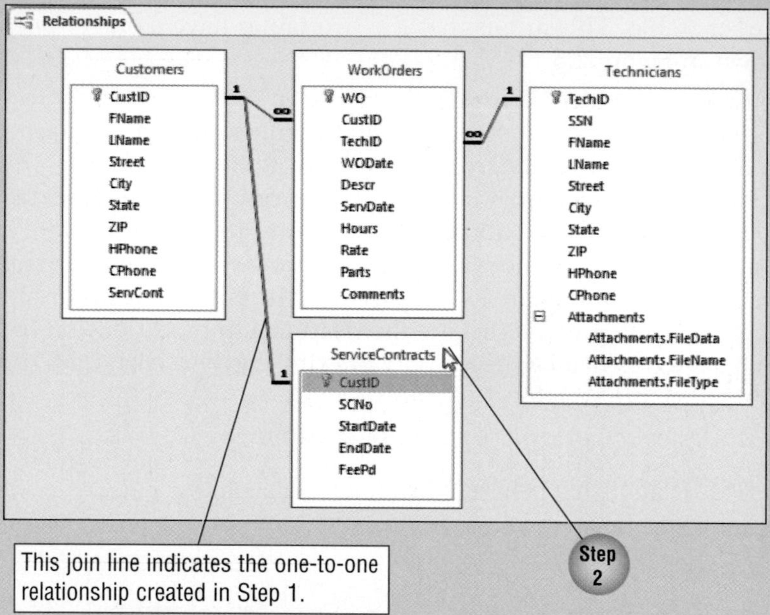

3. Create a relationships report by clicking the Relationship Report button in the Tools group on the RELATIONSHIP TOOLS DESIGN tab.
4. Access displays the report in Print Preview. Click the Print button in the Print group on the PRINT PREVIEW tab and then click OK at the Print dialog box.
5. Close the relationships report for AL2-C2-RSRCompServ.accdb. Click Yes to save the report and click OK to accept the default name at the Save As dialog box.
6. Close the Relationships window.

Establishing a Many-to-Many Relationship

Consider the association between the Customers table and the Technicians table in the RSR Computer Services database. Over time, any individual customer can have computer service work done by many different technicians and any individual technician can perform computer service work at many different customer locations. In other words, a record in the Customers table can be matched to many records in the Technicians table and a record in the Technicians table can be matched to many records in the Customers table. This is an example of a many-to-many relationship. A diagram of the many-to-many relationship between the Customers table and Technicians table is shown in Figure 2.6.

A many-to-many relationship is problematic because it creates duplicate records. If the same customer number is associated with many technicians and vice versa, many duplicates occur in the two tables and Access may experience data conflicts when trying to identify a unique record. To resolve the duplication

Figure 2.6 Many-to-Many Relationship between the Customers Table and Technicians Table

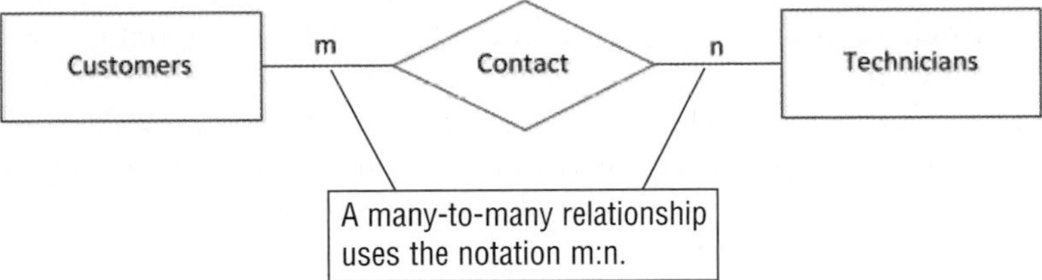

and create unique entries, a third table is used to associate, or link, the many-to-many tables. The third table is called a ***junction table***, and contains the primary key field from each table in the many-to-many relationship as its foreign keys. Using the junction table, two one-to-many relationships are created.

In the Relationships window in Figure 2.7, the WorkOrders table is the junction table. Notice that the WorkOrders table contains two foreign keys: *CustID*, which is the primary key in the Customers table, and *TechID*, which is the primary key in the Technicians table. One-to-many relationships exist between the Customers and WorkOrders tables and the Technicians and WorkOrders tables. These two one-to-many relationships create a many-to-many relationship between the Customers and Technicians tables.

Figure 2.7 Relationships Window Showing a Many-to-Many Relationship between the Customers Table and Technicians Table

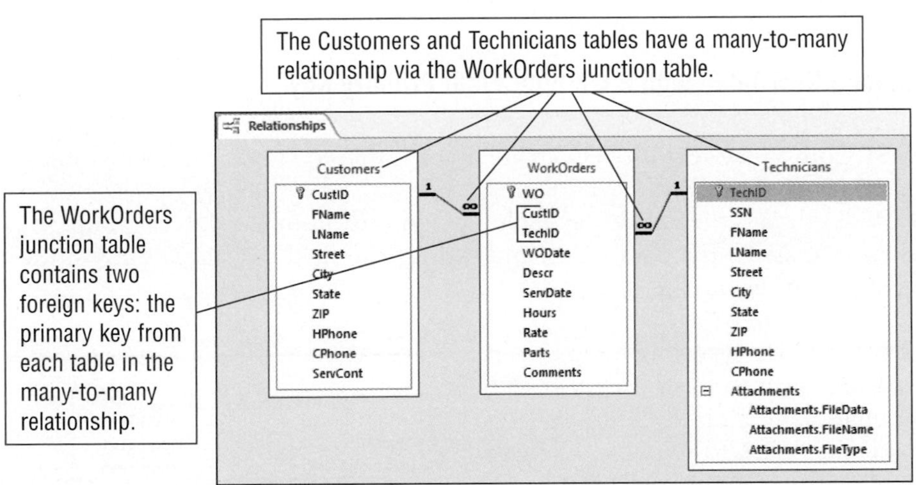

Project 2 Create a Table with a Multiple-Field Primary Key and Lookup Fields — 5 Parts

You will create a new table that requires two fields to uniquely identify each record. To restrict data entry in the table, you will create fields that display a list from which the user selects the field value(s).

Defining a Multiple-Field Primary Key

Quick Steps

Define a Multiple-Field Primary Key

1. Open table in Design view.
2. Select first field.
3. Hold down Shift key (adjacent row) or Ctrl key (nonadjacent row) and select second field.
4. Click Primary Key button.
5. Save table.

Primary Key

HINT

Delete a primary key by opening the table in Design view, activating the primary key field, and then clicking the Primary Key button.

In most tables, one field is designated as the primary key. However, in some situations, a single field may not be guaranteed to hold unique data. Look at the fields in the table shown in Figure 2.8. This is a new table you will create in the RSR Computer Services database to store computer profiles for RSR customers. The company stores the profiles as a service to their clients in case they forget their login information. Technicians can also access the profile data when troubleshooting at a customer's site.

A customer may have more than one computer in his or her home or office and each computer can have a different profile for each username. The *CustID* field will not serve as the primary key field if the customer has more than one record in the Profiles table. However, a combination of the three fields *CustID, CompID,* and *Username* will uniquely identify each record. In this table, you will define all three fields as primary keys. A primary key that is made up of two or more fields is called a ***composite key***.

Figure 2.8 Project 2a Profiles Table

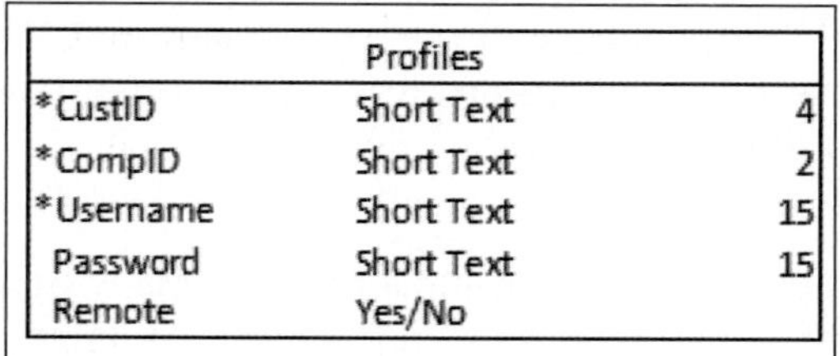

Profiles		
*CustID	Short Text	4
*CompID	Short Text	2
*Username	Short Text	15
Password	Short Text	15
Remote	Yes/No	

Project 2a Creating a New Table with a Multiple-Field Primary Key — Part 1 of 5

1. With **AL2-C2-RSRCompServ.accdb** open, create a new table to store customer profiles by completing the following steps:
   a. Click the CREATE tab and then click the Table Design button in the Tables group.
   b. Type the field names, assign the data types, and change the field sizes according to the data structure shown in Figure 2.8.
2. Hover the mouse pointer over the field selector bar (the blank column to the left of the field names) next to *CustID* until the pointer changes to a black right-pointing arrow and then click to select the field.
3. Hold down the Shift key and then click in the field selector bar next to *Username*. The three adjacent fields *CustID*, *CompID*, and *Username* are now selected.

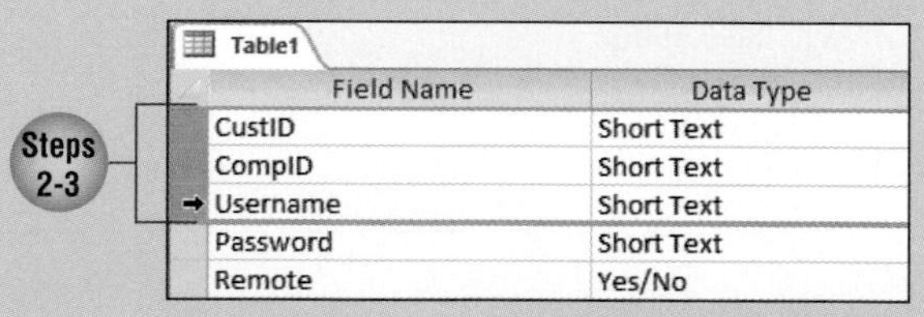

4. Click the Primary Key button in the Tools group on the TABLE TOOLS DESIGN tab. Access displays the primary key icon next to each field name.
5. Click in any data type field to deselect the first three rows.
6. Save the table and name it *Profiles*.
7. Close the table.

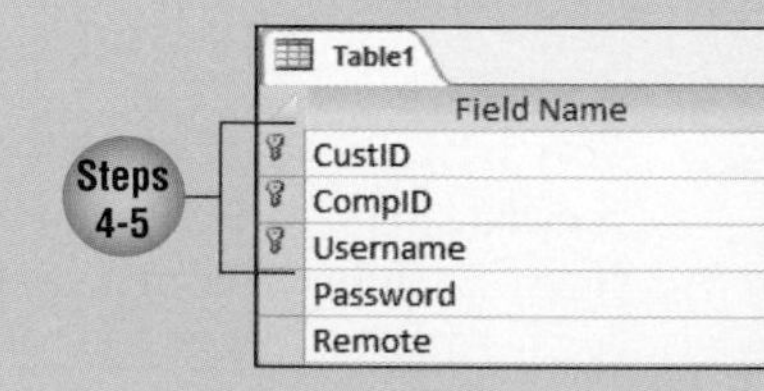

Creating a Field to Look Up Values in Another Table

In Level 1, Chapter 4, you learned how to use the Lookup Wizard to create a lookup field. You can also use the Lookup Wizard to create a lookup field in which you display, in the drop-down list, the values found in records from another table. Lookup fields allow the user to enter data by pointing and clicking, rather than by typing the field's entry.

A lookup field that draws its data from a field in another table can be useful in several ways. Data can be restricted to items within the list, which prevents orphan records, data entry errors, and spelling inconsistencies. The lookup field can also provide the user with more information to help him or her select the correct option. For example, suppose that a lookup field requires the user to select a customer's identification number. Looking at a drop-down list of identification numbers is not very helpful; however, if the lookup field displays the identification number as well as the customer's name, the correct entry is easily identifiable. When the user chooses the field entry based on the name, Access automatically enters the correct identification number.

When using the Lookup Wizard to create a lookup field, make sure to do so before you create relationships. If a relationship already exists between the table for the lookup field and the source data table, Access prompts you to delete the relationship before the Lookup Wizard can run.

Quick Steps

Create a Lookup Field to Another Table

1. Open table in Design view.
2. Click in column of lookup field.
3. Click down-pointing arrow.
4. Click *Lookup Wizard.*
5. Click Next.
6. Choose table and click Next.
7. Choose fields to display in column.
8. Click Next.
9. Choose field by which to sort.
10. Click Next.
11. If necessary, expand column widths.
12. Clear *Hide key column* if desired.
13. Click Next.
14. Choose field value to store in table.
15. Click Next.
16. Click Finish.
17. Click Yes.

Project 2b **Creating a Field to Look Up Data in Another Table** **Part 2 of 5**

1. With **AL2-C2-RSRCompServ.accdb** open, open the Profiles table in Design view.
2. Create a lookup field to select and enter a customer's identification number from a list of customers in the Customers table by completing the following steps:
   a. With *CustID* the active field, click in the *Data Type* column, click the down-pointing arrow that appears, and then click *Lookup Wizard* at the drop-down list.
   b. At the first Lookup Wizard dialog box with *I want the lookup field to get the values from another table or query* selected, click Next.

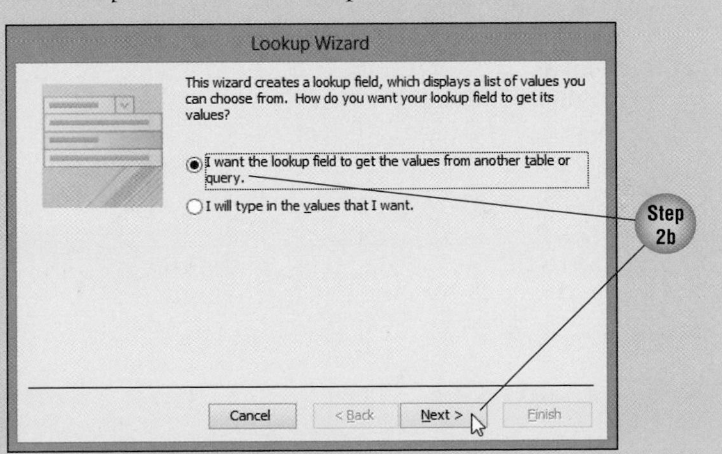

c. At the second Lookup Wizard dialog box with *Table: Customers* already selected in the *Which table or query should provide the values for your lookup field?* list box, click Next.
d. At the third Lookup Wizard dialog box, double-click *FName* in the *Available Fields* list box to move the field to the *Selected Fields* list box.
e. Double-click *LName* in the *Available Fields* list box to move the field to the *Selected Fields* list box and then click Next.
f. At the fourth Lookup Wizard dialog box, click the down-pointing arrow next to the first sort option box, click *LName* at the drop-down list, and then click Next. Notice that you can define up to four sort keys to sort the lookup list and that an Ascending button appears next to each *Sort* option box. You can change the sort order from Ascending to Descending by clicking the Ascending button.
g. At the fifth Lookup Wizard dialog box, expand column widths if necessary to display all of the data. Scroll down the list of entries in the dialog box. Notice that the column widths are sufficient to show all of the text.

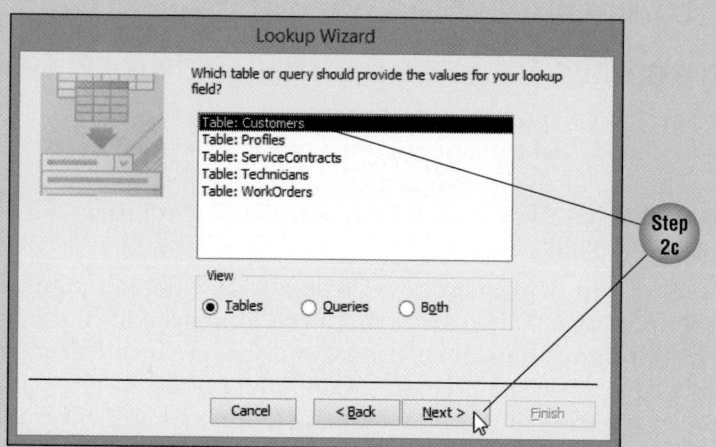

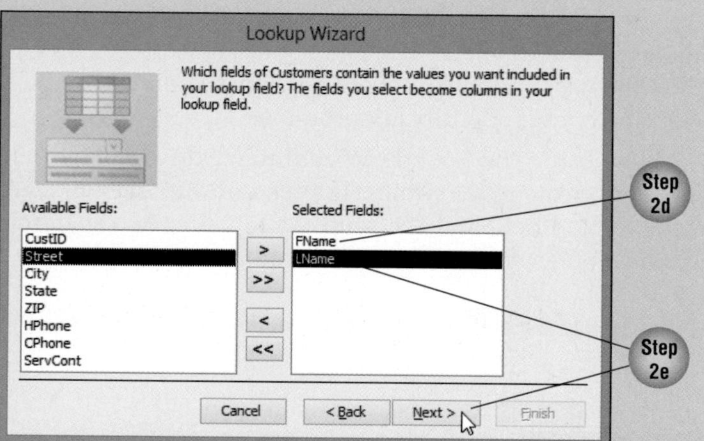

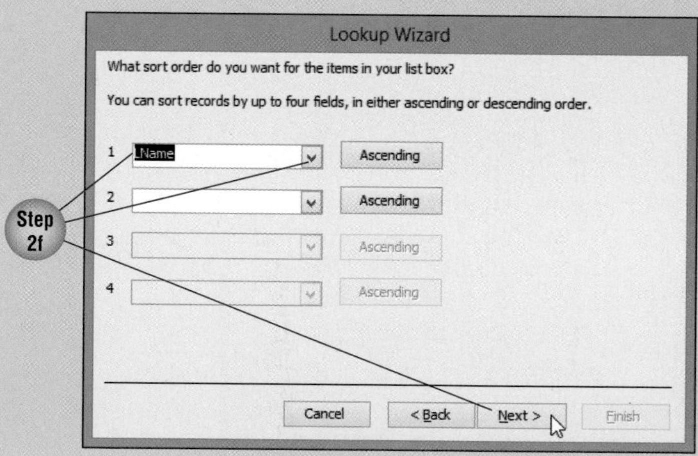

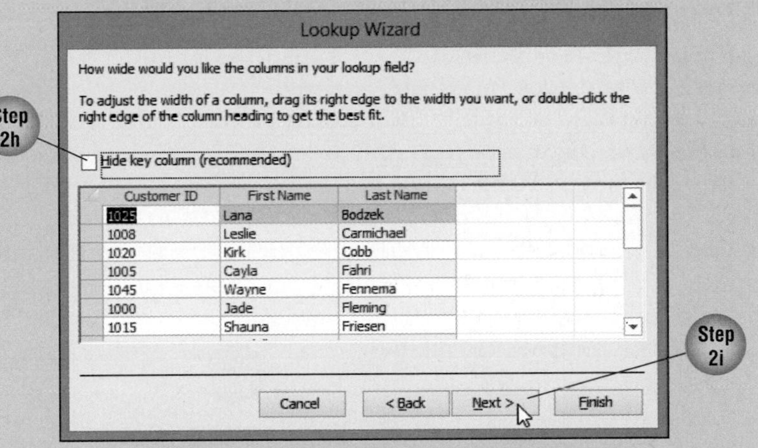

h. To view the customer identification numbers with the names while the list is open in a record, click the *Hide key column (recommended)* check box to remove the check mark. Removing the check mark displays the *CustID* field values as the first column in the lookup list.

i. Click Next.

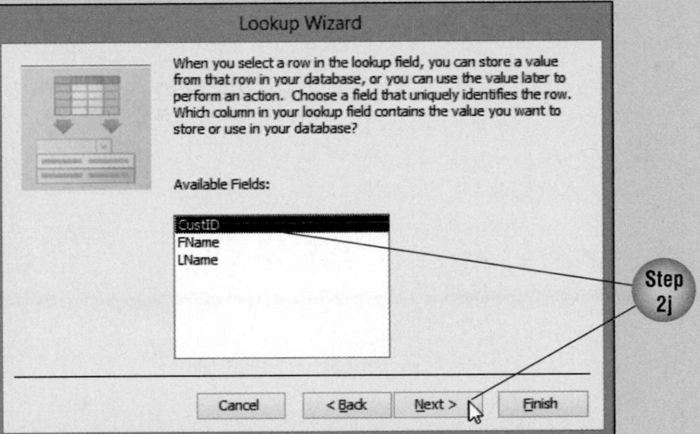

j. At the sixth Lookup Wizard dialog box, choose the field value that you want to store in the table when an entry is selected in the drop-down list. With *CustID* already selected in the Available Fields list box, click Next.

k. At the last Lookup Wizard dialog box, click Finish to accept the existing field name for the lookup field of *CustID*.

l. At the Lookup Wizard message box stating that the table must be saved before relationships can be created, click Yes to save the table. Access automatically creates a relationship between the Customers table and the Profiles table based on the *CustID* field used to create the lookup field. ***Note: In the initial release of Access 2013, the field size for the* CustID *field will change to 255 characters once the Lookup Wizard is finished. If a later Access 2013 Service Pack has been installed on your computer, the field size will remain as 4.***

3. Close the Profiles table.

Project 2c Modifying Lookup List Properties and Using a Lookup List Field in a Record

Part 3 of 5

1. With **AL2-C2-RSRCompServ.accdb** open, open the Profiles table in Design view.
2. Type the following text in the *Caption* property box for each of the following fields:

CustID	Customer ID
CompID	Computer ID
Remote	Remote Access?

3. Modify the lookup field properties to restrict entries in new records to items within the list by completing the following steps:
   a. Make *CustID* the active field.

b. Click the Lookup tab in the *Field Properties* section.

c. Look at the entries in all of the Lookup tab's property boxes. These entries were created by the Lookup Wizard.

d. Double-click in the *Limit To List* property box to change *No* to *Yes*. This means that the field will accept data only from existing customer records. A user will not be able to type in an entry that is not in the list.

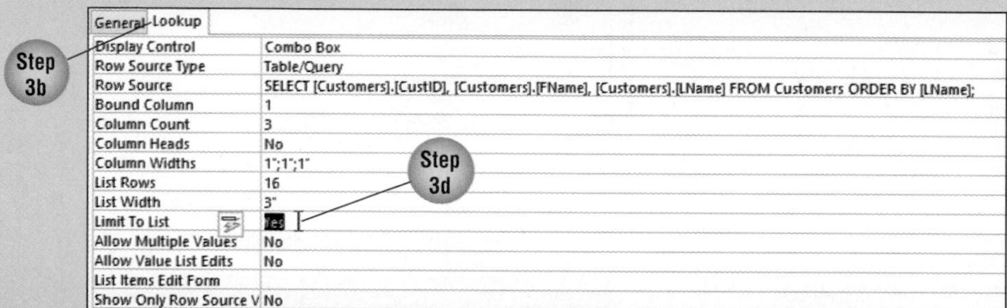

e. Save the table.

4. Switch to Datasheet view.
5. With *Customer ID* in the first row of the datasheet as the active field, click the down-pointing arrow in the field and then click *Jade Fleming* at the drop-down list. Notice that Access inserts *1000* as the field value in the first column since that is the customer number associated with the name you clicked.

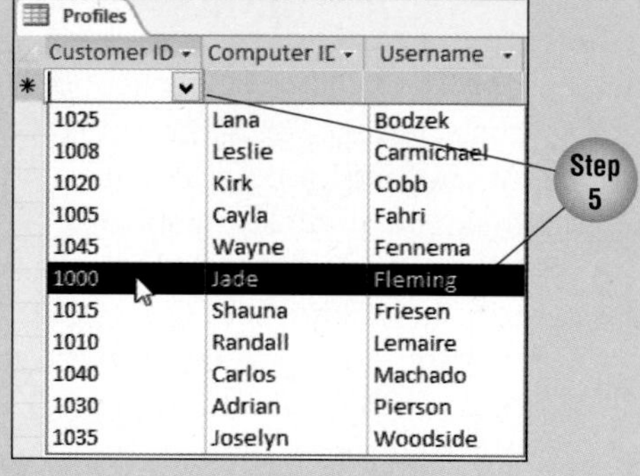

6. Type the remaining data as indicated:

   Computer ID **D1**
   Username **jade**
   Password **P$ck7**
   Remote Access? (Leave blank to indicate *No*.)

7. Adjust all column widths to best fit.

Profiles

Customer ID	Computer ID	Username	Password	Remote Access?
1000	D1	jade	P$ck7	☐

Steps 5-7

8. Print and then close the Profiles datasheet. Click Yes when prompted to save changes to the table layout.

Creating a Field That Allows Multiple Values

HINT

Multiple-value fields are suited to those occasions when you want to store more than one choice from a small list without having to create an advanced database design.

Suppose you want to keep track of the industry certifications a technician has achieved. You could organize this data by creating a separate field for each certification, but this approach might produce a table that requires numerous fields in which only one or two technicians have entries. As an alternative, you can create a single field that displays a list of certifications with check boxes to indicate whether they have been attained.

Look at the fields in the table structure shown in Figure 2.9. In this table, for each technician, you open a list in the *Certifications* field and click the check box next to the applicable certification title. In the *OperatingSys* field, another list can be used to keep track of the operating systems for which the technician is considered an expert.

Figure 2.9 Project 2d TechSkills Table

TechSkills		
*TechID	Short Text	2
Certifications	Short Text	20
OperatingSys	Short Text	20
NetworkSpc	Yes/No	
WebDesign	Yes/No	
Programming	Yes/No	

Use the Lookup Wizard to create a field to store multiple values. You can choose to look up the values in a field in another table or create your own value list. At the last Lookup Wizard dialog box, make sure to click the *Allow Multiple Values* check box to insert a check mark.

Quick Steps

Create a Multiple-Value Lookup Field

1. Open table in Design view.
2. Start Lookup Wizard for desired field.
3. Create list by typing values or binding data to field in another table.
4. At last Lookup Wizard dialog box, insert a check mark in *Allow Multiple Values* check box.
5. Click Finish.
6. Click Yes.

Project 2d Creating a Table with Lookup Fields, Including a Multiple-Value Field Part 4 of 5

1. With **AL2-C2-RSRCompServ.accdb** open, create a new table to store technician competencies by completing the following steps:
   a. Create a new table using Design view.
   b. Type the field names and assign the data types according to the data structure shown in Figure 2.9.
   c. Assign the primary key to the field denoted with an asterisk in Figure 2.9.
   d. Save the table and name it *TechSkills*.
2. Create a lookup field to select a technician from a list of names in the Technicians table by completing the following steps:
   a. Click in the *Data Type* column for the *TechID* field, click the down-pointing arrow that appears, and then click *Lookup Wizard*.
   b. Click Next at the first Lookup Wizard dialog box.
   c. Click *Table: Technicians* and then click Next.
   d. Double-click *FName* in the *Available Fields* list box to move the field to the *Selected Fields* list box.
   e. Double-click *LName* in the *Available Fields* list box and then click Next.
   f. Sort by *LName* and then click Next.
   g. With a check mark in the *Hide key column (recommended)* check box, click Next to accept the current column widths. In this lookup example, you are electing not to show the technician's ID field value. Although you will view and select by name, Access stores the primary key value in the table. *TechID* is considered the bound field and *FName* and *LName* are considered display fields.
   h. Click Finish and then click Yes to save the table.

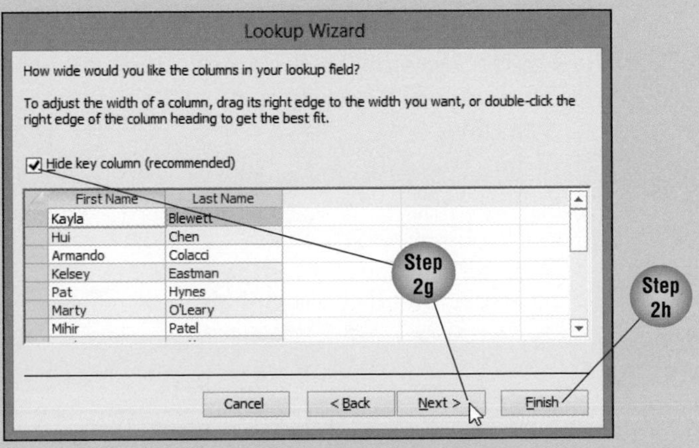

3. Create a lookup field that allows multiple values for certification information by completing the following steps:
   a. Click in the *Data Type* column for the *Certifications* field, click the down-pointing arrow that appears, and then click *Lookup Wizard*.
   b. Click *I will type in the values that I want* and then click Next.
   c. At the second Lookup Wizard dialog box, type the entries in *Col1* as shown at the right.
   d. Click Next.
   e. At the last Lookup Wizard dialog box, click the *Allow Multiple Values* check box to insert a check mark and then click Finish.
   f. At the message box indicating that once the field is set to store multiple values, the action cannot be undone, click Yes to change the *Certifications* field to multiple values.

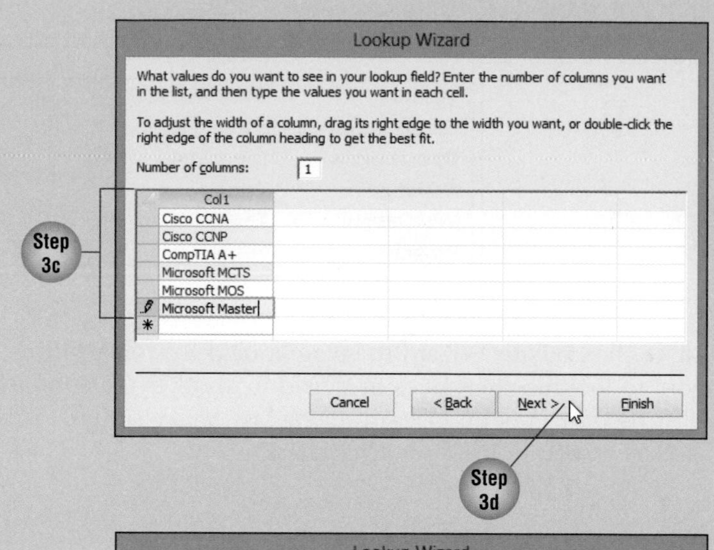

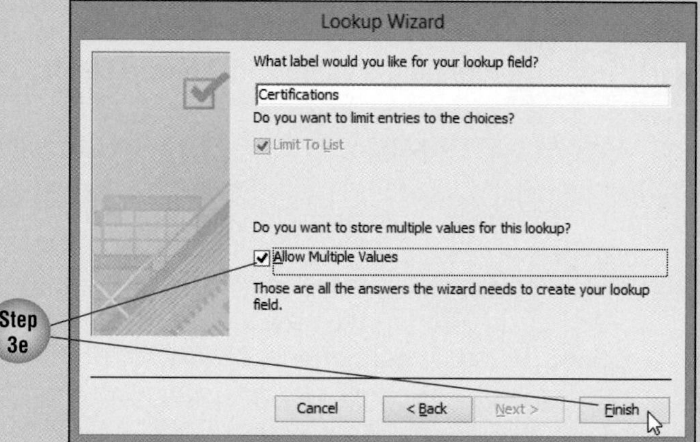

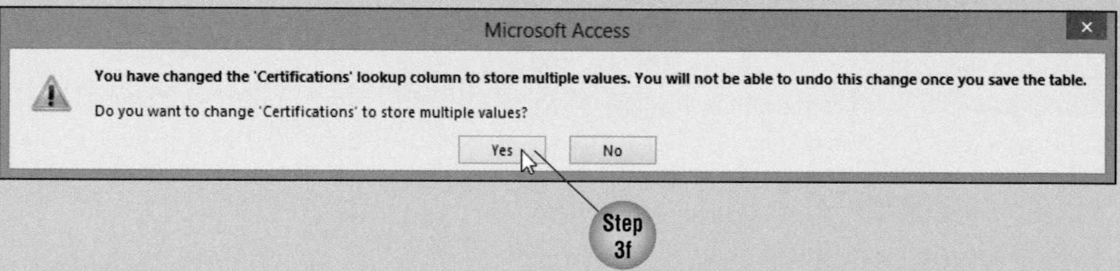

4. Complete steps similar to those in Steps 3a–3f to create a lookup list to store multiple values in the *OperatingSys* field using following value list:
   - Windows 8
   - Windows 7
   - Windows Vista
   - Linux
   - Unix
   - Mac OS X
5. Save and close the TechSkills table.

Project 2e Assigning Multiple Values in a Lookup List

Part 5 of 5

1. With **AL2-C2-RSRCompServ.accdb** open, open the TechSkills table in Design view.
2. Type the following text in the *Caption* property box for each field noted:

TechID	Technician ID
OperatingSys	Operating Systems
NetworkSpc	Network Specialist?
WebDesign	Design Web Sites?
Programming	Programming?

3. Save the table and then switch to Datasheet view.
4. Add a new record to the table by completing the following steps:
   a. With the insertion point positioned in the *Technician ID* column, click the down-pointing arrow and then click *Kelsey Eastman* at the drop-down list. Notice that Access displays the technician's first name in the column. *FName* is considered a display field for this column, but the identification number associated with Kelsey Eastman is stored in the table.
   b. Press Tab and then click the down-pointing arrow in the *Certifications* column.
   c. Since *Certifications* is a multiple-value field, the drop-down list displays with check boxes next to all of the items. Click the *Cisco CCNA* check box and the *Microsoft MCTS* check box to insert check marks and then click OK.
   d. Press Tab and then click the down-pointing arrow in the *Operating System* column.
   e. Click the *Windows 8, Windows 7*, and *Linux* check boxes to insert check marks and then click OK.
   f. Press Tab and then press the spacebar to insert a check mark in the *Network Specialist?* check box.
   g. Press Tab three times to finish the record, leaving the check boxes blank in the *Design Web Sites?* and *Programming?* columns.
5. Adjust the width of all of the columns to best fit.
6. Print the TechSkills table in landscape orientation with left and right margins of 0.25 inch.
7. Close the TechSkills table. Click Yes when prompted to save changes to the layout.

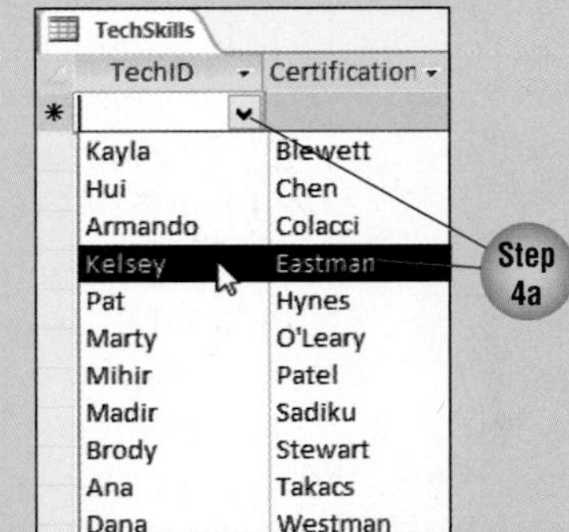

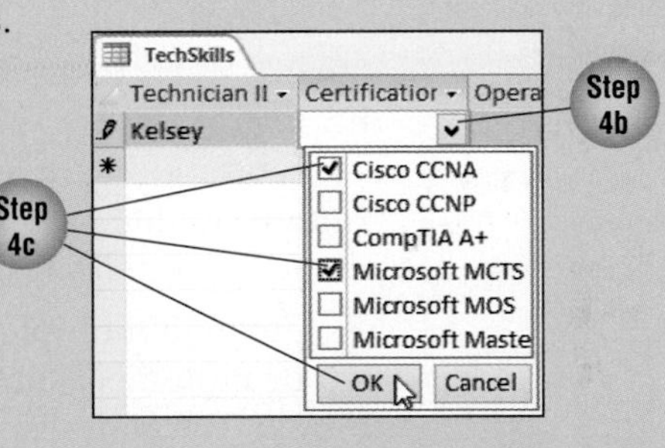

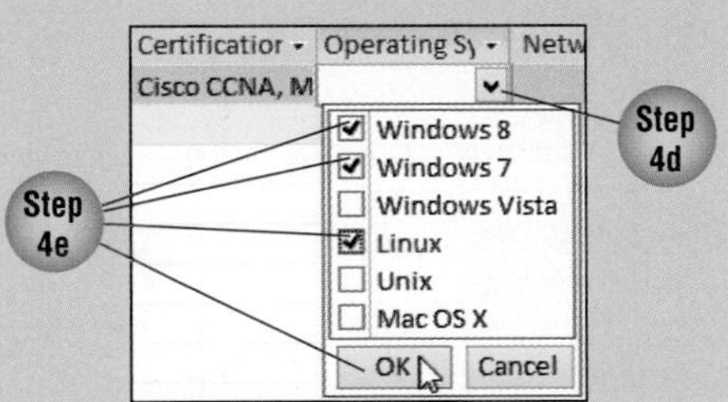

Project 3 Create an Index **1 Part**

You will create indexes to speed up database processing.

Indexes

Quick Steps

Create a Single-Field Index

1. Open table in Design view.
2. Make desired field active.
3. Click in *Indexed* property box.
4. Click down-pointing arrow.
5. Click *Yes (Duplicates OK)* or *Yes (No Duplicates)*.
6. Save table.

Create a Multiple-Field Index

1. Open table in Design view.
2. Click Indexes button.
3. Click in first blank row in *Index Name* column.
4. Type name for index.
5. Press Tab.
6. Click down-pointing arrow in *Field Name* column.
7. Click desired field.
8. If necessary, change sort order.
9. Click in *Field Name* column in next row.
10. Click down-pointing arrow.
11. Click desired field.
12. If necessary, change sort order.
13. Repeat Steps 9–12 until finished.
14. Close Indexes window.

An index cannot be generated for fields with a data type of OLE Object or Attachment.

Creating Indexes

An ***index*** is a list created by Access containing pointers that direct Access to the locations of specific records in a table. A database index is very similar to an index you would find at the back of a book. You search the book's index for a keyword that is associated with the topic you want to find, and the index directs you to the page number(s) in the book that contain information on that topic. You use a book's index because you want to find the information quickly and more directly. Although you cannot see an Access index, it operates in much the same way, reducing the amount of time it takes Access to find a particular record.

Access automatically generates an index for a field designated as the primary key in a table. In a database with a large number of records, identify fields other than the primary key that are often sorted or searched and create indexes for these fields to speed up sorting and searching. For example, in the Customers table in the RSR Computer Services database, creating an index for the *LName* field is a good idea, because the table data will be frequently sorted by last name.

An index can be created to restrict data in a field to unique values. This creates a field similar to a primary key, in that Access will not allow two records to hold the same data. For example, an email field in a table that is frequently searched is a good candidate for an index. To avoid data entry errors in a field that should contain unique values (and is not the primary key), set up the index so that it will not accept duplicates.

Create a multiple-field index if you frequently sort or search a large table by two or more fields at the same time. In Table Design view, click the Indexes button to open the Indexes window, as shown in Figure 2.10, and create an index for a combination of up to 10 fields.

Figure 2.10 Indexes Window

Indexes: Table1

Index Name	Field Name	Sort Order

Index Properties

The name for this index. Each index can use up to 10 fields.

Project 3 Creating Indexes

1. With **AL2-C2-RSRCompServ.accdb** open, open the Customers table in Design view.
2. Create a single-field index for the *ZIP* field by completing the following steps:
   a. Make *ZIP* the active field.
   b. Double-click in the *Indexed* property box to change *No* to *Yes (Duplicates OK)*.
   c. Save the table.

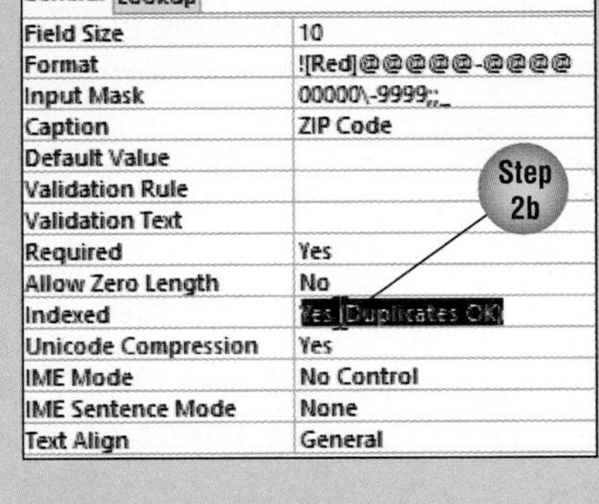

3. Create a multiple-field index for the *LName* and *FName* fields by completing the following steps:
   a. Click the Indexes button in the Show/Hide group on the TABLE TOOLS DESIGN tab.
   b. At the Indexes: Customers window, click in the first blank row in the *Index Name* column (below *ZIP*) and then type **Names**.
   c. Press Tab, click the down-pointing arrow that appears in the *Field Name* column, and then click *LName* at the drop-down list. The sort order for *LName* defaults to *Ascending*.

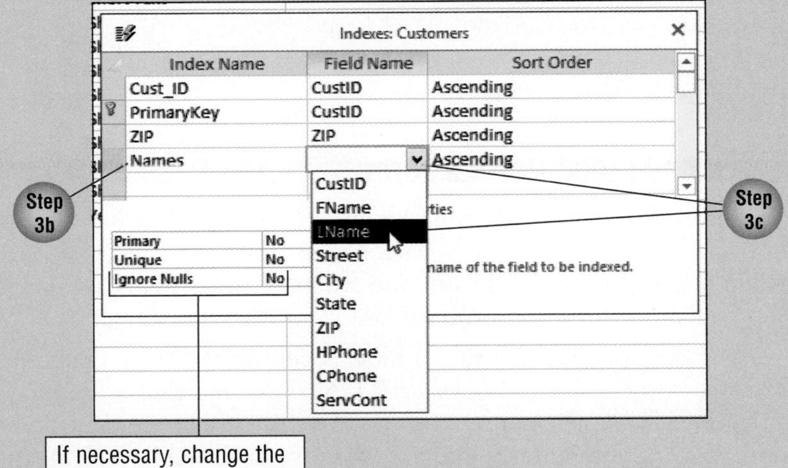

   d. Click in the row in the *Field Name* column below *LName*, click the down-pointing arrow that appears, and then click *FName*.
   e. Close the Indexes: Customers window.
   f. Save the table.
4. Close the Customers table.
5. Close **AL2-C2-RSRCompServ.accdb**.

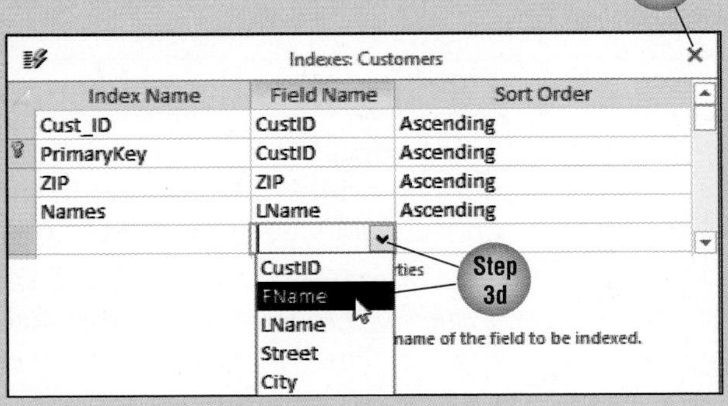

Normalizing a Database

Normalizing a database involves reviewing the database structure and ensuring that the tables are set up to eliminate redundancy. If data redundancy is discovered, the process of normalization often involves splitting fields into smaller units, and/or breaking larger tables down into smaller tables and creating relationships to remove repeating groups of data. Three normalization states are tested: first normal form, second normal form, and third normal form.

Checking First Normal Form

A table meets first normal form when it does not contain any fields that can be broken down into smaller units and when it does not have similar information stored in several fields.

For example, a table that contains a single field called *TechnicianName* that stores the technician's first and last names in the same column is in violation of first normal form. To correct the structure, split *TechnicianName* into two fields, such as *TechLastName* and *TechFirstName*.

A table that has multiple fields set up with each field containing similar data—such as *Week1*, *Week2*, *Week3*, and *Week4*—also violates first normal form. To correct this structure, delete the four week fields and replace them with a single field named *WeekNumber*.

Checking Second Normal Form

Second normal form is of concern only for a table that has a multiple-field primary key (composite key). A table with a composite key meets second normal form when it is in first normal form and when all of its fields are dependent on all of the fields that form the primary key.

For example, assume that a table is defined with two fields that form the primary key: *CustID* and *ComputerID*. Also assume that a field in the same table is titled *EmailAdd*. The contents of the *EmailAdd* field are dependent on the customer only (not the computer). Since *EmailAdd* is not dependent on **both** ***CustID*** **and** *ComputerID*, the table is not in second normal form. To correct the structure, delete the *EmailAdd* field.

Checking Third Normal Form

Third normal form applies to a table that has a single primary key and is in first normal form. If a field exists in the table for which the field value is not dependent on the field value of the primary key, the table is not in third normal form.

For example, assume that a table is defined with a single primary key titled *TechnicianID*. Also assume that fields in the same table are titled *PayCode* and *PayRate*. Finally, assume that a technician's pay rate is dependent on the pay code assigned to him or her. Since the pay rate is dependent on the field value in the pay code field and not on the technician's identification number, the table is not in third normal form. To convert the table to third normal form, delete the *PayRate* field from the table. (The *PayRate* field belongs in another table in the database.)

Chapter Summary

- When building relationships, consider the frequency of matching data in the common field in both tables to determine if the relationship is one-to-many, one-to-one, or many-to-many.
- The most common type of relationship is one-to-many. This type of relationship involves joining tables by dragging the primary key from the "one" table to the foreign key in the "many" table.
- In a one-to-many relationship, only one record for a matching field value exists in the primary table, while many records for the same value can exist in the related table.
- A relationship diagram depicts the two tables joined in the relationship and the type of relationship between the tables.
- At the Edit Relationships dialog box, you can enforce referential integrity, which places restrictions on new data entered into a related table. A record is not allowed in the related table if a matching record does not already exist in the primary table.
- The *Cascade Update Related Fields* option automatically updates all occurrences of the same data in the foreign key field when a change is made to the primary key data.
- The *Cascade Delete Related Records* option automatically deletes related records when a record is deleted from the primary table.
- In a one-to-one relationship, only one record exists with a matching value in the joined field in both tables.
- In a many-to-many relationship, many records can exist with matching values in the joined fields in both tables.
- A junction table is used to create a many-to-many relationship. A junction table contains a minimum of two fields, which are the primary key fields from the two tables in the many-to-many relationship.
- Using a junction table, two one-to-many relationships are joined to form a many-to-many relationship.
- In some tables, two or more fields are used to create the primary key if a single field is not guaranteed to hold unique data.
- A primary key that is made up of two or more fields is called a composite key.
- A lookup field displays a drop-down list in a field, in which the user points and clicks to enter the field value. The list can be generated from records in a related table or by typing in a value list.
- Once you have created the lookup field, use the Lookup tab in the *Field Properties* section in Table Design view to modify individual properties.
- The Limit To List property allows you to restrict entries in the field to items within the lookup list.
- A field that allows multiple entries to be selected from a drop-down list can be created by clicking *Allow Multiple Values* at the final Lookup Wizard dialog box.

- A field that is defined as a multiple-value field cannot be changed back to a single-value field.
- Access displays check boxes next to all of the items in the drop-down list if the field has been set to allow multiple values.
- An index is a list generated by Access that includes pointers that direct Access to the locations of specific records in a table.
- Access creates an index for a primary key field automatically.
- To create a single-field table index, change the Indexed property to *Yes (Duplicates OK)* or *Yes (No Duplicates)*.
- To create multiple-field index, use the Indexes window.
- Normalizing a database involves reviewing the database structure to eliminate redundancy. Three normalization states are checked: first normal form, second normal form, and third normal form.

Commands Review

FEATURE	RIBBON TAB, GROUP	BUTTON
edit relationships	RELATIONSHIP TOOLS DESIGN, Tools	
indexes	TABLE TOOLS DESIGN, Show/Hide	
primary key	TABLE TOOLS DESIGN, Tools	
relationships report	RELATIONSHIP TOOLS DESIGN, Tools	
relationships window	DATABASE TOOLS, Relationships OR TABLE TOOLS DESIGN, Relationships	
show table	RELATIONSHIP TOOLS DESIGN, Relationships	

Concepts Check Test Your Knowledge 

Completion: In the space provided at the right, indicate the correct term, command, or number.

1. This is the term for a field added to a related table for the purpose of creating a relationship that is the primary key in the other table. ________________

2. The Relationships button is found on this tab on the ribbon. ________________

3. Add a table to the Relationships window using this dialog box. ________________

4. At the Edit Relationships dialog box, the two cascade options do not become active until this option is activated. ________________

5. This symbol appears on the join line next to the "many" side of a relationship when referential integrity is activated. ________________

6. To open the Edit Relationships dialog box for an existing relationship, perform this action with the mouse while pointing at the black join line in the Relationships window. ________________

7. This type of relationship exists if only one matching record exists in both tables in the relationship. ________________

8. A many-to-many relationship is created by establishing two one-to-many relationships using a third table referred to by this term. ________________

9. A primary key that is made up of two or more fields is referred to by this term. ________________

10. A lookup field can be restricted to items within the list by setting this property to Yes. ________________

11. Specify a field as a multiple-value field by clicking this check box at the final Lookup Wizard dialog box. ________________

12. Set the Indexed property to this option for an index field that is likely to contain more than one record with the same field value, such as a zip code. ________________

13. Open this window to create an index that uses two or more fields. ________________

14. These are the three normalization states that are tested. ________________

15. If a field exists in a table for which the field value is not dependent on the primary key, the table is not in this normalization state. ________________

Skills Check Assess Your Performance

Assessment 1

CREATE A LOOKUP LIST

1. Open **AL2-C2-ViewIt.accdb** and enable the content.
2. Open all of the tables in Datasheet view and review the tables' fields and records to familiarize yourself with the database. Close all of the tables when finished.
3. Open the Relationships window and close the Show Table dialog box. Notice that no relationships have been created in the database. Close the Relationships window.
4. The *CustID* field in the WebOrders table can be made easier to use by changing it to a lookup list that presents customer names and numbers from the WebCustomers table. Open the WebOrders table in Design view, make *CustID* the active field, and then create a lookup list to display values from another table using the following information:
   a. Display the *CustID*, *FirstName*, and *LastName* fields from the WebCustomers table.
   b. Sort the list in ascending order by the *LastName* field.
   c. Remove the check box from the *Hide key column* check box.
   d. Store the *CustID* value.
   e. Accept the default label of *CustID* for the column.
5. Modify the Lookup property for the *CustID* field that will ensure only items within the list can be entered into the field.
6. Save the table, switch to Datasheet view, and then enter the following record to test the lookup list:

Web Order ID	**10007**
Customer ID	Select *106 Gary Gallagher* in the lookup list.
Date Ordered	**Feb 26 2015**

7. Print the datasheet.
8. Close the WebOrders table.

Assessment

2 CREATE A TABLE WITH A MULTIPLE-FIELD PRIMARY KEY AND LOOKUP LISTS

1. With **AL2-C2-ViewIt.accdb** open, create a new table using Design view to track the videos downloaded by a customer using the following information:

Field Name	Data Type	Field Size	Caption
WebOrdID	Short Text	5	**Web Order ID**
WebProdID	Short Text	7	**Product ID**
Qty	Number	–	**Quantity**

2. A customer can choose to buy more than one video on the same order. When this occurs, the same order number is associated with more than one record in the table. Therefore, the primary key cannot be based on the *WebOrdID* field alone. Assign a multiple-field primary key using both the *WebOrdID* and *WebProdID* fields. The combination of the order identification number and product identification number will uniquely describe each record in the table.
3. Save the table and name it *WebOrderDetails*.
4. Create a lookup list for the *WebOrdID* field that connects to the *WebOrdID* field in the WebOrders table. Add all three of the fields in the WebOrders table to the lookup list, do not specify a sort field, remove the check mark from the *Hide key column* check box, store *WebOrdID* in the field, and then accept the default field name. Modify the Lookup property to ensure only items within the list can be entered into the field.
5. Create a lookup list for the *WebProdID* field that connects to the *WebProdID* field in the WebProducts table. Display the *Product* field sorted in ascending order, make sure the column is wide enough to display the entire video title in the list, hide the key column, and then accept the default field name. Modify the Lookup property to ensure only items within the list can be entered into the field.
6. Save the table and switch to Datasheet view. Add the following records to the WebOrderDetails datasheet to test the lookup lists:

Web Order ID	Product ID	Quantity
10001	To Kill a Mockingbird	1
10001	Blue Hawaii	1
10002	The Great Escape	2
10003	Cool Hand Luke	1
10003	Doctor Zhivago	1
10003	The Longest Day	1
10004	Dial M for Murder	1

7. Adjust all of the column widths to best fit and print the datasheet.
8. Close the WebOrderDetails table. Click Yes when prompted to save changes to the layout.

Assessment

3 EDIT RELATIONSHIPS

1. With **AL2-C2-ViewIt.accdb** open, open the Relationships window to view the relationships created by Access when the lookup lists were created.
2. Resize and move the table field list boxes to the approximate sizes and locations, as shown in Figure 2.11.
3. Edit the relationships as follows:
   a. Edit the one-to-many relationship between the WebCustomers and WebOrders tables to activate referential integrity and the two cascade options.
   b. Edit the one-to-many relationship between the WebOrders and WebOrderDetails tables to activate referential integrity and the two cascade options.
   c. Edit the one-to-many relationship between the WebProducts and WebOrderDetails tables to activate referential integrity and the two cascade options.
4. Create and print a relationships report.
5. On your relationships report printout, write the type of relationship that exists between the WebOrders table and the WebProducts table.
6. Close the relationships report for the **AL2-C2-ViewIt** database. Click Yes to save the report and accept the default name in the Save As dialog box.
7. Close the Relationships window.

Figure 2.11 Assessment 3

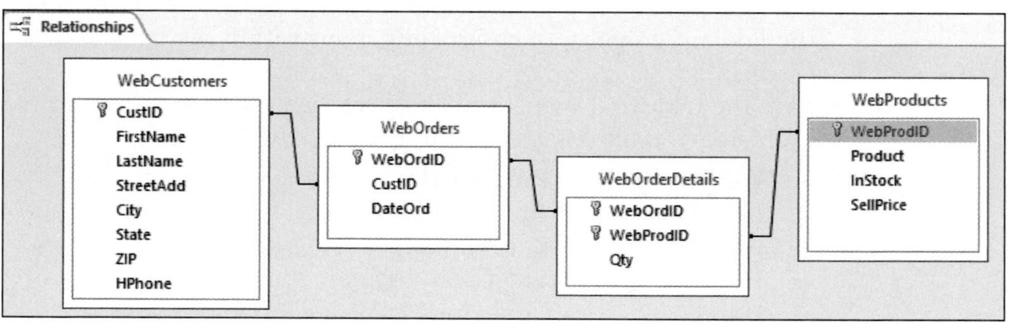

Assessment

4 CREATE A TABLE WITH A ONE-TO-ONE RELATIONSHIP

1. With **AL2-C2-ViewIt.accdb** open, create a new table using Design view to store a customer's credit card information using the following information:

Field Name	Data Type	Field Size	Caption
CustID	Short Text	3	**Customer ID**
CCType	Short Text	20	**Credit Card Type**
CCNumber	Short Text	16	**Credit Card Number**
CCExpMonth	Number	–	**Expiry Month**
CCExpYear	Number	–	**Expiry Year**
EmailAdd	Short Text	30	**Email Address**

2. Assign the primary key to the *CustID* field.
3. Save the table and name it *WebCustPymnt*.
4. Create a lookup list for the *CustID* field that connects to the *CustID* field in the WebCustomers table. Include the *FirstName*, *LastName*, and *HPhone* fields. Sort the list by *LastName* and then by *FirstName*. Remove the check mark from the *Hide key column* check box. Accept all of the other defaults. Modify the Lookup property to ensure only items within the list can be entered into the field.
5. Save the table, switch to Datasheet view, and enter the following record:

Customer ID	Select *106 Gary Gallagher* in the lookup list
Credit Card Type	**Visa**
Credit Card Number	**0009100876453152**
Expiry Month	**7**
Expiry Year	**2017**
Email Address	**garyg@emcp.net**

6. Adjust all of the column widths to best fit and print the datasheet in landscape orientation.
7. Close the WebCustPymnt table. Click Yes when prompted to save changes to the layout.
8. Open the Relationships window and open the Show Table dialog box.
9. Add the WebCustPymnt table to the window. Edit the one-to-one relationship between the WebCustomers and WebCustPymnt tables to activate referential integrity and the two cascade options.
10. If necessary, rearrange the table field list boxes in the Relationships window so you can better see the join line between the WebCustPymnt and WebCustomers tables.
11. Print a relationships report, changing page layout options as necessary to fit the report on one page. Close the relationships report. Click Yes to save the report and type **Relationships-Assessment4** as the report name in the Save As dialog box.
12. Close the Relationships window.
13. Close **AL2-C2-ViewIt.accdb**.

Visual Benchmark Demonstrate Your Proficiency

CREATE LOOKUP LISTS AND EDIT RELATIONSHIPS

1. Open **AL2-C2-PawsParadise.accdb**.
2. This database is similar to the Visual Benchmark database created in Chapter 1, but an additional table has been created and several records have been added to the database. Spend a few moments familiarizing yourself with the tables and records.
3. Create the following lookup lists, making sure the field value saved is always the primary key field:
   a. In the Dogs table, look up the kennel category in the KennelCategories table. Make sure the *Hide key column* check box contains a check mark.
   b. In the Dogs table, look up the customer number in the DogOwners table. Remove the check mark from the *Hide key column* check box.
   c. In the Reservations table, look up the customer number in the DogOwners table. Remove the check mark from the *Hide key column* check box.
4. Open the Relationships window and edit the relationships to activate referential integrity and both cascade options for each relationship.
5. Rearrange and move the table field list boxes as necessary so that your Relationships window appears similar to the one shown in Figure 2.12.
6. Create and print a relationships report.
7. Save the relationships report using the default name and then close the report and the Relationships window.
8. Close **AL2-C2-PawsParadise.accdb**.

Figure 2.12 Visual Benchmark Relationships Window

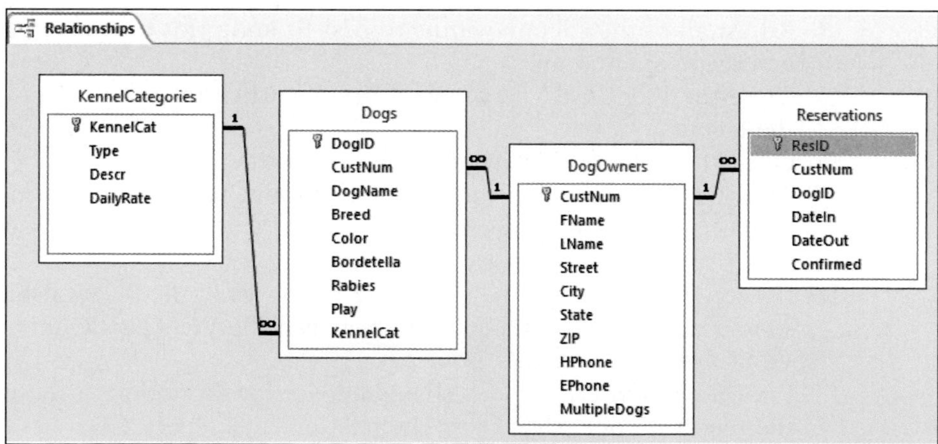

Case Study Apply Your Skills

Part 1

You are working as an intern at Hillsdale Realty. The intern that worked there before you started developing a database for use in for managing sales agents, listings, sales, and commission quotas. The previous intern did not have time to finish the database, however. Open **AL2-C2-HillsdaleRealty.accdb** and enable the content. Open all of the tables and review the fields and records to familiarize yourself with the database.

The Agents table is not in first normal form. The field named *AgentName* contains both the first and last names of each sales agent. To improve the table design, modify the table so that two separate fields are used for representative names. Add captions to the name fields. Correct the data in the datasheet so the names are correctly split into the two columns. Print the revised Agents table datasheet with all of the column widths adjusted to best fit. Close the table.

Part 2

You decide to improve the efficiency of data entry by creating lookup lists as follows:

- In the Listings table, you want to be able to select the correct Agent ID by viewing the agent names in a sorted drop-down list. Display the *AgentID* as the value in the field.
- In the Agents table, you want to be able to select the quota code by viewing all of the quota codes and amounts in a drop-down list. Display the commission quota in the datasheet but store *QuotaID* as the field value. Edit the caption for the field to read *Quota* (instead of *Quota Code*).
- In the SalesAndComm table, you want to be able to select the correct listing number by viewing the listing numbers and addresses from the Listings table. Make sure the column width is wide enough to display all of the street address information. Display *ListingNo* as the value in the field.

Open the Relationships window. If necessary, add all of the tables to the window. Resize and arrange boxes so the join lines between tables are easy to follow and understand. Edit each relationship to activate referential integrity and the two cascade options. Create, print, and save a relationships report. Close the relationships report and close the Relationships window.

Part 3

You have decided to add another table named *Preferences* to the database. Create the table using the information below. You determine the appropriate data types and other field properties.

Field Name	Lookup Lists
ClientID	–
ListingNo	Create a lookup list to the Listings table.
AgentID	Create a lookup list to the Agents table.
Preferences	Create a multiple-value list with the following items: Exclusive listing MLS listing Pre-sale inspection Staging service

A client could have more than one listing at Hillsdale Realtors, so you do not want to use *ClientID* as the primary key. Assign the primary key as a combination of two fields: *ClientID* and *ListingNo*. Add a sample record to the table to test your lookup lists and multiple-value field. Adjust all of the column widths to best fit, print the datasheet, and then close the table, saving the layout. Open the Relationships window, add the new table, and then arrange the layout so that join lines are not overlapping. Edit the relationships among Preferences and Listings and Agents to activate referential integrity and the two cascade options. Create, print, and save a new relationships report named *Relationships-Part3*.

MICROSOFT®
ACCESS®

Advanced Query Techniques

PERFORMANCE OBJECTIVES

Upon successful completion of Chapter 3, you will be able to:

- **Save a filter as a query**
- **Create and run a parameter query to prompt for criteria**
- **Add tables to and remove tables from a query**
- **Create an inner join, left join, and right join to modify query results**
- **Create a self-join to match two fields in the same table**
- **Create a query that includes a subquery**
- **Create a query that uses conditional logic**
- **Assign an alias to a table name and a field name**
- **Select records using a multiple-value field in a query**
- **Create a new table using a make-table query**
- **Remove records from a table using a delete query**
- **Add records to the end of an existing table using an append query**
- **Modify records using an update query**

Tutorials

3.1 Saving a Filter as a Query
3.2 Prompting for Criteria Using a Parameter Query
3.3 Creating a Query with Right Outer Join
3.4 Creating a Self-Join Query
3.5 Creating and Using Subqueries
3.6 Assigning Aliases and Using a Multivalued Field in a Query
3.7 Performing Operations Using Action Queries
3.8 Creating a New Table Using a Query
3.9 Adding and Deleting Records to a Table Using a Query
3.10 Modifying Records Using an Update Query

In this chapter, you will create, save, and run queries that incorporate advanced query features, such as saving a filter as a query, prompting for criteria on single and multiple fields, modifying join properties to view alternative query results, and using action queries to perform operations on groups of records. In addition, you will also create an alias for a table and a field and incorporate subqueries to manage multiple calculations. Model answers for this chapter's projects appear on the following pages.

AL2C3

Note: Before beginning the projects, copy to your storage medium the AL2C3 subfolder from the AL2 folder on the CD that accompanies this textbook and then make AL2C3 the active folder.

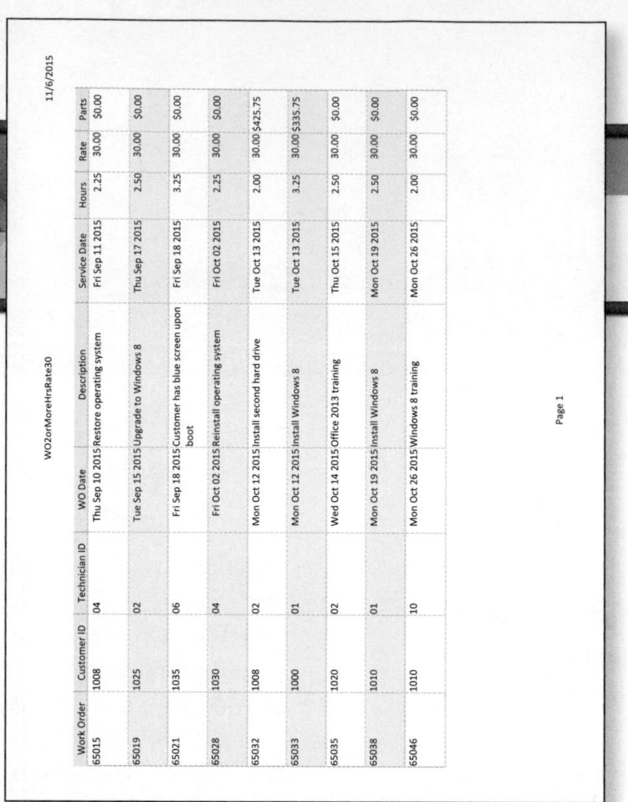

WO2orMoreHrsRate30 11/6/2015

Work Order	Customer ID	Technician ID	WO Date	Description	Service Date	Hours	Rate	Parts
65015	1008	04	Thu Sep 10 2015	Restore operating system	Fri Sep 11 2015	2.25	30.00	$0.00
65019	1025	02	Tue Sep 15 2015	Upgrade to Windows 8	Thu Sep 17 2015	2.50	30.00	$0.00
65021	1035	06	Fri Sep 18 2015	Customer has blue screen upon boot	Fri Sep 18 2015	3.25	30.00	$0.00
65028	1030	04	Fri Oct 02 2015	Reinstall operating system	Fri Oct 02 2015	2.25	30.00	$0.00
65032	1008	02	Mon Oct 12 2015	Install second hard drive	Tue Oct 13 2015	2.00	30.00	$425.75
65033	1000	01	Mon Oct 12 2015	Install Windows 8	Tue Oct 13 2015	3.25	30.00	$335.75
65035	1020	02	Wed Oct 14 2015	Office 2013 training	Thu Oct 15 2015	2.50	30.00	$0.00
65038	1010	01	Mon Oct 19 2015	Install Windows 8	Mon Oct 19 2015	2.50	30.00	$0.00
65046	1010	10	Mon Oct 26 2015	Windows 8 training	Mon Oct 26 2015	2.00	30.00	$0.00

Page 1

Project 1 Select Records Using Filtered Criteria and Prompted Criteria Project 1a, WO2orMoreHrsRate30 Query

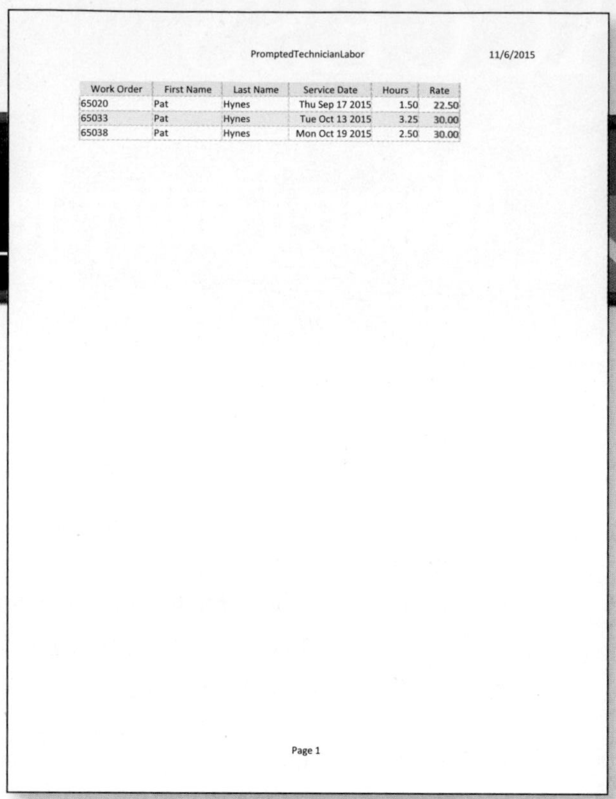

PromptedTechnicianLabor 11/6/2015

Work Order	First Name	Last Name	Service Date	Hours	Rate
65020	Pat	Hynes	Thu Sep 17 2015	1.50	22.50
65033	Pat	Hynes	Tue Oct 13 2015	3.25	30.00
65038	Pat	Hynes	Mon Oct 19 2015	2.50	30.00

Page 1

Project 1b, PromptedTechnicianLabor Query

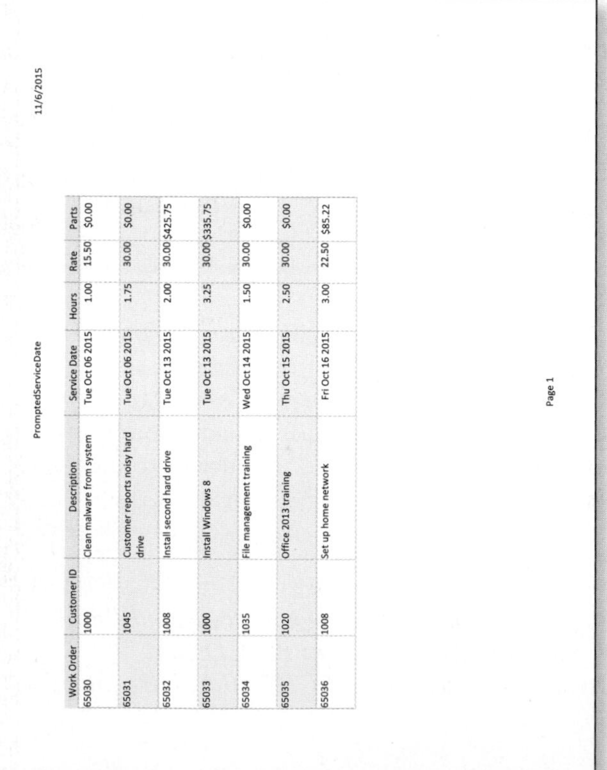

PromptedServiceDate 11/6/2015

Work Order	Customer ID	Description	Service Date	Hours	Rate	Parts
65030	1000	Clean malware from system	Tue Oct 06 2015	1.00	15.50	$0.00
65031	1045	Customer reports noisy hard drive	Tue Oct 06 2015	1.75	30.00	$0.00
65032	1008	Install second hard drive	Tue Oct 13 2015	2.00	30.00	$425.75
65033	1000	Install Windows 8	Tue Oct 13 2015	3.25	30.00	$335.75
65034	1035	File management training	Wed Oct 14 2015	1.50	30.00	$0.00
65035	1020	Office 2013 training	Thu Oct 15 2015	2.50	30.00	$0.00
65036	1008	Set up home network	Fri Oct 16 2015	3.00	22.50	$85.22

Page 1

Project 1c, PromptedServiceDate Query

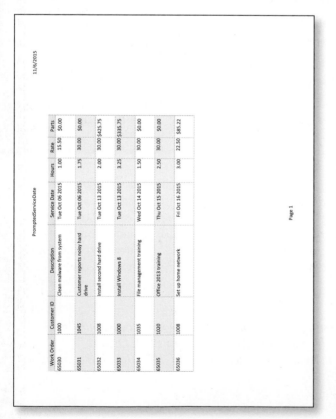

UnassignedWO 11/6/2015

First Name	Last Name	Work Order	WO Date	Description
		65047	Tue Oct 27 2015	Set up automatic backup
		65048	Thu Oct 29 2015	Replace LCD monitor
		65049	Fri Oct 30 2015	Set up dual monitor system
		65050	Fri Oct 30 2015	Reinstall Windows 8
Pat	Hynes	65020	Thu Sep 17 2015	Troubleshoot noisy fan
Pat	Hynes	65033	Mon Oct 12 2015	Install Windows 8
Pat	Hynes	65038	Mon Oct 19 2015	Install Windows 8
Hui	Chen	65014	Thu Sep 10 2015	Replace power supply
Hui	Chen	65019	Tue Sep 15 2015	Upgrade to Windows 8
Hui	Chen	65026	Tue Sep 29 2015	Upgrade memory
Hui	Chen	65032	Mon Oct 12 2015	Install second hard drive
Hui	Chen	65035	Wed Oct 14 2015	Office 2013 training
Kayla	Blewett	65023	Tue Sep 22 2015	Upgrade RAM
Kayla	Blewett	65036	Thu Oct 15 2015	Set up home network
Kayla	Blewett	65041	Thu Oct 22 2015	Bi-annual computer maintenance
Mihir	Patel	65015	Thu Sep 10 2015	Restore operating system
Mihir	Patel	65022	Mon Sep 21 2015	Customer reports screen is fuzzy
Mihir	Patel	65024	Thu Sep 24 2015	Install malware protection
Mihir	Patel	65028	Fri Oct 02 2015	Reinstall operating system
Madir	Sadiku	65037	Mon Oct 19 2015	Bi-annual computer maintenance
Brody	Stewart	65016	Fri Sep 11 2015	Install upgraded video card
Brody	Stewart	65021	Fri Sep 18 2015	Customer has blue screen upon boot
Brody	Stewart	65025	Mon Sep 28 2015	Troubleshoot hard drive noise
Brody	Stewart	65039	Mon Oct 19 2015	Set up automatic backup
Brody	Stewart	65042	Thu Oct 22 2015	File management training
Ana	Takacs	65029	Fri Oct 02 2015	Set up automatic backup
Ana	Takacs	65034	Mon Oct 12 2015	File management training
Ana	Takacs	65044	Fri Oct 23 2015	DVD drive is not working
Marty	O'Leary	65017	Mon Sep 14 2015	Replace DVD drive
Marty	O'Leary	65043	Thu Oct 22 2015	Troubleshoot video fuzziness
Armando	Colacci	65031	Tue Oct 06 2015	Customer reports noisy hard drive
Armando	Colacci	65040	Mon Oct 19 2015	Configure dual monitors
Kelsey	Eastman	65013	Mon Sep 07 2015	Replace keyboard
Kelsey	Eastman	65018	Mon Sep 14 2015	Upgrade Office suite
Kelsey	Eastman	65027	Wed Sep 30 2015	Replace hard drive
Kelsey	Eastman	65046	Mon Oct 26 2015	Windows 8 training
Dana	Westman	65012	Mon Sep 07 2015	Bi-annual computer maintenance
Dana	Westman	65030	Tue Oct 06 2015	Clean malware from system
Dana	Westman	65045	Fri Oct 23 2015	Set up automatic backup

Page 1

Project 2 Modify Query Results by Changing the Join Property
Project 2c, UnassignedWO Query

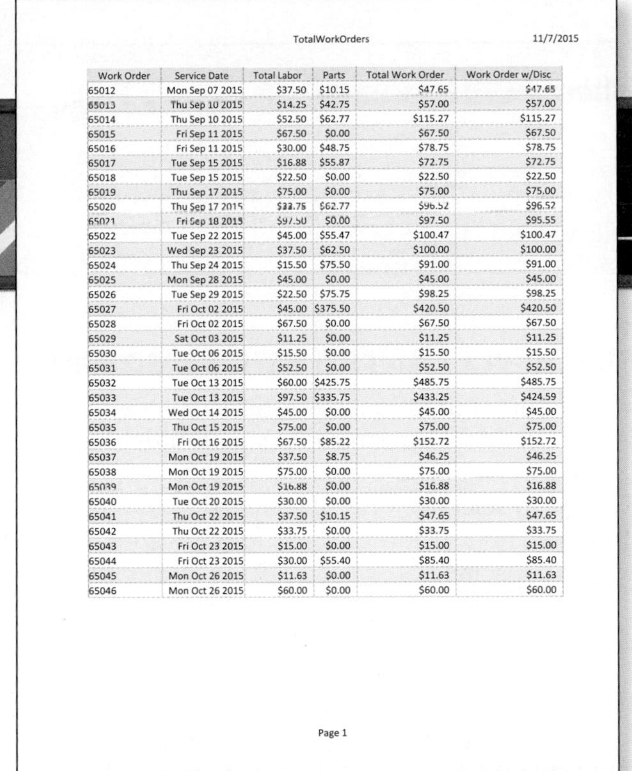

TotalWorkOrders 11/7/2015

Work Order	Service Date	Total Labor	Parts	Total Work Order	Work Order w/Disc
65012	Mon Sep 07 2015	$37.50	$10.15	$47.65	$47.65
65013	Thu Sep 10 2015	$14.25	$42.75	$57.00	$57.00
65014	Thu Sep 10 2015	$52.50	$62.77	$115.27	$115.27
65015	Fri Sep 11 2015	$67.50	$0.00	$67.50	$67.50
65016	Fri Sep 11 2015	$30.00	$48.75	$78.75	$78.75
65017	Tue Sep 15 2015	$16.88	$55.87	$72.75	$72.75
65018	Tue Sep 15 2015	$22.50	$0.00	$22.50	$22.50
65019	Thu Sep 17 2015	$75.00	$0.00	$75.00	$75.00
65020	Thu Sep 17 2015	$33.75	$62.77	$96.52	$96.52
65021	Fri Sep 18 2015	$97.50	$0.00	$97.50	$95.55
65022	Tue Sep 22 2015	$45.00	$55.47	$100.47	$100.47
65023	Wed Sep 23 2015	$37.50	$62.50	$100.00	$100.00
65024	Thu Sep 24 2015	$15.50	$75.50	$91.00	$91.00
65025	Mon Sep 28 2015	$45.00	$0.00	$45.00	$45.00
65026	Tue Sep 29 2015	$22.50	$75.75	$98.25	$98.25
65027	Fri Oct 02 2015	$45.00	$375.50	$420.50	$420.50
65028	Fri Oct 02 2015	$67.50	$0.00	$67.50	$67.50
65029	Sat Oct 03 2015	$11.25	$0.00	$11.25	$11.25
65030	Tue Oct 06 2015	$15.50	$0.00	$15.50	$15.50
65031	Tue Oct 06 2015	$52.50	$0.00	$52.50	$52.50
65032	Tue Oct 13 2015	$60.00	$425.75	$485.75	$485.75
65033	Tue Oct 13 2015	$97.50	$335.75	$433.25	$424.59
65034	Wed Oct 14 2015	$45.00	$0.00	$45.00	$45.00
65035	Thu Oct 15 2015	$75.00	$0.00	$75.00	$75.00
65036	Fri Oct 16 2015	$67.50	$85.22	$152.72	$152.72
65037	Mon Oct 19 2015	$37.50	$8.75	$46.25	$46.25
65038	Mon Oct 19 2015	$75.00	$0.00	$75.00	$75.00
65039	Mon Oct 19 2015	$16.88	$0.00	$16.88	$16.88
65040	Tue Oct 20 2015	$30.00	$0.00	$30.00	$30.00
65041	Thu Oct 22 2015	$37.50	$10.15	$47.65	$47.65
65042	Thu Oct 22 2015	$33.75	$0.00	$33.75	$33.75
65043	Fri Oct 23 2015	$15.00	$0.00	$15.00	$15.00
65044	Fri Oct 23 2015	$30.00	$55.40	$85.40	$85.40
65045	Mon Oct 26 2015	$11.63	$0.00	$11.63	$11.63
65046	Mon Oct 26 2015	$60.00	$0.00	$60.00	$60.00

Page 1

Project 3 Calculate Work Order Totals

Project 3c, TotalWorkOrders Query

TechniciansOperatingSys 11/7/2015

First Name	Last Name	Oprrating System
Pat	Hynes	Windows 8
Mihir	Patel	Windows 8
Ana	Takacs	Windows 8
Armando	Colacci	Windows 8

Page 1

Project 4 Query a Multiple-Value Field

TechniciansOperatingSys Query

Sept2015WO 11/7/2015

WO	CustID	TechID	WODate	Descr	ServDate	Hours	Rate	Parts
65012	1000	11	9/7/2015	Bi-annual comp	9/7/2015	1.25	$30.00	$10.15
65013	1000	10	9/7/2015	Replace keyboa	9/10/2015	0.5	$28.50	$42.75
65014	1005	02	9/10/2015	Replace power	9/10/2015	1.75	$30.00	$62.77
65015	1008	04	9/10/2015	Restore operati	9/11/2015	2.25	$30.00	$0.00
65016	1010	06	9/11/2015	Install upgrade	9/11/2015	1	$30.00	$48.75
65017	1015	08	9/14/2015	Replace DVD dr	9/15/2015	0.75	$22.50	$55.87
65018	1020	10	9/14/2015	Upgrade Office	9/15/2015	1	$22.50	$0.00
65019	1025	02	9/15/2015	Upgrade to Wi	9/17/2015	2.5	$30.00	$0.00
65020	1030	01	9/17/2015	Troubleshoot n	9/17/2015	1.5	$22.50	$62.77
65021	1035	06	9/18/2015	Customer has b	9/18/2015	3.25	$30.00	$0.00
65022	1040	04	9/21/2015	Customer repo	9/22/2015	1.5	$30.00	$55.47
65023	1045	03	9/22/2015	Upgrade RAM	9/23/2015	1.25	$30.00	$62.50
65024	1005	04	9/24/2015	Install malware	9/24/2015	1	$15.50	$75.50
65025	1010	06	9/28/2015	Troubleshoot h	9/28/2015	1.5	$30.00	$0.00
65026	1025	02	9/29/2015	Upgrade memo	9/29/2015	0.75	$30.00	$75.75

Page 1

Project 5 Modify Records Using Action Queries

Project 5c, Sept2015WO Table

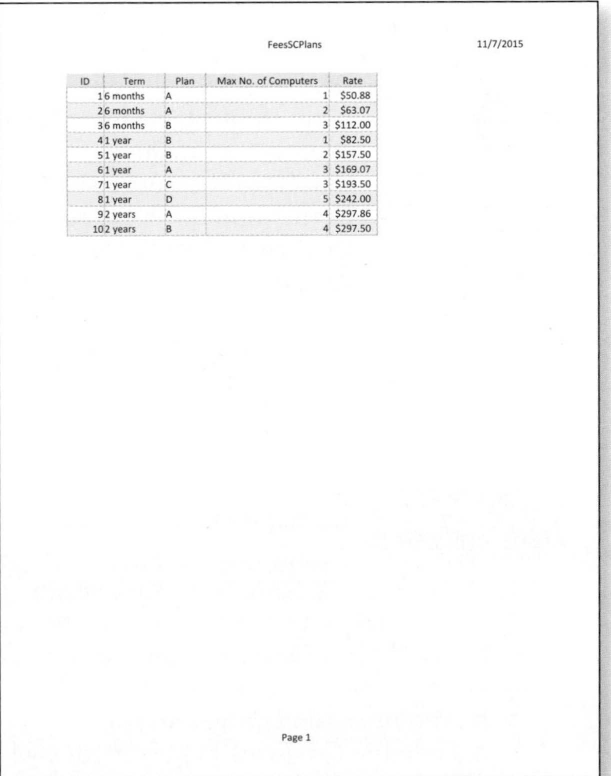

FeesSCPlans 11/7/2015

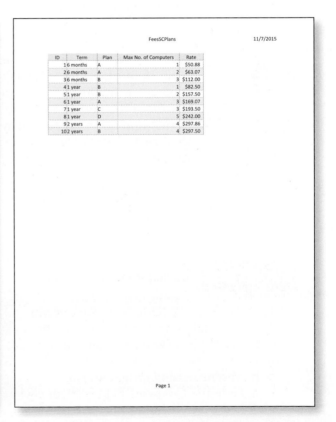

ID	Term	Plan	Max No. of Computers	Rate
1	6 months	A	1	$50.88
2	6 months	A	2	$63.07
3	6 months	B	3	$112.00
4	1 year	B	1	$82.50
5	1 year	B	2	$157.50
6	1 year	A	3	$169.07
7	1 year	C	3	$193.50
8	1 year	D	5	$242.00
9	2 years	A	4	$297.86
10	2 years	B	4	$297.50

Page 1

Project 5d, FeesSCPlans Table

Project 1 Select Records Using Filtered Criteria and Prompted Criteria — 3 Parts

You will create queries to select records by saving a filter's criteria and creating a query that prompts the user for the criteria when the query is run.

Extracting Records Using Select Queries

A ***select query*** is the type of query most often used in Access. Select queries extract records that meet criteria you specify from a single table or multiple tables. The subset of records that a query returns can be edited, viewed, and/or printed. In Query Design view, the criteria used to select records are entered by typing expressions in the *Criteria* row for the required field(s). Access also provides other methods by which query criteria can be specified.

Saving a Filter as a Query

Quick Steps

Save a Filter as a Query
1. Open table.
2. Filter table as desired.
3. Click Advanced button.
4. Click *Filter By Form*.
5. Click Advanced button.
6. Click *Save As Query*.
7. Type desired query name.
8. Click OK.
9. Close Filter By Form datasheet.
10. Close table.

Advanced

A ***filter*** is used in a datasheet or form to temporarily hide records that do not meet specified criteria. For example, you can filter a WorkOrders datasheet to display only those work orders completed on a specified date. The subset of records can be edited, viewed, or printed. Use the Filter by Form feature to filter a datasheet by multiple criteria using a blank datasheet. A filter is active until it is removed or the datasheet or form is closed. When you close a filtered worksheet and then reopen it, all of the records are redisplayed.

If you filter a datasheet and then decide you may want to reuse the criteria, save the filter as a query. You may also want to save a filter as a query if you are more comfortable using filters to select records than you are with typing criteria expressions in Query Design view. To save a filter as a query, click the Advanced button in the Sort & Filter group on the HOME tab and then click *Filter By Form* at the drop-down list to display the criteria. Click the Advanced button again and then click *Save As Query* at the drop-down list. Type a query name at the Save As Query dialog box and then press Enter or click OK. Saving a filter as a query means that all of the columns in the table display in the query results datasheet. Use the Hide Fields feature to remove field(s) from the results.

Project 1a **Saving a Filter as a Query** — **Part 1 of 3**

1. Open **AL2-C3-RSRCompServ.accdb** and enable the contents.
2. Use the Filter by Form feature to display only those service calls that required two or more hours of labor by technicians billed at $30.00 per hour by completing the following steps:
   a. Open the WorkOrders table in Datasheet view.
   b. Minimize the Navigation pane.
   c. Hide the *Comments* field by right-clicking the *Comments* column heading in the datasheet and then clicking *Hide Fields* at the shortcut menu.

d. Click the Advanced button in the Sort & Filter group on the HOME tab and then click *Filter By Form* at the drop-down list.

e. Click in the empty record in the *Hours* column. Type >=2 and then press Tab.

f. With the insertion point positioned in the *Rate* column, click the down-pointing arrow that appears and then click *30* at the drop-down list.

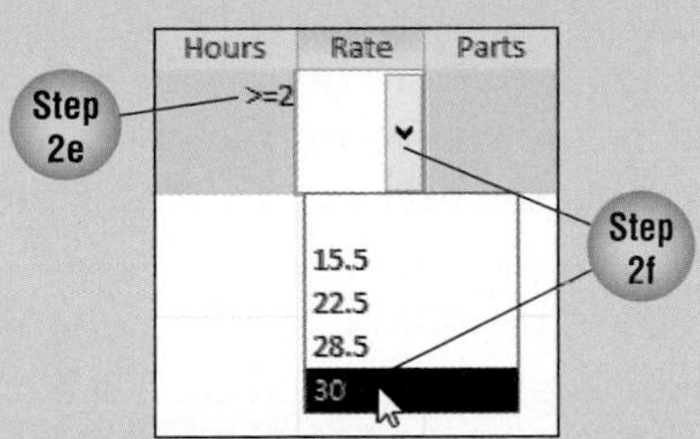

g. Click the Toggle Filter button (which displays the ScreenTip *Apply Filter*) in the Sort & Filter group on the HOME tab. The records that meet the filter conditions are displayed.

3. Review the nine filtered records in the datasheet.
4. Click the Toggle Filter button (which displays the ScreenTip *Remove Filter*) to redisplay all of the records.
5. Click the Advanced button and then click *Filter By Form* at the drop-down list. Notice that the filter criteria in the *Hours* and *Rate* columns are intact.

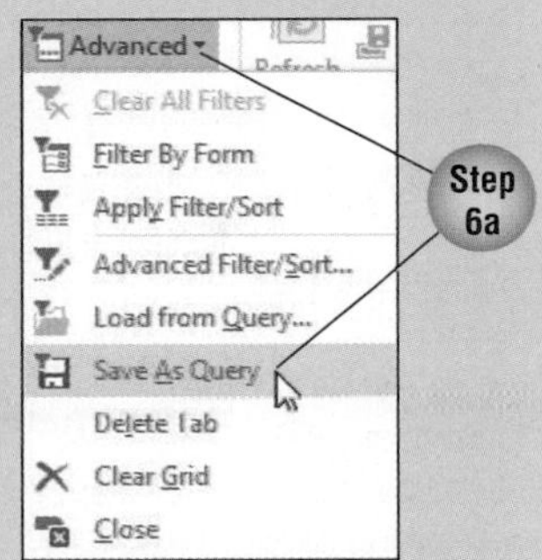

6. Save the filter as a query so that you can reuse the criteria by completing the following steps:
   a. Click the Advanced button and then click *Save As Query* at the drop-down list.
   b. At the Save As Query dialog box, type **WO2orMoreHrsRate30** in the *Query Name* text box and then press Enter or click OK.

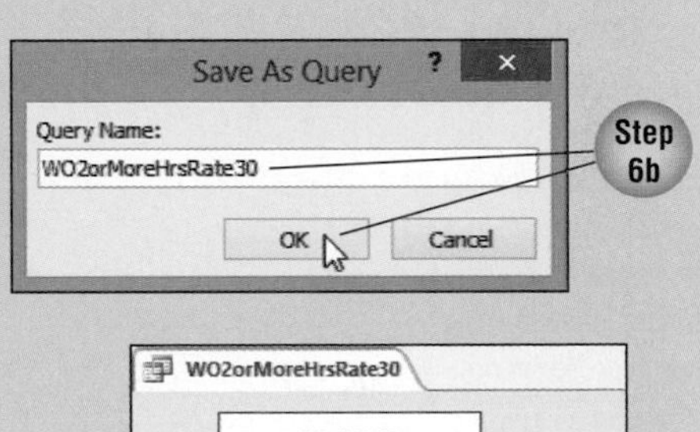

   c. Click the Advanced button and then click *Close* at the drop-down list to close the Filter By Form datasheet.
   d. Close the WorkOrders table. Click No when prompted to save changes to the table design.
7. Expand the Navigation pane.
8. Double-click the query object *WO2orMoreHrsRate30* to open the query and then review the results.
9. Hide the *Comments* column in the query results datasheet.
10. Print the datasheet in landscape orientation with the left and right margins set to 0.5 inch.
11. Switch to Design view. Notice that the query design grid for a query created from a filter includes columns only for those columns for which criteria have been defined.
12. Close the query. Click Yes when prompted to save changes to the query layout.

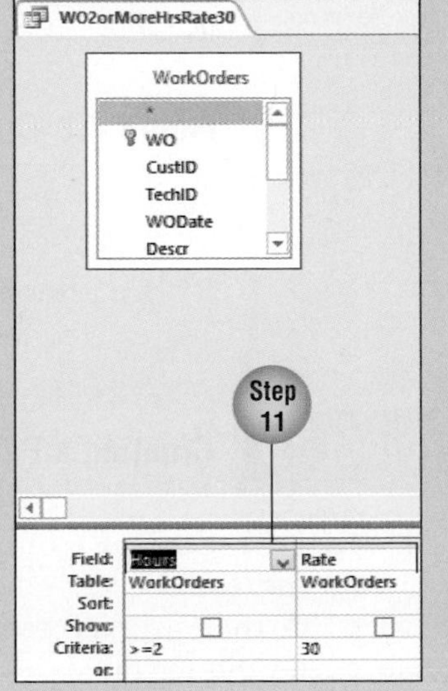

Prompting for Criteria Using a Parameter Query

Quick Steps

Create a Parameter Query

1. Start new query in Design view.
2. Add desired table(s).
3. Close Show Table dialog box.
4. Add desired fields to query design grid.
5. Click in *Criteria* row in field to be prompted.
6. Type message text encased in square brackets.
7. Repeat Steps 5–6 for each additional criterion field.
8. Save query.
9. Close query.

If you are creating a parameter query that will be used by other people, consider adding an example of an acceptable entry in the message. For example, the message *Type the service date in the format mmm-dd-yyyy (example Oct-31-2015)* is more informative than *Type the service date.*

In a ***parameter query***, specific criteria for a field are not stored with the query design. Instead, the field(s) used to select records have a prompt message that displays when the query is run. The prompt message instructs the user to type the criteria by which to select records.

Figure 3.1 illustrates the Enter Parameter Value dialog box that is displayed when a parameter query to select by a technician's name is run. The message that is shown in the dialog box is created in the field for which the criterion will be applied. When the query is run, the user types the criterion at the Enter Parameter Value dialog box and Access selects the records based on the entry. If more than one field contains a parameter, Access prompts the user one field at a time.

A parameter query is useful if you run a query several times on the same field but use different criteria each time. For example, if you needed a list of each technician's work orders, you would have to create a separate query for each technician. This would create several query objects in the Navigation pane. Creating a parameter query that prompts you to enter the technician's name means you only have to create one query.

To create a parameter query, start a new query in Design view and add the desired tables and fields to the query design grid. Type a message enclosed in square brackets to prompt the user for the required criterion in the *Criteria* row of the field to be used to select records. Access does not allow you to include punctuation at the end of the message. The text inside the square brackets is displayed in the Enter Parameter Value dialog box when the query is run. Figure 3.2 displays the entry in the *Criteria* row of the *FName* field that generated the Enter Parameter Value message shown in Figure 3.1.

Figure 3.1 Enter Parameter Value Dialog Box

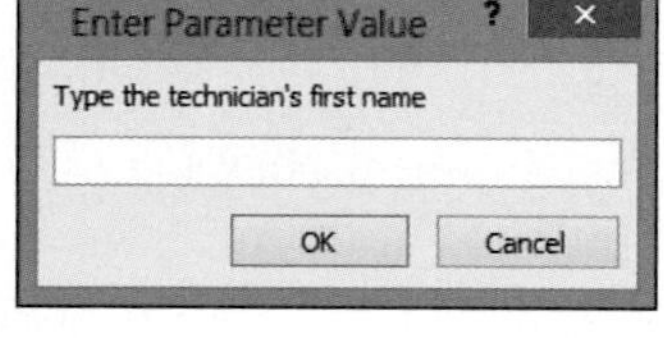

Figure 3.2 Criterion to Prompt for the Name in the *FName* Field

Field:	WO	FName
Table:	WorkOrders	Technicians
Sort:		
Show:	☑	☑
Criteria:		[Type the technician's first name]
or:		

Type a message in square brackets to prompt the user for the criterion by which to select records.

Project 1b **Creating a Parameter Query to Prompt for Technician Names** **Part 2 of 3**

1. With **AL2-C3-RSRCompServ.accdb** open, create a query in Design view to select records from the Technicians table and the WorkOrders table by completing the following steps:
   a. Click the CREATE tab and then click the Query Design button in the Queries group.
   b. At the Show Table dialog box, add the Technicians table and the WorkOrders table to the query.

c. Close the Show Table dialog box.
d. At the top of the query, drag the bottom border of each table's field list box until all of the field names are visible in the box.
e. Double-click the following field names in the Technicians and WorkOrders field list boxes to add the fields to the query design grid (click the field names in the order indicated): *WO*, *FName*, *LName*, *ServDate*, *Hours*, *Rate*.

These fields are added to the query design grid in Step 1e.

Field:	WO	FName	LName	ServDate	Hours	Rate
Table:	WorkOrders	Technicians	Technicians	WorkOrders	WorkOrders	WorkOrders
Sort:						
Show:	☑	☑	☑	☑	☑	☑

2. Click the Run button in the Results group on the QUERY TOOLS DESIGN tab to run the query.
3. Add parameters to select records by a technician's first and last names by completing the following steps:
   a. Switch to Design view.
   b. Click in the *Criteria* row in the *FName* column in the query design grid, type **[Type the technician's first name]**, and then press Enter.
   c. Position the mouse pointer on the vertical line between *FName* and *LName* in the gray field selector bar above the field names until the pointer changes to a left-and-right-pointing arrow with a vertical line in the middle and then double-click to expand the width of the *FName* column so you can see the entire criterion entry.

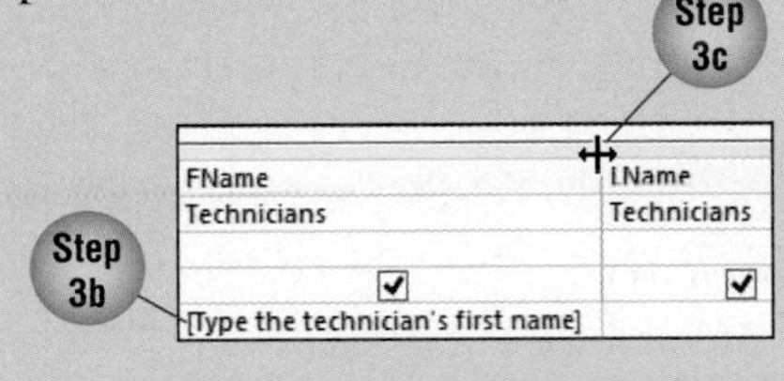

   d. With the insertion point positioned in the *Criteria* row in the *LName* column, type **[Type the technician's last name]** and then press Enter.
   e. Expand the width of the *LName* column so you can see the entire criterion entry.
4. Click the Save button on the Quick Access toolbar, type **PromptedTechnicianLabor** in the *Query Name* text box at the Save As dialog box, and then press Enter or click OK.
5. Close the query.
6. Run the parameter query and extract a list of work orders for the technician named Pat Hynes by completing the following steps:
   a. Double-click the query named *PromptedTechnicianLabor* in the Navigation pane.
   b. Type **pat** at the first Enter Parameter Value dialog box, which displays the message *Type the technician's first name*, and then press Enter or click OK. Note that Access is not case-sensitive for text strings.

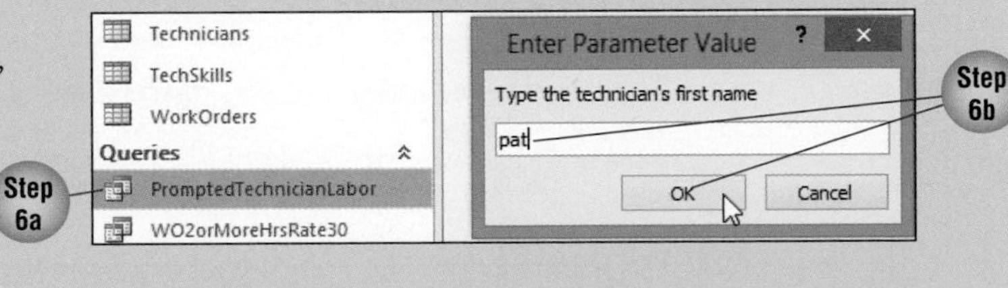

   c. Type **hynes** at the second Enter Parameter Value dialog box, which displays the message *Type the technician's last name*, and then press Enter or click OK.

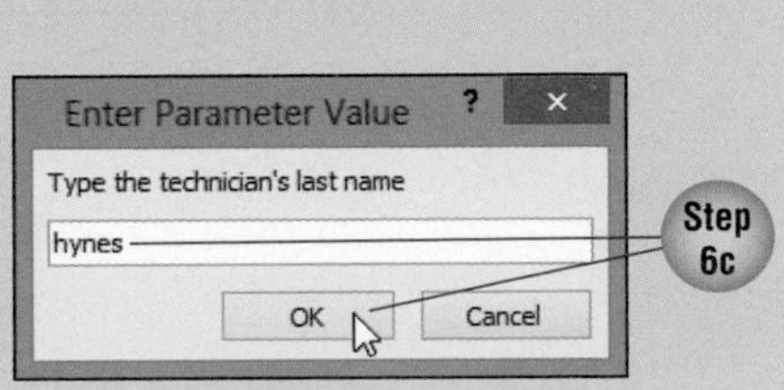

7. Review the records in the query results datasheet.
8. Print the query results datasheet.
9. Close the query.

Project 1c Creating a Parameter Query to Prompt for a Starting and Ending Date Part 3 of 3

1. With **AL2-C3-RSRCompServ.accdb** open, create a parameter query in Design view to prompt the user for the starting and ending dates by which to select records in the WorkOrders table by completing the following steps:
   a. Click the CREATE tab and then click the Query Design button in the Queries group.
   b. At the Show Table dialog box, add the WorkOrders table to the query and then close the dialog box.
   c. Drag the bottom border of the table's field list box until all of the field names are visible.
   d. Add the following fields to the query design grid in this order: *WO, CustID, Descr, ServDate, Hours, Rate, Parts*.
   e. Click in the *Criteria* row in the *ServDate* column, type the entry **Between [Type starting date] And [Type ending date]**, and then press Enter.

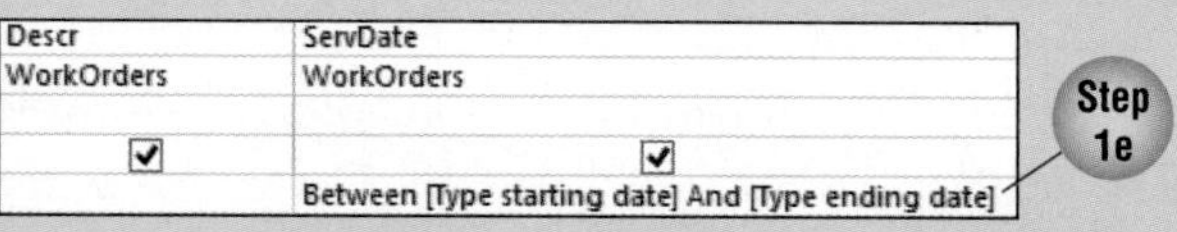

   f. Expand the *ServDate* column width until the entire criterion entry is visible.
2. Save the query, type **PromptedServiceDate** at the Save As dialog box, and then press Enter or click OK.
3. Close the query.
4. Double-click *PromptedServiceDate* in the Navigation pane. At the first Enter Parameter Value dialog box, with *Type starting date* displayed, type **October 5, 2015** and then press Enter or click OK. At the second Enter Parameter Value dialog box, with *Type ending date* displayed, type **October 16, 2015** and then press Enter or click OK.

PromptedServiceDate

Work Order	Customer ID	Description	Service Date	Hours	Rate	Parts
65030	1000	Clean malware from system	Tue Oct 06 2015	1.00	15.50	$0.00
65031	1045	Customer reports noisy hard drive	Tue Oct 06 2015	1.75	30.00	$0.00
65032	1008	Install second hard drive	Tue Oct 13 2015	2.00	30.00	$425.75
65033	1000	Install Windows 8	Tue Oct 13 2015	3.25	30.00	$335.75
65034	1035	File management training	Wed Oct 14 2015	1.50	30.00	$0.00
65035	1020	Office 2013 training	Thu Oct 15 2015	2.50	30.00	$0.00
65036	1008	Set up home network	Fri Oct 16 2015	3.00	22.50	$85.22

Records within the date range October 5, 2015 to October 16, 2015 are selected in Step 4.

5. Print the query results datasheet in landscape orientation.
6. Close the query.

Project 2 Modify Query Results by Changing the Join Property

5 Parts

You will create and modify queries that obtain various results based on changing the join properties for related tables.

Modifying Join Properties in a Query

The term ***join properties*** refers to the manner in which Access matches the field values in the common field between the two tables in a relationship. The method used determines how many records are selected for inclusion in the query results datasheet. Access provides for three join types in a relationship: an inner join, left outer join, and right outer join. By default, Access uses an inner join between the tables, which means that records are selected for display in a query only when a match on the joined field value exists in both tables. If a record exists in either table with no matching record in the other table, the record is not displayed in the query results datasheet. This means that in some cases, you may not see all of the records from both tables when you run a query.

HINT

You can edit a relationship if you always want the join type to be a left or right outer join. To do this, click the Join Type button in the Edit Relationships dialog box to open the Join Properties dialog box. Select the desired join type and then click OK.

Specifying the Join Type

Double-click the black join line between tables in a query to open the Join Properties dialog box, shown in Figure 3.3. By default, option 1, referred to as an ***inner join***, is selected. In an inner join, only those records for which the primary key field value in the primary table matches a foreign key field value in the related table are displayed.

Options 2 and 3 are referred to as ***outer joins***. Option 2 is a ***left outer join.*** In this type of join, the primary table (referred to as the *left table*) displays all of the rows, whereas the related table (referred to as the *right table*) shows only rows with matching values in the foreign key field. For example, examine the query results datasheet shown in Figure 3.4 on the next page. This query was created with the Technicians and TechSkills tables. All of the technician records are shown in the datasheet, but notice that some technician records display with empty field values for the columns from the TechSkills table. These records reflect the technicians who have not yet had any information entered in the TechSkills table. In a left outer join, all of the records from the primary table in the relationship are shown in the query results datasheet

Quick Steps

Create a Query with a Left Outer Join

1. Create new query in Design view.
2. Add tables to query window.
3. Double-click join line between tables.
4. Select option 2.
5. Click OK.
6. Add desired fields to query design grid.
7. Save and run query.

HINT

Changing the join type at a query window does not alter the join type for other objects based on the relationship. The revised join property applies to the query only.

Figure 3.3 Join Properties Dialog Box

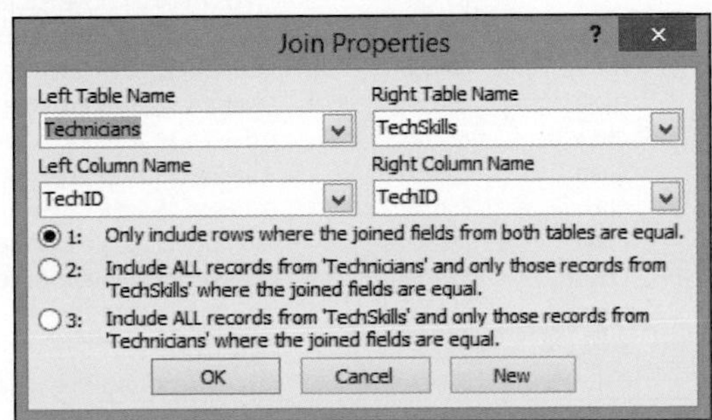

Figure 3.4 Left Outer Join Example

	First Name	Last Name	Certifications	Operating Systems	Network Specialist?	Design Websites?	Programming?
	Pat	Hynes	Cisco CCNP, CompTIA A+, Microsoft MCTS	Linux, Unix, Windows 7, Windows 8	☑	☐	☑
	Hui	Chen	Cisco CCNP, CompTIA A+	Linux, Unix, Windows 7	☑	☑	☐
	Kayla	Blewett			■	■	■
	Mihir	Patel	CompTIA A+, Microsoft MCTS	Unix, Windows 8, Windows Vista	☐	☐	☑
	Madir	Sadiku	CompTIA A+, Microsoft MCTS	Mac OS X, Windows 7, Windows Vista	☐	☐	☐
	Brody	Stewart			■	■	■
	Ana	Takacs	Cisco CCNA	Mac OS X, Windows 8	☑	☐	☑
	Marty	O'Leary	Cisco CCNP	Linux, Unix	☑	☑	☐
	Armando	Colacci	Microsoft Master	Windows 7, Windows 8, Windows Vista	☐	☐	☑
	Kelsey	Eastman	Cisco CCNA, Microsoft MCTS	Linux, Windows 7, Windows Vista	☑	☑	☐
	Dana	Westman			■	■	■
*					■	■	■

Left outer join query results show blank related *TechSkills* fields for those technicians who do not yet have records in the TechSkills table.

Quick Steps

Create a Query with a Right Outer Join

1. Create new query in Design view.
2. Add tables to query window.
3. Double-click join line between tables.
4. Select option *3*.
5. Click OK.
6. Add desired fields to query design grid.
7. Save and run query.

Option 3 is a ***right outer join.*** In this type of join, the related table (right table) shows all of the rows, whereas the primary table (left table) shows only rows with matching values in the common field. For example, examine the partial query results datasheet shown in Figure 3.5. This datasheet illustrates 15 of the 39 records in the query results datasheet from the Technicians and WorkOrders tables. Notice that the first four records have no technician first or last name. These are the work orders that have not yet been assigned to a technician. In a right outer join, all of the records from the related table in the relationship are shown in the query results datasheet. In a left or right outer join, Access displays an arrow at the end of the join line pointing to the table that shows only matching rows.

To illustrate the difference in query results when no change is made to the join type, examine the query results datasheet shown in Figure 3.6. This is the datasheet you will create in Project 2a. In this project, you will create a list with the technician names and qualifications. Compare the number of records shown in Figure 3.6 with the number of records shown in Figure 3.4. Notice that fewer records display in the datasheet in Figure 3.6. Since an inner join displays only those records for which matching entries exists in both tables, records from either table that do not have matching records in the other table are not displayed. Understanding that an inner join (the default join type) may not display all of the records that exist in the tables when you run a query is important.

Figure 3.5 Right Outer Join Example

First Name	Last Name	Work Order	WO Date	Description
		65047	Tue Oct 27 2015	Set up automatic backup
		65048	Thu Oct 29 2015	Replace LCD monitor
		65049	Fri Oct 30 2015	Set up dual monitor system
		65050	Fri Oct 30 2015	Reinstall Windows 8
Pat	Hynes	65020	Thu Sep 17 2015	Troubleshoot noisy fan
Pat	Hynes	65033	Mon Oct 12 2015	Install Windows 8
Pat	Hynes	65038	Mon Oct 19 2015	Install Windows 8
Hui	Chen	65014	Thu Sep 10 2015	Replace power supply
Hui	Chen	65019	Tue Sep 15 2015	Upgrade to Windows 8
Hui	Chen	65026	Tue Sep 29 2015	Upgrade memory
Hui	Chen	65032	Mon Oct 12 2015	Install second hard drive
Hui	Chen	65035	Wed Oct 14 2015	Office 2013 training
Kayla	Blewett	65023	Tue Sep 22 2015	Upgrade RAM
Kayla	Blewett	65036	Thu Oct 15 2015	Set up home network
Kayla	Blewett	65041	Thu Oct 22 2015	Bi-annual computer maintenance

Right outer join query results show blank related technician fields for those work orders that have yet to be assigned to a technician.

Figure 3.6 Inner Join Example

First Name	Last Name	Certifications	Operating Systems	Network Specialist?	Design Websites?	Programming?
Pat	Hynes	Cisco CCNP, CompTIA A+, Microsoft MCTS	Linux, Unix, Windows 7, Windows 8	☑	☐	☑
Hui	Chen	Cisco CCNP, CompTIA A+	Linux, Unix, Windows 7	☑	☑	☐
Mihir	Patel	CompTIA A+, Microsoft MCTS	Unix, Windows 8, Windows Vista	☐	☐	☑
Madir	Sadiku	CompTIA A+, Microsoft MCTS	Mac OS X, Windows 7, Windows Vista	☐	☐	☐
Ana	Takacs	Cisco CCNA	Mac OS X, Windows 8	☑	☐	☑
Marty	O'Leary	Cisco CCNP	Linux, Unix	☑	☑	☐
Armando	Colacci	Microsoft Master	Windows 7, Windows 8, Windows Vista	☐	☐	☑
Kelsey	Eastman	Cisco CCNA, Microsoft MCTS	Linux, Windows 7, Windows Vista	☑	☑	☐
*						

An inner join displays a record from either table only when a matching value in the joined field exists in the other table. No blank records appear in the query results. However, notice that you are not viewing all of the records in the technicians table.

Project 2a Selecting Records in a Query Using an Inner Join

Part 1 of 4

1. With **AL2-C3-RSRCompServ.accdb** open, create a query in Design view to display a list of technicians that notes each technician's skill specialties by completing the following steps:
   a. Create a new query in Design view. At the Show Table dialog box, add the Technicians and TechSkills tables. Close the Show Table dialog box and then drag the bottom border of each table's field list box until all of the field names are visible in the box.
   b. Double-click the black join line between the two tables to open the Join Properties dialog box.

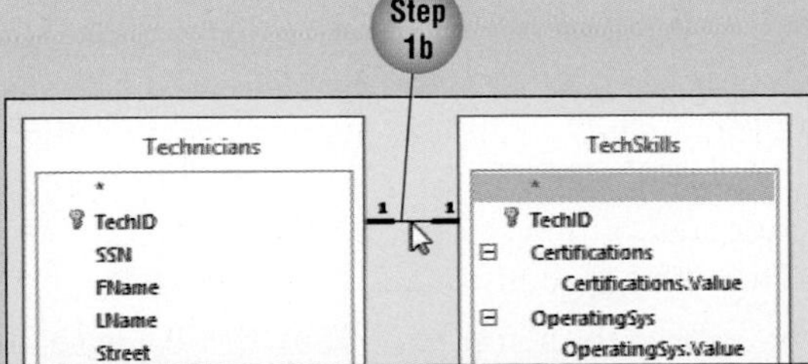

   c. At the Join Properties dialog box, notice that option *1* is selected by default. Option 1 selects records only when the joined fields from both tables are equal. This represents an inner join. Click OK.
   d. Add the following fields to the query design grid in order: *FName, LName, Certifications, OperatingSys, NetworkSpc, WebDesign, Programming.*
   e. Run the query.

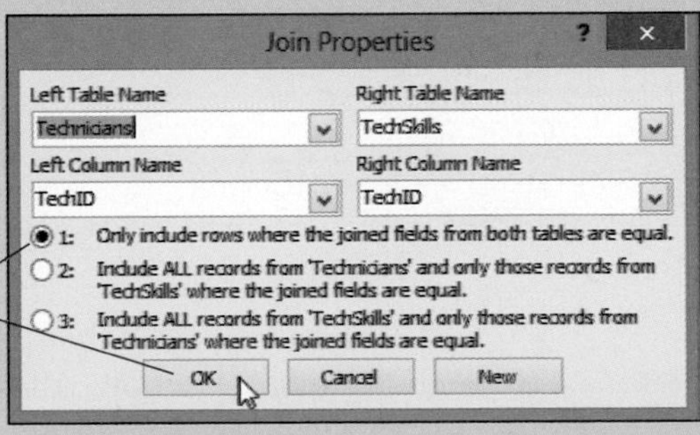

2. Minimize the Navigation pane and then compare your results with the query results datasheet displayed in Figure 3.6.
3. Save the query and type **TechnicianSpecialties** as the query name.
4. Close the query.
5. Expand the Navigation pane.

Project 2b **Selecting Records in a Query Using a Left Outer Join** **Part 2 of 4**

1. With **AL2-C3-RSRCompServ.accdb** open, modify the TechnicianSpecialties query to a left outer join to check whether any technicians have not had any information entered in the TechSkills table by completing the following steps:
   a. Right-click the TechnicianSpecialties query and then click *Design View* at the shortcut menu.
   b. Right-click the black join line between the two tables and then click *Join Properties* at the shortcut menu.
   c. At the Join Properties dialog box, click option 2 and then click OK. Option 2 includes all of the records from the Technicians table and only those records from TechSkills for which the joined fields are equal. The left table (Technicians) is the table that will show all of the records. If a technician does not have a matching record in the other table, the columns display empty fields next to the technician's name.
   d. Notice that the join line between the two tables now displays with an arrow pointing to the joined field in the TechSkills table.
   e. Run the query.
2. Minimize the Navigation pane and then compare your results with the query results datasheet displayed in Figure 3.4 on page 76. Notice that 11 records display in this datasheet, whereas only 8 records displayed in the query results from Project 2a.
3. Click the FILE tab and then click the *Save As* Option. At the Save As backstage area, click *Save Object As* in the *File Types* section and then click the Save As button. At the Save As dialog box, type **AllTechnicianSkills** in the *Save 'TechnicianSpecialties' to* text box and then press Enter or click OK.
4. Close the query.
5. Expand the Navigation pane.

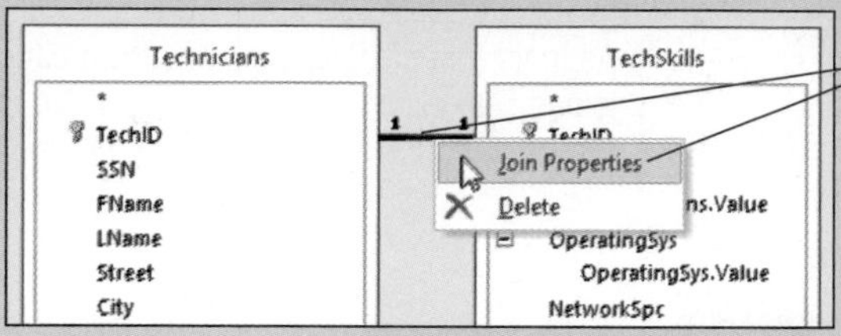

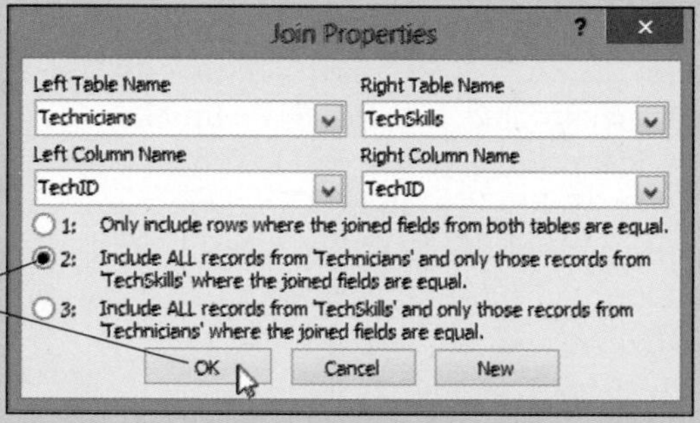

Do not assume that a left join always occurs with the table that is the left table in the query window. Although Technicians was the left table in the Project 2b query window, the term *left* refers to the table that represents the "one" side (primary table) in the relationship.

Adding Tables to and Removing Tables from a Query

Show Table

Open a query in Design view to add a table to a query. Click the Show Table button in the Query Setup group on the QUERY TOOLS DESIGN tab and then add the desired table using the Show Table dialog box. Close the Show Table dialog box when finished.

To remove a table from a query, click any field within the table field list box to activate the table in the query window and then press Delete. The table is removed from the window and all of the fields associated with the table that were added to the query design grid are automatically removed. You can also remove a table by right-clicking the table in the query window and then clicking *Remove Table* at the shortcut menu.

Project 2c **Selecting Records in a Query Using a Right Outer Join** **Part 3 of 4**

1. With **AL2-C3-RSRCompServ.accdb** open, modify an existing query to create a new query to check for work orders that have not been assigned to a technician by completing the following steps:
   a. Open the TechnicianSpecialties query in Design view.
   b. Right-click the *TechSkills* table name in the Table fields list box in the query window and then click *Remove Table* at the shortcut menu. Notice that the last five columns are removed from the query design grid along with the table.

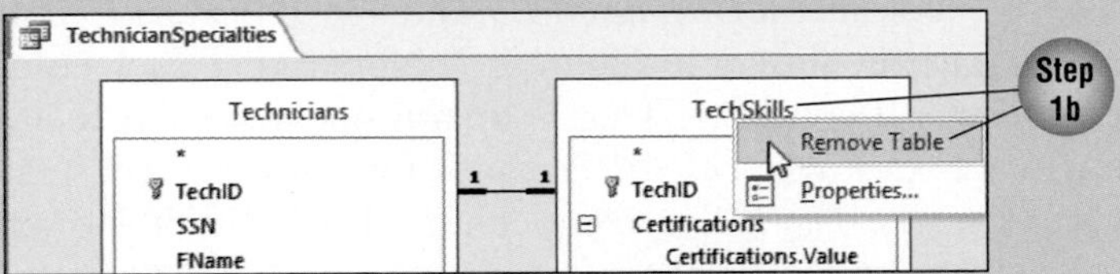

   c. Click the Show Table button in the Query Setup group on the QUERY TOOLS DESIGN tab.
   d. At the Show Table dialog box, double-click *WorkOrders* in the Tables list, click the Close button, and then drag the bottom border of the WorkOrders table field list box until all of the fields are visible in the box.
   e. Double-click the black join line between the two tables.
   f. At the Join Properties dialog box, click option 3 and then click OK. Option 3 includes all of the records from the WorkOrders table and only those records from the Technicians table for which the joined fields are equal. The right table (WorkOrders) is the table that will show all of the records. If a work order does not have a matching record in the other table, the columns display empty fields for the technician names.

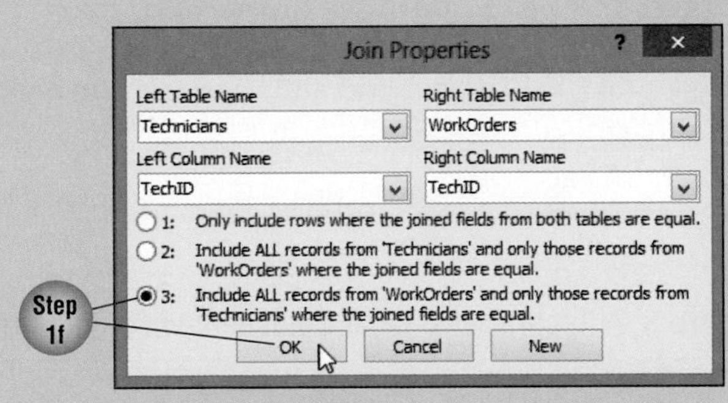

   g. Notice that the join line between the two tables now displays with an arrow pointing to the joined field in the Technicians table.
   h. Add the following fields from the WorkOrders table to the query design grid in this order: *WO*, *WODate*, *Descr*.
2. Click the FILE tab and then click the *Save As* option. At the Save As backstage area, click *Save Object As* in the *File Types* section and then click the Save As button. At the Save As dialog box, type **UnassignedWO** in the *Save 'TechnicianSpecialties' to* text box and then press Enter or click OK.
3. Run the query.

4. Compare your results with the partial query results datasheet shown in Figure 3.5 on page 76. Notice that the first four records in the query results datasheet have empty fields in the *First Name* and *Last Name* columns.
5. Double-click the right column boundary of the *Description* column to adjust the column width and then print the query results datasheet with the right margin set to 0.5 inch.
6. Close the query. Click Yes to save changes.

Quick Steps

Create a Self-Join Query

1. Create query in Design view.
2. Add two copies of table to query.
3. Right-click second table name.
4. Click *Properties.*
5. Click in *Alias* property box and delete existing table name.
6. Type alias table name.
7. Close Property Sheet.
8. Drag field name from left table to field name with matching values in right table.
9. Add fields as required to query design grid.
10. Run query.
11. Save query.

In a self-join query, the two fields joined must have the same data type.

Do not assume that a right join always occurs with the table that is the right table in the query window. Although WorkOrders was the right table in the Project 2c query window, *right* refers to the table that represents the *many* side (related table) in the relationship.

Creating a Self-Join Query

Assume that you have a table in which two fields contain similar field values. For example, look at the *Technician ID* and *Tier 2 Supervisor* columns in the Technicians table datasheet shown in Figure 3.7. Notice that each column contains a technician's ID number. Tier 2 supervisors are senior technicians who are called in when a work order is too complex for a regular technician to solve. The ID number in the *Tier 2 Supervisor* column is the ID of the senior technician who is assigned to the technician.

You may find it more informative to view the list of technicians with the Tier 2 supervisor's last name instead of his or her ID number. If you have a table that has matching values in two separate fields, you can create a ***self-join query,*** which creates a relationship between fields in the same table. To create a self-join query, add two copies of the same table to the query window. Name the second occurrence of the table using the original table name with *_1* added to the end. You can assign an alias to the second table to provide it with a more descriptive name in the query. Next, join the two tables by dragging the field with matching values from one table field list to the other. Add the required fields to the query design grid and then run the query.

Figure 3.7 Technicians Table Datasheet with Fields Used in Self-Join Query

Technician ID	SSN	First Name	Last Name	Street Address	City	State	ZIP Code	Home Phone	Cell Phone	(attachment)	Tier 2 Supervisor
01	000-45-5368	Pat	Hynes	206-31 Woodland Street	Detroit	MI	48202-1138	313-555-6874	313-555-6412	(1)	03
02	000-47-3258	Hui	Chen	12905 Hickory Street	Detroit	MI	48205-3462	313-555-7468	313-555-5234	(1)	06
03	000-62-7468	Kayla	Blewett	1310 Jarvis Street	Detroit	MI	48220-2011	313-555-3265	313-555-6486	(1)	
04	000-33-1485	Mihir	Patel	8213 Elgin Street	Detroit	MI	48234-4092	313-555-7458	313-555-6385	(1)	11
05	000-48-7850	Madir	Sadiku	8190 Kenwood Street	Detroit	MI	48220-1132	313-555-6327	313-555-8569	(1)	03
06	000-75-8412	Brody	Stewart	3522 Moore Place	Detroit	MI	48208-1032	313-555-7499	313-555-3625	(1)	
07	000-55-1248	Ana	Takacs	14902 Hampton Court	Detroit	MI	48215-3616	313-555-6142	313-555-4586	(0)	11
08	000-63-1247	Marty	O'Leary	14000 Vernon Drive	Detroit	MI	48237-1320	313-555-9856	313-555-4125	(0)	11
09	000-84-1254	Armando	Colacci	17302 Windsor Avenue	Detroit	MI	48224-2257	313-555-9641	313-555-8796	(0)	06
10	000-43-5789	Kelsey	Eastman	550 Montclair Street	Detroit	MI	48214-3274	313-555-6315	313-555-7411	(2)	06
11	000-65-4185	Dana	Westman	18101 Keeler Streeet	Detroit	MI	48223-1322	313-555-5488	313-555-4158	(0)	
*										(0)	

These two fields contain technician ID numbers. Tier 2 supervisors are senior-level technicians who are assigned to handle complex cases for regular technicians.

Creating an Alias for a Table

An *alias* is an additional name to use to reference a table in a query. The alias is temporary and applies to the query only. Generally, you create an alias if you want to assign a shorter name to a table (or a more descriptive name, in the case of a self-join query). For example, one of the tables that you will use in the query in Project 2d is named *Technicians_1*. You can assign the table a more descriptive name, such as *Supervisors*, to more accurately describe the second table's role in the query.

To assign an alias to a table, right-click the table name in the query window and then click *Properties* at the shortcut menu to open the Property Sheet task pane. Click in the *Alias* property box, delete the existing table name, and then type the name by which you want to reference the table. Access replaces all occurrences of the table name in the query design grid with the alias.

Quick Steps

Create an Alias for a Table

1. Open query in Design view.
2. Right-click table name in query window.
3. Click *Properties*.
4. Click *Alias* property box.
5. Delete existing table name.
6. Type alias name.
7. Press Tab.

Project 2d **Creating a Self-Join Query** **Part 4 of 4**

1. With **AL2-C3-RSRCompServ.accdb** open, create a self-join query to display the last name of the Tier 2 supervisor, instead of his or her ID number, by completing the following steps:
   a. Create a new query in Design view.
   b. At the Show Table dialog box, double-click *Technicians* in the list box twice to add two copies of the Technicians table to the query and then close the Show Table dialog box. Notice that the second copy of the table is named *Technicians_1*.
   c. Drag the bottom borders of both table field list boxes down until all of the field names are visible.
   d. Create an alias for the second table by completing the following steps:
      1) Right-click the *Technicians_1* table name.
      2) Click *Properties* at the shortcut menu.
      3) Select and delete the current name in the *Alias* property box in the Property Sheet task pane.
      4) Type **Supervisors** and then close the Property Sheet task pane.

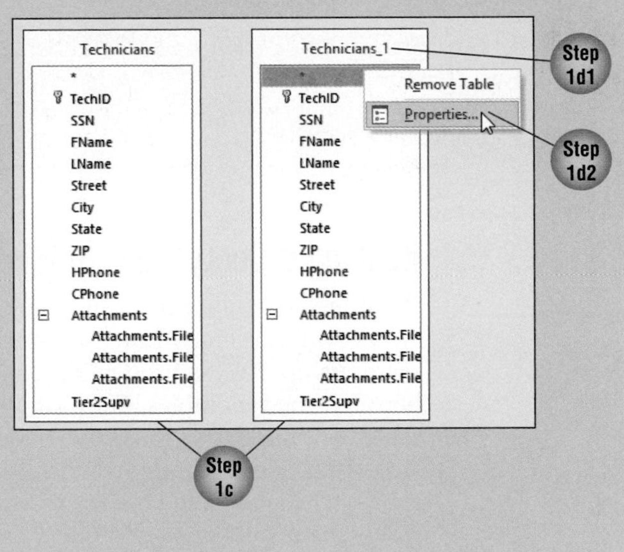

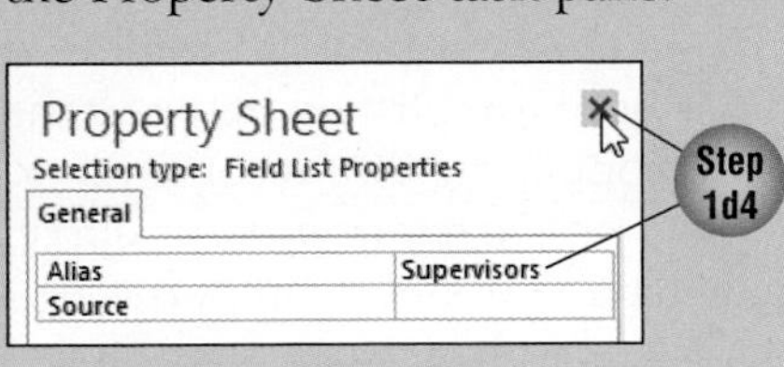

e. Drag the field named *Tier2Supv* from the Technicians table field list box at the left to the field named *TechID* in the Supervisors table field list box at the right. This creates a join line between the two tables.
f. Add the *FName* and *LName* fields from the Technicians table to the query design grid.
g. Add the *LName* field from the Supervisors table to the query design grid.

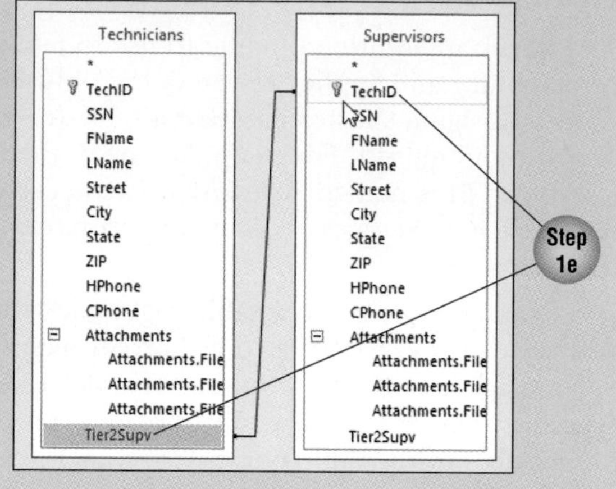

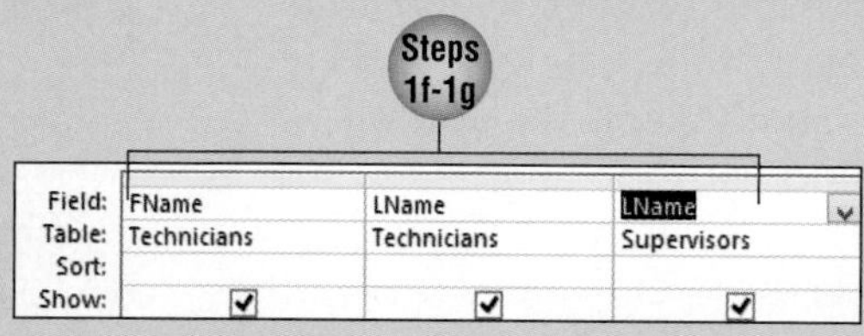

Field:	FName	LName	LName
Table:	Technicians	Technicians	Supervisors
Sort:			
Show:	☑	☑	☑

2. Run the query. The last names displayed in the second *Last Name* column represent the *Tier2Supv* names.
3. Switch to Design view.
4. Right-click the second *LName* column (from the Supervisors table) and then click *Properties* at the shortcut menu. Click in the *Caption* property box in the Property Sheet task pane, type **Tier 2 Supervisor**, and then close the Property Sheet task pane.
5. Save the query. Type **Tier2Supervisors** at the Save As dialog box and then press Enter or click OK.
6. Run the query.
7. Double-click the right column boundary of the *Tier 2 Supervisor* column to adjust the width and then compare your results to the datasheet shown at the right.
8. Close the query. Click Yes to save changes.

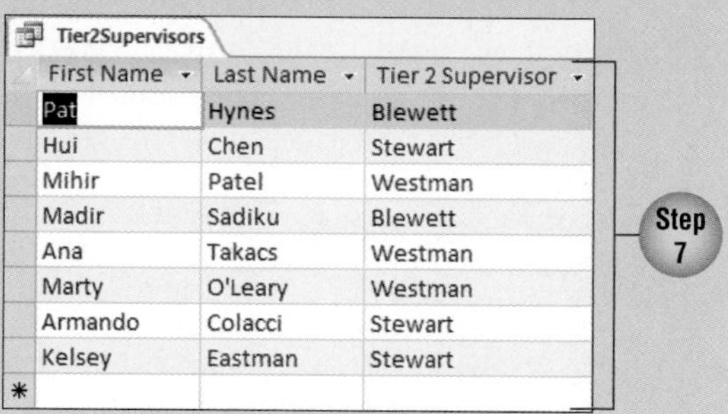

First Name	Last Name	Tier 2 Supervisor
Pat	Hynes	Blewett
Hui	Chen	Stewart
Mihir	Patel	Westman
Madir	Sadiku	Blewett
Ana	Takacs	Westman
Marty	O'Leary	Westman
Armando	Colacci	Stewart
Kelsey	Eastman	Stewart

Running a Query with No Established Relationship

If a query is created from two tables for which no join has been established, Access will not know how to relate the records in the tables. When there is no relationship, Access produces a datasheet representing every combination of records between the two tables. For example, if one table contains 20 records, the other table contains 10 records, and no join has been established between the tables, Access produces a query results datasheet containing 200 records (20 × 10). This type of query is called a ***cross product query*** or ***Cartesian product query***. In most cases, the results of such a query provide data that serves no purpose.

If you add two tables to a query and no join line appears, create a join by dragging a field from one table to a compatible field in the other table. The two fields should contain the same data type and be logically related in some way. If no join can logically be established, a many-to-many relationship exists between the tables, and you may need to add a junction table to the query.

Project 3 Calculate Work Order Totals — 3 Parts

You will use a subquery nested within another query to calculate the total amount earned from each work order. You will also use conditional logic to apply a discount if certain criteria are met.

Creating and Using Subqueries

When performing multiple calculations based on numeric fields, you may decide to create a separate query for each individual calculation and then use subqueries to generate the final total. A ***subquery*** is a query nested inside another query. Using subqueries to break the calculations into individual objects allows you to reuse a calculated field in multiple queries. For example, assume that you want to calculate the total amount for each work order. The WorkOrders table contains fields with the number of hours for each service call, the labor rate, and the total value of the parts used. To find the total for each work order, you need to calculate the total labor by multiplying the hours times the rate and then add the parts value to the total labor value. However, you may want the total labor value to be in a separate query so that you can perform other calculations, such as finding the average, maximum, or minimum labor on work orders. To be able to reuse the total labor value, you will need to create the calculated field in its own query.

Once the query is created to calculate the total labor, you can nest the query inside another query to add the labor to the parts to calculate the total for each work order. Creating subqueries provides you with the flexibility to reuse calculations, thus avoiding duplication of effort and reducing the potential for calculation errors.

In Level 1, Chapter 3, you learned how to insert a calculated field in a query. Recall that the format for inserting an equation in a query is to type in a blank *Field* row the desired field name followed by a colon and then the equation with field names in square brackets—for example, *Total:[Sales]+[SalesTax]*.

Quick Steps

Create a Subquery
1. Start new query in Design view.
2. At Show Table dialog box, click Queries tab.
3. Double-click query to be used as subquery.
4. Add other queries or tables as required.
5. Close Show Table dialog box.
6. Add fields as required.
7. Save and run query.

Subqueries are not restricted to use in nested calculations. Use a subquery for any combination of fields that you want to be able to reuse in multiple queries.

Project 3a Creating a Query to Calculate Total Labor — Part 1 of 3

1. With **AL2-C3-RSRCompServ.accdb** open, create a query to calculate the total labor for each work order by completing the following steps:
   a. Create a new query in Design view. At the Show Table dialog box, add the WorkOrders table to the query window and then close the Show Table dialog box.
   b. Drag the bottom border of the WorkOrders table field list box down until all of the fields are visible.
   c. Add the following fields to the query design grid in this order: *WO, ServDate, Hours, Rate*.
   d. Click in the blank *Field* row next to *Rate* in the query design grid and then click the Builder button in the Query Setup group on the QUERY TOOLS DESIGN tab.
   e. In the Expression Builder dialog box, type **TotalLabor:[Hours]*[Rate]** and then click OK.
   f. Expand the width of the calculated column until you can see the entire formula in the *Field* row.

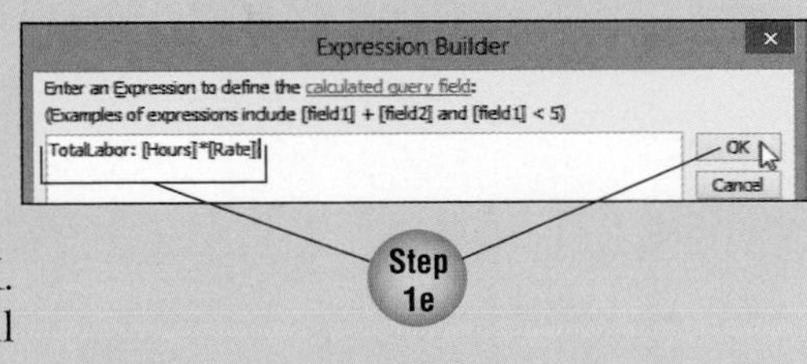

2. Run the query and view the query results. Notice that the *Total Labor* column does not display a consistent number of decimal values.
3. Switch to Design view.
4. Format the *Total Labor* column by completing the following steps:
   a. Activate the field by clicking anywhere within the *Total Labor* field row.
   b. Click the Property Sheet button in the Show/Hide group on the QUERY TOOLS DESIGN tab.
   c. Click in the *Format* property box in the Property Sheet task pane, click the down-pointing arrow that appears, and then click *Standard* at the drop-down list.
   d. Type **Total Labor** in the *Caption* property box.
   e. Close the Property Sheet task pane.

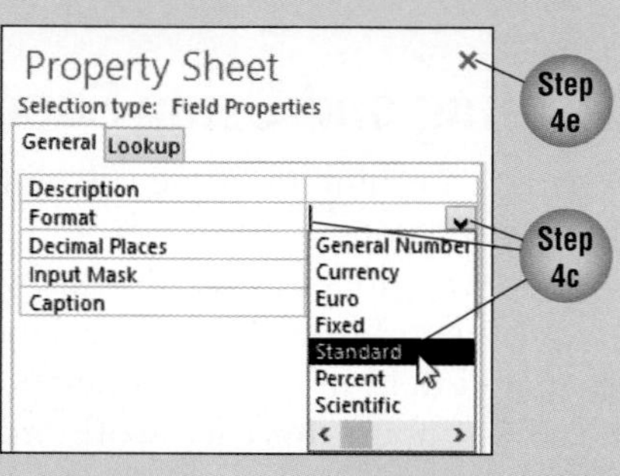

5. Save the query. Type **TotalLabor** at the Save As dialog box and then press Enter or click OK.
6. Run the query. Notice that the last four rows contain no values, because the service calls have not yet been completed.
7. Switch to Design view. Click in the *Criteria* row in the *Hours* column, type **>0**, and then press Enter.
8. Save the revised query and then run the query.
9. Close the query.

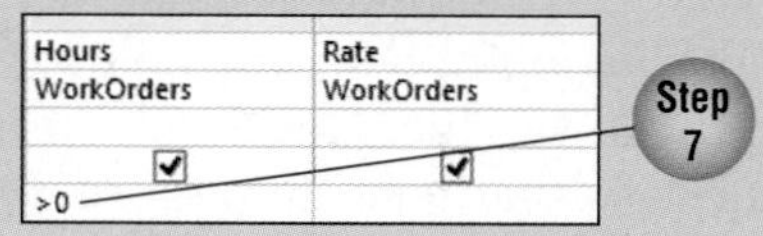

Project 3b Creating a Subquery

Part 2 of 3

1. With **AL2-C3-RSRCompServ.accdb** open, create a new query to calculate the total value of each work order using the TotalLabor query as a subquery by completing the following steps:
   a. Create a new query in Design view.
   b. At the Show Table dialog box, click the Queries tab.
   c. Double-click *TotalLabor* in the queries list.
   d. Click the Tables tab.
   e. Double-click *WorkOrders* in the tables list and then close the Show Table dialog box. Notice that Access has automatically joined the two objects on the *WO* field.

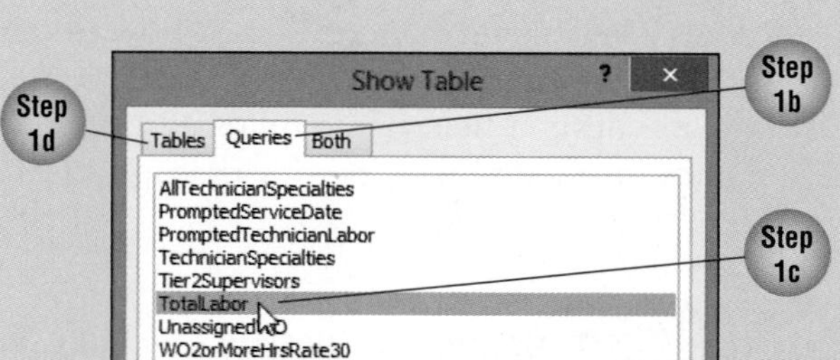

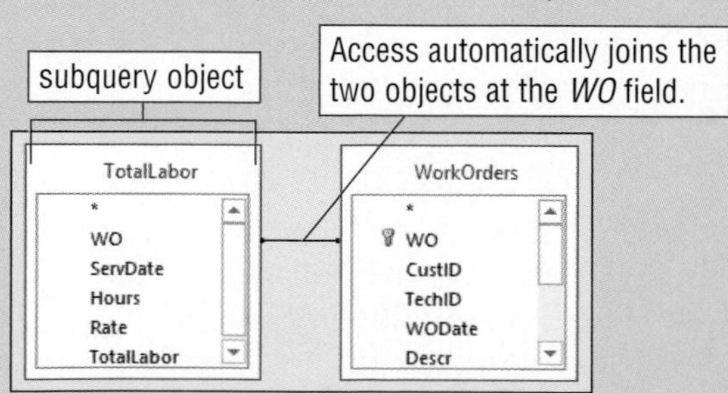

2. Add fields from the TotalLabor subquery and from the WorkOrders table by completing the following steps:
   a. Double-click the asterisk (*) at the top of the TotalLabor table field list box. Access adds the entry *TotalLabor.** to the first column in the query design grid. This entry adds all of the fields from the query. Individual columns do not display in the grid, but when you run the query, the datasheet will show all fields.

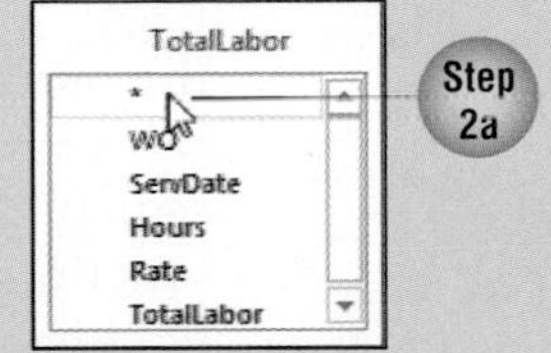

   b. Run the query. Notice that the query results datasheet shows all five columns from the TotalLabor query.
   c. Switch to Design view. You decide to apply the Currency format to the *Total Labor* column in this new query. To do this, you need to add the column to the query design grid as an individual field and not as a group.
   d. Right-click in the field selector bar (the gray bar above the *Field* row) for the *TotalLabor.** column and then click *Cut* at the shortcut menu to remove the column from the design grid.
   e. Add the following fields from the TotalLabor query field list box to the query design grid in this order: *WO*, *ServDate*, *TotalLabor*.
   f. Format the *TotalLabor* column by applying the Currency format.
   g. Drag the bottom border of the WorkOrders table field list box down until all of the fields are visible and then double-click *Parts* to add the field to the query design grid.
3. Create a calculated field to add the total labor and parts by completing the following steps:
   a. Click in the blank *Field* row next to *Parts* in the query design grid, type **TotalWorkOrder:[TotalLabor]+[Parts]**, and then press Enter.
   b. Expand the width of the *TotalWorkOrder* column until the entire formula is visible.
   c. Format the *TotalWorkOrder* column by applying the Currency format.
   d. Type **Total Work Order** in the *Caption* property box.
   e. Close the Property Sheet task pane.

Parts	TotalWorkOrder: [TotalLabor]+[Parts]
WorkOrders	

Step 3b

Step 3a

4. Save the query. Type **TotalWorkOrders** at the Save As dialog box and then press Enter or click OK. Run the query.
5. Double-click the column boundary for the *TotalWorkOrder* column to adjust the column width.

TotalWorkOrders

Work Order	Service Date	Total Labor	Parts	Total Work Order
65012	Mon Sep 07 2015	$37.50	$10.15	$47.65
65013	Thu Sep 10 2015	$14.25	$42.75	$57.00
65014	Thu Sep 10 2015	$52.50	$62.77	$115.27

Step 5

6. Close the query. Click Yes to save changes.

Smaller queries and subqueries are useful because they are easier to build and troubleshoot than large queries. Subqueries are also useful when you need to create a complex query—you can create subqueries to build and test sections individually and then combine the subqueries into the final larger query.

Using Conditional Logic

Using conditional logic in an Access query is similar to using a logical formula in Excel. Using conditional logic requires Access to perform a calculation based on the outcome of a logical or conditional test. One calculation is performed if the test proves true and another calculation is performed if the test proves false. The structure of the IF function is *=IIF(logical_test,value_if_true,value_if_false)*. Logical functions are also similar to calculated fields in Access in that you type the desired field name followed by a colon and field names are encased in square brackets.

In Project 3c, you will process a 2% discount on the total cost of the work order if the cost of the labor is greater than $80. You will use the following IF function to calculate this discount, where *Labor>80* is the field that will store the discounted total: *Labor>80:IIF([TotalLabor]>80,[TotalWorkOrder]-([TotalWorkOrder]*.02),[TotalWorkOrder])*.

To determine whether to provide a discount, Access first tests the value of the record in the *TotalLabor field* to see if it is greater than $80. If the condition proves true, Access populates the *Labor>80* field with the value from the *TotalWorkOrder* field minus 2%. This is the discounted total that the customer owes. If the value in the *Total Labor* field is not greater than $80, the condition proves false and Access populates the *Labor>80* field with the same value that appears in the *TotalWorkOrder* field, since the work order did not qualify for a discount.

Figure 3.8 shows the TotalWorkOrders query after the IF function above has been applied. For work order 65021, the value in the *TotalLabor* field is $97.50. Since this value is greater than $80, the test is true and Access returns the value_if_true value, or the value in the *TotalWorkOrder* field minus 2% of the value ($97.50 - $1.95 = $95.55). For work order 65012, the value in the *TotalLabor* field is $37.50. Since the test is false, Access returns the value_if_false value, or the value in the *TotalWorkOrder* field ($47.65).

Figure 3.8 Project 3c TotalWorkOrders Query in Datasheet View

TotalWorkOrders

Work Order	Service Date	Total Labor	Parts	Total Work Order	Work Order w/Disc
65012	Mon Sep 07 2015	$37.50	$10.15	$47.65	$47.65
65013	Thu Sep 10 2015	$14.25	$42.75	$57.00	$57.00
65014	Thu Sep 10 2015	$52.50	$62.77	$115.27	$115.27
65015	Fri Sep 11 2015	$67.50	$0.00	$67.50	$67.50
65016	Fri Sep 11 2015	$30.00	$48.75	$78.75	$78.75
65017	Tue Sep 15 2015	$16.88	$55.87	$72.75	$72.75
65018	Tue Sep 15 2015	$22.50	$0.00	$22.50	$22.50
65019	Thu Sep 17 2015	$75.00	$0.00	$75.00	$75.00
65020	Thu Sep 17 2015	$33.75	$62.77	$96.52	$96.52
65021	Fri Sep 18 2015	$97.50	$0.00	$97.50	$95.55
65022	Tue Sep 22 2015	$45.00	$55.47	$100.47	$100.47
65023	Wed Sep 23 2015	$37.50	$62.50	$100.00	$100.00

The caption *Work Order w/Disc* was added to the *Labor>80* field.

Since the *Total Labor* value is less than $80, Access returns the value from the *Total Work Order* field in the *Work Order w/Disc* field.

Since the *Total Labor* value is greater than $80, Access subtracts 2% from the *Total Work Order* field and displays this value in the *Work Order w/Disc* field.

Project 3c Creating a Query Using Conditional Logic

Part 3 of 3

1. With **AL2-C3-RSRCompServ.accdb** open, open the TotalWorkOrders query in Design view.
2. Modify the TotalWorkOrders query to calculate a 2% discount if the total labor costs are greater than $80 by completing the following steps:
   a. Right-click in the blank field row next to *TotalWorkOrder* in the query design grid and then click *Zoom* at the drop-down list.

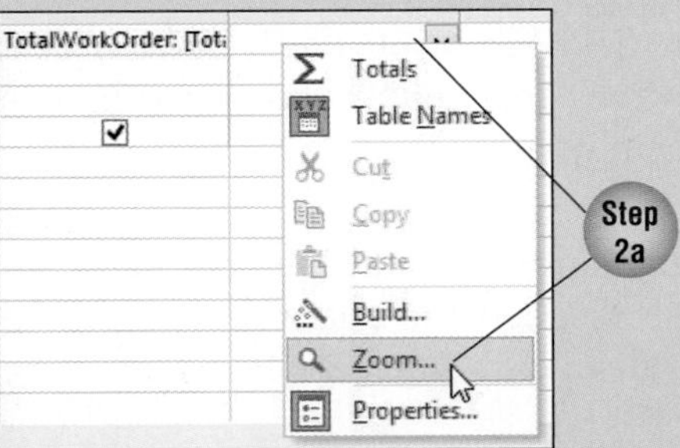

   b. Type **Labor>80:IIF([TotalLabor]>80,[TotalWorkOrder]-([TotalWorkOrder]*.02), [TotalWorkOrder])** and then press Enter or click OK.

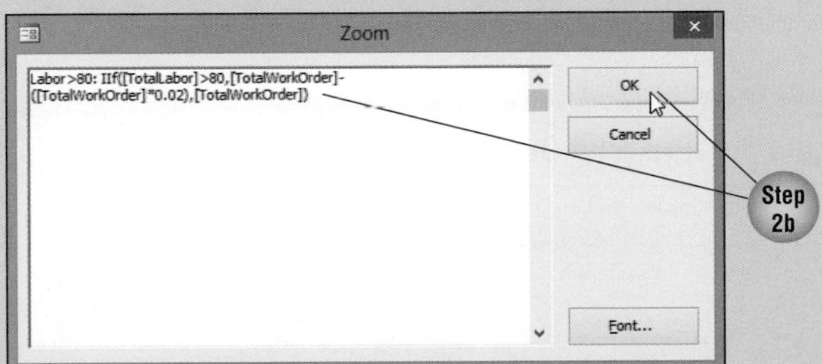

   c. Run the query.
3. Switch to Design view, open the Property Sheet task pane for the *Labor>80* column, and then make the following changes:
   a. Apply the Currency format.
   b. Type **Work Order w/Disc** in the *Caption* property box.
   c. Close the Property Sheet task pane.
4. Run the query.
5. Double-click the right boundary line of the *Work Order w/Disc* column to adjust the column width.
6. Print the query results datasheet with the right margins set to 0.5 inch.
7. Close the query. Click Yes to save changes.

Project 4 Query a Multiple-Value Field — 1 Part

You will select records using a multiple-value field in a query.

Selecting Records Using a Multiple-Value Field

Quick Steps

Show a Multiple-Value Field in Separate Rows in a Query

1. Open query in Design view.
2. Click in *Field* box of multiple-value field in design grid.
3. Move insertion point to end of field name.
4. Type period (.).
5. Press Enter to accept *.Value*.
6. Save query.

You learned to create and use multiple-value fields in Chapter 2. In a query, a multiple-value field can display as it does in a table datasheet, with the multiple field values in the same column separated by commas, or each field value can be shown in a separate row.

To show each value in a separate row, add *.Value* at the end of the multiple-value field name and then add the field name in the *Field* box in the query design grid. Figure 3.9 displays the query design grid for the query you will use in Project 4 that displays each entry in the *OperatingSys* field in a separate row in the datasheet.

To select records using criteria in a multiple-value field, type the criteria using the same procedures you would use for a single-value field. For example, in the TechnicianSpecialties query, typing *Windows 8* in the *Criteria* row in the *OperatingSys* column causes Access to return the records of any technician with Windows 8 as one of the multiple field values.

Figure 3.9 Project 4 Query Design Grid

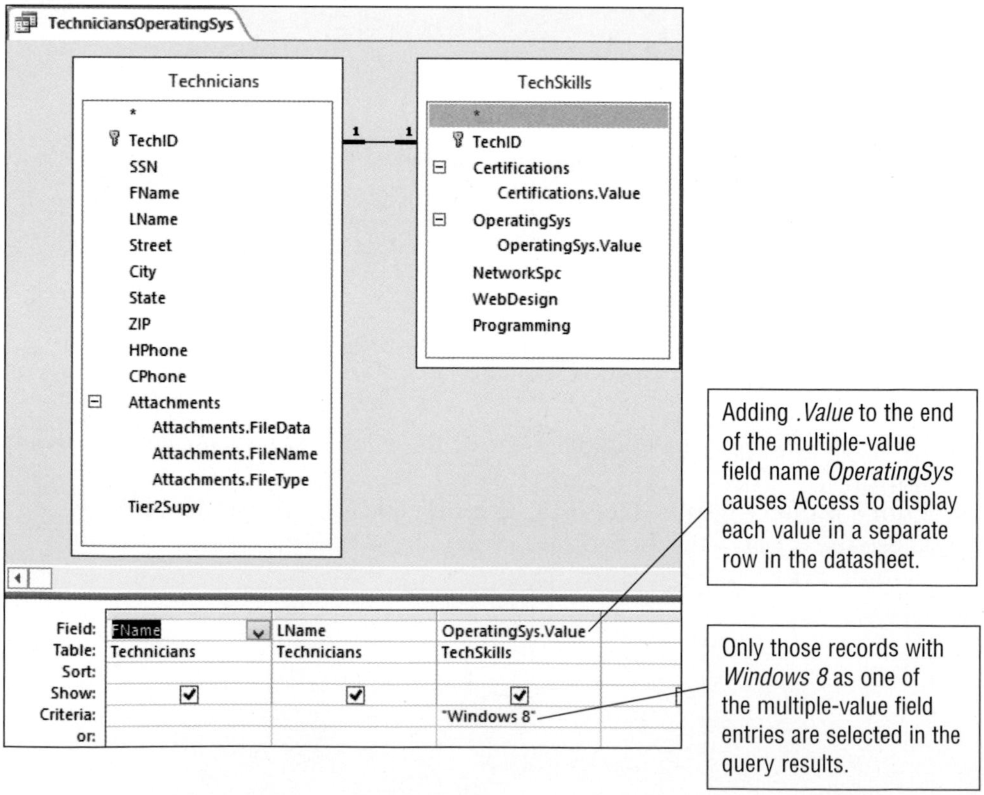

Project 4 Using a Multiple-Value Field in a Query

1. With **AL2-C3-RSRCompServ.accdb** open, open the TechnicianSpecialties query in Design view.
2. Right-click in the field selector bar above the *Certifications* field and then click *Cut* at the shortcut menu to remove the field from the query design grid.

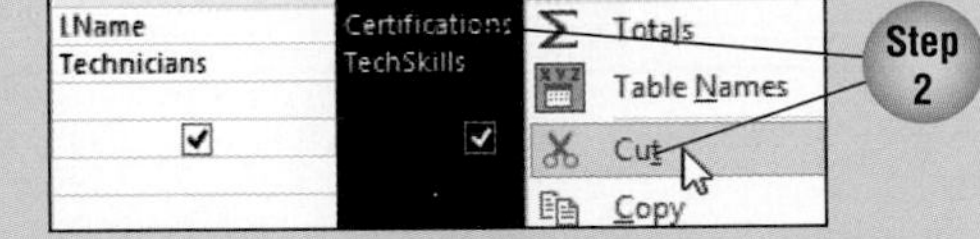

3. Delete the *NetworkSpc*, *WebDesign*, and *Programming* columns from the query design grid. Refer to Step 2.
4. Run the query. Notice that each record in the *Operating Systems* column displays the multiple values separated by commas.
5. Switch to Design view.
6. Click in the *OperatingSys* field box in the query design grid, move the insertion point to the end of the field name, and then type a period (.). Access automatically adds *.Value* to the end of the name in the *Field* box. Press Enter to accept *.Value* at the end of the field name. ***Note: When creating a query from scratch, drag the multiple-value field name with the .Value property already attached from the table's field list box to the query design grid.***

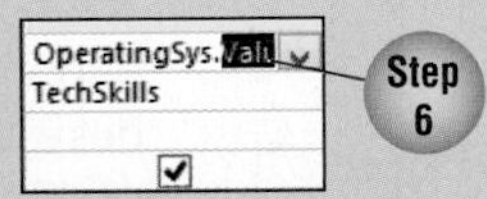

7. Click the FILE tab and then click the *Save As* option. At the Save As backstage area, click *Save Object As* in the *File Types* section and then click the Save As button. At the Save As dialog box, type **TechniciansOperatingSys** in the *Save 'TechnicianSpecialties' to* text box and then press Enter or click OK.
8. Run the query. Notice that each entry in the multiple-value field is now displayed in a separate row.
9. Switch to Design view.
10. Click in the *Criteria* row in the *OperatingSys.Value* column in the query design grid, type **Windows 8**, and then press Enter.

OperatingSys.Value
TechSkills
"Windows 8"
Step 10

11. Run the query. Notice that the column title for the multiple-value field in the query results datasheet is now *TechSkills.OperatingSys.Value*. Change the column heading for the field by completing the following steps:
    a. Switch to Design view.
    b. Click anywhere within the *OperatingSys.Value* field box in the query design grid.
    c. Press F4 to open the Property Sheet task pane.
    d. Click in the *Caption* property box, type **Operating System**, and then press Enter.
    e. Close the Property Sheet task pane.

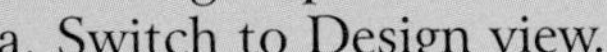

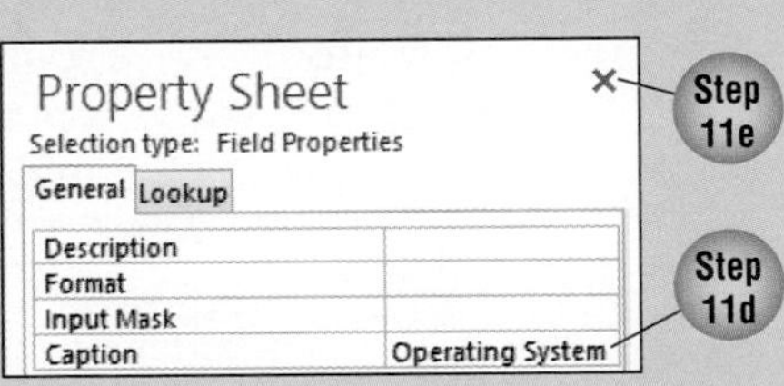

12. Run the query.

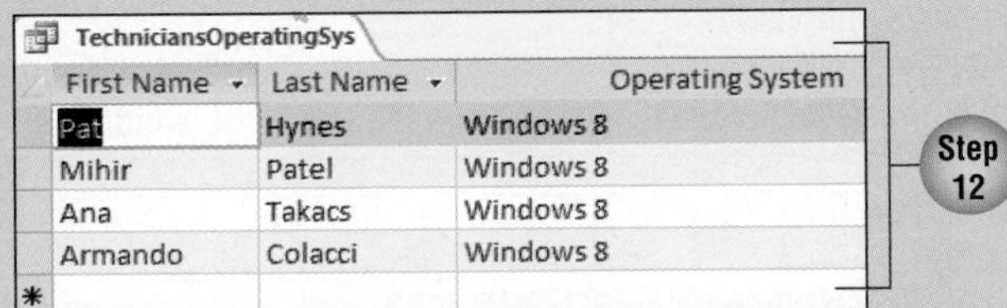
TechniciansOperatingSys

First Name	Last Name	Operating System
Pat	Hynes	Windows 8
Mihir	Patel	Windows 8
Ana	Takacs	Windows 8
Armando	Colacci	Windows 8

Step 12

13. Print the query results datasheet and then close the query. Click Yes to save changes.

Project 5 Modify Records Using Action Queries — 4 Parts

You will create a new table, add and delete records, and update field values using action queries.

Performing Operations Using Action Queries

An ***action query*** is used to perform an operation on a group of records. Building an action query is similar to building a select query, but with the extra step of specifying the action to perform on the group of selected records. Four types of action queries are available, as described in Table 3.1.

To create an action query, first build a select query by adding tables, fields, and criteria to the query design grid. Run the select query to make sure the desired group of records is targeted for action. Once you are satisfied that the correct records will be modified, change the query type using the Make Table, Append, Update, or Delete buttons in the Query Type group on the QUERY TOOLS DESIGN tab, shown in Figure 3.10.

Clicking the Run button once the query type has been changed to an action query causes Access to perform the make-table, append, update, or delete operation. Once an action query has been run, the results cannot be reversed.

Table 3.1 Action Query Types

Query Type	*Description*
make table	A new table is created from selected records in an existing table—for example, a new table that combines fields from two other tables in the database.
append	Selected records are added to the end of an existing table. This action is similar to performing a copy and paste.
update	A global change is made to the selected group of records based on an update expression—for example, the labor rate can be increased by 10% in one step.
delete	The selected group of records is deleted from a table.

Figure 3.10 Query Type Group on the QUERY TOOLS DESIGN Tab

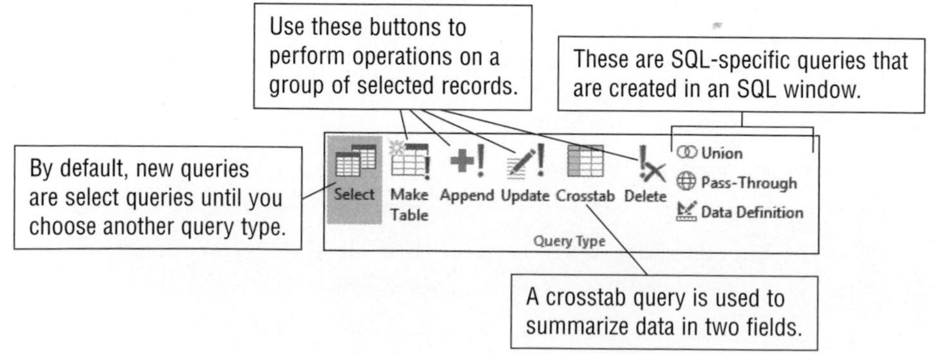
Use these buttons to perform operations on a group of selected records.
These are SQL-specific queries that are created in an SQL window.
By default, new queries are select queries until you choose another query type.
Select
Make Table
Append
Update
Crosstab
Delete
Union
Pass-Through
Data Definition
Query Type
A crosstab query is used to summarize data in two fields.

Creating a New Table Using a Query

A ***make-table query*** creates a new table from selected records in the same database or another database. This type of query is useful for creating a history table before purging old records that are no longer required. The history table can be placed in the same database or in another database used as an archive copy.

Once you have created a select query that will extract the records you want to copy to a new table, click the Make Table button in the Query Type group on the QUERY TOOLS DESIGN tab to open the Make Table dialog box, shown in Figure 3.11. Enter a table name, choose the destination database, and then click OK. Once you have run a make-table query, do not double-click the query name in the Navigation pane, because doing so instructs Access to run the query again. Open the query in Design view to make changes to the criteria and/or query type if you need to run the query again.

Quick Steps

Create a Make-Table Query

1. Create query in Design view.
2. Add desired table(s) to query.
3. Add desired fields to query design grid.
4. If necessary, enter criteria to select records.
5. Run query.
6. Switch to Design view.
7. Click Make Table button.
8. Type table name.
9. If necessary, select destination database.
10. Click OK.
11. Run query.
12. Click Yes.
13. Save query.

Make Table

Figure 3.11 Make Table Dialog Box

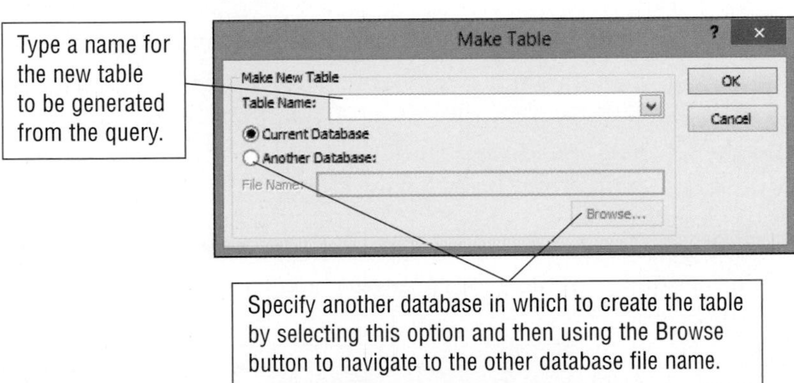

Project 5a **Creating a New Table Using a Query** **Part 1 of 4**

1. With **AL2-C3-RSRCompServ.accdb** open, create a select query to select all of the work order records for September 1, 2015 through September 15, 2015 by completing the following steps:
   a. Create a new query in Design view. Add the WorkOrders table to the query window and then close the Show Table dialog box. Drag the bottom border of the table field list box until you can see all of the field names.
   b. Double-click the WorkOrders table field list box title bar. This selects all of the records within the table.
   c. Position the mouse pointer anywhere within the selected field names in the field list box and then drag the pointer to the first column in the query design grid. All of the fields in the table are added to the query design grid.
   d. Click in the *Criteria* row in the *ServDate* column, type **Between September 1, 2015 and September 15, 2015**, and then press Enter.

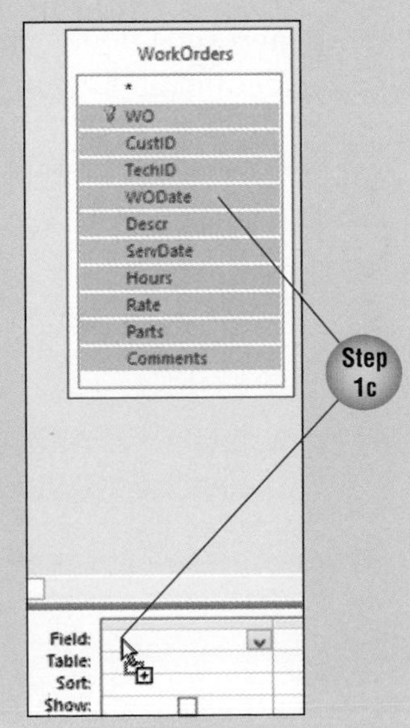

e. Run the query. The query results datasheet displays seven records.

Step 1e

Work Order	Customer ID	Technician ID	WO Date	Description
65012	1000	11	Mon Sep 07 2015	Bi-annual computer maintenance
65013	1000	10	Mon Sep 07 2015	Replace keyboard
65014	1005	02	Thu Sep 10 2015	Replace power supply
65015	1008	04	Thu Sep 10 2015	Restore operating system
65016	1010	06	Fri Sep 11 2015	Install upgraded video card
65017	1015	08	Mon Sep 14 2015	Replace DVD drive
65018	1020	10	Mon Sep 14 2015	Upgrade Office suite

f. You decide you do not need to archive the *Comments* field data. Switch to Design view and then delete the *Comments* column from the query design grid.

2. Make a new table from the selected records and store the table in a history database to be used for archiving purposes by completing the following steps:
   a. If necessary, switch to Design view.
   b. Click the Make Table button in the Query Type group on the QUERY TOOLS DESIGN tab.
   c. With the insertion point positioned in the *Table Name* text box, type **Sept2015WO**.
   d. Click the *Another Database* option and then click the Browse button.
   e. At the Make Table dialog box, navigate to the AL2C3 folder on your storage medium and then double-click the file named ***AL2-C3-RSRCompServHistory.accdb***.

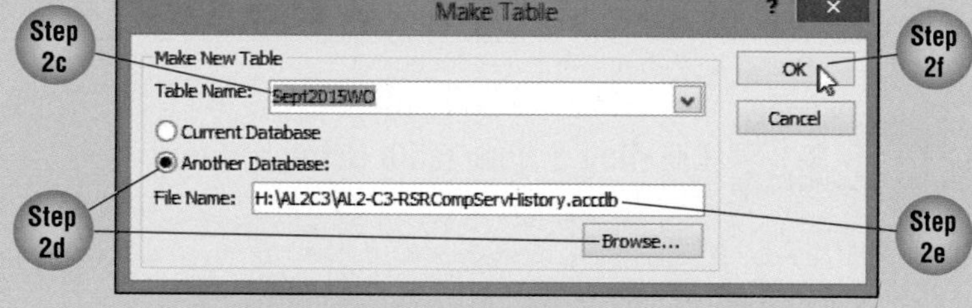

   f. Click OK.
   g. Run the query.
   h. Click Yes at the Microsoft Access message box indicating that you are about to paste seven rows to a new table.
3. Save the query. Type **Sept2015MakeTable** at the Save As dialog box and then press Enter or click OK.
4. Close the query.
5. Close **AL2-C3-RSRCompServ.accdb**.
6. Open **AL2-C3-RSRCompServHistory.accdb** and enable the content. Click OK to continue if a message appears stating that Access has to update object dependencies.
7. Open the Sept2015WO table in Datasheet view.
8. Review the records that were copied to the new table from the make-table query.
9. Close the table.
10. Close **AL2-C3-RSRCompServHistory.accdb**.

Deleting a Group of Records Using a Query

A ***delete query*** is used to delete, in one step, a group of records that meet specified criteria. You can use this action query in any instance in which the records to be deleted can be selected using a criteria statement. Using a query to remove the records is more efficient and reduces the chances of removing a record in error, which can happen when the records are deleted manually.

The make-table query used in Project 5a created a duplicate copy of the records in the new table. The original records still exist in the WorkOrders table. The make-table query used to archive the records can be changed to a delete query and then used to remove the records from the original table.

In the Navigation pane, action query names display with a black exclamation mark next to an icon that indicates the type of action that will be performed when the query is run.

Quick Steps

Create a Delete Query

1. Create query in Design view.
2. Add desired table to query.
3. Add desired fields to query design grid.
4. Enter criteria to select records.
5. Run query.
6. Switch to Design view.
7. Click Delete button.
8. Run query.
9. Click Yes.
10. Save query.

Delete

Project 5b **Deleting Records Using a Query** **Part 2 of 4**

1. Open **AL2-C3-RSRCompServ.accdb** and enable the content.
2. Right-click *Sept2015MakeTable* in the Queries group in the Navigation pane and then click *Design View* at the shortcut menu.
3. Click the Delete button in the Query Type group on the QUERY TOOLS DESIGN tab.
4. Click the FILE tab and then click the *Save As* option. At the Save As backstage area, click *Save Object As* in the *File Types* section and then click the Save As button. At the Save As dialog box, type **Sept2015Delete** in the *Save 'Sept2015MakeTable' to* text box and then press Enter or click OK.
5. With the QUERY TOOLS DESIGN tab selected, run the query.
6. At the Microsoft Access message box indicating that you are about to delete seven rows from the table and informing you that the action cannot be reversed, click Yes to delete the selected records.

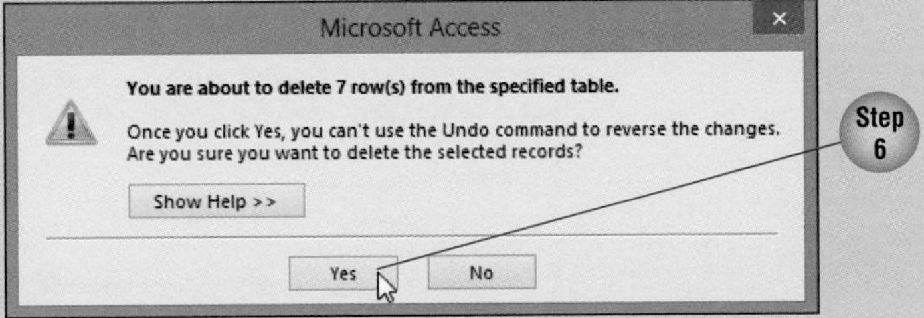

7. Close the query.
8. Open the WorkOrders table. Notice that no records have a service date that occurred before September 15, 2015.
9. Close the table.

▼ Quick Steps

Create an Append Query

1. Create query in Design view.
2. Add desired table to query.
3. Add desired fields to query design grid.
4. Enter criteria to select records.
5. Run query.
6. Switch to Design view.
7. Click Append button.
8. Type table name.
9. Select destination database.
10. Click OK.
11. Run query.
12. Click Yes.
13. Save query.

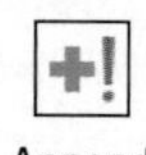

Append

Adding Records to a Table Using a Query

An ***append query*** is used to copy a group of records from one or more tables to the end of an existing table. Consider using an append query in any situation in which you want to make a duplicate copy of records. For example, in Project 5a, the make-table query was used to create a new table to store archived records. Once the table exists, you can use append queries to copy subsequent archived records to the end of the existing history table.

Clicking the Append button in the Query Type group on the QUERY TOOLS DESIGN tab causes the Append dialog box to open with the same options as the Make Table dialog box, as shown in Figure 3.12. The receiving table should have the same structure as the query from which the records are selected.

Figure 3.12 Append Dialog Box

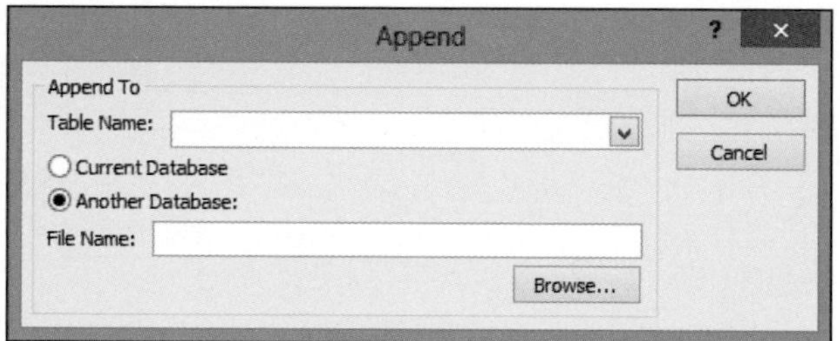

Project 5c **Adding Records to a Table Using a Query** **Part 3 of 4**

1. With **AL2-C3-RSRCompServ.accdb** open, open the Sept2015MakeTable query in Design view.
2. Modify the criteria to select work order records for the last half of September 2015 by completing the following steps:
   a. Expand the width of the *ServDate* column until you can see the entire criteria statement.
   b. Click in the *Criteria* row in the *ServDate* column, insert and delete text as necessary to modify the criteria statement to read *Between #9/16/2015# And #9/30/2015#*, and then press Enter.

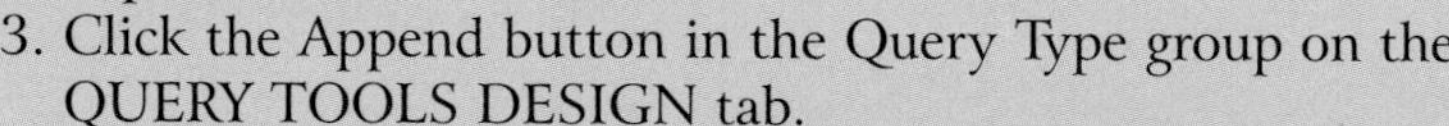

3. Click the Append button in the Query Type group on the QUERY TOOLS DESIGN tab.
4. Since the query is being changed from a make-table query, Access inserts the same table name and database that were used to create the table in Project 5a. Click OK to accept the table name *Sept2015WO* and the file name *AL2-C3-RSRCompServHistory.accdb*.

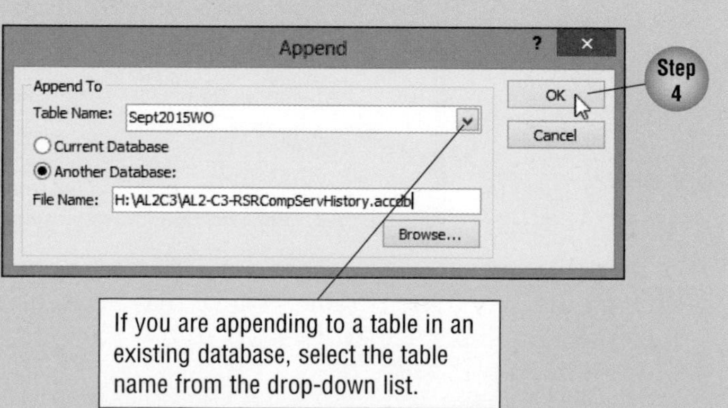

5. Click the FILE tab and then click the *Save As* option. At the Save As backstage area, click *Save Object As* in the *File Types* section and then click the Save As button. At the Save As dialog box, type **Sept2015Append** in the *Save 'Sept2015MakeTable' to* text box and then press Enter or click OK.
6. With the QUERY TOOLS DESIGN tab selected, run the query.
7. Click Yes at the Microsoft Access message box indicating that you are about to append eight rows and that the action cannot be undone.
8. Close the query.
9. Close **AL2-C3-RSRCompServ.accdb**.
10. Open **AL2-C3-RSRCompServHistory.accdb**.
11. Open the Sept2015WO table and then print the datasheet in landscape orientation.
12. Close the table.
13. Close **AL2-C3-RSRCompServHistory.accdb**.

Modifying Records Using an Update Query

When you need to make a change to a group of records that can be selected in a query, and the change to be incorporated is the same for all of the records, you can instruct Access to modify the data using an ***update query***. Making a global change using an update query is efficient and reduces the potential for errors that can occur from the manual editing of multiple records. You can increase or decrease fields such as quotas, rates, and selling prices by adding or subtracting specific amounts or by multiplying by desired percentages.

Clicking the Update button in the Query Type group on the QUERY TOOLS DESIGN tab causes an *Update To* row to appear in the query design grid. Click in the *Update To* box in the column to be modified and then type the expression that will change the field values as needed. Run the query to make the global change.

Quick Steps

Create an Update Query
1. Create query in Design view.
2. Add desired table to query.
3. Add desired fields to query design grid.
4. Enter criteria to select records.
5. Run query.
6. Switch to Design view.
7. Click Update button.
8. Click in *Update To* box in field to be changed.
9. Type update expression.
10. Run query.
11. Click Yes.
12. Save query.

Update

Project 5d **Changing Service Plan Rates Using an Update Query** **Part 4 of 4**

1. Open **AL2-C3-RSRCompServ.accdb** and enable the content.
2. Open the FeesSCPlans table and review the current values in the *Rate* column. For example, notice that the current rate for Plan A's six-month term for one computer is $48.00. Close the table when you are finished reviewing the current rates.
3. Create an update query to increase the Plan A service contract rates by 6% by completing the following steps:
   a. Create a new query in Design view.
   b. Add the FeesSCPlans table to the query and then close the Show Table dialog box.
   c. Add the *Plan* and *Rate* fields to the query design grid.

d. Click in the *Criteria* row in the *Plan* column, type A, and then click in the *Criteria* row in the next column in the query design grid. ***Note: The AutoComplete feature will show a list of functions as soon as you type A. You can ignore the AutoComplete drop-down list, since you are not entering a mathematical expression for the criteria. However, pressing Enter causes Access to add Abs to the*** **Criteria** ***row. Clicking in another box in the query design grid will remove the AutoComplete drop-down list.***

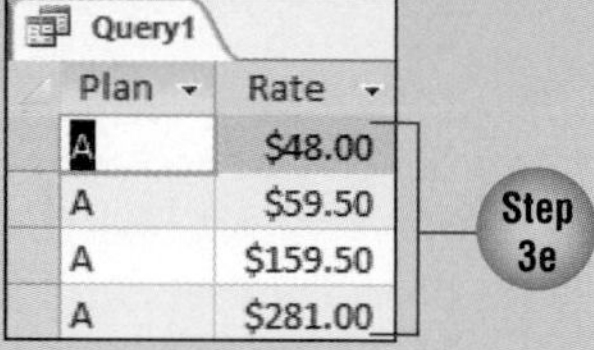

e. Run the query. Review the four records shown in the query results datasheet.

f. Switch to Design view.

g. Click the Update button in the Query Type group on the QUERY TOOLS DESIGN tab. Access adds a row labeled *Update To* in the query design grid between the *Table* and *Criteria* rows.

h. Click in the *Update To* row in the *Rate* column, type **[Rate]*1.06**, and then press Enter.

4. Save the query. Type **RateUpdate** at the Save As dialog box and then press Enter or click OK.
5. Run the query. Click Yes at the Microsoft Access message that says you are about to update four rows.
6. Close the query.
7. Open the FeesSCPlans table. Notice that the rate values for Plan A records have increased. For example, the value in the *Rate* column for Plan A's six-month term for one computer is now $50.88. Print the datasheet.
8. Close the table and then close **AL2-C3-RSRCompServ.accdb**.

Create a backup copy of the database before running an action query.

Exercise caution when running any action query, since the queries make changes to database tables. For example, in Project 5d, if you ran the update query a second time, the rates for the Plan A service plans would increase another 6%. Once changed, the rates cannot be undone. To reverse the update, you would need to create a mathematical expression in a new update query to remove 6% from the prices.

Chapter Summary

- A filter can be saved as a query by displaying the filter criteria in a Filter By Form window, clicking the Advanced button, and then clicking *Save As Query* at the drop-down list.
- Parameter queries prompt the user for the criteria by which to select records when the query is run.
- To create a parameter query, type a prompt message enclosed in square brackets in the *Criteria* row in the field you want to use to select records.

- Changing the join property can alter the number of records that are displayed in the query results datasheet.
- An inner join selects records only if a matching value is found in the joined field in both tables.
- A left outer join selects all of the records from the left table and matching records from the related table. Empty fields display if no matching records exist in the related table.
- Click the Show Table button in the Query Setup group on the QUERY TOOLS DESIGN tab to add a table or query to the query window.
- Remove a table from the query by clicking a field within the table's field list box and pressing the Delete key or by right-clicking the table and clicking *Remove Table* at the shortcut menu.
- A right outer join selects all of the records from the right table and matching records from the primary table. Empty fields display if no matching records exist in the primary table.
- A self-join query is created by adding two copies of the same table to the query window and joining the tables on a field containing matching field values.
- An alias is another name that is used to reference a table in a query.
- Right-click a table name in the query window, click *Properties* at the shortcut menu, and then enter the alias for the table in the *Alias* property box at the Property Sheet task pane.
- A query that contains two tables that are not joined creates a cross product or Cartesian product query. This means that Access creates records for every possible combination from both tables, the results of which are generally not meaningful.
- A subquery is a query nested inside another query. Use subqueries to break down a complex query into manageable units. For example, a query with multiple calculations can be created by combining subqueries in which each calculation is built individually.
- Another reason for using subqueries is to be able to reuse a smaller query in many other queries, avoiding the need to keep recreating the same structure.
- Create select queries on multiple-value fields using the same methods you use for single-field criteria.
- Adding *.Value* to the end of a multiple-value field name in the *Field* box in the query design grid causes Access to place each field value in a separate row in the query results datasheet.
- A make-table query creates a new table in the active database or another database with the structure defined in the query design grid and containing records selected by a criteria statement.
- Delete a group of records in one step by creating and running a delete query.
- Add a group of records to the bottom of an existing table in the active database or another database using an append query.
- An update query allows you to make a global change to records by entering an expression such as a mathematical formula in the query design grid.

Commands Review

FEATURE	RIBBON TAB, GROUP	BUTTON
advanced filter options	HOME, Sort & Filter	
append query	QUERY TOOLS DESIGN, Query Type	
create query in Design view	CREATE, Queries	
delete query	QUERY TOOLS DESIGN, Query Type	
make-table query	QUERY TOOLS DESIGN, Query Type	
run query	QUERY TOOLS DESIGN, Results	
show table	QUERY TOOLS DESIGN, Query Setup	
update query	QUERY TOOLS DESIGN, Query Type	

Concepts Check Test Your Knowledge

Completion: In the space provided at the right, indicate the correct term, command, or number.

1. Click this button at a Filter By Form datasheet to save the filter's criteria as a query. ____________________
2. This is the name for a query that prompts the user to type the criteria in a dialog box when the query is run. ____________________
3. Double-clicking the black join line between tables in a query window opens this dialog box. ____________________
4. This join type displays all of the records from the related table and empty fields if no matching record exists in the primary table. ____________________
5. Click this button in the Query Setup group on the QUERY TOOLS DESIGN tab to add a table to an existing query. ____________________
6. This is the term for a query in which two copies of the same table are added to the query window and joined by two fields in the same table that contain matching field values. ____________________

7. This is the term used to describe another name with which to reference a table in a query. __________

8. This is the term for a query in which two tables are used in the query window with no join established to connect one table to the other. __________

9. This term describes a query nested inside another query. __________

10. Add this to the end of a multiple-value field name in the *Field* box in the query design grid to display each field value in a separate row. __________

11. Queries that perform operations on selected records are referred to by this term. __________

12. Create this type of query to create a new table from existing records in the active database or an archive database. __________

13. This type of query removes a group of records that meet specified criteria. __________

14. This query adds a group of records to the end of an existing table in the active database or another database. __________

15. Create this type of query to increase the prices in all records by 10%. __________

Skills Check Assess Your Performance

Assessment 1

EXTRACT RECORDS USING A FILTER AND PROMPTED QUERIES

1. Open **AL2-C3-ViewIt.accdb** and enable the content.
2. Open the WebCustomers table.
3. Using the Filter By Form feature, display only those customers who reside in Burlington with zip codes that begin with 05401. ***Hint: Type* 05401* *in the* ZIP *field to specify only the first five characters in the ZIP code. The asterisk is a wildcard character that allows you to filter by specifying only a portion of the field value.***
4. Save the filter as a query named *CustBurlington05401*.
5. Close the Filter By Form datasheet and close the table. Click No when prompted to save changes to the table design.
6. Open the CustBurlington05401 query.
7. Print the query results datasheet in landscape orientation and then close the query.

8. Create a new query in Design view using the following specifications:
   a. Add the tables WebOrderDetails, WebOrders, and WebProducts to the query.
   b. Add the fields *WebOrderID* (WebOrders table), *DateOrd*, *Qty*, and *Product* to the query design grid.
   c. Create a parameter query to prompt the user to type the title of the movie in the *Product* column. The prompt should be *Type the movie title*.
   d. Save the query, name it *PromptedMovie*, and then close the query.
9. Run the PromptedMovie query. Type **The Longest Day** at the Enter Parameter Value dialog box. Print the query results datasheet and then close the query.
10. Open the PromptedMovie query in Design view. Use Save As to name the query *PromptedOrderDates*. Delete the prompt message in the *Product* column. Create a parameter query to prompt the user to type beginning and ending dates to view Web orders in the *DateOrd* column. The prompts should be *Type starting date* and *Type ending date*. Save and then close the query.
11. Run the PromptedOrderDates query. Type **February 1, 2015** as the beginning date and **February 28, 2015** as the ending date. Print the query results datasheet and then close the query.

Assessment 2

MODIFY JOIN PROPERTIES

SNAP Grade It

1. With **AL2-C3-ViewIt.accdb** open, create a new query in Design view using the following specifications:
   a. Add the WebCustomers and WebOrders tables to the query.
   b. Add the fields *CustID*, *FirstName*, *LastName*, and *WebOrderID* to the query design grid. ***Note: Add* CustID *from the WebCustomers table.***
   c. Modify the join type between the WebCustomers table and WebOrders table to a left outer join.
   d. Save the query and name it *CustWebOrders*.
2. Run the query. Print the query results datasheet and then close the query.
3. Create a new query in Design view using the following specifications:
   a. Add the WebOrderDetails and WebProducts tables to the query.
   b. Add the fields *WebOrdID*, *WebProdID*, and *Product* to the query design grid. ***Note: Add* WebProdID *from the WebProducts table*.**
   c. Modify the join type between the WebProducts table and the WebOrderDetails table to a left outer join.
   d. Save the query and name it *WebProductOrders*.
4. Run the query. Print the query results datasheet and then close the query.

Assessment

3 ADD A TABLE TO A QUERY AND CREATE AND USE A SUBQUERY TO PERFORM CALCULATIONS

1. With **AL2-C3-ViewIt.accdb** open, open the CustWebOrders query in Design view, use Save As to name the new query *WebSalesWithTotal*, and then modify the query as follows:
   a. Modify the join type between the WebCustomers table and WebOrders table to an inner join.
   b. Add the WebOrderDetails table and WebProducts table to the query.
   c. Add the fields named *DateOrd*, *Qty*, *Product*, and *SellPrice* to the query design grid.
   d. Delete the *CustID* field from the query.
   e. Create a calculated field with the column label *TotalSale* that multiplies the quantity ordered times the selling price. Change the caption to *Total Sale*.
2. Save and then run the query. Print the query results datasheet with the left and right margins set to 0.5 inch and then close the query.
3. Create a new query in Design view that calculates the total sale with tax as follows:
   a. Nest the WebSalesWithTotal query in the new query.
   b. Add the fields *WebOrdID*, *DateOrd*, and *TotalSale* to the query design grid.
   c. Create a calculated field with the column label *Tax* that multiples the value in the *TotalSale* column times 0.06 (decimal equivalent of 6%). Format the calculated column by applying the *Standard* format.
   d. Create a second calculated column with the column label *TotalSaleWithTax* that adds the *TotalSale* column to the *Tax* column. Change the caption to *Total Sale With Tax*.
   e. Save the query and name it *WebSalesWithTotalAndTax*.
4. Run the query. Double-click the right column boundary for the last column in the query results datasheet to display the entire field heading and then print the query results datasheet with the left and right margins set to 0.5 inch. Close the query, saving the changes.

Assessment

4 USE ACTION QUERIES TO ARCHIVE RECORDS AND UPDATE SELLING PRICES

1. With **AL2-C3-ViewIt.accdb** open, open the WebSalesWithTotal query in Design view, use Save As to name the new query *Feb2015SalesMakeTable*, and then modify the query as follows:
   a. Delete the *SellPrice* and *TotalSale* columns from the query design grid.
   b. Use the *Between* expression to add a criterion to select the records for sales during the month of February 2015.
   c. Run the query to make sure the correct records are being selected.
   d. Change the query to a make-table query, name the new table *Feb2015WebSales*, and archive it in the current database.
   e. Save, run, and then close the query.
2. Open the Feb2015WebSales table. Adjust column widths as necessary and then print the datasheet. Close the table, saving the changes to the layout.
3. Open the Feb2015SalesMakeTable query in Design view, use Save As to name the new query *Feb2015SalesDelete*, and then modify the query as follows:
   a. Change the query to a delete query.
   b. Remove the WebCustomers, WebOrderDetails, and WebProducts tables from the query.
   c. Save the query, run the query, and then close the query window.
4. Open the WebSalesWithTotal query. Print the query results datasheet in landscape orientation with left and right margins set to 0.5 inch and then close the query.
5. Create a new query in Design view to update the selling prices of movies with Web product IDs between CV-1026 and CV-1029 as follows:
   a. Add the WebProducts table to the query.
   b. Add the *WebProdID* and *SellPrice* fields to the query design grid.
   c. Change the query to an update query and add a formula that will add $1.05 to the selling price of each movie that has a Web product ID between CV-1026 and CV-1029.
   d. Save the query and name it *PriceUpdate*.
   e. Run the query and then close the query window.
6. Open the WebProducts table. Print the datasheet and then close the table.
7. Close **AL2-C3-ViewIt.accdb**.

Visual Benchmark Demonstrate Your Proficiency

CALCULATE DAYS BOARDED AND AMOUNT DUE USING NESTED QUERIES

1. Open **AL2-C3-PawsParadise.accdb**.
2. Review the query results datasheet shown in Figure 3.13. This query is the result of nesting a query within a query. Create the calculations as follows:
   a. Create the first query to calculate the number of days a dog is boarded in the kennel. Show in the query results the reservation ID, the customer's name, the dog's name, and the two date fields. Calculate the number of days the dog was boarded. Save the query and name it *DaysBoarded*.

b. Nest DaysBoarded in a new query. Add the Dogs and KennelCategories tables to the query. Join the DaysBoarded query to the Dogs table on the common *DogName* field. Add the fields to the query design grid as shown in Figure 3.13 and then calculate the amount due for each reservation.

c. Sort and format the query results as shown in Figure 3.13. The font used is 11-point Arial Narrow. The alternate row color used is Maroon 1, which is from the *Standard Colors* section of the color palette. ***Note: The first row is not formatted differently from the remainder of the datasheet; the row displays with a different row color because the first row is selected.*** Save the query and name it *ReservationTotals*.

3. Print the ReservationTotals query results datasheet in landscape orientation with the left and right margins set to 0.5 inch.
4. Close the query.
5. Close **AL2-C3-PawsParadise.accdb**.

Figure 3.13 Visual Benchmark

Reservation	First Name	Last Name	Dog's Name	Date In	Date Out	Days Boarded	Kennel Type	Daily Rate	Amount Due
1	Shawn	Jenkins	Abby	11/9/2015	11/12/2015	3	V.I.P. Suite	$38.50	$115.50
2	Shawn	Jenkins	Winnie	11/9/2015	11/12/2015	3	V.I.P. Suite	$38.50	$115.50
3	Sean	Gallagher	Tank	11/10/2015	11/13/2015	3	V.I.P. Suite	$38.50	$115.50
4	Sofia	Ramos	Apollo	11/11/2015	11/18/2015	7	Indoor/Outdoor Suite	$25.50	$178.50
5	Sofia	Ramos	Murphy	11/11/2015	11/18/2015	7	Indoor/Outdoor Suite	$25.50	$178.50
6	Dina	Lombardi	Niko	11/12/2015	11/16/2015	4	Indoor/Outdoor Suite	$25.50	$102.00
7	Natale	Rizzo	Dallas	11/12/2015	11/14/2015	2	Indoor/Outdoor Suite	$25.50	$51.00
8	James	Chung	Lassie	11/12/2015	11/13/2015	1	Deluxe Suite	$29.50	$29.50
9	Bernard	Jedicke	Kosmo	11/12/2015	11/13/2015	1	Day Care Boarding	$16.50	$16.50
10	Bernard	Jedicke	Sierra	11/12/2015	11/13/2015	1	Day Care Boarding	$16.50	$16.50
11	Bernard	Jedicke	Emma	11/12/2015	11/13/2015	1	Day Care Boarding	$16.50	$16.50
12	Carlotta	Sanchez	Scrappy	11/13/2015	11/19/2015	6	Deluxe Suite	$29.50	$177.00
13	Michael	Mancini	Harley	11/13/2015	11/23/2015	10	Indoor/Outdoor Suite	$25.50	$255.00
14	Glen	Waters	Barney	11/14/2015	11/29/2015	15	Indoor/Outdoor Suite	$25.50	$382.50
15	Lenora	Diaz	Zack	11/14/2015	11/17/2015	3	Indoor/Outdoor Suite	$25.50	$76.50
16	Maeve	Murphy	King	11/15/2015	11/19/2015	4	V.I.P. Suite	$38.50	$154.00
17	Valerie	McTague	Chloe	11/16/2015	11/19/2015	3	Deluxe Suite	$29.50	$88.50
18	Nadia	Costa	Bailey	11/17/2015	11/24/2015	7	Deluxe Suite	$29.50	$206.50
19	Juan	Torres	Taffy	11/17/2015	11/21/2015	4	V.I.P. Suite	$38.50	$154.00
20	Liam	Doherty	Zeus	11/18/2015	11/23/2015	5	V.I.P. Suite	$38.50	$192.50
21	Dillon	Farrell	Chico	11/18/2015	11/22/2015	4	Indoor/Outdoor Suite	$25.50	$102.00
22	Diane	Ye	Elvis	11/20/2015	11/25/2015	5	Indoor/Outdoor Suite	$25.50	$127.50
23	Lorenzo	Rivera	Fifi	11/22/2015	11/27/2015	5	V.I.P. Suite	$38.50	$192.50
24	Lorenzo	Rivera	Lucky	11/22/2015	11/27/2015	5	Indoor/Outdoor Suite	$25.50	$127.50
25	Bernard	Jedicke	Kosmo	11/26/2015	11/27/2015	1	Day Care Boarding	$16.50	$16.50
26	Bernard	Jedicke	Sierra	11/26/2015	11/27/2015	1	Day Care Boarding	$16.50	$16.50
27	Bernard	Jedicke	Emma	11/26/2015	11/27/2015	1	Day Care Boarding	$16.50	$16.50

Case Study Apply Your Skills

Part 1

You are continuing your work as an intern at Hillsdale Realty. The office manager has requested a series of printouts with information from the database. Open **AL2-C3-HillsdaleRealty.accdb** and enable the content. Design, create, save, run, and print query results to provide the required information. You determine an appropriate descriptive name for each query.

- Produce a list of sales by agent that includes the date of sale, address, sale price, and commission rate. Sort the query results by the agent's last name and then by date of sale, sorting both fields in ascending order.
- Modify the first query to allow the office manager to type the agent's name when she runs the query, which will allow viewing individual sales reports by agent. To test your query, run the query using the agent name *Cecilia Ortega*. Save the revised query using a new name.
- Produce a list that shows each agent and his or her clients. Show the client ID, client first name, and client last name next to each agent's name. The manager wants to see which agents have not yet signed any clients, so you need to make sure the query results show all agents.
- Produce a list of agents that shows each agent's co-broker agent. The Agents table contains a field named *CoBroker*. This field is the agent ID for the person assigned to co-broker listings. The office manager has requested a list that shows the agent's last name, instead of his or her ID number, in the *CoBroker* field. Sort the list in ascending order by AgentLName. ***Hint: Create a self-join query and remember to use the alias and caption properties to rename the table and the column that will display the co-broker agent last name.***
- Modify the first query to add a column to calculate the amount of commission that will be owed on the sale by multiplying the sale price times the commission rate. Save the revised query using a new name.
- Use a query to update all of the commission quota values to add 15%. After updating the values, create a new query to show each agent and his or her respective commission quota. Sort the list in ascending order by agent last name.

Part 2

Help

The office manager would like to see the five highest sale prices to date. Research in Help how to create a top-values query using the *Return* option box in the Query Setup group. Using the information you learned in Help, modify the first query created in Part 1 to produce the top-five list. Save the revised query using a new name and print the query results. ***Hint: Remove the sorting from the original query and then sort by sale price in descending order before converting the query to a top-five values query.***

Part 3

The office manager would like to review the client preferences for each listing with each preference on a separate line. Include in the list the date of the listing, street address, client's name, and client's telephone number. Add criteria to select only those records for cases in which the client has requested a pre-sale inspection or staging service for his or her listing. Save and print the query.

MICROSOFT® ACCESS®

Creating and Using Custom Forms

PERFORMANCE OBJECTIVES

Upon successful completion of Chapter 4, you will be able to:

- **Create a custom form in Design view using all three form sections**
- **Add fields individually and as a group**
- **Move, size, and format control objects**
- **Change the tab order of fields**
- **Create tabbed pages in a form and insert a subform on each page**
- **Add and format a calculation to a custom form**
- **Group and ungroup multiple controls**
- **Adjust the alignment and spacing of controls**
- **Add graphics to a form**
- **Anchor a control to a position in a form**
- **Create a datasheet form**
- **Modify form properties to restrict actions allowed in records**
- **Create a blank form**
- **Add list boxes to a form**
- **Sort records in a form and locate a record using a wildcard character**

Tutorials

4.1 Creating Custom Forms Using Design View
4.2 Binding a Table to a Form and Adding Fields
4.3 Moving, Resizing, and Formatting Control Objects
4.4 Changing the Tab Order of Fields
4.5 Adding a Tab Control and a Subform
4.6 Adding Subforms and a New Page to the Tab Control
4.7 Adding Calculations to a Form in Design View
4.8 Grouping, Aligning, and Spacing Controls
4.9 Creating a Datasheet Form and Modifying Form Properties
4.10 Sorting and Finding Records in a Form

Forms provide an interface for data entry and maintenance that allows end users to work more efficiently with data stored in the underlying tables. For example, a form can be designed with a layout that uses the screen space more effectively than the tabular layout of a datasheet. A form can also include fields from multiple tables, allowing data to be entered in one object but used to update several tables. Generally, database designers provide forms for end users to perform data maintenance and restrict access to tables to protect the structure and integrity of the database. In this chapter, you will learn how to build custom forms. Model answers for this chapter's projects appear on the following page.

Note: Before beginning the projects, copy to your storage medium the AL2C4 subfolder from the AL2 folder on the CD that accompanies this textbook and then make AL2C4 the active folder.

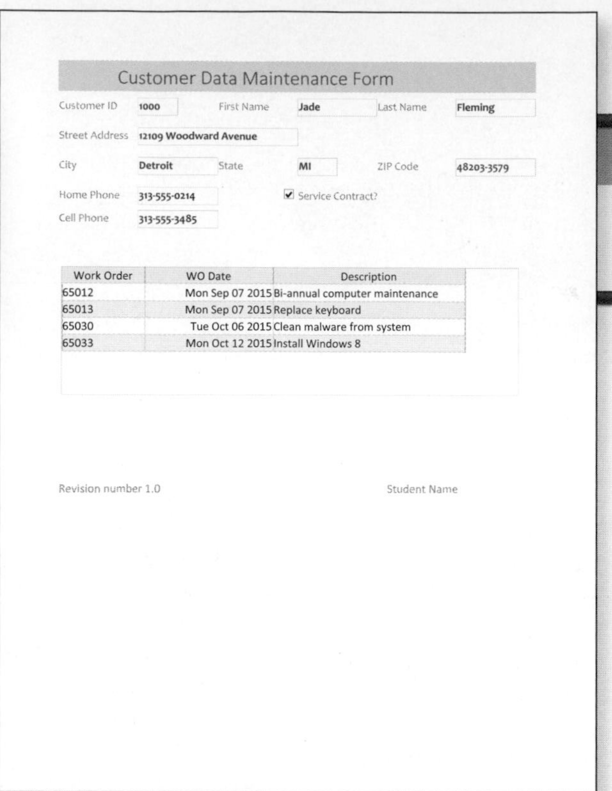

Work Order	WO Date	Description
65012	Mon Sep 07 2015	Bi-annual computer maintenance
65013	Mon Sep 07 2015	Replace keyboard
65030	Tue Oct 06 2015	Clean malware from system
65033	Mon Oct 12 2015	Install Windows 8

Project 1 Design and Create a Custom Form

CustMaintenance Form

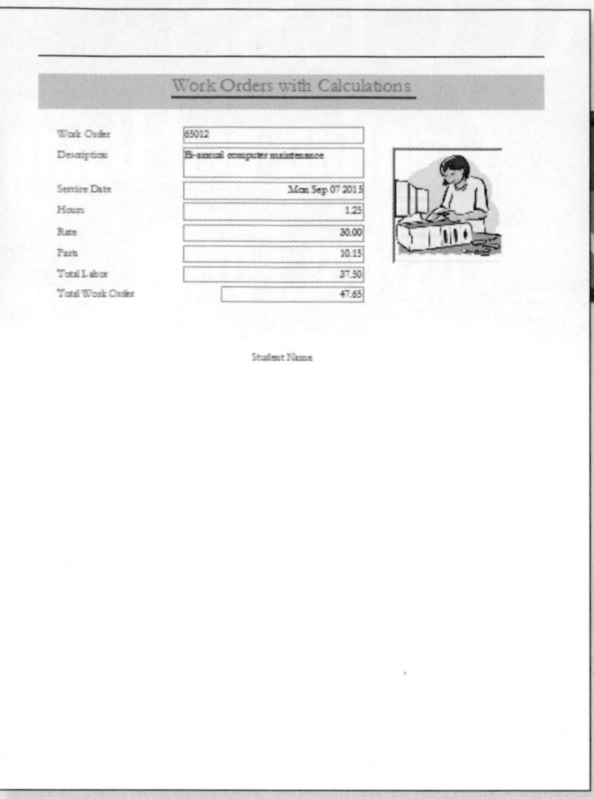

Project 2 Create a New Form with Calculations and Graphics

WorkOrders Form

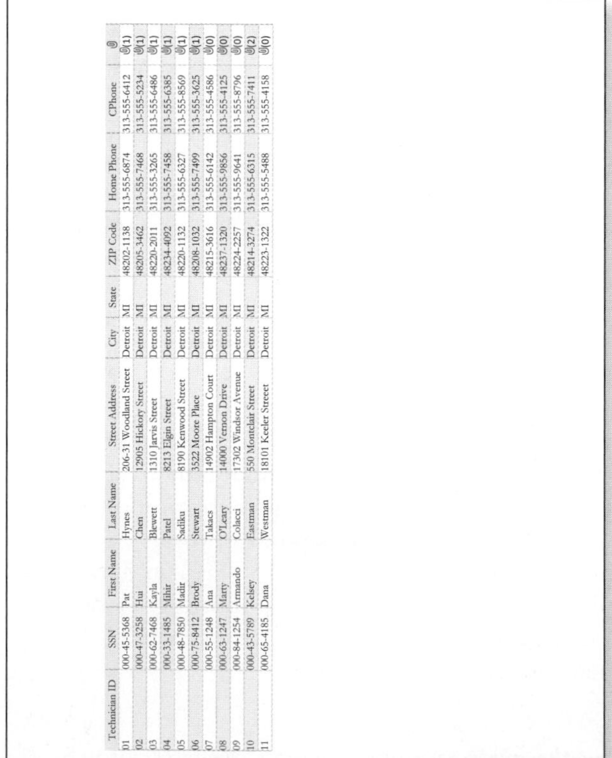

Technician ID	SSN	First Name	Last Name	Street Address	City	State	ZIP Code	Home Phone	CPhone	📎
01	000-45-5368	Pat	Hynes	206-31 Woodland Street	Detroit	MI	48202-1138	313-555-6874	313-555-6412	(1)
02	000-47-3258	Hui	Chen	12905 Hickory Street	Detroit	MI	48205-3462	313-555-7468	313-555-5234	(1)
03	000-62-7468	Kayla	Blewett	1310 Jarvis Street	Detroit	MI	48220-2011	313-555-3265	313-555-6486	(1)
04	000-33-1485	Mihir	Patel	8213 Elgin Street	Detroit	MI	48234-4092	313-555-7458	313-555-6385	(1)
05	000-48-7850	Madir	Sadiku	8190 Kenwood Street	Detroit	MI	48220-1132	313-555-6327	313-555-8569	(1)
06	000-75-8412	Brody	Stewart	3522 Moore Place	Detroit	MI	48208-1032	313-555-7499	313-555-3625	(1)
07	000-55-1248	Ana	Takacs	14902 Hampton Court	Detroit	MI	48215-3616	313-555-6142	313-555-4586	(0)
08	000-63-1247	Marty	O'Leary	14000 Vernon Drive	Detroit	MI	48237-1320	313-555-9856	313-555-4125	(0)
09	000-84-1254	Armando	Colacci	17302 Windsor Avenue	Detroit	MI	48224-2257	313-555-9641	313-555-8796	(0)
10	000-43-5789	Kelsey	Eastman	550 Montclair Street	Detroit	MI	48214-3274	313-555-6315	313-555-7411	(2)
11	000-65-4185	Dana	Westman	18101 Keeler Streeet	Detroit	MI	48223-1322	313-555-5488	313-555-4158	(0)

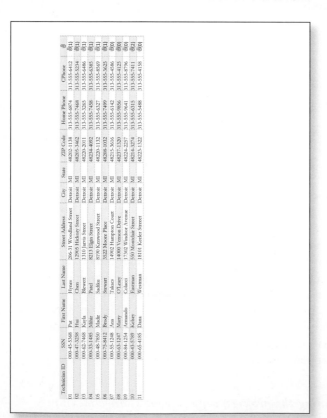

Project 3 Create a Restricted-Use Form

Technicians Form

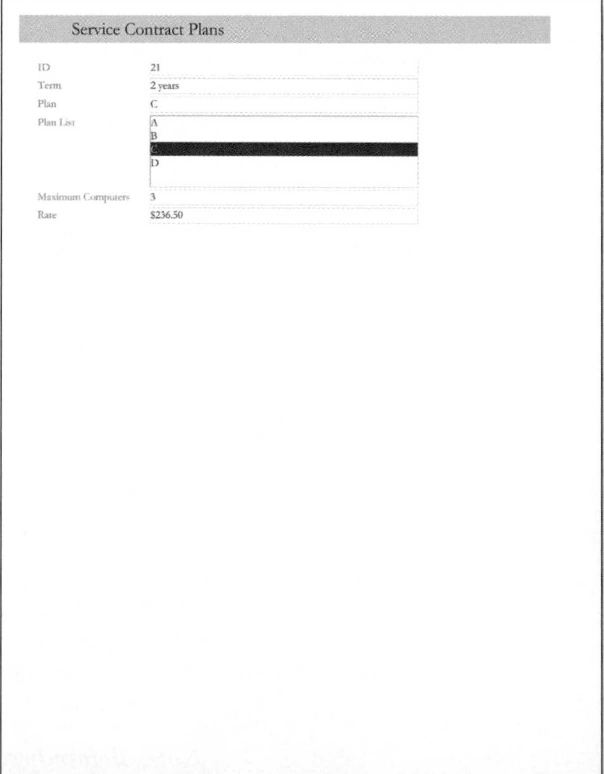

Project 4 Create a Blank Form with Lists

SCPlans Form

Project 1 Design and Create a Custom Form 7 Parts

You will create a custom form in Design view that includes subforms in tabbed pages to provide a single object in which data stored in four tables can be entered, viewed, and printed.

Creating Custom Forms Using Design View

Quick Steps

Start a New Form in Design View
1. Click CREATE tab.
2. Click Form Design button.

Form Design

Access provides several tools that allow you to build a form quickly, such as the Form tool, the Split Form tool, and the Form Wizard. A form generated using one of these tools can be modified in Layout view or Design view to customize the content, format, or layout. If you require a form with several custom options, you can begin in Design view and build the form from scratch. Click the CREATE tab and then click the Form Design button in the Forms group to begin a new form using the Design view window, as shown in Figure 4.1.

In Design view, the form displays the *Detail* section, which is used to display fields from the table associated with the form. Objects are added to the form using buttons in the Controls, Header/Footer, and Tools groups on the FORM DESIGN TOOLS DESIGN tab, shown in Figure 4.2 on the next page.

Figure 4.1 Form Design View

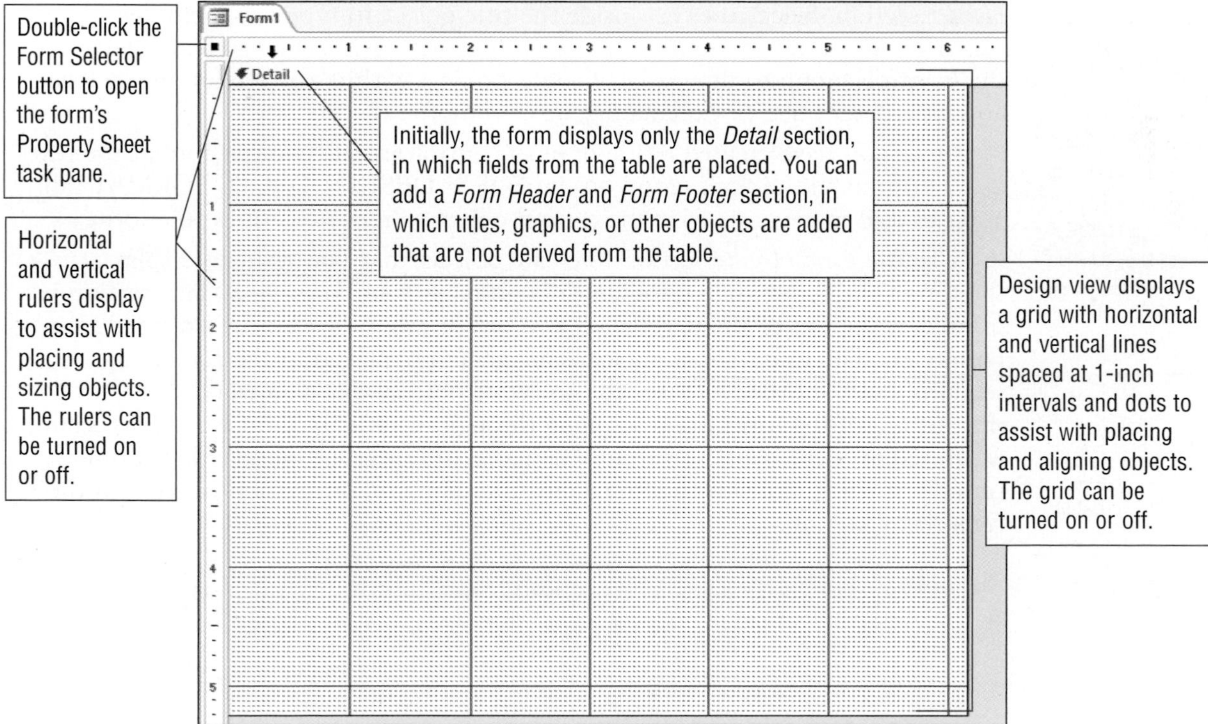

Double-click the Form Selector button to open the form's Property Sheet task pane.
Horizontal and vertical rulers display to assist with placing and sizing objects. The rulers can be turned on or off.
Form1
Detail
Initially, the form displays only the *Detail* section, in which fields from the table are placed. You can add a *Form Header* and *Form Footer* section, in which titles, graphics, or other objects are added that are not derived from the table.
Design view displays a grid with horizontal and vertical lines spaced at 1-inch intervals and dots to assist with placing and aligning objects. The grid can be turned on or off.

Figure 4.2 Controls, Header/Footer, and Tools Groups on FORM DESIGN TOOLS DESIGN Tab

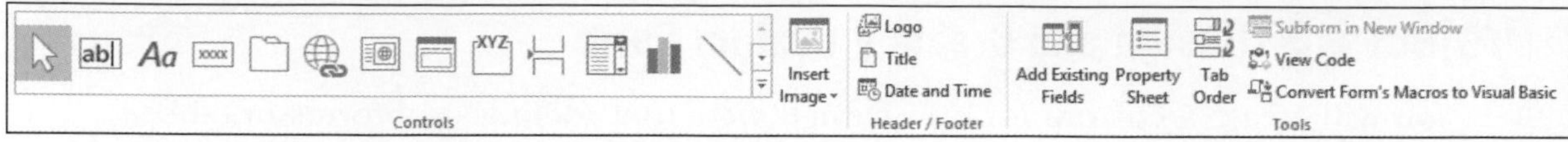

Understanding Bound, Unbound, and Calculated Control Objects

Before starting a new custom form in Design view, it is a good idea to sketch the rough layout of the form on a piece of paper. Doing this will help you place the fields and determine other objects you need to create.

As you begin to build a custom form, you need to understand the three types of control objects that can be created in a form. A ***control object*** in a form may be bound, unbound, or calculated. ***Bound objects*** draw and display data in the control from the field in the table associated with the control. In other words, the content that is displayed in the control object in Form view is drawn from a field in a record in a table. ***Unbound objects*** are used to display text or graphics and do not rely on a table for their content. For example, an object that contains a clip art image to enhance the visual appearance of a form or an object that contains the hours of business for informational purposes are both unbound objects. A ***calculated object*** displays the result of a mathematical formula. Totals and percentages are examples of calculated objects.

Creating Titles and Label Objects

Quick Steps

Add a Form Title
1. Open form in Design view.
2. Click Title button.
3. Type title text.
4. Press Enter.

Add a Label Object
1. Open form in Design view.
2. Click Label button.
3. Drag to create object of desired height and width.
4. Type label text.
5. Press Enter.

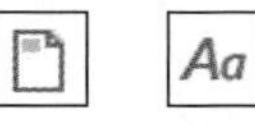

Click the Title button in the Header/Footer group on the FORM DESIGN TOOLS DESIGN tab to display the *Form Header* and *Form Footer* sections and automatically insert a label object with the name of the form inside the *Form Header* section. Select the text inside the title object to type new text, delete existing text, or otherwise modify the default title text. Click the Label button in the Controls group to draw a label control object within any section in the form and type descriptive or explanatory text inside the object.

Once you have created a title or label control object, you can format the text using buttons in the Font group on the FORM DESIGN TOOLS FORMAT tab. You can also move and resize the control object to reposition it on the form.

Use the *Form Header* section to create objects that you want to display at the top of the form when scrolling through records in Form view. This section is printed at the top of the page when a record or group of records is printed from Form view. Titles and company logos are generally placed in the *Form Header* section. Use the *Form Footer* section to create objects that you want to display at the bottom of the form when scrolling through records in Form view. This section is printed at the end of a printout when a record or group of records is printed from Form view. Consider adding a creation date and/or revision number in the *Form Footer* section.

Project 1a Starting a New Form Using Design View and Adding a Title and Label Object Part 1 of 7

1. Open **AL2-C4-RSRCompServ.accdb** and enable the content.
2. Click the CREATE tab and then click the Form Design button in the Forms group.

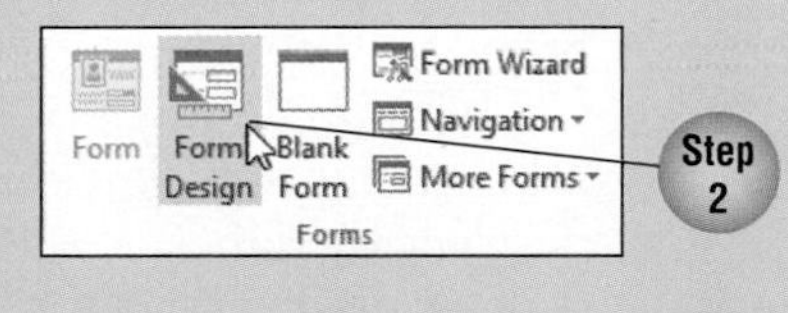

3. Add a title in the *Form Header* section of the form and then center the text within the object by completing the following steps:
   a. With the FORM DESIGN TOOLS DESIGN tab active, click the Title button in the Header/Footer group. Access displays the *Form Header* section above the *Detail* section and inserts a title object with the text *Form1* selected.

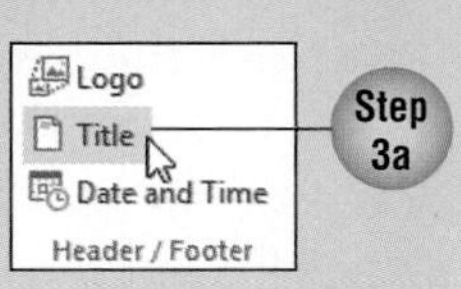

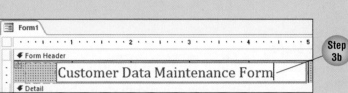

   b. With the insertion point positioned in the title object and *Form1* selected, type **Customer Data Maintenance Form**. Notice that the background behind the title object is shaded blue and the color of the text is blue as well. The colors and fonts that appear in controls are dependent on the current theme. The Office theme is the default theme for a database.
   c. Press Enter.
   d. With the title object selected (as indicated by the orange border around the title text), click the FORM DESIGN TOOLS FORMAT tab and then click the Center button in the Font group.
4. Scroll down the form until you see the *Form Footer* section.
5. Position the mouse pointer at the bottom border of the form's grid until the pointer changes to an up-and-down-pointing arrow with a horizontal line in the middle and then drag the bottom of the form down to the 0.5-inch position on the vertical ruler.

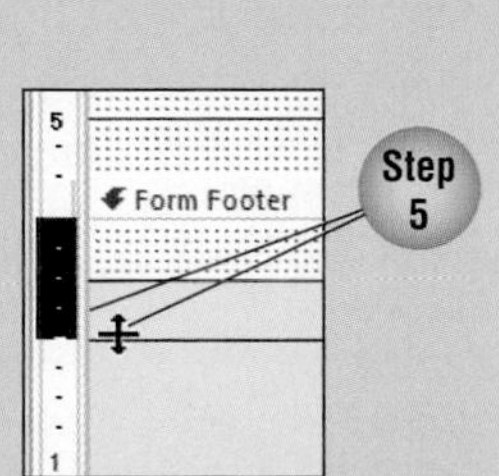

6. Add a label control object at the left edge of the form footer that contains a revision number and another at the right edge of the form footer that contains your name by completing the following steps:
   a. Click the FORM DESIGN TOOLS DESIGN tab and then click the Label button in the Controls group (third button from the left).
   b. Position the crosshairs with the label icon attached at the left side of the *Form Footer* section and then drag to draw a label control object of the approximate height and width shown at the right. When you release the mouse, the insertion point appears inside the label control object.
   c. Type **Revision number 1.0** and then press Enter.

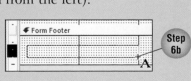

d. Create another label control object at the right side of the *Form Footer* section that is similar in height and width to the one shown below, type your first and last names inside the label control object, and then press Enter. Refer to Steps 6a through 6c if you need help with this step.

Step 6d

e. Click in any blank area of the form to deselect the label control object.

7. Click the Save button on the Quick Access toolbar, type **CustMaintenance** in the *Form Name* text box at the Save As dialog box, and then press Enter or click OK.

Step 7

Quick Steps

Connect a Table to a Form

1. Open form in Design view.
2. Double-click Form Selector button.
3. Click Data tab in Property Sheet task pane.
4. Click down-pointing arrow in *Record Source* property box.
5. Click desired table.
6. Close Property Sheet task pane.

Add Fields to a Form

1. Click Add Existing Fields button.
2. Drag field name from Field List task pane to desired location in *Detail* section.

OR

1. Click first field name in Field List task pane.
2. Hold down Shift key.
3. Click last field name in Field List task pane.
4. Drag selected fields from Field List task pane to desired location in *Detail* section.

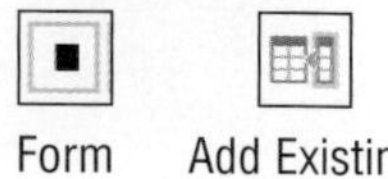

Form Selector   Add Existing Fields

Adding Fields to a Form

Before you can add fields to the *Detail* section, you must first connect a table to the form. Specify the table that will be connected with the form using the Record Source property on the Data tab of the form's Property Sheet task pane. To do this, double-click the Form Selector button, which is located above the vertical ruler and left of the horizontal ruler, to open the form's Property Sheet task pane at the right side of the work area. Click the Data tab, click the down-pointing arrow in the *Record Source* property box, click the desired table at the drop-down list, and then close the Property Sheet task pane.

To add fields to the form, click the Add Existing Fields button in the Tools group on the FORM DESIGN TOOLS DESIGN tab to open the Field List task pane. Select and drag individual or groups of field names from the Field List task pane to the *Detail* section of the form. Release the mouse button when the mouse pointer is near the location in the *Detail* section at which you want to display the data. For each field added to the form, Access inserts two control objects. A label control object is placed at the left of where you release the mouse button and a text box control object is placed at the right. The label control object contains the field name or a caption, if a caption was entered in the *Caption* property box. The text box control object is bound to the field and displays table data from the record in Form view. Figure 4.3 displays the fields from the Customers table that you will add to the CustMaintenance form in Project 1b.

Figure 4.3 Fields from Customers Table Added to CustMaintenance Form in Project 1b

Project 1b Connecting a Table to a Form and Adding Fields Part 2 of 7

1. With **AL2-C4-RSRCompServ.accdb** open and the CustMaintenance form open in Design view, scroll up to the top of the form in the work area.
2. Connect the Customers table to the form by completing the following steps:
   a. Double-click the Form Selector button (which displays as a black or blue square) located at the top of the vertical ruler and left of the horizontal ruler to open the form's Property Sheet task pane.
   b. Click the Data tab in the Property Sheet task pane.
   c. Click the down-pointing arrow in the *Record Source* property box and then click *Customers* at the drop-down list.
   d. Close the Property Sheet task pane.
3. Add fields individually from the Customers table to the *Detail* section of the form by completing the following steps:
   a. Click the Add Existing Fields button in the Tools group on the FORM DESIGN TOOLS DESIGN tab. The Field List task pane opens at the right side of the work area.
   b. Position the mouse pointer on the right border of the form's grid until the pointer changes to a left-and-right-pointing arrow with a vertical line in the middle and then drag the right edge of the form to the 6.5-inch position on the horizontal ruler.

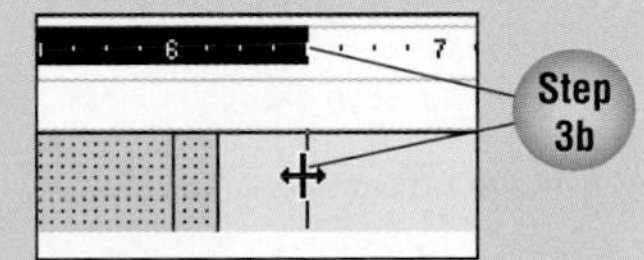

   c. If necessary, click *CustID* in the Field List task pane to select the field and then drag the field name to the *Detail* section, releasing the mouse button when the pointer is near the top of the section at the 1-inch position on the horizontal ruler.

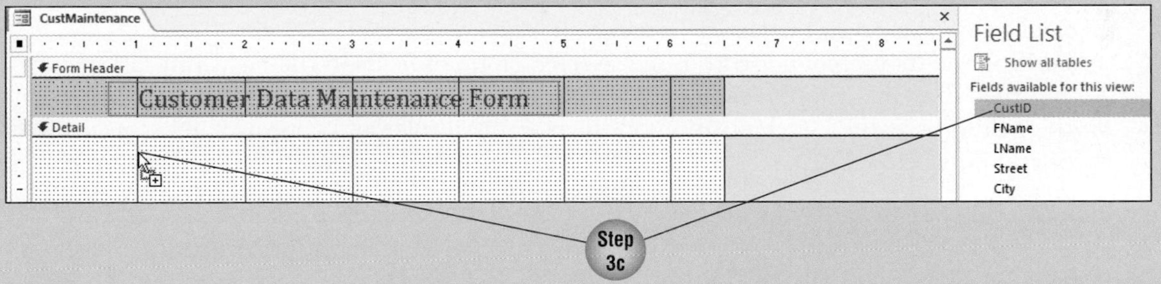

   d. Click to select *FName* in the Field List task pane and then drag the field to the same vertical position as *CustID* in the *Detail* section, releasing the mouse button when the pointer is at the 3-inch position on the horizontal ruler.
   e. Click to select *LName* in the Field List task pane and then drag the field to the same vertical position as *CustID* in the *Detail* section, releasing the mouse button when the pointer is at the 5-inch position on the horizontal ruler.

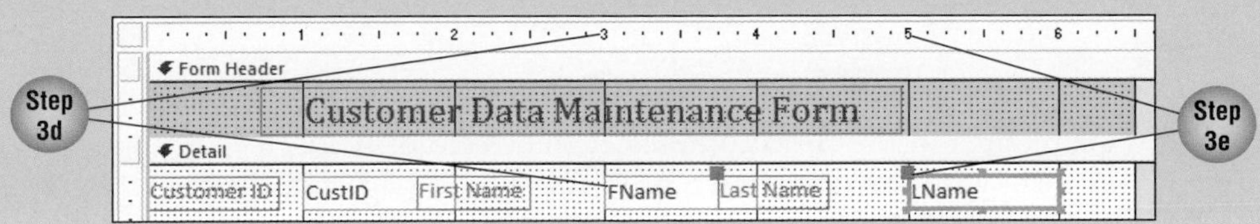

f. Drag the *Street* field from the Field List task pane to the *Detail* section below *CustID*, releasing the mouse button when the pointer is at the 1-inch position on the horizontal ruler and approximately three rows of grid dots below *CustID*.
g. Drag the *City* field from the Field List task pane to the *Detail* section below *Street*, releasing the mouse button when the pointer is at approximately the 1-inch position on the horizontal ruler and approximately three rows of grid dots below *Street*.
h. Drag the *State* field from the Field List task pane to the *Detail* section at the same horizontal position as *City*, releasing the mouse button when the pointer is at the 3-inch position on the horizontal ruler.
i. Drag the *ZIP* field from the Field List task pane to the *Detail* section at the same horizontal position as *City*, releasing the mouse button when the pointer is at the 5-inch position on the horizontal ruler.

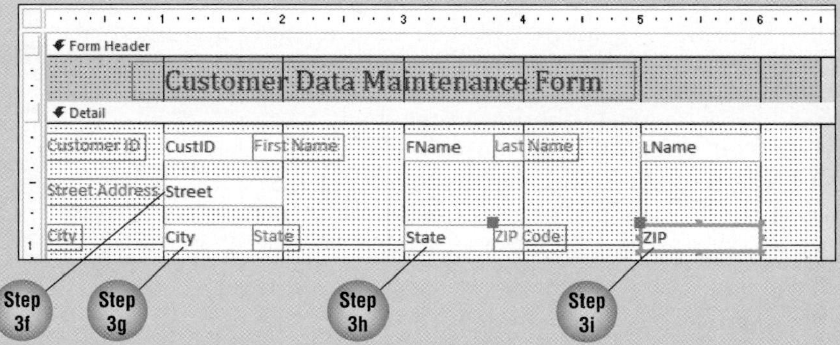

4. Add a group of fields from the Customers table to the *Detail* section of the form by completing the following steps:
   a. Click the *HPhone* field name in the Field List task pane.
   b. Hold down the Shift key and then click the *ServCont* field name in the Field List task pane. When you hold down the Shift key, Access selects all of the fields from the first field name clicked to the last field name clicked.
   c. Position the mouse pointer within the selected group of fields in the Field List task pane and then drag the group to the *Detail* section below *City*, releasing the mouse button when the pointer is at the 1-inch position on the horizontal ruler and approximately three rows of grid dots below *City*.

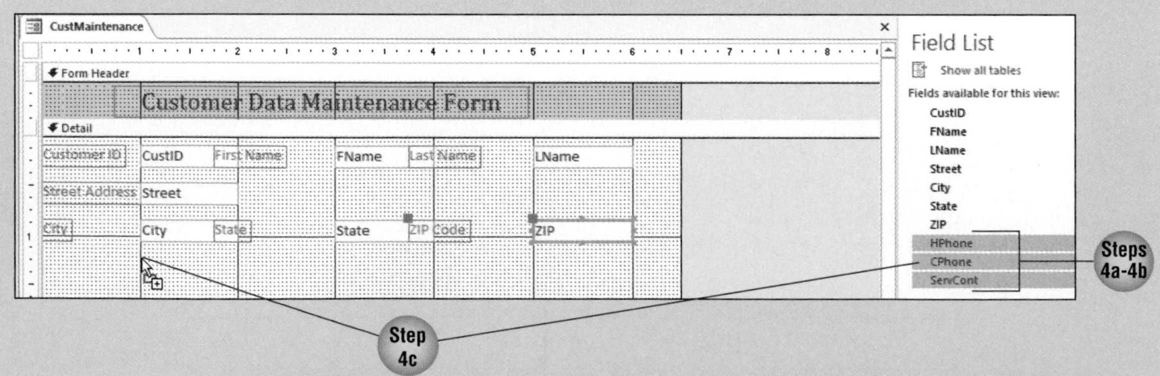

5. Click in any blank area of the form to deselect the group of fields.
6. Compare your form with the one shown in Figure 4.3 on page 110.
7. Click the Save button on the Quick Access toolbar.
8. Close the Field List task pane.

Moving and Resizing Control Objects

Once you have placed fields in a form, you can move or resize objects to change the layout. In Project 1b, you saw that Access places two control objects for each field in the form. A label control object, which contains the caption or field name, is placed to the left of a text box control object, which displays the field value from the record (or a blank entry box when adding a new record). Click the label control object or text box control object for the field you want to move or resize and the object is surrounded by an orange border with eight handles. Access displays a large, dark gray square (called the *move handle*) at the top left of the label control object or text box control object for the selected field.

Point to the orange border around the selected control object until the mouse pointer displays with the four-headed arrow move icon attached and then drag the field to the new position on the form. Access moves both the label control and text box control objects to the new location. If you want to move a selected label control or text box control independently from its connected object, point to the large, dark gray move handle at the top left of either control and use it to drag the control object to the new position, as shown in Figure 4.4.

To resize a selected control object, point to one of the sizing handles (the small orange squares) on the border of the selected object until the pointer displays with an up-and-down-pointing arrow, a left-and-right-pointing arrow, or a two-headed diagonal arrow. Drag the arrow to resize the height and/or width.

By default, the Snap to Grid feature is turned on in Design view. This feature pulls a control to the nearest grid point when an object is moved or resized. If you want to move or resize an object in small increments, you may want to turn off this feature. To do this, click the FORM DESIGN TOOLS ARRANGE tab, click the Size/Space button in the Sizing & Ordering group, and then click *Snap to Grid* at the drop-down list. Snap to Grid is a toggle feature, which means it is turned on or off by clicking the button.

Figure 4.4 Moving Control Objects in Design View

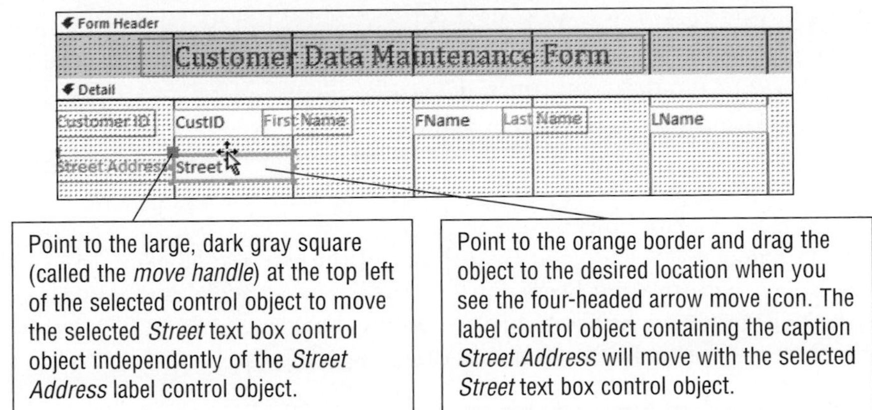
Form Header
Customer Data Maintenance Form
Detail
Customer ID
CustID
First Name
FName
Last Name
LName
Street Address
Street
Point to the large, dark gray square (called the *move handle*) at the top left of the selected control object to move the selected *Street* text box control object independently of the *Street Address* label control object.
Point to the orange border and drag the object to the desired location when you see the four-headed arrow move icon. The label control object containing the caption *Street Address* will move with the selected *Street* text box control object.

Quick Steps

Move Objects in Design View
1. Select control object.
2. Drag using orange border or move handle to desired location.

Resize Objects in Design View
1. Select control object.
2. Drag middle top, bottom, left, or right sizing handle to resize height or width.

OR
1. Select control object.
2. Drag corner sizing handle to resize height and width at same time.

Toggle Snap to Grid On or Off
1. Click FORM DESIGN TOOLS ARRANGE tab.
2. Click Size/Space button.
3. Click *Snap to Grid*.

Size/Space

HINT

Do not be overly concerned with exact placement and alignment as you begin to add fields to a form. You will learn how to use alignment and spacing tools in the FORM DESIGN TOOLS ARRANGE tab to assist with layout.

▼ Quick Steps

Format Multiple Controls Using the Shift Key

1. In Design view, click to select first control object.
2. Shift + click remaining control objects.
3. Click desired formatting options.
4. Deselect controls.

Format Multiple Controls Using a Selection Rectangle

1. In Design view, position pointer above top left control to be formatted.
2. Drag down and right to draw rectangle around controls.
3. Release mouse.
4. Click desired formatting options.
5. Deselect controls.

Conditional Formatting

Themes

Formatting Controls

Use the buttons in the Font group on the FORM DESIGN TOOLS FORMAT tab to change the font, font size, font color, background color, or alignment and to apply bold, italic, or underline formatting to the selected control object. Use the Conditional Formatting button in the Control Formatting group to apply conditional formatting to the selected object.

Format multiple control objects at the same time by holding down the Shift key while clicking individual controls. You can also select multiple objects inside the rectangle by using the mouse pointer to draw a selection rectangle around a group of controls.

Apply a theme to the form by clicking the Themes button on the FORM DESIGN TOOLS DESIGN tab. The theme controls the default colors and fonts for objects in the form. You can change the color and fonts used in a form with the Colors and Fonts buttons in the Themes group. A theme applied to one form is applied to all of the forms and reports in the database.

Project 1c **Moving and Resizing Controls** **Part 3 of 7**

1. With **AL2-C4-RSRCompServ.accdb** open and the CustMaintenance form open in Design view, preview the form to determine what controls need to be moved or resized by clicking the View button in the Views group on the FORM DESIGN TOOLS DESIGN tab. (Make sure to click the button and not the button arrow.)
2. The form is displayed in Form view with data from the first record displayed in the text box control objects. Notice that some label control objects overlap text box control objects and that the street address in the first record is not entirely displayed.
3. Click the Design View button in the view area at the right side of the Status bar.
4. Move the controls for those objects that are overlapping other objects by completing the following steps:
   a. Click the *First Name* label control object.
   b. Point to the large, dark gray move handle at the top left of the selected label control object until the pointer displays with the four-headed arrow move icon attached and then drag right to the 2-inch position on the horizontal ruler. Notice that the connected *FName* text box control object does not move, because you are dragging using the move handle.

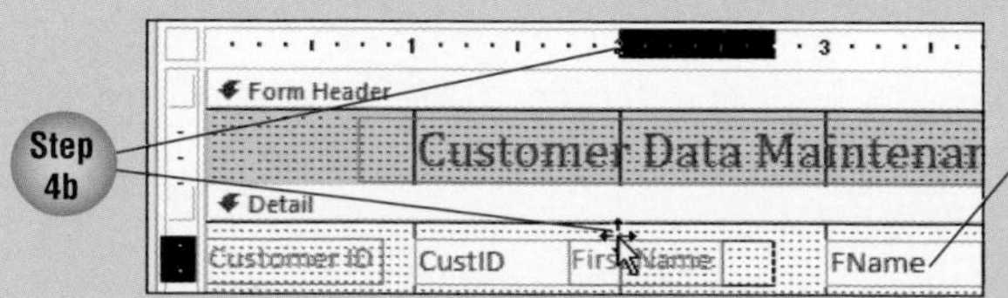

The connected *FName* text box control does not move when you drag the label control object using the move handle.

c. Click the *Last Name* label control object and then use the move handle to drag right to the 4-inch position on the horizontal ruler.
d. Move the *State* label control object right to the 2-inch position on the horizontal ruler.
e. Move the *ZIP Code* label control object right to the 4-inch position on the horizontal ruler.

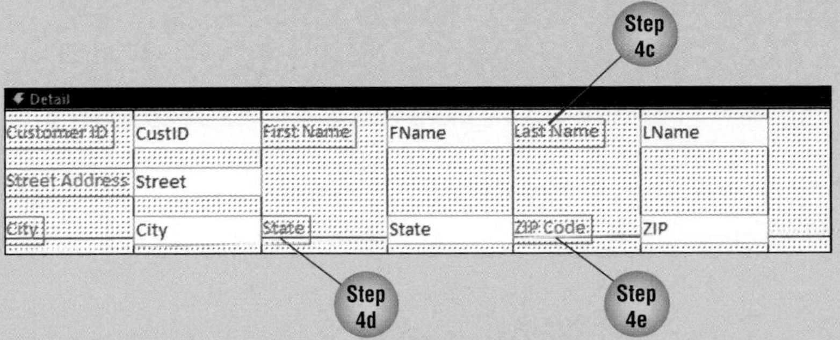

f. Click in any blank area to deselect the *ZIP Code* label control.

5. Click the *Street* text box control object and then drag the right middle sizing handle right to the 3-inch position on the horizontal ruler.

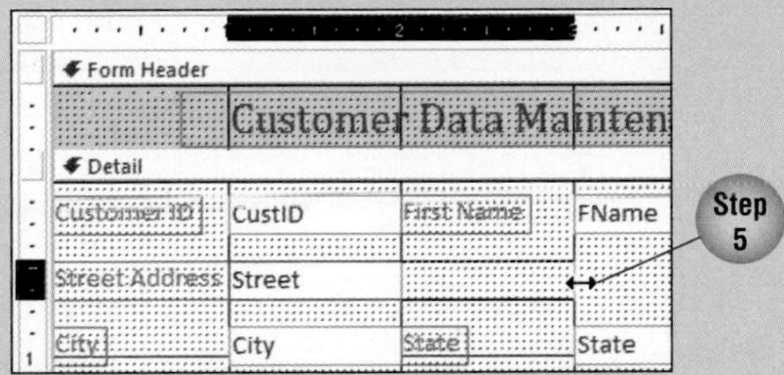

6. Click the *State* text box control object and then drag the right middle sizing handle left to the 3.5-inch position on the horizontal ruler. (Since the *State* field displays only two characters, this control object can be made smaller.)
7. Resize the *CustID* text box control so that the right edge of the control is at the 1.5-inch position on the horizontal ruler.
8. Click the *Service Contract?* label control object. Point to any area of the selected object's orange border (not on a sizing handle) and then drag the object until the left edge is at the 3-inch position on the horizontal ruler, adjacent to the *HPhone* field. Notice that both the label control object and text box control object moved, since you dragged the border rather than the move handle.

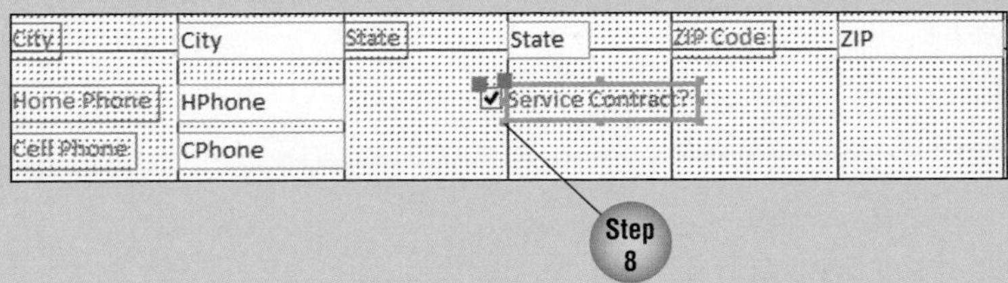

9. Deselect the *Service Contract?* control object.
10. Save the form.

Project 1d Formatting Multiple Controls

Part 4 of 7

1. With **AL2-C4-RSRCompServ.accdb** open and the CustMaintenance form open in Design view, click the View button to preview the form in Form view.
2. Scroll through a few records in the form and then switch back to Design view.
3. Format multiple controls using a selection rectangle by completing the following steps:
   a. Position the arrow pointer in the top left corner of the *Detail* section (above the *Customer ID* label control object), drag down and to the right until you have drawn a rectangle around all of the controls in the section, and then release the mouse.

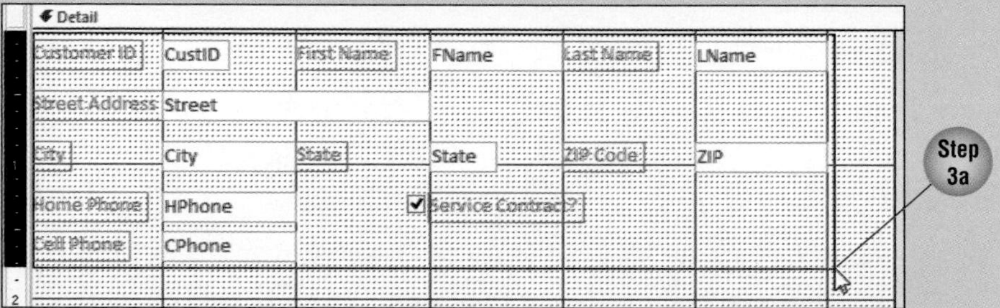

   b. Notice that all of the objects contained within the rectangle are selected.

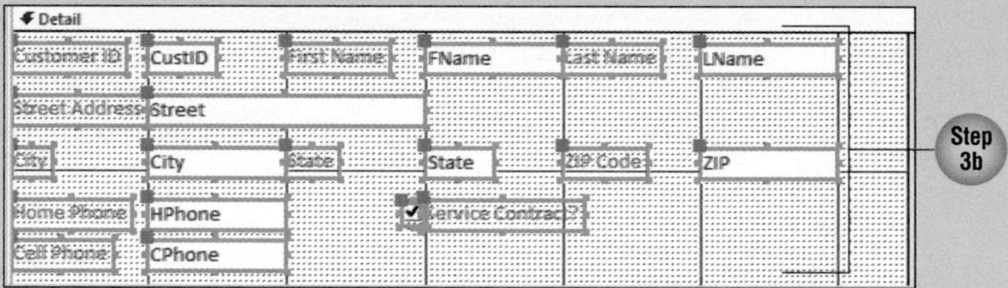

   c. Use the Font button in the Font group on the FORM DESIGN TOOLS FORMAT tab to change the font to Candara.
   d. Use the Font Size button to change the font size to 10 points.
   e. Click in any blank area to deselect the controls.
4. Apply formatting to multiple controls at once by completing the following steps:
   a. Click the *CustID* text box control object.
   b. Hold down the Shift key and then click each of the other text box control objects in the *Detail* section.

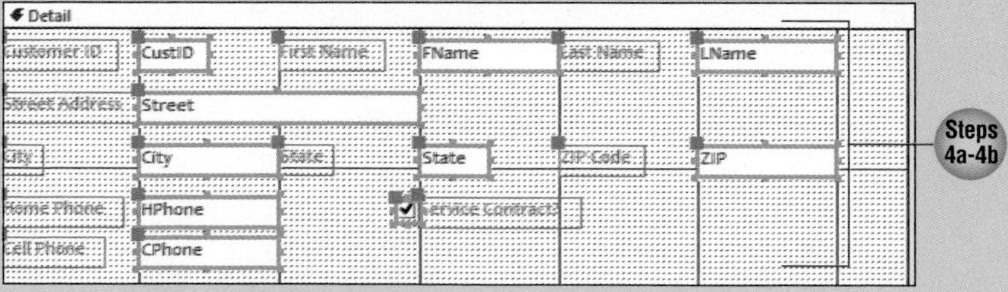

c. Click the Font Color button arrow in the Font group on the FORM DESIGN TOOLS FORMAT tab and then click *Dark Red* at the color palette (first option in the last row).
d. Click the Bold button.
e. Click in any blank area to deselect the controls.

5. Click the FORM DESIGN TOOLS DESIGN tab and then switch to Form view to view the formatting changes applied to the form.
6. Switch to Design view and then save the form.

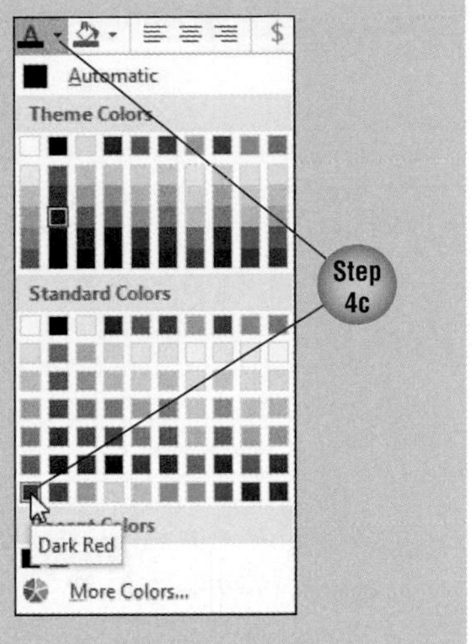

Automatic
Theme Colors
Standard Colors
Dark Red
More Colors...
Step 4c

Changing the Tab Order of Fields

Tab order refers to the order in which fields are selected when you press the Tab key while entering data in Form view. You do not have to enter data into a record in the order in which the fields are presented. Click the Tab Order button in the Tools group on the FORM DESIGN TOOLS DESIGN tab to open the Tab Order dialog box, shown in Figure 4.5.

The order of fields in the *Custom Order* list box in the Tab Order dialog box is the order in which the fields will be selected when the Tab key is pressed in a record in Form view. To change the tab order of the fields, position the pointer in the gray field selector bar next to the field name that you want to move until the pointer displays as a black right-pointing arrow and then click to select the field. Drag the selected field up or down to the desired position. Click OK when you have finished reorganizing the fields. To quickly set the tab order as left-to-right and top-to-bottom, click the Auto Order button at the bottom of the Tab Order dialog box.

Quick Steps

Change the Tab Order of Fields

1. Open form in Design view.
2. Click Tab Order button.
3. Click in gray field selector bar next to field name.
4. Drag field to desired location.
5. Repeat Steps 3–4 as required.
6. Click OK.

Tab Order

Figure 4.5 Tab Order Dialog Box

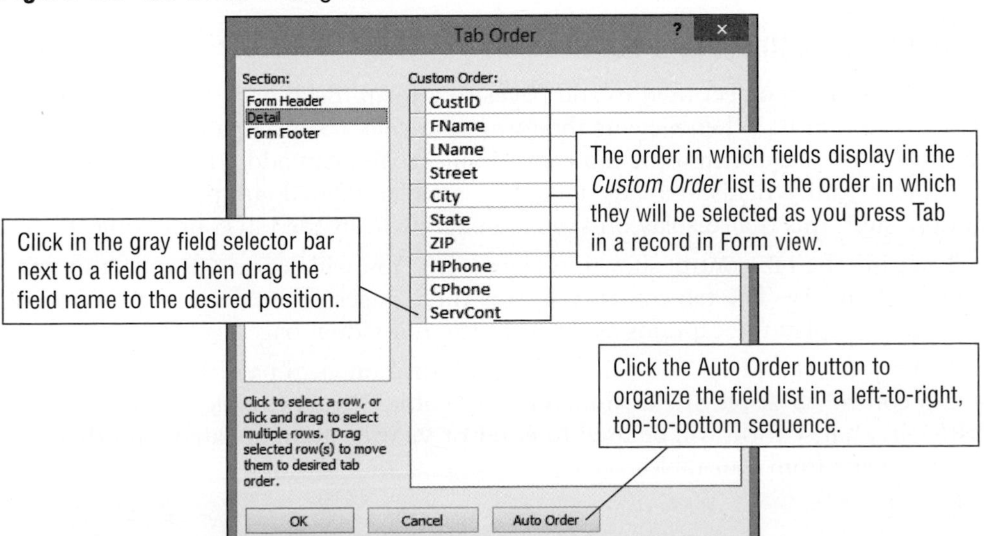

Tab Order
Section:
Form Header
Detail
Form Footer
Custom Order:
CustID
FName
LName
Street
City
State
ZIP
HPhone
CPhone
ServCont
Click to select a row, or click and drag to select multiple rows. Drag selected row(s) to move them to desired tab order.
OK
Cancel
Auto Order
Click in the gray field selector bar next to a field and then drag the field name to the desired position.
The order in which fields display in the Custom Order list is the order in which they will be selected as you press Tab in a record in Form view.
Click the Auto Order button to organize the field list in a left-to-right, top-to-bottom sequence.

Project 1e Changing the Tab Order of Fields

Part 5 of 7

1. With **AL2-C4-RSRCompServ.accdb** database open and the CustMaintenance form open in Design view, click the View button to display the form in Form view.
2. With the insertion point positioned in the *CustID* field in the first record in the table, press the Tab key seven times. As you press Tab, notice that the fields are selected in a left-to-right, top-to-bottom sequence.
3. With the insertion point positioned in the *HPhone* field, press Tab. Notice that the selected field moves down to the *CPhone* field instead of moving right to the *ServCont* field.
4. With the insertion point in the *CPhone* field, press Tab to move to the *ServCont* field.
5. Switch to Design view.
6. Change the tab order of the fields so that the *ServCont* field is selected after the *HPhone* field by completing the following steps:
   a. Click the Tab Order button in the Tools group on the FORM DESIGN TOOLS DESIGN tab.
   b. At the Tab Order dialog box, hover the mouse pointer over the gray field selector bar next to *ServCont* until the pointer displays as a black right-pointing arrow.
   c. Click to select the field.
   d. With the pointer now displayed as a white arrow in the field selector bar, drag *ServCont* up until the black horizontal line indicating the location to which the field will be moved is positioned between *HPhone* and *CPhone* in the *Custom Order* list and then release the mouse button.
   e. Click OK. Note that since the tabs follow the left-to-right, top-to-bottom sequence, you could have also created this tab order by clicking the Auto Order button in the Tab Order dialog box.
7. Switch to Form view.
8. Press the Tab key nine times to move through the fields in the first record. Notice that when you reach the *HPhone* field and press Tab, the *ServCont* field becomes active instead of the *CPhone* field.
9. Switch to Design view.
10. Save the form.

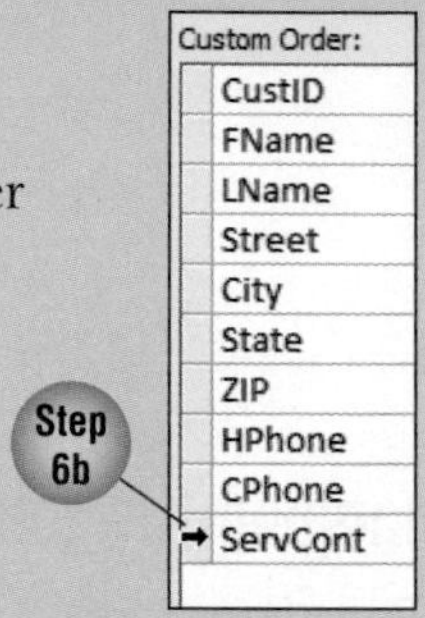

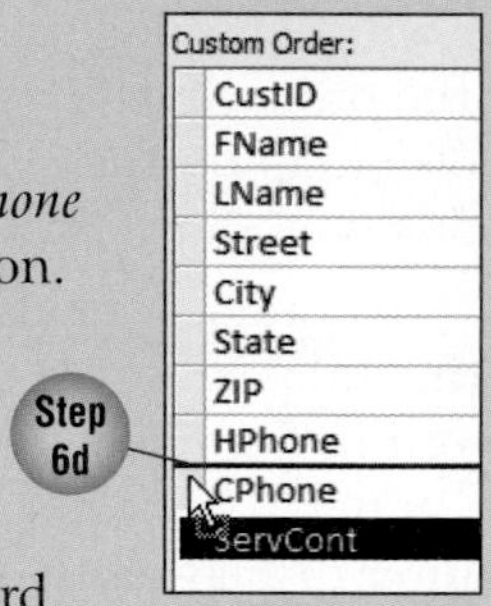

Adding a Tab Control to a Form

A ***tab control*** is an object used to add pages to a form. Each page displays with a tab at the top of it. When viewing the form, you click the page tab to display the contents of the page within the tab control object. You can add a tab control to a form to organize fields in a large table into smaller, related groups or to insert multiple subforms that display on separate pages within the tab control object.

Examine the tab control shown in Figure 4.6. You will create this object in Projects 1f and 1g. The tab control contains three pages. The tabs across the top of the control display the captions assigned to the individual pages.

In Projects 1f and 1g, you will create a subform on each page within the tab control to display fields from a related table. When completed, the CustMaintenance form will be used to enter or view customer-related data that includes fields from four tables.

Figure 4.6 Tab Control with Three Pages Created in Projects 1f and 1g

A tab displays at the top of each page added to a tab control object. Click the tab to display the contents of the page in the tab control.

Profiles | Service Contracts | Work Orders

Computer ID	Username	Password	Remote Access?
D1	jade	P$ck7	☐
*			☐

Record: 1 of 1 No Filter Search

To add a tab control object to a form, click the Tab Control button in the Controls group on the FORM DESIGN TOOLS DESIGN tab. Position the crosshairs with the tab control icon attached in the top left of the area of the *Detail* section where you want to begin the tab control and then drag down and to the right to draw the control. When you release the mouse button, the tab control object initially displays with two pages, as shown in Figure 4.7.

Change the text displayed in the tab at the top of the page by editing the text in the *Caption* property box in the page's Property Sheet task pane. Add fields or create subforms on each page as needed. Add a page to the tab control by right-clicking an existing tab in the tab control object and then clicking *Insert Page* at the shortcut menu. Remove a page from the tab control by right-clicking the tab to be deleted and then clicking *Delete Page* at the shortcut menu.

Quick Steps

Add a Tab Control to a Form

1. Open form in Design view.
2. Click Tab Control button.
3. Position crosshairs in *Detail* section at desired location.
4. Drag down and right to draw object.
5. Release mouse.

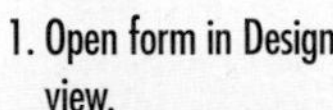

Change a Page Caption

1. Click desired tab in tab control.
2. Click Property Sheet button.
3. Click in *Caption* property box.
4. Type desired text.
5. Close Property Sheet task pane.

Add a Page to a Tab Control

1. Right-click existing tab in tab control.
2. Click *Insert Page*.

Delete a Page from a Tab Control

1. Right-click tab of page to delete.
2. Click *Delete Page*.

Tab Control

Figure 4.7 New Tab Control Object with Two Pages

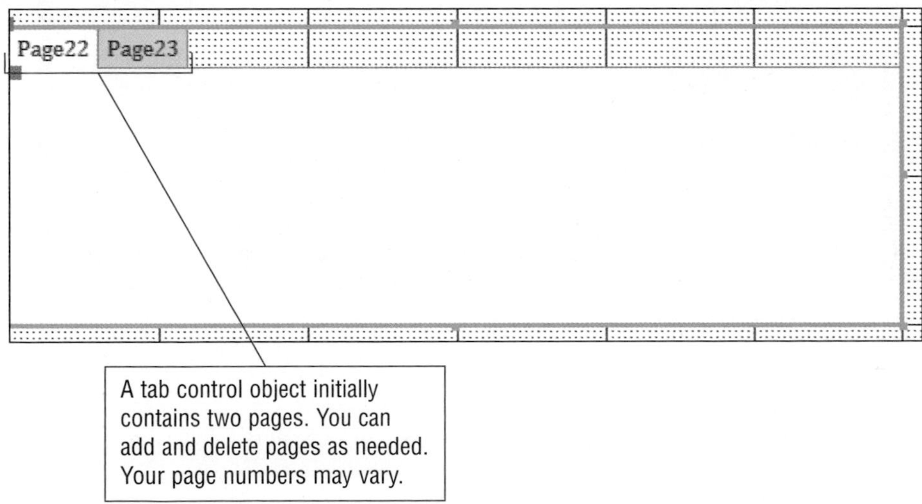
Page22
Page23
A tab control object initially contains two pages. You can add and delete pages as needed. Your page numbers may vary.

Creating a Subform

Quick Steps

Create a Subform

1. Click desired page tab in tab control.
2. Make sure Use Control Wizards is toggled on.
3. Click More button in Controls group.
4. Click Subform/Subreport button.
5. Click crosshairs inside selected page.
6. Click Next.
7. Choose table and fields.
8. Click Next.
9. Click Next.
10. Click Finish.
11. Delete subform label control object.
12. Move and resize subform object as required.

Subform/Subreport

Use Control Wizards

The Subform/Subreport button in the Controls group on the FORM DESIGN TOOLS DESIGN tab is used to add a subform to a form. Create a ***subform*** to display fields from another related table within the existing form. The form in which a subform is created is called the ***main form***.

Adding a related table as a subform creates a control object within the main form that can be moved, formatted, and resized independently of other objects. The subform displays as a datasheet within the main form in Form view. Data can be entered or updated in the subform while the main form is being viewed. Before you click the Subform/Subreport button, make sure the Use Control Wizards button in the Controls group is toggled on so that you can add the subform using the Subform Wizard, as shown in Figure 4.8. The Use Control Wizards button displays with a pink background when the feature is active.

A subform is stored as a separate object outside the main form. You will notice an additional form name (with *subform* at the end of it) in the Navigation pane when you finish the steps in the Subform Wizard. Do not delete a subform object from the Navigation pane. If the subform object is deleted, the main form will no longer display the fields from the related table in the tab control.

Figure 4.8 First Subform Wizard Dialog Box

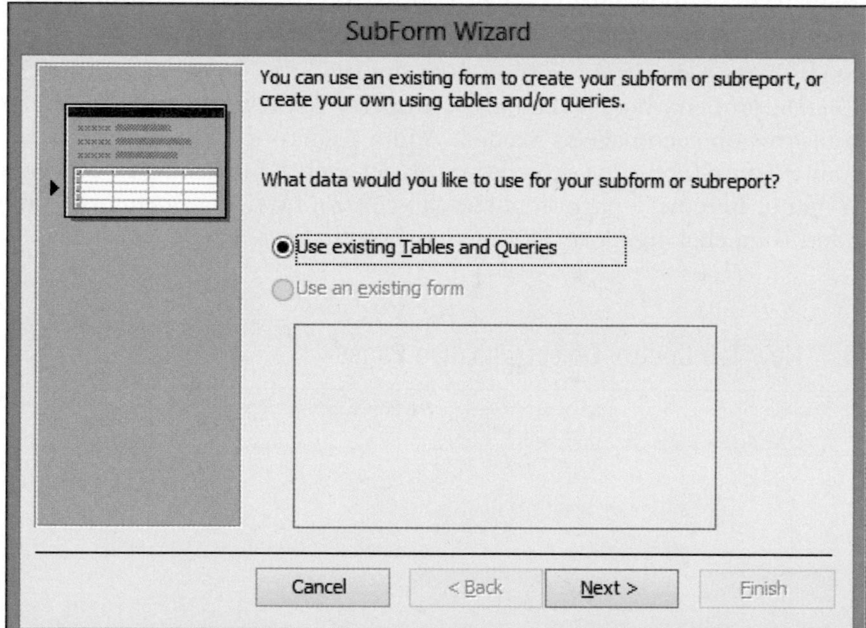
SubForm Wizard
You can use an existing form to create your subform or subreport, or create your own using tables and/or queries.
What data would you like to use for your subform or subreport?
Use existing Tables and Queries
Use an existing form
Cancel
< Back
Next >
Finish

Project 1f Adding a Tab Control and Subform Part 6 of 7

1. With **AL2-C4-RSRCompServ.accdb** open and the CustMaintenance form open in Design view, add a tab control object to the form by completing the following steps:
   a. Click the Tab Control button in the Controls group on the FORM DESIGN TOOLS DESIGN tab. The Tab Control button is the fifth button from the left in the Controls group.
   b. Position the crosshairs with the tab control icon attached at the left edge of the grid in the *Detail* section at the 2-inch position on the vertical ruler. Drag down to the 4-inch position on the vertical ruler and right to the 6-inch position on the horizontal ruler and then release the mouse button.

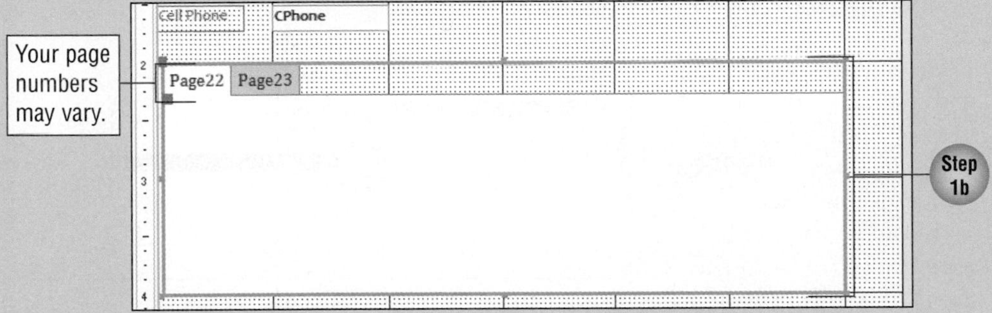

2. Change the page caption and add a subform to the first page within the tab control by completing the following steps:
   a. Click the first tab in the tab control that displays *Pagexx*, where *xx* is the page number to select the page. (For example, click *Page22* in the image shown above.)
   b. Click the Property Sheet button in the Tools group.
   c. Click the Format tab in the Property Sheet task pane, click in the *Caption* property box, type **Profiles**, and then close the Property Sheet task pane. The tab displays the caption text in place of *Pagexx*.

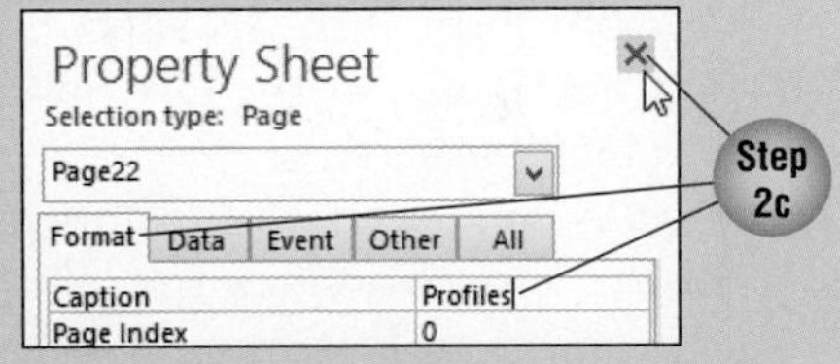

   d. By default, the Use Control Wizards feature is toggled on in the Controls group. Click the More button in the Controls group to expand the Controls group and view two rows of buttons and the Controls drop-down list. View the current status of the Use Control Wizards button. If the button displays with a pink background, the feature is active. If the button is pink, click in a blank area to remove the expanded Controls list. If the feature is not active (displays with a white background), click the Use Control Wizards button to turn on the feature.
   e. Click the More button in the Controls group and then click the Subform/Subreport button at the expanded Controls list.

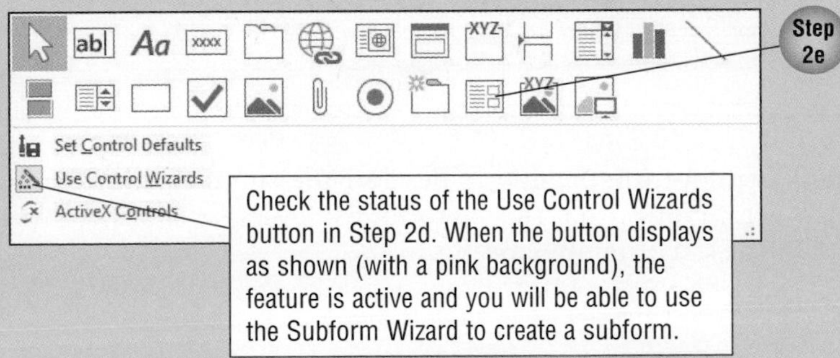

f. Move the crosshairs with the subform icon attached to the Profiles page in the tab control. The background of the page turns black. Click the mouse to start the SubForm Wizard.

g. At the first SubForm Wizard dialog box, with *Use existing Tables and Queries* already selected, click Next.

h. At the second SubForm Wizard dialog box, select the table and fields to be displayed in the subform by completing the following steps:

   1) Click the down-pointing arrow next to the *Tables/Queries* option box and then click *Table: Profiles* at the drop-down list.

   2) Move all of the fields except *CustID* from the *Available Fields* list box to the *Selected Fields* list box.

   3) Click Next.

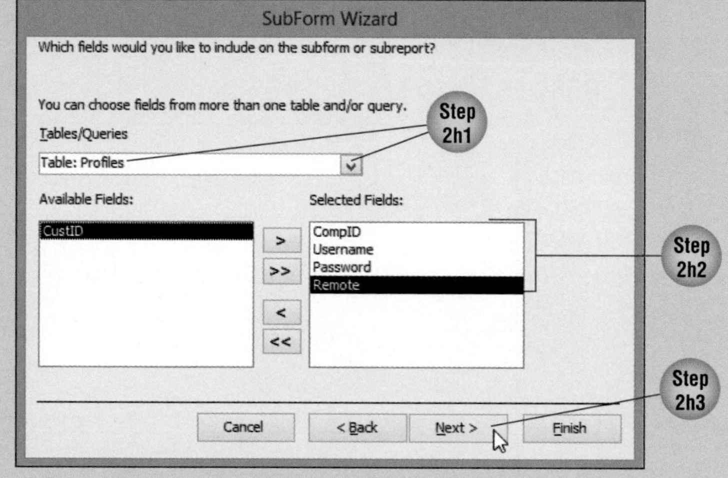

i. At the third SubForm Wizard dialog box, with *Show Profiles for each record in Customers using CustID* selected, click Next. Since a relationship has been created between two tables with *CustID* as the joined field, Access knows the field that links records in the main form with the subform.

j. Click Finish at the last SubForm Wizard dialog box to accept the default subform name *Profiles subform*.

3. Access creates the subform within the active page in the tab control with a label control object above it. Click the label control object displaying the text *Profiles subform* to select the object and then press Delete.

4. Click the edge of the subform control object to display the orange border and sizing handles and then use the techniques you learned in Project 1c to move and resize the object so that the subform fills the tab control object as shown below.

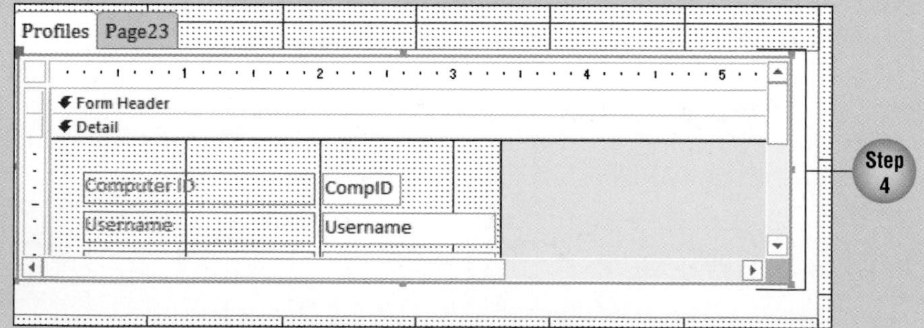

5. Click in a blank area outside the grid to deselect the subform control object and then switch to Form view. Notice that the subform displays as a datasheet within the tab control object in the CustMaintenance form.

6. In the field names row in the datasheet, position the mouse pointer on the boundary lines that separate the columns and then double-click to adjust each column's width to best fit.

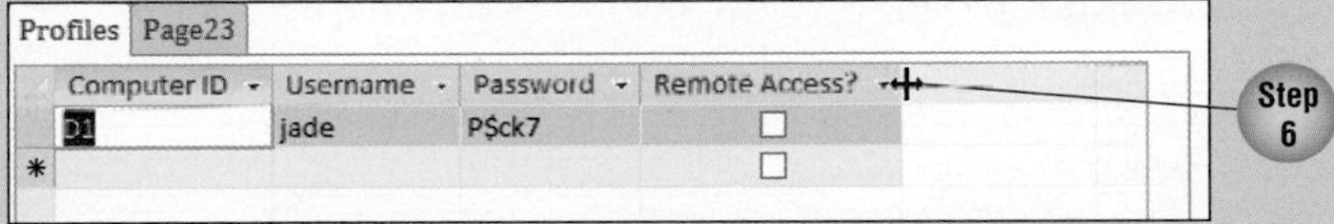

7. Notice that two sets of navigation buttons are displayed: one set at the bottom of the main form (just above the Status bar) and another set at the bottom of the datasheet in the subform. Use the navigation buttons at the bottom of the main form to scroll through a few records and watch the fields update in both the main form and subform as you move to the next customer record.
8. Switch to Design view.
9. Save the form.
10. In the Navigation pane, notice that a form object exists with the name *Profiles subform*. Subforms are separate objects within the database. If the main form is closed, you can still open the subform to edit data.

In Design view, the controls within the subform display one below another, but in Form view, the subform displays using a datasheet layout. If desired, you can change the Default View property in the subform's Property Sheet task pane to *Single Form*. This view matches the layout of the controls in Design view to the layout of the fields in Form view. The fields display one below another in a single column in Form view.

To do this, open the subform's Property Sheet task pane by double-clicking the Form Selector button at the top of the vertical ruler and to the left of the horizontal ruler in the subform control object in Design view. Click the down-pointing arrow in the Default View property in the Format tab and then click *Single Form* at the drop-down list.

Project 1g Adding More Subforms and Adding a New Page to the Tab Control — Part 7 of 7

1. With **AL2-C4-RSRCompServ.accdb** open and the CustMaintenance form open in Design view, change the caption for the second page in the tab control to *Service Contracts* by completing steps similar to those in Steps 2a–2c of Project 1f.
2. With the Service Contracts page selected in the tab control, add a subform to display the fields from the ServiceContracts table on the page by completing the following steps:
   a. Click the More button in the Controls group and then click the Subform/Subreport button in the expanded Controls group.
   b. Click inside the selected Service Contracts page in the tab control.
   c. Click Next at the first SubForm Wizard dialog box.
   d. At the second SubForm Wizard dialog box, change the table displayed in the *Tables/Queries* option box to *Table: ServiceContracts*.
   e. Move all of the fields from the table, except the *CustID* field, to the *Selected Fields* list box.
   f. Click Next.
   g. At the third SubForm Wizard dialog box, with *Show ServiceContracts for each record in Customers using CustID* selected, click Next.
   h. Click Finish at the last SubForm Wizard dialog box to accept the default subform name *ServiceContracts subform*.

3. Select and then delete the label control object above the subform (displays the text *ServiceContracts subform*).
4. Click the subform control object to display the orange border and sizing handles and then move and resize the form as shown below.

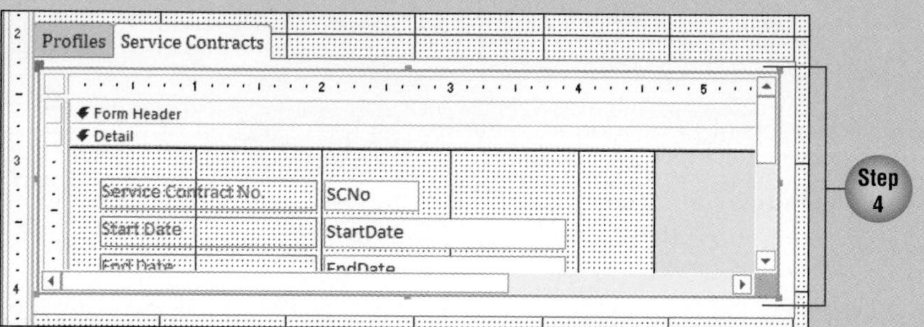

5. Deselect the subform control object and then switch to Form view.
6. Click the Service Contracts tab and then adjust the column width for each column in the datasheet to best fit.

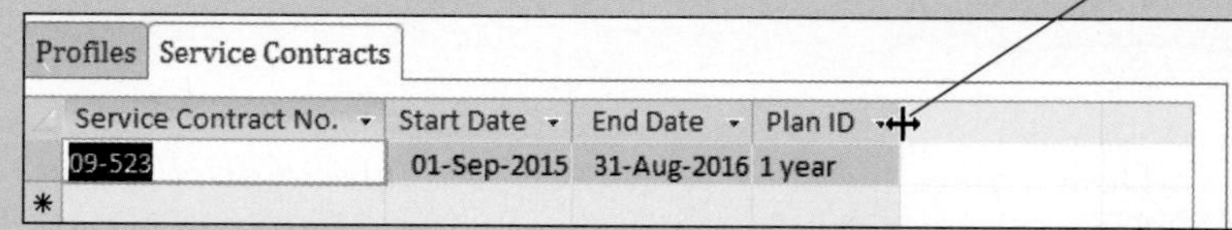

7. Switch to Design view and then save the form.
8. Add a new page to the tab control and add a subform to display selected fields from the WorkOrders table in the new page by completing the following steps:
   a. Right-click the Service Contracts tab and then click *Insert Page* at the shortcut menu.
   b. With the new page already selected, display the Property Sheet task pane, type **Work Orders** as the page caption, and then close the Property Sheet task pane.
   c. Click the More button in the Controls group and then click the Subform/Subreport button. Click inside the selected Work Orders page. Create a subform to display selected fields from the WorkOrders table by completing the following steps:
      1) Click Next at the first SubForm Wizard dialog box.
      2) At the second SubForm Wizard dialog box, change the table displayed in the *Tables/Queries* option box to *Table: WorkOrders*.
      3) Move the following fields from the *Available Fields* list box to the *Selected Fields* list box:
         WO
         WODate
         Descr
      4) Click Next.
      5) Click Next at the third SubForm Wizard dialog box.
      6) Click Finish at the last SubForm Wizard dialog box to accept the default subform name.
9. Select and then delete the label control object above the subform (displays the text *WorkOrders subform*).
10. Click the subform control object to display the orange border and sizing handles and then move and resize the form as shown at the right.

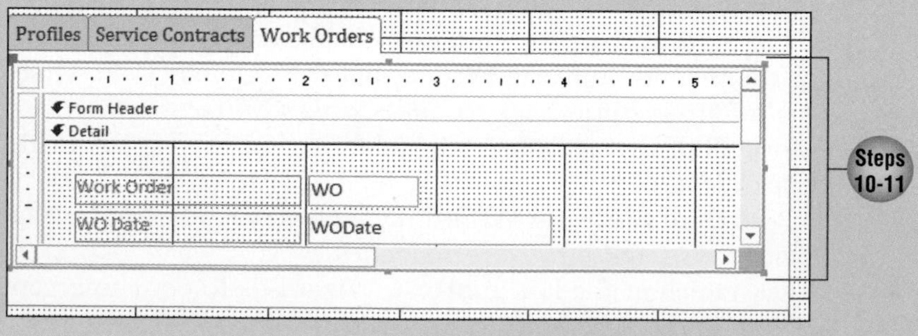

11. Access automatically extends the form's width and widens the tab control object if a table with many fields is added to a subform. If necessary, select the tab control object and decrease the width so that the right edge of the tab control is at the 6-inch position on the horizontal ruler. If necessary, decrease the width of the form so that the right edge of the grid is at the 6.5-inch position on the horizontal ruler. ***Hint: If Access resizes the tab control to the edge of the form, you may have to temporarily widen the grid to see the middle sizing handle at the right edge of the tab control object.***
12. Deselect the subform control object and then switch to Form view.
13. While viewing the form, you decide the title would look better if it was not centered. Switch to Design view, click the Title control object in the *Form Header* section, click the FORM DESIGN TOOLS FORMAT tab, and then click the Align Left button in the Font group.
14. Click the FORM DESIGN TOOLS DESIGN tab and then switch to Form view.
15. Click the Work Orders tab and adjust the column width for each column in the datasheet to best fit. Compare your CustMaintenance form with the one shown in Figure 4.9.
16. Print only the selected record. To do this, open the Print dialog box, click *Selected Record(s)* in the *Print Range* section, and then click OK.
17. Save and then close the CustMaintenance form.

Figure 4.9 Completed CustMaintenance Form

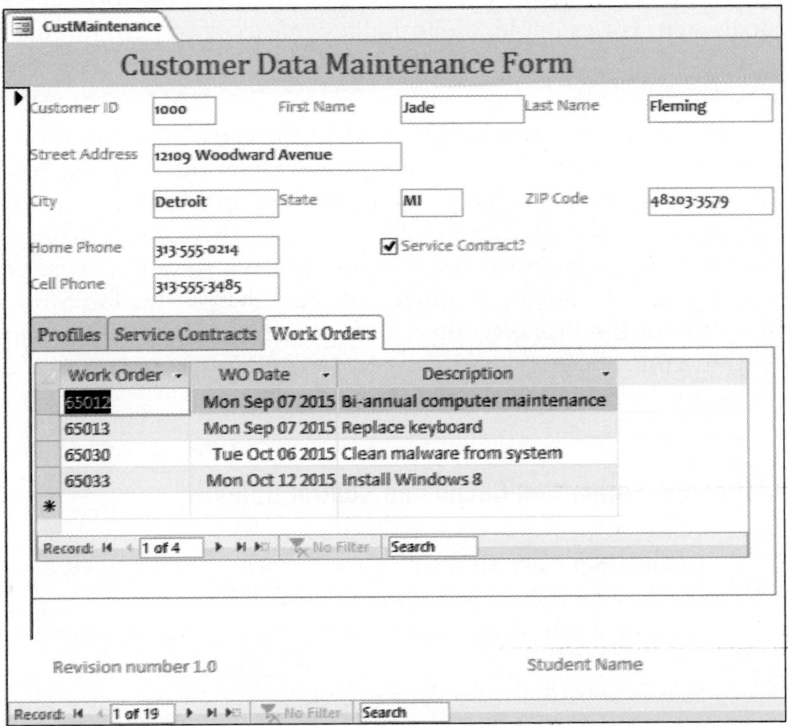

Adding the tab control with a separate page displaying a subform for each table related to the Customers table in the CustMaintenance form allowed you to create one object that can be used to view and update fields in multiple tables.

Project 2 Create a New Form with Calculations and Graphics — 4 Parts

You will create a new form using the Form Wizard, add two calculations to the form, use features that assist with alignment and spacing of multiple control objects, and add graphics to the form.

Adding Calculations to a Form in Design View

Quick Steps

Add a Calculated Control to a Form

1. Open form in Design view.
2. Click Text Box button.
3. Position crosshairs in *Detail* section at desired location.
4. Drag to create control object of required height and width.
5. Release mouse.
6. Click in text box control.
7. Type formula.
8. Press Enter.
9. Delete text in label control object.
10. Type label text and press Enter.

Text Box

To display a calculated value in a form, you can create a query that includes a calculated column and then create a new form based on that query. Alternatively, you can create a calculated control object in an existing form using Design view.

To do this, click the Text Box button in the Controls group on the FORM DESIGN TOOLS DESIGN tab and then drag the crosshairs in the *Detail* section to create a control object the approximate height and width required to show the calculation. Access displays a text box control with *Unbound* inside the object and a label control to the left displaying *Textxx* (where *xx* is the text box object number). A calculated control is considered an unbound object, since the data displayed in the control is not drawn from a stored field value in a record. Click inside the text box control object (*Unbound* disappears) and then type the formula, beginning with an equals sign. For example, the formula *=[Hours]*[Rate]* multiplies the value in the *Hours* field times the value in the *Rate* field. Field names in a formula are enclosed in square brackets.

Edit the label control object next to the calculated control to add a descriptive name that identifies the calculated value. Open the Property Sheet task pane for the calculated control object and apply the *Fixed*, *Standard*, or *Currency* format, as appropriate for the calculated value. Since the data displayed in calculated controls is based on formulas, you do not need to tab to these controls when entering data or moving through a record. Change the Tab Stop property in the Other tab of the Property Sheet task pane from *Yes* to *No* to avoid stopping at any text box control object.

Project 2a Adding and Formatting Calculated Control Objects — Part 1 of 4

1. With **AL2-C4-RSRCompServ.accdb** open, use the Form Wizard to create a new form based on the WorkOrders table by completing the following steps:
   a. Click *WorkOrders* in the Tables group in the Navigation pane and then click the CREATE tab.
   b. Click the Form Wizard button in the Forms group.
   c. With *Table: WorkOrders* selected in the *Table/Queries* option box, complete the steps in the Form Wizard as follows:
      1) Move the *WO*, *Descr*, *ServDate*, *Hours*, *Rate*, and *Parts* fields from the *Available Fields* list box to the *Selected Fields* list box and then click Next.
      2) With *Columnar* selected as the layout option, click Next.
      3) With *WorkOrders* the default text in the *What title do you want for your form?* text box, click *Modify the form's design* at the last dialog box and then click Finish.

2. With the WorkOrders form displayed in Design view, change the theme and add a calculated control object to display the total labor for the work order by completing the following steps:
   a. Click the Themes button in the Themes group on the FORM DESIGN TOOLS DESIGN tab and then click *Organic* (the second option in the second row) at the drop-down gallery.
   b. Position the pointer on the top border of the gray *Form Footer* section bar until the pointer displays as an up-and-down-pointing arrow with a horizontal line in the middle and then drag down just below the 3-inch position on the vertical ruler. (The 3-inch mark will not appear until you drag the border below it and release the mouse button.) Doing this creates more grid space in the *Detail* section, to which you can add controls.

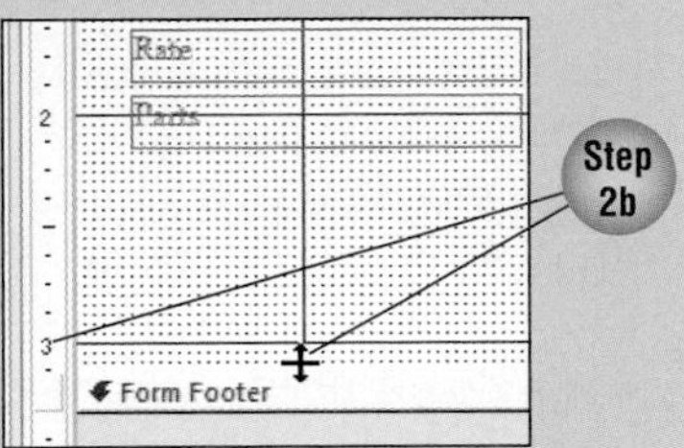

   c. Click the Text Box button in the Controls group.
   d. Position the crosshairs with the text box icon attached below the *Parts* text box control, drag to create an object of the approximate height and width shown at the right, and then release the mouse button.

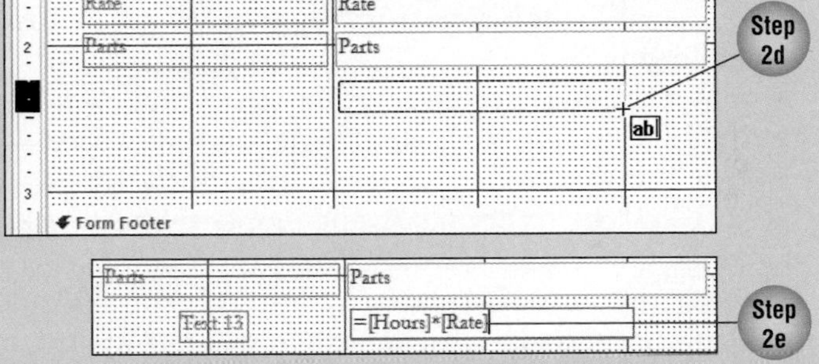

   e. Click in the text box control (which displays *Unbound*) and then type **=[Hours]*[Rate]**.

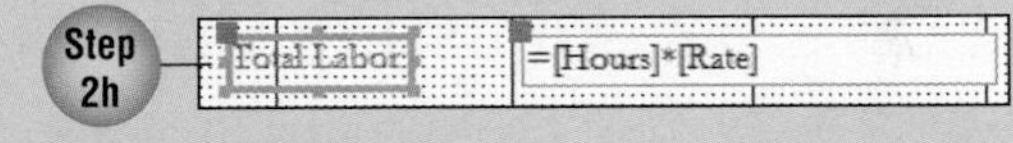

   f. Press Enter.
   g. With the calculated control object selected, click the Property Sheet button in the Tools group. With the Format tab in the Property Sheet task pane active, click the down-pointing arrow in the *Format* property box, click *Standard* at the drop-down list, and then close the Property Sheet task pane. By default, calculated values display right-aligned in Form view.
   h. Click to select the label control object to the left of the calculated control object (which displays *Textxx* [where *xx* is the text box label number]). Click inside the selected label control object a second time to place the insertion point. Delete *Textxx*, type **Total Labor**, and then press Enter. Notice that the label control automatically expands to accommodate the width of the typed text.

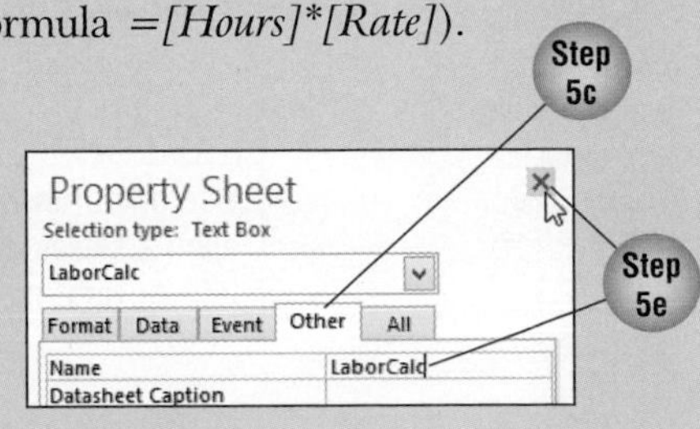

3. With the FORM DESIGN TOOLS DESIGN tab selected, click the View button to display the form in Form view and scroll through a few records to view the calculated field. Do not be concerned with the size, position, alignment, and/or spacing of the controls, since the format will be fixed in a later project.
4. Switch to Design view and then save the form.
5. A calculated control object can be used as a field in another formula. To do this, reference the calculated object in the formula by its Name property enclosed in square brackets. Change the name for the calculated object created in Step 2 to a more descriptive name by completing the following steps:
   a. Click the calculated control object (which displays the formula *=[Hours]*[Rate]*).
   b. Click the Property Sheet button in the Tools group.
   c. Click the Other tab in the Property Sheet task pane.
   d. Select and delete the existing text (which displays *Textxx* [where *xx* is the text box number]) in the *Name* property box.
   e. Type **LaborCalc** and then close the Property Sheet task pane.

6. Add another calculated control object to the form to include labor and parts and determine the total value for the work order by completing the following steps:
   a. Click the Text Box button.
   b. Position the crosshairs with the text box icon attached below the calculated control created in Step 2, drag to create an object the approximate height and width as the first calculated control, and then release the mouse button.
   c. Click in the text box control (which displays *Unbound*), type **=[LaborCalc]+[Parts]**, and then press Enter.
   d. Apply the Currency format to the calculated control. Refer to Step 2g if you need assistance with this step.
   e. Type **Total Work Order** in the label control object. Refer to Step 2h if you need assistance with this step.

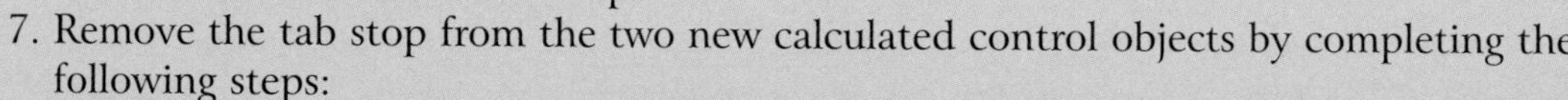

Step 6e
Total Labor
=[Hours]*[Rate]
Total Work Order
=[LaborCalc]+[Parts]
Steps 6a-6d

7. Remove the tab stop from the two new calculated control objects by completing the following steps:
   a. Press and hold the Shift button as you click the calculated control objects that display the formulas *=[Hours]*[Rate]* and *=[LaborCalc]+[Parts]*.
   b. Click the Property Sheet button in the Tools group.
   c. Click the Other tab in the Property Sheet task pane.
   d. Double-click *Yes* in the *Tab Stop* property box to change it to *No*.
8. Save the form. Display the form in Form view and then scroll through a few records to view the calculations. Tab through a record and notice that when you press Tab after the *Parts* field, the insertion point does not stop at *Total Labor* or *Total Work Order*, and instead moves to the next record.
9. Switch to Design view.

Adjusting Objects for Consistency in Appearance

When working in Design view, use the tools that Access provides for positioning, aligning, sizing, and spacing multiple controls to create forms with a uniform and consistent appearance. Locate these tools using the Size/Space and Align buttons in the Sizing & Ordering group on the FORM DESIGN TOOLS ARRANGE tab.

Aligning Multiple Controls at the Same Position

Quick Steps

Align Multiple Objects
1. In Design view, select desired control objects.
2. Click FORM DESIGN TOOLS ARRANGE tab.
3. Click Align button.
4. Click desired option at drop-down list.
5. Deselect controls.

Align

The options in the Align button drop-down list in the Sizing & Ordering group on the FORM DESIGN TOOLS ARRANGE tab are shown in Figure 4.10. You can use these options to align multiple selected controls at the same horizontal or vertical position and save the work of adjusting each control individually.

Figure 4.10 Alignment Options in Drop-Down List at Align Button

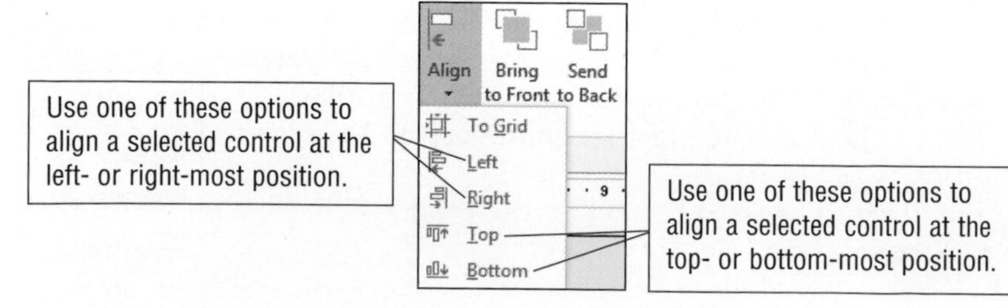

Align
Bring to Front
Send to Back
To Grid
Left
Right
Top
Bottom
Use one of these options to align a selected control at the left- or right-most position.
Use one of these options to align a selected control at the top- or bottom-most position.

Adjusting the Sizing and Spacing between Controls

The options provided by the Size/Space button on the Sizing & Ordering group on the FORM DESIGN TOOLS ARRANGE tab are shown in Figure 4.11. You can use these options to assist with the consistent sizing of controls and spacing between controls. Use options in the *Size* section of the drop-down list to adjust the height or width to the tallest, shortest, widest, or narrowest of the selected control objects. Use options in the *Spacing* section to adjust the horizontal and vertical spacing between controls, increase or decrease the space, or provide equal spaces between all of the selected objects.

You will find these tools helpful when you create a new form by adding controls manually to the grid or after editing an existing form because they allow you to change the space between controls easily after adding or deleting objects. To adjust the spacing by moving individual control objects would be too time consuming.

Quick Steps

Adjust the Spacing between Objects

1. In Design view, select desired control objects.
2. Click FORM DESIGN TOOLS ARRANGE tab.
3. Click Size/Space button.
4. Click desired option in *Spacing* section.
5. Deselect controls.

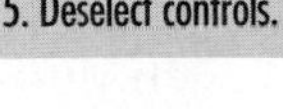

Size/Space

Figure 4.11 Size and Spacing Options in Size/Space Button Drop-Down List

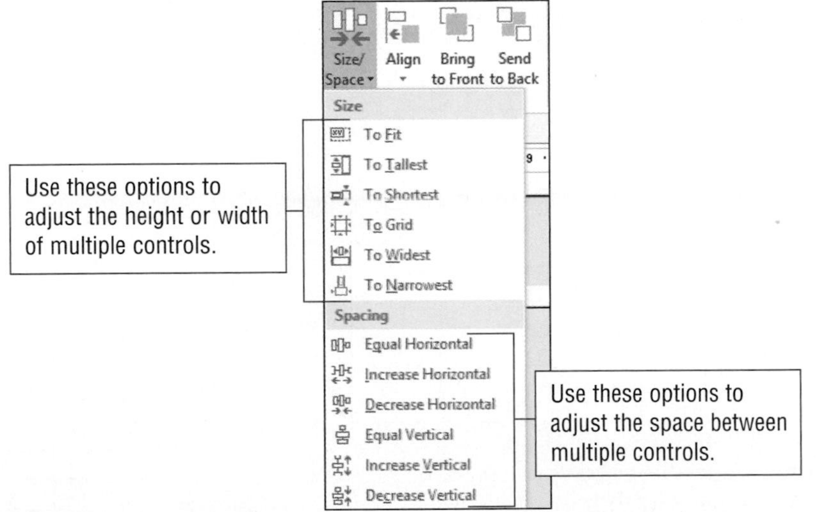

Project 2b **Sizing, Aligning, and Spacing Multiple Controls** **Part 2 of 4**

1. With **AL2-C4-RSRCompServ.accdb** open and the WorkOrders form open in Design view, edit the title in the *Form Header* section to *Work Orders with Calculations* and then widen the control object to fit the title on one line.
2. With the title control object still selected, position the mouse pointer on the orange border until the pointer changes to the four-headed arrow move icon and then drag the control to the approximate center of the *Form Header* section.

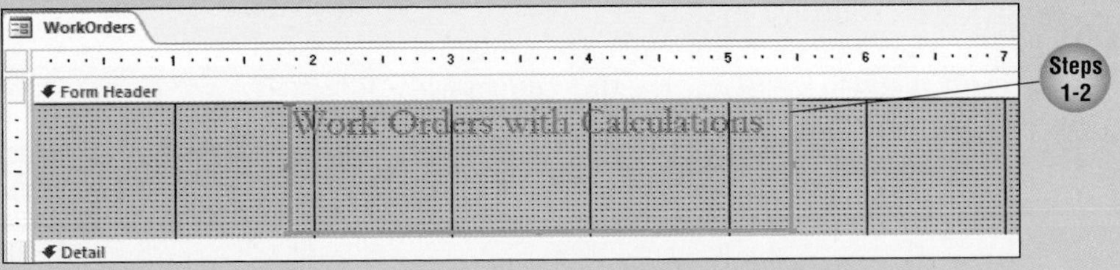

3. Point to the bottom gray border in the *Form Footer* section bar until the pointer displays as an up-and-down-pointing arrow with a horizontal line in the middle and then drag down approximately 0.5 inch to create space in the *Form Footer* section. Create a label control object with your name in the center of the *Form Footer* section.

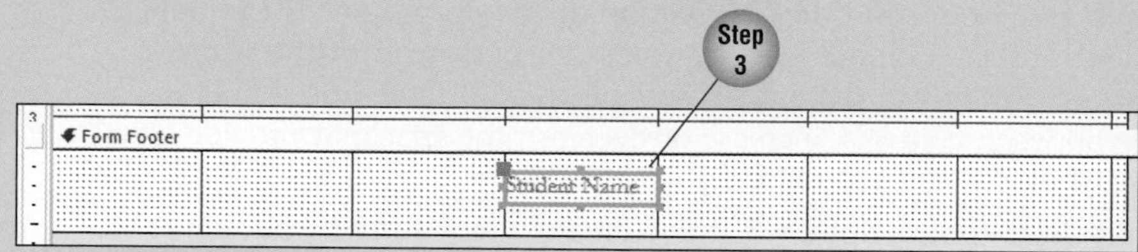

4. Click to select the *Descr* text box control object and then drag the right middle sizing handle left until the control is resized to approximately the 4.5-inch position on the horizontal ruler.
5. Press and hold down Shift as you click the six text box control objects for the fields above the two calculated controls. Click the FORM DESIGN TOOLS ARRANGE tab, click the Size/Space button in the Sizing & Ordering group, and then click *To Widest* at the drop-down list. The six text box control objects are now all the same width, with the width set to fit of the widest selected object.

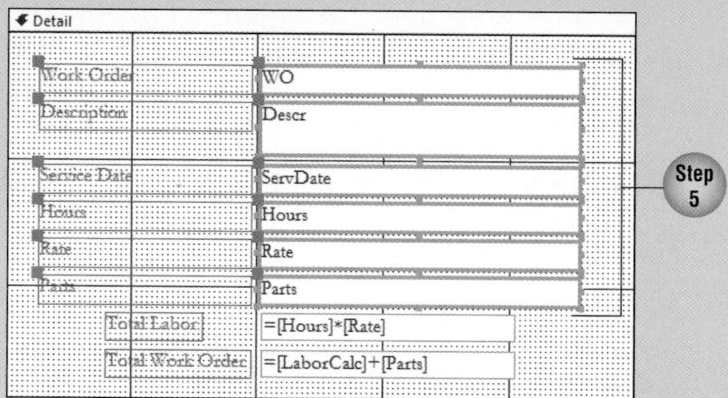

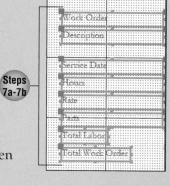

6. Click in any blank area to deselect the controls.
7. Use the Align button to align multiple controls by completing the following steps:
   a. Draw a selection rectangle around all of the label control objects at the left side of the form. This selects all eight label controls.
   b. Click the Align button in the Sizing & Ordering group and then click *Left* at the drop-down list. All of the label control objects align at the left edge of the left-most control.
   c. Deselect the controls.
   d. Draw a selection rectangle around all of the text box control objects at the right of the form to select all eight text box controls.
   e. Click the Align button in the Sizing & Ordering group and then click *Right* at the drop-down list. All of the control objects align at the right edge of the right-most control.
   f. Deselect the controls.

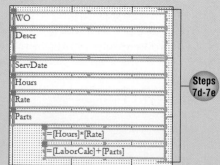

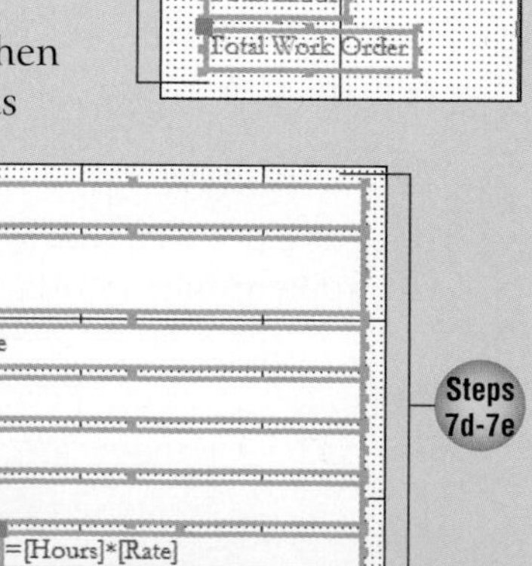

WO
Descr
ServDate
Hours
Rate
Parts
=[Hours]*[Rate]
=[LaborCalc]+[Parts]
Steps 7d-7e

8. Adjust the vertical spaces between controls to make all of the control objects equally spaced in the *Detail* section by completing the following steps:
   a. Draw a selection rectangle around all of the control objects in the *Detail* section.
   b. Click the Size/Space button and then click *Equal Vertical* in the *Spacing* section of the drop-down list. All of the control objects are now separated by the same amount of vertical space.
   c. Deselect the controls.

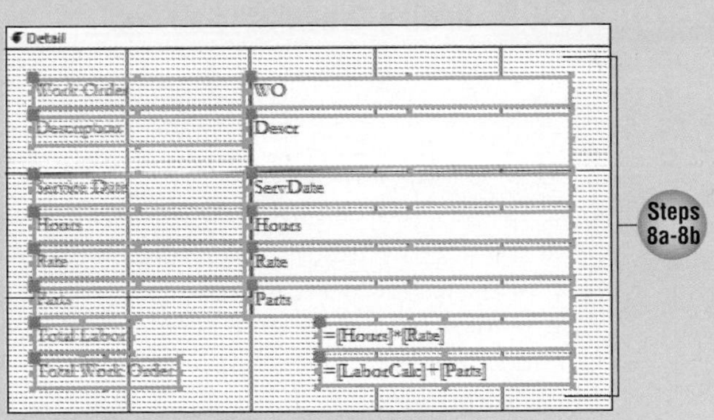

9. Save the form.
10. Display the form in Form view and then scroll through a few records to view the revised alignment and spacing options. The numeric fields will be formatted in Project 2c to align the numbers correctly.
11. Switch to Design view.

Adding Graphics to a Form in Design View

A picture that is saved in a graphic file format can be added to a form using the Logo button or Insert Image button in the Controls group on the FORM DESIGN TOOLS DESIGN tab. Click the Logo button and Access opens the Insert Picture dialog box. Navigate to the drive and/or folder in which the graphic file is stored and then double-click the image file name. Access automatically adds the image to the left side of the *Form Header* section. Move and/or resize the image as needed. Access supports the BMP, GIF, JPEG, JPG, and PNG graphic file formats for a logo control object.

Logo

Use the Insert Image button to place the picture in another section or to draw a larger control object to hold the picture. Click the Insert Image button and then click *Browse* at the drop-down list to open the Insert Picture dialog box. Navigate to the drive and/or folder in which the graphic file is stored and then double-click the image file name. Next, position the crosshairs with the image icon attached at the location in the form where you want to place the image and then drag the crosshairs to draw a control object of the approximate height and width desired. Access supports the GIF, JPEG, JPG, and PNG file formats for an image control object.

Insert Image

Use the Line button in the Controls group to draw horizontal or vertical lines in a form. Hold down the Shift key while dragging to draw a straight line. Once you have drawn the line, use the Shape Outline button in the Control Formatting group on the FORM DESIGN TOOLS FORMAT tab to modify the line thickness, line type, and line color.

You can also add clip art images to a form. Access does not provide a clip art button in the Controls group. However, you can insert a clip art image in a Microsoft Word document and then use standard Windows commands to copy the image to the Clipboard task pane and paste it into a form. Access inserts the clip art in an unbound control object.

Quick Steps

Add Clip Art to a Form
1. Open form in Design view.
2. Start Microsoft Word.
3. Locate and insert desired clip art image into document.
4. Copy clip art image to Clipboard task pane.
5. Switch to Microsoft Access.
6. Paste image into desired form section.
7. Move and resize as required.
8. If necessary, display Property Sheet task pane and change Size Mode property.

Line

Project 2c Adding Graphics to a Form

1. With **AL2-C4-RSRCompServ.accdb** open and the WorkOrders form open in Design view, start Microsoft Word and open a new blank document.

Step 2c

2. Locate and insert a clip art image in the document and then copy and paste the image to the form in Microsoft Access by completing the following steps:
   a. At a blank Word document screen, click the INSERT tab and then click the Online Pictures button in the Illustrations group.
   b. At the Insert Pictures window, type **computer repairs** in the text box to the right of *Office.com Clip Art* and then press Enter.
   c. Scroll down the results list box and then double-click the image shown above and to the right to insert it in the current document. If the image shown is not available, select a similar alternative image.
   d. Right-click the clip art image in the Word document and then click *Copy* at the shortcut menu.
   e. Click the Microsoft Access button on the Taskbar.
   f. Right-click in the *Detail* section of the form and then click *Paste* at the shortcut menu. Access inserts the image and displays the orange border with selection handles.

Build Event...
Tab Order...
Paste
Fill/Back Color
Alternate Fill/Back Color
Ruler
Grid
Page Header/Footer
Form Header/Footer
Form Properties
Properties

Step 2f

   g. Move and resize the image to the approximate position and size shown at the right. (Your size and image may vary.) Notice that when you resize the control object, Access cuts off parts of the image as you make the control object smaller. This action reflects the default Clip property for the object. You will correct this in Step 3.

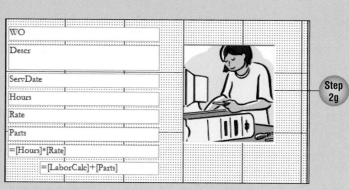

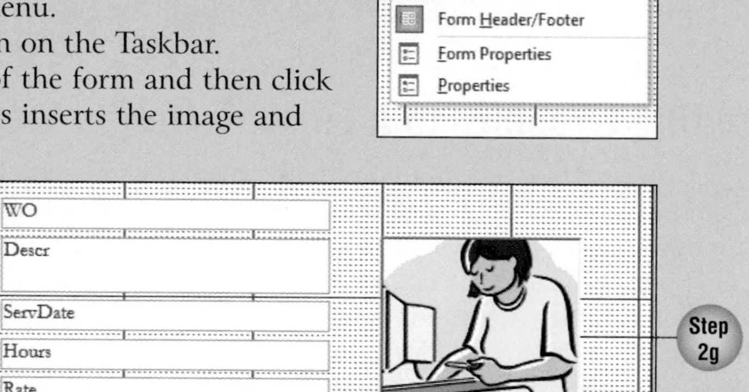

   h. Right-click the Microsoft Word button on the Taskbar and then click *Close Window*. Click Don't Save when prompted to save the document. Click No if prompted to make the Clipboard contents available for other applications.

3. Right-click the clip art image at the right side of the *Detail* section in the form and then click *Properties* at the shortcut menu. If necessary, make Format the active tab in the Property Sheet task pane. Click in the *Size Mode* property box (displays *Clip*), click the down-pointing arrow that appears, and then click *Zoom* at the drop-down list. Close the Property Sheet task pane. Changing the Size Mode property to *Zoom* instructs Access to resize the image within the control object while maintaining the original proportions of height and width. The *Size Mode* drop-down list also contains the *Stretch* option. Use this option to stretch the image to fit the height and width of the control object. Note that using *Stretch* may skew the appearance of the image.

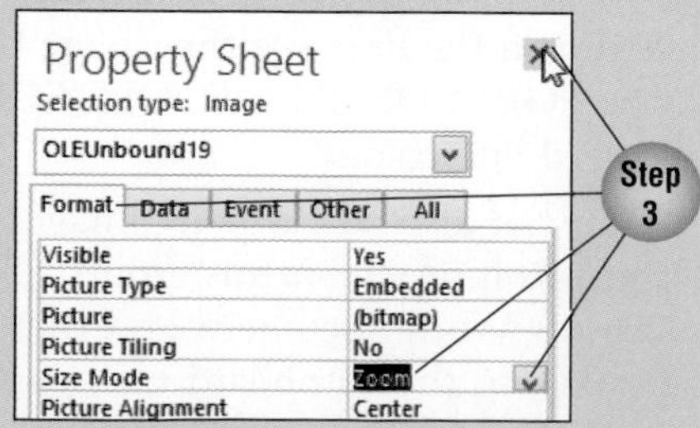

4. Deselect the control object containing the clip art image and then display the form in Form view. You decide that adding a line below the title will improve the form's appearance. Draw and modify the line by completing the following steps:
   a. Switch to Design view and then click the Line button in the Controls group.
   b. Position the crosshairs with the line icon attached below the title in the *Form Header* section beginning a few rows of grid dots below the first letter in the title, hold down the Shift key, drag to the right, release the mouse button below the last letter in the title, and then release the Shift key.
   c. Click the FORM DESIGN TOOLS FORMAT tab, click the Shape Outline button in the Control Formatting group, point to *Line Thickness* at the drop-down list, and then click *3 pt* (fourth option from the top).

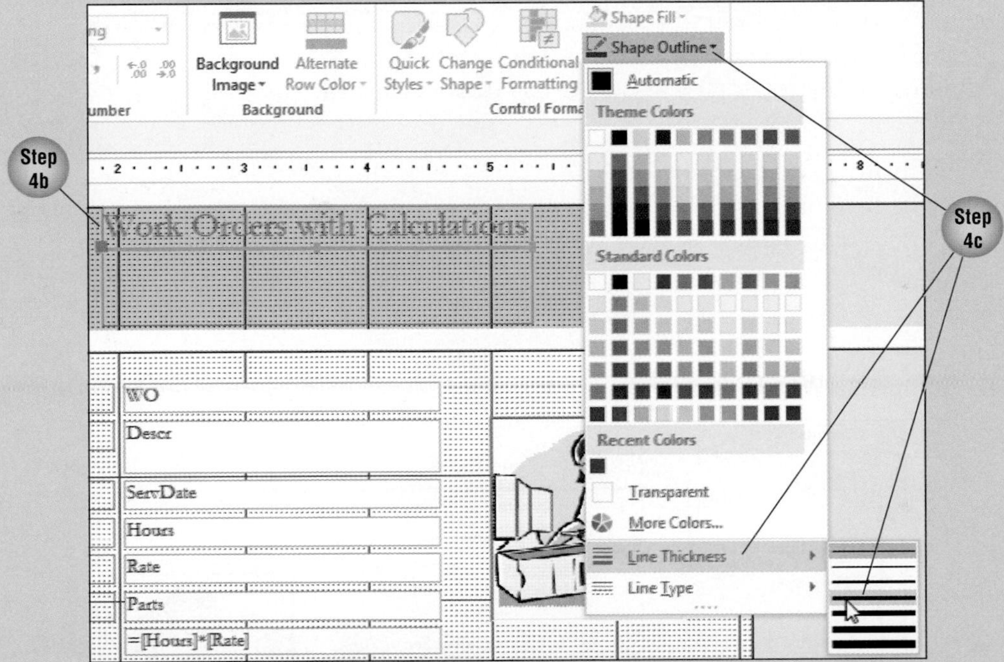

   d. With the line object still selected, click the Shape Outline button and then click the *Dark Red* color (first option in last row of *Standard Colors*).
   e. Deselect the line object.
5. Display the form in Form view to see the line under the title.
6. Switch to Design view. If desired, adjust the length and/or position of the line.
7. Adjust the alignment and formatting options of numeric fields by completing the following steps:
   a. Press and hold down Shift as you click to select the *Hours*, *Rate*, *Parts*, and both calculated text box control objects.
   b. Click the FORM DESIGN TOOLS FORMAT tab and then click the Align Right button in the Font group.
   c. Deselect the controls.
   d. Press and hold down Shift as you click the *Parts* text box control object and the bottom calculated control object that displays the formula *=[LaborCalc]+[Parts]*.
   e. Click the FORM DESIGN TOOLS DESIGN tab and then click the Property Sheet button in the Tools group. Change the Format property to *Standard* and then close the Property Sheet task pane.
   f. Deselect the controls.

8. Click to select the title text in the *Form Header* section and then drag the bottom middle sizing handle up to decrease the height of the control object to approximately 0.4 inch on the vertical ruler. You may need to drag the bottom border of the Form Header section down in order to select the sizing handle.
9. Position the pointer on the top of the gray *Detail* section bar until the pointer displays as an up-and-down-pointing arrow with a horizontal line in the middle and then drag up to decrease the height of the *Form Header* section to approximately 0.5 inch on the vertical ruler.

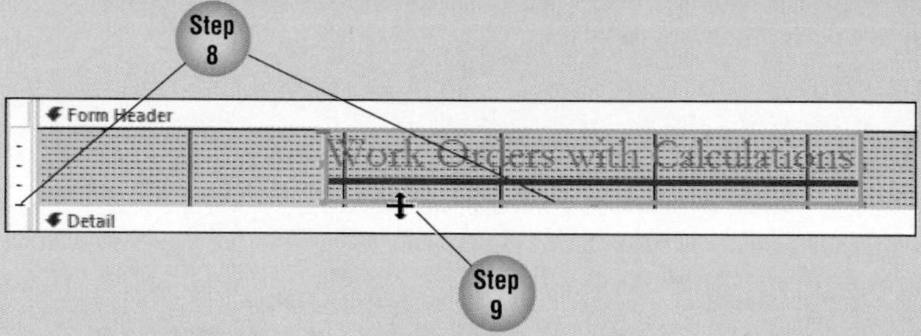

10. Save the form.
11. Display the form in Form view and compare your form with the one shown in Figure 4.12.
12. Print the selected record only with the left and right margins both set to 0.5 inch.
13. Close the form.

Figure 4.12 Completed WorkOrders Form

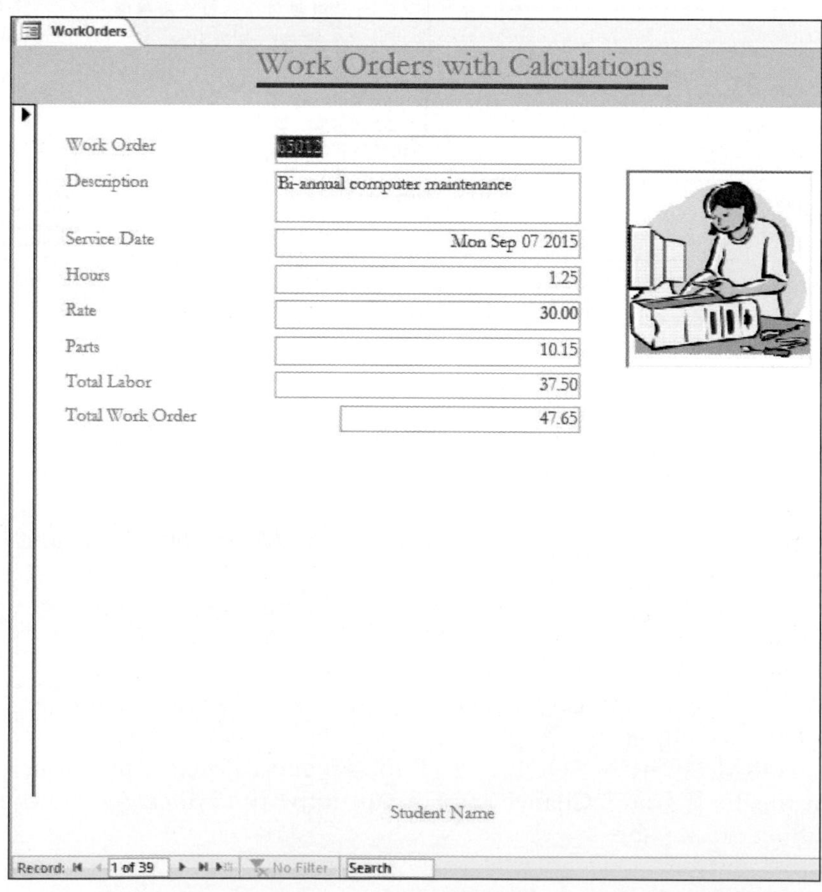

Anchoring Controls to a Form

A control object in a form can be anchored to a section or another control object using the Anchoring button in the Position group on the FORM DESIGN TOOLS ARRANGE tab. When a control object is anchored, its position is maintained when the form is resized. For example, if a clip art image is anchored to the top right of the *Detail* section, when the form is resized in Form view, the image automatically moves in conjunction with the new form size so that the original distance between the image and top right of the *Detail* section is maintained. If the image is not anchored and the form is resized, the position of the image relative to the edges of the form can change.

By default, *Top Left* is selected as the anchor position for each control object in a form. To change the anchor position, select the object(s), click the FORM DESIGN TOOLS ARRANGE tab, click the Anchoring button, and then click one of these options: *Stretch Down*, *Bottom Left*, *Stretch Across Top*, *Stretch Down and Across*, *Stretch Across Bottom*, *Top Right*, *Stretch Down and Right*, or *Bottom Right*. Click the option that represents how you want the object to move as the form is resized. Note that some options will cause a control object to resize as well as move when the form is changed.

Quick Steps

Anchor a Control to a Form

1. Open form in Design view.
2. Select control object(s) to be anchored.
3. Click FORM DESIGN TOOLS ARRANGE tab.
4. Click Anchoring button.
5. Click desired anchor position.
6. Deselect object.
7. Save form.

Anchoring

Project 2d **Anchoring an Image to a Position within a Section** **Part 4 of 4**

1. With **AL2-C4-RSRCompServ.accdb** open, open the WorkOrders form in Form view.
2. Switch to Design view.
3. Anchor the clip art image to the top of the *Detail* section of the form by completing the following steps:
   a. Click to select the clip art image.
   b. Click the FORM DESIGN TOOLS ARRANGE tab.
   c. Click the Anchoring button in the Position group.
   d. Click *Stretch Across Top* at the drop-down list.

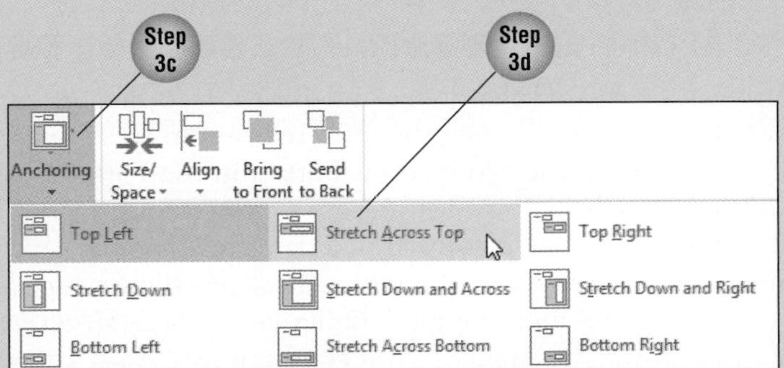

   e. Take note of the distance between the top border of the selected clip art image and the top of the *Detail* section.

4. Display the form in Form view. Notice that the image has shifted up and become stretched across the top of the *Detail* section, yet it has maintained the distance between the top of the control object's boundary and the top of the *Detail* section.

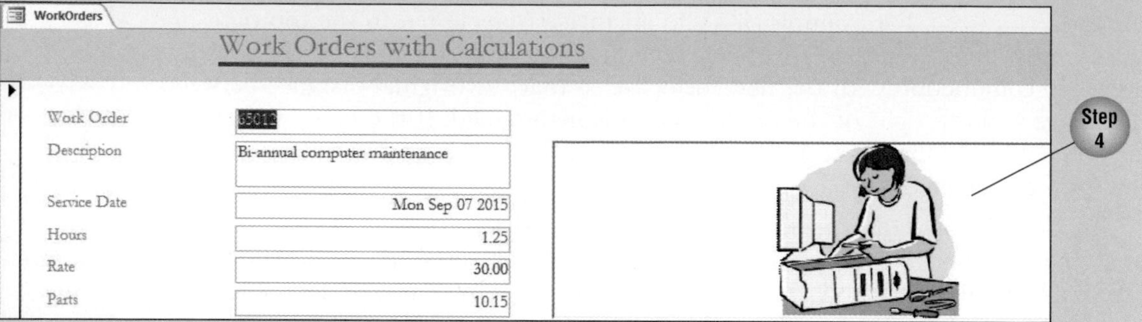

5. Click the FILE tab and then click the *Save As* option. At the Save As backstage area, click *Save Object As* in the *File Types* section and then click the Save As button. At the Save As dialog box, type **WorkOrdersAnchored** in the *Save 'WorkOrders' to* text box and then press Enter or click OK.
6. Close the form.

Project 3 Create a Restricted-Use Form — 1 Part

You will create a datasheet form for use in entering information into a table and set the form's properties to prevent records from being deleted.

Quick Steps

Create a Datasheet Form
1. Select table in Navigation pane.
2. Click CREATE tab.
3. Click More Forms button.
4. Click *Datasheet*.
5. Save form.

Restrict Record Actions for a Form
1. Open form in Design view.
2. Double-click Form Selector button.
3. Click Data tab.
4. Change *Allow Additions, Allow Deletions, Allow Edits,* or *Allow Filters* to *No*.
5. Close Property Sheet task pane.
6. Save form.

Creating a Datasheet Form and Restricting Form Actions

A form can be created that looks just like the datasheet of a table. With the table for which you want to create the form selected in the Navigation pane, click the CREATE tab, click the More Forms button in the Forms group, and then click *Datasheet* at the drop-down list. Access creates a form including all of the fields from the selected table presented in a datasheet layout. Although the datasheet form has the look and feel of a table datasheet, the form object prevents end users from accessing and modifying the underlying table's structure.

Using options available in the Data tab of a form's Property Sheet, as shown in Figure 4.13, you can restrict the actions that can be performed while a form is displayed in Form view. For example, you can prevent new records from being added and/or existing records from being deleted, edited, and/or filtered. Setting the Data Entry property to *Yes* means the end user will see only a blank form when the form is opened. A data entry form is intended to be used only to add new records. The user is prevented from scrolling through existing records in the form.

Figure 4.13 Form Property Sheet Task Pane with Data Tab Selected

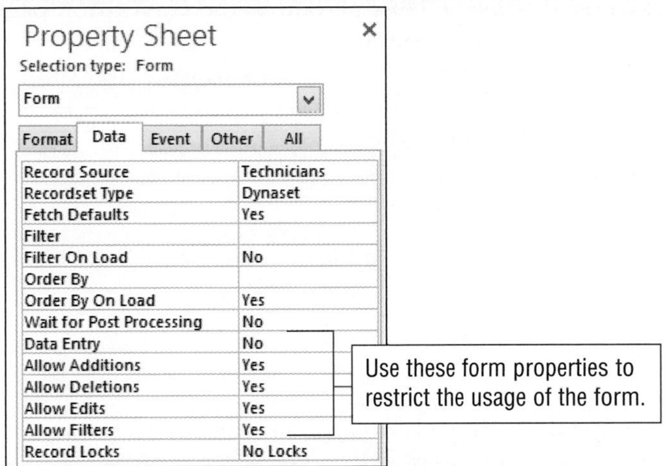

Project 3 Creating a Datasheet Form and Preventing Record Deletions

Part 1 of 1

1. With **AL2-C4-RSRCompServ.accdb** open, click *Technicians* in the Tables group in the Navigation pane and then click the CREATE tab.
2. Click the More Forms button in the Forms group and then click *Datasheet* at the drop-down list.
3. Review the Technicians form in the work area. Notice that the form resembles a table datasheet.
4. Switch to Design view.
5. Modify the properties of the Technicians form to prevent users from deleting records by completing the following steps:
   a. Click in a blank area to deselect the controls.
   b. Double-click the Form Selector button located at the top of the vertical ruler and to the left of the horizontal ruler to open the form's Property Sheet task pane.
   c. Click the Data tab.
   d. Double-click in the *Allow Deletions* property box to change *Yes* to *No*.
   e. Close the Property Sheet task pane.
6. Click the Save button and then click OK to accept *Technicians* as the form name.
7. Click the View button arrow in the Views group on the FORM DESIGN TOOLS DESIGN tab. Notice that *Datasheet View* and *Design View* are the only views available. The *Form View* option is not available at the drop-down list or in the View buttons at the right side of the Status bar.
8. Click in a blank area to close the drop-down list and then close the form.

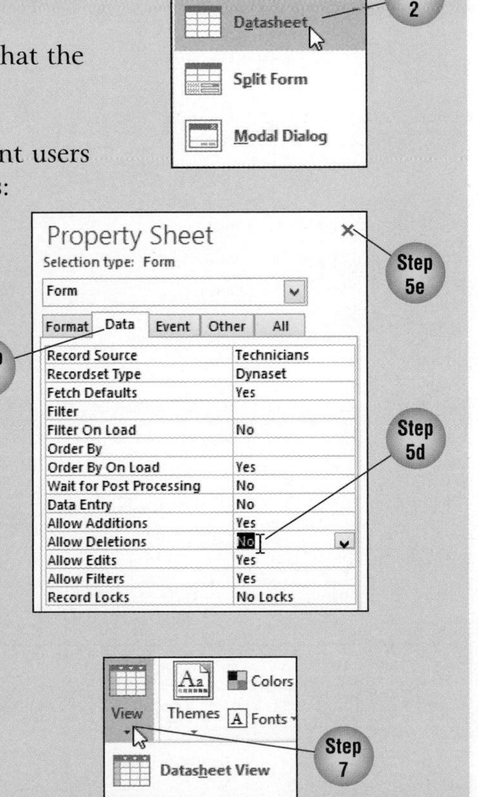

9. Double-click *Technicians* in the Forms group in the Navigation pane. Be careful to open the form object and not the table object.
10. Click in the record selector bar next to the first row in the datasheet (for technician ID 01) to select the record.
11. Click the HOME tab and then look at the Delete button in the Records group. Notice that the Delete button is dimmed. This feature is unavailable because the *Allow Deletions* property box is set to *No*.

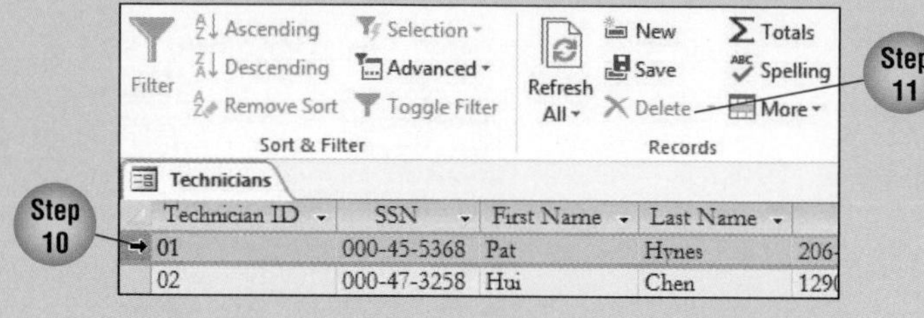

12. Adjust the column widths to best fit, print the first page of the Technicians form in landscape orientation, and then close the form.
13. Right-click *Technicians* in the Forms group in the Navigation pane and then click *Layout View* at the shortcut menu. Notice that the datasheet form displays in a columnar layout in Layout view. The Technicians table includes a field named *Attachments*. In this field in the first record, a picture of the technician has been attached to the record. In Layout view, Access automatically opens the image file and displays the contents.

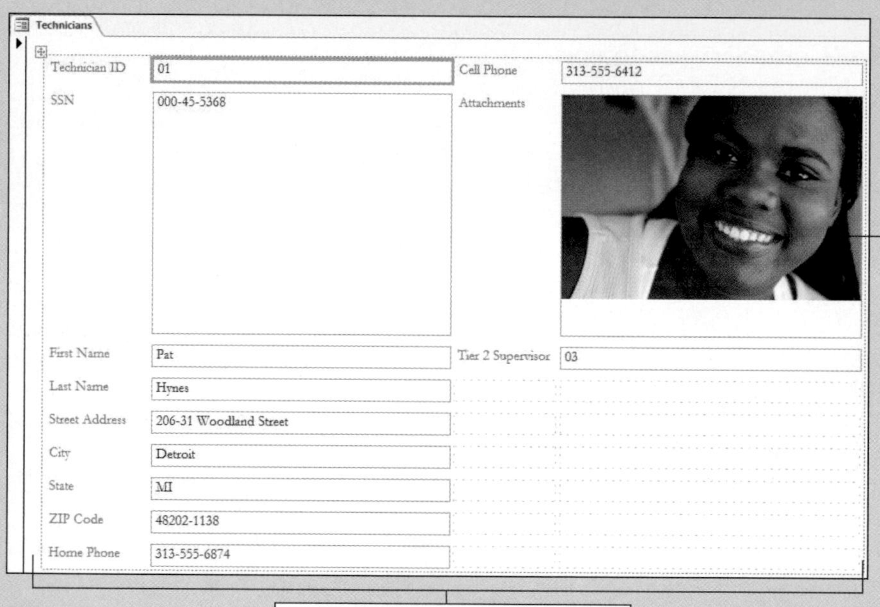

The *Attachments* field automatically displays an attached image file if one has been added.

In Layout view, the datasheet form displays in a columnar layout.

14. Close the form.

Project 4 Create a Blank Form with Lists — 1 Part

You will use the Blank Form tool to create a new form for maintaining the service plan fees table named *FeesSCPlans*. In the form, you will create list boxes to provide an easy way to enter data for new service contract plans.

Creating a Form Using the Blank Form Tool

To quickly build a form that contains a small number of fields, use the Blank Form tool. A blank form begins with no controls or formatting and displays as a blank white page in Layout view.

To begin a new form, click the CREATE tab and then click the Blank Form button in the Forms group. Access opens the Field List task pane at the right side of the work area. Expand the list for the desired table and then add fields to the form as needed. If the Field List task pane displays with no table names, click the Show all tables hyperlink at the top of the pane.

Quick Steps

Create a Blank Form
1. Click CREATE tab.
2. Click Blank Form button.
3. Expand field list for desired table.
4. Drag fields to form as needed.
5. Add title, format, or make other design changes as needed.
6. Save form.

Add a List Box
1. Open form in Layout or Design view.
2. Click List Box button in Controls group.
3. Click within form at desired location.
4. Create values within List Box Wizard.
5. Save form.

Add a Combo Box
1. Open form in Layout or Design view.
2. Click Combo Box button in Controls group.
3. Click within form at desired location.
4. Create values within Combo Box Wizard.
5. Save form.

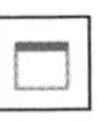
Blank Form

List Box

Combo Box

Adding a List Box to a Form

A ***list box*** displays a list of values for a field within the control object. In Form view, the user can easily see the entire list for the field. You can create the list of values when you create the control object or instruct Access to populate the list using values from a table or query. When you add a list box control to the form, the List Box Wizard begins (as long as the Use Control Wizards button is toggled on). Within the List Box Wizard, you specify the values to be shown within the list box.

Adding a Combo Box to a Form

A ***combo box*** is similar to a list box, but it includes a text box within the control object so that the user can either type the value for the field or click the down-pointing arrow to display field values in a drop-down list and click the desired value. As happens when adding a list box, when you add a combo box control to the form, the Combo Box Wizard begins (as long as the Use Control Wizards button is toggled on). Within the Combo Box Wizard, you specify the values to be shown within the drop-down list.

Project 4 **Creating a Blank Form with List Boxes** **Part 1 of 1**

1. With **AL2-C4-RSRCompServ.accdb** open, click the CREATE tab and then click the Blank Form button in the Forms group.
2. If the Field List task pane at the right side of the work area does not display the table names, click the Show all tables hyperlink. Otherwise, proceed to Step 3.
3. Add fields from the FeesSCPlans table to the form by completing the following steps:
   a. Click the plus symbol (+) next to the FeesSCPlans table to expand the field list.
   b. Click the first field, named *ID*, in the Field List task pane and then drag the field to the top left of the form.
   c. Click the second field, named *Term*, in the Field List task pane, hold down the Shift key, and then click the last field, *Rate*, in the Field List task pane to select the remaining fields in the FeesSCPlans table.
   d. Position the mouse pointer within the selected field names and then drag the group of fields to the form below the *ID* field. Release the mouse when you see the pink bar displayed below *ID*.
   e. With the four fields added to the table still selected, hold down the Shift key and then click the *ID* field.

f. Position the mouse pointer on the orange border at the right of any of the selected label control objects until the pointer changes to a left-and-right-pointing arrow and then drag the right edge of the label control objects to the right until you can read all of the label text, as shown below.

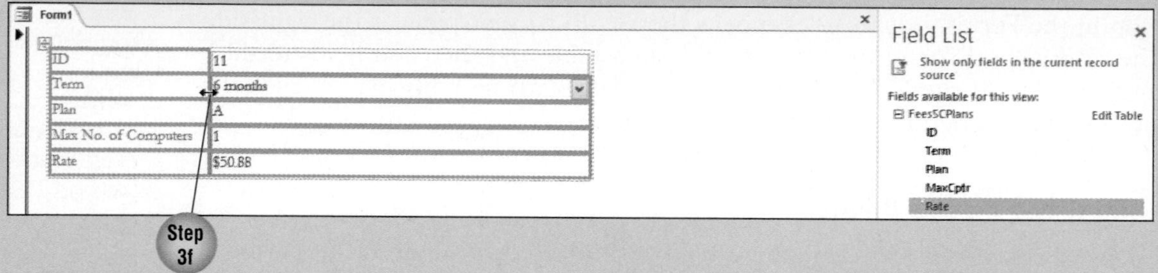

4. Add a list box control object to show the plan letters in a list by completing the following steps:
   a. Click the List Box button in the Controls group on the FORM LAYOUT TOOLS DESIGN tab.
   b. Position the pointer with the list box icon attached below the *Plan* field text box control object in the form. Click the mouse when you see the pink bar displayed between *A* and *1* in the right column. The List Box Wizard starts when you release the mouse.

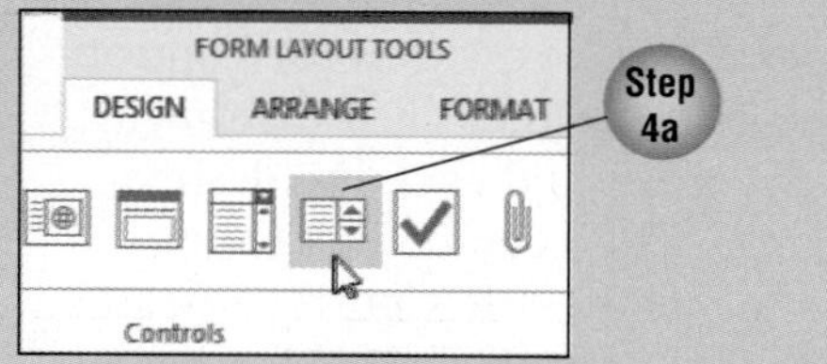

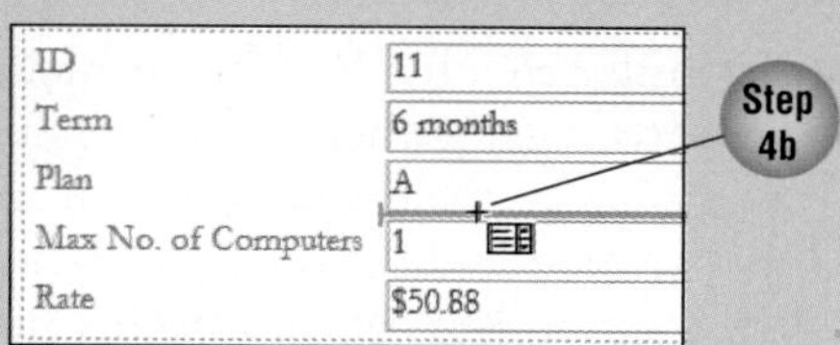

   c. At the first List Box Wizard dialog box, click *I will type in the values that I want* and then click Next.

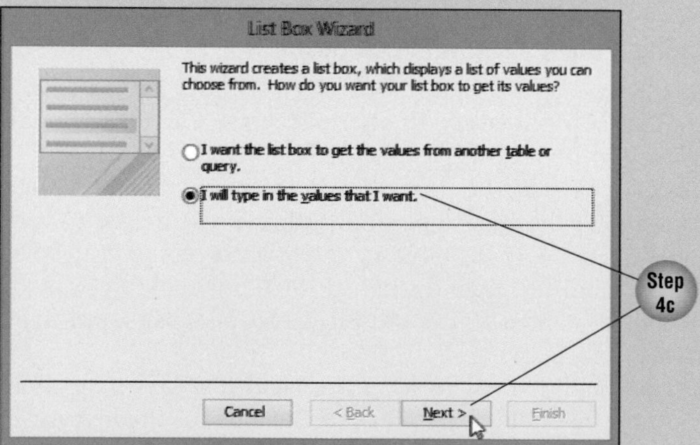

d. At the second List Box Wizard dialog box, click in the first cell below *Col1*, type **A**, and then press the Tab key.

e. Type **B**, press Tab, type **C**, press Tab, type **D**, and then click Next.

f. At the third List Box Wizard dialog box, click *Store that value in this field*, click the down-pointing arrow at the right of the option box, and then click *Plan* at the drop-down list.

g. Click Next.

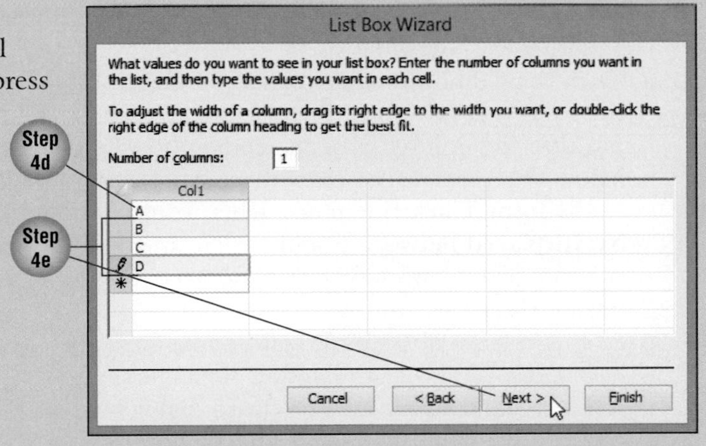

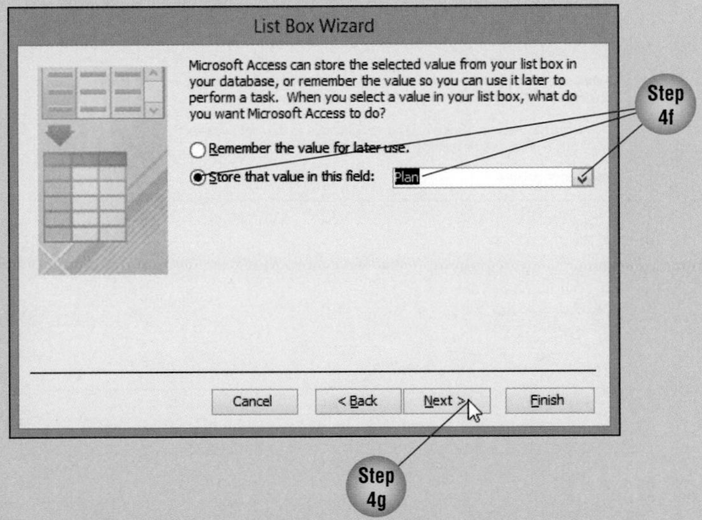

h. At the last List Box Wizard dialog box, with the current text already selected in the *What label would you like for your list box?* text box, type **PlanList** and then click Finish. Access adds the list box to the form, displaying all of the values you entered in the list.

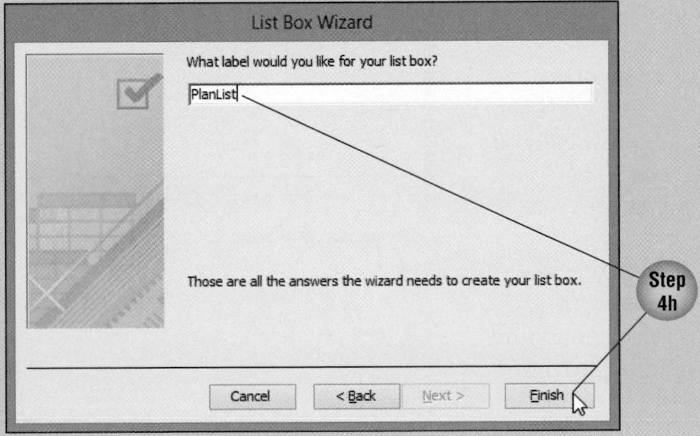

5. Add a combo box control object to enter the maximum number of computers in a plan by completing the following steps:
   a. Click the Combo Box button in the Controls group on the FORM LAYOUT TOOLS DESIGN tab.
   b. Position the pointer with the combo box icon attached below the *Max No. of Computers* text box control object in the form. Click the mouse when you see the pink bar displayed between *1* and *$50.88* in the right column. The Combo Box Wizard starts when you release the mouse button.
   c. At the first Combo Box Wizard dialog box, click *I will type in the values that I want* and then click Next.
   d. At the second Combo Box Wizard dialog box, click in the first cell below *Col1*, type **1**, and then press Tab.
   e. Type **2**, press Tab, type **3**, press Tab, type **4**, press Tab, type **5**, and then click Next.

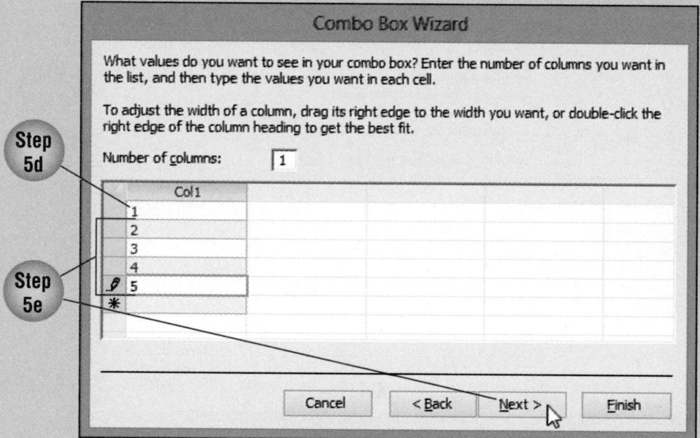

   f. At the third Combo Box Wizard dialog box, click *Store that value in this field*, click the down-pointing arrow at the right of the option box, click *MaxCptr* at the drop down list, and then click Next.
   g. At the last Combo Box Wizard dialog box, with the current text already selected in the *What label would you like for your combo box?* text box, type **CptrList** and then click Finish. Access adds the combo box to the form, displaying a value and a drop-down arrow at the right side of the text box.

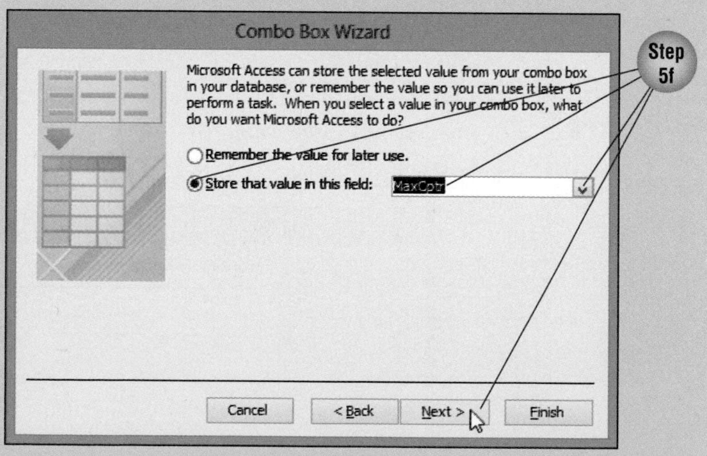

6. Double-click the label for the combo box added in Step 5 (which currently reads *CptrList*), select the text if it is not selected, and then type **Maximum Computers**. Edit the label for the list box added in Step 4 (which currently reads *PlanList*) to add a space between *Plan* and *List*.
7. Right-click the label control object above the combo box (displays the text *Max No. of Computers*) and then click *Select Entire Row* at the shortcut menu. Press Delete to remove the selected row from the form.
8. Click the Title button in the Header/Footer group on the FORM LAYOUT TOOLS DESIGN tab and then type the text **Service Contract Plans**.
9. Save the form and name it *SCPlans*.
10. Switch to Form view and then scroll through the records in the form.
11. Add a new form to the table by completing the following steps:
    a. Click the New button in the Records group on the HOME tab.
    b. Press Tab to move past the *ID* field, since this field is an AutoNumber field.
    c. Click the down-pointing arrow at the right of the *Term* field and then click *2 years* at the drop-down list.
    d. Click *C* in the *Plan List* list box. Notice that *C* is entered into the *Plan* field text box control object when you click the letter *C* in the list box.
    e. Click the down-pointing arrow at the right of the *Maximum Computers* field combo box and then click *3* at the drop-down list.
    f. Click in the *Rate* text box and then type **236.50**.
12. Print the selected record and then close the form.

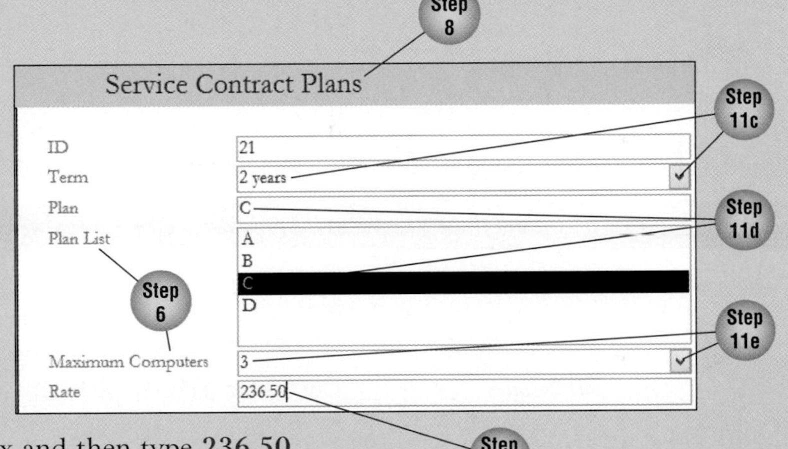

Project 5 Sort and Find Records within a Form — 1 Part

You will open a custom-built form and use the form to sort and find records by using a wildcard character and searching backward by date.

Sorting and Finding Records in Forms

One of the advantages of using a form for data entry and maintenance is that the form displays a single record at a time within the work area. Seeing one record at a time reduces the likelihood of editing the wrong record, because you can focus on the current record and not be distracted by other records. In a table with many records, quickly finding the specific record that you need to maintain or view is important. Use the Sort and Find features to move to the desired record quickly.

Quick Steps

Find Records Using a Wildcard

1. Open form in Form view.
2. Click in field by which to search.
3. Click Find button.
4. Type search string including asterisk for any variable text.
5. Click Find Next.
6. Continue clicking Find Next until search is finished.
7. Click OK.
8. Close Find and Replace dialog box.

Find

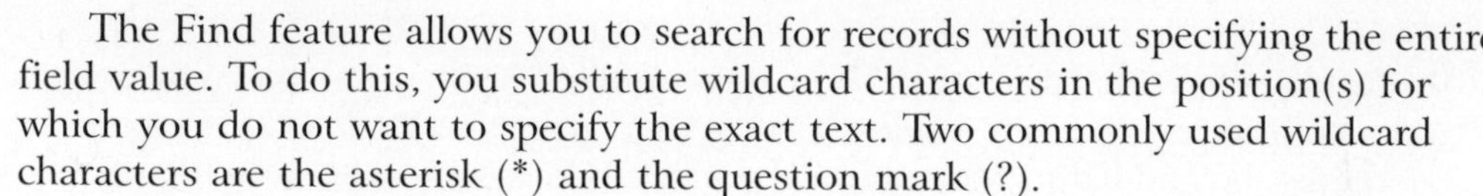

The Find feature allows you to search for records without specifying the entire field value. To do this, you substitute wildcard characters in the position(s) for which you do not want to specify the exact text. Two commonly used wildcard characters are the asterisk (*) and the question mark (?).

For example, suppose that you want to search for a record by a person's last name, but you are not sure of the correct spelling. Use the asterisk wildcard character in a position for which one or more characters vary. Use the question mark wildcard character in a fixed-width word for which you want to view all of the records with the same number of characters in the field. In this case, substitute one question mark for each character not specified. Table 4.1 provides examples of how you can use the asterisk and question mark wildcard characters. In Project 5, you will use the asterisk wildcard character to locate customer records for a specified street.

Table 4.1 Examples of Using Wildcard Characters with Find Feature

Find What Entry	In This Field	Will Find
104?	*Customer ID*	Customer records with customer IDs that begin with 104 and have one more character, such as 1041, 1042, 1043, and so on up to 1049.
4820?	*ZIP Code*	Customer records with zip codes that begin with 4820 and have one more character, such as 48201, 48202, and so on.
650??	*Work Order*	Work order records with work order numbers that begin with 650 and have two more characters, such as 65023, 65035, 65055, and so on.
313*	*Home Phone*	Customer records with telephone numbers that begin with the 313 area code.
Peter*	*Last Name*	Customer records with last names that begin with Peter and have any number of characters following, such as Peters, Peterson, Petersen, Peterovski, and so on.
4820*	*ZIP Code*	Customer records with zip codes that begin with 4820 and have any number of characters following, such as 48201 and 48203-4841.
oak	*Street Address*	Customer records with street addresses that have oak within them, such as 1755 Oak Drive, 12-234 Oak Street, and 9 Oak Boulevard.

Project 5 Sorting and Finding Records in a Form

Part 1 of 1

1. With **AL2-C4-RSRCompServ.accdb** open, open the CustMaintenance form in Form view.
2. Click in the *Last Name* field and then click the Ascending button in the Sort & Filter group on the HOME tab. The records are now arranged in ascending alphabetical order by customer last name. Scroll through a few records in the form, watching the last names to confirm the new sorted order.

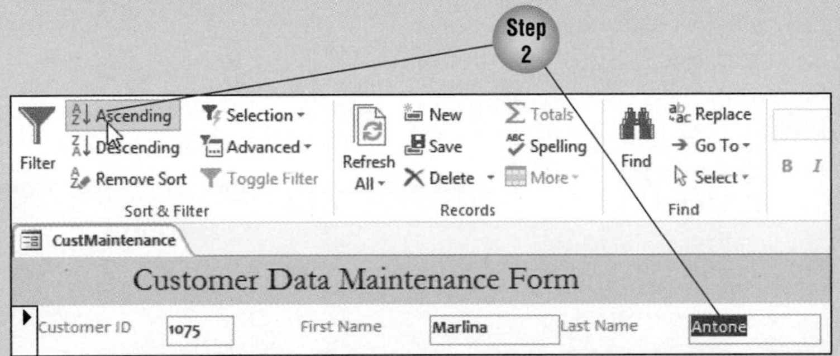

3. Assume that you now need to locate the name of the customer who resides on Roselawn Street. You do not know the exact house number or the customer's name. Complete the following steps to find the record using a wildcard character in the criterion:
   a. Click the First record button in the Record Navigation bar to return to record 1 and then click in the *Street Address* field.
   b. Click the Find button in the Find group.
   c. With the insertion point positioned in the *Find What* text box, type ***roselawn*** and then click the Find Next button. The entry **roselawn** means "Find any record in which any number of characters before roselawn and any number of characters after roselawn exist in the active field." Access displays the first record in the form in which a match was found.

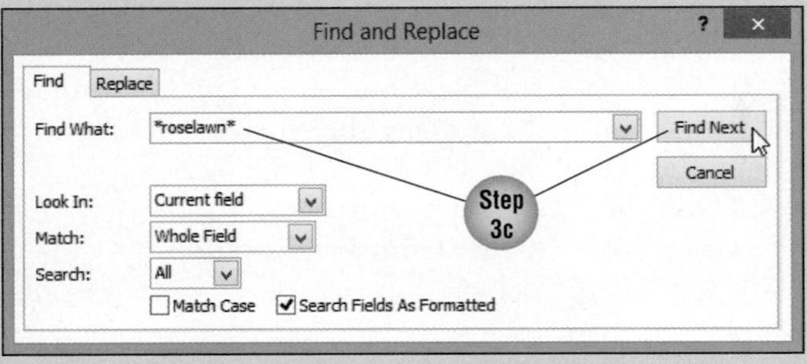

   d. Click the Find Next button to see if any other records exist for customers on Roselawn Street.
   e. At the Microsoft Access message box indicating that Access has finished searching the records, click OK.
   f. Close the Find and Replace dialog box.
4. Close the CustMaintenance form.
5. Open the WorkOrders form in Form view.
6. Click in the *Service Date* field and then click the Descending button in the Sort & Filter group to sort the records from the most recent service date to the oldest service date. Scroll through a few records in the form, watching the service dates to confirm the new sorted order.

7. Find the records for work orders completed on October 19, 2015, by completing the following steps:
   a. Click the First record button in the Record Navigation bar to return to record 1 and then click the Find button. The insertion point should still be positioned in the *Service Date* field.
   b. With the existing text in the *Find What* text box already selected, type **10/19/2015**.
   c. Click the down-pointing arrow next to the *Search* list box and then click *Down* at the drop-down list. (Because the records are arranged in descending order, you need Access to search in a downward direction.)
   d. Click the *Search Fields As Formatted* check box to remove the check mark. (Because the date entered in the *Find What* text box does not match the date format in the *Service Date* field, this check box must be cleared or Access will not match any records.)
   e. Click the Find Next button. Access moves to the first record for the specified date (*Work Order 65039*). If necessary, drag the Find and Replace dialog box down to the bottom of the work area so you can view the record details.
   f. Click the Find Next button. Access moves to the next record (*Work Order 65038*).
   g. Click the Find Next button. Access moves to the next record (*Work Order 65037*).
   h. Click the Find Next button. At the Microsoft Access message box indicating that Access has finished searching the records, click OK.
   i. Close the Find and Replace dialog box.
8. Close the WorkOrders form.
9. Close **AL2-C4-RSRCompServ.accdb**.

Quick Steps

Remove Sort
1. Open form in Form view.
2. Click Remove Sort button.

Remove Sort

Once a form has been sorted, Access displays the records in the sorted order whenever the form is opened. To remove a sort and have the order revert to the order of the primary key, open the form in Form view and then click the Remove Sort button (which displays the ScreenTip *Clear All Sorts*) in the Sort & Filter group on the HOME tab. Access clears the sort order and the table records are rearranged in ascending order by the primary key field value.

In this chapter, you have learned techniques for building a custom form using Design view. As you learned in Project 2, you can create a form using one of the form tools, such as the Form Wizard, and then make changes to the form in Design view. As you become more experienced with Access, you will likely use a combination of three methods to build custom forms: a form tool to build the basic table and field structure of the form; Layout view to apply formatting options, add a title and logo, and make other appearance changes; and Design view to add advanced control objects, such as tab controls, subforms, and calculations.

Chapter Summary

- A new form in Design view initially displays only the *Detail* section, which is where fields are placed to display record data.
- A *Form Header* section and a *Form Footer* section can be added to a form. Objects placed in the *Form Header* section display at the top of the form or print at the beginning of a printout of records from Form view. Objects placed in the *Form Footer* section display at the bottom of the form or print at the end of a printout of records from Form view.
- A form can contain three types of control objects: bound, unbound, and calculated.
- Click the Title button to display the *Form Header* and *Form Footer* sections and add a label control object in the *Form Header* section that contains the form name.
- Click the Label button in the Controls group to add a label control object containing unbound text to any section within the form.
- Double-click the Form Selector button in Design view to open the form's Property Sheet task pane and specify the table to be bound to the form in the Record Source property.
- Once a table has been associated with a form, click the Add Existing Fields button to open the Field List task pane.
- To add fields to a form, drag individual field names or a group of selected field names from the Field List task pane to the *Detail* section in the form.
- Use the move handle (the large, dark gray square at the top left of the selected control) to move a selected object independently of the control's associated label control or text box control.
- Use buttons in the Font group on the FORM DESIGN TOOLS FORMAT tab to apply formatting options to selected controls.
- Multiple control objects can be selected in Design view by drawing a selection rectangle around a group of adjacent control objects or holding down the Shift key while clicking controls.
- Open the Tab Order dialog box to change the order in which fields are selected as you press Tab to move from field to field in Form view.
- A tab control object in a form allows you to organize groups of related fields in pages.
- Click the Subform/Subreport button in the controls group to create a subform in a page within a tab control object.
- Create a calculated control object in a form using the Text Box button in the Controls group.
- Type a formula in a text box control object (which displays *Unbound*) beginning with an equals sign (=). Field names within the formula are enclosed in square brackets.
- Use the Size/Space and Align buttons in the Sizing & Ordering group on the FORM DESIGN TOOLS ARRANGE tab to resize, align, or adjust spacing between multiple selected control objects.

- Images can be added to a form in Design view using the Logo button in the Header/Footer group or Insert Image button in the Controls group.
- Draw a horizontal or vertical line in a form using the Line button in the Controls group. To draw a straight line, hold down the Shift key while dragging.
- Use the Shape Outline button on the FORM DESIGN TOOLS FORMAT tab to adjust a line's thickness, type, or color.
- Clip art images can be copied to the clipboard from another Microsoft Office program, such as Microsoft Word, and then pasted to a form in Design view.
- Change a control object's Size Mode property to resize an image within a control object while maintaining the original proportions of height and width.
- A control object can be anchored to a position in a form so that the object's position relative to the edges of the form is maintained when the form is resized.
- A datasheet form is a form that looks like a table datasheet.
- Modify properties in the Data tab of a form's Property Sheet task pane to restrict the actions a user can perform when viewing records in Form view.
- The Blank Form tool in the Forms group on the CREATE tab creates a new form with no controls or format applied. The form opens as a blank, white page in Layout view with the Field List task pane opened at the right of the work area.
- A list box control object displays all of the list values inside a rectangular-shaped control object in the form. Field values can be added to the list within the List Box Wizard by typing the values or selecting fields from a table or query.
- A combo box control object displays a text box along with a down-pointing arrow to a drop-down list of field values. The user can type the field value into the text box or click the down-pointing arrow to pick the field value from a list. Field values are added within the Combo Box Wizard by typing the values or selecting fields from a table or query.
- Sort a form in Form view by clicking in the field by which to sort records and then clicking the Ascending button or Descending button.
- Click in a field by which to search records in Form view, click the Find button, and then enter the search criterion in the *Find What* text box. Typing an asterisk or question mark in the criterion allows you to search records using a wildcard character for variable data.

Commands Review

FEATURE	RIBBON TAB, GROUP	BUTTON	KEYBOARD SHORTCUT
add existing fields	FORM DESIGN TOOLS DESIGN, Tools		
adjust size of multiple controls	FORM DESIGN TOOLS ARRANGE, Sizing & Ordering		
align multiple controls at same position	FORM DESIGN TOOLS ARRANGE, Sizing & Ordering		
anchor controls to form	FORM DESIGN TOOLS ARRANGE, Position		
blank form	CREATE, Forms		
change tab order of fields	FORM DESIGN TOOLS DESIGN, Tools		
combo box control object	FORM LAYOUT TOOLS DESIGN, Controls		
create datasheet form	CREATE, Forms		
Design view	HOME, Views OR FORM DESIGN TOOLS DESIGN, Views		
equal spacing between controls	FORM DESIGN TOOLS ARRANGE, Sizing & Ordering		
find	HOME, Find		Ctrl + F
Form view	HOME, Views OR FORM DESIGN TOOLS DESIGN, Views		
insert image	FORM DESIGN TOOLS DESIGN, Controls		
label control object	FORM DESIGN TOOLS DESIGN, Controls	Aa	
line	FORM DESIGN TOOLS DESIGN, Controls		
list box control object	FORM DESIGN TOOLS DESIGN, Controls		
Property Sheet task pane	FORM DESIGN TOOLS DESIGN, Tools		F4
sort ascending order	HOME, Sort & Filter		
sort descending order	HOME, Sort & Filter		
subform	FORM DESIGN TOOLS DESIGN, Controls		
tab control object	FORM DESIGN TOOLS DESIGN, Controls		
text box control object	FORM DESIGN TOOLS DESIGN, Controls	ab|	
title	FORM DESIGN TOOLS DESIGN, Header/Footer		

Concepts Check Test Your Knowledge 

Completion: In the space provided at the right, indicate the correct term, command, or number.

1. A new form created in Design view initially displays only this section. ____________
2. These three types of control objects are found in a form. ____________
3. Before you can add fields to a table, you must first connect the table to the form in this property box in the form's Property Sheet task pane. ____________
4. The large, dark gray square at the top left of a selected control is referred to by this name. ____________
5. Hold down this key while clicking controls to select multiple control objects to be formatted. ____________
6. Open this dialog box to change the order in which fields are selected when the Tab key is pressed in Form view. ____________
7. Add this object to the bottom of a form to display subforms as individual pages. ____________
8. Make sure this feature is active in the Controls group before clicking the Subform/Subreport button so that the Subform Wizard is available. ____________
9. Click this button in the Controls group to add a calculation to a form. ____________
10. The *Equal Vertical* option is located at the drop-down list for this button on the FORM DESIGN TOOLS ARRANGE tab. ____________
11. For a control object containing a clip art image, change this property to *Zoom* to proportionately adjust the image to the height and width of the resized object. ____________
12. The *Datasheet* form is available at the drop-down list for this button in the Forms group on the CREATE tab. ____________
13. Click this tab in a form's Property Sheet task pane to locate the *Allow Deletions* property box. ____________
14. This form tool opens as a blank, white page in Layout view. ____________
15. These two controls are used to add list boxes to a form. ____________
16. Type this entry in the *Find What* text box to search for all of the records in the active field that begin with the zip code 48221 and have any four-character extension. ____________

Skills Check Assess Your Performance

Assessment

1 CREATE A CUSTOM FORM USING DESIGN VIEW

SNAP Grade It

1. Open **AL2-C4-ViewIt.accdb** and enable the content.
2. Create a query named *CustWebOrders* using the following specifications:
   a. Add the WebOrderDetails, WebOrders, and WebProducts tables to the query.
   b. Add the following fields first from the WebOrders table, then from the WebOrderDetails table, and then from the WebProducts table.

WebOrders Table	**WebOrderDetails Table**	**WebProducts Table**
WebOrdID	Qty	Product
CustID		SellPrice
DateOrd		

   c. Run the query and then close the query results datasheet.
3. Create a new form called *WebCustOrders* using Design view and then build the form using the following specifications:
   a. Expand the width of the form in the grid to the 6.5-inch position on the horizontal ruler.
   b. Add a title object in the *Form Header* section and then type the text **Web Customer Orders**. Use the move handle that displays at the top left of the selected title control to move the title until the first letter (W) is at approximately the 1.5-inch position on the horizontal ruler.
   c. Add your name in a label control object centered in the *Form Footer* section.
   d. Apply the Retrospect theme.
   e. Connect the WebCustomers table to the form and add all of the fields to the *Detail* section in the layout shown in Figure 4.14. Adjust the widths of the control objects as shown. Remember to use the Size/Space and Align buttons to position multiple controls at the same horizontal or vertical position and adjust spacing between controls.

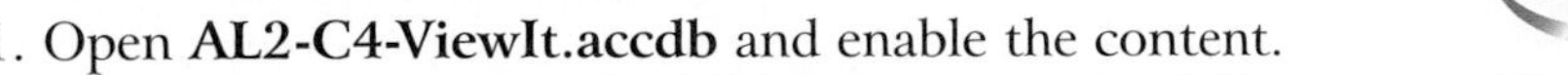

Figure 4.14 Assessment 1

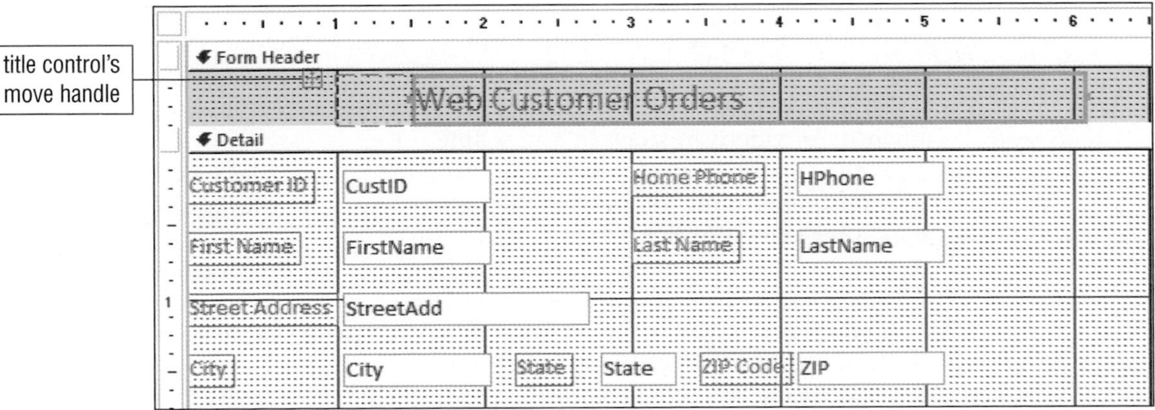

f. Change the tab order of the fields so the *HPhone* field is selected after the *CustID* field.

g. Add a tab control object below the existing fields with a height of approximately 2 inches and a width that extends to the right edge of the form.

1) On the first page, change the caption to *Web Orders* and add all of the fields from the CustWebOrders query in a subform. Delete the subform label control object. Delete the label control object and text box control object for the *CustID* field in the subform and then move the remaining fields up to fill in the space. Move and resize the subform to fit the width of the page. Autofit column widths in Form view to view all of the columns within the page.

2) On the second page, change the caption to *Payment Information* and add all of the fields except *Cust ID* and *EmailAdd* from the WebCustPymnt table in a subform. Delete the subform label control object and move and resize the subform to fit the width of the page. Autofit column widths in Form view to view all of the columns within the page.

4. Apply bold formatting to the label control objects and Green, Accent 6, Lighter 80% (second row, last column in the *Theme* colors) background color to the text box control objects.
5. Save the form.
6. Print the form in Form view with the first record displayed and the Web Orders page active.
7. Close the form.

Assessment 2

CREATE A FORM USING THE FORM WIZARD; ADD A CALCULATION AND GRAPHICS

1. With **AL2-C4-ViewIt.accdb** open, create a new form using the Form Wizard as follows:
   a. Select all of the fields from the WebProducts table.
   b. Apply the Columnar format.
   c. Accept the default form name *WebProducts*.
2. View the completed form in Form view.
3. Switch to Design view and edit the form to resemble the one shown in Figure 4.15 using the following additional information:
   a. The *Retail Value* field is a calculated field that uses a formula to multiply the quantity of videos in stock by the selling price.
   b. Find the clip art image by searching using the keyword *Movies*. Choose a suitable alternative image if the image shown is not available on the computer you are using.
   c. Apply the Maroon 5 font color for the title text and lines (available in the *Standard Colors* section of the color palette).
   d. Use your best judgment in selecting other formatting options to match the form in Figure 4.15 as closely as possible.
4. Print the form in Form view with the first record displayed.
5. Save and close the form.

Figure 4.15 Assessment 2

WebProducts Retail Value

Product ID	CV-1001
Product	Abbot & Costello Go to Mars
In Stock	2
Selling Price	$15.95
Retail Value	$31.90

Student Name

Assessment 3

CREATE A RESTRICTED-USE FORM

1. With **AL2-C4-ViewIt.accdb** open, create a Datasheet form using the WebCustPymnt table.
2. Modify the form so that records cannot be deleted when using the form.
3. Display the form in Datasheet view with the HOME tab active and a record selected.
4. Using the Insert Screenshot command or the Print Screen key with the Paste feature, insert a screenshot of the screen with the Delete button dimmed while the record is selected.
5. Paste the screenshot into a blank Word document. Type your name, the chapter number, assessment number, and any other identification information required by your instructor above or below the screenshot.
6. Print the document.
7. Save the Word document and name it **AL2-C4-ViewItForm.**
8. Exit Word.
9. Save the form using the default form name *WebCustPymnt* and then close the form.

Assessment

4 CREATE A CUSTOM FORM USING THE BLANK FORM TOOL AND ADD A LIST BOX

1. With **AL2-C4-ViewIt.accdb** open, create a new form using the Blank Form tool that adds all of the fields from the WebCustomers table. Widen the labels column so that all of the label text is visible in the form.
2. Add a list box control object between the *City* and *State* fields. Type the values into the list as follows:

   Burlington
   Charlotte
   Colchester

   Store the values in the field named *City* and accept the default label for the control object at the last List Box Wizard dialog box.
3. Delete the label control object for the list box.
4. Add a title to the form with the text *Customer Maintenance Form*. Resize the title control object to just fit the text. Add your name in a label control object centered in the *Form Footer* section.
5. Save the form and name it *WebCustomerMaintenance*.
6. Switch to Form view and then add the following new record to the WebCustomers table:

Customer ID	**121**
First Name	**Morgan**
Last Name	**Kalil**
Street Address	**29011 Greenbush Road**
City	(Click *Charlotte* in the list box.)
State	(Accept the default value of *VT*.)
ZIP Code	**05445-9314**
Home Phone	**802-555-9185**

7. Print the selected record for the new customer and then close the form.
8. Close **AL2-C4-ViewIt.accdb**.

Visual Benchmark Demonstrate Your Proficiency

CREATE A CUSTOM RESERVATIONS FORM

1. Open **AL2-C4-PawsParadise.accdb**.
2. Review the form shown in Figure 4.16 below and Figure 4.17 on the next page. This form was created from scratch in Design view. Create the form using your best judgment for alignment, spacing, sizing, and position of controls and follow these specifications:
   a. Connect the Reservations table to the main form.
   b. Apply the Ion Boardroom theme.
   c. Apply the Dark Blue line color and set the line thickness to 3 points. Select the *Dark Blue* line thickness.
   d. The days boarded value is calculated by subtracting the two date fields.
   e. Default View property (Format tab) for each subform was changed from Datasheet to Single Form. This view displays the fields one below the other instead of in a tabular arrangement. ***Hint: Create the subform by including the linked common field in the Subform Wizard dialog box so that the correct relationship between the main form and subform is established. Then delete the extra controls while editing the subform object.***
3. Save the form naming it *Reservations*.
4. Display the form in Form view and then print the first record only.
5. Close the form and then close **AL2-C4-PawsParadise.accdb**.

Figure 4.16 Visual Benchmark Custom Form with Dog Information Tab Displayed

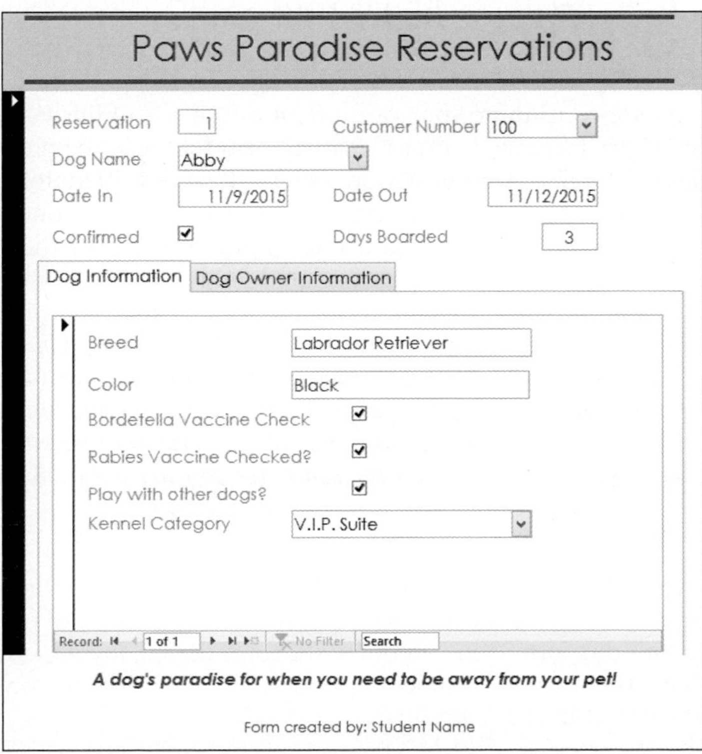

Figure 4.17 Visual Benchmark Custom Form with Dog Owner Information Tab Displayed

Case Study Apply Your Skills

Part 1

You are continuing your work as an intern with Hillsdale Realty. The office manager has asked you to create a form for easier data entry and maintenance of listings and sales information. Open **AL2-C4-HillsdaleRealty.accdb** and enable the content. Design and create a form similar to the one shown in Figure 4.18 using the Listings and SalesAndComm tables. Apply the Organic theme and orange colors. Include the calculated field at the bottom of the subform. Do not stop at any calculated fields and modify the tab order of the fields to match the arrangement of the fields in Figure 4.18. ***Hints: Change the default view for the subform to Single Form and add a calculated control in the subform control object that multiplies the sale price times the commission rate. Search for the clip art image using the keywords* for sale*; choose another suitable image if the one shown is not available on the computer you are using.*** Save the form and name it appropriately. Print the first record in the form.

Part 2

The office manager would like to have another form that displays the information from the Agents table along with the clients related to each agent. Design and create this form. You determine the form design, layout, and formatting options. Save the form and name it appropriately. Print the form with the first record displayed in the main form.

Figure 4.18 Case Study Part 1

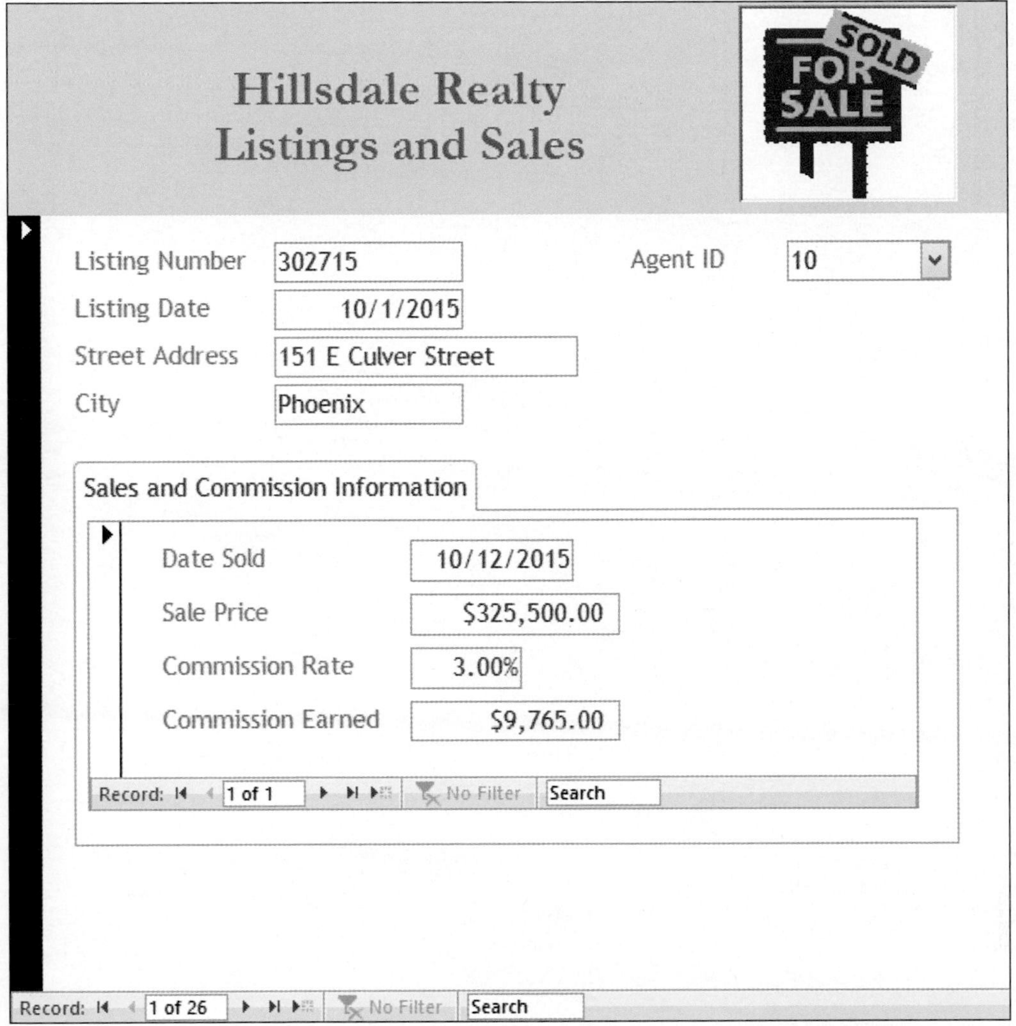

Part 3

Open the main form created in Part 1. While viewing the form, you realize that the Record Navigation bar at the bottom of the subform is not needed, since a listing will have only one sale record. Remove the Record Navigation bar in the subform by opening the subform's Property Sheet task pane. At the Format tab, change the Navigation Buttons property to *No*. Close the Property Sheet task pane and then display the form in Form view. Notice that the subform no longer displays a Record Navigation bar. Save the revised form. Take a screenshot of the revised form using the Insert Screenshot command or the Print Screen key with the Paste feature. Paste the screenshot into a new Word document. Type your name, the chapter number, and any other identifying information required by your instructor above or below the screenshot. Print the Word document. Save the Word document as **AL2-C4-CS-P3-HillsdaleRealty** and then exit Word.

UNIT 1

MICROSOFT® ACCESS® Performance Assessment

Note: The Student Resources CD does not include an Access Level 2, Unit 1 subfolder of files because no data files are required for the Unit 1 assessments. You will create all of the files yourself. Before beginning the assessments, create a folder for the new files and name it AL1U1.

Assessing Proficiency

In this unit, you have learned to design advanced tables that incorporate best practices in database design. You have created tables with multiple-field primary keys, multiple-value fields, attachment fields, and lookup fields to retrieve data from another table. You have learned to modify the join type in a relationship to achieve various query results and understand the concept of normalization as it applies to table design. You have created select queries, parameter queries, and action queries. Finally, you have learned how to use Design view to build a custom form that includes calculations, multiple pages, and subforms.

Assessment 1 Create Tables for a Property Management Database

1. Create a new database named **AL2-U1-BenchmarkPropMgt.accdb**.
2. Create the tables shown in Figure U1.1 to store residential building management and tenant information, including setting the primary key and assigning data types and field sizes. Leave field sizes at the default setting for those fields that do not have a field size specified in Figure U1.1.
3. Close any tables that have been left open.

Figure U1.1 Assessment 1

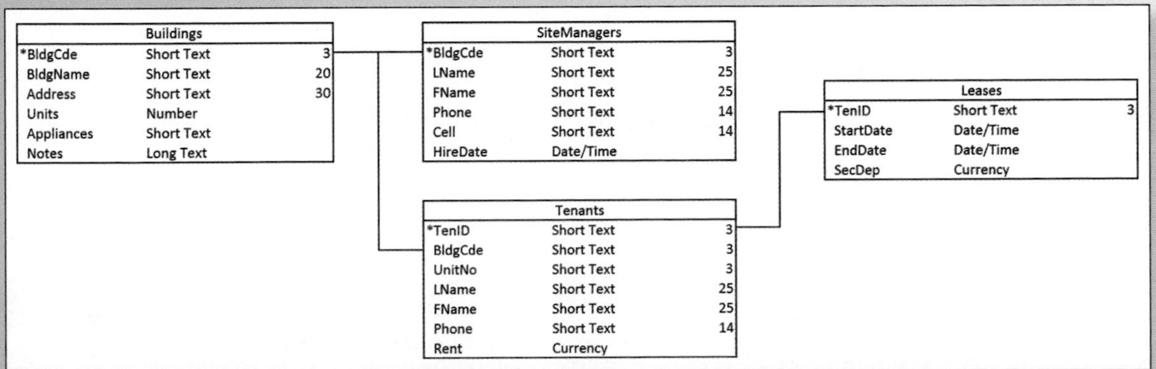

4. Open the Access Options dialog box and then click the *Compact on Close* check box with the Current Database pane active to make sure the file size is optimized each time you close the database. Click OK at the message saying that you must close and reopen the current database for the option to take effect.
5. Close **AL2-U1-BenchmarkPropMgt.accdb**.

Assessment 2 Add Captions and Modify Field Properties

1. Open the **AL2-U1-BenchmarkPropMgt.accdb** database, enable the contents, and then create captions for the fields as follows:

Buildings Table

Field Name	Caption
BldgCde	Bldg Code
BldgName	Name

Leases Table

Field Name	Caption
TenID	Tenant ID
StartDate	Start Date
EndDate	End Date
SecDep	Security Deposit

SiteManagers Table

Field Name	Caption
BldgCde	Bldg Code
LName	Last Name
FName	First Name
Phone	Telephone
Cell	Cell Phone
HireDate	Hire Date

Tenants Table

Field Name	Caption
TenID	Tenant ID
BldgCde	Bldg Code
UnitNo	Unit No
LName	Last Name
FName	First Name
Phone	Telephone

2. Make *UnitNo* in the Tenants table a required field, including disallowing zero-length strings.
3. Create a custom format for all of the date fields that displays dates in the short date format, with leading zeros for months and days. Use slashes (/) to separate the sections in the date—for example, *01/05/2015*.
4. Create the following custom input masks:
   a. For the *BldgCde* field in the Buildings table, require three digits and display an underscore character as the placeholder. Do not store the display characters.
   b. For the *TenID* field in the Tenants table, require three digits and display an underscore character as the placeholder. Do not store the display characters.

c. In each date field, create an input mask that will require dates to be entered using the short date format created in Step 3 with all digits required. Do not store the display characters. ***Hints: Use the Input Mask Wizard to create the first input mask, modify the code created by the wizard to change optional digits to required digits, and then copy and paste the input mask codes to the other two date fields.***
d. Require all of the telephone numbers to include the area code, with hyphens between sections of the number. Display the pound symbol (#) as the placeholder character. (See the hint provided for Step 4c.) Do not store the display characters.

5. Enable rich text formatting in the *Notes* field in the Buildings table.
6. Make *995.00* the default value in the *Rent* field in the Tenants table.
7. Save and then close all of the tables.

Assessment 3 Add Records

1. With **AL2-U1-BenchmarkPropMgt.accdb** open, add the following records:

Buildings Table

Field	Record 1	Record 2	Record 3
Bldg Code	**115**	**120**	**125**
Name	**Coventry Park**	**Mornington Place**	**Bayview Towers**
Address	**33 Westview Road**	**1100 Forrester Lane**	**12 Lakeview Circle**
Units	**38**	**60**	**110**
Appliances	(leave blank)	(leave blank)	(leave blank)
Notes	**New roof in 2014**	**Furnace and air conditioning units under warranty until 2018**	**Parking lot resurfaced in 2013**

Leases Table

Field	Record 1	Record 2	Record 3
Tenant ID	**101**	**102**	**103**
Start Date	**01 01 2015**	**02 01 2015**	**02 01 2015**
End Date	**12 31 2015**	**01 31 2016**	**01 31 2016**
Security Deposit	**995**	**995**	**1125**

SiteManagers Table

Field	Record 1	Record 2	Record 3
Bldg Code	**115**	**120**	**125**
Last Name	**Jenkins**	**Hernandez**	**Doxtator**
First Name	**Blair**	**Maria**	**Cody**
Telephone	**800 555 3485**	**800 555 8675**	**800 555 9677**
Cell Phone	**800 555 3748**	**800 555 3996**	**800 555 7795**
Hire Date	**02 08 2010**	**04 23 2013**	**09 15 2014**

Tenants Table

Field	Record 1	Record 2	Record 3
Tenant ID	**101**	**102**	**103**
Bldg Code	**115**	**115**	**115**
Unit No	**110**	**215**	**320**
Last Name	**Chen**	**Ayoub**	**Reiser**
First Name	**Wei**	**Mona**	**Helena**
Telephone	**519 555 8776**	**519 555 2286**	**519 555 7668**
Rent	**995**	**995**	**1125**

2. Apply bold formatting and the red font color to the years entered in the *Notes* field in each record.
3. For each table, adjust the column widths until all of the data is entirely visible. Print each table, adjusting print options as necessary to fit each table on one page.
4. Save and then close all of the tables.

Assessment 4 Create Lookup Lists and Edit Relationships

1. With **AL2-U1-BenchmarkPropMgt.accdb** open, create the following lookup lists to display values from another table:
   a. In the SiteManagers table, create a lookup field for *BldgCde* that displays the building codes and names from the Buildings table. Sort the list by building name and show the key column. Widen the column displaying the building names to accommodate longer names that may be added to the table in the future. Store the *BldgCde* value in the field.
   b. In the Tenants table, create a lookup field for *BldgCde* using the same specifications as for Step 1a.
   c. In the Leases table, create a lookup field for *TenID* that displays the tenant IDs, first names, and last names from the Tenants table. Sort the list by last name and show the key column. Store the *TenID* value in the field.
2. Create a multiple-value lookup field for the *Appliances* field in the Buildings table that contains the following items:

   Refrigerator
   Stove
   Microwave
   Dishwasher
   Washer
   Dryer

3. Edit the three records to populate the *Appliances* field as follows:

Bldg Code	*Appliances*
115	Refrigerator, Stove, Microwave
120	Refrigerator, Stove, Microwave, Dishwasher
125	Refrigerator, Stove, Washer, Dryer

4. Adjust the field width of the *Appliances* column to best fit, change the width of the *Notes* column to 35 characters, change the row height to 30 points, and then print the Buildings table in landscape orientation with the left and right margins set to 0.25 inch.
5. Close the Buildings table, saving changes to the table layout.
6. Open the Relationships window. Edit all of the relationships to turn on referential integrity and the two cascade options.
7. Arrange the table field list boxes in the window to show the relationships with the primary tables on the left and related tables on the right. Make sure no join lines overlap so that each relationship is easily distinguished from the others. Create, save, and then print a relationships report using the default report name.
8. Close the relationship report window and relationships window.

Assessment 5 Create Select Queries

1. With **AL2-U1-BenchmarkPropMgt.accdb** open, design and create the following select queries:
   a. A PromptedTenant query that displays the *BldgCde* and *BldgName* fields from the Buildings table and the *UnitNo*, *FName*, *LName*, and *Phone* fields from the Tenants table. Include prompts to specify the building name and unit number criteria when the query is run.
   b. A PromptedLease query that displays the *TenID* from the Tenants table; the *BldgName* from the Buildings table; the *UnitNo*, *FName*, and *LName* fields from the Tenants table; and the *StartDate*, *EndDate*, and *SecDep* fields from the Leases table. Include prompts to specify the starting date and ending date criteria when the query is run.
   c. A TenantsList query that displays the *BldgCde* and *BldgName* fields from the Buildings table and the *UnitNo*, *FName*, *LName*, and *Rent* fields from the Tenants table. Sort in ascending order by building name. Modify the join properties to show all of the records from the Buildings table in a left outer join.
   d. A BuildingsList query that displays all of the fields in the Buildings table except the *Notes* field. Show each entry in the multiple-value *Appliances* field in a separate row in the query results datasheet and assign the field the caption *Supplied Appliances*.
2. Run the PromptedTenant query. Type **coventry park** when prompted for the building name and **110** when prompted for the unit number. Print the query results datasheet and then close the query.
3. Run the PromptedLease query. Type **02/01/2015** when prompted for the starting date and **01/31/2016** when prompted for the ending date. Print the query results datasheet in landscape orientation and then close the query.
4. Run the TenantsList query, print the query results datasheet, and then close the query.
5. Run the BuildingsList query, print the query results datasheet in landscape orientation, and then close the query.

Assessment 6 Calculate in a Query and Use an Update Query to Increase Rents

1. With **AL2-U1-BenchmarkPropMgt.accdb** open, create a query to calculate the total rental income from each unit as follows:
   a. Open the TenantsList query in Design view and use Save Object As to name the query *RentalIncome*.
   b. Modify the join properties to show records only when the joined fields are equal in both tables using an inner join.
   c. Add a calculated field to the query with the column heading *AnnualRent* that calculates 12 months of rental income. Change the caption to *Annual Rent*.
   d. Run the query and add a *Total* row in the query results datasheet with a Sum function in the *Rent* and *Annual Rent* columns.
   e. Print the query results datasheet in landscape orientation and then close the query, saving the changes.
2. Create an update query named *RentIncrease* to increase all of the rents by 4%. Run the query.
3. Close the RentIncrease query.
4. Open the RentalIncome query, print the query results datasheet in landscape orientation, and then close the query.

Assessment 7 Design and Create Forms

1. With **AL2-U1-BenchmarkPropMgt.accdb** open, design and create a form to enter data into the Buildings table as a main form with the SiteManagers table in a subform. Name the main form *BldgsAndMgrs*. You determine the form design, layout, and formatting options. Include an appropriate clip art image in the form. Add your name in the *Form Footer* section. Print the first record in the Buildings table displayed in Form view.
2. Design and create a form to enter data into the Tenants table as a main form with the Leases table in a subform, similar to the one shown in Figure U1.2. Name the form *TenantsAndLeases*. Modify the tab order to move in this order: *Tenant ID*, *Bldg Code*, *Unit No*, *Telephone*, *First Name*, *Last Name*, and *Rent*. Remove the tab stop from *Annual Rent*, as it is a calculated control. Use your best judgment to match the color formatting with the theme colors. Add labels and graphics as shown. (Note that the subform does not show a Record Navigation bar. Refer to Case Study Part 3, on page 157 in Chapter 4, if you need help turning off the bar.)
3. Print all of the records using the TenantsAndLeases form and then close the form, saving the changes.
4. Close **AL2-U1-BenchmarkPropMgt.accdb**.

Figure U1.2 Assessment 7, Step 2

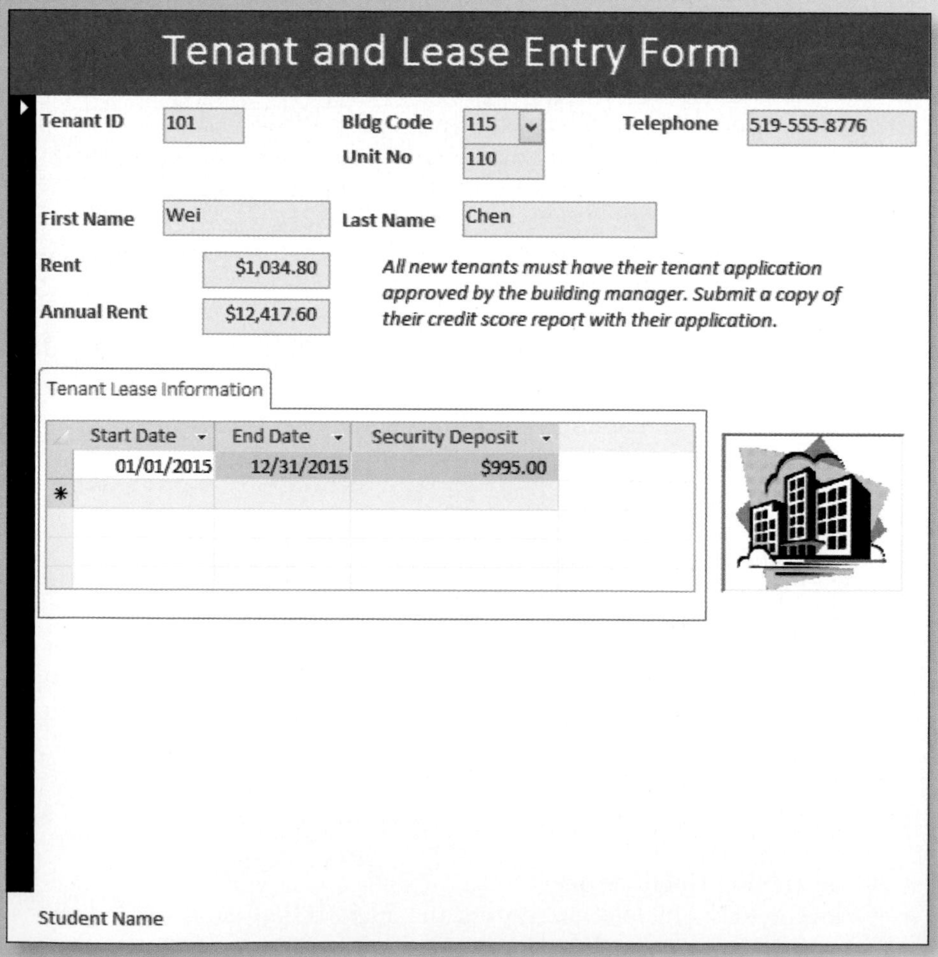

Writing Activities

The following activities give you the opportunity to practice your writing skills while demonstrating an understanding of some of the important Access features you have mastered in this unit. Use correct grammar, appropriate word choices, and clear sentence constructions when required.

Activity 1 Design Tables for Parking Information in the Property Management Database

The office manager at Benchmark Property Management would like to add tables to **AL2-U1-BenchmarkPropMgt.accdb** to store information about assigned parking at each building. Design and create one table to store parking rates and another table to track rental information for each parking spot using the information provided below. Create two lookup fields in the assigned parking table: one to look up the correct parking rate in the Rates table and another to look up the tenant's ID in the Tenants table. Add at least three records to test your tables.

Use the following information to assist you with the table design:

Parking Rates

- Coventry Park charges $30 per month for parking.
- Mornington Place charges $41 per month for parking.
- Bayview Towers charges $58 per month for parking.

Assigned Parking Table

- Include fields to store the vehicle make, model, color, and license plate number of the tenant's vehicle that will be parked in the spot.
- Include a field to store the date the tenant began renting the spot.

In Microsoft Word, document your table design by including each table's name and the fields created in each table, including the data type and field properties that you set (such as field size, caption, input mask, and so on). Indicate the primary key(s) in each table by typing an asterisk preceding the field name. Save the Word document and name it **AL2-U1-Act1-BenchmarkPropMgt**. Print the document and then exit Word.

Activity 2 Design Tables for a Soccer League Database

You are assisting the volunteer registration coordinator for a local soccer league. The registration coordinator would like to create an Access database in which to store information about this season's soccer players so that he can extract reports by age category to develop team lists and generate financial reports for the league treasurer. Design and create tables in a new database named **AL2-U1-SoccerRegn.accdb**. The registration coordinator has given you a sample registration form to help you design the tables. Refer to the sample form shown in Figure U1.3 on the next page.

Figure U1.3 Writing Activity 2

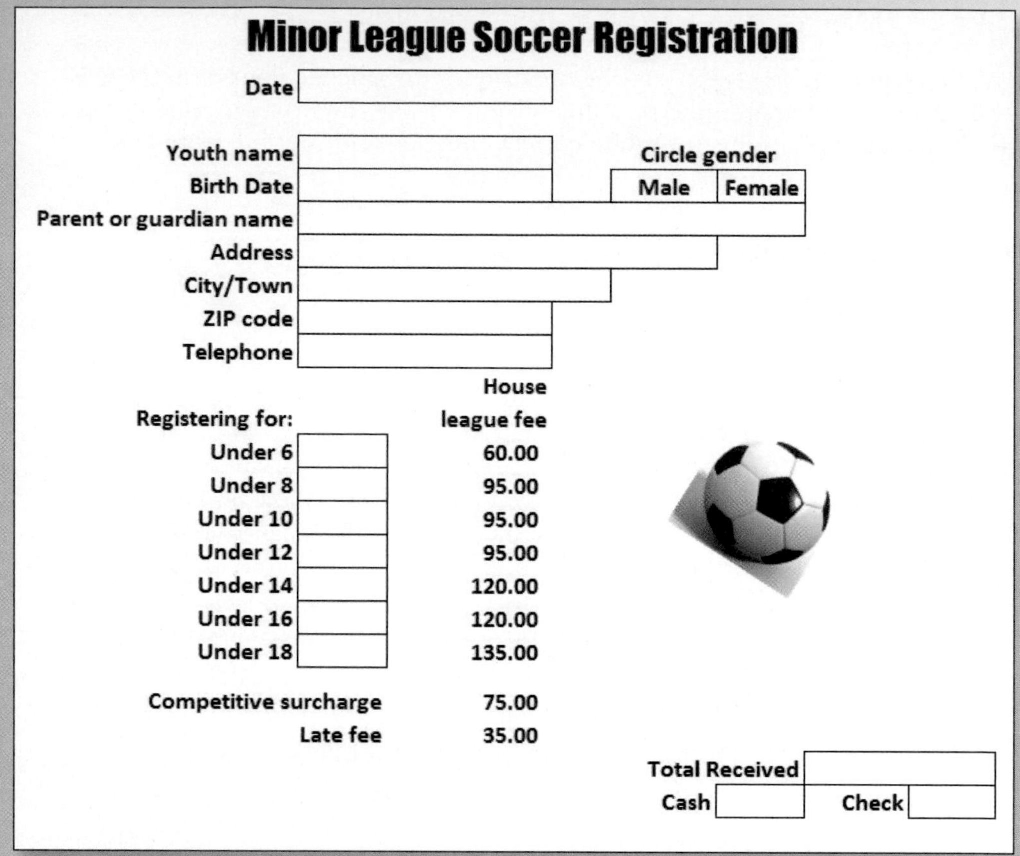

Minor League Soccer Registration

Date

Youth name
Birth Date
Parent or guardian name
Address
City/Town
ZIP code
Telephone

Circle gender: Male | Female

Registering for:		House league fee
Under 6		60.00
Under 8		95.00
Under 10		95.00
Under 12		95.00
Under 14		120.00
Under 16		120.00
Under 18		135.00
Competitive surcharge		75.00
Late fee		35.00

Total Received

Cash | Check

Create one data entry form to enter information into the tables and add at least five records to test your table and form design. Print all of the records using the form. Design and create a prompted query that will print a list of soccer players selecting records by age category. Design and create another query to print the names of the soccer players registered for the current season, including the registration fee paid. Add a *Total* row in the query results datasheet to show the total registration fees collected. Run each query to test your query design and print the query results datasheets.

In Microsoft Word, create a one-page quick reference guide for the registration coordinator and treasurer that provides instructions on how to open the database and use the data entry form, prompted query, and registration fee query. Include in your instructions how to print objects in the database, including how to print a selected form. Save the Word document and name it **AL2-U1-Act2-SoccerRegistration**. Print the document and then exit Word.

Internet Research

Plan Your Volunteer Work

You want to volunteer each week after school but are not sure which organization is a good fit with your skills and interests. As you begin to consider where you would like to donate your time and expertise, you decide to use your newly learned Access skills to develop a volunteer organization database that you can share with your friends and relatives.

To create your database, research five to eight organizations in your area that need volunteers on a regular basis. Pick a variety of organizations so that most people will find at least one organization in the database that appeals to them. Design tables in Access in a new database named **AL2-U1-VolunteerOrg.accdb** to store each organization's name, address, telephone number, and volunteer coordinator (if applicable). Include a field with notes about the organization's mission. Look for annual fund-raising events at which volunteers are needed and include an Events table related to the organization. Design and create a form for data entry and use the form to input records for the organizations that you researched. Print all of the records using the form.

Using Microsoft Word, create a brief document with instructions for your friends and relatives on how to open the database, browse records using the form, and print information. Save and then print the document, naming it **AL2-U1-VolunteerInfo**.

MICROSOFT®

ACCESS®

Level 2

Unit 2 ■ Advanced Reports, Access Tools, and Customizing Access

MICROSOFT® ACCESS®

Creating and Using Custom Reports

PERFORMANCE OBJECTIVES

Upon successful completion of Chapter 5, you will be able to:

- **Create a custom report in Design view using all five report sections**
- **Move, size, format, and align control objects**
- **Insert a subreport into a report**
- **Add page numbers and date and time controls**
- **Add graphics to a report**
- **Group records including adding functions and totals**
- **Add and format a calculated field to a custom report**
- **Modify section or group properties to control print options**
- **Create and modify charts in a report**
- **Create a blank report**
- **Add hyperlinks and list boxes to a report**
- **Change the shape of a tab control**
- **Change the tab order of fields**
- **Insert a subform into a report**

Tutorials

5.1 Creating Custom Reports Using Design View
5.2 Connecting a Table or Query to a Report and Adding Fields
5.3 Moving Control Objects to Another Section
5.4 Inserting a Subreport
5.5 Formatting Controls in a Report
5.6 Grouping Records in a Report
5.7 Creating a Report with a Grouping Level Using the Report Wizard
5.8 Adding and Formatting a Calculated Field
5.9 Adding Functions to a Group; Keeping a Group Together
5.10 Modifying Section Properties; Inserting a Chart
5.11 Creating a Report Using the Blank Report Tool

Reports are used to generate printouts from the tables in a database. Although you can use the Print feature to print data from a table datasheet, query results datasheet, or form, you cannot customize or change the formatting of the data in these printouts. The Report feature provides tools and options that can be used to control the content and formatting to produce professional-quality reports that serve particular purposes. In this chapter, you will learn how to build custom reports. Model answers for this chapter's projects appear on the following pages.

AL2C5

Note: Before beginning the projects, copy to your storage medium the AL2C5 subfolder from the AL2 folder on the CD that accompanies this textbook and then make AL2C5 the active folder.

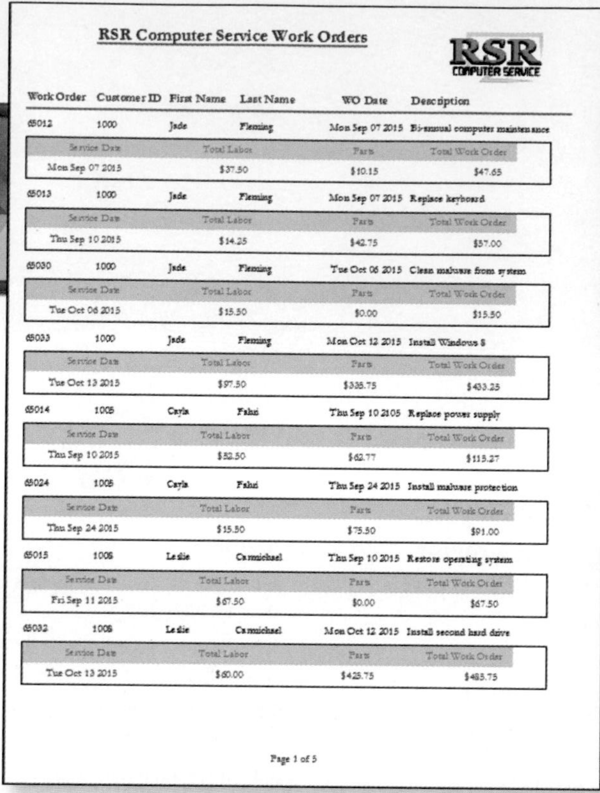

RSR Computer Service Work Orders

RSR COMPUTER SERVICE

Work Order	Customer ID	First Name	Last Name	WO Date	Description	Service Date	Total Labor	Parts	Total Work Order
65012	1000	Jade	Fleming	Mon Sep 07 2015	Bi-annual computer maintenance	Mon Sep 07 2015	$37.50	$10.15	$47.65
65013	1000	Jade	Fleming	Mon Sep 07 2015	Replace keyboard	Thu Sep 10 2015	$14.25	$42.75	$57.00
65030	1000	Jade	Fleming	Tue Oct 06 2015	Clean malware from system	Tue Oct 06 2015	$15.50	$0.00	$15.50
65033	1000	Jade	Fleming	Mon Oct 12 2015	Install Windows 8	Tue Oct 13 2015	$97.50	$335.75	$433.25
65014	1005	Cayla	Fahri	Thu Sep 10 2105	Replace power supply	Thu Sep 10 2015	$52.50	$62.77	$115.27
65024	1005	Cayla	Fahri	Thu Sep 24 2015	Install malware protection	Thu Sep 24 2015	$15.50	$75.50	$91.00
65015	1008	Leslie	Carmichael	Thu Sep 10 2015	Restore operating system	Fri Sep 11 2015	$67.50	$0.00	$67.50
65032	1008	Leslie	Carmichael	Mon Oct 12 2015	Install second hard drive	Tue Oct 13 2015	$60.00	$425.75	$485.75

Page 1 of 5

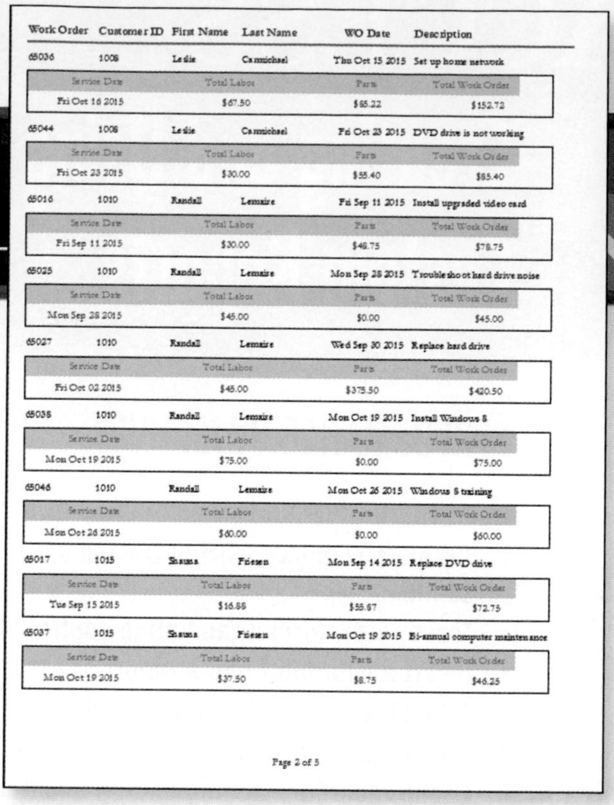

Work Order	Customer ID	First Name	Last Name	WO Date	Description	Service Date	Total Labor	Parts	Total Work Order
65036	1008	Leslie	Carmichael	Thu Oct 15 2015	Set up home network	Fri Oct 16 2015	$67.50	$85.22	$152.72
65044	1008	Leslie	Carmichael	Fri Oct 23 2015	DVD drive is not working	Fri Oct 23 2015	$30.00	$55.40	$85.40
65016	1010	Randall	Lemaire	Fri Sep 11 2015	Install upgraded video card	Fri Sep 11 2015	$30.00	$48.75	$78.75
65025	1010	Randall	Lemaire	Mon Sep 28 2015	Troubleshoot hard drive noise	Mon Sep 28 2015	$45.00	$0.00	$45.00
65027	1010	Randall	Lemaire	Wed Sep 30 2015	Replace hard drive	Fri Oct 02 2015	$45.00	$375.50	$420.50
65038	1010	Randall	Lemaire	Mon Oct 19 2015	Install Windows 8	Mon Oct 19 2015	$75.00	$0.00	$75.00
65046	1010	Randall	Lemaire	Mon Oct 26 2015	Windows 8 training	Mon Oct 26 2015	$60.00	$0.00	$60.00
65017	1015	Shauna	Friesen	Mon Sep 14 2015	Replace DVD drive	Tue Sep 15 2015	$16.88	$55.87	$72.75
65037	1015	Shauna	Friesen	Mon Oct 19 2015	Bi-annual computer maintenance	Mon Oct 19 2015	$37.50	$8.75	$46.25

Page 2 of 5

Projects 1 and 2 Design and Create a Custom Report; Add Features and Enhance a Report Project 2b, WorkOrders Report

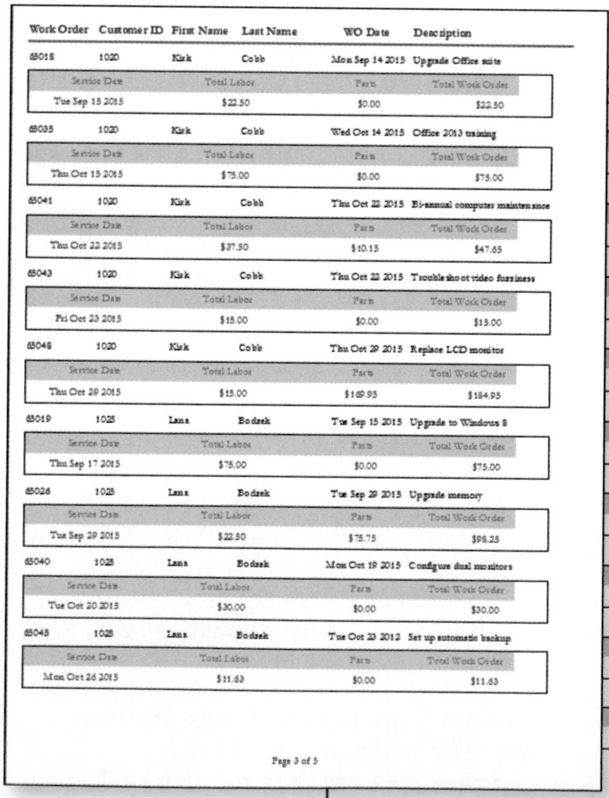

Work Order	Customer ID	First Name	Last Name	WO Date	Description	Service Date	Total Labor	Parts	Total Work Order
65018	1020	Kirk	Cobb	Mon Sep 14 2015	Upgrade Office suite	Tue Sep 15 2015	$22.50	$0.00	$22.50
65035	1020	Kirk	Cobb	Wed Oct 14 2015	Office 2013 training	Thu Oct 15 2015	$75.00	$0.00	$75.00
65041	1020	Kirk	Cobb	Thu Oct 22 2015	Bi-annual computer maintenance	Thu Oct 22 2015	$37.50	$10.15	$47.65
65043	1020	Kirk	Cobb	Thu Oct 22 2015	Troubleshoot video fuzziness	Fri Oct 23 2015	$15.00	$0.00	$15.00
65048	1020	Kirk	Cobb	Thu Oct 29 2015	Replace LCD monitor	Thu Oct 29 2015	$15.00	$169.95	$184.95
65019	1025	Lana	Bodzek	Tue Sep 15 2015	Upgrade to Windows 8	Thu Sep 17 2015	$75.00	$0.00	$75.00
65026	1025	Lana	Bodzek	Tue Sep 29 2015	Upgrade memory	Tue Sep 29 2015	$22.50	$75.75	$98.25
65040	1025	Lana	Bodzek	Mon Oct 19 2015	Configure dual monitors	Tue Oct 20 2015	$30.00	$0.00	$30.00
65045	1025	Lana	Bodzek	Tue Oct 23 2012	Set up automatic backup	Mon Oct 26 2015	$11.63	$0.00	$11.63

Page 3 of 5

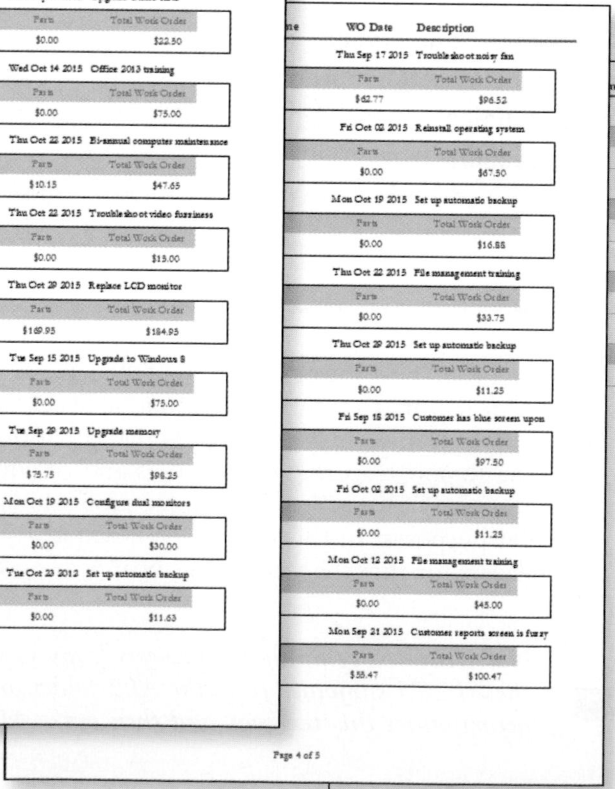

WO Date	Description	Parts	Total Work Order
Thu Sep 17 2015	Troubleshoot noisy fan	$62.77	$96.52
Fri Oct 02 2015	Reinstall operating system	$0.00	$67.50
Mon Oct 19 2015	Set up automatic backup	$0.00	$16.88
Thu Oct 22 2015	File management training	$0.00	$33.75
Thu Oct 29 2015	Set up automatic backup	$0.00	$11.25
Fri Sep 18 2015	Customer has blue screen upon	$0.00	$97.50
Fri Oct 02 2015	Set up automatic backup	$0.00	$11.25
Mon Oct 12 2015	File management training	$0.00	$45.00
Mon Sep 21 2015	Customer reports screen is fuzzy	$35.47	$100.47

Page 4 of 5

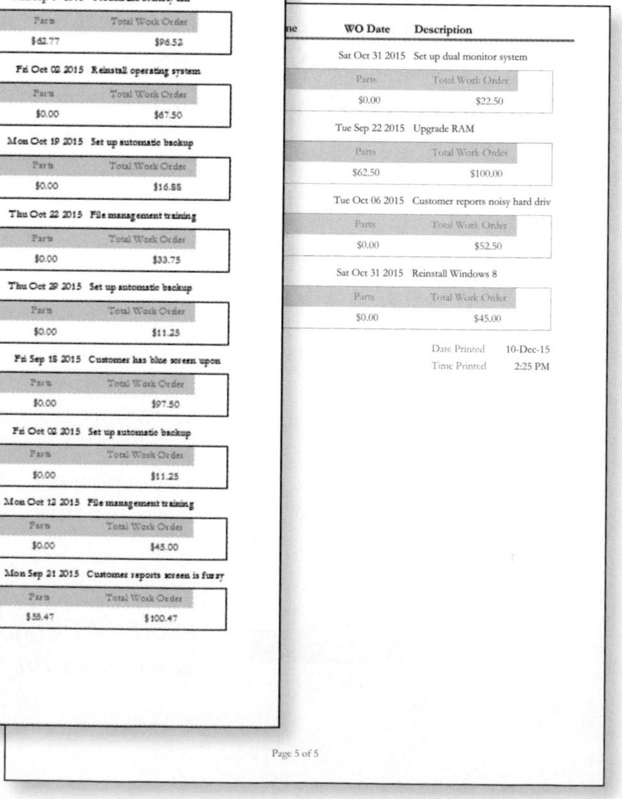

WO Date	Description	Parts	Total Work Order
Sat Oct 31 2015	Set up dual monitor system	$0.00	$22.50
Tue Sep 22 2015	Upgrade RAM	$62.50	$100.00
Tue Oct 06 2015	Customer reports noisy hard driv	$0.00	$52.50
Sat Oct 31 2015	Reinstall Windows 8	$0.00	$45.00

Date Printed 10-Dec-15
Time Printed 2:25 PM

Page 5 of 5

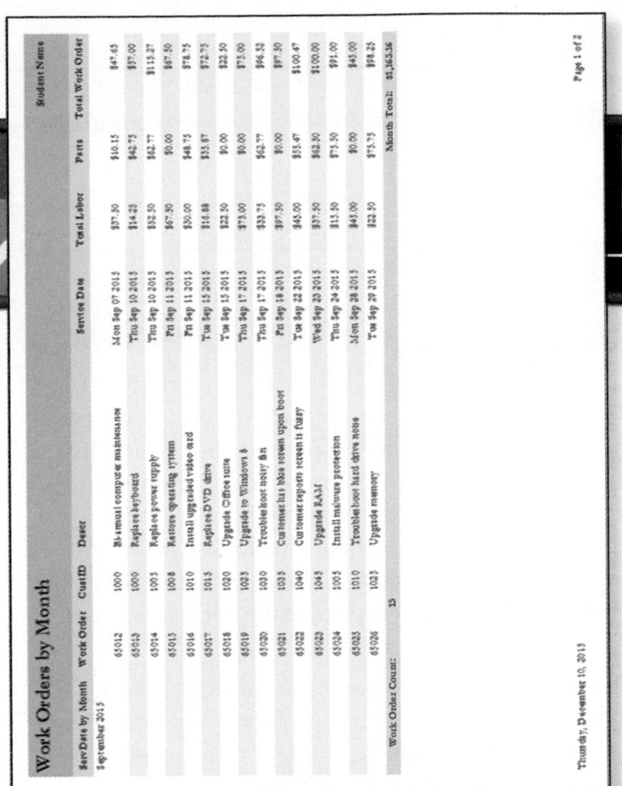

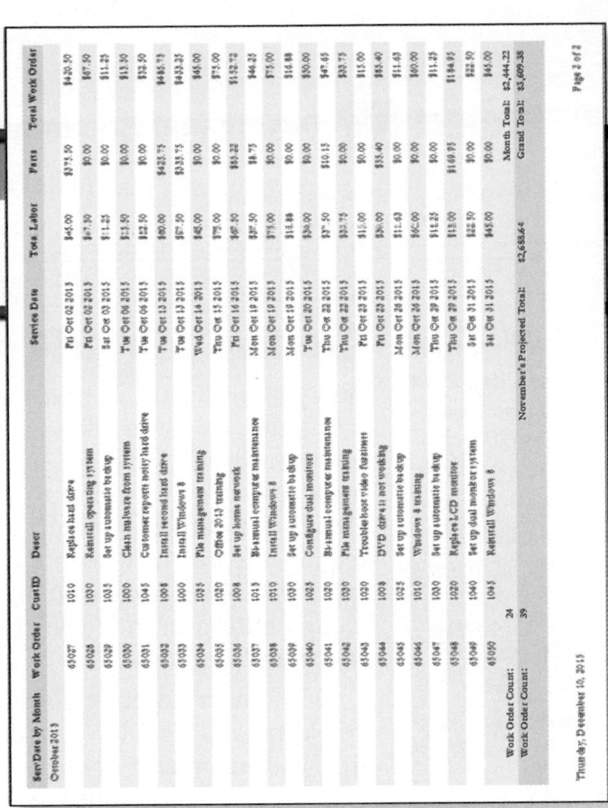

Projects 3 and 4 Group Records and Add Functions to Count and Sum; Modify Section and Group Properties

Project 4, WorkOrdersbyMonth Report

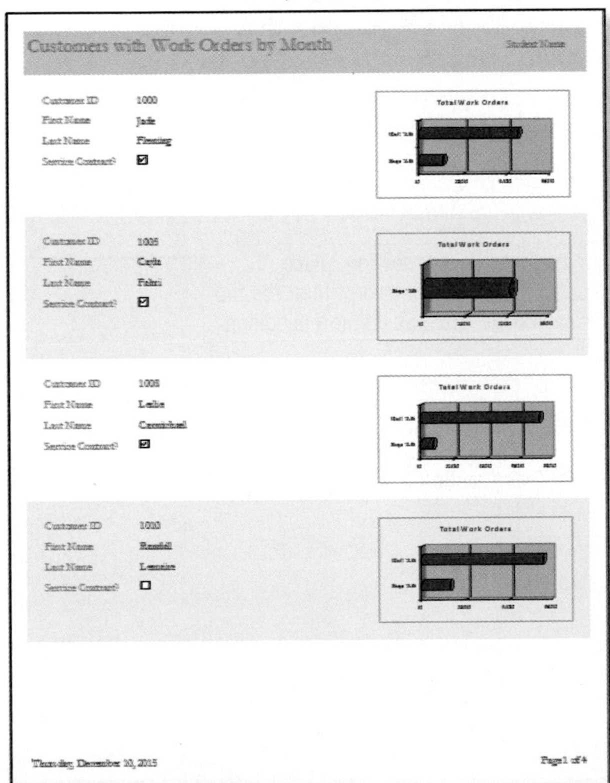

Project 5 Create and Format a Chart

Project 5b, CustomersWOChart Report

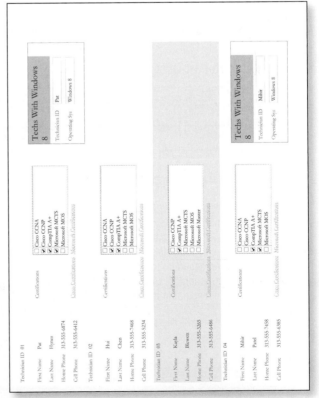

Project 6 Create a Blank Report with Hyperlinks and a LIst

TechCertifications Report

Project 1 Design and Create a Custom Report **5 Parts**

You will create a custom report in Design view with fields from two tables and insert a subreport.

Quick Steps

Start a New Report in Design View
1. Click CREATE tab.
2. Click Report Design button.

Add a Report Title
1. Open report in Design view.
2. Click Title button.
3. Type title text.
4. Press Enter.

Add a Label Object
1. Open report in Design view.
2. Click Label button.
3. Drag to create object of desired height and width.
4. Type label text.
5. Press Enter.

Report Design

Creating Custom Reports Using Design View

Access provides the Report tool and the Report Wizard to help you create reports. Using these features allows you to quickly build a report that you can later modify in Layout view or Design view to customize the content, format, or layout. In most cases, you will want to use one of the report tools to generate the report structure and then customize the report in a different view. However, if you require a report with several custom options, you can begin in Design view and build the report from scratch. Click the CREATE tab and then click the Report Design button in the Reports group to create a new report using Design view, as shown in Figure 5.1.

Creating a custom report in Design view involves using the same techniques that you learned in Chapter 4 for designing and building a custom form. You will add a title; connect a table or query to the report; add fields; and align, move, resize, and format controls the same way you would when customizing a form.

A report can contain up to five sections, each of which is described in Table 5.1. You can also add *Group Header* and *Group Footer* sections, which you can use to group records that contain repeating values in a field, such as a department or city. You will learn how to use these additional sections in Project 3. A report that is grouped by more than one field can have multiple *Group Header* and *Group Footer* sections.

Figure 5.1 Report Design View

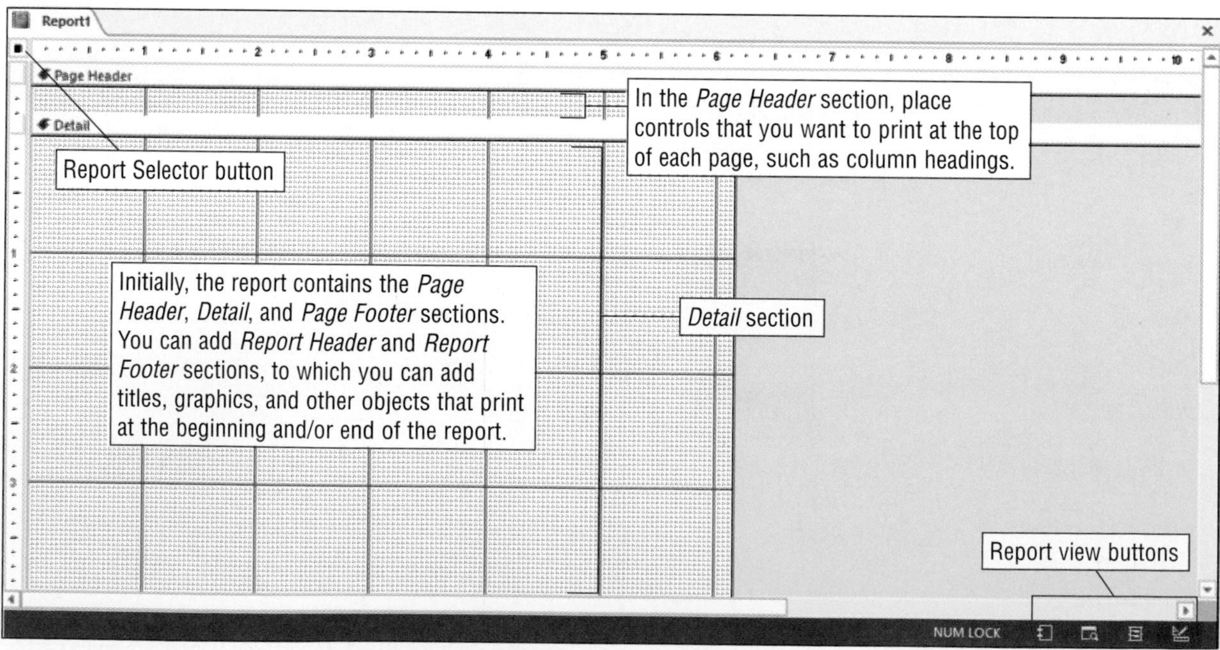

Table 5.1 Report Sections

Report Section	***Description***
Report Header	Content prints at the beginning of the report. Add controls to this section for the report title and company logo or another image.
Page Header	Content prints at the top of each page in the report. Add controls to this section for column headings in a tabular report format.
Detail	Add controls to this section for the fields from the table or query that make up the body of the report.
Page Footer	Content prints at the bottom of each page in the report. Add a control to this section to print a page number at the bottom of each page.
Report Footer	Content prints at the end of the report. Add a control in this section to print a grand total or perform another function, such as calculating the average, maximum, minimum, or count.

Project 1a Starting a New Report Using Design View and Adding a Title and Label Object

Part 1 of 5

1. Open **AL2-C5-RSRCompServ.accdb** and enable the content.
2. Click the CREATE tab and then click the Report Design button in the Reports group.

Step 2
Report
Report Design
Blank Report
Report Wizard
Labels
Reports

3. Add a title in the *Report Header* section of the report by completing the following steps:
   a. With the REPORT DESIGN TOOLS DESIGN tab active, click the Title button in the Header/Footer group. Access adds the *Report Header* section above the *Page Header* section and places a title object containing the selected text *Report1*.
   b. Type **RSR Computer Service Work Orders** and then press Enter.

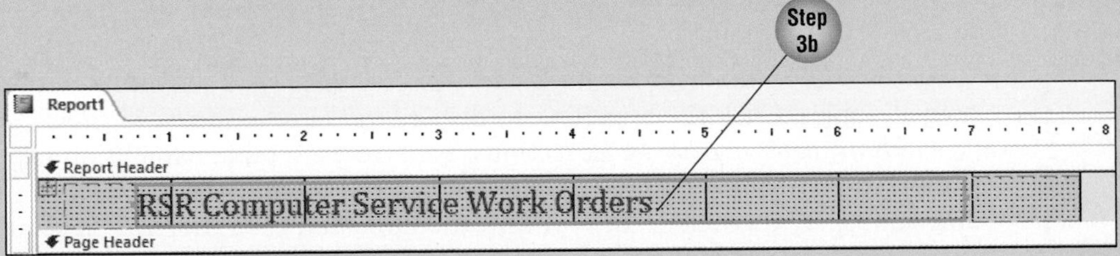

4. With the title control object still selected, click the REPORT DESIGN TOOLS FORMAT tab and then click the Center button in the Font group.
5. Drag the right edge of the report grid until it is aligned at the 8-inch position on the horizontal ruler.

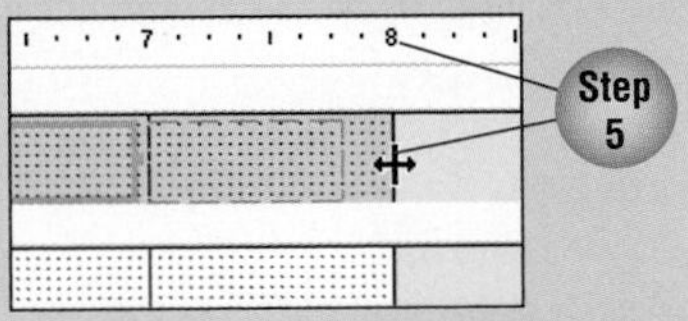

6. Scroll down the report until you can see the *Page Footer* and *Report Footer* sections. The *Report Footer* section was added to the design grid at the same time the *Report Header* section was added when the title was created in Step 3.

7. Drag the bottom edge of the *Report Footer* section down until the bottom of the report is aligned at the 0.5-inch position in the vertical ruler.
8. Click the REPORT DESIGN TOOLS DESIGN tab and then click the Label button in the Controls group. Add a label control object containing your first and last names at the left side of the *Report Footer* section.
9. Click in any blank area of the report to deselect the label control object.
10. Save the report and name it *WorkOrders*.

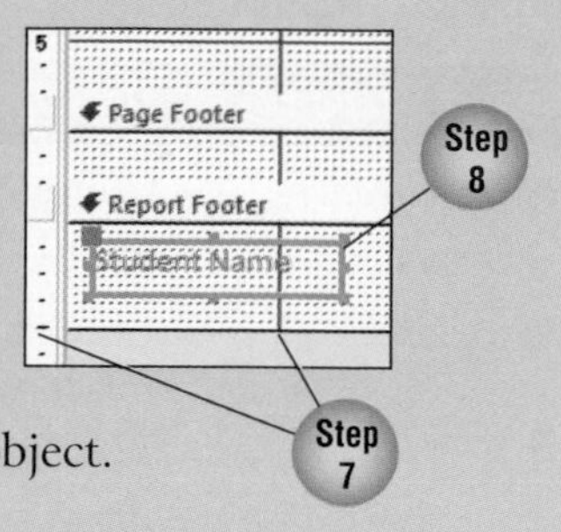

Connecting a Table or Query to a Report and Adding Fields

Quick Steps

Connect a Table or Query to a Report
1. Open report in Design view.
2. Double-click Report Selector button.
3. Click Data tab in Property Sheet task pane.
4. Click down-pointing arrow in *Record Source* property box.
5. Click desired table or query.
6. Close Property Sheet task pane.

Add Fields to a Report
1. Click Add Existing Fields button.
2. Drag field name(s) from Field List task pane to *Detail* section.

Add a Field from a Related Table
1. Open Field List task pane.
2. Click Show all tables hyperlink.
3. Click expand button next to desired table name in *Fields available in related tables* section.
4. Drag field name from related table list to *Detail* section.

Report Selector

Add Existing Fields

A new report that is started in Design view does not have a table or query associated with it. To view data in the report, Access needs to know the source from which to draw its data. As you would with a form, you connect a table or query to the report using the Record Source property in the report's Property Sheet task pane. Make sure to complete this step before you add fields to the *Detail* section.

The steps to connect a table or query to a report are the same as the steps to connect a table to a form. Double-click the Report Selector button located above the vertical ruler and to the left of the horizontal ruler to open the report's Property Sheet task pane. Click the Data tab and then select the table or query name in the drop-down list at the *Record Source* property box. Display the Field List task pane and then drag individual fields or a group of fields from the table or query to the *Detail* section. After adding the fields, you can move and resize the control objects as needed.

The Field List task pane displays in one of two states: showing one section only, with the fields from the table or query associated with the report, or showing two additional sections, with fields from other tables in the database. If the Field List task pane contains only the fields from the associated table or query, you can add fields from other tables by displaying other table names in the database within the Field List task pane.

At the top of the Field List task pane, Access displays a hyperlink with the text Show all tables. Click the hyperlink to display the *Fields available in related tables* and *Fields available in other tables* sections. Next to each table name is an expand button, which displays as a plus symbol. Click the expand button next to a table name to display the fields stored within the table and then drag the field name(s) to the *Detail* section of the report. You will perform these steps in Project 1b.

Project 1b Connecting a Table to a Report and Adding Fields

Part 2 of 5

1. With **AL2-C5-RSRCompServ.accdb** open and the WorkOrders report open in Design view, scroll up to the top of the report in the work area.
2. Connect the WorkOrders table to the report so that Access knows which fields to display in the Field List task pane by completing the following steps:
   a. Double-click the Report Selector button located at the top of the vertical ruler and to the left of the horizontal ruler to open the report's Property Sheet task pane.
   b. Click the Data tab in the Property Sheet task pane, click the down-pointing arrow in the *Record Source* property box, and then click *WorkOrders* at the drop-down list.
   c. Close the Property Sheet task pane.

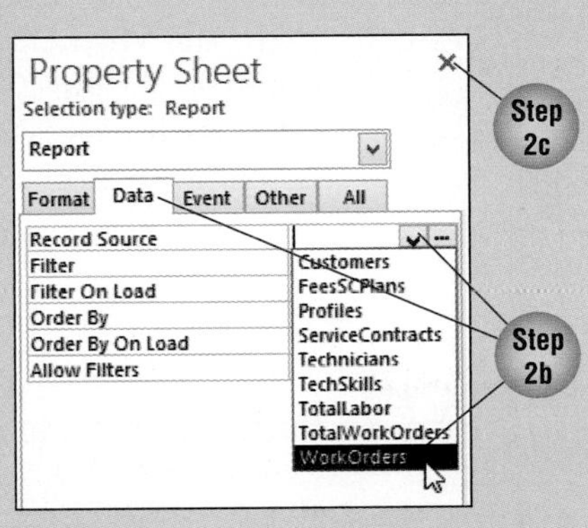

3. Click the Add Existing Fields button in the Tools group on the REPORT DESIGN TOOLS DESIGN tab to open the Field List task pane.
4. Add fields from the WorkOrders table and related fields from the Customers table by completing the following steps:
   a. Click the Show all tables hyperlink at the top of the Field List task pane. Access adds two sections to the pane. One section contains related tables and the other contains other tables in the database that do not have established relationships with the report's table. Next to each table name is an expand button (plus symbol), which is used to display field names for the table. ***Note: Skip this step if the hyperlink at the top of the Field List task pane displays Show only fields in the current record source. This means that the other sections have already been added to the pane.***

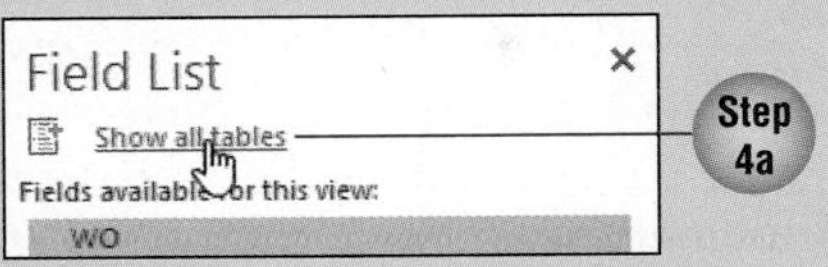

   b. Click the expand button next to *Customers* in the *Fields available in related tables* section of the Field List task pane. Access expands the list to display the field names in the Customers table.

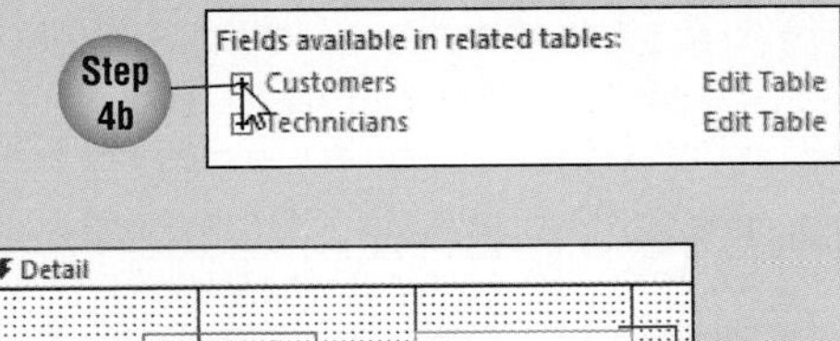

   c. Drag the *WO*, *CustID*, *WODate*, and *Descr* fields from the WorkOrders table to the design grid as shown at the right.
   d. Drag the *FName* and *LName* fields from the Customers table to the design grid as shown at the right. Notice that the Customers table and field names move to the *Fields available for this view* section in the Field List task pane once you add the first field from the Customers table to the *Detail* section.

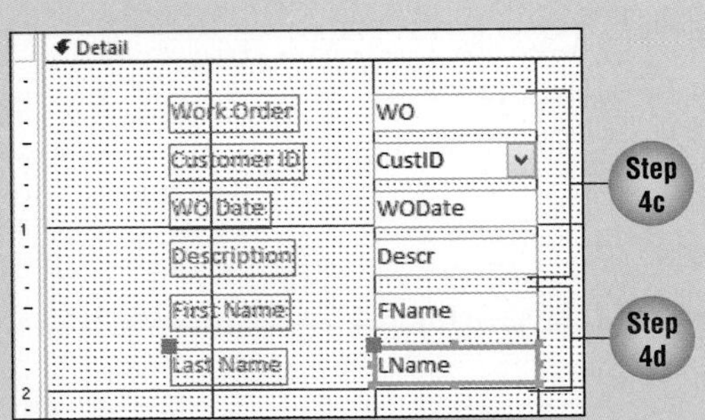

5. Close the Field List task pane.
6. Save the report.

Quick Steps

Move Controls to Another Section

1. Open report in Design view.
2. Select controls to be moved.
3. Click HOME tab.
4. Click Cut button.
5. Click bar of section to which to move controls.
6. Click Paste button.
7. Deselect controls.

Moving Control Objects to Another Section

When a field is added to the *Detail* section of a report, a label control object containing the caption or field name is placed to the left of a text box control object that displays the field value from the record when the report is viewed or printed. Recall from Chapter 4 that the same thing happens when you customize a form.

In the WorkOrders report, the label control object for each field needs to be moved to the *Page Header* section so that the field names or captions print at the top of each page as column headings. In Project 1c, you will cut the controls from the *Detail* section and paste them into the *Page Header* section.

Project 1c Moving Controls to Another Section — Part 3 of 5

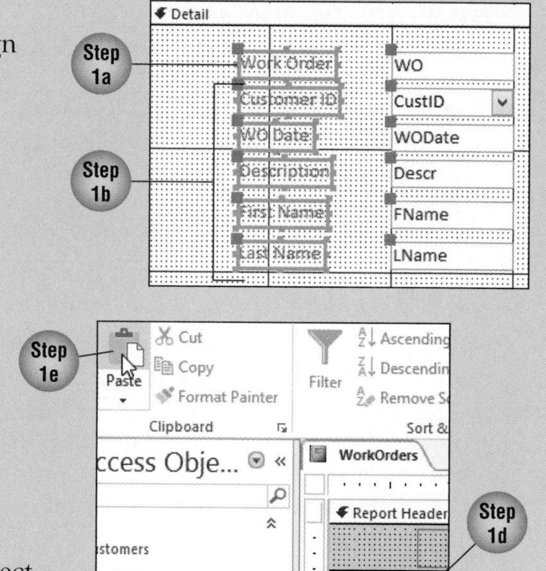

1. With **AL2-C5-RSRCompServ.accdb** open and the WorkOrders report open in Design view, move the label control objects from the *Detail* section to the *Page Header* section by completing the following steps:
   a. Click to select the *Work Order* label control object.
   b. Hold down Shift and click to select each of the other label control objects.
   c. Click the HOME tab and then click the Cut button in the Clipboard group.
   d. Click the *Page Header* section bar.
   e. Click the Paste button in the Clipboard group. (Do not click the button arrow.) Access pastes the label control objects and expands the *Page Header* section.
   f. Deselect the controls.
2. Click to select the *Customer ID* label control object and then move the control to the top of the *Page Header* section next to the *Work Order* label control object by hovering the mouse pointer over the *Customer ID* label control object until the four-headed arrow move icon displays and then dragging the object to the location shown at the right.
3. Move the remaining four label control objects to the top of the *Page Header* section in the order shown in the image at the top of the next page by completing a step similar to Step 2.

4. Drag the top of the *Detail* section bar up until the top of the bar is aligned at the bottom edge of the label control objects in the *Page Header* section, as shown below.

5. Save the report.

Applying a Theme

Apply a theme to a report using the Themes button on the REPORT DESIGN TOOLS DESIGN tab. The theme sets the default colors and fonts for the report. The themes available in Access align with the themes available in Word, Excel, and PowerPoint, allowing you to maintain the same consistent look in your Access reports that you have in your documents, worksheets, and presentations. Note that changing a theme for one report in a database automatically changes the theme for all of the reports and forms in the database.

Quick Steps

Apply a Theme

1. Open report in Design view.
2. Click REPORT DESIGN TOOLS DESIGN tab.
3. Click Themes button.
4. Click desired theme.

Themes

Project 1d **Moving Controls, Resizing Controls, and Applying a Theme** **Part 4 of 5**

1. With **AL2-C5-RSRCompServ.accdb** open and the WorkOrders report open in Design view, move each text box control object in the *Detail* section below their associated label control objects in the *Page Header* section so that the field values will align below the correct column headings in the report, as shown below.

2. Click the REPORT DESIGN TOOLS DESIGN tab, click the View button arrow in the Views group, and then click *Print Preview* at the drop-down list. (Note that there is also a Print Preview button in the view area at the right side of the Status bar.) Notice that the field value in the *WO Date* column displays pound symbols (#), indicating that the field's text box control object needs to be widened. ***Note: If you receive an error message with the text* The section width is greater than the page width, *click OK.***

View Themes Colors Fonts

Report View

Print Preview

Layout View

Design View

Step 2

3. Return to Design view by clicking the Design View button in the view area at the right side of the Status bar, next to the Zoom slider.

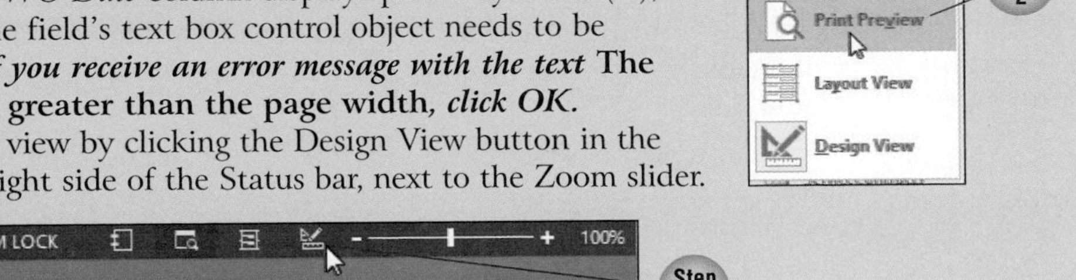

4. Resize the *WODate* text box control in the *Detail* section so that the right edge of the control meets the left edge of the *Descr* text box control object.
5. Resize the *Descr* text box control in the *Detail* section so that the right edge of the control is aligned at approximately the 7.5-inch position on the horizontal ruler.
6. Deselect the *Descr* control object.
7. Click the Themes button in the Themes group on the REPORT DESIGN TOOLS DESIGN tab and then click *Organic* at the drop-down gallery (second option in the second row).

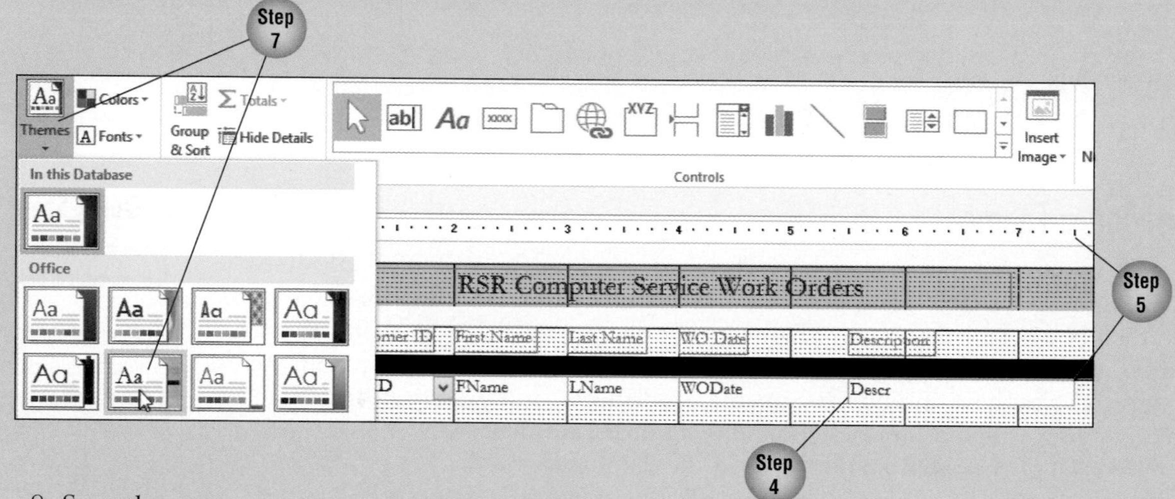

8. Save the report.
9. Display the report in Print Preview to review the changes made in this project. Switch back to Design view when finished. ***Note: Do not be concerned if you see only one record in the report. Currently, the* Detail *section is sized so that only one record can fit on a page. This will be corrected in the next project.***

Quick Steps

Insert a Subreport

1. Open report in Design view.
2. Make sure *Use Control Wizards* is active.
3. Click Subform/Subreport button.
4. Drag crosshairs to desired height and width in *Detail* section.
5. Click Next.
6. Choose table or query and fields.
7. Click Next.
8. Choose field by which to link main report with subreport.
9. Click Next.
10. Click Finish.

Subform/Subreport

Inserting a Subreport

A ***subreport*** is a report that is inserted inside another report. Similar to a nested query, a subreport allows you to reuse a group of fields, formatting, and calculations in more than one report without having to recreate the setup each time.

The Subform/Subreport button in the Controls group on the REPORT DESIGN TOOLS DESIGN tab is used to insert a subreport into a report. The report into which the subreport is inserted is called the ***main report***. Adding a related table or query as a subreport creates a control object within the main report that can be moved, formatted, and resized independently of the other control objects. Make sure the Use Control Wizards button is toggled on in the expanded Controls group before you click the Subform/Subreport button. This will enable you to add the subreport using the SubReport Wizard, as shown in Figure 5.2.

A subreport is stored as a separate object outside the main report. You will notice an additional report name in the Navigation pane with *subreport* at the end. Do not delete a subreport object in the Navigation pane. If the subreport object is deleted, the main report will no longer be able to display the fields from the related table or query in the report.

Figure 5.2 First Dialog Box in SubReport Wizard

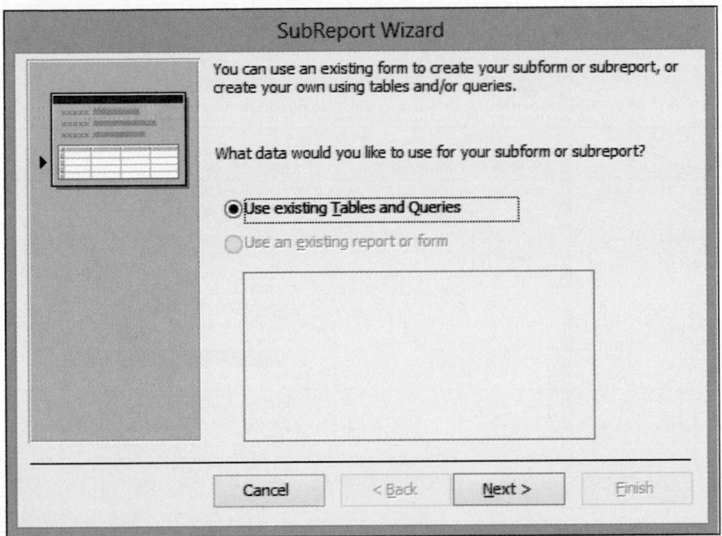
SubReport Wizard
You can use an existing form to create your subform or subreport, or create your own using tables and/or queries.
What data would you like to use for your subform or subreport?
Use existing Tables and Queries
Use an existing report or form
Cancel
< Back
Next >
Finish

Project 1e Inserting a Subreport

Part 5 of 5

1. With **AL2-C5-RSRCompServ.accdb** open and the WorkOrders report open in Design view, insert a subreport into the WorkOrders report with fields from a query for the service date, labor, and parts for each work order by completing the following steps:
   a. By default, the Use Control Wizards button is toggled on in the Controls group. Click the More button in the Controls group to expand the Controls group and view three rows of buttons and the Controls drop-down list. View the current status of the Use Control Wizards button—if it displays with a pink background, the feature is active. If the button is pink, click in a blank area to close the expanded Controls list. If the feature is not active (displays with a white background), click the Use Control Wizards button to turn on the feature.
   b. Click the More button in the Controls group and then click the Subform/Subreport button.
   c. Move the crosshairs with the subreport icon attached to the *Detail* section below the *WO* text box control object and then drag down and to the right to create a subreport object of the approximate height and width shown below. When you release the mouse, the SubReport Wizard begins.

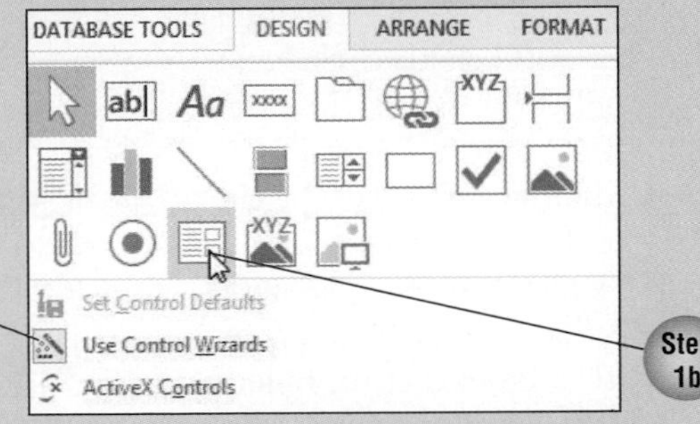
DATABASE TOOLS
DESIGN
ARRANGE
FORMAT
Set Control Defaults
Use Control Wizards
ActiveX Controls
A pink background means the Use Control Wizards button is toggled on. Check the status and click the button to turn on the feature if necessary in Step 1a.
Step 1b

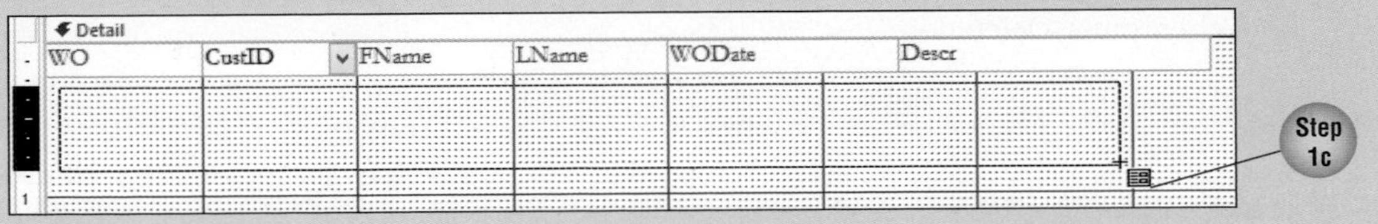
Detail
WO
CustID
FName
LName
WODate
Descr
Step 1c

d. With *Use existing Tables and Queries* already selected at the first SubReport Wizard dialog box, click Next.

e. At the second SubReport Wizard dialog box, select the query fields to be displayed in the subreport by completing the following steps:

1) Click the down-pointing arrow next to the *Tables/ Queries* option box and then click *Query: TotalWorkOrders* at the drop-down list.
2) Move all of the fields from the *Available Fields* list box to the *Selected Fields* list box.
3) Click Next.

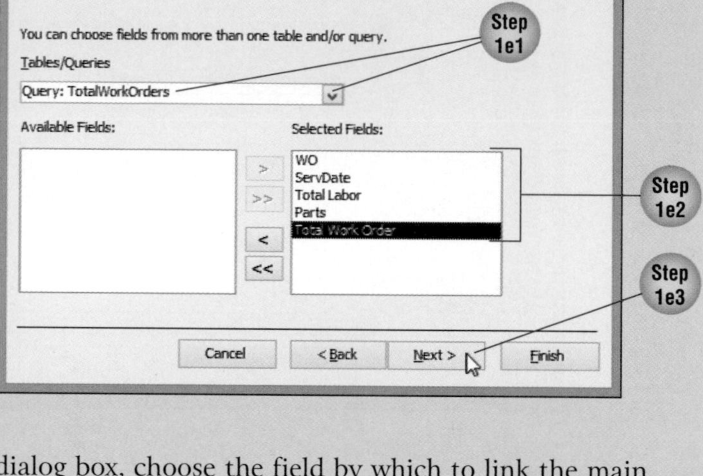

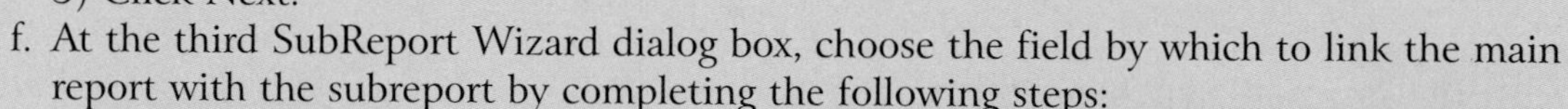

f. At the third SubReport Wizard dialog box, choose the field by which to link the main report with the subreport by completing the following steps:

1) With *Choose from a list* and the first option in the list box selected, read the description of the linked field that displays below the list box. The text indicates that the main report will be linked to the subreport using the *CustID* field. This is not the correct field—you want your report to show the service date, labor, and parts based on the work order number.
2) Click the second option in the list box and then read the text below the list box.
3) Since the second option indicates the two reports will be linked using the *WO* field, click Next.

g. Click Finish at the last SubReport Wizard dialog box to accept the default subreport name *TotalWorkOrders subreport*.

2. Access inserts the subreport with a label control object above it that contains the name of the subreport. Click the label control displaying the text *TotalWorkOrders subreport* to select the object and then press Delete.

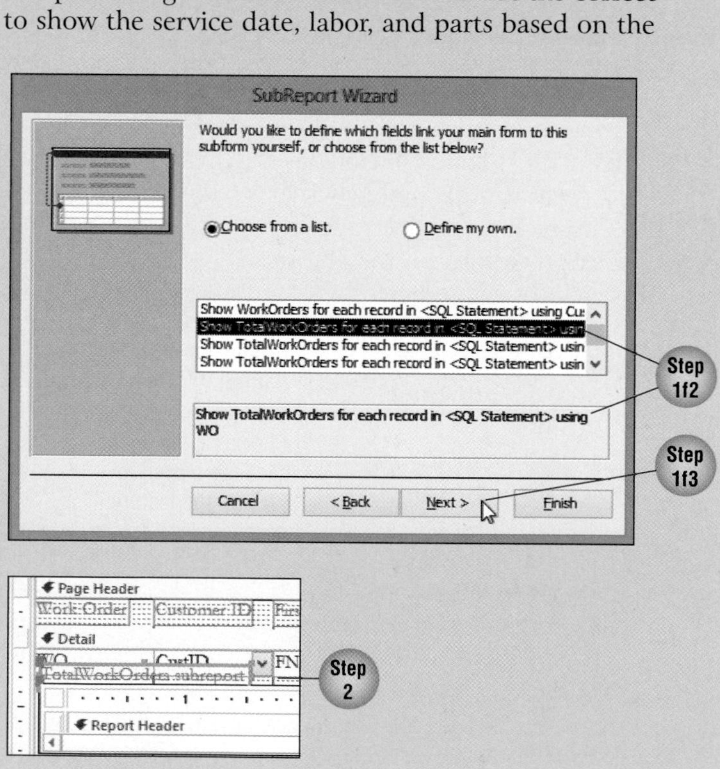

3. Click the Report View button in the Views group on the REPORT DESIGN TOOLS DESIGN tab. Note that a Report View button is also located in the View group at the right side of the Status bar (the first button). Report view is not the same as Print Preview. Report view displays the report with data in the fields and is useful for viewing reports within the database. However, this view does not show how the report will look when printed. For printing purposes, always use Print Preview to resize and adjust control objects.
4. Notice that the work order number in the subreport is the same work order number that is displayed in the first record in the main report.

The main report and subreport are correctly linked by the *WO* field.

WorkOrders

RSR Computer Service Work Orders

Work Order	Customer ID	First Name	Last Name	WO Date	Description
65012	1000	Jade	Fleming	Mon Sep 07 2015	Bi-annual computer maintenance

Work Order	Service Date	Total Labor	Parts	Total Work Order
65012	Mon Sep 07 2015	$37.50	$10.15	$47.65

5. Switch back to Design view.
6. Now that you know the subreport is linked correctly to the main report, you do not need to display the work order number in the subreport. Delete the work order number control objects in the subreport by completing the following steps:
   a. Click to select the subreport control object and then drag the bottom middle sizing handle down to increase the height of the subreport until you can see all of the controls in the *Report Header* and *Detail* sections.
   b. Click to select the *Work Order* label control object in the *Report Header* section, hold down Shift, and then click the *WO* text box control object in the *Detail* section in the subreport.

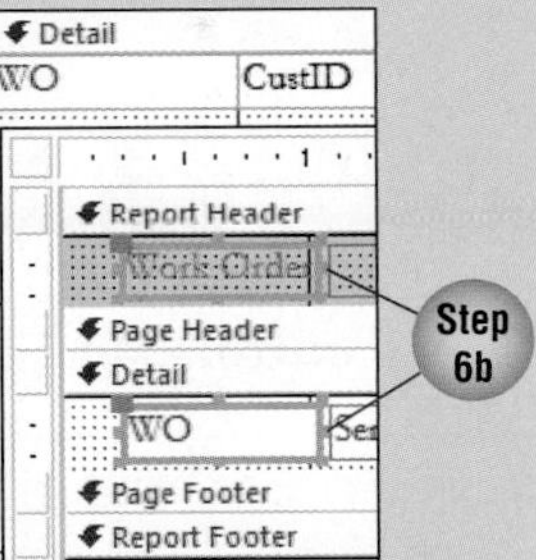

   c. Press Delete.
   d. Select all of the label control objects in the *Report Header* section and all of the text box control objects in the *Detail* section. Move the control objects to the left so that the left edges of the *Service Date* control objects are at the left margin. Click outside the subreport to deselect the control objects.
7. Click to select the subreport control object and then drag the bottom middle sizing handle of the control up until the height of the subreport is approximately 0.5 inch.
8. Scroll down the report until you can see the *Page Footer* section bar.
9. Drag the top of the *Page Footer* section bar up until the section bar is just below the subreport control object in the *Detail* section, as shown below.

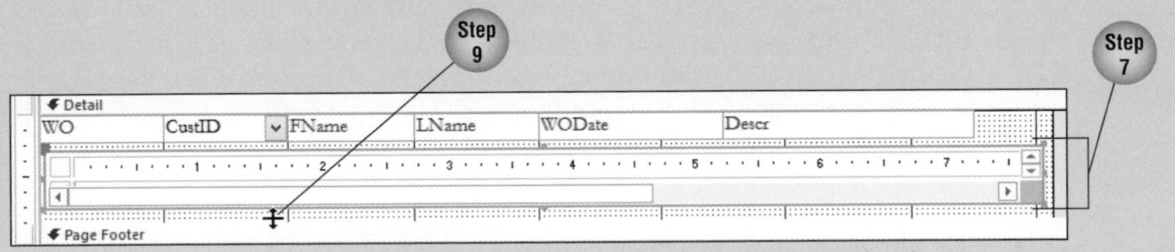

10. Save the report and then switch to Report view to view the revised report. Resizing the *Detail* section in Step 9 allows more records and related subreport records to display on the page because the spaces between sections are reduced.

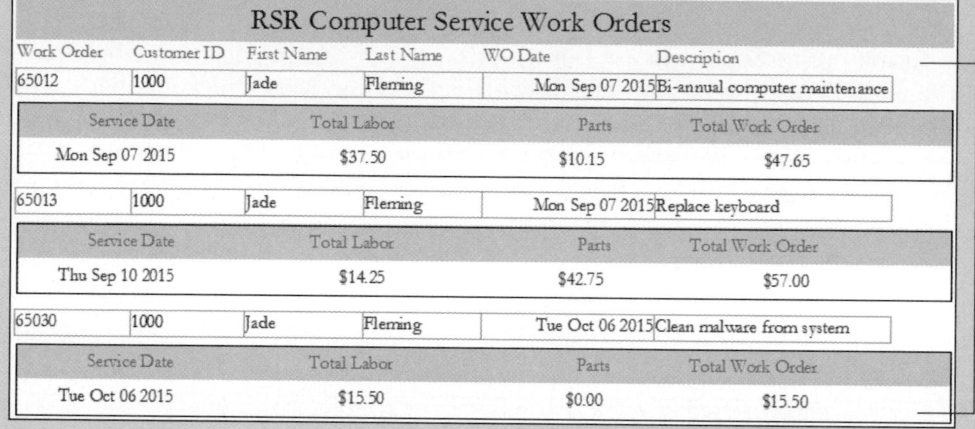

Reducing the height of the *Detail* section allows Access to display more records on the page.

11. Close the report.

Project 2 Add Features and Enhance a Report — 2 Parts

You will modify the WorkOrders report to add page numbers, date and time controls, and graphics.

Adding Page Numbers and Date and Time Controls to a Report

Quick Steps

Add Page Numbers
1. Open Report in Design view.
2. Click Page Numbers button.
3. Select desired format, position, and alignment options.
4. Click OK.

Page Numbers

When you create a report using the Report tool, page numbers and the current date and time are automatically added to the top right of the report. The Report Wizard automatically inserts the current date at the bottom left and page numbers at the bottom right of the report.

In Design view, you can add page numbers to a report using the Page Numbers button in the Header/Footer group on the REPORT DESIGN TOOLS DESIGN tab. Click the button to open the Page Numbers dialog box, shown in Figure 5.3. Choose the desired format, position, and alignment for the page number and then click OK. Access inserts a control object in the *Page Header* or *Page Footer* section, depending on the *Position* option selected in the dialog box. Including page numbers in a report is a good idea in case the pages become shuffled and need to be put back into sequential order.

Add the current date and/or time in the *Report Header* section by clicking the Date and Time button in the Header/Footer group to open the Date and Time dialog box, shown in Figure 5.4. By default, both the *Include Date* and *Include Time* check boxes contain check marks. Access creates one control object for the desired date format and a separate control object for the desired time format. Access places the date control object above the time control object, with both aligned at the right edge of the *Report Header* section. Once the controls have been inserted, you can move them to another section in the report. Adding a date and/or time control means that the current date and/or time the report is printed will be included on the printout. This information tells readers of the report whether the information they are seeing is current. At a minimum, you should always include a date control. Depending on the end user's needs, the time control may or may not be necessary.

Quick Steps

Add the Date and/or Time

1. Open report in Design view.
2. Click Date and Time button.
3. Select desired date and/or time options.
4. Click OK.

Date and Time

Figure 5.3 Page Numbers Dialog Box

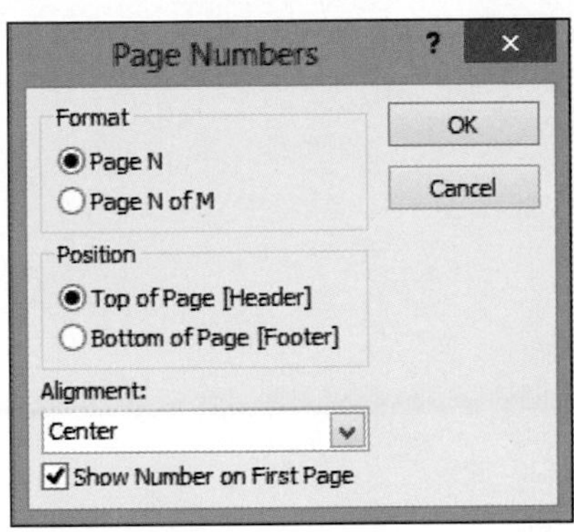

Figure 5.4 Date and Time Dialog Box

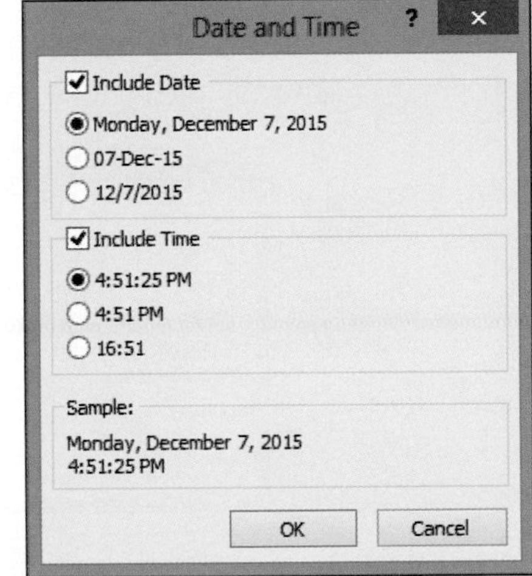

Project 2a Adding Page Numbers and the Date and Time to a Report

Part 1 of 2

1. With **AL2-C5-RSRCompServ.accdb** open, right-click *WorkOrders* in the Report group in the Navigation pane and then click *Design View* at the shortcut menu.
2. When the subreport was inserted in Project 1e, the width of the report may have been automatically extended beyond the page width. Look at the Report Selector button. If a green diagonal triangle displays in the upper left corner of the button, correct the page width by completing the following steps. Skip this step if the Report Selector button does not display with a green diagonal triangle.
   a. Click the subreport control object to display the orange border and sizing handles. Point to the orange border and then drag the subreport control object left until the left edge of the control object is at the left edge of the *Detail* section. Next, drag the right middle sizing handle left to decrease the subreport width until the right edge of the subreport control object is aligned with the right edge of the *Descr* text box control object above it.

b. Click the green triangle to display the error-checking options button and then click the button to display the drop-down list of options.

c. Click *Remove Extra Report Space* at the drop-down list to automatically decrease the width of the report. Notice that the green diagonal triangle is removed from the Report Selector button once the report width has been corrected.

3. Add page numbers at the bottom center of each page by completing the following steps:

   a. Click the Page Numbers button in the Header/Footer group on the REPORT DESIGN TOOLS DESIGN tab.

   b. Click *Page N of M* in the *Format* section of the Page Numbers dialog box.

   c. Click *Bottom of Page [Footer]* in the *Position* section.

   d. With *Alignment* set to *Center* and a check mark in the *Show Number on First Page* check box, click OK. Access adds a control object in the center of the *Page Footer* section with the codes required to print the page numbers in the desired format.

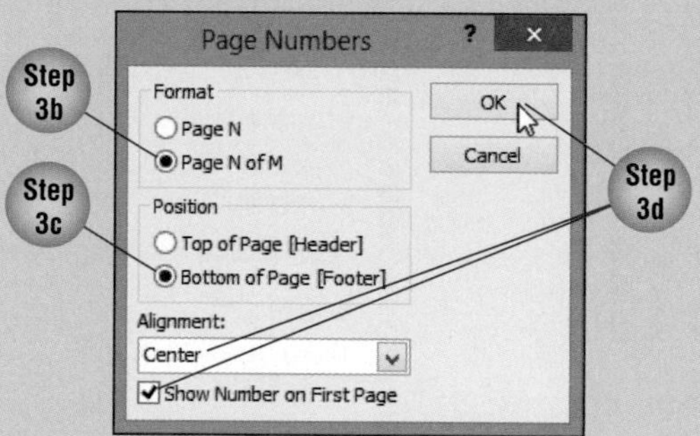

4. Add the current date and time to the end of the report along with a label control object containing the text *Date and Time Printed:* by completing the following steps:

   a. Click the Date and Time button in the Header/Footer group on the REPORT DESIGN TOOLS DESIGN tab.

   b. Click the second option in the *Include Date* section in the Date and Time dialog box, which displays the date in the format *dd-mmm-yy*—for example, *07-Dec-15*.

   c. Click the second option in the *Include Time* section, which displays the time in the format *hh:mm AM/PM*—for example, *2:40 PM*.

   d. Click OK. Access adds two control objects, one above the other, at the right side of the *Report Header* section with the date code *=Date()* and time code *=Time()*.

   e. Select the date and time control objects added to the *Report Header* section. Click the HOME tab and then click the Cut button in the Clipboard group.

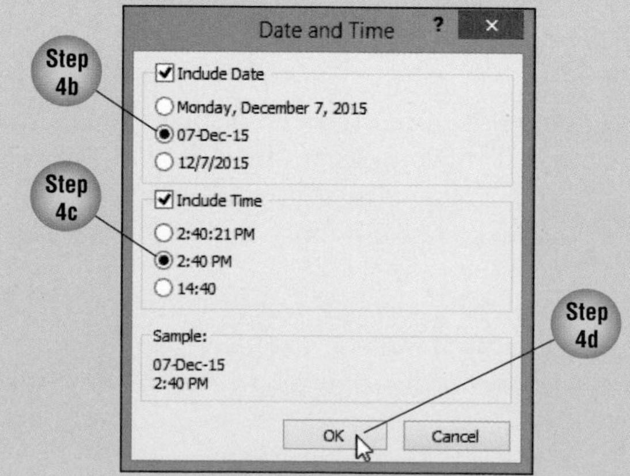

f. Click the *Report Footer* section bar and then click the Paste button in the Clipboard group. Access pastes the two objects at the left side of the *Report Footer* section. With the date and time control objects still selected, position the mouse pointer on the orange border until the pointer displays with the four-headed arrow move icon and then drag the controls to the right side of the *Report Footer* section, aligning the right edge of the controls near the right edge of the report grid.

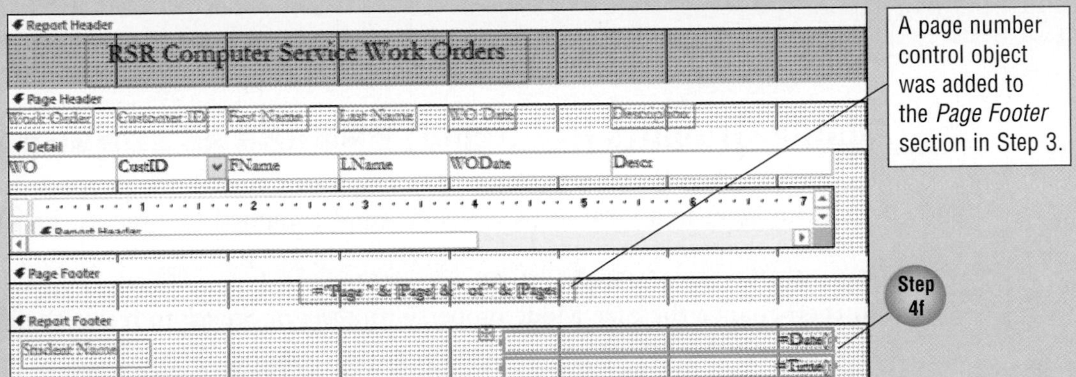

g. Resize and then move the date and time controls to arrange them as shown at the right.

h. Create the two label control objects, type the text **Date Printed:** and **Time Printed:**, and then position them to the left of the date control object and the time control object, as shown at the right.

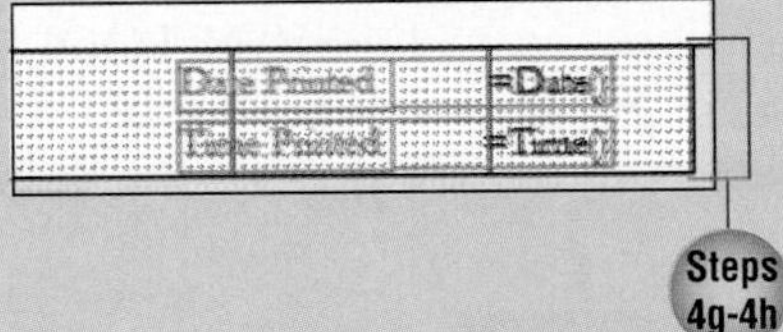

5. Save the report and then display Print Preview.
6. Scroll to the bottom of the first page to view the page number.
7. Click the Last Page button in the Page Navigation bar to scroll to the last page in the report and view the date and time.
8. Notice that in Print Preview, the subreport data is being cut off at the right edge of the report, meaning that the total work order value is not visible. Exit Print Preview to switch back to Design view.
9. Adjust the size and placement of the subreport control objects by completing the following steps:
   a. Since the subreport's control objects are not visible within the WorkOrders report, it is easier to work within the separate TotalWorkOrders subreport to make changes to its contents. Close the WorkOrders report.
   b. Right-click the *TotalWorkOrders* subreport in the Navigation pane and then click *Design View* at the shortcut menu.
   c. Press Ctrl + A to select all of the objects. (Ctrl + A is the shortcut for Select All.)
   d. Position the mouse pointer on the edge of any selected control until the four-headed arrow move icon appears and then drag the controls to the left edge of the report grid.
   e. Click in any blank area to deselect the controls and then drag the right edge of the grid left to approximately the 7-inch position on the horizontal ruler.

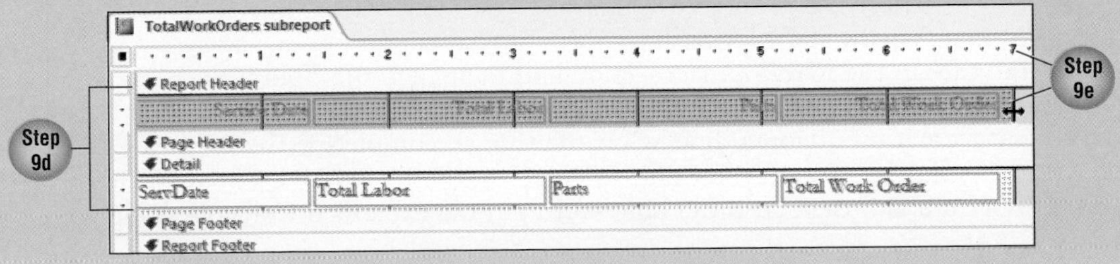

f. Click to select the *Parts* label control object in the *Page Header* section and then drag the right middle sizing handle left until the right edge of the control aligns at the 5-inch position on the horizontal ruler.

10. Save and close the TotalWorkOrders subreport.
11. Open the WorkOrders report. Notice that the subreport data is no longer cut off at the right side.
12. Display the report in Design view.

Adding Graphics to a Report

The same techniques that you learned in Chapter 4 for adding pictures or clip art or drawing lines in a form in Design view can be applied to a report. Recall from Chapter 4 that when a control object containing a clip art is resized, parts of the image can be cut off. Display the Property Sheet task pane for the clip art object and then change the Size Mode property to *Zoom* or *Stretch* to resize the image to the height and width of the control object.

A company logo or other company artwork that is available in a standard picture file format (such as .gif, .jpg, or .png) can be inserted in an image control object. Click the Insert Image button in the Controls group on the REPORT DESIGN TOOLS DESIGN tab, browse to the drive and folder containing the image, double-click the image file name, and then drag to create an image control object of the desired height and width within the report.

Insert Image

Project 2b **Adding Graphics and Formatting Controls** **Part 2 of 2**

1. With **AL2-C5-RSRCompServ.accdb** open and the WorkOrders report open in Design view, insert a company logo in the report by completing the following steps:
   a. Position the mouse pointer on the top of the *Page Header* section bar until the pointer displays an up-and-down-pointing arrow with a horizontal line in the middle and then drag down approximately 0.5 inch to increase the height of the *Report Header* section.
   b. Click the Insert Image button in the Controls group on the REPORT DESIGN TOOLS DESIGN tab and then click *Browse* at the drop-down list.
   c. At the Insert Picture dialog box, navigate to the drive and/or folder for the AL2C5 data files on your storage medium and then double-click the file named ***RSRlogo.png***.
   d. Position the crosshairs with the image icon attached at the top of the *Report Header* section near the 6-inch position on the horizontal ruler and then drag to create an image control object of the approximate height and width shown.

2. Select the title in the *Report Header* section and then click the Bold button in the Font group on the REPORT DESIGN TOOLS FORMAT tab.
3. Draw and format a horizontal line below the title by completing the following steps:
   a. Click the More button in the Controls group on the REPORT DESIGN TOOLS DESIGN tab and then click the Line button in the expanded Controls group.

b. Position the crosshairs with the line icon attached below the first letter in the title in the *Report Header* section, hold down the Shift key, drag to the right, release the mouse below the last letter in the title, and then release the Shift key.
c. Click the REPORT DESIGN TOOLS FORMAT tab and then click the Shape Outline button in the Control Formatting group.
d. Point to *Line Thickness* and then click *3 pt* (fourth option).
e. With the line still selected, click the Shape Outline button, click *Blue-Gray, Accent 3* (seventh option in the first row of the *Theme Colors* section), and then deselect the line.

4. Draw and format a horizontal line below the report's column headings by completing the following steps:
   a. Drag the top of the *Detail* section bar down approximately 0.25 inch to add grid space in the *Page Header* section.
   b. Click the REPORT DESIGN TOOLS DESIGN tab, click the More button in the Controls group, and then click the Line button in the expanded Controls group.
   c. Draw a straight horizontal line that extends the width of the report along the bottom of the label control objects in the *Page Header* section.
   d. Click the Shape Outline button on the REPORT DESIGN TOOLS FORMAT tab, point to *Line Thickness*, and then click *2 pt*. Change the line color to the same blue-gray you applied to the line below the report title.
   e. Deselect the line.

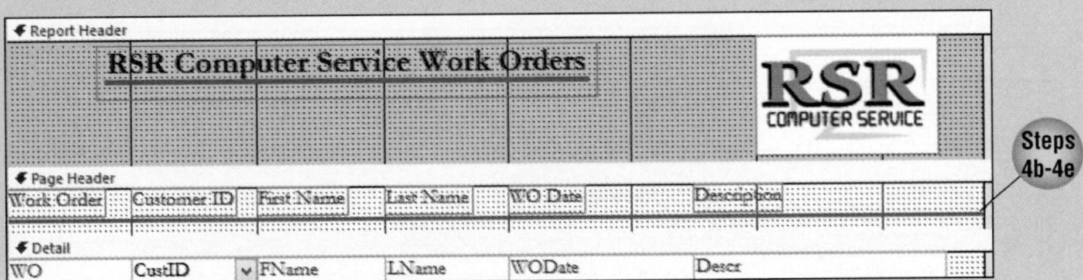

5. Format, move, and resize control objects as follows:
   a. Select all of the label control objects in the *Page Header* section, apply bold formatting, change the font size to 12 points, and then apply the Blue-Gray, Accent 3, Darker 50% font color (seventh option in the last row of the *Theme Colors* section).
   b. Resize the controls as needed to show all of the label text after increasing the font size.
   c. Move the report title and the line below it until the first *R* in the title is aligned at the 1-inch position on the horizontal ruler.
   d. Move the *WO Date* label control object in the *Page Header* section until the left edge of the object is aligned at the 4.5-inch position on the horizontal ruler.
   e. Click the *Report Header* section bar, click the Shape Fill button in the Control Formatting group on the REPORT DESIGN TOOLS FORMAT tab, and then click *White, Background 1* (first option in the first row of the *Theme Colors* section).
   f. Select all of the text box control objects in the *Detail* section. Open the Property Sheet task pane, click the Format tab, click in the *Border Style* property box, click the down-pointing arrow that appears, and then click *Transparent* at the drop-down list. This removes the border around the data in the fields.

g. With all of the text box control objects still selected, click the *Fore Color* property box on the Format tab of the Property Sheet task pane. Click the Build button to open the color palette and then click *Black, Text 1* (second option in the first row of the *Theme Colors* section).

h. Deselect the text box control objects and then select the *WODate* text box control object. Click in the *Width* property box in the Property Sheet task pane, change *1.5* to *1.4*, and then close the Property Sheet task pane.

6. Display the report in Report view.
7. Compare your report with the partial report shown in Figure 5.5. If necessary, return to Design view; make adjustments to the format, alignment, or position of control objects; and then redisplay the report in Report view.
8. Save the report.
9. Print the report. ***Note: This report is five pages long. Check with your instructor before printing it.***
10. Close the WorkOrders report.

Figure 5.5 Partial View of Completed WorkOrders Report

RSR Computer Service Work Orders

RSR COMPUTER SERVICE

Work Order	Customer ID	First Name	Last Name	WO Date	Description
65012	1000	Jade	Fleming	Mon Sep 07 2015	Bi-annual computer maintenance

Service Date	Total Labor	Parts	Total Work Order
Mon Sep 07 2015	$37.50	$10.15	$47.65

Work Order	Customer ID	First Name	Last Name	WO Date	Description
65013	1000	Jade	Fleming	Mon Sep 07 2015	Replace keyboard

Service Date	Total Labor	Parts	Total Work Order
Thu Sep 10 2015	$14.25	$42.75	$57.00

Work Order	Customer ID	First Name	Last Name	WO Date	Description
65030	1000	Jade	Fleming	Tue Oct 06 2015	Clean malware from system

Service Date	Total Labor	Parts	Total Work Order
Tue Oct 06 2015	$15.50	$0.00	$15.50

Project 3 Group Records and Add Functions to Count and Sum

3 Parts

You will create a new report using the Report Wizard and then modify the report in Design view to add count and sum functions.

Grouping Records and Adding Functions and a Calculated Field in a Report

A field that contains repeated values—such as a department, city, or name—is an appropriate field on which to group records in a report. For example, you could organize a report to show all of the records for the same department or city. By summarizing the records by a common field value, you can also add totals using functions to calculate the sum, average, maximum, minimum, or count for each group. For example, a report similar to the partial report shown in Figure 5.6 that organizes work orders by customer allows the owners of RSR Computer Service to see which customer has provided the most revenue to their service business. In this report, the *CustID* field (column heading *Customer ID*) is used to group the records and a Sum function has been added to each group.

As you learned in Level 1, Chapter 6, you can use the Report Wizard to group records in a report. At the Report Wizard dialog box, shown in Figure 5.7, you can double-click a field name in the field list box to add a grouping level. The preview window updates to display the grouped field in blue. More than one grouping level can be added to a report. If you change your mind after adding a grouping level, use the Remove Field button (the button with the left-pointing arrow) to remove the grouped level. Use the Priority buttons (the buttons with up-pointing and down-pointing arrows) to change the grouping order when you have multiple grouped fields.

If you created a report using the Report Wizard and did not specify a grouping level, you can group records after the report has been generated using Layout view or Design view. In Layout view, click the Group & Sort button in

Quick Steps

Group Records Using the Report Wizard

1. Click CREATE tab.
2. Click Report Wizard button.
3. Choose table or query and fields.
4. Click Next.
5. If necessary, remove default grouped field name.
6. Double-click field name by which to group records.
7. Click Next.
8. Choose field(s) by which to sort.
9. Click Next.
10. Choose layout options.
11. Click Next.
12. Enter title for report.
13. Click Finish.

Figure 5.6 Example Report with Work Order Records Grouped by Customer

RSR COMPUTER SERVICE

Work Orders by Customer

09-Dec-15
4:54 PM

Customer ID	First Name	Last Name	Work Order	Description	Service Date	Total Work Order
1000	Jade	Fleming	65012	Bi-annual computer maintenance	Mon Sep 07 2015	$47.65
			65013	Replace keyboard	Thu Sep 10 2015	$57.00
			65030	Clean malware from system	Tue Oct 06 2015	$15.50
			65033	Install Windows 8	Tue Oct 13 2015	$433.25
					Customer Total:	$553.40
1005	Cayla	Fahri	65014	Replace power supply	Thu Sep 10 2015	$115.27
			65024	Install malware protection	Thu Sep 24 2015	$91.00
					Customer Total:	$206.27
1008	Leslie	Carmichael	65015	Restore operating system	Fri Sep 11 2015	$67.50
			65032	Install second hard drive	Tue Oct 13 2015	$485.75
			65036	Set up home network	Fri Oct 16 2015	$152.72
			65044	DVD drive is not working	Fri Oct 23 2015	$85.40
					Customer Total:	$791.37

The report is grouped on the *CustID* field (displays with column heading *Customer ID*), allowing owners to see how many calls were made to each customer and how much revenue each customer generated.

Figure 5.7 Grouping by a Field Using the Report Wizard

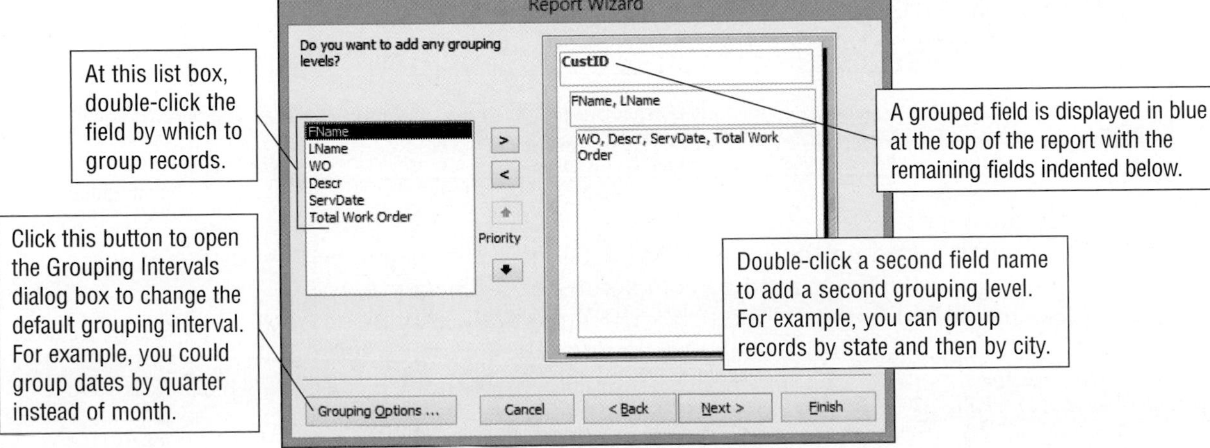

Report Wizard
Do you want to add any grouping levels?
FName
LName
WO
Descr
ServDate
Total Work Order
Priority
CustID
FName, LName
WO, Descr, ServDate, Total Work Order
Grouping Options ...
Cancel
< Back
Next >
Finish
At this list box, double-click the field by which to group records.
Click this button to open the Grouping Intervals dialog box to change the default grouping interval. For example, you could group dates by quarter instead of month.
A grouped field is displayed in blue at the top of the report with the remaining fields indented below.
Double-click a second field name to add a second grouping level. For example, you can group records by state and then by city.

Use Layout view to group records using the Group, Sort, and Total pane, because Access will do all of the work for you after you select the group field. In Design view, Access creates the *Group Header* section but does not automatically place the field's text box control within the group section. You have to do that manually.

Group & Sort

the Grouping & Totals group on the REPORT LAYOUT TOOLS DESIGN tab. In Design view, click the Group & Sort button in the Grouping & Totals group on the REPORT DESIGN TOOLS DESIGN tab. Clicking the button in either view opens the Group, Sort, and Total pane, shown in Figure 5.8, at the bottom of the work area. Click the Add a group button and then click the field name by which to group records in the pop-up list.

Figure 5.8 Group, Sort, and Total Pane

Group, Sort, and Total ×

Add a group   Add a sort

Project 3a Creating a Report with a Grouping Level Using the Report Wizard Part 1 of 3

1. With **AL2-C5-RSRCompServ.accdb** open, modify the TotalWorkOrders query to add two fields you want to include in a report by completing the following steps:
   a. Open the TotalWorkOrders query in Design view.
   b. Drag the *CustID* field from the *WorkOrders* table field list box to the *Field* option box in the second column in the query design grid. *ServDate* and other fields will shift right to accommodate the new field.
   c. Drag the *Descr* field from the *WorkOrders* table field list box to the *Field* option box in the third column in the query design grid.
   d. Save the revised query.
   e. Run the query.

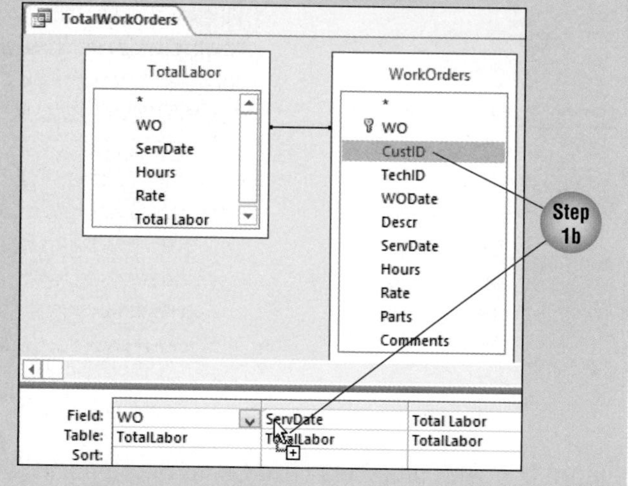

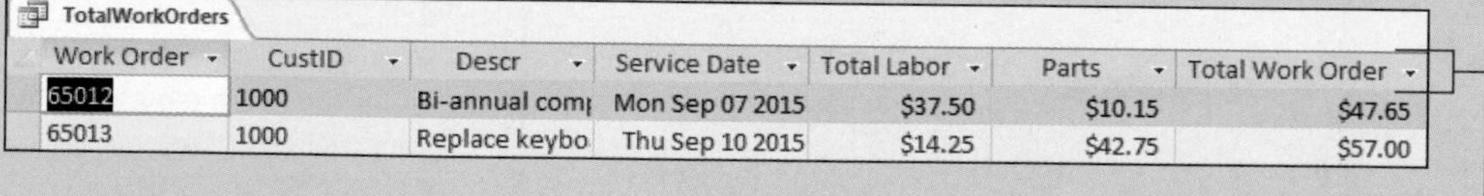

TotalWorkOrders

Work Order	CustID	Descr	Service Date	Total Labor	Parts	Total Work Order
65012	1000	Bi-annual comp	Mon Sep 07 2015	$37.50	$10.15	$47.65
65013	1000	Replace keybo	Thu Sep 10 2015	$14.25	$42.75	$57.00

In Step 1e, you run the revised query with the new fields added.

   f. Close the query.
2. Create a report based on the TotalWorkOrders query that is grouped by service date by month using the Report Wizard by completing the following steps:
   a. Click the CREATE tab and then click the Report Wizard button in the Reports group.
   b. At the first Report Wizard dialog box with *Query: TotalWorkOrders* already selected in the *Tables/Queries* option box, move all of the fields from the *Available Fields* list box to the *Selected Fields* list box and then click Next.

c. At the second Report Wizard dialog box, specify that you want the report grouped by the *ServDate* field by completing the following steps:

1) With *CustID* displayed in blue in the preview section, indicating that the report will be grouped by customer number, click the Remove field button (the left-pointing arrow) to remove the grouping level.
2) Double-click *ServDate* in the field list box to add a grouping level by the service date field. By default, Access groups a date field by month.
3) With the preview section now displaying that the report will be grouped by *ServDate by Month*, click Next.

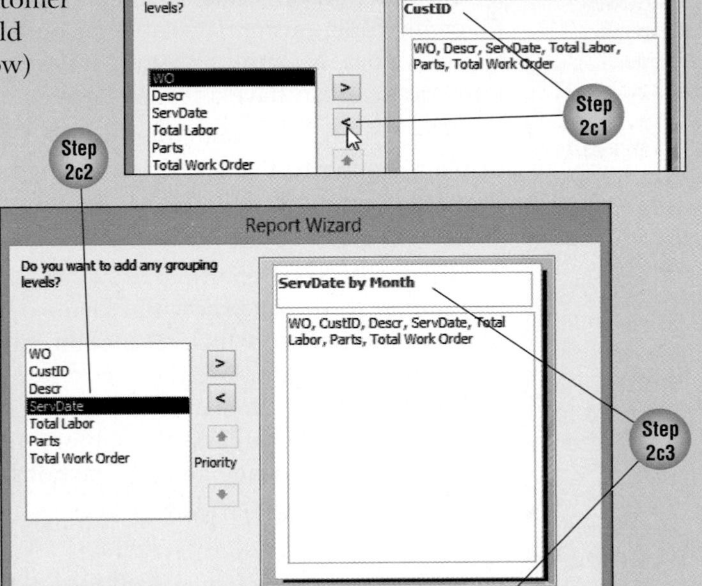

d. At the third Report Wizard dialog box, click the down-pointing arrow at the right of the first sort option box, click *WO* at the drop-down list to sort each group by work order number in ascending order and then click Next.

e. At the fourth Report Wizard dialog box, click *Landscape* in the *Orientation* section and then click Next.

f. At the last Report Wizard dialog box, select the existing text in the *What title do you want for your report?* text box, type **WorkOrdersbyMonth**, and then click Finish.

3. Minimize the Navigation pane.
4. Preview the report and then switch to Layout view or Design view. Edit the text in the report title and column heading labels and adjust column widths as necessary until the report looks similar to the one shown below. The Organic theme was applied in Project 2. Modify the colors for the *Report Header* and *Page Header* sections to most closely match the theme colors shown below.

Work Orders by Month

ServDate by Month	Work Order	CustID	Descr	Service Date	Total Labor	Parts	Total Work Order
September 2015							
	65012	1000	Bi-annual computer maintenance	Mon Sep 07 2015	$37.50	$10.15	$47.65
	65013	1000	Replace keyboard	Thu Sep 10 2015	$14.25	$42.75	$57.00
	65014	1005	Replace power supply	Thu Sep 10 2015	$52.50	$62.77	$115.27
	65015	1008	Restore operating system	Fri Sep 11 2015	$67.50	$0.00	$67.50
	65016	1010	Install upgraded video card	Fri Sep 11 2015	$30.00	$48.75	$78.75
	65017	1015	Replace DVD drive	Tue Sep 15 2015	$16.88	$55.87	$72.75
	65018	1020	Upgrade Office suite	Tue Sep 15 2015	$22.50	$0.00	$22.50
	65019	1025	Upgrade to Windows 8	Thu Sep 17 2015	$75.00	$0.00	$75.00
	65020	1030	Troubleshoot noisy fan	Thu Sep 17 2015	$33.75	$62.77	$96.52

5. Save the report.

Adding Functions to a Group

Quick Steps

Add Functions to a Group

1. Open report in Design view or Layout view.
2. Click Group & Sort button.
3. Click More Options button.
4. Click down-pointing arrow next to *with no totals*.
5. Choose field in *Total On* list box.
6. Choose function in *Type* list box.
7. If desired, click *Show Grand Total* check box.
8. If desired, click *Show group subtotal as % of Grand Total* check box.
9. Click *Show subtotal in group header* or *Show subtotal in group footer* check box.
10. Repeat Steps 5–9 as needed for other fields.
11. Click outside *Totals* option box.
12. Close Group, Sort, and Total pane.

When a report is grouped, the Group, Sort, and Total pane can be used to add a calculation below a numeric field at the end of each group. You can also add a function to more than one field within the group. For example, you can calculate a Sum function on a sales field and a Count function on an invoice field. The following functions are available for numeric fields: Sum, Average, Count Records, Count Values, Maximum, Minimum, Standard Deviation, and Variance. A non-numeric field can have a Count Records or Count Values function added.

The Group, Sort, and Total pane for a report with an existing grouping level displays similar to the one shown in Figure 5.9. Click the More Options button next to the group level to which a total is to be added to expand the available group options.

Click the down-pointing arrow next to *with no totals* to open a *Totals* option box similar to the one shown in Figure 5.10. Use the option boxes within this box to select the field to which a function should be added and the type of aggregate function to calculate. Use the check boxes to choose to add a grand total to the end of the report, calculate group subtotals as a percentage of the grand total, and decide whether to add the subtotal function to the *Group Header* or *Group Footer* section. Continue adding functions to other fields as needed and then click outside the *Totals* option box to close it.

Figure 5.9 Group, Sort, and Total Pane with a Grouping Level Added

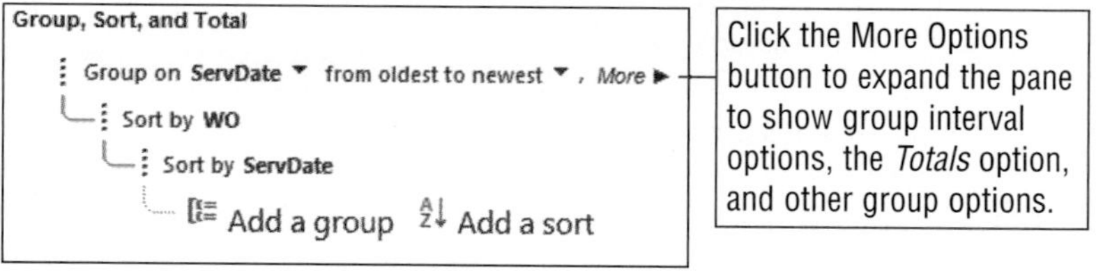

Figure 5.10 *Totals* Option Box in Group, Sort, and Total Pane

Click here in the expanded options list to open the *Totals* option box, in which you specify the field(s) and function(s) to add to the report. You can also add functions to calculate a grand total at the end of the report and group totals as a percentage of the grand total.

Group, Sort, and Total

Group on ServDate from oldest to newest, by month, with no totals

with a header section, without a footer section, do not keep group toge

Less ◀

Sort by WO

Sort by ServDate

Totals

Total On WO

Type Count Values

Show Grand Total

Show group subtotal as % of Grand Total

Show subtotal in group header

Show subtotal in group footer

Apply formatting options such as bold, color, and borders (in the Property Sheet task pane) to totals to make them stand out in a report. For totals without a border style, use the Line tool to underline them. For example, draw two lines below a grand total to create a double underline.

Project 3b Adding Functions to a Report

Part 2 of 3

1. With **AL2-C5-RSRCompServ.accdb** open, display the WorkOrdersbyMonth report in Design view.
2. Add two functions at the end of each month to show the number of work orders and the total value of the work orders by completing the following steps:
   a. In the Grouping & Totals group on the REPORT DESIGN TOOLS DESIGN tab, click the Group & Sort button.
   b. At the Group, Sort, and Total pane located at the bottom of the work area, click the More Options button next to *from oldest to newest* in the *Group on ServDate* group options.
   c. Click the down-pointing arrow next to *with no totals* in the expanded group options.
   d. At the *Totals* option box with *WO* selected in the *Total On* option box, specify the type of function and the placement of the result by completing the following steps:
      1) Click the down-pointing arrow next to *Type* and then click *Count Records* at the drop-down list.
      2) Click the *Show Grand Total* check box to insert a check mark. Access adds a Count function in a control object in the *Report Footer* section below the *WO* column.
      3) Click the *Show subtotal in group footer* check box to insert a check mark. Access displays a new section with the title *ServDate Footer* in the section bar below the *Detail* section and inserts a Count function in a control object below the *WO* column.

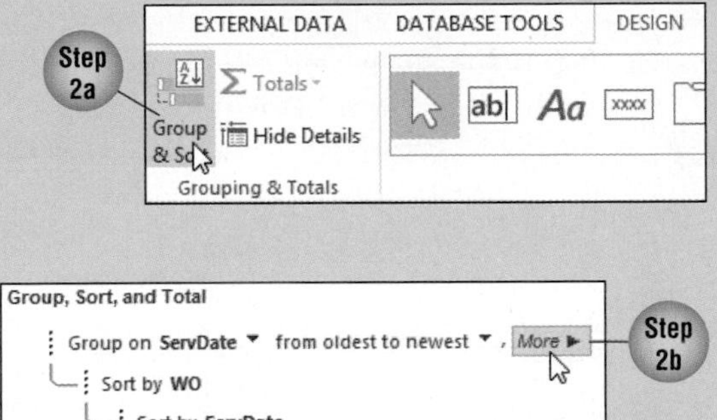

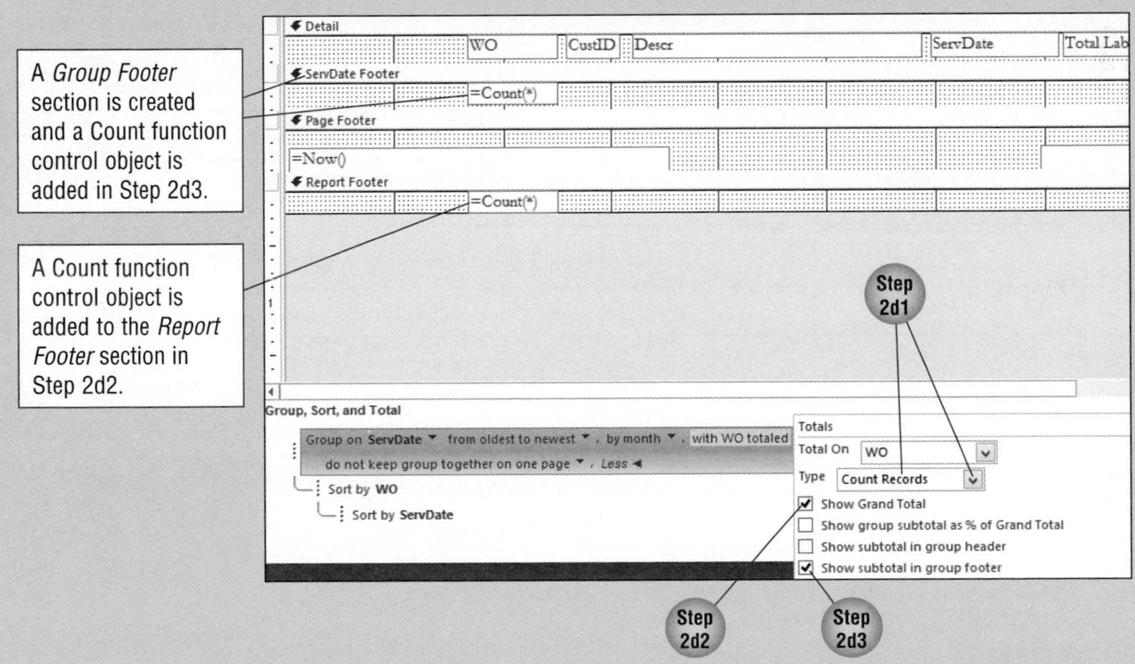

e. With the *Totals* option box still open, click the down-pointing arrow next to *Total On* and then click *Total Work Order* at the drop-down list. The *Type* option defaults to *Sum* for a numeric field.
f. Click the *Show Grand Total* check box to insert a check mark. Access adds a Sum function in a control object in the *Report Footer* section.
g. Click the *Show subtotal in group footer* check box to insert a check mark. Access adds a Sum function in a control object in the *ServDate Footer* section.

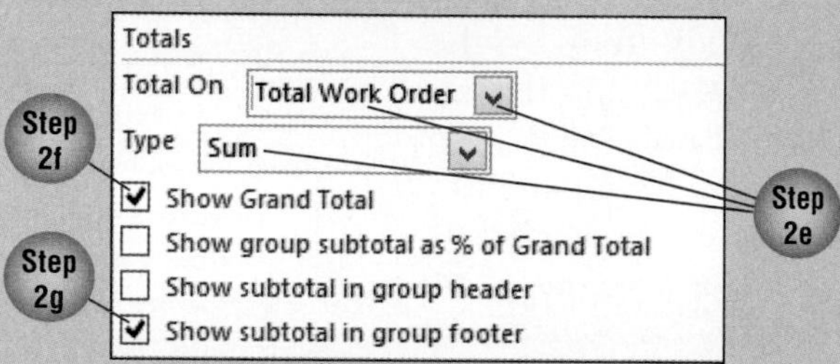

h. Click outside the *Totals* option box to close the box.
3. Click the Group & Sort button to close the Group, Sort, and Total pane.
4. Review the two Count functions and two Sum functions added to the report in Design view.
5. Display the report in Print Preview to view the calculated results. Notice that the printout requires two pages and that the report's grand totals print on page 2. Also notice that Access added the Sum function below the Count function rather than at the bottom of the *Total Work Order* column.
6. Close Print Preview to switch back to Design view.
7. Click to select the Sum function control object in the *ServDate Footer* section and then hold down Shift as you click to select the Sum function control object in the *Report Footer* section. Position the mouse pointer on the orange border of one of the selected control objects and then drag to move the two objects simultaneously to the right below the Total Work Order object in the *Detail* section.

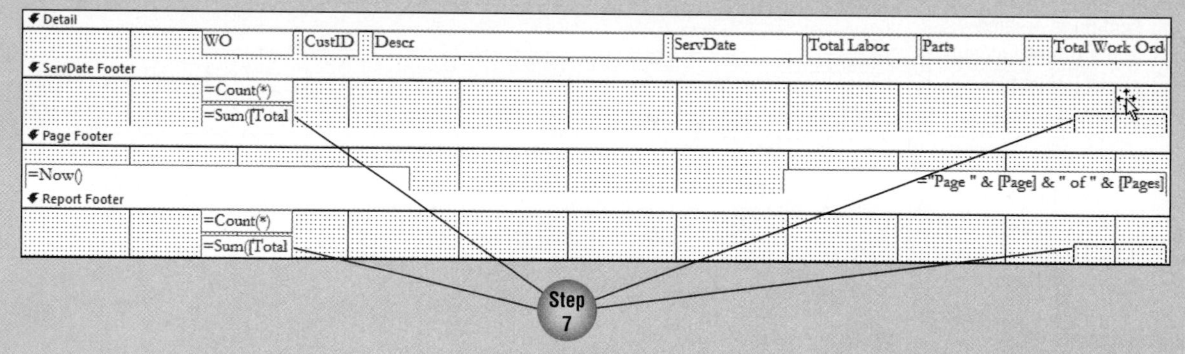

8. Add a label control object to the left of the Count function in the *ServDate Footer* section that displays the text *Work Order Count:* and another label control object to the left of the Sum function that displays the text *Month Total:*. Apply bold formatting and the red font color and right-align the text in the two label control objects. Resize and align the two labels as necessary. ***Note: Access displays an error flag on the two label control objects, indicating that these objects are not associated with another control object. You can ignore these error flags, since the labels have been added for descriptive text only.***
9. Move the Sum function control object and *Month Total* label control object up until they are at the same horizontal position as the Count function and then decrease the height of the *ServDate Footer* section as shown below.

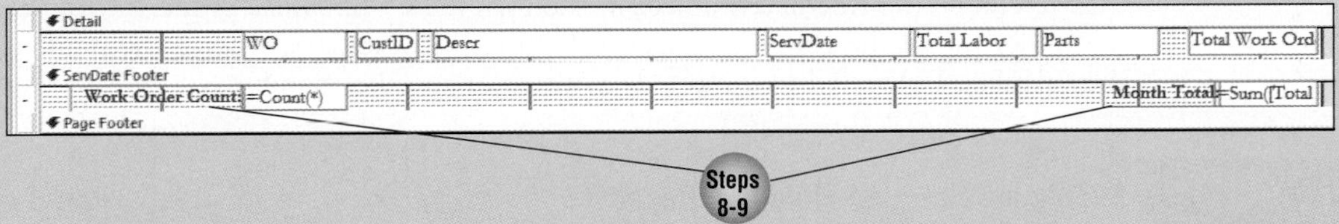

10. Display the report in Print Preview to view the labels. If necessary, return to Design view to make further size and alignment adjustments.

Step 10

ServDate by Month	Work Order	CustID	Descr	Service Date	Total Labor	Parts	Total Work Order
September 2015							
	65012	1000	Bi-annual computer maintenance	Mon Sep 07 2015	$37.50	$10.15	$47.65
	65013	1000	Replace keyboard	Thu Sep 10 2015	$14.25	$42.75	$57.00
	65014	1005	Replace power supply	Thu Sep 10 2015	$52.50	$62.77	$115.27
	65015	1008	Restore operating system	Fri Sep 11 2015	$67.50	$0.00	$67.50
	65016	1010	Install upgraded video card	Fri Sep 11 2015	$30.00	$48.75	$78.75
	65017	1015	Replace DVD drive	Tue Sep 15 2015	$16.88	$55.87	$72.75
	65018	1020	Upgrade Office suite	Tue Sep 15 2015	$22.50	$0.00	$22.50
	65019	1025	Upgrade to Windows 8	Thu Sep 17 2015	$75.00	$0.00	$75.00
	65020	1030	Troubleshoot noisy fan	Thu Sep 17 2015	$33.75	$62.77	$96.52
	65021	1035	Customer has blue screen upon boot	Fri Sep 18 2015	$97.50	$0.00	$97.50
	65022	1040	Customer reports screen is fuzzy	Tue Sep 22 2015	$45.00	$55.47	$100.47
	65023	1045	Upgrade RAM	Wed Sep 23 2015	$37.50	$62.50	$100.00
	65024	1005	Install malware protection	Thu Sep 24 2015	$15.50	$75.50	$91.00
	65025	1010	Troubleshoot hard drive noise	Mon Sep 28 2015	$45.00	$0.00	$45.00
	65026	1025	Upgrade memory	Tue Sep 29 2015	$22.50	$75.75	$98.25
Work Order Count:	15					Month Total:	$1,165.16

11. With the report displayed in Design view, select the Sum function control object in the *Report Footer* section and move the control up until it is positioned at the same horizontal position as the Count function below the *WO* column.
12. Click to select the *Work Order Count*: label control object, hold down Shift, click to select the *Month Total*: label control object, click the HOME tab, and then click the Copy button in the Clipboard group. Click the *Report Footer* section bar and then click the Paste button in the Clipboard group. Move and align the copied labels as shown below. Edit the *Month Total*: label control object to *Grand Total*: as shown.

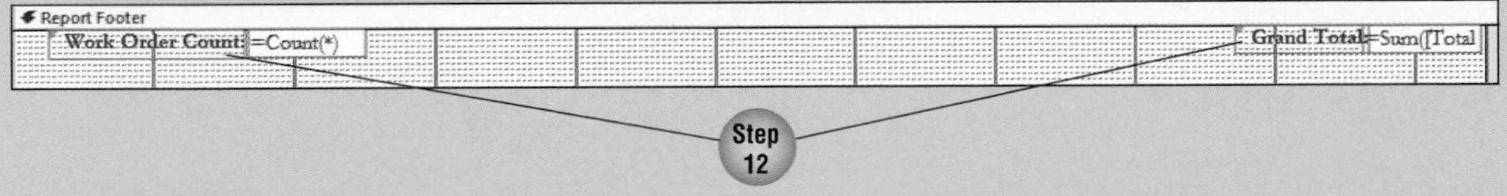

13. Display the report in Report view. Scroll to the bottom of the page to view the labels next to the grand totals. If necessary, return to Design view to make further size and alignment adjustments and then save and close the report.

Adding a Calculated Field to a Report

You have several options for adding a calculated field to a report, as you do when adding a calculated field to a form. You can create a query that includes a calculated column and then create a new report based on the query, or you can create a calculated control object in an existing report using Design view. A calculated value can be placed in any section of the report. To create a calculated control in a report, follow the same steps you learned in Chapter 4 for adding a calculated control to a form. Remember that field names in a formula are enclosed in square brackets.

A calculated control object can be used as a field in another formula. To do this, reference the calculated object in the formula by its *Name* property (found on the Other tab of the Property Sheet task pane). If necessary, change the name of the calculated objected to a more descriptive or succinct name.

Project 3c Adding a Calculated Field to a Report — Part 3 of 3

1. With **AL2-C5-RSRCompServ.accdb** open, display the WorkOrdersbyMonth report in Design view, and create a calculated control object to project the value of November's work orders, assuming that the value for November will be a 10% increase over the value for October.
2. Change the name of the text box control object that contains the summed value of October's work orders to a shortened name by completing the following steps:
   a. Click the control object that contains the summed monthly value (displays part of the formula *=Sum([Total Work Order])*) in the *ServDate Footer* section.
   b. Click the Property Sheet button in the Tools group.
   c. Click the Other tab in the Property Sheet task pane.
   d. Select and delete the existing text (displays *AccessTotalsTotal Work Order1*), type **MonthlyTotal**, and then close the Property Sheet task pane.
3. Add a calculated text box control object to the *Report Footer* section by completing the following steps:
   a. Click the Text Box button in the Controls group.
   b. Position the crosshairs with the text box icon attached at the 6-inch mark on the horizontal ruler in the *Report Footer* section. Drag to create an object that is approximately 2 inches wide by 0.25 inches tall at the same vertical position as the other objects in the *Report Footer* section and then release the mouse.
   c. Click in the text box control (displays *Unbound*), type **=[MonthlyTotal]*1.1**, and then press Enter.

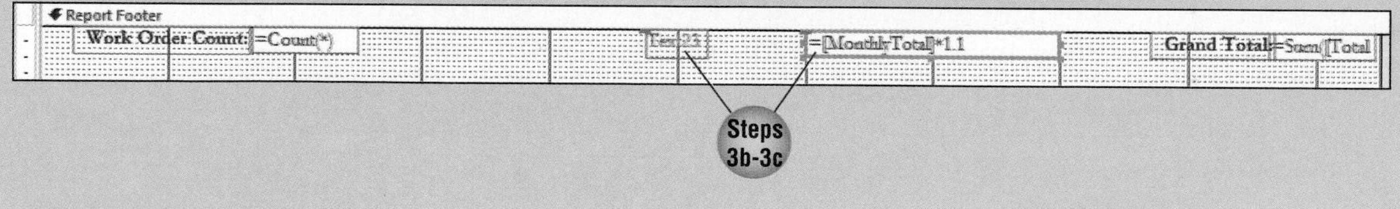

d. Format the calculated control using the Currency number format.
e. Select the entry in the label control object (displays *Textxx,* where *xx* is the text box object number) and then type **November's Projected Total:**.
f. Apply bold formatting and the red font color to the text in both objects.
g. Resize the text box control that contains the new formula until the left edge of the control is aligned at approximately the 7-inch position on the horizontal ruler.
h. Resize the label control that contains the text *November's Projected Total:* until the right edge of the control object meets the left edge of the text box control object, as shown below. Right-align the text in the label control object.

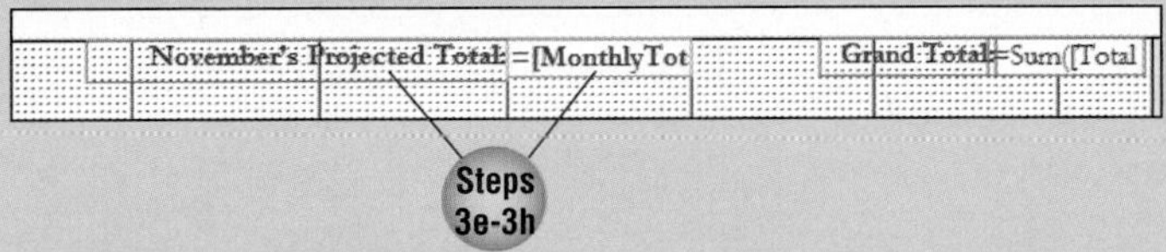

4. Display the report in Report view. Scroll to the bottom of the page to view the calculated field. If necessary, return to Design view to make further size and alignment adjustments and then save and close the report. Further changes to the report will be made in Project 4.
5. Redisplay the Navigation pane.

Project 4 Modify Section and Group Properties — 1 Part

You will change a report's page setup and then modify section and group properties to control print options.

Modifying Section Properties

A report has a Property Sheet, each control object within a report has a Property Sheet, and each section within a report has a Property Sheet. Section properties control whether the section is visible when printed, along with the section's height, background color, special effects, and so on.

Figure 5.11 on the next page displays the Format tab in the Property Sheet task pane for the *Report Header* section. Some of the options can be changed without opening the Property Sheet task pane. For example, you can increase or decrease the height of a section by dragging the top or bottom of a gray section bar in Design view. You can also set the background color using the Fill/Back Color button in the Font group on the REPORT DESIGN TOOLS FORMAT tab.

Quick Steps

Modify Section Properties
1. Open report in Design view.
2. Double-click gray section bar.
3. Change desired properties.
4. Close Property Sheet task pane.

Figure 5.11 *Report Header* Section Property Sheet Task Pane with Format Tab Selected

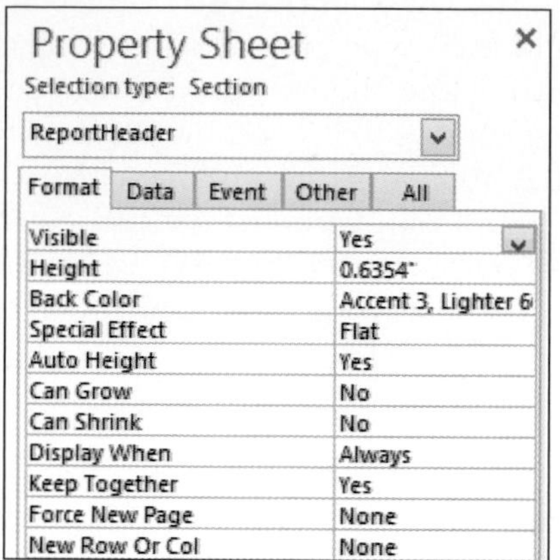

Quick Steps

Keep a Group Together on One Page

1. Open report in Design view or Layout view.
2. Click Group & Sort button.
3. Click More Options button.
4. Click down-pointing arrow next to *do not keep group together on one page.*
5. Click desired print option.
6. Close Group, Sort, and Total pane.

Use the Keep Together property to ensure that a section does not split over two pages due to a page break. If necessary, Access starts printing the section at the top of the next page. However, if the section is longer than can fit on one page, Access continues printing the section on the following page. In that case, you can decrease margins and/or apply a smaller font size to fit the text for the section all on one page.

Use the Force New Page property to insert a page break before a section begins *(Before Section)*, after a section is finished *(After Section)*, or before and after a section *(Before & After)*.

Keeping a Group Together on the Same Page

Open the Group, Sort, and Total pane and click the More Options button for a group to specify whether you want to keep an entire group together on the same page. By default, Access does not keep a group together. Click the down-pointing arrow next to *do not keep group together on one page* and then click the desired option, as shown in Figure 5.12.

Figure 5.12 Group, Sort, and Total Pane with Keep Group Together Print Options

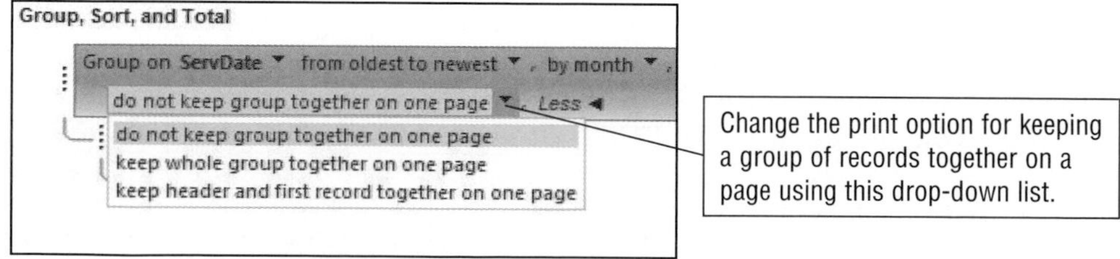

Project 4 Modifying Section Properties and Keeping a Group Together

Part 1 of 1

1. With **AL2-C5-RSRCompServ.accdb** open, display the WorkOrdersbyMonth report in Print Preview and then click the Zoom button (not the button arrow) in the Zoom group to change the zoom to view an entire page within the window.
2. Click the Next Page button in the Page Navigation bar to view page 2 of the report, which shows the grand totals.
3. Switch to Design view and then minimize the Navigation pane.
4. Change the section properties for the *Group Footer* and *Report Footer* sections displaying the Count and Sum functions and control objects by completing the following steps:
   a. Double-click the *ServDate Footer* section bar to open the section's Property Sheet task pane.
   b. Click in the *Back Color* property box and then click the Build button to open the color palette.
   c. Click *Blue-Gray, Accent 3, Lighter 80%* (seventh option in the second row of the *Theme Colors* section).
   d. Close the Property Sheet task pane.
   e. Select the Count function control object and the Sum function control object in the *ServDate Footer* section and then change the font color to red and apply bold formatting.
   f. With the Count and Sum function control objects still selected, right-click one of the selected controls, point to *Fill/Back Color* at the shortcut menu, and then click *Transparent*. The background color applied in Step 4c will now display behind the calculations.
   g. Double-click the *Report Footer* section bar, change the Back Color property to the same color as the *ServDate Footer* section (see Steps 4b and 4c), and then close the Property Sheet task pane.
   h. Apply the formatting in Steps 4e and 4f to the Count and Sum function control objects in the *Report Footer* section.
   i. Right-click the text box control object containing the formula *=[MonthlyTotal]*1.1* and then click *Properties* at the shortcut menu. Change the Back Style property to *Transparent* and the Border Style property to *Transparent*. Close the Property Sheet task pane.

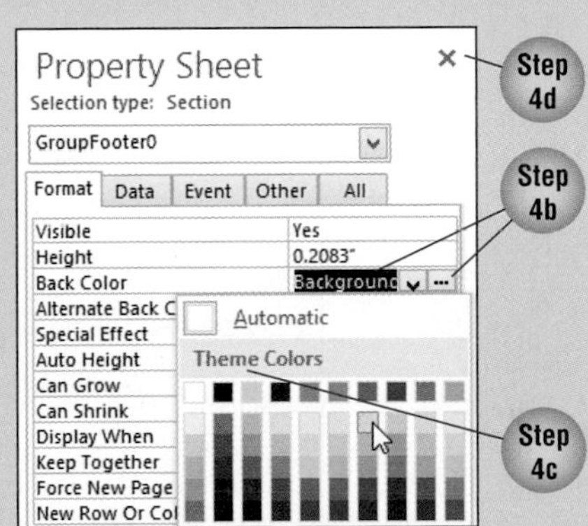

5. Print each month's work orders on a separate page by completing the following steps:
   a. Click the Group & Sort button on the REPORT DESIGN TOOLS DESIGN tab.
   b. Click the More Options button in the Group, Sort, and Total pane.
   c. Click the down-pointing arrow next to *do not keep group together on one page* and then click *keep whole group together on one page* at the drop-down list.
   d. Close the Group, Sort, and Total pane.

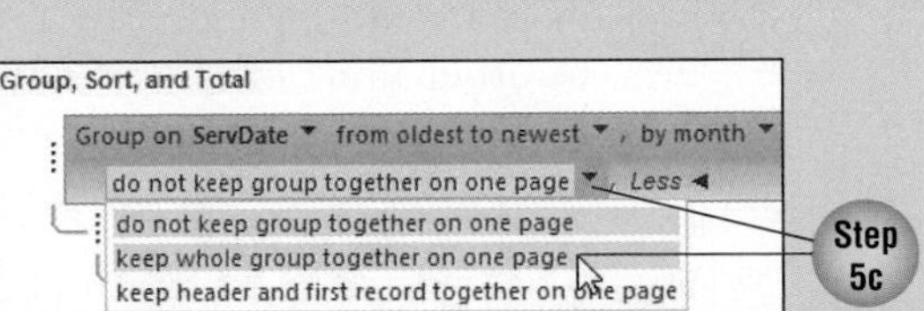

6. Create a label control object at the top right of the *Report Header* section with your first and last names. Apply bold formatting to the label control object and select the *Blue-Gray, Accent 3, Darker 50%* font color (seventh option in the last row of the *Theme Colors* section).
7. Display the report in Print Preview and then change the zoom to view an entire page within the window. Compare your report with the one shown in Figure 5.13 on the next page. Scroll to page 2 to view all of October's work orders on the same page.
8. Save, print, and then close the report.
9. Redisplay the Navigation pane.

Figure 5.13 Page 1 of Completed Report in Project 4

Work Orders by Month — Student Name

ServDate by Month	Work Order	CustID	Descr	Service Date	Total Labor	Parts	Total Work Order
September 2015							
	65012	1000	Bi-annual computer maintenance	Mon Sep 07 2015	$37.50	$10.15	$47.65
	65013	1000	Replace keyboard	Thu Sep 10 2015	$14.25	$42.75	$57.00
	65014	1005	Replace power supply	Thu Sep 10 2015	$52.50	$62.77	$115.27
	65015	1008	Restore operating system	Fri Sep 11 2015	$67.50	$0.00	$67.50
	65016	1010	Install upgraded video card	Fri Sep 11 2015	$30.00	$48.75	$78.75
	65017	1015	Replace DVD drive	Tue Sep 15 2015	$16.88	$55.87	$72.75
	65018	1020	Upgrade Office suite	Tue Sep 15 2015	$22.50	$0.00	$22.50
	65019	1025	Upgrade to Windows 8	Thu Sep 17 2015	$75.00	$0.00	$75.00
	65020	1030	Troubleshoot noisy fan	Thu Sep 17 2015	$33.75	$62.77	$96.52
	65021	1035	Customer has blue screen upon boot	Fri Sep 18 2015	$97.50	$0.00	$97.50
	65022	1040	Customer reports screen is fuzzy	Tue Sep 22 2015	$45.00	$55.47	$100.47
	65023	1045	Upgrade RAM	Wed Sep 23 2015	$37.50	$62.50	$100.00
	65024	1005	Install malware protection	Thu Sep 24 2015	$15.50	$75.50	$91.00
	65025	1010	Troubleshoot hard drive noise	Mon Sep 28 2015	$45.00	$0.00	$45.00
	65026	1025	Upgrade memory	Tue Sep 29 2015	$22.50	$75.75	$98.25
Work Order Count:	15					Month Total:	$1,165.16

Thursday, December 10, 2015 — Page 1 of 2

Project 5 Create and Format a Chart — 2 Parts

You will create and format a chart in a customers report to show the total parts and labor on work orders by month.

Inserting and Editing a Chart in a Report

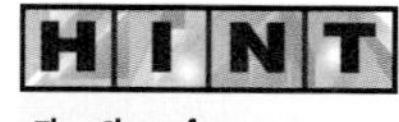

The Chart feature in Access is not the same Chart tool that is included in Word, Excel, and PowerPoint.

A chart can be added to a report to graphically display numerical data from another table or query. The chart is linked to a field in the report that is common to both objects. Access summarizes and graphs the data from the charted table or query based on the fields you select for each record in the report.

Inserting a Chart

Insert Chart

With a report open in Design view, increase the height or width of the *Detail* section to make room for the chart, click the Insert Chart button in the Controls group on the REPORT DESIGN TOOLS DESIGN tab, and then drag the crosshairs with the chart icon attached to create the approximate height and width of the chart. When you release the mouse, Access launches the Chart Wizard with six dialog boxes that guide you through the steps of creating a chart. The first Chart Wizard dialog box is shown in Figure 5.14.

Figure 5.14 First Chart Wizard Dialog Box

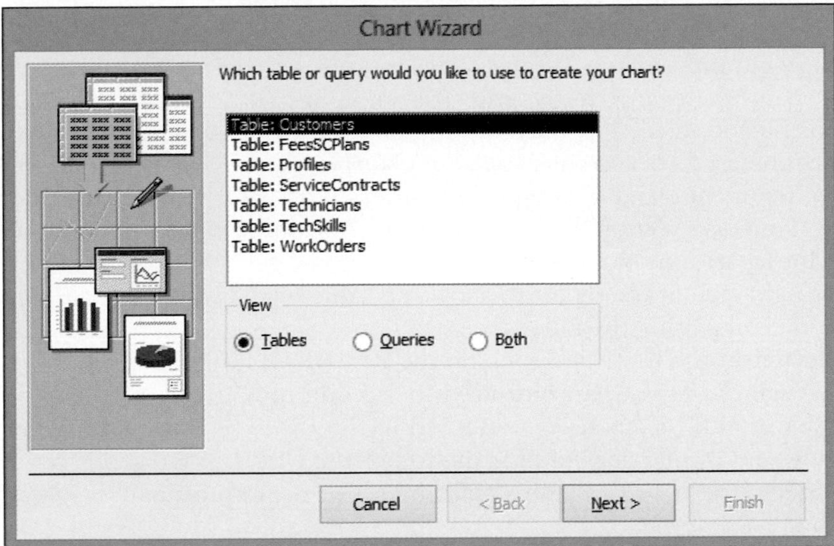

In Project 5, you will use the Chart Wizard to insert a chart in a customer report that depicts the total value of work orders for each customer by month. The data for the chart will be drawn from a related query. A chart can also be inserted into a form and formatted by completing steps similar to those in Projects 5a and 5b.

Quick Steps

Insert a Chart in a Report

1. Open report in Design view.
2. Click Insert Chart button.
3. Drag to create control object of desired height and width.
4. Select table or query for chart data.
5. Click Next.
6. Add fields to use in chart.
7. Click Next.
8. Click desired chart type.
9. Click Next.
10. Add fields as needed to chart layout.
11. Click Preview Chart.
12. Close Sample Preview window.
13. Click Next.
14. Select field to link report with chart.
15. Click Next.
16. Type chart name.
17. Click Finish.

Project 5a Creating a Report and Inserting a Chart

Part 1 of 2

1. With **AL2-C5-RSRCompServ.accdb** open, create a new report using the Report Wizard by completing the following steps:
   a. Click *Customers* in the Tables group in the Navigation pane, click the CREATE tab, and then click the Report Wizard button.
   b. At the first Report Wizard dialog box with *Table: Customers* selected in the *Tables/Queries* option box, move *CustID*, *FName*, *LName*, and *ServCont* from the *Available Fields* list box to the *Selected Fields* list box and then click Next.
   c. At the second Report Wizard dialog box, with no group field selected, click Next.
   d. Click Next at the third Report Wizard dialog to choose not to sort the report.
   e. Click *Columnar* at the fourth Report Wizard dialog box and then click Next.
   f. Click at the end of the current text in the *What title do you want for your report?* text box, type **WOChart** so that the report title is *CustomersWOChart*, and then click Finish.
2. Minimize the Navigation pane and display the report in Design view.
3. To minimize the number of pages printed, change the page layout of the report to two columns by completing the following steps:
   a. Delete the date and page number control objects in the *Page Footer* section.
   b. Drag the right side of the grid to the left to meet the right edge of the *LName* text box control object. The grid will be approximately 3.8 inches wide.
   c. Click the Columns button in the Page Layout group on the REPORT DESIGN TOOLS PAGE SETUP tab, change *1* to *2* in the *Number of Columns* text box, and then click OK.
   d. Switch to Print Preview and review the report.

4. There is not enough room to place a chart showing the value of the work orders for each customer. Switch the report back to one column by completing the following steps:
   a. Close Print Preview and press Ctrl + Z three times to undo the deletion of the two text box control objects and the change in the grid size.
   b. Click the Columns button in the Page Layout group on the REPORT DESIGN TOOLS PAGE SETUP tab, change 2 to 1 in the *Number of Columns* text box, and then click OK.
5. Select the text in the report title and then type **Customers with Work Orders by Month**.
6. Drag the top of the *Page Footer* section bar down until the bottom of the *Detail* section is positioned at the 2-inch position on the vertical ruler.
7. Insert a chart at the right side of the report to show the value of the work orders for each customer by month by completing the following steps:
   a. Click the More button in the Controls group on the REPORT DESIGN TOOLS DESIGN tab and then click the Chart button in the second row.
   b. Position the crosshairs with the chart icon attached in the *Detail* section at the 5-inch position on the horizontal ruler aligned near the top of the *CustID* control object and then drag down and to the right to create a chart object of the approximate height and width shown below.

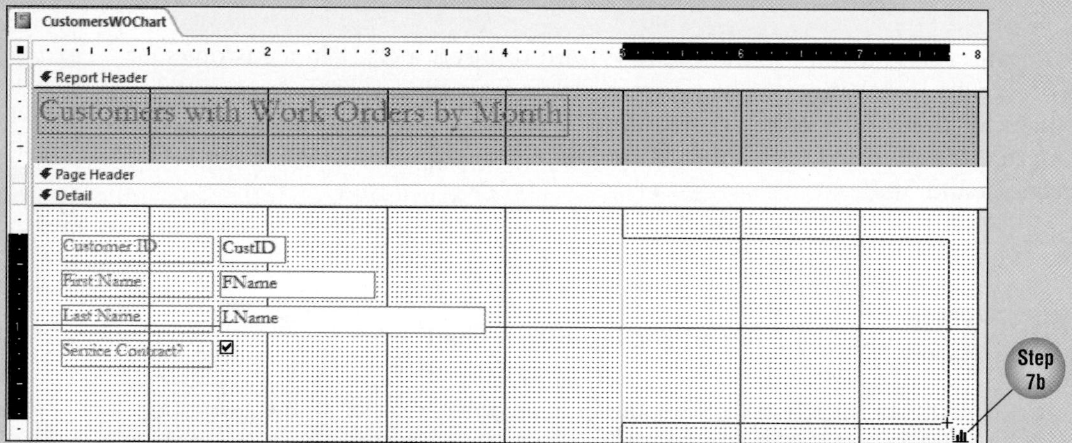

   c. At the first Chart Wizard dialog box, click *Queries* in the *View* section, click *Query: TotalWorkOrders* in the list box, and then click Next.

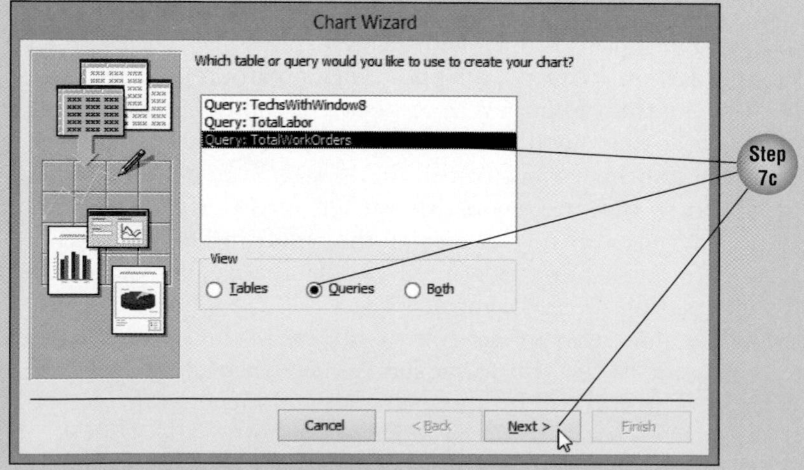

d. At the second Chart Wizard dialog box, double-click *ServDate* and *Total Work Order* in the *Available Fields* list box to move the fields to the *Fields for Chart* list box and then click Next.

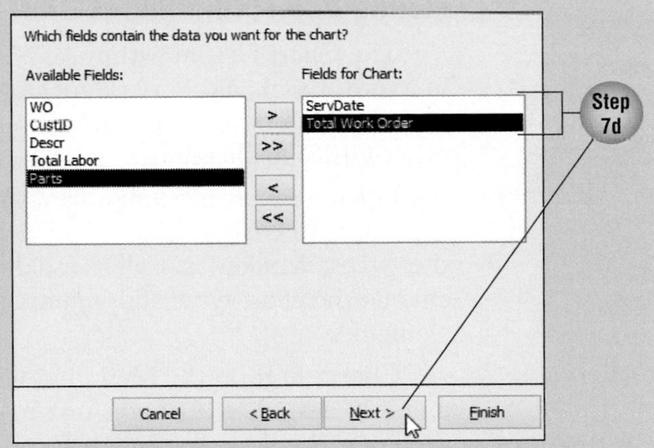

e. At the third Chart Wizard dialog box, click the second chart type in the first row (*3-D Column Chart*) and then click Next.

f. At the fourth Chart Wizard dialog box, look at the fields that Access has already placed to lay out the chart. Since only two fields were added, Access automatically used the numeric field with a Sum function as the data series for the chart and the date field as the *x*-axis category axis. Click Next.

g. At the fifth Chart Wizard dialog box, notice that Access has correctly detected the field to link records in the Customers report with the chart (based on the TotalWorkOrders query) as *CustID*. Click Next.

h. At the last Chart Wizard dialog box, click Finish. Access inserts a chart within the height and width of the chart control. The chart displayed in the control in Design view is not the actual chart based on the query data; it is only a sample to show the chart elements.

8. Display the report in Print Preview and scroll through the four pages in the report. Customers for which an empty chart displays have no work order data to be graphed.

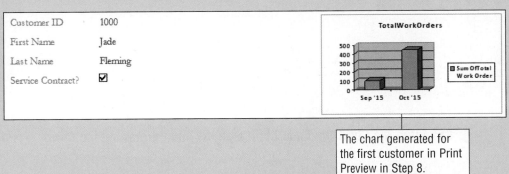

The chart generated for the first customer in Print Preview in Step 8.

9. Save and close the report and then redisplay the Navigation pane.

Quick Steps

Change Chart Options
1. Open report in Design view.
2. Double-click chart.
3. Click Chart on Menu bar.
4. Click *Chart Options*.
5. Click desired tab.
6. Change options.
7. Click OK.

Change the Chart Type
1. Open report in Design view.
2. Double-click chart.
3. Click Chart on Menu bar.
4. Click *Chart Type*.
5. Click desired chart type in list box.
6. Click desired chart subtype.
7. Click OK.

Format a Chart Element
1. Open report in Design view.
2. Double-click chart.
3. Right-click chart element.
4. Click *Format*.
5. Change format options as desired.
6. Click OK.

Editing and Formatting a Chart

The Chart feature within Access is not the same Chart tool that is available in Word, Excel, and PowerPoint. Access uses the Microsoft Graph application for charts, which means the editing and formatting processes are different than in other Office applications.

Open a report in Design view and then double-click a chart object to edit the chart. In chart-editing mode, a Menu bar and a toolbar display at the top of the Access window, as well as a datasheet for the chart in the work area. You can change the chart type; add, remove, or change chart options; and format chart elements.

Click Chart on the Menu bar and then click *Chart Options* at the drop-down menu to add, delete, or edit text in chart titles and add or remove chart axes, gridlines, the legend, data labels, or a data table at the Chart Options dialog box. Click *Chart Type* at the Chart drop-down menu to open the Chart Type dialog box and choose a different type of chart, such as a bar chart or pie chart.

Right-click an object within a chart—such as the chart title, legend, chart area, or data series—and a format option displays in the shortcut menu for the selected chart element. Click the format option to open a Format dialog box for the selected element. Make the desired changes and then click OK.

When you have finished editing the chart, click outside the chart object to exit chart-editing mode. Sometimes Access displays a sample chart within the control object in chart-editing mode instead of the actual chart, which can make editing specific chart elements difficult if your chart does not match the sample. If this occurs, exit chart-editing mode, close and reopen the report in Design view, or switch views to cause Access to update the chart displayed in the control object.

Project 5b **Changing the Chart Type and Chart Options and Formatting the Chart** **Part 2 of 2**

1. With **AL2-C5-RSRCompServ.accdb** open, display the CustomersWOChart report in Design view.
2. Change the chart type, edit the chart title, and remove the chart legend by completing the following steps:
   a. Double-click within the chart to open the chart in chart-editing mode. Access displays a datasheet with the chart and opens the Microsoft Graph application, in which charts are edited.
   b. Click Chart on the Menu bar and then click *Chart Type*.

Chart Help
Chart Type...
Chart Options...
Add Trendline...
3-D View...
Step 2b

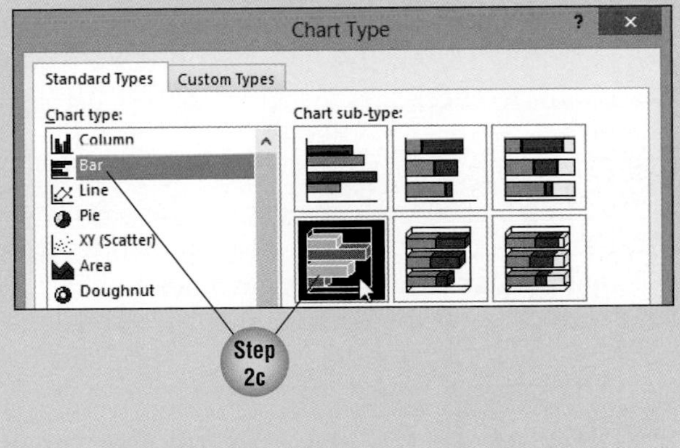

c. At the Chart Type dialog box with the Standard Types tab selected, click *Bar* in the *Chart type* list box and then click the first chart in the second row in the *Chart sub-type* section.
d. Click OK.
e. Click Chart on the Menu bar and then click *Chart Options*.
f. At the Chart Options dialog box with the Titles tab selected, edit the text in the *Chart title* text box by inserting spaces between the words so the title text reads *Total Work Orders*.
g. Click the Legend tab.
h. Click the *Show legend* check box to remove the check mark. Since there is only one data series, the chart title sufficiently describes the data and the legend is not necessary.
i. Click OK.

3. Format the bars in the chart to change the shape and colors by completing the following steps. ***Note: If the chart shown is not the actual chart but a sample chart showing multiple data bars, click outside the chart object to exit chart-editing mode, save, and then close the report. Reopen the report in Report view, switch to Design view, and then double-click the chart to open Microsoft Graph.***
   a. Right-click the bar in the chart and then click *Format Data Series* at the shortcut menu.
   b. At the Format Data Series dialog box, click the Shape tab.
   c. Click *4* in the *Bar shape* section (cylinder shape).
   d. Click the Patterns tab.
   e. Click the bright blue color square (last option in the last row).
   f. Click OK.
4. Right-click the chart title, click *Format Chart Title* at the shortcut menu, click the Font tab, apply the Red color (first option in the third row of the drop-down list), and then click OK.
5. Click outside the chart object to exit Microsoft Graph.
6. Create a label control object with your first and last names in the *Report Header* section with the right edge of the control aligned with the right edge of the chart.
7. Display the report in Print Preview. ***Note: Your x-axis values may be in different increments.***

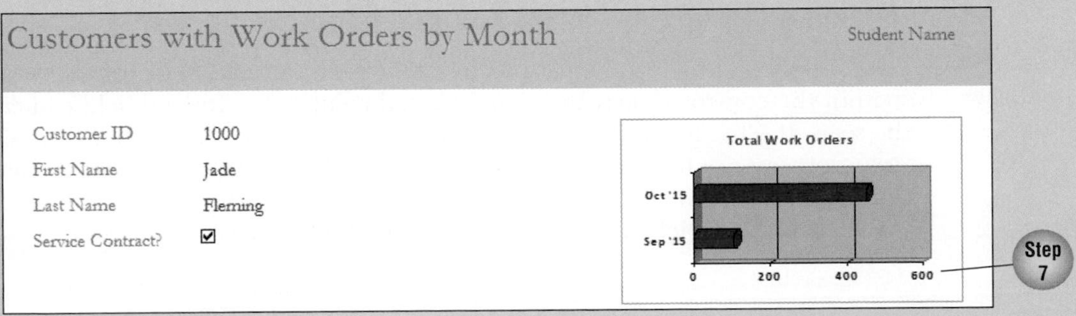

8. Save and then print only the first page of the report.
9. Open the Customers table, modify the data source by inserting a check mark in the *Service Contract?* check box for Kirk Cobb (Customer ID 1020), and then close the Customers table.
10. Go to page 2 of the report. Notice that the information for Kirk Cobb has not been updated. To refresh the data, either switch to another view and then go back to Print Preview, or close the report and open it again. Go to page 2, verify that the data has been updated, and then close the report.

Project  Create a Blank Report with Hyperlinks, a List, and a Subform **1 Part**

You will use the Blank Report tool to create a new report for viewing technician certifications. In the report, you will reorder the tab fields, create a list box inside a tab control, change the shape of the tab control, and add hyperlinks and a subform.

Creating a Report Using the Blank Report Tool

Quick Steps

Create a Blank Report

1. Click CREATE tab.
2. Click Blank Report button.
3. Expand field list for desired table.
4. Drag fields to report as needed.
5. Add a title, control objects, or format or make other design changes as needed.
6. Save report.

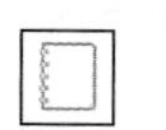

Blank Report

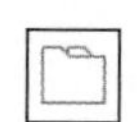

Tab Control

List Box

A blank report created with the Blank Report tool begins with no controls or formatting and displays as a blank white page in Layout view, similar to a form created with the Blank Form tool you learned about in Chapter 4. Click the CREATE tab and then click the Blank Report button in the Reports group to begin a new report. Access opens the Field List task pane at the right side of the work area. Expand the list for the desired table and then add fields to the report as needed. If the Field List task pane displays with no table names, click the Show all tables hyperlink at the top of the task pane.

Adding a Tab Control to a Report

In Chapter 4, you learned how to add a tab control to a form that allowed you to display fields from different tables in pages. In Form view, you displayed a page by clicking the page tab. Similarly, a tab control can be used in a report to display fields from the same table or a different table in pages. To create a tab control in a report, follow the steps you learned in Chapter 4 for adding a tab control to a form.

Adding a List Box or Combo Box to a Report

Like a list box in a form, a list box in a report displays a list of values for a field within the control object. In Report view, the entire list for the field can easily be seen. If a list is too long for the size of the list box control, scroll bars display that you can use to scroll up or down the list when viewing the report. Although you cannot edit the data in a report, you can use a list box to view all of the field values and see which value has been selected for the current record.

A combo box added to a report does not display as a list. However, the field value that was entered into the field from the associated table, query, or form is shown in the combo box control object. Since you cannot edit the data in a report, the combo box field is not shown as a drop-down list. A combo box can be changed to display as a list box within the report. In this case, the list box displays all of the field values, with the value stored in the current record shown selected within the list. A list box or a combo box can be added to a report by following the steps you learned in Chapter 4 for adding a list box or combo box to a form.

Combo Box

Adding Hyperlinks to a Report

With the Hyperlink button in the Controls group on the REPORT LAYOUT TOOLS DESIGN tab, you can create a link in a report to a web page, picture, email address, or program. Click the Hyperlink button and then click within the report at the desired location to open the Insert Hyperlink dialog box, in which you provide the text to display in the control object and the address to which the object should be linked. Use the Places bar at the left of the Insert Hyperlink dialog box to choose to link to an existing file or web page, another object within the database, or an email address.

Quick Steps

Add a Hyperlink to Report

1. Open report in Layout view or Design view.
2. Click Hyperlink button in Controls group.
3. Click in desired location with report.
4. Type text to display in control in *Text to display* text box.
5. Type URL in *Address* text box.
6. Click OK.

Change the Shape of a Control Object

1. Open report in Layout view.
2. Click to select control object.
3. Click REPORT LAYOUT TOOLS FORMAT tab.
4. Click Change Shape button.
5. Click desired shape.

Hyperlink

Changing the Shape of a Control Object

The Change Shape button in the Control Formatting group on the REPORT LAYOUT TOOLS FORMAT tab contains a drop-down list with eight shape options. You can use the shape options to modify the appearance of a command button, toggle button, navigation button, or tab control. Select the control object you want to modify, click the Change Shape button, and then click the desired shape at the drop-down list.

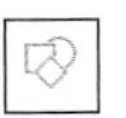
Change Shape

Changing the Tab Order of Fields

In Chapter 4, you learned how to open the Tab Order dialog box and change the order in which the tab key moves from field to field. In a report, you can change the order in which the tab key moves from field to field in Report view. Although you do not add, delete, or edit data in Report view, you may want to use the tab key to move within a report. Display the report in Design view, click the Tab Order button in the Tools group on the REPORT DESIGN TOOLS DESIGN tab, and then drag the fields up or down the *Custom Order* list as desired.

Tab Order

Adding a Subform to a Report

A subform can be added to a report using the Subform/Subreport button in the Control group on the REPORT DESIGN TOOLS DESIGN tab. (You used this method in Project 1e.) With the report in Design view, another method to create a subform is to drag the form from the Navigation pane to the desired location in the report. After the form has been placed in the report, check the Link Master Fields and Link Child Fields properties in the Property Sheet to ensure that the record sources are related using the fields that are to be linked.

Project 6 Creating a Blank Report with Hyperlinks, a List, and a Subform

Part 1 of 1

1. With **AL2-C5-RSRCompServ.accdb** open, click the CREATE tab and then click the Blank Report button in the Reports group.
2. If the Field List task pane at the right side of the work area does not display the table names, click the Show all tables hyperlink. If the table names are displayed, proceed to Step 3.
3. Add fields from the Technicians table and a tab control object to the report by completing the following steps:
   a. Click the plus symbol (+) next to the *Technicians* table name to expand the field list.
   b. Click *TechID* in the Field List task pane and then drag the field to the top left of the report.
   c. Right-click the *Technician ID* column, point to *Layout* at the shortcut menu, and then click *Stacked*. A stacked layout is better suited to this report, in which you want to show each technician's certifications next to his or her name in a tab control object.
   d. Drag the *FName* field from the Field List task pane below the first *Technician ID* text box control object. Release the mouse when you see the pink bar below the *01* text box control object next to *Technician ID*.

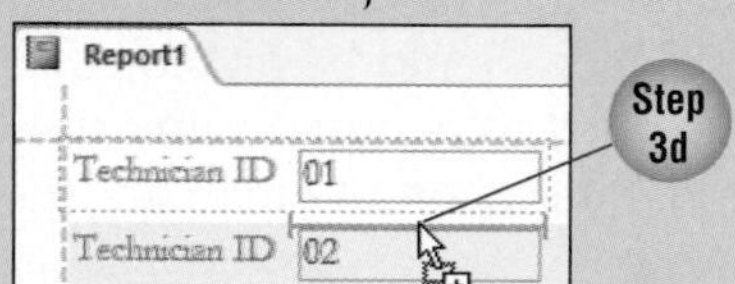

   e. Drag the *LName* field from the Field List task pane below the first *First Name* text box control object. Release the mouse when the pink bar displays below *Pat*.
   f. Click the Tab Control button in the Controls group on the REPORT LAYOUT TOOLS DESIGN tab.
   g. Position the mouse pointer with the tab control icon attached at the right of the first *Technician ID* text box control in the report. Click the mouse when you see the pink bar displayed at the right of the *01* text box control object.

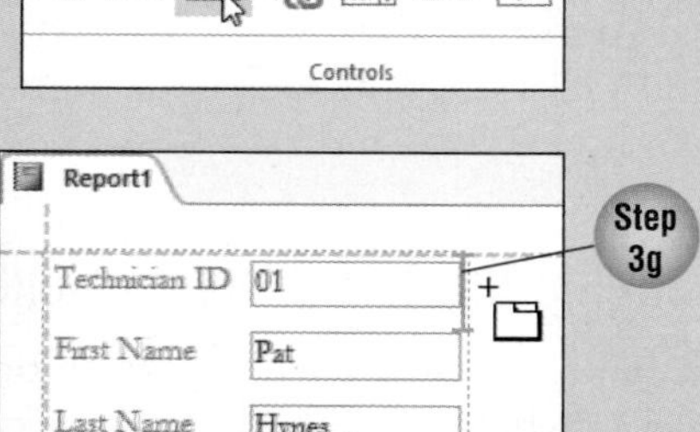

   h. Right-click the selected tab control object, point to *Layout*, and then click *Remove Layout* at the shortcut menu.
   i. Select the *HPhone* and *CPhone* fields in the Field List task pane and then drag the two fields below the *Last Name* text box control object. Release the mouse when the pink bar displays below *Hynes*.
   j. Double-click the first *Pagexx* tab (where *xx* is the page number) in the tab control object at the right of the report to select the tab control object. Point to the bottom orange border of the selected tab control object until the pointer displays as an up-and-down-pointing arrow and then drag the bottom of the object down until it aligns with the bottom of the *Cell Phone* control object.

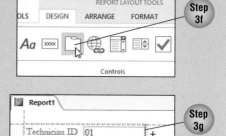

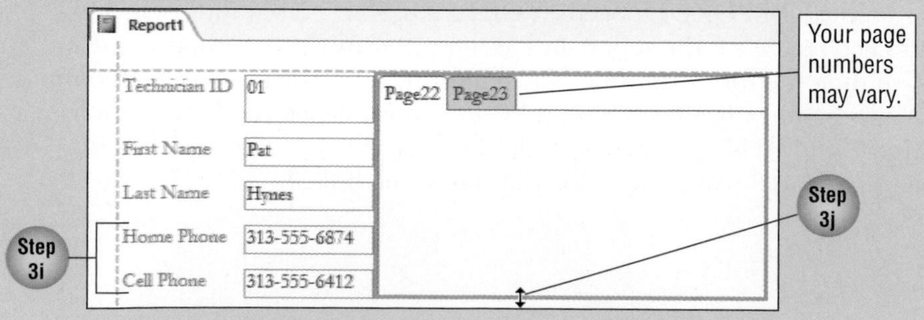

4. Add a field from the TechSkills table to the tab control object and change the control to a list box by completing the following steps:
   a. Click the plus symbol (+) next to the *TechSkills* table name in the *Fields available in related tables* section of the Field List task pane to expand the list.
   b. Click to select the *Certifications* field name and then drag the field to the first page in the tab control, next to *Technician ID 01*.
   c. Access inserts the field in the page with both the label control object and text box control object selected. To change the field to display as a list box, click to select only the text box control object (displays *Cisco CCNP, CompTIA A+,* and *Microsoft MCTS* in the first record).
   d. Right-click the selected text box control object, point to *Change To*, and then click *List Box* at the shortcut menu.

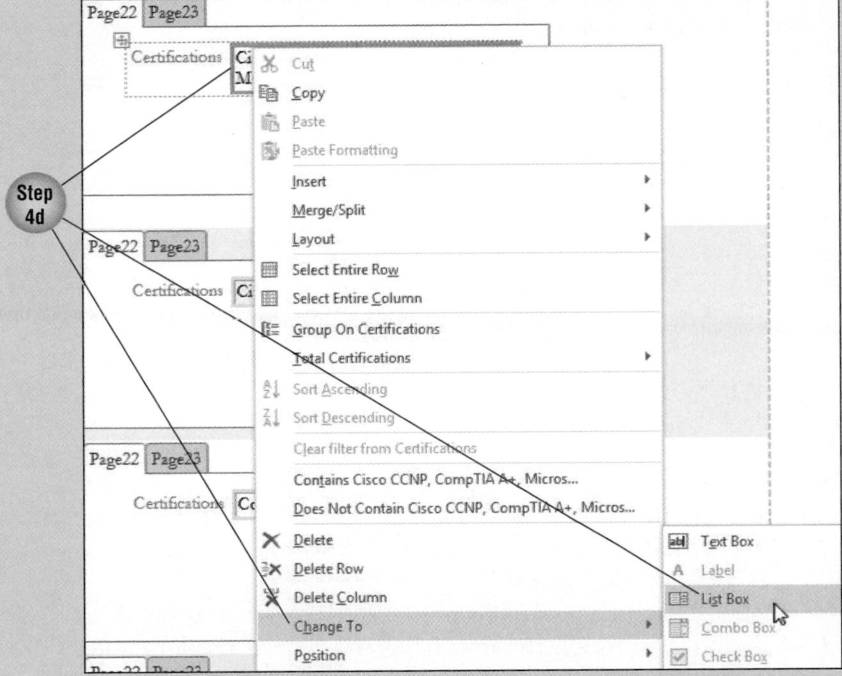

5. Add hyperlinks to the bottom of the tab control by completing the following steps:
   a. Click the Hyperlink button in the Controls group on the REPORT LAYOUT TOOLS DESIGN tab.
   b. Position the mouse pointer with the hyperlink icon attached below *Certifications* in the tab control object. Click the mouse when the pink bar displays.
   c. At the Insert Hyperlink dialog box, click in the *Text to display* text box and then type **Cisco Certifications**.
   d. Click in the *Address* text box, type **www.cisco.com/web/learning/netacad/course_catalog/index.html**, and then click OK.
   e. Drag the right orange border of the hyperlink control object to the right until all of the text displays within the control object.

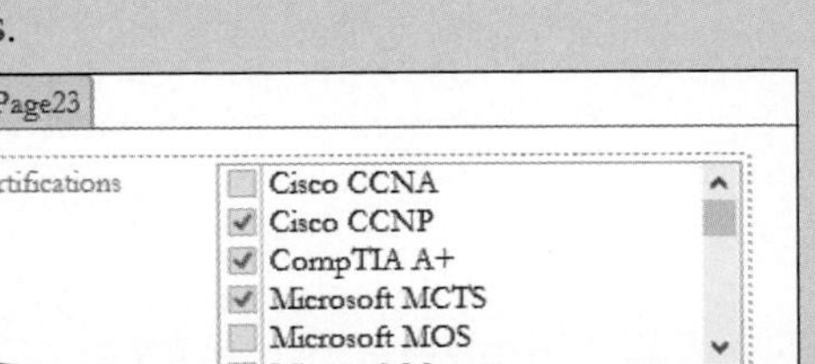

f. Add a second hyperlink control object below the list box in the tab control object that displays the text *Microsoft Certifications* and links to the address *www.microsoft.com/learning/en/us/certification/cert-overview.aspx* by completing steps similar to those in Steps 5a–5d.

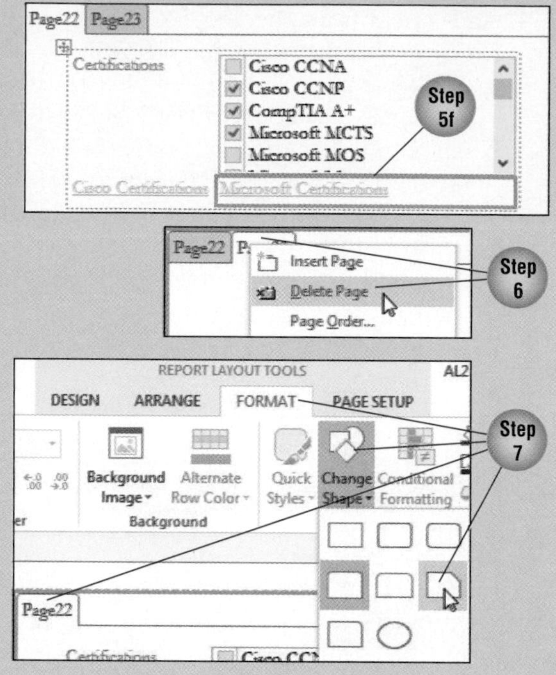

6. Click the second page in the tab control to select it, right-click, and then click *Delete Page* at the shortcut menu. Do not be concerned if Access displays the first page with an empty list box. The screen will refresh at the next step.
7. Double-click over *Pagexx* (where *xx* is the page number) in the tab control to select the entire tab control object. Click the REPORT LAYOUT TOOLS FORMAT tab, click the Change Shape button in the Control Formatting group, and then click *Snip Single Corner Rectangle* at the drop-down list (last option in the second row of shapes).
8. Click to select *Pagexx* (where *xx* is the page number), click the REPORT LAYOUT TOOLS DESIGN tab, and then click the Property Sheet button to open the Property Sheet task pane. With *Selection type: Page* displayed at the top of the Property Sheet task pane, click in the *Caption* property box, type **Technician's Certifications**, and then close the Property Sheet task pane.
9. Right-click the *Technician ID* text box control object (displays *01*) and then click *Select Entire Column* at the shortcut menu. Click the REPORT LAYOUT TOOLS FORMAT tab, click the Shape Outline button, and then click *Transparent* at the drop-down list.
10. Save the report and name it *TechCertifications*.
11. Switch to Report view. Click in the first *Technician ID* text box and press Tab four times to see how the Tab key moves through the first fields in order at the left side of the report.
12. Switch to Design view. You want the Tab key to move to the technician's last name first and then to the first name. Change the tab order of the fields by completing the following steps:
    a. Click the Tab Order button in the Tools group on the REPORT DESIGN TOOLS DESIGN tab.
    b. At the Tab Order dialog box, click in the bar next to *LName* in the *Custom Order* section to select the field and then drag the field to the top of the list until the black line displays above *TechID*.
    c. Drag *TechID* to the bottom of the list.
    d. Click OK.

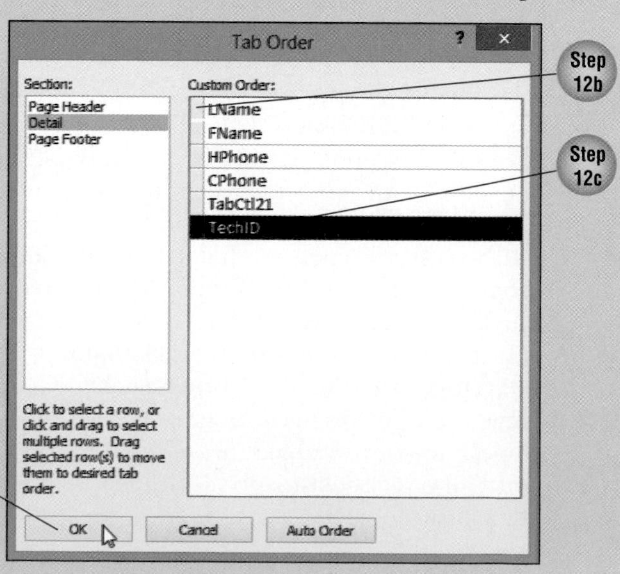

13. Save the revised form and then switch to Report view. Press Tab. Notice that the first field selected is the *Last Name* field. Press Tab a second time. Notice that the selected field moves to *First Name*. Press Tab two more times to watch the selected fields move to the *Home Phone* and *Cell Phone* fields below the *Last Name* field.
14. Click the Cisco Certifications hyperlink to open an Internet Explorer window and display the Cisco Courses & Certifications web page.
15. Close the browser window and then click the Microsoft Certifications hyperlink to display the Microsoft Certification Overview web page in a browser window.
16. Close the browser window and then display the report in Design view.
17. Add a subform to the report by completing the following steps:
    a. Click the TechWithWindows8 form in the Navigation pane and then drag it to the right of the tab control object as shown at the right. 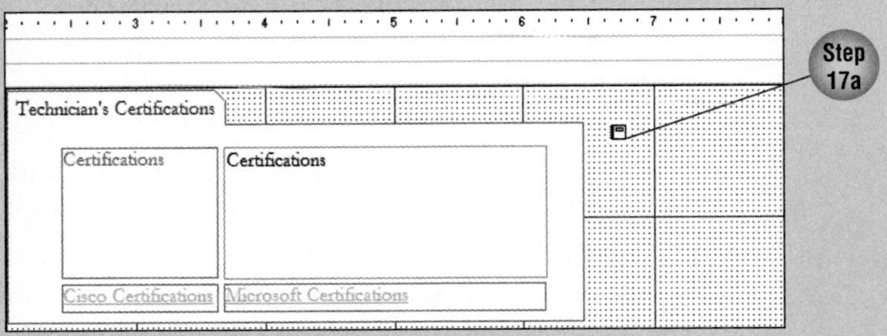
    b. Access inserts the subform with a label control object above it that contains the name of the subform. Click the label control displaying the text *TechsWithWindows8* to select it and then press Delete.

18. Link the fields to relate a field in the subform to a field in the report by completing the following steps:
    a. Click the subform to select it and then press F4 to display the Property Sheet task pane.
    b. Click the Data tab. Notice that the *Link Master Fields* and *Link Child Fields* property boxes are blank, as no fields are linked.
    c. Click in the Link Master Fields property box and then click the ellipsis to open the Subreport Field Linker.
    d. Click OK to accept the linking of the *TechID* field and then close the Property Sheet task pane.

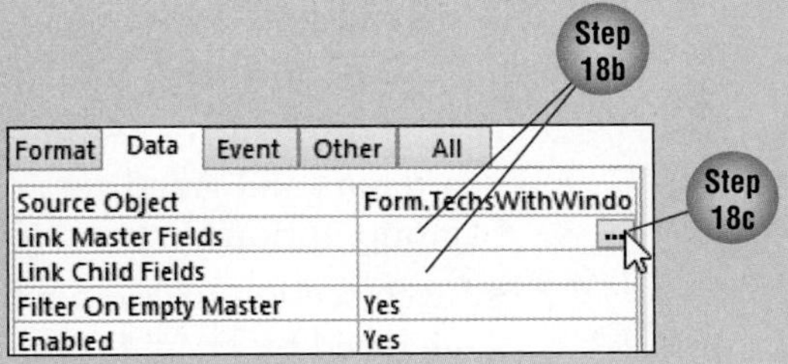

19. Save the revised form and display the report in Print Preview.
20. Switch the report to Landscape, print only the first page of the report and then close Print Preview.
21. Save and close the TechCertifications report and then close **AL2-C5-RSRCompServ.accdb**.

In this chapter, you learned how to build a custom report from scratch using Design view. You also created reports using the Report Wizard and Blank Report tool and used options in Design view and Layout view to customize the reports. As you become more comfortable with reports, explore other tools available in Layout View and Design view using the Design, Arrange, Format, and Page Setup tabs. More features are available to assist you with creating professional quality reports.

Chapter Summary

- A report generally contains five sections: *Report Header, Page Header, Detail, Page Footer,* and *Report Footer*.
- Drag a field or group of fields from the Field List task pane to the *Detail* section of the report, which represents the body of the report.
- An additional *Group Header* section and *Group Footer* section can be added if the report is grouped by a field containing repeating values, such as a department or city.
- Click the CREATE tab and click the Report Design button to build a custom report from scratch.
- Connect a table or query to a report using the *Record Source* property box in the Data tab of the report's Property Sheet task pane.
- Place label control objects to be used as column headings in a tabular report within the *Page Header* section in Design view.
- A related table or query can be inserted as a subreport within a main report. A subreport is stored as a separate object outside the main report.
- Click the Page Numbers button in the Header/Footer group to open the Page Numbers dialog box, in which you specify the format, position, and alignment options for page numbers in a report.
- The current date and/or time can be added as a control object within the *Report Header* section using the Date and Time button in the Header/Footer group.
- Add pictures or clip art images and draw lines in a report using the same techniques that you learned for adding graphics to a form.
- A report can be grouped by a field at the Report Wizard or by opening the Group, Sort, and Total pane.
- Functions such as Sum, Average, and Count can be added to each group within a report and grand totals can be added to the end of a report by expanding the group options in the Group, Sort, and Total pane.
- Each section within a report has a set of properties that can be viewed or changed by opening the section's Property Sheet task pane.
- The Keep Together property for a section is used to prevent a section from being split by a page break.
- The Force New Page property in a section's Property Sheet can be used to automatically insert a page break before a section begins, after a section ends, or before and after a section.
- At the Group, Sort, and Total pane, you can specify to keep an entire group together on the same page.
- A report can be formatted into multiple columns using the Columns button in the REPORT DESIGN TOOLS PAGE SETUP tab.
- A chart can be added to a report to graphically display numerical data from another table or query related to the report.

- Open a report in Design view, click the Chart button in the Controls group to create a chart control object in a report or form, and then use the Chart Wizard to generate the chart.
- Double-click a chart control object in Design view to edit the chart using Microsoft Graph by changing the chart type; adding, removing, or changing chart options; and formatting chart elements.
- The Blank Report tool in the Reports group in the CREATE tab creates a new report with no controls or format applied. The report opens as a blank, white page in Layout view, with the Field List task pane opened at the right of the work area.
- A tab control and list box can be added to a blank report using the same techniques you learned for adding these controls to a form.
- Use the Hyperlink button to create a link in a report to a web page, picture, email address, or program.
- The shape of a command button, toggle button, navigation button, or tab control can be modified using the Change Shape button in the Control Formatting group of the REPORT LAYOUT TOOLS FORMAT tab.
- You can alter the order of the fields in which the Tab key will move within a report at the Tab Order dialog box. Display a report in Design view to access the Tab Order button in the Tools group on the REPORT DESIGN TOOLS DESIGN tab.
- To add a subform to a report, drag the subform from the Navigation pane to the desired location in the report that is displayed in Design view.
- After a subform has been added, check the Link Master Fields and Link Child Fields properties in the Property Sheet to ensure that the record sources are related.

Commands Review

FEATURE	RIBBON TAB, GROUP	BUTTON
add existing fields	REPORT DESIGN TOOLS DESIGN, Tools	
blank report	CREATE, Reports	
change shape of selected control	REPORT LAYOUT TOOLS FORMAT, Control Formatting	
date and time	REPORT DESIGN TOOLS DESIGN, Header/Footer	
Design view	REPORT DESIGN TOOLS DESIGN, Views	
group and sort	REPORT DESIGN TOOLS DESIGN, Grouping & Totals	
insert chart	REPORT DESIGN TOOLS DESIGN, Controls	
insert hyperlink	REPORT LAYOUT TOOLS DESIGN, Controls	
insert image	REPORT DESIGN TOOLS DESIGN, Controls	
page numbers	REPORT DESIGN TOOLS DESIGN, Header/Footer	
Property Sheet task pane	REPORT DESIGN TOOLS DESIGN, Tools	
report design	CREATE, Reports	
Report view	REPORT DESIGN TOOLS DESIGN, Views	
Report Wizard	CREATE, Reports	
subreport	REPORT DESIGN TOOLS DESIGN, Controls	
tab control	REPORT LAYOUT TOOLS DESIGN, Controls	
tab order	REPORT DESIGN TOOLS DESIGN, Tools	
theme	REPORT DESIGN TOOLS DESIGN, Themes	
title	REPORT DESIGN TOOLS DESIGN, Header/Footer	

Concepts Check Test Your Knowledge 

Completion: In the space provided at the right, indicate the correct term, command, or number.

1. Add controls in this section to print grand totals at the end of a report. ____________________
2. Double-click this button to open the Property Sheet task pane for a report. ____________________
3. The Subform/Subreport button is found in this group on the REPORT DESIGN TOOLS DESIGN tab. ____________________
4. The Page Numbers button is located in this group on the REPORT DESIGN TOOLS DESIGN tab. ____________________
5. If the date and time are added to a report using the Date and Time dialog box, Access creates the control objects in this report section. ____________________
6. At the Report Wizard dialog box, Access displays a grouped field in this color in the preview section. ____________________
7. Grouping can be added to an existing report by opening this pane. ____________________
8. Click this button to expand the group options for a grouped field to add a Sum function to each group. ____________________
9. Modify this section property to instruct Access to insert a page break after the section is finished printing. ____________________
10. Double-click this element in report Design view to open the Property Sheet task pane for a section. ____________________
11. Use this button in the expanded Controls group to insert a bar chart into a report. ____________________
12. Launch the Microsoft Graph application to edit a chart by performing this action with the mouse. ____________________
13. When finished editing a chart, exit Microsoft Graph by performing this action with the mouse. ____________________
14. This report tool opens as a blank, white page in Layout view. ____________________
15. Click this button to create a control object within a report that will display a web page when clicked. ____________________
16. This button in the Control Formatting group on the REPORT LAYOUT TOOLS FORMAT tab can be used to change the shape of a selected control. ____________________

Skills Check Assess Your Performance

Assessment 1

CREATE A CUSTOM REPORT USING DESIGN VIEW

SNAP Grade It

1. Open **AL2-C5-ViewIt.accdb** and enable the content.
2. Create a new report using the Report Design button and build the report using the following specifications:
   a. Add a title in the *Report Header* section with the text **Web Products and Sales**.
   b. Add your name in a label control object in the center of the *Report Footer* section.
   c. Connect the WebProducts table to the report. Add all of the fields from the table to the report.
   d. Move the label control objects for each field from the *Detail* section to the *Page Header* section, arranging the controls horizontally in the order the fields appeared in the table. Place the objects as follows:

Field Label	Position of left edge of label control object on the horizontal ruler
Product ID	left margin
Product	2-inch mark
In Stock	4.25-inch mark
Selling Price	5-inch mark

   e. Resize the *Page Header* section when finished so that the extra space is removed.
   f. Align each text box control object in the *Detail* section below the object's associated label control object in the *Page Header* section as follows.

Text Box Control Object	Position of left edge of text box control object on the horizontal ruler
WebProdID	left margin
Product	1-inch mark
Instock	4-inch mark
SellPrice	5-inch mark

   g. Use Report view to check the alignment and width of controls to make sure that data is not truncated in any of the control objects. Make adjustments as needed in Design view or Layout view.
   h. Apply the *Retrospect* theme. Apply bold formatting to the title.
   i. Insert a subreport into the *Detail* section using the following specifications. ***Hint: You may first need to adjust the height of the* Detail *section to make room for the subreport if you have been using Layout view.***
      1) Use the WebSaleswithTotal query and add the fields to the subreport in this order: *CustID*, *WebOrdID*, *DateOrd*, *WebProdID*, and *Qty*.
      2) Accept the default link option to link the main report to the subreport by the *WebProdID* field.

3) Accept the default subreport name.
4) Edit the text in the subreport label control object to *Web Sales*.
5) View the report to ensure the data is properly linked.
6) Remove the *WebProdID* field (including the associated label control object) from the subreport, since this data is duplicated in the main report, and then move the *Qty* field (including the associated label control object) left to fill in the space.
7) Move and/or resize the subreport control object as desired.

j. Resize the *Detail* section so the section ends just below the subreport.
k. Apply 12-point bold formatting to the *WebProdID, Product, InStock,* and *SellPrice* fields in the *Detail* section.
l. Make any additional adjustments to the position, height, width, alignment, or formatting of any control objects that you think will improve the appearance of the report, but do not add any further elements, as you will continue to work on this report in the next assessment.

3. Save the report and name it *WebProductsWithSales*.
4. Print and then close the report.

Assessment 2

ENHANCE THE REPORT

1. With **AL2-C5-ViewIt.accdb** open, display the WebProductsWithSales report in Design view.
2. Add a page number to the bottom left of each page using the *Page N of M* format.
3. Add the current date to the bottom right of each page, aligning the right edge of the control in the *Page Footer* section at the 7-inch position on the horizontal ruler. Use the third option.
4. Insert an appropriate clip art image to the top right of the report, resizing the image to a suitable height and width and aligning the right edge of the image at the 7-inch position on the horizontal ruler. Adjust the position of the report title to center it vertically left of the clip art image and horizontally within the title control object.
5. Draw a horizontal line under the report title. Change the line thickness to 2 points and apply the Tan, Accent 5, Darker 50% line color (second-to-last option in the last row of the *Theme Colors* section).
6. Change all four margins for the report to 0.5 inch.
7. The diagonal, green triangle appears on the Report Selector button after the margins are changed. Click the Error Checking button and then click *Select the Control Farthest to the Right*. This will remove the drop-down list and select the control object at the right edge of the report that would prevent resizing the grid to remove extra space. The control selected is part of the date and time controls that were added within the title placeholder in Step 3. Drag the right middle sizing handle of the selected control left to decrease the control's width, aligning the control at the right edge of the clip art image. Click the Error Checking button again and then click *Remove Extra Report Space* at the drop-down list.
8. Save the report.
9. Print only the first page of the revised report and then close the report.

Assessment 3

CREATE A NEW REPORT WITH GROUPING AND TOTALS

1. With **AL2-C5-ViewIt.accdb** open, create a new report using the Report Wizard as follows:
   a. Use the WebSalesWithTotal query and add all of the fields to the report except *CustID* and *WebProdID*.
   b. Group by the *DateOrd* field by month.
   c. Click Next to leave the sort field blank.
   d. Apply the Stepped layout option in landscape orientation.
   e. Edit the report title to *WebSalesByDate*.
2. Preview both pages of the report and then switch to Design view.
3. Add your name in a label control object at the left edge of the *Report Footer* section.
4. Open the Group, Sort, and Total pane and make the following changes:
   a. Add a Sum function to each month's *Total Sale* column. Show a grand total at the end of the report and a subtotal in the group footer.
   b. Add a sort by the *LastName* field.
5. Add an appropriate label next to the Sum function in the *DateOrd Footer* section and next to the Sum function in the *Report Footer* section.
6. Edit the report title to *Web Sales by Date* and edit the *DateOrd by Month* label to *Month*.
7. Display the report in Print Preview and note any column widths that need to be adjusted or labels that need to be edited to display the entire entry. Switch to Design view or Layout view and adjust column widths as necessary so that all of the data is entirely visible. Change *Quantity* to *Qty*.
8. Change the top and bottom margins to 0.75 inch and then print the report.
9. Save and then close the report.

Assessment 4

CREATE AND FORMAT A NEW REPORT WITH A CHART

1. With **AL2-C5-ViewIt.accdb** open, create a new report using the Report Wizard as follows:
   a. Use the WebCustomers table and add the customer number, customer name, and home telephone fields to the report.
   b. Do not group or sort the report.
   c. Apply the Columnar layout option in portrait orientation.
   d. Edit the report title to *WebCustomersWithChart*.
2. Preview the report.
3. Switch to Design view.
4. Insert a chart at the right side of the page next to each customer record using the following information:
   a. Use the WebSalesWithTotal query.
   b. Add the *DateOrd* and *Total Sale* fields to the chart field list.
   c. Select a bar chart style. You determine which bar chart style to use.
   d. Accept the default chart layout that Access creates with *DateOrd by month* as the *x*-axis labels and *SumOfTotal Sale* as the value axis.
   e. Accept *CustID* as the linked field for the report and chart.
   f. Edit the title for the chart to *Web Sales*.

5. Preview the report with the bar chart and then switch to Design view.
6. Edit the chart as follows:
   a. Change the chart type to a clustered column with a 3-D visual effect.
   b. Delete the legend.
   c. Change the color of the columns to dark purple (fifth column from the left, second row from the bottom).
7. Edit the report title to *Customers with Web Sales Chart*.
8. Add your name in a label control object at the bottom left of the report.
9. Make any other formatting changes you think will improve the appearance of the report.
10. Print only the first page of the report.
11. Save and then close the report.

Assessment 5

CREATE A CUSTOM REPORT USING THE BLANK REPORT TOOL

1. With **AL2-C5-ViewIt.accdb** open, create a new report using the Blank Report tool.
2. Add the first field named *CustID* from the WebCustomers table and then apply the Stacked layout to the report.
3. Add the remaining fields from the WebCustomers table below the *Customer ID* field. Make sure you release the mouse with the pink bar displayed below *101* for the first *Customer ID*.
4. Widen the labels column so that *Street Address* does not wrap to a second line in the label column.
5. Insert a tab control object at the right of the *Customer ID* field. Make sure you click the mouse when the pink bar displays at the right of *101*.
6. Remove the layout from the tab control column and then lengthen the tab control object to align with the bottom of the *Home Phone* field.
7. Expand the field list for the *WebCustPymnt* table and then add the following fields to the tab control object:
   CCType
   CCNumber
   CCExpMonth
   CCExpYear
8. Select all of the label control objects in the tab control and widen the objects so that all of the label text is visible.
9. Save the report and name it *CustomersWithCreditCards*.
10. Delete the second page in the tab control and then change the shape of the selected tab control object to be *Round Single Corner Rectangle*.
11. Change the caption of the page in the tab control to *Credit Card Details*.
12. Insert a title at the top of the report with the text *Customers with Payment Information*.
13. Print only the first page of the report.
14. Save and close the report and then close **AL2-C5-ViewIt.accdb**.

Visual Benchmark Demonstrate Your Proficiency

CREATE CUSTOM RESERVATIONS REPORT WITH TOTALS

1. Open **AL2-C5-PawsParadise.accdb** and enable the content.
2. Review the partial report shown in Figure 5.15. This report was created based on the Dog Owners table, with the Dogs table added as a subreport. Create the report with the subreport with the following specifications and using your best judgment for formatting options as well as alignment, spacing, sizing, and position of controls:
   a. Apply the Ion Boardroom theme.
   b. Substitute another suitable clip art image if the one shown is not available.
   c. Add the current date and add page numbers to the bottom of each page.
   d. Edit the labels in the subreport as shown in Figure 5.15.
   e. Add your name in the *Report Footer* section.
3. Save the report, naming it *DogOwnersWithDogs*.
4. Preview the report. If necessary, return to Layout view or Design view to make adjustments. When finished, save and print the report.
5. Close the report and then close **AL2-C5-PawsParadise.accdb**.

Figure 5.15 Partial View of Completed Visual Benchmark Report

Dog Owners with Dogs

Customer Number	First Name	Last Name	Home Telephone	Emergency Telephone
100	Shawn	Jenkins	(814) 555-8446	(814) 555-7469

Dog's Name	Breed	Color	Bordetella Vaccine?	Rabies Vaccine?	Play with other dogs?	Kennel Category
Abby	Labrador Retriever	Black	Yes	Yes	Yes	V.I.P. Suite
Winnie	Cocker Spaniel	Buff	Yes	Yes	Yes	V.I.P. Suite

Customer Number	First Name	Last Name	Home Telephone	Emergency Telephone
110	Valerie	McTague	(814) 555-3456	(814) 555-1495

Dog's Name	Breed	Color	Bordetella Vaccine?	Rabies Vaccine?	Play with other dogs?	Kennel Category
Chloe	Poodle	White	Yes	Yes	No	Deluxe Suite

Customer Number	First Name	Last Name	Home Telephone	Emergency Telephone
115	Glen	Waters	(814) 555-7496	(814) 555-6124

Dog's Name	Breed	Color	Bordetella Vaccine?	Rabies Vaccine?	Play with other dogs?	Kennel Category
Barney	Pug	Black	No	No	No	Indoor/Outdoor Suite

Customer Number	First Name	Last Name	Home Telephone	Emergency Telephone
120	Sofia	Ramos	(814) 555-6523	(814) 555-8769

Dog's Name	Breed	Color	Bordetella Vaccine?	Rabies Vaccine?	Play with other dogs?	Kennel Category
Apollo	Greyhound	Cream	Yes	Yes	Yes	Indoor/Outdoor Suite
Murphy	Bichon Frise	White	Yes	Yes	No	Indoor/Outdoor Suite

Case Study Apply Your Skills

Part 1

Continuing your work as an intern at Hillsdale Realty, your next task is to create reports for management. Open **AL2-C5-HillsdaleRealty.accdb** and enable the content. For each report created, add your name in a label control object in the *Report Footer* section. The first report has been requested by the office manager. She uses the SalesByAgentWithComm query frequently but has asked for a report that provides the information in a more useful format. Specifically, the office manager would like the report to be organized with each individual agent's sales together, showing the total value of sales and commissions earned for that agent and sorted by the date the listing sold. The office manager would also like to see grand totals and the percentage of the grand total that each agent has achieved for the sale prices and commissions earned. Design and create the report, including features such as page numbers, date and time controls, and graphics. Save the report and name it appropriately. Print the report with the top and bottom margins set to 0.5 inch and making sure that an entire group is kept together on the same page.

Part 2

The office manager would like a printout of the listings with the clients' preferences and the agents attached to the listings grouped by the city. (Note that not all of the listings have a preferences record but the office manager wants to see all of the listings on the report.) You determine an appropriate sort order within each city's group of records. Design and create the report. Save the report and name it appropriately. Print the report with a top margin of 0.75 inch and make sure that an entire group is kept together on the same page. ***Hint: Consider first creating a query with the relevant fields needed from the Listings, Preferences, and Agents tables and then base the report on the query. For one of the relationships in the query, you will need to modify the join properties.***

Part 3

The accountant would like a report that shows the number of days a listing that has sold was on the market, as well as the average number of days it took to sell a listing by city. Design and create the report. Save the report and name it appropriately. Print the report with the top and bottom margins set to 0.75 inch. ***Hint: Create a query using the Listings and SalesAndComm tables that includes a calculated field for the number of days a listing was on the market and then base the report on the query.***

Part 4

Help

In Access Help, research how to create a summary report (a report without the record details shown within a group). The accountant would like a compacted version of the report created for the office manager in Part 1 that shows the totals only for an individual agent. Open the report created in Part 1 and use *Save Object As* to create a copy of the report. You determine an appropriate new name. In the new copy of the report, modify the design as needed to create the report for the accountant. Print the new report, changing page setup options as needed to fit the entire report on one page. Save and close the report. Close **AL2-C5-HillsdaleRealty.accdb**.

MICROSOFT® ACCESS®

Using Access Tools and Managing Objects

PERFORMANCE OBJECTIVES

Upon successful completion of Chapter 6, you will be able to:

- **Create a new database using a template**
- **Add a group of objects to a database using an Application Parts template**
- **Save a database as a template**
- **Create a new form using an Application Parts Blank Form**
- **Create a form to be used as a template in a database**
- **Create a table by copying the structure of another table**
- **Evaluate a table using the Table Analyzer Wizard**
- **Evaluate a database using the Performance Analyzer**
- **Split a database**
- **Print documentation about a database using the Database Documenter**
- **Rename and delete objects**

Tutorials

6.1 Creating a Database Using a Template
6.2 Creating a Table Using a Table Template
6.3 Copying a Table Structure to a New Table
6.4 Modifying a Table Using the Table Analyzer Wizard
6.5 Optimizing Performance Using the Performance Analyzer
6.6 Splitting a Database
6.7 Documenting a Database
6.8 Renaming and Deleting Objects

Access provides tools to assist you with creating and managing databases and objects within databases. Templates are provided that can be used to create a new database or a new table and/or a related group of objects. Blank form templates provide you with a predefined layout and may include a form title and command buttons. If none of the predefined templates suits your needs, you can create your own template. Access provides wizards to assist with analyzing tables and databases to improve performance. A database can be split into two files to store the tables separately from the queries, forms, and reports. The Database Documenter can be used to print a report that provides details about objects and their properties. In this chapter, you will learn how to use these Access tools and how to rename and delete objects in the Navigation pane. Model answers for this chapter's projects appear on the following pages.

AL2C6

Note: Before beginning the projects, copy to your storage medium the AL2C6 subfolder from the AL2 folder on the CD that accompanies this textbook and then make AL2C6 the active folder.

12/7/2015 Page 1 of 1

Full Alphabetical Contact List

Ariel Grayson E-mail Map Grayson Accounting Services
17399 Windsor Avenue Accountant
Detroit, MI 48214-3274 USA ariel@emcp.net

Business	Home	Mobile
800-555-4988	313-555-6811	313-555-9648

Project 1 Create a New Database Using a Template

Project 1b, ContactDetails Report

Contact List

Contact Name	Company	Phone Number		Address
S				
Terry Silver	Cityscape Electronics	Mobile:	313-555-3442	3700 Woodward Avenue
	Sales Manager	Business:	800-555-4968	Detroit, MI 48201-2006
	terry_s@emcp.net	Home:		
		Fax:	800-555-6941	

Project 2 Create Objects Using a Template

Project 2a, ContactList Report

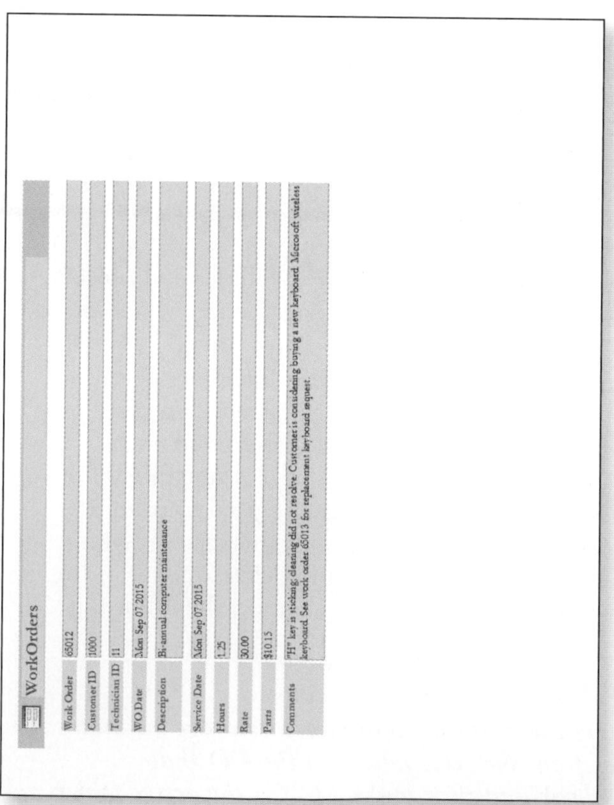

WorkOrders

Work Order	65012
Customer ID	1000
Technician ID	11
WO Date	Mon Sep 07 2015
Description	Bi-annual computer maintenance
Service Date	Mon Sep 07 2015
Hours	1.25
Rate	30.00
Parts	$10.15
Comments	"H" key is sticking; cleaning did not resolve. Customer is considering buying a new keyboard. Microsoft wireless keyboard. See work order 65013 for replacement keyboard request.

Project 2c, WorkOrders Form

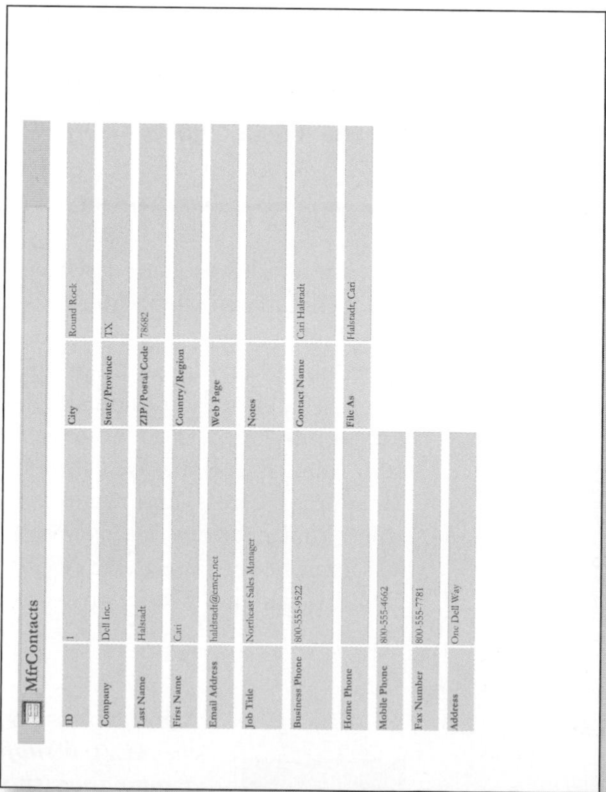

MfrContacts

ID	1	City	Round Rock
Company	Dell Inc.	State/Province	TX
Last Name	Halstadt	ZIP/Postal Code	78682
First Name	Cari	Country/Region	
Email Address	halstadt@emcp.net	Web Page	
Job Title	Northeast Sales Manager	Notes	
Business Phone	800-555-9522	Contact Name	Cari Halstadt
Home Phone		File As	Halstadt, Cari
Mobile Phone	800-555-4662		
Fax Number	800-555-7781		
Address	One Dell Way		

Project 3 Copy Table Structure

MfrContacts Form

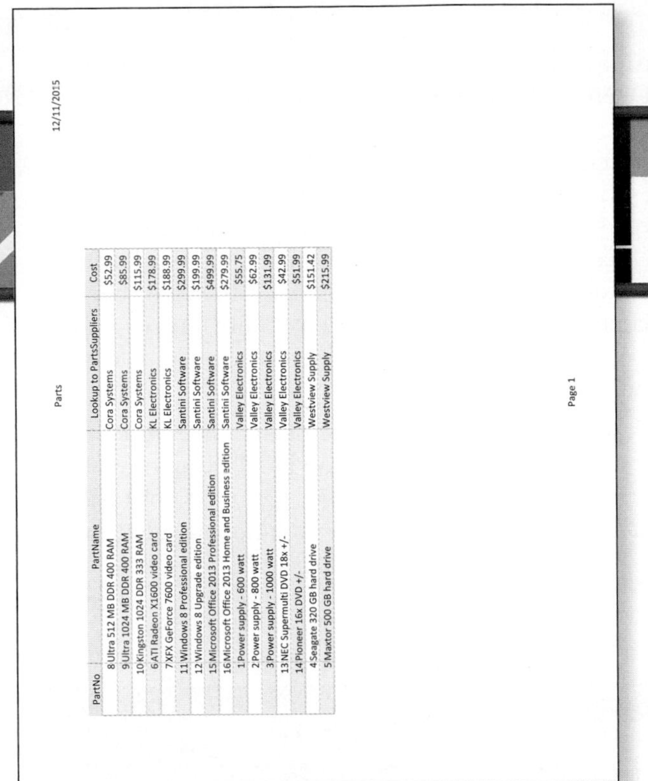

12/11/2015 Parts

PartNo	PartName	Lookup to PartsSuppliers	Cost
8	Ultra 512 MB DDR 400 RAM	Cora Systems	$52.99
9	Ultra 1024 MB DDR 400 RAM	Cora Systems	$85.99
10	Kingston 1024 DDR 333 RAM	Cora Systems	$115.99
6	ATI Radeon X1600 video card	KL Electronics	$178.99
7	XFX GeForce 7600 video card	KL Electronics	$188.99
11	Windows 8 Professional edition	Santini Software	$299.99
12	Windows 8 Upgrade edition	Santini Software	$199.99
15	Microsoft Office 2013 Professional edition	Santini Software	$499.99
16	Microsoft Office 2013 Home and Business edition	Santini Software	$279.99
1	Power supply - 600 watt	Valley Electronics	$55.75
2	Power supply - 800 watt	Valley Electronics	$62.99
3	Power supply - 1000 watt	Valley Electronics	$131.99
13	NEC Supermulti DVD 18x +/-	Valley Electronics	$42.99
14	Pioneer 16x DVD +/-	Valley Electronics	$51.99
4	Seagate 320 GB hard drive	Westview Supply	$151.42
5	Maxtor 500 GB hard drive	Westview Supply	$215.99

Page 1

H:\AL2C6\AL2-C6-RSRCompServ_be.accdb Monday, December 7, 2015
Table: PartsSuppliers Page: 1

Properties

DateCreated:	12/7/2015 6:26:29 PM	LastUpdated:	12/7/2015 6:26:29 PM
RecordCount:	5	Updatable:	True

Columns

Name		Type	Size
Supplier		Short Text	255
AllowZeroLength:	False		
AppendOnly:	False		
Attributes:	Variable Length		
CollatingOrder:	General		
DataUpdatable:	False		
OrdinalPosition:	0		
Required:	False		
SourceField:	Supplier		
SourceTable:	PartsSuppliers		
ID		Long Integer	4
AllowZeroLength:	False		
AppendOnly:	False		
Attributes:	Fixed Size, Auto-Increment		
CollatingOrder:	General		
DataUpdatable:	False		
OrdinalPosition:	1		
Required:	False		
SourceField:	ID		
SourceTable:	PartsSuppliers		

Relationships

PartsSuppliersPartsAndCosts

PartsSuppliers: ID — 1 ∞ — PartsAndCosts: PartsSuppliers_ID

Attributes: Enforced, Cascade Updates
RelationshipType: One-To-Many

Project 4 Use Access Tools to Optimize and Document a Database

Project 4a, Parts Query

Project 4d, PartsSuppliers Definition Report

Project 1 Create a New Database Using a Template — 2 Parts

You will create a new database using one of the database templates supplied with Access, as well as create your own template.

Creating a New Database Using a Template

At the Open or New backstage area, you can create a new database using one of the professionally designed templates provided by Microsoft. The database templates provide a complete series of objects, including predefined tables, forms, reports, queries, and relationships. You can use a template as provided and immediately start entering data or you can base a new database on a template and modify the objects to suit your needs. If a template exists for a database application that you need, you can save time by creating the database based on one of the template designs.

Along with desktop templates, Access 2013 contains templates for creating apps. These apps require you to have Microsoft SharePoint to share your data with other users. (SharePoint is a server application that allows for collaboration on and sharing of documents.)

Quick Steps

Create a Database from a Template
1. Start Access.
2. Click desired template.
3. Click Browse button.
4. Navigate to drive and/or folder.
5. Edit file name as required.
6. Click OK.
7. Click Create button.

To create a new database using a template, start Access and then click one of the available templates in the Open backstage area. If Access is already open, click one of the available templates at the New backstage area. When you click the desired template, a preview appears, similar to what is shown in Figure 6.1. The name of the template provider, a description, and the rating are displayed in the preview. Use the directional arrows on either side of the preview to move through the other available templates. Once you have chosen a template, click the Browse button to navigate to the drive and/or folder in which you want to store the database and then type a file name at the *File Name* text box. This returns you to the previous screen, with the new database file name entered below the *File Name* text box. Click the Create button to create the database.

If none of the sample templates are suited to the type of database you want to create, close the preview and search for templates online by clicking one of the hyperlinked suggested searches (such as Assets, Business, or Contacts) or type a subject in the *Search for online templates* text box. Templates are downloaded from Office.com.

Figure 6.1 Available Templates in the New Backstage Area

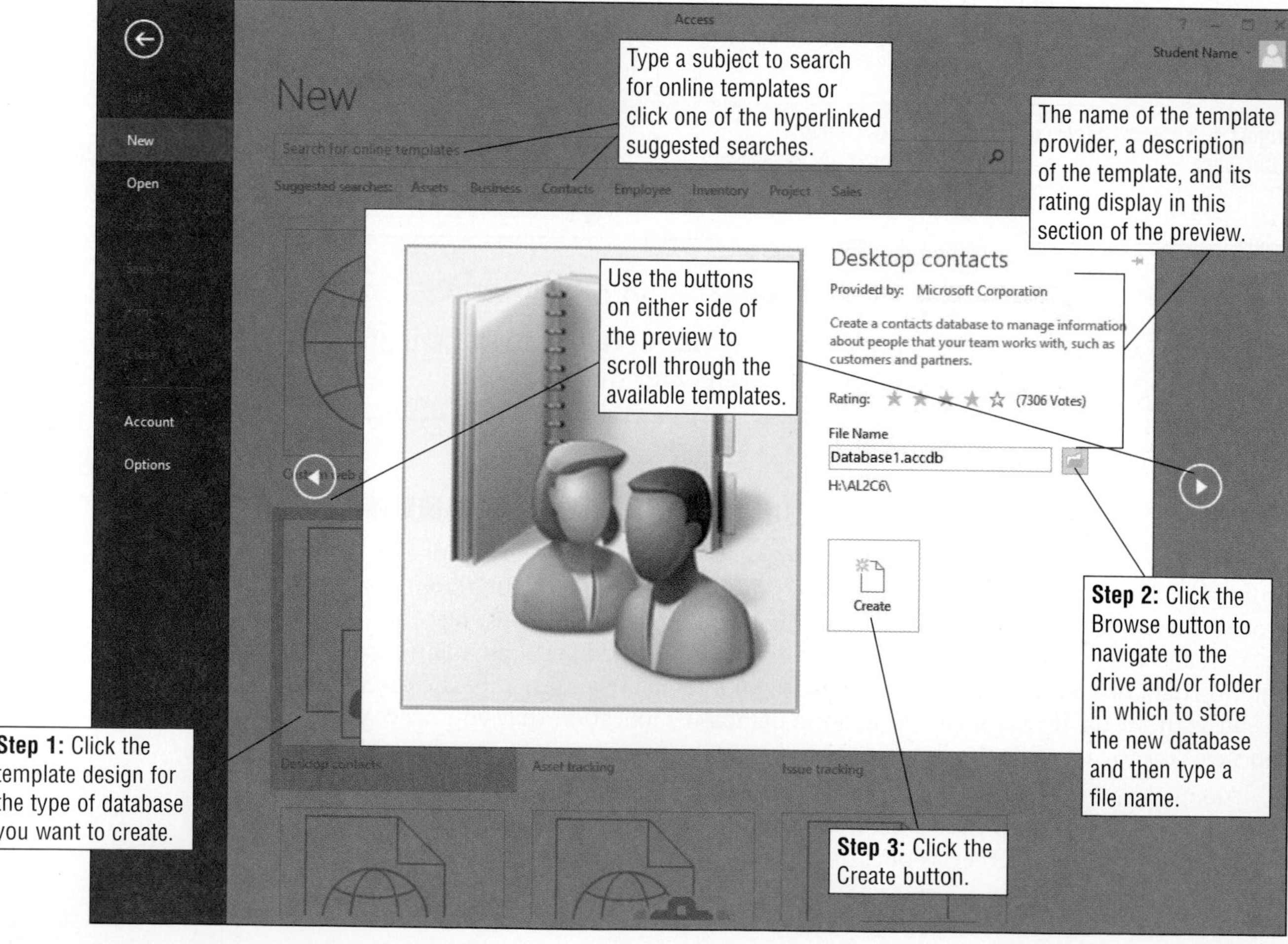
Type a subject to search for online templates or click one of the hyperlinked suggested searches.
The name of the template provider, a description of the template, and its rating display in this section of the preview.
Use the buttons on either side of the preview to scroll through the available templates.
Step 1: Click the template design for the type of database you want to create.
Step 2: Click the Browse button to navigate to the drive and/or folder in which to store the new database and then type a file name.
Step 3: Click the Create button.
New
Open
Account
Options
Desktop contacts
Provided by: Microsoft Corporation
Create a contacts database to manage information about people that your team works with, such as customers and partners.
Rating: (7306 Votes)
File Name
Database1.accdb
H:\AL2C6\
Create

Project 1a Creating a New Contacts Database Using a Template — Part 1 of 3

1. Start Microsoft Access 2013.
2. At the Open backstage area, click the *Desktop contacts* template.
3. Click the Browse button (which displays as a file folder icon) next to the *File Name* text box in the template preview.
4. At the File New Database dialog box, navigate to the AL2C6 folder on your storage medium, select the current entry in the *File name* text box, and then type **AL2-C6-Contacts**.
5. Click OK.

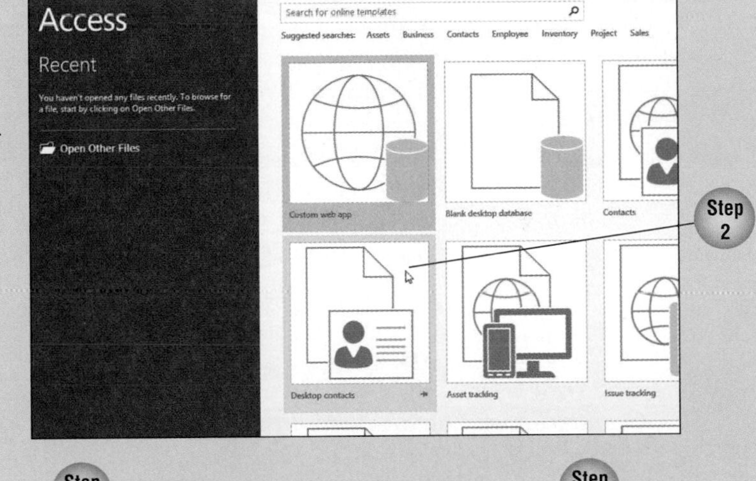

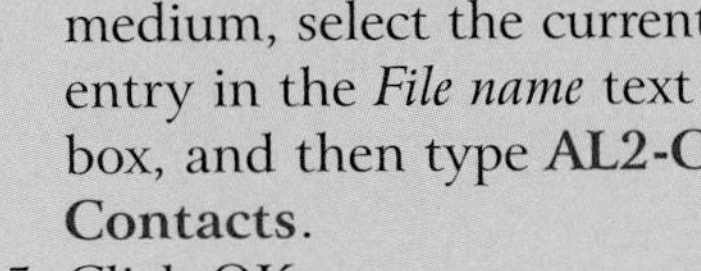

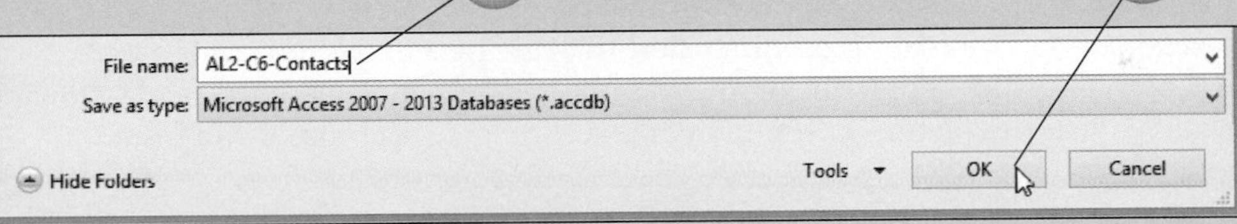

6. Click the Create button.
7. The database is created with all of the objects from the template loaded into the current window and the Contact List form open. A Getting Started with Contacts form appears, containing videos and links to information on using this database. Click the *Show Getting Started when this database is opened* check box to remove the check mark. If the box is left checked, this form will open every time you open the database. Close the Getting Started with Contacts form.

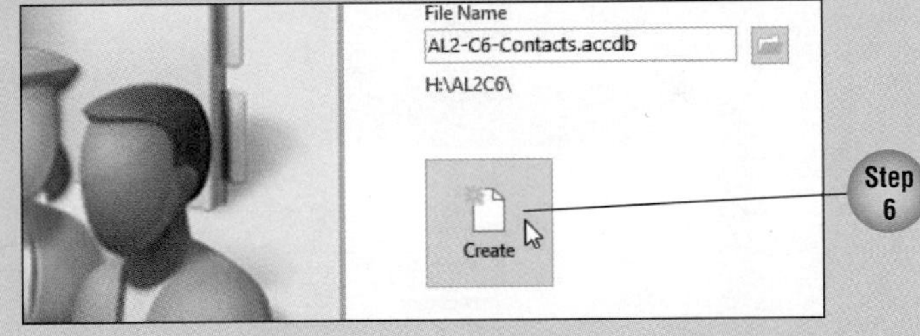

8. Click the Enable Content button in the message bar. Notice that the Title bar contains the text *Contact Management Database* rather than the name of the database, *Contacts.accdb*. In Chapter 7, you will learn how to change the Title bar to display a more descriptive title for your database.
9. Review the list of objects that Access has created for you in the Navigation pane and then double-click to open the Contacts table.
10. Scroll right to view all of the fields in the Contacts table and then close the table.
11. Review the Contact List form that is open in the work area.

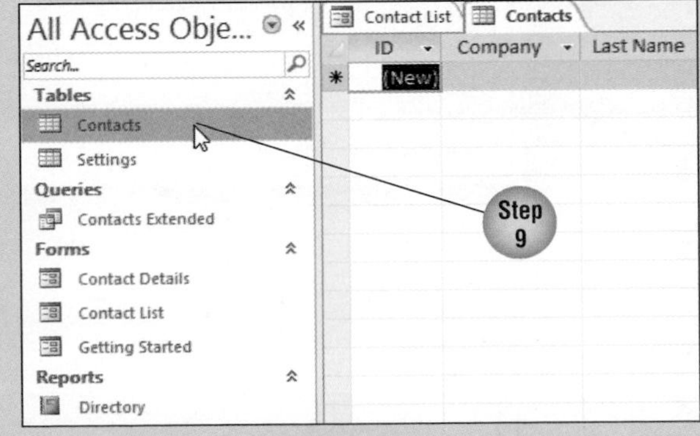

Project 1b Entering and Viewing Data in the Contacts Database Part 2 of 3

1. With **AL2-C6-Contacts.accdb** open, close the Contact List form and open the Contact Details form. In Form view, add the following record to modify the data source using the form:

First Name	Ariel
Last Name	Grayson
Company	Grayson Accounting Services
Job Title	Accountant
Business Phone	800-555-4988
Home Phone	313-555-9648
Mobile Phone	313-555-6811
Fax Number	800-555-3472
Street	17399 Windsor Avenue
City	Detroit
State/Province	MI
Zip/Postal Code	48214-3274
Country/Region	USA ***Note: Press Tab or Enter three times after this field to move to the* E-mail *field.***
E-mail	ariel@emcp.net
Web Page	www.emcp.net/grayson
Notes	Ariel recommended to RSR by Pat Hynes.

2. Add a picture of the contact using the *Attachments* field by completing the following steps:
   a. Double-click the picture in the Images placeholder at the top of the form.

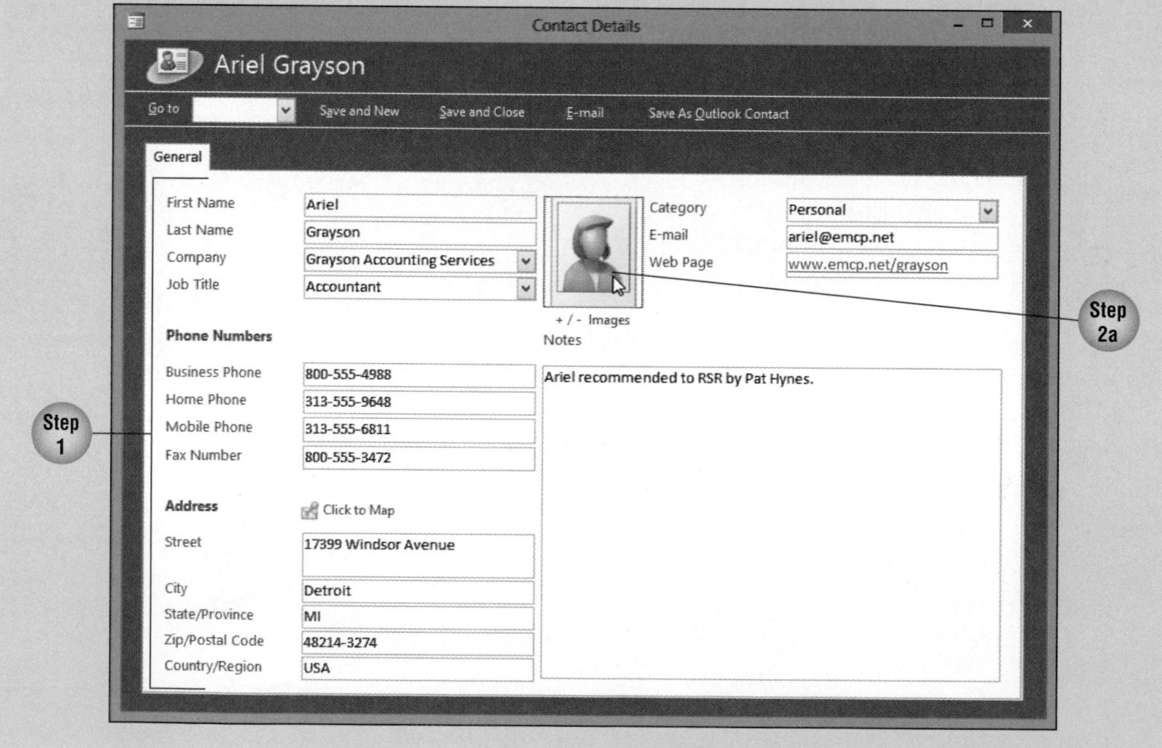

b. At the Attachments dialog box, click the Add button.
c. At the Choose File dialog box, navigate to the AL2C6 folder on your storage medium.
d. Double-click ***ArielGrayson.jpg*** to add the file to the Attachments dialog box and then click OK.

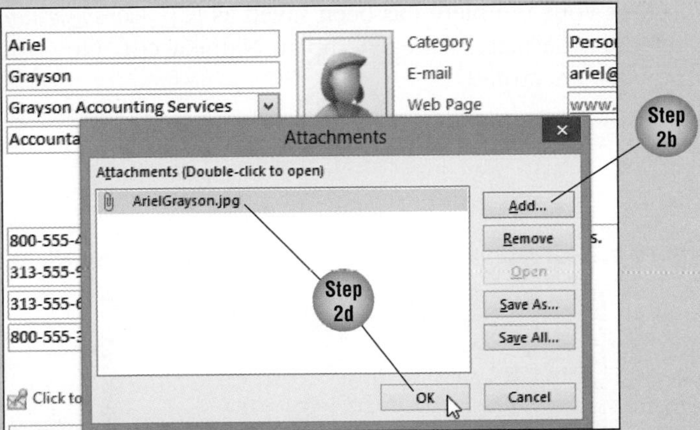

e. Notice that the picture now displays in the form. If you had selected a Word document in the Attachments dialog box, a Word icon would display instead.

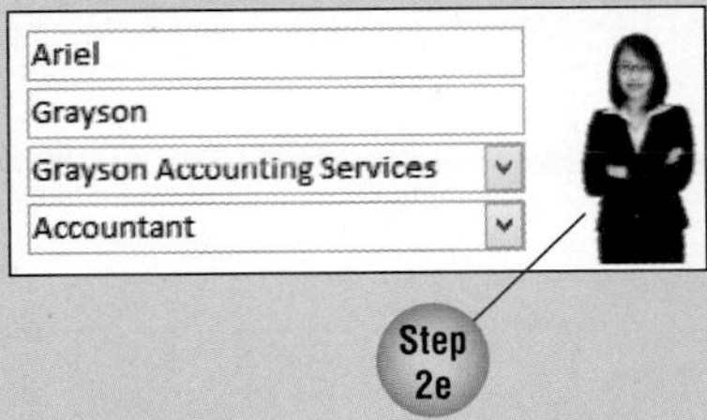

3. Click the Close button to close the form. ***Note: Do not use the Save and Close button located at the top of the form, as macro errors may occur.***
4. Double-click *Directory* in the Reports group in the Navigation pane. Review the report.
5. Display the report in Print Preview and then print the report.
6. Close Print Preview and then close the *Directory* report.

Saving a Database as a Template

If none of the existing templates meet your needs and you often find yourself creating the same database structure, you may want to create your own template. As with other Microsoft applications, using a template in Access can help save you time and effort. To create a database template, you can either create the whole database yourself, or you can modify an existing database based on a template and then save it as a new template.

Quick Steps

Save a Database as a Template
1. Open database.
2. Make desired changes.
3. Click FILE tab.
4. Click *Save As.*
5. Click Browse button.
6. Change *Save as type* to *Template (*.accdt).*
7. Type information in Contact Management dialog box.
8. Click OK twice.

To save a database as a template, click the FILE tab and then click the *Save As* option. With *Save Database As* selected in the *File Types* section, click *Template (*.accdt)* in the *Database File Types* section and then click the Save As button. Fill in the Create New Template from This Database dialog box, shown in Figure 6.2, and then click OK. Click OK at the Contact Management Database dialog box telling you that your template has been saved as [c]\Users*username*\AppData\Roaming\Microsoft\Templates\Access\TemplateName.accdt. Note the location where the templates are stored.

Figure 6.2 Create New Template from This Database Dialog Box

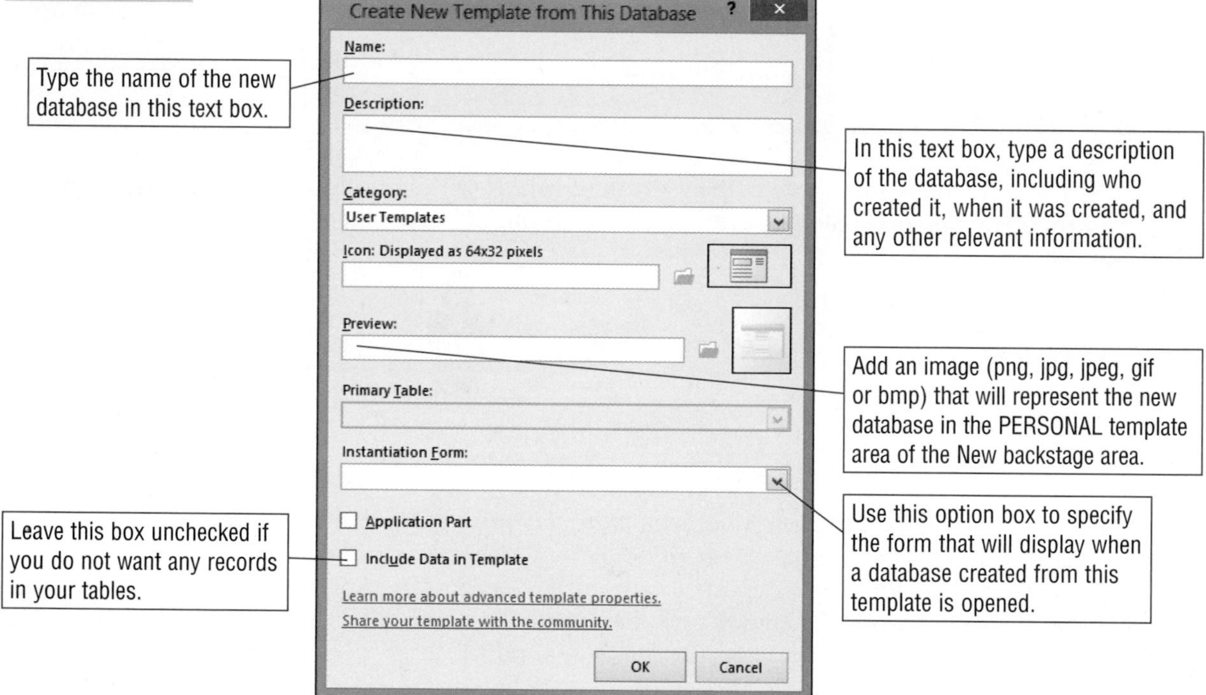
Create New Template from This Database
Name:
Description:
Category:
User Templates
Icon: Displayed as 64x32 pixels
Preview:
Primary Table:
Instantiation Form:
Application Part
Include Data in Template
Learn more about advanced template properties.
Share your template with the community.
OK
Cancel
Type the name of the new database in this text box.
In this text box, type a description of the database, including who created it, when it was created, and any other relevant information.
Add an image (png, jpg, jpeg, gif or bmp) that will represent the new database in the PERSONAL template area of the New backstage area.
Use this option box to specify the form that will display when a database created from this template is opened.
Leave this box unchecked if you do not want any records in your tables.

Project 1c Saving a Database as a Template — Part 3 of 3

1. With **AL2-C6-Contacts.accdb** open, open the Contact List form in Design view and then delete all of the information in the upper right corner of the form. You can individually click each object and press Delete to remove them one by one, or you can draw a selection rectangle around all of the objects and then press Delete to remove them all at once. Save and close the form.
2. Save the revised database as a template by completing the following steps:
   a. Click the FILE tab.
   b. Click *Save As*.
   c. Click *Template(*.accdt)* in the *Database File Types* section.
   d. Click the Save As button.

e. At the Create New Template from this Database dialog box, enter data as follows:

Name:	**CustomContacts**
Description:	**Created by [Student Name] on [current date].** (Substitute your name for [Student Name] and today's date for [current date].)
Preview:	Click the Browse button, navigate to the AL2C6 data folder, and then double-click ***CustomizedContacts.png***.

3. Click OK.

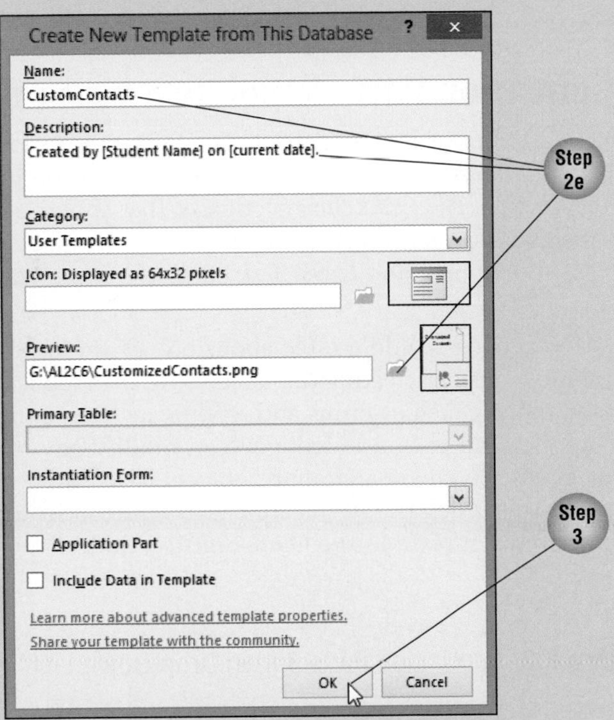

4. Click OK.
5. Close **AL2-C6-Contacts.accdt**.
6. To view the new template, click the FILE tab and then click *PERSONAL*. The CustomContacts template you created is shown with CustomizedContacts.png as the image. Click the Back button.

Using a Custom Template

To use a template that you created yourself, click the FILE tab and then click *New*. At the New backstage area, click *PERSONAL*. This opens the PERSONAL template area. Double-click the name of the desired template to open it.

Deleting a Custom Template

To delete a custom template, use the Open dialog box to navigate to [c]\Users\ *username*\AppData\Roaming\Microsoft\Templates\Access\. Right-click the name of the template that you want to delete and then click *Delete* at the shortcut menu. Click Cancel to close the Open dialog box.

Project 2 Create Objects Using a Template — 3 Parts

You will use Application Parts templates to create a series of objects in an existing database. You will also define a form as a template for all new forms in a database.

Creating Objects Using an Application Parts Template

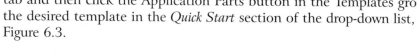

Access 2013 provides templates for prebuilt objects that can be inserted into an existing database using the Application Parts button in the Templates group on the CREATE tab. The *Quick Start* section of the Application Parts button drop-down list includes *Comments*, which creates a table; *Contacts*, which creates a table, a query, forms, and reports; and *Issues*, *Tasks*, and *Users*, each of which creates a table and two forms.

HINT
You can create your own Application Parts template by copying an object you will reuse in other databases to a new database and then saving the database as a template at the Save As backstage area.

If you need to add a table about one of the topics listed above to an existing database, consider creating the table using the Application Parts template, because related objects such as forms and reports are also automatically generated. Once the application part is added, you can modify any of the object designs to suit your needs. To create a group of objects based on a template, click the CREATE tab and then click the Application Parts button in the Templates group. Click the desired template in the *Quick Start* section of the drop-down list, as shown in Figure 6.3.

Figure 6.3 Application Parts Button Drop-Down List

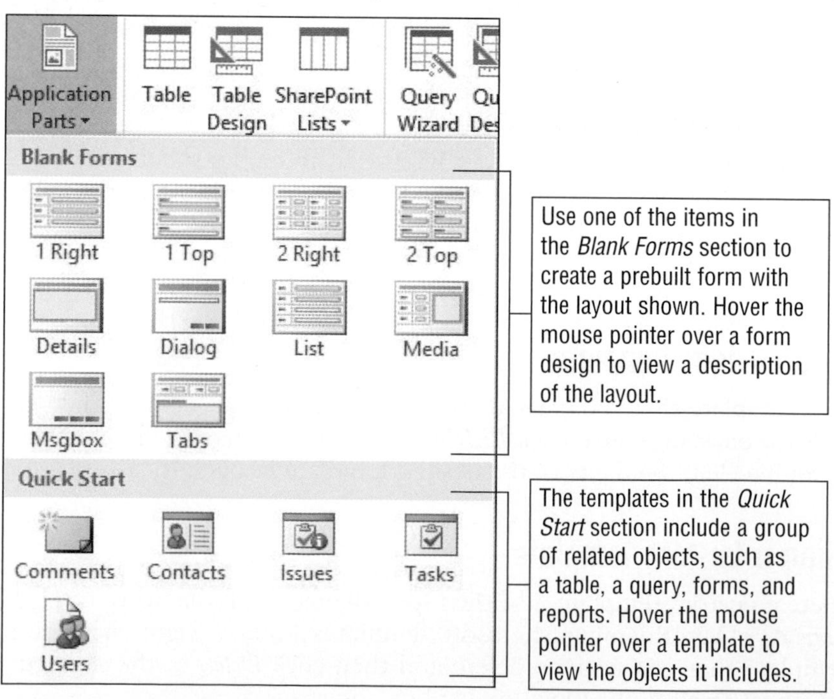

Application Parts
Table
Table Design
SharePoint Lists
Query Wizard
Blank Forms
1 Right
1 Top
2 Right
2 Top
Details
Dialog
List
Media
Msgbox
Tabs
Quick Start
Comments
Contacts
Issues
Tasks
Users
Use one of the items in the *Blank Forms* section to create a prebuilt form with the layout shown. Hover the mouse pointer over a form design to view a description of the layout.
The templates in the *Quick Start* section include a group of related objects, such as a table, a query, forms, and reports. Hover the mouse pointer over a template to view the objects it includes.

Access opens the Create Relationship Wizard to guide you through creating the relationship for the new table. Decide in advance of creating the new table what relationship, if any, will exist between the new table and an existing table in the database. At the first Create Relationship dialog box, shown in Figure 6.4, click the first option if the new table will be the "many" table in a one-to-many relationship. Use the drop-down list to choose the "one" table and then click Next. If the new table will be the "one" table in a one-to-many relationship, click the second option, use the drop-down list to choose the "many" table, and then click Next.

At the second Create Relationship dialog box, enter the settings for the lookup column between the two tables. Choose the field to use to join the tables, choose a sort order if desired, assign the name of the lookup column, and then click the Create button. If the new table will not be related to any of the existing tables in the database, choose the *There is no relationship* option at the first Create Relationship dialog box and then click the Create button.

Quick Steps

Create Objects Using an Application Parts Template

1. Open database.
2. Click CREATE tab.
3. Click Application Parts button.
4. Click desired template.
5. Choose relationship options.
6. Add data or modify objects as required.

Application Parts

Figure 6.4 First Dialog Box in the Create Relationship Wizard

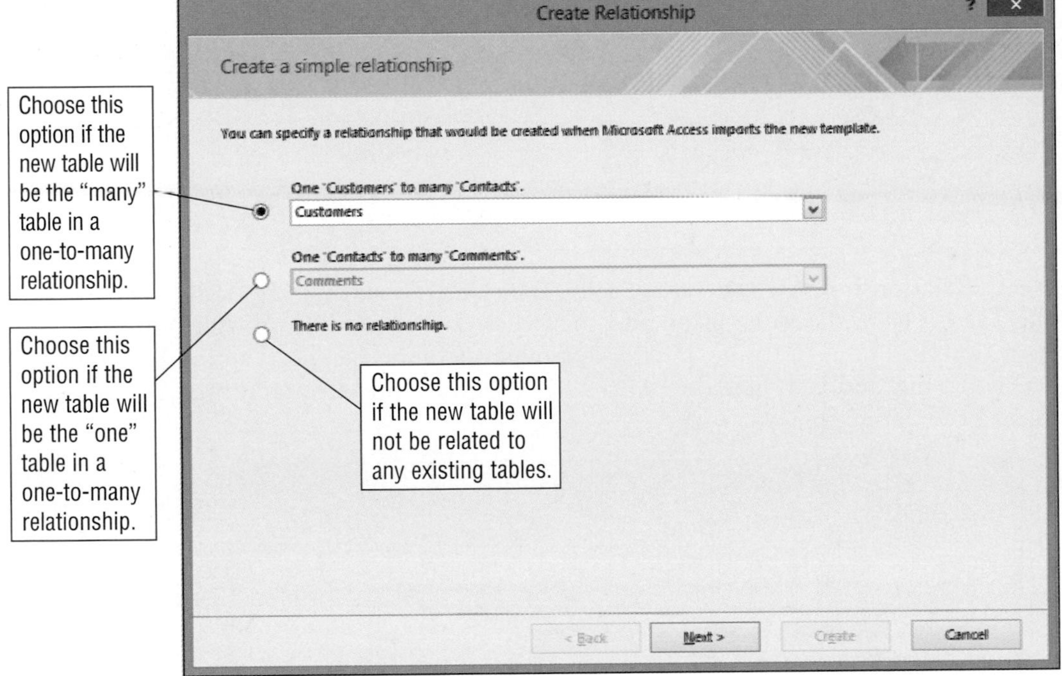
Create Relationship
Create a simple relationship
You can specify a relationship that would be created when Microsoft Access imports the new template.
One 'Customers' to many 'Contacts'.
Customers
One 'Contacts' to many 'Comments'.
Comments
There is no relationship.
< Back
Next >
Create
Cancel
Choose this option if the new table will be the "many" table in a one-to-many relationship.
Choose this option if the new table will be the "one" table in a one-to-many relationship.
Choose this option if the new table will not be related to any existing tables.

Project 2a Creating a Contacts Table, a Query, Forms, and Reports Using a Template Part 1 of 3

1. Open **AL2-C6-RSRCompServ.accdb** and enable the content.
2. Use a template to create a new table, a query, forms, and reports related to contacts by completing the following steps:
   a. Click the CREATE tab.
   b. Click the Application Parts button in the Templates group and then click *Contacts* in the *Quick Start* section of the drop-down list.

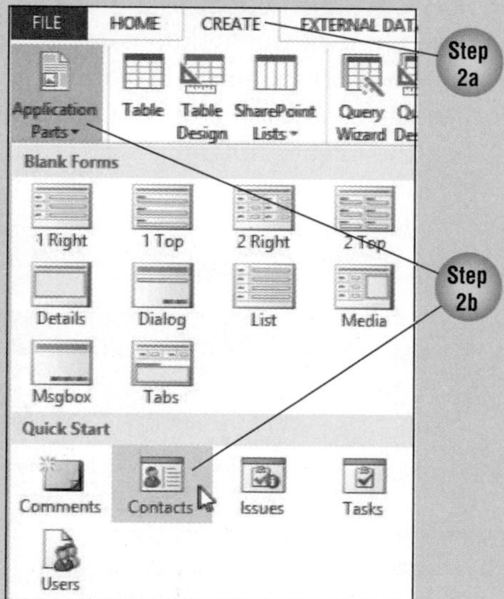

   c. The Create Relationship Wizard starts. At the first Create Relationship dialog box, click the *There is no relationship* option and then click the Create button. Access imports a Contacts table; a ContactsExtended query; ContactDetails, ContactDS, and ContactList forms; and ContactAddressBook, ContactList, and ContactPhoneBook reports into the database.

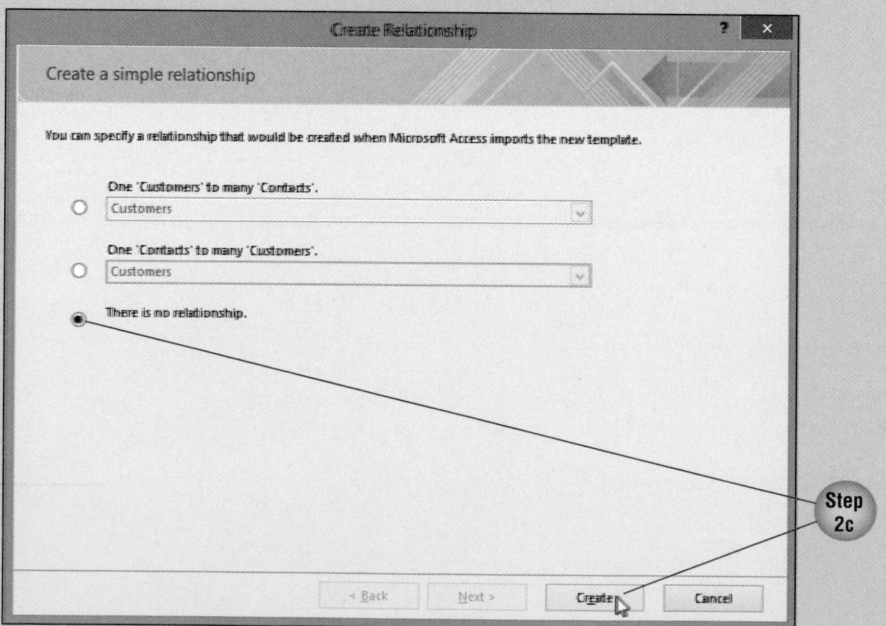

3. Double-click *Contacts* in the Tables group in the Navigation pane. Scroll to the right to view all of the fields in the new table and then close the table.
4. Double-click *ContactDetails* in the Forms group in the Navigation pane.
5. Enter the following record using the ContactDetails form:

First Name	**Terry**
Last Name	**Silver**
Job Title	**Sales Manager**
Company	**Cityscape Electronics** ***Note: Press Tab twice or Enter twice after this field to move to the E-mail field.***
E-mail	**terry_s@emcp.net**
Web Page	**www.emcp.net/cityscape**
Business Phone	**800-555-4968**
Fax	**800-555-6941**
Home Phone	(leave blank)
Mobile Phone	**313-555-3442**
Address	**3700 Woodward Avenue**
City	**Detroit**
State/Province	**MI**
ZIP/Postal Code	**48201-2006**
Country/Region	(leave blank)
Notes	(leave blank)

6. Click the Save & Close button at the top right of the form.

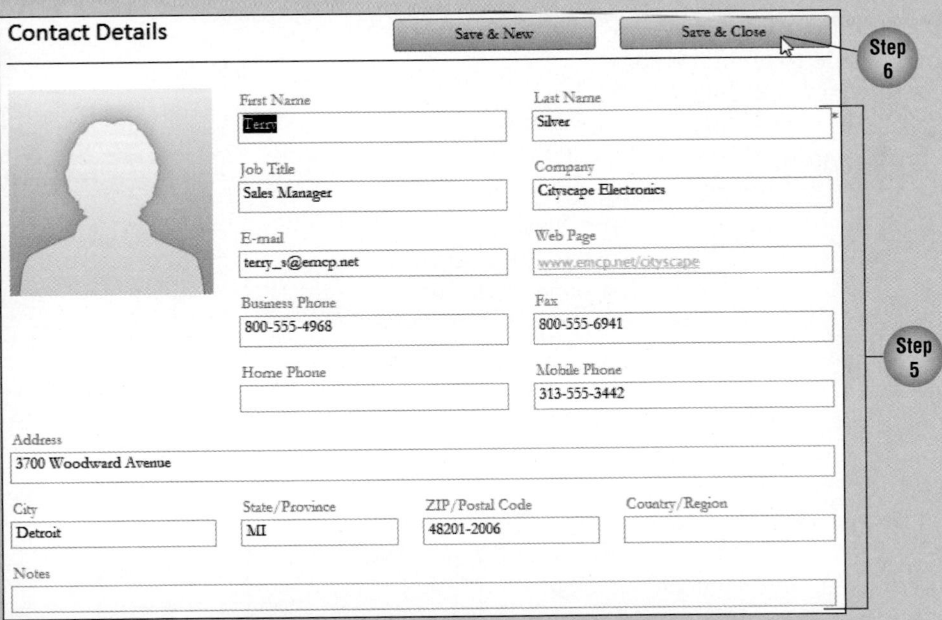

7. Open the ContactList report.
8. Display the report in Print Preview and then print the report.
9. Close Print Preview and then close the ContactList report.

Quick Steps

Create a Form Using a Blank Application Parts Form
1. Click CREATE tab.
2. Click Application Parts button.
3. Click desired blank form layout.
4. Add fields to form.
5. Customize form as needed.
6. Save form.

Application Parts also includes various blank form layouts, which make the task of creating a new form easier by allowing you to pick a layout that has already been defined. The *Blank Forms* section of the Application Parts button drop-down list contains ten prebuilt blank forms. Most of the forms contain command buttons that perform actions such as saving changes or saving and closing the form. Hovering the mouse pointer over a blank form option at the Application Parts button drop-down list displays a description of the form's layout in a ScreenTip. When you click a blank form option, Access creates the form object using a predefined form name. For example, if you click *1 Right*, Access creates a form named *SingleOneColumnRightLabels*. Locate the form name in the Navigation pane and then open the form in Layout view or Design view to customize it as needed.

Each Application Parts form has a control layout applied so that all of the form's controls move and resize together. Remove the control layout to make individual size adjustments. To do this, in Design view, select all of the controls and then click the Remove Layout button in the Table group on the FORM DESIGN TOOLS ARRANGE tab.

Project 2b Creating a New Form Using an Application Parts Blank Form — Part 2 of 3

1. With **AL2-C6-RSRCompServ.accdb** open, use an Application Parts blank form to create a new form for maintaining records in the Parts table by completing the following steps:
   a. If necessary, click the CREATE tab.
   b. Click the Applications Parts button in the Templates group and then click *1 Right* in the *Blank Forms* section of the drop-down list. Access creates a form named *SingleOneColumnRightLabels*.
   c. If necessary, position the mouse pointer on the right border of the Navigation pane until the pointer changes to a left-and-right-pointing arrow and then drag right to widen the Navigation pane until you can read all of the object names.
   d. Double-click *SingleOneColumnRightLabels* in the Forms group in the Navigation pane.

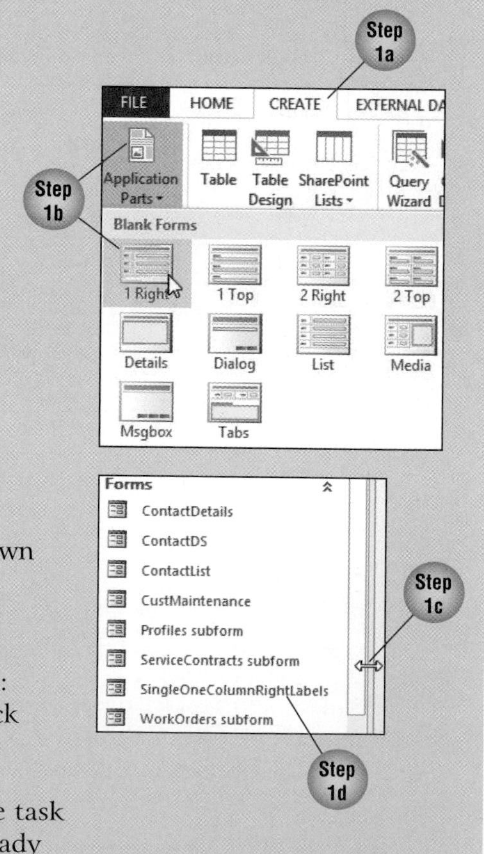

2. Switch to Layout view.
3. Click to select the *Field1* label control object. Hold down Shift, click to select the *Field2*, *Field3*, and *Field4* label control objects, and then press Delete.
4. Associate the Parts table with the form and add fields from the Parts table by completing the following steps:
   a. If the Field List task pane is not currently open, click the Add Existing Fields button in the Tools group on the FORM LAYOUT TOOLS DESIGN tab.
   b. Click the Show all tables hyperlink at the top of the task pane. Skip this step if your Field List task pane already displays all of the table names in the database.
   c. Click the plus symbol (+) next to *Parts* in the Field List task pane to expand the list and show all of the fields in the Parts table.

d. Drag the *PartNo* field to the second column in the row shown at the right.

e. Drag the remaining fields *PartName*, *Supplier*, and *Cost* below *PartNo* as shown below and to the right.

5. With the *Cost* field selected, drag the bottom orange border of the control up to decrease the height of the control object so that the bottom border is approximately 0.5 inch below the label text.

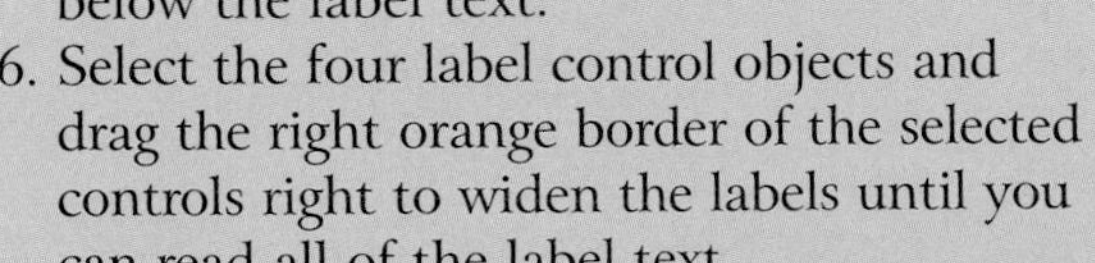

6. Select the four label control objects and drag the right orange border of the selected controls right to widen the labels until you can read all of the label text.

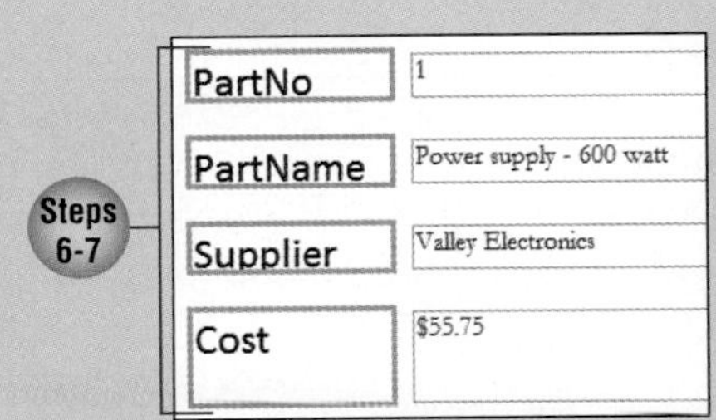

7. With the four label control objects still selected, click the FORM LAYOUT TOOLS ARRANGE tab, click the Control Padding button in the Position group, and then click *Wide* at the drop-down list.
8. Double-click the form title to place the insertion point inside the title text, delete *Form Title*, type **Repair Parts**, and then press Enter.
9. Make formatting changes to the form as follows:
   a. Select the two command buttons at the top right of the form (Save and Save & Close), click the FORM LAYOUT TOOLS FORMAT tab, click the Quick Styles button, and then click *Intense Effect - Blue-Gray, Accent 3*.
   b. Select the *Repair Parts* title control object and apply the Blue-Gray, Accent 3 font color (seventh option in the first row of the *Theme Colors* section).
   c. Apply the Blue-Gray, Accent 3 font color to the four label control objects.
   d. Apply the Blue-Gray, Accent 3 Lighter 80% background color (seventh option in the second row of the *Theme Colors* section) to the four text box control objects adjacent to the labels.

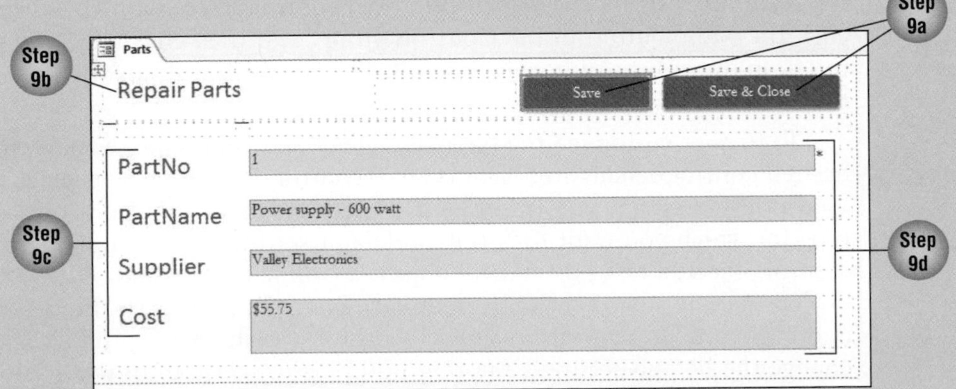

   e. Click in a blank area of the form to deselect the four text box control objects.

10. Click the FILE tab, click the *Save As* option, click *Save Object As,* and then click the Save As button. Type **Parts** in the *Save 'SingleOneColumnRightLabels' to* text box at the Save As dialog box and then click OK.
11. Click the HOME tab and then switch to Form view.
12. Scroll through a few records in the Parts form and then click the Save & Close button at the top right of the form. Your record may look different than the one shown below.

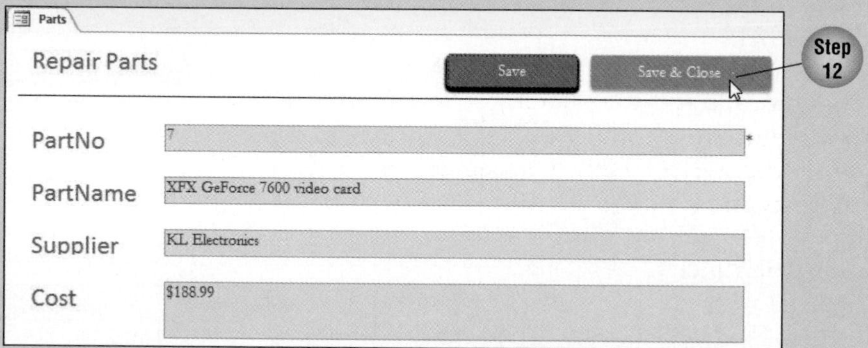

13. The SingleOneColumnRightLabels form is no longer needed. Click *SingleOneColumnRightLabels* in the Forms group in the Navigation pane and then press Delete. Answer Yes to the question *Do you want to permanently delete the form 'SingleOneColumnRightLabels'?*

Setting Form Control Defaults and Creating a User-Defined Form Template

Quick Steps

Create a User-Defined Form Template
1. Create new form in Design view.
2. Add control object to form.
3. Format control object as desired.
4. Click More button in Control group.
5. Click *Set Control Defaults.*
6. Repeat Steps 2–5 for each type of control to be used.
7. Save form, naming it *Normal.*

Using a standard design for all of the forms in a database is an effective way of ensuring consistency and portraying a professional image. For example, you may want all label control objects in your forms to be formatted as 14-point blue text on a gray background. However, changing these options manually in each form is time consuming and may lead to inconsistencies, so you can choose to customize the default settings instead.

The *Set Control Defaults* option at the Controls drop-down list allows you to change the default properties for all of the new labels in a form. To do this, open the form in Design view, format one label control object with the desired settings, click the More button in the Controls group, and then click *Set Control Defaults* at the drop-down list. All new labels added to the form will now be formatted with the options you have defined.

To further customize the database, create a form template that will set the desired control defaults for each type of control object that you place on a form. To do this, open a new form in Design view and create one control object of each type for which you want to specify a default setting. For example, add a label control object, a text box control object, a command button, and a list box control object, making sure that you format each control object with the desired colors and backgrounds. As you finish each control, use the *Set Control Defaults* option to change the default settings. Another option is to select all of the controls after you have finished the form and then perform one *Set Control Defaults* command. When you are finished, save the form using the name *Normal*. The Normal form becomes the template for all new forms in the database. Existing forms retain their initial formatting, unless you change them manually.

Delete the Normal form if you want to go back to using the standard default options for control objects in forms.

Project 2c Creating and Using a User-Defined Form Template — Part 3 of 3

1. With **AL2-C6-RSRCompServ.accdb** open, create a form template for the database by completing the following steps:
   a. Click the CREATE tab and then click the Form Design button in the Forms group.
   b. Click the Themes button in the Themes group. Notice that the database uses the Organic theme for any new forms.
   c. Click the Label button in the Controls group on the FORM DESIGN TOOLS DESIGN tab, draw a label in the *Detail* section, type **Sample Label Text**, and then press Enter. Do not be concerned with the position and size of the label object at this time, since you are using this control object only to set new default formatting options.
   d. Click the FORM DESIGN TOOLS FORMAT tab. Apply bold formatting and change the font color to *Blue-Gray, Accent 3* (seventh option in the first row of the *Theme Colors* section) and the background color to *Blue-Gray, Accent 3, Lighter 80%* (seventh option in the second row of the *Theme Colors* section).

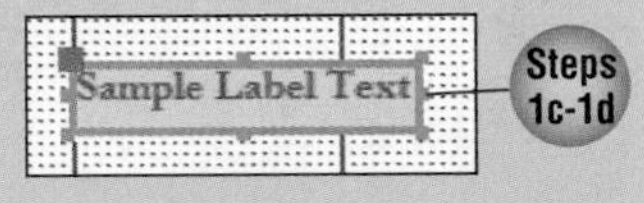

   e. Click the FORM DESIGN TOOLS DESIGN tab, click the Text Box button in the Controls group, and then draw a text box control object in the *Detail* section. Format the text box control object and its associated label control object as follows:
      1) To the label control object, apply bold formatting and the same font and background colors that you applied to the label control object in Step 1d.
      2) Select the text box control object (displays *Unbound*) and apply the same background color you applied to the label control object in Step 1d.
   f. Click the FORM DESIGN TOOLS DESIGN tab, click the Combo Box button in the Controls group, and then draw a combo box in the *Detail* section. If the Combo Box Wizard begins, click Cancel. Format the combo box control object using the same options you applied to the text box control object in Steps 1e1 and 1e2.
   g. Press Ctrl + A to select all of the control objects in the form.
   h. Click the FORM DESIGN TOOLS DESIGN tab, click the More button in the Controls group and then click *Set Control Defaults*.

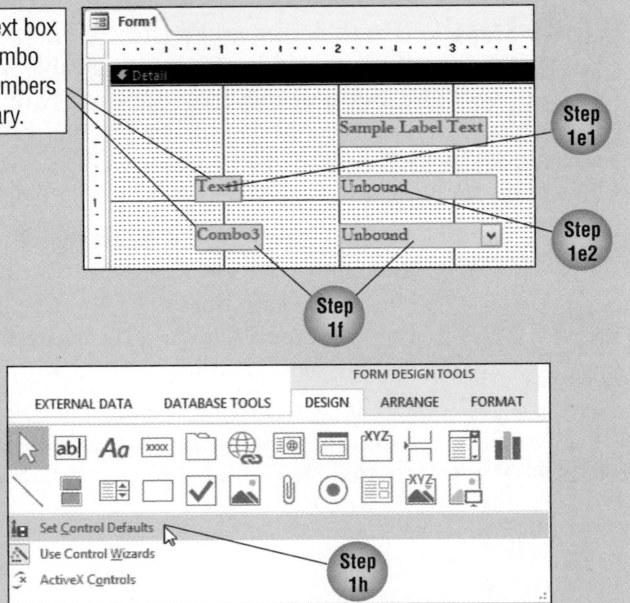

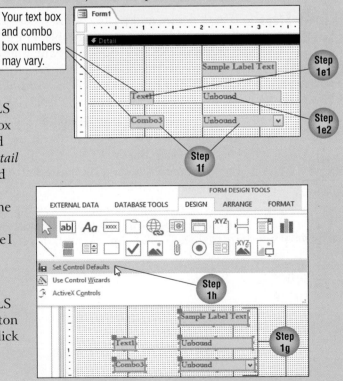

2. Save the form and name it *Normal*.
3. Close the Normal form. Normal becomes the form template for AL2-C6-RSRCompServ.accdb. Any new form created will have labels, text boxes, and combo boxes formatted as specified in Step 1.

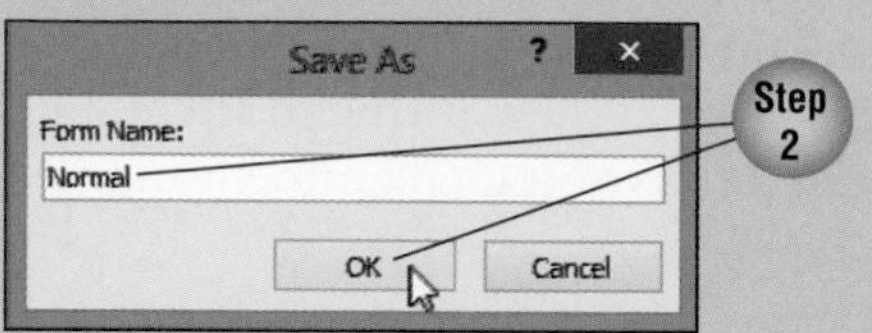

4. Click *WorkOrders* in the Tables group in the Navigation pane, click the CREATE tab, and then click the Form button in the Forms group. The new WorkOrders form uses the formatting applied to the labels, text boxes, and combo boxes in the Normal form template.
5. With the first record displayed in the WorkOrders form in Form view, open the Print dialog box. Click the Setup button located at the bottom left of the Print dialog box and then click the Columns tab at the Page Setup dialog box. Select the current value in the *Width* text box in the *Column Size* section, type 8, and then click OK. Click *Selected Record(s)* in the *Print Range* section of the Print dialog box and then click OK.
6. Close the WorkOrders form. Click Yes when prompted to save changes to the design of the form and then click OK to accept the default form name *WorkOrders*.

Project 3 Copy Table Structure — 1 Part

You will create a new table to store contact information for manufacturer sales representatives by copying an existing table's field names and field properties.

Copying a Table's Structure to Create a New Table

Quick Steps

Copy Table Structure
1. Select table.
2. Click Copy button.
3. Click Paste button.
4. Type new table name.
5. Click *Structure Only*.
6. Click OK.

HINT

If a new table will be similar to an existing table, you can save time by copying the existing table's structure and then adding, deleting, and modifying fields in Design view.

Use the copy and paste commands to create a new table that uses the same or similar fields as an existing table. For example, in Project 3, you will copy the Contacts table structure to create a new table for manufacturer contacts that you want to maintain separately from other contact records. Since the fields needed for manufacturer contact records are the same as those that already exist for the other contact records, you can base the new table on the existing table.

To copy a table's structure, click the existing table name in the Navigation pane and then click the Copy button in the Clipboard group on the HOME tab. Next, click the Paste button in the Clipboard group. When a table has been copied to the Clipboard, clicking the Paste button causes the Paste Table As dialog box to appear, as shown in Figure 6.5.

Type the desired name for the new table in the *Table Name* text box, click *Structure Only* in the *Paste Options* section, and then click OK. Once you have created the table, you can add, delete, or modify fields as needed.

Figure 6.5 Paste Table As Dialog Box

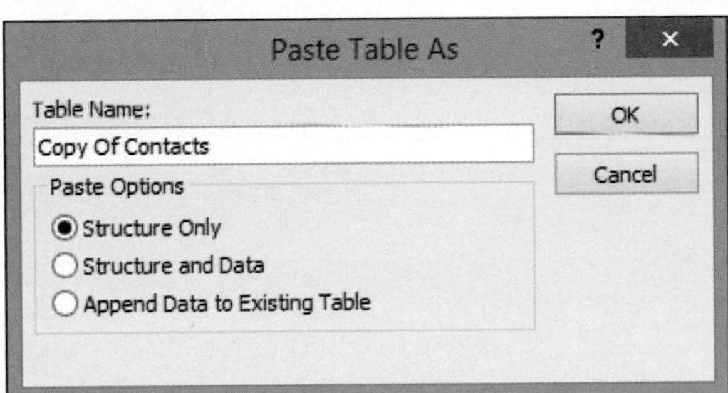

Project 3 Copying a Table Structure to Create a New Table

Part 1 of 1

1. With **AL2-C6-RSRCompServ.accdb** open, click *Contacts* in the Tables group in the Navigation pane.
2. Click the HOME tab and then click the Copy button in the Clipboard group.
3. Click the Paste button in the Clipboard group. (Do not click the Paste button arrow.)
4. At the Paste Table As dialog box, type **MfrContacts** in the *Table Name* text box, click *Structure Only* in the *Paste Options* section, and then press Enter or click OK.

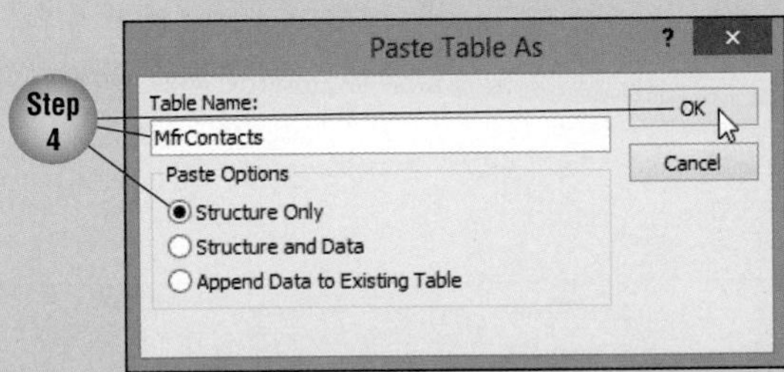

5. Open the MfrContacts table. The table structure contains the same fields as the Contacts table.
6. Enter the following data in a new record using Datasheet view. Press Tab or Enter to move past the remaining fields after *ZIP/Postal Code* and finish the record.

ID	(AutoNumber)
Company	**Dell Inc.**
Last Name	**Haldstadt**
First Name	**Cari**
Email Address	**haldstadt@emcp.net**
Job Title	**Northeast Sales Manager**
Business Phone	**800-555-9522**
Home Phone	(leave blank)
Mobile Phone	**800-555-4662**
Fax Number	**800-555-7781**
Address	**One Dell Way**
City	**Round Rock**
State/Province	**TX**
ZIP/Postal Code	**78682**

7. Close the table.

8. With *MfrContacts* selected in the Tables group in the Navigation pane, click the CREATE tab and then click the Form button in the Forms group. The form should appear similar to the image shown below.

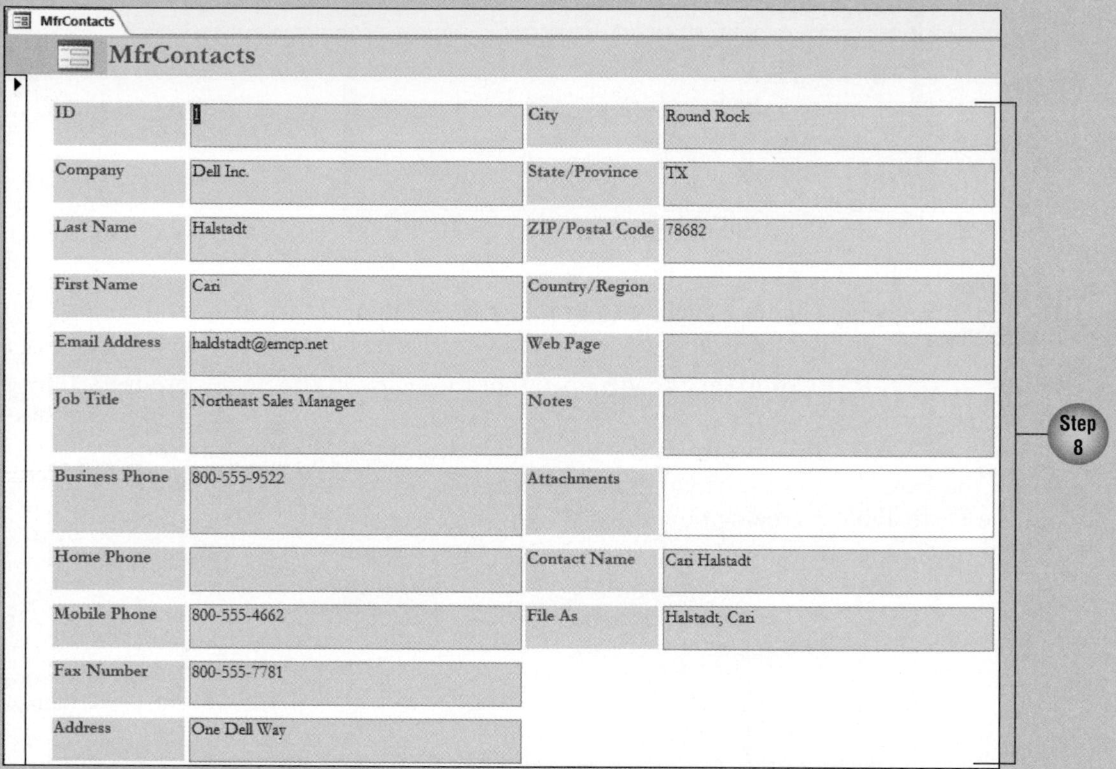

9. Select the label control object and text box control object for the *Attachments* field. Press Delete.
10. To move the *Contact Name* and *File As* fields up one spot, select the label and text box control objects for both of these fields and then click the Move Up button in the Move group on the FORM LAYOUT TOOLS ARRANGE tab.
11. Click the FILE tab, click the *Print* option, and then click Print Preview to display the form in Print Preview. Change the page orientation to landscape and the left and right margins to 1 inch and then close Print Preview.
12. Save the form using the default name *MfrContacts*.
13. Print the selected record and then close the form.

Project 4 Use Access Tools to Optimize and Document a Database — 5 Parts

You will use the Table Analyzer Wizard to improve a table's design and the Performance Analyzer to optimize database design, and you will split a database by separating tables from queries, forms, and reports. Finally, you will use the Database Documenter to print a report that documents the table structure.

Modifying a Table Using the Table Analyzer Wizard

Repeating information within a table can result in inconsistencies and wasted storage space. The Table Analyzer Wizard is used to examine a table and determine if duplicate information can be split into smaller related tables to improve the table design. The wizard suggests fields that can be separated into a new table and remain related to the original table with a lookup field. You can accept the proposed solutions or modify the suggestions.

In Project 4a, you will use the Table Analyzer Wizard in a new Parts table. The table was created to store information about parts that are commonly used by the technicians at RSR Computer Services. Access will examine the table and propose that the *Supplier* field be moved to a separate table. The reason this change will improve the design is that several parts records can be associated with the same supplier. In the current table design, the supplier name is typed into a field in each record. Since several parts are associated with each supplier name, the field contains many duplicate entries that take up more storage space than necessary. Furthermore, entering the same data more than once increases the potential for introducing errors in records, which could result in a query producing incorrect results.

To begin the Table Analyzer Wizard, click the DATABASE TOOLS tab and then click the Analyze Table button in the Analyze group. Doing this opens the first Table Analyzer Wizard dialog box, shown in Figure 6.6. The first two dialog boxes in the wizard explain what the Table Analyzer can do to improve the table design. At the third dialog box in the wizard, you select the table you want to analyze. At the fourth dialog box, you can either choose to let the wizard decide which fields to group in the smaller tables, or you can split the tables manually by dragging and dropping fields.

The wizard looks for fields with repetitive data and then suggests a solution. You confirm the grouping of fields and primary keys in the new tables, and, at the final step in the wizard, you can elect to have Access create a query so that the fields in the split tables are presented together in a datasheet that resembles the original table.

Quick Steps

Evaluate a Table with the Table Analyzer Wizard

1. Click DATABASE TOOLS tab.
2. Click Analyze Table button.
3. Click Next.
4. Click Next.
5. Click table name.
6. Click Next.
7. If necessary, click *Yes, let wizard decide.*
8. Click Next.
9. Confirm grouping of fields in proposed tables.
10. Rename each table.
11. Click Next.
12. Confirm and/or set primary key in each table.
13. Click Next.
14. If necessary, click *Yes, create the query.*
15. Click Finish.
16. Close Help window.
17. Close query.

Analyze Table

The Table Analyzer Wizard helps you normalize a table.

Figure 6.6 First Table Analyzer Wizard Dialog Box

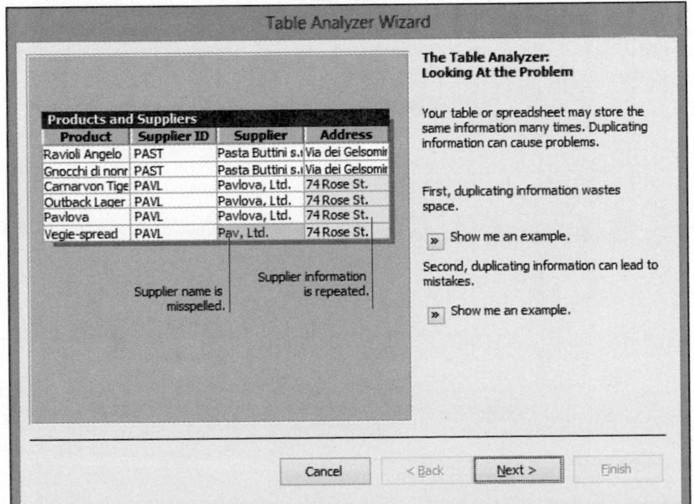

Project 4a Splitting a Table Using the Table Analyzer Wizard Part 1 of 5

1. With **AL2-C6-RSRCompServ.accdb** open, open the Parts table in Datasheet view and review the table structure and data. Notice that the table includes four fields: *PartNo*, *PartName*, *Supplier*, and *Cost*. Also notice that the supplier names are repeated in the *Supplier* field.
2. Close the Parts table.
3. Use the Table Analyzer Wizard to evaluate the Parts table design by completing the following steps:
   a. Click the DATABASE TOOLS tab.
   b. Click the Analyze Table button in the Analyze group.
   c. Read the information at the first Table Analyzer Wizard dialog box and then click Next.
   d. Read the information at the second Table Analyzer Wizard dialog box and then click Next.
   e. With *Parts* selected in the *Tables* list box at the third Table Analyzer Wizard dialog box, click Next.
   f. At the fourth Table Analyzer Wizard dialog box, with *Yes, let the wizard decide* selected for *Do you want the wizard to decide what fields go in what tables?*, click Next.
   g. At the fifth Table Analyzer Wizard dialog box, look at the two tables the wizard is proposing. Notice that the *Supplier* field has been moved to a new table with a one-to-many relationship has been created between the table and the supplier names (the "one") and a new table with the remaining fields (the "many"). Access names the new tables *Table1* and *Table2* and asks two questions: *Is the wizard grouping information correctly?* and *What name do you want for each table?* ***Note: If necessary, resize the table list boxes to see the proposed fields.***
   h. The proposed tables have the fields grouped correctly. Double-click the Table1 Title bar to give the table a new name.

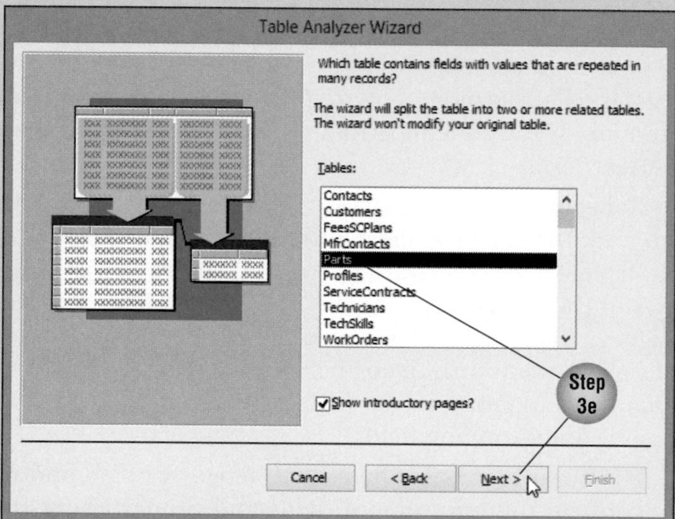

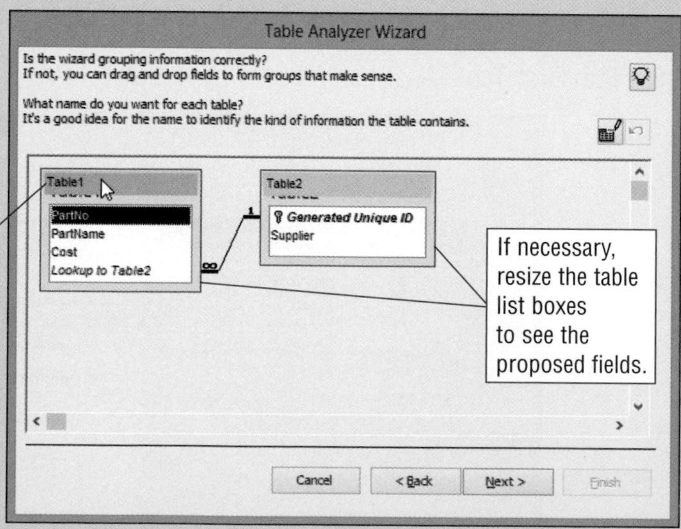

i. Type **PartsAndCosts** in the *Table Name* text box and then press Enter or click OK.

j. Click the Table2 Title bar and then click the Rename Table button located near the top right of the dialog box, above the table list boxes. Type **PartsSuppliers** in the *Table Name* text box and then press Enter or click OK.

k. Click Next.

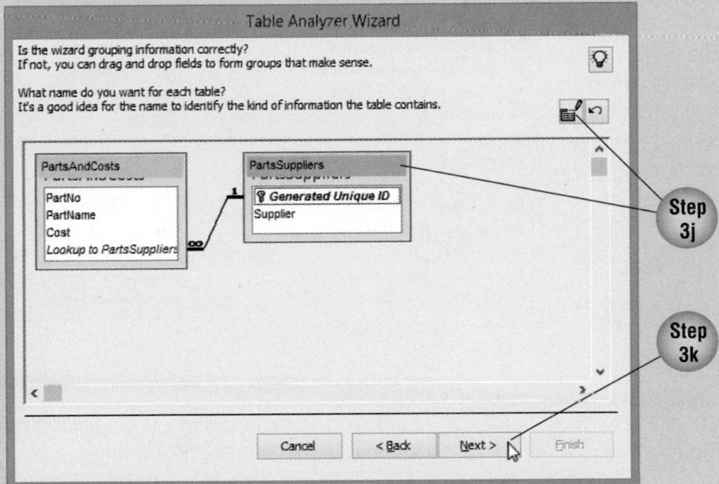

l. At the sixth Table Analyzer Wizard dialog box, the unique identifier, or primary key, for each table is set and/or confirmed. The primary key fields are displayed in bold in the table list boxes. Notice that the PartsAndCosts table does not have a primary key defined. Click *PartNo* in the *PartsAndCosts* table field list box and then click the Primary Key button located near the top right of the dialog box. Access sets *PartNo* as the primary key field, displays a key icon, and applies bold formatting to the field name.

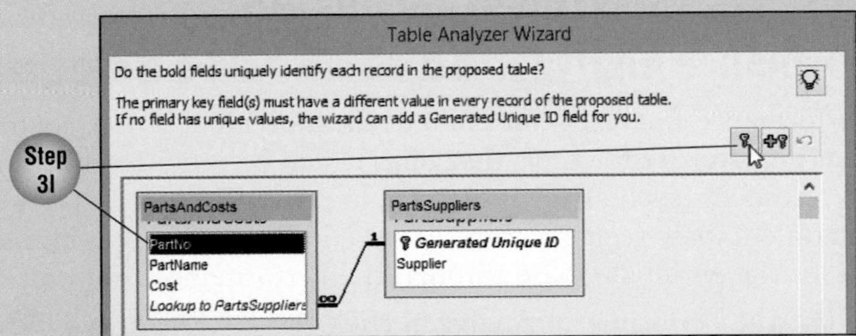

m. Click Next.

n. At the last Table Analyzer Wizard dialog box, you can choose to have Access create a query with the original table name that includes the fields from the new tables. Creating the query means that existing forms or reports that were based on the original table will still operate. With *Yes, create the query* selected, click Finish. Access renames the original table *Parts_OLD*, creates the query with the name *Parts*, and opens the Parts query results datasheet with the Access Help window in the foreground.

o. Close the Help window.

4. Examine the Parts query datasheet and the object names added in the Navigation pane, including the new tables PartsAndCosts and PartsSuppliers along with the original table, Parts_OLD. The Parts query looks just like the original table you opened in Step 1, with the exception of the additional field named *Lookup to PartsSupplier*. The lookup field displays the supplier name, which is also displayed in the original *Supplier* field. The second *Supplier* field can be deleted from the query.
5. Switch to Design view and delete the *Supplier* field.

All Access Objects

Search...

Tables: Contacts, Customers, FeesSCPlans, MfrContacts, Parts_OLD, PartsAndCosts, PartsSuppliers, Profiles, ServiceContracts, Technicians, TechSkills, WorkOrders

Queries: ContactsExtended, Parts

The original tables were renamed and new tables were created through the Table Analyzer Wizard

Parts

PartNo	PartName	Lookup to PartsSuppliers	Supplier	Cost
3	Ultra 512 MB DDR 400 RAM	Cora Systems	Cora Systems	$52.99
9	Ultra 1024 MB DDR 400 RAM	Cora Systems	Cora Systems	$85.99
10	Kingston 1024 DDR 333 RAM	Cora Systems	Cora Systems	$115.99
6	ATI Radeon X1600 video card	KL Electronics	KL Electronics	$178.99
7	XFX GeForce 7600 video card	KL Electronics	KL Electronics	$188.99
1	Windows 8 Professional edition	Santini Software	Santini Software	$299.99
2	Windows 8 Upgrade edition	Santini Software	Santini Software	$199.99
5	Microsoft Office 2013 Professional edition	Santini Software	Santini Software	$499.99
6	Microsoft Office 2013 Home and Business edition	Santini Software	Santini Software	$279.99
1	Power supply - 600 watt	Valley Electronics	Valley Electronics	$55.75
2	Power supply - 800 watt	Valley Electronics	Valley Electronics	$62.99
3	Power supply - 1000 watt	Valley Electronics	Valley Electronics	$131.99
13	NEC Supermulti DVD 18x +/-	Valley Electronics	Valley Electronics	$42.99
14	Pioneer 16x DVD +/-	Valley Electronics	Valley Electronics	$51.99
4	Seagate 320 GB hard drive	Westview Supply	Westview Supply	$151.42
5	Maxtor 500 GB hard drive	Westview Supply	Westview Supply	$215.99
(New)				

This query was created to resemble the original table.

Lookup to PartsSuppliers and *Supplier* display the same information. You delete the *Supplier* field from the query in Step 5.

6. Save the revised query. Switch to Datasheet view, adjust all of the column widths to best fit, and then print the query results datasheet in landscape orientation.
7. Close the query, saving changes to the layout.

Optimizing Performance Using the Performance Analyzer

Quick Steps

Optimize Database Performance
1. Click DATABASE TOOLS tab.
2. Click Analyze Performance button.
3. Click All Object Types tab.
4. Click Select All button.
5. Click OK.
6. Review *Analysis Results* items.
7. Optimize desired recommendations or suggestions.
8. Click Close button.

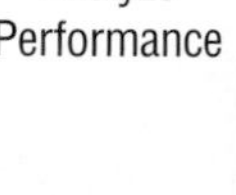

Analyze Performance

The Performance Analyzer can evaluate an individual object, a group of objects, or an entire database for ways that objects can be modified to optimize the use of system resources (such as memory) and improve the speed of data access. If you find that a database seems to run slowly, consider running tables, queries, forms, reports, or the entire database through the Performance Analyzer.

To use the Performance Analyzer, click the DATABASE TOOLS tab and then click the Analyze Performance button in the Analyze group to open the Performance Analyzer dialog box, shown in Figure 6.7. Select an object type tab, click the check box next to an object to have the object analyzed, and then click OK. You can select multiple objects or click the Select All button to select all of the objects in the current tab for analysis. To evaluate the entire database, click the All Object Types tab and then click the Select All button. Click OK to begin the analysis.

Figure 6.7 Performance Analyzer Dialog Box

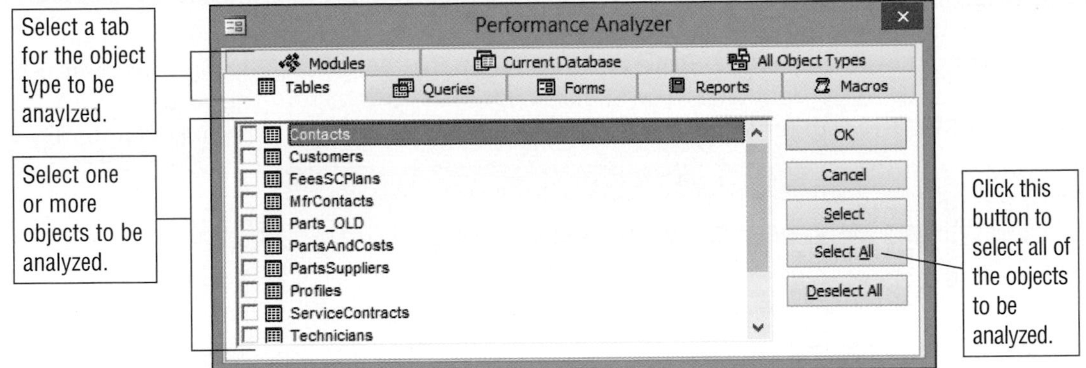

Three types of results are presented to optimize the selected objects: recommendation, suggestion, and idea. Click an item in the *Analysis Results* list box to read a description of the proposed optimization method in the *Analysis Notes* section. Click a recommendation or suggestion in the *Analysis Results* list box and then click the Optimize button to instruct Access to carry out the recommendation or suggestion. Access will modify the object and mark the item as fixed when completed. The Performance Analyzer may provide ideas to improve the design, such as assigning a different data type for a field based on the type of data that has been entered into records or creating relationships between tables that are not already related.

Before running the Performance Analyzer, make sure all objects you want to analyze are closed. If they are open, the Performance Analyzer will skip them.

Project 4b Analyzing a Database to Improve Performance — Part 2 of 5

1. With **AL2-C6-RSRCompServ.accdb** open, use the Performance Analyzer to evaluate the database by completing the following steps:
   a. If necessary, click the DATABASE TOOLS tab.
   b. Click the Analyze Performance button in the Analyze group.
   c. At the Performance Analyzer dialog box, click the All Object Types tab.
   d. Click the Select All button.
   e. Click OK. The Performance Analyzer displays the name of each object as the object is evaluated and presents a full list of results when the analysis is finished.

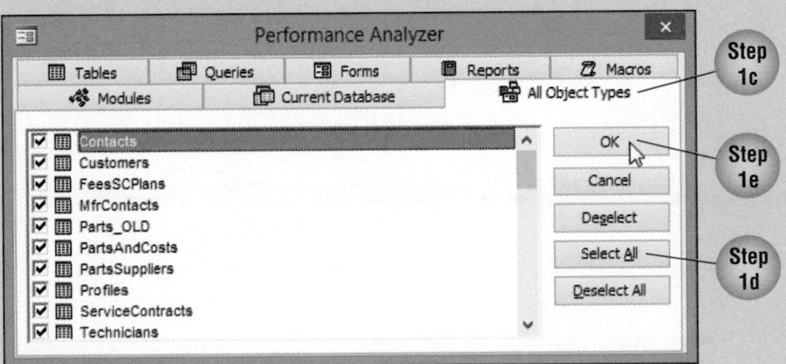

2. Review the items in the *Analysis Results* list box and then optimize a relationship by completing the following steps:
   a. Click the first entry in the *Analysis Results* list box (contains the text *Application: Save your application as an MDE file*) and then read the description of the idea in the *Analysis Notes* section. (You will learn about saving an application as an MDE file in the next chapter.)

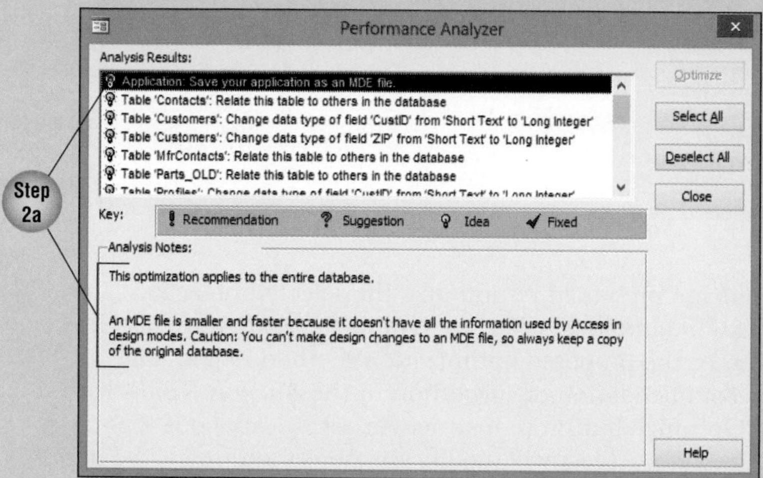

   b. Click the fifth entry in the *Analysis Results* list box (contains the text *Table "MfrContacts": Relate this table to others in the database*) and then read the description of the idea in the *Analysis Notes* section. The contact information stored in this table is for manufacturer sales representatives and cannot be related to any other tables.
   c. Scroll down the *Analysis Results* list box and then click the item with the green question mark (representing a suggestion) with the text *Table 'WorkOrders': Relate to table 'WorkOrders'*. Read the description of the suggestion in the *Analysis Notes* section. Note that the optimization will benefit the TotalWorkOrders query. This optimization refers to a query that contains a subquery with two levels of calculations. The suggestion is to create a relationship to speed up the query calculations.
   d. Click the Optimize button.

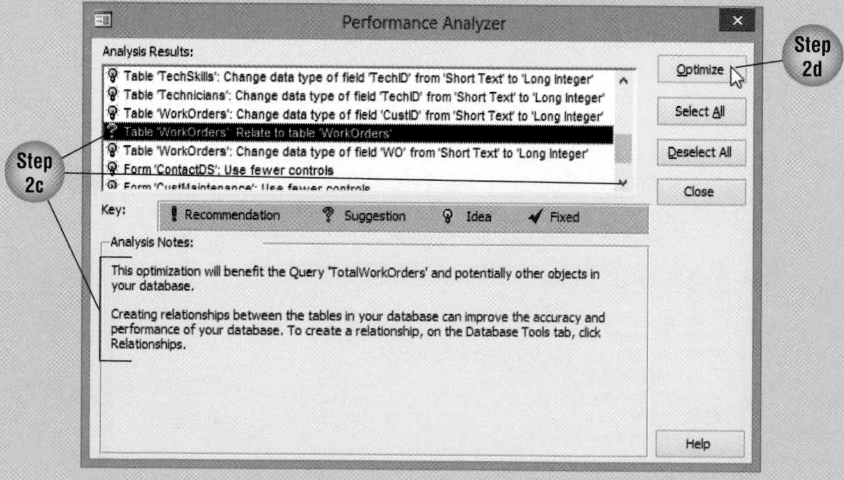

e. Access creates the relationship and changes the question mark next to the item in the *Analysis Results* list box to a check mark (✓). The check mark indicates that the item has been fixed.

f. Click the the last item in the *Analysis Results* list box (contains the text *Form 'CustMaintenance': Use fewer controls*) and then read the description of the idea, which is to break the form into multiple forms, retaining information that is used often in the existing form. Information viewed less often would be split out into individual forms. To implement this optimization idea, you would need to redesign the form.

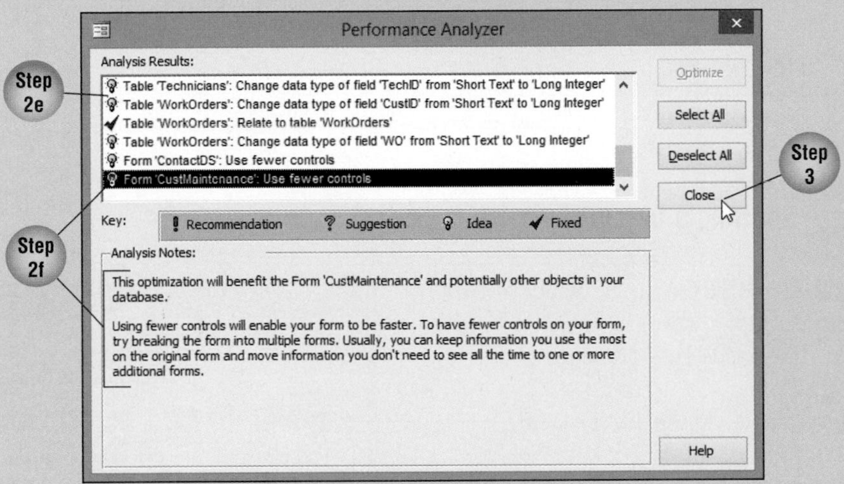

3. Click the Close button to close the Performance Analyzer dialog box.

Splitting a Database

If a database is placed on a network where multiple users can access it simultaneously, the speed with which the data is accessed may decrease. One way to improve performance is to split the database into two files. The file containing the tables (called the ***back-end database***) is stored in the network share folder, while the other file, containing the queries, forms, and reports (called the ***front-end database***), is stored on individual end-user computers. The end users can create and/or customize their own queries, forms, and reports to serve their individual purposes. The front-end database contains tables linked to the back-end data, so all end users update a single data source.

To split an existing database into back-end and front-end databases, Access provides the Database Splitter Wizard. Click the DATABASE TOOLS tab and then click the Access Database button in the Move Data group to open the first Database Splitter Wizard dialog box, shown in Figure 6.8 on the next page.

Click the Split Database button to open the Create Back-end Database dialog box and navigate to the drive and/or folder where you want to store the database file containing the original tables. By default, Access uses the original database file name with *_be* added to the end (before the file extension). Change the file name if desired and then click the Split button. Access moves the table objects to the back-end file, creates links to the back-end tables in the front-end file, and then displays a message that the database was successfully split.

Quick Steps

Split a Database

1. Click DATABASE TOOLS tab.
2. Click Access Database button.
3. Click Split Database button.
4. If necessary, navigate to desired drive and/or folder.
5. If necessary, edit file name.
6. Click Split button.
7. Click OK.

Access Database

Figure 6.8 First Database Splitter Wizard Dialog Box

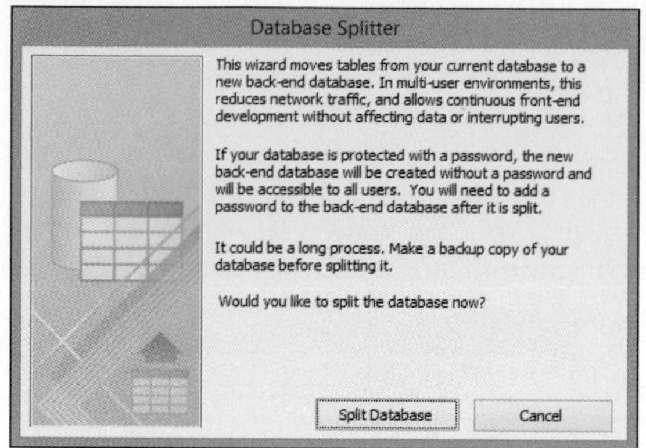

Consider making a backup copy of the database before you split the file, in case you need to restore the database to its original state.

Project 4c Splitting a Database

Part 3 of 5

1. With **AL2-C6-RSRCompServ.accdb** open, split the database to create back-end and front-end databases by completing the following steps:
   a. If necessary, click the DATABASE TOOLS tab.
   b. Click the Access Database button in the Move Data group.
   c. At the first Database Splitter Wizard dialog box, click the Split Database button.
   d. At the Create Back-end Database dialog box, navigate to thesame folder as the original database (AL2C6). With the default file name *AL2-C6-RSRCompServ_be.accdb*, click the Split button.

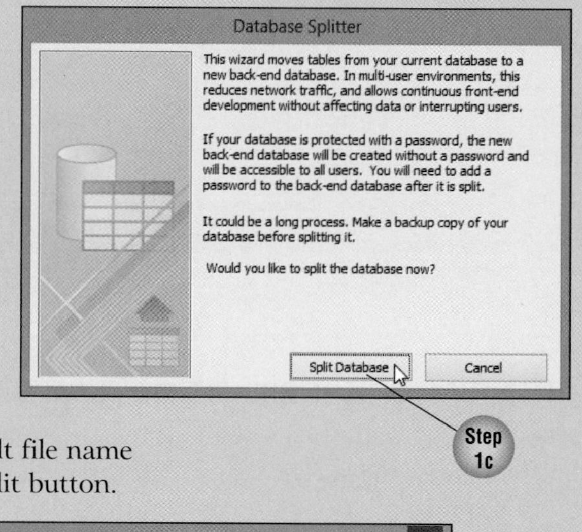

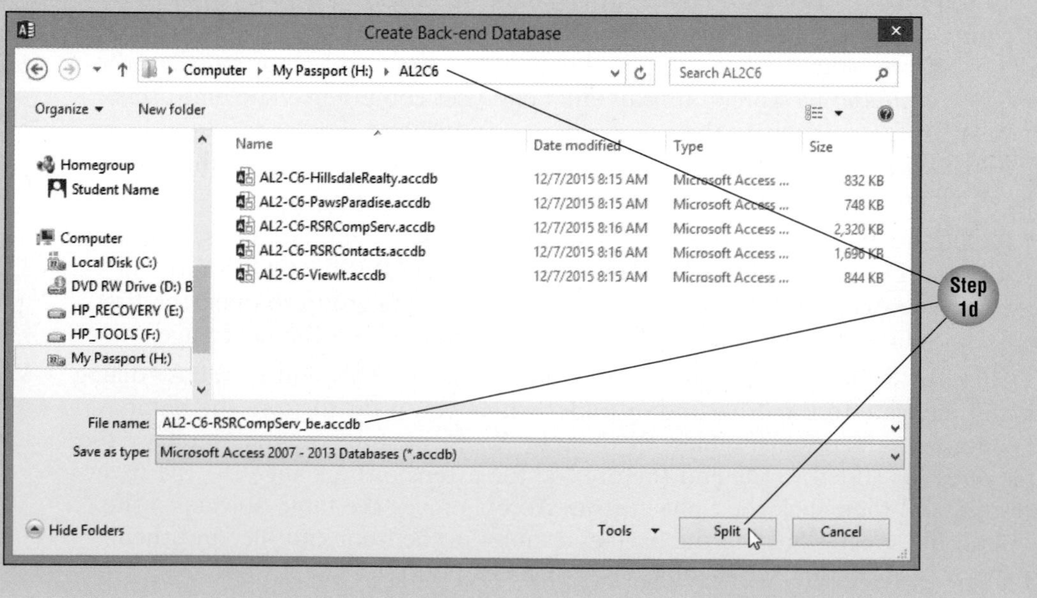

e. Click OK at the Database Splitter message box indicating that the database was successfully split.
2. When the database was split, Access moved the tables to the back-end file and created links to the tables in the front-end file. Notice that each table name in the Navigation pane is preceded by a right-pointing arrow. The arrow indicates that the table is a linked object. Opening a linked table causes Access to retrieve the records from the back-end database to display in the table datasheet. Double-click the linked Contacts table datasheet to open it and review the data.
3. Switch to Design view. Click *Company* in the *Field Name* list, change the field size to 50 characters, and then click the Save button. Access displays a message indicating that the operation is not supported for this type of object. Since the table is linked to an external source, Access will not let you make changes to the table design. Click OK and then close the table without saving the changes.

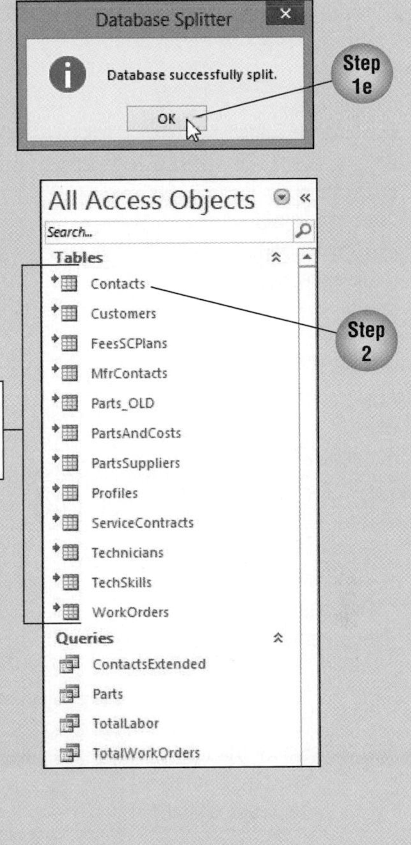

An arrow indicates that a table is linked to an external source.

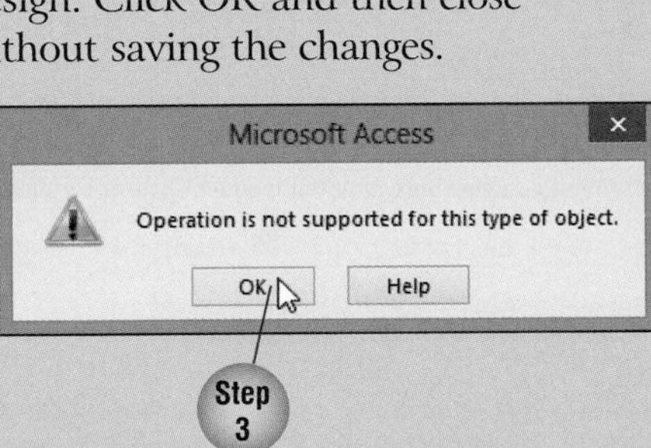

4. Close **AL2-C6-RSRCompServ.accdb**.
5. Open **AL2-C6-RSRCompServ_be.accdb** and enable the content.
6. Notice that the back-end database file contains only the tables. Open the Customers table in Datasheet view and review the data.
7. Switch to Design view. Notice that in the back-end database, you can switch to Design view to make changes without receiving the message box you saw in Step 3, because this database contains the original source table.
8. Close the table.

Another reason to split a database is to overcome the file size restriction in Access 2013. Database specifications for Access 2013 place the maximum file size at 2 gigabytes, but this size includes space needed by Access to open system objects while working with the database, which means the actual maximum file size is even less. However, the size restriction does not include links to external data sources. By splitting a database, you can extend the size beyond the 2-gigabyte limitation.

Documenting a Database

Quick Steps

Print Object Documentation

1. Click DATABASE TOOLS tab.
2. Click Database Documenter button.
3. Click Options button.
4. Choose desired report options.
5. Click OK.
6. Click desired object name.
7. Click OK.
8. Print report.
9. Close report.

Database Documenter

Access provides the Database Documenter feature, which allows you to print a report with details about the definition of a database object. This report can be used as hard-copy documentation of a table's structure with field properties or documentation regarding a query, form, or report definition. You can also include relationship diagrams for all of the defined relationships for the table. Relationship options are documented below each relationship diagram.

It is a good idea to store a database documentation report in a secure place. That way, if the data gets corrupted or another disaster strikes, you will have the information needed to manually repair, rebuild, or otherwise recreate the database.

Click the DATABASE TOOLS tab and then click the Database Documenter button in the Analyze group to open the Documenter dialog box, shown in Figure 6.9. As you did for the Performance Analyzer, insert a check mark in the check box next to the name of object for which you want to generate a report and then click OK.

Figure 6.9 Documenter Dialog Box

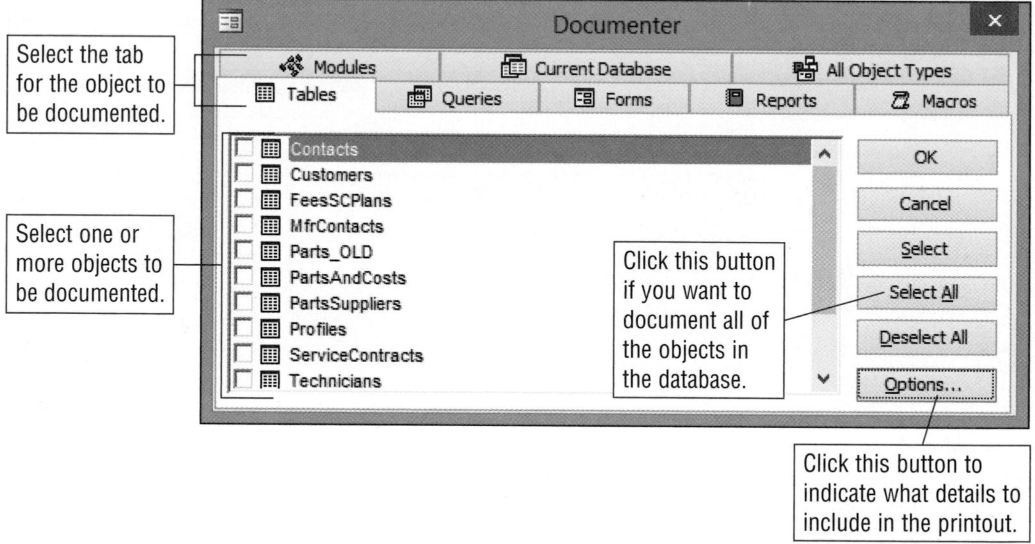

Project 4d **Generating a Table Definition Documentation Report** **Part 4 of 5**

1. With **AL2-C6-RSRCompServ_be.accdb** open, generate a report providing details of the table structure, field properties, and relationships for an individual table by completing the following steps:
   a. Click the DATABASE TOOLS tab.
   b. In the Analyze group, click the Database Documenter button.
   c. At the Documenter dialog box, click the Options button.

d. At the Print Table Definition dialog box, click the *Permissions by User and Group* check box in the *Include for Table* section to remove the check mark.
e. Make sure *Names, Data Types, Sizes, and Properties* is selected in the *Include for Fields* section.
f. Click *Nothing* in the *Include for Indexes* section.
g. Click OK.
h. With Tables the active tab in the Documenter dialog box, click the *PartsSuppliers* check box to insert a check mark.
i. Click OK.

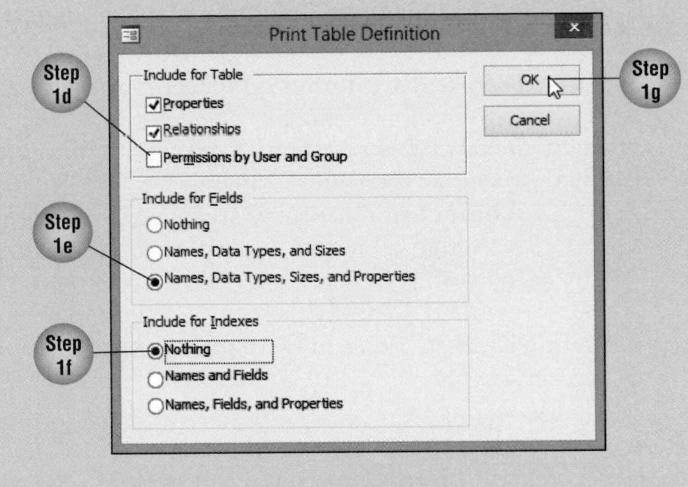

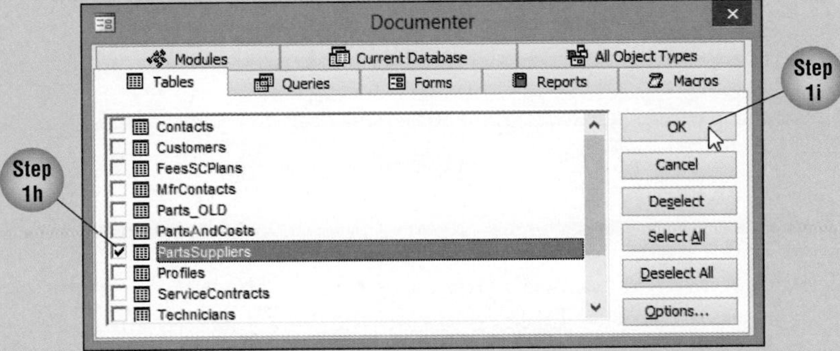

2. Access generates the table definition report and displays the report in Print Preview. Print the report.
3. Notice that the Save option is dimmed. You cannot save a report generated by the Database Documenter. Click the Close Print Preview button in the Close Preview group on the PRINT PREVIEW tab.

Renaming and Deleting Objects

As part of managing a database, you may decide to rename or delete objects within the database file. To do this, right-click the object name in the Navigation pane and then click *Rename* or *Delete* at the shortcut menu. You can also delete an object from a database by selecting the object in the Navigation pane and then pressing Delete. Click Yes at the Microsoft Access message box that displays asking you to confirm that you want to delete the object. Consider making a backup copy of a database before renaming or deleting objects in case you want to restore the database to its previous state.

Be cautious when renaming or deleting objects that have dependencies to other objects. For example, if you delete a table and a query exists that is dependent on fields within the table you deleted, the query will no longer run. You will need to edit in Design view any query, form, or report that references a renamed table.

Quick Steps

Rename an Object
1. Right-click object in Navigation pane.
2. Click *Rename*.
3. Type new name.
4. Press Enter.

Delete an Object
1. Right-click object in Navigation pane.
2. Click *Delete*.
3. Click Yes.

Project 4e Renaming and Deleting Database Objects Part 5 of 5

1. With **AL2-C6-RSRCompServ_be.accdb** open, rename the MfrContacts table by completing the following steps:
   a. Right-click *MfrContacts* in the Tables group in the Navigation pane.
   b. Click *Rename* at the shortcut menu.
   c. Type **ManufacturerContacts** and then press Enter.

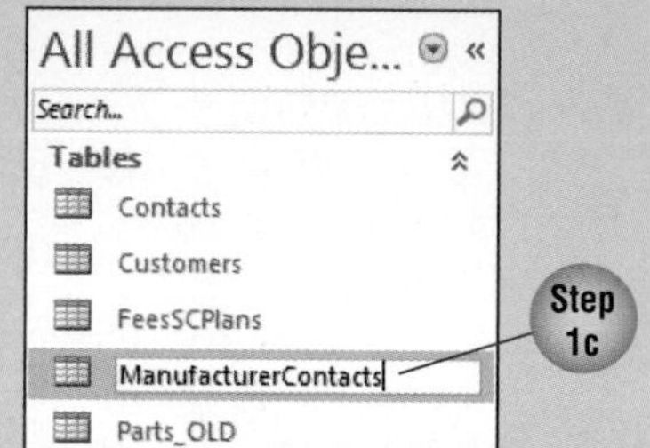

2. Delete the original table that was split using the Table Analyzer Wizard in Project 4a by completing the following steps:
   a. Right-click *Parts_OLD* in the Tables group in the Navigation pane.
   b. Click *Delete* at the shortcut menu.
   c. Click Yes at the Microsoft Access message box asking if you want to delete the table *Parts_OLD*.

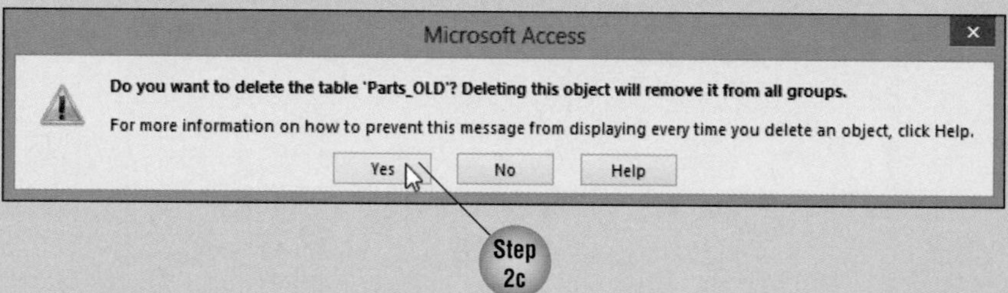

3. Close **AL2-C6-RSRCompServ_be.accdb**.
4. Open **AL2-C6-RSRCompServ.accdb** (the front-end database) and enable the content.
5. Double-click *MfrContacts* in the Tables group in the Navigation pane. Because the table was renamed in Step 1, Access can no longer find the source data. At the Microsoft Access message box informing you that the database engine cannot find the input table, click OK. The link will have to be recreated to establish a new connection to the renamed table. (You will learn how to link to an external table in Chapter 8.)

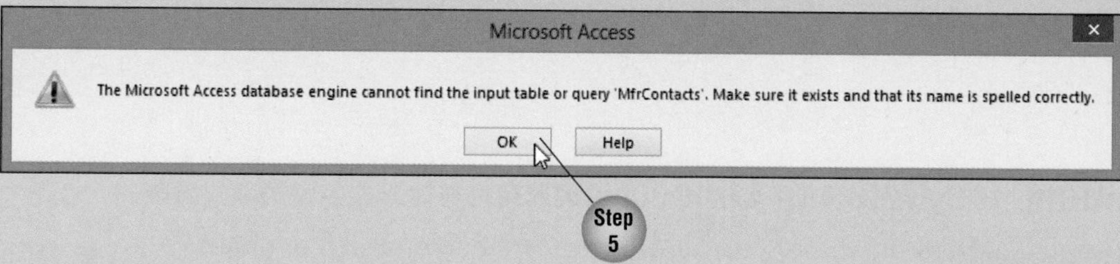

6. Double-click *Parts_OLD* in the Tables group in the Navigation pane. Because this table was deleted in Step 2, the same message appears. Click OK to close the message box.

7. Right-click *Parts_OLD* in the Tables group in the Navigation pane and then click *Delete* at the shortcut menu. Click Yes at the Microsoft Access message box asking if you want to remove the link.

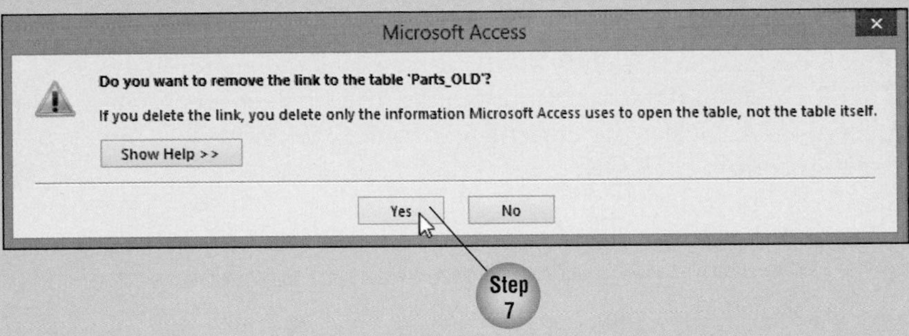

8. Delete the ContactPhoneBook report by completing the following steps:
   a. Click *ContactPhoneBook* in the Reports group in the Navigation pane.
   b. Press Delete.
   c. Click Yes at the Microsoft Access message box asking if you want to permanently delete the report.

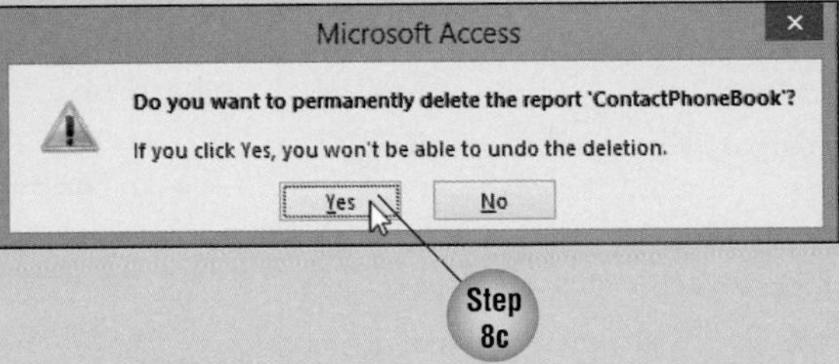

9. Close **AL2-C6-RSRCompServ.accdb**.

Creating Databases Using Templates, Application Parts, Quick Start, and Wizards

In earlier versions of Access, a wizard walked you through the steps of creating a customized database. Access 2013 comes with many ways to effectively create and customize a database, similar to those available in the wizard in earlier versions. Start by creating a database from one of the predefined templates as demonstrated in Project 1, or by using the Blank desktop database template you learned about in Chapter 1.

Tables, queries, forms and reports can be added using one or more of the following wizards or Quick Start options. You learned in Project 2 that Application Parts templates can be used to add tables, queries, forms and reports depending upon the option you choose in the *Quick Start* section of the Application Parts drop-down list. In Level 1, Chapter 1, the *Quick Start* section of the More Fields drop-down list allowed you to quickly add a group of related fields to a table in one easy step. For example, if you click the *Address* option, Access inserts *Address*, *City*, *StateProvince*, *ZIPPostal* and *CountryRegion* fields. The short text data type and a caption have been assigned to each field. Once you have created tables in your database, use the Query Wizard, Form Wizard and Report Wizard to efficiently generate queries, forms and reports. You have used the Query, Form, and Report Wizards throughout Level 1 and Level 2.

Project 5 Create a Database Using Templates, Application Parts, Quick Start and Wizards

Part 1 of 1

1. Complete the following steps to create a new database and save it to an external drive. ***Note: If you do not have an external drive, or if you already save to an external drive, save the database to the AL2C6 folder on your storage medium.***
   a. At the Open backstage area click the *Blank desktop database* template.
   b. At the Blank Desktop database window, click the Browse button and then navigate to your external drive. Select the current text in the *File Name* text box, type **AL2-C6-ConvTask**, and then click OK.
   c. Click the Create button.
2. Close the Table1 blank table datasheet.
3. Use a template to create a new table and two new forms by completing the following steps:
   a. Click the CREATE tab.
   b. Click the Application Parts button in the Templates group and then click *Tasks* in the *Quick Start* section of the drop-down list.
4. Click Enable Content.
5. You want to keep track of the employees who are responsible for each task, so you decide to create an Employees table to hold name and address information by completing the following steps:
   a. Click the Table button in the Tables group to create a new table.
   b. With the TABLE TOOLS FIELDS tab selected, click the More Fields button in the Add & Delete group. Scroll down the list and then click *Name*. *Last Name* and *First Name* fields are added.
   c. Click the blank field under the *Click to Add* field, click the More Fields button, scroll down the list, and then click *Address*. Five fields related to the employee's address are added. ***Note: If you do not click the blank field under the Click to Add field, the First Name field will be out of order.***

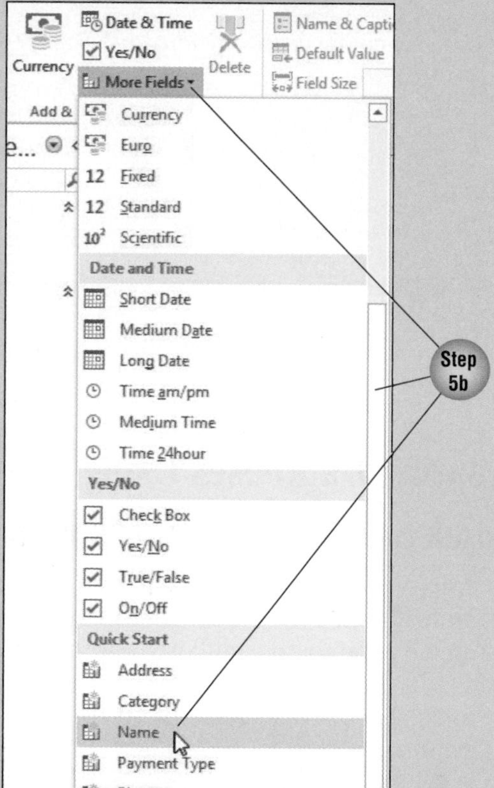

6. Save the table and name it *Employees*.
7. Switch to Design view and then change the name and data type of the primary key from *ID* and AutoNumber to *EmpID* and Short Text. Delete the *Country Region* field. Save the table.
8. Add yourself as an employee. Type **E10** for your *EmpID* value and then close the table.
9. Open the Tasks table and then add the field *EmpID* after the *Active* field.

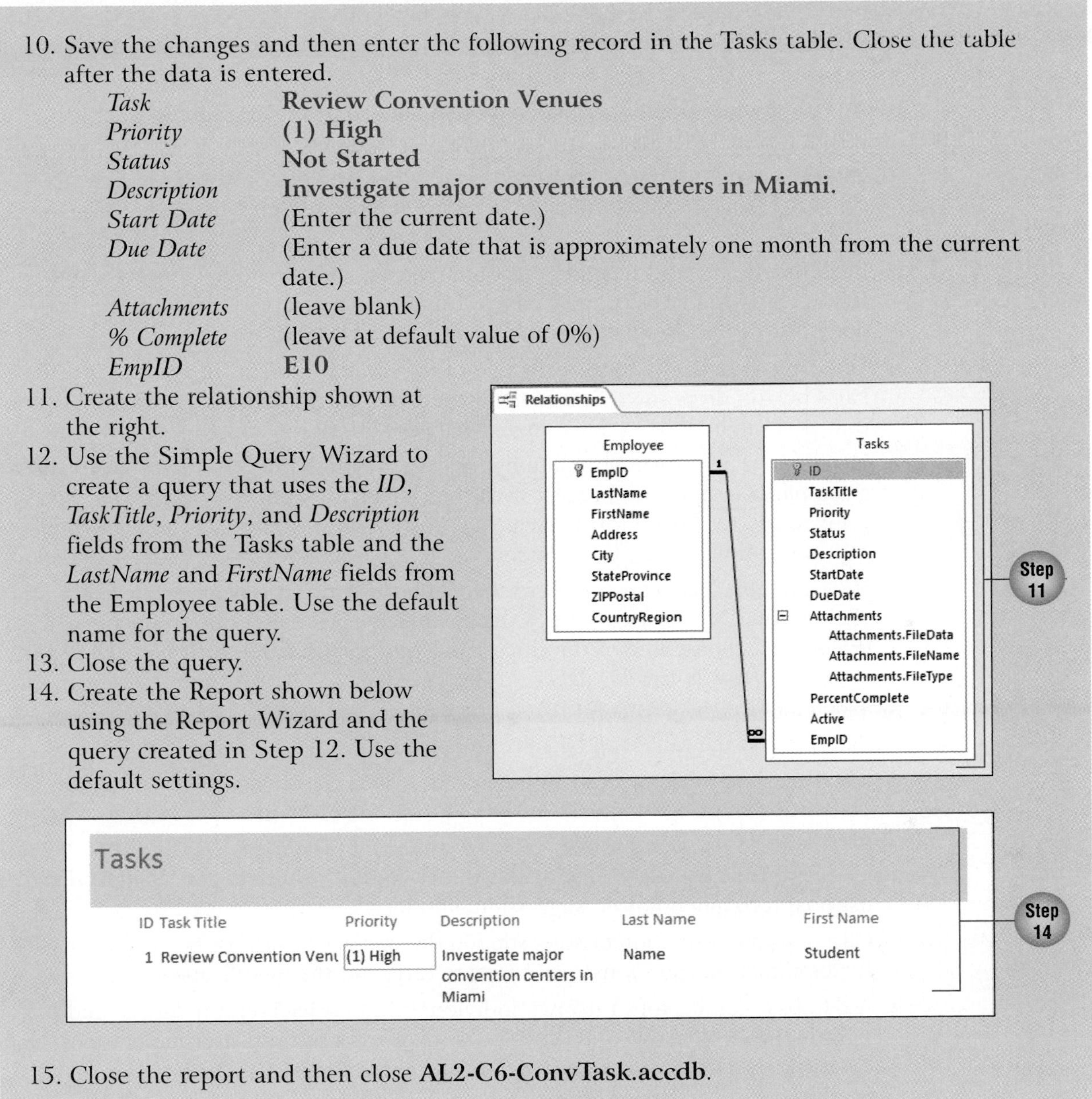

10. Save the changes and then enter the following record in the Tasks table. Close the table after the data is entered.

Task	**Review Convention Venues**
Priority	**(1) High**
Status	**Not Started**
Description	**Investigate major convention centers in Miami.**
Start Date	(Enter the current date.)
Due Date	(Enter a due date that is approximately one month from the current date.)
Attachments	(leave blank)
% Complete	(leave at default value of 0%)
EmpID	**E10**

11. Create the relationship shown at the right.
12. Use the Simple Query Wizard to create a query that uses the *ID*, *TaskTitle*, *Priority*, and *Description* fields from the Tasks table and the *LastName* and *FirstName* fields from the Employee table. Use the default name for the query.
13. Close the query.
14. Create the Report shown below using the Report Wizard and the query created in Step 12. Use the default settings.

15. Close the report and then close **AL2-C6-ConvTask.accdb**.

In this chapter, you have learned to use some of the tools that Access provides to create a new database, create new tables and related objects, improve database and individual object design and performance, and document a database. You have also learned how to rename and delete objects.

Chapter Summary

- Access provides predefined database templates that include tables, queries, forms, and reports for use in creating a new database.
- You can choose a database template from sample templates stored on your computer or you can download a database template from Microsoft Office Online.
- Predefined table and related object templates for Comments; Contacts; and Issues, Tasks, and Users are available from the Application Parts button drop-down list in the Templates group on the CREATE tab.
- You can create a new form using one of the 10 blank forms in the Application Parts button drop-down list. Most of the blank forms include command buttons that perform actions such as saving changes and saving and closing the form.
- Define your own form template by creating a form named *Normal* that includes a sample of each control object with the formatting options applied that you want to use for future forms. Select all of the controls and use the *Set Control Defaults* option to save the new settings.
- When a table has been copied to the Clipboard from the Navigation pane, clicking the Paste button causes the Paste Table As dialog box to open. At this dialog box, choose one of the three options: *Structure Only*, *Structure and Data*, or *Append Data to Existing Table*.
- The Table Analyzer Wizard is used to evaluate a table for repeated data and determine if the table can be split into smaller related tables.
- The Performance Analyzer can be used to evaluate a single object, group of objects, or an entire database for ways to optimize the use of system resources or disk space.
- The Performance Analyzer provides three types of results in the *Analysis Results* list box: recommendation, suggestion, and idea.
- Click a recommendation or suggestion in the *Analysis Results* list box and then click the Optimize button to instruct Access to carry out the modification.
- A database can be split into two individual files—a back-end database and a front-end database—to improve performance for a multi-user database or overcome the maximum database file size restriction.
- To split a database using the Database Splitter Wizard, begin by clicking the Access Database button in the Move Data group on the DATABASE TOOLS tab.
- Access provides the Database Documenter feature, which is used to obtain hard-copy reports providing object definitions and field or control properties.
- Rename an object by right-clicking the object name in the Navigation pane, clicking *Rename* at the shortcut menu, typing a new name, and then pressing Enter.
- Delete an object by right-clicking the object name in the Navigation pane, clicking *Delete* at the shortcut menu, and then clicking Yes at the message box asking if you want to delete the object.

Commands Review

FEATURE	RIBBON TAB, GROUP	BUTTON	KEYBOARD SHORTCUT
Application Parts template	CREATE, Templates		
Database Documenter	DATABASE TOOLS, Analyze		
Paste Table As	HOME, Clipboard		Ctrl + V
Performance Analyzer	DATABASE TOOLS, Analyze		
split database	DATABASE TOOLS, Move Data		
Table Analyzer Wizard	DATABASE TOOLS, Analyze		

Concepts Check

Test Your Knowledge

Completion: In the space provided at the right, indicate the correct term, command, or number.

1. To create a new database using a template, click on one of the available templates in either of these backstage areas. ________________
2. A predefined table with related objects to store information about Contacts can be imported into the current database using this button in the Templates group on the CREATE tab. ________________
3. Access provides 10 prebuilt forms, each with a defined layout and most including titles and command buttons, in this section of the Application Parts button drop-down list. ________________
4. Give a form this name to use it as a template for all new forms. ________________
5. Clicking the Paste button after copying a table in the Navigation pane causes this dialog box to open. ________________
6. This wizard analyzes a table for repeated information and suggests how the table can be split into smaller, related tables. ________________
7. Optimize a database using this button in the Analyze group on the DATABASE TOOLS tab. ________________

8. List the three types of results provided by the Performance Analyzer to optimize selected objects. ________________

9. Click an item in the *Analysis Results* list box and read a description of the optimization method in this section of the Performance Analyzer dialog box. ________________

10. A database can be split into a front-end database file and a back-end database file using this button in the Move Data group on the DATABASE TOOLS tab. ________________

11. When a database has been split, the back-end database file contains these objects. ________________

12. When a database has been split, the front-end database file contains links to these objects. ________________

13. Open this dialog box to print a report with a table's definition and field properties. ________________

14. Rename a database object in the Navigation pane by performing this action. ________________

15. Remove a selected object from the database by pressing this key. ________________

Skills Check Assess Your Performance

Assessment

1 CREATE A NEW DATABASE USING A TEMPLATE

1. Create a new database named **AL2-C6-Assets.accdb** using the Desktop asset tracking template. Close the Getting Started with Assets form. Enable the content.
2. Spend a few moments opening and viewing various objects within the database. Close all of the objects when you are finished, including the Asset List form.
3. Open the Contact Details form, add the following record using the form, and then close the form. Substitute your names in the *First Name* and *Last Name* fields. Leave the fields blank after the *Business Phone*.

First Name	**Student's First Name**
Last Name	**Student's Last Name**
Company	**River Assets**
Job Title	(leave blank)
Business Phone	**212-555-5559**

4. Open the Asset Details form, add the following records using the form, and then close the form.

Item	**Web Server**
Category	**(1) Category**
Manufacturer	**Edge Industries**
Model	**TrueEdge 6500**
Acquired Date	(Enter the current date.)
Purchase Price	**1850.00**
Current Value	**1850.00**
Condition	(Click *(1) Great* at the drop-down list.)
Location	(Click *(1) Location* at the drop-down list.)
Owner	(Click your name at the drop-down list.)
Retired Date	(leave blank)
Description	(leave blank)
Attachments	(attach **WebServer.jpg**)

Item	**Workstation**
Category	**(1) Category**
Manufacturer	**Edge Industries**
Model	**EdgeConnect 100**
Acquired Date	(enter the current date)
Purchase Price	**985.00**
Current Value	**985.00**
Condition	(Click *(1) Great* at the drop-down list.)
Location	(Click *(1) Location* at the drop-down list.)
Owner	(Click your name at the drop-down list.)
Retired Date	(leave blank)
Attachments	(attach **Workstation.jpg**)
Description	(leave blank)

5. Print the two records as displayed in the Asset Details form.
6. Close the form and then close **AL2-C6Assets.accdb**.

Assessment

2 CREATE A TABLE USING AN APPLICATIONS PARTS TEMPLATE

1. Open **AL2-C6-ViewIt.accdb** and enable the content.
2. Create a new group of objects related to Tasks using the Tasks Application Part. When the Create Relationship Wizard starts, specify no relationship.
3. Using the TaskDetails form, add a record using the following information. Substitute your name for *Student Name* in the *Description* field.

Task	**Set up backup Web server**
Status	**Not Started**
Priority	**(1) High**
Start Date	Enter the current date
Due Date	Enter a due date that is one week from the current date
Attachments	(leave blank)
% Complete	(leave at default value of 0%)
Description	**Configure hot server to be on standby in event of failover. Assigned to Student Name.**

4. Click the Save and Close button.
5. Open the Tasks table to view the record added to the table using the form in Step 3. Close the table.
6. Print the selected record using the TaskDetails form.
7. Close the form.

Assessment

3 USE ACCESS TOOLS TO IMPROVE DESIGN AND PERFORMANCE

1. With **AL2-C6-ViewIt.accdb** open, use the Table Analyzer Wizard to analyze the WebCustPymnt table using the following information:
   a. Rename the new table that includes all of the fields except the *CCType* field as *WebCustCreditCards*.
   b. Rename the new table that includes the *CCType* field as *CreditCardTypes*.
   c. Choose an appropriate field for the primary key in the WebCustCreditCards table.
   d. If the wizard determines that the Discover card is a typographical error, choose (*Leave as is*) at the *Correction* drop-down list and then click Next.
   e. Create the query.
2. Close the Help window.
3. Delete the *CCType* field in the WebCustPymnt query. Adjust all of the column widths to best fit and print the query results datasheet with left and right margins of 0.25 inch.
4. Close the query, saving the layout changes.
5. Delete the WebCustPymnt_OLD table.
6. Split the database to create front-end database and back-end database. Accept the default file name for the back-end database.
7. Close **AL2-C6-ViewIt.accdb**.
8. Open **AL2-C6-ViewIt_be.accdb** and enable the content.
9. Generate and print a report that provides the table and field property definitions for the CreditCardTypes table. Include the relationships in the report.
10. Close **AL2-C6-ViewIt_be.accdb**.

Visual Benchmark Demonstrate Your Proficiency

1 CREATE A TABLE TO STORE GROOMERS' INFORMATION

1. Open **AL2-C6-PawsParadise.accdb** and enable the content.
2. Review the table shown in Figure 6.10 and create the new table in the database by copying the structure of the DogOwners table.
3. Modify the table design as needed, add the records shown in the figure, and then rename the table as shown.
4. Adjust all of the column widths and print the table.
5. Close the table.

2 CREATE A FORM TEMPLATE

1. With **AL2-C6-PawsParadise.accdb** open, examine the control objects in the form named *Normal*, shown in Figure 6.11. Create a Normal form to be used as a template with the three control objects shown. Apply the Lavender, Accent 5, Lighter 80% font color, bold font formatting, and the Lavender, Accent 5, Lighter 80% background color.
2. Create a new form for the Groomers table using the Form button in the Forms group on the CREATE tab. Decrease the width of the form title and text box control objects in the form so that one form will fit on one page and then print only the first form.
3. Save the Groomers form, accepting the default name *Groomers*.
4. Close the form and then close **AL2-C6-PawsParadise.accdb**.

Figure 6.10 Visual Benchmark 1

Groomers

Groomer ID	First Name	Last Name	Street Address	City	State	ZIP Code	Home Telephone	Hourly Rate
01	Max	Lahey	715 Irish Hollow	Smethport	PA	16749-	(814) 555-6253	$28.50
02	Juan	Modesta	117 Spring Drive	Bradford	PA	16701-	(814) 555-3845	$28.50
03	Pat	O'Connor	147 Lamont Drive	Bradford	PA	16701-	(814) 555-2118	$31.50
04	Greg	Walczak	22 Foster Square	Allegheny	PA	15212-	(814) 555-7448	$35.50
05	Melissa	Cochrane	140 Congress Street	Bradford	PA	16701-	(814) 555-6489	$28.50
*				Bradford	PA			

Figure 6.11 Visual Benchmark 2

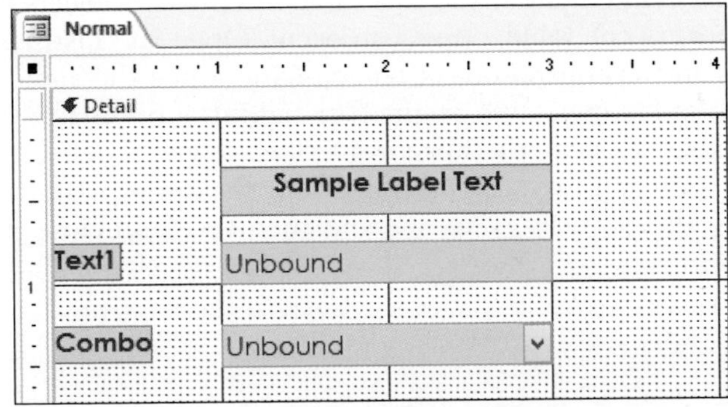

Case Study Apply Your Skills

Part 1

As an intern at Hillsdale Realty, you have been building a listings, sales, and commission database over the past weeks. You decide to create a new database to store information about home shows and conferences that Hillsdale Realty attends as an exhibitor. To save time developing new objects, download the Desktop Event Management template to create a new database in the AL2C6 folder on your storage medium named **AL2-C6-HillsdaleShows.accdb**. Enable the content and then add the following two trade show events to the database using the Event List form:

- The three-day Homebuilders Association Trade Show begins April 14, 2015, at the Phoenix Convention Center.
- The four-day Green Home Design Conference begins October 26, 2015, at the University of Phoenix Hohokam Campus.

The office manager likes the idea of tracking the trade shows in the database and would like you to create a similar table to keep track of conferences that agents attend as visitors. Close the Event List form and display the Navigation pane. Change the Navigation pane view to display objects by *Object Type*. Next, copy the structure of the Events table to create a new table named *AgentConferences*. Modify the AgentConferences table to delete the *Attachments* field and add a new field to store the number of people the company will send to the show. Create a form for the AgentConferences table using the Form button and add the following record:

- Five employees will attend the three-day Window and Door Manufacturers Association Annual Conference that begins November 9, 2015, at the Georgia International Convention Center.

Preview the AgentConferences form in Print Preview. If necessary, make adjustments to fit the form on one page. Print the AgentConferences form with the first record displayed. Save and close the form. Open the Event Details report. Print and then close the report. Close **AL2-C6-HillsdaleShows.accdb**.

Part 2

You want to see how Access tools can help you improve the database design of the database you have been building. Open **AL2-C6-HillsdaleRealty.accdb** and enable the content. Use the Table Analyzer Wizard to analyze the Listings table. Accept the proposed table split, create appropriate table names, assign primary key fields, and create the query. Modify the query as needed to remove duplicate columns. Sort the query in ascending order by the *ListDate* field. Print the query results datasheet with all of the column widths adjusted to best fit. Delete the original table with *_OLD* in the name.

When changes are made to a table after other objects are created that are dependent on the table, errors can occur. Open the ListingsAndSales form. Notice the error in the control object named *City*. Since the Table Analyzer Wizard split the original Listings table on the *City* field, the original field added to the form no longer exists. Display the form in Design view and delete the *City* control object. Display the Field List task pane and add the appropriate field to the form. Size and align the controls as needed and then save and close the form.

Part 3

Use the Performance Analyzer to analyze the entire database. When the Listings table was split in Part 2, the relationships between the original Listings table and other objects were removed, leaving the new split table not related to any other table. Select and optimize entries in the *Analysis Results* list box that will create the relationships between the new Listings table and other objects.

Next, notice that all of the fields that store identification numbers—such as *AgentID*, *ClientID*, *ListingNo*, and *QuotaID*—have the idea proposed that the data type should be changed from Text to Long Integer. Long Integer is not actually a data type but a field size setting for a numeric field. Research data types in Access Help. Specifically, find out the difference between assigning a field the Text data type and Number data type. Using Microsoft Word, compose a memo to your instructor that includes the following information:

- An explanation of the use of the Text data type
- An explanation of the use of the Number data type
- Your recommendation of which data type should be used for the four *ID* fields in the database and why

Save the memo and name it **AL2-C6-HillsdaleDBAnalysisMemo.docx**. Print the memo and exit Word. In the database, open the Relationships window. Delete the original Listings table from the window and display the new Listings table name to show the relationships created when the database was optimized. Rearrange the table field list boxes so that the join lines are easy to follow and generate a relationships report. Print the relationships report. Save and close the relationships report and then close **AL2-C6-HillsdaleRealty.accdb**.

MICROSOFT®

ACCESS®

Automating, Customizing, and Securing Access

PERFORMANCE OBJECTIVES

Upon successful completion of Chapter 7, you will be able to:

- **Create, run, edit, and delete a macro**
- **Assign a macro to a command button on a form**
- **View macro code created for a command button in a form's Property Sheet task pane**
- **Convert a macro to Visual Basic**
- **Create and edit a Navigation form**
- **Change database startup options**
- **Show and hide the Navigation pane**
- **Customize the Navigation pane by hiding objects**
- **Define error-checking options**
- **Import and export customizations**
- **Customize the ribbon**

Tutorials

7.1 Creating and Editing a Macro
7.2 Creating a Command Button to Run a Macro
7.3 Creating a Navigation Form
7.4 Adding a Command Button to a Navigation Form
7.5 Limiting Ribbon Tabs and Menus in a Database
7.6 Customizing the Navigation Pane
7.7 Configuring Error Checking Options
7.8 Importing and Exporting Customizations
7.9 Customizing the Ribbon

Macros are used to automate repetitive tasks and to store these actions so that they can be executed by clicking a button in a form. A Navigation form is a form used as a menu that provides an interface between the end user and objects within the database file. In this chapter, you will learn how to automate a database using macros and a Navigation form. You will also learn how to customize the Access environment. A model answer for this chapter's Project 3 appears on the following page.

AL2C7

Note: Before beginning the projects, copy to your storage medium the AL2C7 subfolder from the AL2 folder on the CD that accompanies this textbook and then make AL2C7 the active folder.

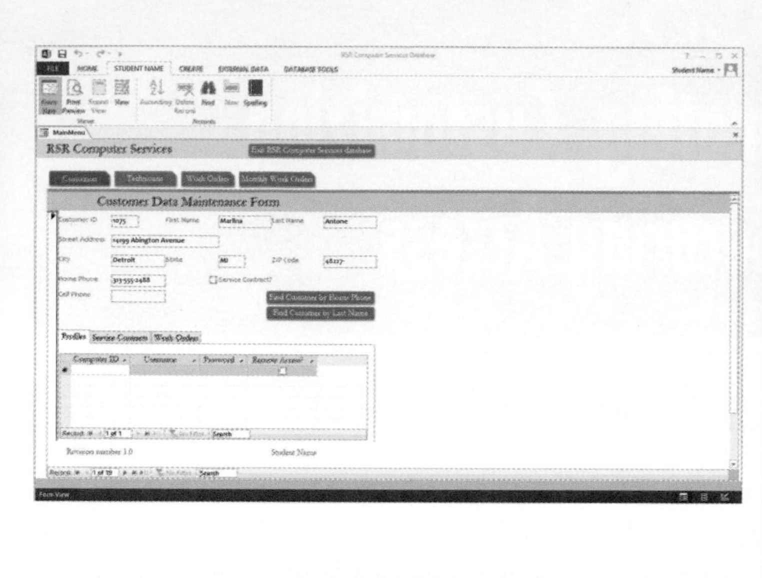

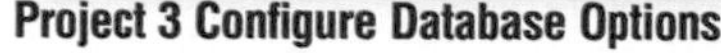

Project 3 Configure Database Options

Project 3d, Customized Database Startup Options, Navigation Pane, and Custom Ribbon Tab

Project 1 Create Macros and Assign Macros to Command Buttons — 8 Parts

You will create macros to automate routine tasks and add macros to command buttons in forms that run the macros.

Creating a Macro

For a complex macro, begin by working through the steps you want to save. Write down all of the parameters as you go before attempting to create the macro.

A ***macro*** is a series of instructions stored in a sequence that can be recalled and carried out whenever the need arises. A macro is generally created for a task that is never varied and that is repeated frequently. For example, you might create a macro to open a query, form, or report. The macro object stores a series of instructions (called ***actions***) in the sequence in which they are to be performed. Macros appear as objects within the Navigation pane. Macros that open a query, form, or report can be run by double-clicking the macro name in the Navigation pane.

Not all macros can be run by this method, however. Some need to be assigned to a button that you click in order to run the macro. For example, you can create a macro in a form that automates the process of finding a record by the last name field. The macro will contain two instructions: to move to the field in which the last name is stored and to open the Find dialog box. In general, a macro that does not include an instruction with the query, form, or report name in it must be assigned to a button. Otherwise, an error message will appear stating that the object is not currently selected or is not in the active view.

To create a macro, click the CREATE tab and then click the Macro button in the Macros & Code group. This opens the Macro Builder window, shown in Figure 7.1. Click the down-pointing arrow at the right side of the *Add New Action* option box and then click the desired instruction at the drop-down list. As an alternative, you can add an action using the Action Catalog task pane, as described in Figure 7.1.

Each new action entered into the Macro Builder window is associated with a set of ***arguments*** that displays once the action has been added. Similar to the field properties displayed in Table Design view, the arguments displayed in the *Action Arguments* section vary depending on the active action that has been expanded in the Macro Builder window. Figure 7.2 displays the action arguments for the OpenForm action.

The OpenForm action is used to open a form. Within the *Action Arguments* section, specify the name of the form to open and the view in which the form is to be presented. You can choose to open the form in Form view, Datasheet view, Layout view, Design view, or Print Preview. Use the Filter Name or Where Condition argument to restrict the records displayed in the report.

The Data Mode argument is used to place editing restrictions on records while the form is open. You can open the form in Add mode to only allow adding new records (users cannot view existing records); Edit mode to allow records to be added, edited, or deleted; or Read Only mode to only allow records to be viewed. The Window Mode argument is used to instruct Access to open the form in Normal mode (the way you normally view forms in the work area), Hidden mode (form is hidden), Icon mode (form opens minimized), or Dialog mode (form opens in a separate window similar to a dialog box).

Quick Steps

Create a Macro

1. Click CREATE tab.
2. Click Macro button.
3. Click *Add New Action* option box arrow.
4. Click desired action.
5. Enter arguments as required in *Action Arguments* section.
6. Click Save button.
7. Type name for macro.
8. Press Enter.
9. Repeat Steps 3–6 as needed.

Run a Macro

Double-click macro name in Navigation pane.

OR

1. Right-click macro name.
2. Click *Run.*

Macro

Figure 7.1 Macro Builder Window

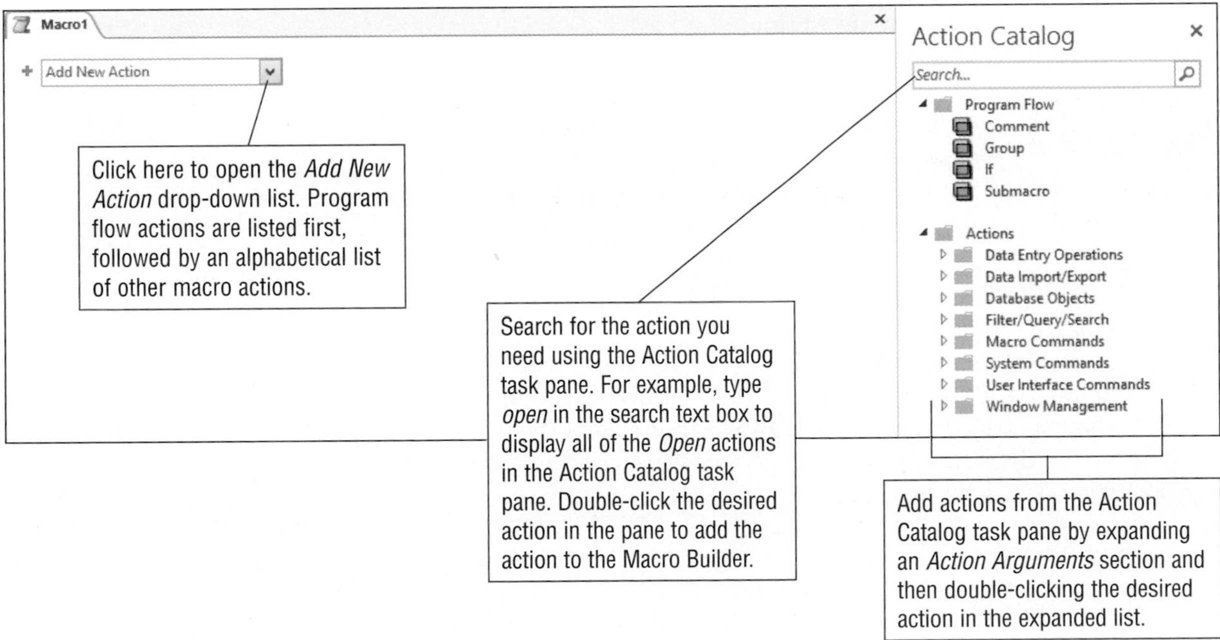

Figure 7.2 Macro Builder Window with Action Arguments for OpenForm Action

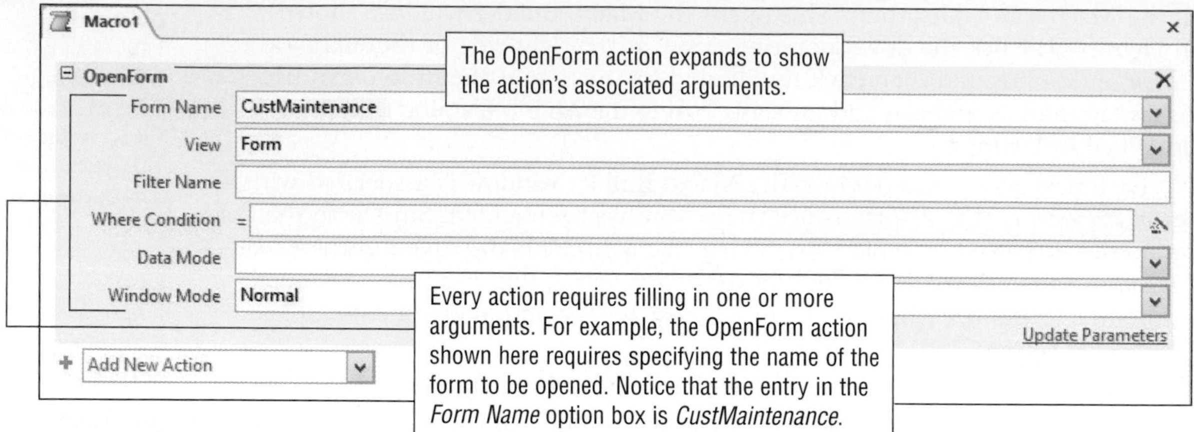

HINT

Hovering the mouse pointer over the entry box for an argument allows you to read a description of the argument and the available parameters in a ScreenTip.

To create a macro with multiple actions, use the *Add New Action* option box to add the second action below the first action. Access executes the actions in the order they appear in the Macro Builder window. In Project 1a, you will create a macro with multiple actions that will instruct Access to open a form, make active a control within the form, and then open the Find dialog box to search for a record.

The GoToControl action is used to make active a control within a form or report and the RunMenuCommand action is used to execute an Access command. For each action, a single argument specifies the name of the control to move to and the name of the command you want to run.

As you add actions to the Macro Builder window, you can expand and collapse the *Action Arguments* section as needed. When several actions have been added to the Macro Builder window, collapsing arguments allows you to focus on the current action you are editing.

Project 1a Creating a Macro to Open a Form and Find a Record **Part 1 of 8**

1. Open **AL2-C7-RSRCompServ.accdb** and enable the content. Create a macro to open the TechMaintenance form by completing the following steps:
   a. Click the CREATE tab.
   b. Click the Macro button in the Macros & Code group.
   c. At the Macro Builder window, click the down-pointing arrow at the right of the *Add New Action* option box, scroll down the list, and then click *OpenForm*. Access adds the action and opens the *Action Arguments* section. Most actions require at least one action argument.

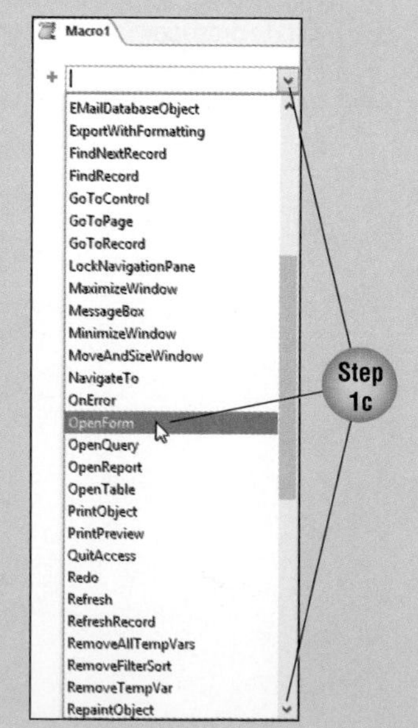

d. Click the down-pointing arrow at the right of the *Form Name* option box in the *Action Arguments* section and then click *TechMaintenance* at the drop-down list.

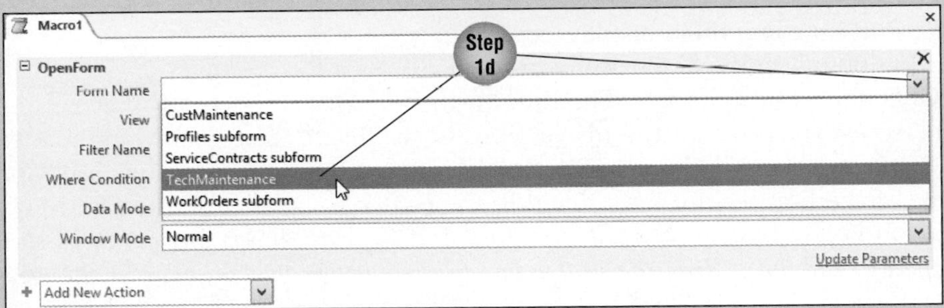

2. Add additional instructions to move to the field for the technician's last name and then open the Find dialog box by completing the following steps:
   a. Click the down-pointing arrow at the right of the *Add New Action* option box, scroll down the list, and then click *GoToControl*. Notice that only one action argument is required for the *GoToControl* action.
   b. Click in the *Control Name* text box in the *Action Arguments* section and then type **LName**. (Entering the name of the field that you want to make active in the form is required.)

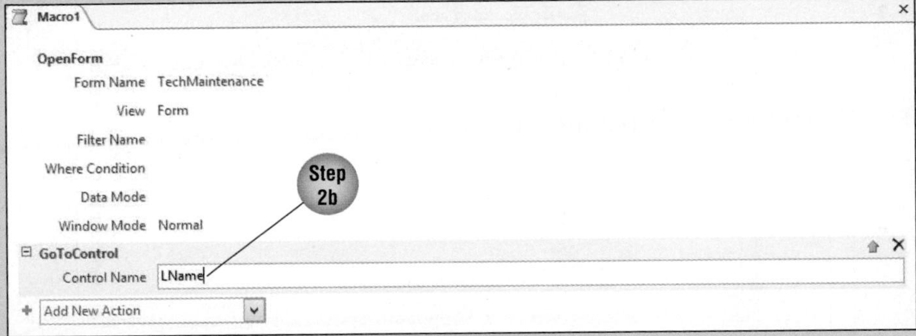

   c. Click the down-pointing arrow at the right of the *Add New Action* option box, scroll down the list, and then click *RunMenuCommand*.
   d. Click the down-pointing arrow at the right of the *Command* option box, scroll down the list, and then click *Find*.

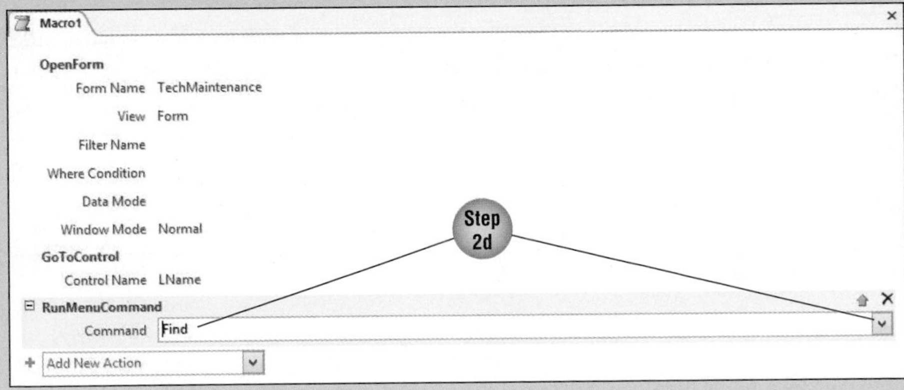

3. Click the Save button on the Quick Access toolbar, type **FormFindTech** in the *Macro Name* text box at the Save As dialog box, and then press Enter or click OK.

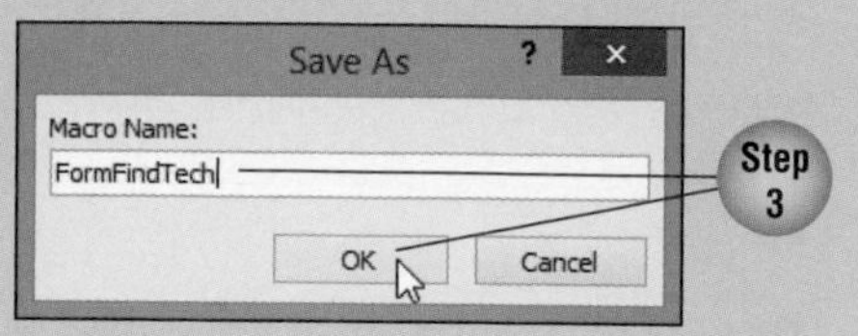

4. Click the Run button (which displays as a red exclamation point) in the Tools group on the MACRO TOOLS DESIGN tab. The Run button instructs Access to carry out the instructions in the macro. The TechMaintenance form opens, the *Last Name* field is active, and the Find and Replace dialog box appears with the last name of the first technician entered in the *Find What* text box. Type **Sadiku** and then click the Find Next button. ***Note: If the Find and Replace dialog box overlaps the* Last Name *field in the form, drag the dialog box to the bottom or right edge of the work area.***

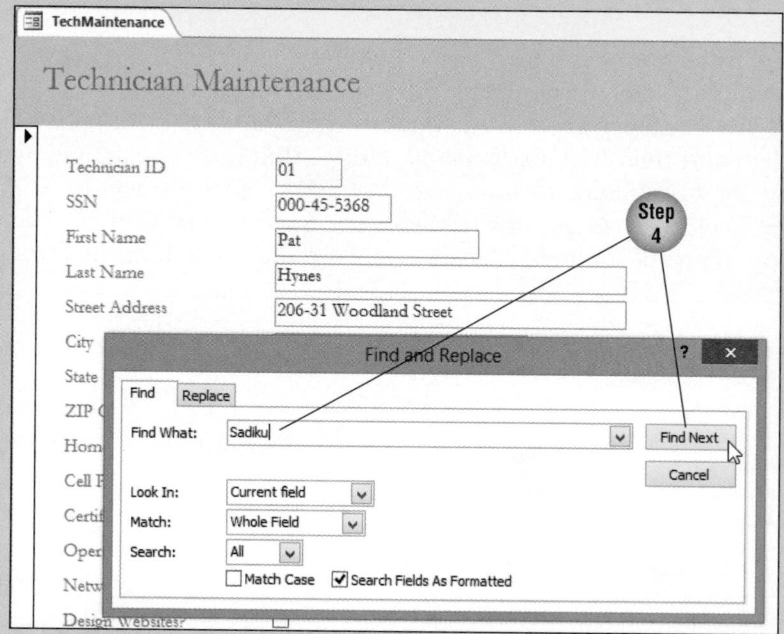

5. Access moves to record 5. Close the Find and Replace dialog box. Notice that the last name text is selected in the form. Read the data displayed in the form for the technician named Madir Sadiku.
6. Close the form.
7. At the Macro Builder window, click the Close button located at the top right of the work area, to the left of the Action Catalog task pane. This closes the FormFindTech macro. Notice that a Macros group has been added to the Navigation pane and that FormFindTech appears as an object below this new group name.

You can also create a macro by dragging and dropping an object name from the Navigation pane into the *Add New Action* option box in a Macro Builder window. By default, Access creates an OpenTable, OpenQuery, OpenForm, or OpenReport action depending on the object you dragged to the window. The object name is also automatically entered in the *Action Arguments* section.

Project 1b Creating a Macro by Dragging and Dropping an Object — Part 2 of 8

1. With **AL2-C7-RSRCompServ.accdb** open, use the drag and drop method to create a macro to open the CustMaintenance form by completing the following steps:
   a. Click the CREATE tab.
   b. Click the Macro button in the Macros & Code group.
   c. Position the mouse pointer on the CustMaintenance form name in the Navigation pane, hold down the left mouse button, drag the object name to the *Add New Action* option box in the Macro Builder window, and then release the mouse. Access inserts an OpenForm action with *CustMaintenance* entered in the *Form Name* option box.
2. Click the Save button, type **FormCustMaint**, and then press Enter or click OK.

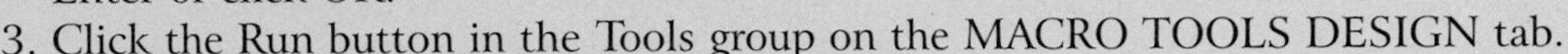

3. Click the Run button in the Tools group on the MACRO TOOLS DESIGN tab.
4. Close the form.
5. Close the macro by clicking the Close button located at the top right of the work area and to the left of the Action Catalog task pane.

Project 1c Creating a Macro Using the Action Catalog Task Pane — Part 3 of 8

1. With **AL2-C7-RSRCompServ.accdb** open, use the Action Catalog task pane to create a macro to find a record in a form by making active the home telephone field and then opening the Find dialog box by completing the following steps.
   Note: This macro will be assigned to a button in Projects 1e and 1f. An error will occur if you try to run the macro by double-clicking it in the Navigation pane.
   a. Click the CREATE tab.
   b. Click the Macro button in the Macros & Code group.
   c. Click the expand button (which displays as a white triangle) next to *Database Objects* in the *Actions* list in the Action Catalog task pane to expand the category and display the actions available for changing controls or objects in the database. ***Note: If you accidentally closed the Action Catalog task pane in a previous Macro Builder window and the task pane does not redisplay in the new Macro Builder window, you can restore the task pane by clicking the Action Catalog button in the Show/Hide group on the Macro Tools Design tab.***
   d. Double-click *GoToControl* at the expanded *Database Objects* actions list in the Action Catalog task pane to add the action to the Macro Builder window.

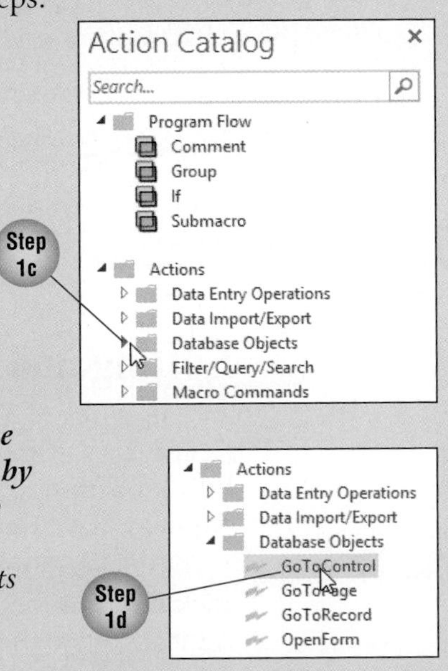

e. With the insertion point positioned in the *Control Name* text box in the Macro Builder window, type **HPhone**.
f. Click in the search text box at the top of the Action Catalog task pane and then type **Run**. As you type, Access displays available actions in the Action Catalog task pane that begin with the text you type.
g. Double-click *RunMenuCommand* in the *Macro Commands* list in the Action Catalog task pane.
h. With the insertion point positioned in the *Command* text box in the Macro Builder window, type **Find**.
i. Click the Save button on the Quick Access toolbar.
j. At the Save As dialog box, type **HPhoneFind** and then press Enter or click OK.
k. Close the HPhoneFind macro.

2. Use the Action Center catalog to create a macro to close the current database and exit Access by completing the following steps:
   a. Click the CREATE tab and then click the Macro button.
   b. Click the box at the right of the search text box in the Action Catalog task pane to clear *Run* from the search text box and redisplay all of the Action Catalog categories.
   c. Click the expand button (which displays as a white triangle) next to *System Commands* in the *Actions* list in the Action Catalog task pane.
   d. Double-click *QuitAccess* in the expanded *System Commands* actions list.
   e. With *Save All* as the default argument in the *Options* option box, click the Save button on the Quick Access toolbar.
   f. Type **ExitRSRdb** at the Save As dialog box and then press Enter or click OK.
3. Close the ExitRSRdb macro.

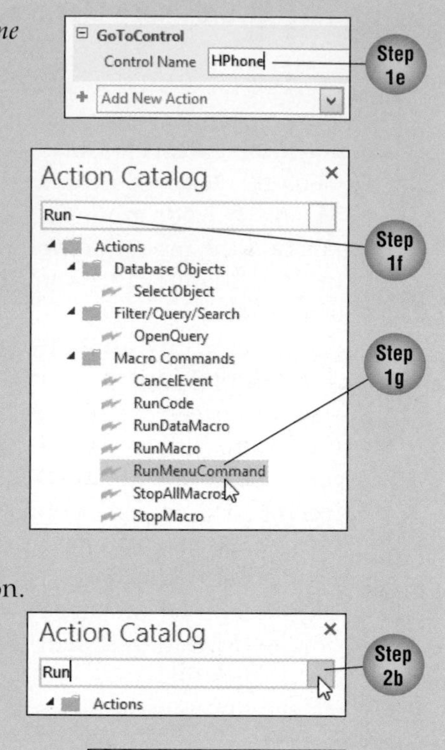

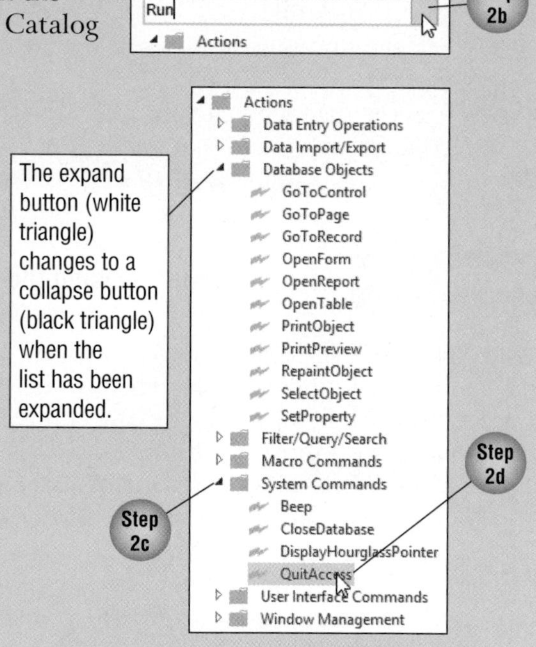

Editing and Deleting a Macro

To edit a macro, right-click the macro name in the Navigation pane and then click *Design View* at the shortcut menu. The macro opens in the Macro Builder window. Edit an action and/or its arguments, insert new actions, and/or delete actions as required. Save the revised macro and close the Macro Builder window when finished.

To delete a macro, right-click the macro name in the Navigation pane and then click *Delete* at the shortcut menu. At the Microsoft Access dialog box asking if you want to delete the macro, click Yes.

Project 1d Editing and Deleting a Macro Part 4 of 8

1. With **AL2-C7-RSRCompServ.accdb** open, assume you decide that the macro to find a technician record will begin with the TechMaintenance form already opened. This means that you have to delete the first macro instruction to open the TechMaintenance form in the FormFindTech macro. To do this, complete the following steps:
   a. If necessary, scroll down the Navigation pane to view the macro object names.
   b. Right-click *FormFindTech* in the Macros group in the Navigation pane and then click *Design View* at the shortcut menu. The macro opens in the Macro Builder window.
   c. Position the mouse pointer over the OpenForm action in the Macro Builder window. As you point to an action in the Macro Builder window, Access displays a collapse indicator at the left of the action to allow you to collapse the *Action Arguments* section; a green down-pointing arrow at the right to allow you to move the action; and a black X to delete the action.

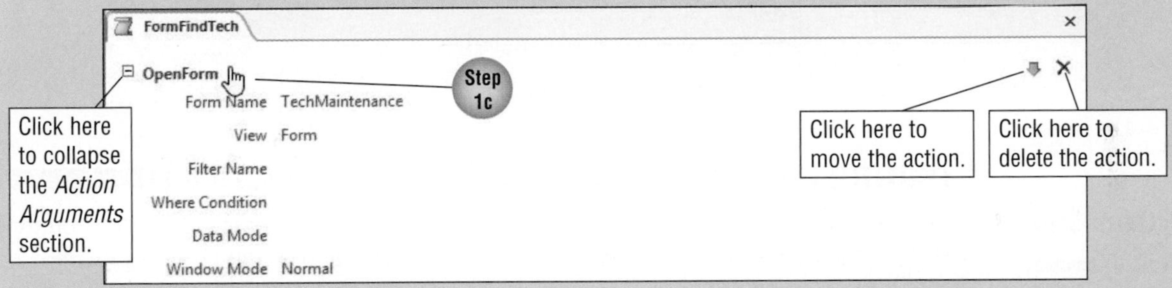

   d. Click the black X at the right side of the Macro Builder window across from *OpenForm*. The action is removed from the Macro Builder window. ***Note: If the buttons at the right side of the Macro Builder window disappear as you move the mouse to the right, move the pointer up so it is on the same line as* OpenForm *to redisplay the buttons.***

2. Save the revised macro. ***Note: This macro can no longer be run by double-clicking it in the Navigation pane. As mentioned earlier, an error will occur. The macro will be assigned to a button in Projects 1e and 1f.***
3. Close the macro.
4. The revised macro contains two instructions that activate the *LName* control and then open the Find dialog box. This macro can be used in any form that contains a field named *LName*; therefore, you decide to rename the macro. To do this, right-click *FormFindTech* in the Navigation pane, click *Rename* at the shortcut menu, type **LNameFind**, and then press Enter.

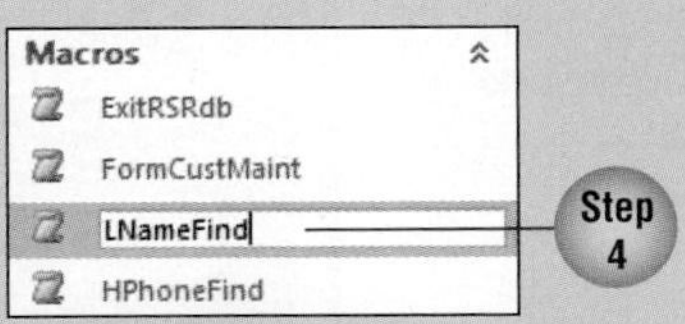

5. Delete the FormCustMaint macro by completing the following steps:
   a. Right-click *FormCustMaint* in the Navigation pane and then click *Delete* at the shortcut menu.
   b. At the Microsoft Access dialog box asking if you want to delete the macro, click Yes.

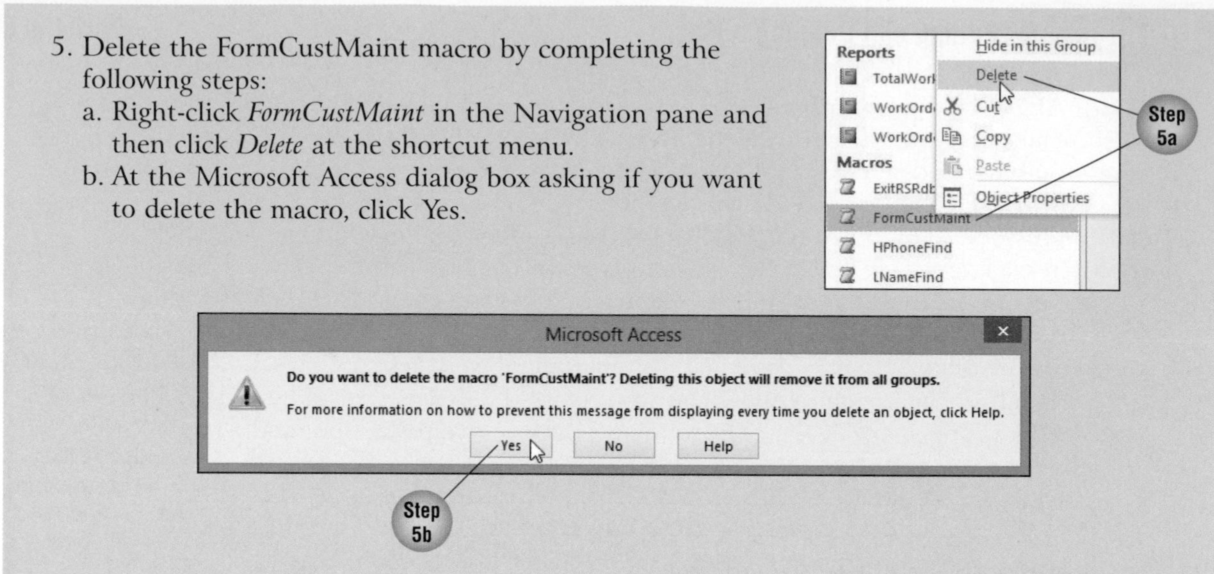

Reports
TotalWork
WorkOrd
WorkOrd
Macros
ExitRSRdb
FormCustMaint
HPhoneFind
LNameFind
Hide in this Group
Delete
Cut
Copy
Paste
Object Properties
Step 5a
Microsoft Access
Do you want to delete the macro 'FormCustMaint'? Deleting this object will remove it from all groups.
For more information on how to prevent this message from displaying every time you delete an object, click Help.
Yes
No
Help
Step 5b

Creating a Command Button to Run a Macro

Quick Steps

Create a Command Button in a Form

1. Open form in Design view.
2. Click Button button.
3. Drag to create button.
4. Click *Miscellaneous.*
5. Click *Run Macro.*
6. Click Next.
7. Click desired macro name.
8. Click Next.
9. Click *Text.*
10. Select current text in *Text* text box.
11. Type desired text to appear on button.
12. Click Next.
13. Type name for command button.
14. Click Finish.

Button

A macro can be assigned to a button in a form so that the macro can be executed with a single mouse click. This method of running macros makes them more accessible and efficient.

To add a button to a form to be used to run a macro, open the form in Design view. Click the Button button in the Controls group on the FORM DESIGN TOOLS DESIGN tab and then drag to create a button in the desired form section. When you release the mouse, the Command Button Wizard launches (if the Use Control Wizards feature is active).

At the first Command Button Wizard dialog box, shown in Figure 7.3, begin by choosing the type of command to assign to the button. Click *Miscellaneous* in the *Categories* list box, click *Run Macro* in the *Actions* list box, and then click Next. At the second Command Button Wizard dialog box, choose the name of the macro to assign to the button. At the third dialog box, shown in Figure 7.4, specify text or a picture to display on the face of the button. When you enter text

Figure 7.3 First Command Button Wizard Dialog Box

Command Button Wizard

Sample:

What action do you want to happen when the button is pressed?

Different actions are available for each category.

Categories: Record Navigation, Record Operations, Form Operations, Report Operations, Application, Miscellaneous

Actions: Auto Dialer, Print Table, Run Macro, Run Query

Cancel | < Back | Next > | Finish

Select the *Miscellaneous* category and the *Run Macro* action to assign a macro to the button at the first Command Button Wizard dialog box.

Figure 7.4 Third Command Button Wizard Dialog Box

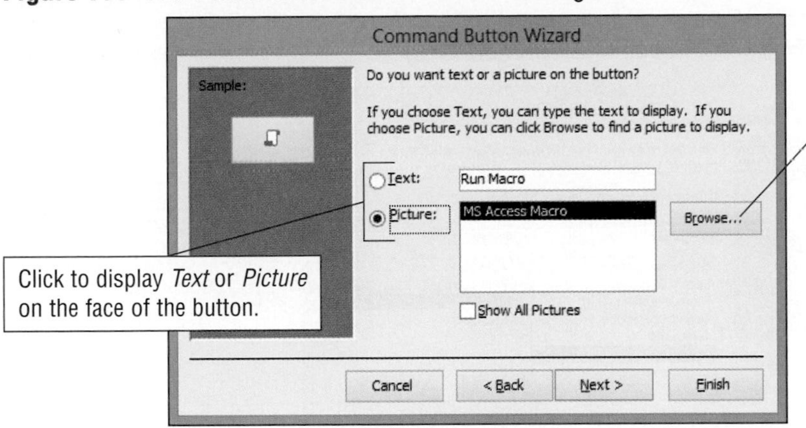

or select a picture file, the button in the *Sample* section of the dialog box updates to show how the button will appear. At the last Command Button Wizard dialog box, assign a name to associate with the command button and then click Finish.

HINT

An action can be assigned to a command button without using a macro. Explore the categories and actions for each category at the first Command Button Wizard dialog box.

Project 1e Creating a Button and Assigning a Macro to a Button in a Form — Part 5 of 8

1. With **AL2-C7-RSRCompServ.accdb** open, create a command button to run the macro to locate a technician record by last name in the TechMaintenance form by completing the following steps:
   a. Open the TechMaintenance form in Design view. To make room for the new button in the *Form Header* section, click to select the control object with the title text and then drag the right middle sizing handle to the left until the right edge is at approximately the 3.5-inch mark on the horizontal ruler.
   b. By default, the Use Control Wizards button is toggled on in the Controls group. Click the More button in the Controls group on the FORM DESIGN TOOLS DESIGN tab. If the Use Control Wizards button displays with a pink background, the feature is active. If the button is pink, click in a blank area to close the expanded Controls group. If the feature is not active (displays with a white background), click the Use Control Wizards button to turn on the feature.
   c. Click the Button button in the Controls group.
   d. Position the crosshairs with the button icon attached in the *Form Header* section, drag to create a button of the approximate height and width shown at the right, and then release the mouse.

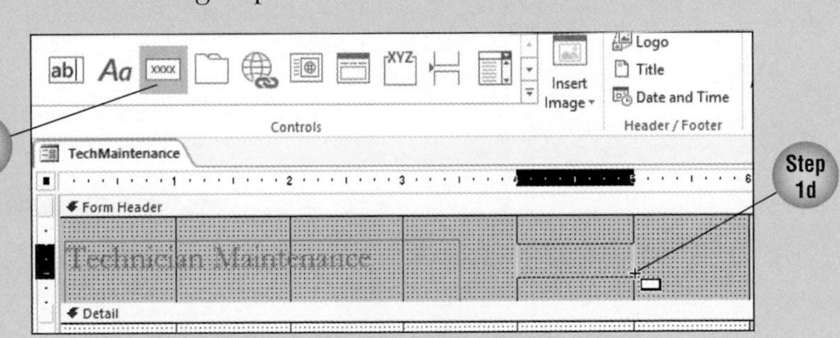

e. At the first Command Button Wizard dialog box, click *Miscellaneous* in the *Categories* list box.
f. Click *Run Macro* in the *Actions* list box and then click Next.

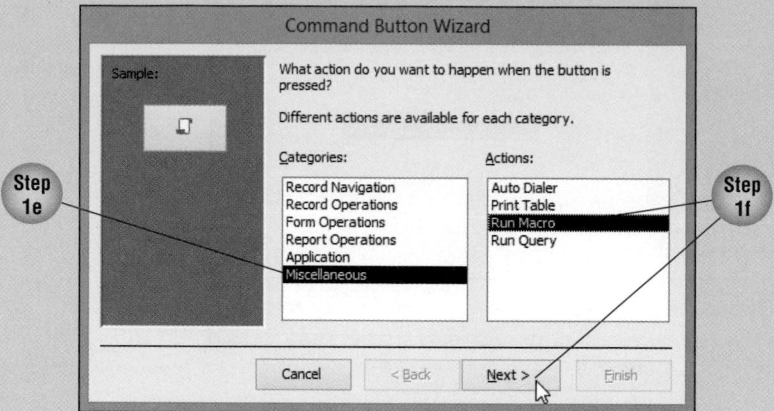

g. At the second Command Button Wizard dialog box, click *LNameFind* in the *What macro would you like the command button to run?* list box and then click Next.

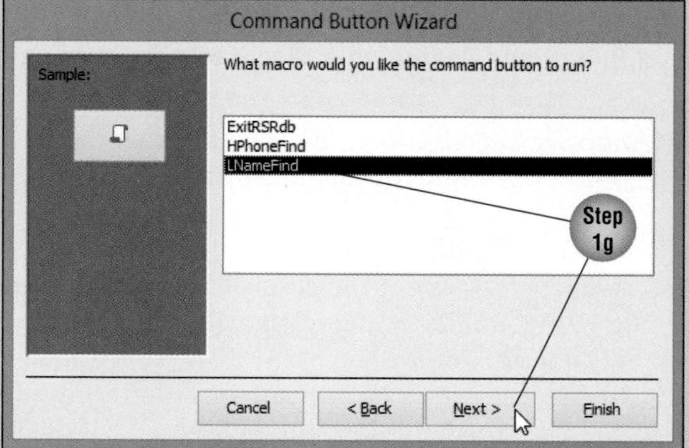

h. At the third Command Button Wizard dialog box, click the *Text* option.
i. Select the current text in the *Text* text box, type **Find Technician by Last Name**, and then click Next.

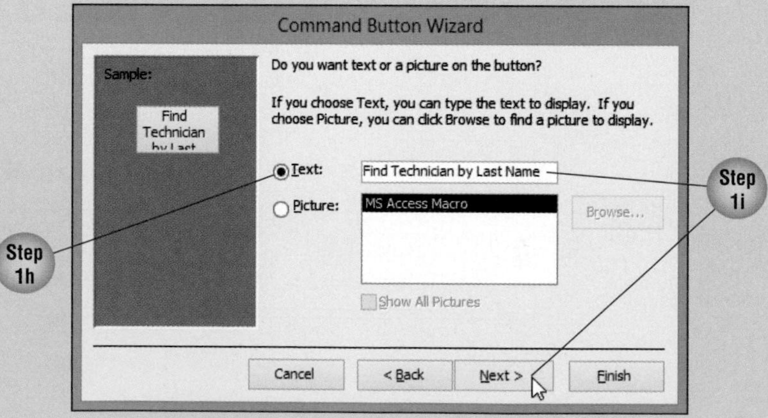

j. With *Command##* (where ## is the number of the command button) already selected in the *What do you want to name the button?* text box, type **FindTechRec** and then click Finish. Access automatically resizes the width of the button to accommodate the text to be displayed on its face.

2. Save the revised form.
3. Switch to Form view.
4. Click the Find Technician by Last Name button to run the macro.
5. Type **Colacci** in the *Find What* text box at the Find and Replace dialog box and then press Enter or click the Find Next button. Access makes record 9 active.
6. Close the Find and Replace dialog box.
7. Close the form.

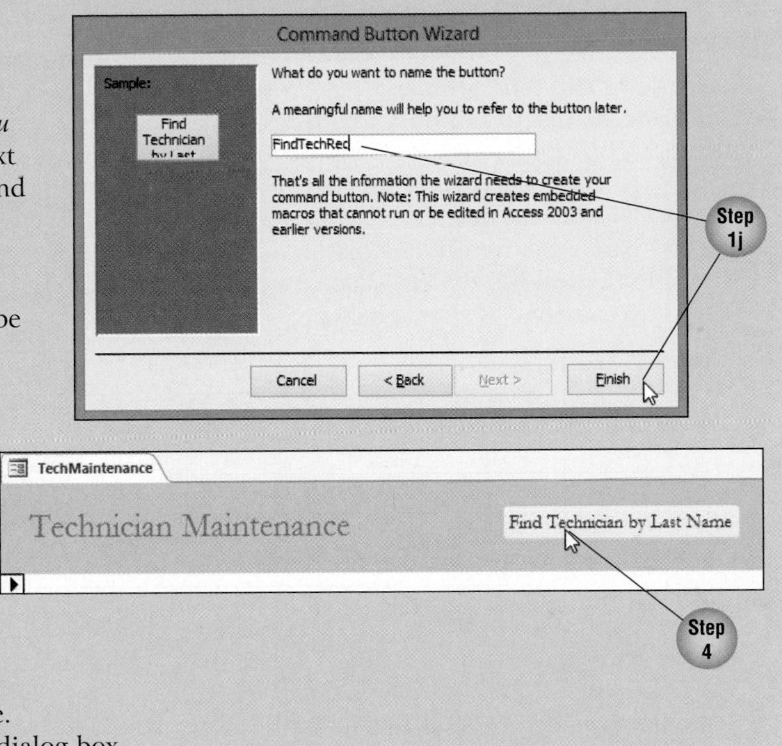

Project 1f Creating Two Command Buttons and Assigning Macros to the Buttons Part 6 of 8

1. With **AL2-C7-RSRCompServ.accdb** open, create a command button to run the macro to find a record by the home telephone number field in the CustMaintenance form by completing the following steps:
   a. Open the CustMaintenance form in Design view.
   b. Click the Button button in the Controls group on the FORM DESIGN TOOLS DESIGN tab.
   c. Position the crosshairs with the button icon attached in the *Detail* section below the *Service Contract?* label control object, drag to create a button of the approximate height and width shown at the right, and then release the mouse.
   d. Click *Miscellaneous* in the *Categories* list box, click *Run Macro* in the *Actions* list box, and then click Next.
   e. Click *HPhoneFind* and then click Next.
   f. Click *Text*, select the current text in the *Text* text box, type **Find Customer by Home Phone**, and then click Next.

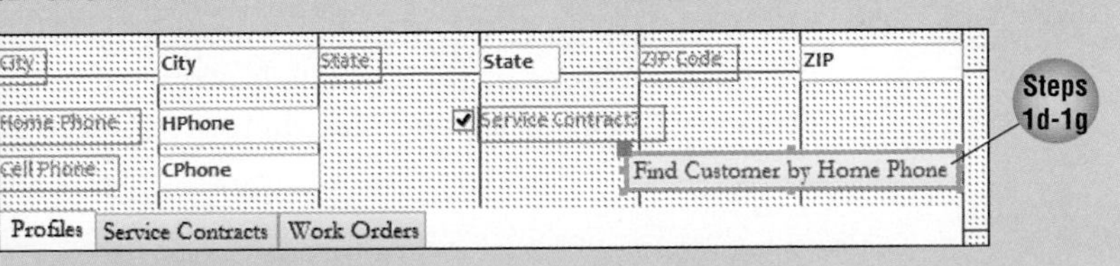

   g. Type **FindByPhone** and then click Finish.

2. Save the revised form.
3. If necessary, move the tab control group down so the top of the object is at the 2.25-inch mark on the vertical ruler. Create a second button below the button you created in Step 1 to run the macro to find a record by the last name by completing steps similar to those in Steps 1b through 1g and using the following additional information:
   - Select *LNameFind* as the macro to assign to the button.
   - Display the text *Find Customer by Last Name* on the button.
   - Name the button *FindByLName*.
4. Apply the Intense Effect - Blue-Gray, Accent 3 quick style. Resize, align, and then position the two buttons as shown below.

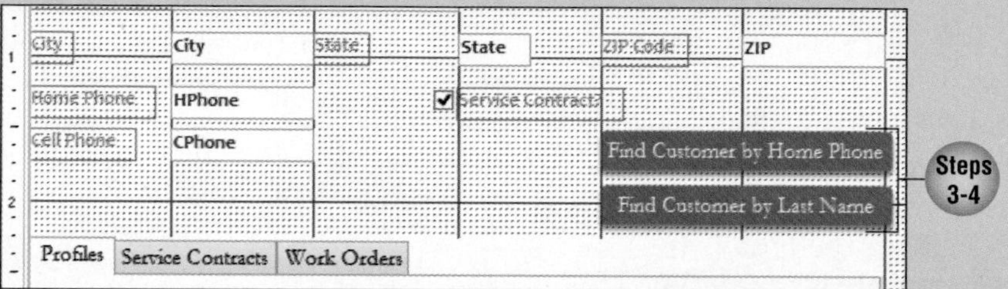

5. Save the revised form.
6. Switch to Form view.
7. Click the Find Customer by Home Phone button, type **313-555-7486** at the Find and Replace dialog box, and then press Enter or click Find Next. Close the dialog box and review the record for Customer ID 1025.
8. Click the Find Customer by Last Name button, type **Antone** at the Find and Replace dialog box, and then press Enter or click Find Next. Close the dialog box and review the record for Customer ID 1075.
9. Close the CustMaintenance form.

Viewing an Embedded Macro

Quick Steps

View the Macro Code for a Command Button

1. Open form in Design view.
2. Click to select command button.
3. Display Property Sheet task pane.
4. Click Event tab.
5. Click Build button in *On Click* property box.

The Command Button Wizard used in Projects 1e and 1f created an embedded macro in the Property Sheet task pane for the button. An ***embedded macro*** is a macro stored within a form, report, or control that is run when a specific event, such as clicking a button, occurs.

Embedded macros are not objects that you can see in the Navigation pane. To view an embedded macro, open the command button's Property Sheet task pane and then click the Event tab. In the *On Click* property box, you will see *[Embedded Macro]*. Click the Build button (which displays three dots) at the right side of the *On Click* property box to open the Macro Builder window with the macro actions displayed. The macro and macro actions were created for you by the Command Button Wizard.

To delete an embedded macro, open the Property Sheet task pane, select *[Embedded Macro]* in the On Click property box, and then press Delete. Close the Property Sheet task pane and then save the form.

Project 1g Viewing Macro Actions Created by the Command Button Wizard — Part 7 of 8

1. With **AL2-C7-RSRCompServ.accdb** open, view the macro actions you embedded in a command button when you used the Command Button Wizard by completing the following steps:
   a. Open the CustMaintenance form in Design view.
   b. Click to select the Find Customer by Home Phone command button.
   c. Click the Property Sheet button in the Tools group on the FORM DESIGN TOOLS DESIGN tab or press F4.
   d. Click the Event tab in the Command Button Property Sheet task pane.
   e. Notice that the text in the *On Click* property box reads *[Embedded Macro]*.
   f. Click the Build button (which displays three dots) in the *On Click* property box. When you click the Build button, Access opens the Macro Builder window for the macro that was embedded in the command button.
   g. Notice that the name of the macro created for you by the Command Button Wizard is *CustMaintenance: FindByPhone: On Click*. The macro's name is made up of the form name, followed by the button name with which the macro is associated, and then the event that causes the macro to run (*On Click*).
   h. Review the macro actions in the Macro Builder window. Notice that the macro action is *RunMacro* and that the name of the macro you selected at the second Command Button Wizard dialog box, *HPhoneFind*, appears in the *Macro Name* option box.
   i. Click the Close button in the Close group on the MACRO TOOLS DESIGN tab.

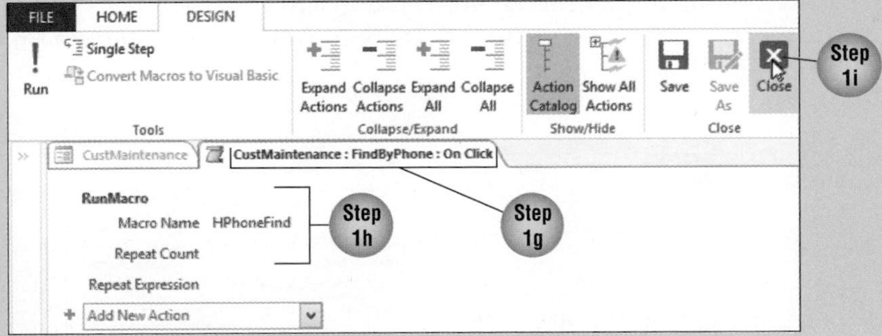

2. With the Property Sheet task pane still open, click to select the Find Customer by Last Name command button and then click the Build button in the *On Click* property box on the Event tab in the Property Sheet task pane.
3. Review the embedded macro name and macro actions in the Macro Builder window and then click the Close button in the Close group on the MACRO TOOLS DESIGN tab.
4. Close the CustMaintenance form.

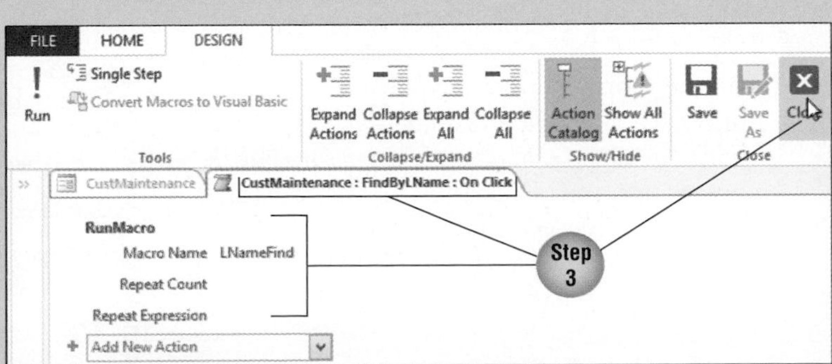

Converting Macros to Visual Basic

Quick Steps

Convert a Macro to Visual Basic
1. Open macro in Design view.
2. Click Convert Macros to Visual Basic button.
3. Click Convert button.
4. Click OK.

Convert Macros to Visual Basic

Creating and using macros enables you to add automation and functionality within Access without having to learn how to write programming code. In the Microsoft Office suite, Visual Basic for Applications (VBA) is the programming language used to build custom applications that operate within Word, Excel, PowerPoint, and Access. The macros used so far in this chapter have been simple enough that they do not need VBA programming. However, when automating more complex tasks, a developer may prefer to write a program using VBA.

A quick method for starting a VBA program is to create a macro and then convert it to VBA code. To do this, open the macro in the Macro Builder window and then click the Convert Macros to Visual Basic button in the Tools group on the MACRO TOOLS DESIGN tab. Access opens a Microsoft Visual Basic window with the VBA code for the macro. When you convert an embedded macro, Access also changes the property box in the Property Sheet task pane for the form, report, or control to run the VBA procedure instead of the macro.

Project 1h Converting a Macro to Visual Basic for Applications — Part 8 of 8

1. With **AL2-C7-RSRCompServ.accdb** open, convert a macro to VBA by completing the following steps:
   a. Right-click *HPhoneFind* in the Macros group in the Navigation pane and then click *Design View* at the shortcut menu. The Macro Builder window opens with the macro actions and arguments for the HPhoneFind macro.
   b. Click the Convert Macros to Visual Basic button in the Tools group on the MACRO TOOLS DESIGN tab.

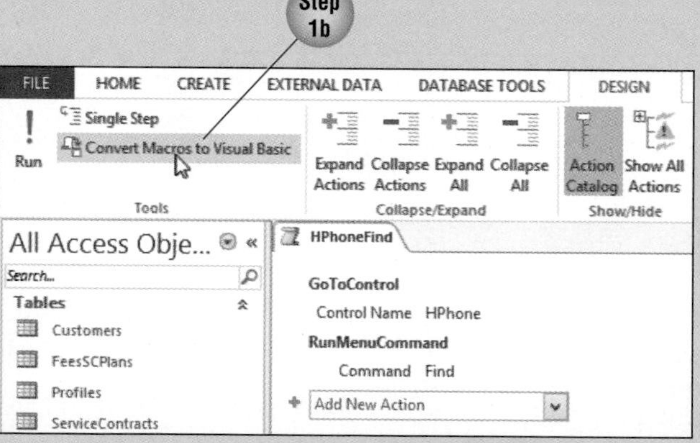

   c. At the Convert macro: HPhoneFind dialog box with the *Add error handling to generated functions* and *Include macro comments* check boxes selected, click the Convert button.
   d. At the *Convert macros to Visual Basic* message box alerting you that the conversion has finished, click OK.

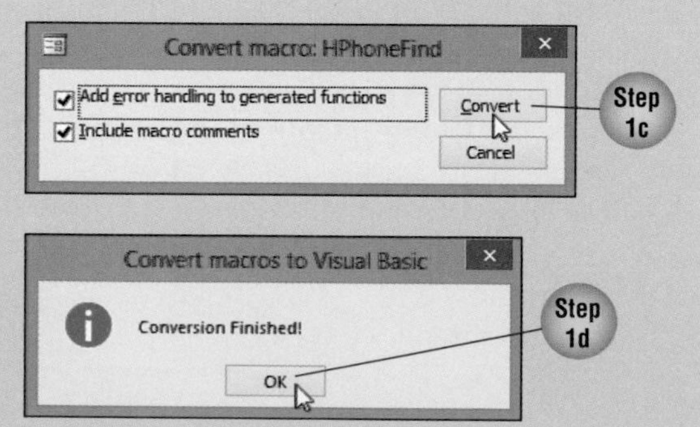

2. Access opens a Microsoft Visual Basic for Applications window when the macro is converted and displays the converted event procedure below the expanded *Modules* folder in the Project pane. If necessary, drag the right border of the Project pane to the right to expand the pane so you can read the entire converted macro name and then double-click the macro name to open the event procedure in its class module window.
3. Read the VBA code and then close the Converted Macro-HPhoneFind (Code) window.

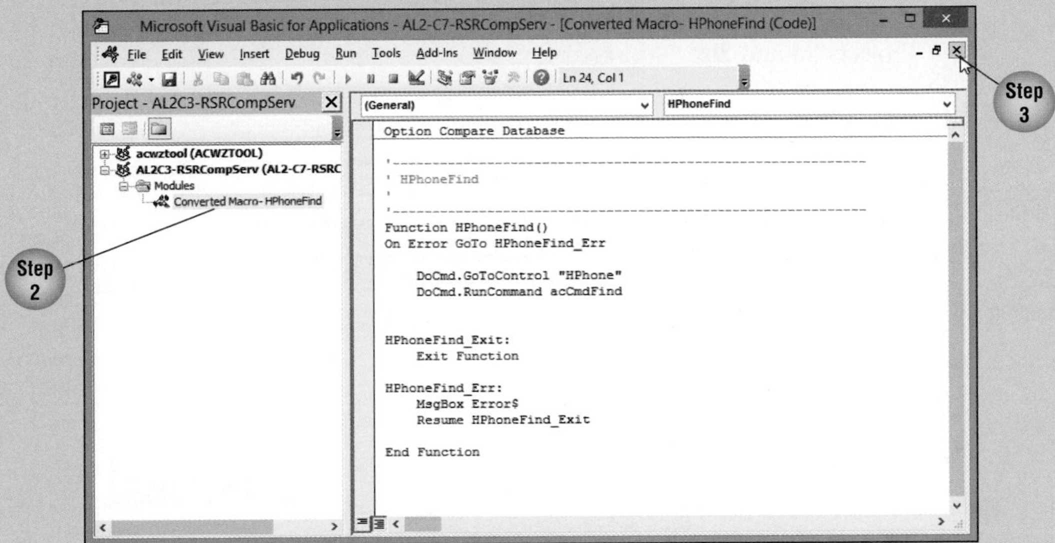

4. Click File on the Menu bar and then click *Close and Return to Microsoft Access* at the drop-down menu.
5. Close the HPhoneFind Macro Builder window.

Project 2 Create a Navigation Form — 2 Parts

You will create a Navigation form to be used as a main menu for the RSR Computer Services database.

Creating a Navigation Form

Database files are often accessed by multiple users who need to use them for specific purposes, such as updating customer records and entering details related to completed work orders. These individuals may not know much about database applications and may want an easy method for completing data entry or maintenance tasks. End users can open the forms and reports needed to update, view, and print data using a Navigation form as a menu. A Navigation form has tabs along the top, left, or right. It can be set to display automatically when the database file is opened so end users do not need to choose which objects to open from the Navigation pane.

Quick Steps

Create a Navigation Form

1. Click CREATE tab.
2. Click Navigation button.
3. Click desired form style.
4. Drag form or report name to *[Add New]* in Navigation Form window.
5. Repeat Step 4 as needed.
6. Click Save.
7. Type form name.
8. Press Enter.

Navigation

To create a Navigation form, click the CREATE tab and then click the Navigation button in the Forms group. At the Navigation button drop-down list, choose the type of form you want to create by selecting the option in the drop-down list that positions the tabs where you want them to appear. A Navigation Form window opens with a title and a tab bar. Access displays *[Add New]* in the first tab in the form. Drag a form or report from the Navigation pane to *[Add New]* in the Navigation Form window to add a form or report to the form. Continue dragging form and/or report names from the Navigation pane to *[Add New]* in the Navigation Form window in the order you want them to appear. Figure 7.5 illustrates the Navigation form you will create in Projects 2a and 2b.

Figure 7.5 Navigation Form for Projects 2a and 2b

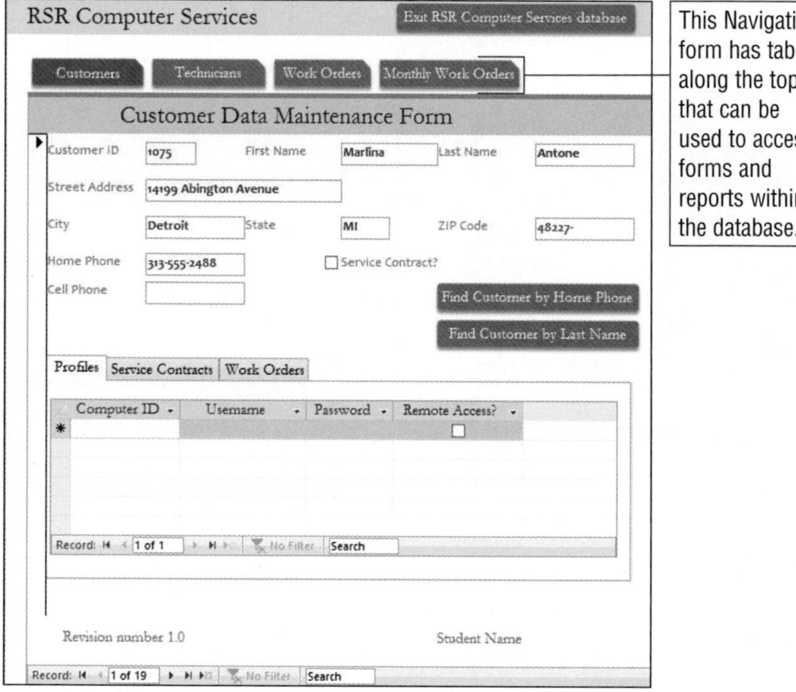

Project 2a Creating a Navigation Form

Part 1 of 2

1. With **AL2-C7-RSRCompServ.accdb** open, create a Navigation form with tabs along the top for accessing forms and reports by completing the following steps:
   a. Click the CREATE tab.
   b. Click the Navigation button in the Forms group.
   c. Click *Horizontal Tabs* at the drop-down list. Access opens a Navigation Form window with a Field List task pane at the right side of the work area. The horizontal tab across the top of the form is selected and *[Add New]* displays in the first tab.

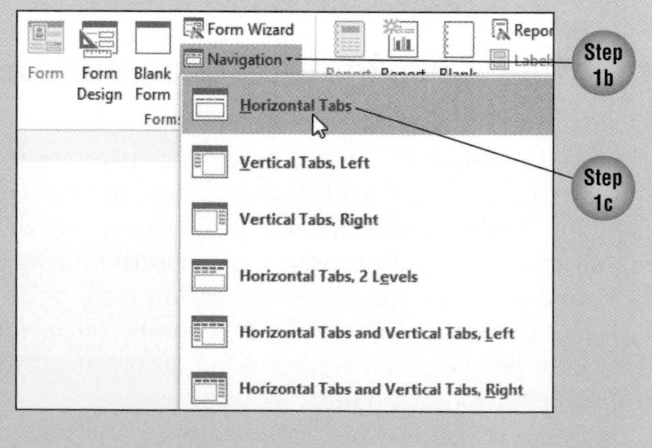

d. Position the mouse pointer on the CustMaintenance form name in the Navigation pane, hold down the left mouse button, drag the form name to *[Add New]* in the Navigation form, and then release the mouse button. Access adds the CustMaintenance form to the first tab in the form and displays a new tab with *[Add New]* to the right of the CustMaintcnance tab.

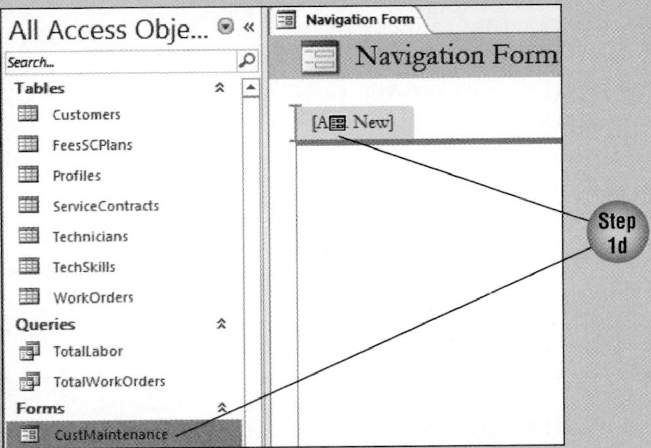

e. Drag the TechMaintenance form name from the Navigation pane to the second tab (which displays *[Add New]*).

f. Drag the WorkOrders report name from the Navigation pane to the third tab (which displays *[Add New]*).

g. Drag the WorkOrdersbyMonth report name from the Navigation pane to the fourth tab (which displays *[Add New]*).

2. Close the Field List task pane at the right side of the work area.
3. Click the Save button on the Quick Access toolbar. At the Save As dialog box, type **MainMenu** in the *Form Name* text box and then press Enter or click OK.
4. Switch to Form view.
5. Click each tab along the top of the Navigation form to view each form or report in the work area. Leave the form open for the next project.

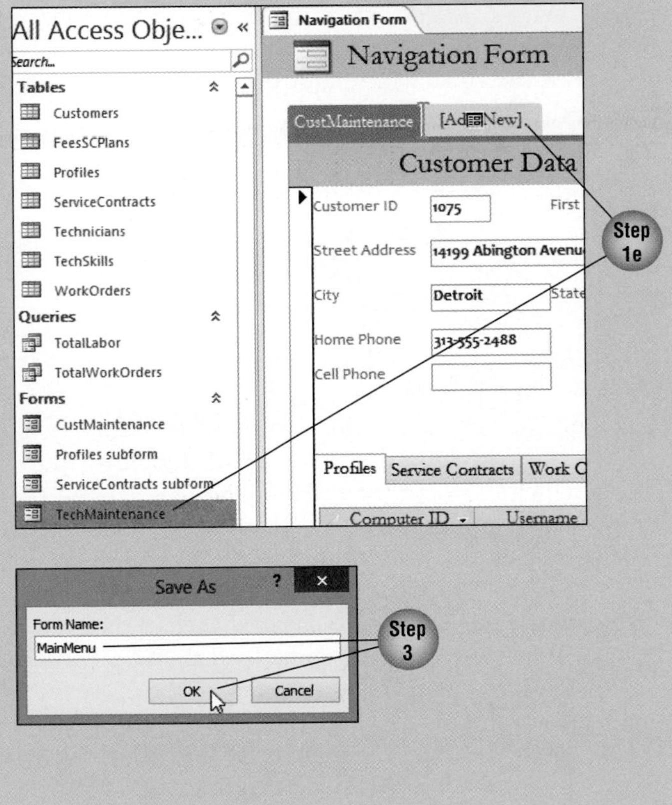

A Navigation form can be edited in Layout view or Form view using all of the tools and techniques you learned in Chapter 4 for working with forms. Consider changing the title, adding a logo and/or a command button, or renaming tabs to customize the Navigation form.

Project 2b Adding a Command Button to a Navigation Form and Editing the Form Part 2 of 2

1. With **AL2-C7-RSRCompServ.accdb** open and the MainMenu form displayed in the work area, add a command button to the Navigation form by completing the following steps:
   a. Switch to Design view.
   b. Select the *Form Header* section bar and then click the FORM DESIGN TOOLS FORMAT tab. Change the fill color of the *Form Header* section to *Blue-Gray, Accent 3, Lighter 80%* (seventh column in the second row in the *Theme Colors* section).
   c. Resize the title control object in the *Form Header* section to align the right edge of the object at approximately the 3-inch position on the horizontal ruler.
   d. Click the Button button in the Controls group on the FORM DESIGN TOOLS DESIGN tab and drag to create a button the approximate height and width shown in the *Form Header* section.

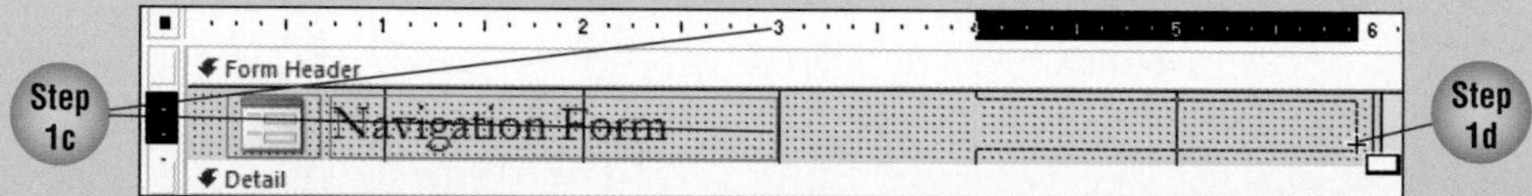

   e. At the first Command Button Wizard dialog box, select *Miscellaneous* in the *Categories* list box and *Run Macro* in the *Actions* list box and then click Next.
   f. With *ExitRSRdb* already selected in the *Macros* list box at the second Command Button Wizard dialog box, click Next.
   g. At the third Command Button Wizard dialog box, click *Text*, select the current entry in the *Text* text box, type **Exit RSR Computer Services database**, and then click Next.
   h. Type **Exitdb** at the last Command Button Wizard dialog box and then click Finish.

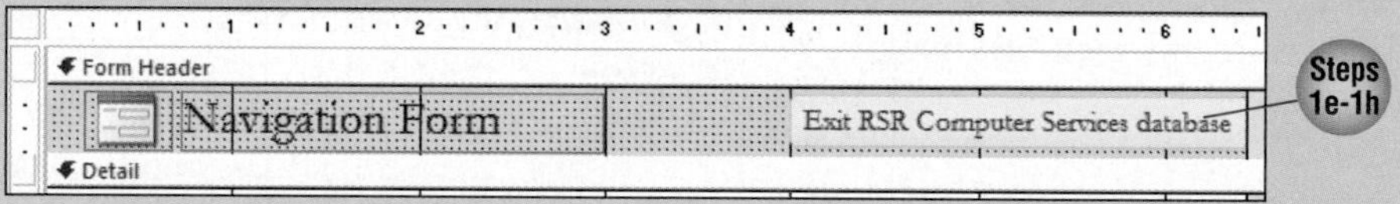

2. Click to select the logo container object at the left of the title in the *Form Header* section and then press Delete.
3. Edit the text in the Title control object in the *Form Header* section to *RSR Computer Services*.
4. Relabel the tabs along the top of the Navigation form by completing the following steps:
   a. Click to select the *CustMaintenance* tab and then click the Property Sheet button in the Tools group on the FORM DESIGN TOOLS DESIGN tab.
   b. Click the Format tab in the Property Sheet task pane, select the current text in the *Caption* property box, and then type **Customers**.
   c. Click the *TechMaintenance* tab, select the current text in the *Caption* property box in the Property Sheet task pane, and then type **Technicians**.
   d. Click the *WorkOrders* tab, click in the *Caption* property box, and then insert a space between *Work* and *Orders* so that the tab name displays as *Work Orders*.
   e. Click the *WorkOrdersbyMonth* tab, select the current text in the *Caption* property box, and then type **Monthly Work Orders**.
   f. Close the Property Sheet task pane.

5. Select the four named tabs plus the [Add New] tab and then make the following formatting changes:
   a. Change the shape to *Snip Single Corner Rectangle.*
   b. Apply the Intense Effect - Blue-Gray, Accent 3 quick style.
6. Select the Exit RSR Computer Services database button and apply the Intense Effect - Blue-Gray, Accent 3 quick style.

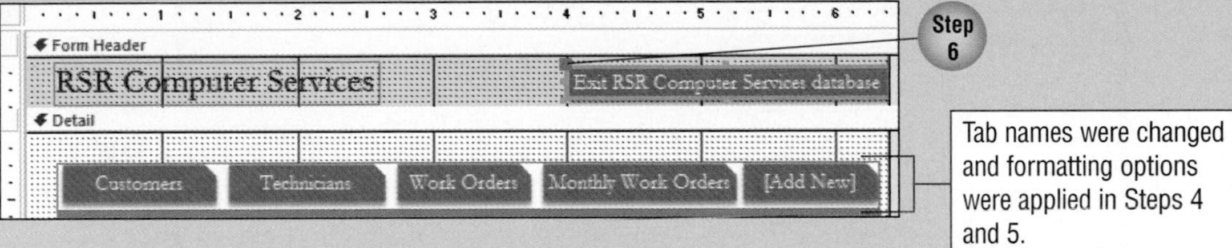

7. Save the revised form and then switch to Form view.
8. Compare your form with the one shown in Figure 7.5 on page 284.

Project 3 Configure Database Options — 6 Parts

You will configure database options for the active database and configure error-checking options for all databases. You will also customize the ribbon.

Customizing the Access Environment

Click the FILE tab and then click *Options* to open the Access Options dialog box, which you can use to customize the Access environment. You can specify options for all databases or just the current database. You can also define behavior for certain keys and set the default margins for printing. You can set a form to display automatically whenever the database file is opened. You can also choose to show or hide the Navigation pane in the current database. For example, if you have created a Navigation form that you want to use to provide limited access to only a certain group of objects, you can hide the Navigation pane. A database can be set to open by default in shared use or exclusive use. *Exclusive use* means the file is restricted to one individual user.

Figure 7.6 on the next page displays the Access Options dialog box with *Current Database* selected in the left pane. With options for the current database displayed, you can define a startup form to open automatically when the database is opened. In Project 3a, you will configure the current database to display the MainMenu form when the database is opened. You will also specify an application title to display in the Title bar when the database is open. In Project 3b, you will customize the Navigation pane.

Quick Steps

Set a Startup Form
1. Click FILE tab.
2. Click *Options.*
3. Click *Current Database* in left pane.
4. Click down-pointing arrow next to *Display Form.*
5. Click desired form.
6. Click OK.

Specify an Application Title
1. Click FILE tab.
2. Click *Options.*
3. Click *Current Database* in left pane.
4. Click in *Application Title* text box.
5. Type desired title.
6. Click OK.

Figure 7.6 Access Options Dialog Box with Current Database Pane Selected

Customize the active database using options in this section.
Removing this check mark hides the Navigation pane in the current database.
Click this button to open the Navigation Options dialog box, in which you can customize the Navigation pane.

Project 3a Specifying a Startup Form and Application Title **Part 1 of 6**

1. With **AL2-C7-RSRCompServ.accdb** open, specify an application title to display in the Title bar and choose a form to display automatically when the database file is opened by completing the following steps:
   a. Click the FILE tab.
   b. Click *Options* to open the Access Options dialog box.
   c. Click *Current Database* in the left pane.
   d. Click in the *Application Title* text box in the Application Options section and then type **RSR Computer Services Database**.
   e. Click the down-pointing arrow next to the *Display Form* option box (which currently displays *[none]*) and then click *MainMenu* at the drop-down list.
2. Click OK.
3. Click OK at the Microsoft Access message box indicating that you must close and reopen the database for the options to take effect.

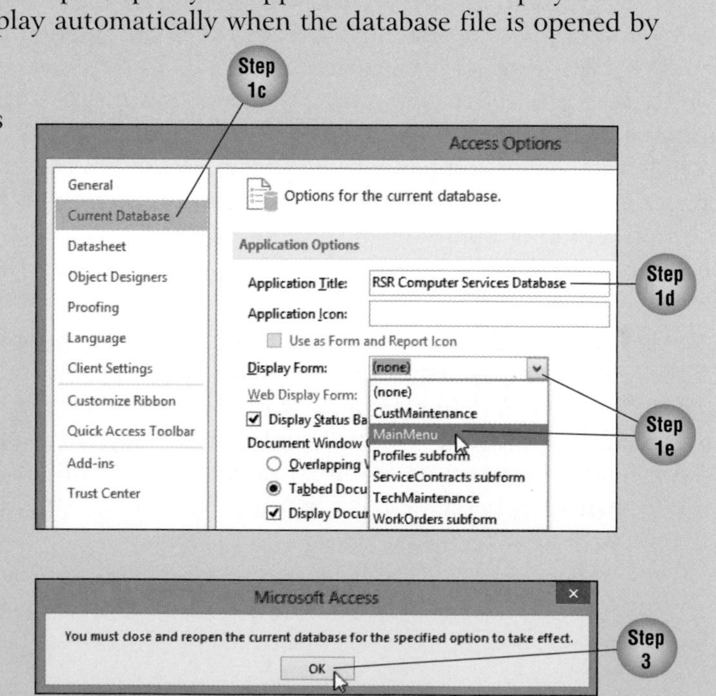

4. Close **AL2-C7-RSRCompServ.accdb**.
5. Reopen **AL2-C7-RSRCompServ.accdb**. The MainMenu form displays automatically in the work area and the Title bar displays the application title *RSR Computer Services Database*.

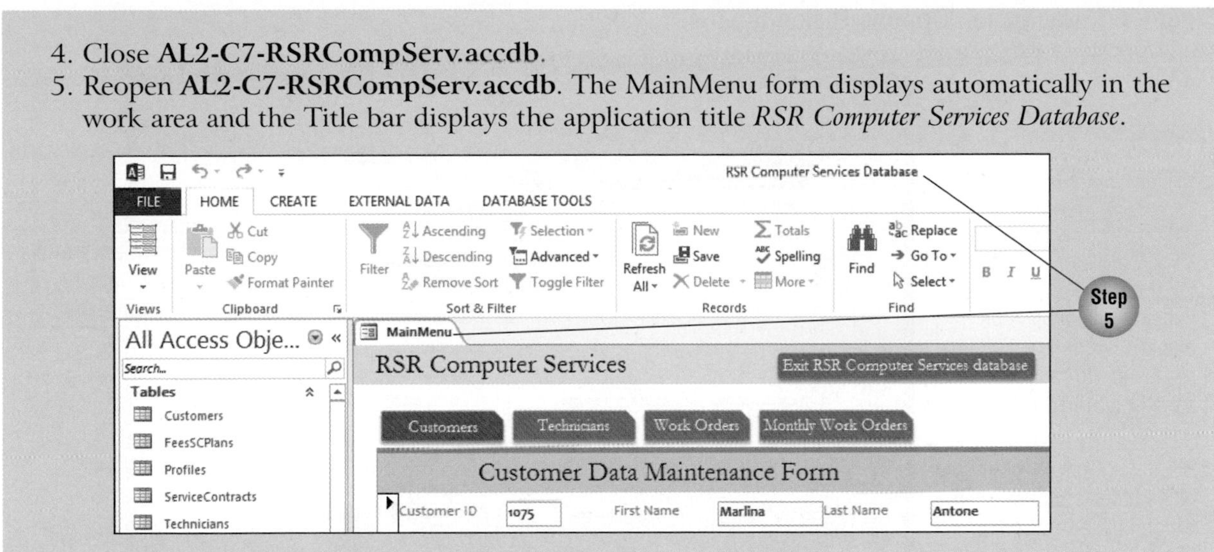

Limiting Ribbon Tabs and Menus in a Database

In addition to securing a database by displaying a startup form that provides limited access to objects, you may also want to limit access to options in the ribbon and menus. Preventing an end user from seeing the full ribbon and shortcut menus allows you to avoid accidental changes that could occur if someone switches views and edits or deletes objects without knowing the full impact of these changes.

To limit others' access, display the Access Options dialog box and select *Current Database* in the left pane. Scroll down the dialog box to the *Ribbon and Toolbar Options* section. Click to remove the check marks from the *Allow Full Menus* and *Allow Default Shortcut Menus* check boxes and then click OK. When the database is closed and reopened, only the HOME tab will be available in the ribbon. The FILE tab backstage area will only display print options. You will not be able to switch views and right-clicking will not show a shortcut menu.

If you need to work within the database and have access to the full ribbon and menus, you can bypass the startup options by holding down the Shift key while double-clicking the file name to open the database.

Quick Steps

Customize the Navigation Pane
1. Click FILE tab.
2. Click *Options*.
3. Click *Current Database* in left pane.
4. Click Navigation Options button.
5. Select desired options.
6. Click OK.
7. Click OK.

Hide the Navigation Pane
1. Click FILE tab.
2. Click *Options*.
3. Click *Current Database* in left pane.
4. Clear *Display Navigation Pane* check box.
5. Click OK.
6. Click OK.

Customizing the Navigation Pane

When a startup form is used in a database, you may want to hide the Navigation pane to prevent users from accidentally making changes to other objects. To hide the Navigation pane, open the Access Options dialog box, click *Current Database* in the left pane, and then click to remove the check mark from the *Display Navigation Pane* check box in the *Navigation* section.

Click the Navigation Options button in the *Navigation* section to open the Navigation Options dialog box, shown in Figure 7.7 on the next page. At this dialog box, you can choose to hide individual objects or groups of objects, set display options for the pane, and define whether objects can be opened using a single or double mouse click. For example, to prevent changes from being made to the table design, you can hide the Tables group.

Press F11 to display a hidden Navigation pane.

Figure 7.7 Navigation Options Dialog Box

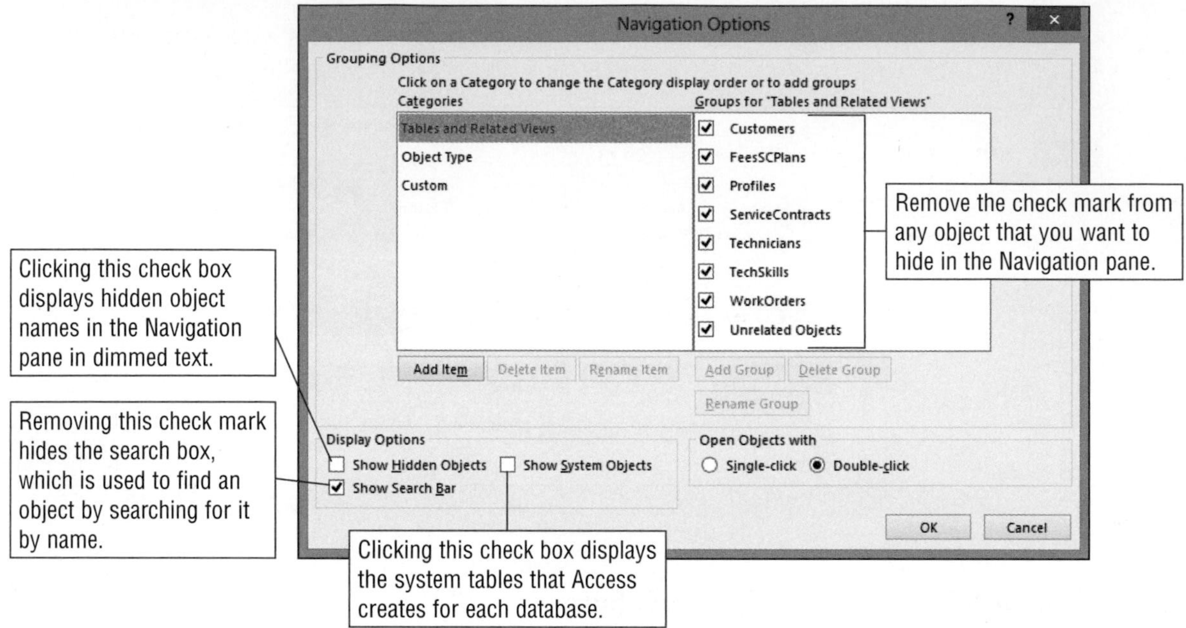

Project 3b Customizing the Navigation Pane

Part 2 of 6

1. With **AL2-C7-RSRCompServ.accdb** open, customize the Navigation pane to hide all of the table, macro, and module objects by completing the following steps:
   a. Click the FILE tab and then click *Options*.
   b. If necessary, click *Current Database* in the left pane. Click the Navigation Options button in the *Navigation* section. (You may need to scroll down to view the *Navigation* section.)
   c. Click *Object Type* in the *Categories* list box.
   d. Click the *Tables* check box in the *Groups for "Object Type"* list box to remove the check mark.
   e. Remove the check mark from the *Macros* check box.
   f. Remove the check mark from the *Modules* check box.
   g. Click OK to close the Navigation Options dialog box.

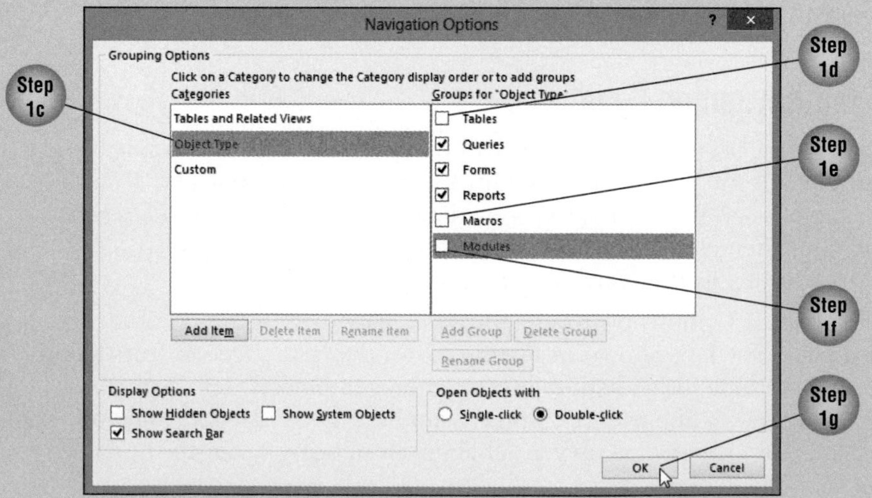

h. Click OK to close the Access Options dialog box.
i. Click OK at the message box that says you must close and reopen the current database for the specified option to take effect.

2. Notice that the Tables, Macros, and Modules groups are hidden in the Navigation pane.

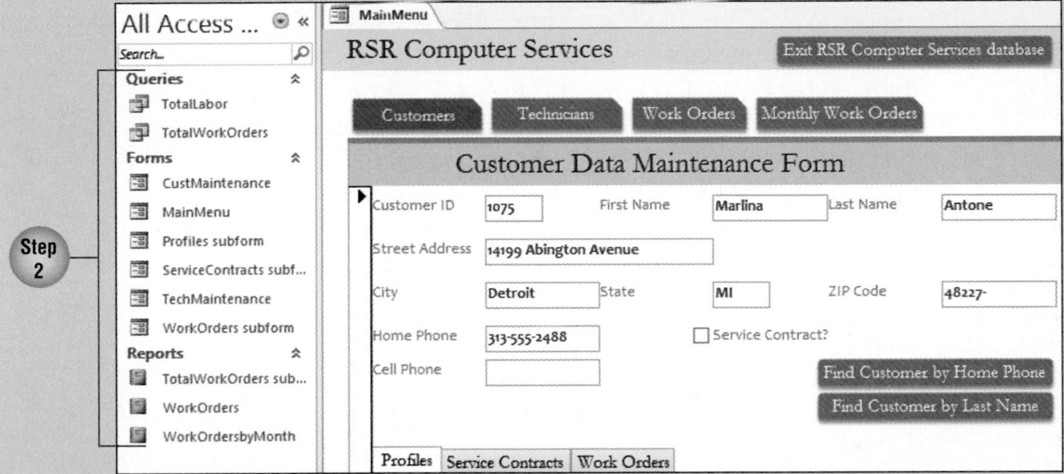

3. After reviewing the customized Navigation pane, you decide that the database will be more secure if the pane is hidden when the database is opened. To do this, complete the following steps:
   a. Click the FILE tab and then click *Options*.
   b. With *Current Database* already selected in the left pane, click the *Display Navigation Pane* check box in the *Navigation* section to remove the check mark.
   c. Click OK.
   d. Click OK at the message box indicating that you must close and reopen the database for the option to take effect.

Step 3b

Navigation

Display Navigation Pane

Navigation Options...

4. Close **AL2-C7-RSRCompServ.accdb**.
5. Reopen **AL2-C7-RSRCompServ.accdb**. The Navigation pane is hidden and the MainMenu form is open in the work area.

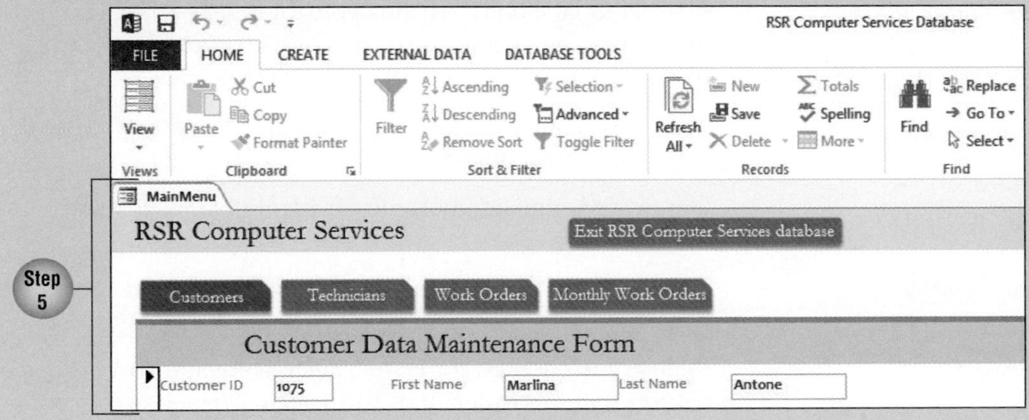

Configuring Error-Checking Options

Quick Steps

Customize Error-Checking Options

1. Click FILE tab.
2. Click *Options.*
3. Click *Object Designers* in left pane.
4. Scroll down to *Error checking in form and report design view* section.
5. Click to remove check marks as desired.
6. Click OK.

Recall from Chapter 5 that a green diagonal triangle displayed in the Report Selector button when the report width was wider than the page would allow. Clicking the error-checking options button allowed you to access tools to fix the report automatically. A green triangle also appeared in a new label that you added to a report to describe another control. Access flagged the label as an error because the label control object was not associated with another object.

By default, Access has error checking turned on and all error-checking options active. To configure error-checking options in Access, open the Access Options dialog box and select *Object Designers* in the left pane. Scroll down the right pane to locate the *Error checking in form and report design view* section, shown in Figure 7.8. Remove the check marks in the check boxes for those options you want to disable and then click OK. Table 7.1 provides a description of each option.

Figure 7.8 Error-Checking Options in Access

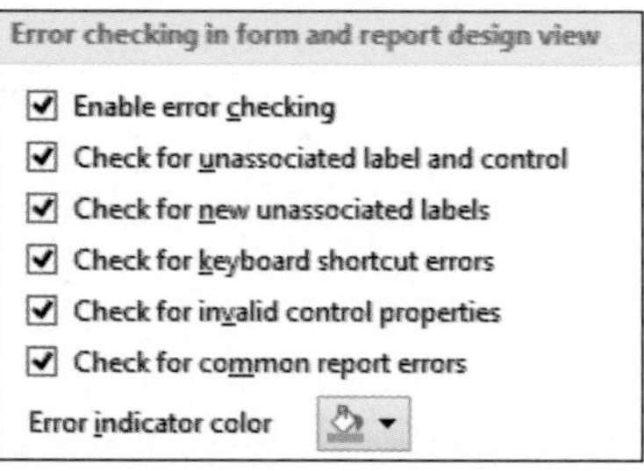

Table 7.1 Error-Checking Options

Error-Checking Option	*Description*
Enable error checking	Error checking can be turned on or off in forms and reports. An error is indicated by a green triangle in the upper left corner of a control.
Check for unassociated label and control	A selected label and text box control object are checked to make sure the two objects are associated. A Trace Error button appears if Access detects an error.
Check for new unassociated labels	New label control objects are checked for association with a text box control object.
Check for keyboard shortcut errors	Duplicate keyboard shortcuts or invalid shortcuts are flagged.
Check for invalid control properties	Invalid properties, formula expressions, and field names are flagged.
Check for common report errors	Reports are checked for errors, such as invalid sort orders and reports that are wider than the selected paper size.
Error indicator color	A green triangle indicates an error in a control. Click the Color Picker button to change to a different color.

Project 3c Customizing Error-Checking Options — Part 3 of 6

1. With **AL2-C7-RSRCompServ.accdb** open, assume that you frequently add label control objects to forms and reports in which you include explanatory text for users. You decide to customize the error-checking options to prevent Access from flagging these independent label controls as errors. To do this, complete the following steps:
   a. Click the FILE tab and then click *Options*.
   b. Click *Object Designers* in the left pane.
   c. Scroll down the right pane to the *Error checking in form and report design view* section.
   d. Click the *Check for new unassociated labels* check box to remove the check mark.
   e. Click OK.
   f. Click OK.

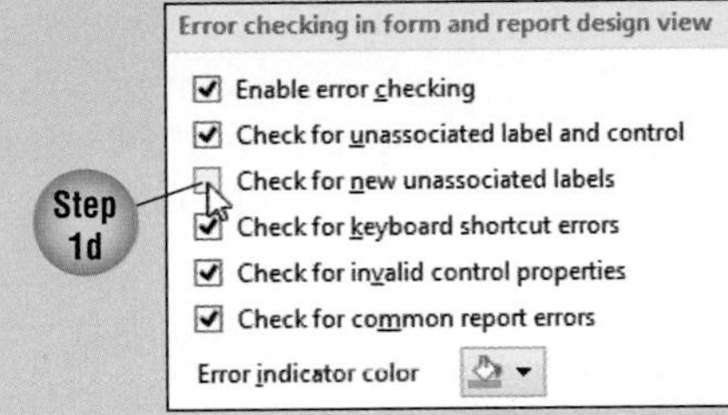

Customizing the Ribbon

You can customize the ribbon by creating a new tab. Within the new tab, you can add groups and then add buttons within the groups. To customize the ribbon, click the FILE tab and then click *Options*. At the Access Options dialog box, click *Customize Ribbon* in the left pane. Options for customizing the ribbon are shown in Figure 7.9.

To save mouse clicks, consider creating a custom tab that includes the buttons you use on a regular basis.

Figure 7.9 Access Options Dialog Box with *Customize Ribbon* Selected

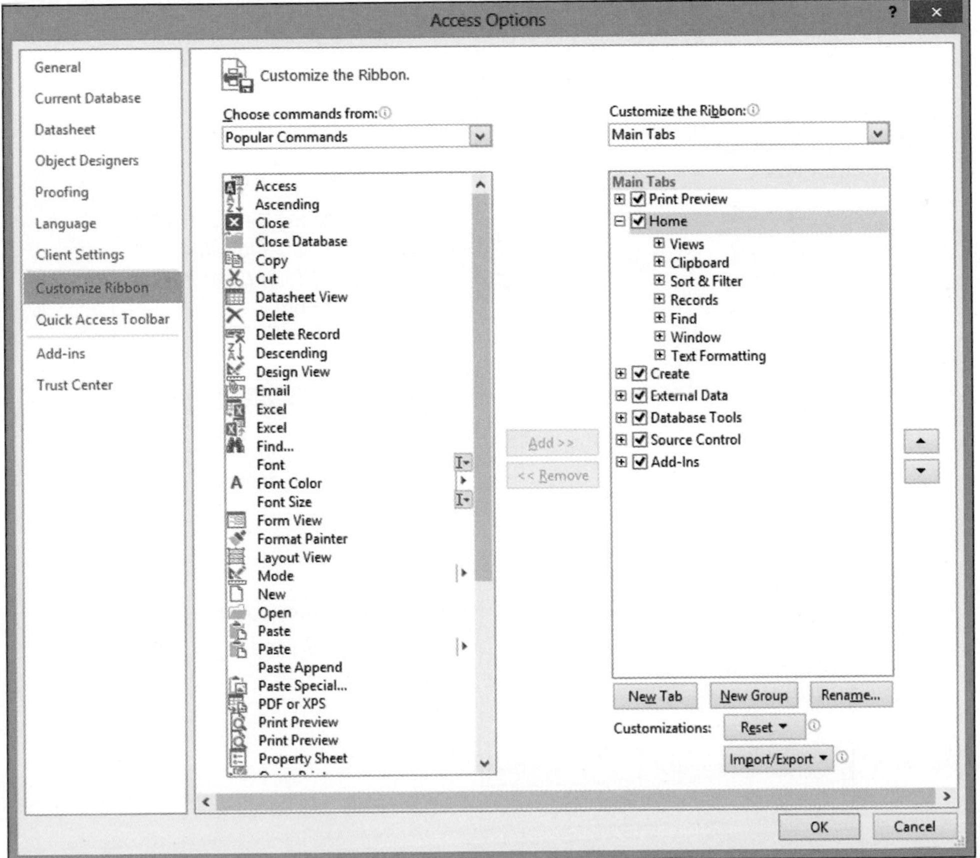

The commands shown in the left list box in Figure 7.9 are dependent on the current option selected in the *Choose commands from* option box above it. Click the down-pointing arrow at the right of the current option (*Popular Commands*) to select from a variety of command lists, such as *Commands Not in the Ribbon* and *All Commands*. The tabs shown in the right list box are dependent on the current option selected in the *Customize the Ribbon* option box. Click the down-pointing arrow at the right of the current option (*Main Tabs*) to select *All Tabs*, *Main Tabs*, or *Tool Tabs*.

You can create a new group in an existing tab and add buttons within the new group. You can also create a new tab, create a new group within the tab, and then add buttons to the new group.

Creating a New Tab

Quick Steps

Create a New Tab and Group

1. Click FILE tab.
2. Click *Options*.
3. Click *Customize Ribbon* in left pane.
4. Click tab name to precede new tab.
5. Click New Tab button.

Add a New Group to an Existing Tab

1. Click FILE tab.
2. Click *Options*.
3. Click *Customize Ribbon* in left pane.
4. Click tab name with which new group is associated.
5. Click New Group button.

To create a new tab, click the tab name in the *Main Tabs* list box that you want the new tab to follow and then click the New Tab button located below the *Main Tabs* list box. Doing this inserts a new tab in the list box, along with a new group below the new tab, as shown in Figure 7.10. If you selected the wrong tab name before clicking the New Tab button, you can move the new tab up or down the list box. To do this, click *New Tab (Custom)* and then click the Move Up or Move Down buttons that display at the right side of the dialog box.

Figure 7.10 New Tab and Group Created in the Customize Ribbon Pane at the Access Options Dialog Box

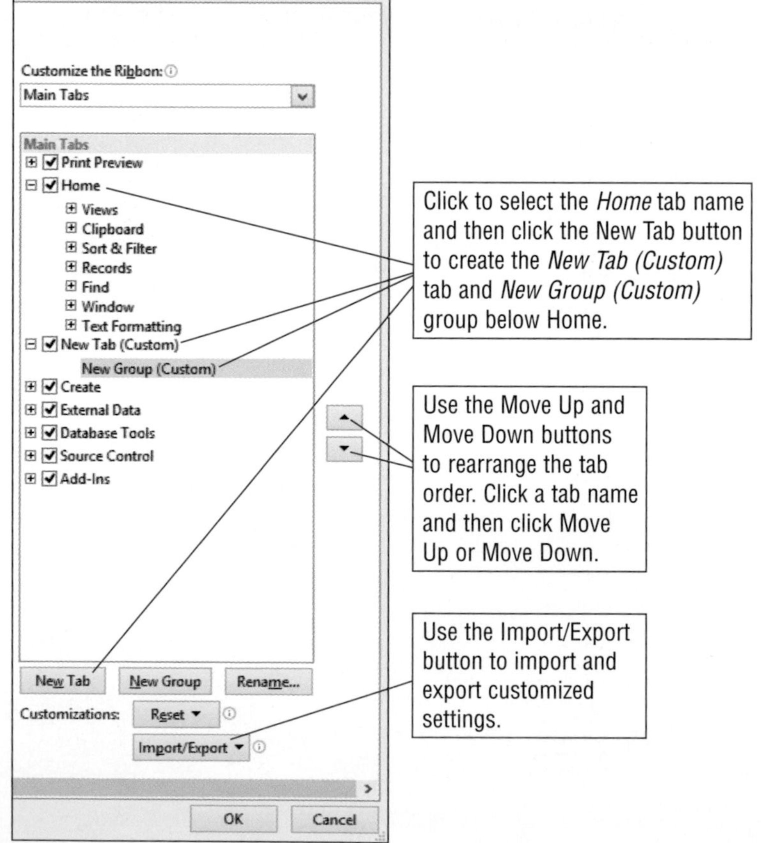
Customize the Ribbon:
Main Tabs
Main Tabs
Print Preview
Home
Views
Clipboard
Sort & Filter
Records
Find
Window
Text Formatting
New Tab (Custom)
New Group (Custom)
Create
External Data
Database Tools
Source Control
Add-Ins
New Tab
New Group
Rename...
Customizations:
Reset
Import/Export
OK
Cancel
Click to select the Home tab name and then click the New Tab button to create the New Tab (Custom) tab and New Group (Custom) group below Home.
Use the Move Up and Move Down buttons to rearrange the tab order. Click a tab name and then click Move Up or Move Down.
Use the Import/Export button to import and export customized settings.

Renaming a Tab or Group

Rename a tab by clicking the tab name in the *Main Tabs* list box and then clicking the Rename button located below the *Main Tabs* list box. At the Rename dialog box, type the desired name for the tab and then press Enter or click OK. You can also display the Rename dialog box by right-clicking the tab name and then clicking *Rename* at the shortcut menu.

Complete similar steps to rename a group. The Rename dialog box for a group name or command name contains a *Symbol* list box as well as a *Display name* text box, but the symbols are more useful for identifying new buttons than they are for new groups. Type the new name for the group in the *Display name* text box and then press Enter or click OK.

Quick Steps

Rename a Tab or Group
1. Click FILE tab.
2. Click *Options.*
3. Click *Customize Ribbon* in left pane.
4. Click tab or group to be renamed.
5. Click Rename button.
6. Type new name.
7. Press Enter.

Add Buttons to a Group
1. Click FILE tab.
2. Click *Options.*
3. Click *Customize Ribbon* in left pane.
4. Click group name in which to insert new button.
5. Change *Choose commands from* to desired command list.
6. Scroll down and click desired command.
7. Click Add button.

Adding Buttons to a Tab Group

Add commands to a tab by clicking the group name within the tab, clicking the desired command in the list box at the left, and then clicking the Add button that displays between the two list boxes. Remove commands in a similar manner, but click the Remove button instead.

Exporting Customizations

You or your instructor may already have taken the time to customize the ribbon in Access. To be able to restore your customizations after you make changes to the ribbon in Project 3e, you will save (export) your settings in Project 3d. In Project 3f, you will reinstall (import) your customizations.

To save your current ribbon settings, click the FILE tab and then click *Options*. At the Access Options dialog box, click *Customize Ribbon* in the left pane. Click the Import/Export button in the lower right hand corner of the Access Options dialog box. Click *Export all customizations* to save the file with the custom settings. You can then use this file to reinstall the saved settings or to install the customized settings on a different computer. To import the saved settings, click the Import/Export button and then click *Import customization file*. Locate the file and reinstall the customized settings.

Project 3d Exporting Customizations — Part 4 of 6

1. With **AL2-C7-RSRCompServ.accdb** open, save the current ribbon settings to the desktop by completing the following steps:
   a. Click the FILE tab and then click *Options*.
   b. Click *Customize Ribbon* in the left pane of the Access Options dialog box.
   c. Click the Import/Export button located in the bottom right of the Access Options dialog box.
   d. Click *Export all customizations* at the drop-down list.
   e. Click *Desktop* in the *Favorites* list at the left side of the File Save dialog box.
   f. Change the file name to **AL2-C7-P3-AccessCustomizations.exportedUI** and then click the Save button.
   g. Click OK twice.

Project 3e Customizing the Ribbon Part 5 of 6

1. With **AL2-C7-RSRCompServ.accdb** open, customize the ribbon by adding a new tab and two new groups on the tab by completing the following steps:
   a. Click the FILE tab and then click *Options*.
   b. Click *Customize Ribbon* in the left pane of the Access Options dialog box.
   c. Click *Home* in the *Main Tabs* list box.
   d. Click the New Tab button located below the list box. (This inserts a new tab below *Home* and a new group below the new tab.)
   e. With *New Group (Custom)* selected below *New Tab (Custom)*, click the New Group button that displays below the list box. (This inserts another new group below the new tab.)

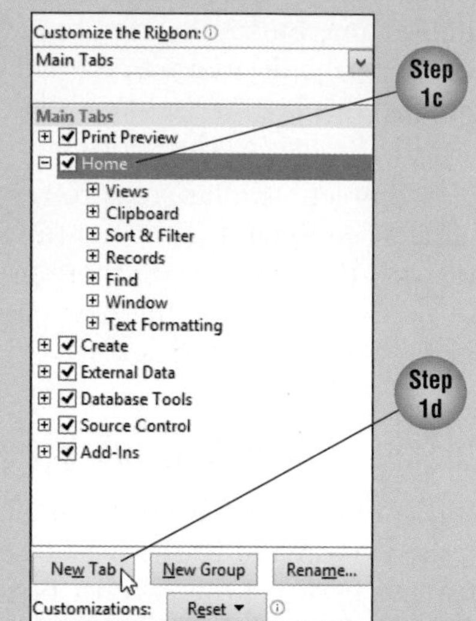

2. Rename the tab and groups by completing the following steps:
   a. Click to select *New Tab (Custom)* in the *Main Tabs* list box.
   b. Click the Rename button that displays below the list box.
   c. At the Rename dialog box, type your first and last names in all caps and then press Enter or click OK.
   d. Click to select the first *New Group (Custom)* group name that displays below the new tab.
   e. Click the Rename button.
   f. At the Rename dialog box, type **Views** in the *Display name* text box and then press Enter or click OK. The Rename dialog box for a group or button displays symbols in addition to the *Display name* text box. You will apply a symbol to a button in a later step.
   g. Right-click the *New Group (Custom)* group name below *Views (Custom)* and then click *Rename* at the shortcut menu.
   h. Type **Records** in the *Display name* text box at the Rename dialog box and then press Enter or click OK.

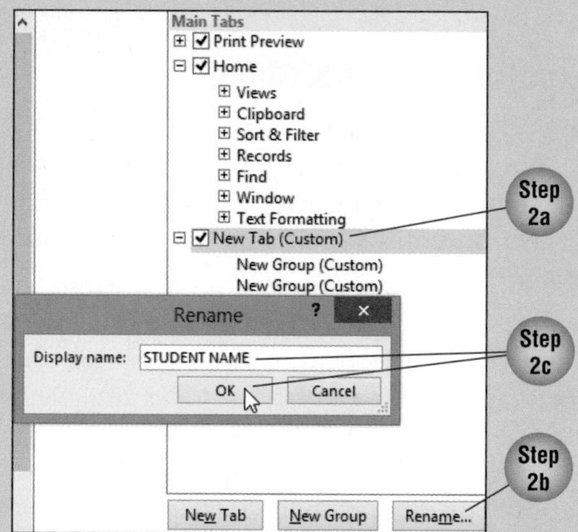

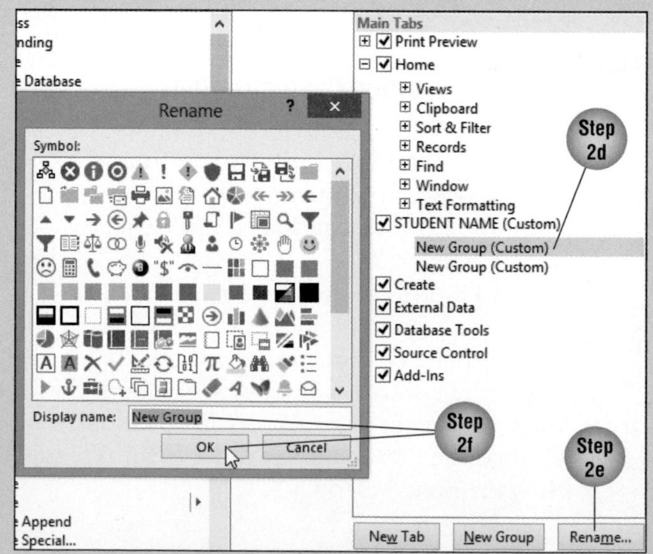

3. Add buttons to the Views (Custom) group by completing the following steps:
   a. Click to select *Views (Custom)* in the *Main Tabs* list box.
   b. With *Popular Commands* selected in the *Choose commands from* option box, click *Form View* in the list box and then click the Add button between the two list boxes. This inserts the command below the *Views (Custom)* group name.
   c. Scroll down the *Popular Commands* list box and double-click the second *Print Preview* option, which displays the ScreenTip *Popular Commands | Print Preview (FilePrintPreview)*. ***Note: The commands are organized in alphabetical order.***
   d. Click *Report View* in the *Popular Commands* list box and then click the Add button.
   e. Scroll to the bottom of the *Popular Commands* list box, click *View*, and then click the Add button.

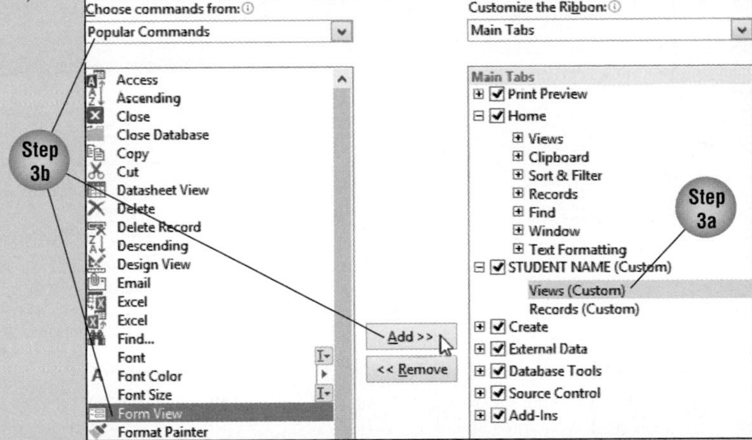

4. Add buttons to the Records (Custom) group by completing the following steps:
   a. Click to select *Records (Custom)* in the *Main Tabs* list box.
   b. Click the down-pointing arrow at the right of the *Choose commands from* option box (which currently displays *Popular Commands*) and then click *All Commands* at the drop-down list.
   c. Scroll down the *All Commands* list box, click *Ascending*, and then click the Add button.
   d. Scroll down the *All Commands* list box (the list displays alphabetically), click *Delete Record*, and then click the Add button.
   e. Scroll down the *All Commands* list box, click *Find*, and then click the Add button.
   f. Scroll down the *All Commands* list box, click *New* (displays the ScreenTip *Home Tab | Records | New (GoToNewRecord)*), and then click the Add button.
   g. Scroll down the *All Commands* list box, click *Spelling*, and then click the Add button.

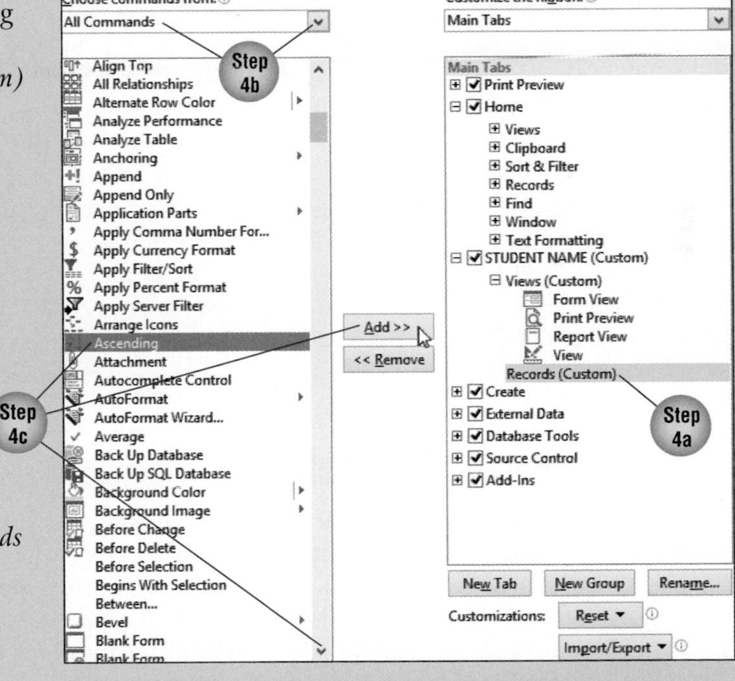

5. Change the symbol for the Spelling button by completing the following steps:
   a. Right-click *Spelling* below *Records (Custom)* in the *Main Tabs* list box.
   b. Click *Rename* at the shortcut menu.
   c. At the Rename dialog box, click the purple book icon in the *Symbol* list box (fourth icon in the seventh row) and then click OK.

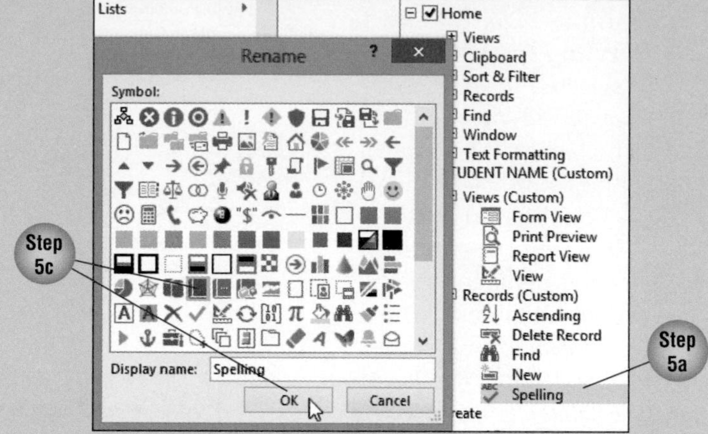

6. Click OK to close the Access Options dialog box.
7. Click OK at the message saying that you must close and reopen the database for the option to take effect.
8. Use buttons in the custom tab to change views and start a spelling check in a form by completing the following steps:
   a. Click the Technicians tab at the top of the MainMenu form.
   b. Click the custom tab with your name and then click the Print Preview button in the Views group.
   c. Click the Form View button in the Views group to switch back to the form.
   d. Click in the *Last Name* field and then click the Spelling button.
   e. Click the Cancel button at the Spelling dialog box.
   f. Click the Customers tab at the top of the MainMenu form.
9. Insert a screenshot of the database window showing the custom tab in a new Microsoft Word document using either the Screenshot button in the Illustrations group on the INSERT tab or the Print Screen key and the Paste feature. Type your name a few lines below the screen image and add any other identifying information as instructed (for example, the chapter number and project number).
10. Save the Microsoft Word document and name it **AL2-C7-P3-CustomRibbon**.
11. Print **AL2-C7-P3-CustomRibbon.docx** and then exit Word.

Resetting the Ribbon

Restore the original ribbon by clicking the Reset button that displays below the *Main Tabs* list box in the Access Options dialog box with *Customize Ribbon* selected in the left pane. Clicking the Reset button displays the following options: *Reset only selected Ribbon tab* and *Reset all customizations*. Click *Reset all customizations* to restore the ribbon to its original settings and then click Yes at the Microsoft Office message box that displays the message *Delete all Ribbon and Quick Access Toolbar customizations for this program?*

To restore your ribbon(s) with your institution's customized settings, you will need to import the settings you exported in Project 3d. Click the Import/Export button in the lower right corner of the Access Options dialog box and then click *Import customization file* at the drop-down list. Locate the file and reinstall the customized settings.

Project 3f Restoring the Ribbon

Part 6 of 6

1. Import the customization file saved in Project 3d to reset the ribbon to your institution's original settings by completing the following steps:
   a. Click the FILE tab and then click *Options* to open the Access Options dialog box.
   b. If necessary, click *Customize Ribbon* in the left pane.
   c. Click the Import/Export button in the bottom right corner of the dialog box.
   d. Click *Import customization file* at the drop-down list.
   e. Click *Desktop* in the *Favorites* list at the left of the File Open dialog box.
   f. Click **AL2-C7-P3-AccessCustomizations.exportedUI**.
   g. Click Open.
   h. Click Yes at the Microsoft Office message box that appears.
   i. Click OK to close the Access Options dialog box.
   j. Click OK at the message that displays saying that you must close and reopen the database for the option to take effect.
2. If **AL2-C7-RSRCompServ.accdb** is open, close it.

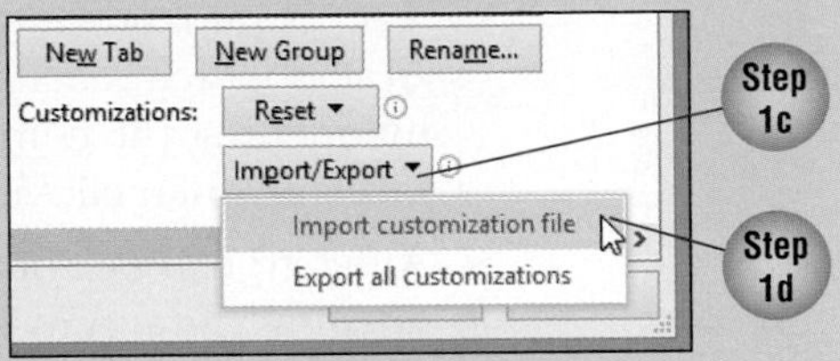

New Tab | New Group | Rename...
Customizations: Reset ▾
Import/Export ▾
Import customization file
Export all customizations
Step 1c
Step 1d

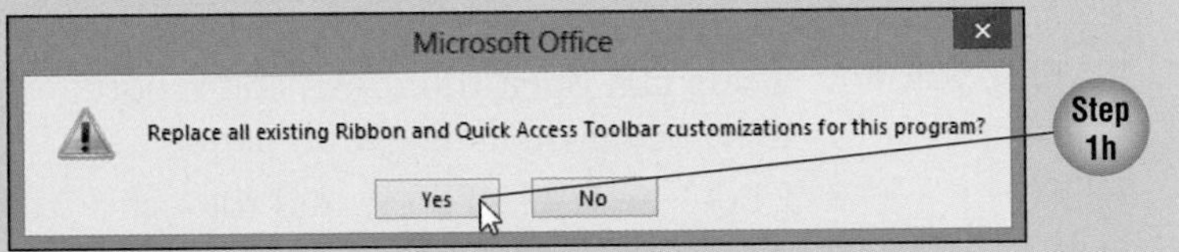

Microsoft Office
Replace all existing Ribbon and Quick Access Toolbar customizations for this program?
Yes | No
Step 1h

In this chapter, you have learned techniques to automate and customize an Access database. As you gain more experience with Access, explore further customizations that allow you to change the behaviors of actions and keys while editing. Also consider experimenting with other macro actions, such as using the OpenQuery action to automate queries.

Chapter Summary

- A macro is used to automate actions within a database, such as opening a form or report.
- Click the CREATE tab and then click the Macro button in the Macros & Code group to open a Macro Builder window, in which you create the actions you want to store.
- Add a macro action using the *Add New Action* option box or Action Catalog task pane.
- Action arguments are parameters for the action, such as the object name, mode in which the object opens, and other restrictions placed on the action.
- The available arguments displayed in the *Action Arguments* section are dependent on the active action.
- Most macros can be run by clicking the Run button in the Macro Builder window or by double-clicking the macro name in the Navigation pane.
- A macro can also be created by dragging and dropping an object name from the Navigation pane to the *Add New Action* option box in the Macro Builder window.

- Edit a macro by right-clicking the macro name and clicking *Design View* at the shortcut menu.
- A macro can be assigned to a button in a form to allow running the macro with a single click.
- Use the Button tool to create a command button in a form.
- The Command Button Wizard creates an embedded macro for you that tells Access which macro to run when the button is clicked. You can view the macro by opening the command button's Property Sheet task pane, clicking the Event tab, and then clicking the Build button in the *On Click* property box.
- A macro can be converted to Visual Basic for Applications (VBA) code by opening the macro in the Macro Builder window and then clicking the Convert Macros to Visual Basic button in the Tools group on the MACRO TOOLS DESIGN tab.
- A Navigation form with tabs along the top, left, or right is used as a menu. Users can open the forms and reports in the database by clicking a tab, rather than using the Navigation pane.
- Click the CREATE tab and then click the Navigation button to create a Navigation form. Choose the desired form style at the drop-down list and then drag and drop form and/or report names from the Navigation pane to *[Add New]* in the tab bar.
- A form can be set to display automatically whenever the database is opened at the *Display Form* option box in the Access Options dialog box with *Current Database* selected in the left pane.
- Change the title that appears in the Title bar for the active database by typing an entry in the *Application Title* text box at the Access Options dialog box with *Current Database* selected in the left pane.
- You can set options for the Navigation pane, such as hiding individual objects and groups of objects, at the Navigation Options dialog box.
- Hide the Navigation pane by clearing the *Display Navigation Pane* check box at the Access Options dialog box with *Current Database* selected in the left pane.
- Change default error-checking options in the Access Options dialog box with *Object Designers* selected in the left pane.
- You can customize the ribbon by creating a new tab, creating a new group within the new tab, and then adding buttons within the new group.
- To customize the ribbon, open the Access Options dialog box and click *Customize Ribbon* in the left pane.
- Create a new ribbon tab by clicking the tab name that will precede the new tab and then clicking the New Tab button. A new group is automatically added with the new tab.
- Rename a custom tab by clicking to select the tab name, clicking the Rename button, typing a new name, and then pressing Enter or clicking OK. Rename a group using a similar process.
- Add buttons within a group by clicking the group name, selecting the desired command in the commands list box, and then clicking the Add button located between the two list boxes.
- Restore the ribbon to the default by clicking the Reset button located near the bottom right of the Access Options dialog box with *Customize Ribbon* selected and then clicking *Reset all customizations* at the drop-down list.

Commands Review

FEATURE	RIBBON TAB, GROUP	BUTTON
convert macros to Visual Basic for Applications	MACRO TOOLS DESIGN, Tools	
create command button	FORM DESIGN TOOLS DESIGN, Controls	
create macro	CREATE, Macros & Code	
create Navigation form	CREATE, Forms	
customize Navigation pane	FILE, Options	
run macro	MACRO TOOLS DESIGN, Tools	!

Concepts Check Test Your Knowledge

Completion: In the space provided at the right, indicate the correct term, command, or number.

1. This is the name of the window in which you create actions with associated action arguments for a macro. ____________________
2. Add a macro action at the *Add New Action* option box or in this pane. ____________________
3. To make Access display the Find dialog box in a macro, choose this action in the *Add New Action* option box. ____________________
4. Drag a form name from the Navigation pane to the *Add New Action* option box to insert this macro action. ____________________
5. Edit a macro by right-clicking the macro name in the Navigation pane and selecting this option at the shortcut menu. ____________________
6. At the first Command Button Wizard dialog box, click this option in the *Categories* list box to locate the *Run Macro* action. ____________________
7. This type of macro is not shown as a macro object within the Navigation pane. ____________________
8. When a macro has been converted to Visual Basic for Applications (VBA), Access opens this window. ____________________
9. This type of form is used to create a menu to allow end users to select forms and reports by clicking tabs. ____________________

10. Open this dialog box to specify a display form to open whenever the database is opened. ________________

11. Hide the Tables group in the Navigation pane by opening this dialog box. ________________

12. Click this option in the left pane at the Access Options dialog box to change an error-checking option. ________________

13. Click this option in the left pane at the Access Options dialog box to create a custom ribbon tab. ________________

14. Click this button in the *Customize Ribbon* section in the Access Options dialog box to save the current ribbon settings. ________________

Skills Check Assess Your Performance

Assessment 1

CREATE AND RUN MACROS

1. Open **AL2-C7-ViewIt.accdb** and enable the content.
2. Create the following macros. Run each macro to make sure it works properly and then close it.
   a. Create a macro named RPTWebOrders that opens the report named WebOrdersByProd—use the macro action *OpenReport*. In the *Action Arguments* section, change *Report* in the View Option argument option box to *Print Preview*.
   b. Create a macro named RPTWebSales to open the WebSalesByDate report in Report view.
   c. Create a macro named FORMCustOrd that opens the WebCustOrders form in Form view, activates the control named *LastName*, and then opens the Find dialog box. Test the macro using the customer last name *Gallagher*.
3. Open the RPTWebOrders macro in Design view. Click the FILE tab, click the *Print* option, and then click *Print* at the Print backstage area. At the Print Macro Definition dialog box, remove check marks as necessary until only the *Actions and Arguments* check box is checked and then click OK. Close the Macro Builder window.
4. Print the FORMCustOrd macro and RPTWebSales macro by completing a step similar to Step 3.

Assessment 2

EDIT A MACRO AND ASSIGN MACROS TO COMMAND BUTTONS

1. With **AL2-C7-ViewIt.accdb** open, edit the FORMCustOrd macro to remove the *OpenForm* action. Save and close the revised macro. Rename the FORMCustOrd macro in the Navigation pane as *FINDLastName*.

2. Create command buttons to run macros as follows:
   a. Open the WebCustOrders form in Design view and then create a command button at the right side of the title in the *Form Header* section that runs the FINDLastName macro. You determine the appropriate text to display on the face of the button and a name for the command button. Format the button using the *Light 1 Outline, Colored Fill-Green, Accent 6* quick style. Save and close the form.
   b. Open the WebProducts form in Design view and create two command buttons as follows:
      - A button at the left side of the form that runs the RPTWebOrders macro
      - A button at the right side of the form that runs the RPTWebSales macro

      Place each button at the bottom of the *Detail* section. You determine the appropriate text to display on the face of each button as well as a name for each button. Format each button with the quick style used in Step 2a. Save and then close the form.
3. Open each form, test the button(s) to make sure the correct form or report displays, and then close each form or report.
4. Open the WebCustOrders form in Form view. Insert a screen shot of the database window showing the custom button in a new Microsoft Word document using either the Screenshot button in the Illustrations group on the INSERT tab or the Print Screen key and the Paste feature. Next, switch back to Access and open the WebProducts form in Form view. Insert a screenshot of the database window below the first image in the Microsoft Word document. Type your name a few lines below the screen images and add any other identifying information as instructed. Save the Microsoft Word document and name it **AL2-C7-A2-FormWindows**. Print **AL2-C7-A2-FormWindows.docx** and then exit Word.
5. Close both forms.

Assessment 3

CREATE A NAVIGATION FORM AND CONFIGURE DATABASE OPTIONS

1. With the **AL2-C7-ViewIt.accdb** database open, create a Navigation form using the following information:
   a. Apply the Vertical Tabs, Left style.
   b. Add the WebCustOrders form as the first tab.
   c. Add the WebProducts form as the second tab.
   d. Add the WebOrdersByProd report as the third tab.
   e. Add the WebSalesByDate report as the fourth tab.
   f. Save the form, naming it *MainMenu*.
2. In Layout view or Design view, edit the MainMenu Navigation form as follows:
   a. Delete the logo container object.
   b. Edit the text in the *Title* control object to read *View It Classic Videos* and resize the object so the right edge of the control ends just after the title text. In other words, adjust the width of the control object so it is only as wide as it needs to be to display the title text.
   c. Apply the Light 1 Outline, Colored Fill - Green, Accent 6 quick style to all of the tabs, including the *[Add New]* tab.
   d. Change the Caption property for the first tab to *Customer Orders*.
   e. Change the Caption property for the second tab to *Classic Products*.
   f. Change the Caption property for the third tab to *Orders by Product*.
   g. Change the Caption property for the fourth tab to *Sales by Month*.

3. Create a new macro named *ExitDB* that will save all objects when exiting Access. Assign the macro to a command button placed in the *Form Header* section of the MainMenu form. You determine the appropriate text to display on the face of the button and a name for the command button. Format it with the same Quick Style used for the tabs. Save and close the MainMenu form.
4. Set the MainMenu form as the startup display form.
5. Create an application title for the database with the text *ViewIt Classic Videos Web Orders Database.*
6. Hide the Navigation pane.
7. Turn on the *Check for new unassociated labels* error-checking option. ***Note: Skip this step if you did not complete Project 3c, in which this option was turned off.***
8. Close and then reopen the database to test your startup options. Click each tab in the MainMenu form to make sure the correct form or report displays.
9. With the database open at the MainMenu form and the Customer Orders tab selected so that the two new groups are displayed, insert a screenshot of the database window in a new Microsoft Word document using either the Screenshot button in the Illustrations group on the INSERT tab or the Print Screen key and the Paste feature. Type your name a few lines below the screenshot and add any other identifying information as instructed. Save the Microsoft Word document and name it **AL2-C7-A3-MainMenu**. Print **AL2-C7-A3-MainMenu.docx** and then exit Word.

Assessment 4

CUSTOMIZE THE RIBBON

1. With **AL2-C7-ViewIt.accdb** open, export your customizations to your storage medium in the AL2C7 subfolder. Save the file as **AL2-C7-A4-ViewItCustomizations.exportedUI.**
2. Add a new tab between the HOME tab and CREATE tab. Rename the tab using your first and last names in uppercase letters. Add a new group to the new tab so that there are two new groups in total. Rename the first group *Formatting* and the second group *Maintenance*.
3. Select *All Commands* in the *Choose commands from* option box and then add the Font Color, Format Cells, Format Painter, and Line Color buttons to the Formatting group.
4. Select *File Tab* in the *Choose commands from* option box and then add the Access 2002-2003 Database, Back Up Database, and Compact & Repair Database buttons to the Maintenance group.
5. With the database open at the MainMenu form, insert a screenshot of the database window showing the custom tab in a new Microsoft Word document using either the Screenshot button in the Illustrations group on the INSERT tab or the Print Screen key and the Paste feature. Type your name a few lines below the screenshot and add any other identifying information as instructed. Save the Microsoft Word document and name it **AL2-C7-A4-CustomizedRibbon**. Print **AL2-C7-A4-CustomizedRibbon.docx** and then exit Word.
6. Import the customization file saved in Step 1 to reset the ribbon back to your institution's settings.
7. Use the exit button in the MainMenu form to exit the database.

Visual Benchmark Demonstrate Your Proficiency

AUTOMATE AND CUSTOMIZE A RESERVATION DATABASE

1. Open **AL2-C7-PawsParadise.accdb** and enable the content.
2. Review the database window shown in Figure 7.11. Create the Navigation form as shown, including the command buttons and required macros assigned to the command buttons. Set the required startup and Navigation pane options.
3. Check with your instructor for instructions on whether to print the macros and a screen image of the database window.

Figure 7.11 Visual Benchmark

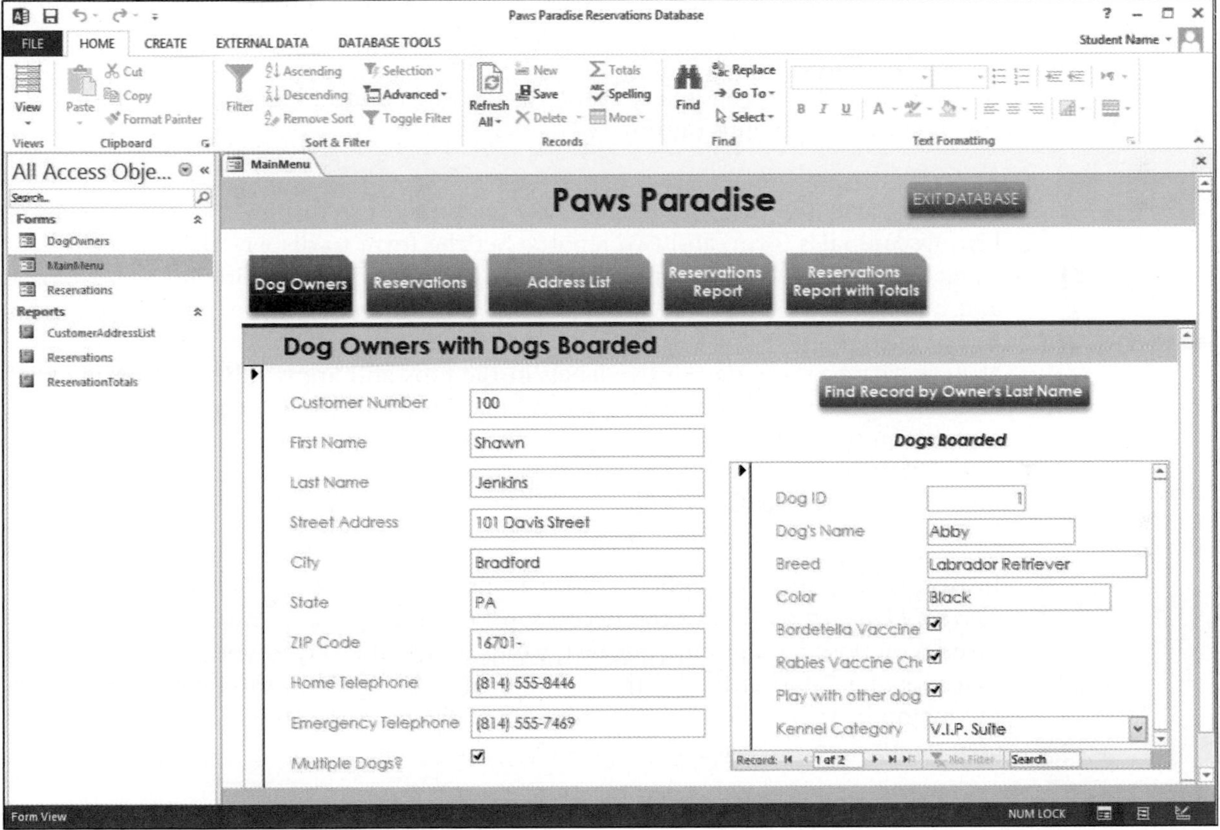

Case Study Apply Your Skills

Part 1

As you near completion of your work as an intern at Hillsdale Realty, you decide to automate the database to make the application easier for the next intern to use. Open **AL2-C7-HillsdaleRealty.accdb** and enable the content. Create three macros to accomplish the tasks in the bulleted list. You determine the appropriate macro names.

- Move to the *AgentLName* control and open the Find dialog box.
- Move to the *ListingNo* control and open the Find dialog box.
- Save all objects when exiting the database.

Assign the first macro as a command button in the Agents form. Assign the second macro as a command button in the ListingsAndSales form. In both forms, determine where to position the button, what text to display on the button, and the button name. Check with your instructor for instructions on whether to print the macros and a screen image of the Agents form and ListingsAndSales form, showing each command button.

Part 2

Create a navigation form to be used as a main menu to display the Agents form, ListingsAndSales form, and two reports. Set the form to display automatically when the database is opened. Add an appropriate application title for the database and hide the tables, queries, and macros in the Navigation pane. Assign the macro to exit the database as a button in the main menu form. Edit the main menu form as necessary to show descriptive labels in the tabs and apply other formatting enhancements. Close and reopen the database to test your startup options. Test each menu tab to make sure each option works. Check with your instructor for instructions on whether to print a screen image of the database window with the main menu form displayed.

Part 3

In Access Help, research other options available to customize Access in the *Current Database* section of the Access Options dialog box. Using Microsoft Word, compose a memo in your own words and addressed to your instructor that provides information on three options not discussed in this chapter. Save the memo in Word and name it **AL2-C7-CS-P3-PackageMemo.docx**. Print the memo and then exit Word.

MICROSOFT® ACCESS®

Integrating Access Data

PERFORMANCE OBJECTIVES

Upon successful completion of Chapter 8, you will be able to:

- **Create and restore a backup database file**
- **Create an ACCDE database file**
- **View Trust Center settings**
- **Import data from another Access database**
- **Link to a table in another Access database**
- **Determine when to import from versus link to external sources**
- **Reset or refresh links using Linked Table Manager**
- **Import data from a text file**
- **Save import specifications**
- **Export data in an Access table or query as a text file**
- **Save and run export specifications**
- **Export an object as an XPS document**
- **Create a database in an older format**

SNAP

Tutorials

8.1 Creating and Restoring a Backup Database File
8.2 Creating an ACCDE Database File
8.3 Viewing Trust Center Settings
8.4 Importing Data from Another Access Database
8.5 Linking to a Table in Another Access Database
8.6 Importing Data to Access from a Text File
8.7 Saving and Repeating a Saved Import Process
8.8 Exporting Access Data to a Text File
8.9 Saving and Repeating Saved Export Specifications
8.10 Publishing Database Objects as PDF or XPS Files

Integrating Access data with other applications in the Microsoft Office suite is easily accomplished with buttons on the EXTERNAL DATA tab. These buttons allow you to export data to and import data from Word and Excel. Data can be exchanged between the Microsoft programs with the formatting and data structure intact. In some cases, however, you may need to exchange data between Access and a non-Microsoft program. In this chapter, you will learn how to create and restore a backup database file, how to integrate data between individual Access database files, and how to import and export data in a text file format that is recognized by nearly all applications. You will also learn how to prevent changes to the design of objects and how to publish an Access object as an XPS file, which is an XML document format. Model answers for this chapter's projects appear on the following page.

Note: Before beginning the projects, copy to your storage medium the AL2C8 subfolder from the AL2 folder on the CD that accompanies this textbook and then make AL2C8 the active folder.

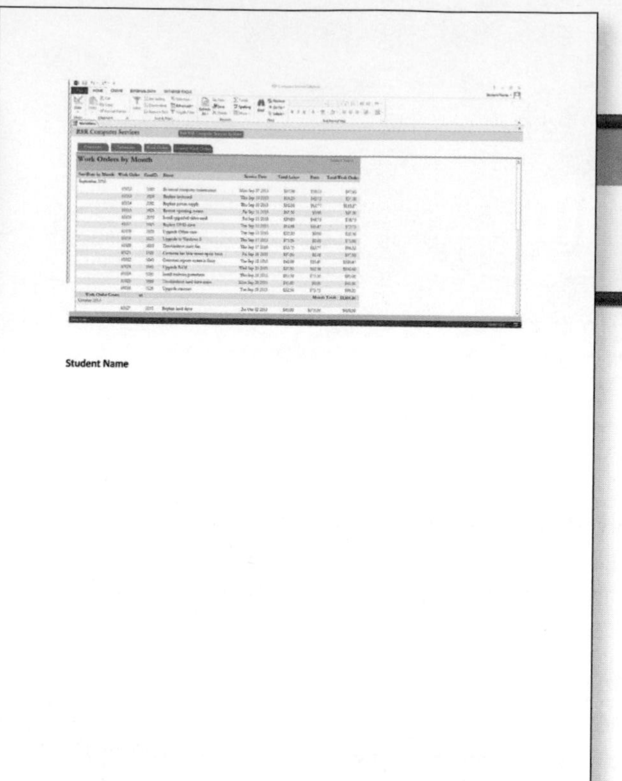

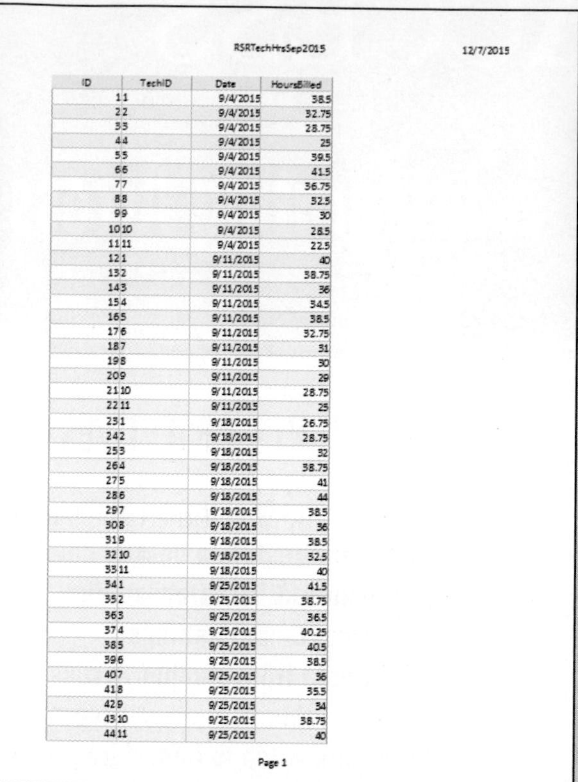

RSRTechHrsSep2015 12/7/2015

ID	TechID	Date	HoursBilled
1	1	9/4/2015	38.5
2	2	9/4/2015	32.75
3	3	9/4/2015	28.75
4	4	9/4/2015	25
5	5	9/4/2015	39.5
6	6	9/4/2015	41.5
7	7	9/4/2015	36.75
8	8	9/4/2015	32.5
9	9	9/4/2015	30
10	10	9/4/2015	28.5
11	11	9/4/2015	22.5
12	1	9/11/2015	40
13	2	9/11/2015	38.75
14	3	9/11/2015	36
15	4	9/11/2015	34.5
16	5	9/11/2015	38.5
17	6	9/11/2015	32.75
18	7	9/11/2015	31
19	8	9/11/2015	30
20	9	9/11/2015	29
21	10	9/11/2015	28.75
22	11	9/11/2015	25
23	1	9/18/2015	26.75
24	2	9/18/2015	28.75
25	3	9/18/2015	32
26	4	9/18/2015	38.75
27	5	9/18/2015	41
28	6	9/18/2015	44
29	7	9/18/2015	38.5
30	8	9/18/2015	36
31	9	9/18/2015	38.5
32	10	9/18/2015	32.5
33	11	9/18/2015	40
34	1	9/25/2015	41.5
35	2	9/25/2015	38.75
36	3	9/25/2015	36.5
37	4	9/25/2015	40.25
38	5	9/25/2015	40.5
39	6	9/25/2015	38.5
40	7	9/25/2015	36
41	8	9/25/2015	35.5
42	9	9/25/2015	34
43	10	9/25/2015	38.75
44	11	9/25/2015	40

Page 1

Project 1 Make an ACCDE Database File

Project 1b, ACCDE Database File, Dimmed Icons on Ribbon

Project 2d, Imported RSRTechHoursSep2015 Table

```
TotalWorkOrders.txt
WO,CustID,Descr,ServDate,Total Labor,Parts,Total Work Order
65012,1000,Bi-annual computer maintenance,9/7/2015 0:00:00,37.50,$10.15,$47.65
65013,1000,Replace keyboard,9/10/2015 0:00:00,14.25,$42.75,$57.00
65014,1005,Replace power supply,9/10/2015 0:00:00,52.50,$62.77,$115.27
65015,1008,Restore operating system,9/11/2015 0:00:00,67.50,$0.00,$67.50
65016,1010,Install upgraded video card,9/11/2015 0:00:00,30.00,$48.75,$78.75
65017,1015,Replace DVD drive,9/15/2015 0:00:00,16.87,$55.87,$72.75
65018,1020,Upgrade Office suite,9/15/2015 0:00:00,22.50,$0.00,$22.50
65019,1025,Upgrade to Windows 8,9/17/2015 0:00:00,75.00,$0.00,$75.00
65020,1030,Troubleshoot noisy fan,9/17/2015 0:00:00,33.75,$62.77,$96.52
65021,1035,Customer has blue screen upon boot,9/18/2015 0:00:00,97.50,$0.00,$97.50
65022,1040,Customer reports screen is fuzzy,9/22/2015 0:00:00,45.00,$55.47,$100.47
65023,1045,Upgrade RAM,9/23/2015 0:00:00,37.50,$62.50,$100.00
65024,1005,Install malware protection,9/24/2015 0:00:00,15.50,$75.50,$91.00
65025,1010,Troubleshoot hard drive noise,9/28/2015 0:00:00,45.00,$0.00,$45.00
65026,1025,Upgrade memory,9/29/2015 0:00:00,22.50,$75.75,$98.25
65027,1010,Replace hard drive,10/2/2015 0:00:00,45.00,$375.50,$420.50
65028,1030,Reinstall operating system,10/2/2015 0:00:00,67.50,$0.00,$67.50
65029,1035,Set up automatic backup,10/3/2015 0:00:00,11.25,$0.00,$11.25
65030,1000,Clean malware from system,10/6/2015 0:00:00,15.50,$0.00,$15.50
65031,1045,Customer reports noisy hard drive,10/6/2015 0:00:00,52.50,$0.00,$52.50
65032,1008,Install second hard drive,10/13/2015 0:00:00,60.00,$425.75,$485.75
65033,1000,Install Windows 8,10/13/2015 0:00:00,97.50,$335.75,$433.25
65034,1035,File management training,10/14/2015 0:00:00,45.00,$0.00,$45.00
65035,1020,Office 2013 training,10/15/2015 0:00:00,75.00,$0.00,$75.00
65036,1008,Set up home network,10/16/2015 0:00:00,67.50,$85.22,$152.72
65037,1015,Bi-annual computer maintenance,10/19/2015 0:00:00,37.50,$8.75,$46.25
65038,1010,Install Windows 8,10/19/2015 0:00:00,75.00,$0.00,$75.00
65039,1030,Set up automatic backup,10/19/2015 0:00:00,16.87,$0.00,$16.88
65040,1025,Configure dual monitors,10/20/2015 0:00:00,30.00,$0.00,$30.00
65041,1020,Bi-annual computer maintenance,10/22/2015 0:00:00,37.50,$10.15,$47.65
65042,1030,File management training,10/22/2015 0:00:00,33.75,$0.00,$33.75
65043,1020,Troubleshoot video fuzziness,10/23/2015 0:00:00,15.00,$0.00,$15.00
65044,1008,DVD drive is not working,10/23/2015 0:00:00,30.00,$55.40,$85.40
65045,1025,Set up automatic backup,10/26/2015 0:00:00,11.62,$0.00,$11.63
65046,1010,Windows 8 training,10/26/2015 0:00:00,60.00,$0.00,$60.00
65047,1030,Set up automatic backup,10/29/2015 0:00:00,11.25,$0.00,$11.25
65048,1020,Replace LCD monitor,10/29/2015 0:00:00,15.00,$169.95,$184.95
65049,1040,Set up dual monitor system,10/31/2015 0:00:00,22.50,$0.00,$22.50
65050,1045,Reinstall Windows 8,10/31/2015 0:00:00,45.00,$0.00,$45.00

Page 1
```

```
TotalLabor.txt
WO     ServDate              Hours   Rate     Total Labor
65012  9/7/2015 0:00:00      1.25    $30.00   37.50
65013  9/10/2015 0:00:00     0.50    $28.50   14.25
65014  9/10/2015 0:00:00     1.75    $30.00   52.50
65015  9/11/2015 0:00:00     2.25    $30.00   67.50
65016  9/11/2015 0:00:00     1.00    $30.00   30.00
65017  9/15/2015 0:00:00     0.75    $22.50   16.87
65018  9/15/2015 0:00:00     1.00    $22.50   22.50
65019  9/17/2015 0:00:00     2.50    $30.00   75.00
65020  9/17/2015 0:00:00     1.50    $22.50   33.75
65021  9/18/2015 0:00:00     3.25    $30.00   97.50
65022  9/22/2015 0:00:00     1.50    $30.00   45.00
65023  9/23/2015 0:00:00     1.25    $30.00   37.50
65024  9/24/2015 0:00:00     1.00    $15.50   15.50
65025  9/28/2015 0:00:00     1.50    $30.00   45.00
65026  9/29/2015 0:00:00     0.75    $30.00   22.50
65027  10/2/2015 0:00:00     1.50    $30.00   45.00
65028  10/2/2015 0:00:00     2.25    $30.00   67.50
65029  10/3/2015 0:00:00     0.50    $22.50   11.25
65030  10/6/2015 0:00:00     1.00    $15.50   15.50
65031  10/6/2015 0:00:00     1.75    $30.00   52.50
65032  10/13/2015 0:00:00    2.00    $30.00   60.00
65033  10/13/2015 0:00:00    3.25    $30.00   97.50
65034  10/14/2015 0:00:00    1.50    $30.00   45.00
65035  10/15/2015 0:00:00    2.50    $30.00   75.00
65036  10/16/2015 0:00:00    3.00    $22.50   67.50
65037  10/19/2015 0:00:00    1.25    $30.00   37.50
65038  10/19/2015 0:00:00    2.50    $30.00   75.00
65039  10/19/2015 0:00:00    0.75    $22.50   16.87
65040  10/20/2015 0:00:00    1.00    $30.00   30.00
65041  10/22/2015 0:00:00    1.25    $30.00   37.50
65042  10/22/2015 0:00:00    1.50    $22.50   33.75
65043  10/23/2015 0:00:00    0.50    $30.00   15.00
65044  10/23/2015 0:00:00    1.00    $30.00   30.00
65045  10/26/2015 0:00:00    0.75    $15.50   11.62
65046  10/26/2015 0:00:00    2.00    $30.00   60.00
65047  10/29/2015 0:00:00    0.50    $22.50   11.25
65048  10/29/2015 0:00:00    0.50    $30.00   15.00
65049  10/31/2015 0:00:00    0.75    $30.00   22.50
65050  10/31/2015 0:00:00    1.50    $30.00   45.00

Page 1
```

Project 3 Export Access Data to a Text File

Project 3a, Exported TotalWorkOrders Query

Project 3b, Exported TotalLabor Query

Project 1 Maintain and Secure a Database — 3 Parts

You will back up and restore a database and secure a database by making an ACCDE file. You will also explore the default settings in the Trust Center.

Creating and Restoring a Backup File

Before you make any major changes to your database, such as running action queries or modifying table structures, it is a good idea to back up your database. Certain changes made to a database cannot be reversed. For example, if you run a delete query to remove the work orders for the month of September, the work orders cannot be reinstated. If field sizes are changed and made too small, the data truncated cannot be restored if the table has been saved. The data will be lost, unless a backup exists.

You may also consider backing up your database on a regular basis to minimize any data loss that may occur due to system failures or design mistakes. Once you have created a backup database, you can use it to restore the entire database or to import a specific object. You will learn how to restore the entire database in Project 1 and how to import objects in Project 2.

To create a backup of your database, click the FILE tab and then click the *Save As* option. Click *Back Up Database* in the *Advanced* section of the Save As backstage area and then click the Save As button. (Access closes any open objects.) Navigate to or create a folder to store your backup databases and then click the Save button. Notice that the current date is added to the end of the file name.

To replace a database with a backup copy, copy the backup database from the backup folder and then paste it in the same folder as the database you want to replace. Delete the database you want to replace and rename the backup database as desired.

Quick Steps

Back Up a Database
1. Click FILE.
2. Click *Save As*.
3. Click *Back Up Database*.
4. Click Save As.
5. Navigate to the appropriate folder.
6. Click Save.

Project 1a Creating and Restoring a Backup File — Part 1 of 3

1. Open **AL2-C8-RSRCompServ.accdb** and enable the content.
2. Create a backup database file by completing the following steps:
   a. Click the FILE tab and then click the *Save As* option.
   b. Click *Back Up Database* in the *Advanced* section.
   c. Click the Save As button.

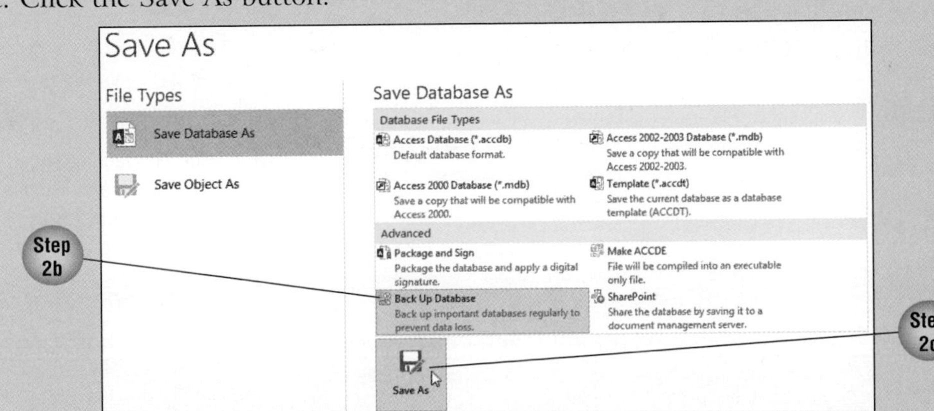

d. The backup file is named **AL2-C8-RSRCompServ_yyyy-mm-dd.accdb**, where *yyyy-mm-dd* represents the year, month, and day the backup is created. (Your date will differ from the one shown below.) With the default location the AL2C8 folder on your storage medium, click the New folder button.
e. With *New folder* selected, type **DatabaseBackUps** and then press Enter.
f. Click the Open button to open the folder.

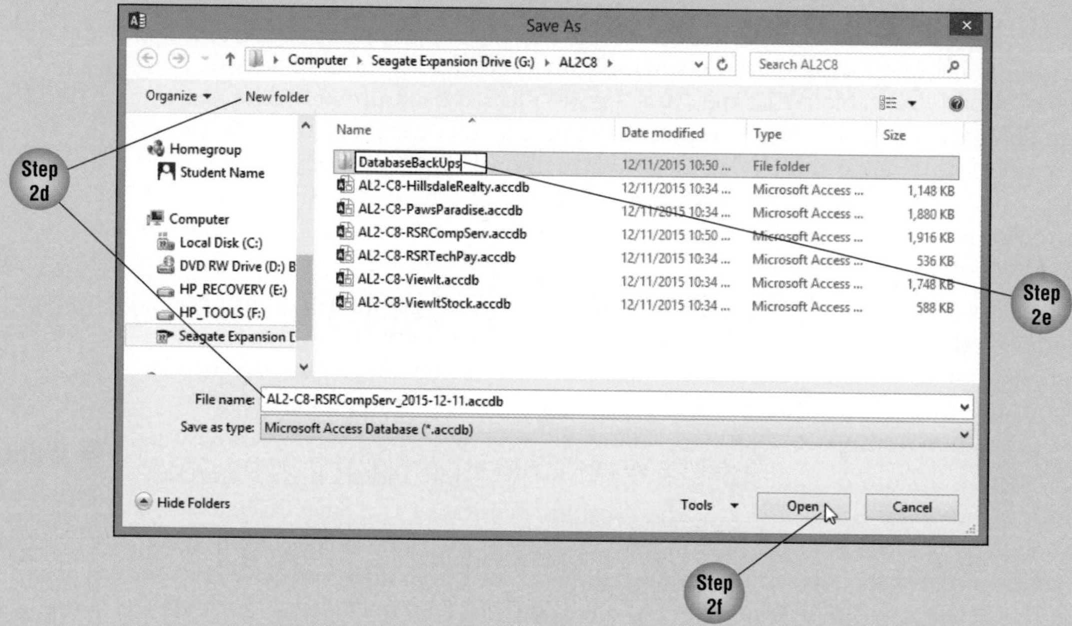

g. Click Save.

3. With **AL2-C8-RSRCompServ** open, open the Customers table in Design view, click *City*, and then change the field size from 25 characters to 5 characters. Save the table.
4. Answer Yes to the alert warning that some data may be lost.

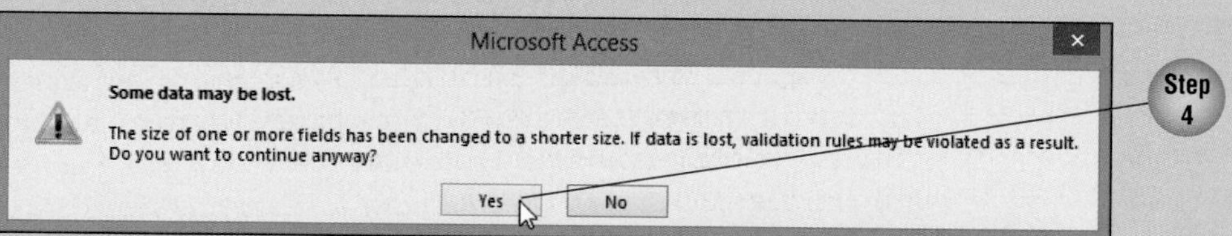

5. Switch to Datasheet view and look at the data in the *City* column. The last two letters were permanently deleted from *Detroit*. Notice that the Undo button on the Quick Access toolbar is dimmed, indicating that this change cannot be reversed.

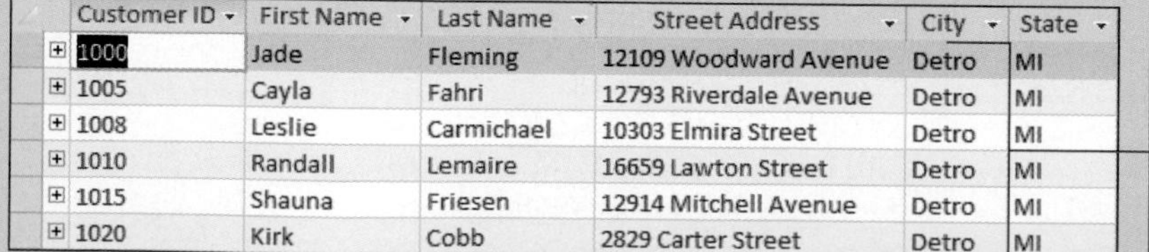

Customer ID	First Name	Last Name	Street Address	City	State
1000	Jade	Fleming	12109 Woodward Avenue	Detro	MI
1005	Cayla	Fahri	12793 Riverdale Avenue	Detro	MI
1008	Leslie	Carmichael	10303 Elmira Street	Detro	MI
1010	Randall	Lemaire	16659 Lawton Street	Detro	MI
1015	Shauna	Friesen	12914 Mitchell Avenue	Detro	MI
1020	Kirk	Cobb	2829 Carter Street	Detro	MI

The field size for the *City* field has been changed to 5 characters. The last two letters in Detroit have been permanently deleted.

6. Close **AL2-C8-RSRCompServ.accdb** and then close Access.

7. Restore the backup copy of the database by completing the following steps:
   a. Move your mouse to the bottom left corner of the screen and then click the Start button.
   b. At the Start screen, start typing **file explorer**. When the File Explorer icon displays below the *Apps* heading, press Enter. (Depending on your operating system, these steps may vary.)
   c. Navigate to the DatabaseBackUps folder in the AL2C8 folder on your storage medium and then right-click ***AL2-C8-RSRCompServ_yyyy-mm-dd.accdb***, where *yyyy-mm-dd* represents the year, month, and day the backup was created.
   d. Click *Copy* at the shortcut menu.
   e. Click *AL2C8* in the Address bar.

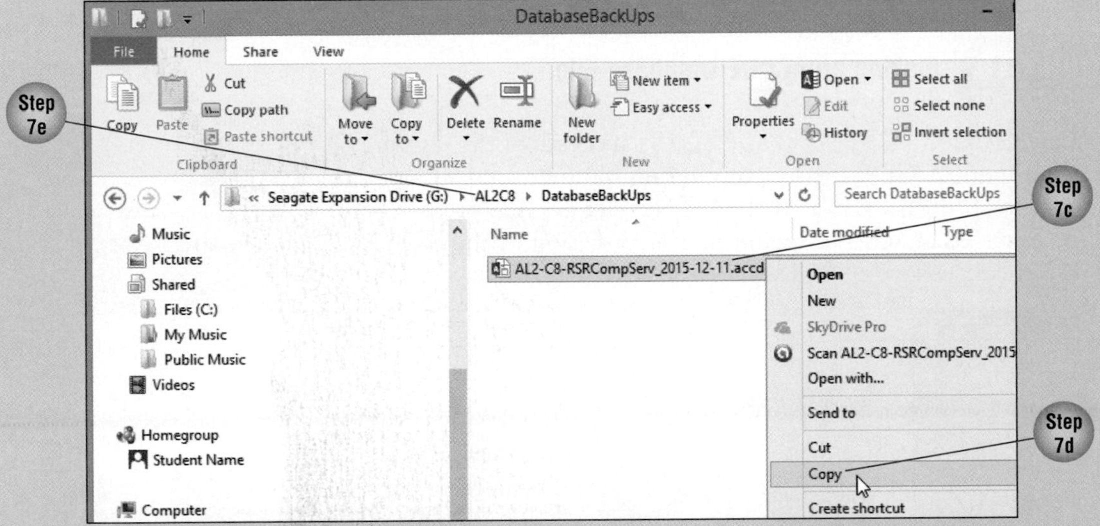

   f. Right-click a blank area of the content pane and then click *Paste* at the shortcut menu.
   g. Right-click ***AL2-C8-RSRCompServ.accdb*** and then click *Delete* at the shortcut menu.
   h. Right-click ***AL2-C8-RSRCompServ_yyyy-mm-dd.accdb*** and then click *Rename* at the shortcut menu.
   i. Delete *_yyyy-mm-dd* and then press Enter.
8. Open **AL2-C8-RSRCompServ.accdb**, enable the content if necessary, and then open the Customers table. Verify that *Detroit* is displayed in the *City* field and then close the table.
9. Close **AL2-C8-RSRCompServ.accdb.**

Creating an ACCDE Database File

In Chapter 6, you learned how to split a database into two files to create a front-end database and a back-end database. Using this method allowed you to improve performance and protect the table objects from changes by separating them from the queries, forms, and reports. Another method you can use to protect an Access database is to create an ACCDE file. In an ACCDE file, end users are prevented from making changes to the design of objects. An Access database stored as an ACCDE file is a locked-down version of the database and therefore does not provide access to Design view or Layout view. In addition, if the database contains any Visual Basic for Applications (VBA) code, the code cannot be modified or changed.

Quick Steps

Create an ACCDE File
1. Open database.
2. Click FILE tab.
3. Click *Save As*.
4. Click *Make ACCDE*.
5. Click Save As button.
6. Navigate to required drive and/or folder.
7. Type name in *File name* text box.
8. Click Save button.

To save an Access database as an ACCDE file, click the FILE tab and then click the *Save As* option. Click the *Make ACCDE* option in the *Advanced* section of the Save As backstage area. Next, click the Save As button to open the Save As dialog box. Navigate to the drive and/or folder in which to save the database, type the desired file name in the *File name* text box, and then click the Save button. Once the file is created, move the original database with the .accdb extension to a secure location and provide end users with the path to the ACCDE file for daily use.

Project 1b Making an ACCDE Database File Part 2 of 3

1. Open **AL2-C8-RSRNavPane.accdb** and enable the content.
2. Create an ACCDE file by completing the following steps:
   a. Click the FILE tab and then click the *Save As* option.
   b. Click *Make ACCDE* in the *Advanced* section of the Save As backstage area.
   c. Click the Save As button.

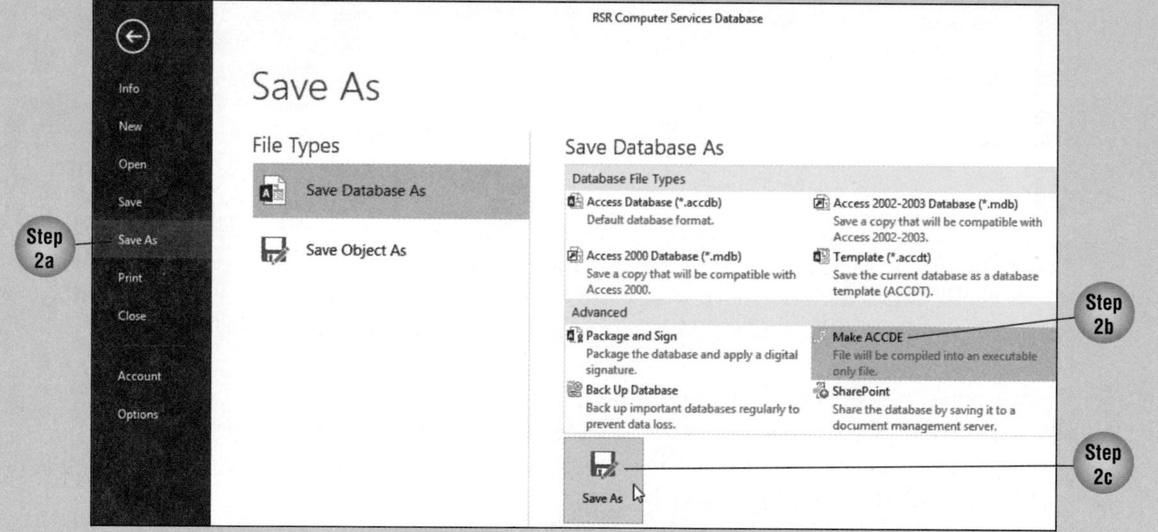

   d. At the Save As dialog box, with the default location the AL2C8 folder on your storage medium and ***AL2-C8-RSRNavPane.accde*** in the *File name* text box, click the Save button.

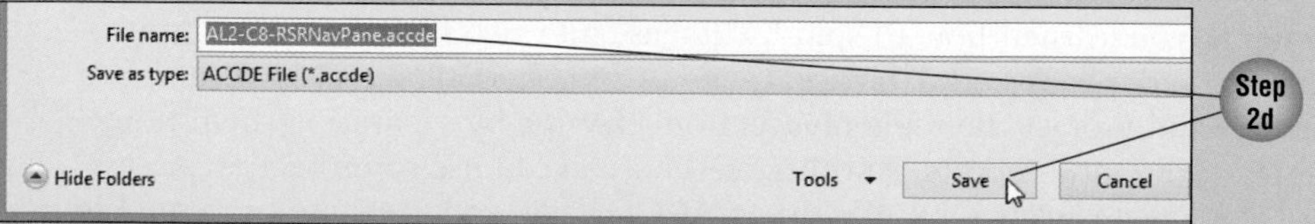

3. Close **AL2-C8-RSRNavPane.accdb**.
4. Open **AL2-C8-RSRNavPane.accde**.

5. At the Microsoft Access Security Notice dialog box informing you that the file might contain unsafe content, click the Open button.
6. With Customers the active tab in the MainMenu form and the Customer Data Maintenance Form open in Form view, click the HOME tab if necessary. Notice that the View button in the Views group is dimmed.

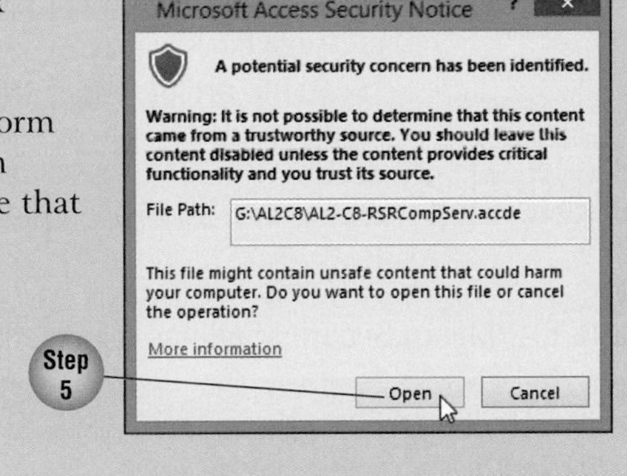

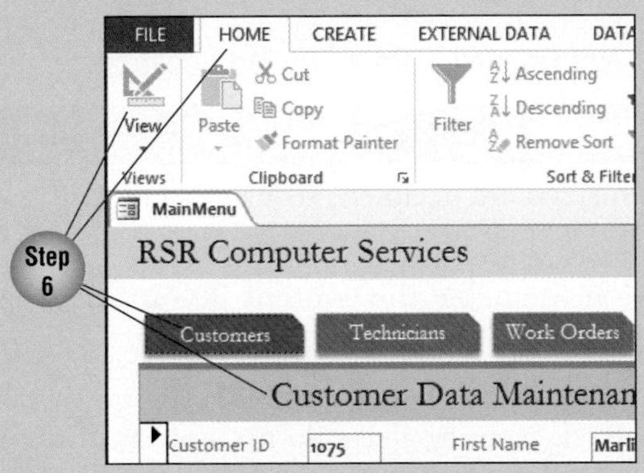

7. Click the Monthly Work Orders tab in the MainMenu form to view the Work Orders by Month report. Notice that the View button on the HOME tab is still dimmed. Also notice that only one view button is available in the view area at the right side of the Status bar.
8. Insert a screen shot of the database window in a new Microsoft Word document using either the Screenshot button in the Illustrations group on the INSERT tab or the Print Screen key with Paste. Type your name a few lines below the screen image and add any other identifying information as instructed.
9. Save the Microsoft Word document and name it **AL2-C8-P1-ACCDEWindow.docx**.
10. Print **AL2-C8-P1-ACCDEWindow.docx** and then exit Word.
11. Close **AL2-C8-RSRNavPane.accde**.

Viewing Trust Center Settings for Access

In Access, the Trust Center is set to block unsafe content when you open a database file. As you have been working with Access, you have closed the security warning that appears in the message bar when you open a database by clicking the Enable Content button. Access provides the Trust Center in which you can view and/or modify the security options that are in place to protect your computer from malicious content.

Quick Steps

View Trust Center Options

1. Click FILE tab.
2. Click *Options*.
3. Click *Trust Center* in left pane.
4. Click Trust Center Settings button.
5. Click desired trust center category in left pane.
6. View and/or modify required options.
7. Click OK twice.

The Trust Center maintains a *Trusted Locations* list, in which the content stored is considered to be from trusted sources. You can add a path to the trusted locations list and Access will treat any files opened from the drive and folder as safe. Databases opened from trusted locations do not display the security warning in the message bar and do not have content blocked.

Before the macros are enabled for a database, the Trust Center checks for a valid and current digital signature signed by an entity that is stored in the *Trusted Publishers* list. The *Trusted Publishers* list is maintained by you on the computer you are using. A trusted publisher is added to the list when you enable the content from an authenticated source and click the *Trust all content from this publisher* option. Depending on the active macro security setting, if the Trust Center cannot match

Changing the macro security setting in Access does not affect the setting in other Microsoft programs, such as Word and Excel.

the digital signature information with an entity in the *Trusted Publishers* list, or if the macro does not contain a digital signature, the security warning displays in the message bar.

Table 8.1 describes the four options available for macro security. The default macro security option is *Disable all macros with notification*. In some cases, you may decide to change the default macro security setting by opening the Trust Center dialog box. You will explore the Trust Center in Project 1c.

Table 8.1 Macro Security Settings for Databases Not Opened from a Trusted Location

Macro Setting	Description
Disable all macros without notification	All macros are disabled; security alerts will not appear.
Disable all macros with notification	All macros are disabled; security alert appears with the option to enable the content if you trust the source of the file. This is the default setting.
Disable all macros except digitally signed macros	A macro that does not contain a digital signature is disabled; security alerts do not appear. If the macro is digitally signed by a publisher in your *Trusted Publishers* list, the macro is allowed to run. If the macro is digitally signed by a publisher not in your *Trusted Publishers* list, you receive a security alert.
Enable all macros (not recommended; potentially dangerous code can run)	All macros are allowed; security alerts do not appear.

Project 1c Exploring Trust Center Settings — Part 3 of 3

1. To explore current settings in the Trust Center, complete the following steps:
   a. Click the Open Other Files hyperlink at the bottom of the *Recent* list and then click *Options*.
   b. Click *Trust Center* in the left pane of the Access Options dialog box.
   c. Click the Trust Center Settings button in the *Microsoft Access Trust Center* section.

Add-ins
Trust Center
Step 1b
Microsoft Trustworthy Computing
Microsoft Access Trust Center
The Trust Center contains security and privacy settings. These settings help keep your computer secure. We recommend that you do not change these settings.
Trust Center Settings...
Step 1c

d. At the Trust Center dialog box, click *Macro Settings* in the left pane.
e. Review the options in the *Macro Settings* section. Notice which option is active on the computer you are using. The default option is *Disable all macros with notification*. ***Note: The security setting on the computer you are using may be different from the default option. Do not change the security setting without the permission of your instructor.***
f. Click *Trusted Publishers* in the left pane. If any publishers have been added to the list on the computer you are using, their names will appear in the list box. If the list box is empty, no trusted publishers have been added.

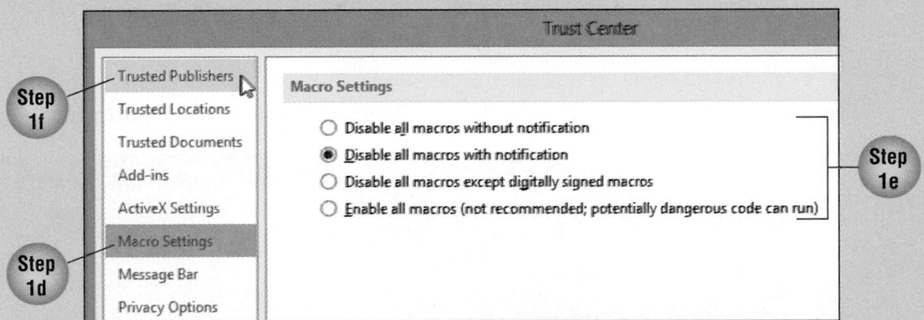

g. Click *Trusted Locations* in the left pane. Review the path and description of any folder in the *Trusted Locations* list. By default, Access adds the folder created upon installation of Microsoft Access that contains the wizard database templates provided by Microsoft. Additional folders that have been added by a system administrator or network administrator may also appear.
h. Click OK to close the Trust Center dialog box.

2. Click OK to close the Access Options dialog box.

Project 2 Import and Merge Data from External Sources — 4 Parts

You will link and import data from a table in another Access database and a comma delimited text file. You will also save import specifications for an import routine that you expect to repeat often.

Importing and Merging Data from Another Access Database

Data stored in another Access database can be merged into the active database by importing a copy of the source object(s). You can choose to copy multiple objects, including the relationships between tables. When importing, you can specify to import only the definition or both the definition and the data.

In Chapter 3, you learned to merge data from tables that contain the same fields by using an Append query to add selected records to the end of an existing table. You learned in Project 1 that you should back up your database before you make any major changes to it (such as merging the data), as some changes cannot be undone. If problems arise as a result of making changes to a database, you can either restore the entire database or import only the damaged table from the backup copy that you created.

Quick Steps

Import Objects from an Access Database

1. Open destination database.
2. Click EXTERNAL DATA tab.
3. Click Import Access database button.
4. Click Browse button.
5. If necessary, navigate to drive and/or folder.
6. Double-click source file name.
7. Click OK.
8. Select desired import object(s).
9. Click OK.
10. Click Close.

Import Access Database

If an object with the same name as an imported table already exists in the destination database, Access does not overwrite the existing object. Instead, it adds *1* to the end of the imported object's name.

To begin an import operation, click the EXTERNAL DATA tab and then click the Import Access database button (which displays the text *Access*) in the Import group to open the Get External Data - Access Database dialog box, shown in Figure 8.1. Specify the source database containing the object(s) you want to import by clicking the Browse button to open the File Open dialog box. Navigate to the drive and/or folder containing the source database and then double-click the desired Access database file name to insert the database file name in the *File name* text box. With the *Import tables, queries, forms, reports, macros, and modules into the current database* option selected by default, click OK. This opens the Import Objects dialog box, shown in Figure 8.2. Select the objects to be imported, change options if necessary, and then click OK.

Figure 8.1 Get External Data - Access Database Dialog Box with Import Option Selected

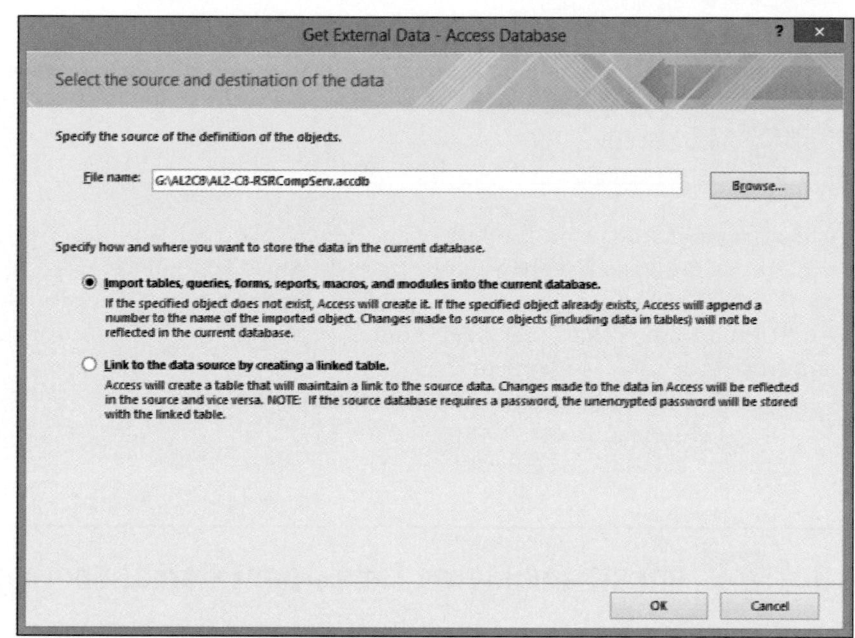

Figure 8.2 Import Objects Dialog Box

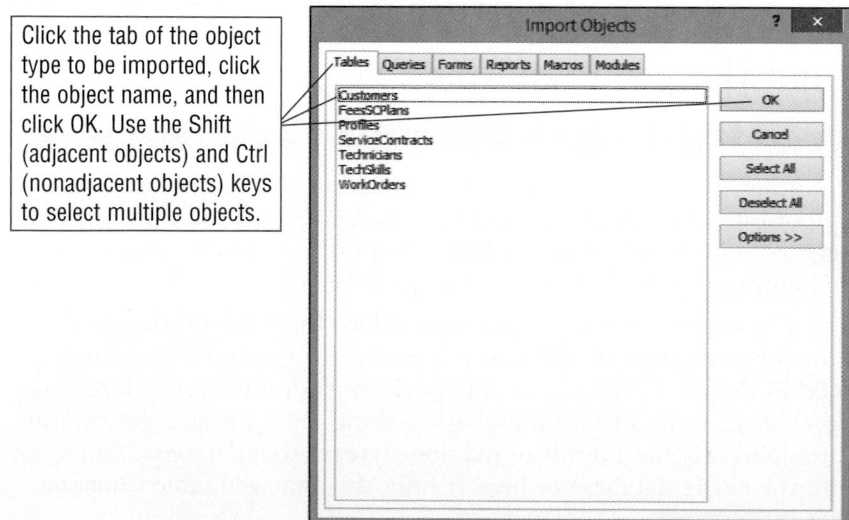

Click the Options button to display the *Import*, *Import Tables*, and *Import Queries* options, shown in Figure 8.3. By default, Access imports relationships between tables as well as their structure definition and data. It also imports a query as a query, as opposed to importing a query as a table. Select or deselect the options as required before clicking OK to begin the import operation.

If you import a query, form, or report, make sure that you also import the tables associated with the object.

Figure 8.3 Import Objects Dialog Box with Options Displayed

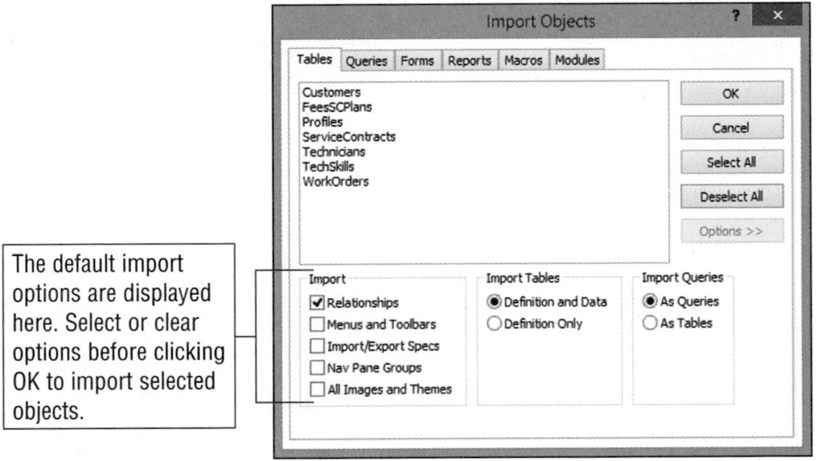

The default import options are displayed here. Select or clear options before clicking OK to import selected objects.

Project 2a Importing a Form and Table from Another Access Database

Part 1 of 4

1. Open **AL2-C8-RSRTechPay.accdb** and enable the content.
2. Merge the RSRCompServe database with the RSRTechPay database by importing the WorkOrders table and TechMaintenance form from **AL2-C8-RSRCompServ.accdb**. Import the two objects by completing the following steps:
   a. Click the EXTERNAL DATA tab.
   b. Click the Import Access database button (displays the text *Access*) in the Import & Link group.
   c. At the Get External Data - Access Database dialog box, click the Browse button.
   d. At the File Open dialog box, double-click ***AL2-C8-RSRCompServ.accdb***. ***Note: Navigate to the AL2C8 folder on your storage medium, if necessary.***
   e. With the *Import tables, queries, forms, reports, macros, and modules into the current database* option already selected, click OK.

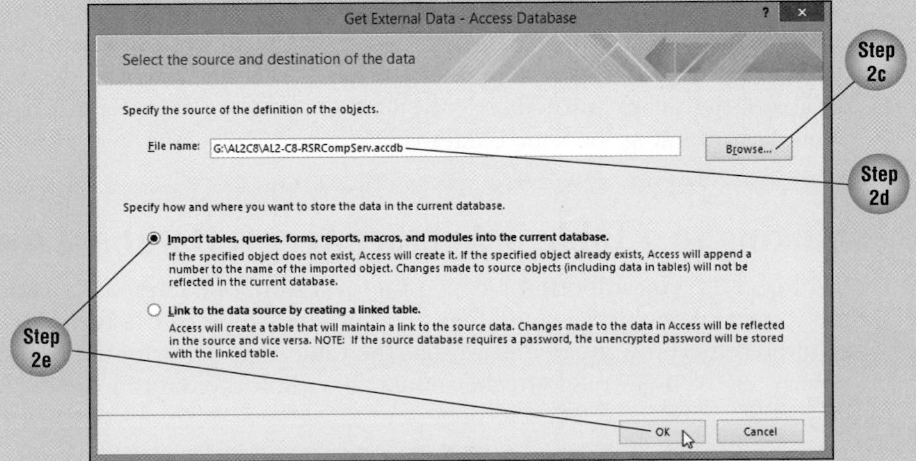

f. At the Import Objects dialog box, with the Tables tab selected, click *WorkOrders* in the Tables list box.
g. Click the Forms tab.
h. Click *TechMaintenance* in the Forms list box and then click OK.
i. At the Get External Data - Access Database dialog box, with the *Save import steps* check box empty, click Close.

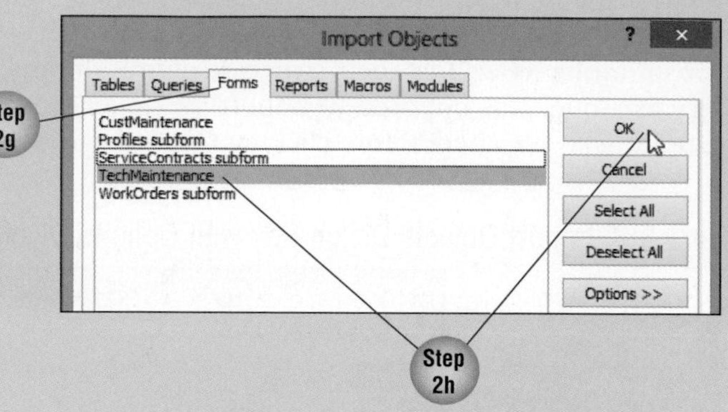

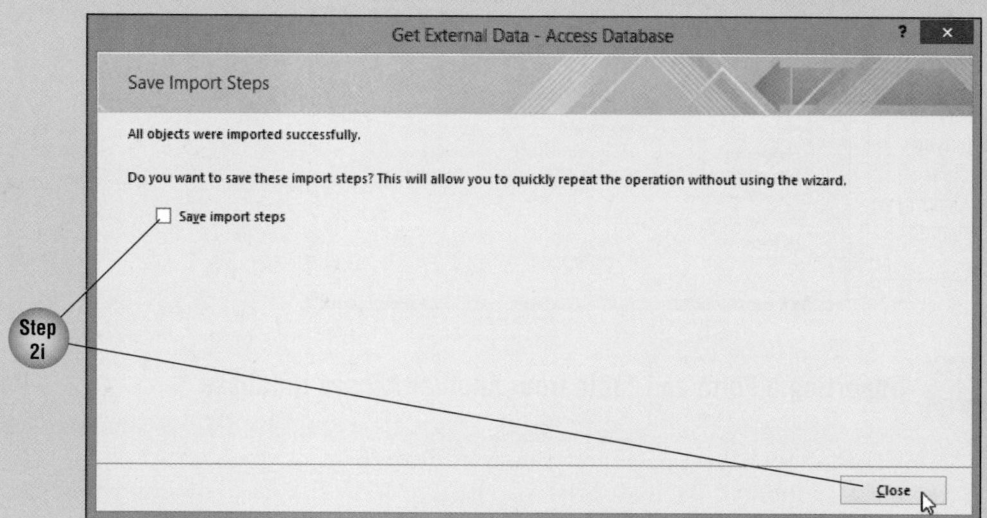

3. Access imports the WorkOrders table and the TechMaintenance form and adds the object names to the Navigation pane. The form will not be operational until after Project 2b, because the tables needed to populate data in the form do not yet reside in the database. You did not import the dependent tables in this project because you want the tables that contain the records to be linked.

You can also copy an object by opening two copies of Access: one with the source database opened and the other with the destination database opened. With the source database window active, right-click the source object in the Navigation pane and then click *Copy*. Switch to the window containing the destination database, right-click in the Navigation pane, and then click *Paste*. Close the Access window containing the source database.

Linking to a Table in Another Access Database

In Project 2a, you imported a copy of a form from one database to another. If the source form object is modified, the imported copy of the form object will not be altered. If you want to ensure that the table in the destination database will inherit any changes made to the source table, link the data in the object when you import it.

To create a linked table in the destination database, click the EXTERNAL DATA tab and then click the Import Access database button. Click the Browse button, navigate to the drive and/or folder in which the source database is stored, and then double-click the source database file name. Click the *Link to the data source by creating a linked table* option at the Get External Data - Access Database dialog box and then click OK, as shown in Figure 8.4.

The Link Tables dialog box, shown in Figure 8.5, contains the *Tables* list box, from which you select the tables to be linked. You can use Shift or Ctrl to select multiple tables to link in one step. Linked tables are indicated in the Navigation pane with blue right-pointing arrows.

Quick Steps

Link to a Table in Another Database

1. Open destination database.
2. Click EXTERNAL DATA tab.
3. Click Import Access database button.
4. Click Browse button.
5. If necessary, navigate to drive and/or folder.
6. Double-click source file name.
7. Click *Link to the data source by creating a linked table.*
8. Click OK.
9. Select desired table(s).
10. Click OK.

Figure 8.4 Get External Data - Access Database Dialog Box with Link Option Selected

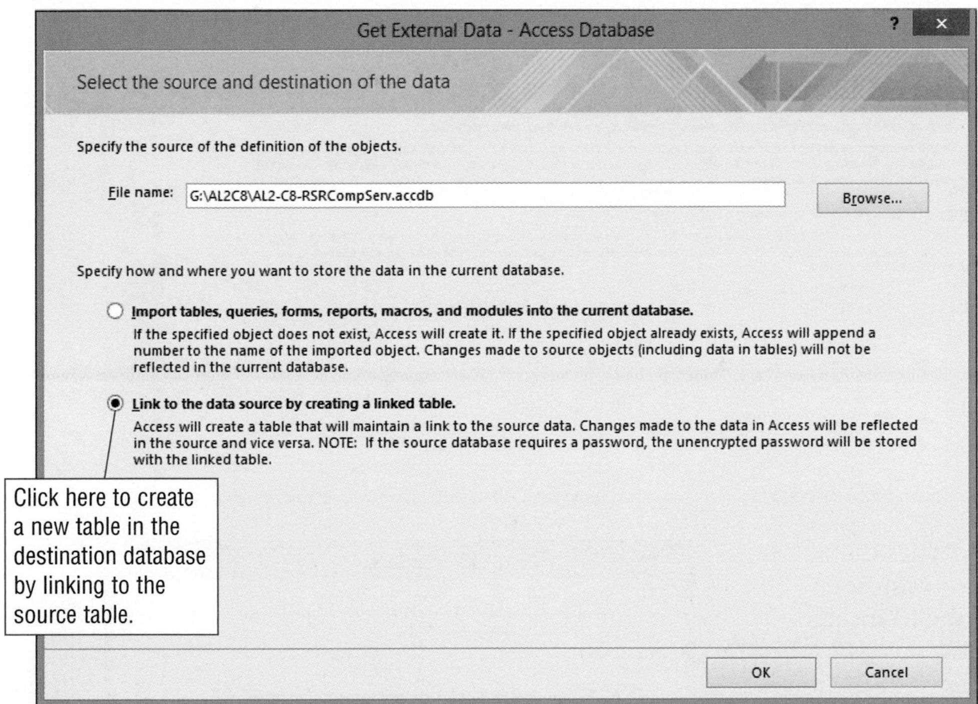

Figure 8.5 Link Tables Dialog Box

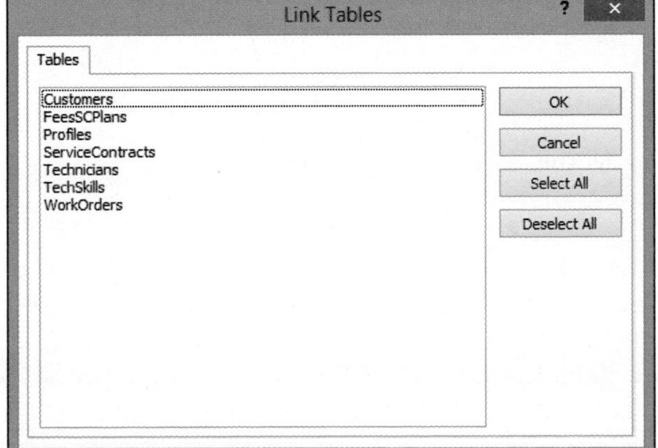

Project 2b Linking to Tables in Another Access Database Part 2 of 4

1. With **AL2-C8-RSRTechPay.accdb** open, link to two tables in **AL2-C8-RSRCompServ.accdb** by completing the following steps:
   a. With the EXTERNAL DATA tab still active, click the Import Access database button.
   b. Click the Browse button and then double-click ***AL2-C8-RSRCompServ.accdb***.
   c. Click the *Link to the data source by creating a linked table* option and then click OK.

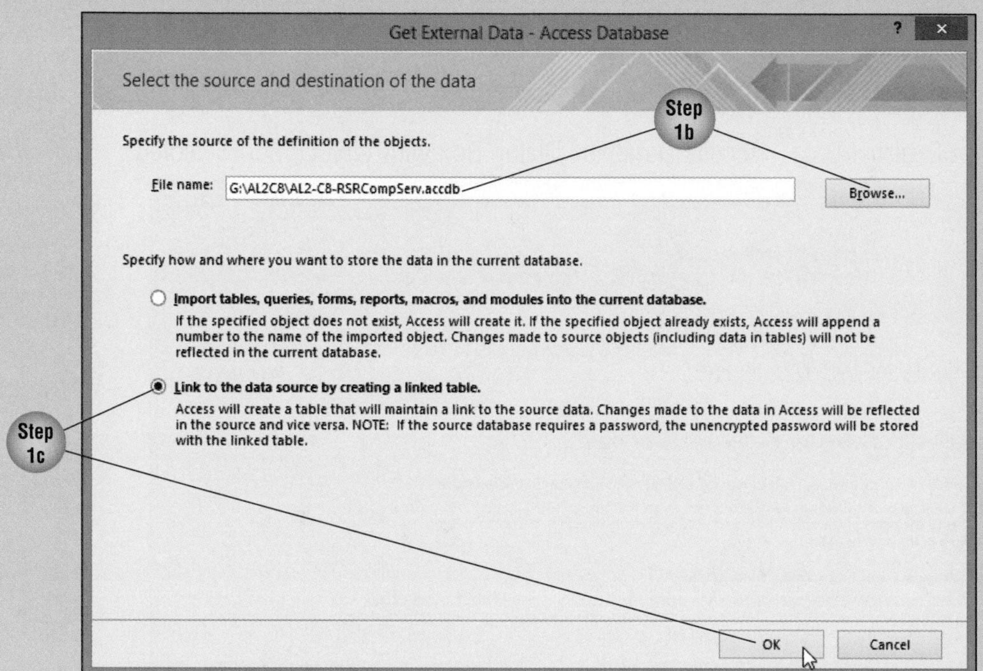

   d. At the Link Tables dialog box, click *Technicians* in the list box.
   e. Hold down the Shift key and then click *TechSkills* in the list box.
   f. Click OK. Access links the two tables to the source database and adds the table names to the Navigation pane. Each linked table displays with a blue right-pointing arrow next to the table icon.

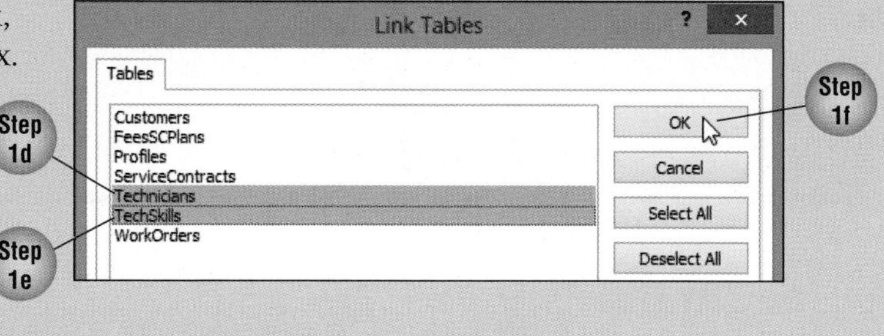

2. Double-click *TechMaintenance* in the Forms group in the Navigation pane to view the form with the first record displayed.
3. Double-click *Technicians* in the Tables group in the Navigation pane to view the table datasheet and then close the datasheet.
4. Double-click *TechSkills* in the Tables group in the Navigation pane to view the table datasheet and then close the datasheet.

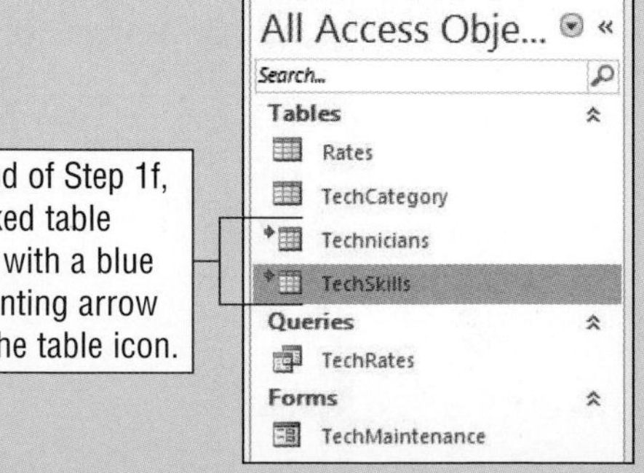

At the end of Step 1f, each linked table displays with a blue right-pointing arrow next to the table icon.

When a table is linked, the source data does not reside in the destination database. Opening a linked table causes Access to update the datasheet with the information in the source table in the other database. You can edit the source data in either the source table or the linked table in the destination database—either way, the changes will be reflected in both tables.

Choosing whether to Import or Link to Source Data

If the source data is not likely to change, you should import it. Keep in mind, however, that since importing creates copies of the data in two locations, changes or updates to the data must be made in both copies. Making the changes twice increases the risk of making a data entry error or forgetting to make an update in one or the other location.

If the source data is updated frequently, link to it so that you only have to make changes once. Since linked data exists only in the source location, the potential for making an error or missing an update is reduced.

You may also choose to link to the data source when several different databases require a common table, such as an Inventory table. To duplicate the table in each database is inefficient and wastes disk space. Also, there is a potential for error if individual databases are not refreshed with updated data. Given these risks, it makes more sense to link rather than import. In this scenario, a master Inventory table in a separate, shared database will be linked to all of the other databases that need to use the data.

Resetting a Link Using the Linked Table Manager

When a table has been linked to another database, Access stores the full path to the source database file name along with the linked table name. Changing the database file name or folder location for the source database means that the linked table will no longer function. Access provides the Linked Table Manager dialog box, shown in Figure 8.6, to allow you to reset or refresh a table's link to reconnect to the data source.

To refresh a link to a table, click the Linked Table Manager button in the Import & Link group on the EXTERNAL DATA tab to open the Linked Table Manager dialog box. Click the check box next to the link you want to refresh and then click OK. Access displays a message box stating that the link was successfully refreshed or provides a dialog box in which you can navigate to the new location for the data source.

Quick Steps

Refresh a Link

1. Click EXTERNAL DATA tab.
2. Click Linked Table Manager button.
3. Click Select All button or click check boxes for desired links.
4. Click OK.
5. Navigate to drive and/or folder.
6. Double-click source database file name.
7. Click OK.
8. Click Close button.

Linked Table Manager

Figure 8.6 Linked Table Manager Dialog Box

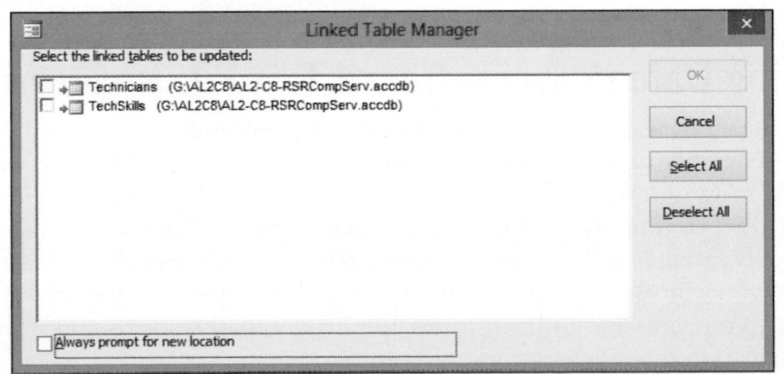

Project 2c **Refreshing a Link** **Part 3 of 4**

1. With **AL2-C8-RSRTechPay.accdb** open, change the location of **AL2-C8-RSRCompServ.accdb** by completing the following steps:
   a. Click the FILE tab, click *Open*, and then locate your AL2C8 folder on your storage medium.
   b. Click the Browse button.
   c. Right-click ***AL2-C8-RSRCompServ.accdb*** in the file list box and then click *Cut* at the shortcut menu.
   d. At the Open dialog box, double-click the *DatabaseBackUps* folder.
   e. Right-click in a blank area of the file list box and then click *Paste*.
   f. Close the Open dialog box. Because the location of the source database has been moved, the linked tables are no longer connected to the correct location.
   g. Click the Back button.
2. Refresh the links to the two tables by completing the following steps:
   a. If necessary, click the EXTERNAL DATA tab.
   b. Click the Linked Table Manager button in the Import & Link group.
   c. At the Linked Table Manager dialog box, click the Select All button to select all linked objects.
   d. Click OK. Access attempts to refresh the links. Because the source database has been moved, Access displays a dialog box for you to select the new location.

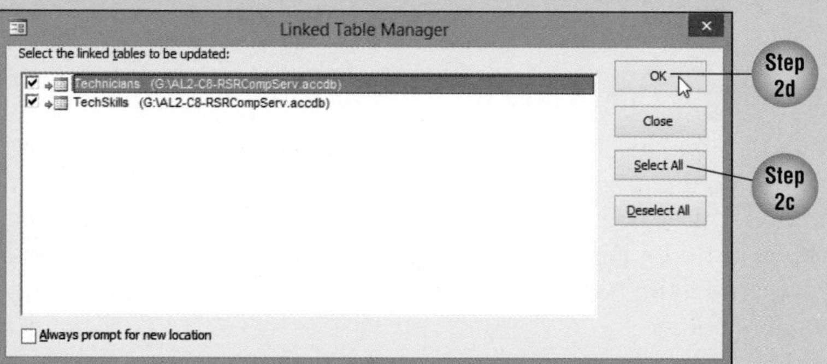

   e. At the Select New Location of Technicians dialog box, locate and then double-click ***AL2-C8-RSRCompServ.accdb***.
   f. Click OK at the Linked Table Manager message box that indicates that all selected links were successfully refreshed.

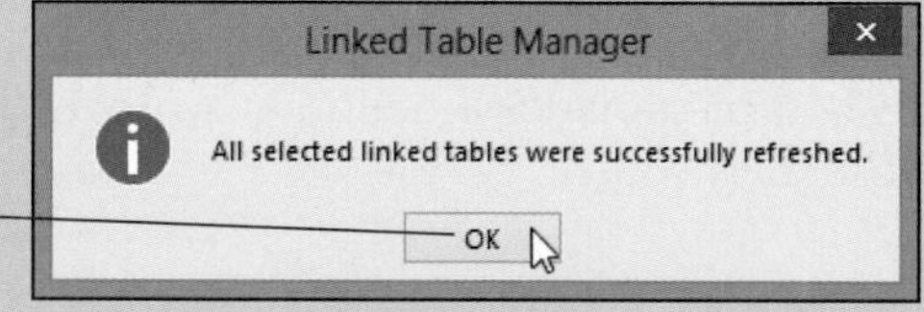

3. Click the Close button at the Linked Table Manager dialog box.

HINT

If you need to use data from a program that is not compatible with Access, check the source program's export options for a text file format, as most programs can export data in this format.

Importing Data to Access from a Text File

Text files are often used to exchange data between dissimilar programs, since the file format is recognized by nearly all applications. Text files contain no formatting and consist only of letters, numbers, punctuation symbols, and a few control characters. Two commonly used text file formats separate fields with a tab character (***delimited file format***) and a comma (***comma separated file format***). A partial view of the text file you will use in Project 2d is shown in a Notepad window in Figure 8.7. If necessary, you can view and edit a text file in Notepad prior to importing if the source application inserts characters you want to delete.

Figure 8.7 Project 2d Partial View of Text File Contents in Notepad

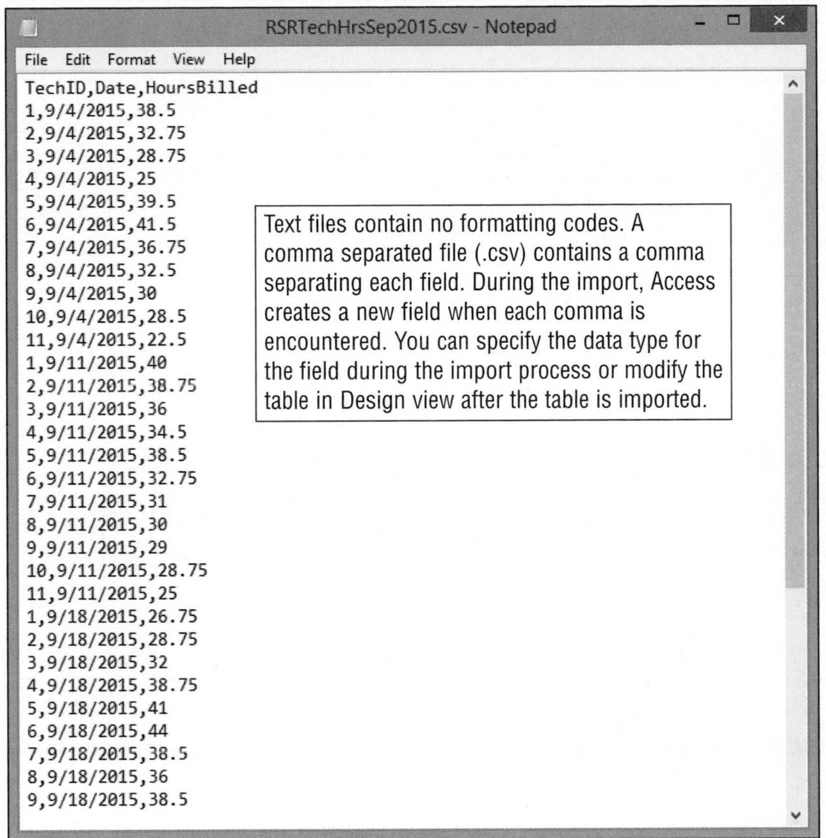
RSRTechHrsSep2015.csv - Notepad
File Edit Format View Help
TechID,Date,HoursBilled
1,9/4/2015,38.5
2,9/4/2015,32.75
3,9/4/2015,28.75
4,9/4/2015,25
5,9/4/2015,39.5
6,9/4/2015,41.5
7,9/4/2015,36.75
8,9/4/2015,32.5
9,9/4/2015,30
10,9/4/2015,28.5
11,9/4/2015,22.5
1,9/11/2015,40
2,9/11/2015,38.75
3,9/11/2015,36
4,9/11/2015,34.5
5,9/11/2015,38.5
6,9/11/2015,32.75
7,9/11/2015,31
8,9/11/2015,30
9,9/11/2015,29
10,9/11/2015,28.75
11,9/11/2015,25
1,9/18/2015,26.75
2,9/18/2015,28.75
3,9/18/2015,32
4,9/18/2015,38.75
5,9/18/2015,41
6,9/18/2015,44
7,9/18/2015,38.5
8,9/18/2015,36
9,9/18/2015,38.5
Text files contain no formatting codes. A comma separated file (.csv) contains a comma separating each field. During the import, Access creates a new field when each comma is encountered. You can specify the data type for the field during the import process or modify the table in Design view after the table is imported.

Quick Steps

Import Data from a Comma Separated Text File

1. Click EXTERNAL DATA tab.
2. Click Import text file button.
3. Click Browse button.
4. If necessary, navigate to drive and/or folder.
5. Double-click .csv file name.
6. Click OK.
7. Click Next.
8. If applicable, click *First Row Contains Field Names* check box.
9. Click Next.
10. Choose primary key field.
11. Click Next.
12. Click Finish.

Save Import Specifications

1. At last Get External Data dialog box, click *Save import steps*.
2. If necessary, edit name in *Save as* text box.
3. Type description in *Description* text box.
4. Click Save Import button.

To import a text file into Access, click the Import text file button (which displays the text *Text File*) in the Import & Link group on the EXTERNAL DATA tab. Access opens the Get External Data - Text File dialog box, which is similar to the dialog box used to import data from another Access database. When importing a text file, Access adds an append option in addition to the import and link options in the *Specify how and where you want to store the data in the current database* section. Click the Browse button to navigate to the location of the source file and double-click the source file name to launch the Import Text Wizard, which guides you through the import process using four dialog boxes.

text file

Saving and Repeating Import Specifications

You can save import specifications for an import routine you are likely to repeat. The last step in the Get External Data - Text File dialog box displays a *Save import steps* check box. Click the check box to expand the dialog box to display the *Save as* and *Description* text boxes. Type a unique name to assign to the import routine and a brief description of the steps. Click the Save Import button to complete the import and store the specifications. Click the *Create Outlook Task* check box if you want to create an Outlook task that you can set up as a recurring item for an import or export operation that you repeat at fixed intervals.

Project 2d Importing Data from a Comma Separated Text File and Saving Import Specifications

Part 4 of 4

1. With **AL2-C8-RSRTechPay.accdb** open, select a text file to import that contains the weekly hours billed for each technician for the month of September 2015 by completing the following steps:
   a. If necessary, click the EXTERNAL DATA tab.
   b. Click the Import text file button (displays the text *Text File*) in the Import & Link group.
   c. At the Get External Data - Text File dialog box, click the Browse button.
   d. At the File Open dialog box, navigate to the AL2C8 folder on your storage medium, if necessary.
   e. Double-click the file named ***RSRTechHrsSep2015.csv***.
   f. With *Import the source data into a new table in the current database* already selected, click OK. This launches the Import Text Wizard.

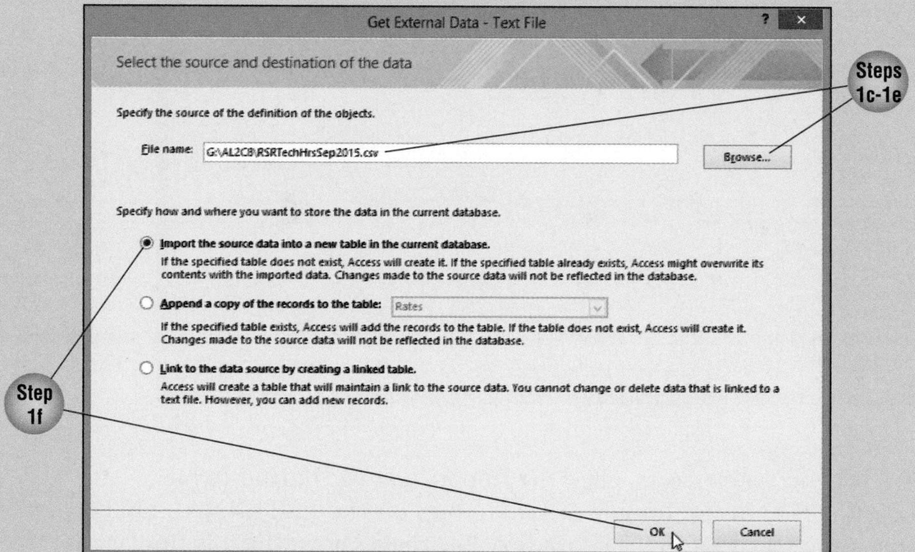

2. Import the comma separated data using the Import Text Wizard by completing the following steps:
   a. At the first Import Text Wizard dialog box, with *Delimited* selected as the format, notice that the preview window in the lower half of the dialog box displays a sample of the data in the source text file. Delimited files use commas or tabs as separators while fixed width files use spaces. Click Next.

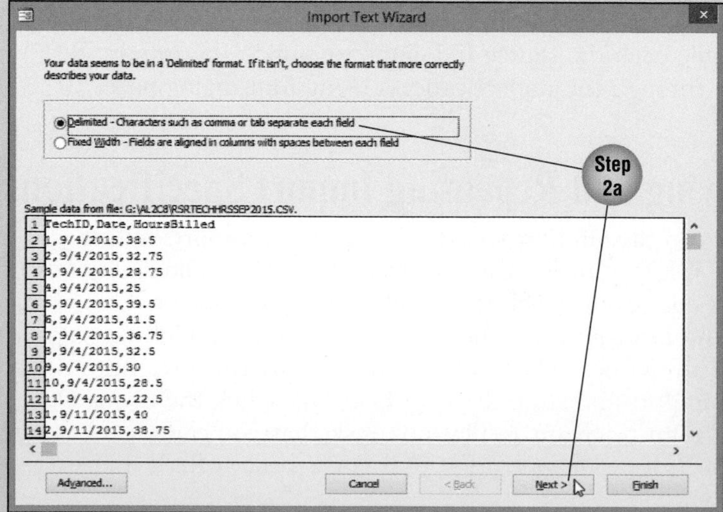

b. At the second Import Text Wizard dialog box with *Comma* already selected as the delimiter, click the *First Row Contains Field Names* check box. Notice that the preview section already shows the data set in columns, similar to a table datasheet. Click Next.

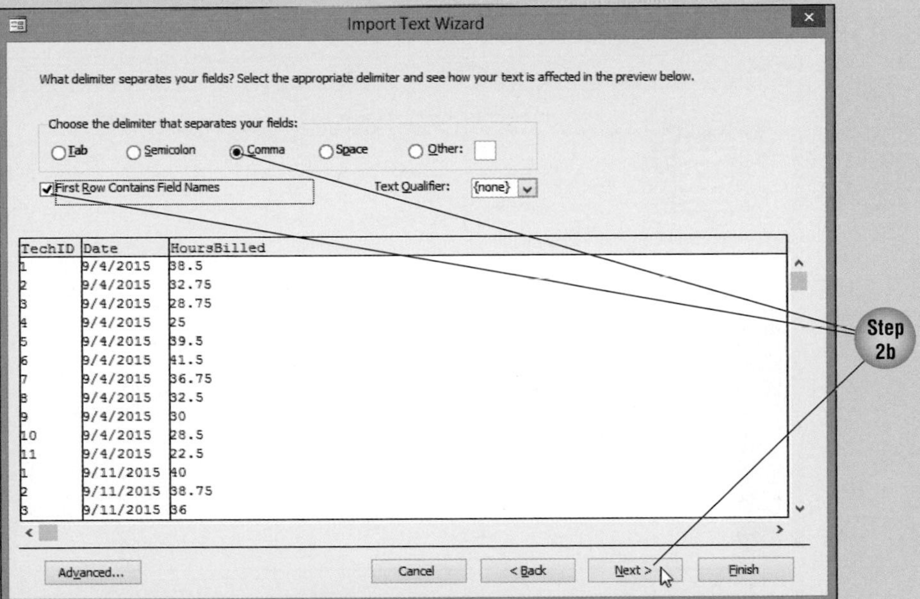

c. At the third Import Text Wizard dialog box, with the *TechID* column in the preview section selected, click the down-pointing arrow next to *Data Type* in the *Field Options* section and then click *Short Text* at the drop-down list.

d. Click Next.

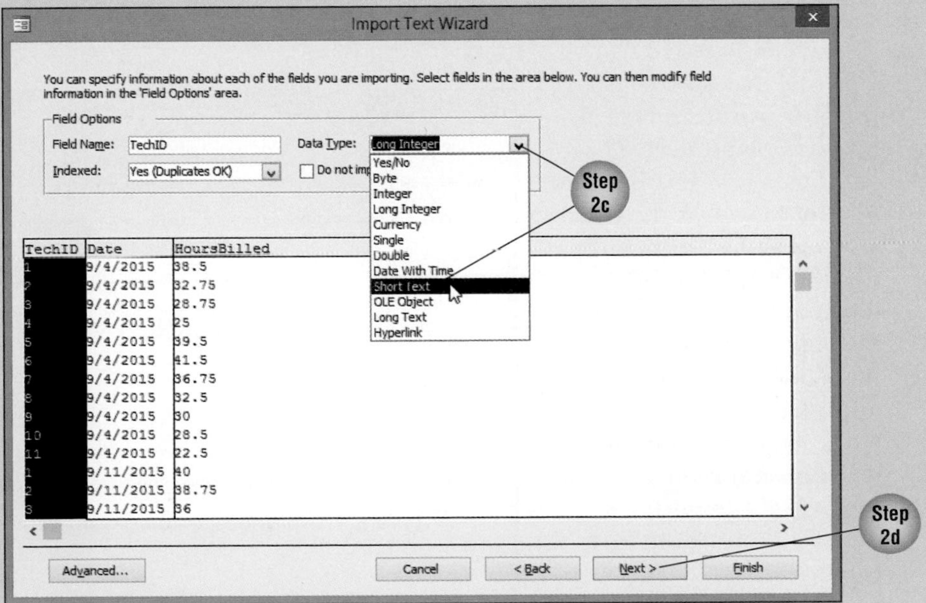

e. At the fourth Import Text Wizard dialog box, with *Let Access add primary key* already selected, notice that Access has added a column in the preview section with the field title *ID*. The column added by Access is defined as an AutoNumber field, in which each row in the text file is numbered sequentially to make the row unique. The ID for any new record added to the table will automatically be incremented by one. Click Next.

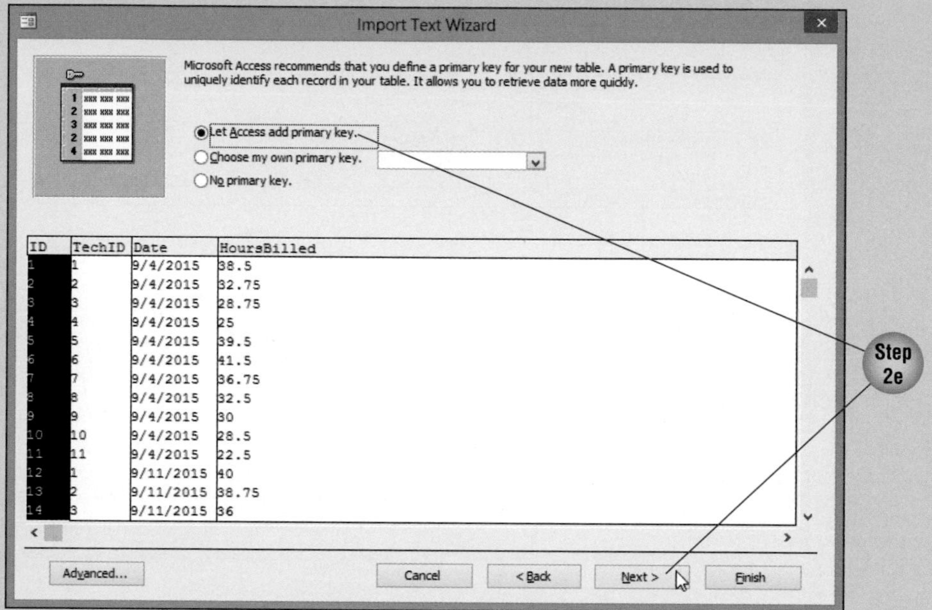

f. At the last Import Text Wizard dialog box, with *RSRTechHrsSep2015* entered in the *Import to Table* text box, click Finish.

3. Save the import specifications in case you want to run this import again by completing the following steps:
   a. At the Get External Data - Text File dialog box, click the *Save import steps* check box. This causes the *Save as* and *Description* text boxes to appear, as well as the *Create an Outlook Task* section. By default, Access creates a name in the *Save as* text box and *Import* precedes the file name containing the imported data.
   b. Click in the *Description* text box and then type **CSV file with weekly hours billed by technicians**.
   c. Click the Save Import button.

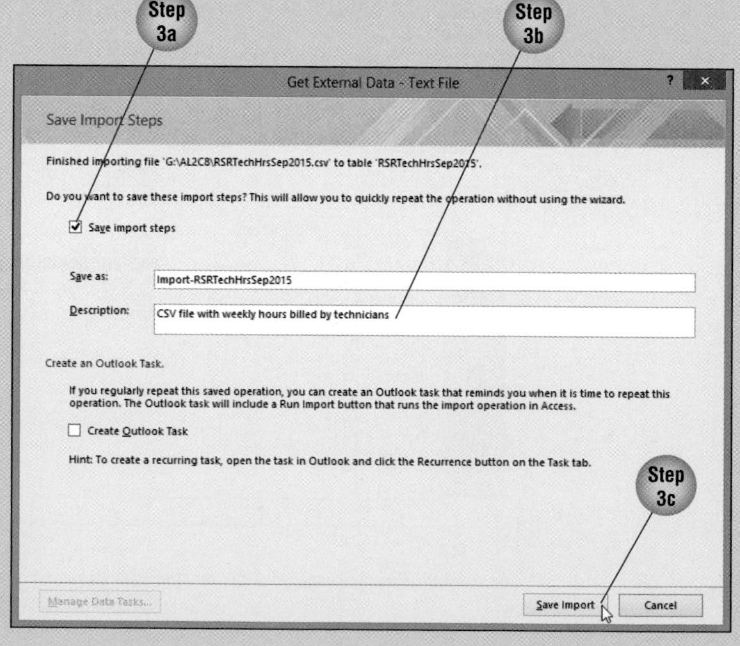

4. Double-click *RSRTechHoursSep2015* in the Tables group in the Navigation pane to open the table datasheet.
5. Print the datasheet with the bottom margin set to 0.5 inch and then close the datasheet.
6. Close **AL2-C8-RSRTechPay.accdb**.

Once an import routine has been saved, you can repeat the import process by opening the Manage Data Tasks dialog box with the Saved Imports tab selected, as shown in Figure 8.8. To do this, click the EXTERNAL DATA tab and then click the Saved Imports button in the Import & Link group. Click the desired import name and then click the Run button to instruct Access to repeat the import operation.

Saved Imports

Figure 8.8 Manage Data Tasks Dialog Box with Saved Imports Tab Selected

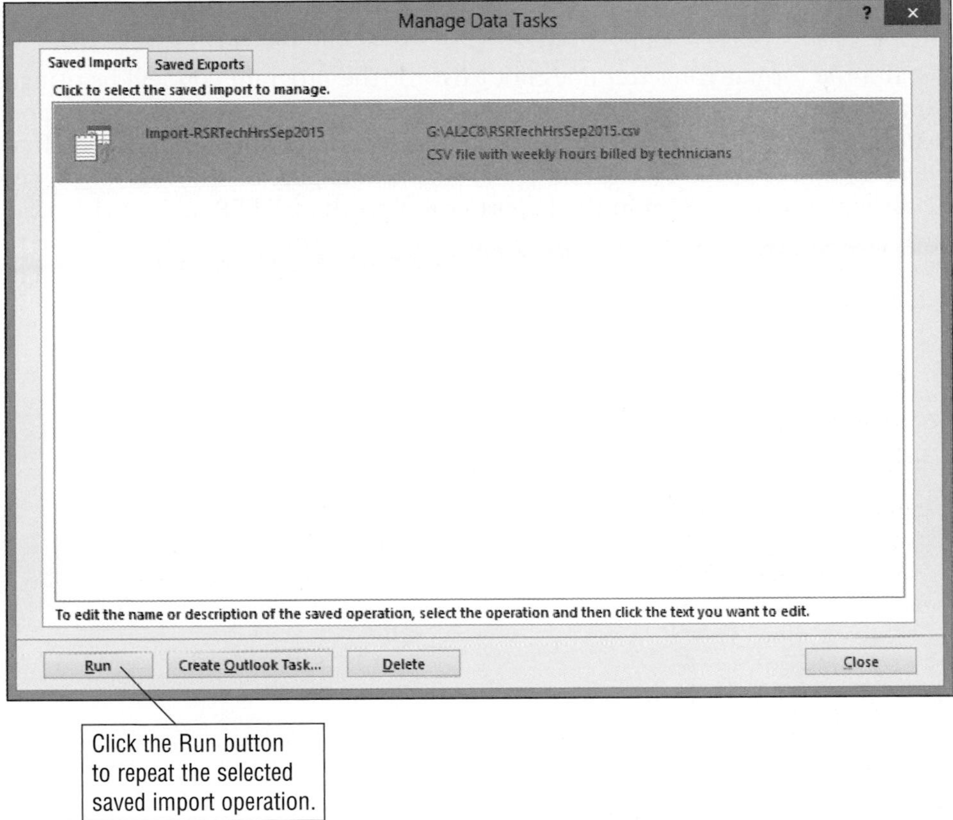

Project 3 Export Access Data to a Text File — 2 Parts

You will export a query as a comma delimited text file and another query as a tab delimited text file, including saving the second export steps so you can repeat the export operation.

Quick Steps

Export Data to a Text File

1. Select object in Navigation pane.
2. Click EXTERNAL DATA tab.
3. Click Export to text file button.
4. Click Browse button.
5. If necessary, navigate to desired drive and/or folder.
6. If necessary, change file name.
7. Click Save button.
8. Click OK.
9. Click Next.
10. Choose delimiter character.
11. If appropriate, click *Include Field Names on First Row* check box.
12. If appropriate, choose *Text Qualifier* character.
13. Click Next.
14. If necessary, change *Export to File* path and/or name.
15. Click Finish.
16. Click Close button.

Export to text file

Exporting Access Data to a Text File

The Export group on the EXTERNAL DATA tab contains buttons you can use to export Access data from a table, query, form, or report to other applications, such as Excel and Word. If you need to work with data from Access in a program that is not part of the Microsoft Office suite, click the More button in the Export group to see if a file format converter exists for the application you will be using. For example, the More button contains options to export in Word, SharePoint List, ODBC Database, and HTML Document format. (Unlike previous versions, Access 2013 does not support exporting to dBase file formats.)

If a file format converter does not exist for the program you will be using, export the data as a text file, since most applications recognize and can import a text data file. Access includes the Export Text Wizard, which is launched after you select an object in the Navigation pane, click the Export to text file button (which displays the text *Text File*) in the Export group on the EXTERNAL DATA tab, and then specify the name of the exported text file and where to store it. The steps in the Export Text Wizard are similar to those in the Import Text Wizard, which you used in Project 2d.

Project 3a Exporting a Query as a Text File — Part 1 of 2

1. Display the Open dialog box and then use cut and paste to move **AL2-C8-RSRCompServ .accdb** back to the AL2C8 folder on your storage medium.
2. Open **AL2-C8-RSRCompServ.accdb** and, if necessary, enable the content.
3. Export the TotalWorkOrders query as a text file by completing the following steps:
   a. Select the TotalWorkOrders query in the Navigation pane.
   b. Click the EXTERNAL DATA tab.
   c. Click the Export to text file button (which displays the text *Text File*) in the Export group.

d. At the Export - Text File dialog box, click the Browse button.
e. At the File Save dialog box, navigate to the AL2C8 folder on your storage medium, if necessary.
f. With the default file name *TotalWorkOrders.txt* in the *File name* text box, click the Save button.
g. Click OK.

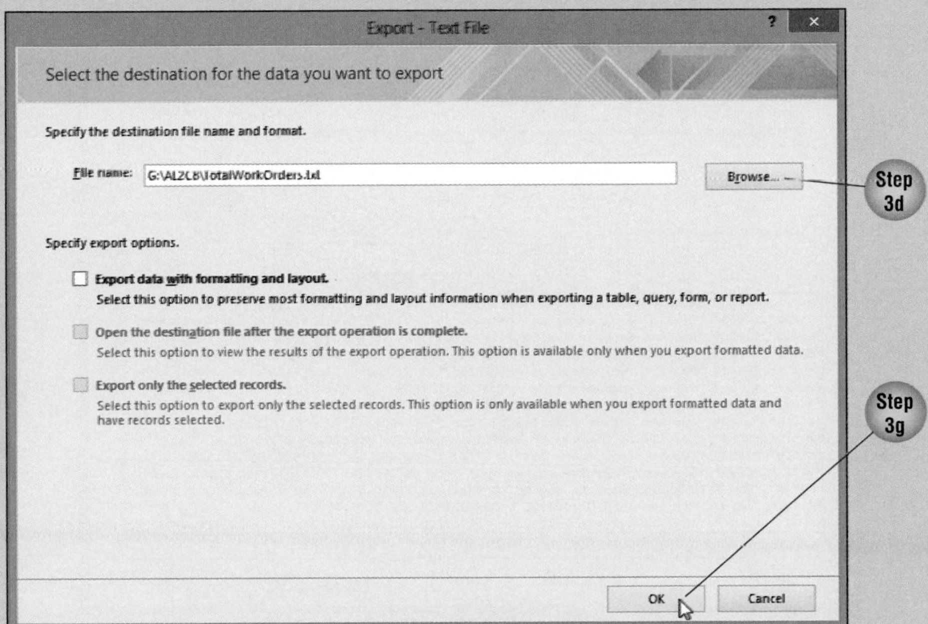

h. At the first Export Text Wizard dialog box, with *Delimited* selected as the format, notice in the preview section of the dialog box that commas separate the fields and that data in a field defined with the Text data type is enclosed in quotation marks. Click Next.

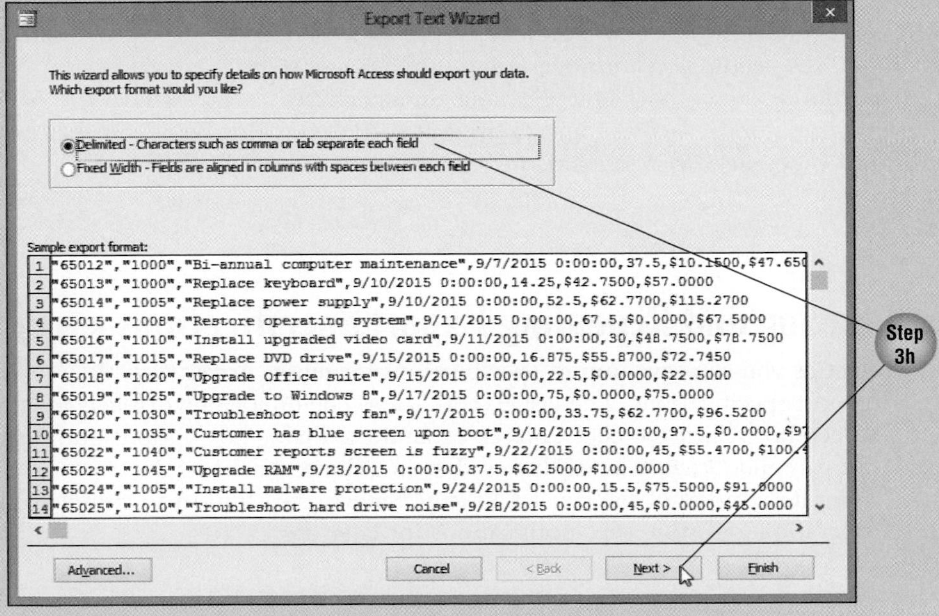

i. At the second Export Text Wizard dialog box, with *Comma* selected as the delimiter character that separates the fields, click the *Include Field Names on First Row* check box to insert a check mark. Access adds a row containing the field names to the top of the data in the preview section. Each field name is enclosed in quotation marks.

j. Click the down-pointing arrow next to the *Text Qualifier* option box and then click *{none}* at the drop-down list. Access removes all of the quotation marks from the text data in the preview section.

k. Click Next.

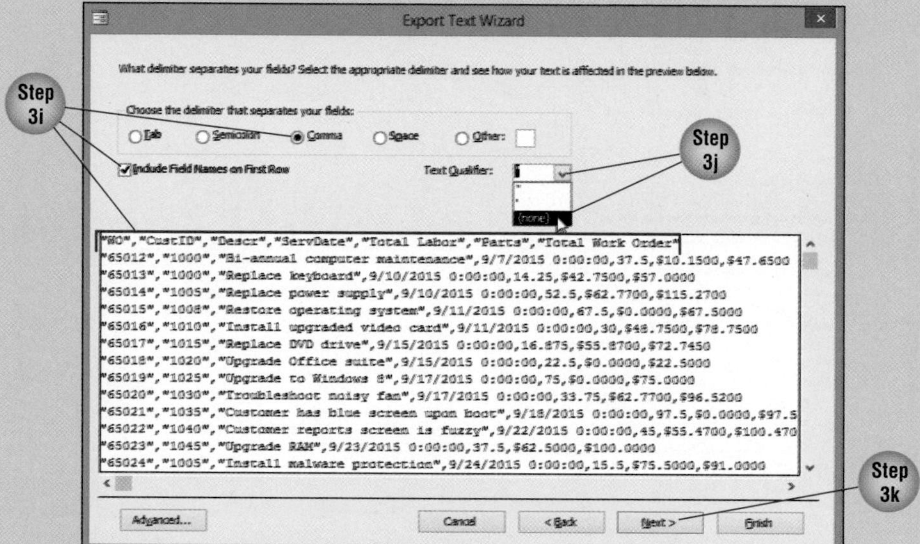

l. At the last Export Text Wizard dialog box, with *[d]:\AL2C8\TotalWorkOrders.txt* (where *[d]* is the drive for your storage medium) entered in the *Export to File* text box, click Finish.

m. Click the Close button to close the dialog box without saving the export steps.

4. Open Notepad and view the text file by completing the following steps:
   a. Move your mouse to the bottom left corner of the screen and then click the Start button. At the Start screen, start typing **notepad**. When *Notepad* displays below the *Apps* heading, press Enter. (Depending on your operating system, these steps may vary).
   b. At a blank Notepad window, click File and then click *Open*. Navigate to the AL2C8 folder on your storage medium and then double-click the **TotalWorkOrders.txt**.
5. Click File and then click *Print* to print the exported text file.
6. Exit Notepad.

Saving and Repeating Export Specifications

Quick Steps

Save Export Specifications
1. At last Export - Text File dialog box, click *Save export steps* check box.
2. Verify file name.
3. Type description in *Description* text box.
4. Click Save Export button.

Just as you can save import specifications for reuse, Access also allows you to save export specifications. The last Export - Text File dialog box displays a *Save export steps* check box. Click the check box to expand the dialog box options and display the *Save as* and *Description* text boxes. Type a unique name for the export routine and a brief description of the steps. Click the Save Export button to complete the export operation and store the specifications for later use.

Project 3b Exporting a Query as a Text File and Saving Export Steps Part 2 of 2

1. With **AL2-C8-RSRCompServ.accdb** open, export the TotalLabor query as a text file using tabs as the delimiter characters by completing the following steps:
   a. Select the TotalLabor query in the Navigation pane.
   b. Click the Export to text file button in the Export group on the EXTERNAL DATA tab.
   c. With *[d]:\AL2C8\TotalLabor.txt* (where *[d]* is the drive for your storage medium) entered in the *File name* text box, click OK.
   d. Complete the steps of the Export Text Wizard as follows:
      1) With *Delimited* selected in the first dialog box, click Next.
      2) At the second dialog box, choose *Tab* as the delimiter character, click the *Include Field Names on First Row* check box to insert a check mark, change the *Text Qualifier* option to *{none}*, and then click Next.
      3) Click Finish.

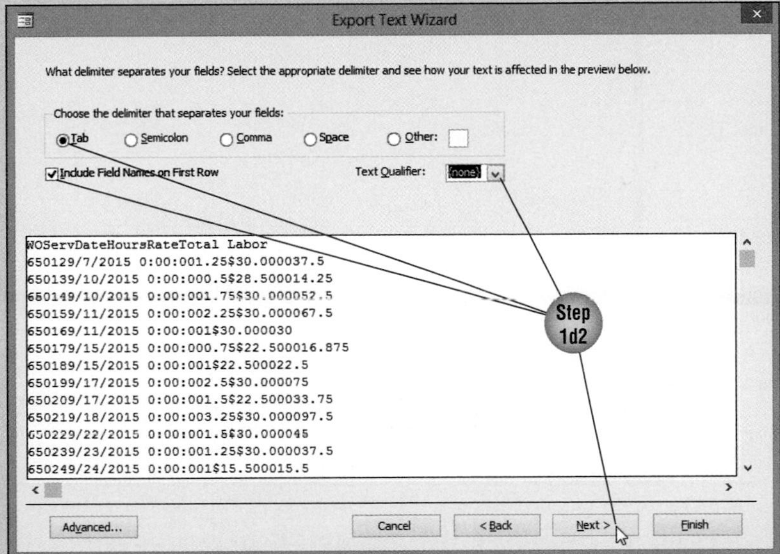

   e. At the Export - Text File dialog box, click the *Save export steps* check box to insert a check mark.
   f. Click in the *Description* text box and then type **TotalLabor query for RSR Computer Service work orders as a text file.**
   g. Click the Save Export button.
2. Start Notepad.
3. At a blank Notepad window, open **TotalLabor.txt**.
4. Print **TotalLabor.txt** and then exit Notepad.

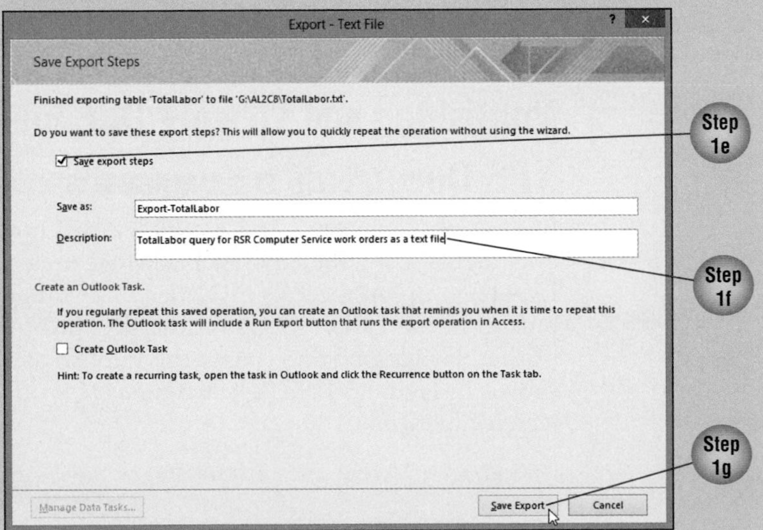

Saved Exports

Once you have saved an export routine, you can repeat the export process by clicking the Saved Exports button in the Export group on the EXTERNAL DATA tab. This opens the Manage Data Tasks dialog box with the Saved Exports tab selected, as shown in Figure 8.9. Click the desired export name in the dialog box and then click the Run button to instruct Access to repeat the export operation.

Figure 8.9 Manage Data Tasks Dialog Box with Saved Exports Tab Selected

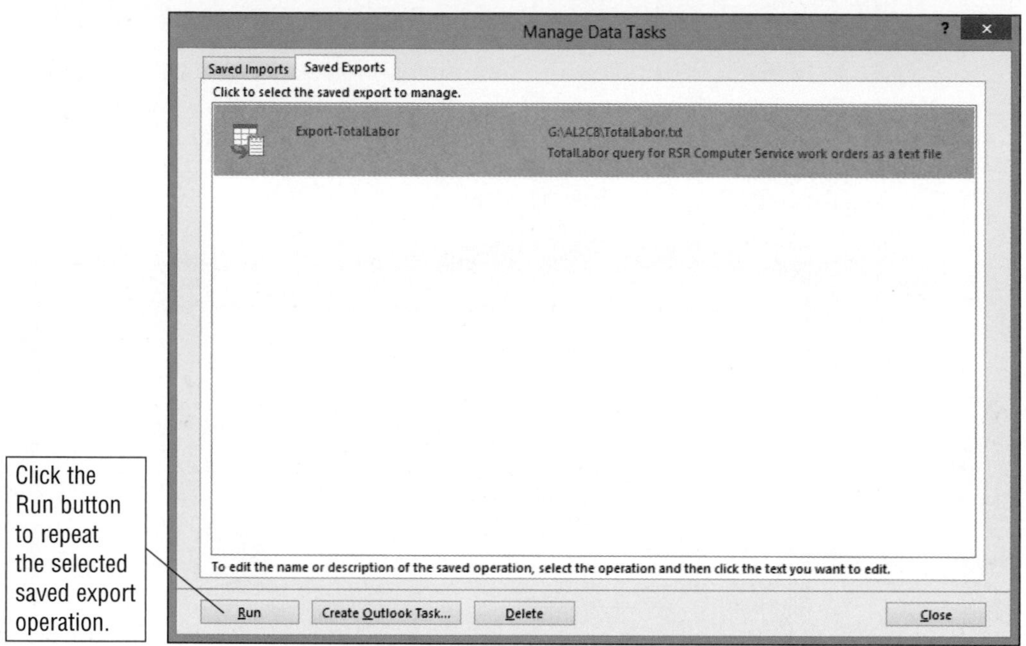

Project 4 Export a Database Object as an XPS Document — 1 Part

You will export and publish a report as an XPS file.

Publishing and Viewing Database Objects as XPS Documents

PDF or XPS

In Level 1, Chapters 7 and 8, you learned how to export database objects as PDF documents using the Save As backstage area and the PDF or XPS button in the Export group on the EXTERNAL DATA tab. Recall that clicking the PDF or XPS button in the Export group on the EXTERNAL DATA tab with an object selected in the Navigation pane causes the Publish as PDF or XPS dialog box to open, as shown in Figure 8.10. Use the *Save as type* option box at this dialog box to choose which file format you want to use.

Figure 8.10 Publish as PDF or XPS Dialog Box

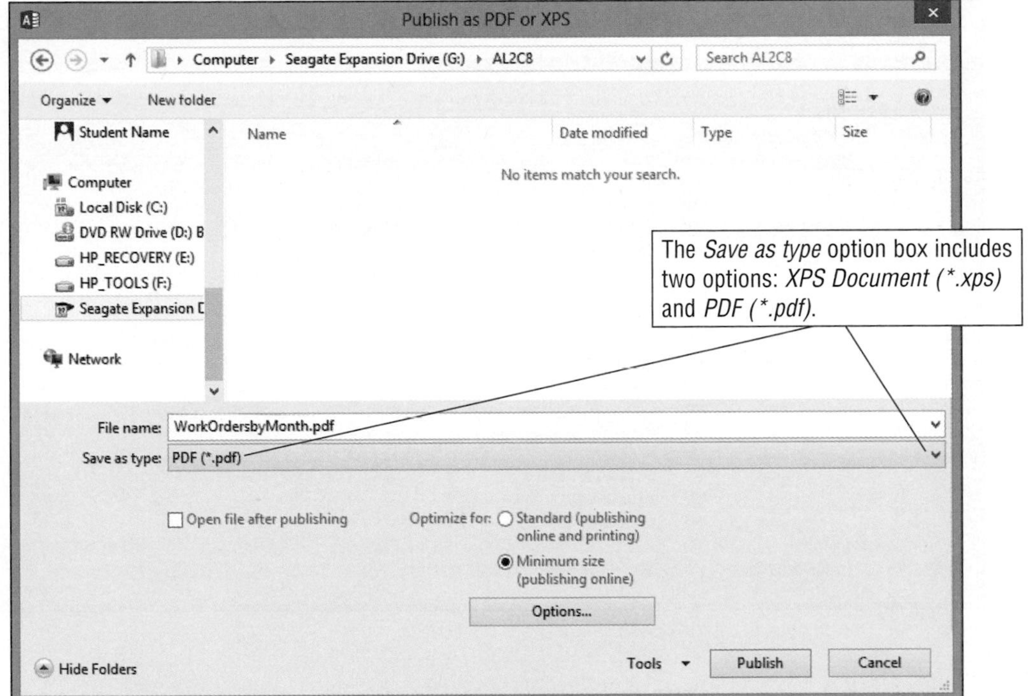

Recall from Level 1, Chapter 7 that XPS stands for *XML paper specification*, which is a fixed-layout format with all formatting preserved. This means that when a file is shared electronically and viewed or printed, the recipients of the file see the formatting as it appeared in Access and cannot easily change the data. The *Save as type* option box in the Publish as PDF or XPS dialog box also includes the *PDF* option. PDF stands for *portable document format*, which is another fixed-layout format that preserves all formatting and is used for file-sharing purposes.

Once you have selected the desired file format in the Publish as PDF or XPS dialog box, navigate to the desired drive and/or folder in which the file should be stored and then change the file name, if necessary. Click the Publish button to create the file.

Similar to how you need the Adobe Reader program to view PDF files, you need a viewer to read an XPS document. The viewer is provided by Microsoft and is included with Windows Vista, Windows 7, and Windows 8. The WorkOrdersbyMonth.xps document created in Project 4 is shown in an XPS Viewer window in Figure 8.11 on the next page.

Quick Steps

Publish an Object as an XPS Document

1. Select object in Navigation pane.
2. Click EXTERNAL DATA tab.
3. Click PDF or XPS button.
4. If necessary, navigate to desired drive and/or folder.
5. If necessary, change file name.
6. Change *Save as type* to *XPS*.
7. Click Publish button.
8. Click Close button.

Figure 8.11 WorkOrdersbyMonth.xps Opened in XPS Viewer Window

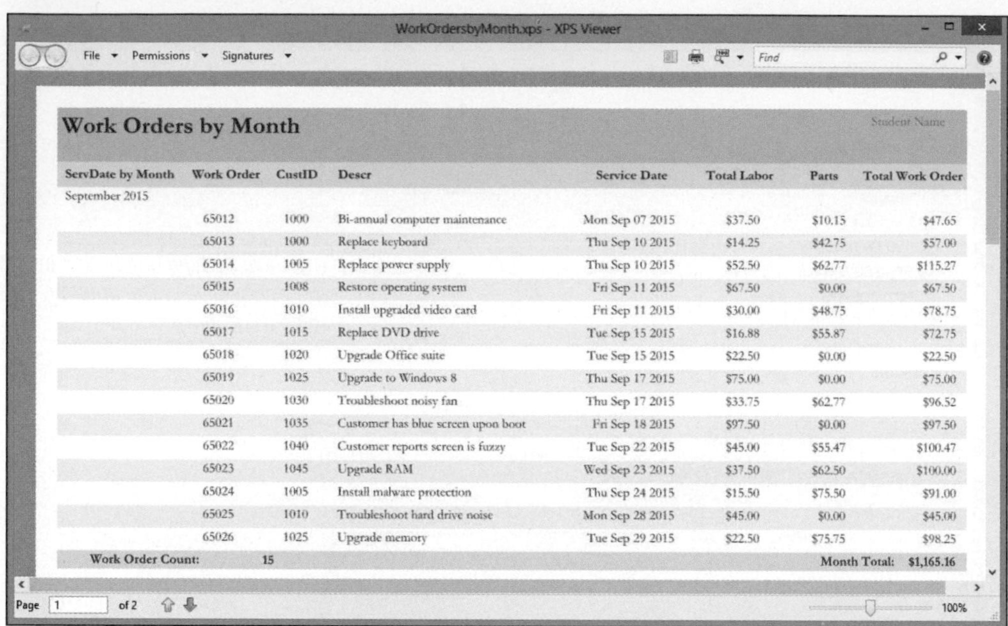

WorkOrdersbyMonth.xps - XPS Viewer

Work Orders by Month Student Name

ServDate by Month	Work Order	CustID	Descr	Service Date	Total Labor	Parts	Total Work Order
September 2015							
	65012	1000	Bi-annual computer maintenance	Mon Sep 07 2015	$37.50	$10.15	$47.65
	65013	1000	Replace keyboard	Thu Sep 10 2015	$14.25	$42.75	$57.00
	65014	1005	Replace power supply	Thu Sep 10 2015	$52.50	$62.77	$115.27
	65015	1008	Restore operating system	Fri Sep 11 2015	$67.50	$0.00	$67.50
	65016	1010	Install upgraded video card	Fri Sep 11 2015	$30.00	$48.75	$78.75
	65017	1015	Replace DVD drive	Tue Sep 15 2015	$16.88	$55.87	$72.75
	65018	1020	Upgrade Office suite	Tue Sep 15 2015	$22.50	$0.00	$22.50
	65019	1025	Upgrade to Windows 8	Thu Sep 17 2015	$75.00	$0.00	$75.00
	65020	1030	Troubleshoot noisy fan	Thu Sep 17 2015	$33.75	$62.77	$96.52
	65021	1035	Customer has blue screen upon boot	Fri Sep 18 2015	$97.50	$0.00	$97.50
	65022	1040	Customer reports screen is fuzzy	Tue Sep 22 2015	$45.00	$55.47	$100.47
	65023	1045	Upgrade RAM	Wed Sep 23 2015	$37.50	$62.50	$100.00
	65024	1005	Install malware protection	Thu Sep 24 2015	$15.50	$75.50	$91.00
	65025	1010	Troubleshoot hard drive noise	Mon Sep 28 2015	$45.00	$0.00	$45.00
	65026	1025	Upgrade memory	Tue Sep 29 2015	$22.50	$75.75	$98.25
Work Order Count:	15					Month Total:	$1,165.16

Page 1 of 2 100%

Project 4 Exporting a Report as an XPS Document Part 1 of 1

1. With **AL2-C8-RSRCompServ.accdb** open, export the WorkOrdersbyMonth report as an XPS document by completing the following steps:
   a. Select the WorkOrdersbyMonth report in the Navigation pane.
   b. Click the PDF or XPS button in the Export group on the EXTERNAL DATA tab.
   c. At the Publish as PDF or XPS dialog box, navigate to the AL2C8 folder, if necessary.
   d. With *WorkOrdersbyMonth* entered in the *File name* text box, publish the report as an XPS document by completing the following steps:
      1) If necessary, click the *Save as type* option and then click *XPS Document (*.xps)*.
      2) If necessary, click the *Open file after publishing* check box to remove the check mark.
      3) Click the Publish button.

Step 1d1

File name: WorkOrdersbyMonth.xps
Save as type: XPS Document (*.xps)
Open file after publishing
Optimize for: Standard (publishing online and printing)
Minimum size (publishing online)
Options...
Step 1d2
Step 1d3
Hide Folders
Tools
Publish
Cancel

   e. Click the Close button at the Export - XPS dialog box to close the dialog box without saving the export steps.
2. Click the Close button in the upper right hand corner to close Access.

Project 5 Create a Database in an Older Format — 1 Part

You will create a database in an older format.

Creating a Database in an Older Format

In Level 1, Chapter 7, you learned that Access 2013, Access 2010, and Access 2007 databases save with the file extension *.accdb* and cannot be opened with earlier versions of Access. If you need to open one of these databases in an earlier version of Access, you will need to save the database in an earlier version by clicking the *Microsoft Access Database (2002-2003)(*.mdb)* button or the *Access 2000 Database (*.mdb)* button in the *Save Database As* section of the Save As backstage area. The database saves with the .mdb file extension. If you know before you create a database that you need to save it using the .mdb file extension, you can create the database in an older format rather then resaving it later.

To create a database in an older format, click the FILE tab. At the Access 2013 opening screen, click the *Blank desktop database* template and then navigate to your storage medium. Type the name of the database and then click the *Save as type* option. Choose *Microsoft Access Databases (2002-2003 format)(*.mdb)* or *Microsoft Access Databases (2000 format) (*.mdb)*.

If most of your databases need to be created in an earlier version of Access, consider changing the default file format to an earlier version. The default can be changed in the *Default File format for Blank Database* option box in the General section of the Access Options dialog box.

Project 5 Creating a Database in an Older Format — Part 1 of 1

1. Open Access.
2. At the Access 2013 opening screen, complete the following steps to create a new database in the 2002-2003 format:
   a. Click the *Blank desktop database* template.
   b. At the Blank desktop database window that displays, click the Browse button, navigate to the AL2C8 folder on your storage medium, select the current text in the *File name* text box, and then type **AL2-C8-RSR2003**.
   c. Click the *Save as type* option, click *Microsoft Access Databases (2002-2003 format)(*.mdb)*, and then click OK.
   d. Click the Create button located below the *File Name* text box.
3. Close **AL2-C8-RSR2003.mdb** and then close Access.

In this chapter, you have learned to back up and restore data, secure an Access database, import and merge data from another Access database, and import and export using a text file format to exchange data between Access and non-Microsoft programs. To distribute Access data with formatting preserved in a non-editable format, you learned how to export and publish an object as a PDF or XPS document. Finally, you learned how to create a database in an earlier version of Access.

Chapter Summary

- Use options at the Save As backstage area to create backup database files on a regular basis. This will help to minimize any data loss due to system failures or design mistakes.
- Create a backup copy of your database before making any major changes to the database.
- An ACCDE database file is a locked-down version of a database, in which objects are prevented from being opened in Design view or Layout view. Create an ACCDE database file at the Save As backstage area.
- Open the Access Options dialog box, click *Trust Center* in the left pane, and then click the Trust Center Settings button to view and/or modify Trust Center options.
- An object in another Access database can be imported into the active database using the Import Access database button in the Import & Link group on the EXTERNAL DATA tab.
- If the source object is a table, you can choose to import or link to the source table.
- In a linked table, the data is not copied into the active database—it resides only in the source database.
- You can edit source data in a linked table in the source database or in the destination database.
- Use an import routine if the source data is not likely to require changes or updates.
- Link to source data that requires frequent changes to reduce the potential for making data entry mistakes or missing updates.
- You may also decide to link to a source table that is shared among several different databases within an organization.
- Access stores the full path to the source database when a table is linked. If you move the location of the source database, the links will need to be refreshed.
- A text file is often used to exchange data between dissimilar programs, because a text file is recognized by nearly all applications.
- Import a text file into an Access database by clicking the Import text file button in the Import & Link group on the EXTERNAL DATA tab.
- When a text file is selected for import, Access launches the Text Import Wizard, which guides you through the steps to import the text into a table.
- If an import operation is repeated often, consider saving the import steps so that you can run the import routine without having to perform each step every time you import.
- Open the Manage Data Tasks dialog box to run a saved import by clicking the Saved Imports button in the Import & Link group on the EXTERNAL DATA tab.

- Export Access data in a text file format using the Export Text Wizard by clicking the Export to text file button in the Export group on the EXTERNAL DATA tab.
- Within the Export Text Wizard, you are prompted to choose the text format, delimiter character, field names, text qualifier symbols, export path, and file name.
- You can save export steps at the last Export - Text File dialog box to repeat an export operation.
- Click the Saved Exports button in the Export group on the EXTERNAL DATA tab to run a saved export routine.
- Access includes a feature that allows you to save an object as an XPS or PDF document to distribute Access data with formatting preserved in a non-editable format.
- Publish an object by selecting the object name in the Navigation pane and then clicking the PDF or XPS button in the Export group on the EXTERNAL DATA tab.
- Create a database in a previous version of Access using the *Save as type* option in the File New Database dialog box.

Commands Review

FEATURE	RIBBON TAB, GROUP	BUTTON
create ACCDE file	FILE, *Save As*	
export data as text file	EXTERNAL DATA, Export	
import or link data from Access database	EXTERNAL DATA, Import & Link	
import data from text file	EXTERNAL DATA, Import & Link	
Linked Table Manager	EXTERNAL DATA, Import & Link	
export object as XPS document	EXTERNAL DATA, Export	
saved exports	EXTERNAL DATA, Export	
saved imports	EXTERNAL DATA, Import & Link	

Concepts Check Test Your Knowledge

Completion: In the space provided at the right, indicate the correct term, command, or number.

1. Do this on a regular basis to minimize the risk of data loss due to system failures or design mistakes. ____________________
2. Save a database as this type of file to disallow Design view and Layout view for the database objects. ____________________
3. View and/or change the macro security setting at this dialog box. ____________________
4. Click this button at the Import Objects dialog box to choose whether or not relationships between tables will be imported. ____________________
5. Click this option at the Get External Data - Access Database dialog box to create a table in which changes to data are automatically updated in the source or destination database. ____________________
6. Data that will not likely be changed should be brought into the active database from another database using this method. ____________________
7. Data that will be updated frequently should be brought into the active database from another database using this method. ____________________
8. If the location of a source database has moved, refresh the link to the source table by opening this dialog box. ____________________
9. This type of file format is used to exchange data between programs for which an application-specific file format converter is not available. ____________________
10. A file in which fields are separated by commas has this file extension. ____________________
11. Click this check box at the last Get External Data dialog box to store the steps used in the import process for use of the routine at a future date. ____________________
12. The Export Text Wizard is launched from this button in the Export group on the EXTERNAL DATA tab. ____________________
13. XPS is a file format that stands for this type of document specification. ____________________

Skills Check Assess Your Performance

Assessment 1

IMPORT AND LINK OBJECTS FROM ANOTHER ACCESS DATABASE

SNAP Grade It

1. Open **AL2-C8-ViewItStock.accdb** and enable the content.
2. Using **AL2-C8-ViewIt.accdb** as the data source, integrate the following objects into the active database:
   a. Import the WebProducts form.
   b. Link to the WebProducts, WebOrders, and WebOrderDetails tables.
3. Display the Relationships window, add the WebProducts table, and then create a relationship between the WebProducts and WebProductsCost tables using the *WebProdID* field. Save and close the Relationships window.
4. Modify the WebProducts form as follows:
   a. Open the form in Design view.
   b. Delete the *Retail Value* label and text box control objects at the bottom of the form. This will leave the form with four fields: *Product ID*, *Product*, *In Stock*, and *Selling Price*.
   c. Display the Field List task pane and show all of the tables in the pane. Expand the field list for the WebProductsCost table.
   d. Add the *CostPrice* field below the *Selling Price* field in the form.
   e. Align, resize, and format the field as necessary so the cost price displays similarly to the selling price.
   f. Change the form title to *Inventory Stock and Pricing*.
5. Save the revised form, print the first record, and then close the form.
6. Open the WebProdCostsWithSupp query in Design view and modify it as follows:
   a. Add the WebProducts table to the query.
   b. Add the *SellPrice* field to the query design grid, placing the field between the *Product* and *CostPrice* columns.
   c. Add a calculated column at the right of the *CostPrice* column named *GrossProfit* that subtracts the cost price from the selling price. Change the caption to *Gross Profit*.
7. Save the revised query and then run the query.
8. Print the query in landscape orientation and then close the query.

Assessment 2

IMPORT A TEXT FILE

SNAP Grade It

1. With **AL2-C8-ViewItStock.accdb** open, make a backup copy and then append records from a text file using the following information:
   - Name the backup database file **AL2-C8-ViewItStock_yyyy-mm-dd.accdb**, where *yyyy-mm-dd* represents today's date. Save this database in your DatabaseBackUps folder, created in Project 1a.
   - The data source file is named **WebProducts.csv**.
   - Append a copy of the records to the end of the existing WebProductsCost table.
   - Save the import steps using the default name and type the following description: **Import of new classic video titles from WebProducts.csv**.
2. Open the WebProductsCost table and print the table datasheet.
3. Close the datasheet.
4. Close **AL2-C8-ViewItStock.accdb**.

Assessment 3

EXPORT AND PUBLISH ACCESS DATA

1. Open **AL2-C8-ViewIt.accdb** and enable the content.
2. Export the CustWebOrders query to a comma delimited text file using the following information:
   - Include the field names and remove the quotation marks.
   - Save the export steps and type the following description: **Export the customers' web orders to a text file**.
3. Open Notepad and then open and print **CustWebOrders.txt**.
4. Exit Notepad.

Assessment 4

SECURE THE DATABASE

1. With **AL2-C8-ViewIt.accdb** open, save a copy of the database as an ACCDE file in the same folder and using the same file name.
2. Close **AL2-C8-ViewIt.accdb**.
3. Open **AL2-C8-ViewIt.accde**.
4. Insert a screenshot of the database window in a new Microsoft Word document using the Screenshot button in the Illustrations group on the INSERT tab or the Print Screen key with the Paste feature. Type your name a few lines below the screenshot and add any other identifying information as instructed. Save the Microsoft Word document and name it **AL2-C8-A4-ViewItACCDE.docx**. Print **AL2-C8-A4-ViewItACCDE.docx** and then exit Word.
5. Close the **AL2-C8-ViewIt.accde** database.

Visual Benchmark Demonstrate Your Proficiency

ANALYZE RESERVATION DATABASE

1. Open **AL2-C8-PawsParadise.accdb** and enable the content.
2. Using **AL2-C8-PawsGroomers.accdb** as the data source, integrate the following objects into the active database:
   a. Import the Groomers form.
   b. Link to the Groomers table.
3. Modify the Groomers form as shown in Figure 8.12. Search using the phrase *pet grooming* to find the clip art.
4. Save a copy of the database as an ACCDE database.
5. Close **AL2-C8-PawsParadise.accdb**.
6. Open **AL2-C8-PawsParadise.accde**. Check with your instructor for instructions on whether to print a screen image of the database window, as shown below.
7. Close **AL2-C8-PawsParadise.accde**.

Figure 8.12 Visual Benchmark

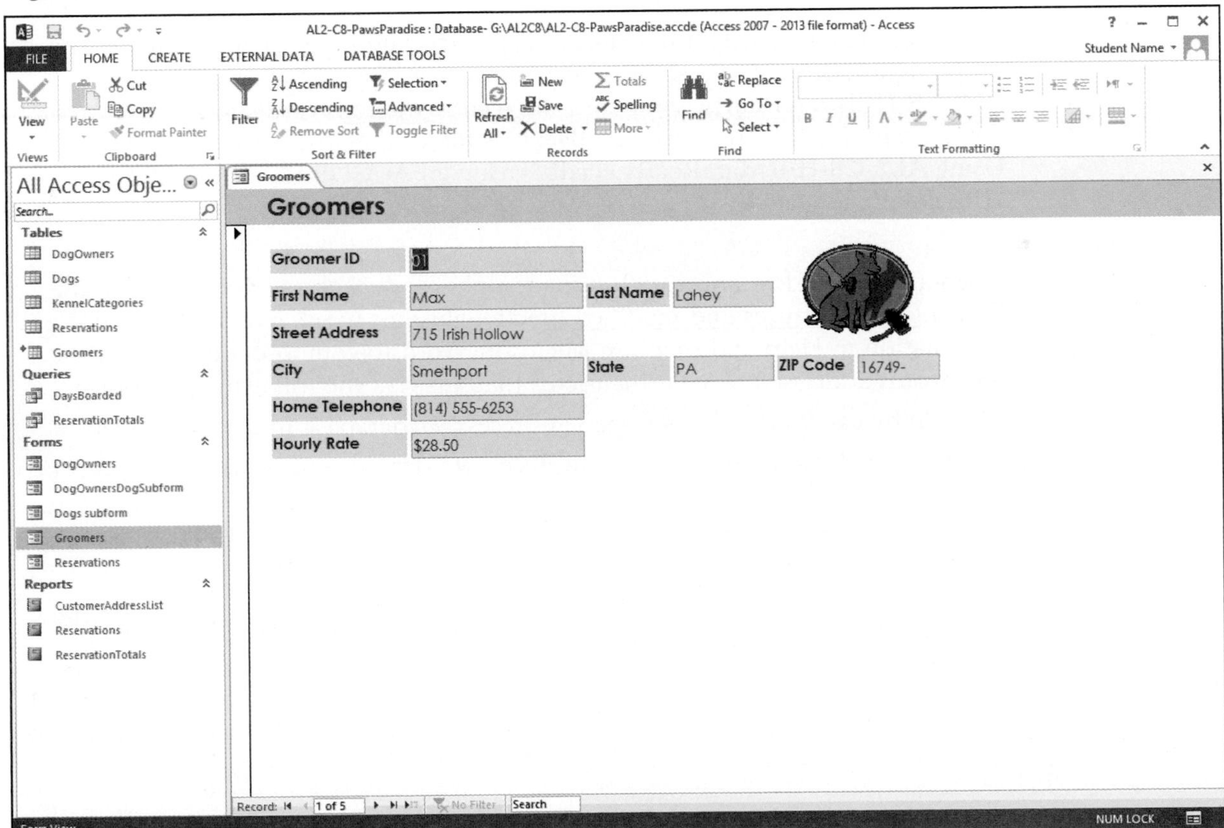

Case Study Apply Your Skills

Part 1

The office manager at Hillsdale Realty would like to export the Listings table data from the database for use in a custom software package that accepts comma separated data files. Open **AL2-C8-HillsdaleRealty.accdb** and enable the content. Create a text file for the office manager, including field names and quotations marks as text qualifiers. Save the export steps, because the office manager has told you that this data exchange file will be required often. Print the text file for your records.

The CEO has requested an electronic copy of the SalesAndCommissions report. The CEO is not familiar with Access and has asked you to send the report with the formatting it would have when displayed in Access, but in a file that can be opened on her laptop, which does not have the Microsoft Office suite. Publish the report as an XPS document using the default name and send the report to your professor as an email attachment using an appropriate subject line and message. Do not save the export steps. ***Note: Check with your instructor for alternate instructions before emailing the file, in case he or she would prefer that you submit the XPS file in a different manner.***

Part 2

The office manager at Hillsdale Realty has asked you to assist her with backing up the HillsdaleRealty database. Create a backup copy of the database, name it **AL2-C8-HillsdaleRealty_yyyy-mm-dd.accdb** (where *yyyy-mm-dd* is the current date), and place it in the DatabaseBackUps folder that you created in Project 1a. Using **AL2-C8-HillsdaleRealty.accdb**, create an ACCDE file called **AL2-C8-HillsdaleRealty.accde.**

Part 3

Open a Help window and search using the phrase *discontinued features*. Click the Discontinued features and modified functionality in Access hyperlink. Read the information in Help and then use Microsoft Word to compose a memo in your own words addressed to your instructor that answers the following questions:

- Why can you no longer open an Access 97 database in Access 2013?
- What do you have to do to an Access 97 database to be able to open it in Access 2013?
- Why is there no longer an option to create PivotCharts and PivotTables in Access 2013?

Save the memo in Word and name it **AL2-C8-CS-P3-DiscontinuedMemo.docx**. Print the memo and then exit Word.

MICROSOFT® ACCESS® Performance Assessment

Note: Before beginning unit assessments, copy to your storage medium the AL2U2 subfolder from the AL2 folder on the CD that accompanies this textbook and then make AL2U2 the active folder.

Assessing Proficiency

In this unit, you have learned to design and create reports with grouping, sorting, totals, and subreports; to use Access tools to analyze tables and improve database efficiency; to automate a database using macros and a Navigation form; to configure startup options and customize the database and Navigation pane; and to integrate Access data with other programs.

Assessment 1 Import Data from Text Files and Create Reports for a Property Management Database

1. Open **AL2-U2-BenchmarkPropMgt.accdb** from the AL2U2 folder on your storage medium and enable the content. In this unit, you will continue working with the residential property management database that you started in Unit 1. The database design and objects have since been modified based on feedback from the property manager and office staff.
2. Create a folder called *DatabaseBackUps* in the AL2U2 folder. Make a backup copy of the database and place it in the new folder. Name the backup database **AL2-U2-BenchmarkPropMgt_yyyy-mm-dd**, where *yyyy-mm-dd* represents today's date.
3. With **AL2-U2-BenchmarkPropMgt.accdb** open, import data into tables from two text files as follows. Save each set of import specifications for future use. Use the default name and determine an appropriate description for each set of import steps.
   a. Append the data in the **TenantsU2.csv** text file to the Tenants table.
   b. Append the data in the **LeasesU2.csv** text file to the Leases table.
4. Design and create reports as follows:
   a. Design and create a report based on the LeasesByBldg query with all of the fields included except the building code field. Group the records by the building name and sort by unit number within each group. Name the report *BuildingsAndLeases*. Include the current date and page numbers in the page footer. Add your name as the report designer in the report footer and insert an appropriate clip art image in the report header. You determine the remaining layout and formatting elements, including a descriptive report title.

b. Design and create a report based on the RentalIncome query with all of the fields included, except for the building code field. Group the records by the building name and sort by unit number within each group. Name the report *IncomeByBuilding*. Sum the rent and annual rent columns and count the unit numbers. Show the statistics in the group footer and as grand totals at the end of the report. Include appropriate labels to describe the statistics and format the values to a suitable numeric format, if necessary. Add your name as the report designer in the report footer and insert an appropriate clip art image in the report header. You determine the remaining layout and formatting elements including a descriptive report title.

5. Print the BuildingAndLeases and IncomeByBuilding reports.

Assessment 2 Use Access Tools to Improve the Property Management Database Design

1. With **AL2-U2-BenchmarkPropMgt.accdb** open, use the Performance Analyzer feature to analyze all of the objects in the database. In the *Analysis Results* list, use the Optimize button to fix each Suggestion item. (A Suggestion item displays with a green question mark.)
2. Use the Database Splitter to split the database into two files to create a back-end database. Accept the default file name at the Create Back-end Database dialog box.
3. Close **AL2-U2-BenchmarkPropMgt.accdb**.
4. Open **AL2-U2-BenchmarkPropMgt_be.accdb** and enable the content.
5. Use the Database Documenter feature to generate a table definition report for the Leases table. Change the options as follows: Set *Include for Table* to *Properties* and *Relationships*; set *Include for Fields* to *Names, Data Types, and Sizes*; and set *Include for Indexes* to *Nothing*. Print and then close the report.
6. Close **AL2-U2-BenchmarkPropMgt_be.accdb**.

Assessment 3 Automate the Property Management Database with Macros and Command Buttons

1. Open **AL2-U2-BenchmarkPropMgt.accdb** and, if necessary, enable the content.
2. Create the following macros. After creating each macro, run the macro to make sure it works properly, print each macro's definition, and then close the macro.
   a. Create a QLeasesByTenant macro that opens the LeasesByTenant query in Datasheet view and Edit mode. Use the macro action *OpenQuery*.
   b. Create a QLeaseTerms macro that opens the LeaseTermsAndDeposits query in Datasheet view and Edit mode. Use the macro action *OpenQuery*.
   c. Create a RBldLeases macro that opens the BuildingsAndLeases report in report view. Use the macro action OpenReport.
   d. Create a RIncome macro that opens the IncomeByBuilding report in report view. Use the macro action OpenReport.
3. Open the BldgsAndMgrs form in Design view.
4. Create two command buttons in the *Form Header* section: one that runs the RBldgLeases macro and another that runs the RIncome macro. You determine the placement of the buttons within the section, the text to display on the face of each button, and a name to assign each button.

5. Test each button to make sure the macro displays the correct report. Insert a screenshot of the BldgsAndMgrs form with the buttons displayed in a new Microsoft Word document using the Screenshot button in the Illustrations group on the INSERT tab or the Print Screen key with the Paste feature. Type your name a few lines below the screenshot and add any other identifying information as instructed. Print the document and then exit Word without saving.
6. Make sure all objects are closed.

Assessment 4 Create a Navigation Form and Configure Startup Options for the Property Management Database

1. With **AL2-U2-BenchmarkPropMgt.accdb** open, create a Navigation form named *MainMenu* using the Horizontal Tabs style with forms and reports in the following tab order:
    - BldgsAndMgrs form
    - TenantsAndLeases form
    - BuildingsAndLeases report
    - IncomeByBuilding report
2. Edit the form title and delete the logo container object. You determine appropriate text to replace *Navigation Form*.
3. Edit the tab captions. You determine appropriate text for each tab.
4. Create a macro named *ExitDB* that saves all objects when quitting Access and then create a command button at the right end of the MainMenu *Form Header* section that runs the macro. You determine the text to display on the face of the button and a name for the button.
5. Display the form in Form view and then click each tab to make sure the correct form or report displays.
6. Set the MainMenu form to display as the startup form, add an appropriate application title for the database, and then hide the Navigation pane.
7. Close and then reopen **AL2-U2-BenchmarkPropMgt.accdb**.
8. Insert a screenshot of the database in a new Microsoft Word document using the Screenshot button in the Illustrations group on the INSERT tab or the Print Screen key with the Paste feature. Type your name a few lines below the screenshot and add any other identifying information as instructed. Print the Word document and then exit Word without saving.

Assessment 5 Configure Security for the Property Management Database

1. With **AL2-U2-BenchmarkPropMgt.accdb** open, make an ACCDE file from the database, saving the copy in the same folder and using the same file name.
2. Close **AL2-U2-BenchmarkPropMgt.accdb**.
3. Open **AL2-U2-BenchmarkPropMgt.accde**.
4. Change the database startup option to display the Navigation pane with the tables and macros hidden.
5. Close and then reopen **AL2-U2-BenchmarkPropMgt.accde**.
6. Insert a screenshot of the database in a new Microsoft Word document using the Screenshot button in the Illustrations group on the INSERT tab or the Print Screen key with the Paste feature. Type your name a few lines below the screenshot and add any other identifying information as instructed. Print the Word document and then exit Word without saving.

Assessment 6 Export and Publish Data from the Property Management Database

1. With **AL2-U2-BenchmarkPropMgt.accde** open, export the LeaseTermsAndDeposits query as a text file using the default name and making sure that the file is saved in the AL2U2 folder on your storage medium. Include the field names in the first row and remove the quotation marks. Do not save the export steps.
2. Open Notepad, open **LeaseTermsAndDeposits.txt**, and then print the text file.
3. Exit Notepad.
4. Publish the IncomeByBuilding report as an XPS document named **AL2-U2-BenchmarkRentInc.xps**, making sure the file is saved in the AL2U2 folder on your storage medium. Do not save the export steps.
5. Open **AL2-U2-BenchmarkRentInc.xps** in an XPS Viewer window and then print the report.
6. Click the button that you created to exit the database.

Writing Activities

The following activities give you the opportunity to practice your writing skills while demonstrating an understanding of some of the important Access features you have mastered in this unit. Use correct grammar, appropriate word choices, and clear sentence constructions.

Activity 1 Create a New Database for Renovation Contracts by Importing Data

You work for a home renovation contractor who operates as a sole proprietor. The contractor has an old computer in his basement that he has been using to keep invoices and other records for renovation contracts. The computer is from the Windows XP operating system era, and the software on it is no longer being sold or updated. The contractor was able to copy data from the old system into a tab delimited text file named **DavisRenos.txt**.

Create a new Access database named **AL2-U2-DavisRenos.accdb** and import the data from the old system into a new table. Modify the table design after importing to apply the Currency format to the *Amount* field. Design and create a form based on the table to be used for entering new records. Also design and create a report to print the records, including a total for the *Invoice Amount* column. The contractor is not familiar with Access and would like you to create a user-friendly menu that can be used to add new records via the form you designed and to view the report. Create the menu using a Navigation form and configure startup options so that the menu is the only object displayed in the work area when the database is opened. Test your menu to make sure each tab functions correctly. Using Microsoft Word, compose a quick reference instruction page for the contractor that instructs him on how to open the database, add a new record, view and print the report, and exit the database. Save the Word document and name it **AL2-U2-Act1-DavisRenos**. Print the document.

Activity 2 Design and Publish a Report for a Painting Franchise

You are helping a friend who has started a student painting franchise to earn money over the summer. Your friend has asked for your help in designing a database to store job information and revenue earned from jobs completed over the summer. Create a new database named **AL2-U2-StudentPainters.accdb**. Design and create tables to store the records for painting contract jobs that include the date the job is completed; the invoice number; the homeowner name, address, and telephone number; and the contract price. Enter at least ten records into the tables. Design a report to print the records in ascending order by date completed. Include statistics at the bottom of the report that provide your friend with the maximum, minimum, average, and total of the contract price field. Include appropriate titles and other report elements. Add your name in the footer as the report designer. Publish and print the report as an XPS document named **AL2-U2-PaintingContracts.xps**.

Internet Research

Buying a Home

You plan on buying a home within the next few years. While you save money for this investment, you decide to maintain a database of the homes offered for sale within the area you are interested in buying. Design and create tables and relationships in a new database named **AL2-U2-Homes4Sale.accdb**. Include fields to store data that will be of interest to you, such as the address, asking price, style of home (condominium, ranch, two story, semi-detached, etc.), number of bedrooms, number of bathrooms, type of heating/cooling system, property taxes, and basement and garage information. Design and create a form to be used to enter information into the tables. Search the Internet to find at least five listings within the area you wish to live and then use the form to enter information for each listing. Design and create a report that groups the records by style of home. Calculate the average list price at the end of each group and at the end of the report. Include five hyperlinked control objects that will link to the web pages from which you retrieved the information for the listings. Include appropriate titles and other report elements. Add your name in the footer as the report designer. Publish and print the report as an XPS document named **AL2-U2-AvgHousePrices.xps**.

Job Study

Meals on Wheels Database

You are a volunteer working in the office of your local Meals on Wheels organization. Meals on Wheels delivers nutritious, affordable meals to citizens in need of the service, such as seniors, convalescents, and people with disabilities. The organization requires volunteers using their own vehicles to drive to the meal depot, pick up the meals, and deliver them to clients' homes. The volunteer coordinator has expressed an interest in using an Access database to better organize and plan volunteer delivery routes. Create a new database named **AL2-U2-MealsOnWheels.accdb**. Design and create tables and relationships according to the instructions below. Remember to apply best practices in database design to minimize data redundancy and validate data whenever possible to ensure accuracy.

- Include fields for the client name, address, telephone, gender, age, reason for requiring meals (senior, convalescent, or disability), meals required (breakfast, lunch, dinner), date service started, and estimated length of service required.
- Include fields for the volunteer name, address, telephone, gender, age, date started, availability by day and by meal (breakfast, lunch, dinner), and receipt of police check clearance.
- Incorporate in your design assignments for the client and the volunteer to the quadrant of the city or town in which each is located. The volunteer coordinator divides the city or town by north, south, east, and west and tries to match drivers with clients in the same quadrant.
- Include other information you think will be important to the volunteer coordinator for this service.

Create a user-defined form template so that all of your forms have a consistent look. Design and create forms to be used to enter the information into the tables and then use the forms to enter at least eight client records and five volunteer records. Make sure you enter records for both clients and volunteers in all four quadrants and for all three meals (breakfast, lunch, dinner).

Design and create queries to extract records of clients and volunteers within the same quadrant. Include in the query results datasheet the information you think will be useful to the volunteer coordinator in setting up route schedules. Design and create reports based on the queries. Print the reports.

Create a main menu for the database to provide access to the forms and reports. Configure startup options to display an application title and the main menu form and to hide the tables in the Navigation pane when the database is opened. Close the database and then reopen it. In Word, use the Screenshot button in the Illustrations group on the INSERT tab or the Print Screen key with the Paste feature to capture an image of the Access window. Print the image from Word and then exit Word without saving.

Index

D

E

F

G

H

I

J

K

L

Q

R

S

T

U

V

W

X

Y

Z

Access 2013 Feature	Ribbon Tab, Group/Option	Button, Option	Keyboard Shortcut
Advanced Filter options	HOME, Sort & Filter		
append query	QUERY TOOLS DESIGN, Query Type		
Application Parts	CREATE, Templates		
close Access			Alt + F4
close database	FILE, *Close*		
copy	HOME, Clipboard		Ctrl + C
create ACCDE file	FILE, *Save As*		
create table	CREATE, Tables		
customize Access options or Navigation Pane	FILE, *Options*		
cut	HOME, Clipboard		Ctrl + X
delete query	QUERY TOOLS DESIGN, Query Type		
delete record	HOME, Records		
Design view	HOME, Views OR TABLE TOOLS FIELDS, Views		
export object to PDF or XPS	EXTERNAL DATA, Export		
export object to Excel	EXTERNAL DATA, Export		
export object to Word	EXTERNAL DATA, Export		
filter	HOME, Sort & Filter		
Find	HOME, Find		Ctrl + F
form	CREATE, Forms		
Form Wizard	CREATE, Forms		
Help		?	
import Excel data	EXTERNAL DATA, Import & Link		
import Access data	EXTERNAL DATA, Import & Link		

Access 2013 Feature	Ribbon Tab, Group/Option	Button, Option	Keyboard Shortcut
Labels Wizard	CREATE, Reports		
macro	CREATE, Macros & Code		
Make Table query	QUERY TOOLS DESIGN, Query Type		
Navigation Forms	CREATE, Forms		
new record	HOME, Records		Ctrl + +
paste	HOME, Clipboard		Ctrl + V
Performance Analyzer	DATABASE TOOLS, Analyze		
primary key	TABLE TOOLS DESIGN, Tools		
Property Sheet	FORM DESIGN TOOLS DESIGN, Tools OR REPORT DESIGN TOOLS DESIGN OR Tools, QUERY TOOLS DESIGN, Show/Hide OR TABLE TOOLS DESIGN, Show/Hide		F4
Query Design	CREATE, Queries		
Query Wizard	CREATE, Queries		
Relationships window	DATABASE TOOLS, Relationships		
report	CREATE, Reports		
Report Design	CREATE, Reports		
Report Wizard	CREATE, Reports		
sort records ascending	HOME, Sort & Filter		
sort records descending	HOME, Sort & Filter		
spelling checker	HOME, Records		F7
split database	DATABASE TOOLS, Move Data		
Table Analyzer Wizard	DATABASE TOOLS, Analyze		
Total row	HOME, Records	Σ	
update query	QUERY TOOLS DESIGN, Query Type